UNIFORM TRUST AND ESTATE STATUTES

2018–2019 Edition

Compiled and Edited by

THOMAS P. GALLANIS

Allan D. Vestal Chair in Law
Associate Dean for Research
University of Iowa

FOUNDATION
PRESS

© 1987, 1989, 1991, 1992, 1994, 1995, 2001–2004 FOUNDATION PRESS
© 2005, 2007–2012 THOMSON REUTERS/FOUNDATION PRESS
© 2013 LEG, Inc. d/b/a West Academic Publishing
© 2015–2017 LEG, Inc. d/b/a West Academic
© 2018 LEG, Inc. d/b/a West Academic
    444 Cedar Street, Suite 700
    St. Paul, MN 55101
    1-877-888-1330

Printed in the United States of America

ISBN: 978-1-64020-923-7

[No claim of copyright is made for official U.S. government statutes, rules or regulations.]

PREFACE

This book contains the full statutory texts of the principal Uniform Acts pertaining to trusts and estates. It also reproduces the official comments for the substantive articles of the Uniform Probate Code (Articles II and VI); for the Uniform Trust Code; and for most of the other Uniform Acts. The statutes are arranged into three parts.

———

Part One, Probate Statutes, primarily contains the Uniform Probate Code (UPC), incorporating all subsequent amendments. The most recent amendments were adopted by the Uniform Law Commission in 2018.

Part One also contains the United Kingdom Inheritance (Provision for Family and Dependants) Act 1975, as amended through March 2018. The broad discretion that the Act devolves upon the court in the distribution of decedents' estates provides a striking contrast with the emphasis on fixed shares in the UPC's arrangements for intestate succession and elective shares.

———

Part Two of this book, devoted to Trust Statutes, begins with the Uniform Trust Code (originally enacted in 2000). The text incorporates all subsequent amendments to this Code. The most recent amendments were adopted in 2018.

This book no longer contains the Uniform Trustee Powers Act, the substance of which has been recodified within the Uniform Trust Code.

Part Two also contains the Uniform Directed Trust Act (2017); the Uniform Trust Decanting Act (2015, with amendments in 2018 to conform it to the Uniform Directed Trust Act); the Uniform Principal and Income Act (1997, with amendments in 2008); the Uniform Prudent Investor Act (1994); and the Uniform Custodial Trust Act (1987).

———

Part Three, containing other Uniform and Model Acts, is chronologically organized — most recent to least recent — and contains the Uniform Parentage Act (2017); the Revised Uniform Fiduciary Access to Digital Assets Act (2015); the Uniform Powers of Appointment Act (2013); the Uniform Premarital and Marital Agreements Act (2012); the Model Protection of Charitable Assets Act (2011); the Revised Uniform Anatomical Gift Act (2006); the Uniform Prudent Management of Institutional Funds Act (2006); the Uniform Health-Care Decisions Act (1993); the Uniform Simultaneous Death Act (1993); the Uniform Fraudulent Transfer Act (1984, as amended in 2014 and renamed the Uniform Voidable Transactions Act); the Uniform Transfers to Minors Act (1983, with 1986 amendments); and the Model Marital Property Act (1983).

———

To make the book more useful, interspersed are some selected provisions from former versions of various Uniform Acts, especially former versions of UPC Article II. Also interspersed are a few provisions from the new Restatements — the Restatement (Third) of Trusts and the Restatement (Third) of Property: Wills and Other Donative Transfers. These insertions are positioned immediately below the comparable provisions of the current text and, to prevent confusion, are set off in a bordered format.

Uniform Acts and Restatements are copyrighted respectively by the Uniform Law Commission and the American Law Institute. Gratitude is extended to these organizations for granting permission to reproduce these Acts and Restatement provisions.

———

It is a pleasure to thank Professors John H. Langbein and Lawrence W. Waggoner, who compiled and edited this book through 2009-2010, and the law school's administrative services supervisor, Amanda Bibb, for her help in the preparation of this edition.

Thomas P. Gallanis

March 2018

SUMMARY OF CONTENTS

TABLE OF CONTENTS

PART THREE: OTHER UNIFORM ACTS

UNIFORM TRUST AND ESTATE STATUTES

2018–2019 Edition

PART ONE: PROBATE STATUTES

Uniform Probate Code (1969, with Subsequent Amendments)

United Kingdom Inheritance (Provision for Family and Dependants) Act 1975 (with Subsequent Amendments)

UNIFORM PROBATE CODE

OFFICIAL TEXT
WITH AMENDMENTS THROUGH 2017

Official Text and Comments Approved by the National Conference of Commissioners on Uniform State Laws

———

AN ACT

Relating to affairs of decedents, missing persons, protected persons, minors, incapacitated persons and certain others and constituting the Uniform Probate Code; consolidating and revising aspects of the law relating to wills and intestacy and the administration and distribution of estates of decedents, missing persons, protected persons, minors, incapacitated persons and certain others; ordering the powers and procedures of the court concerned with the affairs of decedents and certain others; providing for the validity and effect of certain non-testamentary transfers, contracts and deposits which relate to death and appear to have testamentary effect; providing certain procedures to facilitate enforcement of testamentary and other trusts; making uniform the law with respect to decedents and certain others; and repealing inconsistent legislation.

ARTICLE I
GENERAL PROVISIONS, DEFINITIONS AND PROBATE JURISDICTION OF COURT

Table of Sections

PART 1
SHORT TITLE, CONSTRUCTION, GENERAL PROVISIONS

PART 2
DEFINITIONS

PART 3
SCOPE, JURISDICTION AND COURTS

PART 4
NOTICE, PARTIES AND REPRESENTATION IN ESTATE LITIGATION AND OTHER MATTERS

PART 1
SHORT TITLE, CONSTRUCTION, GENERAL PROVISIONS

§ 1-101. Short Title. This [act] shall be known and may be cited as the Uniform Probate Code.

§ 1-102. Purposes; Rule of Construction.

(a) This [code] shall be liberally construed and applied to promote its underlying purposes and policies.

(b) The underlying purposes and policies of this [code] are:

(1) to simplify and clarify the law concerning the affairs of decedents, missing persons, protected persons, minors and incapacitated persons;

(2) to discover and make effective the intent of a decedent in distribution of his property;

(3) to promote a speedy and efficient system for liquidating the estate of the decedent and making distribution to his successors;

(4) to facilitate use and enforcement of certain trusts;

(5) to make uniform the law among the various jurisdictions.

§ 1-103. Supplementary General Principles of Law Applicable. Unless displaced by the particular provisions of this [code], the principles of law and equity supplement its provisions.

§ 1-104. Severability. If any provision of this [code] or the application thereof to any person or circumstances is held invalid, the invalidity shall not affect other provisions or applications of the [code] which can be given effect without the invalid provision or application, and to this end the provisions of this [code] are declared to be severable.

§ 1-105. Construction Against Implied Repeal. This [code] is a general act intended as a unified coverage of its subject matter and no part of it shall be deemed impliedly repealed by subsequent legislation if it can reasonably be avoided.

§ 1-106. Effect of Fraud and Evasion. Whenever fraud has been perpetrated in connection with any proceeding or in any statement filed under this [code] or if fraud is used to avoid or circumvent the provisions or purposes of this [code], any person injured thereby may obtain appropriate relief against the perpetrator of the fraud or restitution from any person (other than a bona fide purchaser) benefitting from the fraud, whether innocent or not. Any proceeding must be commenced within two years after the discovery of the fraud, but no proceeding may be brought against one not a perpetrator of the fraud later than five years after the time of commission of the fraud. This section has no bearing on remedies relating to fraud practiced on a decedent during his lifetime which affects the succession of his estate.

§ 1-107. Evidence of Death or Status. In addition to the rules of evidence in courts of general jurisdiction, the following rules relating to a determination of death and status apply:

(1) Death occurs when an individual [is determined to be dead under the Uniform Determination of Death Act (1978/1980)] [has sustained either (i) irreversible cessation of circulatory and respiratory functions or (ii) irreversible cessation of all functions of the entire brain, including the brain stem. A determination of death must be made in accordance with accepted medical standards].

(2) A certified or authenticated copy of a death certificate purporting to be issued by an official or agency of the place where the death purportedly occurred is prima facie evidence of the fact, place,

date, and time of death and the identity of the decedent.

(3) A certified or authenticated copy of any record or report of a governmental agency, domestic or foreign, that an individual is missing, detained, dead, or alive is prima facie evidence of the status and of the dates, circumstances, and places disclosed by the record or report.

(4) In the absence of prima facie evidence of death under paragraph (2) or (3), the fact of death may be established by clear and convincing evidence, including circumstantial evidence.

(5) An individual whose death is not established under the preceding paragraphs who is absent for a continuous period of five years, during which he [or she] has not been heard from, and whose absence is not satisfactorily explained after diligent search or inquiry, is presumed to be dead. His [or her] death is presumed to have occurred at the end of the period unless there is sufficient evidence for determining that death occurred earlier.

(6) In the absence of evidence disputing the time of death stated on a document described in paragraph (2) or (3), a document described in paragraph (2) or (3) that states a time of death 120 hours or more after the time of death of another individual, however the time of death of the other individual is determined, establishes by clear and convincing evidence that the individual survived the other individual by 120 hours.

§ 1-108. Acts by Holder of General Power. For the purpose of granting consent or approval with regard to the acts or accounts of a personal representative or trustee, including relief from liability or penalty for failure to post bond, to register a trust, or to perform other duties, and for purposes of consenting to modification or termination of a trust or to deviation from its terms, the sole holder or all coholders of a presently exercisable general power of appointment, including one in the form of a power of amendment or revocation, are deemed to act for beneficiaries to the extent their interests (as objects, takers in default, or otherwise) are subject to the power.

§ 1-109. Cost of Living Adjustment of Certain Dollar Amounts.

(a) In this section:

(1) "CPI" means the Consumer Price Index (Annual Average) for All Urban Consumers (CPI-U): U.S. City Average—All items, reported by the Bureau of Labor Statistics, United States Department of Labor or its successor or, if the index is discontinued, an equivalent index reported by a federal authority. If no such index is reported, the term means the substitute index chosen by [insert appropriate state agency]; and

(2) "Reference base index" means the CPI for calendar year [insert year immediately preceding the year in which this section takes effect].

(b) The dollar amounts stated in Sections 2-102, [2-102A,] 2-202(b), 2-402, 2-403, 2-405, and 3-1201 apply to the estate of a decedent who died in or after [insert year in which this section takes effect], but for the estate of a decedent who died after [insert year after the year in which this section takes effect], these dollar amounts must be increased or decreased if the CPI for the calendar year immediately preceding the year of death exceeds or is less than the reference base index. The amount of any increase or decrease is computed by multiplying each dollar amount by the percentage by which the CPI for the calendar year immediately preceding the year of death exceeds or is less than the reference base index. If any increase or decrease produced by the computation is not a multiple of $100, the increase or decrease is rounded down, if an increase, or up, if a decrease, to the next multiple of $100, but for the purpose of Section 2-405, the periodic installment amount is the lump-sum amount divided by 12. If the CPI for [insert year immediately before the effective date of this section] is changed by the Bureau of Labor Statistics, the reference base index must be revised using the rebasing factor reported by the Bureau of Labor Statistics, or other comparable data if a rebasing factor is not reported.

[(c) Before February 1, [insert year after the year in which this section takes effect], and before February 1 of each succeeding year, the [insert appropriate state agency] shall publish a cumulative list, beginning with the dollar amounts effective for the estate of a decedent who died in [insert year after the year in which this section takes effect], of each dollar amount as increased or decreased under this section.]

Legislative Note: *To establish and maintain uniformity among the states, an enacting state that enacted the sections listed in subsection (b) before 2008 should bring those dollar amounts up to date. To adjust for inflation, these amounts were revised in 2008. Between 1990 (when these amounts were previously adjusted for inflation) and 2008, the consumer price index (CPI) increased about 50 percent. As a result, the following increases in the UPC's specific dollar amounts were adopted in 2008 and should be adopted by a state that enacted these sections before 2008:*

Section 2-102(2) should be amended to change $200,000 to $300,000; Section 2-102(3) should be amended to change $150,000 to $225,000; and Section 2-102(4) should be amended to change $100,000 to $150,000. Section 2-102A, if enacted instead of Section 2-102, should be amended accordingly.

Section 2-201(b) should be amended to change $50,000 to $75,000.

Section 2-402 should be amended to change $15,000 to $22,500; Section 2-403 should be amended to change $10,000 to $15,000; and Section 2-405 should be amended to change $18,000 to $27,000 and to change $1,500 to $2,250.

A state enacting these sections after 2008 should adjust the dollar figures for changes in the cost of living that have occurred between 2008 and the effective date of the new enactment.

Comment

Automatic Adjustments for Inflation. Added in 2008, Section 1-109 operates in conjunction with the inflation adjustments of the dollar amounts listed in subsection (b) also adopted in 2008. Section 1-109 was added to make it unnecessary in the future for the ULC or individual enacting states to continue to amend the UPC periodically to adjust the dollar amounts for inflation. This section provides for an automatic adjustment of each of the above dollar amounts annually.

In each January, the Bureau of Labor Statistics of the U.S. Department of Labor reports the CPI (annual average) for the preceding calendar year. The information can be obtained by telephone (202/691-5200) or on the Bureau's website <http://www.bls.gov/cpi>.

Subsection (c) tasks an appropriate state agency, such as the Department of Revenue, to issue an official cumulative list of the adjusted amounts beginning in January of the year after the effective date of the act. This subsection is bracketed because some enacting states might not have a state agency that could appropriately be assigned the task of issuing updated amounts. Such an enacting state might consider tasking the state supreme court to issue a court rule each year making the appropriate adjustment.

PART 2
DEFINITIONS

§ 1-201. General Definitions.

Subject to additional definitions contained in the subsequent [articles] that are applicable to specific [articles,] [parts,] or sections, and unless the context otherwise requires, in this Code:

(1) "Agent" includes an attorney in fact under a durable or nondurable power of attorney, an individual authorized to make decisions concerning another's health care, and an individual authorized to make decisions for another under a natural death act.

(2) "Application" means a written request to the Registrar for an order of informal probate or appointment under [Part] 3 of [Article] III.

(3) "Beneficiary", as it relates to a trust beneficiary, includes a person who has any present or future interest, vested or contingent, and also includes the owner of an interest by assignment or other transfer; as it relates to a charitable trust, includes any person entitled to enforce the trust; as it relates to a "beneficiary of a beneficiary designation", refers to a beneficiary of an insurance or annuity policy, of an account with POD designation, of a security registered in beneficiary form (TOD), or of a pension, profitsharing, retirement, or similar benefit plan, or other nonprobate transfer at death; and, as it relates to a "beneficiary designated in a governing instrument," includes a grantee of a deed, a devisee, a trust beneficiary, a beneficiary of a beneficiary designation, a donee, appointee, or taker in default of a power of appointment, or a person in whose favor a power of attorney or a power held in any individual, fiduciary, or representative capacity is exercised.

(4) "Beneficiary designation" refers to a governing instrument naming a beneficiary of an insurance or annuity policy, of an account with POD designation, of a security registered in beneficiary form (TOD), or of a pension, profitsharing, retirement, or similar benefit plan, or other nonprobate transfer at death.

(5) "Child" includes an individual entitled to take as a child under this [code] by intestate succession from the parent whose relationship is involved and excludes a person who is only a stepchild, a foster child, a grandchild, or any more remote descendant.

(6) "Claims", in respect to estates of decedents and protected persons, includes liabilities of the decedent or protected person, whether arising in contract, in tort, or otherwise, and liabilities of the estate which arise at or after the death of the decedent or after the appointment of a conservator, including funeral expenses and expenses of administration. The term does not include estate or inheritance taxes, or demands or disputes regarding title of a decedent or protected person to specific assets alleged to be included in the estate.

(7) "Conservator" is as defined in Section 5-102.

(8) "Court" means the [......... Court or branch] in this state having jurisdiction in matters relating to the affairs of decedents.

(9) "Descendant" of an individual means all of his [or her] descendants of all generations, with the relationship of parent and child at each generation being determined by the definition of child and parent contained in this [code].

(10) "Devise", when used as a noun, means a testamentary disposition of real or personal property and, when used as a verb, means to dispose of real or personal property by will.

(11) "Devisee" means a person designated in a will to receive a devise. For the purposes of Article III, in the case of a devise to an existing trust or trustee, or to a trustee or trust described by will, the trust or trustee is the devisee and the beneficiaries are not devisees.

(12) "Distributee" means any person who has received property of a decedent from his [or her] personal representative other than as a creditor or purchaser. A testamentary trustee is a distributee only to the extent of distributed assets or increment thereto remaining in his [or her] hands. A beneficiary of a testamentary trust to whom the trustee has distributed property received from a personal representative is a distributee of the personal representative. For the purposes of this provision, "testamentary trustee" includes a trustee to whom assets are transferred by will, to the extent of the devised assets.

(13) "Estate" includes the property of the decedent, trust, or other person whose affairs are subject to this [code] as originally constituted and as it exists from time to time during administration.

(14) "Exempt property" means that property of a decedent's estate which is described in Section 2-403.

(15) "Fiduciary" includes a personal representative, guardian, conservator, and trustee.

(16) "Foreign personal representative" means a personal representative appointed by another jurisdiction.

(17) "Formal proceedings" means proceedings conducted before a judge with notice to interested persons.

(18) "Governing instrument" means a deed, will, trust, insurance or annuity policy, account with POD designation, security registered in beneficiary form (TOD), transfer on death (TOD) deed, pension, profitsharing, retirement, or similar benefit plan, instrument creating or exercising a power of appointment or a power of attorney, or a dispositive, appointive, or nominative instrument of any similar type.

(19) "Guardian" is as defined in Section 5-102.

(20) "Heirs", except as controlled by Section 2-711, means persons, including the surviving spouse and the state, who are entitled under the statutes of intestate succession to the property of a decedent.

(21) "Incapacitated person" means an individual described in Section 5-102.

(22) "Informal proceedings" means those conducted without notice to interested persons by an officer of the court acting as a registrar for probate of a will or appointment of a personal representative.

(23) "Interested person" includes heirs, devisees, children, spouses, creditors, beneficiaries, and any others having a property right in or claim against a trust estate or the estate of a decedent, ward, or protected person. It also includes persons having priority for appointment as personal representative, and other fiduciaries representing interested persons. The meaning as it relates to particular persons may vary from time to time and must be determined according to the particular purposes of, and matter involved in, any proceeding.

(24) "Issue" of an individual means descendant.

(25) "Joint tenants with the right of survivorship" and "community property with the right of survivorship" includes coowners of property held under circumstances that entitle one or more to the whole of the property on the death of the other or others, but excludes forms of coownership registration in which the underlying ownership of each party is in proportion to that party's contribution.

(26) "Lease" includes an oil, gas, or other mineral lease.

(27) "Letters" includes letters testamentary, letters of guardianship, letters of administration, and letters of conservatorship.

(28) "Minor" has the meaning described in Section 5-102.

(29) "Mortgage" means any conveyance, agreement, or arrangement in which property is encumbered or used as security.

(30) "Nonresident decedent" means a decedent who was domiciled in another jurisdiction at the time of his [or her] death.

(31) "Organization" means a corporation, business trust, estate, trust, partnership, joint venture, association, government, or governmental subdivision or agency, or any other legal or commercial entity.

(32) "Parent" includes any person entitled to take, or who would be entitled to take if the child died without a will, as a parent under this [code] by intestate succession from the child whose relationship is in question and excludes any person who is only a stepparent, foster parent, or grandparent.

(33) "Payor" means a trustee, insurer, business entity, employer, government, governmental agency or subdivision, or any other person authorized or obligated by law or a governing instrument to make payments.

(34) "Person" means an individual or an organization.

(35) "Personal representative" includes executor, administrator, successor personal representative, special administrator, and persons who perform substantially the same function under the law governing their status. "General personal representative" excludes special administrator.

(36) "Petition" means a written request to the court for an order after notice.

(37) "Proceeding" includes action at law and suit in equity.

(38) "Property" includes both real and personal property or any interest therein and means anything that may be the subject of ownership.

(39) "Protected person" is as defined in Section 5-102.

(40) "Protective proceeding" means a proceeding under [Part] 4 of [Article] V.

(41) "Record" means information that is inscribed on a tangible medium or that is stored in an electronic or other medium and is retrievable in perceivable form

(42) "Registrar" refers to the official of the court designated to perform the functions of Registrar as provided in Section 1-307.

(43) "Security" includes any note, stock, treasury stock, bond, debenture, evidence of indebtedness, certificate of interest or participation in an oil, gas, or mining title or lease or in payments out of production under such a title or lease, collateral trust certificate, transferable share, voting trust certificate or, in general, any interest or instrument commonly known as a security, or any certificate of interest or participation, any temporary or interim certificate, receipt, or certificate of deposit for, or any warrant or right to subscribe to or purchase, any of the foregoing.

(44) "Settlement", in reference to a decedent's estate, includes the full process of administration, distribution, and closing.

(45) "Sign" means, with present intent to authenticate or adopt a record other than a will:

　　(A) to execute or adopt a tangible symbol; or

　　(B) to attache to or logically associate with the record an electronic symbol, sound, or process.

(46) "Special administrator" means a personal representative as described by Sections 3-614 through 3-618.

(47) "State" means a state of the United States, the District of Columbia, the Commonwealth of Puerto Rico, or any territory or insular possession subject to the jurisdiction of the United States.

(48) "Successor personal representative" means a personal representative, other than a special administrator, who is appointed to succeed a previously appointed personal representative.

(49) "Successors" means persons, other than creditors, who are entitled to property of a decedent under his [or her] will or this [code].

(50) "Supervised administration" refers to the proceedings described in Article III, Part 5.

(51) "Survive" means that an individual has neither predeceased an event, including the death of another individual, nor is deemed to have predeceased an event under Section 2-104 or 2-702. The term includes its derivatives, such as "survives", "survived", "survivor", "surviving."

(52) "Testacy proceeding" means a proceeding to establish a will or determine intestacy.

(53) "Testator" includes an individual of either sex.

(54) "Trust" includes an express trust, private or charitable, with additions thereto, wherever and however created. The term also includes a trust created or determined by judgment or decree under which the trust is to be administered in the manner of an express trust. The term excludes other constructive trusts and excludes resulting trusts, conservatorships, personal representatives, trust accounts as defined in [Article] VI, custodial arrangements pursuant to [each state should list its legislation, including that relating to [gifts] [transfers] to minors, dealing with special custodial situations], business trusts providing for certificates to be issued to beneficiaries, common trust funds, voting trusts, security arrangements, liquidation trusts, and trusts for the primary purpose of paying debts, dividends, interest, salaries, wages, profits, pensions, or employee benefits of any kind, and any

arrangement under which a person is nominee or escrowee for another.

(55) "Trustee" includes an original, additional, or successor trustee, whether or not appointed or confirmed by court.

(56) "Ward" means an individual described in Section 5-102.

(57) "Will" includes codicil and any testamentary instrument that merely appoints an executor, revokes or revises another will, nominates a guardian, or expressly excludes or limits the right of an individual or class to succeed to property of the decedent passing by intestate succession.

[FOR ADOPTION IN COMMUNITY PROPERTY STATES]

[(58) "Separate property" (if necessary, to be defined locally in accordance with existing concept in adopting state).

(59) "Community property" (if necessary, to be defined locally in accordance with existing concept in adopting state).]

PART 3
SCOPE, JURISDICTION AND COURTS

§ 1-301. Territorial Application. Except as otherwise provided in this [code], this [code] applies to (1) the affairs and estates of decedents, missing persons, and persons to be protected, domiciled in this state, (2) the property of nonresidents located in this state or property coming into the control of a fiduciary who is subject to the laws of this state, (3) incapacitated persons and minors in this state, (4) survivorship and related accounts in this state, and (5) trusts subject to administration in this state.

§ 1-302. Subject Matter Jurisdiction.

(a) To the full extent permitted by the constitution, the court has jurisdiction over all subject matter relating to

(1) estates of decedents, including construction of wills and determination of heirs and successors of decedents, and estates of protected persons;

(2) protection of minors and incapacitated persons; and

(3) trusts.

(b) The court has full power to make orders, judgments and decrees and take all other action necessary and proper to administer justice in the matters which come before it.

(c) The court has jurisdiction over protective proceedings and guardianship proceedings.

(d) If both guardianship and protective proceedings as to the same person are commenced or pending in the same court, the proceedings may be consolidated.

§ 1-303. Venue; Multiple Proceedings; Transfer.

(a) Where a proceeding under this [code] could be maintained in more than one place in this state, the court in which the proceeding is first commenced has the exclusive right to proceed.

(b) If proceedings concerning the same estate, protected person, ward, or trust are commenced in more than one court of this state, the court in which the proceeding was first commenced shall continue to hear the matter, and the other courts shall hold the matter in abeyance until the question of venue is decided, and if the ruling court determines that venue is properly in another court, it shall transfer the proceeding to the other court.

(c) If a court finds that in the interest of justice a proceeding or a file should be located in another court of this state, the court making the finding may transfer the proceeding or file to the other court.

§ 1-304. Practice in Court. Unless specifically provided to the contrary in this [code] or unless inconsistent with its provisions, the rules of civil procedure including the rules concerning vacation of orders and appellate review govern formal proceedings under this [code].

§ 1-305. Records and Certified Copies. The [Clerk of Court] shall keep a record for each decedent, ward, protected person or trust involved in any document which may be filed with the court under this [code], including petitions and applications, demands for notices or bonds, trust registrations, and of any orders or responses relating thereto by the Registrar or court, and establish and maintain a system for indexing, filing or recording which is sufficient to enable users of the records to obtain adequate information. Upon payment of the fees required by law the clerk must issue certified copies of any probated wills, letters issued to personal representatives, or any other record or paper filed or recorded. Certificates relating to probated wills must indicate whether the decedent was domiciled in this state and whether the probate was formal or informal. Certificates relating to letters must show the date of appointment.

§ 1-306. Jury Trial.

(a) If duly demanded, a party is entitled to trial by jury in [a formal testacy proceeding and] any proceeding in which any controverted question of fact arises as to which any party has a constitutional right to trial by jury.

(b) If there is no right to trial by jury under subsection (a) or the right is waived, the court in its discretion may call a jury to decide any issue of fact, in which case the verdict is advisory only.

§ 1-307. Registrar; Powers. The acts and orders which this [code] specifies as performable by the Registrar may be performed either by a judge of the court or by a person, including the clerk, designated by the court by a written order filed and recorded in the office of the court.

§ 1-308. Appeals. Appellate review, including the right to appellate review, interlocutory appeal, provisions as to time, manner, notice, appeal bond, stays, scope of review, record on appeal, briefs, arguments and power of the appellate court, is governed by the rules applicable to the appeals to the [Supreme Court] in equity cases from the [court of general jurisdiction], except that in proceedings where jury trial has been had as a matter of right, the rules applicable to the scope of review in jury cases apply.

§ 1-309. Qualifications of Judge. A judge of the court must have the same qualifications as a judge of the [court of general jurisdiction.]

§ 1-310. Oath or Affirmation on Filed Documents. Except as otherwise specifically provided in this [code] or by rule, every document filed with the court under this [code] including applications, petitions, and demands for notice, shall be deemed to include an oath, affirmation, or statement to the effect that its representations are true as far as the person executing or filing it knows or is informed, and penalties for perjury may follow deliberate falsification therein.

PART 4
NOTICE, PARTIES AND REPRESENTATION IN ESTATE LITIGATION AND OTHER MATTERS

§ 1-401. Notice; Method and Time of Giving.

(a) If notice of a hearing on any petition is required and except for specific notice requirements as otherwise provided, the petitioner shall cause notice of the time and place of hearing of any petition to be given to any interested person or his attorney if he has appeared by attorney or requested that notice be sent to his attorney. Notice shall be given:

(1) by mailing a copy thereof at least 14 days before the time set for the hearing by certified, registered or ordinary first class mail addressed to the person being notified at the post office address given in his demand for notice, if any, or at his office or place of residence, if known;

(2) by delivering a copy thereof to the person being notified personally at least 14 days before the time set for the hearing; or

(3) if the address, or identity of any person is not known and cannot be ascertained with reasonable diligence, by publishing at least once a week for 3 consecutive weeks, a copy thereof in a newspaper having general circulation in the county where the hearing is to be held, the last publication of which is to be at least 10 days before the time set for the hearing.

(b) The court for good cause shown may provide for a different method or time of giving notice for any hearing.

(c) Proof of the giving of notice shall be made on or before the hearing and filed in the proceeding.

§ 1-402. Notice; Waiver.
A person, including a guardian ad litem, conservator, or other fiduciary, may waive notice by a writing signed by him or his attorney and filed in the proceeding. A person for whom a guardianship or other protective order is sought, a ward, or a protected person may not waive notice.

§ 1-403. Pleadings; When Parties Bound By Others; Notice.
In formal proceedings involving trusts or estates of decedents, minors, protected persons, or incapacitated persons, and in judicially supervised settlements, the following rules apply:

(1) Interests to be affected must be described in pleadings that give reasonable information to owners by name or class, by reference to the instrument creating the interests or in another appropriate manner.

(2) A person is bound by an order binding another in the following cases:

(A) An order binding the sole holder or all coholders of a power of revocation or a presently exercisable general power of appointment, including one in the form of a power of amendment, binds other persons to the extent their interests as objects, takers in default, or otherwise are subject to the power.

(B) To the extent there is no conflict of interest between them or among persons represented:

(i) an order binding a conservator binds the person whose estate the conservator controls;

(ii) an order binding a guardian binds the ward if no conservator of the ward's estate has been appointed;

(iii) an order binding a trustee binds beneficiaries of the trust in proceedings to probate a will establishing or adding to a trust, to review the acts or accounts of a former fiduciary, and in proceedings involving creditors or other third parties;

(iv) an order binding a personal representative binds persons interested in the undistributed assets of a decedent's estate in actions or proceedings by or against the estate; and

(v) an order binding a sole holder or all coholders of a general testamentary power of appointment binds other persons to the extent their interests as objects, takers in default, or otherwise are subject to the power.

(C) Unless otherwise represented, a minor or an incapacitated, unborn, or unascertained person is bound by an order to the extent the person's interest is adequately represented by another party having a substantially identical interest in the proceeding.

(3) If no conservator or guardian has been appointed, a parent may represent a minor child.

(4) Notice is required as follows:

(A) The notice prescribed by Section 1-401 must be given to every interested person or to one who can bind an interested person as described in paragraph (2)(A) or (B). Notice may be given both to a person and to another who may bind the person.

(B) Notice is given to unborn or unascertained persons who are not represented under paragraph (2)(A) or (B) by giving notice to all known persons whose interests in the proceedings are substantially identical to those of the unborn or unascertained persons.

(5) At any point in a proceeding, a court may appoint a guardian ad litem to represent the interest of a minor, an incapacitated, unborn, or unascertained person, or a person whose identity or address is unknown, if the court determines that representation of the interest otherwise would be inadequate. If not precluded by conflict of interests, a guardian ad litem may be appointed to represent several persons or interests. The court shall state its reasons for appointing a guardian ad litem as a part of the record of the proceeding.

ARTICLE II
INTESTACY, WILLS, AND DONATIVE TRANSFERS

Table of Sections

PART 1
INTESTATE SUCCESSION

PART 2
ELECTIVE SHARE OF SURVIVING SPOUSE

PART 3
SPOUSE AND CHILDREN UNPROVIDED FOR IN WILLS

PART 4
EXEMPT PROPERTY AND ALLOWANCES

PART 5
WILLS, WILL CONTRACTS, AND CUSTODY AND
DEPOSIT OF WILLS

PART 6
RULES OF CONSTRUCTION APPLICABLE ONLY TO WILLS

PART 7
RULES OF CONSTRUCTION APPLICABLE TO WILLS AND OTHER GOVERNING INSTRUMENTS

PART 8
GENERAL PROVISIONS CONCERNING PROBATE AND NONPROBATE TRANSFERS

PART 9
STATUTORY RULE AGAINST PERPETUITIES; HONORARY TRUSTS

PART 10
UNIFORM INTERNATIONAL WILLS ACT (1977)

PART 11
UNIFORM DISCLAIMER OF PROPERTY
INTERESTS ACT (1999/2006)

§ 2-1116.   Application to Existing Relationships.
§ 2-1117.   Relation to Electronic Signatures in Global and National Commerce Act.

———

ARTICLE II
INTESTACY, WILLS, AND DONATIVE TRANSFERS

Prefatory Note

The Uniform Probate Code was originally promulgated in 1969.

1990 Revisions. In 1990, Article II underwent significant revision. The 1990 revisions were the culmination of a systematic study of the Code conducted by the Joint Editorial Board for the Uniform Probate Code (now named the Joint Editorial Board for Uniform Trust and Estate Acts) and a special Drafting Committee to Revise Article II. The 1990 revisions concentrated on Article II, which is the article that covers the substantive law of intestate succession; spouse's elective share; omitted spouse and children; probate exemptions and allowances; execution and revocation of wills; will contracts; rules of construction; disclaimers; and the effect of homicide and divorce on succession rights; and the rule against perpetuities and honorary trusts.

Themes of the 1990 Revisions. In the twenty or so years between the original promulgation of the Code and 1990, several developments occurred that prompted the systematic round of review. Four themes were sounded: (1) the decline of formalism in favor of intent-serving policies; (2) the recognition that will substitutes and other inter-vivos transfers have so proliferated that they now constitute a major, if not the major, form of wealth transmission; (3) the advent of the multiple-marriage society, resulting in a significant fraction of the population being married more than once and having stepchildren and children by previous marriages and (4) the acceptance of a partnership or marital-sharing theory of marriage.

The 1990 revisions responded to these themes. The multiple-marriage society and the partnership/marital-sharing theory were reflected in the revised elective-share provisions of Part 2. As the General Comment to Part 2 explained, the revised elective share granted the surviving spouse a right of election that implemented the partnership/marital-sharing theory of marriage.

The children-of-previous-marriages and stepchildren phenomena were reflected most prominently in the revised rules on the spouse's share in intestacy.

The proliferation of will substitutes and other inter-vivos transfers was recognized, mainly, in measures tending to bring the law of probate and nonprobate transfers into greater unison. One aspect of this tendency was reflected in the restructuring of the rules of construction. Rules of construction are rules that supply presumptive meaning to dispositive and similar provisions of governing instruments. See Restatement (Third) of Property: Wills and Other Donative Transfers § 11.3 (2003). Part 6 of the pre-1990 Code contained several rules of construction that applied only to wills. Some of those rules of construction appropriately applied only to wills; provisions relating to lapse, testamentary exercise of a power of appointment, and ademption of a devise by satisfaction exemplify such rules of construction. Other rules of construction, however, properly apply to all governing instruments, not just wills; the provision relating to inclusion of adopted persons in class gift language exemplifies this type of rule of construction. The 1990 revisions divided pre-1990 Part 6 into two parts – Part 6, containing rules of construction for wills only; and Part 7, containing rules of construction for wills and other governing instruments. A few new rules of construction were also added.

In addition to separating the rules of construction into two parts, and adding new rules of construction, the revocation-upon-divorce provision (Section 2-804) was substantially revised so that divorce not only revokes testamentary devises, but also nonprobate beneficiary designations, in favor of the former spouse. Another feature of the 1990 revisions was a new section (Section 2-503) that brought the execution formalities for wills more into line with those for nonprobate transfers.

2008 Revisions. In 2008, another round of revisions was adopted. The principal features of the 2008 revisions are summarized as follows:

Inflation Adjustments. Between 1990 and 2008, the Consumer Price Index rose by somewhat more than 50 percent. The 2008 revisions raised the dollar amounts by 50 percent in Article II Sections 2-102, 2-

102A, 2-201, 2-402, 2-403, and 2-405, and added a new cost of living adjustment section — Section 1-109.

Intestacy. Part 1 on intestacy was divided into two subparts: Subpart 1 on general rules of intestacy and subpart 2 on parent-child relationships. For details, see the General Comment to Part 1.

Execution of Wills. Section 2-502 was amended to allow notarized wills as an alternative to wills that are attested by two witnesses. That amendment necessitated minor revisions to Section 2-504 on self-proved wills and to Section 3-406 on the effect of notarized wills in contested cases.

Class Gifts. Section 2-705 on class gifts was revised in a variety of ways, as explained in the revised Comment to that section.

Reformation and Modification. New Sections 2-805 and 2-806 brought the reformation and modification sections now contained in the Uniform Trust Code into the Uniform Probate Code.

Historical Note. This Prefatory Note was revised in 2008.

Legislative Note: *References to spouse or marriage appear throughout Article II. States that recognize civil unions, domestic partnerships, or similar relationships between unmarried individuals should add appropriate language wherever such references or similar references appear.*

States that do not recognize such relationships between unmarried individuals, or marriages between same-sex partners, are urged to consider whether to recognize the spousal-type rights that partners acquired under the law of another jurisdiction in which the relationship was formed but who die domiciled in this state. Doing so would not be the equivalent of recognizing such relationships in this state but simply allowing those who move to and die in this state to retain the rights they previously acquired elsewhere. See Christine A. Hammerle, Note, Free Will to Will? A Case for the Recognition of Intestacy Rights for Survivors to a Same-Sex Marriage or Civil Union, 104 Mich. L. Rev. 1763 (2006).

PART 1
INTESTATE SUCCESSION

General Comment

The pre-1990 Code's basic pattern of intestate succession, contained in Part 1, was designed to provide suitable rules for the person of modest means who relies on the estate plan provided by law. The 1990 and 2008 revisions were intended to further that purpose, by fine tuning the various sections and bringing them into line with developing public policy and family relationships.

1990 Revisions. The principal features of the 1990 revisions were:

1. So-called negative wills were authorized, under which the decedent who dies intestate, in whole or in part, can by will disinherit a particular heir.

2. A surviving spouse was granted the whole of the intestate estate, if the decedent left no surviving descendants and no parents or if the decedent's surviving descendants are also descendants of the surviving spouse and the surviving spouse has no descendants who are not descendants of the decedent. The surviving spouse receives the first $200,000 plus three-fourths of the balance if the decedent left no surviving descendants but a surviving parent. The surviving spouse receives the first $150,000 plus one-half of the balance of the intestate estate, if the decedent's surviving descendants are also descendants of the surviving spouse but the surviving spouse has one or more other descendants. The surviving spouse receives the first $100,000 plus one-half of the balance of the intestate estate, if the decedent has one or more surviving descendants who are not descendants of the surviving spouse. (To adjust for inflation, these dollar figures and other dollar figures in Article II were increased by fifty percent in 2008.)

3. A system of representation called per capita at each generation was adopted as a means of more faithfully carrying out the underlying premise of the pre-1990 UPC system of representation. Under the per-capita-at-each-generation system, all grandchildren (whose parent has predeceased the intestate) receive equal shares.

4. Although only a modest revision of the section dealing with the status of adopted children and children born of unmarried parents was then made, the question was under continuing review and it was anticipated that further revisions would be

forthcoming in the future.

5. The section on advancements was revised so that it applies to partially intestate estates as well as to wholly intestate estates.

2008 Revisions. As noted in Item 4 above, it was recognized in 1990 that further revisions on matters of status were needed. The 2008 revisions fulfilled that need. Specifically, the 2008 revisions contained the following principal features:

Part 1 Divided into Two Subparts. Part 1 was divided into two subparts: Subpart 1 on general rules of intestacy and Subpart 2 on parent-child relationships.

Subpart 1: General Rules of Intestacy. Subpart 1 contains Sections 2-101 (unchanged), 2-102 (dollar figures adjusted for inflation), 2-103 (restyled and amended to grant intestacy rights to certain stepchildren as a last resort before the intestate estate escheats to the state), 2-104 (amended to clarify the requirement of survival by 120 hours as it applies to heirs who are born before the intestate's death and those who are in gestation at the intestate's death), 2-105 (unchanged), 2-106 (unchanged), 2-107 (unchanged), 2-108 (deleted and matter dealing with heirs in gestation at the intestate's death relocated to 2-104), 2-109 (unchanged), 2-110 (unchanged), 2-111 (unchanged), 2-112 (unchanged), 2-113 (unchanged), and 2-114 (deleted and replaced with a new section addressing situations in which a parent is barred from inheriting).

Subpart 2: Parent-Child Relationships. New Subpart 2 contains several new or substantially revised sections. New Section 2-115 contains definitions of terms that are used in Subpart 2. New Section 2-116 is an umbrella section declaring that, except as otherwise provided in Section 2-119(b) through (e), if a parent-child relationship exists or is established under this subpart 2, the parent is a parent of the child and the child is a child of the parent for purposes of intestate succession. Section 2-117 continues the rule that,

except as otherwise provided in Sections 2-120 and 2-121, a parent-child relationship exists between a child and the child's genetic parents, regardless of their marital status. Regarding adopted children, Section 2-118 continues the rule that adoption establishes a parent-child relationship between the adoptive parents and the adoptee for purposes of intestacy. Section 2-119 addresses the extent to which an adoption severs the parent-child relationship with the adoptee's genetic parents. New Sections 2-120 and 2-121 turn to various parent-child relationships resulting from assisted reproductive technologies in forming families. As one researcher reported: "Roughly 10 to 15 percent of all adults experience some form of infertility." Debora L. Spar, The Baby Business 31 (2006). Infertility, coupled with the desire of unmarried individuals to have children, have led to increased questions concerning children of assisted reproduction. Sections 2-120 and 2-121 address inheritance rights in cases of children of assisted reproduction, whether the birth mother is the one who parents the child or is a gestational carrier who bears the child for an intended parent or intended parents. As two authors have noted: "Parents, whether they are in a married or unmarried union with another, whether they are a single parent, whether they procreate by sexual intercourse or by assisted reproductive technology, are entitled to the respect the law gives to family choice." Charles P. Kindregan, Jr. & Maureen McBrien, Assisted Reproductive Technology: A Lawyer's Guide to Emerging Law and Science 6-7 (2006). The final section, new Section 2-122, provides that nothing contained in Subpart 2 should be construed as affecting application of the judicial doctrine of equitable adoption.

Historical Note. This General Comment was revised in 2008.

SUBPART 1. GENERAL RULES

§ 2-101. Intestate Estate.

(a) Any part of a decedent's estate not effectively disposed of by will passes by intestate succession to the decedent's heirs as prescribed in this [code], except as modified by the decedent's will.

(b) A decedent by will may expressly exclude or limit the right of an individual or class to succeed to property of the decedent passing by intestate succession. If that individual or a member of that class survives the decedent, the share of the decedent's intestate estate to which that individual or class would have succeeded passes as if that individual or each member of that class had disclaimed his [or her] intestate share.

Comment

Purpose of Revision. The amendments to subsection (a) are stylistic, not substantive.

New subsection (b) authorizes the decedent, by will, to exclude or limit the right of an individual or class to share in the decedent's intestate estate, in effect disinheriting that individual or class. By specifically authorizing so-called negative wills, subsection (b) reverses the usually accepted common-law rule, which defeats a testator's intent for no sufficient reason. See Note, "The Intestate Claims of Heirs Excluded by Will: Should 'Negative Wills' Be Enforced?", 52 U.Chi. L. Rev. 177 (1985).

Whether or not in an individual case the decedent's will has excluded or limited the right of an individual or class to take a share of the decedent's intestate estate is a question of construction. A clear case would be one in which the decedent's will expressly states that an individual is to receive none of the decedent's estate. Examples would be testamentary language such as "my brother, Hector, is not to receive any of my property" or "Brother Hector is disinherited."

Another rather clear case would be one in which the will states that an individual is to receive only a nominal devise, such as "I devise $50.00 to my brother, Hector, and no more."

An individual need not be identified by name to be excluded. Thus, if brother Hector is the decedent's only brother, Hector could be identified by a term such as "my brother." A group or class of relatives (such as "my brothers and sisters") can also be excluded under this provision.

Subsection (b) establishes the consequence of a disinheritance—the share of the decedent's intestate estate to which the disinherited individual or class would have succeeded passes as if that individual or class had disclaimed the intestate share. Thus, if the decedent's will provides that brother Hector is to receive $50.00 and no more, Hector is entitled to the $50.00 devise (because Hector is not treated as having predeceased the decedent for purposes of testate

succession), but the portion of the decedent's intestate estate to which Hector would have succeeded passes as if Hector had disclaimed his intestate share. The consequence of a disclaimer by Hector of his intestate share is governed by Section 2-1106(b)(3)(A), which provides that Hector's intestate share passes to Hector's descendants by representation.

Example: G died partially intestate. G is survived by brother Hector, Hector's 3 children (X, Y, and Z), and the child (V) of a deceased sister. G's will excluded Hector from sharing in G's intestate estate.

Solution: V takes half of G's intestate estate. X, Y, and Z split the other half, i.e., they take 1/6 each. Sections 2-103(3); 2-106; 2-1106(b)(3)(A). Had Hector not been excluded by G's will, the share to which Hector would have succeeded would have been 1/2. Under Section 2-1106(b)(3)(A), that half, not the whole of G's intestate estate, is what passes to Hector's descendants by representation as if Hector had disclaimed his intestate share.

Note that if brother Hector had actually predeceased G, or was treated as if he predeceased G by reason of not surviving G by 120 hours (see Section 2-104), then no consequence flows from Hector's disinheritance: V, X, Y, and Z would each take 1/4 of G's intestate estate under sections 2-103(3) and 2-106.

2002 Amendment Relating to Disclaimers. In 2002, the Code's former disclaimer provision (Section 2-801) was replaced by the Uniform Disclaimer of Property Interests Act, which is incorporated into the Code as Part 11 of Article II (Sections 2-1101 to 2-1117). The statutory references in this Comment to former Section 2-801 have been replaced by appropriate references to Part 11. Updating these statutory references has not changed the substance of this Comment.

Former (Pre-1990) Version

§ 2-101. [Intestate Estate.] Any part of the estate of a decedent not effectively disposed of by his will passes to his heirs as prescribed in the following sections of this Code.

---

§ 2-102. Share of Spouse.

The intestate share of a decedent's surviving spouse is:

    (1) the entire intestate estate if:

        (A) no descendant or parent of the decedent survives the decedent; or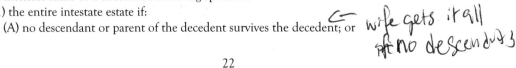

(B) all of the decedent's surviving descendants are also descendants of the surviving spouse and there is no other descendant of the surviving spouse who survives the decedent;

(2) the first [$300,000], plus three-fourths of any balance of the intestate estate, if no descendant of the decedent survives the decedent, but a parent of the decedent survives the decedent;

(3) the first [$225,000], plus one-half of any balance of the intestate estate, if all of the decedent's surviving descendants are also descendants of the surviving spouse and the surviving spouse has one or more surviving descendants who are not descendants of the decedent;

(4) the first [$150,000], plus one-half of any balance of the intestate estate, if one or more of the decedent's surviving descendants are not descendants of the surviving spouse.

Comment

Purpose and Scope of 1990 Revisions. This section was revised in 1990 to give the surviving spouse a larger share than the pre-1990 UPC. If the decedent leaves no surviving descendants and no surviving parent or if the decedent does leave surviving descendants but neither the decedent nor the surviving spouse has other descendants, the surviving spouse is entitled to all of the decedent's intestate estate.

If the decedent leaves no surviving descendants but does leave a surviving parent, the decedent's surviving spouse receives the first $300,000 plus three-fourths of the balance of the intestate estate.

If the decedent leaves surviving descendants and if the surviving spouse (but not the decedent) has other descendants, and thus the decedent's descendants are unlikely to be the exclusive beneficiaries of the surviving spouse's estate, the surviving spouse receives the first $225,000 plus one-half of the balance of the intestate estate. The purpose is to assure the decedent's own descendants of a share in the decedent's intestate estate when the estate exceeds $225,000.

If the decedent has other descendants, the surviving spouse receives $150,000 plus one-half of the balance. In this type of case, the decedent's descendants who are not descendants of the surviving spouse are not natural objects of the bounty of the surviving spouse.

Note that in all the cases where the surviving spouse receives a lump sum plus a fraction of the balance, the lump sums must be understood to be in addition to the probate exemptions and allowances to which the surviving spouse is entitled under Part 4. These can add up to a minimum of $64,500.

Under the pre-1990 Code, the decedent's surviving spouse received the entire intestate estate only if there were neither surviving descendants nor parents. If there were surviving descendants, the descendants to one-half of the balance of the estate in excess of $50,000 (for example, $25,000 in a $100,000 estate). If there were no surviving descendants, but there was a surviving parent or parents, the parent or parents took that one-half of the balance in excess of $50,000.

2008 Cost-of-Living Adjustments. As revised in 1990, the dollar amount in paragraph (2) was $200,000, in paragraph (3) was $150,000, and in paragraph (4) was $100,000. To adjust for inflation, these amounts were increased in 2008 to $300,000, $225,000, and $150,000 respectively. The dollar amounts in these paragraphs are subject to annual cost-of-living adjustments under Section 1-109.

References. The theory of this section is discussed in Waggoner, "The Multiple- Marriage Society and Spousal Rights Under the Revised Uniform Probate Code", 76 Iowa L. Rev. 223, 229-35 (1991).

Empirical studies support the increase in the surviving spouse's intestate share, reflected in the revisions of this section. The studies have shown that testators in smaller estates (which intestate estates overwhelmingly tend to be) tend to devise their entire estates to their surviving spouses, even when the couple has children. See C. Shammas, M. Salmon & M. Bahlin, Inheritance in America from Colonial Times to the Present 184-85 (1987); M. Sussman, J. Cates & D. Smith, The Family and Inheritance (1970); Browder, "Recent Patterns of Testate Succession in the United States and England", 67 Mich. L. Rev. 1303, 1307-08 (1969); Dunham, "The Method, Process and Frequency of Wealth Transmission at Death", 30 U. Chi. L. Rev. 241, 252 (1963); Gibson, "Inheritance of Community Property in Texas—A Need for Reform", 47 Texas L. Rev. 359, 364-66 (1969); Price, "The Transmission of Wealth at Death in a Community Property Jurisdiction", 50 Wash. L. Rev. 277, 283, 311-17 (1975). See also Fellows, Simon & Rau, "Public Attitudes About Property Distribution at Death and Intestate Succession Laws in the United States", 1978 Am. B. F. Research J. 319, 355-68; Note, "A Comparison of

Iowans' Dispositive Preferences with Selected Provisions of the Iowa and Uniform Probate Codes", 63 Iowa L. Rev. 1041, 1091-92 (1978).

Cross Reference. See Section 2-802 for the

definition of spouse, which controls for purposes of intestate succession.

Historical Note. This Comment was revised in 2008.

Former (1990) Version

§ 2-102. Share of Spouse.

The intestate share of a decedent's surviving spouse is:

(1) the entire intestate estate if:

(A) no descendant or parent of the decedent survives the decedent; or

(B) all of the decedent's surviving descendants are also descendants of the surviving spouse and there is no other descendant of the surviving spouse who survives the decedent;

(2) the first [$200,000], plus three-fourths of any balance of the intestate estate, if no descendant of the decedent survives the decedent, but a parent of the decedent survives the decedent;

(3) the first [$150,000], plus one-half of any balance of the intestate estate, if all of the decedent's surviving descendants are also descendants of the surviving spouse and the surviving spouse has one or more surviving descendants who are not descendants of the decedent;

(4) the first [$100,000], plus one-half of any balance of the intestate estate, if one or more of the decedent's surviving descendants are not descendants of the surviving spouse.

Former (Pre-1990) Version

§ 2-102. [Share of the Spouse].

The intestate share of the surviving spouse is:

(1) if there is no surviving issue or parent of the decedent, the entire intestate estate;

(2) if there is no surviving issue but the decedent is survived by a parent or parents, the first [$50,000], plus one-half of the balance of the intestate estate;

(3) if there are surviving issue all of whom are issue of the surviving spouse also, the first [$50,000], plus one-half of the balance of the intestate estate;

(4) if there are surviving issue one or more of whom are not issue of the surviving spouse, one-half of the intestate estate.

Restatement (Third) of Property: Wills and Other Donative Transfers (1999)

§ 2.5, Comment g. Domestic partner. A developing question is the right of the domestic partner of an unmarried intestate decedent to be treated as a surviving spouse for purposes of intestacy or otherwise to be entitled to an intestate share. A few states have, by statute, granted intestacy rights to the surviving domestic partner of an unmarried decedent dying intestate, but the statutes differ in detail and in whether they extend rights only to partners of the same sex or only to partners of the opposite sex....

As of the date of publication of this volume of the Restatement, the American Law Institute has not taken a position on the status of a domestic partner. The question may come before the Institute in a future draft of the Principles of the Law of Family Dissolution: Analysis and Recommendations. To the extent that a domestic partner is treated as having the status of a spouse, conferring rights on such a partner on the dissolution of the relationship, the domestic partner who remains in that relationship with the decedent until the decedent's death should be treated as a legal spouse for purposes of intestacy.

[Editor's Note: In 2000, the American Law Institute approved a provision of the Principles of the Law of Family Dissolution treating a domestic partner, as defined in § 6.03 of that project, as a spouse for purposes of dissolution of the relationship.]

[ALTERNATIVE PROVISION FOR COMMUNITY PROPERTY STATES]

[§ 2-102A. Share of Spouse.

(a) The intestate share of a decedent's surviving spouse in separate property is:

(1) the entire intestate estate if:

(A) no descendant or parent of the decedent survives the decedent; or

(B) all of the decedent's surviving descendants are also descendants of the surviving spouse and there is no other descendant of the surviving spouse who survives the decedent;

(2) the first [$300,000], plus three-fourths of any balance of the intestate estate, if no descendant of the decedent survives the decedent, but a parent of the decedent survives the decedent;

(3) the first [$225,000], plus one-half of any balance of the intestate estate, if all of the decedent's surviving descendants are also descendants of the surviving spouse and the surviving spouse has one or more surviving descendants who are not descendants of the decedent;

(4) the first [$150,000], plus one-half of any balance of the intestate estate, if one or more of the decedent's surviving descendants are not descendants of the surviving spouse.

(b) The one-half of community property belonging to the decedent passes to the [surviving spouse] as the intestate share.]

Comment

The brackets around the term "surviving spouse" in subsection (b) indicate that states are free to adopt a different scheme for the distribution of the decedent's half of the community property, as some community property states have done.

2008 Cost-of-Living Adjustments. As revised in 1990, the dollar amount in subsection (a)(2) was $200,000, in (a)(3) was $150,000, and in (a)(4) was $100,000. To adjust for inflation, these amounts were increased in 2008 to $300,000, $225,000, and $150,000 respectively. The dollar amounts in these paragraphs are subject to annual cost-of-living adjustments under Section 1-109.

Historical Note. This Comment was revised in 2008.

§ 2-103. Share of Heirs other than Surviving Spouse.

(a) Any part of the intestate estate not passing to a decedent's surviving spouse under Section 2-102, or the entire intestate estate if there is no surviving spouse, passes in the following order to the individuals who survive the decedent:

(1) to the decedent's descendants by representation;   *Kids*

(2) if there is no surviving descendant, to the decedent's parents equally if both survive, or to the surviving parent if only one survives;   *Parents*

(3) if there is no surviving descendant or parent, to the descendants of the decedent's parents or either of them by representation;   *Siblings*

(4) if there is no surviving descendant, parent, or descendant of a parent, but the decedent is survived on both the paternal and maternal sides by one or more grandparents or descendants of grandparents: *Grandparents or grandparent kids*

(A) half to the decedent's paternal grandparents equally if both survive, to the surviving paternal grandparent if only one survives, or to the descendants of the decedent's paternal grandparents or either of them if both are deceased, the descendants taking by representation; and

(B) half to the decedent's maternal grandparents equally if both survive, to the surviving maternal grandparent if only one survives, or to the descendants of the decedent's maternal grandparents or either of them if both are deceased, the descendants taking by representation;

(5) if there is no surviving descendant, parent, or descendant of a parent, but the decedent is survived by one or more grandparents or descendants of grandparents on the paternal but not the maternal side, or on the maternal but not the paternal side, to the decedent's relatives on the side with

one or more surviving members in the manner described in paragraph (4).

(b) If there is no taker under subsection (a), but the decedent has: *surviving step children*

(1) one deceased spouse who has one or more descendants who survive the decedent, the estate or part thereof passes to that spouse's descendants by representation; or

(2) more than one deceased spouse who has one or more descendants who survive the decedent, an equal share of the estate or part thereof passes to each set of descendants by representation.

descendants of step children

Comment

This section provides for inheritance by descendants of the decedent, parents and their descendants, and grandparents and collateral relatives descended from grandparents; in line with modern policy, it eliminates more remote relatives tracing through great-grandparents.

1990 Revisions. The 1990 revisions were stylistic and clarifying, not substantive. The pre-1990 version of this section contained the phrase "if they are all of the same degree of kinship to the decedent they take equally (etc.)." That language was removed. It was unnecessary and confusing because the system of representation in Section 2-106 gives equal shares if the decedent's descendants are all of the same degree of kinship to the decedent.

The word "descendants" replaced the word "issue"

in this section and throughout the 1990 revisions of Article II. The term issue is a term of art having a biological connotation. Now that inheritance rights, in certain cases, are extended to adopted children, the term descendants is a more appropriate term.

2008 Revisions. In addition to making a few stylistic changes, which were not intended to change meaning, the 2008 revisions divided this section into two subsections. New subsection (b) grants inheritance rights to descendants of the intestate's deceased spouse(s) who are not also descendants of the intestate. The term deceased spouse refers to an individual to whom the intestate was married at the individual's death.

Historical Note. This Comment was revised in 2008.

Former (Pre-1990) Version

§ 2-103. [Shares of Heirs Other Than Surviving Spouse.] The part of the intestate estate not passing to the surviving spouse under Section 2-102, or the entire intestate estate if there is no surviving spouse, passes as follows:

(1) to the issue of the decedent; if they are all of the same degree of kinship to the decedent they take equally, but if of unequal degree, then those of more remote degree take by representation;

(2) if there is no surviving issue, to his parent or parents equally;

(3) if there is no surviving issue or parent, to the issue of the parents or either of them by representation;

(4) if there is no surviving issue, parent or issue of a parent, but the decedent is survived by one or more grandparents or issue of grandparents, half of the estate passes to the paternal grandparents if both survive, or to the surviving paternal grandparent, or to the issue of the paternal grandparents if both are deceased, the issue taking equally if they are all of the same degree of kinship to the decedent, but if of unequal degree those of more remote degree take by representation; and the other half passes to the maternal relatives in the same manner; but if there be no surviving grandparent or issue of grandparent on either the paternal or the maternal side, the entire estate passes to the relatives on the other side in the same manner as the half.

---

 120 hours

§ 2-104. Requirement of Survival by 120 Hours; Individual in Gestation.

(a) **[Requirement of Survival by 120 Hours; Individual in Gestation.]** For purposes of intestate succession, homestead allowance, and exempt property, and except as otherwise provided in subsection (b), the following rules apply:

(1) An individual born before a decedent's death who fails to survive the decedent by 120 hours is deemed to have predeceased the decedent. If it is not established by clear and convincing evidence that an individual born before the decedent's death survived the decedent by 120 hours, it is deemed

that the individual failed to survive for the required period.

(2) An individual in gestation at a decedent's death is deemed to be living at the decedent's death if the individual lives 120 hours after birth. If it is not established by clear and convincing evidence that an individual in gestation at the decedent's death lived 120 hours after birth, it is deemed that the individual failed to survive for the required period.

(b) [Section Inapplicable if Estate Would Pass to State.] This section does not apply if its application would cause the estate to pass to the state under Section 2-105.

Comment

This section avoids multiple administrations and in some instances prevents the property from passing to persons not desired by the decedent. See Halbach &Waggoner, The UPC's New Survivorship and Antilapse Provisions, 55 Alb. L. Rev. 1091, 1094-1099 (1992). The 120-hour period will not delay the administration of a decedent's estate because Sections 3-302 and 3-307 prevent informal issuance of letters for a period of five days from death. Subsection (b) prevents the survivorship requirement from defeating inheritance by the last eligible relative of the intestate who survives for any period.

In the case of a surviving spouse who survives the 120-hour period, the 120-hour requirement of survivorship does not disqualify the spouse's intestate share for the federal estate-tax marital deduction. See Int.Rev.Code § 2056(b)(3).

2008 Revisions. In 2008, this section was reorganized, revised, and combined with former Section 2-108. What was contained in former Section 2-104 now appears as subsections (a)(1) and (b). What was contained in former Section 2-108 now appears as subsection (a)(2). Subsections (a)(1) and (a)(2) now distinguish between an individual who was born before the decedent's death and an individual who was in gestation at the decedent's death. With respect to an individual who was born before the decedent's death, it must be established by clear and convincing evidence that the individual survived the decedent by 120 hours. For a comparable provision applicable to wills and other governing instruments, see Section 2-702. With respect to an individual who was in gestation at the decedent's death, it must be established by clear and convincing evidence that the individual lived for 120 hours after birth. For a comparable provision applicable to wills and other governing instruments, see Section 2-705(g).

Historical Note. This Comment was revised in 2008.

Former (1990) Version

§ 2-104. Requirement that Heir Survive Decedent for 120 Hours. An individual who fails to survive the decedent by 120 hours is deemed to have predeceased the decedent for purposes of homestead allowance, exempt property, and intestate succession, and the decedent's heirs are determined accordingly. If it is not established by clear and convincing evidence that an individual who would otherwise be an heir survived the decedent by 120 hours, it is deemed that the individual failed to survive for the required period. This section is not to be applied if its application would result in a taking of intestate estate by the state under Section 2-105.

§ 2-108. Afterborn Heirs. An individual in gestation at a particular time is treated as living at that time if the individual lives 120 hours or more after birth.

§ 2-105. No Taker. If there is no taker under the provisions of this [article], the intestate estate passes to the state.

§ 2-106. Representation.

(a) **[Definitions.]** In this section:

(1) "Deceased descendant", "deceased parent", or "deceased grandparent" means a descendant, parent, or grandparent who either predeceased the decedent or is deemed to have predeceased the decedent under Section 2-104.

(2) "Surviving descendant" means a descendant who neither predeceased the decedent nor is

Equally near, Equally dear
- any remaining share is divided by descendants who's parents did not take! See Next page for Example →

deemed to have predeceased the decedent under Section 2-104.

(b) [Decedent's Descendants.] If, under Section 2-103(a)(1), a decedent's intestate estate or a part thereof passes "by representation" to the decedent's descendants, the estate or part thereof is divided into as many equal shares as there are (i) surviving descendants in the generation nearest to the decedent which contains one or more surviving descendants and (ii) deceased descendants in the same generation who left surviving descendants, if any. Each surviving descendant in the nearest generation is allocated one share. The remaining shares, if any, are combined and then divided in the same manner among the surviving descendants of the deceased descendants as if the surviving descendants who were allocated a share and their surviving descendants had predeceased the decedent.

[handwritten margin note: Change from previous manner]

(c) [Descendants of Parents or Grandparents.] If, under Section 2-103(a)(3) or (4), a decedent's intestate estate or a part thereof passes "by representation" to the descendants of the decedent's deceased parents or either of them or to the descendants of the decedent's deceased paternal or maternal grandparents or either of them, the estate or part thereof is divided into as many equal shares as there are (i) surviving descendants in the generation nearest the deceased parents or either of them, or the deceased grandparents or either of them, that contains one or more surviving descendants and (ii) deceased descendants in the same generation who left surviving descendants, if any. Each surviving descendant in the nearest generation is allocated one share. The remaining shares, if any, are combined and then divided in the same manner among the surviving descendants of the deceased descendants as if the surviving descendants who were allocated a share and their surviving descendants had predeceased the decedent.

Comment

Purpose and Scope of Revisions. This section is revised to adopt the system of representation called per capita at each generation. The per-capita-at-each-generation system is more responsive to the underlying premise of the original UPC system, in that it always provides equal shares to those equally related; the pre-1990 UPC achieved this objective in most but not all cases. (See Variation 4, below, for an illustration of this point.) In addition, a recent survey of client preferences, conducted by Fellows of the American College of Trust and Estate Counsel, suggests that the per-capita-at-each-generation system of representation is preferred by most clients. See Young, "Meaning of 'Issue' and 'Descendants,'" 13 ACTEC Probate Notes 225 (1988). The survey results were striking: Of 761 responses, 541 (71.1%) chose the per-capita-at-each-generation system; 145 (19.1%) chose the per-stirpes system, and 70 (9.2%) chose the pre-1990 UPC system.

To illustrate the differences among the three systems, consider a family, in which G is the intestate. G has 3 children, A, B, and C. Child A has 3 children, U, V, and W. Child B has 1 child, X. Child C has 2 children, Y and Z. Consider four variations.

Variation 1: All three children survive G.

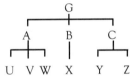

Solution: All three systems reach the same result: A, B, and C take 1/3 each.

Variation 2: One child, A, predeceases G; the other two survive G.

[handwritten margin note: Split 1/3 share]

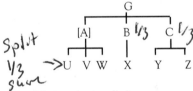

Solution: Again, all three systems reach the same result: B and C take 1/3 each; U, V, and W take 1/9 each.

Variation 3: All three children predecease G.

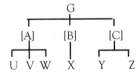

Solution: The pre-1990 UPC and the 1990 UPC systems reach the same result: U, V, W, X, Y, and Z take 1/6 each.

The per-stirpes system gives a different result: U, V, and W take 1/9 each; X takes 1/3 ; and Y and Z take 1/6 each.

Variation 4: Two of the three children, A and B, predecease G; C survives G.

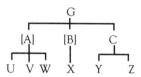

Solution: In this instance, the 1990 UPC system (per capita at each generation) departs from the pre-1990 UPC system. Under the 1990 UPC system, C takes 1/3 and the other two 1/3 shares are combined into a single share (amounting to 2/3 of the estate) and distributed as if C, Y and Z had predeceased G; the result is that U, V, W, and X take 1/6 each.

Although the pre-1990 UPC rejected the per-stirpes system, the result reached under the pre-1990 UPC was aligned with the per-stirpes system in this instance: C would have taken 1/3, X would have taken 1/3, and U, V, and W would have taken 1/9 each.

The 1990 UPC system furthers the purpose of the pre-1990 UPC. The pre-1990 UPC system was premised on a desire to provide equality among those equally related. The pre-1990 UPC system failed to achieve that objective in this instance. The 1990 system (per-capita-at-each-generation) remedies that defect in the pre-1990 system.

Reference. Waggoner, "A Proposed Alternative to the Uniform Probate Code's System for Intestate Distribution among Descendants", 66 Nw.U.L. Rev. 626 (1971).

Effect of Disclaimer. By virtue of Section 2-1106(b)(3)(A), an heir cannot use a disclaimer to effect a change in the division of an intestate's estate.

To illustrate this point, consider the following example:

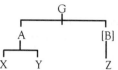

As it stands, G's intestate estate is divided into two equal parts: A takes half and B's child, Z, takes the other half. Suppose, however, that A files a disclaimer under Section 2-1105. A cannot affect the basic division of G's intestate estate by this maneuver. Section 2-1106(b)(3)(A) provides that "the disclaimed interest passes as if the disclaimant had died immediately before the time of distribution [except that] if, by law ..., the descendants of the disclaimant would share in the disclaimed interest by any method of representation had the disclaimant died before the time of distribution, the disclaimed interest passes only to the descendants of the disclaimant who survive the time of distribution." In this example, the "disclaimed interest" is A's share (1/2) of G's estate; thus the 1/2 interest renounced by A devolves to A's children, X and Y, who take 1/4 each.

If Section 2-1106(b)(3)(A) had provided that G's "estate" is to be divided as if A predeceased G, A could have used his disclaimer to increase the share going to his children from 1/2 to 2/3 (1/3 for each child) and to decrease Z's share to 1/3. The careful wording of Section 2-1106(b)(3)(A), however, prevents A from manipulating the result by this method.

2002 Amendment Relating to Disclaimers. In 2002, the Code's former disclaimer provision (Section 2-801) was replaced by the Uniform Disclaimer of Property Interests Act, which is incorporated into the Code as Part 11 of Article 2 (Sections 2-1101 to 2-1117). The statutory references in this Comment to former Section 2-801 have been replaced by appropriate references to Part 11. Updating these statutory references has not changed the substance of this Comment.

Former (Pre-1990) Version

§ 2-106. [Representation.] If representation is called for by this Code, the estate is divided into as many shares as there are surviving heirs in the nearest degree of kinship and deceased persons in the same degree who left issue who survive the decedent, each surviving heir in the nearest degree receiving one share and the share of each deceased person in the same degree being divided among his issue in the same manner.

---

§ 2-107. Kindred of Half Blood. Relatives of the half blood inherit the same share they would inherit if they were of the whole blood.

§ 2-108. [Reserved.]

§ 2-109. Advancements.

(a) If an individual dies intestate as to all or a portion of his [or her] estate, property the decedent gave during the decedent's lifetime to an individual who, at the decedent's death, is an heir is treated as an advancement against the heir's intestate share only if (i) the decedent declared in a contemporaneous writing or the heir acknowledged in writing that the gift is an advancement or (ii) the decedent's contemporaneous writing or the heir's written acknowledgment otherwise indicates that the gift is to be taken into account in computing the division and distribution of the decedent's intestate estate.

(b) For purposes of subsection (a), property advanced is valued as of the time the heir came into possession or enjoyment of the property or as of the time of the decedent's death, whichever first occurs.

(c) If the recipient of the property fails to survive the decedent, the property is not taken into account in computing the division and distribution of the decedent's intestate estate, unless the decedent's contemporaneous writing provides otherwise.

(Handwritten margin note: If advance must be in writing saying so otherwise its a gift presumed)

Comment

Purpose of the 1990 Revisions. This section was revised so that an advancement can be taken into account with respect to the intestate portion of a partially intestate estate.

Other than these revisions, and a few stylistic and clarifying amendments, the original content of the section is maintained, under which the common law relating to advancements is altered by requiring written evidence of the intent that an inter-vivos gift be an advancement.

The statute is phrased in terms of the donee being an heir "at the decedent's death." The donee need not be a prospective heir at the time of the gift. For example, if the intestate, G, made an inter-vivos gift intended to be an advancement to a grandchild at a time when the intestate's child who is the grandchild's parent is alive, the grandchild would not then be a prospective heir. Nevertheless, if G's intent that the gift be an advancement is contained in a written declaration or acknowledgment as provided in subsection (a), the gift is regarded as an advancement if G's child (who is the grandchild's parent) predeceases G, making the grandchild an heir.

To be an advancement, the gift need not be an outright gift; it can be in the form of a will substitute, such as designating the donee as the beneficiary of the intestate's life-insurance policy or the beneficiary of the remainder interest in a revocable inter-vivos trust.

Most inter-vivos transfers today are intended to be absolute gifts or are carefully integrated into a total estate plan. If the donor intends that any transfer during the donor's lifetime be deducted from the donee's share of the donor's estate, the donor may either execute a will so providing or, if he or she intends to die intestate, charge the gift as an advance by a writing within the present section.

This section applies to advances to the decedent's spouse and collaterals (such as nephews and nieces) as well as to descendants.

Computation of Shares—Hotchpot Method. This section does not specify the method of taking an advancement into account in distributing the decedent's intestate estate. That process, called the hotchpot method, is provided by the common law. The hotchpot method is illustrated by the following example.

Example: G died intestate, survived by his wife (W) and his three children (A, B, and C) by a prior marriage. G's probate estate is valued at $190,000. During his lifetime, G had advanced A $50,000 and B $10,000. G memorialized both gifts in a writing declaring his intent that they be advancements.

Solution. The first step in the hotchpot method is to add the value of the advancements to the value of G's probate estate. This combined figure is called the hotchpot estate.

In this case, G's hotchpot estate preliminarily comes to $250,000 ($190,000 + $50,000 + $10,000). W's intestate share of a $250,000 estate under Section 2-102(4) is $200,000 ($150,000 + 1/2 of $100,000). The remaining $50,000 is divided equally among A, B, and C, or $16,667 each. This calculation reveals that A has received an advancement greater than the share to which he is entitled; A can retain the $50,000 advancement, but is not entitled to any additional amount. A and A's $50,000 advancement are therefore disregarded and the process is begun over.

Once A and A's $50,000 advancement are disregarded, G's revised hotchpot estate is $200,000 ($190,000 + $10,000). W's intestate share is $175,000 ($150,000 + 1/2 of $50,000). The remaining $25,000 is divided equally between B and C, or $12,500 each. From G's intestate estate, B receives $2,500 (B already having received $10,000 of his ultimate $12,500 share as an advancement); and C receives $12,500. The final division of G's probate estate is $175,000 to W, zero to A, $2,500 to B, and $12,500 to C.

Effect if Advancee Predeceases the Decedent; Disclaimer. If a decedent had made an advancement to a person who predeceased the decedent, the last sentence of Section 2-109 provides that the advancement is not taken into account in computing the intestate share of the recipient's descendants (unless the decedent's declaration provides otherwise). The rationale is that there is no guarantee that the recipient's descendants received the advanced property or its value from the recipient's estate.

To illustrate the application of the last sentence of Section 2-109, consider this case: During her lifetime, G had advanced $10,000 to her son, A. G died intestate, leaving a probate estate of $50,000. G was survived by her daughter, B, and by A's child, X. A predeceased G.

G's advancement to A is disregarded. G's $50,000 intestate estate is divided into two equal shares, half ($25,000) going to B and the other half ($25,000) going to A's child, X.

Now, suppose that A survived G. In this situation, of course, the advancement to A is taken into account

in the division of G's intestate estate. Under the hotchpot method, illustrated above, G's hotchpot estate is $60,000 (probate estate of $50,000 plus advancement to A of $10,000). A takes half of this $60,000 amount, or $30,000, but is charged with already having received $10,000 of it. Consequently, A takes only a 2/5 share ($20,000) of G's intestate estate, and B takes the remaining 3/5 share ($30,000).

Note that A cannot use a disclaimer under Section 2-1105 in effect to give his child, X, a larger share than A was entitled to. Under Section 2-1106(b)(3)(A), the effect of a disclaimer by A is that the disclaimant's "interest" devolves to A's descendants as if the disclaimant had predeceased the decedent. The "interest" that A renounced was a right to a 2/5 share of G's estate, not a 1/2 share. Consequently, A's 2/5 share ($20,000) passes to A's child, X.

2002 Amendment Relating to Disclaimers. In 2002, the Code's former disclaimer provision (Section 2-801) was replaced by the Uniform Disclaimer of Property Interests Act, which is incorporated into the Code as Part 11 of Article 2 (Sections 2-1101 to 2-1117). The statutory references in this Comment to former Section 2-801 have been replaced by appropriate references to Part 11. Updating these statutory references has not changed the substance of this Comment.

2008 Cost-of-Living Adjustment. As revised in 1990, the dollar amount in Section 2-102(4) was $100,000. To adjust for inflation, that amount was increased in 2008 to $150,000. The Example in this Comment was revised in 2008 to reflect that increase.

Historical Note. This Comment was revised in 2002 and 2008.

Former (Pre-1990) Version

§ 2-110. [Advancements.] If a person dies intestate as to all his estate, property which he gave in his lifetime to an heir is treated as an advancement against the latter's share of the estate only if declared in a contemporaneous writing by the decedent or acknowledged in writing by the heir to be an advancement. For this purpose the property advanced is valued as of the time the heir came into possession or enjoyment of the property or as of the time of death of the decedent, whichever first occurs. If the recipient of the property fails to survive the decedent, the property is not taken into account in computing the intestate share to be received by the recipient's issue, unless the declaration or acknowledgment provides otherwise.

---

§ 2-110. Debts to Decedent. A debt owed to a decedent is not charged against the intestate share of any individual except the debtor. If the debtor fails to survive the decedent, the debt is not taken into account in computing the intestate share of the debtor's descendants.

Comment

Section 2-110 supplements Section 3-903, Right of Retainer.

Effect of Disclaimer. Section 2-1106(b)(3)(A) prevents a living debtor from using the combined effects of the last sentence of Section 2-110 and a disclaimer to avoid a setoff. Although Section 2-110 provides that, if the debtor actually fails to survive the decedent, the debt is not taken into account in computing the intestate share of the debtor's descendants, the same result is not produced when a living debtor disclaims. Section 2-1106(b)(3)(A) provides that the "interest" disclaimed, not the decedent's estate as a whole, devolves as though the disclaimant predeceased the decedent. The "interest"

disclaimed by a living debtor is the share the debtor would have taken had he or she not disclaimed his or her intestate share minus the debt.

2002 Amendment Relating to Disclaimers. In 2002, the Code's former disclaimer provision (Section 2-801) was replaced by the Uniform Disclaimer of Property Interests Act, which is incorporated into the Code as Part 11 of Article 2 (Sections 2-1101 to 2-1117). The statutory references in this Comment to former Section 2-801 have been replaced by appropriate references to Part 11. Updating these statutory references has not changed the substance of this Comment.

§ 2-111. Alienage.

§ 2-111. Alienage. No individual is disqualified to take as an heir because the individual or an individual through whom he [or she] claims is or has been an alien.

Comment

This section eliminates the ancient rule that an alien cannot acquire or transmit land by descent, a rule based on the feudal notions of the obligations of the tenant to the king. Although there never was a

corresponding rule as to personalty, the present section is phrased in light of the basic premise of the Code that distinctions between real and personal property should be abolished.

[§ 2-112. Dower and Curtesy Abolished.

[§ 2-112. Dower and Curtesy Abolished. The estates of dower and curtesy are abolished.]

Comment

The provisions of this Code replace the common-law concepts of dower and curtesy and their statutory counterparts. Those estates provided both a share in intestacy and a protection against disinheritance.

In states that have previously abolished dower and curtesy, or where those estates have never existed, the above section should be omitted.

§ 2-113. Individuals Related to Decedent Through Two Lines.

§ 2-113. Individuals Related to Decedent Through Two Lines. An individual who is related to the decedent through two lines of relationship is entitled to only a single share based on the relationship that would entitle the individual to the larger share.

Comment

This section prevents double inheritance. It has potential application in a case in which a deceased person's brother or sister marries the spouse of the decedent and adopts a child of the former marriage; if the adopting parent died thereafter leaving the

child as a natural and adopted grandchild of its grandparents, this section prevents the child from taking as an heir from the grandparents in both capacities.

§ 2-114. Parent Barred from Inheriting in Certain Circumstances.

§ 2-114. Parent Barred from Inheriting in Certain Circumstances.

(a) A parent is barred from inheriting from or through a child of the parent if:

(1) the parent's parental rights were terminated and the parent-child relationship was not judicially reestablished; or

(2) the child died before reaching [18] years of age and there is clear and convincing evidence that immediately before the child's death the parental rights of the parent could have been terminated

under law of this state other than this [code] on the basis of nonsupport, abandonment, abuse, neglect, or other actions or inactions of the parent toward the child.

(b) For the purpose of intestate succession from or through the deceased child, a parent who is barred from inheriting under this section is treated as if the parent predeceased the child.

Comment

2008 Revisions. In 2008, this section replaced former Section 2-114(c), which provided: "(c) Inheritance from or through a child by either natural parent or his [or her] kindred is precluded unless that natural parent has openly treated the child as his [or hers], and has not refused to support the child."

Subsection (a)(1) recognizes that a parent whose parental rights have been terminated is no longer legally a parent.

Subsection (a)(2) addresses a situation in which a parent's parental rights were not actually terminated. Nevertheless, a parent can still be barred from inheriting from or through a child if the child died before reaching [18] years of age and there is clear and convincing evidence that immediately before the child's death the parental rights of the parent could have been terminated under law of this state other than this [code], but only if those parental rights could have been terminated on the basis of nonsupport, abandonment, abuse, neglect, or other actions or inactions of the parent toward the child.

Statutes providing the grounds for termination of parental rights include: Ariz. Rev. Stat. Ann. § 8-533; Conn. Gen. Stat. § 45a-717; Del. Code Ann. tit. 13 § 1103; Fla. Stat. Ann. § 39.806; Iowa Code § 600A.8; Kan. Stat. Ann. § 38-2269; Mich. Comp. L. Ann. § 712A.19b; Minn. Stat. Ann. § 260C.301; Miss. Code Ann. § 93-15-103; Mo. Rev. Stat. § 211.447; Tex. Fam. Code §§ 161.001 to .007.

Former (1990) Version

§ 2-114. Parent and Child Relationship.

   * * * *

(c) Inheritance from or through a child by either natural parent or his [or her] kindred is precluded unless that natural parent has openly treated the child as his [or hers], and has not refused to support the child.

Former (Pre-1990) Version

§ 2-109. [Meaning of Child and Related Terms.] If, for purposes of intestate succession, a relationship of parent and child must be established to determine succession by, through, or from a person,

   * * * *

(2) * * * * a person is the child of its parents regardless of the marital status of its parents and the parent and child relationship may be established under the [Uniform Parentage Act].

   Alternative subsection (2) for states that have not adopted the Uniform Parentage Act.

[(2) * * * * a person born out of wedlock is a child of the mother. That person is also a child of the father, if:

   (i) the natural parents participated in a marriage ceremony before or after the birth of the child, even though the attempted marriage is void; or

   (ii) the paternity is established by an adjudication before the death of the father or is established thereafter by clear and convincing proof, but the paternity established under this subparagraph is ineffective to qualify the father or his kindred to inherit from or through the child unless the father has openly treated the child as his, and has not refused to support the child.]

Restatement (Third) of Property: Wills and Other Donative Transfers (1999)

§ 2.5 Parent and Child Relationship. For purposes of intestate succession by, from, or through an individual:

(1) An individual is the child of his or her genetic parents, whether or not they are married to each other, except as otherwise provided in paragraph (2) or (5) or as other facts and circumstances warrant a different result.

(2) An adopted individual is a child of his or her adoptive parent or parents.

   (A) If the adoption removes the child from the families of both of the genetic parents, the child is not a

---

child of either genetic parent.

(B) If the adoption is by a relative of either genetic parent, or by the spouse or surviving spouse of such a relative, the individual remains a child of both genetic parents.

(C) If the adoption is by a stepparent, the adopted stepchild is not only a child of the adoptive stepparent but is also a child of the genetic parent who is married to the stepparent. Under several intestacy statutes, including the Uniform Probate Code, the adopted stepchild is also a child of the other genetic parent for purposes of inheritance from and through that parent, but not for purposes of inheritance from or through the child.

(3) A stepchild who is not adopted by his or her stepparent is not the stepparent's child.

(4) A foster child is not a child of his or her foster parent or parents.

(5) A parent who has refused to acknowledge or has abandoned his or her child, or a person whose parental rights have been terminated, is barred from inheriting from or through the child.

SUBPART 2. PARENT-CHILD RELATIONSHIP

§ 2-115. Definitions. In this [subpart]:

(1) "Adoptee" means an individual who is adopted.

(2) "Assisted reproduction" means a method of causing pregnancy other than sexual intercourse.

(3) "Divorce" includes an annulment, dissolution, and declaration of invalidity of a marriage.

(4) "Functioned as a parent of the child" means behaving toward a child in a manner consistent with being the child's parent and performing functions that are customarily performed by a parent, including fulfilling parental responsibilities toward the child, recognizing or holding out the child as the individual's child, materially participating in the child's upbringing, and residing with the child in the same household as a regular member of that household.

(5) "Genetic father" means the man whose sperm fertilized the egg of a child's genetic mother. If the father-child relationship is established under the presumption of paternity under [insert applicable state law], the term means only the man for whom that relationship is established.

(6) "Genetic mother" means the woman whose egg was fertilized by the sperm of a child's genetic father.

(7) "Genetic parent" means a child's genetic father or genetic mother.

(8) "Incapacity" means the inability of an individual to function as a parent of a child because of the individual's physical or mental condition.

(9) "Relative" means a grandparent or a descendant of a grandparent.

Legislative Note: States that have enacted the Uniform Parentage Act (2000, as amended) should replace "applicable state law" in paragraph (5) with "Section 201(b)(1), (2), or (3) of the Uniform Parentage Act (2000), as amended". Two of the principal features of Articles 1 through 6 of the Uniform Parentage Act (2000, as amended) are (i) the presumption of paternity and the procedure under which that presumption can be disproved by adjudication and (ii) the acknowledgment of paternity and the procedure under which that acknowledgment can be rescinded or challenged. States that have not enacted similar provisions should consider whether such provisions should be added as part of Section 2-115(5). States that have not enacted the Uniform Parentage Act (2000, as amended) should also make sure that applicable state law authorizes parentage to be established after the death of the alleged parent, as provided in the Uniform Parentage Act § 509 (2000, as amended), which provides: "For good cause shown, the court may order genetic testing of a deceased individual."

Comment

Scope. This section sets forth definitions that apply   for purposes of the intestacy rules contained in

Subpart 2 (Parent-Child Relationship).

Definition of "Adoptee". The term "adoptee" is not limited to an individual who is adopted as a minor but includes an individual who is adopted as an adult.

Definition of "Assisted Reproduction". The definition of "assisted reproduction" is copied from the Uniform Parentage Act § 102. Current methods of assisted reproduction include intrauterine insemination (previously and sometimes currently called artificial insemination), donation of eggs, donation of embryos, in-vitro fertilization and transfer of embryos, and intracytoplasmic sperm injection.

Definition of "Functioned as a Parent of the Child". The term "functioned as a parent of the child" is derived from the Restatement (Third) of Property: Wills and Other Donative Transfers. The Reporter's Note No. 4 to § 14.5 of the Restatement lists the following parental functions:

Custodial responsibility refers to physical custodianship and supervision of a child. It usually includes, but does not necessarily require, residential or overnight responsibility.

Decisionmaking responsibility refers to authority for making significant life decisions on behalf of the child, including decisions about the child's education, spiritual guidance, and health care.

Caretaking functions are tasks that involve interaction with the child or that direct, arrange, and supervise the interaction and care provided by others. Caretaking functions include but are not limited to all of the following:

(a) satisfying the nutritional needs of the child, managing the child's bedtime and wake-up routines, caring for the child when sick or injured, being attentive to the child's personal hygiene needs including washing, grooming, and dressing, playing with the child and arranging for recreation, protecting the child's physical safety, and providing transportation;

(b) directing the child's various developmental needs, including the acquisition of motor and language skills, toilet training, self-confidence, and maturation;

(c) providing discipline, giving instruction in manners, assigning and supervising chores, and performing other tasks that attend to the child's needs for behavioral control and self-restraint;

(d) arranging for the child's education, including remedial or special services appropriate to the child's needs and interests, communicating with teachers and counselors, and supervising homework;

(e) helping the child to develop and maintain appropriate interpersonal relationships with peers, siblings, and other family members;

(f) arranging for health-care providers, medical follow-up, and home health care;

(g) providing moral and ethical guidance;

(h) arranging alternative care by a family member, babysitter, or other child-care provider or facility, including investigation of alternatives, communication with providers, and supervision of care.

Parenting functions are tasks that serve the needs of the child or the child's residential family. Parenting functions include caretaking functions, as defined [above], and all of the following additional functions:

(a) providing economic support;

(b) participating in decisionmaking regarding the child's welfare;

(c) maintaining or improving the family residence, including yard work, and house cleaning;

(d) doing and arranging for financial planning and organization, car repair and maintenance, food and clothing purchases, laundry and dry cleaning, and other tasks supporting the consumption and savings needs of the household;

(e) performing any other functions that are customarily performed by a parent or guardian and that are important to a child's welfare and development.

Ideally, a parent would perform all of the above functions throughout the child's minority. In cases falling short of the ideal, the trier of fact must balance both time and conduct. The question is, did the individual perform sufficient parenting functions over a sufficient period of time to justify concluding that the individual functioned as a parent of the child. Clearly, insubstantial conduct, such as an occasional gift or social contact, would be insufficient. Moreover, merely obeying a child support order would not, by itself, satisfy the requirement. Involuntarily providing support is inconsistent with functioning as a parent of the child.

The context in which the question arises is also relevant. If the question is whether the individual claiming to have functioned as a parent of the child inherits from the child, the court might require more substantial conduct over a more substantial period of time than if the question is whether a child inherits from an individual whom the child claims functioned as his or her parent.

Definition of "Genetic Father". The term "genetic

father" means the man whose sperm fertilized the egg of a child's genetic mother. If the father-child relationship is established under the presumption of paternity recognized by the law of this state, the term means only the man for whom that relationship is established. As stated in the Legislative Note, a state that has enacted the Uniform Parentage Act (2000/2002) should insert a reference to Section 201(b)(1), (2), or (3) of that Act.

Definition of "Relative". The term "relative" does not include any relative no matter how remote but is limited to a grandparent or a descendant of a grandparent, as determined under this Subpart 2.

§ 2-116. Effect of Parent-Child Relationship. Except as otherwise provided in Section 2-119(b) through (e), if a parent-child relationship exists or is established under this [subpart], the parent is a parent of the child and the child is a child of the parent for the purpose of intestate succession.

Comment

Scope. This section provides that if a parent-child relationship exists or is established under any section in Subpart 2, the consequence is that the parent is a parent of the child and the child is a child of the parent for the purpose of intestate succession by, from, or through the parent and the child. The exceptions in Section 2-119(b) through (e) refer to cases in which a parent-child relationship exists but only for the purpose of the right of an adoptee or a descendant of an adoptee to inherit from or through one or both genetic parents.

§ 2-117. No Distinction Based on Marital Status. Except as otherwise provided in Sections 2-114, 2-119, 2-120, or 2-121, a parent-child relationship exists between a child and the child's genetic parents, regardless of the parents' marital status.

Comment

Scope. This section, adopted in 2008, provides the general rule that a parent-child relationship exists between a child and the child's genetic parents, regardless of the parents' marital status. Exceptions to this general rule are contained in Sections 2-114 (Parent Barred from Inheriting in Certain Circumstances), 2-119 (Adoptee and Adoptee's Genetic Parents), 2-120 (Child Conceived by Assisted Reproduction Other than Child Born to Gestational Carrier), and 2-121 (Child Born to Gestational Carrier).

This section replaces former Section 2-114(a), which provided: "(a) Except as provided in subsections (b) and (c), for purposes of intestate succession by, through, or from a person, an individual is the child of his [or her] natural parents, regardless of their marital status. The parent and child relationship may be established under [the Uniform Parentage Act] [applicable state law] [insert appropriate statutory reference]."

Defined Terms. *Genetic parent* is defined in Section 2-115 as the child's genetic father or genetic mother. *Genetic mother* is defined as the woman whose egg was fertilized by the sperm of a child's genetic father. *Genetic father* is defined as the man whose sperm fertilized the egg of a child's genetic mother.

Former (1990) Version

§ 2-114. Parent and Child Relationship.

(a) Except as provided in subsections (b) and (c), for purposes of intestate succession by, through, or from a person, an individual is the child of his [or her] natural parents, regardless of their marital status. The parent and child relationship may be established under [the Uniform Parentage Act] [applicable state law] [insert appropriate statutory reference].

* * * *

> **Former (Pre-1990) Version**
>
> **§ 2-109. [Meaning of Child and Related Terms.]** If, for purposes of intestate succession, a relationship of parent and child must be established to determine succession by, through, or from a person,
>
> (1) * * * *
>
> (2) * * * * a person is the child of its parents regardless of the marital status of its parents and the parent and child relationship may be established under the [Uniform Parentage Act].
>
> *Alternative subsection (2) for states that have not adopted the Uniform Parentage Act.*
>
> [(2) * * * * a person born out of wedlock is a child of the mother. That person is also a child of the father, if:
>
> (i) the natural parents participated in a marriage ceremony before or after the birth of the child, even though the attempted marriage is void; or
>
> (ii) the paternity is established by an adjudication before the death of the father or is established thereafter by clear and convincing proof, but the paternity established under this subparagraph is ineffective to qualify the father or his kindred to inherit from or through the child unless the father has openly treated the child as his, and has not refused to support the child.]

§ 2-118. Adoptee and Adoptee's Adoptive Parent or Parents.

(a) [Parent-Child Relationship Between Adoptee and Adoptive Parent or Parents.] A parent-child relationship exists between an adoptee and the adoptee's adoptive parent or parents.

(b) [Individual in Process of Being Adopted by Married Couple; Stepchild in Process of Being Adopted by Stepparent.] For purposes of subsection (a):

(1) an individual who is in the process of being adopted by a married couple when one of the spouses dies is treated as adopted by the deceased spouse if the adoption is subsequently granted to the decedent's surviving spouse; and

(2) a child of a genetic parent who is in the process of being adopted by a genetic parent's spouse when the spouse dies is treated as adopted by the deceased spouse if the genetic parent survives the deceased spouse by 120 hours.

(c) [Child of Assisted Reproduction or Gestational Child In Process of Being Adopted.] If, after a parent-child relationship is established between a child of assisted reproduction and a parent under Section 2-120 or between a gestational child and a parent under Section 2-121, the child is in the process of being adopted by the parent's spouse when that spouse dies, the child is treated as adopted by the deceased spouse for the purpose of subsection (b)(2).

Comment

2008 Revisions. In 2008, this section and Section 2-119 replaced former Section 2-114(b), which provided: "(b) An adopted individual is the child of his [or her] adopting parent or parents and not of his [or her] natural parents, but adoption of a child by the spouse of either natural parent has no effect on (i) the relationship between the child and that natural parent or (ii) the right of the child or a descendant of the child to inherit from or through the other natural parent". The 2008 revisions divided the coverage of former Section 2-114(b) into two sections. Subsection (a) of this section covered that part of former Section 2-114(b) that provided that an adopted individual is the child of his or her adopting parent or parents. Section 2-119(a) and (b)(1) covered that part of former Section 2-114(b) that provided that an adopted individual is not the child of his natural parents, but adoption of a child by the spouse of either natural parent has no effect on the relationship between the child and that natural parent or (ii) the right of the child or a descendant of the child to inherit from or through the other natural parent.

The 2008 revisions also added subsections (b)(2) and (c), which are explained below.

Data on Adoptions. Official data on adoptions are not regularly collected. Partial data are sometimes available from the Children's Bureau of the U.S. Department of Health and Human Services, the U.S. Census Bureau, and the Evan B. Donaldson Adoption Institute.

For an historical treatment of adoption, from ancient Greece, through the Middle Ages, 19th- and 20th-century America, to open adoption and international adoption, see Debora L. Spar, The Baby Business ch. 6 (2006) and sources cited therein.

Defined Term. *Adoptee* is defined in Section 2-115 as an individual who is adopted. The term is not limited to an individual who is adopted as a minor but includes an individual who is adopted as an adult.

Subsection (a): Parent-Child Relationship Between Adoptee and Adoptive Parent or Parents. Subsection (a) states the general rule that adoption creates a parent-child relationship between the adoptee and the adoptee's adoptive parent or parents.

Subsection (b)(1): Individual in Process of Being Adopted by Married Couple. If the spouse who subsequently died had filed a legal proceeding to adopt the individual before the spouse died, the individual is "in the process of being adopted" by the deceased spouse when the spouse died. However, the phrase "in the process of being adopted" is not intended to be limited to that situation, but is intended to grant flexibility to find on a case by case basis that the process commenced earlier.

Subsection (b)(2): Stepchild in Process of Being Adopted by Stepparent. If the stepparent who subsequently died had filed a legal proceeding to adopt the stepchild before the stepparent died, the stepchild is "in the process of being adopted" by the deceased stepparent when the stepparent died. However, the phrase "in the process of being adopted" is not intended to be limited to that situation, but is intended to grant flexibility to find on a case by case basis that the process commenced earlier.

Subsection (c): Child of Assisted Reproduction or Gestational Child in Process of Being Adopted. Subsection (c) provides that if, after a parent-child relationship is established between a child of assisted reproduction and a parent under Section 2-120 or between a gestational child and a parent under Section 2-121, the child is in the process of being adopted by the parent's spouse when that spouse dies, the child is treated as adopted by the deceased spouse for the purpose of subsection (b)(2). An example would be a situation in which an unmarried mother or father is the parent of a child of assisted reproduction or a gestational child, and subsequently marries an individual who then begins the process of adopting the child but who dies before the adoption becomes final. In such a case, subsection (c) provides that the child is treated as adopted by the deceased spouse for the purpose of subsection (b)(2). The phrase "in the process of being adopted" carries the same meaning under subsection (c) as it does under subsection (b)(2).

Former (1990) Version

§ 2-114. Parent and Child Relationship.

(a) * * * *.

(b) An adopted individual is the child of his [or her] adopting parent or parents and not of his [or her] natural parents, but adoption of a child by the spouse of either natural parent has no effect on (i) the relationship between the child and that natural parent or (ii) the right of the child or a descendant of the child to inherit from or through the other natural parent.

Former (Pre-1990) Version

§ 2-109. [Meaning of Child and Related Terms.] If, for purposes of intestate succession, a relationship of parent and child must be established to determine succession by, through, or from a person,

(1) an adopted person is the child of an adopting parent and not of the natural parents except that adoption of a child by the spouse of a natural parent has no effect on the relationship between the child and either natural parent.

* * * *

---

§ 2-119. Adoptee and Adoptee's Genetic Parents.

(a) **[Parent-Child Relationship Between Adoptee and Genetic Parents.]** Except as otherwise provided in subsections (b) through (e), a parent-child relationship does not exist between an adoptee and the adoptee's genetic parents.

(b) **[Stepchild Adopted by Stepparent.]** A parent-child relationship exists between an individual who is adopted by the spouse of either genetic parent and:

(1) the genetic parent whose spouse adopted the individual; and

(2) the other genetic parent, but only for the purpose of the right of the adoptee or a descendant of the adoptee to inherit from or through the other genetic parent.

(c) **[Individual Adopted by Relative of a Genetic Parent.]** A parent-child relationship exists between both genetic parents and an individual who is adopted by a relative of a genetic parent, or by the spouse or surviving spouse of a relative of a genetic parent, but only for the purpose of the right of the adoptee or a descendant of the adoptee to inherit from or through either genetic parent.

(d) **[Individual Adopted After Death of Both Genetic Parents.]** A parent-child relationship exists between both genetic parents and an individual who is adopted after the death of both genetic parents, but only for the purpose of the right of the adoptee or a descendant of the adoptee to inherit through either genetic parent.

(e) **[Child of Assisted Reproduction or Gestational Child Who Is Subsequently Adopted.]** If, after a parent-child relationship is established between a child of assisted reproduction and a parent or parents under Section 2-120 or between a gestational child and a parent or parents under Section 2-121, the child is adopted by another or others, the child's parent or parents under Section 2-120 or 2-121 are treated as the child's genetic parent or parents for the purpose of this section.

Comment

2008 Revisions. In 2008, this section and Section 2-118 replaced former Section 2-114(b), which provided: "(b) An adopted individual is the child of his [or her] adopting parent or parents and not of his [or her] natural parents, but adoption of a child by the spouse of either natural parent has no effect on (i) the relationship between the child and that natural parent or (ii) the right of the child or a descendant of the child to inherit from or through the other natural parent".The 2008 revisions divided the coverage of former Section 2-114(b) into two sections. Section 2-118(a) covered that part of former Section 2-114(b) that provided that an adopted individual is the child of his or her adopting parent or parents. Subsections (a) and (b) of this section covered that part of former Section 2-114(b) that provided that an adopted individual is not the child of his natural parents, but adoption of a child by the spouse of either natural parent has no effect on the relationship between the child and that natural parent or (ii) the right of the child or a descendant of the child to inherit from or through the other natural parent.

The 2008 revisions also added subsections (c), (d), and (e), which are explained below.

Defined Terms. Section 2-119 uses terms that are defined in Section 2-115.

Adoptee is defined in Section 2-115 as an individual who is adopted. The term is not limited to an individual who is adopted as a minor, but includes an individual who is adopted as an adult.

Genetic parent is defined in Section 2-115 as the child's genetic father or genetic mother. *Genetic mother* is defined as the woman whose egg was fertilized by the sperm of a child's genetic father. *Genetic father* is defined as the man whose sperm fertilized the egg of a child's genetic mother.

Relative is defined in Section 2-115 as a grandparent or a descendant of a grandparent.

Subsection (a): Parent-Child Relationship Between Adoptee and Adoptee's Genetic Parents. Subsection (a) states the general rule that a parent-child relationship does not exist between an adopted child and the child's genetic parents. This rule recognizes that an adoption severs the parent-child relationship between the adopted child and the child's genetic parents. The adoption gives the adopted child a replacement family, sometimes referred to in the case law as "a fresh start". For further elaboration of this theory, see Restatement (Third) of Property: Wills and Other Donative Transfers § 2.5(2)(A) & cmts. d & e (1999). Subsection (a) also states, however, that there are exceptions to this general rule in subsections (b) through (d).

Subsection (b): Stepchild Adopted by Stepparent. Subsection (b) continues the so-called "stepparent exception" contained in the Code since its original promulgation in 1969. When a stepparent adopts his or her stepchild, Section 2-118 provides that the adoption creates a parent-child relationship between the child and his or her adoptive stepparent. Section 2-119(b)(1) provides that a parent-child relationship continues to exist between the child and the child's genetic parent whose spouse adopted the child. Section 2-119(b)(2) provides that a parent-child relationship also continues to exist between an adopted stepchild and his or her other genetic parent (the noncustodial genetic parent) for purposes of inheritance from and through that genetic parent, but not for purposes of inheritance by the other genetic parent and his or her relatives from or through the adopted stepchild.

Example 1–Post-Widowhood Remarriage. A and B were married and had two children, X and Y. A died, and B married C. C adopted X and Y. Under subsection (b)(1), X and Y are treated as B's children and under Section 2-118(a) as C's children for all purposes of inheritance. Under subsection (b)(2), X and Y are treated as A's children for purposes of inheritance from and through A but not for purposes of inheritance from or through X or Y. Thus, if A's father, G, died intestate, survived by X and Y and by G's daughter (A's sister), S, G's heirs would be S, X, and Y. S would take half and X and Y would take one-fourth each.

Example 2–Post-Divorce Remarriage. A and B were married and had two children, X and Y. A and B got divorced, and B married C. C adopted X and Y. Under subsection (b)(1), X and Y are treated as B's children and under Section 2-118(a) as C's children for all purposes of inheritance. Under subsection (b)(2), X and Y are treated as A's children for purposes of inheritance from and through A. On the other hand, neither A nor any of A's relatives can inherit from or through X or Y.

Subsection (c): Individual Adopted by Relative of a Genetic Parent. Under subsection (c), a child who is adopted by a maternal or a paternal relative of either genetic parent, or by the spouse or surviving spouse of such a relative, remains a child of both genetic parents.

Example 3. F and M, a married couple with a four-year old child, X, were badly injured in an automobile accident. F subsequently died. M, who was in a vegetative state and on life support, was unable to care for X. Thereafter, M's sister, A, and A's husband, B, adopted X. F's father, PGF, a widower, then died intestate. Under subsection (c), X is treated as PGF's grandchild (F's child).

Subsection (d): Individual Adopted After Death of Both Genetic Parents. Usually, a post-death adoption does not remove a child from contact with the genetic families. When someone with ties to the genetic family or families adopts a child after the deaths of the child's genetic parents, even if the adoptive parent is not a relative of either genetic parent or a spouse or surviving spouse of such a relative, the child continues to be in a parent-child relationship with both genetic parents. Once a child has taken root in a family, an adoption after the death of both genetic parents is likely to be by someone chosen or approved of by the genetic family, such as a person named as guardian of the child in a deceased parent's will. In such a case, the child does not become estranged from the genetic family. Such an adoption does not "remove" the child from the families of both genetic parents. Such a child continues to be a child of both genetic parents, as well as a child of the adoptive parents.

Example 4. F and M, a married couple with a four-year-old child, X, were involved in an automobile accident that killed F and M. Neither M's parents nor F's father (F's mother had died before the accident) nor any other relative was in a position to take custody of X. X was adopted by F and M's close friends, A and B, a married couple approximately of the same ages as F and M. F's father, PGF, a widower, then died intestate. Under subsection (d), X is treated as PGF's grandchild (F's child). The result would be the same if F's or M's will appointed A and B as the guardians of the person of X, and A and B subsequently successfully petitioned to adopt X.

Subsection (e): Child of Assisted Reproduction or Gestational Child Who Is Subsequently Adopted. Subsection (e) puts a child of assisted reproduction and a gestational child on the same footing as a genetic child for purposes of this section. The results in Examples 1 through 4 would have been the same had the child in question been a child of assisted reproduction or a gestational child.

Former (1990) Version

§ 2-114. Parent and Child Relationship.

   * * * *

(b) An adopted individual is the child of his [or her] adopting parent or parents and not of his [or her] natural parents, but adoption of a child by the spouse of either natural parent has no effect on (i) the relationship between the child and that natural parent or (ii) the right of the child or a descendant of the child to inherit from or through the other natural parent.

Former (Pre-1990) Version

§ 2-109. [Meaning of Child and Related Terms.] If, for purposes of intestate succession, a relationship of parent and child must be established to determine succession by, through, or from a person,

(1) an adopted person is the child of an adopting parent and not of the natural parents except that adoption of a child by the spouse of a natural parent has no effect on the relationship between the child and either natural parent.

* * * *

§ 2-120. Child Conceived by Assisted Reproduction Other than Child Born to Gestational Carrier.

(a) **[Definitions.]** In this section:

(1) "Birth mother" means a woman, other than a gestational carrier under Section 2-121, who gives birth to a child of assisted reproduction. The term is not limited to a woman who is the child's genetic mother.

(2) "Child of assisted reproduction" means a child conceived by means of assisted reproduction by a woman other than a gestational carrier under Section 2-121.

(3) "Third-party donor" means an individual who produces eggs or sperm used for assisted reproduction, whether or not for consideration. The term does not include:

(A) a husband who provides sperm, or a wife who provides eggs, that are used for assisted reproduction by the wife;

(B) the birth mother of a child of assisted reproduction; or

(C) an individual who has been determined under subsection (e) or (f) to have a parent-child relationship with a child of assisted reproduction.

(b) **[Third-Party Donor.]** A parent-child relationship does not exist between a child of assisted reproduction and a third-party donor.

(c) **[Parent-Child Relationship with Birth Mother.]** A parent-child relationship exists between a child of assisted reproduction and the child's birth mother.

(d) **[Parent-Child Relationship with Husband Whose Sperm Were Used During His Lifetime by His Wife for Assisted Reproduction.]** Except as otherwise provided in subsections (i) and (j), a parent-child relationship exists between a child of assisted reproduction and the husband of the child's birth mother if the husband provided the sperm that the birth mother used during his lifetime for assisted reproduction.

(e) **[Birth Certificate: Presumptive Effect.]** A birth certificate identifying an individual other than the birth mother as the other parent of a child of assisted reproduction presumptively establishes a parent-child relationship between the child and that individual.

(f) **[Parent-Child Relationship with Another.]** Except as otherwise provided in subsections (g), (i), and (j), and unless a parent-child relationship is established under subsection (d) or (e), a parent-child relationship exists between a child of assisted reproduction and an individual other than the birth mother who consented to assisted reproduction by the birth mother with intent to be treated as the other parent of the child. Consent to assisted reproduction by the birth mother with intent to be treated as the other parent of the child is established if the individual:

(1) before or after the child's birth, signed a record that, considering all the facts and circumstances, evidences the individual's consent; or

(2) in the absence of a signed record under paragraph (1):

41

(A) functioned as a parent of the child no later than two years after the child's birth;

(B) intended to function as a parent of the child no later than two years after the child's birth but was prevented from carrying out that intent by death, incapacity, or other circumstances; or

(C) intended to be treated as a parent of a posthumously conceived child, if that intent is established by clear and convincing evidence.

(g) [Record Signed More than Two Years after the Birth of the Child: Effect.] For the purpose of subsection (f)(1), neither an individual who signed a record more than two years after the birth of the child, nor a relative of that individual who is not also a relative of the birth mother, inherits from or through the child unless the individual functioned as a parent of the child before the child reached [18] years of age.

(h) [Presumption: Birth Mother is Married or Surviving Spouse.] For the purpose of subsection (f)(2), the following rules apply:

(1) If the birth mother is married and no divorce proceeding is pending, in the absence of clear and convincing evidence to the contrary, her spouse satisfies subsection (f)(2)(A) or (B).

(2) If the birth mother is a surviving spouse and at her deceased spouse's death no divorce proceeding was pending, in the absence of clear and convincing evidence to the contrary, her deceased spouse satisfies subsection (f)(2)(B) or (C).

(i) [Divorce Before Placement of Eggs, Sperm, or Embryos.] If a married couple is divorced before placement of eggs, sperm, or embryos, a child resulting from the assisted reproduction is not a child of the birth mother's former spouse, unless the former spouse consented in a record that if assisted reproduction were to occur after divorce, the child would be treated as the former spouse's child.

(j) [Withdrawal of Consent Before Placement of Eggs, Sperm, or Embryos.] If, in a record, an individual withdraws consent to assisted reproduction before placement of eggs, sperm, or embryos, a child resulting from the assisted reproduction is not a child of that individual, unless the individual subsequently satisfies subsection (f).

(k) [When Posthumously Conceived Child Treated as in Gestation.] If, under this section, an individual is a parent of a child of assisted reproduction who is conceived after the individual's death, the child is treated as in gestation at the individual's death for purposes of Section 2-104(a)(2) if the child is:

(1) in utero not later than 36 months after the individual's death; or

(2) born not later than 45 months after the individual's death.

Legislative Note: States are encouraged to enact a provision requiring genetic depositories to provide a consent form that would satisfy subsection (f)(1). See Cal. Health & Safety Code § 1644.7 and .8 for a possible model for such a consent form.

Comment

Data on Children of Assisted Reproduction. The Center for Disease Control (CDC) of the U.S. Department of Health and Human Services collects data on children of assisted reproduction (ART). See Center for Disease Control, 2004 Assisted Reproductive Technology Success Rates (Dec. 2006) (2004 CDC Report), available at http://www.cdc.gov/ART/ART2004. The data, however, is of limited use because the definition of ART used in the CDC Report excludes intrauterine (artificial) insemination (2004 CDC Report at 3),

which is probably the most common form of assisted reproductive procedures. The CDC estimates that in 2004 ART procedures (excluding intrauterine insemination) accounted for slightly more than one percent of total U.S. births. 2004 CDC Report at 13. According to the Report: "The number of infants born who were conceived using ART increased steadily between 1996 and 2004. In 2004, 49,458 infants were born, which was more than double the 20,840 born in 1996." 2004 CDC Report at 57. "The average age of women using ART services in 2004 was

36. The largest group of women using ART services were women younger than 35, representing 41% of all ART cycles carried out in 2004. Twenty-one percent of ART cycles were carried out among women aged 35-37, 19% among women aged 38-40, 9% among women aged 41-42, and 9% among women older than 42." 2004 CDC Report at 15. Updates of the 2004 CDC Report are to be posted at http://www.cdc.gov/ART/ART2004.

AMA Ethics Policy on Posthumous Conception. The ethics policies of the American Medical Association concerning artificial insemination by a known donor state that "[i]f semen is frozen and the donor dies before it is used, the frozen semen should not be used or donated for purposes other than those originally intended by the donor. If the donor left no instructions, it is reasonable to allow the remaining partner to use the semen for intrauterine insemination but not to donate it to someone else. However, the donor should be advised of such a policy at the time of donation and be given an opportunity to override it." Am. Med. Assn. Council on Ethical & Judicial Affairs, Code of Medical Ethics: Current Opinions E-2.04 (Issued June 1993; updated December 2004).

Subsection (a): Definitions. Subsection (a) defines the following terms:

Birth mother is defined as the woman (other than a gestational carrier under Section 2-121) who gave birth to a child of assisted reproduction.

Child of assisted reproduction is defined as a child conceived by means of assisted reproduction by a woman other than a gestational carrier under Section 2-121.

Third-party donor. The definition of third-party donor is based on the definition of "donor" in the Uniform Parentage Act § 102.

Other Defined Terms. In addition to the terms defined in subsection (a), this section uses terms that are defined in Section 2-115.

Assisted reproduction is defined in Section 2-115 as a method of causing pregnancy other than sexual intercourse.

Divorce is defined in Section 2-115 as including an annulment, dissolution, and declaration of invalidity of a marriage.

Functioned as a parent of the child is defined in Section 2-115 as behaving toward a child in a manner consistent with being the child's parent and performing functions that are customarily performed by a parent, including fulfilling parental responsibilities toward the child, recognizing or holding out the child as the individual's child, materially participating in the child's upbringing, and residing with the child in the same household as a regular member of that household. See also the Comment to Section 2-115 for additional explanation of the term.

Genetic father is defined in Section 2-115 as the man whose sperm fertilized the egg of a child's genetic mother.

Genetic mother is defined as the woman whose egg was fertilized by the sperm of the child's genetic father.

Incapacity is defined in Section 2-115 as the inability of an individual to function as a parent of a child because of the individual's physical or mental condition.

Subsection (b): Third-Party Donor. Subsection (b) is consistent with the Uniform Parentage Act § 702. Under subsection (b), a third-party donor does not have a parent-child relationship with a child of assisted reproduction, despite the donor's genetic relationship with the child.

Subsection (c): Parent-Child Relationship With Birth Mother. Subsection (c) is in accord with Uniform Parentage Act Section 201 in providing that a parent-child relationship exists between a child of assisted reproduction and the child's birth mother. The child's birth mother, defined in subsection (a) as the woman (other than a gestational carrier) who gave birth to the child, made the decision to undergo the procedure with intent to become pregnant and give birth to the child. Therefore, in order for a parent-child relationship to exist between her and the child, no proof that she consented to the procedure with intent to be treated as the parent of the child is necessary.

Subsection (d): Parent-Child Relationship with Husband Whose Sperm Were Used During His Lifetime By His Wife for Assisted Reproduction. The principal application of subsection (d) is in the case of the assisted reproduction procedure known as intrauterine insemination husband (IIH), or, in older terminology, artificial insemination husband (AIH). Subsection (d) provides that, except as otherwise provided in subsection (i), a parent-child relationship exists between a child of assisted reproduction and the husband of the child's birth mother if the husband provided the sperm that were used during his lifetime by her for assisted reproduction and the husband is the genetic father of the child. The exception contained in subsection (i) relates to the withdrawal of consent in a record before the placement of eggs, sperm, or embryos. Note that subsection (d) only applies if the husband's sperm were used during his lifetime by his wife to cause a pregnancy by assisted reproduction. Subsection (d) does not apply to posthumous conception.

Subsection (e): Birth Certificate: Presumptive Effect. A birth certificate will name the child's birth mother as mother of the child. Under subsection (c), a parent-child relationship exists between a child of assisted reproduction and the child's birth mother. Note that the term "birth mother" is a defined term in subsection (a) as not including a gestational carrier as defined in Section 2-121.

Subsection (e) applies to the individual, if any, who is identified on the birth certificate as the child's other parent. Subsection (e) grants presumptive effect to a birth certificate identifying an individual other than the birth mother as the other parent of a child of assisted reproduction. In the case of unmarried parents, federal law requires that states enact procedures under which "the name of the father shall be included on the record of birth," but only if the father and mother have signed a voluntary acknowledgment of paternity or a court or an administrative agency of competent jurisdiction has issued an adjudication of paternity. See 42 U.S.C. § 666(a)(5)(D). This federal statute is included as an appendix to the Uniform Parentage Act.

The federal statute applies only to unmarried opposite-sex parents. Section 2-120(e)'s presumption, however, could apply to a same-sex couple if state law permits a woman who is not the birth mother to be listed on the child's birth certificate as the child's other parent. Even if state law does not permit that listing, the woman who is not the birth mother could be the child's parent by adoption of the child (see Section 2-118) or under subsection (f) as a result of her consent to assisted reproduction by the birth mother "with intent to be treated as the other parent of the child," or by satisfying the "function as a parent" test in subsection (f)(2).

Section 2-120 does not apply to same-sex couples that use a gestational carrier. For same-sex couples using a gestational carrier, the parent-child relationship can be established by adoption (see Section 2-118 and Section 2-121(b)), or it can be established under Section 2-121(d) if the couple enters into a gestational agreement with the gestational carrier under which the couple agrees to be the parents of the child born to the gestational carrier. It is irrelevant whether either intended parent is a genetic parent of the child. See Section 2-121(a)(4).

Subsection (f): Parent-Child Relationship with Another. In order for someone other than the birth mother to have a parent-child relationship with the child, there needs to be proof that the individual consented to assisted reproduction by the birth mother with intent to be treated as the other parent of the child. The other individual's genetic material might or might not have been used to create the pregnancy. Except as otherwise provided in this section, merely depositing genetic material is not, by itself, sufficient to establish a parent-child relationship with the child.

Subsection (f)(1): Signed Record Evidencing Consent, Considering All the Facts and Circumstances, to Assisted Reproduction with Intent to Be Treated as the Other Parent of the Child. Subsection (f)(1) provides that a parent-child relationship exists between a child of assisted reproduction and an individual other than the birth mother who consented to assisted reproduction by the birth mother with intent to be treated as the other parent of the child. Consent to assisted reproduction with intent to be treated as the other parent of the child is established if the individual signed a record, before or after the child's birth, that considering all the facts and circumstances evidences the individual's consent. Recognizing consent in a record not only signed before the child's birth but also at any time after the child's birth is consistent with the Uniform Parentage Act §§ 703 and 704.

As noted, the signed record need not explicitly express consent to the procedure with intent to be treated as the other parent of child, but only needs to evidence such consent considering all the facts and circumstances. An example of a signed record that would satisfy this requirement comes from In re Martin B., 841 N.Y.S.2d 207 (Sur. Ct. 2007). In that case, the New York Surrogate's Court held that a child of posthumous conception was included in a class gift in a case in which the deceased father had signed a form that stated: "In the event of my death I agree that my spouse shall have the sole right to make decisions regarding the disposition of my semen samples. I authorize repr. lab to release my specimens to my legal spouse [naming her]." Another form he signed stated: "I, [naming him], hereby certify that I am married or intimately involved with [naming her] and the cryopreserved specimens stored at repr. lab will be used for future inseminations of my wife/intimate partner." Although these forms do not explicitly say that the decedent consented to the procedure with intent to be treated as the other parent of the child, they do evidence such consent in light of all of the facts and circumstances and would therefore satisfy subsection (f)(1).

Subsection (f)(2): Absence of Signed Record Evidencing Consent. Ideally an individual other than the birth mother who consented to assisted reproduction by the birth mother with intent to be treated as the other parent of the child will have signed a record that satisfies subsection (f)(1). If not, subsection (f)(2) recognizes that actions speak as loud as words. Under subsection (f)(2), consent to assisted reproduction by the birth mother with intent to be treated as the other parent of the child is established if the individual functioned as a parent of the child no later than two years after the child's birth. Under subsection (f)(2)(B), the same result applies if the evidence establishes that the individual had that intent but death, incapacity, or other circumstances prevented the individual from carrying out that intent. Finally, under subsection (f)(2)(C), the same result applies if it can be established by clear and convincing evidence that the individual intended to be treated as a parent of a posthumously conceived child.

Subsection (g): Record Signed More than Two Years after the Birth of the Child: Effect. Subsection (g) is designed to prevent an individual who has never functioned as a parent of the child from signing a record in order to inherit from or through the child or in order to make it possible for a relative of the individual to inherit from or through the child. Thus, subsection (g) provides that, for purposes of subsection (f)(1), an individual who signed a record more than two years after the birth of the child, or a relative of that individual, does not inherit from or through the child unless the individual functioned as a parent of the child before the child reached the age of [18].

Subsection (h): Presumption: Birth Mother is Married or Surviving Spouse. Under subsection (h), if the birth mother is married and no divorce proceeding is pending, then in the absence of clear and convincing evidence to the contrary, her spouse satisfies subsection (f)(2)(A) or (B) or if the birth mother is a surviving spouse and at her deceased spouse's death no divorce proceeding was pending, then in the absence of clear and convincing evidence to the contrary, her deceased spouse satisfies subsection (f)(2)(B) or (C).

Subsection (i): Divorce Before Placement of Eggs, Sperm, or Embryos. Subsection (i) is derived from the Uniform Parentage Act § 706(b).

Subsection (j): Withdrawal of Consent Before Placement of Eggs, Sperm, or Embryos. Subsection (j) is derived from Uniform Parentage Act Section 706(a). Subsection (j) provides that if, in a record, an individual withdraws consent to assisted reproduction before placement of eggs, sperm, or embryos, a child resulting from the assisted reproduction is not a child of that individual, unless the individual subsequently satisfies the requirements of subsection (f).

Subsection (k): When Posthumously Conceived Gestational Child Treated as in Gestation. Subsection (k) provides that if, under this section, an individual is a parent of a gestational child who is conceived after the individual's death, the child is treated as in gestation at the individual's death for purposes of Section 2-104(a)(2) if the child is either (1) in utero no later than 36 months after the individual's death or (2) born no later than 45 months after the individual's death. Note also that Section 3-703 gives the decedent's personal representative authority to take account of the possibility of posthumous conception in the timing of all or part of the distribution of the estate.

The 36-month period in subsection (k) is designed to allow a surviving spouse or partner a period of grieving, time to make up his or her mind about whether to go forward with assisted reproduction, and a reasonable allowance for unsuccessful attempts to achieve a pregnancy. The 36-month period also coincides with Section 3-1006, under which an heir is allowed to recover property improperly distributed or its value from any distributee during the later of three years after the decedent's death or one year after distribution. If the assisted-reproduction procedure is performed in a medical facility, the date when the child is in utero will ordinarily be evidenced by medical records. In some cases, however, the procedure is not performed in a medical facility, and so such evidence may be lacking. Providing an alternative of birth within 45 months is designed to provide certainty in such cases. The 45-month period is based on the 36-month period with an additional nine months tacked on to allow for a typical period of pregnancy.

§ 2-121. Child Born to Gestational Carrier.

(a) **[Definitions.]** In this section:

(1) "Gestational agreement" means an enforceable or unenforceable agreement for assisted

reproduction in which a woman agrees to carry a child to birth for an intended parent, intended parents, or an individual described in subsection (e).

(2) "Gestational carrier" means a woman who is not an intended parent and gives birth to a child under a gestational agreement. The term is not limited to a woman who is the child's genetic mother.

(3) "Gestational child" means a child born to a gestational carrier under a gestational agreement.

(4) "Intended parent" means an individual who entered into a gestational agreement providing that the individual will be the parent of a child born to a gestational carrier by means of assisted reproduction. The term is not limited to an individual who has a genetic relationship with the child.

(b) [Court Order Adjudicating Parentage: Effect.] A parent-child relationship is conclusively established by a court order designating the parent or parents of a gestational child.

(c) [Gestational Carrier.] A parent-child relationship between a gestational child and the child's gestational carrier does not exist unless the gestational carrier is:

(1) designated as a parent of the child in a court order described in subsection (b); or

(2) the child's genetic mother and a parent-child relationship does not exist under this section with an individual other than the gestational carrier.

(d) [Parent-Child Relationship With Intended Parent or Parents.] In the absence of a court order under subsection (b), a parent-child relationship exists between a gestational child and an intended parent who:

(1) functioned as a parent of the child no later than two years after the child's birth; or

(2) died while the gestational carrier was pregnant if:

(A) there were two intended parents and the other intended parent functioned as a parent of the child no later than two years after the child's birth;

(B) there were two intended parents, the other intended parent also died while the gestational carrier was pregnant, and a relative of either deceased intended parent or the spouse or surviving spouse of a relative of either deceased intended parent functioned as a parent of the child no later than two years after the child's birth; or

(C) there was no other intended parent and a relative of or the spouse or surviving spouse of a relative of the deceased intended parent functioned as a parent of the child no later than two years after the child's birth.

(e) [Gestational Agreement After Death or Incapacity.] In the absence of a court order under subsection (b), a parent-child relationship exists between a gestational child and an individual whose sperm or eggs were used after the individual's death or incapacity to conceive a child under a gestational agreement entered into after the individual's death or incapacity if the individual intended to be treated as the parent of the child. The individual's intent may be shown by:

(1) a record signed by the individual which considering all the facts and circumstances evidences the individual's intent; or

(2) other facts and circumstances establishing the individual's intent by clear and convincing evidence.

(f) [Presumption: Gestational Agreement After Spouse's Death or Incapacity.] Except as otherwise provided in subsection (g), and unless there is clear and convincing evidence of a contrary intent, an individual is deemed to have intended to be treated as the parent of a gestational child for purposes of subsection (e)(2) if:

(1) the individual, before death or incapacity, deposited the sperm or eggs that were used to conceive the child;

(2) when the individual deposited the sperm or eggs, the individual was married and no divorce proceeding was pending; and

(3) the individual's spouse or surviving spouse functioned as a parent of the child no later than

two years after the child's birth.

(g) **[Subsection (f) Presumption Inapplicable.]** The presumption under subsection (f) does not apply if there is:

(1) a court order under subsection (b); or

(2) a signed record that satisfies subsection (e)(1).

(h) **[When Posthumously Conceived Gestational Child Treated as in Gestation.]** If, under this section, an individual is a parent of a gestational child who is conceived after the individual's death, the child is treated as in gestation at the individual's death for purposes of Section 2-104(a)(2) if the child is:

(1) in utero not later than 36 months after the individual's death; or

(2) born not later than 45 months after the individual's death.

(i) **[No Effect on Other Law.]** This section does not affect law of this state other than this [code] regarding the enforceability or validity of a gestational agreement.

Comment

Subsection (a): Definitions. Subsection (a) defines the following terms:

Gestational agreement. The definition of gestational agreement is based on the Comment to Article 8 of the Uniform Parentage Act, which states that the term "gestational carrier" "applies to both a woman who, through assisted reproduction, performs the gestational function without being genetically related to a child, and a woman who is both the gestational and genetic mother. The key is that an agreement has been made that the child is to be raised by the intended parents." The Comment also points out that "The [practice in which the woman is both the gestational and genetic mother] has elicited disfavor in the ART community, which has concluded that the gestational carrier's genetic link to the child too often creates additional emotional and psychological problems in enforcing a gestational agreement."

Gestational carrier is defined as a woman who is not an intended parent and who gives birth to a child under a gestational agreement. The term is not limited to a woman who is the child's genetic mother.

Gestational child is defined as a child born to a gestational carrier under a gestational agreement.

Intended parent is defined as an individual who entered into a gestational agreement providing that the individual will be the parent of a child born to a gestational carrier by means of assisted reproduction. The term is not limited to an individual who has a genetic relationship with the child.

Other Defined Terms. In addition to the terms defined in subsection (a), this section uses terms that are defined in Section 2-115.

Child of assisted reproduction is defined in Section 2-115 as a method of causing pregnancy other than sexual intercourse.

Divorce is defined in Section 2-115 as including an annulment, dissolution, and declaration of invalidity of a marriage.

Functioned as a parent of the child is defined in Section 2-115 as behaving toward a child in a manner consistent with being the child's parent and performing functions that are customarily performed by a parent, including fulfilling parental responsibilities toward the child, recognizing or holding out the child as the individual's child, materially participating in the child's upbringing, and residing with the child in the same household as a regular member of that household. See also the Comment to Section 2-115 for additional explanation of the term.

Genetic mother is defined as the woman whose egg was fertilized by the sperm of the child's genetic father.

Incapacity is defined in Section 2-115 as the inability of an individual to function as a parent of a child because of the individual's physical or mental condition.

Relative is defined in Section 2-115 as a grandparent or a descendant of a grandparent.

Subsection (b): Court Order Adjudicating Parentage: Effect. A court order issued under Section 807 of the Uniform Parentage Act (UPA) would qualify as a court order adjudicating parentage for purposes of subsection (b). UPA Section 807 provides:

UPA Section 807. Parentage under Validated Gestational Agreement.

(a) Upon birth of a child to a gestational carrier, the intended parents shall file notice with the court that a child has been born to the gestational carrier within 300 days after assisted reproduction. Thereupon, the court shall issue an order:

(1) confirming that the intended parents are the parents of the child ;

(2) if necessary, ordering that the child be surrendered to the intended parents; and

(3) directing the [agency maintaining birth records] to issue a birth certificate naming the intended parents as parents of the child.

(b) If the parentage of a child born to a gestational carrier is alleged not to be the result of assisted reproduction, the court shall order genetic testing to determine the parentage of the child.

(c) If the intended parents fail to file notice required under subsection (a), the gestational carrier or the appropriate state agency may file notice with the court that a child has been born to the gestational carrier within 300 days after assisted reproduction. Upon proof of a court order issued pursuant to Section 803 validating the gestational agreement, the court shall order the intended parents are the parents of the child and are financially responsible for the child.

Subsection (c): Gestational Carrier. Under subsection (c), the only way that a parent-child relationship exists between a gestational child and the child's gestational carrier is if she is (1) designated as a parent of the child in a court order described in subsection (b) or (2) the child's genetic mother and a parent-child relationship does not exist under this section with an individual other than the gestational carrier.

Subsection (d): Parent-Child Relationship With Intended Parent or Parents. Subsection (d) only applies in the absence of a court order under subsection (b). If there is no such court order, subsection (b) provides that a parent-child relationship exists between a gestational child and an intended parent who functioned as a parent of the child no later than two years after the child's birth. A parent-child also exists between a gestational child and an intended parent if the intended parent died while the gestational carrier was pregnant, but only if (A) there were two intended parents and the other intended parent functioned as a parent of the child no later than two years after the child's birth; (B) there were two intended parents, the other intended parent also died while the gestational carrier was pregnant, and a relative of either deceased intended parent or the spouse or surviving spouse of a relative

of either deceased intended parent functioned as a parent of the child no later than two years after the child's birth; or (C) there was no other intended parent and a relative of or the spouse or surviving spouse of a relative of the deceased intended parent functioned as a parent of the child no later than two years after the child's birth.

Subsection (e): Gestational Agreement After Death or Incapacity. Subsection (e) only applies in the absence of a court order under subsection (b). If there is no such court order, a parent-child relationship exists between a gestational child and an individual whose sperm or eggs were used after the individual's death or incapacity to conceive a child under a gestational agreement entered into after the individual's death or incapacity if the individual intended to be treated as the parent of the child. The individual's intent may be shown by a record signed by the individual which considering all the facts and circumstances evidences the individual's intent or by other facts and circumstances establishing the individual's intent by clear and convincing evidence.

Subsections (f) and (g): Presumption: Gestational Agreement After Spouse's Death or Incapacity. Subsection (f) and (g) are connected. Subsection (f) provides that unless there is clear and convincing evidence of a contrary intent, an individual is deemed to have intended to be treated as the parent of a gestational child for purposes of subsection (e)(2) if (1) the individual, before death or incapacity, deposited the sperm or eggs that were used to conceive the child, (2) when the individual deposited the sperm or eggs, the individual was married and no divorce proceeding was pending; and (3) the individual's spouse or surviving spouse functioned as a parent of the child no later than two years after the child's birth.

Subsection (g) provides, however, that the presumption under subsection (f) does not apply if there is a court order under subsection (b) or a signed record that satisfies subsection (e)(1).

Subsection (h): When Posthumously Conceived Gestational Child is Treated as in Gestation. Subsection (h) provides that if, under this section, an individual is a parent of a gestational child who is conceived after the individual's death, the child is treated as in gestation at the individual's death for purposes of Section 2-104(a)(2) if the child is either (1) in utero not later than 36 months after the individual's death or (2) born not later than 45 months after the individual's death. Note also that Section 3-703 gives the decedent's personal representative authority to take account of the possibility of posthumous conception in the timing of the distribution of part or all of the estate.

The 36-month period in subsection (g) is designed to allow a surviving spouse or partner a period of grieving, time to make up his or her mind about whether to go forward with assisted reproduction, and a reasonable allowance for unsuccessful attempts to achieve a pregnancy. The three-year period also coincides with Section 3-1006, under which an heir is allowed to recover property improperly distributed or its value from any distributee during the later of

three years after the decedent's death or one year after distribution. If the assisted-reproduction procedure is performed in a medical facility, the date when the child is in utero will ordinarily be evidenced by medical records. In some cases, however, the procedure is not performed in a medical facility, and so such evidence may be lacking. Providing an alternative of birth within 45 months is designed to provide certainty in such cases. The 45-month period is based on the 36-month period with an additional nine months tacked on to allow for a typical period of pregnancy.

§ 2-122. Equitable Adoption. This [subpart] does not affect the doctrine of equitable adoption.

Comment

On the doctrine of equitable adoption, see Restatement (Third) of Property: Wills and Other Donative Transfers § 2.5, cmt. k & Reporter's Note No. 7 (1999).

PART 2
ELECTIVE SHARE OF SURVIVING SPOUSE

General Comment

The elective share of the surviving spouse was fundamentally revised in 1990 and was reorganized and clarified in 1993 and 2008. The main purpose of the revisions is to bring elective-share law into line with the contemporary view of marriage as an economic partnership. The economic partnership theory of marriage is already implemented under the equitable-distribution system applied in both the common-law and community-property states when a marriage ends in divorce. When a marriage ends in death, that theory is also already implemented under the community-property system and under the system promulgated in the Model Marital Property Act. In the common-law states, however, elective-share law has not caught up to the partnership theory of marriage.

The general effect of implementing the partnership theory in elective-share law is to increase the entitlement of a surviving spouse in a long-term marriage in cases in which the marital assets were disproportionately titled in the decedent's name; and to decrease or even eliminate the entitlement of a surviving spouse in a long-term marriage in cases in which the marital assets were more or less equally titled or disproportionately titled in the surviving spouse's name. A further general effect is to decrease or even eliminate the entitlement of a surviving spouse in a short-term, later-in-life marriage (typically

a post-widowhood remarriage) in which neither spouse contributed much, if anything, to the acquisition of the other's wealth, except that a special supplemental elective-share amount is provided in cases in which the surviving spouse would otherwise be left without sufficient funds for support.

The Partnership Theory of Marriage

The partnership theory of marriage, sometimes also called the marital-sharing theory, is stated in various ways. Sometimes it is thought of "as an expression of the presumed intent of husbands and wives to pool their fortunes on an equal basis, share and share alike." M. Glendon, The Transformation of Family Law 131 (1989). Under this approach, the economic rights of each spouse are seen as deriving from an unspoken marital bargain under which the partners agree that each is to enjoy a half interest in the fruits of the marriage, i.e., in the property nominally acquired by and titled in the sole name of either partner during the marriage (other than in property acquired by gift or inheritance). A decedent who disinherits his or her surviving spouse is seen as having reneged on the bargain. Sometimes the theory is expressed in restitutionary terms, a return-of-contribution notion. Under this approach, the law grants each spouse an entitlement to compensation for non-monetary contributions to the marital enterprise, as "a recognition of the activity of one spouse in the home and to compensate not only for this activity but for opportunities lost." Id. See also American Law Institute, Principles of Family Dissolution § 4.09 Comment c (2002).

No matter how the rationale is expressed, the community-property system, including that version of community law promulgated in the Model Marital Property Act, recognizes the partnership theory, but it is sometimes thought that the common-law system denies it. In the ongoing marriage, it is true that the basic principle in the common-law (title-based) states is that marital status does not affect the ownership of property. The regime is one of separate property. Each spouse owns all that he or she earns. By contrast, in the community-property states, each spouse acquires an ownership interest in half the property the other earns during the marriage. By granting each spouse upon acquisition an immediate half interest in the earnings of the other, the community-property regimes directly recognize that the couple's enterprise is in essence collaborative.

The common-law states, however, also give effect or purport to give effect to the partnership theory when a marriage is dissolved by divorce. If the marriage ends in divorce, a spouse who sacrificed his or her financial-earning opportunities to contribute so-called domestic services to the marital enterprise (such as child rearing and homemaking) stands to be recompensed. All states now follow the equitable-distribution system upon divorce, under which "broad discretion [is given to] trial courts to assign to either spouse property acquired during the marriage, irrespective of title, taking into account the circumstances of the particular case and recognizing the value of the contributions of a nonworking spouse or homemaker to the acquisition of that property. Simply stated, the system of equitable distribution views marriage as essentially a shared enterprise or joint undertaking in the nature of a partnership to which both spouses contribute–directly and indirectly, financially and nonfinancially–the fruits of which are distributable at divorce." J. Gregory, The Law of Equitable Distribution ¶ 1.03, at p. 1-6 (1989).

The other situation in which spousal property rights figure prominently is disinheritance at death. The original (pre-1990) Uniform Probate Code, along with almost all other non-UPC common-law states, treats this as one of the few instances in American law where the decedent's testamentary freedom with respect to his or her title-based ownership interests must be curtailed. No matter what the decedent's intent, the original Uniform Probate Code and almost all of the non-UPC common-law states recognize that the surviving spouse does have some claim to a portion of the decedent's estate. These statutes provide the spouse a so-called forced share. The forced share is expressed as an option that the survivor can elect or let lapse during the administration of the decedent's estate, hence in the UPC the forced share is termed the "elective" share.

Elective-share law in the common-law states, however, has not caught up to the partnership theory of marriage. Under typical American elective-share law, including the elective share provided by the original Uniform Probate Code, a surviving spouse may claim a one-third share of the decedent's estate–not the 50 percent share of the couple's combined assets that the partnership theory would imply.

Long-term Marriages. To illustrate the discrepancy between the partnership theory and conventional elective-share law, consider first a long-term marriage, in which the couple's combined assets were accumulated mostly during the course of the marriage. The original elective-share fraction of one-third of the decedent's estate plainly does not implement a partnership principle. The actual result depends on which spouse happens to die first and on how the property accumulated during the marriage was nominally titled.

Example 1–Long-term Marriage under Conventional Forced-share Law. Consider A and B, who were married in their twenties or early thirties; they never divorced, and A died at age, say, 70, survived by B. For whatever reason, A left a will entirely disinheriting B.

Throughout their long life together, the couple managed to accumulate assets worth $600,000, marking them as a somewhat affluent but hardly wealthy couple.

Under conventional elective-share law, B's ultimate entitlement depends on the manner in which these $600,000 in assets were nominally titled as between them. B could end up much poorer or much richer than a 50/50 partnership principle would suggest. The reason is that under conventional elective-share law, B has a claim to one-third of A's "estate."

Marital Assets Disproportionately Titled in Decedent's Name; Conventional Elective-share Law Frequently Entitles Survivor to Less Than Equal Share of Marital Assets. If all the marital assets were titled in A's name, B's claim against A's estate would only be for $200,000—well below B's $300,000 entitlement produced by the partnership/marital-sharing principle.

If $500,000 of the marital assets were titled in A's name, B's claim against A's estate would still only be for $166,667 (1/3 of $500,000), which when combined with B's "own" $100,000 yields a $266,667 cut for B—still below the $300,000 figure produced by the partnership/marital-sharing principle.

Marital Assets Equally Titled; Conventional Elective-share Law Entitles Survivor to Disproportionately Large Share. If $300,000 of the marital assets were titled in A's name, B would still have a claim against A's estate for $100,000, which when combined with B's "own" $300,000 yields a $400,000 cut for B—well above the $300,000 amount to which the partnership/marital-sharing principle would lead.

Marital Assets Disproportionately Titled in Survivor's Name; Conventional Elective-share Law Entitles Survivor to Magnify the Disproportion. If only $200,000 were titled in A's name, B would still have a claim against A's estate for $66,667 (1/3 of $200,000), even though B was already overcompensated as judged by the partnership/marital-sharing theory.

Short-term, Later-in-Life Marriages. Short-term marriages, particularly the post-widowhood remarriage occurring later in life, present different considerations. Because each spouse in this type of marriage typically comes into the marriage owning assets derived from a former marriage, the one-third fraction of the decedent's estate far exceeds a 50/50 division of assets acquired during the marriage.

Example 2–Short-term, Later-in-Life Marriage under Conventional Elective-share Law. Consider B and C. A year or so after A's death, B married C. Both B and C are in their seventies, and after five years of marriage, B dies survived by C. Both B and C have adult children and a few grandchildren by their prior marriages, and each naturally would prefer to leave most or all of his or her property to those children.

The value of the couple's combined assets is $600,000, $300,000 of which is titled in B's name (the decedent) and $300,000 of which is titled in C's name (the survivor).

For reasons that are not immediately apparent, conventional elective-share law gives the survivor, C, a right to claim one-third of B's estate, thereby shrinking B's estate (and hence the share of B's children by B's prior marriage to A) by $100,000 (reducing it to $200,000) while supplementing C's assets (which will likely go to C's children by C's prior

marriage) by $100,000 (increasing their value to $400,000).

Conventional elective-share law, in other words, basically rewards the children of the remarried spouse who manages to outlive the other, arranging for those children a windfall share of one-third of the "loser's" estate. The "winning" spouse who chanced to survive gains a windfall, for this "winner" is unlikely to have made a contribution, monetary or otherwise, to the "loser's" wealth remotely worth one-third.

The Redesigned Elective Share

The redesigned elective share is intended to bring elective-share law into line with the partnership theory of marriage.

In the long-term marriage illustrated in Example 1, the effect of implementing a partnership theory is to increase the entitlement of the surviving spouse when the marital assets were disproportionately titled in the decedent's name; and to decrease or even eliminate the entitlement of the surviving spouse when the marital assets were more or less equally titled or disproportionately titled in the surviving spouse's name. Put differently, the effect is both to reward the surviving spouse who sacrificed his or her financial-earning opportunities in order to contribute so-called domestic services to the marital enterprise and to deny an additional windfall to the surviving spouse in whose name the fruits of a long-term marriage were mostly titled.

In the short-term, later-in-life marriage illustrated in Example 2, the effect of implementing a partnership theory is to decrease or even eliminate the entitlement of the surviving spouse because in such a marriage neither spouse is likely to have contributed much, if anything, to the acquisition of the other's wealth. Put differently, the effect is to deny a windfall to the survivor who contributed little to the decedent's wealth, and ultimately to deny a windfall to the survivor's children by a prior marriage at the expense of the decedent's children by a prior marriage. Bear in mind that in such a marriage, which produces no children, a decedent who disinherits or largely disinherits the surviving spouse may not be acting so much from malice or spite toward the surviving spouse, but from a natural instinct to want to leave most or all of his or her property to the children of his or her former, long-term marriage. In hardship cases, however, as explained later, a special supplemental elective-share amount is provided when the surviving spouse would otherwise be left without sufficient funds for support.

2008 Revisions. When first promulgated in the early 1990s, the statute provided that the "elective-share percentage" increased annually according to a graduated schedule. The "elective-share percentage" ranged from a low of 0 percent for a marriage of less than one year to a high of 50 percent for a marriage of 15 years or more. The "elective-share percentage" did double duty. The system equated the "elective-share percentage" of the couple's combined assets with 50 percent of the marital-property portion of the couple's assets—the assets that are subject to equalization under the partnership theory of marriage. Consequently, the elective share effected the partnership theory rather indirectly. Although the schedule was designed to represent by approximation a constant fifty percent of the marital-property portion of the couple's assets (the augmented estate), it did not say so explicitly.

The 2008 revisions are designed to present the system in a more direct form, one that makes the system more transparent and therefore more understandable. The 2008 revisions disentangle the elective-share percentage from the system that approximates the marital-property portion of the augmented estate. As revised, the statute provides that the "elective-share percentage" is always 50 percent, but it is not 50 percent of the augmented estate but 50 percent of the "marital-property portion" of the augmented estate. The marital-property portion of the augmented estate is computed by approximation—by applying the percentages set forth in a graduated schedule that increases annually with the length of the marriage (each "marital-portion percentage" being double the percentage previously set forth in the "elective-share percentage" schedule). Thus, for example, under the former system, the elective-share amount in a marriage of 10 years was 30 percent of the augmented estate. Under the revised system, the elective-share amount is 50 percent of the marital-property portion of the augmented estate, the marital-property portion of the augmented estate being 60 percent of the augmented estate.

The primary benefit of these changes is that the statute, as revised, presents the elective-share's implementation of the partnership theory of marriage in a direct rather than indirect form, adding clarity and transparency to the system. An important byproduct of the revision is that it facilitates the inclusion of an alternative provision for enacting states that want to implement the partnership theory of marriage but prefer not to define the marital-property portion by approximation but by

classification. Under the deferred marital-property approach, the marital-property portion consists of the value of the couple's property that was acquired during the marriage other than by gift or inheritance. (See below.)

The 2008 revisions are based on a proposal presented in Waggoner, "The Uniform Probate Code's Elective Share: Time for a Reassessment," 37 U. Mich. J. L. Reform 1 (2003), an article that gives a more extensive explanation of the rationale of the 2008 revisions.

Specific Features of the Redesigned Elective Share

Because ease of administration and predictability of result are prized features of the probate system, the redesigned elective share implements the marital-partnership theory by means of a mechanically determined approximation system. Under the redesigned elective share, there is no need to identify which of the couple's property was earned during the marriage and which was acquired prior to the marriage or acquired during the marriage by gift or inheritance. For further discussion of the reasons for choosing this method, see Waggoner, "Spousal Rights in Our Multiple-Marriage Society: The Revised Uniform Probate Code," 26 Real Prop. Prob. & Tr. J. 683 (1992).

Section 2-202(a)–The "Elective-share Amount." Under Section 2-202(a), the elective-share amount is equal to 50 percent of the value of the "marital-property portion of the augmented estate." The marital-property portion of the augmented estate, which is determined under Section 2-203(b), increases with the length of the marriage. The longer the marriage, the larger the "marital-property portion of the augmented estate." The sliding scale adjusts for the correspondingly greater contribution to the acquisition of the couple's marital property in a marriage of 15 years than in a marriage of 15 days. Specifically, the "marital-property portion of the augmented estate" starts low and increases annually according to a graduated schedule until it reaches 100 percent. After one year of marriage, the marital-property portion of the augmented estate is six percent of the augmented estate and it increases with each additional year of marriage until it reaches the maximum 100 percent level after 15 years of marriage.

Section 2-203(a)–the "Augmented Estate." The elective-share percentage of 50 percent is applied to the value of the "marital-property portion of the augmented estate." As defined in Section 2-203, the "augmented estate" equals the value of the couple's *combined* assets, not merely the value of the assets nominally titled in the decedent's name.

More specifically, the "augmented estate" is composed of the sum of four elements:

Section 2-204—the value of the decedent's net probate estate;

Section 2-205—the value of the decedent's nonprobate transfers to others, consisting of will-substitute-type inter-vivos transfers made by the decedent to others than the surviving spouse;

Section 2-206—the value of the decedent's nonprobate transfers to the surviving spouse, consisting of will-substitute-type inter-vivos transfers made by the decedent to the surviving spouse; and

Section 2-207—the value of the surviving spouse's net assets at the decedent's death, plus any property that would have been in the surviving spouse's nonprobate transfers to others under Section 2-205 had the surviving spouse been the decedent.

Section 2-203(b)—the "Marital-property portion" of the Augmented Estate. Section 2-203(b) defines the marital-property portion of the augmented estate.

Section 2-202(a)—the "Elective-share Amount." Section 2-202(a) requires the elective-share percentage of 50 percent to be applied to the value of the marital-property portion of the augmented estate. This calculation yields the "elective-share amount"—the amount to which the surviving spouse is entitled. If the elective-share percentage were to be applied only to the marital-property portion of the decedent's assets, a surviving spouse who has already been overcompensated in terms of the way the marital-property portion of the couple's assets have been nominally titled would receive a further windfall under the elective-share system. The marital-property portion of the couple's assets, in other words, would not be equalized. By applying the elective-share percentage of 50 percent to the marital-property portion of the augmented estate (the couple's combined assets), the redesigned system denies any significance to how the spouses took title to particular assets.

Section 2-209—Satisfying the Elective-share Amount. Section 2-209 determines how the elective-share amount is to be satisfied. Under Section 2-209, the decedent's net probate estate and nonprobate transfers to others are liable to contribute to the satisfaction of the elective-share amount only to the extent the elective-share amount is not fully satisfied by the sum of the following amounts:

Subsection (a)(1)—amounts that pass or have passed from the decedent to the surviving spouse by testate or intestate succession and amounts included in the augmented estate under Section 2-206, i.e., the value of the decedent's nonprobate transfers to the surviving spouse; and

Subsection (a)(2)—the marital-property portion of amounts included in the augmented estate under Section 2-207.

If the combined value of these amounts equals or exceeds the elective-share amount, the surviving spouse is not entitled to any further amount from recipients of the decedent's net probate estate or nonprobate transfers to others, unless the surviving spouse is entitled to a supplemental elective-share amount under Section 2-202(b).

Example 3—15-Year or Longer Marriage under Redesigned Elective Share; Marital Assets Disproportionately Titled in Decedent's Name. A and B were married to each other more than 15 years. A died, survived by B. A's will left nothing to B, and A made no nonprobate transfers to B. A made nonprobate transfers to others in the amount of $100,000 as defined in Section 2-205.

	Augmented Estate	Marital-Property Portion (100%)
A's net probate estate	$300,000	$300,000
A's nonprobate transfers to others	$100,000	$100,000
A's nonprobate transfers to B	$0	$0
B's assets and nonprobate transfers to others	$200,000	$200,000
Augmented Estate	$600,000	$600,000

Elective-Share Amount (50 % of Marital-Property portion)..................................$300,000
Less Amount Already Satisfied.................$200,000
Unsatisfied Balance...........................$100,000

Under Section 2-209(a)(2), the full value of B's assets ($200,000) counts first toward satisfying B's entitlement. B, therefore, is treated as already having received $200,000 of B's ultimate entitlement of

$300,000. Section 2-209(c) makes A's net probate estate and nonprobate transfers to others liable for the unsatisfied balance of the elective-share amount, $100,000, which is the amount needed to bring B's own $200,000 up to $300,000.

Example 4—15-Year or Longer Marriage under Redesigned Elective Share; Marital Assets Disproportionately Titled in Survivor's Name. As in Example 3, A and B were married to each other more than 15 years. A died, survived by B. A's will left nothing to B, and A made no nonprobate transfers to B. A made nonprobate transfers to others in the amount of $50,000 as defined in Section 2-205.

	Augmented Estate	Marital-Property Portion (100%)
A's net probate estate	$150,000	$150,000
A's nonprobate transfers to others	$50,000	$50,000
A's nonprobate transfers to B	$0	$0
B's assets and nonprobate transfers to others	$400,000	$400,000
Augmented Estate	$600,000	$600,000

Elective-Share Amount (50% of Marital-Property portion)............................$300,000
Less Amount Already Satisfied..................$400,000
Unsatisfied Balance.............................. $0

Under Section 2-209(a)(2), the full value of B's assets ($400,000) counts first toward satisfying B's entitlement. B, therefore, is treated as already having received more than B's ultimate entitlement of $300,000. B has no claim on A's net probate estate or nonprobate transfers to others.

In a marriage that has lasted less than 15 years, only a portion of the survivor's assets—not all—count toward making up the elective-share amount. This is because, in these shorter-term marriages, the marital-property portion of the survivor's assets under Section 2-203(b) is less than 100% and, under Section 2-209(a)(2), the portion of the survivor's assets that count toward making up the elective-share amount is limited to the marital-property portion of those assets.

To explain why this is appropriate requires further elaboration of the underlying theory of the redesigned system. The system avoids the classification and tracing-to-source problems in determining the marital-property portion of the couple's assets. This is accomplished under Section 2-203(b) by applying an ever-increasing percentage, as the length of the marriage increases, to the couple's combined assets without regard to when or how those assets were acquired. By approximation, the redesigned system equates the marital-property portion of the couple's combined assets with the couple's marital assets—assets subject to equalization under the partnership/marital-sharing theory. Thus, in a marriage that has endured long enough for the marital-property portion of their assets to be 60% under Section 2-203(b), 60% of each spouse's assets are treated as marital assets. Section 2-209(a)(2) therefore counts only 60% of the survivor's assets toward making up the elective-share amount.

Example 5—Under 15-Year Marriage under the Redesigned Elective Share; Marital Assets Disproportionately Titled in Decedent's Name. A and B were married to each other more than 5 but less than 6 years. A died, survived by B. A's will left nothing to B, and A made no nonprobate transfers to B. A made nonprobate transfers to others in the amount of $100,000 as defined in Section 2-205.

	Augmented Estate	Marital-Property Portion (30%)
A's net probate estate	$300,000	$90,000
A's nonprobate transfers to others	$100,000	$30,000
A's nonprobate transfers to B	$0	$0
B's assets and nonprobate transfers to others	$200,000	$60,000
Augmented Estate	$600,000	$180,000

Elective-Share Amount (50% of Marital-Property portion)....................................$90,000
Less Amount Already Satisfied...................$60,000
Unsatisfied Balance...........................$30,000

Under Section 2-209(a)(2), the marital-property portion of B's assets (30% of $200,000, or $60,000) counts first toward satisfying B's entitlement. B, therefore, is treated as already having received $60,000 of B's ultimate entitlement of $90,000. Under Section 2-209(c), B has a claim on A's net probate estate and nonprobate transfers to others of $30,000.

Deferred Marital-Property Alternative

By making the elective share percentage a flat 50 percent of the marital-property portion of the augmented estate, the 2007 revision disentangles the elective share percentage from the approximation schedule, thus allowing the marital-property portion of the augmented estate to be defined either by the approximation schedule or by the deferred-marital-property approach. Although one of the benefits of the 2007 revision is added clarity, an important byproduct of the revision is that it facilitates the inclusion of an alternative provision for enacting states that prefer a deferred marital-property approach. See Alan Newman, Incorporating the Partnership Theory of Marriage into Elective-Share Law: the Approximation System of the Uniform Probate Code and the Deferred-Community-Property Alternative, 49 Emory L.J. 487 (2000).

The Support Theory

The partnership/marital-sharing theory is not the only driving force behind elective-share law. Another theoretical basis for elective-share law is that the spouses' mutual duties of support during their joint lifetimes should be continued in some form after death in favor of the survivor, as a claim on the decedent's estate. Current elective-share law implements this theory poorly. The fixed fraction, whether it is the typical one-third or some other fraction, disregards the survivor's actual need. A one-third share may be inadequate to the surviving spouse's needs, especially in a modest estate. On the other hand, in a very large estate, it may go far beyond the survivor's needs. In either a modest or a large estate, the survivor may or may not have ample independent means, and this factor, too, is disregarded in conventional elective-share law. The redesigned elective share system implements the support theory by granting the survivor a supplemental elective-share amount related to the survivor's actual needs. In implementing a support rationale, the length of the marriage is quite irrelevant. Because the duty of support is founded upon status, it arises at the time of the marriage.

Section 2-202(b)–the "Supplemental Elective-share Amount." Section 2-202(b) is the provision that implements the support theory by providing a supplemental elective-share amount of $75,000. The $75,000 figure is bracketed to indicate that individual states may wish to select a higher or lower amount.

In satisfying this $75,000 amount, the surviving spouse's own titled-based ownership interests count first toward making up this supplemental amount; included in the survivor's assets for this purpose are amounts shifting to the survivor at the decedent's death and amounts owing to the survivor from the decedent's estate under the accrual-type elective-share apparatus discussed above, but excluded are (1) amounts going to the survivor under the Code's probate exemptions and allowances and (2) the survivor's Social Security benefits (and other governmental benefits, such as Medicare insurance coverage). If the survivor's assets are less than the $75,000 minimum, then the survivor is entitled to whatever additional portion of the decedent's estate is necessary, up to 100 percent of it, to bring the survivor's assets up to that minimum level. In the case of a late marriage, in which the survivor is perhaps aged in the mid-seventies, the minimum figure plus the probate exemptions and allowances (which under the Code amount to a minimum of another $64,500) is pretty much on target—in conjunction with Social Security payments and other governmental benefits—to provide the survivor with a fairly adequate means of support.

Example 6–Supplemental Elective-share Amount. After A's death in Example 1, B married C. Five years later, B died, survived by C. B's will left nothing to C, and B made no nonprobate transfers to C. B made no nonprobate transfers to others as defined in Section 2-205.

	Augmented Estate	Marital-Property Portion (30%)
B's net probate estate	$90,000	$27,000
B's nonprobate transfers to others	$0	$0
B's nonprobate transfers to C	$0	$0
C's assets and nonprobate transfers to others	$10,000	$3,000
Augmented Estate	$100,000	$30,000

Elective-Share Amount (50% of Marital-Property portion) $15,000
Less Amount Already Satisfied $3,000
Unsatisfied Balance. $12,000

Solution under Redesigned Elective Share. Under Section 2-209(a)(2), $3,000 (30%) of C's assets count first toward making up C's elective-share amount; under Section 2-209(c), the remaining $12,000 elective-share amount would come from B's net probate estate.

Application of Section 2-202(b) shows that C is entitled to a supplemental elective-share amount. The calculation of C's supplemental elective-share amount begins by determining the sum of the amounts described in sections:

2-207	$10,000
2-209(a)(1)	0
Elective-share amount payable from decedent's probate estate under Section 2-209(c)	$12,000
Total	$22,000

The above calculation shows that C is entitled to a supplemental elective-share amount under Section 2-202(b) of $53,000 ($75,000 minus $22,000). The supplemental elective-share amount is payable entirely from B's net probate estate, as prescribed in Section 2-209(c).

The end result is that C is entitled to $65,000 ($12,000 + $53,000) by way of elective share from B's net probate estate (and nonprobate transfers to others, had there been any). Sixty-five thousand dollars is the amount necessary to bring C's $10,000 in assets up to $75,000.

Decedent's Nonprobate Transfers to Others

The pre-1990 Code made great strides toward preventing "fraud on the spouse's share." The problem of "fraud on the spouse's share" arises when the decedent seeks to evade the spouse's elective share by engaging in various kinds of nominal inter-vivos transfers. To render that type of behavior ineffective, the original Code adopted the augmented-estate concept, which extended the elective-share entitlement to property that was the subject of specified types of inter-vivos transfer, such as revocable inter-vivos trusts.

In the redesign of the elective share, the augmented-estate concept has been strengthened. The pre-1990 Code left several loopholes ajar in the augmented estate—a notable one being life insurance the decedent buys, naming someone other than his or her surviving spouse as the beneficiary. With appropriate protection for the insurance company that pays off before receiving notice of an elective-share claim, the redesigned elective-share system includes these types of insurance policies in the augmented estate as part of the decedent's nonprobate transfers to others under Section 2-205.

Historical Note. This General Comment was revised in 1993 and in 2008.

2008 Legislative Note. States that have previously enacted the UPC elective share need not amend their enactment, except that (1) the supplemental elective-share amount under Section 2-202(b) should be increased to $75,000, (2) the amendment to Section 2-205(3) relating to gifts within two years of death should be adopted, and (3) Section 2-209(e) should be added so that the unsatisfied balance of the elective-share or supplemental elective-share amount is treated as a general pecuniary devise for purposes of Section 3-904.

§ 2-201. Definitions. In this [part]:

(1) As used in sections other than Section 2-205, "decedent's nonprobate transfers to others" means the amounts that are included in the augmented estate under Section 2-205.

(2) "Fractional interest in property held in joint tenancy with the right of survivorship", whether the fractional interest is unilaterally severable or not, means the fraction, the numerator of which is one and the denominator of which, if the decedent was a joint tenant, is one plus the number of joint tenants who survive the decedent and which, if the decedent was not a joint tenant, is the number of joint tenants.

(3) "Marriage", as it relates to a transfer by the decedent during marriage, means any marriage of the decedent to the decedent's surviving spouse.

(4) "Nonadverse party" means a person who does not have a substantial beneficial interest in the trust or other property arrangement that would be adversely affected by the exercise or nonexercise of the power that he [or she] possesses respecting the trust or other property arrangement. A person having a general power of appointment over property is deemed to have a beneficial interest in the property.

(5) "Power" or "power of appointment" includes a power to designate the beneficiary of a

beneficiary designation.

(6) "Presently exercisable general power of appointment" means a power of appointment under which, at the time in question, the decedent, whether or not he [or she] then had the capacity to exercise the power, held a power to create a present or future interest in himself [or herself], his [or her] creditors, his [or her] estate, or creditors of his [or her] estate, and includes a power to revoke or invade the principal of a trust or other property arrangement.

(7) "Property" includes values subject to a beneficiary designation.

(8) "Right to income" includes a right to payments under a commercial or private annuity, an annuity trust, a unitrust, or a similar arrangement.

(9) "Transfer", as it relates to a transfer by or of the decedent, includes:

(A) an exercise or release of a presently exercisable general power of appointment held by the decedent,

(B) a lapse at death of a presently exercisable general power of appointment held by the decedent, and

(C) an exercise, release, or lapse of a general power of appointment that the decedent created in himself [or herself] and of a power described in Section 2-205(2)(B) that the decedent conferred on a nonadverse party.

§ 2-202. Elective Share.

(a) [Elective-Share Amount.] The surviving spouse of a decedent who dies domiciled in this state has a right of election, under the limitations and conditions stated in this [part], to take an elective-share amount equal to 50 percent of the value of the marital-property portion of the augmented estate.

(b) [Supplemental Elective-Share Amount.] If the sum of the amounts described in Sections 2-207, 2-209(a)(1), and that part of the elective-share amount payable from the decedent's net probate estate and nonprobate transfers to others under Section 2-209(c) and (d) is less than [$75,000], the surviving spouse is entitled to a supplemental elective-share amount equal to [$75,000], minus the sum of the amounts described in those sections. The supplemental elective-share amount is payable from the decedent's net probate estate and from recipients of the decedent's nonprobate transfers to others in the order of priority set forth in Section 2-209(c) and (d).

(c) [Effect of Election on Statutory Benefits.] If the right of election is exercised by or on behalf of the surviving spouse, the surviving spouse's homestead allowance, exempt property, and family allowance, if any, are not charged against but are in addition to the elective-share and supplemental elective-share amounts.

(d) [Non-Domiciliary.] The right, if any, of the surviving spouse of a decedent who dies domiciled outside this state to take an elective share in property in this state is governed by the law of the decedent's domicile at death.

Comment

Pre-1990 Provision. The pre-1990 provisions granted the surviving spouse a one-third share of the augmented estate. The one-third fraction was largely a carryover from common-law dower, under which a surviving widow had a one-third interest for life in her deceased husband's land.

Purpose and Scope of Revisions. The revision of this section is the first step in the overall plan of implementing a partnership or marital-sharing theory of marriage, with a support theory back-up.

Subsection (a). Subsection (a) implements the partnership theory by providing that the elective-share amount is 50 percent of the value of the marital-property portion of the augmented estate. The augmented estate is defined in Section 2-203(a) and the marital-property portion of the augmented estate is defined in Section 2-203(b).

Subsection (b). Subsection (b) implements the support theory of the elective share by providing a [$75,000] supplemental elective-share amount, in case the surviving spouse's assets and other entitlements are below this figure.

Subsection (c). The homestead, exempt property, and family allowances provided by Article II, Part 4, are not charged to the electing spouse as a part of the elective share. Consequently, these allowances may be distributed from the probate estate without reference to whether an elective share right is asserted.

Cross Reference. To have the right to an elective share under subsection (a), the decedent's spouse must survive the decedent. Under Section 2-702(a), the requirement of survivorship is satisfied only if it can be established that the spouse survived the decedent by 120 hours.

Historical Note. This Comment was revised in 1993 and 2008.

§ 2-203. Composition of the Augmented Estate; Marital-Property Portion.

(a) Subject to Section 2-208, the value of the augmented estate, to the extent provided in Sections 2-204, 2-205, 2-206, and 2-207, consists of the sum of the values of all property, whether real or personal, movable or immovable, tangible or intangible, wherever situated, that constitute:

    (1) the decedent's net probate estate;

    (2) the decedent's nonprobate transfers to others;

    (3) the decedent's nonprobate transfers to the surviving spouse; and

    (4) the surviving spouse's property and nonprobate transfers to others.

Alternative A

(b) The value of the marital-property portion of the augmented estate consists of the sum of the values of the four components of the augmented estate as determined under subsection (a) multiplied by the following percentage:

If the decedent and the spouse were married to each other:	The percentage is:
Less than 1 year	3%
1 year but less than 2 years	6%
2 years but less than 3 years	12%
3 years but less than 4 years	18%
4 years but less than 5 years	24%
5 years but less than 6 years	30%
6 years but less than 7 years	36%
7 years but less than 8 years	42%
8 years but less than 9 years	48%
9 years but less than 10 years	54%
10 years but less than 11 years	60%
11 years but less than 12 years	68%
12 years but less than 13 years	76%
13 years but less than 14 years	84%
14 years but less than 15 years	92%
15 years or more	100%

Alternative B

(b) The value of the marital-property portion of the augmented estate equals the value of that portion of the augmented estate that would be marital property at the decedent's death under [the Model Marital Property Act] [copy in definition from Model Marital Property Act, including the presumption that all property is marital property] [copy in other definition chosen by the enacting state.

End of Alternatives

Comment

Subsection (a) operates as an umbrella section identifying the augmented estate as consisting of the sum of the values of four components. On the decedent's side are the values of (1) the decedent's net probate estate (Section 2-204) and (2) the decedent's nonprobate transfers to others (Section 2-205). Straddling between the decedent's side and the surviving spouse's side is the value of (3) the decedent's nonprobate transfers to the surviving spouse (Section 2-206). On the surviving spouse's side are the values of (4) the surviving spouse's net assets and the surviving spouse's nonprobate transfers to others (Section 2-207). Under Section 2-202(a), the elective-share percentage is 50 percent of the value of the marital-property portion of the augmented estate.

Subsection (b) contains alternative provisions. Alternative A is for states that wish to define the marital-property portion of the augmented estate by approximation based on the length of the marriage. Alternative B is for states that wish to define the marital-property portion of the estate in derms of a deferred marital property approach such as the Model Marital Property Act (1983).

Alternative A provides a schedule for determining

the marital-property portion of the value of the four components of the augmented estate. The schedule deems by approximation that 100 percent of the components of the augmented estate is marital property after 15 years of marriage. Government data indicate that the median length of a first marriage that does not end in divorce is 46.3 years, the median length of a post-divorce remarriage that does not end in divorce is 35.1 years, and the median length of a post-widowhood remarriage that does not end in divorce is 14.4 years. Enacting states may determine that this data supports lengthening the schedule in subsection (b) to 20 or even 25 years. See Lawrence W. Waggoner, The Uniform Probate Code's Elective Share: Time for a Reassessment, 37 U. Mich. J. L. Reform 1, 11-29 (2003).

Alternative B is provided for states that decide not to define the marital-property portion of the augmented estate by approximation, but rather in terms of property actually acquired during the marriage other than by gift or inheritance. See Waggoner, supra, at 30-32.

Historical Note. This Comment was added in 1993 and revised in 2008 and 2011.

§ 2-204. Decedent's Net Probate Estate.
The value of the augmented estate includes the value of the decedent's probate estate, reduced by funeral and administration expenses, homestead allowance, family allowances, exempt property, and enforceable claims.

Comment

This section, which in the 1990 version appeared as a paragraph of a single, long section defining the augmented estate, establishes as the first component of the augmented estate the value of the decedent's probate estate, reduced by funeral and administration expenses, homestead allowance (Section 2-402), family allowances (Section 2-404), exempt property (Section 2-403), and enforceable claims. The term "claims" is defined in Section 1-201 as including "liabilities of the decedent or protected person whether arising in contract, in tort, or otherwise, and liabilities of the estate which arise at or after the death

of the decedent or after the appointment of a conservator, including funeral expenses and expenses of administration. The term does not include estate or inheritance taxes, or demands or disputes regarding title of a decedent or protected person to specific assets alleged to be included in the estate."

Various aspects of Section 2-204 are illustrated by Examples 10, 11, and 12 in the Comment to Section 2-205, below.

Historical Note. This Comment was added in 1993.

§ 2-205. Decedent's Nonprobate Transfers to Others.
The value of the augmented estate includes the value of the decedent's nonprobate transfers to others, not included under Section 2-204, of any of the following types, in the amount provided respectively for each type of transfer:

(1) Property owned or owned in substance by the decedent immediately before death that passed outside probate at the decedent's death. Property included under this category consists of:

(A) Property over which the decedent alone, immediately before death, held a presently exercisable general power of appointment. The amount included is the value of the property subject to the power, to the extent the property passed at the decedent's death, by exercise, release, lapse, in default, or otherwise, to or for the benefit of any person other than the decedent's estate or surviving spouse.

(B) The decedent's fractional interest in property held by the decedent in joint tenancy with the right of survivorship. The amount included is the value of the decedent's fractional interest, to the extent the fractional interest passed by right of survivorship at the decedent's death to a surviving joint tenant other than the decedent's surviving spouse.

(C) The decedent's ownership interest in property or accounts held in POD, TOD, or co-ownership registration with the right of survivorship. The amount included is the value of the decedent's ownership interest, to the extent the decedent's ownership interest passed at the decedent's death to or for the benefit of any person other than the decedent's estate or surviving spouse.

(D) Proceeds of insurance, including accidental death benefits, on the life of the decedent, if the decedent owned the insurance policy immediately before death or if and to the extent the decedent alone and immediately before death held a presently exercisable general power of appointment over the policy or its proceeds. The amount included is the value of the proceeds, to the extent they were payable at the decedent's death to or for the benefit of any person other than the decedent's estate or surviving spouse.

(2) Property transferred in any of the following forms by the decedent during marriage:

(A) Any irrevocable transfer in which the decedent retained the right to the possession or enjoyment of, or to the income from, the property if and to the extent the decedent's right terminated at or continued beyond the decedent's death. The amount included is the value of the fraction of the property to which the decedent's right related, to the extent the fraction of the property passed outside probate to or for the benefit of any person other than the decedent's estate or surviving spouse.

(B) Any transfer in which the decedent created a power over income or property, exercisable by the decedent alone or in conjunction with any other person, or exercisable by a nonadverse party, to or for the benefit of the decedent, creditors of the decedent, the decedent's estate, or creditors of the decedent's estate. The amount included with respect to a power over property is the value of the property subject to the power, and the amount included with respect to a power over income is the value of the property that produces or produced the income, to the extent the power in either case was exercisable at the decedent's death to or for the benefit of any person other than the decedent's surviving spouse or to the extent the property passed at the decedent's death, by exercise, release, lapse, in default, or otherwise, to or for the benefit of any person other than the decedent's estate or surviving spouse. If the power is a power over both income and property and the preceding sentence produces different amounts, the amount included is the greater amount.

(3) Property that passed during marriage and during the two-year period next preceding the decedent's death as a result of a transfer by the decedent if the transfer was of any of the following types:

(A) Any property that passed as a result of the termination of a right or interest in, or power over, property that would have been included in the augmented estate under paragraph (1)(A), (B), or (C), or under paragraph (2), if the right, interest, or power had not terminated until the decedent's death. The amount included is the value of the property that would have been included under those paragraphs if the property were valued at the time the right, interest, or power terminated, and is included only to the extent the property passed upon termination to or for the benefit of any person other than the decedent or the decedent's estate, spouse, or surviving spouse. As used in this subparagraph, "termination", with respect to a right or interest in property, occurs when the right or interest terminated by the terms of the governing instrument or the decedent transferred or relinquished the right or interest, and, with respect to a power over property, occurs when the power terminated by exercise, release, lapse, default, or otherwise, but, with respect to a power described in paragraph (1)(A), "termination" occurs when the power terminated by exercise or release, but not otherwise.

(B) Any transfer of or relating to an insurance policy on the life of the decedent if the proceeds would have been included in the augmented estate under paragraph (1)(D) had the transfer not occurred. The amount included is the value of the insurance proceeds to the extent the proceeds were payable at the decedent's death to or for the benefit of any person other than the decedent's estate or surviving spouse.

(C) Any transfer of property, to the extent not otherwise included in the augmented estate, made to or for the benefit of a person other than the decedent's surviving spouse. The amount included is the value of the transferred property to the extent the transfers to any one donee in either of the two years exceeded [$12,000] [the amount exludable from taxable gifts under 26 U.S.C. Section 2503(b) [or its successor] on the date next preceding the date of the decedent's death.]

Legislative Note: In paragraph (3)(C), use the first alternative in the brackets if the second alternative is considered an unlawful delegation of legislative power.

Comment

This section, which in the 1990 version appeared in substance as a paragraph of a single, long section defining the augmented estate, establishes as the second component of the augmented estate the value of the decedent's nonprobate transfers to others. In the 1990 version, the term "reclaimable estate" was used rather than the term "nonprobate transfers to others".

This component is divided into three basic categories: (1) property owned or owned in substance by the decedent immediately before death that passed outside probate to persons other than the surviving spouse; (2) property transferred by the decedent during marriage that passed outside probate to persons other than the surviving spouse; and (3) property transferred by the decedent during marriage and during the two-year period next preceding the decedent's death. Various aspects of each category and each subdivision within each category are discussed and illustrated below.

Paragraph (1)–Property Owned or Owned in Substance by the Decedent. This category covers property that the decedent owned or owned in substance immediately before death and that passed outside probate at the decedent's death to a person or persons other than the surviving spouse. Property owned by the decedent's surviving spouse does not include the value of enhancements to the surviving spouse's earning capacity (e.g., the value of a law, medical, or business degree.

Paragraph (1) subdivides this category into four specific components:

(A) Property over which the decedent alone, immediately before death, held a presently exercisable general power of appointment. The amount included is the value of the property subject to the power, to the extent the property passed at the decedent's death, by exercise, release, lapse, in default, or otherwise, to or for the benefit of any person other than the decedent's estate or surviving spouse.

(B) The decedent's fractional interest in property held by the decedent in joint tenancy with the right of survivorship. The amount included is the value of the decedent's fractional interest, to the extent the fractional interest passed by right of survivorship at the decedent's death to a surviving joint tenant other than the decedent's surviving spouse.

(C) The decedent's ownership interest in property or accounts held in POD, TOD, or co-ownership registration with the right of survivorship. The amount included is the value of the decedent's ownership interest, to the extent the decedent's ownership interest passed at the decedent's death to or for the benefit of any person other than the decedent's estate or surviving spouse.

(D) Proceeds of insurance, including accidental death benefits, on the life of the decedent, if the decedent owned the insurance policy immediately before death or if and to the extent the decedent alone and immediately before death held a presently exercisable general power of appointment over the policy or its proceeds. The amount included is the value of the proceeds, to the extent they were payable at the decedent's death to or for the benefit of any person other than the decedent's estate or surviving spouse.

With one exception for nonseverable joint tenancies (see Example 4 below), each of the above components covers a type of asset of which the decedent could have become the full, technical owner by merely exercising his or her power of appointment, incident of ownership, or right of severance or withdrawal. Had the decedent exercised these powers or rights to become the full, technical owner, the decedent could have controlled the devolution of these assets by his or her will; by not exercising these powers or rights, the decedent allowed the assets to pass outside probate to persons other than the surviving spouse. Thus, *in effect,* property covered by these components passes at the decedent's death by nonprobate transfer from the decedent to others. This is what justifies including these components in the augmented estate without regard to the person who *created* the decedent's substantive ownership interest, whether the decedent or someone else, and without regard to when it was created, whether before or after the decedent's marriage.

Although the augmented estate under the pre-1990 Code did not include life insurance, annuities, etc., payable to other persons, the revisions do include their value; this move recognizes that such arrangements were, under the pre-1990 Code, used to deplete the estate and reduce the spouse's elective-share entitlement.

Various aspects of paragraph (1) are illustrated by the following examples. Other examples illustrating various aspects of this paragraph are Example 19 in this Comment, below, and Examples 20 and 21 in the Comment to Section 2-206, below. In each of the following examples, G is the decedent and S is the decedent's surviving spouse.

Example 1–General Testamentary Power. G's mother, M, created a testamentary trust, providing for the income to go to G for life, remainder in corpus to such persons, including G, G's creditors, G's estate, or the creditors of G's estate, as G by will appoints; in default of appointment, to X. G died, survived by S and X. G's will did not exercise his power in favor of S.

The value of the corpus of the trust at G's death is not included in the augmented estate under paragraph (1)(A), regardless of whether G exercised the power in favor of someone other than S or let the

power lapse, so that the trust corpus passed in default of appointment to X. Section 2-205(1)(A) only applies to presently exercisable general powers; G's power was a general testamentary power. (Note that paragraph (2)(B) does cover property subject to a general testamentary power, but only if the power was created by G during marriage. G's general testamentary power was created by M and hence not covered by paragraph (2)(B).

Example 2–Nongeneral Power and "5-and-5" Power. G's father, F, created a testamentary trust, providing for the income to go to G for life, remainder in corpus to such persons, except G, G's creditors, G's estate, or the creditors of G's estate, as G by will appoints; in default of appointment, to X. G was also given a noncumulative annual power to withdraw an amount equal to the greater of $5,000 or five percent of the trust corpus. G died, survived by S and X. G did not exercise her power in favor of S.

G's power over the remainder interest does not cause inclusion of the value of the full corpus in the augmented estate under paragraph (1)(A) because that power was a nongeneral power.

The value of the greater of $5,000 or five percent of the corpus of the trust at G's death is included in the augmented estate under paragraph (1)(A), to the extent that that property passed at G's death, by exercise, release, lapse, in default, or otherwise, to or for the benefit of any person other than the decedent's estate or surviving spouse, because that portion of the trust corpus was subject to a presently exercisable general power of appointment held by G immediately before G's death. No additional amount is included, however, whether G exercised the withdrawal power or allowed it to lapse in the years prior to G's death. (Note that paragraph (3)(A) is inapplicable to this case. That paragraph only applies to property subject to powers created by the decedent during marriage that lapse within the two-year period next preceding the decedent's death.)

Example 3–Revocable Inter-Vivos Trust. G created a revocable inter-vivos trust, providing for the income to go to G for life, remainder in corpus to such persons, except G, G's creditors, G's estate, or the creditors of G's estate, as G by will appoints; in default of appointment, to X. G died, survived by S and X. G never exercised his power to revoke, and the corpus of the trust passed at G's death to X.

Regardless of whether G created the trust before or after marrying S, the value of the corpus of the trust at G's death is included in the augmented estate under paragraph (1)(A) because, immediately before G's death, the trust corpus was subject to a presently exercisable general power of appointment (the power to revoke: see Section 2-201(6)) held by G.

(Note that if G created the trust during marriage, paragraph (2)(B) also requires inclusion of the value of the trust corpus. Because these two subparagraphs overlap, and because both subparagraphs include the same value, Section 2-208(c) provides that the value of the trust corpus is included under one but not both subparagraphs.)

Example 4–Joint Tenancy. G, X, and Y owned property in joint tenancy. G died, survived by S, X, and Y.

Because G's fractional interest in the property immediately before death was one-third, and because that one-third fractional interest passed by right of survivorship to X and Y at G's death, one-third of the value of the property at G's death is included in the augmented estate under paragraph (1)(B). This is the result whether or not under local law G had the unilateral right to sever her fractional interest. See Section 2-201(2).

Example 5–TOD Registered Securities and POD Account. G registered securities that G owned in TOD form. G also contributed all the funds in a savings account that G registered in POD form. X was designated to take the securities and Y was designated to take the savings account on G's death. G died, survived by S, X, and Y.

Because G was the sole owner of the securities immediately before death (see Sections 6-302 and 6-306), and because ownership of the securities passed to X upon G's death (see Section 6-307), the full value of the securities at G's death is included in the augmented estate under paragraph (1)(C). Because G contributed all the funds in the savings account, G's ownership interest in the savings account immediately before death was 100 percent (see Section 6-211). Because that 100 percentage ownership interest passed by right of survivorship to Y at G's death, the full value of the account at G's death is included in the augmented estate under paragraph (1)(C).

Example 6–Joint Checking Account. G, X, and Y were registered as co-owners of a joint checking account. G contributed 75 percent of the funds in the account. G died, survived by S, X, and Y.

G's ownership interest in the account immediately before death, determined under Section 6-211, was 75 percent of the account. Because that percentage ownership interest passed by right of survivorship to X and Y at G's death, 75 percent of the value of the account at G's death is included in the augmented estate under paragraph (1)(C).

Example 7–Joint Checking Account. G's mother, M, added G's name to her checking account so that G could pay her bills for her. M contributed all the funds in the account. The account was registered in co-ownership form with right of survivorship. G died, survived by S and M.

Because G had contributed none of his own funds to the account, G's ownership interest in the account immediately before death, determined under Section 6-211, was zero. Consequently, no part of the value of the account at G's death is included in the augmented estate under paragraph (1)(C).

Example 8–Life Insurance. G, as owner of a life-insurance policy insuring her life, designated X and Y as the beneficiaries of that policy. G died owning the policy, survived by S, X, and Y.

The full value of the proceeds of that policy is included in the augmented estate under paragraph (1)(D).

Paragraph (2)–Property Transferred by the Decedent During Marriage. This category covers property that the decedent transferred in specified forms during "marriage" (defined in Section 2-201(3) as "any marriage of the decedent to the decedent's surviving spouse"). If the decedent and the surviving spouse were married to each other more than once, transfers that took place during any of their marriages to each other count as transfers during marriage.

The word "transfer", as it relates to a transfer by or of the decedent, is defined in Section 2-201(10), as including "(A) an exercise or release of a presently exercisable general power of appointment held by the decedent, (B) a lapse at death of a presently exercisable general power of appointment held by the decedent, and (C) an exercise, release, or lapse of a general power of appointment that the decedent created in himself [or herself] and of a power described in Section 2-205(2)(B) that the decedent conferred on a nonadverse party."

Paragraph (2) covers the following specific forms of transfer:

(A) Any irrevocable transfer in which the decedent

retained the right to the possession or enjoyment of, or to the income from, the property if and to the extent the decedent's right terminated at or continued beyond the decedent's death. The amount included is the value of the fraction of the property to which the decedent's right related, to the extent the fraction of the property passed outside probate to or for the benefit of any person other than the decedent's estate or surviving spouse.

(B) Any transfer in which the decedent created a power over income or property, exercisable by the decedent alone or in conjunction with any other person, or exercisable by a nonadverse party, to or for the benefit of the decedent, creditors of the decedent, the decedent's estate, or creditors of the decedent's estate. The amount included with respect to a power over property is the value of the property subject to the power, and the amount included with respect to a power over income is the value of the property that produces or produced the income, to the extent the power in either case was exercisable at the decedent's death to or for the benefit of any person other than the decedent's surviving spouse or to the extent the property passed at the decedent's death, by exercise, release, lapse, in default, or otherwise, to or for the benefit of any person other than the decedent's estate or surviving spouse. If the power is a power over both income and property and the preceding sentence produces different amounts, the amount included is the greater amount.

Various aspects of paragraph (2) are illustrated by the following examples. Other examples illustrating various aspects of this paragraph are Examples 1 and 3, above, and Example 22 in the Comment to Section 2-206, below. In the following examples, as in the examples above, G is the decedent and S is the decedent's surviving spouse.

Example 9–Retained Income Interest for Life. Before death, and during marriage, G created an irrevocable inter-vivos trust, providing for the income to be paid annually to G for life, then for the corpus of the trust to go to X. G died, survived by S and X.

The value of the corpus of the trust at G's death is included in the augmented estate under paragraph (2)(A). This paragraph applies to a retained income interest that terminates at the decedent's death, as here. The amount included is the value of the property that passes outside probate to any person other than the decedent's estate or surviving spouse, which in this case is the full value of the corpus that passes outside probate to X.

Had G retained the right to only one-half of the income, with the other half payable to Y for G's lifetime, only one half of the value of the corpus at G's death would have been included under paragraph (2)(A) because that paragraph specifies that "the amount included is the value of the fraction of the property to which the decedent's right related." Note, however, that if G had created the trust within two years before death, paragraph (3)(C) would require the inclusion of the value at the date the trust was established of the other half of the income interest for G's life and of the remainder interest in the other half of the corpus, each value to be reduced by as much as $12,000 as appropriate under the facts, taking into account other gifts made to Y and to X in the same year, if any.

Example 10–Retained Unitrust Interest for a Term. Before death, and during marriage, G created an irrevocable inter-vivos trust, providing for a fixed percentage of the value of the corpus of the trust (determined annually) to be paid annually to G for 10 years, then for the corpus of the trust (and any accumulated income) to go to X. G died six years after the trust was created, survived by S and X.

The full value of the corpus at G's death is included in the augmented estate under a combination of Sections 2-204 and 2-205(2)(A).

Section 2-205(2)(A) requires the inclusion of the commuted value of X's remainder interest at G's death. This paragraph applies to a retained income interest, which under Section 2-201(8) includes a unitrust interest. Moreover, Section 2-205(2)(A) not only applies to a retained income interest that terminates at the decedent's death, but also applies to a retained income interest that continues beyond the decedent's death, as here. The amount included is the value of the interest that passes outside probate to a person other than the decedent's estate or surviving spouse, which in this case is the commuted value of X's remainder interest at G's death.

Section 2-204 requires the inclusion of the commuted value of the remaining four years of G's unitrust interest because that interest passes through G's probate estate to G's devisees or heirs.

Because both the four-year unitrust interest and the remainder interest that directly succeeds it are included in the augmented estate, there is no need to derive separate values for X's remainder interest and for G's remaining unitrust interest. The sum of the two values will equal the full value of the corpus, and that is the value that is included in the augmented estate. (Note, however, that for purposes of Section 2-209 (Sources from Which Elective Share Payable), it might become necessary to derive separate values for these two interests.)

Had the trust been revocable, the end-result would have been the same. The only difference would be that the revocability of the trust would cause paragraph (2)(A) to be inapplicable, but would also cause overlapping application of paragraphs (1)(A) and (2)(B) to X's remainder interest. Because each of these paragraphs yields the same value, Section 2-208(c) would require the commuted value of X's remainder interest to be included in the augmented estate under any one, but only one, of them. Note that neither paragraphs (1)(A) nor (2)(B) would apply to G's remaining four-year term because that four-year term would have passed to G's estate by lapse of G's power to revoke. As above, the commuted value of G's remaining four-year term would be included in the augmented estate under Section 2-204, obviating the need to derive separate valuations of G's four-year term and X's remainder interest.

Example 11–Personal Residence Trust. Before death, and during marriage, G created an irrevocable inter-vivos trust of G's personal residence, retaining the right to occupy the residence for 10 years, then for the residence to go to X. G died six years after the trust was created, survived by S and X.

The full value of the residence at G's death is included in the augmented estate under a combination of Sections 2-204 and 2-205(2)(A).

Section 2-205(2)(A) requires the inclusion of the commuted value of X's remainder interest at G's death. This paragraph applies to a retained right to possession that continues beyond the decedent's death, as here. The amount included is the value of the interest that passes outside probate to a person other than the decedent's estate or surviving spouse, which in this case is the commuted value of X's remainder interest at G's death.

Section 2-204 requires the inclusion of the commuted value of G's remaining four-year term because that interest passes through G's probate estate to G's devisees or heirs.

As in Example 10, there is no need to derive separate valuations of the remaining four-year term and the remainder interest that directly succeeds it. The sum of the two values will equal the full value of

the residence at G's death, and that is the amount included in the augmented estate. (Note, however, that *for purposes of Section 2-209 (Sources from Which Elective Share Payable)*, it might become necessary to derive separate values for these two interests.)

Example 12–Retained Annuity Interest for a Term. Before death, and during marriage, G created an irrevocable inter-vivos trust, providing for a fixed dollar amount to be paid annually to G for 10 years, then for half of the corpus of the trust to go to X; the other half was to remain in trust for an additional five years, after which time the remaining corpus was to go to X. G died 14 years after the trust was created, survived by S and X.

The value of the one-half of the corpus of the trust remaining at G's death is included in the augmented estate under a combination of Sections 2-204 and 2-205(2)(A). The other one-half of the corpus of the trust that was distributed to X four years before G's death is not included in the augmented estate.

Section 2-205(2)(A) requires the inclusion of the commuted value of X's remainder interest in half of the corpus of the trust. This section applies to a retained income interest, which under Section 2-201(8), includes an annuity interest that continues beyond the decedent's death, as here. The amount included is the value of the interest that passes outside probate to a person other than the decedent's estate or surviving spouse, which in this case is the commuted value of X's remainder interest at G's death.

Section 2-204 requires the inclusion of the commuted value of the remaining one year of G's annuity interest in half of the corpus of the trust, which passed through G's probate estate to G's devisees or heirs.

There is no need to derive separate valuations of G's remaining annuity interest and X's remainder interest that directly succeeds it. The sum of the two values will equal the full value of the remaining one-half of the corpus of the trust at G's death, and that is the amount included in the augmented estate. (Note, however, that *for purposes of Section 2-209 (Sources from Which Elective Share Payable)*, it might become necessary to derive separate values for these two interests.)

Had G died eleven years after the trust was created, so that the termination of half of the trust would have occurred within the two-year period next preceding G's death, the value of the half of the corpus of the trust that was distributed to X 10 years after the trust was created would also have been included in the augmented estate under Section 2-205(3)(A).

Example 13–Commercial Annuity. Before G's death, and during marriage, G purchased three commercial annuities from an insurance company. Annuity One was a single-life annuity that paid a fixed sum to G annually and that contained a refund feature payable to X if G died within 10 years. Annuity Two was a single-life annuity that paid a fixed sum to G annually, but contained no refund feature. Annuity Three was a self and survivor annuity that paid a fixed sum to G annually for life, and then paid a fixed sum annually to X for life. G died six years after purchasing the annuities, survived by S and X.

Annuity One: The value of the refund payable to X at G's death under Annuity One is included in the augmented estate under paragraph (2)(A). G retained an income interest, as defined in Section 2-201(8), that terminated at G's death. The amount included is the value of the interest that passes outside probate to a person other than the decedent's estate or surviving spouse, which in this case is the refund amount to which X is entitled.

Annuity Two: Annuity Two does not cause any value to be included in the augmented estate because it expired at G's death; although G retained an income interest, as defined in Section 2-201(8), that terminated at G's death, nothing passed outside probate to any person other than G's estate or surviving spouse.

Annuity Three: The commuted value at G's death of the annuity payable to X under Annuity Three is included in the augmented estate under paragraph (2)(A). G retained an income interest, as defined in Section 2-201(8), that terminated at G's death. The amount included is the value of the interest that passes outside probate to a person other than the decedent's estate or surviving spouse, which in this case is the commuted value of X's right to the annuity payments for X's lifetime.

Example 14–Joint Power. Before death, and during marriage, G created an inter-vivos trust, providing for the income to go to X for life, remainder in corpus at X's death to X's then-living descendants, by representation; if none, to a specified charity. G retained a power, exercisable only with the consent of X, allowing G to withdraw all or any portion of the corpus at any time during G's lifetime. G died without exercising the power, survived by S and X.

The value of the corpus of the trust at G's death is

included in the augmented estate under paragraph (2)(B). This paragraph applies to a power created by the decedent over the corpus of the trust that is exercisable by the decedent "in conjunction with any other person", who in this case is X. Note that the fact that X has an interest in the trust that would be adversely affected by the exercise of the power in favor of G is irrelevant. The amount included is the full value of the corpus of the trust at G's death because the power related to the full corpus of the trust and the full corpus passed at the decedent's death, by lapse or default of the power, to a person other than the decedent's estate or surviving spouse–X, X's descendants, and the specified charity.

Example 15–Power in Nonadverse Party. Before death, and during marriage, G created an inter-vivos trust, providing for the income to go to X for life, remainder in corpus to X's then-living descendants, by representation; if none, to a specified charity. G conferred a power on the trustee, a bank, to distribute, in the trustee's complete and uncontrolled discretion, all or any portion of the trust corpus to G or to X. One year before G's death, the trustee distributed $50,000 of trust corpus to G and $40,000 of trust corpus to X. G died, survived by S and X.

The full value of the portion of the corpus of the trust remaining at G's death is included in the augmented estate under paragraph (2)(B). This paragraph applies to a power created by the decedent over the corpus of the trust that is exercisable by a "nonadverse party." As defined in Section 2-201(4), the term "nonadverse party" is "a person who does not have a substantial beneficial interest in the trust or other property arrangement that would be adversely affected by the exercise or nonexercise of the power that he [or she] possesses respecting the trust or other property arrangement." The trustee in this case is a nonadverse party. The amount included is the full value of the corpus of the trust at G's death because the trustee's power related to the full corpus of the trust and the full corpus passed at the decedent's death, by lapse or default of the power, to a person other than the decedent's estate or surviving spouse–X, X's descendants, and the specified charity.

In addition to the full value of the remaining corpus at G's death, an additional amount is included in the augmented estate because of the $40,000 distribution of corpus to X within two years before G's death. As defined in Section 2-201(9), a transfer of the decedent includes the exercise "of a power described in Section 2-205(2)(B) that the decedent conferred on a nonadverse party." Consequently, the $40,000 distribution to X is considered to be a transfer of the decedent within two years before death, and is included in the augmented estate under paragraph (3)(C) to the extent it exceeded $12,000 of the aggregate gifts to X that year. If no other gifts were made to X in that year, the amount included would be $28,000 ($40,000–$12,000).

Paragraph (3)–Property Transferred by the Decedent During Marriage and During the Two-Year Period Next Preceding the Decedent's Death. This paragraph—called the two-year rule—requires inclusion in the augmented estate of the value of property that the decedent transferred in specified forms during marriage and within two years of death. The word "transfer", as it relates to a transfer by or of the decedent, is defined in Section 2-201(9), as including "(A) an exercise or release of a presently exercisable general power of appointment held by the decedent, (B) a lapse at death of a presently exercisable general power of appointment held by the decedent, and (C) an exercise, release, or lapse of a general power of appointment that the decedent created in himself [or herself] and of a power described in Section 2-205(2)(B) that the decedent conferred on a nonadverse party."

The two-year rule of paragraph (3) covers the following specific forms of transfer:

(A) Any property that passed as a result of the termination of a right or interest in, or power over, property that would have been included in the augmented estate under paragraph (1)(A), (B), or (C), or under paragraph (2), if the right, interest, or power had not terminated until the decedent's death. The amount included is the value of the property that would have been included under those paragraphs if the property were valued at the time the right, interest, or power terminated, and is included only to the extent the property passed upon termination to or for the benefit of any person other than the decedent or the decedent's estate, spouse, or surviving spouse. As used in this subparagraph, "termination", with respect to a right or interest in property, occurs when the right or interest terminated by the terms of the governing instrument or the decedent transferred or relinquished the right or interest, and, with respect to a power over property, occurs when the power terminated by exercise, release, lapse, default, or otherwise, but, with respect to a power

described in paragraph (1)(A), "termination" occurs when the power terminated by exercise or release, but not otherwise.

(B) Any transfer of or relating to an insurance policy on the life of the decedent if the proceeds would have been included in the augmented estate under paragraph (1)(D) had the transfer not occurred. The amount included is the value of the insurance proceeds to the extent the proceeds were payable at the decedent's death to or for the benefit of any person other than the decedent's estate or surviving spouse.

(C) Any transfer of property, to the extent not otherwise included in the augmented estate, made to or for the benefit of a person other than the decedent's surviving spouse. The amount included is the value of the transferred property to the extent the aggregate transfers to any one donee in either of the two years exceeded $12,000.

Various aspects of paragraph (3) are illustrated by the following examples. Other examples illustrating various aspects of this paragraph are Examples 2, 9, 12, 14, and 15, above, and Examples 33 and 34 in the Comment to Section 2-207, below. In the following examples, as in the examples above, G is the decedent and S is the decedent's surviving spouse.

Example 16–Retained Income Interest Terminating Within Two Years Before Death. Before death, and during marriage, G created an irrevocable inter-vivos trust, providing for the income to go to G for 10 years, then for the corpus of the trust to go to X. G died 11 years after the trust was created, survived by S and X. G was married to S when the trust terminated.

The full value of the corpus of the trust at the date of its termination is included in the augmented estate under paragraph (3)(A). The full value of the corpus at death would have been included in the augmented estate under paragraph (2)(A) had G's income interest not terminated until death; G's income interest terminated within the two-year period next preceding G's death; G was married to S when the trust was created and when the income interest terminated; and the trust corpus upon termination passed to a person other than S, G, or G's estate.

Example 17–Personal Residence Trust Terminating Within Two Years Before Death. Before death, and during marriage, G created an irrevocable inter-vivos trust of G's personal residence, retaining the right to occupy the residence for ten years, then for the residence to go to X. G died eleven years after the trust was created, survived by S and X. G was married to S when the right to possession terminated.

The full value of the residence at the date the trust terminated is included in the augmented estate under paragraph (3)(A). The full value of the residence would have been included in the augmented estate under paragraph (2)(A) had G's right to possession not terminated until death; G's right to possession terminated within the two-year period next preceding G's death; G was married to S when the trust was created and when the right to possession terminated; and the residence passed upon termination to a person other than S, G, or G's estate.

Example 18–Irrevocable Assignment of Life-Insurance Policy Within Two Years Before Death. In Example 8, G irrevocably assigned the life-insurance policy to X and Y within two years preceding G's death. G was married to S when the policy was assigned. G died, survived by S, X, and Y.

The full value of the proceeds are included in the augmented estate under paragraph (3)(B). The full value of the proceeds would have been included in the augmented estate under paragraph (1)(D) had G owned the policy at death; G assigned the policy within the two-year period next preceding G's death; G was married to S when the policy was assigned; and the proceeds were payable to a person other than S or G's estate.

Example 19–Property Purchased in Joint Tenancy Within Two Years Before Death. Within two years before death, and during marriage, G and X purchased property in joint tenancy; G contributed

$75,000 of the $100,000 purchase price and X contributed $25,000. G died, survived by S and X.

Regardless of when or by whom the property was purchased, the value at G's death of G's fractional interest of one-half is included in the augmented estate under paragraph (1)(B) because G's half passed to X as surviving joint tenant. Because the property was purchased within two years before death, and during marriage, and because G's contribution exceeded the value of G's fractional interest in the property, the excess contribution of $25,000 constitutes a gift to X within the two-year period next preceding G's death. Consequently, an additional $13,000 ($25,000 minus $12,000) is included in the augmented estate under paragraph (3)(C) as a gift to X.

Had G provided all of the $100,000 purchase price, then paragraph (3)(C)would require $38,000 ($50,000 minus $12,000) to be included in the augmented estate (in addition to the inclusion of one-half the value of the property at G's death under paragraph (1)(B)).

Had G provided one-half or less of the $100,000 purchase price, then G would not have made a gift to X within the two-year period next preceding G's death. Half the value of the property at G's death would still be included in the augmented estate under paragraph (1)(B), however.

Cross Reference. On obtaining written spousal consent to assure qualification for the charitable deduction for charitable remainder trusts or outright charitable donations, see the Comment to Section 2-208.

Historical Note. This Comment was added in 1993 and revised in 2008.

§ 2-206. Decedent's Nonprobate Transfers to the Surviving Spouse.

Excluding property passing to the surviving spouse under the federal Social Security system, the value of the augmented estate includes the value of the decedent's nonprobate transfers to the decedent's surviving spouse, which consist of all property that passed outside probate at the decedent's death from the decedent to the surviving spouse by reason of the decedent's death, including:

(1) the decedent's fractional interest in property held as a joint tenant with the right of survivorship, to the extent that the decedent's fractional interest passed to the surviving spouse as surviving joint tenant,

(2) the decedent's ownership interest in property or accounts held in co-ownership registration with the right of survivorship, to the extent the decedent's ownership interest passed to the surviving spouse as surviving co-owner, and

(3) all other property that would have been included in the augmented estate under Section 2-205(1) or (2) had it passed to or for the benefit of a person other than the decedent's spouse, surviving spouse, the decedent, or the decedent's creditors, estate, or estate creditors.

Comment

This section, which in the 1990 version appeared in substance as a paragraph of a single, long section defining the augmented estate, establishes as the third component of the augmented estate the value of the decedent's nonprobate transfers to the decedent's surviving spouse. Under this section, the decedent's nonprobate transfers to the decedent's surviving spouse consist of all property that passed outside probate at the decedent's death from the decedent to the surviving spouse by reason of the decedent's death, including:

(1) the decedent's fractional interest in property held as a joint tenant with the right of survivorship, to the extent that the decedent's fractional interest passed to the surviving spouse as surviving joint tenant,

(2) the decedent's ownership interest in property or accounts held in co-ownership registration with the right of survivorship, to the extent the decedent's ownership interest passed to the surviving spouse as surviving co-owner, and

(3) all other property that would have been included in the augmented estate under Section 2-205(1) or (2) had it passed to or for the benefit of a person other than the decedent's spouse, surviving spouse, the decedent, or the decedent's creditors, estate, or estate creditors.

Property passing to the surviving spouse under the federal Social Security system is excluded.

Various aspects of Section 2-206 are illustrated by the following examples. In these examples, as in the examples in the Comment to Section 2-205, above, G is the decedent and S is the decedent's surviving spouse.

Example 20—Tenancy by the Entirety. G and S own property in tenancy by the entirety. G died, survived by S.

Because the definition in Section 1-201 of "joint tenants with the right of survivorship" includes tenants by the entirety, the provisions of Section 2-206 relating to joint tenancies with right of survivorship apply to tenancies by the entirety.

In total, therefore, the full value of the property is included in the augmented estate—G's one-half under Section 2-206(1) and S's one-half under Section 2-207(a)(1)(A).

Section 2-206(1) requires the inclusion of the value of G's one-half fractional interest because it passed to S as surviving joint tenant.

Section 2-207(a)(1)(A) requires the inclusion of S's one-half fractional interest. Because G was a joint tenant immediately before G's death, S's fractional interest, for purposes of Section 2-207, is determined immediately before G's death, disregarding the fact that G predeceased S. Immediately before G's death, S's fractional interest was then a one-half fractional interest. Despite Section 2-205(1)(B), none of S's fractional interest is included under Section 2-207(a)(2) because that provision does not apply to fractional interests that are included under Section 2-207(a)(1)(A). Consequently, the value of S's one-half interest is included under Section 2-207(a)(1)(A) but not under Section 2-207(a)(2).

Example 21—Joint Tenancy. G, S, and X own property in joint tenancy. G died more than two years after the property was titled in that form, survived by S and X.

In total, two-thirds of the value of the property at G's death is included in the augmented estate—one-sixth under Section 2-205, one-sixth under Section 2-206, and one-third under Section 2-207.

Section 2-205(1)(B) requires the inclusion of half of the value of G's one-third fractional interest because that half passed by right of survivorship to X.

Section 2-206(1) requires the inclusion of the value of the other half of G's one-third fractional interest because that half passed to S as surviving joint tenant.

Section 2-207(a)(1)(A) requires the inclusion of the value of S's one-third interest. Because G was a joint tenant immediately before G's death, S's fractional interest, for purposes of Section 2-207, is determined immediately before G's death, disregarding the fact that G predeceased S. Immediately before G's death, S's fractional interest was then a one-third fractional interest. Despite Section 2-205(1)(B), none of S's fractional interest is included under Section 2-207(a)(2) because that provision does not apply to fractional interests that are included under Section 2-207(a)(1)(A). Consequently, the value of S's one-third fractional interest is included in the augmented estate under Section 2-207(a)(1)(A) but not under Section 2-207(a)(2).

Example 22—Income Interest Passing to Surviving Spouse. Before death, and during marriage, G created an irrevocable inter-vivos trust, providing for the income to go to G for life, then for the income to go to S for life, then for the corpus of the trust to go to

X. G died, survived by S and X.

The full value of the corpus of the trust at G's death is included in the augmented estate under a combination of Sections 2-205 and 2-206.

Section 2-206(3) requires the inclusion of the commuted value of S's income interest. Note that, although S owns the income interest as of G's death, the value of S's income interest is not included under Section 2-207 because Section 2-207 only includes property interests that are not included under Section 2-206.

Section 2-205(2)(A) requires the inclusion of the commuted value of X's remainder interest.

Example 23–Corpus Passing to Surviving Spouse. Before death, and during marriage, G created an irrevocable inter-vivos trust, providing for the income to go to G for life, then for the corpus of the trust to go to S. G died, survived by S.

The value of the corpus of the trust at G's death is included in the augmented estate under Section 2-206(3). Note that, although S owns the corpus as of G's death, the value of S's ownership interest in the corpus is not included under Section 2-207 because Section 2-207 only includes property interests that are not included under Section 2-206.

Example 24–TOD Registered Securities, POD Account, *and Life Insurance Payable to Surviving Spouse.* In Examples 5 and 8 in the Comment to Section 2-205, G designated S to take the securities on death, registered S as the beneficiary of the POD savings account, and named S as the beneficiary of the life-insurance policy.

The same values that were included in the augmented estate under Section 2-205(1) in those examples are included in the augmented estate under Section 2-206.

Example 25–Joint Checking Account. G and S were registered as co-owners of a joint checking account. G contributed 75 percent of the funds in the account and S contributed 25 percent of the funds. G died, survived by S.

G's ownership interest in the account immediately before death, determined under Section 6-211, was 75 percent of the account. Because that percentage ownership interest passed by right of survivorship to S at G's death, 75 percent of the value of the account at G's death is included in the augmented estate under Section 2-206. The remaining 25 percent of the account is included in the augmented estate under Section 2-207.

Historical Note. This Comment was added in 1993 and revised in 2008.

§ 2-207. Surviving Spouse's Property and Nonprobate Transfers to Others.

(a) **[Included Property.]** Except to the extent included in the augmented estate under Section 2-204 or 2-206, the value of the augmented estate includes the value of:

(1) property that was owned by the decedent's surviving spouse at the decedent's death, including:

(A) the surviving spouse's fractional interest in property held in joint tenancy with the right of survivorship,

B) the surviving spouse's ownership interest in property or accounts held in co-ownership registration with the right of survivorship, and

C) property that passed to the surviving spouse by reason of the decedent's death, but not including the spouse's right to homestead allowance, family allowance, exempt property, or payments under the federal Social Security system; and

(2) property that would have been included in the surviving spouse's nonprobate transfers to others, other than the spouse's fractional and ownership interests included under subsection (a)(1)(A) or (B), had the spouse been the decedent.

(b) **[Time of Valuation.]** Property included under this section is valued at the decedent's death, taking the fact that the decedent predeceased the spouse into account, but, for purposes of subsection (a)(1)(A) and (B), the values of the spouse's fractional and ownership interests are determined immediately before the decedent's death if the decedent was then a joint tenant or a co-owner of the property or accounts. For purposes of subsection (a)(2), proceeds of insurance that would have been included in the spouse's nonprobate transfers to others under Section 2-205(1)(D) are not valued as if he [or she] were deceased.

(c) **[Reduction for Enforceable Claims.]** The value of property included under this section is reduced by enforceable claims against the surviving spouse.

Comment

This section, which in the 1990 version appeared in substance as a paragraph of a single, long section defining the augmented estate, establishes as the fourth component of the augmented estate the value of property owned by the surviving spouse at the decedent's death plus the value of amounts that would have been includible in the surviving spouse's nonprobate transfers to others had the spouse been the decedent, reduced by enforceable claims against that property or that spouse, as provided in Sections 2-207(c) and 2-208(b)(1). Property owned by the decedent's surviving spouse does not include the value of enhancements to the surviving spouse's earning capacity (e.g., the value of a law, medical, or business degree).

Note that amounts that would have been includible in the surviving spouse's nonprobate transfers to others under Section 2-205(1)(D) are not valued as if he or she were deceased. Thus, if, at the decedent's death, the surviving spouse owns a $1 million life-insurance policy on his or her life, payable to his or her sister, that policy would not be valued at its face value of $1 million, but rather could be valued under the method used in the federal estate tax under Treas. Reg. § 20.2031-8.

The purpose of combining the estates and nonprobate transfers of both spouses is to implement a partnership or marital-sharing theory. Under that theory, there is a fifty/fifty split of the property acquired by both spouses. Hence the redesigned elective share includes the survivor's net assets in the augmented-estate entity. (Under a different rationale, no longer appropriate under the redesigned system, the pre-1990 version of Section 2-202 also added the value of property owned by the surviving spouse, but only to the extent the owned property had been derived from the decedent. An incidental benefit of the redesigned system is that this tracing-to-source feature of the pre-1990 version is eliminated.)

Various aspects of Section 2-207 are illustrated by the following examples. Other examples illustrating various aspects of this section are Examples 20, 21, 22, 23, and 25 in the Comment to Section 2-206. In the following examples, as in the examples in the Comments to Sections 2-205 and 2-206, above, G is the decedent and S is the decedent's surviving spouse.

Example 26—Inter-Vivos Trust Created by Surviving Spouse; Corpus Payable to Spouse at Decedent's Death. Before G's death, and during marriage, S created an irrevocable inter-vivos trust, providing for the income to go to G for life, then for the corpus of the trust to go to S. G died, survived by S.

The value of the corpus of the trust at G's death is included in the augmented estate under Section 2-207(a)(1) as either an interest owned by S at G's death or as an interest that passed to the spouse by reason of G's death.

Example 27—Inter-Vivos Trust Created by Another; Income Payable to Spouse for Life. Before G's death, X created an irrevocable inter-vivos trust, providing for the income to go to S for life, then for the income to go to G for life, then for the corpus of the trust to go to Y. G died, survived by S and Y.

The commuted value of S's income interest as of G's death is included in the augmented estate under Section 2-207(a), as a property interest owned by the surviving spouse at the decedent's death.

Example 28—Inter-Vivos Trust Created by Another; Income Payable to Spouse for Life. Before G's death, X created an irrevocable inter-vivos trust, providing for the income to go to G for life, then for the income to go to S for life, then for the corpus of the trust to go to Y. G died, survived by S and Y.

The commuted value of S's income interest at the decedent's death is included in the augmented estate under Section 2-207(a)(1), as either a property interest owned by the surviving spouse at the decedent's death or a property interest that passed to the surviving spouse by reason of the decedent's death.

Example 29—Life Insurance on Decedent's Life Owned by Surviving Spouse; Proceeds Payable to Spouse. Before G's death, S bought a life-insurance policy on G's life, naming S as the beneficiary. G died, survived by S.

The value of the proceeds of the life-insurance policy is included in the augmented estate under Section 2-207(a)(1), as property owned by the surviving spouse at the decedent's death.

Example 30—Life Insurance on Decedent's Life Owned by Another; Proceeds Payable to Spouse. Before G's death, X bought a life-insurance policy on G's life, naming S as the beneficiary. G died, survived by S.

71

The value of the proceeds of the life-insurance policy is included in the augmented estate under Section 2-207(a)(1)(C), as property that passed to the surviving spouse by reason of the decedent's death.

Example 31–Joint Tenancy Between Spouse and Another. S and Y own property in joint tenancy. G died, survived by S and Y.

The value of S's one-half fractional interest at G's death is included in the augmented estate under Section 2-207(a)(1)(A). Despite Section 2-205(1)(B), none of S's fractional interest is included under Section 2-207(a)(2) because that provision does not apply to fractional interests required to be included under Section 2-207(a)(1)(A). Consequently, the value of S's one-half is included under Section 2-207(a)(1)(A) but not under Section 2-207(a)(2).

Example 32–Inter-Vivos Trust with Retained Income Interest Created by Surviving Spouse. Before G's death, and during marriage, S created an irrevocable inter-vivos trust, providing for the income to go to S for life, then for the income to go to G for life, then for the corpus of the trust to go to X. G died, survived by S and X.

The value of the trust corpus at G's death is included in the augmented estate under Section 2-207(a)(2) because, if S were the decedent, that value would be included in the spouse's nonprobate transfers to others under Section 2-205(2)(A). Note that property included under Section 2-207 is valued at the decedent's death, taking the fact that the decedent predeceased the spouse into account. Thus, G's remainder in income for life is extinguished, and the full value of the corpus is included in the augmented estate under Section 2-207(a)(2). The commuted value of S's income interest would also be included under Section 2-207(a)(1) but for the fact that Section 2-208(c) provides that when two provisions apply to the same property interest, the interest is not included under both provisions, but is included under the provision yielding the highest value. Consequently, since Section 2-207(a)(2) yields a higher value (the full corpus) than Section 2-207(a)(1) (the income interest), and since the income interest is part of the value of the corpus, and hence both provisions apply to the same property interest, the full corpus is included under Section 2-207(a)(2) and nothing is included under Section 2-207(a)(1).

Example 33–Inter-Vivos Trust Created by Decedent; Income to Surviving Spouse. More than two years before G's death, and during marriage, G created an irrevocable inter-vivos trust, providing for the income to go to S for life, then for the corpus of the trust to go to X. G died, survived by S and X.

The commuted value of S's income interest as of G's death is included in the augmented estate under Section 2-207. If G had created the trust within the two-year period next preceding G's death, the commuted value of X's remainder interest as of the date of the creation of the trust (less $12,000, assuming G made no other gifts to X in that year) would also have been included in the augmented estate under Section 2-205(3)(C).

Example 34–Inter-Vivos Trust Created by Surviving Spouse; No Retained Interest or Power. More than two years before G's death, and during marriage, S created an irrevocable inter-vivos trust, providing for the income to go to G for life, then for the corpus of the trust to go to Y. G died, survived by S and Y.

The value of the trust is not included in the augmented estate. If S had created the trust within the two-year period next preceding G's death, the commuted value of Y's remainder interest as of the date of the creation of the trust (less $12,000, assuming no other gifts to Y in that year) would have been included in the augmented estate under Section 2-207(a)(2) because if S were the decedent, the value of the remainder interest would have been included in S's nonprobate transfers to others under Section 2-205(3)(C).

Historical Note. This Comment was added in 1993 and revised in 2008.

§ 2-208. Exclusions, Valuation, and Overlapping Application.

(a) [**Exclusions.**] The value of any property is excluded from the decedent's nonprobate transfers to others:

(1) to the extent the decedent received adequate and full consideration in money or money's worth for a transfer of the property; or

(2) if the property was transferred with the written joinder of, or if the transfer was consented to in writing before or after the transfer by, the surviving spouse.

(b) [Valuation.] The value of property:

(1) included in the augmented estate under Section 2-205, 2-206, or 2-207 is reduced in each category by enforceable claims against the included property; and

(2) includes the commuted value of any present or future interest and the commuted value of amounts payable under any trust, life insurance settlement option, annuity contract, public or private pension, disability compensation, death benefit or retirement plan, or any similar arrangement, exclusive of the federal Social Security system.

(c) [Overlapping Application; No Double Inclusion.] In case of overlapping application to the same property of the paragraphs or subparagraphs of Section 2-205, 2-206, or 2-207, the property is included in the augmented estate under the provision yielding the greatest value, and under only one overlapping provision if they all yield the same value.

Comment

Subsection (a). This subsection excludes from the decedent's nonprobate transfers to others the value of any property (1) to the extent that the decedent received adequate and full consideration in money or money's worth for a transfer of the property or (2) if the property was transferred with the written joinder of, or if the transfer was consented to in writing before or after the transfer by, the surviving spouse.

Consenting to Split-Gift Treatment Not Consent to the Transfer. Spousal consent to split-gift treatment under I.R.C. § 2513 does not constitute written joinder of or consent to the transfer by the spouse for purposes of subsection (a).

Obtaining the Charitable Deduction for Transfers Coming Within Section 2-205(2) or (3). Because, under Section 2-201(8), the term "right to income" includes a right to payments under an annuity trust or a unitrust, the value of a charitable remainder trust established by a married grantor without written spousal consent or joinder would be included in the decedent's nonprobate transfers to others under Section 2-205(2)(A). Consequently, a married grantor planning to establish a charitable remainder trust is advised to obtain the written consent of his or her spouse to the transfer, as provided in Section 2-208(a), in order to be assured of qualifying for the charitable deduction.

Similarly, outright gifts made by a married donor within two years preceding death are included in the augmented estate under Section 2-205(3)(C) to the extent that the aggregate gifts to any one donee exceed $10,000 the amount excludable from taxable gifts under 26 U.S.C. Section 2503(b) [or its successor] on the date next preceding the date of the decedent's death (or, if referring to federal law is considered an unlawful delegation of legislative power, $12,000) in either of the two years. Consequently, a married donor planning to donate more than that amount to any charitable organization within a twelve-month period is advised to obtain the written consent of his or her spouse to the transfer, as provided in Section 2-208(a), in order to be assured of qualifying for the charitable deduction.

Spousal Waiver of ERISA Benefits. Under the Employee Retirement Income Security Act (ERISA), death benefits under an employee benefit plan subject to ERISA must be paid in the form of an annuity to the surviving spouse. A married employee wishing to designate someone other than the spouse must obtain a waiver from the spouse. As amended in 1984 by the Retirement Equity Act, ERISA requires each employee benefit plan subject to its provisions to provide that an election of a waiver shall not take effect unless

(1) the spouse of the participant consents in writing to such election,

(2) such election designates a beneficiary (or form of benefits) which may not be changed without spousal consent (or the consent of the spouse expressly permits designation by the participant without any requirement of further consent by the spouse), and

(3) the spouse's consent acknowledges the effect of such election and is witnessed by a plan representative or a notary public.

See 29 U.S.C. § 1055(c) (1988); Int.Rev.Code § 417(a). Any spousal waiver that complies with these requirements would satisfy Section 2-208(a) and would serve to exclude the value of the death benefits from the decedent's nonprobate transfers to others.

Cross Reference. See also Section 2-213 and Comment.

Subsection (c). The application of subsection (c) is illustrated in Example 32 in the Comment to Section

2-207.

1993. Subsection (a) was amended in 2008 by adding the phrase "before or after the transfer."

§ 2-209. Sources from Which Elective Share Payable.

(a) [Elective-Share Amount Only.] In a proceeding for an elective share, the following are applied first to satisfy the elective-share amount and to reduce or eliminate any contributions due from the decedent's net probate estate and recipients of the decedent's nonprobate transfers to others:

(1) amounts included in the augmented estate under Section 2-204 which pass or have passed to the surviving spouse by testate or intestate succession and amounts included in the augmented estate under Section 2-206; and

(2) the marital-property portion of amounts included in the augmented estate under Section 2-207.

(b) [Marital-Property Portion.] The marital-property portion under subsection (a)(2) is computed by multiplying the value of the amounts included in the augmented estate under Section 2-207 by the percentage of the augmented estate set forth in the schedule in Section 2-203(b) appropriate to the length of time the spouse and the decedent were married to each other.

(c) [Unsatisfied Balance of Elective-Share Amount; Supplemental Elective-Share Amount.] If, after the application of subsection (a), the elective-share amount is not fully satisfied, or the surviving spouse is entitled to a supplemental elective-share amount, amounts included in the decedent's net probate estate, other than assets passing to the surviving spouse by testate or intestate succession, and in the decedent's nonprobate transfers to others under Section 2-205(1), (2), and (3)(B) are applied first to satisfy the unsatisfied balance of the elective-share amount or the supplemental elective-share amount. The decedent's net probate estate and that portion of the decedent's nonprobate transfers to others are so applied that liability for the unsatisfied balance of the elective-share amount or for the supplemental elective-share amount is apportioned among the recipients of the decedent's net probate estate and of that portion of the decedent's nonprobate transfers to others in proportion to the value of their interests therein.

(d) [Unsatisfied Balance of Elective-Share and Supplemental Elective-Share Amounts.] If, after the application of subsections (a) and (c), the elective-share or supplemental elective-share amount is not fully satisfied, the remaining portion of the decedent's nonprobate transfers to others is so applied that liability for the unsatisfied balance of the elective-share or supplemental elective-share amount is apportioned among the recipients of the remaining portion of the decedent's nonprobate transfers to others in proportion to the value of their interests therein.

(e) [Unsatisfied Balance Treated as General Pecuniary Devise.] The unsatisfied balance of the elective-share or supplemental elective-share amount as determined under subsection (c) or (d) is treated as a general pecuniary devise for purposes of Section 3-904.

Comment

Section 2-209 is an integral part of the overall redesign of the elective share. It establishes the priority to be used in determining the sources from which the elective-share amount is payable.

Subsection (a). Subsection (a) applies only to the elective-share amount determined under Section 2-202(a), not to the supplemental elective-share amount determined under Section 2-202(b). Under subsection (a), the following are counted first toward satisfying the elective-share amount (to the extent they are included in the augmented estate):

(1) amounts included in the augmented estate under Section 2-204 which pass or have passed to the surviving spouse by testate or intestate succession and amounts included in the augmented estate under Section 2-206, i.e., the value of the decedent's nonprobate transfers to the surviving spouse, including the proceeds of insurance (including accidental death benefits) on the life of the decedent and benefits payable under a retirement plan in which the decedent was a participant, but excluding property passing under

the Federal Social Security system; and

(2) the marital-property portion of amounts included in the augmented estate under Section 2-207.

Under subsection (b), the marital-property portion of amounts included in the augmented estate under Section 2-207 is computed by multiplying the value of the amounts included in the augmented estate under Section 2-207 by the percentage of the augmented estate set forth in the schedule in Section 2-203(b) appropriate to the length of time the spouse and the decedent were married to each other.

If the combined value of the amounts described in subsection (a)(1) and (2) equals or exceeds the elective-share amount, the surviving spouse is not entitled to any further amount from the decedent's probate estate or recipients of the decedent's nonprobate transfers to others, unless the surviving spouse is entitled to a supplemental elective-share amount under Section 2-202(b).

Subsections (c) and (d). Subsections (c) and (d) apply to both the elective-share amount and the supplemental elective-share amount, if any. As to the elective-share amount determined under Section 2-202(a), the decedent's probate estate and nonprobate transfers to others become liable only if and to the extent that the amounts described in subsection (a) are insufficient to satisfy the elective-share amount. The decedent's probate estate and nonprobate transfers to others are fully liable for the supplemental elective-share amount determined under Section 2-202(b), if any.

Subsections (c) and (d) establish a layer of priority within the decedent's net probate estate (other than assets passing to the surviving spouse by testate or intestate succession) and nonprobate transfers to others. The decedent's probate estate and that portion of the decedent's nonprobate transfers to others that are included in the augmented estate

under Section 2-205(1), (2), and 3(B) are liable first. Only if and to the extent that those amounts are insufficient does the remaining portion of the decedent's nonprobate transfers to others become liable.

Note that the exempt property and allowances provided by Sections 2-401, 2-402, and 2-403 are not charged against, but are in addition to, the elective-share and supplemental elective-share amounts.

The provision that the spouse is charged with amounts that would have passed to the spouse but were disclaimed was deleted in 1993. That provision was introduced into the Code in 1975, prior to the addition of the QTIP provisions in the marital deduction of the federal estate tax. At that time, most devises to the surviving spouse were outright devises and did not require actuarial computation. Now, many if not most devises to the surviving spouse are in the form of an income interest that qualifies for the marital deduction under the QTIP provisions, and these devises require actuarial computations that should be avoided whenever possible.

The word "equitably" is eliminated from subsections (c) and (d) because it has caused confusion about whether it grants discretion to the court to apportion liability for the unsatisfied balance among the recipients of the decedent's net probate estate and of that portion of the decedent's nonprobate transfers to others in some proportion other than in proportion to the value of their interests therein. The intent of including that word in the earlier version was merely to describe the prescribed apportionment as "equitable", not to grant authority to vary the prescribed apportionment.

Historical Note. This Comment was revised in 1993 and 2008.

§ 2-210. Personal Liability of Recipients.

(a) Only original recipients of the decedent's nonprobate transfers to others, and the donees of the recipients of the decedent's nonprobate transfers to others, to the extent the donees have the property or its proceeds, are liable to make a proportional contribution toward satisfaction of the surviving spouse's elective-share or supplemental elective-share amount. A person liable to make contribution may choose to give up the proportional part of the decedent's nonprobate transfers to him [or her] or to pay the value of the amount for which he [or she] is liable.

(b) If any section or part of any section of this [part] is preempted by federal law with respect to a payment, an item of property, or any other benefit included in the decedent's nonprobate transfers to others, a person who, not for value, receives the payment, item of property, or any other benefit is obligated to return the payment, item of property, or benefit, or is personally liable for the amount of the payment or the value of that item of property or benefit, as provided in Section 2-209, to the person who would have been entitled to it were that section or part of that section not preempted.

Comment

Federal Preemption of State Law. See the Comment to Section 2-804 for a discussion of federal preemption.

Historical Note. This Comment was added in 2014.

§ 2-211. Proceeding for Elective Share; Time Limit.

(a) Except as provided in subsection (b), the election must be made by filing in the court and mailing or delivering to the personal representative, if any, a petition for the elective share within nine months after the date of the decedent's death, or within six months after the probate of the decedent's will, whichever limitation later expires. The surviving spouse must give notice of the time and place set for hearing to persons interested in the estate and to the distributees and recipients of portions of the augmented estate whose interests will be adversely affected by the taking of the elective share. Except as provided in subsection (b), the decedent's nonprobate transfers to others are not included within the augmented estate for the purpose of computing the elective share, if the petition is filed more than nine months after the decedent's death.

(b) Within nine months after the decedent's death, the surviving spouse may petition the court for an extension of time for making an election. If, within nine months after the decedent's death, the spouse gives notice of the petition to all persons interested in the decedent's nonprobate transfers to others, the court for cause shown by the surviving spouse may extend the time for election. If the court grants the spouse's petition for an extension, the decedent's nonprobate transfers to others are not excluded from the augmented estate for the purpose of computing the elective-share and supplemental elective-share amounts, if the spouse makes an election by filing in the court and mailing or delivering to the personal representative, if any, a petition for the elective share within the time allowed by the extension.

(c) The surviving spouse may withdraw his [or her] demand for an elective share at any time before entry of a final determination by the court.

(d) After notice and hearing, the court shall determine the elective-share and supplemental elective-share amounts, and shall order its payment from the assets of the augmented estate or by contribution as appears appropriate under Sections 2-209 and 2-210. If it appears that a fund or property included in the augmented estate has not come into the possession of the personal representative, or has been distributed by the personal representative, the court nevertheless shall fix the liability of any person who has any interest in the fund or property or who has possession thereof, whether as trustee or otherwise. The proceeding may be maintained against fewer than all persons against whom relief could be sought, but no person is subject to contribution in any greater amount than he [or she] would have been under Sections 2-209 and 2-210 had relief been secured against all persons subject to contribution.

(e) An order or judgment of the court may be enforced as necessary in suit for contribution or payment in other courts of this state or other jurisdictions.

Comment

This section is revised to coordinate the terminology with that used in revised Section 2-205 and with the fact that an election can be made by a conservator, guardian, or agent on behalf of a surviving spouse, as provided in Section 2-212(a).

Historical Note. This Comment was revised in 1993.

§ 2-212. Right of Election Personal to Surviving Spouse; Incapacitated Surviving Spouse.

(a) [**Surviving Spouse Must Be Living at Time of Election.**] The right of election may be exercised only by a surviving spouse who is living when the petition for the elective share is filed in the court under Section 2-211(a). If the election is not exercised by the surviving spouse personally, it may be exercised on the surviving spouse's behalf by his [or her] conservator, guardian, or agent under the authority of a power of attorney.

Alternative A

(b) [**Incapacitated Surviving Spouse.**] If the election is exercised on behalf of a surviving spouse who is an incapacitated person, that portion of the elective-share and supplemental elective-share amounts due from the decedent's probate estate and recipients of the decedent's nonprobate transfers to others under Section 2-209(c) and (d) must be placed in a custodial trust for the benefit of the surviving spouse under the provisions of the [Enacting state] Uniform Custodial Trust Act, except as modified below. For the purposes of this subsection, an election on behalf of a surviving spouse by an agent under a durable power of attorney is presumed to be on behalf of a surviving spouse who is an incapacitated person. For purposes of the custodial trust established by this subsection, (i) the electing guardian, conservator, or agent is the custodial trustee, (ii) the surviving spouse is the beneficiary, and (iii) the custodial trust is deemed to have been created by the decedent spouse by written transfer that takes effect at the decedent spouse's death and that directs the custodial trustee to administer the custodial trust as for an incapacitated beneficiary.

(c) [**Custodial Trust.**] For the purposes of subsection (b), the [Enacting state] Uniform Custodial Trust Act must be applied as if Section 6(b) thereof were repealed and Sections 2(e), 9(b), and 17(a) were amended to read as follows:

(1) Neither an incapacitated beneficiary nor anyone acting on behalf of an incapacitated beneficiary has a power to terminate the custodial trust; but if the beneficiary regains capacity, the beneficiary then acquires the power to terminate the custodial trust by delivering to the custodial trustee a writing signed by the beneficiary declaring the termination. If not previously terminated, the custodial trust terminates on the death of the beneficiary.

(2) If the beneficiary is incapacitated, the custodial trustee shall expend so much or all of the custodial trust property as the custodial trustee considers advisable for the use and benefit of the beneficiary and individuals who were supported by the beneficiary when the beneficiary became incapacitated, or who are legally entitled to support by the beneficiary. Expenditures may be made in the manner, when, and to the extent that the custodial trustee determines suitable and proper, without court order but with regard to other support, income, and property of the beneficiary [exclusive of] [and] benefits of medical or other forms of assistance from any state or federal government or governmental agency for which the beneficiary must qualify on the basis of need.

(3) Upon the beneficiary's death, the custodial trustee shall transfer the unexpended custodial trust property in the following order: (i) under the residuary clause, if any, of the will of the beneficiary's predeceased spouse against whom the elective share was taken, as if that predeceased spouse died immediately after the beneficiary; or (ii) to that predeceased spouse's heirs under Section 2-711 of [this state's] Uniform Probate Code.

Alternative B

(b) [**Incapacitated Surviving Spouse.**] If the election is exercised on behalf of a surviving spouse who is an incapacitated person, the court must set aside that portion of the elective-share and supplemental elective-share amounts due from the decedent's probate estate and recipients of the decedent's nonprobate transfers to others under Section 2-209(c) and (d) and must appoint a trustee to administer that property for the support of the surviving spouse. For the purposes of this subsection, an election on behalf of a surviving spouse by an agent under a durable power of attorney is presumed to be on behalf of a surviving spouse who is an incapacitated person. The trustee must administer the trust in accordance with the following terms and such additional terms as the court determines appropriate:

(1) Expenditures of income and principal may be made in the manner, when, and to the extent that the trustee determines suitable and proper for the surviving spouse's support, without court order but with regard to other support, income, and property of the surviving spouse [exclusive of] [and] benefits of medical or other forms of assistance from any state or federal government or governmental agency for which the surviving spouse must qualify on the basis of need.

(2) During the surviving spouse's incapacity, neither the surviving spouse nor anyone acting on behalf of the surviving spouse has a power to terminate the trust; but if the surviving spouse regains capacity, the surviving spouse then acquires the power to terminate the trust and acquire full ownership of the trust property free of trust, by delivering to the trustee a writing signed by the surviving spouse declaring the termination.

(3) Upon the surviving spouse's death, the trustee shall transfer the unexpended trust property in the following order: (i) under the residuary clause, if any, of the will of the predeceased spouse against whom the elective share was taken, as if that predeceased spouse died immediately after the surviving spouse; or (ii) to the predeceased spouse's heirs under Section 2-711.

End of Alternatives

Comment

Subsection (a). Subsection (a) is revised to make it clear that the right of election may be exercised only by or on behalf of a living surviving spouse. If the election is not made by the surviving spouse personally, it can be made on behalf of the surviving spouse by the spouse's conservator, guardian, or agent. In any case, the surviving spouse must be alive when the election is made. The election cannot be made on behalf of a deceased surviving spouse.

Alternative A: Subsections (b) and (c). If the election is made on behalf of a surviving spouse who is an "incapacitated person", as defined in section 5-103(7), that portion of the elective-share and supplemental elective-share amounts which, under Section 2-209(c) and (d), are payable from the decedent's probate estate and nonprobate transfers to others must go into a custodial trust under the Uniform Custodial Trust Act, as adjusted in subsection (c).

If the election is made on behalf of the surviving spouse by his or her guardian or conservator, the surviving spouse is by definition an "incapacitated person." If the election is made by the surviving spouse's agent under a durable power of attorney, the surviving spouse is presumed to be an "incapacitated person"; the presumption is rebuttable.

The terms of the custodial trust are governed by the Uniform Custodial Trust Act, except as adjusted in subsection (c).

The custodial trustee is authorized to expend the custodial trust property for the use and benefit of the surviving spouse to the extent the custodial trustee considers it advisable. In determining the amounts, if any, to be expended for the spouse's benefit, the custodial trustee is directed to take into account the spouse's other support, income, and property; these items would include governmental benefits such as Social Security and Medicare.

Bracketed language in subsection (c)(2) (and in Alternative subsection (b)(1)) gives enacting states a choice as to whether governmental benefits for which the spouse must qualify on the basis of need, such as Medicaid, are also to be considered. If so, the enacting state should include the bracketed word "and" but not the bracketed phrase "exclusive of" in its enactment; if not, the enacting state should include the bracketed phrase "exclusive of" and not include the bracketed word "and" in its enactment.

At the surviving spouse's death, the remaining custodial trust property does not go to the surviving spouse's estate, but rather under the residuary clause of the will of the predeceased spouse whose probate estate and nonprobate transfers to others were the source of the property in the custodial trust, as if the predeceased spouse died immediately after the surviving spouse. In the absence of a residuary clause, the property goes to the predeceased spouse's heirs. See Section 2-711.

Alternative B: Subsection (b). For states that have not enacted the Uniform Custodial Trust Act, an

Alternative subsection (b) is provided under which the court must set aside that portion of the elective-share and supplemental elective-share amounts which, under Section 2-209(c) and (d), are due from the decedent's probate estate and nonprobate transfers to others and must appoint a trustee to administer that property for the support of the surviving spouse, in accordance with the terms set forth in Alternative subsection (b).

Planning for an Incapacitated Surviving Spouse Not Disrupted. Note that the portion of the elective-share or supplemental elective-share amounts that go into the custodial or support trust is that portion due from the decedent's probate estate and nonprobate transfers to others under Section 2-209(c) and (d). These amounts constitute the involuntary transfers to the surviving spouse under the elective-share system.

Amounts voluntarily transferred to the surviving spouse under the decedent's will, by intestacy, or by nonprobate transfer, if any, do not go into the custodial or support trust. Thus, estate planning measures deliberately established for a surviving spouse who is incapacitated are not disrupted. For example, the decedent's will might establish a trust that qualifies for or that can be elected as qualifying for the federal estate tax marital deduction. Although the value of the surviving spouse's interests in such a trust count toward satisfying the elective-share amount under Section 2-209(a)(1), the trust itself is not dismantled by virtue of Section 2-212(b) in order to force that property into the nonqualifying custodial or support trust.

Rationale. The approach of this section is based on a general expectation that most surviving spouses are, at the least, generally aware of and accept their decedents' overall estate plans and are not antagonistic to them. Consequently, to elect the elective share, and not have the disposition of that part of it that is payable from the decedent's probate estate and nonprobate transfers to others under Section 2-209(c) and (d) governed by subsections (b) and (c), the surviving spouse must not be an incapacitated person. When the election is made by or on behalf of a surviving spouse who is not an incapacitated person, the surviving spouse has personally signified his or her opposition to the decedent's overall estate plan.

If the election is made on behalf of a surviving spouse who is an incapacitated person, subsections (b) and (c) control the disposition of that part of the elective-share amount or supplemental elective-share amount payable under Section 2-209(c) and (d) from the decedent's probate estate and nonprobate transfers to others. The purpose of subsections (b) and (c), generally speaking, is to assure that that part of the elective share is devoted to the personal economic benefit and needs of the surviving spouse, but not to the economic benefit of the surviving spouse's heirs or devisees.

Historical Note. This Comment was revised in 1993 and 2008.

§ 2-213. Effect of Premarital or Marital Agreement on Right to Elect and Other Rights.

(a) In this section, "agreement" includes a subsequent agreement that affirms, modifies, or waives an earlier agreement.

(b) The right of election of a surviving spouse and the rights of the surviving spouse to homestead allowance, exempt property, and family allowance, or any of them, may be affirmed, modified, or waived only by a written agreement signed by the surviving spouse, before or after marriage. The agreement is enforceable without consideration.

(c) An agreement under subsection (b) is not enforceable if the surviving spouse proves that:

(1) the agreement was involuntary or the result of duress;

(2) the surviving spouse did not have access to independent legal representation under subsection (d);

(3) unless the surviving spouse had independent legal representation when the agreement was executed, the agreement did not include an explanation in plain language of the rights under subsection (b) being affirmed, modified, or waived; or

(4) before signing the agreement, the surviving spouse did not receive adequate financial disclosure under subsection (e).

(d) A surviving spouse had access to independent legal representation if:

(1) before signing an agreement, the surviving spouse had a reasonable time to:

(A) decide whether to retain a lawyer to provide independent legal representation; and

(B) locate a lawyer to provide independent legal representation, obtain the lawyer's advice, and consider the advice provided; and

(2) the other spouse was represented by a lawyer and the surviving spouse had the financial ability to retain a lawyer or the other spouse agreed to pay the reasonable fees and expenses of independent legal representation.

(e) A surviving spouse had adequate financial disclosure under this section if the surviving spouse:

(1) received a reasonably accurate description and good-faith estimate of the value of the property, liabilities, and income of the other spouse;

(2) expressly waived, in a separate signed record, the right to financial disclosure beyond the disclosure provided; or

(3) had adequate knowledge or a reasonable basis for having adequate knowledge of the information described in paragraph (1).

(f) A court may refuse to enforce a term of an agreement under subsection (b) if, in the context of the agreement taken as a whole[:]

[(1)] the term was unconscionable at the time of signing[; or

(2) enforcement of the term would result in substantial hardship for the surviving spouse because of a material change in circumstances arising after the agreement was signed].

(g) An issue of unconscionability [or substantial hardship] of an agreement is for decision by the court as a matter of law.

(h) Unless an agreement under subsection (b) provides to the contrary, a waiver of "all rights", or equivalent language, in the property or estate of a present or prospective spouse or a complete property settlement entered into after or in anticipation of separation or divorce is a waiver of all rights of elective share, homestead allowance, exempt property, and family allowance by the spouse in the property of the other spouse and a renunciation of all benefits that would otherwise pass to the renouncing spouse by intestate succession or by virtue of any will executed before the waiver or property settlement.

Legislative Note: *Subsection (b) places the burden of proof on the party challenging a premarital or marital agreement affecting marital property rights at death. Amendments are required if a state wants to place the burden of proof on a party seeking to enforce the agreement.*

If a state wants to permit review for "substantial hardship" at the time of the enforcement, the state should include the bracketed language in subsections (f) and (g).

Comment

This section incorporates the standards by which the validity of a premarital or marital agreement is determined under the Uniform Premarital and Marital Agreements Act (UPMAA). As stated in that act's prefatory note, "[t]he general approach of [the UPMAA] is that parties should be free, within broad limits, to choose the financial terms of their marriage. The limits are those of due process in formation, on the one hand, and certain minimal standards of substantive fairness, on the other."

For examples of public policy constraints on the enforcement of the substantive terms of premarital and marital agreements, see UPMAA Sections 9(e) and 10. This section does not override those constraints, though they primarily concern rights at divorce rather than at death.

The Legislative Note on the burden of proof is explained as follows in the prefatory note to the UPMAA: "[B]ecause few states put the burden of proof on the party seeking enforcement of marital (and, more rarely, premarital) agreements, a Legislative Note suggests [the need for] alternative language to reflect that burden of proof" if a state so wishes.

The bracketed language in subsections (f) and (g) and the corresponding reference in the Legislative Note are explained as follows in the prefatory note to the UPMAA: "Because a significant minority of states authorizes some form of fairness review based on the parties' circumstances at the time the agreement is to be enforced, a bracketed provision ... offers the option of refusing enforcement based on a finding of substantial hardship at the time of enforcement." Extensive research by the drafting committee for the UPMAA located no appellate authority applying this fairness review (at the time of enforcement) to a surviving spouse's rights at the first spouse's death. Nevertheless, to be consistent with the language of the UPMAA, the bracketed language is included in this section.

Effect of Premarital Agreement or Waiver on ERISA Benefits. As amended in 1984 by the Retirement Equity Act, ERISA requires each employee benefit plan subject to its provisions to provide that an election of a waiver shall not take effect unless

(1) the spouse of the participant consents in writing to such election,

(2) such election designates a beneficiary (or form of benefits) which may not be changed without spousal consent (or the consent of the spouse expressly permits designation by the participant without any requirement of further consent by the spouse), and

(3) the spouse's consent acknowledges the effect of such election and is witnessed by a plan representative or a notary public.

See 29 U.S.C. § 1055(c) (1988); Int.Rev.Code § 417(a). See also Robins v. Geisel, 666 F.Supp.2d 463 (D. N.J. 2009) (waiver in premarital agreement did not qualify as a waiver under ERISA); Strong v. Dubin, 901 N.Y.S.2d 214 (N.Y. App. Div. 2010) (waiver in premarital agreement conformed with ERISA's requirements and was held enforceable).

In Hurwitz v. Sher, 982 F.2d 778 (2d Cir.1992), the court held that a premarital agreement was not an effective waiver of a wife's claims to spousal death benefits under a qualified profit sharing plan in which the deceased husband was the sole participant.

The premarital agreement provided, in part, that "each party hereby waives and releases to the other party and to the other party's heirs, executor, administrators and assigns any and all rights and causes of action which may arise by reason of the marriage between the parties ... with respect to any property, real or personal, tangible or intangible ... now owned or hereafter acquired by the other party, as fully as though the parties had never married...." The court held that the premarital agreement was not an effective waiver because it "did not designate a beneficiary and did not acknowledge the effect of the waiver as required by ERISA." 982 F.2d at 781. Although the district court had held that the premarital agreement was also ineffective because the wife was not married to the participant when she signed the agreement, the Second Circuit "reserve[d] judgment on whether the [premarital] agreement might have operated as an effective waiver if its only deficiency were that it had been entered into before marriage." Id. at 781 n. 3. The court did, however, quote Treas. Reg. § 1.401(a)-20 (1991), which specifically states that "an agreement entered into prior to marriage does not satisfy the applicable consent requirements...." Id. at 762.

Cross Reference. See also Section 2-208 and Comment.

2002 Amendment Relating to Disclaimers. In 2002, the Code's former disclaimer provision (Section 2-801) was replaced by the Uniform Disclaimer of Property Interests Act, which is incorporated into the Code as Part 11 of Article 2 (Sections 2-1101 to 2-1117). The statutory references in this Comment to former Section 2-801 have been replaced by appropriate references to Part 11. Updating these statutory references has not changed the substance of this Comment.

2016 Amendment. This section was amended in 2016 to conform it with the Uniform Premarital and Marital Agreements Act.

Historical Note. This Comment was revised in 1993, 2002, and 2016.

Restatement (Third) of Property: Wills and Other Donative Transfers (2003)

§ 9.4 Premarital or Marital Agreement

(a) The elective share and other statutory rights accruing to a surviving spouse may be waived, wholly or partially, or otherwise altered, before or during marriage, by a written agreement that was signed by both parties. An agreement that was entered into before marriage is a premarital agreement. An agreement that was entered into during marriage is a marital agreement. Consideration is not necessary to the enforcement of a premarital or a marital agreement.

(b) For a premarital or a marital agreement to be enforceable against the surviving spouse, the enforcing party must show that the surviving spouse's consent was informed and was not obtained by undue influence or duress.

(c) A rebuttable presumption arises that the requirements of subsection (b) are satisfied, shifting the burden of proof to the surviving spouse to show that his or her consent was not informed or was obtained by undue influence or duress, if the enforcing party shows that:

(1) before the agreement's execution, (i) the surviving spouse knew, at least approximately, the decedent's assets and asset values, income, and liabilities; or (ii) the decedent or his or her representative provided in timely fashion to the surviving spouse a written statement accurately disclosing the decedent's significant assets and asset values, income, and liabilities; and either

(2) the surviving spouse was represented by independent legal counsel; or

(3) if the surviving spouse was not represented by independent legal counsel, (i) the decedent or the decedent's representative advised the surviving spouse, in timely fashion, to obtain independent legal counsel, and if the surviving spouse was needy, offered to pay for the costs of the surviving spouse's representation; and (ii) the agreement stated, in language easily understandable by an adult of ordinary intelligence with no legal training, the nature of any rights or claims otherwise arising at death that were altered by the agreement, and the nature of that alteration.

§ 2-214. Protection of Payors and Other Third Parties.

(a) Although under Section 2-205 a payment, item of property, or other benefit is included in the decedent's nonprobate transfers to others, a payor or other third party is not liable for having made a payment or transferred an item of property or other benefit to a beneficiary designated in a governing instrument, or for having taken any other action in good faith reliance on the validity of a governing instrument, upon request and satisfactory proof of the decedent's death, before the payor or other third party received written notice from the surviving spouse or spouse's representative of an intention to file a petition for the elective share or that a petition for the elective share has been filed. A payor or other third party is liable for payments made or other actions taken after the payor or other third party received written notice of an intention to file a petition for the elective share or that a petition for the elective share has been filed.

(b) A written notice of intention to file a petition for the elective share or that a petition for the elective share has been filed must be mailed to the payor's or other third party's main office or home by registered or certified mail, return receipt requested, or served upon the payor or other third party in the same manner as a summons in a civil action. Upon receipt of written notice of intention to file a petition for the elective share or that a petition for the elective share has been filed, a payor or other third party may pay any amount owed or transfer or deposit any item of property held by it to or with the court having jurisdiction of the probate proceedings relating to the decedent's estate, or if no proceedings have been commenced, to or with the court having jurisdiction of probate proceedings relating to decedents' estates located in the county of the decedent's residence. The court shall hold the funds or item of property and, upon its determination under Section 2-211(d), shall order disbursement in accordance with the determination. If no petition is filed in the court within the specified time under Section 2-211(a) or, if filed, the demand for an elective share is withdrawn under Section 2-211(c), the court shall order disbursement to the designated beneficiary. Payments or transfers to the court or deposits made into court discharge the payor or other third party from all claims for amounts so paid or the value of property so transferred or deposited.

(c) Upon petition to the probate court by the beneficiary designated in a governing instrument, the court may order that all or part of the property be paid to the beneficiary in an amount and subject to conditions consistent with this [part].

Comment

This section provides protection to "payors" and other third parties who made payments or took any other action before receiving written notice of the spouse's intention to make an election under this part or that an election has been made. The term "payor" is defined in Section 1-201 as meaning "a trustee, insurer, business entity, employer, government, governmental agency or subdivision, or any other person authorized or obligated by law or a governing instrument to make payments."

Historical Note. Although this Comment was added in 1993, the substance of the Comment previously appeared as the last paragraph of the Comment to Section 2-202, 8 U.L.A. 92, 93 (Supp.1992).

Former (Pre-1990) Version of the Elective Share

§ 2-201. [Right to Elective Share.]

(a) If a married person domiciled in this state dies, the surviving spouse has a right of election to take an elective share of one-third of the augmented estate under the limitations and conditions hereinafter stated.

(b) If a married person not domiciled in this state dies, the right, if any, of the surviving spouse to take an elective share in property in this state is governed by the law of the decedent's domicile at death.

§ 2-202. [Augmented Estate.] The augmented estate means the estate reduced by funeral and administrative expenses, homestead allowance, family allowances and exemptions, and enforceable claims, to which is added the sum of the following amounts:

(1) The value of property transferred to anyone other than a bona fide purchaser by the decedent at any time during marriage, to or for the benefit of any person other than the surviving spouse, to the extent that the decedent did not receive adequate and full consideration in money or money's worth for the transfer, if the transfer is of any of the following types:

(i) any transfer under which the decedent retained at the time of his death the possession or enjoyment of, or right to income from, the property;

(ii) any transfer to the extent that the decedent detained at the time of his death a power, either alone or in conjunction with any other person, to revoke or to consume, invade or dispose of the principal for his own benefit;

(iii) any transfer whereby property is held at the time of decedent's death by decedent and another with right of survivorship;

(iv) any transfer made to a donee within two years of death of the decedent to the extent that the aggregate transfers to any one donee in either of the years exceed $3,000.00.

Any transfer is excluded if made with the written consent or joinder of the surviving spouse. Property is valued as of the decedent's death except that property given irrevocably to a donee during lifetime of the decedent is valued as of the date the donee came into possession or enjoyment if that occurs first. Nothing herein shall cause to be included in the augmented estate any life insurance, accident insurance, joint annuity, or pension payable to a person other than the surviving spouse.

(2) The value of property owned by the surviving spouse at the decedent's death, plus the value of property transferred by the spouse at any time during marriage to any person other than the decedent which would have been includible in the spouse's augmented estate if the surviving spouse had predeceased the decedent to the extent the owned or transferred property is derived from the decedent by any means other than testate or intestate succession without a full consideration in money or money's worth. For purposes of this paragraph:

(i) Property derived from the decedent includes, but is not limited to, any beneficial interest of the surviving spouse in a trust created by the decedent during his lifetime, any property appointed to the spouse by the decedent's exercise of a general or special power of appointment also exercisable in favor of others than the spouse, any proceeds of insurance (including accidental death benefits) on the life of the decedent attributable to premiums paid by him, any lump sum immediately payable and the commuted value of the proceeds of annuity contracts under which the decedent was the primary annuitant attributable to premiums paid by him, the commuted value of amounts payable after the decedent's death under any public or private pension, disability compensation, death benefit or retirement plan, exclusive of the Federal Social Security system, by reason of service performed or disabilities incurred by the decedent, any property held at the time of decedent's death by decedent and the surviving spouse with right of survivorship, any property held by decedent and transferred by contract to the surviving spouse by reason of the decedent's death and the value of the share of the surviving spouse resulting from rights in community property in this or any other state formerly owned with the decedent. Premiums paid by the decedent's employer, his partner, a partnership of which he was a member, or his creditors, are deemed to have been paid by the decedent.

(ii) Property owned by the spouse at the decedent's death is valued as of the date of death. Property transferred by the spouse is valued at the time the transfer became irrevocable, or at the decedent's death, whichever occurred first. Income earned by included property prior to the decedent's death is not treated as property derived from the decedent.

(iii) Property owned by the surviving spouse as of the decedent's death, or previously transferred by the surviving spouse, is presumed to have been derived from the decedent except to the extent that the surviving spouse establishes that it was derived from another source.

(3) For purposes of this section a bona fide purchaser is a purchaser for value in good faith and without notice of any adverse claim. Any recorded instrument on which a state documentary fee is noted pursuant to [insert appropriate reference] is prima facie evidence that the transfer described therein was made to a bona fide purchaser.

§ 2-203. [Right of Election Personal to Surviving Spouse]. The right of election of the surviving spouse may be exercised only during his lifetime by him. In the case of a protected person, the right of election may be exercised only by order of the court in which protective proceedings as to his property are pending, after finding that exercise is necessary to provide adequate support for the protected person during his probable life expectancy.

§ 2-204. [Waiver of Right to Elect and of Other Rights]. The right of election of a surviving spouse and the rights of the surviving spouse to homestead allowance, exempt property and family allowance, or any of them, may be waived, wholly or partially, before or after marriage, by a written contract, agreement or waiver signed by the party waiving after fair disclosure. Unless it provides to the contrary, a waiver of "all rights" (or equivalent language) in the property or estate of a present or prospective spouse or a complete property settlement entered into after or in anticipation of separation or divorce is a waiver of all rights to elective share, homestead allowance, exempt property and family allowance by each spouse in the property of the other and a renunciation by each of all benefits which would otherwise pass to him from the other by intestate succession or by virtue of the provisions of any will executed before the waiver or property settlement.

§ 2-205. [Proceeding for Elective Share; Time Limit].

(a) The surviving spouse may elect to take his elective share in the augmented estate by filing in the Court and mailing or delivering to the personal representative, if any, a petition for the elective share within 9 months after the date of death, or within 6 months after the probate of the decedent's will, whichever limitation last expires. However, non-probate transfers, described in Section 2-202(1), shall not be included within the augmented estate for the purpose of computing the elective share, if the petition is filed later than 9 months after death.

The Court may extend the time for election as it sees fit for cause shown by the surviving spouse before the time for election has expired.

(b) The surviving spouse shall give notice of the time and place set for hearing to persons interested in the estate and to the distributees and recipients of portions of the augmented net estate whose interests will be adversely affected by the taking of the elective share.

(c) The surviving spouse may withdraw his demand for an elective share at any time before entry of a final determination by the Court.

(d) After notice and hearing, the Court shall determine the amount of the elective share and shall order its payment from the assets of the augmented net estate or by contribution as appears appropriate under Section 2-207. If it appears that a fund or property included in the augmented net estate has not come into the possession of the personal representative, or has been distributed by the personal representative, the Court nevertheless shall fix the liability of any person who has any interest in the fund or property or who has possession thereof, whether as trustee or otherwise. The proceeding may be maintained against fewer than all persons against whom relief could be sought, but no person is subject to contribution in any greater amount than he would have been if relief had been secured against all persons subject to contribution.

(e) The order or judgment of the Court may be enforced as necessary in suit for contribution or payment in other courts of this state or other jurisdictions.

§ 2-206. [Effect of Election on Benefits by Will or Statute]. A surviving spouse is entitled to homestead allowance, exempt property, and family allowance, whether or not he elects to take an elective share.

§ 2-207. [Charging Spouse With Gifts Received; Liability of Others for Balance of Elective Share].

(a) In the proceeding for an elective share, values included in the augmented estate which pass or have passed to the surviving spouse, or which would have passed to the spouse but were renounced, are applied first to satisfy the elective share and to reduce any contributions due from other recipients of transfers included in the augmented estate. For purposes of this subsection, the electing spouse's beneficial interest in any life estate or in any trust shall be computed as if worth one half of the total value of the property subject to the life estate, or of the trust estate, unless higher or lower values for these interests are established by proof.

(b) Remaining property of the augmented estate is so applied that liability for the balance of the elective share of the surviving spouse is equitably apportioned among the recipients of the augmented estate in proportion to the value of their interests therein.

(c) Only original transferees from, or appointees of, the decedent and their donees, to the extent the donees have the property or its proceeds, are subject to the contribution to make up the elective share of the surviving spouse. A person liable to contribution may choose to give up the property transferred to him or to pay its value as of the time it is considered in computing the augmented estate.

PART 3
SPOUSE AND CHILDREN UNPROVIDED FOR IN WILLS

§ 2-301. Entitlement of Spouse; Premarital Will.

(a) If a testator's surviving spouse married the testator after the testator executed his [or her] will, the surviving spouse is entitled to receive, as an intestate share, no less than the value of the share of the estate he [or she] would have received if the testator had died intestate as to that portion of the testator's estate, if any, that neither is devised to a child of the testator who was born before the testator married the surviving spouse and who is not a child of the surviving spouse nor is devised to a descendant of such a child or passes under Sections 2-603 or 2-604 to such a child or to a descendant of such a child, unless:

(1) it appears from the will or other evidence that the will was made in contemplation of the testator's marriage to the surviving spouse;

(2) the will expresses the intention that it is to be effective notwithstanding any subsequent marriage; or

(3) the testator provided for the spouse by transfer outside the will and the intent that the transfer be in lieu of a testamentary provision is shown by the testator's statements or is reasonably inferred from the amount of the transfer or other evidence.

(b) In satisfying the share provided by this section, devises made by the will to the testator's surviving spouse, if any, are applied first, and other devises, other than a devise to a child of the testator who was born before the testator married the surviving spouse and who is not a child of the surviving spouse or a devise or substitute gift under Sections 2-603 or 2-604 to a descendant of such a child, abate as provided in Section 3-902.

Comment

Purpose and Scope of the Revisions. This section applies only to a premarital will, a will executed prior to the testator's marriage to his or her surviving spouse. If the decedent and the surviving spouse were married to each other more than once, a premarital will is a will executed by the decedent at any time when they were not married to each other but not a will executed during a prior marriage. This section reflects the view that the intestate share of the spouse in that portion of the testator's estate not devised to certain of the testator's children, under trust or not, (or that is not devised to their descendants, under trust or not, or does not pass to their descendants under the antilapse statute) is what the testator would want the spouse to have if he or she had thought about the relationship of his or her old will to the new situation.

Under this section, a surviving spouse who married the testator after the testator executed his or her will may be entitled to a certain minimum amount of the testator's estate. The surviving spouse's entitlement under this section, if any, is granted automatically; it need not be elected. If the surviving spouse exercises his or her right to take an elective share, amounts provided under this section count toward making up the elective-share amount by virtue of the language in subsection (a) stating that the amount provided by this section is treated as "an intestate share." Under Section 2-209(a)(1), amounts passing to the surviving spouse by intestate succession count first toward making up the spouse's elective-share amount.

Subsection (a). Subsection (a) is revised to make it clear that a surviving spouse who, by a premarital will, is devised, under trust or not, less than the share of the testator's estate he or she would have received had the testator died intestate as to that part of the estate, if any, not devised to certain of the testator's children, under trust or not, (or that is not devised to their descendants, under trust or not, or does not pass to their descendants under the antilapse statute) is entitled to be brought up to that share. Subsection (a) was amended in 1993 to make it clear that any lapsed devise that passes under Section 2-604 to a child of the testator by a prior marriage, rather than only to a descendant of such a child is covered.

Example. G's will devised the residue of his estate "to my two children, A and B, in equal shares." A and B are children of G's prior marriage. G is survived by A and by G's new spouse, X. B predeceases G, without leaving any descendants who survived G by 120 hours. Under Section 2-604, B's half of the residue passes to G's child, A. A is a child of the testator's prior marriage but not a descendent of B. X's right under Section 2-301 are to take an intestate share in that portion of G's estate not covered by the residuary clause.

The pre-1990 version of Section 2-301 was titled "*Omitted* Spouse", and the section used phrases such as "*fails* to provide" and "*omitted* spouse." The implication of the title and these phrases was that the section was inapplicable if the person the decedent later married was a devisee in his or her premarital will. It was clear, however, from the underlying purpose of the section that this was not intended. The courts recognized this and refused to interpret the section that way, but in doing so they have been forced to say that a premarital will containing a devise to the person to whom the testator was married at death could still be found to "fail to provide" for the survivor *in the survivor's capacity as spouse.* See Estate of Christensen, 665 P.2d 646 (Utah 1982); Estate of Ganier, 418 So.2d 256 (Fla.1982); Note, "The Problem of the 'Un-omitted' Spouse Under Section 2-301 of the [Pre-1990] Uniform Probate Code", 52 U.Chi.L. Rev. 481 (1985). By making the existence and amount of a premarital devise to the spouse irrelevant, the revisions of subsection (a) make the operation of the statute more purposive.

Subsection (a)(1), (2), and (3) Exceptions. The moving party has the burden of proof on the exceptions contained in subsections (a)(1), (2), and (3). For a case interpreting the language of subsection (a)(3), see Estate of Bartell, 776 P.2d 885 (Utah 1989). This section can be barred by a premarital agreement, marital agreement, or waiver as provided in Section 2-213.

Subsection (b). Subsection (b) is also revised to provide that the value of any premarital devise to the surviving spouse, equitable or legal, is used first to satisfy the spouse's entitlement under this section, before any other devises suffer abatement. This revision is made necessary by the revision of subsection (a): If the existence or amount of a premarital devise to the surviving spouse is irrelevant, any such devise must be counted toward and not be in addition to the ultimate share to which the spouse is entitled. Normally, a devise in favor of the person whom the testator later marries will be a specific or general devise, not a residuary devise. The effect under the pre-1990 version of subsection (b) was that the surviving spouse could take the intestate share under Section 2-301, which in the pre-1990 version was satisfied out of the residue (under the rules of abatement in Section 3-902), plus the devise in his or her favor. The revision of subsection (b) prevents this "double dipping", so to speak.

Reference. The theory of this section is discussed in Waggoner, "Spousal Rights in Our Multiple-Marriage Society: The Revised Uniform Probate Code." 26 Real Prop. Prob. & Tr. J. 683, 748-51 (1992).

Historical Note. This Comment was revised in 1993. For the prior version, see 8 U.L.A. 101 (Supp. 1992).

Former (Pre-1990) Version

§ 2-301. [Omitted Spouse.]

(a) If a testator fails to provide by will for his surviving spouse who married the testator after the execution of the will, the omitted spouse shall receive the same share of the estate he would have received if the decedent left no will unless it appears from the will that the omission was intentional or the testator provided for the spouse by transfer outside the will and the intent that the transfer be in lieu of a testamentary provision is shown by statements of the testator or from the amount of the transfer or other evidence.

(b) In satisfying a share provided by this section, the devises made by the will abate as provided in Section 3-902.

---

§ 2-302. Omitted Children.

(a) Except as provided in subsection (b), if a testator fails to provide in his [or her] will for any of his [or her] children born or adopted after the execution of the will, the omitted after-born or after-adopted child receives a share in the estate as follows:

(1) If the testator had no child living when he [or she] executed the will, an omitted after-born or after-adopted child receives a share in the estate equal in value to that which the child would have received had the testator died intestate, unless the will devised all or substantially all of the estate to the other parent of the omitted child and that other parent survives the testator and is entitled to take under the will.

(2) If the testator had one or more children living when he [or she] executed the will, and the will devised property or an interest in property to one or more of the then-living children, an omitted after-born or after-adopted child is entitled to share in the testator's estate as follows:

(A) The portion of the testator's estate in which the omitted after-born or after-adopted child is entitled to share is limited to devises made to the testator's then-living children under the will.

(B) The omitted after-born or after-adopted child is entitled to receive the share of the testator's estate, as limited in subparagraph (A), that the child would have received had the testator included all omitted after-born and after-adopted children with the children to whom devises were made under the will and had given an equal share of the estate to each child.

(C) To the extent feasible, the interest granted an omitted after-born or after-adopted child under this section must be of the same character, whether equitable or legal, present or future, as that devised to the testator's then-living children under the will.

(D) In satisfying a share provided by this paragraph, devises to the testator's children who were living when the will was executed abate ratably. In abating the devises of the then-living children, the court shall preserve to the maximum extent possible the character of the testamentary plan adopted by the testator.

(b) Neither subsection (a)(1) nor subsection (a)(2) applies if:

(1) it appears from the will that the omission was intentional; or

(2) the testator provided for the omitted after-born or after-adopted child by transfer outside the will and the intent that the transfer be in lieu of a testamentary provision is shown by the testator's statements or is reasonably inferred from the amount of the transfer or other evidence.

(c) If at the time of execution of the will the testator fails to provide in his [or her] will for a living child solely because he [or she] believes the child to be dead, the child is entitled to share in the estate as if the child were an omitted after-born or after-adopted child.

(d) In satisfying a share provided by subsection (a)(1), devises made by the will abate under Section 3-902.

Comment

This section provides for both the case where a child was born or adopted after the execution of the will and not foreseen at the time and thus not provided for in the will, and the rare case where a testator omits one of his or her children because of the mistaken belief that the child is dead. For the purpose of this section, the term "child" refers to a child who would take under a class gift created in the testator's will. See Section 2-705.

Basic Purposes and Scope of 1990 Revisions. This section was substantially revised in 1990. The revisions had two basic objectives. The first was to provide that a will that devised, under trust or not, all or substantially all of the testator's estate to the other parent of the omitted child prevents an after-born or after-adopted child from taking an intestate share if none of the testator's children was living when he or she executed the will. (Under this rule, the other parent must survive the testator and be entitled to take under the will.)

Under the pre-1990 Code, such a will prevented the omitted child's entitlement only if the testator had one or more children living when he or she executed the will. The rationale for the revised rule is found in the empirical evidence (cited in the Comment to Section 2-102) that suggests that even testators with children tend to devise their entire estates to their surviving spouses, especially in smaller estates. The testator's purpose is not to disinherit the children; rather, such a will evidences a purpose to trust the surviving parent to use the property for the benefit of the children, as appropriate. This attitude of trust of the surviving parent carries over to the case where none of the children have been born when the will is executed.

The second basic objective of the 1990 revisions was to provide that if the testator had children when he or she executed the will, and if the will made provision for one or more of the then-living children, an omitted after-born or after-adopted child does not take a full intestate share (which might be substantially larger or substantially smaller than given to the living children). Rather, the omitted after-born or after-adopted child participates on a pro rata basis in the property devised, under trust or not, to the then-living children.

A more detailed description of the revised rules follows.

No Child Living When Will Executed. If the testator had no child living when he or she executed the will, subsection (a)(1) provides that an omitted after-born or after-adopted child receives the share he or she would have received had the testator died intestate, unless the will devised, under trust or not, all or substantially all of the estate to the other parent of the omitted child. If the will did devise, under trust or not, all or substantially all of the estate to the other parent of the omitted child, and if that other parent survives the testator and is entitled to take under the will, the omitted after-born or after-adopted child receives no share of the estate. In the case of an after-adopted child, the term "other parent" refers to the other adopting parent. (The other parent of the omitted child might survive the testator, but not be entitled to take under the will because, for example, that devise, under trust or not, to the other parent was revoked under Section 2-803 or 2-804.)

One or More Children Living When Will Executed. If the testator had one or more children living when the will was executed, subsection (a)(2), which implements the second basic objective stated above, provides that an omitted after-born or after-adopted child only receives a share of the testator's estate if the testator's will devised property or an equitable or legal interest in property to one or more of the children living at the time the will was executed; if not, the omitted after-born or after-adopted child receives nothing.

Subsection (a)(2) is modeled on N.Y. Est. Powers & Trusts Law § 5-3.2. Subsection (a)(2) is illustrated by the following example.

Example. When G executed her will, she had two living children, A and B. Her will devised $7,500 to each child. After G executed her will, she had another child, C.

C is entitled to $5,000. $2,500 (1/3 of $7,500) of C's entitlement comes from A's $7,500 devise (reducing it to $5,000); and $2,500 (1/3 of $7,500) comes from B's $7,500 devise (reducing it to $5,000).

Variation. If G's will had devised $10,000 to A and $5,000 to B, C would be entitled to $5,000. $3,333 (1/3 of $10,000) of C's entitlement comes from A's $10,000 devise (reducing it to $6,667); and $1,667 (1/3 of $5,000) comes from B's $5,000 devise (reducing it to $3,333).

Subsection (b) Exceptions. To preclude operation of subsection (a)(1) or (2), the testator's will need not make any provision, even nominal in amount, for a testator's present or future children; under subsection (b)(1), a simple recital in the will that the testator intends to make no provision for then living children or any the testator thereafter may have would be sufficient.

For a case applying the language of subsection (b)(2), in the context of the omitted spouse provision, see Estate of Bartell, 776 P.2d 885 (Utah 1989).

The moving party has the burden of proof on the elements of subsections (b)(1) and (2).

Subsection (c). Subsection (c) addresses the problem that arises if at the time of execution of the will the testator fails to provide in his or her will for a living child solely because he or she believes the child to be dead. Extrinsic evidence is admissible to determine whether the testator omitted the living child solely because he or she believed the child to be dead. Cf. Section 2-601, Comment. If the child was omitted solely because of that belief, the child is entitled to share in the estate as if the child were an omitted after-born or after-adopted child.

Abatement Under Subsection (d). Under subsection (d) and Section 3-902, any intestate estate would first be applied to satisfy the intestate share of an omitted after-born or after-adopted child under subsection (a)(1).

Historical Note. This Comment was revised in 1993 and 2010.

Former (Pre-1990) Version

§ 2-302. [Pretermitted Children.]

(a) If a testator fails to provide in his will for any of his children born or adopted after the execution of his will, the omitted child receives a share in the estate equal in value to that which he would have received if the testator had died intestate unless:

(1) it appears from the will that the omission was intentional;

(2) when the will was executed the testator had one or more children and devised substantially all his estate to the other parent of the omitted child; or

(3) the testator provided for the child by transfer outside the will and the intent that the

transfer be in lieu of a testamentary provision is shown by statements of the testator or from

the amount of the transfer or other evidence.

(b) If at the time of execution of the will the testator fails to provide in his will for a living child solely because he believes the child to be dead, the child receives a share in the estate equal in value to that which he would have received if the testator had died intestate.

(c) In satisfying a share provided by this section, the devises made by the will abate as provided in Section 3-902.

PART 4
EXEMPT PROPERTY AND ALLOWANCES

General Comment

For decedents who die domiciled in this state, this part grants various allowances to the decedent's surviving spouse and certain children. The allowances have priority over unsecured creditors of the estate and persons to whom the estate may be devised by will. If there is a surviving spouse, all of the allowances described in this part, which (as revised to adjust for inflation) total $25,000, plus whatever is allowed to the spouse for support during administration, normally pass to the spouse. If the surviving spouse and minor or dependent children live apart from one another, the minor or dependent children may receive some of the support allowance. If there is no surviving spouse, minor or dependent children become entitled to the homestead exemption of $15,000 and to support allowances. The exempt property section confers rights on the spouse, if any, or on all children, to $10,000 in certain chattels, or funds if the unencumbered value of chattels is below the $10,000 level. This provision is designed in part to relieve a personal representative of the duty to sell household chattels when there are children who will have them.

These family protection provisions supply the basis for the important small estate provisions of Article III, Part 12.

States adopting the Code may see fit to alter the dollar amounts suggested in these sections, or to vary the terms and conditions in other ways so as to accommodate existing traditions. Although creditors of estates would be aided somewhat if all family exemption provisions relating to probate estates were the same throughout the country, there is probably less need for uniformity of law regarding these provisions than for any of the other parts of this article. Still, it is quite important for all states to limit their homestead, support allowance and exempt property provisions, if any, so that they apply only to estates of decedents who were domiciliaries of the state.

Cross Reference. Notice that under Section 2-104 a spouse or child claiming under this part must survive the decedent by 120 hours.

§ 2-401. Applicable Law.
This [part] applies to the estate of a decedent who dies domiciled in this state. Rights to homestead allowance, exempt property, and family allowance for a decedent who dies not domiciled in this state are governed by the law of the decedent's domicile at death.

§ 2-402. Homestead Allowance.
A decedent's surviving spouse is entitled to a homestead allowance of [$22,500]. If there is no surviving spouse, each minor child and each dependent child of the decedent is entitled to a homestead allowance amounting to [$22,500] divided by the number of minor and dependent children of the decedent. The homestead allowance is exempt from and has priority over all claims against the estate. Homestead allowance is in addition to any share passing to the surviving spouse or minor or dependent child by the will of the decedent, unless otherwise provided, by intestate succession, or by way of elective share.

Comment

As originally adopted in 1969, the bracketed dollar amount was $5,000. To adjust for inflation, the bracketed amount was increased to $15,000 in 1990.

See Section 2-802 for the definition of "spouse", which controls in this part. Also, see Section 2-104. Waiver of homestead is covered by Section 2-213. "Election" between a provision of a will and homestead is not required unless the will so provides.

A set dollar amount for homestead allowance was dictated by the desirability of having a certain level below which administration may be dispensed with or be handled summarily, without regard to the size of allowances under Section 2-404. The "small estate" line is controlled largely, though not entirely, by the size of the homestead allowance. This is because Part 12 of Article III dealing with small estates rests on the assumption that the only justification for keeping a decedent's assets from his creditors is to benefit the decedent's spouse and children.

Another reason for a set amount is related to the fact that homestead allowance may prefer a decedent's minor or dependent children over his or her other children. It was felt desirable to minimize the consequence of application of an arbitrary age line among children of the decedent.

[§ 2-402A. Constitutional Homestead.
The value of any constitutional right of homestead in the family home received by a surviving spouse or child must be charged against the spouse or child's

homestead allowance to the extent the family home is part of the decedent's estate or would have been but for the homestead provision of the constitution.]

Comment

This optional section is designed for adoption only in states with a constitutional homestead provision. The value of the surviving spouse's constitutional right of homestead may be considerably less than the full value of the family home if the constitution gives him or her only a terminable life estate enjoyable in common with minor children.

§ 2-403. Exempt Property. In addition to the homestead allowance, the decedent's surviving spouse is entitled from the estate to a value, not exceeding $15,000 in excess of any security interests therein, in household furniture, automobiles, furnishings, appliances, and personal effects. If there is no surviving spouse, the decedent's children are entitled jointly to the same value. If encumbered chattels are selected and the value in excess of security interests, plus that of other exempt property, is less than $15,000, or if there is not $15,000 worth of exempt property in the estate, the spouse or children are entitled to other assets of the estate, if any, to the extent necessary to make up the $15,000 value. Rights to exempt property and assets needed to make up a deficiency of exempt property have priority over all claims against the estate, but the right to any assets to make up a deficiency of exempt property abates as necessary to permit earlier payment of homestead allowance and family allowance. These rights are in addition to any benefit or share passing to the surviving spouse or children by the decedent's will, unless otherwise provided, by intestate succession, or by way of elective share.

Comment

As originally adopted in 1969, the dollar amount exempted was set at $3,500. To adjust for inflation, the amount was increased to $10,000 in 1990.

Unlike the exempt amount described in Sections 2-402 and 2-404, the exempt amount described in this section is available in a case in which the decedent left no spouse but left only adult children. The provision in this section that establishes priorities is required because of possible difference between beneficiaries of the exemptions described in this section and those described in Sections 2-402 and 2-404.

Section 2-213 covers waiver of exempt property rights. This section indicates that a decedent's will may put a spouse to an election with reference to exemptions, but that no election is presumed to be required.

§ 2-404. Family Allowance.

(a) In addition to the right to homestead allowance and exempt property, the decedent's surviving spouse and minor children whom the decedent was obligated to support and children who were in fact being supported by the decedent are entitled to a reasonable allowance in money out of the estate for their maintenance during the period of administration, which allowance may not continue for longer than one year if the estate is inadequate to discharge allowed claims. The allowance may be paid as a lump sum or in periodic installments. It is payable to the surviving spouse, if living, for the use of the surviving spouse and minor and dependent children; otherwise to the children, or persons having their care and custody. If a minor child or dependent child is not living with the surviving spouse, the allowance may be made partially to the child or his [or her] guardian or other person having the child's care and custody, and partially to the spouse, as their needs may appear. The family allowance is exempt from and has priority over all claims except the homestead allowance.

(b) The family allowance is not chargeable against any benefit or share passing to the surviving spouse or children by the will of the decedent, unless otherwise provided, by intestate succession, or by way of elective share. The death of any person entitled to family allowance terminates the right to allowances not yet paid.

Comment

The allowance provided by this section does not qualify for the marital deduction under the federal estate tax because the interest is a non-deductible terminable interest. A broad code must be drafted to provide the best possible protection for the family in all cases, even though this may not provide desired tax advantages for certain larger estates. In the estates falling in the federal estate tax bracket where careful planning may be expected, it is important to the operation of formula clauses that the family allowance be clearly deductible or clearly non-deductible. With the section clearly creating a non-deductible interest, estate planners can create a plan that will operate with certainty. Finally, in order to facilitate administration of this allowance without court supervision it is necessary to provide a fairly simple and definite framework.

In determining the amount of the family allowance, account should be taken of both the previous standard of living and the nature of other resources available to the family to meet current living expenses until the estate can be administered and assets distributed. While the death of the principal income producer may necessitate some change in the standard of living, there must also be a period of adjustment. If the surviving spouse has a substantial income, this may be taken into account. Whether life insurance proceeds payable in a lump sum or periodic installments were intended by the decedent to be used for the period of adjustment or to be conserved as capital may be considered. A living trust may provide the needed income without resorting to the probate estate.

Obviously, need is relative to the circumstances, and what is reasonable must be decided on the basis of the facts of each individual case. Note, however, that under the next section the personal representative may not determine an allowance of more than $2,250 per month for one year; a court order would be necessary if a greater allowance is reasonably necessary.

Historical Note. This Comment was revised in 2010 to reflect the increase in the amount of the allowance.

§ 2-405. Source, Determination, and Documentation.

(a) If the estate is otherwise sufficient, property specifically devised may not be use to satisfy rights to homestead allowance or exempt property. Subject to this restriction, the surviving spouse, guardians of minor children, or children who are adults may select property of the estate as homestead allowance and exempt property. The personal representative may make those selections if the surviving spouse, the children, or the guardians of the minor children are unable or fail to do so within a reasonable time or there is no guardian of a minor child. The personal representative may execute an instrument or deed of distribution to establish the ownership of property taken as homestead allowance or exempt property. The personal representative may determine the family allowance in a lump sum not exceeding $27,000 or periodic installments not exceeding $2,250 per month for one year, and may disburse funds of the estate in payment of the family allowance and any part of the homestead allowance payable in cash. The personal representative or an interested person aggrieved by any selection, determination, payment, proposed payment, or failure to act under this section may petition the court for appropriate relief, which may include a family allowance other than that which the personal representative determined or could have determined.

(b) If the right to an elective share is exercised on behalf of a surviving spouse who is an incapacitated person, the personal representative may add any unexpended portions payable under the homestead allowance, exempt property, and family allowance to the trust established under Section 2-212(b).

Comment

Scope and Purpose of Revision. As originally adopted in 1969, the maximum family allowance the personal representative was authorized to determine without court order was a lump sum of $6,000 or periodic installments of $500 per month for one year.

To adjust for inflation, the amounts were increased in 1990 to $18,000 and $1,500 respectively and in 2008 to $22,500 and $2,250. The dollar amount in this section is subject to annual cost-of-living adjustments under Section 1-109.

A new subsection (b) was added to provide for the case where the right to an elective share is exercised on behalf of a surviving spouse who is an incapacitated person. In that case, the personal representative is authorized to add any unexpended portions under the homestead allowance, exempt property, and family allowance to the custodial trust established by Section 2-212(b).

If Domiciliary Assets Insufficient. Note that a domiciliary personal representative can collect against out of state assets if domiciliary assets are insufficient.

Cross References. See Sections 3-902, 3-906 and 3-907.

Historical Note. This Comment was revised in 1993 and 2008.

PART 5
WILLS, WILL CONTRACTS, AND CUSTODY AND DEPOSIT OF WILLS

General Comment

Part 5 of Article II was retitled in 1990 to reflect the fact that it now includes the provisions on will contracts (pre-1990 Section 2-701) and on custody and deposit of wills (pre-1990 Sections 2-901 and 2-902).

Part 5 deals with capacity and formalities for execution and revocation of wills. The basic intent of the pre-1990 sections was to validate wills whenever possible. To that end, the minimum age for making wills was lowered to eighteen, formalities for a written and attested will were reduced, holographic wills written and signed by the testator were authorized,

choice of law as to validity of execution was broadened, and revocation by operation of law was limited to divorce or annulment. In addition, the statute also provided for an optional method of execution with acknowledgment before a public officer (the self-proved will).

These measures have been retained, and the purpose of validating wills whenever possible has been strengthened by the addition of a new section, Section 2-503, which allows a will to be upheld despite a harmless error in its execution.

§ 2-501. Who May Make Will.
An individual 18 or more years of age who is of sound mind may make a will.

Comment

This section states a uniform minimum age of eighteen for capacity to execute a will. "Minor" is defined in Section 1-201, and may involve an age different from that prescribed here.

Restatement (Third) of Property: Wills and Other Donative Transfers (2003)

§ 8.1 Requirement of Mental Capacity

(a) A person must have mental capacity in order to make or revoke a donative transfer.

(b) If the donative transfer is in the form of a will, a revocable will substitute, or a revocable gift, the testator or donor must be capable of knowing and understanding in a general way the nature and extent of his or her property, the natural objects of his or her bounty, and the disposition that he or she is making of that property, and must also be capable of relating these elements to one another and forming an orderly desire regarding the disposition of the property.

(c) If the donative transfer is in the form of an irrevocable gift, the donor must have the mental capacity necessary to make or revoke a will and must also be capable of understanding the effect that the gift may have on the future financial security of the donor and of anyone who may be dependent on the donor.

---

§ 2-502. Execution; Witnessed or Notarized Wills; Holographic Wills.

(a) **[Witnessed or Notarized Wills.]** Except as provided in subsection (b) and in Sections 2-503, 2-506, and 2-513, a will must be:

(1) in writing;

(2) signed by the testator or in the testator's name by some other individual in the testator's

conscious presence and by the testator's direction; and

(3) either:

(A) signed by at least two individuals, each of whom signed within a reasonable time after the individual witnessed either the signing of the will as described in paragraph (2) or the testator's acknowledgment of that signature or acknowledgment of the will; or

(B) acknowledged by the testator before a notary public or other individual authorized by law to take acknowledgments.

(b) **[Holographic Wills.]** A will that does not comply with subsection (a) is valid as a holographic will, whether or not witnessed, if the signature and material portions of the document are in the testator's handwriting.

(c) **[Extrinsic Evidence.]** Intent that the document constitute the testator's will can be established by extrinsic evidence, including, for holographic wills, portions of the document that are not in the testator's handwriting.

Holograph

Property & Benefues

In writng

Comment

Subsection (a): Witnessed or Notarized Wills. Three formalities for execution of a witnessed or notarized will are imposed. Subsection (a)(1) requires the will to be in writing. Any reasonably permanent record is sufficient. See Restatement (Third) of Property: Wills and Other Donative Transfers § 3.1 cmt. i (1999).

Under subsection (a)(2), the testator must sign the will or some other individual must sign the testator's name in the testator's presence and by the testator's direction. If the latter procedure is followed, and someone else signs the testator's name, the so-called "conscious presence" test is codified, under which a signing is sufficient if it was done in the testator's conscious presence, i.e., within the range of the testator's senses such as hearing; the signing need not have occurred within the testator's line of sight. For application of the "conscious-presence" test, see Restatement (Third) of Property: Wills and Other Donative Transfers § 3.1 cmt. n (1999); Cunningham v. Cunningham, 83 N.W. 58 (Minn. 1900) (conscious-presence requirement held satisfied where "the signing was within the sound of the testator's voice; he knew what was being done ..."); Healy v. Bartless, 59 A. 617 (N.H. 1904) (individuals are in the decedent's conscious presence "whenever they are so near at hand that he is conscious of where they are and of what they are doing, through any of his senses, and where he can readily see them if he is so disposed."); Demaris' Estate, 110 P.2d 571 (Or. 1941) ("[W]e do not believe that sight is the only test of presence. We are convinced that any of the senses that a testator possesses, which enable him to know whether another is near at hand and what he is doing, may be employed by him in determining whether [an individual is] in his [conscious] presence

...").

Signing may be by mark, nickname, or initials, subject to the general rules relating to that which constitutes a "signature." See Restatement (Third) of Property: Wills and Other Donative Transfers § 3.1 cmt. j (1999). There is no requirement that the testator "publish" the document as his or her will, or that he or she request the witnesses to sign, or that the witnesses sign in the presence of the testator or of each other. The testator may sign the will outside the presence of the witnesses, if he or she later acknowledges to the witnesses that the signature is his or hers (or that his or her name was signed by another) or that the document is his or her will. An acknowledgment need not be expressly stated, but can be inferred from the testator's conduct. Norton v. Georgia Railroad Bank & Tr. Co., 285 S.E.2d 910 (Ga. 1982).

There is no requirement that the testator's signature be at the end of the will; thus, if the testator writes his or her name in the body of the will and intends it to be his or her signature, the statute is satisfied. See Restatement (Third) of Property: Wills and Other Donative Transfers § 3.1 cmts. j & k (1999).

Subsection (a)(3) requires that the will either be (A) signed by at least two individuals, each of whom witnessed at least one of the following: (i) the signing of the will; (ii) the testator's acknowledgment of the signature; or (iii) the testator's acknowledgment of the will; or (B) acknowledged by the testator before a notary public or other individual authorized by law to take acknowledgments. Subparagraph (B) was added in 2008 in order to recognize the validity of notarized wills.

Under subsection (a)(3)(A), the witnesses must sign

94

as witnesses (see, e.g., Mossler v. Johnson, 565 S.W.2d 952 (Tex. Civ.App. 1978)), and must sign within a reasonable time after having witnessed the testator's act of signing or acknowledgment. There is, however, no requirement that the witnesses sign before the testator's death. In a particular case, the reasonable-time requirement could be satisfied even if the witnesses sign after the testator's death.

Under subsection (a)(3)(B), a will, whether or not it is properly witnessed under subsection (a)(3)(A), can be acknowledged by the testator before a notary public or other individual authorized by law to take acknowledgments. Note that a signature guarantee is not an acknowledgment before a notary public or other person authorized by law to take acknowledgments. The signature guarantee program, which is regulated by federal law, is designed to facilitate transactions relating to securities. See 17 C.F.R. § 240.17Ad-15.

Allowing notarized wills as an optional method of execution addresses cases that have begun to emerge in which the supervising attorney, with the client and all witnesses present, circulates one or more estate-planning documents for signature, and fails to notice that the client or one of the witnesses has unintentionally neglected to sign one of the documents. See, e.g., Dalk v. Allen, 774 So.2d 787 (Fla. Dist. Ct. App. 2000); Sisson v. Park Street Baptist Church, 24 E.T.R.2d 18 (Ont. Gen. Div. 1998). This often, but not always, arises when the attorney prepares multiple estate-planning documents — a will, a durable power of attorney, a health-care power of attorney, and perhaps a revocable trust. It is common practice, and sometimes required by state law, that the documents other than the will be notarized. It would reduce confusion and chance for error if all of these documents could be executed with the same formality.

In addition, lay people (and, sad to say, some lawyers) think that a will is valid if notarized, which is not true under non-UPC law. See, e.g., Estate of Saueressig, 136 P.3d 201 (Cal. 2006). In Estate of Hall, 51 P.3d 1134 (Mont. 2002), a notarized but otherwise unwitnessed will was upheld, but not under the pre-2008 version of Section 2-502, which did not authorize notarized wills. The will was upheld under the harmless-error rule of Section 2-503. There are also cases in which a testator went to his or her bank to get the will executed, and the bank's notary notarized the document, mistakenly thinking that notarization made the will valid. Cf., e.g., Orrell v. Cochran, 695 S.W.2d 552 (Tex. 1985). Under non-

UPC law, the will is usually held invalid in such cases, despite the lack of evidence raising any doubt that the will truly represented the decedent's wishes.

Other uniform acts affecting property or person do not require either attesting witnesses or notarization. See, e.g., Uniform Trust Code Section 402(a)(2); Uniform Power of Attorney Act Section 105; Uniform Health-Care Decisions Act Section 2(f).

A will that does not meet the requirements of subsection (a) may be valid under subsection (b) as a holograph or under the harmless-error rule of Section 2-503.

Subsection (b): Holographic Wills. This subsection authorizes holographic wills. On holographic wills, see Restatement (Third) of Property: Wills and Other Donative Transfers § 3.2 (1999). Subsection (b) enables a testator to write his or her own will in handwriting. There need be no witnesses. The only requirement is that the signature and the material portions of the document be in the testator's handwriting.

By requiring only the "material portions of the document" to be in the testator's handwriting (rather than requiring, as some existing statutes do, that the will be "entirely" in the decedent's handwriting), a holograph may be valid even though immaterial parts such as date or introductory wording are printed, typed, or stamped.

A valid holograph can also be executed on a printed will form if the material portions of the document are handwritten. The fact, for example, that the will form contains printed language such as "I give, devise, and bequeath to _____" does not disqualify the document as a holographic will, as long as the testator fills out the remaining portion of the dispositive provision in his or her own hand.

Subsection (c): Extrinsic Evidence. Under subsection (c), testamentary intent can be shown by extrinsic evidence, including for holographic wills the printed, typed, or stamped portions of the form or document. Handwritten alterations, if signed, of a validly executed nonhandwritten will can operate as a holographic codicil to the will. If necessary, the handwritten codicil can derive meaning, and hence validity as a holographic codicil, from nonhandwritten portions of the document. See Restatement (Third) of Property: Wills and Other Donative Transfers § 3.2 cmt. g (1999). This position intentionally contradicts Estate of Foxley, 575 N.W.2d 150 (Neb. 1998), a decision condemned in Reporter's Note No. 4 to the Restatement as a decision that "reached a manifestly unjust result".

2008 Revisions. In 2008, this section was amended by adding subsection (a)(3)(B). Subsection (a)(3)(B) and its rationale are discussed in Waggoner, The UPC Authorizes Notarized Wills, 34 ACTEC J. 58 (2008).

Historical Note. This Comment was revised in 2008.

Former (1990) Version

§ 2-502. Execution; Witnessed Wills; Holographic Wills.

(a) Except as provided in subsection (b) and in Sections 2-503, 2-506, and 2-513, a will must be:

(1) in writing;

(2) signed by the testator or in the testator's name by some other individual in the testator's conscious presence and by the testator's direction; and

(3) signed by at least two individuals, each of whom signed within a reasonable time after he [or she] witnessed either the signing of the will as described in paragraph (2) or the testator's acknowledgment of that signature or acknowledgment of the will.

(b) A will that does not comply with subsection (a) is valid as a holographic will, whether or not witnessed, if the signature and material portions of the document are in the testator's handwriting.

(c) Intent that the document constitute the testator's will can be established by extrinsic evidence, including, for holographic wills, portions of the document that are not in the testator's handwriting.

Former (Pre-1990) Version

§ 2-502. [Execution.] Except as provided for holographic wills, writings within Section 2-513, and wills within Section 2-506, every will shall be in writing signed by the testator or in the testator's name by some other person in the testator's presence and by his direction, and shall be signed by at least 2 persons each of whom witnessed either the signing or the testator's acknowledgment of the signature or of the will.

§ 2-503. [Holographic Will.] A will which does not comply with Section 2-502 is valid as a holographic will, whether or not witnessed, if the signature and the material provisions are in the handwriting of the testator.

Military Will

10 U.S.C. § 1044d. Military testamentary instruments: requirement for recognition by States.

(a) **Testamentary Instruments to Be Given Legal Effect.** A military testamentary instrument—

(1) is exempt from any requirement of form, formality, or recording before probate that is provided for testamentary instruments under the laws of a State; and

(2) has the same legal effect as a testamentary instrument prepared and executed in accordance with the laws of the State in which it is presented for probate.

(b) **Military Testamentary Instruments.** For purposes of this section, a military testamentary instrument is an instrument that is prepared with testamentary intent in accordance with regulations prescribed under this section and that—

(1) is executed in accordance with subsection (c) by (or on behalf of) a person, as a testator, who is eligible for military legal assistance;

(2) makes a disposition of property of the testator; and

(3) takes effect upon the death of the testator.

(c) **Requirements for Execution of Military Testamentary Instruments.** An instrument is valid as a military testamentary instrument only if—

(1) the instrument is executed by the testator (or, if the testator is unable to execute the instrument personally, the instrument is executed in the presence of, by the direction of, and on behalf of the testator);

(2) the instrument is executed in the presence of a military legal assistance counsel acting as presiding attorney;

> (3) the instrument is executed in the presence of at least two disinterested witnesses (in addition to the presiding attorney), each of whom attests to witnessing the testator's execution of the instrument by signing it; and
>
> (4) the instrument is executed in accordance with such additional requirements as may be provided in regulations prescribed under this section.

§ 2-503. Harmless Error. Although a document or writing added upon a document was not executed in compliance with Section 2-502, the document or writing is treated as if it had been executed in compliance with that section if the proponent of the document or writing establishes by clear and convincing evidence that the decedent intended the document or writing to constitute:

(1) the decedent's will,

(2) a partial or complete revocation of the will,

(3) an addition to or an alteration of the will, or

(4) a partial or complete revival of his [or her] formerly revoked will or of a formerly revoked portion of the will.

Comment

Purpose of New Section. By way of dispensing power, this new section allows the probate court to excuse a harmless error in complying with the formal requirements for executing or revoking a will. The measure accords with legislation in force in the Canadian province of Manitoba and in several Australian jurisdictions. The Uniform Laws Conference of Canada approved a comparable measure for the Canadian Uniform Wills Act in 1987.

Legislation of this sort was enacted in the state of South Australia in 1975. The experience there has been closely studied by a variety of law reform commissions and in the scholarly literature. See, e.g., Law Reform Commission of British Columbia, Report on the Making and Revocation of Wills (1981); New South Wales Law Reform Commission, Wills: Execution and Revocation (1986); Langbein, Excusing Harmless Errors in the Execution of Wills: A Report on Australia's Tranquil Revolution in Probate Law, 87 Colum. L. Rev. 1 (1987). A similar measure has been in effect in Israel since 1965 (see British Columbia Report, supra, at 44-46; Langbein, supra, at 48-51).

Consistent with the general trend of the revisions of the UPC, Section 2-503 unifies the law of probate and nonprobate transfers, extending to will formalities the harmless error principle that has long been applied to defective compliance with the formal requirements for nonprobate transfers. See, e.g., Annot., 19 A.L.R.2d 5 (1951) (life insurance beneficiary designations).

Evidence from South Australia suggests that the dispensing power will be applied mainly in two sorts of cases. See Langbein, supra, at 15-33. When the testator misunderstands the attestation requirements of Section 2-502(a) and neglects to obtain one or both witnesses, new Section 2-503 permits the proponents of the will to prove that the defective execution did not result from irresolution or from circumstances suggesting duress or trickery—in other words, that the defect was harmless to the purpose of the formality. The measure reduces the tension between holographic wills and the two-witness requirement for attested wills under Section 2-502(a). Ordinarily, the testator who attempts to make an attested will but blunders will still have achieved a level of formality that compares favorably with that permitted for holographic wills under the Code.

The other recurrent class of case in which the dispensing power has been invoked in South Australia entails alterations to a previously executed will. Sometimes the testator adds a clause, that is, the testator attempts to interpolate a defectively executed codicil. More frequently, the amendment has the character of a revision—the testator crosses out former text and inserts replacement terms. Lay persons do not always understand that the execution and revocation requirements of Section 2-502 call for fresh execution in order to modify a will; rather, lay persons often think that the original execution has continuing effect.

By placing the burden of proof upon the proponent of a defective instrument, and by requiring the proponent to discharge that burden by clear and convincing evidence (which courts at the trial and appellate levels are urged to police with rigor), Section 2-503 imposes procedural standards appropriate to the seriousness of the issue. Experience in Israel and South Australia strongly supports the view that a dispensing power like Section 2-503 will not breed litigation. Indeed, as an Israeli judge reported to the British Columbia Law Reform Commission, the dispensing power "actually prevents a great deal of unnecessary litigation", because it eliminates disputes about technical lapses and limits the zone of dispute to the functional question of whether the instrument correctly expresses the testator's intent. British Columbia Report, supra, at 46.

The larger the departure from Section 2-502 formality, the harder it will be to satisfy the court that the instrument reflects the testator's intent. Whereas the South Australian and Israeli courts lightly excuse breaches of the attestation requirements, they have never excused noncompliance with the requirement that a will be in writing, and they have been extremely reluctant to excuse noncompliance with the signature requirement. See Langbein, supra, at 23-29, 49-50. The main circumstance in which the South Australian courts have excused signature errors has been in the recurrent class of cases in which two wills are prepared for simultaneous execution by two testators, typically husband and wife, and each mistakenly signs the will prepared for the other. E.g., Estate of Blakely, 32 S.A.S.R. 473 (1983). Recently, the New York Court of Appeals remedied such a case without aid of statute, simply on the ground "what has occurred is so obvious, and what was intended so clear." In re Snide, 52 N.Y.2d 193, 196, 418 N.E.2d 656, 657, 437 N.Y.S.2d 63, 64 (1981).

Section 2-503 means to retain the intent-serving benefits of Section 2-502 formality without inflicting intent-defeating outcomes in cases of harmless error.

Reference. The rule of this section is supported by the Restatement (Third) of Property: Wills and Other Donative Transfers § 3.3 (1999).

Restatement (Third) of Property: Wills and Other Donative Transfers (1999)

§ 3.3 Excusing Harmless Errors. A harmless error in executing a will may be excused if the proponent establishes by clear and convincing evidence that the decedent adopted the document as his or her will.

---

§ 2-504. Self-Proved Will.

(a) A will that is executed with attesting witnesses may be simultaneously executed, attested, and made self-proved, by acknowledgment thereof by the testator and affidavits of the witnesses, each made before an officer authorized to administer oaths under the laws of the state in which execution occurs and evidenced by the officer's certificate, under official seal, in substantially the following form:

I, _____, the testator, sign my name to this instrument this ___ day of _____, ____, and being first duly sworn, do hereby declare to the undersigned authority that I sign and execute this instrument as my will and that I sign it willingly (or willingly direct another to sign for me), that I execute it as my free and voluntary act for the purposes therein expressed, and that I am [18] years of age or older, of sound mind, and under no constraint or undue influence.

_____
Testator

We, _____, _____, the witnesses, sign our names to this instrument, being first duly sworn, and do hereby declare to the undersigned authority that the testator signs and executes this instrument as (his)(her) will and that (he)(she) signs it willingly (or willingly directs another to sign for (him)(her), and that each of us, in the presence and hearing of the testator, hereby signs this will as witness to the testator's signing, and that to the best of our knowledge the testator is eighteen years of age or older, of sound mind, and under no constraint or undue influence.

_____
Witness

_____
Witness

State of _____
County of _____

     Subscribed, sworn to and acknowledged before me by _____, the testator, and subscribed and sworn to before me by _____, and _____, witness, this ____ day of _____, _____.

(Seal)   (Signed) _____

                                                 (Official capacity of officer)

     (b) A will that is executed with attesting witnesses may be made self-proved at any time after its execution by the acknowledgment thereof by the testator and the affidavits of the witnesses, each made before an officer authorized to administer oaths under the laws of the state in which the acknowledgment occurs and evidenced by the officer's certificate, under official seal, attached or annexed to the will in substantially the following form:

State of _____
County of _____
     We, _____, _____, and _____, the testator and the witnesses, respectively, whose names are signed to the attached or foregoing instrument, being first duly sworn, do hereby declare to the undersigned authority that the testator signed and executed the instrument as the testator's will and that (he)(she) had signed willingly (or willingly directed another to sign for (him)(her), and that (he)(she) executed it as (his)(her) free and voluntary act for the purposes therein expressed, and that each of the witnesses, in the presence and hearing of the testator, signed the will as witness and that to the best of (his)(her) knowledge the testator was at that time [18] years of age or older, of sound mind, and under no constraint or undue influence.

                                               _____
                                                    Testator

                                               _____
                                                    Witness

                                               _____
                                                    Witness

     Subscribed, sworn to and acknowledged before me by _____, the testator, and subscribed and sworn to before me by _____, and _____, witnesses, this ____ day of _____, ____.

(Seal)   (Signed) _____

                                                   (Official capacity of officer)

     (c) A signature affixed to a self-proving affidavit attached to a will is considered a signature affixed to the will, if necessary to prove the will's due execution.

Comment

     A self-proved will may be admitted to probate as provided in Sections 3-303, 3-405, and 3-406 without the testimony of any attesting witness, but otherwise it is treated no differently from a will not self proved. Thus, a self-proved will may be contested (except in regard to questions of proper execution), revoked, or amended by a codicil in exactly the same fashion as a will not self proved. The procedural advantage of a self-proved will is limited to formal testacy proceedings because Section 3-303, which deals with informal probate, dispenses with the necessity of testimony of witnesses even though the instrument is not self proved under this section.

Subsection (c) was added in 1990 to counteract an unfortunate judicial interpretation of similar self-proving will provisions in a few states, under which a signature on the self-proving affidavit was held not to constitute a signature on the will, resulting in invalidity of the will in cases in which the testator or witnesses got confused and only signed on the self-proving affidavit. See Mann, Self-proving Affidavits and Formalism in Wills Adjudication, 63 Wash. U. L.Q. 39 (1985); Estate of Ricketts, 773 P.2d

93 (Wash.Ct.App.1989).

2008 Revision. Section 2-502(a) was amended in 2008 to add an optional method of execution by having a will notarized rather than witnessed by two attesting witnesses. The amendment to Section 2-502 necessitated amending this section so that it only applies to a will that is executed with attesting witnesses.

Historical Note. This Comment was revised in 2008.

§ 2-505. Who May Witness.

(a) An individual generally competent to be a witness may act as a witness to a will.

(b) The signing of a will by an interested witness does not invalidate the will or any provision of it.

Comment

This section carries forward the position of the pre-1990 Code. The position adopted simplifies the law relating to interested witnesses. Interest no longer disqualifies a person as a witness, nor does it invalidate or forfeit a gift under the will. Of course, the purpose of this change is not to foster use of interested witnesses, and attorneys will continue to use disinterested witnesses in execution of wills. But the rare and innocent use of a member of the testator's family on a home-drawn will is not penalized.

This approach does not increase appreciably the

opportunity for fraud or undue influence. A substantial devise by will to a person who is one of the witnesses to the execution of the will is itself a suspicious circumstance, and the devise might be challenged on grounds of undue influence. The requirement of disinterested witnesses has not succeeded in preventing fraud and undue influence; and in most cases of undue influence, the influencer is careful not to sign as a witness, but to procure disinterested witnesses.

Under Section 3-406, an interested witness is competent to testify to prove execution of the will.

§ 2-506. Choice of Law as to Execution. A written will is valid if executed in compliance with Section 2-502 or 2-503 or if its execution complies with the law at the time of execution of the place where the will is executed, or of the law of the place where at the time of execution or at the time of death the testator is domiciled, has a place of abode, or is a national.

Comment

This section permits probate of wills in this state under certain conditions even if they are not executed in accordance with the formalities of Section 2-502 or 2-503. Such wills must be in writing but otherwise are valid if they meet the requirements for execution of the law of the place where the will is executed (when it is executed in another state or country) or the law of testator's domicile, abode or nationality at either the time of execution or at the time of death. Thus, if testator is domiciled in state 1 and executes a typed will merely by signing it without witnesses in state 2

while on vacation there, the court of this state would recognize the will as valid if the law of either state 1 or state 2 permits execution by signature alone. Or if a national of Mexico executes a written will in this state which does not meet the requirements of Section 2-502 but meets the requirements of Mexican law, the will would be recognized as validly executed under this section. The purpose of this section is to provide a wide opportunity for validation of expectations of testators.

§ 2-507. Revocation by Writing or by Act.

(a) A will or any part thereof is revoked:

(1) by executing a subsequent will that revokes the previous will or part expressly or by

[handwritten annotations:]

Writing
- Express - Explicitly revoke prior wills
- Implied
     Bequests Contradict

100

Act
- Original
- terms, Burning, etc
- Done at direction of testator
- doesn't need to touch language

inconsistency; or

> (2) by performing a revocatory act on the will, if the testator performed the act with the intent and for the purpose of revoking the will or part or if another individual performed the act in the testator's conscious presence and by the testator's direction. For purposes of this paragraph, "revocatory act on the will" includes burning, tearing, canceling, obliterating, or destroying the will or any part of it. A burning, tearing, or canceling is a "revocatory act on the will", whether or not the burn, tear, or cancellation touched any of the words on the will.

> (b) If a subsequent will does not expressly revoke a previous will, the execution of the subsequent will wholly revokes the previous will by inconsistency if the testator intended the subsequent will to replace rather than supplement the previous will.

> (c) The testator is presumed to have intended a subsequent will to replace rather than supplement a previous will if the subsequent will makes a complete disposition of the testator's estate. If this presumption arises and is not rebutted by clear and convincing evidence, the previous will is revoked; only the subsequent will is operative on the testator's death.

> (d) The testator is presumed to have intended a subsequent will to supplement rather than replace a previous will if the subsequent will does not make a complete disposition of the testator's estate. If this presumption arises and is not rebutted by clear and convincing evidence, the subsequent will revokes the previous will only to the extent the subsequent will is inconsistent with the previous will; each will is fully operative on the testator's death to the extent they are not inconsistent.

Comment

Purpose and Scope of Revisions. Revocation of a will may be by either a subsequent will or an authorized act done to the document. Revocation by subsequent will cannot be effective unless the subsequent will is valid.

Revocation by Inconsistency. As originally promulgated, this section provided no standard by which the courts were to determine whether in a given case a subsequent will with no revocation clause revokes a prior will, wholly or partly, by inconsistency. Some courts seem to have been puzzled about the standard to be applied. New subsections (b), (c), and (d) codify the workable and common-sense standard set forth in the Restatement (Second) of Property (Donative Transfers) § 34.2 comment b (1991). Under these subsections, the question whether the subsequent will was intended to replace rather than supplement the previous will depends upon whether the second will makes a complete disposition of the testator's estate. If the second will does make a complete disposition of the testator's estate, a presumption arises that the second will was intended to replace the previous will. If the second will does not make a complete disposition of the testator's estate, a presumption arises that the second will was intended to supplement rather than replace the previous will. The rationale is that, when the second will does not make a complete disposition of the testator's estate, the second will is more in the nature

of a codicil to the first will. This standard has been applied in the cases without the benefit of a statutory provision to this effect. E.g., Gilbert v. Gilbert, 652 S.W.2d 663 (Ky.Ct.App.1983).

Example. Five years before her death, G executed a will (Will #1), devising her antique desk to A; $20,000 to B; and the residue of her estate to C. Two years later, A died, and G executed another will (Will #2), devising her antique desk to A's spouse, X; $10,000 to B; and the residue of her estate to C. Will #2 neither expressly revoked Will #1 nor made any other reference to it. G's net probate estate consisted of her antique desk (worth $10,000) and other property (worth $90,000). X, B, and C survived G by 120 hours.

Solution. Will #2 was presumptively intended by G to replace Will #1 because Will #2 made a complete disposition of G's estate. Unless this presumption is rebutted by clear and convincing evidence, Will #1 is wholly revoked; only Will #2 is operative on G's death.

If, however, Will #2 had not contained a residuary clause, and hence had not made a complete disposition of G's estate, "Will #2" is more in the nature of a codicil to Will #1, and the solution would be different. Now, Will #2 would presumptively be treated as having been intended to supplement rather than replace Will #1. In the absence of evidence clearly and convincingly rebutting this presumption, Will #1 would be revoked only to the extent Will #2 is inconsistent with it; both wills would be operative on G's death, to the extent they are not inconsistent. As to the devise of the antique desk, Will #2 is inconsistent with Will #1, and the antique desk would go to X. There being no residuary clause in Will #2, there is nothing in Will #2 that is inconsistent with the residuary clause in Will #1, and so the residue would go to C. The more difficult question relates to the cash devises in the two wills. The question whether they are inconsistent with one another is a question of interpretation in the individual case. Section 2-507 does not establish a presumption one way or the other on that question. If the court finds that the cash devises are inconsistent with one another, i.e., if the court finds that the cash devise in Will #2 was intended to replace rather than supplement the cash devise in Will #1, then B takes $10,000. But, if the court finds that the cash devises are not inconsistent with one another, B would take $30,000.

Revocatory Act. In the case of an act of revocation done to the document, subsection (a)(2) is revised to provide that a burning, tearing, or canceling is a sufficient revocatory act even though the act does not touch any of the words on the will. This is consistent with cases on burning or tearing (e.g., White v. Casten, 46 N.C. 197 (1853) (burning); Crampton v. Osburn, 356 Mo. 125, 201 S.W.2d 336 (1947) (tearing)), but inconsistent with most, but not all, cases on cancellation (e.g., Yont v. Eads, 317 Mass. 232, 57 N.E.2d 531 (1944); Kronauge v. Stoecklein, 33 Ohio App.2d 229, 293 N.E.2d 320 (1972); Thompson v. Royall, 163 Va. 492, 175 S.E. 748 (1934); contra, Warner v. Warner's Estate, 37 Vt. 356 (1864)). By substantial authority, it is held that removal of the testator's signature—by, for example, lining it through, erasing or obliterating it, tearing or cutting it out of the document, or removing the entire signature page—constitutes a sufficient revocatory act to revoke the entire will. Board of Trustees of the University of Alabama v. Calhoun, 514 So.2d 895 (Ala.1987) and cases cited therein.

Subsection (a)(2) is also revised to codify the "conscious-presence" test. As revised, subsection (a)(2) provides that, if the testator does not perform the revocatory act, but directs another to perform the act, the act is a sufficient revocatory act if the other individual performs it in the testator's conscious presence. The act need not be performed in the testator's line of sight. See the Comment to Section

2-502 for a discussion of the "conscious-presence" test.

Revocatory Intent. To effect a revocation, a revocatory act must be accompanied by revocatory intent. Determining whether a revocatory act was accompanied by revocatory intent may involve exploration of extrinsic evidence, including the testator's statements as to intent.

Partial Revocation. This section specifically permits partial revocation.

Dependent Relative Revocation. Each court is free to apply its own doctrine of dependent relative revocation. See generally Palmer, "Dependent Relative Revocation and Its Relation to Relief for Mistake", 69 Mich. L. Rev. 989 (1971). Note, however, that dependent relative revocation should less often be necessary under the revised provisions of the Code. Dependent relative revocation is the law of second best, i.e., its application does not produce the result the testator actually intended, but is designed to come as close as possible to that intent. A precondition to the application of dependent relative revocation is, or should be, good evidence of the testator's actual intention; without that, the court has no basis for determining which of several outcomes comes the closest to that actual intention.

When there is good evidence of the testator's actual intention, however, the revised provisions of the Code would usually facilitate the effectuation of the result the testator actually intended. If, for example, the testator by revocatory act revokes a second will for the purpose of reviving a former will, the evidence necessary to establish the testator's intent to revive the former will should be sufficient under Section 2-509 to effect a revival of the former will, making the application of dependent relative revocation as to the second will unnecessary. If, by revocatory act, the testator revokes a will in conjunction with an effort to execute a new will, the evidence necessary to establish the testator's intention that the new will be valid should, in most cases, be sufficient under Section 2-503 to give effect to the new will, making the application of dependent relative revocation as to the old will unnecessary. If the testator lines out parts of a will or dispositive provision in conjunction with an effort to alter the will's terms, the evidence necessary to establish the testator's intention that the altered terms be valid should be sufficient under Section 2-503 to give effect to the will as altered, making dependent relative revocation as to the lined-out parts unnecessary.

Former (Pre-1990) Version

§ 2-507. [Revocation by Writing or by Act.] A will or any part thereof is revoked

(1) by a subsequent will which revokes the prior will or part expressly or by inconsistency; or

(2) by being burned, torn, canceled, obliterated, or destroyed, with the intent and for the purpose of revoking it by the testator or by another person in his presence and by his direction.

Restatement (Third) of Property: Wills and Other Donative Transfers (1999)

§ 4.3 Ineffective Revocation (Dependent Relative Revocation)

(a) A partial or complete revocation of a will is presumptively ineffective if the testator made the revocation:

(1) in connection with an attempt to achieve a dispositive objective that fails under applicable law, or

(2) because of a false assumption of law, or because of a false belief about an objective fact, that is either recited in the revoking instrument or established by clear and convincing evidence.

(b) The presumption established in subsection (a) is rebutted if allowing the revocation to remain in effect would be more consistent with the testator's probable intention.

---

§ 2-508. Revocation by Change of Circumstances. Except as provided in Sections 2-803 and 2-804, a change of circumstances does not revoke a will or any part of it.

§ 2-509. Revival of Revoked Will.

(a) If a subsequent will that wholly revoked a previous will is thereafter revoked by a revocatory act under Section 2-507(a)(2), the previous will remains revoked unless it is revived. The previous will is revived if it is evident from the circumstances of the revocation of the subsequent will or from the testator's contemporary or subsequent declarations that the testator intended the previous will to take effect as executed.

(b) If a subsequent will that partly revoked a previous will is thereafter revoked by a revocatory act under Section 2-507(a)(2), a revoked part of the previous will is revived unless it is evident from the circumstances of the revocation of the subsequent will or from the testator's contemporary or subsequent declarations that the testator did not intend the revoked part to take effect as executed.

(c) If a subsequent will that revoked a previous will in whole or in part is thereafter revoked by another, later, will, the previous will remains revoked in whole or in part, unless it or its revoked part is revived. The previous will or its revoked part is revived to the extent it appears from the terms of the later will that the testator intended the previous will to take effect.

Comment

Purpose and Scope of Revisions. Although a will takes effect as a revoking instrument when it is executed, it takes effect as a dispositive instrument at death. Once revoked, therefore, a will is ineffective as a dispositive instrument unless it has been revived. This section covers the standards to be applied in determining whether a will (Will #1) that was revoked by a subsequent will (Will #2), either expressly or by inconsistency, has been revived by the revocation of the subsequent will, i.e., whether the revocation of Will #2 (the revoking will) revives Will #1 (the will that Will #2 revoked).

As revised, this section is divided into three subsections. Subsections (a) and (b) cover the effect of revoking Will #2 (the revoking will) by a revocatory act under Section 2-507(a)(2). Under subsection (a), if Will #2 (the revoking will) wholly revoked Will #1, the revocation of Will #2 does not revive Will #1 unless "it is evident from the circumstances of the revocation of [Will #2] or from the testator's contemporary or subsequent declarations that the testator intended [Will #1] to take effect as executed." This standard places the burden of persuasion on the proponent of Will #1 to establish that the decedent's intention was that Will #1 is to be his or her valid will. Testimony regarding the decedent's statements at the time he or she revokes Will #2 or at a later date can be admitted. Indeed, all relevant evidence of intention is to be considered by the court on this question; the open-ended statutory language is not to be undermined by translating it into discrete subsidiary elements, all of which must be met, as the court did in Estate of Boysen, 309 N.W.2d 45 (Minn.1981). See Langbein & Waggoner, "Reforming the Law of Gratuitous Transfers: The New Uniform Probate Code", 55 Alb.L. Rev. 871, 885-87 (1992).

The pre-1990 version of this section did not distinguish between complete and partial revocation. Regardless of whether Will #2 wholly or partly revoked Will #1, the pre-1990 version presumed against revival of Will #1 when Will #2 was revoked by act.

As revised, this section properly treats the two situations as distinguishable. The presumption against revival imposed by subsection (a) is justified because where Will #2 wholly revoked Will #1, the testator understood or should have understood that Will #1 had no continuing effect. Consequently, subsection (a) properly presumes that the testator's act of revoking Will #2 was not accompanied by an intent to revive Will #1.

Subsection (b) establishes the opposite presumption where Will #2 (the revoking will)

revoked Will #1 only in part. In this case, the revocation of Will #2 revives the revoked part or parts of Will #1 unless "it is evident from the circumstances of the revocation of [Will #2] or from the testator's contemporary or subsequent declarations that the testator did not intend the revoked part to take effect as executed." This standard places the burden of persuasion on the party arguing that the revoked part or parts of Will #1 were not revived. The justification is that where Will #2 only partly revoked Will #1, Will #2 is only a codicil to Will #1, and the testator knows (or should know) that Will #1 does have continuing effect. Consequently, subsection (b) properly presumes that the testator's act of revoking Will #2 (the codicil) was accompanied by an intent to revive or reinstate the revoked parts of Will #1.

Subsection (c) covers the effect on Will #1 of revoking Will #2 (the revoking will) by another, later, will (Will #3). Will #1 remains revoked except to the extent that Will #3 shows an intent to have Will #1 effective.

Historical Note. This Comment was revised in 1993. For the prior version, see 8 U.L.A. 118 (Supp.1992).

Former (Pre-1990) Version

§ 2-509. [Revival of Revoked Will.]

(a) If a second will which, had it remained effective at death, would have revoked the first will in whole or in part, is thereafter revoked by acts under Section 2-507, the first will is revoked in whole or in part unless it is evident from the circumstances of the revocation of the second will or from testator's contemporary or subsequent declarations that he intended the first will to take effect as executed.

(b) If a second will which, had it remained effective at death, would have revoked the first will in whole or in part, is thereafter revoked by a third will, the first will is revoked in whole or in part, except to the extent it appears from the terms of the third will that the testator intended the first will to take effect.

---

§ 2-510. **Incorporation by Reference.** A writing in existence when a will is executed may be incorporated by reference if the language of the will manifests this intent and describes the writing sufficiently to permit its identification.

Comment

This section codifies the common-law doctrine of incorporation by reference, except that the sometimes troublesome requirement that the will refer to the document as being in existence when the will was executed has been eliminated.

§ 2-511. **Uniform Testamentary Additions to Trusts Act (1991).**

(a) A will may validly devise property to the trustee of a trust established or to be established (i) during the testator's lifetime by the testator, by the testator and some other person, or by some other person, including a funded or unfunded life insurance trust, although the settlor has reserved any or all rights of ownership of the insurance contracts, or (ii) at the testator's death by the testator's devise to the trustee, if the trust is identified in the testator's will and its terms are set forth in a written instrument, other than a will, executed before, concurrently with, or after the execution of the testator's will or in another individual's will if that other individual has predeceased the testator, regardless of the existence, size, or character of the corpus of the trust. The devise is not invalid because the trust is amendable or revocable, or because the trust was amended after the execution of the will or the testator's death.

(b) Unless the testator's will provides otherwise, property devised to a trust described in subsection (a) is not held under a testamentary trust of the testator, but it becomes a part of the trust to which it is devised, and must be administered and disposed of in accordance with the provisions of the governing instrument setting forth the terms of the trust, including any amendments thereto made before or after the testator's death.

(c) Unless the testator's will provides otherwise, a revocation or termination of the trust before the testator's death causes the devise to lapse.

Comment

This section, which was last revised in 1990, was codified separately in 1991 as the free-standing Uniform Testamentary Additions to Trusts Act (1991). In addition to making a few stylistic changes, several substantive changes to this section were made in the 1990 revision.

As revised, it has been made clear that the "trust" need not have been established (funded with a trust res) during the decedent's lifetime, but can be established (funded with a res) by the devise itself. The pre-1990 version probably contemplated this result and reasonably could be so interpreted (because of the phrase "regardless of the existence ... of the corpus of the trust"). Indeed, a few cases have expressly stated that statutory language like the pre-1990 version of this section authorizes pour-over devises to unfunded trusts. E.g., Clymer v. Mayo, 473 N.E.2d 1084 (Mass.1985); Trosch v. Maryland Nat'l Bank, 32 Md.App. 249, 359 A.2d 564 (1976). The authority of these pronouncements is problematic, however, because the trusts in these cases were so-called "unfunded" life-insurance trusts. An unfunded life-insurance trust is not a trust without a trust res; the trust res in an unfunded life-insurance trust is the contract right to the proceeds of the life-insurance policy conferred on the trustee by virtue of naming the trustee the beneficiary of the policy. See Gordon v. Portland Trust Bank, 201 Or. 648, 271 P.2d 653 (1954) ("[T]he [trustee as the] beneficiary [of the policy] is the owner of a promise to pay the proceeds at the death of the insured...."); Gurnett v. Mutual Life Ins. Co., 356 Ill. 612, 191 N.E. 250 (1934). Thus, the term "unfunded life-insurance trust" does not refer to an unfunded trust, but to a funded trust that has not received additional funding. For further indication of the problematic nature of the idea that the pre-1990 version of this section permits pour-over devises to unfunded trusts, see Estate of Daniels, 665 P.2d 594 (Colo.1983) (pour-over devise failed; before signing the trust instrument, the decedent was advised by counsel that the "mere signing of the trust agreement would not activate it and that, before the trust could come into being, [the decedent] would have to fund it;" decedent then signed the trust agreement and returned it to counsel "to wait for further directions on it;" no further action was taken by the decedent prior to death; the decedent's will devised the residue of her estate to the trustee of the trust, but added that the residue should go elsewhere "if the trust created by said agreement is not in effect at my death.")

Additional revisions of this section are designed to remove obstacles to carrying out the decedent's intention that were contained in the pre-1990 version. These revisions allow the trust terms to be set forth in a written instrument executed after as well as before or concurrently with the execution of the will; require the devised property to be administered in accordance with the terms of the trust as amended after as well as before the decedent's death, even though the decedent's will does not so provide; and allow the decedent's will to provide that the devise is not to lapse even if the trust is revoked or terminated before the decedent's death.

Revision of Uniform Testamentary Additions to Trusts Act. The freestanding Uniform Testamentary Additions to Trusts Act (UTATA) was revised in 1991 in accordance with the revisions to Section 2-511. States that enact Section 2-511 need not enact the UTATA as revised in 1991 and should repeal the original version of the UTATA if previously enacted in the state.

Former (Pre-1990) Version

Former Uniform Testamentary Additions to Trusts Act (1960)

§ 2-511. [Testamentary Additions to Trusts.] A devise or bequest, the validity of which is determinable by the law of this state, may be made by a will to the trustee of a trust established or to be established by the testator or by the testator and some other person or by some other person (including a funded or unfunded life insurance trust, although the trustor has reserved any or all rights of ownership of the insurance contracts) if the trust is identified in the testator's will and its terms are set forth in a written instrument (other than a will) executed before or concurrently with the execution of the testator's will or in the valid last will of a person who has predeceased the testator (regardless of the existence, size, or character of the corpus of the trust). The devise is not invalid because the trust is amendable or revocable, or because the trust was amended after the execution of the will or after the death of the testator. Unless the testator's will provides otherwise, the property so devised (1) is not deemed to be held under a testamentary trust of the testator but becomes a part of the trust to which it is given and (2) shall be administered and disposed of in accordance with the provisions of the instrument or will setting forth the terms of the trust, including any amendments thereto made before the death of the testator (regardless of whether made before or after the execution of the testator's will), and, if the testator's will so provides, including any amendments to the trust made after the death of the testator. A revocation or termination of the trust before the death of the testator causes the devise to lapse.

---

§ 2-512. Events of Independent Significance. A will may dispose of property by reference to acts and events that have significance apart from their effect upon the dispositions made by the will, whether they occur before or after the execution of the will or before or after the testator's death. The execution or revocation of another individual's will is such an event.

§ 2-513. Separate Writing Identifying Devise of Certain Types of Tangible Personal Property. Whether or not the provisions relating to holographic wills apply, a will may refer to a written statement or list to dispose of items of tangible personal property not otherwise specifically disposed of by the will, other than money. To be admissible under this section as evidence of the intended disposition, the writing must be signed by the testator and must describe the items and the devisees with reasonable certainty. The writing may be referred to as one to be in existence at the time of the testator's death; it may be prepared before or after the execution of the will; it may be altered by the testator after its preparation; and it may be a writing that has no significance apart from its effect on the dispositions made by the will.

Comment

Purpose and Scope of Revision. As part of the broader policy of effectuating a testator's intent and of relaxing formalities of execution, this section permits a testator to refer in his or her will to a separate document disposing of tangible personalty other than money. The pre-1990 version precluded the disposition of "evidences of indebtedness, documents of title, and securities, and property used in a trade or business." These limitations are deleted in the revised version, partly to remove a source of confusion in the pre-1990 version, which arose because evidences of indebtedness, documents of title, and securities are not items of tangible personal property to begin with, and partly to permit the disposition of a broader range of items of tangible personal property.

The language "items of tangible personal property" does not require that the separate document specifically itemize each item of tangible personal property covered. The only requirement is that the document described the items covered "with reasonable certainty." Consequently, a document referring to "all my tangible personal property other than money" or to "all my tangible personal property located in my office" or using similar catch-all type of language would normally be sufficient.

The separate document disposing of an item or items of tangible personal property may be prepared after execution of the will, so would not come within Section 2-510 on incorporation by reference. It may even be altered from time to time. The only requirement is that the document be signed by the

106

testator. The pre-1990 version of this section gave effect to an unsigned document if it was in the testator's handwriting. The revisions remove the language giving effect to such an unsigned document. The purpose is to prevent a mere handwritten draft from becoming effective without sufficient indication that the testator intended it to be effective. The signature requirement is designed to prevent mere drafts from becoming effective against the testator's wishes. An unsigned document could still be given effect under Section 2-503, however, if the proponent could carry the burden of proving by clear and convincing evidence that the testator intended the document to be effective.

The typical case covered by this section would be a list of personal effects and the persons whom the decedent desired to take specified items.

Sample Clause. Section 2-513 might be utilized by a clause in the decedent's will such as the following:

"I might leave a written statement or list disposing of items of tangible personal property. If I do and if my written statement or list is found and is identified as such by my Personal Representative no later than 30 days after the probate of this will, then my written statement or list is to be given effect to the extent authorized by law and is to take precedence over any contrary devise or devises of the same item or items of property in this will."

Section 2-513 only authorizes disposition of tangible personal property "not otherwise specifically disposed of by the will." The sample clause above is consistent with this restriction. By providing that the written statement or list takes precedence over any contrary devise in the will, a contrary devise is made conditional upon the written statement or list not contradicting it; if the written statement or list does contradict a devise in the will, the will does not otherwise specifically dispose of the property. If, however, the clause in the testator's will does not provide that the written statement or list is to take precedence over any contrary devise in the will (or contain a provision having similar effect), then the written statement or list is ineffective to the extent it purports to dispose of items of property that were otherwise specifically disposed of by the will.

Former (Pre-1990) Version

§ 2-513. [Separate Writing Identifying Bequest of Tangible Property.] Whether or not the provisions relating to holographic wills apply, a will may refer to a written statement or list to dispose of items of tangible personal property not otherwise specifically disposed of by the will, other than money, evidences of indebtedness, documents of title, and securities, and property used in trade or business. To be admissible under this section as evidence of the intended disposition, the writing must either be in the handwriting of the testator or be signed by him and must describe the items and the devisees with reasonable certainty. The writing may be referred to as one to be in existence at the time of the testator's death; it may be prepared before or after the execution of the will; it may be altered by the testator after its preparation; and it may be a writing which has no significance apart from its effect upon the dispositions made by the will.

---

§ 2-514. Contracts Concerning Succession. A contract to make a will or devise, or not to revoke a will or devise, or to die intestate, if executed after the effective date of this [article], may be established only by (i) provisions of a will stating material provisions of the contract, (ii) an express reference in a will to a contract and extrinsic evidence proving the terms of the contract, or (iii) a writing signed by the decedent evidencing the contract. The execution of a joint will or mutual wills does not create a presumption of a contract not to revoke the will or wills.

Comment

Section Relocated. In the 1969 Code, Section 2-514 appeared as Section 2-701. The 1990 amendments relocated this section to make room for Part 7, which was added in 1990. No substantive revision was made.

The purpose of this section is to tighten the methods by which contracts concerning succession may be proved. Oral contracts not to revoke wills have given rise to must litigation in a number of states; and in many states if two persons execute a single document as their joint will, this gives rise to a presumption that the parties had contracted not to revoke the will except by consent of both.

This section requires that either the will must set

forth the material provisions of the contract, or the will must make express reference to the contract and extrinsic evidence prove the terms of the contract, or there must be a separate writing signed by the decedent evidencing the contract. Oral testimony regarding the contract is permitted if the will makes reference to the contract, but this provision of the statute is not intended to affect normal rules regarding admissibility of evidence.

This section does not preclude recovery in quantum meruit for the value of services rendered the testator.

Historical Note. This Comment was revised in 2010.

§ 2-515. Deposit of Will with Court in Testator's Lifetime.

A will may be deposited by the testator or the testator's agent with any court for safekeeping, under rules of the court. The will must be sealed and kept confidential. During the testator's lifetime, a deposited will must be delivered only to the testator or to a person authorized in writing signed by the testator to receive the will. A conservator may be allowed to examine a deposited will of a protected testator under procedures designed to maintain the confidential character of the document to the extent possible, and to ensure that it will be resealed and kept on deposit after the examination. Upon being informed of the testator's death, the court shall notify any person designated to receive the will and deliver it to that person on request; or the court may deliver the will to the appropriate court.

Comment

Many states already have statutes permitting deposit of wills during a testator's lifetime. Most of these statutes have elaborate provisions governing purely administrative matters: how the will is to be enclosed in a sealed wrapper, what is to be endorsed on the wrapper, the form of receipt or certificate given to the testator, the fee to be charged, how the will is to be opened after testator's death and who is to be notified. Under this section, details have been left to court rule, except as other relevant statutes such as one governing fees may apply.

It is, of course, vital to maintain the confidential nature of deposited wills. However, this obviously does not prevent the opening of the will after the death of the testator if necessary in order to determine the executor or other interested persons to be notified. Nor should it prevent opening the will to microfilm for confidential record storage, for example. These matters could again be regulated by court rule.

The provision permitting examination of a will of a protected person by the conservator supplements Section 5-411.

§ 2-516. Duty of Custodian of Will; Liability.

After the death of a testator and on request of an interested person, a person having custody of a will of the testator shall deliver it with reasonable promptness to a person able to secure its probate and if none is known, to an appropriate court. A person who wilfully fails to deliver a will is liable to any person aggrieved for any damages that may be sustained by the failure. A person who wilfully refuses or fails to deliver a will after being ordered by the court in a proceeding brought for the purpose of compelling delivery is subject to penalty for contempt of court.

Comment

In addition to a Registrar or clerk, a person authorized to accept delivery of a will from a custodian may be a universal successor or other person authorized under the law of another nation to carry out the terms of a will.

§ 2-517. Penalty Clause for Contest.

A provision in a will purporting to penalize an interested person for contesting the will or instituting other proceedings relating to the estate is unenforceable if probable cause exists for instituting proceedings.

Comment

This section replicates Section 3-905.

PART 6
RULES OF CONSTRUCTION APPLICABLE ONLY TO WILLS

General Comment

Parts 6 and 7 address a variety of construction problems that commonly occur in wills, trusts, and other types of governing instruments. All of the "rules" set forth in these parts yield to a finding of a contrary intention and are therefore rebuttable presumptions.

The rules of construction set forth in Part 6 apply only to wills. The rules of construction set forth in Part 7 apply to wills and other governing instruments.

The sections in Part 6 deal with such problems as death before the testator (lapse), the inclusiveness of the will as to property of the testator, effect of failure of a gift in the will, change in form of securities specifically devised, ademption by reason of fire, sale and the like, exoneration, and exercise of a power of appointment by general language in the will.

§ 2-601. Scope. In the absence of a finding of a contrary intention, the rules of construction in this [part] control the construction of a will.

Comment

Purpose and Scope of 1990 Revisions. Common-law rules of construction yield to a finding of a contrary intention. The pre-1990 version of this section provided that the rules of construction in Part 6 yielded only to a "contrary intention indicated by the will." To align the statutory rules of construction in Part 6 with those established at common law, this section was revised in 1990 so that the rules of construction yield to a "finding of a contrary intention." As revised, evidence extrinsic to the will as well as the content of the will itself is admissible for the purpose of rebutting the rules of construction in Part 6.

As originally promulgated, this section began with the sentence: "The intention of a testator as expressed in his will controls the legal effect of his dispositions." This sentence was removed primarily because it was inappropriate and unnecessary in a part of the Code containing rules of construction. Deleting this sentence did not signify a retreat from the widely accepted proposition that a testator's intention controls the legal effect of his or her dispositions.

A further reason for deleting this sentence was that a possible, though unintended, reading of the sentence might have been that it prevented the judicial adoption of a general reformation doctrine for wills, as approved by the American Law Institute in the Restatement (Third) of Property: Wills and Other Donative Transfers § 12.1 (2003), and as advocated in Langbein & Waggoner, "Reformation of Wills on the Ground of Mistake: Change of Direction in American Law?", 130 U.Pa.L. Rev. 521 (1982). Striking this sentence removed that possible impediment to the judicial adoption of a general reformation doctrine for wills as approved by the American Law Institute, as advocated in the Langbein-Waggoner article, and (as of 2008) codified in Section 2-805.

Cross Reference. See Section 8-101(b) for the application of the rules of construction in this part to documents executed prior to the effective date of this article.

Historical Note. This Comment was revised in 2008.

Former (Pre-1990) Version

§ 2-603. [Rules of Construction and Intention.] The intention of a testator as expressed in his will controls the legal effect of his dispositions. The rules of construction expressed in the succeeding sections of this Part apply unless a contrary intention is indicated by the will.

---

§ 2-602. Will May Pass All Property and After-Acquired Property. A will may provide for the passage of all property the testator owns at death and all property acquired by the estate after the testator's death.

Comment

Purpose and Scope of Revision. This section is revised to assure that, for example, a residuary clause in a will not only passes property owned at death that is not otherwise devised, even though the property was acquired by the testator after the will was executed, but also passes property acquired by a testator's estate after his or her death. This reverses a case like Braman Estate, 435 Pa. 573, 258 A.2d 492 (1969), where the court held that Mary's residuary devise to her sister Ruth "or her estate", which had passed to Ruth's estate where Ruth predeceased Mary by about a year, could not go to Ruth's residuary legatee. The court held that Ruth's will had no power to control the devolution of property acquired by Ruth's estate after her death; such property passed, instead, by intestate succession from Ruth. This section, applied to the Braman Estate case, would mean that the property acquired by Ruth's estate after her death would pass under her residuary clause.

The added language also makes it clear that items such as bonuses awarded to an employee after his or her death pass under his or her will.

§ 2-603. Antilapse; Deceased Devisee; Class Gifts.

(a) [Definitions.] In this section:

(1) "Alternative devise" means a devise that is expressly created by the will and, under the terms of the will, can take effect instead of another devise on the happening of one or more events, including survival of the testator or failure to survive the testator, whether an event is expressed in condition-precedent, condition-subsequent, or any other form. A residuary clause constitutes an alternative devise with respect to a nonresiduary devise only if the will specifically provides that, upon lapse or failure, the nonresiduary devise, or nonresiduary devises in general, pass under the residuary clause.

(2) "Class member" includes an individual who fails to survive the testator but who would have taken under a devise in the form of a class gift had he [or she] survived the testator.

(3) "Descendant of a grandparent", as used in subsection (b), means an individual who qualifies as a descendant of a grandparent of the testator or of the donor of a power of appointment under the (i) rules of construction applicable to a class gift created in the testator's will if the devise or exercise of the power is in the form of a class gift or (ii) rules for intestate succession if the devise or exercise of the power is not in the form of a class gift.

(4) "Descendants", as used in the phrase "surviving descendants" of a deceased devisee or class member in subsections (b)(1) and (2), mean the descendants of a deceased devisee or class member who would take under a class gift created in the testator's will.

(5) "Devise" includes an alternative devise, a devise in the form of a class gift, and an exercise of a power of appointment.

(6) "Devisee" includes (i) a class member if the devise is in the form of a class gift, (ii) an individual or class member who was deceased at the time the testator executed his [or her] will as well as an individual or class member who was then living but who failed to survive the testator, and (iii) an appointee under a power of appointment exercised by the testator's will.

(7) "Stepchild" means a child of the surviving, deceased, or former spouse of the testator or of the donor of a power of appointment, and not of the testator or donor.

(8) "Surviving", in the phrase "surviving devisee" or "surviving descendant", means a devisee or a descendant who neither predeceased the testator nor is deemed to have predeceased the testator under Section 2-702. (120 hairs)

(9) "Testator" includes the donee of a power of appointment if the power is exercised in the testator's will.

(b) [Substitute Gift.] If a devisee fails to survive the testator and is a grandparent, a descendant of a grandparent, or a stepchild of either the testator ~~or the donor of a power of~~ appointment exercised by the testator's will, the following apply:

(1) Except as provided in paragraph (4), if the devise is not in the form of a class gift and the deceased devisee leaves surviving descendants, a substitute gift is created in the devisee's surviving descendants. They take by representation the property to which the devisee would have been entitled had the devisee survived the testator.

(2) Except as provided in paragraph (4), if the devise is in the form of a class gift, other than a devise to "issue", "descendants", "heirs of the body", "heirs", "next of kin", "relatives", or "family", or a class described by language of similar import, a substitute gift is created in the surviving descendants of any deceased devisee. The property to which the devisees would have been entitled had all of them survived the testator passes to the surviving devisees and the surviving descendants of the deceased devisees. Each surviving devisee takes the share to which he [or she] would have been entitled had the deceased devisees survived the testator. Each deceased devisee's surviving descendants who are substituted for the deceased devisee take by representation the share to which the deceased devisee would have been entitled had the deceased devisee survived the testator. For the purposes of this paragraph, "deceased devisee" means a class member who failed to survive the testator and left one or more surviving descendants.

(3) For the purposes of Section 2-601, words of survivorship, such as in a devise to an individual "if he survives me", or in a devise to "my surviving children", are not, in the absence of additional evidence, a sufficient indication of an intent contrary to the application of this section.

(4) If the will creates an alternative devise with respect to a devise for which a substitute gift is created by paragraph (1) or (2), the substitute gift is superseded by the alternative devise if:

(A) the alternative devise is in the form of a class gift and one or more members of the class is entitled to take under the will; or

(B) the alternative devise is not in the form of a class gift and the expressly designated devisee of the alternative devise is entitled to take under the will.

(5) Unless the language creating a power of appointment expressly excludes the substitution of the descendants of an appointee for the appointee, a surviving descendant of a deceased appointee of a power of appointment can be substituted for the appointee under this section, whether or not the descendant is an object of the power.

(c) [**More Than One Substitute Gift; Which One Takes.**] If, under subsection (b), substitute gifts are created and not superseded with respect to more than one devise and the devises are alternative devises, one to the other, the determination of which of the substitute gifts takes effect is resolved as follows:

(1) Except as provided in paragraph (2), the devised property passes under the primary substitute gift.

(2) If there is a younger-generation devise, the devised property passes under the younger-generation substitute gift and not under the primary substitute gift.

(3) In this subsection:

(A) "Primary devise" means the devise that would have taken effect had all the deceased devisees of the alternative devises who left surviving descendants survived the testator.

(B) "Primary substitute gift" means the substitute gift created with respect to the primary devise.

(C) "Younger-generation devise" means a devise that (i) is to a descendant of a devisee of the primary devise, (ii) is an alternative devise with respect to the primary devise, (iii) is a devise for which a substitute gift is created, and (iv) would have taken effect had all the deceased devisees who left surviving descendants survived the testator (except the deceased devisee or devisees of the primary devise).

(D) "Younger-generation substitute gift" means the substitute gift created with respect to the younger-generation devise.

Comment

Purpose and Scope. Section 2-603 is a comprehensive antilapse statute that resolves a variety of interpretive questions that have arisen under standard antilapse statutes, including the antilapse statute of the pre-1990 Code.

Theory of Lapse. As explained in Restatement (Third) of Property: Wills and Other Donative Transfers § 1.2 (1999), the common-law rule of lapse is predicated on the principle that a will transfers property at the testator's death, not when the will was executed, and on the principle that property cannot be transferred to a deceased individual. Under the rule of lapse, all devises are automatically and by law conditioned on survivorship of the testator. A devise to a devisee who predeceases the testator fails (lapses); the devised property does not pass to the devisee's estate, to be distributed according to the devisee's will or pass by intestate succession from the devisee. (Section 2-702 modifies the rule of lapse by presumptively conditioning devises on a 120-hour period of survival.)

"Antilapse" Statutes—Rationale of Section 2-603. Statutes such as Section 2-603 are commonly called "antilapse" statutes. An antilapse statute is remedial in nature, tending to preserve equality of treatment among different lines of succession. Although Section 2-603 is a rule of construction, and hence under Section 2-601 yields to a finding of a contrary intention, the remedial character of the statute means that it should be given the widest possible latitude to operate in considering whether the testator had formed a contrary intent. See Restatement (Third) of Property: Wills and Other Donative Transfers § 5.5 cmt. f (1999).

The 120-hour Survivorship Period. In effect, the requirement of survival of the testator's death means survival of the 120-hour period following the testator's death. This is because, under Section 2-702(a), "an individual who is not established to have survived an event ... by 120 hours is deemed to have predeceased the event". As made clear by subsection (a)(8), for the purposes of Section 2-603, the "event" to which Section 2-702(a) relates is the testator's death.

General Rule of Section 2-603—Subsection (b). Subsection (b) states the general rule of Section 2-603. Subsection (b)(1) applies to individual devises; subsection (b)(2) applies to devises in class gift form. For the distinction between an individual devise and a devise in class gift form, see Restatement (Third) of Property: Wills and Other Donative Transfers §§ 13.1, 13.2 (2008). Together, subsections (b)(1) and (2) show that the "antilapse" label is somewhat misleading. Strictly speaking, these subsections do not reverse the common-law rule of lapse. They do not abrogate the law-imposed condition of survivorship, so that devised property passes to the estates of predeceasing devisees. Subsections (b)(1) and (2) leave the law-imposed condition of survivorship intact, but modify the devolution of lapsed devises by providing a statutory substitute gift in the case of specified relatives. The statutory substitute gift is to the devisee's descendants who survive the testator by 120 hours; they take the property to which the devisee would have been entitled had the devisee survived the testator by 120 hours.

Class Gifts. In line with modern policy, subsection (b)(2) continues the pre-1990 Code's approach of expressly extending the antilapse protection to class gifts. Subsection (b)(2) applies to single-generation class gifts (see Restatement (Third) of Property: Wills and Other Donative Transfers §§ 14.1, 14.2 (2008)) in which one or more class members fail to survive the testator (by 120 hours) leaving descendants who survive the testator (by 120 hours) ; in order for the subsection to apply, it is not necessary that any of the class members survive the testator (by 120 hours). Multiple-generation class gifts, i.e., class gifts to "issue", "descendants", "heirs of the body", "heirs", "next of kin", "relatives", "family", or a class described by language of similar import. are excluded, however, because antilapse protection is unnecessary in class gifts of these types. They already contain within themselves the idea of representation, under which a deceased class member's descendants are substituted for him or her. See Sections 2-708, 2-709, 2-711; Restatement (Third) of Property: Wills and Other Donative Transfers §§ 14.3, 14.4 (2008).

"Void" Gifts. By virtue of subsection (a)(6), subsection (b) applies to the so-called "void" gift, where the devisee is dead at the time of execution of the will. Though contrary to some decisions, it seems likely that the testator would want the descendants of a person included, for example, in a class term but dead when the will is made to be treated like the descendants of another member of the class who was alive at the time the will was executed but who dies before the testator.

Protected Relatives. The specified relatives whose devises are protected by this section are the testator's grandparents and their descendants and the testator's stepchildren or, in the case of a testamentary exercise of a power of appointment, the testator's (donee's) or donor's grandparents and their descendants and the testator's or donor's stepchildren. Subsection (a)(3), added by technical amendment in 2008, defines "descendant of a grandparent" as an individual who qualifies as a descendant of a grandparent of the testator or of the donor of a power of appointment under the (i) rules of construction applicable to a class gift created in the testators will if the devise or exercise of the power is in the form of a class gift or (ii) rules for intestate succession if the devise or exercise of the power is not in the form of a class gift.

Section 2-603 extends the "antilapse" protection to devises to the testator's own stepchildren. The term "stepchild" is defined in subsection (a)(7). Antilapse protection is not extended to devises to descendants of the testator's stepchildren or to stepchildren of any of the testator's relatives. As to the testator's own stepchildren, note that under Section 2-804 a devise to a stepchild might be revoked if the testator and the stepchild's adoptive or genetic parent become divorced; the antilapse statute does not, of course, apply to a deceased stepchild's devise if it was revoked by Section 2-804. Subsections (b)(1) and (2) give this result by providing that the substituted descendants take the property to which the deceased devisee or deceased class member would have been entitled if he or she had survived the testator. If a deceased stepchild whose devise was revoked by Section 2-804 had survived the testator, that stepchild would not have been entitled to his or her devise, and so his or her descendants take nothing, either.

Other than stepchildren, devisees related to the testator by affinity are not protected by this section.

Section 2-603 Applicable to Testamentary Exercise of a Power of Appointment Where Appointee Fails to Survive the Testator. Subsections (a)(5), (6), (7), (9), and (b)(5) extend the protection of this section to appointees under a power of appointment exercised by the testator's will. The extension of the antilapse statute to powers of appointment is a step long overdue. The extension is supported by the Restatement (Third) of Property: Wills and Other Donative Transfers § 19.12 (2008).

Substitute Gifts. The substitute gifts provided for by subsections (b)(1) and (2) are to the deceased devisee's descendants. Subsection (a)(4), added by technical amendment in 2008, defines "descendants" as the descendants of a deceased devisee or class member who would take under a class gift created in the testator's will. As such, the rules of construction in Section 2-705 are applicable. The rules of

construction in Section 2-705 are subject to a finding of a contrary intent as described in Section 2-701. A contrary intent to the rules of construction in Section 2-705 could be found, for example, in the definitions section of the testator's will.

The 120-hour survival requirement stated in Section 2-702 does not require descendants who would be substituted for their parent by this section to survive their parent by any set period. Thus, if a devisee who is a protected relative survives the testator by less than 120 hours, the substitute gift is to the devisee's descendants who survive the testator by 120 hours; survival of the devisee by 120 hours is not required.

The statutory substitute gift is divided among the devisee's descendants "by representation", a phrase defined in Section 2-709(b).

Section 2-603 Restricted to Wills. Section 2-603 is applicable only when a devisee of a will predeceases the testator. It does not apply to beneficiary designations in life-insurance policies, retirement plans, or transfer-on-death accounts, nor does it apply to inter-vivos trusts, whether revocable or irrevocable. See, however, Sections 2-706 and 2-707 for rules of construction applicable when the beneficiary of a life-insurance policy, a retirement plan, or a transfer-on-death account predeceases the decedent or when the beneficiary of a future interest is not living when the interest is to take effect in possession or enjoyment.

Contrary Intention—the Rationale of Subsection (b)(3). An antilapse statute is a rule of construction, designed to carry out presumed intention. In effect, Section 2-603 declares that when a testator devises property "to A (a specified relative)", the testator (if he or she had thought further about it) is presumed to have wanted to add: "but if A is not alive (120 hours after my death), I devise the property in A's stead to A's descendants (who survive me by 120 hours)".

Under Section 2-601, the rule of Section 2-603 yields to a finding of a contrary intention. A foolproof means of expressing a contrary intention is to add to a devise the phrase "and not to [the devisee's] descendants". See Restatement (Third) of Property: Wills and Other Donative Transfers § 5.5 cmt. i (1999). In the case of a power of appointment, the phrase "and not to an appointee's descendants" can be added by the donor of the power in the document creating the power of appointment, if the donor does not want the antilapse statute to apply to an appointment under a power. See Restatement

(Third) of Property: Wills and Other Donative Transfers § 19.12 cmts. c & g (2008). In addition, adding to the residuary clause a phrase such as "including all lapsed or failed devises", adding to a nonresiduary devise a phrase such as "if the devisee does not survive me, the devise is to pass under the residuary clause", or adding a separate clause providing generally that "if the devisee of any nonresiduary devise does not survive me, the devise is to pass under the residuary clause" makes the residuary clause an "alternative devise". Under subsection (b)(4), as clarified by technical amendment in 2008, an alternative devise supersedes a substitute gift created by subsection (b)(1) or (2) if: (A) the alternative devise is in the form of a class gift and one or more members of the class is entitled to take under the will; or (B) the alternative devise is not in the form of a class gift and the expressly designated devisee of the alternative devise is entitled to take under the will. See infra Example 3.

A much-litigated question is whether mere words of survivorship—such as in a devise "to my daughter, A, if A survives me" or "to my surviving children"—automatically defeat the antilapse statute. Lawyers who believe that the attachment of words of survivorship to a devise is a foolproof method of defeating an antilapse statute are mistaken. The very fact that the question is litigated so frequently is itself proof that the use of mere words of survivorship is far from foolproof. In addition, the results of the litigated cases are divided on the question. To be sure, many cases hold that mere words of survivorship do automatically defeat the antilapse statute. E.g., Estate of Stroble, 636 P.2d 236 (Kan.Ct.App.1981); Annot., 63 A.L.R.2d 1172, 1186 (1959); Annot., 92 A.L.R. 846, 857 (1934). Other cases, however, and the Restatement (Third) of Property: Wills and Other Donative Transfers § 5.5 cmt. h (1999), reach the opposite conclusion. E.g., Ruotolo v. Tietjen, 890 A.2d 166 (Conn. App. Ct. 2006), aff'd per curiam, 916 A.2d 1 (Conn. 2007) (residuary devise of half of the residue to testator's stepdaughter "if she survives me"; stepdaughter predeceased testator leaving a daughter who survived testator; citing this section and the Restatement, court held that the survival language did not defeat the antilapse statute); Estate of Ulrikson, 290 N.W.2d 757 (Minn. 1980) (residuary devise to testator's brother Melvin and sister Rodine, and "in the event that either one of them shall predecease me, then to the other surviving brother or sister"; Melvin and Rodine predeceased testator, Melvin but not Rodine leaving descendants who

survived testator; court held residue passed to Melvin's descendants under antilapse statute); Detzel v. Nieberding, 219 N.E.2d 327 (Ohio P. Ct. 1966) (devise of $5,000 to sister "provided she be living at the time of my death"; sister predeceased testator; court held $5,000 devise passed under antilapse statute to sister's descendants); Henderson v. Parker, 728 S.W.2d 768 (Tex. 1987) (devise of all of testator's property "unto our surviving children of this marriage"; two of testator's children survived testator, but one child, William, predeceased testator leaving descendants who survived testator; court held that share William would have taken passed to William's descendants under antilapse statute; words of survivorship found ineffective to counteract antilapse statute because court interpreted those words as merely restricting the devisees to those living at the time the will was executed). It may also be noted that the antilapse statutes in some other common-law countries expressly provide that words of survivorship do not defeat the statute. See, e.g., Queensland Succession Act 1981, § 33(2) ("A general requirement or condition that [protected relatives] survive the testator or attain a specified age is not a contrary intention for the purposes of this section").

Subsection (b)(3) adopts the position that mere words of survivorship do not—by themselves, in the absence of additional evidence—lead to automatic defeat of the antilapse statute. As noted in French, "Antilapse Statutes Are Blunt Instruments: A Blueprint for Reform", 37 Hastings L. J. 335, 369 (1985) "courts have tended to accord too much significance to survival requirements when deciding whether to apply antilapse statutes".

A formalistic argument sometimes employed by courts adopting the view that words of survivorship automatically defeat the antilapse statute is that, when words of survivorship are used, there is nothing upon which the antilapse statute can operate; the devise itself, it is said, is eliminated by the devisee's having predeceased the testator. The language of subsections (b)(1) and (2), however, nullify this formalistic argument by providing that the predeceased devisee's descendants take the property to which the devisee would have been entitled had the devisee survived the testator.

Another objection to applying the antilapse statute is that mere words of survivorship somehow establish a contrary intention. The argument is that attaching words of survivorship indicates that the testator thought about the matter and intentionally did not provide a substitute gift to the devisee's descendants.

At best, this is an inference only, which may or may not accurately reflect the testator's actual intention. An equally plausible inference is that the words of survivorship are in the testator's will merely because the testator's lawyer used a will form with words of survivorship. The testator who went to lawyer X and ended up with a will containing devises with a survivorship requirement could by chance have gone to lawyer Y and ended up with a will containing devises with no survivorship requirement—with no different intent on the testator's part from one case to the other.

Even a lawyer's deliberate use of mere words of survivorship to defeat the antilapse statute does not guarantee that the lawyer's intention represents the client's intention. Any linkage between the lawyer's intention and the client's intention is speculative unless the lawyer discussed the matter with the client. Especially in the case of younger-generation devisees, such as the client's children or nieces and nephews, it cannot be assumed that all clients, on their own, have anticipated the possibility that the devisee will predecease the client and will have thought through who should take the devised property in case the never-anticipated event happens.

If, however, evidence establishes that the lawyer did discuss the question with the client, and that the client decided that, for example, if the client's child predeceases the client, the deceased child's children (the client's grandchildren) should not take the devise in place of the deceased child, then the combination of the words of survivorship and the extrinsic evidence of the client's intention would support a finding of a contrary intention under Section 2-601. See Example 1, below. For this reason, Sections 2-601 and 2-603 will not expose lawyers to malpractice liability for the amount that, in the absence of the finding of the contrary intention, would have passed under the antilapse statute to a deceased devisee's descendants. The success of a malpractice claim depends upon sufficient evidence of a client's intention and the lawyer's failure to carry out that intention. In a case in which there is evidence that the client did not want the antilapse statute to apply, that evidence would support a finding of a contrary intention under Section 2-601, thus preventing the client's intention from being defeated by Section 2-603 and protecting the lawyer from liability for the amount that, in the absence of the finding of a contrary intention, would have passed under the antilapse statute to a deceased devisee's descendants.

Any inference about actual intention to be drawn from mere words of survivorship is especially problematic in the case of will substitutes such as life insurance, where it is less likely that the insured had the assistance of a lawyer in drafting the beneficiary designation. Although Section 2-603 only applies to wills, a companion provision is Section 2-706, which applies to will substitutes, including life insurance. Section 2-706 also contains language similar to that in subsection (b)(3), directing that words of survivorship do not, in the absence of additional evidence, indicate an intent contrary to the application of this section. It would be anomalous to provide one rule for wills and a different rule for will substitutes.

The basic operation of Section 2-603 is illustrated in the following example:

Example 1. G's will devised "$10,000 to my surviving children". G had two children, A and B. A predeceased G, leaving a child, X, who survived G by 120 hours. B also survived G by 120 hours.

Solution: Under subsection (b)(2), X takes $5,000 and B takes $5,000. The substitute gift to A's descendant, X, is not defeated by the fact that the devise is a class gift nor, under subsection (b)(3), is it automatically defeated by the fact that the word "surviving" is used.

Note that subsection (b)(3) provides that words of survivorship are not by themselves to be taken as expressing a contrary intention for purposes of Section 2-601. Under Section 2-601, a finding of a contrary intention could appropriately be based on affirmative evidence that G deliberately used the words of survivorship to defeat the antilapse statute. In the case of such a finding, B would take the full $10,000 devise. Relevant evidence tending to support such a finding might be a pre-execution letter or memorandum to G from G's attorney stating that G's attorney used the word "surviving" for the purpose of assuring that if one of G's children were to predecease G, that child's descendants would not take the predeceased child's share under any statute or rule of law.

In the absence of persuasive evidence of a contrary intent, however, the antilapse statute, being remedial in nature, and tending to preserve equality among different lines of succession, should be given the widest possible chance to operate and should be defeated only by a finding of intention that directly contradicts the substitute gift created by the statute. Mere words of survivorship—by themselves—do not directly contradict the statutory substitute gift to the descendants of a deceased devisee. The common law of lapse already conditions all devises on survivorship (and Section 2-702 presumptively conditions all devises on survivorship by 120 hours). As noted above, the antilapse statute does not reverse the law-imposed requirement of survivorship in any strict sense; it merely alters the devolution of lapsed devises by substituting the deceased devisee's descendants in place of those who would otherwise take. Thus, mere words of survivorship merely duplicate the law-imposed survivorship requirement deriving from the rule of lapse, and do not contradict the statutory substitute gift created by subsection (b)(1) or (2).

Subsection (b)(4). Under subsection (b)(4), as clarified by technical amendment in 2008, a statutory substitute gift is superseded if the testator's will expressly provides for its own alternative devisee and if: (A) the alternative devise is in the form of a class gift and one or more members of the class is entitled to take under the will; or (B) the alternative devise is not in the form of a class gift and the expressly designated devisee of the alternative devise is entitled to take under the will. For example, the statute's substitute gift would be superseded in the case of a devise "to A if A survives me; if not, to B", where B survived the testator but A predeceased the testator leaving descendants who survived the testator. Under subsection (b)(4), B, not A's descendants, would take. In the same example, however, it should be noted that A's descendants would take under the statute if B as well as A predeceased the testator, for in that case B (the "expressly designated devisee of the alternative devise") would not be entitled to take under the will. This would be true, even if B left descendants who survived the testator; B's descendants are not "expressly designated devisees of the alternative devise".

It should also be noted that, for purposes of Section 2-601, an alternative devise might indicate a contrary intention even if subsection (b)(4) is inapplicable. To illustrate this point, consider a variation of Example 1. Suppose that in Example 1, G's will devised "$10,000 to my surviving children, but *if none of my children survives me*, to the descendants of deceased children". The alternative devise to the descendants of deceased children would not cause the substitute gift to X to be superseded under subsection (b)(4) because the condition precedent to the alternative devise—"if none of my children survives me"—was not satisfied; one of G's children, B, survived G. Hence the alternative devisees would not be entitled to take under the will. Nevertheless, the italicized language would indicate

that G did not intend to substitute descendants of deceased children unless all of G's children failed to survive G. Thus, although A predeceased G leaving a child, X, who survived G by 120 hours, X would not be substituted for A. B, G's surviving child, would take the whole $10,000 devise.

The above variation of Example 1 is to be distinguished from other variations, such as one in which G's will devised "$10,000 to my surviving children, *but if none of my children survives me*, to my brothers and sisters". The italicized language in this variation would not indicate that G did not intend to substitute descendants of deceased children unless all of G's children failed to survive G. In addition, even if one or more of G's brothers and sisters survived G, the alternative devise would not cause the substitute gift to X to be superseded under subsection (b)(4); the alternative devisees would not be entitled to take under the will because the alternative devise is expressly conditioned on none of G's children surviving G. Thus X would be substituted for A, allowing X and B to divide the $10,000 equally (as in the original version of Example 1).

Subsection (b)(4) is further illustrated by the following examples:

Example 2. G's will devised "$10,000 to my sister, S" and devised "the rest, residue, and remainder of my estate to X-Charity". S predeceased G, leaving a child, N, who survived G by 120 hours.

Solution: S's $10,000 devise goes to N, not to X-Charity. The residuary clause does not create an "alternative devise", as defined in subsection (a)(1), because neither it nor any other language in the will specifically provides that S's $10,000 devise or lapsed or failed devises in general pass under the residuary clause.

Example 3. Same facts as Example 2, except that G's residuary clause devised "the rest, residue, and remainder of my estate, including all failed and lapsed devises, to X-Charity".

Solution: S's $10,000 devise goes to X-Charity, not to N. Under subsection (b)(4), the substitute gift to N created by subsection (b)(1) is superseded. The residuary clause expressly creates an "alternative devise", as defined in subsection (a)(1), in favor of X-Charity and that alternative devisee, X-Charity, is entitled to take under the will.

Example 4. G's will devised "$10,000 to my two children, A and B, or to the survivor of them". A predeceased G, leaving a child, X, who survived G by 120 hours. B also survived G by 120 hours.

Solution: B takes the full $10,000. Because the takers of the $10,000 devise are both named and numbered ("my two children, A and B"), the devise is not in the form of a class gift. See Restatement (Third) of Property: Wills and Other Donative Transfers § 13.2 (2008). The substance of the devise is as if it read "half of $10,000 to A, but if A predeceases me, that half to B if B survives me and the other half of $10,000 to B, but if B predeceases me, that other half to A if A survives me". With respect to each half, A and B have alternative devises, one to the other. Subsection (b)(1) creates a substitute gift to A's descendant, X, with respect to A's alternative devise in each half. Under subsection (b)(4), however, that substitute gift to X with respect to each half is superseded by the alternative devise to B because the alternative devisee, B, survived G by 120 hours and is entitled to take under G's will.

Example 5. G's will devised "$10,000 to my two children, A and B, or to the survivor of them". A and B predeceased G. A left a child, X, who survived G by 120 hours; B died childless.

Solution: X takes the full $10,000. Because the devise itself is in the same form as the one in Example 4, the substance of the devise is as if it read "half of $10,000 to A, but if A predeceases me, that half to B if B survives me and the other half of $10,000 to B, but if B predeceases me, that other half to A if A survives me". With respect to each half, A and B have alternative devises, one to the other. As in Example 4, subsection (b)(1) creates a substitute gift to A's descendant, X, with respect to A's alternative devise in each half. Unlike the situation in Example 4, however, neither substitute gift to X is superseded under subsection (b)(4) by the alternative devise to B because, in this case, the alternative devisee, B, failed to survive G by 120 hours and is therefore not entitled to take either half under G's will.

Note that the order of deaths as between A and B is irrelevant. The phrase "or to the survivor" does not mean the survivor as between them if they both predecease G; it refers to the one who survives G if one but not the other survives G.

Example 6. G's will devised "$10,000 to my son, A, if he is living at my death; if not, to A's children". A predeceased G. A's child, X, also predeceased G. A's other child, Y and X's children, M and N, survived G by 120 hours.

Solution: Half of the devise ($5,000) goes to Y. The other half ($5,000) goes to M and N.

Because A failed to survive G by 120 hours and left descendants who survived G by 120 hours, subsection (b)(1) substitutes A's descendants who survived G by 120 hours for A. But that substitute gift is superseded under subsection (b)(4) by the alternative devise to A's children. Under subsection (b)(4), as clarified by technical amendment in 2008, an alternative devise supersedes a substitute gift if the alternative devise is in the form of a class gift and one or more members of the class is entitled to take under the will. Because the alternative devise is in the form of a class gift (see Restatement (Third) of Property: Wills and Other Donative Transfers § 13.1 (2008), and because one member of the class, Y, survived the testator and is entitled to take, the substitute gift under subsection (b)(1) is superseded.

Because the alternative devise to A's children is in the form of a class gift, however, and because one of the class members, X, failed to survive G by 120 hours and left descendants who survived G by 120 hours, subsection (b)(2) applies and substitutes M and N for X.

Subsection (c). Subsection (c) is necessary because there can be cases in which subsections (b)(1) or (2) create substitute gifts with respect to two or more alternative devises of the same property, and those substitute gifts are not superseded under the terms of subsection (b)(4). Subsection (c) provides the tie-breaking mechanism for such situations.

The initial step is to determine which of the alternative devises would take effect had all the devisees themselves survived the testator (by 120 hours). In subsection (c), this devise is called the "primary devise". Unless subsection (c)(2) applies, subsection (c)(1) provides that the devised property passes under substitute gift created with respect to the primary devise. This substitute gift is called the "primary substitute gift". Thus, the devised property goes to the descendants of the devisee or devisees of the primary devise.

Subsection (c)(2) provides an exception to this rule. Under subsection (c)(2), the devised property does not pass under the primary substitute gift if there is a "younger-generation devise"—defined as a devise that (i) is to a descendant of a devisee of the primary devise, (ii) is an alternative devise with respect to the primary devise, (iii) is a devise for which a substitute gift is created, and (iv) would have taken effect had all the deceased devisees who left surviving descendants survived the testator except the deceased devisee or devisees of the primary devise. If there is a younger-generation devise, the devised property passes under the "younger- generation substitute gift"—defined as the substitute gift created with respect to the younger-generation devise.

Subsection (c) is illustrated by the following examples:

Example 7. G's will devised "$5,000 to my son, A, if he is living at my death; if not, to my daughter, B" and devised "$7,500 to my daughter, B, if she is living at my death; if not, to my son, A". A and B predeceased G, both leaving descendants who survived G by 120 hours.

Solution: A's descendants take the $5,000 devise as substitute takers for A, and B's descendants take the $7,500 devise as substitute takers for B. In the absence of a finding based on affirmative evidence such as described in the solution to Example 1, the mere words of survivorship do not by themselves indicate a contrary intent.

Both devises require application of subsection (c). In the case of both devises, the statute produces a substitute gift for the devise to A and for the devise to B, each devise being an alternative devise, one to the other. The question of which of the substitute gifts takes effect is resolved by determining which of the devisees themselves would take the devised property if both A and B had survived G by 120 hours.

With respect to the devise of $5,000, the primary devise is to A because A would have taken the devised property had both A and B survived G by 120 hours. Consequently, the primary substitute gift is to A's descendants and that substitute gift prevails over the substitute gift to B's descendants.

With respect to the devise of $7,500, the primary devise is to B because B would have taken the devised property had both A and B survived G by 120 hours, and so the substitute gift to B's descendants is the primary substitute gift and it prevails over the substitute gift to A's descendants.

Subsection (c)(2) is inapplicable because there is no younger-generation devise. Neither A nor B is a descendant of the other.

Example 8. G's will devised "$10,000 to my son, A, if he is living at my death; if not, to A's children, X and Y". A and X predeceased G. A's child, Y, and X's children, M and N, survived G by 120 hours.

Solution: Half of the devise ($5,000) goes to Y. The other half ($5,000) goes to M and N. The disposition

of the latter half requires application of subsection (c).

Subsection (b)(1) produces substitute gifts as to that half for the devise of that half to A and for the devise of that half to X, each of these devises being alternative devises, one to the other. The primary devise is to A. But there is also a younger-generation devise, the alternative devise to X. X is a descendant of A, X would take if X but not A survived G by 120 hours, and the devise is one for which a substitute gift is created by subsection (b)(1). So, the younger-generation substitute gift, which is to X's descendants (M and N), prevails over the primary substitute gift, which is to A's descendants (Y, M, and N).

Note that the outcome of this example is the same as in Example 6.

Example 9. Same facts as Example 5, except that both A and B predeceased the testator and both left descendants who survived the testator by 120 hours.

Solution: A's descendants take half ($5,000) and B's descendants take half ($5,000).

As to the half devised to A, subsection (b)(1) produces a substitute gift to A's descendants and a substitute gift to B's descendants (because the language "or to the survivor of them" created an alternative devise in B of A's half). As to the half devised to B, subsection (b)(1) produces a substitute gift to B's descendants and a substitute gift to A's descendants (because the language "or to the survivor of them" created an alternative devise in A of B's half). Thus, with respect to each half, resort must be had to subsection (c) to determine which substitute gift prevails.

Under subsection (c)(1), each half passes under the primary substitute gift. The primary devise as to A's half is to A and the primary devise as to B's half is to B because, if both A and B had survived G by 120 hours, A would have taken half ($5,000) and B would have taken half ($5,000). Neither A nor B is a descendant of the other, so subsection (c)(2) does not apply. Only if one were a descendant of the other would the other's descendant take it all, under the rule of subsection (c)(2).

Technical Amendments. Technical amendments in 2008 added definitions of "descendant of a grandparent" and "descendants" as used in subsections (b)(1) and (2) and clarified subsection (b)(4). The two new definitions resolve questions of status previously unanswered. The technical amendment of subsection (b)(4) makes that subsection easier to understand but does not change its substance.

Reference. This section is discussed in Halbach & Waggoner, "The UPC's New Survivorship and Antilapse Provisions", 55 Alb.L. Rev. 1091 (1992).

Historical Note. This Comment was revised in 1993 and 2008.

Former (Pre-1990) Version

§ 2-605. [Anti-lapse; Deceased Devisee; Class Gifts.] If a devisee who is a grandparent or a lineal descendant of a grandparent of the testator is dead at the time of execution of the will, fails to survive the testator, or is treated as if he predeceased the testator, the issue of the deceased devisee who survive the testator by 120 hours take in place of the deceased devisee and if they are all of the same degree of kinship to the devisee they take equally, but if of unequal degree than those of more remote degree take by representation. One who would have been a devisee under a class gift if he had survived the testator is treated as a devisee for purposes of this section whether his death occurred before or after the execution of the will.

---

§ 2-604. Failure of Testamentary Provision.

(a) Except as provided in Section 2-603, a devise, other than a residuary devise, that fails for any reason becomes a part of the residue.

(b) Except as provided in Section 2-603, if the residue is devised to two or more persons, the share of a residuary devisee that fails for any reason passes to the other residuary devisee, or to other residuary devisees in proportion to the interest of each in the remaining part of the residue.

Comment

This section applies only if Section 2-603 does not produce a substitute taker for a devisee who fails to survive the testator by 120 hours. There is also a special rule for disclaimers contained in Section 2-1106(b)(3)(A); a disclaimed devise may be governed by either Section 2-603 or the present section, depending on the circumstances.

A devise of "all of my estate", or a devise using words of similar import, constitutes a residuary devise for purposes of this section.

Historical Note. This Comment was revised in 1993. For the prior version, see 8 U.L.A. 132 (Supp.1992).

2002 Amendment Relating to Disclaimers. In 2002, the Code's former disclaimer provision (Section 2-801) was replaced by the Uniform Disclaimer of Property Interests Act, which is incorporated into the Code as Part 11 of Article 2 (Sections 2-1101 to 2-1117). The statutory references in this Comment to former Section 2-801 have been replaced by appropriate references to Part 11. Updating these statutory references has not changed the substance of this Comment.

§ 2-605. Increase in Securities; Accessions.

(a) If a testator executes a will that devises securities and the testator then owned securities that meet the description in the will, the devise includes additional securities owned by the testator at death to the extent the additional securities were acquired by the testator after the will was executed as a result of the testator's ownership of the described securities and are securities of any of the following types:

(1) securities of the same organization acquired by reason of action initiated by the organization or any successor, related, or acquiring organization, excluding any acquired by exercise of purchase options;

(2) securities of another organization acquired as a result of a merger, consolidation, reorganization, or other distribution by the organization or any successor, related, or acquiring organization; or

(3) securities of the same organization acquired as a result of a plan of reinvestment.

(b) Distributions in cash before death with respect to a described security are not part of the devise.

Comment

Purpose and Scope of Revisions. The rule of subsection (a), as revised, relates to a devise of securities (such as a devise of 100 shares of XYZ Company), regardless of whether that devise is characterized as a general or specific devise. If the testator executes a will that makes a devise of securities and if the testator then owned securities that meet the description in the will, then the devisee is entitled not only to the described securities to the extent they are owned by the testator at death; the devisee is also entitled to any additional securities owned by the testator at death that were acquired by the testator during his or her lifetime after the will was executed and were acquired as a result of the testator's ownership of the described securities by reason of an action specified in subsections (a)(1), (2), or (3), such as the declaration of stock splits or stock dividends or spinoffs of a subsidiary.

The impetus for these revisions derives from the rule on stock splits enunciated by Bostwick v. Hurstel, 364 Mass. 282, 304 N.E.2d 186 (1973), and now codified in Massachusetts as to actions covered by subsections (a)(1) and (2). Mass. Gen. Laws c. 191, § 1A(4).

Subsection (a) Not Exclusive. Subsection (a) is not exclusive, i.e., it is not to be understood as setting forth the only conditions under which additional securities of the types described in subsections (a)(1) through (3) are included in the devise. For example, the express terms of subsection (a) do not apply to a case in which the testator owned the described securities when he or she executed the will, but later sold (or otherwise disposed of) those securities, and then later purchased (or otherwise acquired) securities that meet the description in the will, following which additional securities of the type or types described in subsections (a)(1), (2), or (3) are acquired as a result of the testator's ownership of the later-acquired securities. Nor do the express terms of subsection (a) apply to a similar (but less likely) case in which the testator did not own the described securities when he or she executed the will, but later purchased (or otherwise acquired) such securities. Subsection (a) does not preclude a court, in an appropriate case, from deciding that additional securities of the type described in subsections (a)(1), (2), or (3) acquired as a result of the testator's ownership of the later-acquired securities pass under the devise in either of these two cases, or in other cases if appropriate.

Subsection (b) codifies existing law that distributions in cash, such as interest, accrued rent, or cash dividends declared and payable as of a record date before the testator's death, do not pass as a part of the devise. It makes no difference whether such cash distributions were paid before or after death. See Section 4 of the Revised Uniform Principal and Income Act.

Cross Reference. The term "organization" is defined in Section 1-201.

Former (Pre-1990) Version

§ 2-607. [Change in Securities; Accessions; Nonademption.]

(a) If the testator intended a specific devise of certain securities rather than the equivalent value thereof, the specific devisee is entitled only to:

(1) as much of the devised securities as is a part of the estate at time of the testator's death;

(2) any additional or other securities of the same entity owned by the testator by reason of action initiated by the entity excluding any acquired by exercise of purchase options;

(3) securities of another entity owned by the testator as a result of a merger, consolidation, reorganization or other similar action initiated by the entity; and

(4) any additional securities of the entity owned by the testator as a result of a plan of reinvestment.

(b) Distributions prior to death with respect to a specifically devised security not provided for in subsection (a) are not part of the specific devise.

Restatement (Third) of Property: Wills and Other Donative Transfers (1999)

§ 5.3 Effect of Stock Splits, Stock Dividends, and Other Distributions on Devises of a Specified Number of Securities. A devise of a specified number of securities carries with it any additional securities acquired by the testator after executing the will to the extent that the post-execution acquisitions resulted from the testator's ownership of the described securities.

§ 2-606. Nonademption of Specific Devises; Unpaid Proceeds of Sale, Condemnation, or Insurance; Sale by Conservator or Agent.

(a) A specific devisee has a right to specifically devised property in the testator's estate at the testator's death and to:

(1) any balance of the purchase price, together with any security agreement, owed by a purchaser at the testator's death by reason of sale of the property;

(2) any amount of a condemnation award for the taking of the property unpaid at death;

(3) any proceeds unpaid at death on fire or casualty insurance on or other recovery for injury to the property;

(4) any property owned by the testator at death and acquired as a result of foreclosure, or obtained in lieu of foreclosure, of the security interest for a specifically devised obligation;

(5) any real property or tangible personal property owned by the testator at death which the testator acquired as a replacement for specifically devised real property or tangible personal property; and

(6) if not covered by paragraphs (1) through (5), a pecuniary devise equal to the value as of its date of disposition of other specifically devised property disposed of during the testator's lifetime but only to the extent it is established that ademption would be inconsistent with the testator's manifested plan of distribution or that at the time the will was made, the date of disposition or otherwise, the testator did not intend ademption of the devise.

(b) If specifically devised property is sold or mortgaged by a conservator or by an agent acting within the authority of a durable power of attorney for an incapacitated principal, or a condemnation award, insurance proceeds, or recovery for injury to the property is paid to a conservator or to an agent acting within the authority of a durable power of attorney for an incapacitated principal, the specific devisee has the right to a general pecuniary devise equal to the net sale price, the amount of the unpaid loan, the condemnation award, the insurance proceeds, or the recovery.

(c) The right of a specific devisee under subsection (b) is reduced by any right the devisee has under subsection (a).

(d) For the purposes of the references in subsection (b) to a conservator, subsection (b) does not apply if, after the sale, mortgage, condemnation, casualty, or recovery, it was adjudicated that the testator's incapacity ceased and the testator survived the adjudication for at least one year.

(e) For the purposes of the references in subsection (b) to an agent acting within the authority of a durable power of attorney for an incapacitated principal, (i) "incapacitated principal" means a principal who is an incapacitated person, (ii) no adjudication of incapacity before death is necessary, and (iii) the acts of an agent within the authority of a durable power of attorney are presumed to be for an incapacitated principal.

Comment

Purpose and Scope of Revisions. Under the "identity" theory followed by most courts, the common-law doctrine of ademption by extinction is that a specific devise is adeemed—rendered ineffective—if the specifically devised property is not owned by the testator at death. In applying the "identity" theory, courts do not inquire into the testator's intent to determine whether the testator's objective in disposing of the specifically devised property was to revoke the devise. The only thing that matters is that the property is no longer owned at death. The application of the "identity" theory of ademption has resulted in harsh results in a number of cases, where it was reasonably clear that the testator did not intend to revoke the devise. Notable examples include McGee v. McGee, 413 A.2d 72 (R.I.1980); Estate of Dungan, 73 A.2d 776 (Del.Ch.1950).

Recently, some courts have begun to break away from the "identity" theory and adopt instead the so-called "intent" theory. E.g., Estate of Austin, 113 Cal.App.3d 167, 169 Cal.Rptr. 648 (1980). The major import of the revisions of this section is to adopt the "intent" theory in subsections (a)(5) and (6).

Subsection (a)(5) does not import a tracing principle into the question of ademption, but rather should be seen as a sensible "mere change in form" principle.

Example 1. G's will devised to X "my 1984 Ford." After she executed her will, she sold her 1984 Ford and bought a 1988 Buick; later, she sold the 1988 Buick and bought a 1993 Chrysler. She still owned the 1993 Chrysler when she died. Under subsection (a)(5), X takes the 1993 Chrysler.

Variation. If G had sold her 1984 Ford (or any of the replacement cars) and used the proceeds to buy shares in a mutual fund, which she owned at death, subsection (a)(5) does not give X the shares in the mutual fund. If G owned an automobile at death as a replacement for her 1984 Ford, however, X would be entitled to that automobile, even though it was bought with funds other than the proceeds of the sale of the 1984 Ford.

Subsection (a)(6) applies only to the extent the specifically devised property is not in the testator's estate at death and its value or its replacement is not covered by the provisions of subsections (a)(1) through (5). In that event, subsection (a)(6) allows the devisee claiming that an ademption has not occurred to establish that the facts and circumstances indicate that ademption of the devise was not intended by the testator or that ademption of the devise is inconsistent with the testator's manifested plan of distribution.

Example 2. G's will devised to his son, A, "that diamond ring I inherited from grandfather" and devised to his daughter, B, "that diamond brooch I inherited from grandmother." After G executed his will, a burglar entered his home and stole the diamond ring (but not the diamond brooch, as it was in G's safety deposit box at his bank).

Under subsection (a)(6), A could likely establish that G intended A's devise to not adeem or that ademption would be inconsistent with G's manifested plan of distribution. In fact, G's equalizing devise to B affirmatively indicates that ademption is inconsistent with G's manifested plan of distribution. The likely result is that, under subsection (a)(6), A would be entitled to the value of the diamond ring.

Example 3. G's will devised her painting titled The Bar by Edouard Manet to X. After executing her will, G donated the painting to a museum. G's deliberate act of giving away the specifically devised property is a fact and circumstance indicating that ademption of the devise was intended. In the absence of persuasive evidence to the contrary, therefore, X would not be entitled to the value of the painting.

Reference. Section 2-606 is discussed in Alexander, "Ademption and the Domain of Formality in Wills Law", 55 Alb.L. Rev. 1067 (1992).

Historical Note. The above Comment was revised in 1993 and 1997. For the prior version, see 8 U.L.A. 134 (Supp.1992).

1997 Technical Amendment. By technical amendment effective July 31, 1997, subsection (a)(6) was substantially revised. Subsection (a)(6) previously provided:

"(a) A specific devisee has a right to the specifically devised property in the testator's estate at death and: * * *

"(6) unless the facts and circumstances indicate that ademption of the devise was intended by the testator or ademption of the devise is consistent with the testator's manifested plan of distribution, the value of the specifically devised property to the extent the specifically devised property is not in the testator's estate at death and its value or its replacement is not covered by paragraphs (1) through (5)."

Of the seven enactments of Section 2-606 as of early 1997, five omitted subsection (a)(6). Attorneys, accustomed to the concept that a specific devise automatically fails if the devised property is not in the testator's estate at death, were confused by the reverse assumption stated in original (a)(6). The confusion was heightened by the fact that (a)(6), stating a general rule, followed five carefully tailored safe harbors. The replacement provision, like the other exceptions, places the burden on the devisee to establish that an ademption has not occurred.

Former (Pre-1990) Version

§ 2-608. [Nonademption of Specific Devises in Certain Cases; Unpaid Proceeds of Sale, Condemnation or Insurance; Sale by Conservator.]

(a) A specific devisee has the right to the remaining specifically devised property and:

(1) any balance of the purchase price (together with any security interest) owing from a purchaser to the testator at death by reason of sale of the property;

(2) any amount of a condemnation award for the taking of the property unpaid at death;

(3) any proceeds unpaid at death on fire or casualty insurance on the property; and

(4) property owned by testator at his death as a result of foreclosure, or obtained in lieu of foreclosure, of the security for a specifically devised obligation.

(b) If specifically devised property is sold by a conservator or an agent acting within the authority of a durable power of attorney for a principal who is under a disability, or if a condemnation award or insurance proceeds are paid to a conservator or an agent acting within the authority of a durable power of attorney for a principal who is under a disability as a result of condemnation, fire, or casualty, the specific devisee has the right to a general pecuniary devise equal to the net sale price, the condemnation award, or the insurance proceeds. This subsection does not apply if after the sale, condemnation or casualty, it is adjudicated that the disability of the testator has ceased and the testator survives the adjudication by one year. The right of the specific devisee under this subsection is reduced by any right he has under subsection (a).

Restatement (Third) of Property: Wills and Other Donative Transfers (1999)

§ 5.2 Failure ("Ademption") of Specific Devises by Extinction

(a) If specifically devised property, in its original or in a changed form, is in the testator's estate at death, the devisee is entitled to the specifically devised property.

(b) If specifically devised property is not in the testator's estate at death, the devisee is entitled to any proceeds remaining unpaid at death of (i) any sale, (ii) any condemnation award, or (iii) any insurance on or other recovery for damage to or loss of the property.

(c) Subject to subsection (b), if specifically devised property is not in the testator's estate at death, the specific devise fails unless failure of the devise would be inconsistent with the testator's intent.

§ 2-607. Nonexoneration. A specific devise passes subject to any mortgage interest existing at the date of death, without right of exoneration, regardless of a general directive in the will to pay debts.

Comment

See Section 3-814 empowering the personal representative to pay an encumbrance under some circumstances; the last sentence of that section makes it clear that such payment does not increase the right of the specific devisee. The present section governs the substantive rights of the devisee. The common-law rule of exoneration of the specific devise is abolished by this section, and the contrary rule is adopted.

For the rule as to exempt property, see Section 2-403.

The rule of this section is not inconsistent with Section 2-606(b). If a conservator or agent for an incapacitated principal mortgages specifically devised property, Section 2-606(b) provides that the specific devisee is entitled to a pecuniary devise equal to the amount of the unpaid loan. Section 2-606(b) does not contradict this section, which provides that the specific devise passes subject to any mortgage interest existing at the date of death, without right of exoneration.

§ 2-608. Exercise of Power of Appointment. In the absence of a requirement that a power of appointment be exercised by a reference, or by an express or specific reference, to the power, a general residuary clause in a will, or a will making general disposition of all of the testator's property, expresses an intention to exercise a power of appointment held by the testator only if (i) the power is a general power exercisable in favor of the powerholder's estate and the creating instrument does not contain an effective gift if the power is not exercised or (ii) the testator's will manifests an intention to include the property subject to the power.

Comment

General Residuary Clause. This section, in conjunction with section 2-601, provides that a general residuary clause (such as "All the residue of my estate, I devise to ...") in the testator's will or a will making general disposition of all of the testator's property (such as "All of my estate, I devise to ...") is presumed to express an intent to exercise a power of appointment only if one or the other of two circumstances or sets of circumstances are satisfied. One such circumstance (whether the power is general or nongeneral) is if the testator's will manifests an intention to include the property subject to the power. A simple example of a residuary clause that manifests such an intention is a so-called "blending" clause, such as "All the residue of my estate, including any property over which I have a power of appointment, I devise to ..."

The other circumstance under which a general residuary clause or a will making general disposition of all of the testator's property is presumed to express an intent to exercise a power is if the power is a general power exercisable in favor of the powerholder's estate and the instrument that created the power does not contain an effective gift over in the event the power is not exercised (a "gift in default"). In well planned estates, a general power of appointment will be accompanied by a gift in default. The gift-in-default clause is ordinarily expected to take effect; it is not merely an after-thought just in case the power is not exercised. The power is not expected to be exercised, and in fact is often conferred mainly to gain a tax benefit—the federal estate-tax marital deduction under Section 2056(b)(5) of the Internal Revenue Code or, now, inclusion of the property in the gross estate of a younger-generation beneficiary under Section 2041 of the Internal Revenue Code, in order to avoid the possibly higher rates imposed by the federal generation-skipping tax. See Blattmachr & Pennell, "Adventures in Generation Skipping, Or How We Learned to Love the 'Delaware Tax Trap,'" 24 Real Prop. Prob. & Tr. J. 75 (1989). A general power should not be exercised in such a case without clear evidence of an intent to appoint.

In poorly planned estates, on the other hand, there may be no gift-in-default clause. In the absence of a gift-in-default clause, it seems better to let the property pass under the powerholder's will than force it to return to the donor's estate, for the reason that the donor died before the powerholder died and it seems better to avoid forcing a reopening of the donor's estate.

Cross Reference. See also Section 2-704 for a provision governing the meaning of a requirement that a power of appointment be exercised by a reference (or by an express or specific reference) to the power.

Historical Note. This section was amended in 2014 to conform it to Section 302 of the Uniform Powers of Appointment Act.

Former (Pre-2014) Version

§ 2-608. Exercise of Power of Appointment. In the absence of a requirement that a power of appointment be exercised by a reference, or by an express or specific reference, to the power, a general residuary clause in a will, or a will making general disposition of all of the testator's property, expresses an intention to exercise a power of appointment held by the testator only if (i) the power is a general power and the creating instrument does not contain a gift if the power is not exercised or (ii) the testator's will manifests an intention to include the property subject to the power.

Former (Pre-1990) Version

§ 2-610. [Exercise of Power of Appointment.] A general residuary clause in a will, or a will making general disposition of all of the testator's property, does not exercise a power of appointment held by the testator unless specific reference is made to the power or there is some other indication of intention to include the property subject to the power.

---

§ 2-609. Ademption by Satisfaction.

(a) Property a testator gave in his [or her] lifetime to a person is treated as a satisfaction of a devise in whole or in part, only if (i) the will provides for deduction of the gift, (ii) the testator declared in a contemporaneous writing that the gift is in satisfaction of the devise or that its value is to be deducted from the value of the devise, or (iii) the devisee acknowledged in writing that the gift is in satisfaction of the devise or that its value is to be deducted from the value of the devise.

(b) For purposes of partial satisfaction, property given during lifetime is valued as of the time the devisee came into possession or enjoyment of the property or at the testator's death, whichever occurs first.

(c) If the devisee fails to survive the testator, the gift is treated as a full or partial satisfaction of the devise, as appropriate, in applying Sections 2-603 and 2-604, unless the testator's contemporaneous writing provides otherwise.

Comment

Scope and Purpose of Revisions. In addition to minor stylistic changes, this section is revised to delete the requirement that the gift in satisfaction of a devise be made to the devisee. The purpose is to allow the testator to satisfy a devise to A by making a gift to B. Consider why this might be desirable. G's will made a $20,000 devise to his child, A. G was a widower. Shortly before his death, G in consultation with his lawyer decided to take advantage of the $10,000 annual gift tax exclusion and sent a check for $10,000 to A and another check for $10,000 to A's spouse, B. The checks were accompanied by a letter from G explaining that the gifts were made for tax purposes and were in lieu of the $20,000 devise to A. The removal of the phrase "to that person" from the statute allows the $20,000 devise to be fully satisfied by the gifts to A and B.

This section parallels Section 2-109 on advancements and follows the same policy of requiring written evidence that lifetime gifts are to be taken into account in the distribution of an estate, whether testate or intestate. Although courts traditionally call this "ademption by satisfaction" when a will is involved, and "advancement" when the estate is intestate, the difference in terminology is not significant.

Some wills expressly provide for lifetime advances by a hotchpot clause. Where the will contains no such clause, this section requires either the testator to declare in writing that the gift is in satisfaction of the devise or its value is to be deducted from the value of the devise or the devisee to acknowledge the same in writing.

To be a gift in satisfaction, the gift need not be an outright gift; it can be in the form of a will substitute, such as designating the devisee as the beneficiary of the testator's life-insurance policy or the beneficiary of the remainder interest in a revocable inter-vivos trust.

Subsection (b) on value accords with Section 2-109 and applies if, for example, property such as stock is given. If the devise is specific, a gift of the specific property to the devisee during lifetime adeems the devise by extinction rather than by satisfaction, and this section would be inapplicable. Unlike the common law of satisfaction, however, specific devises are not excluded from the rule of this section. If, for example, the testator makes a devise of a specific item of property, and subsequently makes a gift of cash or other property to the devisee, accompanied by the requisite written intent that the gift satisfies the devise, the devise is satisfied under this section even if the subject of the specific devise is still in the testator's estate at death (and hence would not be adeemed under the doctrine of ademption by extinction).

Under subsection (c), if a devisee to whom a gift in satisfaction is made predeceases the testator and his or her descendants take under Section 2-603 or 2-604, they take the same devise as their ancestor would have taken had the ancestor survived the testator; if the devise is reduced by reason of this section as to the ancestor, it is automatically reduced as to the devisee's descendants. In this respect, the rule in testacy differs from that in intestacy; see Section 2-109(c).

Former (Pre-1990) Version

§ 2-612. [Ademption by Satisfaction.] Property which a testator gave in his lifetime to a person is treated as a satisfaction of a devise to that person in whole or in part, only if the will provides for deduction of the lifetime gift, or the testator declares in a contemporaneous writing that the gift is to be deducted from the devise or is in satisfaction of the devise, or the devisee acknowledges in writing that the gift is in satisfaction. For purpose of partial satisfaction, property given during lifetime is valued as of the time the devisee came into possession or enjoyment of the property or as of the time of death of the testator, whichever occurs first.

PART 7
RULES OF CONSTRUCTION APPLICABLE TO WILLS AND OTHER GOVERNING INSTRUMENTS

General Comment

Part 7 contains rules of construction applicable to wills and other governing instruments, such as deeds, trusts, appointments, beneficiary designations, and so on. Like the rules of construction in Part 6 (which apply only to wills), the rules of construction in this part yield to a finding of a contrary intention.

Some of the sections in Part 7 are revisions of sections contained in Part 6 of the pre-1990 Code. Although these sections originally applied only to wills, their restricted scope was inappropriate.

Some of the sections in Part 7 are new, having been added to the Code as desirable means of carrying out common intention.

Application to Pre-Existing Governing Instruments. Under Section 8-101(b), for decedents dying after the effective date of enactment, the provisions of this Code apply to governing instruments executed prior to as well as on or after the effective date of enactment. The Joint Editorial Board for the Uniform Probate Code has issued a statement concerning the constitutionality under the Contracts Clause of this feature of the Code. The statement, titled "Joint Editorial Board Statement Regarding the Constitutionality of Changes in Default Rules as Applied to Pre-Existing Documents", can be found at 17 ACTEC Notes 184 (1991) or can be obtained from the Uniform Law Commission, www.uniformlaws.org.

Historical Note. This General Comment was revised in 1993.

Joint Editorial Board Statement Regarding the Constitutionality of Changes in Default Rules as Applied to Pre-Existing Documents
Published in 17 ACTEC Notes 184 (1991)

The Joint Editorial Board for [Uniform Trust and Estate Acts] (JEB) resolves to express its disapproval of the decision of a three-judge panel of the Eighth Circuit Court of Appeals in the case of *Whirlpool Corp. v. Ritter*, 929 F.2d 1318 (8th Cir. 1991). The JEB believes that the *Ritter* opinion is manifestly wrong. Were the error to go unnoticed and be followed elsewhere, it could seriously hamper an important and benign trend toward unifying the law of probate and nonprobate transfers.

The *Ritter* case held unconstitutional as a violation of the Contracts Clause of the federal Constitution an Oklahoma statute that resembles Uniform Probate Code § 2-804 (1990 revision). Both statutes deal with the disposition of life insurance proceeds when there has been a divorce. They provide that when the owner of a contract of life insurance dies after being divorced from the person who is named as the beneficiary in the policy, the designation in favor of the divorced spouse should be treated as having been revoked unless the policy owner expresses a contrary intention. The main purpose of these statutes is to take the same rule that has long been applied to transfers by will and apply it to other revocable transfers effective at death, such as life insurance.

The court in the *Ritter* case held that the Oklahoma statute could only be applied to beneficiary designations that are executed after the effective date of the statute. The court reasoned that when a beneficiary designation in favor of a particular spouse is already in effect at the time that the legislature changes the rule governing the effect of divorce upon a beneficiary designation, the change impermissibly disrupts the insured's expectations and hence impairs the insured's rights under the insurance contract. The court characterized the situation in *Ritter* as an instance of retroactive legislative disturbance of contractual relations, even though the divorce (and, of course, the decedent's death) occurred after the enactment of the statute.

The JEB believes that the court's reasoning is mistaken at several levels.

No impairment of the obligation to pay. It is crucial to understand that a statute such as UPC § 2-804 works no impairment of the insurance company's liability to pay the proceeds due under the policy. A life insurance policy is a third-party beneficiary contract. As such, it is a mixture of contract and donative transfer. The Contracts Clause of the federal Constitution appropriately applies to protect against legislative interference with the contractual component of the policy. In *Ritter* and in comparable cases, there is never a suggestion that the insurance company can escape paying the policy proceeds that are due under the contract. The insurance company interpleads or pays the proceeds into court for distribution to the successful claimant. The divorce statute affects only the donative transfer, the component of the policy that raises no Contracts Clause issue. The precise question in these cases is which of the decedent's potential donee-transferees should receive the proceeds. The JEB is aware of no U.S. Supreme Court authority applying the Contracts Clause to defeat state-law default rules that affect only the choice of a donee under a third-party beneficiary contract.

Intent-serving default rule. The Contracts Clause protects contractual reliance. Because statutes such as UPC § 2-804 serve to implement rather than to defeat the insured's expectation under the insurance contract, the premise for applying the Contracts Clause is wholly without foundation. The rationale for the divorce statutes is that when spouses are sufficiently unhappy with each other that they obtain a divorce, neither is likely to want to transfer his or her property to the survivor on death. These statutes reflect the legislative judgement that when the transferor leaves unaltered a will or trust or insurance beneficiary designation in favor of an ex-spouse, this failure to designate substitute takers more likely that not represents inattention rather than intention.

These statutes do not forbid transfers to the ex-spouse. They propound a default rule, not a rule of mandatory law. Because the normal inference in such circumstances is that the transferor would not want to benefit the ex-spouse, the statutes provide that the transferor whose intention contradicts the norm and who does indeed want to benefit the ex-spouse must express that intention. In the *Ritter* case itself, there was no evidence that the decedent, who had remarried, intended his ex-spouse to receive his insurance benefits.

Application of intent-serving default rules to preexisting documents. The JEB believes that there are sound policy reasons for applying an intent-serving legislative default rule to a revocable document that exists at the time of the enactment, and accordingly, that the Contracts Clause poses no constitutional obstacle to doing so. The distinctive attribute of intent serving default rules is that they represent an attempt to protect rather than defeat the decedent's reliance. In the case of divorce statutes like UPC § 2-804 and its Oklahoma counterpart in *Ritter*, the legislature's enactment responds to two trends, the liberalization of divorce and the spread of nonprobate modes of transfer. The legislature is attempting to identify and implement the default rule that best captures the wishes of the typical citizen, while preserving the right of any affected person to opt out of the legislatively determined rule.

The Contracts Clause has never been read to pose any obstacle to the application of legislatively altered constructional rules to pre-existing donative documents such as revocable trusts that have no contractual component. The JEB believes that there is no justification for extending Contracts Clause concerns to a statute that only affect the donative-transfer component of a life insurance policy, since the statute works no interference with the contractual component of the policy, the company's obligation to pay.

No Supreme Court authority for applying the Contracts Clause to default rules. There is no U.S. Supreme Court authority for the Eighth Circuit's extension of Contracts Clause regulation to legislative default rules. The principal Supreme Court precedent upon which the Eighth Circuit relied in *Ritter* was *Allied Structural Steel Co. v. Spannaus*, 438 U.S. 234 (1978). *Spannaus* held unconstitutional a Minnesota statute that retroactively increased the pension obligations that a company would owe to its workers when the company ceased operations in Minnesota or terminated the plan. By contrast, in *Ritter*, there is no increase, decrease or other interference with the obligation of the insurer to pay the contractual proceeds. The JEB is aware of no authority for the application of the Contracts Clause to state legislation applying altered rules of construction or other default rules to pre-existing documents in any field of law, and especially not in the field of estates, trusts, and donative transfers. See generally J. Nowak & R. Rotunda, *Constitutional Law* § 11.8, at 394 *et seq.* (4th ed. 1991).

It should also be observed that *Ritter* is wholly at variance with the general tolerance that the Supreme Court has shown toward retroactive federal legislation imposing liabilities under the Multiemployer Pension Plan

Amendments Act of 1980 (MEPPA). When an employer withdraws from an underfunded pension plan, MEPPA allows the imposition of significant unforeseen liabilities. In *Pension Benefit Guaranty Corporation v. Gray*, 467 U.S. 717 (1984), and *Connolly v. Pension Benefit Guaranty Corporation*, 475 U.S. 211 (1986), the Court rejected both due process objections to these retroactively imposed MEPPA obligations as well as objections based upon the constitutional protection against uncompensated takings.

ABOUT THE JEB

The Joint Editorial Board for [Uniform Trust and Estate Acts] (JEB) is the oversight panel for the law reform activities of three organizations that promote the improvement of the law in the fields of trusts, estates, probate, and guardianship.

Those organizations are:

(1) The *National Conference of Commissioners on Uniform State Laws*, a body of delegates from each state. The Commissioners draft the uniform laws. The Commission is funded from the contributions of all the state legislatures. Commissioners are appointed by governors or from state legislatures, and include leading practitioners, judges, and law professors.

(2) The *American College of Trust and Estate Counsel*, whose 2,000 elected Fellows comprise the most seasoned experts in trust and estate law.

(3) The *American Bar Association's* Section on Real Property, Probate and Trust Law, the largest body of specialist practitioners in the field.

The JEB is responsible for updating the Uniform Probate Code and other uniform legislation in the field of trusts and estates.

§ 2-701. Scope. In the absence of a finding of a contrary intention, the rules of construction in this [part] control the construction of a governing instrument. The rules of construction in this [part] apply to a governing instrument of any type, except as the application of a particular section is limited by its terms to a specific type or types of provision or governing instrument.

Comment

The rules of construction in this part apply to governing instruments of any type, except as the application of a particular section is limited by its terms to a specific type or types of provision or governing instrument.

The term "governing instrument" is defined in Section 1-201 as "a deed, will, trust, insurance or annuity policy, account with POD designation, security registered in beneficiary form (TOD), pension, profit-sharing, retirement, or similar benefit plan, instrument creating or exercising a power of appointment or a power of attorney, or a dispositive, appointive, or nominative instrument of any similar type."

Certain of the sections in this part are limited in their application to provisions or governing instruments of a certain type or types. Section 2-704, for example, applies only to a governing instrument creating a power of appointment. Section 2-706 applies only to governing instruments that are "beneficiary designations", a term defined in Section 1-201 as referring to "a governing instrument naming a beneficiary of an insurance or annuity policy, of an account with POD designation, of a security registered in beneficiary form (TOD), or of a pension, profit-sharing, retirement, or similar benefit plan, or other nonprobate transfer at death." Section 2-707 applies only to governing instruments creating a future interest under the terms of a trust.

Cross References. See the Comment to Section 2-601.

Historical Note. This Comment was revised in 1993. For the prior version, see 8 U.L.A. 138 (Supp.1992).

§ 2-702. Requirement of Survival by 120 Hours.

(a) [**Requirement of Survival by 120 Hours Under Probate Code.**] For the purposes of this [code], except as provided in subsection (d), an individual who is not established by clear and convincing evidence to have survived an event, including the death of another individual, by 120 hours is deemed to have predeceased the event.

(b) [Requirement of Survival by 120 Hours under Governing Instrument.] Except as provided in subsection (d), for purposes of a provision of a governing instrument that relates to an individual surviving an event, including the death of another individual, an individual who is not established by clear and convincing evidence to have survived the event by 120 hours is deemed to have predeceased the event.

(c) [Co-owners With Right of Survivorship; Requirement of Survival by 120 Hours.] Except as provided in subsection (d), if (i) it is not established by clear and convincing evidence that one of two co-owners with right of survivorship survived the other co-owner by 120 hours, one-half of the property passes as if one had survived by 120 hours and one-half as if the other had survived by 120 hours and (ii) there are more than two co-owners and it is not established by clear and convincing evidence that at least one of them survived the others by 120 hours, the property passes in the proportion that one bears to the whole number of co-owners. For the purposes of this subsection, "co-owners with right of survivorship" includes joint tenants, tenants by the entireties, and other co-owners of property or accounts held under circumstances that entitles one or more to the whole of the property or account on the death of the other or others.

(d) [Exceptions.] Survival by 120 hours is not required if:

(1) the governing instrument contains language dealing explicitly with simultaneous deaths or deaths in a common disaster and that language is operable under the facts of the case;

(2) the governing instrument expressly indicates that an individual is not required to survive an event, including the death of another individual, by any specified period or expressly requires the individual to survive the event by a specified period; but survival of the event or the specified period must be established by clear and convincing evidence;

(3) the imposition of a 120-hour requirement of survival would cause a nonvested property interest or a power of appointment to fail to qualify for validity under Section 2-901(a)(1), (b)(1), or (c)(1) or to become invalid under Section 2-901(a)(2), (b)(2), or (c)(2); but survival must be established by clear and convincing evidence; or

(4) the application of a 120-hour requirement of survival to multiple governing instruments would result in an unintended failure or duplication of a disposition; but survival must be established by clear and convincing evidence.

(e) [Protection of Payors and Other Third Parties.]

(1) A payor or other third party is not liable for having made a payment or transferred an item of property or any other benefit to a beneficiary designated in a governing instrument who, under this section, is not entitled to the payment or item of property, or for having taken any other action in good faith reliance on the beneficiary's apparent entitlement under the terms of the governing instrument, before the payor or other third party received written notice of a claimed lack of entitlement under this section. A payor or other third party is liable for a payment made or other action taken after the payor or other third party received written notice of a claimed lack of entitlement under this section.

(2) Written notice of a claimed lack of entitlement under paragraph (1) must be mailed to the payor's or other third party's main office or home by registered or certified mail, return receipt requested, or served upon the payor or other third party in the same manner as a summons in a civil action. Upon receipt of written notice of a claimed lack of entitlement under this section, a payor or other third party may pay any amount owed or transfer or deposit any item of property held by it to or with the court having jurisdiction of the probate proceedings relating to the decedent's estate, or if no proceedings have been commenced, to or with the court having jurisdiction of probate

proceedings relating to decedents' estates located in the county of the decedent's residence. The court shall hold the funds or item of property and, upon its determination under this section, shall order disbursement in accordance with the determination. Payments, transfers, or deposits made to or with the court discharge the payor or other third party from all claims for the value of amounts paid to or items of property transferred to or deposited with the court.

(f) [Protection of Bona Fide Purchasers; Personal Liability of Recipient.]

(1) A person who purchases property for value and without notice, or who receives a payment or other item of property in partial or full satisfaction of a legally enforceable obligation, is neither obligated under this section to return the payment, item of property, or benefit nor is liable under this section for the amount of the payment or the value of the item of property or benefit. But a person who, not for value, receives a payment, item of property, or any other benefit to which the person is not entitled under this section is obligated to return the payment, item of property, or benefit, or is personally liable for the amount of the payment or the value of the item of property or benefit, to the person who is entitled to it under this section.

(2) If this section or any part of this section is preempted by federal law with respect to a payment, an item of property, or any other benefit covered by this section, a person who, not for value, receives the payment, item of property, or any other benefit to which the person is not entitled under this section is obligated to return the payment, item of property, or benefit, or is personally liable for the amount of the payment or the value of the item of property or benefit, to the person who would have been entitled to it were this section or part of this section not preempted.

Comment

Scope and Purpose of Revision. This section parallels Section 2-104, which requires an heir to survive the intestate by 120 hours in order to inherit.

The scope of this section is expanded to cover all provisions of a governing instrument and this Code that relate to an individual surviving an event (including the death of another individual). As expanded, this section imposes the 120-hour requirement of survival in the areas covered by the Uniform Simultaneous Death Act. By 1993 technical amendment, an anomalous provision exempting securities registered under Part 3 of Article VI (Uniform TOD Security Registration Act) from the 120-hour survival requirement was eliminated. The exemption reflected a temporary concern attributable to UTODSRA's preparation prior to discussion of inserting a 120-hour survival requirement in the freestanding Uniform Simultaneous Death Act (USDA).

In the case of a multiple-party account such as a joint checking account registered in the name of the decedent and his or her spouse with right of survivorship, the 120-hour requirement of survivorship will not, under the facility-of-payment provision of Section 6-222(1), interfere with the surviving spouse's ability to withdraw funds from the account during the 120-hour period following the decedent's death.

Note that subsection (d)(1) provides that the 120-hour requirement of survival is inapplicable if the governing instrument "contains language dealing explicitly with simultaneous deaths or deaths in a common disaster and that language is operable under the facts of the case." The application of this provision is illustrated by the following example.

Example. G died leaving a will devising her entire estate to her husband, H, adding that "in the event he dies before I do, at the same time that I do, or under circumstances as to make it doubtful who died first", my estate is to go to my brother Melvin. H died about 38 hours after G's death, both having died as a result of injuries sustained in an automobile accident.

Under subsection (b), G's estate passes under the alternative devise to Melvin because H's failure to survive G by 120 hours means that H is deemed to have predeceased G. The language in the governing instrument does not, under subsection (d)(1), nullify the provision that causes H, because of his failure to survive G by 120 hours, to be deemed to have predeceased G. Although the governing instrument does contain language dealing with simultaneous deaths, that language is not operable under the facts of the case because H did not die before G, at the same time as G, or under circumstances as to make it doubtful who died first.

Note that subsection (d)(4) provides that the 120-hour requirement of survival is inapplicable if "the application of this section to multiple governing instruments would result in an unintended failure or duplication of a disposition." The application of this provision is illustrated by the following example.

Example. Pursuant to a common plan, H and W executed mutual wills with reciprocal provisions. Their intention was that a $50,000 charitable devise would be made on the death of the survivor. To that end, H's will devised $50,000 to the charity if W predeceased him. W's will devised $50,000 to the charity if H predeceased her. Subsequently, H and W were involved in a common accident. W survived H by 48 hours.

Were it not for subsection (d)(4), not only would the charitable devise in W's will be effective, because H in fact predeceased W, but the charitable devise in H's will would also be effective, because W's failure to survive H by 120 hours would result in her being deemed to have predeceased H. Because this would result in an unintended duplication of the $50,000 devise, subsection (d)(4) provides that the 120-hour requirement of survival is inapplicable. Thus, only the $50,000 charitable devise in W's will is effective.

Subsection (d)(4) also renders the 120-hour requirement of survival inapplicable had H and W died in circumstances in which it could not be established by clear and convincing evidence that either survived the other. In such a case, an appropriate result might be to give effect to the common plan by paying half of the intended $50,000 devise from H's estate and half from W's estate.

Federal Preemption of State Law. See the Comment to Section 2-804 for a discussion of federal preemption.

Revision of Uniform Simultaneous Death Act. The freestanding Uniform Simultaneous Death Act (USDA) was revised in 1991 in accordance with the revisions of this section. States that enact Sections 2-104 and 2-702 need not enact the USDA as revised in 1991 and should repeal the original version of the USDA if previously enacted in the state.

Reference. This section is discussed in Halbach & Waggoner. "The UPC's New Survivorship and Antilapse Provisions", 55 Alb.L. Rev. 1091 (1992).

Historical Note. This Comment was revised in 1993 and 2014.

Former (Pre-1990) Version

§ 2-601. [Requirement That Devisee Survive Testator by 120 Hours.] A devisee who does not survive the testator by 120 hours is treated as if he predeceased the testator, unless the will of decedent contains some language dealing explicitly with simultaneous deaths or deaths in a common disaster, or requiring that the devisee survive the testator or survive the testator for a stated period in order to take under the will.

---

§ 2-703. Choice of Law as to Meaning and Effect of Governing Instrument. The meaning and legal effect of a governing instrument is determined by the local law of the state selected in the governing instrument, unless the application of that law is contrary to the provisions relating to the elective share described in Part 2, the provisions relating to exempt property and allowances described in Part 4, or any other public policy of this state otherwise applicable to the disposition.

Comment

Purpose and Scope of Revisions. The scope of this section is expanded to cover all governing instruments, not just wills. As revised, this section enables the law of a particular state to be selected in the governing instrument for purposes of interpreting the instrument without regard to the location of property covered thereby. So long as local public policy is accommodated, the section should be accepted as necessary and desirable.

Cross Reference. Choice of law rules regarding formal validity of a will are in Section 2-506. See also Sections 3-202 and 3-408.

Historical Note. This Comment was revised in 1993. For the prior version, see 8 U.L.A. 141 (Supp.1992).

§ 2-704. Power of Appointment; Compliance With Specific Reference Requirement. A powerholder's substantial compliance with a formal requirement of appointment imposed in a governing instrument by the donor, including a requirement that the instrument exercising the power of appointment make reference or specific reference to the power, is sufficient if:

(1) the powerholder knows of and intends to exercise the power; and

(2) the powerholder's manner of attempted exercise does not impair a material purpose of the donor in imposing the requirement.

Comment

Rationale of Section. In the creation of powers of appointment, it has become common estate-planning practice to require that the powerholder can exercise the power only by making reference (or express or specific reference) to it. The question of whether the powerholder has made a sufficiently specific reference is much litigated. The precise question often is whether a so-called blanket-exercise clause—a clause referring to "any property over which I have a power of appointment"—constitutes a sufficient reference to a particular power to exercise that power. E.g., First National Bank v. Walker, 607 S.W.2d 469 (Tenn.1980), and cases cited therein.

Section 2-704 adopts a substantial-compliance rule. If it could be shown that the powerholder had knowledge of and intended to exercise the power, the blanket-exercise clause would be sufficient to exercise the power, unless it could be shown that the donor had a material purpose in insisting on the specific-reference requirement.

References and Cross References. See Section 2-

805, under which a powerholder's governing instrument mistakenly omitting a sufficiently specific reference to a particular power of appointment can be reformed to include the necessary reference. See also Langbein & Waggoner, "Reformation of Wills on the Ground of Mistake: Change of Direction in American Law?", 130 U.Pa.L. Rev. 521, 583, n. 223 (1982); Motes/Henes Trust v. Mote, 297 Ark. 380, 761 S.W.2d 938 (1988) (powerholder's intended exercise given effect despite use of blanket-exercise clause); In re Strobel, 149 Ariz. 213, 717 P.2d 892 (1986) (powerholder's intended exercise given effect despite defective reference to power).

See Section 2-608 for a provision governing whether a general residuary clause exercises a power of appointment that does not require a reference (or an express or specific reference) by the powerholder.

2014 Amendment. This section was amended in 2014 to conform it to Section 304 of the Uniform Powers of Appointment Act.

Former (Pre-2014) Version

§ 2-704. Power of Appointment; Meaning of Specific Reference Requirement. If a governing instrument creating a power of appointment expressly requires that the power be exercised by a reference, an express reference, or a specific reference, to the power or its source, it is presumed that the donor's intention, in requiring that the donee exercise the power by making reference to the particular power or to the creating instrument, was to prevent an inadvertent exercise of the power.

---

§ 2-705. Class Gifts Construed to Accord with Intestate Succession; Exceptions.

(a) **[Definitions.]** In this section:

(1) "Adoptee" has the meaning set forth in Section 2-115.

(2) "Child of assisted reproduction" has the meaning set forth in Section 2-120.

(3) "Distribution date" means the time when an immediate or a postponed class gift is to take effect in possession or enjoyment.

(4) "Functioned as a parent of the adoptee" has the meaning set forth in Section 2-115, substituting "adoptee" for "child" in that definition.

(5) "Functioned as a parent of the child" has the meaning set forth in Section 2-115.

(6) "Genetic parent" has the meaning set forth in Section 2-115.

(7) "Gestational child" has the meaning set forth in Section 2-121.

(8) "Relative" has the meaning set forth in Section 2-115.

(b) [**Terms of Relationship.**] A class gift that uses a term of relationship to identify the class members includes a child of assisted reproduction, a gestational child, and, except as otherwise provided in subsections (e) and (f), an adoptee and a child born to parents who are not married to each other, and their respective descendants if appropriate to the class, in accordance with the rules for intestate succession regarding parent-child relationships. For the purpose of determining whether a contrary intention exists under Section 2-701, a provision in a governing instrument that relates to the inclusion or exclusion in a class gift of a child born to parents who are not married to each other but does not specifically refer to a child of assisted reproduction or a gestational child does not apply to a child of assisted reproduction or a gestational child.

(c) [**Relatives by Marriage.**] Terms of relationship in a governing instrument that do not differentiate relationships by blood from those by marriage, such as uncles, aunts, nieces, or nephews, are construed to exclude relatives by marriage, unless:

(1) when the governing instrument was executed, the class was then and foreseeably would be empty; or

(2) the language or circumstances otherwise establish that relatives by marriage were intended to be included.

(d) [**Half-Blood Relatives.**] Terms of relationship in a governing instrument that do not differentiate relationships by the half blood from those by the whole blood, such as brothers, sisters, nieces, or nephews, are construed to include both types of relationships.

(e) [**Transferor Not Genetic Parent.**] In construing a dispositive provision of a transferor who is not the genetic parent, a child of a genetic parent is not considered the child of that genetic parent unless the genetic parent, a relative of the genetic parent, or the spouse or surviving spouse of the genetic parent or of a relative of the genetic parent functioned as a parent of the child before the child reached [18] years of age.

(f) [**Transferor Not Adoptive Parent.**] In construing a dispositive provision of a transferor who is not the adoptive parent, an adoptee is not considered the child of the adoptive parent unless:

(1) the adoption took place before the adoptee reached [18] years of age;

(2) the adoptive parent was the adoptee's stepparent or foster parent; or

(3) the adoptive parent functioned as a parent of the adoptee before the adoptee reached [18] years of age.

(g) [**Class-Closing Rules.**] The following rules apply for purposes of the class-closing rules:

(1) A child in utero at a particular time is treated as living at that time if the child lives 120 hours after birth.

(2) If a child of assisted reproduction or a gestational child is conceived posthumously and the distribution date is the deceased parent's death, the child is treated as living on the distribution date if the child lives 120 hours after birth and was in utero not later than 36 months after the deceased parent's death or born not later than 45 months after the deceased parent's death.

(3) An individual who is in the process of being adopted when the class closes is treated as adopted when the class closes if the adoption is subsequently granted.

Comment

This section facilitates a modern construction of gifts that identify the recipient by reference to a relationship to someone; usually these gifts will be class gifts. The rules of construction contained in this section are substantially consistent with the rules of construction contained in the Restatement (Third) of Property: Wills and Other Donative Transfers §§ 14.5 through 14.9. These sections of the Restatement apply to the treatment for class-gift purposes of an adoptee, a nonmarital child, a child of assisted reproduction, a gestational child, and a relative by marriage.

The rules set forth in this section are rules of construction, which under Section 2-701 are controlling in the absence of a finding of a contrary intention. With two exceptions, Section 2-705 invokes the rules pertaining to intestate succession as rules of construction for interpreting terms of relationship in private instruments.

Subsection (a): Definitions. With one exception, the definitions in subsection (a) rely on definitions contained in intestacy sections. The one exception is the definition of "distribution date," which is relevant to the class-closing rules contained in subsection (g). *Distribution date* is defined as the date when an immediate or postponed class gift takes effect in possession or enjoyment.

Subsection (b): Terms of Relationship. Subsection (b) provides that a class gift that uses a term of relationship to identify the takers includes a child of assisted reproduction and a gestational child, and their respective descendants if appropriate to the class, in accordance with the rules for intestate succession regarding parent-child relationships. As provided in subsection (g), inclusion of a child of assisted reproduction or a gestational child in a class is subject to the class-closing rules. See Examples 11 through 15.

The last sentence of subsection (b) was added by technical amendment in 2010. That sentence is necessary to prevent a provision in a governing instrument that relates to the inclusion or exclusion of a child born to parents who are not married to each other from applying to a child of assisted reproduction or a gestational child, unless the provision specifically refers to such a child. Technically, for example, a posthumously conceived child born to a decedent's surviving widow could be considered a nonmarital child. See e.g., Woodward v. Commissioner of Social Security, 760 N.E.2d 257, 266-67 (Mass. 2002) ("Because death ends a marriage, ... posthumously conceived children are always nonmarital children."). A provision in a will, trust, or other governing instrument that relates to the inclusion or exclusion of a nonmarital child, or to the inclusion or exclusion of a nonmarital child under specified circumstances, was not likely inserted with a child of assisted reproduction or a gestational child in mind. The last sentence of subsection (b) provides that, unless that type of provision specifically refers to a child of assisted reproduction or gestational child, such a provision does not state a contrary intention under Section 2-701 to the rule of construction contained in subsection (b).

Subsection (b) also provides that, except as otherwise provided in subsections (e) and (f), an adoptee and a child born to parents who are not married to each other, and their respective descendants if appropriate to the class, are included in class gifts and other terms of relationship in accordance with the rules for intestate succession regarding parent-child relationships. The subsection (e) exception relates to situations in which the transferor is not the genetic parent of the child. The subsection (f) exception relates to situations in which the transferor is not the adoptive parent of the adoptee. Consequently, if the transferor *is* the genetic or adoptive parent of the child, neither exception applies, and the class gift or other term of relationship is construed in accordance with the rules for intestate succession regarding parent-child relationships. As provided in subsection (g), inclusion of an adoptee or a child born to parents who are not married to each other in a class is subject to the class-closing rules. See Examples 9 and 10.

Subsection (c): Relatives by Marriage. Subsection (c) provides that terms of relationship that do not differentiate relationships by blood from those by marriage, such as "uncles", "aunts", "nieces", or "nephews", are construed to exclude relatives by marriage, unless (1) when the governing instrument was executed, the class was then and foreseeably would be empty or (2) the language or circumstances otherwise establish that relatives by marriage were intended to be included. The Restatement (Third) of Property: Wills and Other Donative Transfers § 14.9 adopts a similar rule of construction. As recognized in both subsection (c) and the Restatement, there are situations in which the circumstances would tend to include a relative by marriage. As provided in subsection (g), inclusion of a relative by marriage in a class is subject to the class-closing rules.

One situation in which the circumstances would tend to establish an intent to include a relative by marriage is the situation in which, looking at the facts existing when the governing instrument was executed, the class was then and foreseeably would be empty unless the transferor intended to include relatives by marriage.

Example 1. G's will devised property in trust, directing the trustee to pay the income in equal shares "to G's children who are living on each income payment date and on the death of G's last surviving child, to distribute the trust property to G's issue then living, such issue to take per stirpes, and if no issue of G is then living, to distribute the trust property to the X Charity." When G executed her will, she was past the usual childbearing age, had no children of her own, and was married to a man who had four children by a previous marriage. These children had lived with G and her husband for many years, but G had never adopted them. Under these circumstances, it is reasonable to conclude that when G referred to her "children" in her will she was referring to her stepchildren. Thus her stepchildren should be included in the presumptive meaning of the gift "to G's children" and the issue of her stepchildren should be included in the presumptive meaning of the gift "to G's issue." If G, at the time she executed her will, had children of her own, in the absence of additional facts, G's stepchildren should not be included in the presumptive meaning of the gift to "G's children" or in the gift to "G's issue."

Example 2. G's will devised property in trust, directing the trustee to pay the income to G's wife W for life, and on her death, to distribute the trust property to "my grandchildren." W had children by a prior marriage who were G's stepchildren. G never had any children of his own and he never adopted his stepchildren. It is reasonable to conclude that under these circumstances G meant the children of his stepchildren when his will gave the future interest under the trust to G's "grandchildren."

Example 3. G's will devised property in trust, directing the trustee to pay the income "to my daughter for life and on her death, to distribute the trust property to her children." When G executed his will, his son had died, leaving surviving the son's wife, G's daughter-in-law, and two children. G had no daughter of his own. Under these circumstances, the conclusion is justified that G's daughter-in-law is the "daughter" referred to in G's will.

Another situation in which the circumstances would tend to establish an intent to include a relative by marriage is the case of reciprocal wills, as illustrated in Example 4, which is based on Martin v. Palmer, 1 S.W.3d 875 (Tex. Ct. App. 1999).

Example 4. G's will devised her entire estate "to my husband if he survives me, but if not, to my nieces and nephews." G's husband H predeceased her. H's will devised his entire estate "to my wife if she survives me, but if not, to my nieces and

nephews." Both G and H had nieces and nephews. In these circumstances, "my nieces and nephews" is construed to include G's nieces and nephews by marriage. Were it otherwise, the combined estates of G and H would pass only to the nieces and nephews of the spouse who happened to survive.

Still another situation in which the circumstances would tend to establish an intent to include a relative by marriage is a case in which an ancestor participated in raising a relative by marriage other than a stepchild.

Example 5. G's will devised property in trust, directing the trustee to pay the income in equal shares "to my nieces and nephews living on each income payment date until the death of the last survivor of my nieces and nephews, at which time the trust shall terminate and the trust property shall be distributed to the X Charity." G's wife W was deceased when G executed his will. W had one brother who predeceased her. G and W took the brother's children, the wife's nieces and nephews, into their home and raised them. G had one sister who predeceased him, and G and W were close to her children, G's nieces and nephews. Under these circumstances, the conclusion is justified that the disposition "to my nieces and nephews" includes the children of W's brother as well as the children of G's sister.

The language of the disposition may also establish an intent to include relatives by marriage, as illustrated in Examples 6, 7, and 8.

Example 6. G's will devised half of his estate to his wife W and half to "my children." G had one child by a prior marriage, and W had two children by a prior marriage. G did not adopt his stepchildren. G's relationship with his stepchildren was close, and he participated in raising them. The use of the plural "children" is a factor indicating that G intended to include his stepchildren in the class gift to his children.

Example 7. G's will devised the residue of his estate to "my nieces and nephews named herein before." G's niece by marriage was referred to in two earlier provisions as "my niece." The previous reference to her as "my niece" indicates that G intended to include her in the residuary devise.

Example 8. G's will devised the residue of her estate "in twenty-five (25) separate equal shares, so that there shall be one (1) such share for each of my nieces and nephews who shall survive me, and one (1) such share for each of my nieces and nephews who shall not survive me but who shall have left a child or children surviving me." G had 22 nieces and nephews by blood or adoption and three nieces and nephews by marriage. The reference to twenty-five nieces and nephews indicates that G intended to include her three nieces and nephews by marriage in the residuary devise.

Subsection (d): Half Blood Relatives. In providing that terms of relationship that do not differentiate relationships by the half blood from those by the whole blood, such as "brothers", "sisters", "nieces", or "nephews", are construed to include both types of relationships, subsection (d) is consistent with the rules for intestate succession regarding parent-child relationships. See Section 2-107 and the phrase "or either of them" in Section 2-103(a)(3) and (4). As provided in subsection (g), inclusion of a half blood relative in a class is subject to the class-closing rules.

Subsection (e): Transferor Not Genetic Parent. The general theory of subsection (e) is that a transferor who is not the genetic parent of a child would want the child to be included in a class gift as a child of the genetic parent only if the genetic parent (or one or more of the specified relatives of the child's genetic parent functioned as a parent of the child before the child reached the age of [18]. As provided in subsection (g), inclusion of a genetic child in a class is subject to the class-closing rules.

Example 9. G's will created a trust, income to G's son, A, for life, remainder in corpus to A's descendants who survive A, by representation. A fathered a child, X; A and X's mother, D, never married each other, and A never functioned as a parent of the child, nor did any of A's relatives or spouses or surviving spouses of any of A's relatives. D later married E; D and E raised X as a member of their household. Because neither A nor any of A's specified relatives ever functioned as a parent of X, X would not be included as a member of the class of A's descendants who take the corpus of G's trust on A's death.

If, however, A executed a will containing a devise to his children or designated his children as beneficiary of his life insurance policy, X would be included in the class. Under Section 2-117, X would be A's child for purposes of intestate succession. Subsection (c) is inapplicable because the transferor, A, is the genetic parent.

Subsection (f): Transferor Not Adoptive Parent. The general theory of subsection (f) is that a transferor who is not the adoptive parent of an adoptee would want the child to be included in a class gift as a child of the adoptive parent only if (1) the adoption took place before the adoptee reached the age of [18]; (2) the adoptive parent was the adoptee's stepparent or foster parent; or (3) the adoptive parent functioned as a parent of the adoptee before the adoptee reached the age of [18]. As provided in subsection (g), inclusion of an adoptee in a class is subject to the class-closing rules.

Example 10. G's will created a trust, income to G's daughter, A, for life, remainder in corpus to A's descendants who survive A, by representation. A and A's husband adopted a 47-year old man, X. Because the adoption did not take place before X reached the age of [18], A was not X's stepparent or foster parent, and A did not function as a parent of X before X reached the age of [18]. X would not be included as a member of the class of A's descendants who take the corpus of G's trust on A's death.

If, however, A executed a will containing a devise to her children or designated her children as beneficiary of her life insurance policy, X would be included in the class. Under Section 2-118, X would be A's child for purposes of intestate succession. Subsection (d) is inapplicable because the transferor, A, is an adoptive parent.

Subsection (g): Class-Closing Rules. In order for an individual to be a taker under a class gift that uses a term of relationship to identify the class members, the individual must (1) qualify as a class member under subsection (b), (c), (d), (e), or (f) and (2) not be excluded by the class-closing rules. For an exposition of the class-closing rules, see Restatement (Third) of Property: Wills and Other Donative Transfers § 15.1. Section 15.1 provides that, "unless the language or circumstances establish that the transferor had a different intention, a class gift that has not yet closed physiologically closes to future entrants on the distribution date if a beneficiary of the class gift is then entitled to distribution."

Subsection (g)(1): Child in Utero. Subsection (g)(1) codifies the well-accepted rule that a child in utero at a particular time is treated as living at that time if the child lives 120 hours after birth.

Subsection (g)(2): Children of Assisted Reproduction and Gestational Children; Class Gift in Which Distribution Date Arises At Deceased Parent's Death. Subsection (g)(2) changes the class-closing rules in one respect. If a child of assisted reproduction (as defined in Section 2-120) or a gestational child (as defined in Section 2-121) is conceived posthumously, and if the distribution date arises at the deceased parent's death, then the child is treated as living on the distribution date if the child lives 120 hours after birth and was either (1) in utero no later than 36 months after the deceased parent's death or (2) born no later than 45 months after the deceased parent's death.

The 36-month period in subsection (g)(2) is designed to allow a surviving spouse or partner a period of grieving, time to make up his or her mind about whether to go forward with assisted reproduction, and a reasonable allowance for unsuccessful attempts to achieve a pregnancy. The 36-month period also coincides with Section 3-1006, under which an heir is allowed to recover property improperly distributed or its value from any distributee during the later of three years after the decedent's death or one year after distribution. If the assisted-reproduction procedure is performed in a medical facility, the date when the child is in utero will ordinarily be evidenced by medical records. In some cases, however, the procedure is not performed in a medical facility, and so such evidence may be lacking. Providing an alternative of birth within 45 months is designed to provide certainty in such cases. The 45-month period is based on the 36-month period with an additional nine months tacked on to allow for a normal period of pregnancy.

Example 11. G, a member of the armed forces, executed a military will under 10 U.S.C. § 1044d shortly before being deployed to a war zone. G's will devised "90 percent of my estate to my wife W and 10 percent of my estate to my children." G also left frozen sperm at a sperm bank in case he should be killed in action. G consented to be treated as the parent of the child within the meaning of Section 2-120(f). G was killed in action. After G's death, W decided to become inseminated with his frozen sperm so she could have his child. If the child so produced was either (1) in utero within 36 months after G's death or (2) born within 45 months after G's death, and if the child lived 120 hours after birth, the child is treated as

living at G's death and is included in the class.

Example 12. G, a member of the armed forces, executed a military will under 10 U.S.C. § 1044d shortly before being deployed to a war zone. G's will devised "90 percent of my estate to my husband H and 10 percent of my estate to my issue by representation." G also left frozen embryos in case she should be killed in action. G consented to be the parent of the child within the meaning of Section 2-120(f). G was killed in action. After G's death, H arranged for the embryos to be implanted in the uterus of a gestational carrier. If the child so produced was either (1) in utero within 36 months after G's death or (2) born within 45 months after the G's death, and if the child lived 120 hours after birth, the child is treated as living at G's death and is included in the class.

Example 13. The will of G's mother created a testamentary trust, directing the trustee to pay the income to G for life, then to distribute the trust principal to G's children. When G's mother died, G was married but had no children. Shortly after being diagnosed with leukemia, G feared that he would be rendered infertile by the disease or by the treatment for the disease, so he left frozen sperm at a sperm bank. G consented to be the parent of the child within the meaning of Section 2-120(f). After G's death, G's widow decided to become inseminated with his frozen sperm so she could have his child. If the child so produced was either (1) in utero within 36 months after G's death or (2) born within 45 months after the G's death, and if the child lived 120 hours after birth, the child is treated as living at G's death and is included in the class under the rule of convenience.

Subsection (g)(2) Inapplicable Unless Child of Assisted Reproduction or Gestational Child is Conceived Posthumously and Distribution Date Arises At Deceased Parent's Death. Subsection (g)(2) only applies if a child of assisted reproduction or a gestational child is conceived posthumously and the distribution date arises at the deceased parent's death. Subsection (g)(2) does not apply if a child of assisted reproduction or a gestational child is not conceived posthumously. It also does not apply if the distribution date arises before or after the deceased parent's death. In cases to which subsection (g)(2) does not apply, the ordinary class-closing rules apply. For purposes of the ordinary class-closing rules, subsection (g)(1) provides that a child in utero at a particular time is treated as living at that time if the child lives 120 hours after birth.

This means, for example, that, with respect to a child of assisted reproduction or a gestational child, a class gift in which the distribution date arises after the deceased parent's death is not limited to a child who is born before or in utero at the deceased parent's death or, in the case of posthumous conception, either (1) in utero within 36 months after the deceased parent's death or (2) born within 45 months after the deceased parent's death. The ordinary class-closing rules would only exclude a child of assisted reproduction or a gestational child if the child was not yet born or in utero on the distribution date (or who was then in utero but who failed to live 120 hours after birth).

A case that reached the same result that would be reached under this section is In re Martin B., 841 N.Y.S.2d 207 (Sur. Ct. 2007). In that case, two children (who were conceived posthumously and were born to a deceased father's widow around three and five years after his death) were included in class gifts to the deceased father's "issue" or "descendants". The children would be included under this section because (1) the deceased father signed a record that would satisfy Section 2-120(f)(1), (2) the distribution dates arose after the deceased father's death, and (3) the children were living on the distribution dates, thus satisfying subsection (g)(1).

Example 14. G created a revocable inter vivos trust shortly before his death. The trustee was directed to pay the income to G for life, then "to pay the income to my wife, W, for life, then to distribute the trust principal by representation to my descendants who survive W." When G died, G and W had no children. Shortly before G's death and after being diagnosed with leukemia, G feared that he would be rendered infertile by the disease or by the treatment for the disease, so he left frozen sperm at a sperm bank. G consented to be the parent of the child within the meaning of Section 2-120(f). After G's death, W decided to become inseminated with G's frozen sperm so that she could have his child. The child, X, was born five years after G's death. W raised X. Upon W's death many years later, X was a grown adult. X is entitled to receive the trust principal, because a parent-child relationship between G and X existed under Section 2-120(f) and X was living on the distribution date.

Example 15. The will of G's mother created a testamentary trust, directing the trustee to pay the income to G for life, then "to pay the income by representation to G's issue from time to time living, and at the death of G's last surviving child, to distribute the trust principal by representation to G's descendants who survive G's last surviving child." When G's mother died, G was married but had no children. Shortly after being diagnosed with leukemia, G feared that he would be rendered infertile by the disease or by the treatment for the disease, so he left frozen sperm at a sperm bank. G consented to be the parent of the child within the meaning of Section 2-120(f). After G's death, G's widow decided to become inseminated with his frozen sperm so she could have his child. If the child so produced was either (1) in utero within 36 months after G's death or (2) born within 45 months after the G's death, and if the child lived 120 hours after birth, the child is treated as living at G's death and is included in the class-gift of income under the rule of convenience. If G's widow later decides to use his frozen sperm to have another child or children, those children would be included in the class-gift of income (assuming they live 120 hours after birth) even if they were not in utero within 36 months after G's death or born within 45 months after the G's death. The reason is that an income interest in class-gift form is treated as creating separate class gifts in which the distribution date is the time of payment of each subsequent income payment. See Restatement (Third) of Property: Wills and Other Donative Transfers § 15.1 cmt. p. Regarding the remainder interest in principal that takes effect in possession on the death of G's last living child, the issue of the posthumously conceived children who are then living would take the trust principal.

Subsection (g)(3). For purposes of the class-closing rules, an individual who is in the process of being adopted when the class closes is treated as adopted when the class closes if the adoption is subsequently granted. An individual is "in the process of being adopted" if a legal proceeding to adopt the individual had been filed before the class closed. However, the phrase "in the process of being adopted" is not intended to be limited to the filing of a legal proceeding, but is intended to grant flexibility to find on a case by case basis that the process commenced earlier.

Reference. For the application of this section to children of assisted reproduction and gestational children, see Sheldon F. Kurtz & Lawrence W.

Waggoner, The UPC Addresses the Class-Gift and Intestacy Rights of Children of Assisted Reproduction Technologies, 35 ACTEC J. 30 (2009).

Historical Note. This Comment was revised in 1993, 2008, and 2010.

Former (1990) Version

§ 2-705. Class Gifts Construed to Accord With Intestate Succession.

(a) Adopted individuals and individuals born out of wedlock, and their respective descendants if appropriate to the class, are included in class gifts and other terms of relationship in accordance with the rules for intestate succession. Terms of relationship that do not differentiate relationships by blood from those by affinity, such as "uncles", "aunts", "nieces", or "nephews", are construed to exclude relatives by affinity. Terms of relationship that do not differentiate relationships by the half blood from those by the whole blood, such as "brothers", "sisters", "nieces", or "nephews", are construed to include both types of relationships.

(b) In addition to the requirements of subsection (a), in construing a dispositive provision of a transferor who is not the natural parent, an individual born to the natural parent is not considered the child of that parent unless the individual lived while a minor as a regular member of the household of that natural parent or of that parent's parent, brother, sister, spouse, or surviving spouse.

(c) In addition to the requirements of subsection (a), in construing a dispositive provision of a transferor who is not the adopting parent, an adopted individual is not considered the child of the adopting parent unless the adopted individual lived while a minor, either before or after the adoption, as a regular member of the household of the adopting parent.

Former (Pre-1990) Version

§ 2-603. [Rules of Construction and Intention.] The intention of a testator as expressed in his will controls the legal effect of his dispositions. The rules of construction expressed in the succeeding sections of this Part [6] apply unless a contrary intention is indicated by the will.

§ 2-611. [Construction of Generic Terms to Accord with Relationships as Defined for Intestate Succession.] Halfbloods, adopted persons, and persons born out of wedlock are included in class gift terminology and terms of relationship in accordance with rules for determining relationships for purposes of intestate succession. [However, a person born out of wedlock is not treated as the child of the father unless the person is openly and notoriously so treated by the father.]

---

§ 2-706. Life Insurance; Retirement Plan; Account with POD Designation; Transfer-on-Death Registration; Deceased Beneficiary.

(a) [**Definitions.**] In this section:

(1) "Alternative beneficiary designation" means a beneficiary designation that is expressly created by the governing instrument and, under the terms of the governing instrument, can take effect instead of another beneficiary designation on the happening of one or more events, including survival of the decedent or failure to survive the decedent, whether an event is expressed in condition-precedent, condition-subsequent, or any other form.

(2) "Beneficiary" means the beneficiary of a beneficiary designation under which the beneficiary must survive the decedent and includes (i) a class member if the beneficiary designation is in the form of a class gift and (ii) an individual or class member who was deceased at the time the beneficiary designation was executed as well as an individual or class member who was then living but who failed to survive the decedent, but excludes a joint tenant of a joint tenancy with the right of survivorship and a party to a joint and survivorship account.

(3) "Beneficiary designation" includes an alternative beneficiary designation and a beneficiary designation in the form of a class gift.

(4) "Class member" includes an individual who fails to survive the decedent but who would have taken under a beneficiary designation in the form of a class gift had he [or she] survived the decedent.

(5) "Descendant of a grandparent", as used in subsection (b), means an individual who qualifies as a descendant of a grandparent of the decedent under the (i) rules of construction applicable to a class gift created in the decedent's beneficiary designation if the beneficiary designation is in the form of a class gift or (ii) rules for intestate succession if the beneficiary designation is not in the form of a class gift.

(6) "Descendants", as used in the phrase "surviving descendants" of a deceased beneficiary or class member in subsections (b)(1) and (2), mean the descendants of a deceased beneficiary or class member who would take under a class gift created in the beneficiary designation.

(7) "Stepchild" means a child of the decedent's surviving, deceased, or former spouse, and not of the decedent.

(8) "Surviving", in the phrase "surviving beneficiary" or "surviving descendant", means a beneficiary or a descendant who neither predeceased the decedent nor is deemed to have predeceased the decedent under Section 2-702.

(b) [**Substitute Gift.**] If a beneficiary fails to survive the decedent and is a grandparent, a descendant of a grandparent, or a stepchild of the decedent, the following apply:

(1) Except as provided in paragraph (4), if the beneficiary designation is not in the form of a class gift and the deceased beneficiary leaves surviving descendants, a substitute gift is created in the beneficiary's surviving descendants. They take by representation the property to which the beneficiary would have been entitled had the beneficiary survived the decedent.

(2) Except as provided in paragraph (4), if the beneficiary designation is in the form of a class gift, other than a beneficiary designation to "issue", "descendants", "heirs of the body", "heirs", "next of kin", "relatives", or "family", or a class described by language of similar import, a substitute gift is created in the surviving descendants of any deceased beneficiary. The property to which the beneficiaries would have been entitled had all of them survived the decedent passes to the surviving beneficiaries and the surviving descendants of the deceased beneficiaries. Each surviving beneficiary takes the share to which he [or she] would have been entitled had the deceased beneficiaries survived the decedent. Each deceased beneficiary's surviving descendants who are substituted for the deceased beneficiary take by representation the share to which the deceased beneficiary would have been entitled had the deceased beneficiary survived the decedent. For the purposes of this paragraph, "deceased beneficiary" means a class member who failed to survive the decedent and left one or more surviving descendants.

(3) For the purposes of Section 2-701, words of survivorship, such as in a beneficiary designation to an individual "if he survives me", or in a beneficiary designation to "my surviving children", are not, in the absence of additional evidence, a sufficient indication of an intent contrary to the application of this section.

(4) If a governing instrument creates an alternative beneficiary designation with respect to a beneficiary designation for which a substitute gift is created by paragraph (1) or (2), the substitute gift is superseded by the alternative beneficiary designation if:

(A) the alternative beneficiary designation is in the form of a class gift and one or more members of the class is entitled to take; or

(B) the alternative beneficiary designation is not in the form of a class gift and the expressly designated beneficiary of the alternative beneficiary designation is entitled to take.

(c) [**More Than One Substitute Gift; Which One Takes.**] If, under subsection (b), substitute gifts are created and not superseded with respect to more than one beneficiary designation and the beneficiary designations are alternative beneficiary designations, one to the other, the determination of which of the substitute gifts takes effect is resolved as follows:

(1) Except as provided in paragraph (2), the property passes under the primary substitute gift.

(2) If there is a younger-generation beneficiary designation, the property passes under the younger-generation substitute gift and not under the primary substitute gift.

(3) In this subsection:

(A) "Primary beneficiary designation" means the beneficiary designation that would have taken effect had all the deceased beneficiaries of the alternative beneficiary designations who left surviving descendants survived the decedent.

(B) "Primary substitute gift" means the substitute gift created with respect to the primary beneficiary designation.

(C) "Younger-generation beneficiary designation" means a beneficiary designation that (i) is to a descendant of a beneficiary of the primary beneficiary designation, (ii) is an alternative beneficiary designation with respect to the primary beneficiary designation, (iii) is a beneficiary designation for which a substitute gift is created, and (iv) would have taken effect had all the deceased beneficiaries who left surviving descendants survived the decedent except the deceased beneficiary or beneficiaries of the primary beneficiary designation.

(D) "Younger-generation substitute gift" means the substitute gift created with respect to the younger-generation beneficiary designation.

(d) [Protection of Payors.]

(1) A payor is protected from liability in making payments under the terms of the beneficiary designation until the payor has received written notice of a claim to a substitute gift under this section. Payment made before the receipt of written notice of a claim to a substitute gift under this section discharges the payor, but not the recipient, from all claims for the amounts paid. A payor is liable for a payment made after the payor has received written notice of the claim. A recipient is liable for a payment received, whether or not written notice of the claim is given.

(2) The written notice of the claim must be mailed to the payor's main office or home by registered or certified mail, return receipt requested, or served upon the payor in the same manner as a summons in a civil action. Upon receipt of written notice of the claim, a payor may pay any amount owed by it to the court having jurisdiction of the probate proceedings relating to the decedent's estate or, if no proceedings have been commenced, to the court having jurisdiction of probate proceedings relating to decedents' estates located in the county of the decedent's residence. The court shall hold the funds and, upon its determination under this section, shall order disbursement in accordance with the determination. Payment made to the court discharges the payor from all claims for the amounts paid.

(e) [Protection of Bona Fide Purchasers; Personal Liability of Recipient.]

(1) A person who purchases property for value and without notice, or who receives a payment or other item of property in partial or full satisfaction of a legally enforceable obligation, is neither obligated under this section to return the payment, item of property, or benefit nor is liable under this section for the amount of the payment or the value of the item of property or benefit. But a person who, not for value, receives a payment, item of property, or any other benefit to which the person is not entitled under this section is obligated to return the payment, item of property, or benefit, or is personally liable for the amount of the payment or the value of the item of property or benefit, to the person who is entitled to it under this section.

(2) If this section or any part of this section is preempted by federal law with respect to a payment, an item of property, or any other benefit covered by this section, a person who, not for value, receives the payment, item of property, or any other benefit to which the person is not entitled under this section is obligated to return the payment, item of property, or benefit, or is personally liable for the amount of the payment or the value of the item of property or benefit, to the person who would have been entitled to it were this section or part of this section not preempted.

Comment

Purpose. This section provides an antilapse statute for "beneficiary designations" under which the beneficiary must survive the decedent. The term "beneficiary designation" is defined in Section 1-201 as "a governing instrument naming a beneficiary of an insurance or annuity policy, of an account with POD designation, of a security registered in beneficiary form (TOD), or of a pension, profit-sharing, retirement, or similar benefit plan, or other nonprobate transfer at death".

The terms of this section parallel those of Section 2-603, except that the provisions relating to payor protection and personal liability of recipients have been added. The Comment to Section 2-603 contains an elaborate exposition of Section 2-603, together with examples illustrating its application. That Comment, in addition to the examples given below, should aid understanding of Section 2-706. For a discussion of the reasons why Section 2-706 should not be preempted by federal law, see the Comment to Section 2-804.

Example 1. G is the owner of a life-insurance policy. When the policy was taken out, G was married to S; G and S had two young children. A and B. G died 45 years after the policy was taken out. S predeceased G, A survived G by 120 hours and B predeceased G leaving three children (X, Y, and Z) who survived G by 120 hours. G's policy names S as the primary beneficiary of the policy, but because S predeceased G, the secondary (contingent) beneficiary designation became operative. The secondary (contingent) beneficiary designation of G's policy states: "equally to the then living children born of the marriage of G and S".

The printed terms of G's policy provide:

"If two or more persons are designated as beneficiary, the beneficiary will be the designated person or persons who survive the Insured, and if more than one survive, they will share equally".

Solution: The printed clause constitutes an "alternative beneficiary designation" for purposes of subsection (b)(4), which supersedes the substitute gift to B's descendants created by subsection (b)(2). A is entitled to all of the proceeds of the policy.

Example 2. The facts are the same as in Example 1, except that G's policy names "A and B" as secondary (contingent) beneficiaries. The printed terms of the policy provide:

"If any designated Beneficiary predeceases the Insured, the interest of such Beneficiary will terminate and shall be shared equally by such of the Beneficiaries as survive the Insured".

Solution: The printed clause constitutes an "alternative beneficiary designation" for purposes of subsection (b)(4), which supersedes the substitute gift to B's descendants created by subsection (b)(1). A is entitled to all of the proceeds of the policy.

Example 3. The facts are the same as Examples 1 or 2, except that the printed terms of the policy do not contain either quoted clause or a similar one.

Solution: Under Section 2-706, A would be entitled to half of the policy proceeds and X, Y, and Z would divide the other half equally.

Example 4. The facts are the same as Example 3, except that the policy has a beneficiary designation that provides that, if the adjacent box is checked, the share of any deceased beneficiary shall be paid "in one sum and in equal shares to the children of that beneficiary who survive". G did not check the box adjacent to this option.

Solution: G's deliberate decision not to check the box providing for the share of any deceased beneficiary to go to that beneficiary's children constitutes a clear indication of a contrary intention for purposes of Section 2-701. A would be entitled to all of the proceeds of the policy.

Example 5. G's life-insurance policy names her niece, A, as primary beneficiary, and provides that if A does not survive her, the proceeds are to go to her niece B, as contingent beneficiary. A predeceased G, leaving children who survived G by 120 hours, B survived G by 120 hours.

Solution: The contingent beneficiary designation constitutes an "alternative beneficiary designation" for purposes of subsection (b)(4), which supersedes the substitute gift to A's descendants created by subsection (b)(1). The proceeds go to B, not to A's children.

Example 6. G's life-insurance policy names her niece, A, as primary beneficiary, and provides that if A does not survive her, the proceeds are to go to her niece B, as contingent beneficiary. The printed terms of the policy specifically state that if neither the primary nor secondary beneficiaries survive the policyholder, the proceeds are payable to the policyholder's estate. A predeceased G, leaving children who survived G by 120 hours, B also predeceased G, leaving children who survived G by 120 hours.

Solution: The second contingent beneficiary designation to G's estate constitutes an "alternative beneficiary designation" for purposes of subsection (b)(4), which supersedes the substitute gifts to A's and B's descendants created by subsection (b)(1). The proceeds go to G's estate, not to A's children or to B's children.

References. This section is discussed in Halbach & Waggoner, "The UPC's New Survivorship and Antilapse Provisions", 55 Alb.L. Rev. 1091 (1992). See also Restatement (Third) of Property: Wills and Other Donative Transfers § 5.5 cmt. p (1999); § 7.2 cmt. k (2003); Lebolt, "Making the Best of *Egelhoff*:

Federal Common Law for ERISA-Preempted Beneficiary Designations", 28 J. Pension Planning & Compliance 29 (Fall 2002); Gallanis, "ERISA and the Law of Succession", 60 Ohio St. L.J. 185 (2004); Rayho, Note, 106 Mich. L. Rev. 373 (2007).

Technical Amendments. Technical amendments in 1993 added language specifically excluding joint and survivorship accounts and joint tenancies with the right of survivorship; this amendment is consistent with the original purpose of the section.

Technical amendments in 2008 added definitions of "descendant of a grandparent" and "descendants" as used in subsections (b)(1) and (2) and clarified subsection (b)(4). The two new definitions resolve questions of status previously unanswered. The technical amendment of subsection (b)(4) makes that subsection easier to understand but does not change its substance.

Historical Note. This Comment was revised in 1993, 2008, and 2014.

§ 2-707. Survivorship with Respect to Future Interests under Terms of Trust; Substitute Takers.

(a) **[Definitions.]** In this section:

(1) "Alternative future interest" means an expressly created future interest that can take effect in possession or enjoyment instead of another future interest on the happening of one or more events, including survival of an event or failure to survive an event, whether an event is expressed in condition-precedent, condition-subsequent, or any other form. A residuary clause in a will does not create an alternative future interest with respect to a future interest created in a nonresiduary devise in the will, whether or not the will specifically provides that lapsed or failed devises are to pass under the residuary clause.

(2) "Beneficiary" means the beneficiary of a future interest and includes a class member if the future interest is in the form of a class gift.

(3) "Class member" includes an individual who fails to survive the distribution date but who would have taken under a future interest in the form of a glass gift had he [or she] survived the distribution date.

(4) "Descendants", in the phrase "surviving descendants" of a deceased beneficiary or class member in subsections (b)(1) and (2), mean the descendants of a deceased beneficiary or class member who would take under a class gift created in the trust.

(5) "Distribution date", with respect to a future interest, means the time when the future interest is to take effect in possession or enjoyment. The distribution date need not occur at the beginning or end of a calendar day, but can occur at a time during the course of a day.

(6) "Future interest" includes an alternative future interest and a future interest in the form of a class gift.

(7) "Future interest under the terms of a trust" means a future interest that was created by a transfer creating a trust or to an existing trust or by an exercise of a power of appointment to an existing trust, directing the continuance of an existing trust, designating a beneficiary of an existing trust, or creating a trust.

(8) "Surviving", in the phrase "surviving beneficiary" or "surviving descendant", means a

beneficiary or a descendant who neither predeceased the distribution date nor is deemed to have predeceased the distribution date under Section 2-702.

   (b) [Survivorship Required; Substitute Gift.] A future interest under the terms of a trust is contingent on the beneficiary's surviving the distribution date. If a beneficiary of a future interest under the terms of a trust fails to survive the distribution date, the following apply:

   (1) Except as provided in paragraph (4), if the future interest is not in the form of a class gift and the deceased beneficiary leaves surviving descendants, a substitute gift is created in the beneficiary's surviving descendants. They take by representation the property to which the beneficiary would have been entitled had the beneficiary survived the distribution date.

   (2) Except as provided in paragraph (4), if the future interest is in the form of a class gift, other than a future interest to "issue", "descendants", "heirs of the body", "heirs", "next of kin", "relatives", or "family", or a class described by language of similar import, a substitute gift is created in the surviving descendants of any deceased beneficiary. The property to which the beneficiaries would have been entitled had all of them survived the distribution date passes to the surviving beneficiaries and the surviving descendants of the deceased beneficiaries. Each surviving beneficiary takes the share to which he [or she] would have been entitled had the deceased beneficiaries survived the distribution date. Each deceased beneficiary's surviving descendants who are substituted for the deceased beneficiary take by representation the share to which the deceased beneficiary would have been entitled had the deceased beneficiary survived the distribution date. For the purposes of this paragraph, "deceased beneficiary" means a class member who failed to survive the distribution date and left one or more surviving descendants.

   (3) For the purposes of Section 2-701, words of survivorship attached to a future interest are not, in the absence of additional evidence, a sufficient indication of an intent contrary to the application of this section. Words of survivorship include words of survivorship that relate to the distribution date or to an earlier or an unspecified time, whether those words of survivorship are expressed in condition-precedent, condition-subsequent, or any other form.

   (4) If the governing instrument creates an alternative future interest with respect to a future interest for which a substitute gift is created by paragraph (1) or (2), the substitute gift is superseded by the alternative future interest if:

      (A) the alternative future interest is in the form of a class gift and one or more members of the class is entitled to take in possession or enjoyment; or

      (B) the alternative future interest is not in the form of a class gift and the expressly designated beneficiary of the alternative future interest is entitled to take in possession or enjoyment.

   (c) [More Than One Substitute Gift; Which One Takes.] If, under subsection (b), substitute gifts are created and not superseded with respect to more than one future interest and the future interests are alternative future interests, one to the other, the determination of which of the substitute gifts takes effect is resolved as follows:

   (1) Except as provided in paragraph (2), the property passes under the primary substitute gift.

   (2) If there is a younger-generation future interest, the property passes under the younger-generation substitute gift and not under the primary substitute gift.

   (3) In this subsection:

      (A) "Primary future interest" means the future interest that would have taken effect had all the deceased beneficiaries of the alternative future interests who left surviving descendants survived the distribution date.

      (B) "Primary substitute gift" means the substitute gift created with respect to the primary future interest.

      (C) "Younger-generation future interest" means a future interest that (i) is to a descendant of a beneficiary of the primary future interest, (ii) is an alternative future interest with respect to the primary future interest, (iii) is a future interest for which a substitute gift is created, and (iv) would have taken effect had all the deceased beneficiaries who left surviving descendants survived the distribution date except the deceased beneficiary or beneficiaries of the primary future interest.

(D) "Younger-generation substitute gift" means the substitute gift created with respect to the younger-generation future interest.

(d) [If No Other Takers, Property Passes Under Residuary Clause or to Transferor's Heirs.] Except as provided in subsection (e), if, after the application of subsections (b) and (c), there is no surviving taker, the property passes in the following order:

(1) if the trust was created in a nonresiduary devise in the transferor's will or in a codicil to the transferor's will, the property passes under the residuary clause in the transferor's will; for purposes of this section, the residuary clause is treated as creating a future interest under the terms of a trust.

(2) if no taker is produced by the application of paragraph (1), the property passes to the transferor's heirs under Section 2-711.

(e) [If No Other Takers and If Future Interest Created by Exercise of Power of Appointment.] If, after the application of subsections (b) and (c), there is no surviving taker and if the future interest was created by the exercise of a power of appointment:

(1) the property passes under the donor's gift-in-default clause, if any, which clause is treated as creating a future interest under the terms of a trust; and

(2) if no taker is produced by the application of paragraph (1), the property passes as provided in subsection (d). For purposes of subsection (d), "transferor" means the donor if the power was a nongeneral power and means the donee if the power was a general power.

Comment

Rationale. The objective of this section is to project the antilapse idea into the area of future interests, thus preventing disinheritance of a descending line that has one or more living members on the distribution date and preventing a share from passing down a descending line that has died out by the distribution date.

Scope. This section applies only to future interests under the terms of a trust. For shorthand purposes, references in this Comment to the term "future interest" refer to a future interest under the terms of a trust. The rationale for restricting this section to future interests under the terms of a trust is that legal life estates in land, followed by indefeasibly vested remainder interests, are still created in some localities, often with respect to farmland. In such cases, the legal life tenant and the person holding the remainder interest can, together, give good title in the sale of the land. If the antilapse idea were injected into this type of situation, the ability of the parties to sell the land would be impaired if not destroyed because the antilapse idea would, in effect, create a contingent substitute remainder interest in the present and future descendants of the person holding the remainder interest.

Structure. The structure of this section substantially parallels the structure of the regular antilapse statute, Section 2-603, and the antilapse-type statute relating to beneficiary designations, Section 2-706.

Common-law Background. At common law, conditions of survivorship are not implied with respect to future interests. The rule against implying a condition of survivorship applies whether the future interest is created in trust or otherwise and whether the future interest is or is not in the form of a class gift. The only exception, where a condition of survivorship is implied at common law, is in the case of a multiple-generation class gift. See Restatement (Third) of Property: Wills and Other Donative Transfers §§ 15.3, 15.4 (2008). For example, in the simple case of a trust, "income to husband, A, for life, remainder to daughter, B", B's interest is not defeated at common law if she predeceases A; B's interest would pass through her estate to her successors in interest (probably either her residuary legatees or heirs: see Waggoner, "The Uniform Probate Code Extends Antilapse-Type Protection to Poorly Drafted Trusts", 94 Mich. L. Rev. 2309, 2331-32 (1996)), who would become entitled to possession when A died. If any of B's successors in interest died before A, the interest held by that deceased successor in interest would likewise pass through his or her estate to his or her successors in interest; and so on. Thus, a benefit of adopting a statutory provision reversing the common-law rule and providing substitute takers is that it prevents cumbersome and costly distributions to and through the estates of deceased beneficiaries of future interests, who may have died long before the distribution date.

Subsection (b). Subsection (b) imposes a condition of survivorship on future interests to the distribution date—defined as the time when the future interest is to take effect in possession or enjoyment. The requirement of survivorship imposed by subsection (b) applies whether or not the deceased beneficiary leaves descendants who survive the distribution date and are takers of a substitute gift provided by subsections (b)(1) or (2). Imposing a condition of survivorship on a future interest when the deceased beneficiary did not leave descendants who survive the distribution date prevents a share from passing down a descending line that has died out by the distribution date. Imposing a condition of survivorship on a future interest when the deceased beneficiary did leave descendants who survive the distribution date, and providing a substitute gift to those descendants, prevents disinheritance of a descending line that has one or more living members on the distribution date.

The 120-hour Survivorship Period. In effect, the requirement of survival of the distribution date means survival of the 120-hour period following the distribution date. This is because, under Section 2-702(a), "an individual who is not established to have survived an event ... by 120 hours is deemed to have predeceased the event". As made clear by subsection (a)(8), for the purposes of Section 2-707, the "event" to which Section 2-702(a) relates is the distribution date.

Note that the "distribution date" need not occur at the beginning or end of a calendar day, but can occur at a time during the course of a day, such as the time of death of an income beneficiary.

References in Section 2-707 and in this Comment to survival of the distribution date should be understood as referring to survival of the distribution date by 120 hours.

Ambiguous Survivorship Language. Subsection (b) serves another purpose. It resolves a frequently litigated question arising from ambiguous language of survivorship, such as in a trust, "income to A for life, remainder in corpus to my surviving children". Although some case law interprets the word "surviving" as merely requiring survival of the testator

(e.g., Nass' Estate, 182 A. 401 (Pa.1936)), the predominant position at common law interprets "surviving" as requiring survival of the life tenant, A. Hawke v. Lodge, 77 A. 1090 (Del.Ch.1910); Restatement (Third) of Property: Wills and Other Donative Transfers §§ 15.3 cmt. f; 15.4 cmt. g (2008). The first sentence of subsection (b), in conjunction with paragraph (3), codifies the predominant common-law/Restatement position that survival relates to the distribution date.

The first sentence of subsection (b), in combination with paragraph (3), imposes a condition of survivorship to the distribution date (the time of possession or enjoyment) even when an express condition of survivorship to an earlier time has been imposed. Thus, in a trust like "income to A for life, remainder in corpus to B, but if B predeceases A, to B's children who survive B", the first sentence of subsection (b) combined with paragraph (3) requires B's children to survive (by 120 hours) the death of the income beneficiary, A.

Rule of Construction. Note that Section 2-707 is a rule of construction. It is qualified by the rule set forth in Section 2-701, and thus it yields to a finding of a contrary intention. Consequently, in trusts like "income to A for life, remainder in corpus to B whether or not B survives A", or "income to A for life, remainder in corpus to B or B's estate", this section would not apply and, should B predecease A, B's future interest would pass through B's estate to B's successors in interest, who would become entitled to possession or enjoyment at A's death.

Classification. Subsection (b) renders a future interest "contingent" on the beneficiary's survival of the distribution date. As a result, future interests are "nonvested" and subject to the Rule Against Perpetuities. To prevent an injustice from resulting because of this, the Uniform Statutory Rule Against Perpetuities, which has a wait-and-see element, is incorporated into the Code as Article II, Part 9.

Substitute Gifts. Section 2-707 not only imposes a condition of survivorship to the distribution date; like its antilapse counterparts, Sections 2-603 and 2-706, it provides substitute takers in cases of a beneficiary's failure to survive the distribution date.

The statutory substitute gift is divided among the devisee's descendants "by representation", a phrase defined in Section 2-709(b). A technical amendment adopted in 2008 added subsection (a)(4), defining the term "descendants".

Subsection (b)(1)—Future Interests Not in the Form of a Class Gift. Subsection (b)(1) applies to non-class gifts, such as the "income to A for life, remainder in corpus to B" trust discussed above. If B predeceases A, subsection (b)(1) creates a substitute gift with respect to B's future interest; the substitute gift is to B's descendants who survive A (by 120 hours).

Subsection (b)(2)—Class Gift Future Interests. Subsection (b)(2) applies to single-generation class gifts, such as in a trust "income to A for life, remainder in corpus to A's children". See Restatement (Third) of Property: Wills and Other Donative Transfers §§ 14.1, 14.2 (2008). Suppose that A had two children, X and Y. X predeceases A; Y survives A (by 120 hours). Subsection (b)(2) creates a substitute gift with respect to any of A's children who fail to survive A (by 120 hours) leaving descendants who survive A (by 120 hours). Thus, if X left descendants who survived A (by 120 hours), those descendants would take X's share; if X left no descendants who survived A (by 120 hours), Y would take it all.

Subsection (b)(2) does not apply to future interests to multiple-generation classes such as "issue", "descendants", "heirs of the body", "heirs", "next of kin", "distributees", "relatives", "family", or the like. The reason is that these types of class gifts have their own internal systems of representation, and so the substitute gift provided by subsection (b)(1) would be out of place with respect to these types of future interests. See Restatement (Third) of Property: Wills and Other Donative Transfers §§ 14.3, 14.4, 15.3 (2008). The first sentence of subsection (b) and subsection (d) do apply, however. For example, suppose a nonresiduary devise "to A for life, remainder to A's issue, by representation". If A leaves issue surviving him (by 120 hours), they take. But if A leaves no issue surviving him (by 120 hours), the testator's residuary devisees are the takers.

Subsection (b)(4). Subsection (b)(4), as clarified by technical amendment in 2008, provides that, if a governing instrument creates an alternative future interest with respect to a future interest for which a substitute gift is created by paragraph (1) or (2), the substitute gift is superseded by the alternative future interest if: (A) the alternative future interest is in the form of a class gift and one or more members of the class is entitled to take in possession or enjoyment; or (B) the alternative future interest is not in the form of a class gift and the expressly designated beneficiary of the alternative future interest is entitled to take in possession or enjoyment. Consider, for example, a trust under which the income is to be paid to A for

life, remainder in corpus to B if B survives A, but if not to C if C survives A. If B predeceases A, leaving descendants who survive A (by 120 hours), subsection (b)(1) creates a substitute gift to those descendants. But, if C survives A (by 120 hours), the alternative future interest in C supersedes the substitute gift to B's descendants. Upon A's death, the trust corpus passes to C.

Subsection (c). Subsection (c) is necessary because there can be cases in which subsections (b)(1) or (2) create substitute gifts with respect to two or more alternative future interests, and those substitute gifts are not superseded under the terms of subsection (b)(4). Subsection (c) provides the tie-breaking mechanism for such situations.

The initial step is to determine which of the alternative future interests would take effect had all the beneficiaries themselves survived the distribution date (by 120 hours). In subsection (c), this future interest is called the "primary future interest". Unless subsection (c)(2) applies, subsection (c)(1) provides that the property passes under substitute gift created with respect to the primary future interest. This substitute gift is called the "primary substitute gift". Thus, the property goes to the descendants of the beneficiary or beneficiaries of the primary future interest.

Subsection (c)(2) provides an exception to this rule. Under subsection (c)(2), the property does not pass under the primary substitute gift if there is a "younger-generation future interest"—defined as a future interest that (i) is to a descendant of a beneficiary of the primary future interest, (ii) is an alternative future interest with respect to the primary future interest, (iii) is a future interest for which a substitute gift is created, and (iv) would have taken effect had all the deceased beneficiaries who left surviving descendants survived the distribution date except the deceased beneficiary or beneficiaries of the primary future interest. If there is a younger-generation future interest, the property passes under the "younger-generation substitute gift"—defined as the substitute gift created with respect to the younger-generation future interest.

Subsection (d). Since it is possible that, after the application of subsections (b) and (c), there are no substitute gifts, a back-stop set of substitute takers is provided in subsection (d)—the transferor's residuary devisees or heirs. Note that the transferor's residuary clause is treated as creating a future interest and, as such, is subject to this section. Note also that the meaning of the back-stop gift to the transferor's heirs is governed by Section 2-711, under which the gift is to the transferor's heirs determined as if the transferor died when A died. Thus there will always be a set of substitute takers, even if it turns out to be the State. If the transferor's surviving spouse has remarried after the transferor's death but before A's death, he or she would not be a taker under this provision.

Examples. The application of Section 2-707 is illustrated by the following examples. Note that, in each example, the "distribution date" is the time of the income beneficiary's death. Assume, in each example, that an individual who is described as having "survived" the income beneficiary's death survived the income beneficiary's death by 120 hours or more.

Example 1. A nonresiduary devise in G's will created a trust, income to A for life, remainder in corpus to B if B survives A. G devised the residue of her estate to a charity. B predeceased A. At A's death, B's child, X, is living.

Solution: On A's death, the trust property goes to X, not to the charity. Because B's future interest is not in the form of a class gift, subsection (b)(1) applies, not subsection (b)(2). Subsection (b)(1) creates a substitute gift with respect to B's future interest; the substitute gift is to B's child, X. Under subsection (b)(3), the words of survivorship attached to B's future interest ("to B if B survives A") do not indicate an intent contrary to the creation of that substitute gift. Nor, under subsection (b)(4), is that substitute gift superseded by an alternative future interest because, as defined in subsection (a)(1), G's residuary clause does not create an alternative future interest. In the normal lapse situation, a residuary clause does not supersede the substitute gift created by the antilapse statute, and the same analysis applies to this situation as well.

Example 2. Same as Example 1, except that B left no descendants who survived A.

Solution: Subsection (b)(1) does not create a substitute gift with respect to B's future interest because B left no descendants who survived A. This brings subsection (d) into operation, under which the trust property passes to the charity under G's residuary clause.

Example 3. G created an irrevocable inter-vivos trust, income to A for life, remainder in corpus to B if B survives A. B predeceased A. At A's death, G and X, B's child, are living.

Solution: X takes the trust property. Because B's future interest is not in the form of a class gift, subsection (b)(1) applies, not subsection (b)(2). Subsection (b)(1) creates a substitute gift with respect to B's future interest; the substitute gift is to B's child, X. Under subsection (b)(3), the words of survivorship ("to B if B survives A") do not indicate an intent contrary to the creation of that substitute gift. Nor, under subsection (b)(4), is the substitute gift superseded by an alternative future interest; G's reversion is not an alternative future interest as defined in subsection (a)(1) because it was not expressly created.

Example 4. G created an irrevocable inter-vivos trust, income to A for life, remainder in corpus to B if B survives A; if not, to C. B predeceased A. At A's death, C and B's child are living.

Solution: C takes the trust property. Because B's future interest is not in the form of a class gift, subsection (b)(1) applies, not subsection (b)(2). Subsection (b)(1) creates a substitute gift with respect to B's future interest; the substitute gift is to B's child, X. Under subsection (b)(3), the words of survivorship ("to B if B survives A") do not indicate an intent contrary to the creation of that substitute gift. But, under subsection (b)(4), the substitute gift to B's child is superseded by the alternative future interest held by C because C, having survived A (by 120 hours), is entitled to take in possession or enjoyment.

Example 5. G created an irrevocable inter-vivos trust income to A for life, remainder in corpus to B, but if B predeceases A, to the person B appoints by will. B predeceased A. B's will exercised his power of appointment in favor of C. C survives A. B's child, X, also survives A.

Solution: B's appointee, C, takes the trust property, not B's child, X. Because B's future interest is not in the form of a class gift, subsection (b)(1) applies, not subsection (b)(2). Subsection (b)(1) creates a substitute gift with respect to B's future interest; the substitute gift is to B's child, X. Under subsection (b)(3), the words of survivorship ("to B if B survives A") do not indicate an intent contrary to the creation of that substitute gift. But, under subsection (b)(4), the substitute gift to B's child is superseded by the alternative future interest held by C because C, having survived A (by 120 hours), is entitled to take in possession or enjoyment. Because C's future interest was created in "a" governing instrument (B's will), it counts as an "alternative future interest".

Example 6. G creates an irrevocable inter-vivos trust, income to A for life, remainder in corpus to A's children who survive A; if none, to B. A's children predecease A, leaving descendants, X and Y, who survive A. B also survives A.

Solution: On A's death, the trust property goes to B, not to X and Y. Because the future interest in A's children is in the form of a class gift (see Restatement (Third) of Property: Wills and Other Donative Transfers § 13.1 (2008)), subsection (b)(2) applies, not subsection (b)(1). Subsection (b)(2) creates a substitute gift with respect to the future interest in A's children; the substitute gift is to the descendants of A's children, X and Y. Under subsection (b)(3), the words of survivorship ("to A's children who survive A") do not indicate an intent contrary to the creation of that substitute gift. But, under subsection (b)(4), the alternative future interest to B supersedes the substitute gift to the descendants of A's children because B survived A.

Alternative Facts: One of A's children, J, survives A; A's other child, K, predeceases A, leaving descendants, X and Y, who survive A. B also survives A.

Solution: J takes half the trust property and X and Y split the other half. Although there is an alternative future interest (in B) and although B did survive A, the alternative future interest was conditioned on none of A's children surviving A. Because that condition was not satisfied, the expressly designated beneficiary of that alternative future interest, B, is not entitled to take in possession or enjoyment. Thus, the alternative future interest in B does not supersede the substitute gift to K's descendants, X and Y.

Example 7. G created an irrevocable inter-vivos trust, income to A for life, remainder in corpus to B if B survives A; if not, to C. B and C predecease A. At A's death, B's child and C's child are living.

Solution: Subsection (b)(1) produces substitute gifts with respect to B's future interest and with respect to C's future interest. B's future interest and C's future interest are alternative future interests, one to the other. B's future interest is expressly conditioned on B's surviving A. C's future interest is conditioned on B's predeceasing A and C's surviving A. The condition that C survive A does not arise from express language in G's trust but from the first sentence of subsection (b); that sentence makes C's future interest contingent on C's surviving A. Thus,

because neither B nor C survived A, neither B nor C is entitled to take in possession or enjoyment. So, under subsection (b)(4), neither substitute gift, created with respect to the future interests in B and C, is superseded by an alternative future interest. Consequently, resort must be had to subsection (c) to break the tie to determine which substitute gift takes effect.

Under subsection (c), B is the beneficiary of the "primary future interest" because B would have been entitled to the trust property had both B and C survived A. Unless subsection (c)(2) applies, the trust property passes to B's child as the taker under the "primary substitute gift".

Subsection (c)(2) would only apply if C's future interest qualifies as a "younger-generation future interest". This depends upon whether C is a descendant of B, for C's future interest satisfies the other requirements necessary to make it a younger-generation future interest. If C was a descendant of B, the substitute gift to C's child would be a "younger-generation substitute gift" and would become effective instead of the "primary substitute gift" to B's descendants. But if C was not a descendant of B, the property would pass under the "primary substitute gift" to B's descendants.

Example 8. G created an irrevocable inter-vivos trust, income to A for life, remainder in corpus to A's children who survive A; if none, to B. All of A's children predecease A. X and Y, who are descendants of one or more of A's children, survive A. B predeceases A, leaving descendants, M and N, who survive A.

Solution: On A's death, the trust property passes to X and Y under the "primary substitute gift", unless B was a descendant of any of A's children.

Subsection (b)(2) produces substitute gifts with respect to A's children who predeceased A leaving descendants who survived A. Subsection (b)(1) creates a substitute gift with respect to B's future interest. A's children's future interest and B's future interest are alternative future interests, one to the other. A's children's future interest is expressly conditioned on surviving A. B's future interest is conditioned on none of A's children surviving A and on B's surviving A. The condition of survivorship as to B's future interest does not arise because of express language in G's trust but because of the first sentence of subsection (b); that sentence makes B's future interest contingent on B's surviving A. Thus, because none of A's children survived A, and because B did not survive A, none of A's children nor B is entitled to take in possession or enjoyment. So, under subsection (b)(4), neither substitute gift—i.e., neither the one created with respect to the future interest in A's children nor the one created with respect to the future interest in B—is superseded by an alternative future interest. Consequently, resort must be had to subsection (c) to break the tie to determine which substitute gift takes effect.

Under subsection (c), A's children are the beneficiaries of the "primary future interest" because they would have been entitled to the trust property had all of them and B survived A. Unless subsection (c)(2) applies, the trust property passes to X and Y as the takers under the "primary substitute gift". Subsection (c)(2) would only apply if B's future interest qualifies as a "younger-generation future interest". This depends upon whether B is a descendant of any of A's children, for B's future interest satisfies the other requirements necessary to make it a "younger-generation future interest". If B was a descendant of one of A's children, the substitute gift to B's children, M and N, would be a "younger-generation substitute gift" and would become effective instead of the "primary substitute gift" to X and Y. But if B was not a descendant of any of A's children, the property would pass under the "primary substitute gift" to X and Y.

Example 9. G's will devised property in trust, income to niece Lilly for life, corpus on Lilly's death to her children; should Lilly die without leaving children, the corpus shall be equally divided among my nephews and nieces then living, the child or children of nieces who may be deceased to take the share their mother would have been entitled to if living.

Lilly never had any children. G had 3 nephews and 2 nieces in addition to Lilly. All 3 nephews and both nieces predeceased Lilly. A child of one of the nephews survived Lilly. One of the nieces had 8 children, 7 of whom survived Lilly. The other niece had one child, who did not survive Lilly. (This example is based on the facts of Bomberger's Estate, 32 A.2d 729 (Pa.1943).)

Solution: The trust property goes to the 7 children of the nieces who survived Lilly. The substitute gifts

created by subsection (b)(2) to the nephew's son or to the nieces' children are superseded under subsection (b)(4) because there is an alternative future interest (the "child or children of nieces who may be deceased") and expressly designated beneficiaries of that alternative future interest (the 7 children of the nieces) are living at Lilly's death and are entitled to take in possession or enjoyment.

Example 10. G devised the residue of his estate in trust, income to his wife, W, for life, remainder in corpus to their children, John and Florence; if either John or Florence should predecease W, leaving descendants, such descendants shall take the share their parent would have taken if living.

G's son, John, survived W. G's daughter, Florence, predeceased W. Florence never had any children. Florence's husband survived W. (This example is based on the facts of Matter of Kroos, 99 N.E.2d 222 (N.Y.1951).)

Solution: John, of course, takes his half of the trust property. Because Florence left no descendants who survived W, subsection (b)(1) does not create a substitute gift with respect to Florence's future interest in her half. Subsection (d)(1) is inapplicable because G's trust was not created in a nonresiduary devise or in a codicil to G's will. Subsection (d)(2) therefore becomes applicable, under which Florence's half goes to G's heirs determined as if G died when W died, i.e., John. See Section 2-711.

Subsection (e). Subsection (e) was added in 1993 to clarify the passing of the property in cases in which the future interest is created by the exercise of a power of appointment.

Technical Amendments. Technical amendments in 2008 added a definition of "descendants" as used in subsections (b)(1) and (2) and clarified subsection (b)(4). The new definition resolves questions of status previously unanswered. The technical amendment of subsection (b)(4) makes that subsection easier to understand but does not change its substance.

Reference. This section is discussed in Halbach & Waggoner, "The UPC's New Survivorship and Antilapse Provisions", 55 Alb.L. Rev. 1091 (1992).

Historical Note. This Comment was revised in 1993 and 2008.

§ 2-708. Class Gifts to "Descendants", "Issue", or "Heirs of the Body"; Form of Distribution if None Specified. If a class gift in favor of "descendants", "issue", or "heirs of the body" does not specify the manner in which the property is to be distributed among the class members, the property is distributed among the class members who are living when the interest is to take effect in possession or enjoyment, in such shares as they would receive, under the applicable law of intestate succession, if the designated ancestor had then died intestate owning the subject matter of the class gift.

Comment

Purpose of New Section. This new section tracks Restatement (1st) of Property § 303(1), and does not accept the position taken in Restatement (Second) of Property, Donative Transfers § 28.2 (1988), under which a per stirpes form of distribution is presumed, regardless of the form of distribution used in the applicable law of intestate succession.

§ 2-709. Representation; Per Capita at Each Generation; Per Stirpes.

(a) [**Definitions.**] In this section:

(1) "Deceased child" or "deceased descendant" means a child or a descendant who either predeceased the distribution date or is deemed to have predeceased the distribution date under Section 2-702.

(2) "Distribution date", with respect to an interest, means the time when the interest is to take effect in possession or enjoyment. The distribution date need not occur at the beginning or end of a calendar day, but can occur at a time during the course of a day.

(3) "Surviving ancestor", "surviving child", or "surviving descendant" means an ancestor, a child, or a descendant who neither predeceased the distribution date nor is deemed to have predeceased the distribution date under Section 2-702.

(b) [**Representation; Per Capita at Each Generation.**] If an applicable statute or a governing instrument calls for property to be distributed "by representation" or "per capita at each generation", the property is divided into as many equal shares as there are (i) surviving descendants in the generation nearest to the designated ancestor which contains one or more surviving descendants (ii) and deceased descendants in the same generation who left surviving descendants, if any. Each surviving descendant in the nearest generation is allocated one share. The remaining shares, if any, are combined and then divided in the same manner among the surviving descendants of the deceased descendants as if the surviving descendants who were allocated a share and their surviving descendants had predeceased the distribution date.

(c) [**Per Stirpes.**] If a governing instrument calls for property to be distributed "per stirpes", the property is divided into as many equal shares as there are (i) surviving children of the designated ancestor and (ii) deceased children who left surviving descendants. Each surviving child, if any, is allocated one share. The share of each deceased child with surviving descendants is divided in the same manner, with subdivision repeating at each succeeding generation until the property is fully allocated among surviving descendants.

(d) [**Deceased Descendant With No Surviving Descendant Disregarded.**] For the purposes of subsections (b) and (c), an individual who is deceased and left no surviving descendant is disregarded, and an individual who leaves a surviving ancestor who is a descendant of the designated ancestor is not entitled to a share.

Comment

Purpose of New Section. This new section provides statutory definitions of "representation", "per capita at each generation", and "per stirpes." Subsection (b) applies to both private instruments and to provisions of applicable statutory law (such as Sections 2-603, 2-706, and 2-707) that call for property to be divided "by representation." The system of representation employed is the same as that which is adopted in Section 2-106 for intestate succession.

Subsection (c)'s definition of "per stirpes" accords with the predominant understanding of the term. In 1993, the phrase "if any" was added to subsection (c) to clarify the point that, under per stirpes, the initial division of the estate is made at the children generation even if no child survives the ancestor.

Historical Note. This Comment was revised in 1993. For the prior version, see 8 U.L.A. 154 (Supp.1992).

§ 2-710. Worthier-Title Doctrine Abolished.

§ 2-710. Worthier-Title Doctrine Abolished. The doctrine of worthier title is abolished as a rule of law and as a rule of construction. Language in a governing instrument describing the beneficiaries of a disposition as the transferor's "heirs", "heirs at law", "next of kin", "distributees", "relatives", or "family", or language of similar import, does not create or presumptively create a reversionary interest in the transferor.

Comment

Purpose of New Section. This new section abolishes the doctrine of worthier title as a rule of law and as a rule of construction.

Cross Reference. See Section 2-711 for a rule of construction concerning the meaning of a disposition to the heirs, etc., of a designated person.

§ 2-711. Interests in "Heirs" and Like.

§ 2-711. Interests in "Heirs" and Like. If an applicable statute or a governing instrument calls for a present or future distribution to or creates a present or future interest in a designated individual's "heirs", "heirs at law", "next of kin", "relatives", or "family", or language of similar import, the property passes to those persons, including the state, and in such shares as would succeed to the designated individual's intestate estate under the intestate succession law of the designated individual's domicile if the designated individual died when the disposition is to take effect in possession or enjoyment. If the designated individual's surviving spouse is living but is remarried at the time the disposition is to take effect in possession or enjoyment, the surviving spouse is not an heir of the designated individual.

Comment

Purpose of New Section. This new section provides a statutory definition of "heirs", etc., when contained in a donative disposition or a statute (such as Section 2-707(h)). This section was amended in 1993 to make it applicable to present as well as future interests in favor of heirs and the like. Application of this section to present interests codifies the position of the Restatement (Second) of Property § 29.4 cmts. c & g (1987).

Cross Reference. See Section 2-710, abolishing the doctrine of worthier title.

Historical Note. This Comment was revised in 1993. For the prior version, see 8 U.L.A. 155 (Supp.1992).

PART 8
GENERAL PROVISIONS CONCERNING PROBATE AND NONPROBATE TRANSFERS

General Comment

Part 8 contains five general provisions that cut across probate and nonprobate transfers. Part 8 previously contained a sixth provision, Section 2-801, which dealt with disclaimers. Section 2-801 was replaced in 2002 by the Uniform Disclaimer of Property Interests Act, which is incorporated into the Code as Part 11 of Article 2 (Sections 2-1101 to 2-1117). To avoid renumbering the other sections in this part, Section 2-801 is reserved for possible future use.

Section 2-802 deals with the effect of divorce and separation on the right to elect against a will, exempt property and allowances, and an intestate share.

Section 2-803 spells out the legal consequence of intentional and felonious killing on the right of the killer to take as heir and under wills and revocable inter-vivos transfers, such as revocable trusts and life-insurance beneficiary designations.

Section 2-804 deals with the consequences of a divorce on the right of the former spouse (and relatives of the former spouse) to take under wills and revocable inter-vivos transfers, such as revocable trusts and life-insurance beneficiary designations.

Sections 2-805 and 2-806, added in 2008, bring the reformation provisions in the Uniform Trust Code into the UPC.

Application to Pre-Existing Governing Instruments. Under Section 8-101(b), for decedents dying after the effective date of enactment, the provisions of this Code apply to governing instruments executed prior to as well as on or after the effective date of enactment. The Joint Editorial Board for the Uniform Probate Code has issued a statement concerning the constitutionality under the Contracts Clause of this feature of the Code. The statement, titled "Joint Editorial Board Statement Regarding the Constitutionality of Changes in Default Rules as Applied to Pre-Existing Documents",

can be found at 17 ACTEC Notes 184 (1991) or can be obtained from the Uniform Law Commission, www.uniformlaws.org.

Historical Note. This General Comment was revised in 1993, 2002, and 2008.

2002 Amendment Relating to Disclaimers. In 2002, the Code's former disclaimer provision (Section 2-801) was replaced by the Uniform Disclaimer of Property Interests Act, which is incorporated into the Code as Part 11 of Article 2 (Sections 2-1101 to 2-1117). The statutory references in this Comment to former Section 2-801 have been replaced by appropriate references to Part 11. Updating these statutory references has not changed the substance of this Comment.

§ 2-801. [Reserved.]

§ 2-802. Effect of Divorce, Annulment, and Decree of Separation.

(a) An individual who is divorced from the decedent or whose marriage to the decedent has been annulled is not a surviving spouse unless, by virtue of a subsequent marriage, he [or she] is married to the decedent at the time of death. A decree of separation that does not terminate the status of spouse is not a divorce for purposes of this section.

(b) For purposes of [Parts] 1, 2, 3, and 4 of this [article], and of Section 3-203, a surviving spouse does not include:

(1) an individual who obtains or consents to a final decree or judgment of divorce from the decedent or an annulment of their marriage, which decree or judgment is not recognized as valid in this state, unless subsequently they participate in a marriage ceremony purporting to marry each to the other or live together as spouses;

(2) an individual who, following an invalid decree or judgment of divorce or annulment obtained by the decedent, participates in a marriage ceremony with a third individual; or

(3) an individual who was a party to a valid proceeding concluded by an order purporting to terminate all marital property rights.

Comment

Clarifying Revision. The only substantive revision of this section is a clarifying revision of subsection (b)(2), making it clear that this subsection refers to an invalid decree of divorce or annulment.

Rationale. Although some existing statutes bar the surviving spouse for desertion or adultery, the present section requires some definitive legal act to bar the surviving spouse. Normally, this is divorce. Subsection (a) states an obvious proposition, but subsection (b) deals with the difficult problem of invalid divorce or annulment, which is particularly frequent as to foreign divorce decrees but may arise as to a local decree where there is some defect in jurisdiction; the basic principle underlying these provisions is estoppel against the surviving spouse.

Where there is only a legal separation, rather than a divorce, succession patterns are not affected; but if the separation is accompanied by a complete property settlement, this may operate under Section 2-213 as a waiver or renunciation of benefits under a prior will and by intestate succession.

Cross Reference. See Section 2-804 for similar provisions relating to the effect of divorce to revoke devises and other revocable provisions to a former spouse.

Historical Note. This Comment was revised in 1993. For the prior version, see 8 U.L.A. 159 (Supp. 1992). Technical amendments to subsection (a) and subsection (b)(1) were made in 2017 to replace "husband and wife" with "spouse" or "spouses."

§ 2-803. Effect of Homicide on Intestate Succession, Wills, Trusts, Joint Assets, Life Insurance, and Beneficiary Designations.

(a) [**Definitions.**] In this section:

(1) "Disposition or appointment of property" includes a transfer of an item of property or any other benefit to a beneficiary designated in a governing instrument.

(2) "Governing instrument" means a governing instrument executed by the decedent.

(3) "Revocable", with respect to a disposition, appointment, provision, or nomination, means one under which the decedent, at the time of or immediately before death, was alone empowered, by law or under the governing instrument, to cancel the designation in favor of the killer, whether or not the decedent was then empowered to designate himself [or herself] in place of his [or her] killer and or the decedent then had capacity to exercise the power.

(b) [**Forfeiture of Statutory Benefits.**] An individual who feloniously and intentionally kills the decedent forfeits all benefits under this [article] with respect to the decedent's estate, including an intestate share, an elective share, an omitted spouse's or child's share, a homestead allowance, exempt property, and a family allowance. If the decedent died intestate, the decedent's intestate estate passes as if the killer disclaimed his [or her] intestate share.

(c) [**Revocation of Benefits Under Governing Instruments.**] The felonious and intentional killing of the decedent:

(1) revokes any revocable (i) disposition or appointment of property made by the decedent to the killer in a governing instrument, (ii) provision in a governing instrument conferring a general or nongeneral power of appointment on the killer, and (iii) nomination of the killer in a governing instrument, nominating or appointing the killer to serve in any fiduciary or representative capacity, including a personal representative, executor, trustee, or agent; and

(2) severs the interests of the decedent and killer in property held by them at the time of the killing as joint tenants with the right of survivorship [or as community property with the right of survivorship], transforming the interests of the decedent and killer into equal tenancies in common.

(d) [**Effect of Severance.**] A severance under subsection (c)(2) does not affect any third-party interest in property acquired for value and in good faith reliance on an apparent title by survivorship in the killer unless a writing declaring the severance has been noted, registered, filed, or recorded in records appropriate to the kind and location of the property which are relied upon, in the ordinary course of transactions involving such property, as evidence of ownership.

(e) [**Effect of Revocation.**] Provisions of a governing instrument are given effect as if the killer disclaimed all provisions revoked by this section or, in the case of a revoked nomination in a fiduciary or representative capacity, as if the killer predeceased the decedent.

(f) [**Wrongful Acquisition of Property.**] A wrongful acquisition of property or interest by a killer not covered by this section must be treated in accordance with the principle that a killer cannot profit from his [or her] wrong.

(g) [**Felonious and Intentional Killing; How Determined.**] After all right to appeal has been exhausted, a judgment of conviction establishing criminal accountability for the felonious and intentional killing of the decedent conclusively establishes the convicted individual as the decedent's killer for purposes of this section. In the absence of a conviction, the court, upon the petition of an interested person, must determine whether, under the preponderance of evidence standard, the individual would be found criminally accountable for the felonious and intentional killing of the decedent. If the court determines that, under that standard, the individual would be found criminally accountable for the felonious and intentional killing of the decedent, the determination conclusively establishes that individual as the decedent's killer for purposes of this section.

(h) [Protection of Payors and Other Third Parties.]

(1) A payor or other third party is not liable for having made a payment or transferred an item of property or any other benefit to a beneficiary designated in a governing instrument affected by an intentional and felonious killing, or for having taken any other action in good faith reliance on the validity of the governing instrument, upon request and satisfactory proof of the decedent's death, before the payor or other third party received written notice of a claimed forfeiture or revocation under this section. A payor or other third party is liable for a payment made or other action taken after the payor or other third party received written notice of a claimed forfeiture or revocation under this section.

(2) Written notice of a claimed forfeiture or revocation under paragraph (1) must be mailed to the payor's or other third party's main office or home by registered or certified mail, return receipt requested, or served upon the payor or other third party in the same manner as a summons in a civil action. Upon receipt of written notice of a claimed forfeiture or revocation under this section, a payor or other third party may pay any amount owed or transfer or deposit any item of property held by it to or with the court having jurisdiction of the probate proceedings relating to the decedent's estate, or if no proceedings have been commenced, to or with the court having jurisdiction of probate proceedings relating to decedents' estates located in the county of the decedent's residence. The court shall hold the funds or item of property and, upon its determination under this section, shall order disbursement in accordance with the determination. Payments, transfers, or deposits made to or with the court discharge the payor or other third party from all claims for the value of amounts paid to or items of property transferred to or deposited with the court.

(i) [Protection of Bona Fide Purchasers; Personal Liability of Recipient.]

(1) A person who purchases property for value and without notice, or who receives a payment or other item of property in partial or full satisfaction of a legally enforceable obligation, is neither obligated under this section to return the payment, item of property, or benefit nor is liable under this section for the amount of the payment or the value of the item of property or benefit. But a person who, not for value, receives a payment, item of property, or any other benefit to which the person is not entitled under this section is obligated to return the payment, item of property, or benefit, or is personally liable for the amount of the payment or the value of the item of property or benefit, to the person who is entitled to it under this section.

(2) If this section or any part of this section is preempted by federal law with respect to a payment, an item of property, or any other benefit covered by this section, a person who, not for value, receives the payment, item of property, or any other benefit to which the person is not entitled under this section is obligated to return the payment, item of property, or benefit, or is personally liable for the amount of the payment or the value of the item of property or benefit, to the person who would have been entitled to it were this section or part of this section not preempted.

Comment

Purpose and Scope of Revisions. This section is substantially revised. Although the revised version does make a few substantive changes in certain subsidiary rules (such as the treatment of multiple party accounts, etc.), it does not alter the main thrust of the pre-1990 version. The major change is that the revised version is more comprehensive than the pre-1990 version. The structure of the section is also changed so that it substantially parallels the structure of Section 2-804, which deals with the effect of divorce on revocable benefits to the former spouse.

The pre-1990 version of this section was bracketed to indicate that it may be omitted by an enacting state without difficulty. The revised version omits the brackets because the Joint Editorial Board/Article II Drafting Committee believes that uniformity is desirable on the question.

As in the pre-1990 version, this section is confined to felonious and intentional killing and excludes the accidental manslaughter killing. Subsection (g) leaves no doubt that, for purposes of this section, a killing can be "felonious and intentional", whether or not the killer has actually been convicted in a criminal prosecution. Under subsection (g), after all right to appeal has been exhausted, a judgment of conviction establishing criminal accountability for the felonious and intentional killing of the decedent conclusively establishes the convicted individual as the decedent's killer for purposes of this section. Acquittal, however, does not preclude the acquitted individual from being regarded as the decedent's killer for purposes of this section. This is because different considerations as well as a different burden of proof enter into the finding of criminal accountability in the criminal prosecution. Hence it is possible that the defendant on a murder charge may be found not guilty and acquitted, but if the same person claims as an heir, devisee, or beneficiary of a revocable beneficiary designation, etc. of the decedent, the probate court, upon the petition of an interested person, may find that, under a preponderance of the evidence standard, he or she would be found criminally accountable for the felonious and intentional killing of the decedent and thus be barred under this section from sharing in the affected property. In fact, in many of the cases arising under this section there may be no criminal prosecution because the killer has committed suicide.

It is now well accepted that the matter dealt with is not exclusively criminal in nature but is also a proper matter for probate courts. The concept that a wrongdoer may not profit by his or her own wrong is a civil concept, and the probate court is the proper forum to determine the effect of killing on succession to the decedent's property covered by this section. There are numerous situations where the same conduct gives rise to both criminal and civil consequences. A killing may result in criminal prosecution for murder and civil litigation by the decedent's family under wrongful death statutes. Another analogy exists in the tax field, where a taxpayer may be acquitted of tax fraud in a criminal prosecution but found to have committed the fraud in a civil proceeding.

The phrases "criminal accountability" and "criminally accountable" for the felonious and intentional killing of the decedent not only include criminal accountability as an actor or direct perpetrator, but also as an accomplice or co-conspirator.

Unlike the pre-1990 version, the revised version contains a subsection protecting payors who pay before receiving written notice of a claimed forfeiture or revocation under this section, and imposing personal liability on the recipient or killer.

The pre-1990 version's provision on the severance of joint tenancies and tenancies by the entirety also extended to "joint and multiple party accounts in banks, savings and loan associations, credit unions and other institutions, and any other form of co-ownership with survivorship incidents." Under subsection (c)(2) of the revised version, the severance applies only to "property held by [the decedent and killer] as joint tenants with the right of survivorship [or as community property with the right of survivorship]." The terms "joint tenants with the right of survivorship" and "community property with the right of survivorship" are defined in Section 1-201. That definition includes tenancies by the entirety, but excludes "forms of co-ownership registration in which the underlying ownership of each party is in proportion to that party's contribution." Under subsection (c)(1), any portion of the decedent's contribution to the co-ownership registration running in favor of the killer would be treated as a revocable and revoked disposition.

Subsection (e) was amended in 1993 to make it clear that the antilapse statute applies in appropriate cases in which the killer is treated as having disclaimed.

Federal Preemption of State Law. See the Comment to Section 2-804 for a discussion of federal preemption.

Cross References. See Section 1-201 for definitions of "beneficiary designated in a governing instrument", "governing instrument", "joint tenants with the right of survivorship", "community property with the right of survivorship", and "payor."

1997 Technical Amendment. By technical amendment effective July 31, 1997, the word "equal" was added to subsection (c)(2) to make it clear that the effect of severing the interests of the decedent and killer is to transform their interests into equal tenancies in common, without regard to the percentage of consideration furnished by either. Although this was the intent of this subsection, the court in Estate of Garland, 928 P.2d 928 (Mont. 1996), misconstrued the original language and held that once the interests were severed and transformed into tenancies in common, the shares "depend on the decedent's and the [killer's] individual contributions to the acquisition and maintenance of the property." This percentage-of-consideration rule is inconsistent with both the general principle of Section 2-803 and with the statutory language. Section 2-803 is based on the principle that while the killer should not gain from the killing, neither should the killer be deprived of the killer's own property. In the case of a joint tenancy, neither the killer nor the victim could by a lawful, unilateral act have severed and become owner of more than his or her fractional interest. This is true even if one joint tenant provided more consideration than another joint tenant. Once property is titled in joint tenancy, any excess consideration provided by one joint tenant constitutes an irrevocable gift to the other joint tenant or tenants. The original statutory language established a fractional-interest rule by providing that the interests that are transformed into tenancies in common are "the [severed] interests of the decedent and killer." This statutory language, as revised, confirms this strict fractioning.

Historical Note. This Comment was revised in 1993, 1997, and 2014.

Former (Pre-1990) Version

[§ 2-803. [Effect of Homicide on Intestate Succession, Wills, Joint Assets, Life Insurance and Beneficiary Designations.]

(a) A surviving spouse, heir or devisee who feloniously and intentionally kills the decedent is not entitled to any benefits under the will or under this Article, and the estate of decedent passes as if the killer had predeceased the decedent. Property appointed by the will of the decedent to or for the benefit of the killer passes as if the killer had predeceased the decedent.

(b) Any joint tenant who feloniously and intentionally kills another joint tenant thereby effects a severance of the interest of the decedent so that the share of the decedent passes as his property and the killer has no rights by survivorship. This provision applies to joint tenancies [and tenancies by the entirety] in real and personal property, joint and multiple-party accounts in banks, savings and loan associations, credit unions and other institutions, and any other form of co-ownership with survivorship incidents.

(c) A named beneficiary of a bond, life insurance policy, or other contractual arrangement who feloniously and intentionally kills the principal obligee or the person upon whose life the policy is issued is not entitled to any benefit under the bond, policy or other contractual arrangement, and it becomes payable as though the killer had predeceased the decedent.

(d) Any other acquisition of property or interest by the killer shall be treated in accordance with the principles of this section.

(e) A final judgment of conviction of felonious and intentional killing is conclusive for purposes of this section. In the absence of a conviction of felonious and intentional killing the Court may determine by a preponderance of evidence whether the killing was felonious and intentional for purposes of this section.

(f) This section does not affect the rights of any person who, before rights under this section have been adjudicated, purchases from the killer for value and without notice property which the killer would have acquired except for this section, but the killer is liable for the amount of the proceeds or the value of the property. Any insurance company, bank, or other obligor making payment according to the terms of its policy or obligation is not liable by reason of this section unless prior to payment it has received at its home office or principal address written notice of a claim under this section.]

Restatement (Third) of Property: Wills and Other Donative Transfers (2003)

§ 8.4 Homicide–The Slayer Rule

(a) A slayer is denied any right to benefit from the wrong. For purposes of this section, a slayer is a person who, without legal excuse or justification, is responsible for the felonious and intentional killing of another.

(b) Whether or not a person is a slayer is determined in a civil proceeding under the preponderance of the evidence standard rather than beyond a reasonable doubt. For purposes of the civil proceeding, however, a final judgment of conviction for the felonious and intentional killing of the decedent in a criminal proceeding conclusively establishes the convicted person as the decedent's slayer.

§ 2-804. Revocation of Probate and Nonprobate Transfers by Divorce; No Revocation by Other Changes of Circumstances.

(a) **[Definitions.]** In this section:

(1) "Disposition or appointment of property" includes a transfer of an item of property or any other benefit to a beneficiary designated in a governing instrument.

(2) "Divorce or annulment" means any divorce or annulment, or any dissolution or declaration of invalidity of a marriage, that would exclude the spouse as a surviving spouse within the meaning of Section 2-802. A decree of separation that does not terminate the status of spouse is not a divorce for purposes of this section.

(3) "Divorced individual" includes an individual whose marriage has been annulled.

(4) "Governing instrument" means a governing instrument executed by the divorced individual before the divorce or annulment of his [or her] marriage to his [or her] former spouse.

(5) "Relative of the divorced individual's former spouse" means an individual who is related to the divorced individual's former spouse by blood, adoption, or affinity and who, after the divorce or annulment, is not related to the divorced individual by blood, adoption, or affinity.

(6) "Revocable", with respect to a disposition, appointment, provision, or nomination, means one under which the divorced individual, at the time of the divorce or annulment, was alone empowered, by law or under the governing instrument, to cancel the designation in favor of his [or her] former spouse or former spouse's relative, whether or not the divorced individual was then empowered to designate himself [or herself] in place of his [or her] former spouse or in place of his [or her] former spouse's relative and whether or not the divorced individual then had the capacity to exercise the power.

(b) **[Revocation Upon Divorce.]** Except as provided by the express terms of a governing instrument, a court order, or a contract relating to the division of the marital estate made between the divorced individuals before or after the marriage, divorce, or annulment, the divorce or annulment of a marriage:

(1) revokes any revocable

(A) disposition or appointment of property made by a divorced individual to his [or her] former spouse in a governing instrument and any disposition or appointment created by law or in a governing instrument to a relative of the divorced individual's former spouse,

(B) provision in a governing instrument conferring a general or nongeneral power of appointment on the divorced individual's former spouse or on a relative of the divorced individual's former spouse, and

(C) nomination in a governing instrument, nominating a divorced individual's former spouse or a relative of the divorced individual's former spouse to serve in any fiduciary or representative capacity, including a personal representative, executor, trustee, conservator, agent, or guardian; and

(2) severs the interests of the former spouses in property held by them at the time of the divorce or annulment as joint tenants with the right of survivorship [or as community property with the right of survivorship], transforming the interests of the former spouses into equal tenancies in common.

(c) **[Effect of Severance.]** A severance under subsection (b)(2) does not affect any third-party interest in property acquired for value and in good faith reliance on an apparent title by survivorship in the survivor of the former spouses unless a writing declaring the severance has been noted, registered, filed, or recorded in records appropriate to the kind and location of the property which are relied upon, in the ordinary course of transactions involving such property, as evidence of ownership.

(d) **[Effect of Revocation.]** Provisions of a governing instrument are given effect as if the former spouse and relatives of the former spouse disclaimed all provisions revoked by this section or, in the case of a revoked nomination in a fiduciary or representative capacity, as if the former spouse and relatives of the former spouse died immediately before the divorce or annulment.

(e) [Revival if Divorce Nullified.] Provisions revoked solely by this section are revived by the divorced individual's remarriage to the former spouse or by a nullification of the divorce or annulment.

(f) [No Revocation for Other Change of Circumstances.] No change of circumstances other than as described in this section and in Section 2-803 effects a revocation.

(g) [Protection of Payors and Other Third Parties.]

(1) A payor or other third party is not liable for having made a payment or transferred an item of property or any other benefit to a beneficiary designated in a governing instrument affected by a divorce, annulment, or remarriage, or for having taken any other action in good faith reliance on the validity of the governing instrument, before the payor or other third party received written notice of the divorce, annulment, or remarriage. A payor or other third party is liable for a payment made or other action taken after the payor or other third party received written notice of a claimed forfeiture or revocation under this section.

(2) Written notice of the divorce, annulment, or remarriage under subsection (g)(1) must be mailed to the payor's or other third party's main office or home by registered or certified mail, return receipt requested, or served upon the payor or other third party in the same manner as a summons in a civil action. Upon receipt of written notice of the divorce, annulment, or remarriage, a payor or other third party may pay any amount owed or transfer or deposit any item of property held by it to or with the court having jurisdiction of the probate proceedings relating to the decedent's estate or, if no proceedings have been commenced, to or with the court having jurisdiction of probate proceedings relating to decedents' estates located in the county of the decedent's residence. The court shall hold the funds or item of property and, upon its determination under this section, shall order disbursement or transfer in accordance with the determination. Payments, transfers, or deposits made to or with the court discharge the payor or other third party from all claims for the value of amounts paid to or items of property transferred to or deposited with the court.

(h) [Protection of Bona Fide Purchasers; Personal Liability of Recipient.]

(1) A person who purchases property from a former spouse, relative of a former spouse, or any other person for value and without notice, or who receives from a former spouse, relative of a former spouse, or any other person a payment or other item of property in partial or full satisfaction of a legally enforceable obligation, is neither obligated under this section to return the payment, item of property, or benefit nor is liable under this section for the amount of the payment or the value of the item of property or benefit. But a former spouse, relative of a former spouse, or other person who, not for value, received a payment, item of property, or any other benefit to which that person is not entitled under this section is obligated to return the payment, item of property, or benefit, or is personally liable for the amount of the payment or the value of the item of property or benefit, to the person who is entitled to it under this section.

(2) If this section or any part of this section is preempted by federal law with respect to a payment, an item of property, or any other benefit covered by this section, a former spouse, relative of the former spouse, or any other person who, not for value, received a payment, item of property, or any other benefit to which that person is not entitled under this section is obligated to return that payment, item of property, or benefit, or is personally liable for the amount of the payment or the value of the item of property or benefit, to the person who would have been entitled to it were this section or part of this section not preempted.

Comment

Purpose and Scope of Revision. The revisions of this section, pre-1990 Section 2-508, intend to unify the law of probate and nonprobate transfers. As originally promulgated, pre-1990 Section 2-508 revoked a predivorce devise to the testator's former spouse. The revisions expand the section to cover "will substitutes" such as revocable inter-vivos trusts, life-insurance and retirement-plan beneficiary designations, transfer-on-death accounts, and other revocable dispositions to the former spouse that the divorced individual established before the divorce (or annulment). As revised, this section also effects a severance of the interests of the former spouses in property that they held at the time of the divorce (or annulment) as joint tenants with the right of survivorship; their co-ownership interests become tenancies in common.

As revised, this section is the most comprehensive provision of its kind, but many states have enacted piecemeal legislation tending in the same direction. For example, Michigan and Ohio have statutes transforming spousal joint tenancies in land into tenancies in common upon the spouses' divorce. Mich.Comp.Laws Ann. § 552.102; Ohio Rev.Code Ann. § 5302.20(c)(5). Ohio, Oklahoma, and Tennessee have recently enacted legislation effecting a revocation of provisions for the settlor's former spouse in revocable inter-vivos trusts. Ohio Rev.Code Ann. § 1339.62; Okla.Stat.Ann. tit. 60, § 175; Tenn.Code Ann. § 35-50-5115 (applies to revocable and irrevocable inter-vivos trusts). Statutes in Michigan, Ohio, Oklahoma, and Texas relate to the consequence of divorce on life-insurance and retirement-plan beneficiary designations. Mich.Comp.Laws Ann. § 552.101; Ohio Rev.Code Ann. § 1339.63; Okla.Stat.Ann. tit. 15, § 178; Tex.Fam.Code §§ 3.632-.633.

The courts have also come under increasing pressure to use statutory construction techniques to extend statutes like the pre-1990 version of Section 2-508 to various will substitutes. In Clymer v. Mayo, 473 N.E.2d 1084 (Mass.1985), the Massachusetts court held the statute applicable to a revocable inter-vivos trust, but restricted its "holding to the particular facts of this case-specifically the existence of a revocable pour-over trust funded entirely at the time of the decedent's death." 473 N.E.2d at 1093. The trust in that case was an unfunded life-insurance trust; the life insurance was employer-paid life insurance. In Miller v. First Nat'l Bank & Tr. Co., 637 P.2d 75 (Okla.1981), the court also held such a statute to be applicable to an unfunded life-insurance trust. The testator's will devised the residue of his estate to the trustee of the life-insurance trust. Despite the absence of meaningful evidence of intent to incorporate, the court held that the pour-over devise incorporated the life-insurance trust into the will be reference, and thus was able to apply the revocation-upon-divorce statute. In Equitable Life Assurance Society v. Stitzel, 1 Pa.Fiduc.2d 316 (C.P.1981), however, the court held a statute similar to the pre-1990 version of Section 2-508 to be inapplicable to effect a revocation of a life-insurance beneficiary designation of the former spouse.

Revoking Benefits of the Former Spouse's Relatives. In several cases, including Clymer v. Mayo, 473 N.E.2d 1084 (Mass.1985), and Estate of Coffed, 387 N.E.2d 1209 (N.Y.1979), the result of treating the former spouse as if he or she predeceased the testator was that a gift in the governing instrument was triggered in favor of relatives of the former spouse who, after the divorce, were no longer relatives of the testator. In the Massachusetts case, the former spouse's nieces and nephews ended up with an interest in the property. In the New York case, the winners included the former spouse's child by a prior marriage. For other cases to the same effect, see Porter v. Porter, 286 N.W.2d 649 (Iowa 1979); Bloom v. Selfon, 555 A.2d 75 (Pa.1989); Estate of Graef, 368 N.W.2d 633 (Wis.1985). Given that, during divorce process or in the aftermath of the divorce, the former spouse's relatives are likely to side with the former spouse, breaking down or weakening any former ties that may previously have developed between the transferor and the former spouse's relatives, seldom would the transferor have favored such a result. This section, therefore, also revokes these gifts.

Consequence of Revocation. The effect of revocation by this section is that the provisions of the governing instrument are given effect as if the divorced individual's former spouse (and relatives of the former spouse) disclaimed all provisions revoked by this section (see Section 2-1106 for the effect of a disclaimer). In the case of a revoked nomination in a fiduciary or representative capacity, the provisions of the governing instrument are given effect as if the former spouse and relatives of the former spouse died immediately before the divorce or annulment. If the divorced individual (or relative of the divorced individual) is the donee of an unexercised power of appointment that is revoked by this section, the gift-in-default clause, if any, is to take effect, to the extent that the gift-in-default clause is not itself revoked by this section.

Federal Preemption of State Law. The Employee Retirement Income Security Act of 1974 (ERISA) federalizes pension and employee benefit law. Section 514(a) of ERISA, 29 U.S.C. § 1144(a), provides that the provisions of Titles I and IV of ERISA "shall supersede any and all State laws insofar as they may now or hereafter relate to any employee benefit plan" governed by ERISA.

ERISA's preemption clause is extraordinarily broad. ERISA Section 514(a) does not merely preempt state laws that conflict with specific provisions in ERISA. Rather, it preempts "any and all State laws" insofar as they "relate to" any ERISA-governed employee benefit plan.

A complex body of case law has arisen concerning the question of whether to apply ERISA Section 514(a) to preempt state law in circumstances in which ERISA supplies no substantive regulation. For example, until 1984, ERISA contained no authorization for the enforcement of state domestic relations decrees against pension accounts, but the federal courts were virtually unanimous in refusing to apply ERISA preemption against such state decrees. See, e.g., American Telephone & Telegraph Co. v. Merry, 592 F.2d 118 (2d Cir.1979). The Retirement Equity Act of 1984 amended ERISA to add Sections 206(d)(3) and 514(b)(7), confirming the judicially created exception for state domestic relations decrees.

The federal courts have been less willing, unfortunately, to defer to state probate law. In Egelhoff v. Egelhoff, 532 U.S. 141 (2001), the U.S. Supreme Court held that the State of Washington's revocation-on-divorce statute (which, like Section 2-804, extends the revocation-on-divorce rule of probate law into the realm of nonprobate transfers) was preempted with respect to ERISA-governed life insurance policies and pension plans. The decision left open the possibility that such assets might remain governed by slayer statutes (such as Section 2-803). Id. at 152. In Mendez-Bellido v. Board of Trustees, 709 F.Supp. 329 (E.D.N.Y.1989), the court applied the New York "slayer-rule" against an ERISA preemption claim, reasoning that "state laws prohibiting murderers from receiving death benefits are relatively uniform ... [and therefore] there is little threat of creating a 'patchwork scheme of regulations'" that ERISA sought to avoid. Id. at 332. For a post-Egelhoff case applying state slayer law to an ERISA-governed insurance plan, see First National Bank & Trust Co. of Mountain Home v. Stonebridge Life Ins. Co., 619 F.3d 951 (8th Cir. 2010).

It is to be hoped that the federal courts will show sensitivity to the primary role of state law in the field of probate and nonprobate transfers. To the extent that the federal courts think themselves unable to craft exceptions to ERISA's preemption language, it

is open to them to apply state law concepts as federal common law. Because the Uniform Probate Code contemplates multistate applicability, it is well suited to be the model for federal common law absorption. See, e.g., Gallanis, "ERISA and the Law of Succession," 65 Ohio St. L. J. 185, 196-197 (2004); Lebolt, "Making the Best of Egelhoff: Federal Common Law for ERISA-Preempted Beneficiary Designations," 28 J. Pension Planning & Compliance 29 (Fall 2002).

Another avenue of reconciliation between ERISA preemption and the primacy of state law in this field is envisioned in subsection (h)(2) of this section. It imposes a personal liability for pension payments that pass to a former spouse or relative of a former spouse. This provision respects ERISA's concern that federal law govern the administration of the plan, while still preventing unjust enrichment that would result if an unintended beneficiary were to receive the pension benefits. Federal law has no interest in working a broader disruption of state probate and nonprobate transfer law than is required in the interest of smooth administration of pension and employee benefit plans.

Regrettably, the U.S. Supreme Court decided in Hillman v. Maretta, 133 S.Ct. 1943 (2013), that a Virginia statute essentially equivalent to subsection (h)(2) of this section was pre-empted by the federal law known as FEGLIA (the Federal Employees' Group Life Insurance Act of 1954), 5 U.S.C. § 8701 et seq. FEGLIA provides that "[t]he provisions of any contract under [FEGLIA] which relate to the nature or extent of coverage or benefits (including payments with respect to benefits) shall supersede and preempt any law of any State ... which relates to group life insurance to the extent that the law or regulation is inconsistent with the contractual provisions." 5 U.S.C. § 8709(d)(1). The Court's decision in Hillman has many unfortunate consequences. First, the decision frustrates the dominant purpose of wealth transfer law, which is to implement the transferor's intention. The result in Hillman, that the decedent's ex-spouse remained entitled to the proceeds of the decedent's life insurance policy purchased through a program established by FEGLIA, frustrates the decedent's intention. Second, the Hillman decision ignores the decades-long trend of unifying the law governing probate and nonprobate transfers. The revocation-on-divorce rule has long been a part of probate law (see, e.g., pre-1990 Section 2-508). In 1990, this section extended the rule of revocation on divorce to nonprobate transfers. Third, the decision in Hillman fosters a division between state- and federally-regulated nonprobate mechanisms. If the decedent in Hillman had purchased a life insurance policy individually, rather than through the FEGLIA program, the policy would have been governed by the Virginia counterpart of this section. For critiques of the Hillman decision, see Langbein, "Destructive Federal Preemption of State Wealth Transfer Law in Beneficiary Designation Cases: Hillman Doubles Down on Egelhoff," 67 Vand. L. Rev. 1665 (2014); Waggoner, "The Creeping Federalization of Wealth-Transfer Law," 67 Vand. L. Rev. 1635 (2014).

Cross References. See Section 1-201 for definitions of "beneficiary designated in a governing instrument", "governing instrument", "joint tenants with the right of survivorship", "community property with the right of survivorship", and "payor."

References. The theory of this section is discussed in Waggoner, "Spousal Rights in Our Multiple-Marriage Society: The Revised Uniform Probate Code", 26 Real Prop. Prob. & Tr. J. 683, 689-701

(1992). See also Langbein, "The Nonprobate Revolution and the Future of the Law of Succession", 97 Harv.L. Rev. 1108 (1984).

1997 Technical Amendment. For an explanation of the 1997 technical amendment, which added the word "equal" to subsection (b)(2), see the Comment to Section 2-803.

2002 Amendment Relating to Disclaimers. In 2002, the Code's former disclaimer provision (Section 2-801) was replaced by the Uniform Disclaimer of Property Interests Act, which is incorporated into the Code as Part 11 of Article II (Sections 2-1101 to 2-1117). The statutory references in this Comment to former Section 2-801 have been replaced by appropriate references to Part 11. Updating these statutory references has not changed the substance of this Comment.

Historical Note. The above Comment was revised in 1993, 2002, and 2014. A technical amendment to subsection (a)(2) was made in 2017 to replace "husband and wife" with "spouse."

Former (Pre-1990) Version

§ 2-508. [Revocation by Divorce; No Revocation by Other Changes of Circumstances.] If after executing a will the testator is divorced or his marriage annulled, the divorce or annulment revokes any disposition or appointment of property made by the will to the former spouse, any provision conferring a general or special power of appointment on the former spouse, and any nomination of the former spouse as executor, trustee, conservator, or guardian, unless the will expressly provides otherwise. Property prevented from passing to a former spouse because of revocation by divorce or annulment passes as if the former spouse failed to survive the decedent, and other provisions conferring some power or office on the former spouse are interpreted as if the spouse failed to survive the decedent. If provisions are revoked solely by this section, they are revived by testator's remarriage to the former spouse. For purposes of this section, divorce or annulment means any divorce or annulment which would exclude the spouse as a surviving spouse within the meaning of Section 2-802(b). A decree of separation which does not terminate the status of husband and wife is not a divorce for purposes of this section. No change of circumstances other than as described in this section revokes a will.

---

§ 2-805. Reformation to Correct Mistakes. The court may reform the terms of a governing instrument, even if unambiguous, to conform the terms to the transferor's intention if it is proved by clear and convincing evidence what the transferor's intention was and that the terms of the governing instrument were affected by a mistake of fact or law, whether in expression or inducement.

Comment

Added in 2008, Section 2-805 is based on Section 415 of the Uniform Trust Code, which in turn was based on Section 12.1 of the Restatement (Third) of Property: Wills and Other Donative Transfers (2003).

Section 2-805 is broader in scope than Section 415 of the Uniform Trust Code because Section 2-805 applies but is not limited to trusts.

Section 12.1, and hence Section 2-805, is explained and illustrated in the Comments to Section 12.1 of

the Restatement and also, in the case of a trust, in the Comment to Section 415 of the Uniform Trust Code.

2010 Amendment. This section was revised by technical amendment in 2010. The amendment better conforms the language of the section to the language of the Restatement (Third) of Property provision on which the section is based.

Restatement (Third) of Property: Wills and Other Donative Transfers (2003)

§ 12.1 Reforming Donative Documents to Correct Mistakes. A donative document, though unambiguous, may be reformed to conform the text to the donor's intention if it is established by clear and convincing evidence (1) that a mistake of fact or law, whether in expression or inducement, affected specific terms of the document; and (2) what the donor's intention was. In determining whether these elements have been established by clear and convincing evidence, direct evidence of intention contradicting the plain meaning of the text as well as other evidence of intention may be considered.

Comment:

a. Scope note. This section only addresses reformation as a method of correcting mistakes in donative documents. It does not address the full range of equitable remedies for correcting mistakes in donative transfers. For example, this section does not address situations such as those in which a donor is entitled to restitution or rescission in equity because the donor was induced by a mistake of fact or law to make a gift that the donor would not have made if the donor had known the truth. Nor does this section address denial of probate or partial denial of probate as a possible remedy for correcting mistakes in wills in appropriate circumstances.

b. Rationale. When a donative document is unambiguous, evidence suggesting that the terms of the document vary from intention is inherently suspect but possibly correct. The law deals with situations of inherently suspicious but possibly correct evidence in either of two ways. One is to exclude the evidence altogether, in effect denying a remedy in cases in which the evidence is genuine and persuasive. The other is to consider the evidence, but guard against giving effect to fraudulent or mistaken evidence by imposing an above-normal standard of proof. In choosing between exclusion and high-safeguard allowance of extrinsic evidence, this Restatement adopts the latter. Only high-safeguard allowance of extrinsic evidence achieves the primary objective of giving effect to the donor's intention. To this end, the full range of direct and circumstantial evidence relevant to the donor's intention described in § 10.2 may be considered in a reformation action.

Equity rests the rationale for reformation on two related grounds: giving effect to the donor's intention and preventing unjust enrichment. The claim of an unintended taker is an unjust claim. Using the equitable remedy of reformation to correct a mistake is necessary to prevent unjustly enriching the mistaken beneficiary at the expense of the intended beneficiary.

c. Historical background. The reformation doctrine for donative documents other than wills is well established. Equity has long recognized that deeds of gift, inter-vivos trusts, life-insurance contracts, and other donative documents can be reformed if it is established by clear and convincing evidence: (1) that a mistake of fact or law, whether in expression or inducement, affected specific terms of the document; and (2) what the donor's intention was. Reformation of these documents is granted, on an adequate showing of proof, even after the death of the donor.

This section unifies the law of wills and will substitutes by applying to wills the standards that govern other donative documents. Until recently, courts have not allowed reformation of wills. The denial of a reformation remedy for wills was predicated on observance of the Statute of Wills, which requires that wills be executed in accordance with certain formalities. See § 3.1. Reforming a will, it was feared, would often require inserting language that was not executed in accordance with the statutory formalities. Section 11.2, however, authorizes inserting language to resolve *ambiguities* in accordance with the donor's intention. As noted in § 11.2, Comment c, modern authority is moving away from insistence on strict compliance with the statutory formalities on the question of initial execution of wills. Section § 3.3 adopts the position a harmless error in executing a will may be excused "if the proponent establishes by clear and convincing evidence that the decedent adopted the document as his or her will." See also Restatement Second, Property (Donative Transfers) § 33.1, Comment g. The Revised Uniform Probate Code § 2-503 also adopts a harmless-error rule. Under the Revised UPC, a document or writing on a document that was not executed in compliance with the statutory formalities is treated as if it had been properly executed "if the proponent of the document or writing establishes by clear-and-convincing evidence that the decedent intended the document or writing to constitute . . . the decedent's will . . . ."

The trend away from insisting on strict compliance with statutory formalities is based on a growing acceptance

---

of the broader principle that mistake, whether in execution or in expression, should not be allowed to defeat intention. A common principle underlies the movement to excuse defective execution: § 11.2, authorizing insertion of language to resolve ambiguities in donative documents; and this section, authorizing reformation of unambiguous donative documents (including wills) to correct mistakes.

The important difference between § 11.2 and this section is the burden of proof. Ambiguity shows that the donative document contains an inadequate expression of the donor's intention. Here, because there is no ambiguity, clear and convincing evidence is required to establish that the document does not adequately express intention.

Recent cases have begun to recognize that wills can be reformed. The Restatement Second, Property (Donative Transfers) § 34.7, Comment *d* also accepted the proposition that wills as well as other donative documents can be reformed to correct mistakes, stating:

"The general law of mistake, under which a mistake may be significant enough to justify the conclusion that the donative transfer should be set aside or reformed, is incorporated herein by reference and made applicable to both wills and other donative documents of transfer."

This section carries forward the position of the Restatement Second by extending the conventional reformation remedy for inter-vivos donative documents to wills, hence to all donative documents.

d. Plain meaning rule disapproved. The so-called plain meaning rule is disapproved to the extent that that rule purports to exclude extrinsic evidence of the donor's intention. The plain meaning, Wigmore noted, "is simply the meaning of the people who did *not* write the document." The objective of the plain meaning rule, to prevent giving effect to mistaken or fraudulent testimony, is sufficiently preserved by subjecting extrinsic evidence that contradicts what appears to be the plain meaning of the text to a higher than normal standard of proof, the clear-and-convincing-evidence standard.

e. Standard of proof—clear and convincing evidence. There are two standards of proof for civil cases—preponderance of the evidence and clear and convincing evidence. This section imposes the clear-and-convincing-evidence standard of proof. Reformation is permissible only if the elements stated in this section are established by clear and convincing evidence.

The normal standard of proof in civil cases is preponderance of the evidence. Under that standard, the evidence must establish a probability that an assertion is true, *i.e.*, that it is more probable than not that the assertion is true. A higher degree of probability is required under the clear-and-convincing-evidence standard. Although this higher standard of proof defies quantification, it is generally agreed that it requires an assertion to be established by a high degree of probability, though not to an absolute or moral certainty or beyond a reasonable doubt.

The standard of proof serves various functions. It alerts potential plaintiffs to the strength of evidence required in order to prevail, instructs the trier of fact regarding the level of confidence needed to find for the plaintiff, and allocates the risk of an erroneous factual determination.

The higher standard of proof under this section imposes a heightened sense of responsibility upon the trier of fact. When the case is tried before a judge, the judge should respond by rendering a thorough, reasoned set of findings that deal with the relevant contested facts. A collateral benefit of requiring clear and convincing proof is that an appellate court will rightly feel free to scrutinize the trial court's work more closely than in the typical preponderance-of-the-evidence review. As a practical matter, this greater scrutiny pressures the trial judge to do an especially careful job.

Absolute certainty about the truth of assertions of fact can seldom be established. Because a determination of fact is based on probability, not certainty, there is always a risk of error. An erroneous factual determination can result in a judgment for the plaintiff when the truth, were it known, would warrant a judgment for the defendant, and vice versa. The higher standard of proof under this section imposes a greater risk of an erroneous factual determination on the party seeking reformation than on the party opposing reformation. Tilting the risk of an erroneous factual determination in this fashion is appropriate because the party seeking reformation is seeking to establish that a donative document does not reflect the donor's intention. This tilt also deters a potential plaintiff from bringing a reformation suit on the basis of insubstantial evidence.

f. Nature of reformation and constructive trust. The grounds stated in this section, if established by clear and convincing evidence, support an order of reformation and, if necessary, other equitable relief such as the imposition of a constructive trust. An order of reformation alters the text of a donative document so that it expresses the intention it was intended to express. Thus, unless otherwise stated, a judicial order of reformation relates back and operates to alter the text as of the date of execution rather than as of the date of the order or any other post-execution date.

If property was previously distributed under the mistaken terms of the document, the court may impose a constructive trust or take other remedial steps in addition to issuing an order of reformation. A constructive trust is an equitable remedy that orders property in the hands of an unintended recipient to be transferred to the intended beneficiary. Thus, the court imposes the constructive trust in favor of the intended beneficiary. Unless otherwise stated, the constructive trust imposed under this section presupposes that the order of reformation relates back and operates to alter the text as of the date of the donor's execution of the document, as described above.

g. Grounds for reformation. In order to support the equitable remedy of reformation, the extrinsic evidence must establish, by clear and convincing evidence, (1) that a mistake of fact or law affected the expression, inclusion, or omission of specific terms of the document and (2) what the donor's actual intention was in a case of mistake in expression or what the donor's actual intention would have been in a case of mistake in the inducement. A petition for reformation can be brought under this section by any interested person, before or after the donor's death.

h. Limitations on the scope of reformation. Reformation is a rule governing mistakes in the content of a donative document, in a case in which the donative document does not say what the transferor meant it to say. Accordingly, reformation is not available to correct a failure to prepare and execute a document (Illustration 1). Nor is reformation available to modify a document in order to give effect to the donor's post-execution change of mind (Illustration 2) or to compensate for other changes in circumstances (Illustration 3).

Illustrations:

1. G decided to leave his estate to his niece, X. G orally communicated his intent to X, mistakenly thinking that he could effectuate his intent in this manner. Thereafter G died intestate, leaving his sister, A, as his sole heir.

Because G did not reduce his testamentary intent to writing and execute it as required by the Statute of Wills, X cannot invoke the reformation doctrine to implement G's true intent. G's mistake did not refer to specific terms in a donative document, because G never executed a document. There is no document to reform.

2. G validly executed a will that devised his estate to his sister, A. After execution, G formed an intent to alter the disposition in favor of A's daughter, X, in the mistaken belief that he could substitute his new intent by communicating it to X orally.

G's oral communication to X does not support a reformation remedy. Although a donative document exists that could be reformed by substituting "X" for "A," the remedy does not lie because G's will was not the product of mistake. The will when executed stated G's intent accurately. G's mistake was his subsequent failure to execute a codicil or a new will to carry out his new intent. This is a mistake of the same sort that G made in Illustration 1 in not making a valid will in the first place.

3. G's will devised his government bonds to his daughter, A, and the residue of his estate to a friend. Evidence shows that the bonds are worth only half of what they were worth at the time of execution of the will and that G would probably have left A more had he known that the bonds would depreciate in value.

This evidence does not support a reformation remedy. G's mistake did not relate to facts that existed when the will was executed.

i. Mistake in expression or inducement. If proved by clear and convincing evidence, a mistake justifies an equitable remedy, whether the mistake is one of expression or inducement. A mistake of expression arises when a donative document includes a term that misstates the donor's intention (Illustration 4), fails to include a term that was intended to be included (Illustration 5), or includes a term that was not intended to be included (Illustration 6). A mistake in the inducement arises when a donative document includes a term that was intended to be included or fails to include a term that was not intended to be included, but the intention to include or not to include the term was the product of a mistake of fact or law (Illustrations 7 and 8).

Illustrations:

4. G's will devised "$1,000 to A." Extrinsic evidence, including the testimony and files of the drafting attorney, shows that there was a mistake in transcription and that G's intention was to devise $10,000 to A.

If this evidence satisfies the clear-and-convincing-evidence standard of proof, the will is reformed to substitute "$10,000" for "$1,000."

5. G created an inter-vivos trust. The trust document did not contain a clause reserving to G a power to revoke the trust. Controlling law provides that a trust is irrevocable in the absence of an expressly retained power to revoke. After G signed the document, G's financial condition changed and G sought to revoke the trust.

Extrinsic evidence shows that G intended to create a revocable trust and so instructed her attorney; and shows that G's attorney mistakenly failed to include the revocation clause.

If this evidence satisfies the clear-and-convincing-evidence standard of proof, the trust document is reformed to insert the mistakenly omitted power to revoke.

6. G's will devised "$1,000 to A." Extrinsic evidence, including the testimony and files of the drafting attorney, shows that there was a mistake in transcription and that G's intention was not to devise any property to A. Although earlier drafts of G's will contained the devise to A, there is evidence that G had instructed his attorney to delete the devise in the final draft and that, by mistake, G's attorney failed to carry out G's instructions.

If this evidence satisfies the clear-and-convincing-evidence standard of proof, the will is reformed to delete the devise to A.

7. G created an inter-vivos trust. The trust document did not contain a clause reserving to G a power to revoke the trust. Controlling law provides that a trust is irrevocable in the absence of an expressly retained power to revoke. After G signed the document, G's financial condition changed and G sought to revoke the trust.

Extrinsic evidence shows that G intended to create a revocable trust and did not understand the need for a revocation clause.

If this evidence satisfies the clear-and-convincing-evidence standard of proof, the trust document is reformed to insert a power to revoke.

8. G created an inter-vivos trust of the bulk of his assets. The trust document did not contain a clause reserving to G a power to revoke the trust. Controlling law provides that a trust is irrevocable in the absence of an expressly retained power to revoke. After G signed the document, G sought to revoke the trust.

Extrinsic evidence shows that G established the trust when he was in line for a high-level position in the federal government. From the press reports he had read, he mistakenly believed that he had to place all of his assets into an irrevocable trust in order to comply with federal policies on public service conflicts of interest. G liquidated much of his property, and placed the bulk of his assets into the irrevocable trust. Subsequently, G learned that federal policies did not require him to transfer his assets to an irrevocable trust.

If this evidence satisfies the clear-and-convincing-evidence standard of proof, the trust document is reformed to insert a power to revoke.

j. Particularity of proof. In order to support an order of reformation or the imposition of a constructive trust, the petitioner must prove, by clear and convincing evidence, both (1) that a mistake of fact or law affected specific terms of the document and (2) what the donor's true intention was. Both elements must be proved with particularity. For example, a claim that "if only my aunt had known how much I loved her, she would have left me more" lacks sufficient particularity to support a petition for remedy. Proof that the donor instructed his or her attorney to "give me an estate plan that incurs the lowest possible tax liability" lacks sufficient particularity to support a reformation remedy.

Notice, however, that the requirement of particularity does not require proof that the donor personally made the mistake nor proof that the donor formulated the exact language needed to carry out his or her intention. A remedy will lie if a mistake of the donor's advisor or drafting agent has affected specific terms of the document by failing properly to formulate the language necessary to carry out the donor's intention. Suppose, for example, that the petitioner proves by clear and convincing evidence that the testator instructed his lawyer to draft a will that devised certain property to child A. A remedy will lie if the lawyer drafted a will that misdescribed the intended property or the intended devisee. The petitioner need not prove that the testator formulated the exact language necessary to carry out his intention, which the testator's lawyer mistakenly failed to include. The testator properly relies upon the lawyer to draft the language necessary to carry out his intention.

k. *Statutory rules of construction.* Just as the requirement of particularity discussed in Comment *j* does not require the petitioner to prove that the donor formulated the exact language necessary to carry out intention, neither does the petitioner need to prove that the donor expressly intended to overcome a statutory rule of construction. Statutes often provide that a particular rule of construction prevails unless the donative document, another specified document, or one of a list of specified documents expressly provides otherwise. See § 11.3. Such rules of construction purport to govern when the document is silent. If the elements of this section are satisfied by clear and convincing evidence, however, a petition for reformation can be sustained to insert language into the document that rebuts the rule of construction. Suppose, for example, that the petitioner proves by clear and convincing evidence that the donor instructed his or her lawyer to draft a will that devised certain property to child, A, but not to A's children if A predeceased the donor leaving children who survived the donor. A remedy will lie if the lawyer drafted a will that failed to include language necessary to defeat the applicable antilapse statute. As reformed under this section, the donor's will defeats the antilapse statute because it includes language expressly contradicting that statutory rule of construction. As stated in Comment *j*, the petitioner need not prove that the donor formulated the exact language necessary to carry out his or her intention and that the donor's lawyer, by mistake, failed to include the donor's language; the donor properly relies upon the lawyer to draft the language necessary to carry out his or her intention.

l. *Donor's signature after having read document does not bar remedy.* Proof that the donor read the document or had the opportunity to read the document before signing it does not preclude an order of reformation or the imposition of a constructive trust. The English Law Reform Committee, in recommending the adoption of a reformation doctrine for wills, stated well the rationale for this position:

"We have also considered whether any special significance ought to be given to cases in which the will has been read over to the testator, perhaps with explanation, and expressly approved by him before execution. In our view it should not. Some testators are inattentive, some find it difficult to understand what their solicitors say and do not like to confess it, and some make little or no attempt to understand. As long as they are assured that the words used carry out their instructions, they are content. Others may follow every word with meticulous attention. It is impossible to generalise, and our view is that reading over is one of the many factors to which the court should pay attention, but that it should have no conclusive effect."

Law Reform Committee, Nineteenth Report: Interpretation of Wills, Cmnd. No. 5301, at 12 (1973).

m. *Defenses: change of position by recipient; bona fide purchaser; laches; etc.* All defenses generally available in equity to a suit to reform a donative document or to impose a constructive trust upon the recipient of property distributed under a donative document are available under this section. For example, a reformation order is ineffective and the imposition of a constructive trust does not lie against a person regarding property that he or she received without giving value therefor if, after receiving the property and without knowledge of the circumstances justifying reformation under this section, the recipient changed position in a way that makes it inequitable to require the recipient to return that property or its value. See Restatement, Restitution §§ 69, 142. See also Restatement Second, Trusts §§ 292, 333; Restatement Second, Contracts § 155 and Comment *f*.

A reformation order is ineffective and the imposition of a constructive trust does not lie against a person regarding property that he or she has received if the recipient gave value therefor without knowledge of the circumstances justifying reformation under this section. See Restatement, Restitution §§ 13, 123, 141, 173, 174.

See also Restatement Second, Trusts §§ 283-320; Restatement Second, Contracts § 155 and Comment *f*.

A person otherwise entitled to reformation or to a constructive trust is barred from recovery if the complainant has failed to bring, or, having brought, has failed to prosecute a suit for so long a time and under such circumstances that it would be inequitable to permit the complainant to prosecute the suit. A cause of action may also be barred by lapse of time because of an applicable statute of limitations. See Restatement, Restitution § 148.

n. Contractual transfers. If a will, trust, beneficiary designation, or similar document is made pursuant to a contract, such as a premarital or postmarital agreement, a divorce settlement, or a will contract, ambiguities in the implementing document of transfer are presumptively resolved in accordance with the transferor's contractual obligation. See § 11.2, Comments *g* and *m*, § 11.3, Comment *k*. If, however, the implementing document of transfer is unambiguous and clearly deviates from the transferor's contractual obligation, the remedy would normally lie in a breach of contract action against the transferor or the transferor's estate. On the other hand, if clear and convincing evidence establishes that the deviation was the product of mistake, the rule of this section supplies an alternative means of curing the breach by reforming the document of transfer to accord with the contract.

§ 2-806. Modification to Achieve Transferor's Tax Objectives.

To achieve the transferor's tax objectives, the court may modify the terms of a governing instrument in a manner that is not contrary to the transferor's probable intention. The court may provide that the modification has retroactive effect.

Comment

Added in 2008, Section 2-806 is based on Section 416 of the Uniform Trust Code, which in turn was based on Section 12.2 of the Restatement (Third) of Property: Wills and Other Donative Transfers (2003).

Section 2-806 is broader in scope than Section 416 of the Uniform Trust Code because Section 2-806 applies but is not limited to trusts.

Section 12.2, and hence Section 2-806, is explained and illustrated in the Comments to Section 12.2 of the Restatement and also, in the case of a trust, in the Comment to Section 416 of the Uniform Trust Code.

Restatement (Third) of Property: Wills and Other Donative Transfers (2003)

§12.2 Modifying Donative documents to Achieve Donor's Tax Objectives. A donative document may be modified, in a manner that does not violate the donor's probable intention, to achieve the donor's tax objectives.

Comment:

a. Scope note. This section authorizes modification of a donative document to achieve the donor's tax objectives, to the extent that the proposed modification does not violate the donor's probable intention. The term modification rather than reformation is used in this section to distinguish the situation covered here from the situation, covered by § 12.1, in which the donative document fails to express the donor's original, particularized intention.

b. Rationale. This section is based on probable intention (see Comment *f*). The rationale for modifying a donative document is that the donor would have desired the modification to be made if he or she had realized that the desired tax objectives would not be achieved. A similar rationale underlies the cy pres doctrine for charitable trusts, the deviation doctrine for private trusts, and the special-purpose reformation doctrine for curing perpetuity violations.

c. Establishing the donor's tax objectives. Modification under this section requires that the donor's tax objectives be established by a preponderance of the evidence. The donor's tax objectives can be established by the express terms of the donative document, by inference from the donative document, or by extrinsic evidence. See § 10.2. The donor's tax objectives can be specific, such as an objective to qualify a disposition for the federal estate tax charitable deduction; or general, such as an objective to minimize taxes.

d. Achieving the donor's tax objectives. Achieving the donor's tax objectives by modifying a donative document is straightforward if the donor's tax objectives concern state taxes, unless controlling state law expressly disallows the governing effect of the modification for state tax purposes.

Achieving the donor's tax objectives is more complicated if the donor's tax objectives concern federal taxes, as they often do. Federal law controls the federal tax consequences of a transaction. From time to time, however, federal law expressly recognizes specified modifications of a donative document as controlling for certain federal tax purposes. Current examples of federal statutory recognition include modifying split-interest charitable trusts in certain cases to qualify the value of the charitable interest for the federal income, gift, or estate tax charitable deduction, modifying trusts for noncitizen spouses in order to qualify them as qualified domestic trusts, and dividing trusts for purposes of the federal generation-skipping transfer tax. The primary purpose of this section is to authorize any modification that is clearly effective under federal law if the donor's tax objectives relate to federal taxes, or that is clearly effective under state law if the donor's tax objectives relate to state taxes, subject to the requirement in either case that the modification not violate the donor's probable intention.

When federal tax law is unclear regarding the tax consequences of a proposed modification, modification to achieve the donor's federal tax objectives is more problematic. Courts should be cautious in granting a requested order of modification in such circumstances. In addition to requiring that the modification not violate the donor's probable intention (see Comment *f*), the proponent of modification bears the burden of showing a reasonable prospect that the proposed modification will be effective for federal tax purposes.

e. Failure to achieve tax objectives need not be related to post-execution change in tax law. Although failure to achieve the donor's tax objectives is often due to a change in the tax law occurring after the document was executed, this section is not restricted to that situation. Federal law sometimes accepts modification in situations in which the tax law did not change after execution. It would be too restrictive, therefore, to limit this section to post-execution changes in tax law.

f. Modification not to violate the donor's probable intention. To be authorized under this section, the proposed modification must not violate the donor's probable intention. In many cases, this requirement is easily satisfied. The modification necessary to achieve the donor's tax objectives may consist merely of an order to divide a trust into two or more trusts, leaving the combined interests of each beneficiary unaffected. Indeed, for some tax purposes, federal law may accept a modification only if it does not change the quality, value, or timing of the interests of the beneficiaries.

In other situations, the modification necessary to achieve the donor's tax objectives may require an alteration of beneficial interests. Such an alteration is acceptable so long as it does not violate the donor's probable intention. In determining the donor's probable intention, the donor's non-tax as well as tax objectives are to be considered. The greater the proposed alteration, the more rigorous the court should be in measuring the requested modification against the donor's probable intention. One measure of the donor's probable intention is the donor's general dispositive plan. Even if it is questionable whether the modification would be consistent with the donor's general dispositive plan, however, the court can still find that it does not violate the donor's probable intention if the detrimentally affected beneficiaries consent to the proposed modification. Such consent makes it more likely that the donor would have approved of the modification, whether or not the modification alters the donor's general dispositive plan.

g. Time when modification becomes effective. Unlike a court-ordered reformation under § 12.1, a court-ordered modification under this section does not necessarily relate back to the date of execution. This is because modification, unlike reformation (see § 12.1), does not give effect to original, particularized intention but to probable intention – to what the donor's intention would probably have been had the donor known that his or her objectives could not be achieved under the donative document as formulated. Under this section, a court-ordered modification takes effect whenever necessary to achieve the purpose for which the modification is ordered.

PART 9
STATUTORY RULE AGAINST PERPETUITIES;
HONORARY TRUSTS

General Comment

Subpart 1 of this part incorporates into the Code the Uniform Statutory Rule Against Perpetuities (USRAP or Uniform Statutory Rule) and Subpart 2 contains an optional section on honorary trusts and trusts for pets. Subpart 2 is under continuing review and, after appropriate study, might subsequently be revised to add provisions affecting certain types of commercial transactions respecting land, such as options in gross, that directly or indirectly restrain alienability.

In codifying Subparts 1 and 2, enacting states may deem it appropriate to locate them at some place other than in the probate code.

SUBPART 1. UNIFORM STATUTORY RULE AGAINST PERPETUITIES (1986/1990)

General Comment

Simplified Wait-and-See/Deferred-Reformation Approach Adopted. The Uniform Statutory Rule reforms the common-law Rule Against Perpetuities (common-law Rule) by adding a simplified wait-and-see element and a deferred-reformation element.

Wait-and-see is a two-step strategy. Step One (Section 2-901(a)(1) preserves the validating side of the common-law Rule. By satisfying the common-law Rule, a nonvested future interest in property is valid at the moment of its creation. Step Two (Section 2-901(a)(2) is a salvage strategy for future interests that would have been invalid at common law. Rather than invalidating such interests at creation, wait-and-see allows a period of time, called the permissible vesting period, during which the nonvested interests are permitted to vest according to the trust's terms.

The traditional method of measuring the permissible vesting period has been by reference to lives in being at the creation of the interest (the measuring lives) plus 21 years. There are, however, various difficulties and costs associated with identifying and tracing a set of actual measuring lives to see which one is the survivor and when he or she dies. In addition, it has been documented that the use of actual measuring lives plus 21 years does not produce a period of time that self-adjusts to each disposition, extending dead-hand control no further than necessary in each case; rather, the use of actual measuring lives (plus 21 years) generates a permissible vesting period whose length almost always exceeds by some arbitrary margin the point of actual vesting in cases traditionally validated by the wait-and-see strategy. The actual-measuring-lives approach, therefore, performs a margin-of-safety function. Given this fact, and given the costs and difficulties associated with the actual-measuring-lives approach, the Uniform Statutory Rule forgoes the use of actual measuring lives and uses instead a permissible vesting period of a flat 90 years.

The philosophy behind the 90-year period is to fix a period of time that approximates the average period of time that would traditionally be allowed by the wait-and-see doctrine. The flat-period-of-years method was not used as a means of increasing permissible dead-hand control by lengthening the permissible vesting period beyond its traditional boundaries. In fact, the 90-year period falls substantially short of the absolute maximum period of time that could theoretically be achieved under the common-law Rule itself, by the so-called "twelve-healthy-babies ploy"— a ploy that would average out to a period of about 115 years,* 25 years or 27.8% longer than the 90 years allowed by USRAP. The fact that the traditional period roughly averages out to a longish-sounding 90 years is a reflection of a quite different phenomenon: the dramatic increase in longevity that society as a whole has experienced in the course of the twentieth century.

The framers of the Uniform Statutory Rule derived the 90-year period as follows. The first point recognized was that if actual measuring lives were to have been used, the length of the permissible vesting

---

*Actuarially, the life expectancy of the longest living member of a group of twelve new-born babies is about 94 years; with the 21-year tack-on period, the "twelve-healthy-babies ploy" would produce, on average, a period of about 115 years (94 + 21).

period would, in the normal course of events, be governed by the life of the youngest measuring life. The second point recognized was that no matter what method is used to identify the measuring lives, the youngest measuring life, in standard trusts, is likely to be the transferor's youngest descendant living when the trust was created.[**] The 90-year period was premised on these propositions. Using four hypothetical families deemed to be representative of actual families, the framers of the Uniform Statutory Rule determined that, on average, the transferor's youngest descendant in being at the transferor's death—assuming the transferor's death to occur between ages 60 and 90, which is when 73 percent of the population die—is about 6 years old. See Waggoner, "Perpetuities: A Progress Report on the Draft Uniform Statutory Rule Against Perpetuities", 20 U.Miami Inst. on Est. Plan. Ch. 7 at 7-17 (1986). The remaining life expectancy of a 6-year-old is about 69 years. The 69 years, plus the 21-year tack-on period, gives a permissible vesting period of 90 years.

Acceptance of the 90-year-period Approach under the Federal Generation- skipping Transfer Tax. Federal regulations, to be promulgated by the U.S. Treasury Department under the generation-skipping transfer tax, will accept the Uniform Statutory Rule's 90-year period as a valid approximation of the period that, on average, would be produced by lives in being plus 21 years. See Temp.Treas.Reg. § 26.2601-1(b)(1)(v)(B)(2) (as to be revised). When originally promulgated in 1988, this regulation was prepared without knowledge of the Uniform Statutory Rule Against Perpetuities, which had been promulgated in 1986; as first promulgated, the regulation only recognized a period measured by actual lives in being plus 21 years. After the 90-year approach of the Uniform Statutory Rule was brought to the attention of the U.S. Treasury Department, the Department issued a letter of intent to amend the regulation to treat the 90-year period as the equivalent of a lives-in-being-plus-21-years period. Letter from Michael J. Graetz, Deputy Assistant Secretary of the Treasury (Tax Policy), to Lawrence J. Bugge,

President, National Conference of Commissioners on Uniform State Laws (Nov. 16, 1990). For further discussion of the coordination of the federal generation-skipping transfer tax with the Uniform Statutory Rule, see the Comment to Section 2-901(e), infra, and the Comment to Section 1(e) of the Uniform Statutory Rule Against Perpetuities.

The 90-year Period Will Seldom be Used Up. Nearly all trusts (or other property arrangements) will terminate by their own terms long before the 90-year permissible vesting period expires, leaving the permissible vesting period to extend unused (and ignored) into the future long after the contingencies have been resolved and the property distributed. In the unlikely event that the contingencies have not been resolved by the expiration of the permissible vesting period, Section 2-903 requires the disposition to be reformed by the court so that all contingencies are resolved within the permissible period.

In effect, wait-and-see with deferred reformation operates similarly to a traditional perpetuity saving clause, which grants a margin-of-safety period measured by the lives of the transferor's descendants in being at the creation of the trust or other property arrangement (plus 21 years).

No New Learning Required. The Uniform Statutory Rule does not require the practicing bar to learn a new and unfamiliar set of perpetuity principles. The effect of the Uniform Statutory Rule on the planning and drafting of documents for clients should be distinguished from the effect on the resolution of actual or potential perpetuity-violation cases. The former affects many more practicing lawyers than the latter.

With respect to the planning and drafting end of the practice, the Uniform Statutory Rule requires no modification of current practice and no new learning. *Lawyers can and should continue to use the same traditional perpetuity-saving/termination clause, using specified lives in being plus 21 years, they used before enactment.* Lawyers should not shift to a "later of" type clause that purports to operate upon the later of (A) 21 years after the death of the survivor of specified lives in being or (B) 90 years. As explained in more detail in the Comment to Section 2-901, such a clause is not effective. If such a "later of" clause is used in a trust that contains a violation of the common-law rule against perpetuities, Section 2-901(a), by itself, would render the clause ineffective, limit the maximum permissible vesting period to 90 years, and render the trust vulnerable to a reformation suit under Section 2-903. Section 2-

---

[**] Under section 2-707, the descendants of a beneficiary of a future interest are presumptively made substitute beneficiaries, almost certainly making those descendants in being at the creation of the interest measuring lives, were measuring lives to have been used.

901(e), however, saves documents using this type of clause from this fate. By limiting the effect of such clauses to the 21-year period following the death of the survivor of the specified lives, subsection (e) in effect transforms this type of clause into a traditional perpetuity-saving/termination clause, bringing the trust into compliance with the common-law rule against perpetuities and rendering it invulnerable to a reformation suit under Section 2-903.

Far fewer in number are those lawyers (and judges) who have an actual or potential perpetuity-violation case. An actual or potential perpetuity-violation case will arise very infrequently under the Uniform Statutory Rule. When such a case does arise, however, lawyers (or judges) involved in the case will find considerable guidance for its resolution in the detailed analysis contained in the commentary accompanying the Uniform Statutory Rule itself. In short, the detailed analysis in the commentary accompanying the Uniform Statutory Rule need not be part of the general learning required of lawyers in the drafting and planning of dispositive documents for their clients. The detailed analysis is supplied in the commentary for the assistance in the resolution of an actual violation. Only then need that detailed analysis be consulted and, in such a case, it will prove extremely helpful.

General References. Fellows, "Testing Perpetuity Reforms: A Study of Perpetuity Cases 1984-89", 25 Real Prop.Prob. & Tr.J. 597 (1991) (testing the various types of perpetuity reform measures and concluding, on the basis of empirical evidence, that the Uniform Statutory Rule is the best opportunity offered to date for a uniform perpetuity law that efficiently and effectively achieves a fair balance between present and future property owners); Waggoner, "The Uniform Statutory Rule Against Perpetuities: Oregon Joins Up", 26 Willamette L. Rev. 259 (1990) (explaining the operation of the Uniform Statutory Rule); Waggoner, "The Uniform Statutory Rule Against Perpetuities: The Rationale of the 90-Year Waiting Period", 73 Cornell L. Rev. 157 (1988) (explaining the derivation of the 90-year period); Waggoner, "The Uniform Statutory Rule Against Perpetuities", 21 Real Prop., Prob. & Tr.J. 569 (1986) (explaining the theory and operation of the Uniform Statutory Rule).

§ 2-901. Statutory Rule Against Perpetuities.

(a) [**Validity of Nonvested Property Interest.**] A nonvested property interest is invalid unless:

(1) when the interest is created, it is certain to vest or terminate no later than 21 years after the death of an individual then alive; or

(2) the interest either vests or terminates within 90 years after its creation.

(b) [**Validity of General Power of Appointment Subject to a Condition Precedent.**] A general power of appointment not presently exercisable because of a condition precedent is invalid unless:

(1) when the power is created, the condition precedent is certain to be satisfied or becomes impossible to satisfy no later than 21 years after the death of an individual then alive; or

(2) the condition precedent either is satisfied or becomes impossible to satisfy within 90 years after its creation.

(c) [**Validity of Nongeneral or Testamentary Power of Appointment.**] A nongeneral power of appointment or a general testamentary power of appointment is invalid unless:

(1) when the power is created, it is certain to be irrevocably exercised or otherwise to terminate no later than 21 years after the death of an individual then alive; or

(2) the power is irrevocably exercised or otherwise terminates within 90 years after its creation.

(d) [**Possibility of Post-death Child Disregarded.**] In determining whether a nonvested property interest or a power of appointment is valid under subsection (a)(1), (b)(1), or (c)(1), the possibility that a child will be born to an individual after the individual's death is disregarded.

(e) [**Effect of Certain "Later-of" Type Language.**] If, in measuring a period from the creation of a trust or other property arrangement, language in a governing instrument (i) seeks to disallow the vesting or termination of any interest or trust beyond, (ii) seeks to postpone the vesting or termination of any interest or trust until, or (iii) seeks to operate in effect in any similar fashion upon, the later of (A) the expiration of a period of time not exceeding 21 years after the death of the survivor of specified lives in being at the creation of the trust or other property arrangement or (B) the expiration of a period of time that exceeds or might exceed 21 years after the death of the survivor of lives in being at the creation of the trust or other property arrangement, that language is inoperative to the extent it produces a period of time that exceeds 21 years after the death of the survivor of the specified lives.

Comment

Section 2-901 codifies the validating side of the common-law Rule and implements the wait-and-see feature of the Uniform Statutory Rule Against Perpetuities. As provided in Section 2-906, this section and the other sections in Subpart 1 of Part 9 supersede the common-law Rule Against Perpetuities (common-law Rule) in jurisdictions previously adhering to it (or repeals any statutory version or variation thereof previously in effect in the jurisdiction). The common-law Rule (or the statutory version or variation thereof) is replaced by the Statutory Rule in Section 2-901 and by the other provisions of Subpart 1 of Part 9.

Section 2-901(a) covers nonvested property interests, and will be the subsection most often applicable. Subsections (b) and (c) cover powers of appointment.

Paragraph (1) of subsections (a), (b), and (c) is a codified version of the validating side of the common-law Rule. In effect, paragraph (1) of these subsections provides that nonvested property interests and powers of appointment that are valid under the common-law Rule Against Perpetuities, including those that are rendered valid because of a perpetuity saving clause, continue to be valid under the Statutory Rule and can be declared so at their inceptions. This means that no new learning is required of competent estate planners: The practice of lawyers who competently draft trusts and other property arrangements for their clients is undisturbed.

Paragraph (2) of subsections (a), (b), and (c) establishes the wait-and-see rule. Paragraph (2) provides that an interest or a power of appointment that is not validated by paragraph (1), and hence would have been invalid under the common-law Rule, is given a second chance: Such an interest is valid if it does not actually remain in existence and nonvested when the 90-year permissible vesting period expires; such a power of appointment is valid if it ceases to be subject to a condition precedent or is no longer exercisable when the permissible 90-year period expires.

Subsection (d). The rule established in subsection (d) deserves a special comment. Subsection (d) declares that the possibility that a child will be born to an individual after the individual's death is to be disregarded. It is important to note that this rule applies only for the purpose of determining the validity of an interest (or a power of appointment) under paragraph (1) of subsection (a), (b), or (c). The rule of subsection (d) does not apply, for example, to questions such as whether a child who is born to an individual after the individual's death qualifies as a taker of a beneficial interest—as a member of a class or otherwise. Neither subsection (d), nor any other provision of Part 9, supersedes the widely accepted common-law principle, codified in Section 2-104, that a child in gestation (a child sometimes described as a child en ventre sa mere) who is later born alive (and, under Section 2-104, lives for 120 hours or more after birth) is regarded as alive during gestation.

The limited purpose of subsection (d) is to solve a perpetuity problem created by advances in medical science. The problem is illustrated by a case such as "to A for life, remainder to A's children who reach 21." When the common-law Rule was developing, the possibility was recognized, strictly speaking, that one or more of A's children might reach 21 more than 21 years after A's death. The possibility existed because A's wife (who might not be a life in being) might be pregnant when A died. If she was, and if the child was born viable a few months after A's death, the child could not reach his or her 21st birthday within 21 years after A's death. The device then invented to validate the interest of A's children was to "extend" the allowable perpetuity period by tacking on a period of gestation, if needed. As a result, the common-law perpetuity period was comprised of three components: (1) a life in being (2) plus 21 years (3) plus a period of gestation, when needed. Today, thanks to sperm banks, frozen embryos, and even the possibility of artificially maintaining the body functions of a deceased pregnant woman long enough to develop the fetus to viability—advances in medical science unanticipated when the common-law Rule was in its developmental stages—having a pregnant wife at death is no longer the only way of having children after death. These medical developments, and undoubtedly others to come, make the mere addition of a period of gestation inadequate as a device to confer initial validity under Section 2-901(a)(1) on the interest of A's children in the above example. The rule of subsection (d), however, does insure the initial validity of the children's interest. Disregarding the possibility that children of A will be born after his death allows A to be the validating life. None of his children, under this assumption, can reach 21 more than 21 years after his death.

Note that subsection (d) subsumes not only the case of children conceived after death, but also the more conventional case of children in gestation at death. With subsection (d) in place, the third component of the common-law perpetuity period is unnecessary and has been jettisoned. The perpetuity period recognized in paragraph (1) of subsections (a), (b), and (c) has only two components: (1) a life in being (2) plus 21 years.

As to the legal status of conceived-after-death children, that question has not yet been resolved. For example, if in the above example A leaves sperm on deposit at a sperm bank and after A's death a woman (A's widow or another) becomes pregnant as a result of artificial insemination, the child or children produced thereby might not be included at all in the class gift. Cf. Restatement (Second) of Property (Donative Transfers) Introductory Note to Ch. 26 (1988). Without trying to predict how that question will be resolved in the future, the best way to handle the problem from the perpetuity perspective is the rule in subsection (d) requiring the possibility of post-death children to be disregarded.

Subsection (e)—Effect of Certain "Later-of" Type Language. Subsection (e) was added to the Uniform Statutory Rule in 1990. It primarily applies to a non-traditional type of "later of" clause (described below). Use of that type of clause might have produced unintended consequences, which are now rectified by the addition of subsection (e).

In general, perpetuity saving or termination clauses can be used in either of two ways. The predominant use of such clauses is as an override clause. That is, the clause is not an integral part of the dispositive terms of the trust, but operates independently of the dispositive terms; the clause provides that all interests must vest no later than at a specified time in the future, and sometimes also provides that the trust must then terminate, but only if any interest has not previously vested or if the trust has not previously terminated. The other use of such a clause is as an integral part of the dispositive terms of the trust; that is, the clause is the provision that directly regulates the duration of the trust. Traditional perpetuity saving or termination clauses do not use a "later of" approach; they mark off the maximum time of vesting or termination only by reference to a 21-year period

following the death of the survivor of specified lives in being at the creation of the trust.

Subsection (e) applies to a non-traditional clause called a "later of" (or "longer of") clause. Such a clause might provide that the maximum time of vesting or termination of any interest or trust must occur no later than the later of (A) 21 years after the death of the survivor of specified lives in being at the creation of the trust or (B) 90 years after the creation of the trust.

Under the Uniform Statutory Rule as originally promulgated, this type of "later of" clause would not achieve a "later of" result. If used as an override clause in conjunction with a trust whose terms were, by themselves, valid under the common-law rule against perpetuities (common-law Rule), the "later of" clause did no harm. The trust would be valid under the common-law Rule as codified in subsection (a)(1) because the clause itself would neither postpone the vesting of any interest nor extend the duration of the trust. But, if used either (1) as an override clause in conjunction with a trust whose terms were not valid under the common-law Rule or (2) as the provision that directly regulated the duration of the trust, the "later of" clause would not cure the perpetuity violation in case (1) and would create a perpetuity violation in case (2). In neither case would the clause qualify the trust for validity at common law under subsection (a)(1) because the clause would not guarantee that all interests will be certain to vest or terminate no later than 21 years after the death of an individual then alive.[*] In any given case, 90 years can turn to be longer than the period produced by the specified-lives-in-being-plus-21-years language.

Because the clause would fail to qualify the trust for validity under the common-law Rule of subsection (a)(1), the nonvested interests in the trust would be

---

[*] By substantial analogous authority, the specified-lives-in-being-plus-21-years prong of the "later of" clause under discussion is not sustained by the separability doctrine (described in Part H of the Comment to § 1 of the Uniform Statutory Rule Against Perpetuities). See, e.g., Restatement of Property § 376 comments e & f & illustration 3 (1944); Easton v. Hall, 323 Ill. 397, 154 N.E. 216 (1926); Thorne v. Continental Nat'l Bank & Trust Co., 305 Ill.App. 222, 27 N.E.2d 302 (1940). The inapplicability of the separability doctrine is also supported by perpetuity policy, as described in the text above.

subject to the wait-and-see element of subsection (a)(2) and vulnerable to a reformation suit under Section 2-903. Under subsection (a)(2), an interest that is not valid at common law is invalid unless it actually vests or terminates within 90 years after its creation. Subsection (a)(2) does not grant such nonvested interests a permissible vesting period of either 90 years or a period of 21 years after the death of the survivor of specified lives in being. Subsection (a)(2) only grants such interests a period of 90 years in which to vest.

The operation of subsection (a), as outlined above, is also supported by perpetuity policy. If subsection (a) allowed a "later of" clause to achieve a "later of" result, it would authorize an improper use of the 90-year permissible vesting period of subsection (a)(2). The 90-year period of subsection (a)(2) is designed to approximate the period that, on average, would be produced by using actual lives in being plus 21 years. Because in any given case the period actually produced by lives in being plus 21 years can be shorter or longer than 90 years, an attempt to utilize a 90-year period in a "later of" clause improperly seeks to turn the 90-year average into a minimum.

Set against this background, the addition of subsection (e) is quite beneficial. Subsection (e) limits the effect of this type of "later of" language to 21 years after the death of the survivor of the specified lives, in effect transforming the clause into a traditional perpetuity saving/termination clause. By doing so, subsection (e) grants initial validity to the trust under the common-law Rule as codified in subsection (a)(1) and precludes a reformation suit under Section 2-903.

Note that subsection (e) covers variations of the "later of" clause described above, such as a clause that postpones vesting until the later of (A) 20 years after the death of the survivor of specified lives in being or (B) 89 years. Subsection (e) does not, however, apply to all dispositions that incorporate a "later of" approach. To come under subsection (e), the specified-lives prong must include a tack-on period of up to 21 years. Without a tack-on period, a "later of" disposition, unless valid at common-law comes under subsection (a)(2) and is given 90 years in which to vest. An example would be a disposition that creates an interest that is to vest upon "the later of the death of my widow or 30 years after my death."

Coordination of the Federal Generation-skipping Transfer Tax with the Uniform Statutory Rule. In 1990, the Treasury Department announced a decision to coordinate the tax regulations under the "grandfathering" provisions of the federal

generation-skipping transfer tax with the Uniform Statutory Rule. Letter from Michael J. Graetz, Deputy Assistant Secretary of the Treasury (Tax Policy), to Lawrence J. Bugge, President, National Conference of Commissioners on Uniform State Laws (Nov. 16, 1990) (hereinafter Treasury Letter).

Section 1433(b)(2) of the Tax Reform Act of 1986 generally exempts ("grandfathers") trusts from the federal generation-skipping transfer tax that were irrevocable on September 25, 1985. This section adds, however, that the exemption shall apply "only to the extent that such transfer is not made out of corpus added to the trust after September 25, 1985." The provisions of Section 1433(b)(2) were first implemented by Temp.Treas.Reg. § 26.2601-1, promulgated by T.D. 8187 on March 14, 1988. Insofar as the Uniform Statutory Rule is concerned, a key feature of that temporary regulation is the concept that the statutory reference to "corpus added to the trust after September 25, 1985" not only covers actual post-9/25/85 transfers of new property or corpus to a grandfathered trust but "constructive" additions as well. Under the temporary regulation as first promulgated, a "constructive" addition occurs if, after 9/25/85, the donee of a nongeneral power of appointment exercises that power "in a manner that may postpone or suspend the vesting, absolute ownership or power of alienation of an interest in property for a period, measured from the date of creation of the trust, extending beyond any life in being at the date of creation of the trust plus a period of 21 years. If a power is exercised by creating another power it will be deemed to be exercised to whatever extent the second power may be exercised." Temp.Treas.Reg. § 26.2601-1(b)(1)(v)(B)(2) (1988).

Because the Uniform Statutory Rule was promulgated in 1986 and applies only prospectively, any "grandfathered" trust would have become irrevocable prior to the enactment of USRAP in any state. Nevertheless, the second sentence of Section 2-905(a) extends USRAP's wait-and-see approach to post-effective-date exercises of nongeneral powers even if the power itself was created prior to USRAP's effective date. Consequently, a post-USRAP-effective-date exercise of a nongeneral power of appointment created in a "grandfathered" trust could come under the provisions of the Uniform Statutory Rule.

The literal wording, then, of Temp.Treas.Reg. § 26.2601-1(b)(1)(v)(B)(2) (1988), as first promulgated, could have jeopardized the grandfathered status of an exempt trust if (1) the trust created a nongeneral power of appointment, (2) the donee exercised that nongeneral power, and (3) USRAP is the perpetuity law applicable to the donee's exercise. This possibility arose not only because the donee's exercise itself might come under the 90-year permissible vesting period of subsection (a)(2) if it otherwise violated the common-law Rule and hence was not validated under subsection (a)(1). The possibility also arose in a less obvious way if the donee's exercise created another nongeneral power. The last sentence of the temporary regulation states that "if a power is exercised by creating another power it will be deemed to be exercised to whatever extent the second power may be exercised."

In late March 1990, the National Conference of Commissioners on Uniform State Laws (NCCUSL) and the Joint Editorial Board for the Uniform Probate Code (JEB-UPC) filed a formal request with the Treasury Department asking that measures be taken to coordinate the regulation with USRAP. By the Treasury Letter referred to above, the Treasury Department responded by stating that it "will amend the temporary regulations to accommodate the 90-year period under USRAP as originally promulgated [in 1986] or as amended [in 1990 by the addition of subsection (e)]." This should effectively remove the possibility of loss of grandfathered status under the Uniform Statutory Rule merely because the donee of a nongeneral power created in a grandfathered trust inadvertently exercises that power in violation of the common-law Rule or merely because the donee exercises that power by creating a second nongeneral power that might, in the future, be inadvertently exercised in violation of the common-law Rule.

The Treasury Letter states, however, that any effort by the donee of a nongeneral power in a grandfathered trust to obtain a "later of" specified-lives-in-being-plus-21-years or 90-years approach will be treated as a constructive addition, unless that effort is nullified by state law. As explained above, the Uniform Statutory Rule, as originally promulgated in 1986 or as amended in 1990 by the addition of subsection (e), nullifies any direct effort to obtain a "later of" approach by the use of a "later of" clause.

The Treasury Letter states that an indirect effort to obtain a "later of" approach would also be treated as a constructive addition that would bring grandfathered status to an end, unless the attempt to obtain the later-of approach is nullified by state law. The Treasury Letter indicates that an indirect effort to obtain a "later of" approach could arise if the donee of a nongeneral power successfully attempts to prolong the duration of a grandfathered trust by switching from a specified-lives-in-being-plus-21-years perpetuity period to a 90-year perpetuity period, or vice versa. Donees of nongeneral powers in grandfathered trusts would therefore be well advised to resist any temptation to wait until it becomes clear or reasonably predictable which perpetuity period will be longer and then make a switch to the longer period if the governing instrument creating the power utilized the shorter period. No such attempted switch and no constructive addition will occur if in each instance a traditional specified- lives-in-being-plus-21-years perpetuity saving clause is used.

Any such attempted switch is likely in any event to be nullified by state law and, if so, the attempted switch will not be treated as a constructive addition. For example, suppose that the original grandfathered trust contained a standard perpetuity saving clause declaring that all interests in the trust must vest no later than 21 years after the death of the survivor of specified lives in being. In exercising a nongeneral power created in that trust, any indirect effort by the donee to obtain a "later of" approach by adopting a 90-year perpetuity saving clause will likely be nullified by subsection (e). If that exercise occurs at a time when it has become clear or reasonably predictable that the 90-year period will prove longer, the donee's exercise would constitute language in a governing instrument that seeks to operate in effect to postpone the vesting of any interest until the later of the specified- lives-in-being-plus-21-years period or 90 years. Under subsection (e), "that language is inoperative to the extent it produces a period of time that exceeds 21 years after the death of the survivor of the specified lives."

Quite apart from subsection (e), the relation-back doctrine generally recognized in the exercise of nongeneral powers stands as a doctrine that could potentially be invoked to nullify an attempted switch from one perpetuity period to the other perpetuity period. Under that doctrine, interests created by the exercise of a nongeneral power are considered created by the donor of that power. See, e.g., Restatement (Second) of Property, Donative Transfers § 11.1 comment b (1986). As such, the maximum vesting period applicable to interests created by the exercise of a nongeneral power would apparently be covered by the perpetuity saving clause in the document that created the power, notwithstanding any different period the donee purports to adopt.

Reference. Section 2-901 is Section 1 of the

Uniform Statutory Rule Against Perpetuities (Uniform Act). For further discussion of this section, with numerous examples illustrating its application, see the Official Comment to Section 1 of the Uniform Act.

Restatement (Third) of Property: Wills and Other Donative Transfers (2011)

Position of the American Law Institute. It is the considered judgment of the American Law Institute that the recent statutory movement allowing the creation of perpetual or near-perpetual trusts is ill advised. The movement to abrogate the Rule Against Perpetuities has not been based on the merits of removing the Rule's curb on excessive dead-hand control. The policy issues associated with allowing perpetual or near-perpetual trusts have not been seriously discussed in the state legislatures. The driving force has been the effort to compete for trust industry (financial services) jobs from other states.

A rule that curbs excessive dead-hand control is deeply rooted in this nation's history and tradition, and for good reason. A 360-year trust created in the year 2010 could endure until the year 2370 and have over 100,000 beneficiaries. A 1000-year trust created in 2010 could terminate in the year 3010 and have millions of beneficiaries. No transferor has enough wisdom to make sound dispositions of property across such vast intervals and for beneficiaries so remote and so numerous. A 1000-year or 360-year trust created in 2010 might incorporate what are currently considered to be flexible provisions for a trust that could last that far into the future. To put that claim into perspective, consider the devices for controlling family wealth through subsequent generations that were available 360 or more years ago, in the year 1650 or earlier. Such devices, drafted before the invention of the typewriter, first took the form of the unbarrable entail and, after the entail became barrable, the strict settlement. These devices became archaic long ago. If that which was considered sophisticated 360 or more years ago is considered primitive today, there is reason to suspect that that which is considered sophisticated today will be considered primitive 360 or more years from now....

§ 27.1 Statement of the Rule Against Perpetuities

(a) A trust or other donative disposition of property is subject to judicial modification under § 27.2 to the extent that the trust or other disposition does not terminate on or before the expiration of the perpetuity period, except that if, upon the expiration of the perpetuity period, the share of a beneficiary is distributable upon reaching a specified age and the beneficiary is then younger than the earlier of the specified age or the age of 30, the beneficiary's share may, without judicial modification, be retained in trust until the beneficiary reaches or dies before reaching the earlier of the specified age or the age of 30.

(b) The perpetuity period expires at the death of the last living measuring life. The measuring lives are as follows:

(1) Except as otherwise provided in paragraph (2), the measuring lives constitute a group composed of the following individuals: the transferor, the beneficiaries of the disposition who are related to the transferor and no more than two generations younger than the transferor, and the beneficiaries of the disposition who are unrelated to the transferor and no more than the equivalent of two generations younger than the transferor.

(2) In the case of a trust or other property arrangement for the sole current benefit of a named individual who is more than two generations younger than the transferor or more than the equivalent of two generations younger than the transferor, the measuring life is the named individual.

Comment:

....

d. The subsection (b)(1) measuring lives. Under subsection (b)(1), the measuring lives constitute a group composed of the following individuals: the transferor, the beneficiaries of the disposition who are related to the transferor and no more than two generations younger than the transferor, and the beneficiaries of the disposition who are unrelated to the transferor and no more than the equivalent of two generations younger than the transferor. Only an individual (i.e., a human) can be a measuring life. A non-human (e.g., an animal or an entity such as a government, corporation, or trust) cannot be a measuring life.

d(1). Transferor. The transferor is a measuring life whether or not the transferor is a beneficiary of the trust or other donative disposition of property. Consequently, the perpetuity period can never expire before the transferor's death.

Identifying the transferor is important, not only because the transferor is a measuring life, but also because the other measuring lives are identified by their relationship to the transferor. As discussed in more detail in Comment *j*, the transferor in the case of a trust or other donative disposition created by the exercise of a power of appointment is the donor of the power, unless the exercised power was a presently exercisable general power. If the exercised power was a presently exercisable general power, the transferor is the donee of the power, whether or not the donee is also the donor. Because a presently exercisable general power is an ownership-equivalent power, the transferor is the donee of the power even if the donee does not exercise the power and the appointive property passes under a gift-in-default clause.

Any attempt to disguise the identity of the true transferor by the use of reciprocal transfers or any other deceptive means is ineffective. For example, if by prearrangement a parent gives money outright to his or her child or exchanges money or property with his or her child for the purpose in either case of creating a trust that the parent would otherwise have created, the transferor of the trust is the parent, not the child.

d(2). Beneficiaries of the trust or other donative disposition of property. Other than the transferor, the subsection (b)(1) measuring lives must be beneficiaries of the trust or other donative disposition of property. For purposes of this category, the term "beneficiaries of the trust or other donative disposition of property" refers to those individuals who take beneficial interests in the trust or other disposition and those individuals who have a power of appointment or have a reversionary interest arising by operation of law or otherwise. The term also includes individuals who have succeeded to an interest of a beneficiary by assignment, inheritance, or otherwise. See Restatement Third, Trusts § 48.

An appointee of a general or a nongeneral power of appointment is a beneficiary. A permissible appointee of a nongeneral power is a beneficiary if the individual is identified by name or is a member of a defined and limited class. See § 19.15, Comment *d*. Similarly, in the case of a discretionary trust, a permissible recipient of income or principal or both is a beneficiary.

As noted above (Comment *d*), a beneficiary must be an individual to be a measuring life. A non-human beneficiary cannot be a measuring life.

e. Beneficiaries related to the transferor who can be subsection (b)(1) measuring lives. The beneficiaries of the trust or other donative disposition of property who are related to the transferor can be measuring lives under subsection (b)(1) only if they are not more than two generations younger than the transferor. It is immaterial whether they were or were not in being at the creation of the interest....

e(2). Adopted child. With one exception (see below), an adoptee is assigned to the generation immediately below the adoptive parent's generation. Consequently, an adoptee is a measuring life if the adoptee is assigned to a generation that is not younger than two generations below the transferor's generation and is a named beneficiary of the trust or other donative disposition of property or a class member under § 14.5 or § 14.6. ...

There is one exception to the rule assigning an adoptee to the generation immediately below the adoptive parent's generation: if, before the adoption, the adoptee was a descendant of the transferor or a descendant of an ancestor of the transferor. In that case, the adoption does not cause the adoptee to be reassigned to a higher generation than his or her previous assignment. For example, if a parent of the transferor adopts a child of the transferor, the child remains assigned to the generation immediately below the transferor.

e(3). Child of assisted reproduction. A child of assisted reproduction is assigned to the generation immediately below the child's parent. Consequently, a child of assisted reproduction is a measuring life if the child is assigned to a generation no younger than two generations below the transferor's generation and is a named beneficiary of the trust or other disposition of property or a class member under § 14.8. ...

e(4). Spouse or domestic partner. A spouse or domestic partner or a surviving spouse or surviving domestic partner of the transferor or of a relative of the transferor is treated as related to the transferor and is assigned to the same generation as his or her spouse or domestic partner. Consequently, a spouse or domestic partner or a surviving spouse or surviving domestic partner is a measuring life if he or she is a beneficiary of the trust or other disposition of property and is married to or partnered with a relative of the transferor who is no younger than two generations below the transferor's generation. Divorce, dissolution of the partnership, or death does not cause the former spouse or domestic partner to be removed from the list of measuring lives, unless the divorce, dissolution, or death causes the former spouse or domestic partner to cease being a beneficiary. For purposes of this Restatement, the term "domestic partner" includes a person who qualifies as a domestic partner under § 6.03 of the Principles of the Law of Family Dissolution: Analysis and Recommendations. The term also includes an unmarried partner under any other relationship entitling the partners to intestacy or other spousal-equivalent rights under applicable law, such as a civil union or domestic partner relationship under the laws of various states.

The generation assignment of a current or former spouse or domestic partner is similar to the generation assignment of a current or former spouse under the federal generation-skipping transfer tax (GST tax). Currently, the GST tax assigns a current or former spouse of the transferor or of a lineal descendant of a grandparent of the transferor to the same generation as the transferor or the transferor's relative. IRC § 2651(c) provides: "An individual who has been married at any time to the transferor shall be assigned to the transferor's generation [and an] individual who has been married at any time to an individual [who is a lineal descendant of a grandparent of the transferor] shall be assigned to the generation of the individual so described."

Marriage or domestic partnership between two beneficiaries who are related to the transferor but in different generations does not change the generation assignment of either beneficiary. ...

f. Beneficiaries who are unrelated to the transferor who can be subsection (b)(1) measuring lives. The beneficiaries of the trust or other donative disposition of property who are unrelated to the transferor can be measuring lives under subsection (b)(1) only if they are not more than the equivalent of two generations younger than the transferor. It is immaterial whether they were in being at the creation of the interest. The generation assignment of individuals who are unrelated to the transferor is determined by the number of years that they are younger than the transferor. This Restatement refers to the federal generation-skipping transfer tax (GST tax) to determine whether an unrelated beneficiary is no more than the equivalent of two generations younger than the transferor. Currently, the GST tax assigns an unrelated beneficiary on the basis of the age difference between the beneficiary and the transferor. IRC § 2651(d) provides that such an individual is "assigned to a generation on the basis of the date of such individual's birth with − (1) an individual born not more than 12 ½ years after the date of the birth of the transferor assigned to the transferor's generation, (2) an individual born more than 12 ½ years but not more than 37 ½ years after the date of the birth of the transferor assigned to the first generation younger than the transferor, and (3) similar rules for a new generation every 25 years."

g. No subsection (b)(1) measuring life other than the transferor. If there is no measuring life under subsection (b)(1) other than the transferor, and there is no subsection (b)(2) measuring life, the transferor is the only measuring life and the perpetuity period expires at the transferor's death. See Comment *d(1).*

h. Beneficiary who can be a subsection (b)(2) measuring life. In the case of a trust or other property arrangement for the sole current benefit of a named individual who is more than two generations younger than the transferor or more than the equivalent of two generations younger than the transferor, the measuring life is the named individual. Requiring the beneficiary to be a named individual is intended to assure that the beneficiary is in being when the trust or other property arrangement is established. Subsection (b)(2) thus facilitates the establishment of a trust or other property arrangement for the sole current benefit of a beneficiary such as a living great-grandchild. If the trust or other property arrangement is created by a transfer from an existing trust or fund, the named individual is the measuring life so long as the named individual was named in the original trust or fund and the transfer occurs on or before the expiration of the perpetuity period under subsection (b)(1).

To qualify as the sole current beneficiary, the individual must be the only one who can then receive or benefit from mandatory or discretionary payments or distributions of income or property. The fact that a trustee, a custodian, or another has discretion to withhold income or property for future distribution to someone else does not disqualify the individual from being the sole current beneficiary and hence the measuring life. The beneficiary is the measuring life only so long as the beneficiary continues to be the sole current beneficiary. If, during the beneficiary's life, the beneficiary ceases being the sole current beneficiary, the beneficiary can no longer be a measuring life and, unless there are subsection (b)(1) measuring lives who are still living, the perpetuity period then expires.

Among the types of trusts or other property arrangements that would satisfy the requirement that the beneficiary be the sole current beneficiary are a special-needs trust, a "529 educational savings plan," a "Coverdale Education Savings Account," a "section 2503(c) trust" for a minor, and a custodianship under the Uniform Transfers to Minors Act, the Uniform Gifts to Minors Act, or the Uniform Custodial Trust Act.

A trust or other donative disposition of property is not subject to judicial modification merely because on or before the expiration of the perpetuity period described in subsection (b)(1) the trust or other disposition divides into one or more trusts or other property arrangements that are described in subsection (b)(2).

i. Share distributable at a specified age beyond expiration of the perpetuity period. Subsection (a) provides an exception to the rule that a trust or other donative disposition is subject to judicial modification to the extent that the trust or other disposition does not terminate on or before the expiration of the perpetuity period. If, upon the expiration of the perpetuity period, the share of a beneficiary is distributable upon reaching a specified age and the beneficiary is then younger than the earlier of the specified age or the age of 30, the beneficiary's share may, without judicial modification, be retained in trust until the beneficiary reaches or dies before reaching the earlier of the specified age or the age of 30. ...

j. Trust or other donative disposition created by the exercise of a power of appointment. In determining whether a trust or other donative disposition created by the exercise of a power of appointment is subject to judicial modification under this section, the question is whether the donor or the donee of the power is the transferor. As noted in Comment *d(1)*, the transferor in the case of a trust or other donative disposition of property created by the exercise of a power of appointment is the donor of the power, unless the exercised power was a presently exercisable general power. If the exercised power was a presently exercisable general power, the transferor is the donee of the power, whether or not the donee is also the donor. On the possibility of determining who is the transferor under the doctrine of selective allocation, see Chapter 19, Part E (§ 19.19).

j(1). Trust or other donative disposition created by the exercise of a presently exercisable general power. In the case of a trust or other donative disposition created by the exercise of a presently exercisable general power, the transferor is the donee of the power, whether or not the donee is also the donor. In the case of a presently exercisable general power, the relation-back doctrine is not followed. See § 17.4, Comment *f(1)*..

j(2). *Unexercised presently exercisable general power.* Because a presently exercisable general power is an ownership-equivalent power, the transferor is the donee of the power even if the donee does not exercise the power and the appointive property passes under a gift-in-default clause. ...

j(3). Trust or other donative disposition created by the exercise of a general testamentary power or a nongeneral power. In the case of a trust or other donative disposition created by the exercise of a general testamentary power or a nongeneral power, general principles of property law adopt the relation-back doctrine. See § 17.4, Comments *f(2)* and *f(3)*; § 19.19, Comment *g*. Under that doctrine, the donor of the power is the transferor of the trust or other donative disposition created by the exercise of the power.

If the trust or other donative disposition was created by the exercise of a nongeneral or testamentary power that was created by the exercise of a nongeneral or a testamentary power, the relation-back doctrine is applied twice and the donor of the first power is the transferor of the trust or other donative disposition created by the second donee's exercise of his or her power.

j(4). Trust or other donative disposition created by the exercise of a fiduciary distributive power. As noted in § 17.1, Comment *g*, a fiduciary distributive power is treated as the equivalent of a nongeneral power of appointment for purposes of the Rule Against Perpetuities. Consequently, the transferor in the case of a trust or other donative disposition of property created by the exercise of a fiduciary distributive power is the donor of the power. ....

§ 2-902. When Nonvested Property Interest or Power of Appointment Created.

(a) Except as provided in subsections (b) and (c) and in Section 2-905(a), the time of creation of a nonvested property interest or a power of appointment is determined under general principles of property law.

(b) For purposes of [Subpart] 1 of this [part], if there is a person who alone can exercise a power created by a governing instrument to become the unqualified beneficial owner of (i) a nonvested property interest or (ii) a property interest subject to a power of appointment described in Section 2-901(b) or (c), the nonvested property interest or power of appointment is created when the power to become the unqualified beneficial owner terminates. [For purposes of [Subpart] 1 of this [part], a joint power with respect to community property or to marital property under the Uniform Marital Property Act held by individuals married to each other is a power exercisable by one person alone.]

(c) For purposes of [Subpart] 1 of this [part], a nonvested property interest or a power of appointment arising from a transfer of property to a previously funded trust or other existing property arrangement is created when the nonvested property interest or power of appointment in the original contribution was created.

Comment

Section 2-902 defines the time when, for purposes of Subpart 1 of Part 9, a nonvested property interest or a power of appointment is created. The period of time allowed by Section 2-901 is measured from the time of creation of the nonvested property interest or power of appointment in question. Section 2-905, with certain exceptions, provides that Subpart 1 of Part 9 applies only to nonvested property interests and powers of appointment created on or after the effective date of Subpart 1 of Part 9.

Subsection (a). Subsection (a) provides that, with certain exceptions, the time of creation of nonvested property interests and powers of appointment is determined under general principles of property law. Because a will becomes effective as a dispositive instrument upon the decedent's death, not upon the execution of the will, general principles of property law determine that a nonvested property interest or a power of appointment created by will is created at the decedent's death. With respect to an inter-vivos transfer, an interest or power is created on the date the transfer becomes effective for purposes of property law generally, normally the date of delivery of the deed or the funding of the trust.

Nonvested Property Interests and Powers of Appointment Created by the Exercise of a Power of Appointment. If a nonvested property interest or a power of appointment was created by the testamentary or inter-vivos exercise of a power of appointment, general principles of property law adopt the "relation-back" doctrine. Under that doctrine, the appointed interests or powers are created when the power was created, not when it was exercised, if the exercised power was a nongeneral power or a general testamentary power. If the nonvested property interest or power of appointment was created by the exercise of a nongeneral or a testamentary power of appointment that was itself created by the exercise of a nongeneral or a testamentary power of

appointment, the relation-back doctrine is applied twice and the nonvested property interest or power of appointment was created when the first power of appointment was created, not when the second power was created or exercised.

Example 1. G's will created a trust that provided for the income to go to G's son, A, for life, remainder to such of A's descendants as A shall by will appoint.

A died leaving a will that exercised his nongeneral power of appointment, providing that the trust is to continue beyond A's death, paying the income to A's daughter, X, for her lifetime, remainder in corpus to such of X's descendants as X shall by will appoint; in default of appointment, to X's descendants who survive X, by representation.

A's exercise of his nongeneral power of appointment gave a nongeneral power of appointment to X and a nonvested property interest to X's descendants. For purposes of Section 2-901, X's power of appointment and the nonvested property interest in X's descendants is deemed to have been "created" at G's death when A's nongeneral power of appointment was created, not at A's death when he exercised his power of appointment.

Suppose that X subsequently dies leaving a will that exercises her nongeneral power of appointment. For purposes of Section 2-901, any nonvested property interest or power of appointment created by an exercise of X's nongeneral power of appointment is deemed to have been "created" at G's death, not at A's death or at X's death.

If the exercised power was a presently exercisable general power, the relation-back doctrine is not followed; the time of creation of the appointed property interests or appointed powers is regarded as the time when the power was irrevocably exercised, not when the power was created.

Example 2. The same facts as Example 1, except that A's will exercised his nongeneral power of appointment by providing that the trust is to continue beyond A's death, paying the income to A's daughter, X, for her lifetime, remainder in corpus to such person or persons, including X, her estate, her creditors, and the creditors of her estate, as X shall appoint; in default of appointment, to X's descendants who survive X, by representation.

A's exercise of his nongeneral power of appointment gave a presently exercisable general power of appointment to X. For purposes of Section 2-901, any nonvested property interest or power of appointment created by an exercise of X's presently exercisable general power of appointment is deemed to be "created" when X irrevocably exercises her power of appointment, not when her power of appointment or A's power of appointment was created.

A's exercise of his nongeneral power also granted a nonvested property interest to X's descendants (under the gift-in-default clause). Were it not for the presently exercisable general power granted to X, the nonvested property interest in X's surviving descendants would, under the relation-back doctrine, be deemed "created" for purposes of Section 2-901 at the time of G's death. However, under Section 2-902(b), the fact that X is granted the presently exercisable general power postpones the time of creation of the nonvested property interest of X's descendants. Under Section 2-902(b), that nonvested property interest is deemed not to have been "created" for purposes of Section 2-901 at G's death but rather when X's presently exercisable general power "terminates." Consequently, the time of "creation" of the nonvested interest of X's descendants is postponed as of the time that X was granted the presently exercisable general power (upon A's death) and continues in abeyance until X's power terminates. X's power terminates by the first to happen of the following: X's irrevocable exercise of her power; X's release of her power; X's entering into a contract to exercise or not to exercise her power; X's dying without exercising her power; or any other action or nonaction that would have the effect of terminating her power.

Subsection (b). Subsection (b) provides that, if one person can exercise a power to become the unqualified beneficial owner of a nonvested property interest (or a property interest subject to a power of appointment described in Section 2-901(b) or 2-901(c)), the time of creation of the nonvested property interest (or the power of appointment) is postponed until the power to become the unqualified beneficial owner ceases to exist. This is in accord with existing common law. The standard example of the application of this subsection is a revocable inter-vivos trust. For perpetuity purposes, both at common law and under Subpart 1 of Part 9, the nonvested property interests and powers of appointment created in the trust are created when the power to revoke expires, usually at the settlor's death. For another example of the application of subsection (b), see the last paragraph of Example 2, above.

Subsection (c). Subsection (c) provides that nonvested property interests and powers of appointment arising out of transfers to a previously funded trust or other existing property arrangement are created when the nonvested property interest or power of appointment arising out of the original contribution was created. This avoids an administrative difficulty that can arise at common law when subsequent transfers are made to an existing irrevocable inter-vivos trust. Arguably, at common law, each transfer starts the period of the Rule running anew as to each transfer. The prospect of staggered periods is avoided by subsection (c). Subsection (c) is in accord with the saving-clause principle of wait-and-see embraced by Part 9. If the irrevocable inter-vivos trust had contained a saving clause, the perpetuity-period component of the clause would be measured by reference to lives in being when the original contribution to the trust was made, and the clause would cover subsequent contributions as well.

Reference. Section 2-902 is Section 2 of the Uniform Statutory Rule Against Perpetuities (Uniform Act). For further discussion of this section, with examples illustrating its application, see the Official Comment to Section 2 of the Uniform Act.

§ 2-903. Reformation. Upon the petition of an interested person, a court shall reform a disposition in the manner that most closely approximates the transferor's manifested plan of distribution and is within the 90 years allowed by Section 2-901(a)(2), 2-901(b)(2), or 2-901(c)(2) if:

(1) a nonvested property interest or a power of appointment becomes invalid under Section 2-901

(statutory rule against perpetuities);

(2) a class gift is not but might become invalid under Section 2-901 (statutory rule against perpetuities) and the time has arrived when the share of any class member is to take effect in possession or enjoyment; or

(3) a nonvested property interest that is not validated by Section 2-901(a)(1) can vest but not within 90 years after its creation.

Comment

Section 2-903 implements the deferred-reformation feature of the Uniform Statutory Rule Against Perpetuities. Upon the petition of an interested person, the court is directed to reform a disposition within the limits of the allowable 90-year period, in the manner deemed by the court most closely to approximate the transferor's manifested plan of distribution, in any one of three circumstances. The "interested person" who would frequently bring the reformation suit would be the trustee.

Section 2-903 applies only to dispositions the validity of which is governed by the wait-and-see element of Section 2-901(a)(2), 2-901(b)(2), or 2-901(c)(2); it does not apply to dispositions that are initially valid under Section 2-901(a)(1), 2-901(b)(1), or 2-901(c)(1)—the codified version of the validating side of the common-law Rule.

Section 2-903 will seldom be applied. Of the fraction of trusts and other property arrangements that fail to meet the requirements for initial validity under the codified version of the validating side of the common-law Rule, almost all of them will have been settled under their own terms long before any of the circumstances requisite to reformation under Section 2-903 arise.

If, against the odds, one of the circumstances requisite to reformation does arise, it will be found easier than perhaps anticipated to determine how best to reform the disposition. The court is given two criteria to work with: (i) the transferor's manifested plan of distribution, and (ii) the allowable 90-year period. Because governing instruments are where transferors manifest their plans of distribution, the imaginary horrible of courts being forced to probe the minds of long-dead transferors will not materialize.

Paragraph (1). The theory of Section 2-903 is to defer the right to reformation until reformation becomes truly necessary. Thus, the basic rule of Section 2-903(1) is that the right to reformation does not arise until a nonvested property interest or a power of appointment becomes invalid; under Section 2-901, this does not occur until the expiration of the 90-year permissible vesting period. This

approach is more efficient than the "immediate cy pres" approach to perpetuity reform because it substantially reduces the number of reformation suits. It also is consistent with the saving-clause principle embraced by the Statutory Rule. Deferring the right to reformation until the permissible vesting period expires is the only way to grant every reasonable opportunity for the donor's disposition to work itself out without premature interference.

Paragraph (2). Although, generally speaking, reformation is deferred until an invalidity has occurred, Section 2-903 grants an earlier right to reformation when it becomes necessary to do so or when there is no point in waiting the full 90-year period out. Thus paragraph (2), which pertains to class gifts that are not yet but still might become invalid under the Statutory Rule, grants a right to reformation whenever the share of any class member whose share had vested within the permissible vesting period might otherwise have to wait out the remaining part of the 90 years before obtaining his or her share. Reformation under this subsection will seldom be needed, however, because of the common practice of structuring trusts to split into separate shares or separate trusts at the death of each income beneficiary, one such separate share or separate trust being created for each of the income beneficiary's then-living children; when this pattern is followed, the circumstances described in paragraph (2) will not arise.

Paragraph (3). Paragraph (3) also grants a right to reformation before the 90-year permissible vesting period expires. The circumstances giving rise to the right to reformation under paragraph (3) occurs if a nonvested property interest can vest but not before the 90-year period has expired. Though unlikely, such a case can theoretically arise. If it does, the interest—unless it terminates by its own terms earlier—is bound to become invalid under Section 2-901 eventually. There is no point in deferring the right to reformation until the inevitable happens. Section 2-903 provides for early reformation in such a case, just in case it arises.

Infectious Invalidity. Given the fact that this section makes reformation mandatory, not discretionary with the court, the common-law doctrine of infectious invalidity is superseded by this section. In a state in which the courts have been particularly zealous about applying the infectious-invalidity doctrine, however, an express codification of the abrogation of this doctrine might be thought desirable. If so, the above section could be made subsection (a), with the following new subsection (b) added: (b) The common-law rule known as the doctrine of infectious invalidity is abolished.

Reference. Section 2-903 is Section 3 of the Uniform Statutory Rule Against Perpetuities (Uniform Act). For further discussion of this section, with examples illustrating its application, see the Official Comment to Section 3 of the Uniform Act.

Restatement (Third) of Property: Wills and Other Donative Transfers (2011)

§ 27.2 Judicial Modification

Upon the petition of an interested person, the court shall modify a disposition that is subject to judicial modification under § 27.1(a). The form of the modification must be in a manner that most closely approximates the transferor's manifested plan of distribution and is within the perpetuity period provided in § 27.1(b).

---

§ 2-904. Exclusions from Statutory Rule Against Perpetuities. Section 2-901 (statutory rule against perpetuities) does not apply to:

(1) a nonvested property interest or a power of appointment arising out of a nondonative transfer, except a nonvested property interest or a power of appointment arising out of

  (A) a premarital or postmarital agreement,

  (B) a separation or divorce settlement,

  (C) a spouse's election,

  (D) a similar arrangement arising out of a prospective, existing, or previous marital relationship between the parties,

  (E) a contract to make or not to revoke a will or trust,

  (F) a contract to exercise or not to exercise a power of appointment,

  (G) a transfer in satisfaction of a duty of support, or

  (H) a reciprocal transfer;

(2) a fiduciary's power relating to the administration or management of assets, including the power of a fiduciary to sell, lease, or mortgage property, and the power of a fiduciary to determine principal and income;

(3) a power to appoint a fiduciary;

(4) a discretionary power of a trustee to distribute principal before termination of a trust to a beneficiary having an indefeasibly vested interest in the income and principal;

(5) a nonvested property interest held by a charity, government, or governmental agency or subdivision, if the nonvested property interest is preceded by an interest held by another charity, government, or governmental agency or subdivision;

(6) a nonvested property interest in or a power of appointment with respect to a trust or other property arrangement forming part of a pension, profit-sharing, stock bonus, health, disability, death benefit, income deferral, or other current or deferred benefit plan for one or more employees, independent contractors, or their beneficiaries or spouses, to which contributions are made for the purpose of distributing to or for the benefit of the participants or their beneficiaries or spouses the property, income, or principal in the trust or other property arrangement, except a nonvested property interest or a power of appointment that is created by an election of a participant or a beneficiary or spouse; or

(7) a property interest, power of appointment, or arrangement that was not subject to the common-law rule against perpetuities or is excluded by another statute of this state.

Comment

This section lists the interests and powers that are excluded from the Statutory Rule Against Perpetuities. This section is in part declaratory of existing common law but in part not. Under paragraph (7), all the exclusions from the common-law Rule recognized at common law and by statute in the state are preserved.

The major departure from existing common law comes in paragraph (1). In line with long-standing scholarly commentary, paragraph (1) excludes nondonative transfers from the Statutory Rule. The Rule Against Perpetuities is an inappropriate instrument of social policy to use as a control of such arrangements. The period of the Rule—a life in being plus 21 years—is suitable for donative transfers only, and this point applies with equal force to the 90-year allowable waiting period under the wait-and-see element of Section 2-901. That period, as noted, represents an approximation of the period of time

that would be produced, on average, by tracing a set of actual measuring lives and adding a 21-year period following the death of the survivor.

Certain types of transactions—although in some sense supported by consideration, and hence arguably nondonative—arise out of a domestic situation, and should not be excluded from the Statutory Rule. To avoid uncertainty with respect to such transactions, paragraph (1) lists and restores such transactions, such as premarital or postmarital agreements, contracts to make or not to revoke a will or trust, and so on, to the donative-transfers category that does not qualify for an exclusion.

Reference. Section 2-904 is Section 4 of the Uniform Statutory Rule Against Perpetuities (Uniform Act). For further discussion of this section, with examples illustrating its application, see the Official Comment to Section 4 of the Uniform Act.

Restatement (Third) of Property: Wills and Other Donative Transfers (2011)

§ 27.3 Exclusions from the Rule Against Perpetuities

The Rule Against Perpetuities does not apply to:

(1) commercial transactions, except that the Rule does apply to a trust or other disposition of property arising out of (a) a premarital or postmarital agreement, (b) a separation or divorce settlement, (c) a spouse's election, (d) a similar arrangement arising out of a prospective, existing, or previous marital relationship between the parties, (e) a contract to make or not to revoke a will or trust, (f) a contract to exercise or not to exercise a power of appointment, (g) a transfer in satisfaction of a duty of support, or (h) a reciprocal transfer;

(2) a trust or other donative disposition of property solely for charitable purposes as defined in Restatement Third, Trusts § 28;

(3) an honorary trust and a trust for the care of an animal if authorized by applicable law;

(4) a trust or other property arrangement forming part of a pension, profit-sharing, stock bonus, health, disability, death benefit, income deferral, or other current or deferred benefit plan for one or more employees, independent contractors, or their beneficiaries or spouses or domestic partners, to which contributions are made for the purpose of distributing to or for the benefit of the participants or their beneficiaries or spouses or domestic partners the property, income, or principal in the trust or other property arrangement, except a trust or other donative disposition of property that is created by an election of a participant or a beneficiary or spouse or domestic partner; and

(5) a trust or other disposition of property, a property interest, a power of appointment, or an arrangement that was not subject to the common-law Rule Against Perpetuities or is excluded by an applicable statute.

---

§ 2-905. Prospective Application.

(a) Except as extended by subsection (b), [Subpart] 1 of this [part] applies to a nonvested property interest or a power of appointment that is created on or after the effective date of [Subpart] 1 of this [part]. For purposes of this section, a nonvested property interest or a power of appointment created by the exercise of a power of appointment is created when the power is irrevocably exercised or when a revocable exercise becomes irrevocable.

(b) If a nonvested property interest or a power of appointment was created before the effective date of [Subpart] 1 of this [part] and is determined in a judicial proceeding, commenced on or after the effective date of [Subpart] 1 of this [part], to violate this state's rule against perpetuities as that rule existed before the effective date of [Subpart] 1 of this [part], a court upon the petition of an interested person may reform the disposition in the manner that most closely approximates the transferor's manifested plan of distribution and is within the limits of the rule against perpetuities applicable when the nonvested property interest or power of appointment was created.

Comment

Section 2-905 provides that, except for Section 2-905(b), this part applies only to nonvested property interests or powers of appointment created on or after the effective date of this subpart. The second sentence of subsection (a) establishes a special rule for nonvested property interests (and powers of appointment) created by the exercise of a power of appointment. The import of this special rule, which applies to the exercise of all types of powers of appointment (general testamentary powers and nongeneral powers as well as presently exercisable general powers), is that all the provisions of this subpart except Section 2-905(b) apply if the donee of a power of appointment exercises the power on or after the effective date of this subpart, whether the donee's exercise is revocable or irrevocable. In addition, all the provisions of subpart 1 except Section 2-905(b) apply if the donee exercised the power before the effective date of this subpart if (i) that pre-effective-date exercise was revocable and (ii) that revocable exercise becomes irrevocable on or after the effective date of this subpart. The special rule, in other words, prevents the common-law doctrine of relation back from inappropriately shrinking the reach of this subpart.

Although the Uniform Statutory Rule does not apply retroactively, Section 2-905(b) authorizes a court to exercise its equitable power of reform instruments that contain a violation of the state's former rule against perpetuities and to which the Uniform Statutory Rule does not apply because the offending property interest or power of appointment was created before the effective date of this subpart. Courts are urged to consider reforming such dispositions by judicially inserting a perpetuity saving clause, because a perpetuity saving clause would probably have been used at the drafting stage of the disposition had it been drafted competently. To obviate any possibility of an inequitable exercise of the equitable power to reform, Section 2-905(b) limits the authority to reform to situations in which the violation of the former rule against perpetuities is determined in a judicial proceeding that is commenced on or after the effective date of this subpart. The equitable power to reform would typically be exercised in the same judicial proceeding in which the invalidity is determined.

Reference. Section 2-905 is Section 5 of the Uniform Statutory Rule Against Perpetuities (Uniform Act). For further discussion of this section, with examples illustrating its application, see the Official Comment to Section 5 of the Uniform Act.

§ 2-906. [Supersession] [Repeal]. [Subpart] 1 of this [part] [supersedes the rule of the common law known as the rule against perpetuities] [repeals (list statutes to be repealed)].

Comment

The first set of bracketed text is provided for states that follow the common-law Rule Against Perpetuities. The second set of bracketed text is provided for the repeal of statutory adoptions of the common-law Rule Against Perpetuities, statutory variations of the common-law Rule Against Perpetuities, or statutory prohibitions on the suspension of the power of alienation for more than a certain period. Some states may find it appropriate to enact both sets of bracketed text by joining them with the word "and." This would be appropriate in states having a statute that declares that the common-law Rule Against Perpetuities is in force in the state except as modified therein.

A cautionary note for states repealing listed statutes: If the statutes to be repealed contain exclusions from the rule against perpetuities, states should consider whether to repeal or retain those exclusions, in light of Section 2-904(7), which excludes from the Uniform Statutory Rule property interests, powers of appointment, and other arrangements "excluded by another statute of this state."

SUBPART 2. [HONORARY TRUSTS]

General Comment

Subpart 2 contains an optional provision on honorary trusts and trusts for pets. If this optional provision is enacted, a new paragraph (8) should be added to Section 2-904 to avoid an overlap or conflict between Subpart 1 of Part 9 (USRAP) and Subpart 2 of Part 9. Paragraph (8) makes it clear that Subpart 2 of Part 9 is the exclusive provision applicable to the property interests or arrangements subjected to a time limit by the provisions of Subpart 2. Paragraph (8) states:

"(8) a property interest or arrangement subjected to a time limit under Subpart 2 of Part 9."

Additionally, the "or" at the end of Section 2-904(6) should be removed and placed after Section 2-904(7).

[Optional provision for validating and limiting the duration of so-called honorary trusts and trusts for pets.]

[§ 2-907. Honorary Trusts; Trusts for Pets.

(a) **[Honorary Trust.]** Subject to subsection (c), if (i) a trust is for a specific lawful noncharitable purpose or for lawful noncharitable purposes to be selected by the trustee and (ii) there is no definite or definitely ascertainable beneficiary designated, the trust may be performed by the trustee for [21] years but no longer, whether or not the terms of the trust contemplate a longer duration.

(b) **[Trust for Pets.]** Subject to this subsection and subsection (c), a trust for the care of a designated domestic or pet animal is valid. The trust terminates when no living animal is covered by the trust. A governing instrument must be liberally construed to bring the transfer within this subsection, to presume against the merely precatory or honorary nature of the disposition, and to carry out the general intent of the transferor. Extrinsic evidence is admissible in determining the transferor's intent.

(c) **[Additional Provisions Applicable to Honorary Trusts and Trusts for Pets.]** In addition to the provisions of subsection (a) or (b), a trust covered by either of those subsections is subject to the following provisions:

(1) Except as expressly provided otherwise in the trust instrument, no portion of the principal or income may be converted to the use of the trustee or to any use other than for the trust's purposes or for the benefit of a covered animal.

(2) Upon termination, the trustee shall transfer the unexpended trust property in the following order:

(A) as directed in the trust instrument;

(B) if the trust was created in a nonresiduary clause in the transferor's will or in a codicil to the transferor's will, under the residuary clause in the transferor's will; and

(C) if no taker is produced by the application of subparagraph (A) or (B), to the transferor's heirs under Section 2-711.

(3) For the purposes of Section 2-707, the residuary clause is treated as creating a future interest under the terms of a trust.

(4) The intended use of the principal or income can be enforced by an individual designated for that purpose in the trust instrument or, if none, by an individual appointed by a court upon application to it by an individual.

(5) Except as ordered by the court or required by the trust instrument, no filing, report, registration, periodic accounting, separate maintenance of funds, appointment, or fee is required by reason of the existence of the fiduciary relationship of the trustee.

(6) A court may reduce the amount of the property transferred, if it determines that that amount substantially exceeds the amount required for the intended use. The amount of the reduction, if any,

passes as unexpended trust property under subsection (c)(2).

(7) If no trustee is designated or no designated trustee is willing or able to serve, a court shall name a trustee. A court may order the transfer of the property to another trustee, if required to assure that the intended use is carried out and if no successor trustee is designated in the trust instrument or if no designated successor trustee agrees to serve or is able to serve. A court may also make such other orders and determinations as shall be advisable to carry out the intent of the transferor and the purpose of this section.]

Comment

Subsection (a) of this section authorizes so-called honorary trusts and places a 21-year limit on their duration. The figure "21" is bracketed to indicate that an enacting state may select a different figure.

Subsection (b) provides more elaborate provisions for a particular type of honorary trust, the trust for the care of domestic or pet animals. Under subsection (b), a trust for the care of a designated domestic or pet animal is valid.

Subsection (b) meets a concern of many pet owners by providing them a means for leaving funds to be used for the pet's care.

Under the Uniform Directed Trust Act (UDTA), approved by the Uniform Law Commission in 2017, a person named by the terms of a trust to enforce the trust qualifies as a "trust director" in a state that adopts the UDTA. See Official Comment to UDTA Section 6, stating in relevant part:

Pet and other noncharitable purpose trust enforcers. Statutes in every state validate a trust for a pet animal and certain other noncharitable purposes. Following Uniform Probate Code § 2-907(c)(4) (1993) and Uniform Trust Code §§ 408(b) and 409(2) (2000), most of these statutes authorize enforcement of the trust by a person named in the terms of the trust. In a state that enacts this act, such a person would be a trust director.

Historical Note. This Comment was revised in 1993 and 2018. For the prior version, see 8 U.L.A. 180 (Supp.1992).

PART 10
UNIFORM INTERNATIONAL WILLS ACT (1977)

Prefatory Note

Introduction. The purpose of the Washington Convention of 1973 concerning international wills is to provide testators with a way of making wills that will be valid as to form in all countries joining the Convention. As proposed by the Convention, the objective would be achieved through uniform local rules of form, rather than through local or international law that makes recognition of foreign wills turn on choice of law rules involving possible application of foreign law. The international will provisions, prepared for the National Conference of Commissioners on Uniform State Laws by the Joint Editorial Board for the Uniform Probate Code which has functioned as a special committee of the Conference for the project, should be enacted by all states, including those that have not accepted the Uniform Probate Code. To that end, this statute is framed both as a free-standing act and as an added part of the Uniform Probate Code. The bracketed headings and numbers fit the proposal into UPC; the others present the proposal as a free-standing act.

Uniform enactment of these provisions will permit the Washington Convention of 1973 to be implemented through state legislation familiar to will draftsmen. Thus, local proof of foreign law and reliance on federal legislation regarding wills can be avoided when foreign wills come into our states to be implemented. Also, the citizens of all states will have a will form available that should greatly reduce perils of proof and risks of invalidity that attend proof of American wills abroad.

....

§ 2-1001. Definitions. In this [part]:

(1) "International will" means a will executed in conformity with Sections 2-1002 through 2-1005.

(2) "Authorized person" and "person authorized to act in connection with international wills" mean

a person who by Section 2-1009, or by the laws of the United States including members of the diplomatic and consular service of the United States designated by Foreign Service Regulations, is empowered to supervise the execution of international wills.

§ 2-1002. International Will; Validity.

(a) A will shall be valid as regards form, irrespective particularly of the place where it is made, of the location of the assets and of the nationality, domicile, or residence of the testator, if it is made in the form of an international will complying with the requirements of this [part].

(b) The invalidity of the will as an international will shall not affect its formal validity as a will of another kind.

(c) This [part] shall not apply to the form of testamentary dispositions made by two or more persons in one instrument.

§ 2-1003. International Will; Requirements.

(a) The will shall be made in writing. It need not be written by the testator himself. It may be written in any language, by hand or by any other means.

(b) The testator shall declare in the presence of two witnesses and of a person authorized to act in connection with international wills that the document is his will and that he knows the contents thereof. The testator need not inform the witnesses, or the authorized person, of the contents of the will.

(c) In the presence of the witnesses, and of the authorized person, the testator shall sign the will or, if he has previously signed it, shall acknowledge his signature.

(d) When the testator is unable to sign, the absence of his signature does not affect the validity of the international will if the testator indicates the reason for his inability to sign and the authorized person makes note thereof on the will. In these cases, it is permissible for any other person present, including the authorized person or one of the witnesses, at the direction of the testator to sign the testator's name for him, if the authorized person makes note of this also on the will, but it is not required that any person sign the testator's name for him.

(e) The witnesses and the authorized person shall there and then attest the will by signing in the presence of the testator.

§ 2-1004. International Will; Other Points of Form.

(a) The signatures shall be placed at the end of the will. If the will consists of several sheets, each sheet will be signed by the testator or, if he is unable to sign, by the person signing on his behalf or, if there is no such person, by the authorized person. In addition, each sheet shall be numbered.

(b) The date of the will shall be the date of its signature by the authorized person. That date shall be noted at the end of the will by the authorized person.

(c) The authorized person shall ask the testator whether he wishes to make a declaration concerning the safekeeping of his will. If so and at the express request of the testator the place where he intends to have his will kept shall be mentioned in the certificate provided for in Section 2-1005.

(d) A will executed in compliance with Section 2-1003 shall not be invalid merely because it does not comply with this section.

§ 2-1005. International Will; Certificate. The authorized person shall attach to the will a certificate to be signed by him establishing that the requirements of this [part] for valid execution of an international will have been complied with. The authorized person shall keep a copy of the certificate and deliver another to the testator. The certificate shall be substantially in the following form:

CERTIFICATE
(Convention of October 26, 1973)

1. I, _____ (name, address and capacity), a person authorized to act in connection with international wills

2. Certify that on _____ (date) at _____ (place)

3. (testator) _____ (name, address, date and place of birth) in my presence and that of the witnesses

4. (a) _____ (name, address, date and place of birth)

   (b) _____ (name, address, date and place of birth)has declared that the attached document is his will and that he knows the contents thereof.

5. I furthermore certify that:

6. (a) in my presence and in that of the witnesses

   (1) the testator has signed the will or has acknowledged his signature previously affixed.

   * following a declaration of the testator stating that he

   (2) was unable to sign his will for the following reason _____, I have mentioned this declaration on the will

   * and the signature has been affixed by _____ (name and address)

7. (b) the witnesses and I have signed the will;

8. *(c) each page of the will has been signed by _____ and numbered;

9. (d) I have satisfied myself as to the identity of the testator and of the witnesses as designated above;

10. (e) the witnesses met the conditions requisite to act as such according to the law under which I am acting;

11. *(f) the testator has requested me to include the following statement concerning the safekeeping of his will:

12. PLACE OF EXECUTION

13. DATE

14. SIGNATURE and, if necessary, SEAL

     * to be completed if appropriate

§ 2-1006. International Will; Effect of Certificate. In the absence of evidence to the contrary, the certificate of the authorized person shall be conclusive of the formal validity of the instrument as a will under this [part]. The absence or irregularity of a certificate shall not affect the formal validity of a will under this [part].

§ 2-1007. International Will; Revocation. The international will shall be subject to the ordinary rules of revocation of wills.

§ 2-1008. Source and Construction. Sections 2-1001 through 2-1007 derive from Annex to Convention of October 26, 1973, Providing a Uniform Law on the Form of an International Will. In interpreting and applying this [part], regard shall be had to its international origin and to the need for uniformity in its interpretation.

§ 2-1009. Persons Authorized to Act in Relation to International Will; Eligibility; Recognition by Authorizing Agency. Individuals who have been admitted to practice law before the courts of this state and who are in good standing as active law practitioners in this state, are hereby declared to be authorized persons in relation to international wills.

[**§ 2-1010. International Will Information Registration.** The [Secretary of State] shall establish a registry system by which authorized persons may register in a central information center, information regarding the execution of international wills, keeping that information in strictest confidence until the death of the maker and then making it available to any person desiring information about any will who presents a death certificate or other satisfactory evidence of the testator's death to the center. Information that may be received, preserved in confidence until death, and reported as indicated is limited to the name, social-security or any other individual-identifying number established by law, address, and date and place of birth of the testator, and the intended place of deposit or safekeeping of the instrument pending the death of the maker. The [Secretary of State], at the request of the authorized person, may cause the information it receives about execution of any international will to be transmitted to the registry system of another jurisdiction as identified by the testator, if that other system adheres to rules protecting the confidentiality of the information similar to those established in this state.]

PART 11
UNIFORM DISCLAIMER OF PROPERTY
INTERESTS ACT (1999/2006)

General Comment

Part 11 incorporates into the Code the Uniform Disclaimer of Property Interests Act (1999/2006) (UDPIA or Act). The UDPIA replaces the Code's former disclaimer provision (Section 2-801). It also replaces three Uniform Acts promulgated in 1978 (Uniform Disclaimer of Property Interests Act, Uniform Disclaimer of Transfers by Will, Intestacy or Appointment Act, and Uniform Disclaimer of Transfers under Nontestamentary Instruments Act). The new Act is the most comprehensive disclaimer statute ever written. It is designed to allow every sort of disclaimer, including those that are useful for tax planning purposes. It does not, however, include a specific time limit on the making of any disclaimer. Because a disclaimer is a refusal to accept, the only bar to a disclaimer should be acceptance of the offer. In addition, in almost all jurisdictions disclaimers can be used for more than tax planning. A proper disclaimer will often keep the disclaimed property from the disclaimant's creditors. In short, the new Act is an enabling statute which prescribes all the rules for refusing a proffered interest in or power over property and the effect of that refusal on the power or interest while leaving the effect of the refusal itself to other law. Section 2-1113(e) explicitly states that a disclaimer may be barred or limited by law other than the Act.

The decision not to include a specific time limit—to "decouple" the disclaimer statute from the time requirement applicable to a "qualified disclaimer" under IRC § 2518—is also designed to reduce confusion. The older Uniform Acts and almost all the current state statutes (many of which are based on those Acts) were drafted in the wake of the passage of IRC § 2518 in 1976. That provision replaced the "reasonable time" requirement of prior law with a requirement that a disclaimer must be made within nine months of the creation of the interest disclaimed if the disclaimer is to be a "qualified disclaimer" which is not regarded as a transfer by the disclaimant. The statutes that were written in response to this new provision of tax law reflected the nine month time limit. Under most of these statutes (including the older Uniform Acts and former Section 2-801) a disclaimer must be made within nine months of the creation of a present interest (for example, as disclaimer of an outright gift under a will must be made within nine months of the decedent's death), which corresponds to the requirement of IRC § 2518. A future interest, however, may be disclaimed within nine months of the time the interest vests in possession or enjoyment (for example, a remainder whether or not contingent on surviving the holder of the life income interest must be disclaimed within nine months of the death of the life income beneficiary). The time limit for future interests does not correspond to IRC § 2518 which generally requires that a qualified disclaimer of a future interest be made within nine months of the interest's creation, no matter how contingent it may then be. The nine-month time limit of the existing statutes really is a trap. While it superficially conforms to IRC

§ 2518, its application to the disclaimer of future interests does not. The removal of all mention of time limits will clearly signal the practitioner that the requirements for a tax qualified disclaimer are set by different law.

The elimination of the time limit is not the only change from current statutes. The Act abandons the concept of "relates back" as a proxy for when a disclaimer becomes effective. Instead, by stating specifically when a disclaimer becomes effective and explicitly stating in Section 2-1105(f) that a disclaimer "is not a transfer, assignment, or release", the Act makes clear the results of refusing property or powers through a disclaimer. Second, UDPIA creates rules for several types of disclaimers that have not been explicitly addressed in previous statutes. The Act provides detailed rules for the disclaimer of interests in jointly held property (Section 2-1107). Such disclaimers have important uses especially in tax planning, but their status under current law is not clear. Furthermore, although current statutes mention the disclaimer of jointly held property, they provide no details. Recent developments in the law of qualified disclaimers of jointly held property make fuller treatment of such disclaimers necessary. Section 2-1108 addresses the disclaimer by trustees of property that would otherwise become part of the trust. The disclaimer of powers of appointment and other powers not held in a fiduciary capacity is treated in Section 2-1109 and disclaimers by appointees, objects, and takers in default of exercise of a power of appointment is the subject of Section 2-1110. Finally, Section 2-1111 provides rules for the disclaimer of powers held in a fiduciary capacity.

§ 2-1101. [Reserved.]

§ 2-1102. Definitions. In this [part]:

(1) "Disclaimant" means the person to whom a disclaimed interest or power would have passed had the disclaimer not been made.

(2) "Disclaimed interest" means the interest that would have passed to the disclaimant had the disclaimer not been made.

(3) "Disclaimer" means the refusal to accept an interest in or power over property.

(4) "Fiduciary" means a personal representative, trustee, agent acting under a power of attorney, or other person authorized to act as a fiduciary with respect to the property of another person.

(5) "Jointly held property" means property held in the name of two or more persons under an arrangement in which all holders have concurrent interests and under which the last surviving holder is entitled to the whole of the property.

(6) "Person" means an individual, corporation, business trust, estate, trust, partnership, limited liability company, association, joint venture, government; governmental subdivision, agency, or instrumentality; public corporation, or any other legal or commercial entity.

(7) "State" means a state of the United States, the District of Columbia, Puerto Rico, the United States Virgin Islands, or any territory or insular possession subject to the jurisdiction of the United States. The term includes an Indian tribe or band, or Alaskan native village, recognized by federal law or formally acknowledged by a state.

(8) "Trust" means:

(A) an express trust, charitable or noncharitable, with additions thereto, whenever and however created; and

(B) a trust created pursuant to a statute, judgment, or decree which requires the trust to be administered in the manner of an express trust.

Comment

The definition of "disclaimant" (paragraph (1)) limits the term to the person who would have received the disclaimed property or power if the disclaimer had not been made. The disclaimant is not necessarily the person making the disclaimer, who may be a guardian, custodian, or other fiduciary acting for the disclaimant or the personal representative of the disclaimant's estate.

The term "disclaimed interest" (paragraph (2)) refers to the subject matter of a disclaimer of an interest in property and provides a compact term the use of which simplifies the drafting of Section 2-1106.

The definition of "disclaimer" (paragraph (3)) expands previous definitions. Prior Uniform Acts provided for a disclaimer of "the right of succession to any property or interest therein" and former Section 2-801 referred to "an interest in or with respect to property or an interest therein." These previously authorized types of disclaimers are continued by the present language referring to "an interest in ... property." The language referring to "power over property" broadens the permissible scope of disclaimers to include any power over property that gives the power-holder a right to control property, whether it be cast in the form of a power of appointment or a fiduciary's management power over property or discretionary power of distribution over income or corpus.

Under the Act, a "fiduciary" (defined in paragraph (4)) is given the power to disclaim except where specifically prohibited by state law or by the document creating the fiduciary relationship. See Section 2-1105(b).

The term "jointly held property" (paragraph (5)) includes not only a traditional joint tenancy but also other property that is "held", but may not be "owned", by two or more persons with a right of survivorship. One form of such property is a joint bank account between parties who are not married to each other which, under the laws of many states, is owned by the parties in proportion to their deposits.

(See Section 6-211(b).) This "holding" concept, as opposed to "owning", may also be true with joint brokerage accounts under the law of some states. *See* Treas. Regs. § 25.2518-2(c)(4).

The terms "person" (paragraph (6)), "state" (paragraph) 7, and "trust" (paragraph (8)) are also defined in Section 1-201 of this Code, but the more modern version of these definitions is included here for ease of reference. For purposes of this part, the definitions in this section control.

The term "trust" (paragraph (8)) means an express trust, whether private or charitable, including a trust created by statute, court judgment or decree which is to be administered in the manner of an express trust. Excluded from the Act's coverage are resulting and constructive trusts, which are not express trusts but remedial devices imposed by law. The Act is directed primarily at express trusts which arise in an estate planning or other donative context, but the definition of "trust" is not so limited. A trust created pursuant to a divorce action would be included, even though such a trust is not donative but is created pursuant to a bargained for exchange. The extent to which even more commercially-oriented trusts are subject to the Act will vary depending on the type of trust and the laws, other than this Act, under which the trust is created. Commercial trusts come in various forms, including trusts created pursuant to a state business trust act and trusts created to administer specified funds, such as to pay a pension or to manage pooled investments. *See* John H. Langbein, The Secret Life of the Trust: The Trust as an Instrument of Commerce, 107 Yale L.J. 165 (1997).

§ 2-1103. Scope. This [part] applies to disclaimers of any interest in or power over property, whenever created.

Former (1993) Version

§ 2-801(g) [Application.] An interest in property that exists on the effective date of this section as to which, if a present interest, the time for filing a disclaimer under this section has not expired or, if a future interest, the interest has not become indefeasibly vested or the taker finally ascertained, may be disclaimed within [nine] months after the effective date of this section.

---

§ 2-1104. Part Supplemented by Other Law.

(a) Unless displaced by a provision of this [part], the principles of law and equity supplement this [part].

(b) This [part] does not limit any right of a person to waive, release, disclaim, or renounce an interest in or power over property under a law other than this [part].

Comment

The supplementation of the provisions of this Act by the principles of law and equity in Section 2-1104(a) is important because this Act is not a complete statement of the law relating to disclaimers. For example, Section 2-1105(b) permits a trustee to disclaim, yet the disclaiming trustee must still adhere to all applicable fiduciary duties. See Restatement (Third) of Trusts § 86 Reporter's Notes to cmt. f. Similarly, the provisions of Section 2-1113 on bars to disclaiming are subject to supplementation by equitable principles. See *Badouh v. Hale*, 22 S.E.3d 392 (Tex. 2000) (invalidating a disclaimer of an expectancy as contrary to equity, on the ground that the putative disclaimant had earlier pledged it to a third party).

Not only are the provisions of this Act supplemented by the principles of law and equity, but under Section 2-1104(b) the provisions of this Act do not preempt other law that creates the right to reject an interest in or power over property. The growth of the law would be unduly restricted were the provisions of the Act completely to displace other law.

Historical Note. This Comment was added in 2010.

Former (1993) Version

§ 2-801(f) [Remedy Not Exclusive.] This section does not abridge the right of a person to waive, release, disclaim, or renounce property or an interest therein under any other statute.

---

§ 2-1105. Power to Disclaim; General Requirements; When Irrevocable.

(a) A person may disclaim, in whole or part, any interest in or power over property, including a power of appointment. A person may disclaim the interest or power even if its creator imposed a spendthrift provision or similar restriction on transfer or a restriction or limitation on the right to disclaim.

(b) Except to the extent a fiduciary's right to disclaim is expressly restricted or limited by another statute of this state or by the instrument creating the fiduciary relationship, a fiduciary may disclaim, in whole or part, any interest in or power over property, including a power of appointment, whether acting in a personal or representative capacity. A fiduciary may disclaim the interest or power even if its creator imposed a spendthrift provision or similar restriction on transfer or a restriction or limitation on the right to disclaim, or an instrument other than the instrument that created the fiduciary relationship imposed a restriction or limitation on the right to disclaim.

(c) To be effective, a disclaimer must be in a writing or other record, declare the disclaimer, describe the interest or power disclaimed, be signed by the person making the disclaimer, and be delivered or filed in the manner provided in Section 2-1112. In this subsection:

(1) "record" means information that is inscribed on a tangible medium or that is stored in an electronic or other medium and is retrievable in perceivable form.

(2) "signed" means, with present intent to authenticate or adopt a record, to;

(A) execute or adopt a tangible symbol; or

(B) attach to or logically associate with the record an electronic sound, symbol, or process.

(d) A partial disclaimer may be expressed as a fraction, percentage, monetary amount, term of years, limitation of a power, or any other interest or estate in the property.

(e) A disclaimer becomes irrevocable when it is delivered or filed pursuant to Section 2-1112 or when it becomes effective as provided in Sections 2-1106 through 2-1111, whichever occurs later.

(f) A disclaimer made under this [part] is not a transfer, assignment, or release.

Comment

Subsections (a) and (b) give both persons (as defined in Section 2-1102(6)) and fiduciaries (as defined in Section 2-1102(4)) a broad power to disclaim both interests in and powers over property. In both instances, the ability to disclaim interests is comprehensive; it does not matter whether the disclaimed interest is vested, either in interest or in possession. For example, Father's will creates a testamentary trust which is to pay income to his descendants and after the running of the traditional perpetuities period is to terminate and be distributed to his descendants then living by representation. If at any time there are no descendants, the trust is to terminate and be distributed to collateral relatives. At the time of Father's death he has many descendants and the possibility of his line dying out and the collateral relatives taking under the trust is remote in the extreme. Nevertheless, under the Act the collateral relatives may disclaim their contingent remainders. (In order to make a qualified disclaimer for tax purposes, however, they must disclaim them within 9 months of Father's death.) Every sort of power may also be disclaimed.

Subsection (a) continues the provisions of current law by making ineffective any attempt to limit the right to disclaim which the creator of an interest or non-fiduciary power seeks to impose on a person. This provision follows from the principle behind all disclaimers—no one can be forced to accept property—and extends that principle to powers over property.

This Act also gives fiduciaries broad powers to disclaim both interests and powers. A fiduciary who may also be a beneficiary of the fiduciary arrangement may disclaim in either capacity. For example, a trustee who is also one of several beneficiaries of a trust may have the power to invade trust principal for the beneficiaries. The trustee may disclaim the power as trustee under Section 2-1111 or may disclaim as a holder of a power of appointment under Section 2-1109. Subsection (b) also gives fiduciaries the right to disclaim in spite of spendthrift or similar restrictions given, but subjects that right to a restriction applicable only to fiduciaries. As a policy matter, the creator of a trust or other arrangement creating a fiduciary relationship should be able to prevent a fiduciary accepting office under the arrangement from altering the parameters of the relationship. This reasoning also applies to fiduciary relationships created by statute such as those governing conservatorships and guardianships. Subsection (b) therefore does not override express restrictions on disclaimers contained in the instrument creating the fiduciary relationship or in other statutes of the state.

Subsection (c) sets forth the formal requirements for a disclaimer. The definition of "record" in this subsection is derived from the Uniform Electronic Transactions Act § 102. The definition recognizes that a disclaimer may be prepared in forms other than typewritten pages with a signature in pen. Because of the novelty of a disclaimer executed in electronic form and the ease with which the term "record" can be confused with recording of documents, the Act does not use the term "record" in isolation but refers to "writing or other record." The delivery requirement is set forth in Section 2-1112.

Subsection (d) specifically allows a partial disclaimer of an interest in property or of a power over property, and gives the disclaimant wide latitude in describing the portion disclaimed. For example, a residuary beneficiary of an estate may disclaim a fraction or percentage of the residue or may disclaim specific property included in the residue (all the shares of X corporation or a specific number of shares). A devisee or donee may disclaim specific acreage or an undivided fraction or carve out a life estate or remainder from a larger interest in real or personal property. (It must be noted, however, that a disclaimer by a devisee or donee which seeks to "carve out" a remainder or life estate is not a "qualified disclaimer" for tax purposes, Treas. Reg. § 25.2518-3(b).)

Subsection (e) makes the disclaimer irrevocable on the later to occur of (i) delivery or filing or (ii) its becoming effective under the section governing the disclaimer of the particular power or interest. A disclaimer must be "irrevocable" in order to be a qualified disclaimer for tax purposes. Since a disclaimer under this Act becomes effective at the time significant for tax purposes, a disclaimer under this Act will always meet the irrevocability requirement for tax qualification. The interaction of the Act and the requirements for a tax qualified disclaimer can be illustrated by analyzing a disclaimer of an interest in a revocable lifetime trust.

Example 1. G creates a revocable lifetime trust which will terminate on G's death and distribute the trust property to G's surviving descendants by representation. G's son, S, determines that he would prefer his share of G's estate to pass to his descendants and executes a disclaimer of his interest in the revocable trust. The disclaimer is then delivered to G (*see* Section 2-1112(e)(3)). The disclaimer is not irrevocable at that time, however, because it will not become effective until G's death when the trust becomes irrevocable (*see* Section 2-1106(b)(1)). Because the disclaimer will not become irrevocable until it becomes effective at G's death, S may recall the disclaimer before G's death and, if he does so, the disclaimer will have no effect.

Subsection (f) restates the long standing rule that a disclaimer is a true refusal to accept and not an act by which the disclaimant transfers, assigns, or releases the disclaimed interest. This subsection states the effect and meaning of the traditional "relation back" doctrine of prior Acts. It also makes it clear that the disclaimed interest passes without direction by the disclaimant, a requirement of tax qualification.

Former (1993) Version

§ 2-801. Disclaimer of Property Interests.

(a) [**Right to Disclaim Interest in Property.**] A person, or the representative of a person, to whom an interest in or with respect to property or an interest therein devolves by whatever means may disclaim it in whole or in part by delivering or filing a written disclaimer under this section. The right to disclaim exists notwithstanding (i) any limitation on the interest of the disclaimant in the nature of a spendthrift provision or similar restriction or (ii) any restriction or limitation on the right to disclaim contained in the governing instrument. For purposes of this subsection, the "representative of a person" includes a personal representative of a decedent, a conservator of a disabled person, a guardian of a minor or incapacitated person, and an agent acting on behalf of the person within the authority of a power of attorney.

(b) . . . .

(c) [**Form of Disclaimer.**] The disclaimer must (i) describe the property or interest disclaimed, (ii) declare the disclaimer and extent thereof, and (iii) be signed by the disclaimant.

---

§ 2-1106. Disclaimer of Interest in Property.

(a) In this section:

(1) "Future interest" means an interest that takes effect in possession or enjoyment, if at all, later than the time of its creation.

(2) "Time of distribution" means the time when a disclaimed interest would have taken effect in possession or enjoyment.

(b) Except for a disclaimer governed by Section 2-1107 or 2-1108, the following rules apply to a disclaimer of an interest in property:

(1) The disclaimer takes effect as of the time the instrument creating the interest becomes irrevocable, or, if the interest arose under the law of intestate succession, as of the time of the intestate's death.

(2) The disclaimed interest passes according to any provision in the instrument creating the interest providing for the disposition of the interest, should it be disclaimed, or of disclaimed interests in general.

(3) If the instrument does not contain a provision described in paragraph (2), the following rules apply:

(A) If the disclaimant is not an individual, the disclaimed interest passes as if the disclaimant did not exist.

(B) If the disclaimant is an individual, except as otherwise provided in subparagraphs (C) and (D), the disclaimed interest passes as if the disclaimant had died immediately before the time of distribution.

(C) If by law or under the instrument, the descendants of the disclaimant would share in the disclaimed interest by any method of representation had the disclaimant died before the time of distribution, the disclaimed interest passes only to the descendants of the disclaimant who survive the time of distribution.

(D) If the disclaimed interest would pass to the disclaimant's estate had the disclaimant died before the time of distribution, the disclaimed interest instead passes by representation to the descendants of the disclaimant who survive the time of distribution. If no descendant of the disclaimant survives the time of distribution, the disclaimed interest passes to those persons, including the state but excluding the disclaimant, and in such shares as would succeed to the transferor's intestate estate under the intestate succession law of the transferor's domicile had the transferor died at the time of distribution. However, if the transferor's surviving spouse is living but is remarried at the time of distribution, the transferor is deemed to have died unmarried at the time of distribution.

(4) Upon the disclaimer of a preceding interest, a future interest held by a person other than the disclaimant takes effect as if the disclaimant had died or ceased to exist immediately before the time of distribution, but a future interest held by the disclaimant is not accelerated in possession or enjoyment.

Comment

Subsection (a) defines two terms that are used only in Section 2-1106. The first, "future interest, is used in Section 2-1106(b)(4) in connection with the acceleration rule.

The second defined term, "time of distribution", is used in determining to whom the disclaimed interest passes (*see* below). Possession or enjoyment is a term of art and means that time at which it is certain to whom the property belongs. It does not mean that the person actually has the property in hand. For example, the time of distribution of present interests created by will and all interests arising under the law of intestate succession is the death of the decedent. At that moment the heir or devisee is entitled to his or her devise or share, and it is irrelevant that time will pass before the will is admitted to probate and that actual receipt of the gift may not occur until the administration of the estate is complete. The time of distribution of present interests created by non-testamentary instruments generally depends on when the instrument becomes irrevocable. Because the recipient of a present interest is entitled to the property as soon as the gift is made, the time of distribution occurs when the creator of the interest can no longer take it back. The time of distribution of a future interest is the time when it comes into possession and the owner of the future interest becomes the owner of a present interest. For example, if B is the owner of the remainder interest in a trust which is to pay income to A for life, the time of distribution of B's remainder is A's death. At that time the trust terminated and B's ownership of the remainder becomes outright ownership of the trust property.

Section 2-1106(b)(1) makes a disclaimer of an interest in property effective as of the time the instrument creating the interest becomes irrevocable or at the decedent's death if the interest is created by intestate succession. A will and a revocable trust are irrevocable at the testator's or settlor's death. Inter vivos trusts may also be irrevocable at their creation or may become irrevocable before the settlor's death. A beneficiary designation is also irrevocable at death, unless it is made irrevocable at an earlier time. This provision continues the provision of Uniform Acts on this subject, but with different wording. Previous Acts have stated that the disclaimer "relates back" to some time before the disclaimed interest was created. The relation back doctrine gives effect to the special nature of the disclaimer as a refusal to accept. Because the disclaimer "relates back", the disclaimant is regarded as never having had an interest in the disclaimed property. A disclaimer by a devisee against whom there is an outstanding judgment will prevent the creditor from reaching the property the debtor would otherwise inherit. This Act continues the effect of the relation back doctrine, not by using the specific words, but by directly stating what the relation back doctrine has been interpreted to mean. Sections 2-1102(3) and 2-1105(f) taken together define a disclaimer as a refusal to accept which is not a transfer or release, and subsection (b)(1) of this section makes the disclaimer effective as of the time the creator cannot revoke the interest. Nothing in the statute, however, prevents the legislatures or the courts from limiting the effect of the disclaimer as refusal doctrine in specific situations or generally. *See* the Comments to Section 2-1113 below.

Section 2-1106(b)(2) allows the creator of the instrument to control the disposition of the disclaimed interest by express provision in the instrument. The provision may apply to a particular interest. "I give to my cousin A the sum of ten thousand dollars ($10,000) and should he disclaim any part of this gift, I give the part disclaimed to my cousin B." The provision may also apply to all disclaimed interests. A residuary clause beginning "I give my residuary estate, including all disclaimed interests to.... " is such a provision.

Sections 2-1106(b)(3)(B), (C), and (D) apply if Section 2-1106(b)(2) does not and if the disclaimant is an individual. Because "disclaimant" is defined as the person to whom the disclaimed interest would have passed had the disclaimer not been made (Section 2-1102(1)), these paragraphs would apply to disclaimers by fiduciaries on behalf of individuals. The general rule is that the disclaimed interest passes as if the disclaimant had died immediately before the time of distribution defined in Section 2-1106(a)(2). The application of this general rule to present interests given to named individuals is illustrated by the following examples:

Example 1(a). T's will devised "ten thousand dollars ($10,000) to my brother, B." B disclaims the entire devise. B is deemed to have predeceased T, and, therefore B's gift has lapsed. If the state's antilapse statute applies, it will direct the passing of the disclaimed interest. Under Section 2-603(b)(1), for example, B's descendants who survive T by 120 hours will take the devise by representation.

Example 1(b). T's will devised "ten thousand dollars ($10,000) to my friend, F." F disclaims the entire devise. F is deemed to predecease T and the gift has lapsed. Few antilapse statutes apply to devises to non-family members. Under Section 2-603(b), which saves from lapse only gifts made to certain relatives, the devise would lapse and pass through the residuary clause of the will.

Example 1(c). T's will devised "ten thousand dollars ($10,000) to my brother, B, but if B does not survive me, to my children." If B disclaims the devise, he will be deemed to have predeceased T and the alternative gift to T's children will dispose of the devise.

Present interests are also given to the surviving members of a class or group of persons. Perhaps the most common example of this gift is a devise of the testator's residuary estate "to my descendants who survive me by representation." Under the system of distribution among multi-generational classes used in Section 2-709, division of the property to be distributed begins in the eldest generation in which there are living people. The following example illustrates a problem that can arise.

Example 2(a). T's will devised "the residue of my estate to my descendants who survive me by representation." T is survived by son S and daughter D. Son has two living children and D has one. S disclaims his interest. The disclaimed interest is one-half of the residuary estate, the interest S would have received had he not disclaimed. Section 2-1106(b)(3)(B) provides that the disclaimed interest passes as if S had predeceased T. If Section 2-1106(b)(3) stopped there, S's children would take one-half of the disclaimed interest and D would take the other half under Section 2-709. S's disclaimer should not have that effect, however, but should pass what he would have taken to his children. Section 2-1106(b)(3)(C) solves the problem. It provides that the entire disclaimed interest passes only to S's descendants because they would share in the interest had S truly predeceased T.

The provision also solves a problem that exists when the disclaimant is the only representative of an older generation.

Example 2(b). Assume the same facts as **Example 2(a)**, but D has predeceased T. T is survived, therefore, by S, S's two children, and D's child. S disclaims. Again, the disclaimed interest is one-half of the residuary estate and it passes as if S had predeceased T. Had S actually predeceased T, the three grandchildren of S would have shared equally in T's residuary estate because they are all in the same generation. Were the three grandchildren to share equally in the disclaimed interest, S's two children would each receive one-third of the one-half while D's child would receive one-third of the one-half in addition to the one-half of the residuary estate received as the representative of his or her late parent. Section 2-1106(b)(3)(C) again applies to insure that S's children receive one-half of the residue, exactly the interest S would have received but for the disclaimer.

The disclaimer of future interests created by will leads to a different problem. The effective date of the disclaimer of the future interest, the testator's death, is earlier in time than the distribution date. This in turn leads to a possible anomaly illustrated by the following example.

Example 3. Father's will creates a testamentary

trust for Mother who is to receive all the income for life. At her death, the trust is to be distributed to Father and Mother's surviving descendants by representation. Mother is survived by son S and daughter D. Son has two living children and D has one. Son decides that he would prefer his share of the trust to pass to his children and disclaims. The disclaimer must be made within nine months of Father's death if it is to be a qualified disclaimer for tax purposes. Under prior Acts and former Section 2-801, the interest would have passed as if Son had predeceased Father. A problem could arise if, at Mother's death, one or more of S's children living at that time were born after Father's death. It would be possible to argue that had S predeceased Father the afterborn children would not exist and that D and S's two children living at the time of Father's death are entitled to all of the trust property.

The problem illustrated in **Example 3** is solved by Section 2-1106(b)(3)(B). The disclaimed interest would have taken effect in possession or enjoyment, that is, Son would be entitled to receive one-half of the trust property, at Mother's death. Under paragraph (3)(B) Son is deemed to have died immediately before Mother's death even though under Section 2-1106(b)(1) the disclaimer is effective as of Father's death. There is no doubt, therefore, that S's children living at the distribution date, whenever born, are entitled to the share of the trust property S would have received and, as **Examples 2(a)** and **2(b)** show, they will take exactly what S would have received but for the disclaimer. Had S actually died before Mother, he would have received nothing at Mother's death whether or not the disclaimer had been made. There is nothing to pass to S's children and they take as representatives of S under the representational scheme in effect.

Future interests may or may not be conditioned on survivorship. The following examples illustrate disclaimers of future interests not expressly conditioned on survival.

Example 4(a). G's revocable trust directs the trustee to pay "ten thousand dollars ($10,000) to the grantor's brother, B" at the termination of the trust on G's death. B disclaims the entire gift immediately after G's death. B is deemed to have predeceased G because it is at G's death that the interest given B will come into possession and enjoyment. Had B not disclaimed he would have received $10,000 at that time. The recipient of the disclaimed interest will be determined by the law that applies to gifts of future interests to persons who die before the interest comes into possession and enjoyment. Traditional analysis would regard the gift to B as a vested interest subject to divestment by G's power to revoke the trust. So long as G has not revoked the gift, the interest would pass through B's estate to B's successors in interest. Yet If B's successors in interest are selected by B's will, the disclaimer cannot be a qualified disclaimer for tax purposes. This problem does not arise in a jurisdiction with Section 2-707(b) because the interest passes not through B's estate but rather to B's descendants who survive G by 120 hours by representation. Because the antilapse mechanism of Section 2-707 is not limited to gifts to relatives, a disclaimer by a friend rather than a brother would have the same result. For jurisdictions without Section 2-707, however, Section 2-1106(b)(3)(D) provides an equivalent solution: a disclaimed interest that would otherwise pass through B's estate instead passes to B's descendants who survive G by representation.

Example 4(b). G's revocable trust directed that on his death the trust property is to be distributed to his three children, A, B, and C. A disclaims immediately after G's death and is deemed to predecease the distribution date, which is G's death. The traditional analysis applies exactly as it does in **Example 4(a)**. The only condition on A's gift would be G's not revoking the trust. A is not explicitly required to survive G. (See *First National Bank of Bar Harbor v. Anthony*, 557 A.2d 957 (Me. 1989).) The interest would pass to A's successors in interest. If those successors are selected by A's will, the disclaimer cannot be a qualified disclaimer for tax purposes. Section 2-707(b) provides that A's interest passes by representation to A's descendants who survive G by 120 hours. For jurisdictions without Section 2-707, Section 2-1106(b)(3)(D) reaches the same result.

Example 4(c). G conveys land "to A for life, remainder to B." B disclaims immediately after the conveyance. Traditional analysis regards B's remainder as vested; it is not contingent on surviving A. This classification is unaffected by whether or not the jurisdiction has adopted Section 2-707, because that section only applies to future interests in trust; it does not apply to future interests not in trust, such as the one in this example created directly in land. To the extent that B's remainder is transmissible through B's estate, B's disclaimer cannot be a qualified disclaimer for tax purposes. Section 2-1106(b)(3)(D) resolves the problem: a disclaimed interest that would otherwise pass through B's estate instead passes as if it were controlled by Sections 2-707 and 2-711. Because Section 2-707 only applies to future interests in trust, jurisdictions enacting Section 2-1106 should enact Section 2-1106(b)(3)(D) whether or not they have enacted Section 2-707.

Section 2-1106(b)(3)(A) provides a rule for the passing of property interests disclaimed by persons other than individuals. Because Section 2-1108 applies to disclaimers by trustees of property that would otherwise pass to the trust, Section 2-1106(b)(3)(A) principally applies to disclaimers by corporations, partnerships, and the other entities listed in the definition of "person" in Section 2-1102(6). A charity, for example, might wish to disclaim property the acceptance of which would be incompatible with its purposes.

Section 2-1106(b)(4) continues the provision of prior Uniform Acts and former Section 2-801 on this subject providing for the acceleration of future interests on the making of the disclaimer, except that future interests in the disclaimant do not accelerate. The workings of Section 2-1106(b)(4) are illustrated by the following examples.

Example 5(a). Father's will creates a testamentary trust to pay income to his son S for his life, and on his death to pay the remainder to S's descendants then living, by representation. If S disclaims his life income interest in the trust, he will be deemed to have died immediately before Father's death. The disclaimed interest, S's income interest, came into possession and enjoyment at

Father's death as would any present interest created by will (*see* **Examples 1(a)**, **(b)**, and **(c)**), and, therefore, the time of distribution is Father's death. If at the income beneficiary of a testamentary trust does not survive the testator, the income interest is not created and the next interest in the trust takes effect. Since the next interest in Father's trust is the remainder in S's descendants, the trust property will pass to S's descendants who survive Father by representation. It is immaterial under the statute that the actual situation at the S's death might be different with different descendants entitled to the remainder.

Example 5(b). Mother's will creates a testamentary trust to pay the income to her daughter D until she reaches age 35 at which time the trust is to terminate and the trust property distributed in equal shares to D and her three siblings. D disclaims her income interest. The remainder interests in her three siblings accelerate and they each receive one-fourth of the trust property. D's remainder interest does not accelerate, however, and she must wait until she is 35 to receive her fourth of the trust property.

2006 Technical Amendment. By technical amendment, subsection (b)(3)(D) was added to resolve the problem of future interests transmissible through the disclaimant's estate. The Comment was correspondingly amended. For the prior version, see 8 U.L.A. 65-69 (Supp. 2005).

Legislative Note. Because Section 2-707 only applies to future interests in trust, and does not apply to legal future interests, states that have enacted Section 2-1106 should enact the 2006 technical amendments whether or not they have enacted Section 2-707.

Former (1993) Version

§ 2-801(d) [Effect of Disclaimer.] The effects of a disclaimer are:

(1) If property or an interest therein devolves to a disclaimant under a testamentary instrument, under a power of appointment exercised by a testamentary instrument, or under the laws of intestacy, and the decedent has not provided for another disposition of that interest, should it be disclaimed, or of disclaimed, or failed interests in general, the disclaimed interest devolves as if the disclaimant had predeceased the decedent, but if by law or under the testamentary instrument the descendants of the disclaimant would share in the disclaimed interest by representation or otherwise were the disclaimant to predecease the decedent, then the disclaimed interest passes by representation, or passes as directed by the governing instrument, to the descendants of the disclaimant who survive the decedent. A future interest that takes effect in possession or enjoyment after the termination

of the estate or interest disclaimed takes effect as if the disclaimant had predeceased the decedent. A disclaimer relates back for all purposes to the date of death of the decedent.

(2) If property or an interest therein devolves to a disclaimant under a nontestamentary instrument or contract and the instrument or contract does not provide for another disposition of that interest, should it be disclaimed, or of disclaimed or failed interests in general, the disclaimed interest devolves as if the disclaimant has predeceased the effective date of the instrument or contract, but if by law or under the nontestamentary instrument or contract the descendants of the disclaimant would share in the disclaimed interest by representation or otherwise were the disclaimant to predecease the effective date of the instrument, then the disclaimed interest passes by representation, or passes as directed by the governing instrument, to the descendants of the disclaimant who survive the effective date of the instrument. A disclaimer relates back for all purposes to that date. A future interest that takes effect in possession or enjoyment at or after the termination of the disclaimed interest takes effect as if the disclaimant had died before the effective date of the instrument or contract that transferred the disclaimed interest.

(3) The disclaimer or the written waiver of the right to disclaim is binding upon the disclaimant or person waiving and all persons claiming through or under either of them.

§ 2-1107. Disclaimer of Rights of Survivorship in Jointly Held Property.

(a) Upon the death of a holder of jointly held property, a surviving holder may disclaim, in whole or part, the greater of:

    (1) a fractional share of the property determined by dividing the number one by the number of joint holders alive immediately before the death of the holder to whose death the disclaimer relates; or

    (2) all of the property except that part of the value of the entire interest attributable to the contribution furnished by the disclaimant.

(b) A disclaimer under subsection (a) takes effect as of the death of the holder of jointly held property to whose death the disclaimer relates.

(c) An interest in jointly held property disclaimed by a surviving holder of the property passes as if the disclaimant predeceased the holder to whose death the disclaimer relates.

Comment

The various forms of ownership in which "joint property", as defined in Section 2-1102(5), can be held include common law joint tenancies and any statutory variation that preserves the right of survivorship. The common law was unsettled whether a surviving joint tenant had any right to renounce his interest in jointly-owned property and if so to what extent. See Casner, Estate Planning, 5th ed. §10.7. Specifically, if A and B owned real estate or securities as joint tenants with right of survivorship and A died, the problem was whether B might disclaim what was given to him originally upon creation of the estate, or, if not, whether he could nevertheless reject the incremental portion derived through the right of survivorship. There was also a question of whether a joint bank account should be treated differently from jointly-owned securities or real estate for the purpose of disclaimer.

This common law of disclaimers of jointly held property must be set against the rapid developments in the law of tax qualified disclaimers of jointly held property. Since the previous Uniform Acts were drafted, the law regarding tax qualified disclaimers of joint property interests has been clarified. Courts have repeatedly held that a surviving joint tenant may disclaim that portion of the jointly held property to which the survivor succeeds by operation of law on the death of the other joint tenant so long as the joint tenancy was severable during the life of the joint tenants (*Kennedy v. Commissioner*, 804 F.2d 1332 (7th Cir 1986), *McDonald v. Commissioner*, 853 F.2d 1494 (9th Cir 1988), *Dancy v. Commissioner*, 872 F.2d 84 (4th Cir 1989).) On December 30, 1997 the Service published T.D. 8744 making final proposed amendments of the Regulations under IRC § 2518 to reflect the decisions regarding disclaimers of joint property interests.

The amended final Regulations, § 25.2518-2(c)(4)(i) allow a surviving joint tenant or tenant by the entireties to disclaim that portion of the tenancy to which he or she succeeds upon the death of the first joint tenant (½ where there are two joint tenants) whether or not the tenancy could have been unilaterally severed under local law and regardless of the proportion of consideration furnished by the disclaimant. The Regulations also create a special rule for joint tenancies between spouses created after July 14, 1988 where the spouse of the donor is not a United States citizen. In that case, the donee spouse may disclaim any portion of the joint tenancy includible in the donor spouse's gross estate under IRC § 2040, which creates a contribution rule. Thus the surviving non-citizen spouse may disclaim all of the joint tenancy property if the deceased spouse provided all the consideration for the tenancy's creation.

The amended final Regulations, § 25.2518-2(c)(4)(iii) also recognize the unique features of joint bank accounts, and allow the disclaimer by a survivor of that part of the account contributed by the decedent, so long as the decedent could have regained that portion during life by unilateral action, bar the disclaimer of that part of the account attributable to the survivor's contributions, and explicitly extend the rule governing joint bank accounts to brokerage and other investment accounts, such as mutual fund accounts, held in joint name.

These developments in the tax law of disclaimers are reflected in subsection (a). The subsection allows a surviving holder of jointly held property to disclaim the greater of the accretive share, the part of the jointly held property which augments the survivor's interest in the property, and all of the property that is not attributable to the disclaimant's contribution to the jointly held property. In the usual joint tenancy or tenancy by the entireties between husband and wife, the survivor will always be able to disclaim one-half of the property. If the disclaimer conforms to the requirements of IRC § 2518, it will be a qualified disclaimer. In addition the surviving spouse can disclaim all of the property attributable to the decedent's contribution, a provision which will allow the non-citizen spouse to take advantage of the contribution rule of the final Regulations. The contribution rule of subsection (a)(2) will also allow surviving holders of joint property arrangements other than joint tenancies to make a tax qualified disclaimer under the rules applicable to those joint arrangements. For example, if A contributes 60% and B contributes 40% to a joint bank account and they allow the interest on the funds to accumulate, on B's death A can disclaim 40% of the account; on A's death B can disclaim 60% of the account. (Note that under subsection (a)(1) A can disclaim up to 50% of the account on B's death because there are two joint account holders, but the disclaimer would not be fully tax qualified. As previously noted, a tax qualified disclaimer is limited to 40% of the account.) If the account belonged to the parties during their joint lives in proportion to their contributions, the disclaimers in this example can be tax qualified disclaimers if all the requirements of IRC § 2518 are met.

Subsection (b) provides that the disclaimer is effective as of the death of the joint holder which triggers the survivorship feature of the joint property arrangement. The disclaimant, therefore, has no interest in and has not transferred the disclaimed interest.

Subsection (c) provides that the disclaimed interest passes as if the disclaimant had predeceased the holder to whose death the disclaimer relates. Where there are two joint holders, a disclaimer by the survivor results in the disclaimed property passing as part of the deceased joint holder's estate because under this subsection, the deceased joint holder is the survivor as to the portion disclaimed. If a married couple owns the family home in joint tenancy, therefore, a disclaimer by the survivor under subsection (a)(1) results in one-half of the home passing through the decedent's estate. The surviving spouse and whoever receives the interest through the decedent's estate are tenants in common in the house. In the proper circumstances, the disclaimed one-half could help to use up the decedent's unified credit. Without the disclaimer, the interest would automatically qualify for the marital deduction, perhaps wasting part of the decedent's applicable exclusion amount.

In a multiple holder joint property arrangement, the disclaimed interest will belong to the other joint holder or holders.

Example 1. A, B, and C make equal contributions to the purchase of Blackacre, to which they take title as joint tenants with right of survivorship. On partition each would receive 1/3 of Blackacre and any of them could convert his or her interest to a 1/3 tenancy in common interest by unilateral severance (which, of course, would have to be accomplished in accordance with state law). On A's death, B and C may each, if they wish, disclaim up to 1/3 of the property under subsection (a)(1). Should one of them disclaim the full 1/3, the disclaimant will be deemed to predecease A.

Assume that B so disclaims. With respect to the 1/3 undivided interest that now no longer belongs to A the only surviving joint holder is C. C therefore owns that 1/3 interest as tenant in common with the joint tenancy. Should C predecease B, the 1/3 tenancy in common interest will pass through C's estate and B will be the sole owner of an undivided 2/3 interest in Blackacre as the survivor of the joint tenancy. Should B predecease C, C will be the sole owner of Blackacre in fee simple absolute.

Alternatively, assume that both B and C make valid disclaimers after A's death. They are both deemed to have predeceased A, A is the sole survivor of the joint tenancy and Blackacre passes through A's estate.

Finally, assume that A provided all the consideration for the purchase of Blackacre. On A's death, B and C can each disclaim the entire property under subsection (a)(2). If they both do so, Blackacre will pass through A's estate. If only one of B or C disclaims the entire property, the one who does not will be the sole owner of Blackacre as the only surviving joint tenant. Such a disclaimer would not be completely tax qualified, however. The Regulations limit a tax qualified disclaimer to no more than 1/3 of the property. If, however, B or C were the first to die, A could still disclaim the 1/3 interest that no longer belongs to the decedent under subsection (a)(1), the disclaimer would be a qualified disclaimer for tax purposes under the Regulations, and the result is that the other surviving joint tenant owns 1/3 of Blackacre as tenant in common with the joint tenancy.

2004 Amendment. This Comment was amended in 2004 to correct an error in the joint bank account example and to provide a more complete explanation for the result in Example 1.

§ 2-1108. Disclaimer of Interest by Trustee.

§ 2-1108. Disclaimer of Interest by Trustee. If a trustee disclaims an interest in property that otherwise would have become trust property, the interest does not become trust property.

Comment

Section 2-1108 deals with disclaimer of a right to receive property into a trust, and thus applies only to trustees. (A disclaimer of a right to receive property by a fiduciary acting on behalf of an individual, such as a personal representative, conservator, guardian, or agent is governed by the section of the statute applicable to the type of interest being disclaimed.) The instrument under which the right to receive the property was created may govern the disposition of the property in the event of a disclaimer by providing for a disposition when the trust does not exist. When the instrument does not make such a provision, the doctrine of resulting trust will carry the property back to the donor. The effect of the actions of co-trustees will depend on the state law governing the action of multiple trustees. Every disclaimer by a trustee must be compatible with the trustee's fiduciary obligations.

§ 2-1109. Disclaimer of Power of Appointment or Other Power Not Held in Fiduciary Capacity.

§ 2-1109. Disclaimer of Power of Appointment or Other Power Not Held in Fiduciary Capacity. If a holder disclaims a power of appointment or other power not held in a fiduciary capacity, the following rules apply:

(1) If the holder has not exercised the power, the disclaimer takes effect as of the time the instrument creating the power becomes irrevocable.

(2) If the holder has exercised the power and the disclaimer is of a power other than a presently exercisable general power of appointment, the disclaimer takes effect immediately after the last exercise of the power.

(3) The instrument creating the power is construed as if the power expired when the disclaimer became effective.

Comment

Section 2-1105(a) authorizes a person to disclaim an interest in or power over property. Section 2-1109 provides rules for disclaimers of powers which are not held in a fiduciary capacity. The most common non-fiduciary power is a power of appointment. Section 2-1105(a) also authorizes the partial disclaimer of a power as well as of an interest. For example, the disclaimer could be of a portion of the power to appoint one's self, while retaining the right to appoint to others. The effect of a disclaimer of a power under Section 2-1109 depends on whether or not the holder has exercised the power and on what sort of power is held. If a holder disclaims a power before exercising it, the power expires and can never be exercised. If the power has been exercised, the power is construed as having expired immediately after its last exercise by the holder. The disclaimer affects only the holder of the power and will not affect other aspects of the power.

Example 1. T creates a testamentary trust to pay the income to A for life, remainder as A shall appoint by will among her descendants living at A's death and four named charities. If A does not exercise her power, the remainder passes to her descendants living at her death by representation. A disclaims the power. The power can no longer be exercised and on A's death the remainder will pass to the takers in default.

§ 2-1110. Disclaimer by Appointee, Object, or Taker in Default of Exercise of Power of Appointment.

(a) A disclaimer of an interest in property by an appointee of a power of appointment takes effect as of the time the instrument by which the holder exercises the power becomes irrevocable.

(b) A disclaimer of an interest in property by an object or taker in default of an exercise of a power of appointment takes effect as of the time the instrument creating the power becomes irrevocable.

Comment

This section governs disclaimers by those who may or do receive an interest in property through the exercise of a power of appointment. At the time of the creation of a power of appointment, the creator of the power, besides giving the power to the holder of the power, can also limit the objects of the power (the permissible appointees of the property subject to the power) and also name those who are to take if the power is not exercised, persons referred to as takers in default.

This section provides rules for disclaimers by all of these persons: subsection (a) is concerned with a disclaimer by a person who actually receives an interest in property through the exercise of a power of appointment, and subsection (b) recognizes a disclaimer by a taker in default or permissible appointee before the power is exercised. These two situations are quite different. An appointee is in the same position as any devisee or beneficiary of a trust. He or she may receive a present or future interest depending on how the holder of the power exercises it. Subsection (a) therefore, makes the disclaimer effective as of the time the instrument exercising the power—giving the interest to the disclaimant—becomes irrevocable. If the holder of the power created an interest in the appointee, the effect of the disclaimer is governed by Section 2-1106. If the holder created another power in the appointee, the effect of the disclaimer is governed by Section 2-1109.

Example 1. Mother's will creates a testamentary trust for daughter D. The trustees are to pay all income to D for her life and have discretion to invade principal for D's maintenance. On D's death she may appoint the trust property by will among her then living descendants. In default of appointment the property is to be distributed by representation to D's descendants who survive her. D is the donee, her descendants are the permissible appointees and the takers in default. D exercises her power by appointing the trust property in three equal shares to her children A, B, and C. The three children are the appointees. A disclaims. Under subsection (a) A's disclaimer is effective as of D's death (the time at which the will exercising the power became irrevocable). Because A disclaimed an interest in property, the effect of the disclaimer is governed by Section 2-1106(b). If D's will makes no provisions for the disposition of the interest should it be disclaimed or of disclaimed interests in general (Section 2-1106(b)(2)), the interest passes as if A predeceased the time of distribution which is D's death. An appointment to a person who is dead at the time of the appointment is ineffective except as provided by an antilapse statute. *See* Restatement, Second, Property (Donative Transfers) § 18.5. The Restatement, Second, Property (Donative Transfers), § 18.6 suggests that any requirement of the antilapse statute that the deceased devisee be related in some way to the testator be applied as if the appointive property were owned either by the donor or the holder of the power. (See also Restatement, Third, Property (Wills and Other Donative Transfers) § 5.5, Comment *l*.) That is the position taken by Section 2-603. Since antilapse statutes usually apply to devises to children and grandchildren, the disclaimed interest would pass to A's descendants by representation.

A taker in default or a permissible object of appointment is traditionally regarded as having a type of future interest. *See* Restatement, Second, Property (Donative Transfers) § 11.2, *Comments c* and *d*. The future interest will come into possession and enjoyment when the question of whether or not the power is to be exercised is resolved. For testamentary powers that time is the death of the holder.

Subsection (b) provides that a disclaimer by an object or taker in default takes effect as of the time the instrument creating the power becomes effective. Because the disclaimant is disclaiming an interest in property, albeit a future interest, the effect of the disclaimer is governed by Section 2-1106. The effect of these rules is illustrated by the following examples.

Example 2(a). The facts are the same as **Example 1**, except A disclaims before D's death and D's will does not exercise the power. Under subsection (b) A's disclaimer is effective as of Mother's death which is the time when the instrument creating the power, Mother's will, became irrevocable. Because A disclaimed an interest in property, the effect of the disclaimer is governed by Section 2-1106(b). If Mother's will makes no provision for the disposition of the interest should it be disclaimed or of disclaimed interests in general (Section 2-1106(b)(2)), the interest passes under Section 2-1106(b)(3) as if the disclaimant had died immediately before the time of distribution. Thus, A is deemed to have died immediately before D's death, which is the time of distribution. If A actually survives D, the disclaimed interest is one-third of the trust property; it will pass as if A predeceased D, and the result is the same as in **Example 1**. If A does predecease D he would have received nothing and there is no disclaimed interest. The disclaimer has no effect on the passing of the trust property.

Example 2(b). The facts are the same as in **Example 2(a)** except D does exercise her power of appointment to give one-third of the trust property to each of her three children, A, B, and C. A's disclaimer means the disclaimed interest will pass as if he predeceased D and the result is the same as in **Example 1**.

In addition, if all the objects and takers in default disclaim before the power is exercised the power of appointment is destroyed. *See* Restatement, Second, Property (Donative Transfers) § 12.1, *Comment g*.

§ 2-1111. Disclaimer of Power Held in Fiduciary Capacity.

(a) If a fiduciary disclaims a power held in a fiduciary capacity which has not been exercised, the disclaimer takes effect as of the time the instrument creating the power becomes irrevocable.

(b) If a fiduciary disclaims a power held in a fiduciary capacity which has been exercised, the disclaimer takes effect immediately after the last exercise of the power.

(c) A disclaimer under this section is effective as to another fiduciary if the disclaimer so provides and the fiduciary disclaiming has the authority to bind the estate, trust, or other person for whom the fiduciary is acting.

Comment

Section 2-1111 governs disclaimers by fiduciaries of powers held in their fiduciary capacity. Examples include a right to remove and replace a trustee or a trustee's power to make distributions of income or principal. Such disclaimers have not been specifically dealt with in prior Uniform Acts although they could prove useful in several situations. A trustee who is also a beneficiary may want to disclaim a power to invade principal for himself for tax purposes. A trustee of a trust for the benefit of a surviving spouse who also has the power to invade principal for the decedent's descendants may wish to disclaim the power in order to qualify the trust for the marital deduction. (The use of a disclaimer in just that situation was approved in *Cleaveland v. U.S.*, 62 A.F.T.R.2d 88-5992, 88-1 USTC ¶ 13,766 (C.D.Ill. 1988).)

The section refers to fiduciary in the singular. It is possible, of course, for a trust to have two or more cotrustees and an estate to have two or more co-personal representatives. This Act leaves the effect of actions of multiple fiduciaries to the general rules in effect in each state relating to multiple fiduciaries. For example, if the general rule is that a majority of trustees can make binding decisions, a disclaimer by two of three co-trustees of a power is effective. A dissenting co-trustee could follow whatever procedure state law prescribes for disassociating him or herself from the action of the majority. A sole trustee burdened with a power to invade principal for a group of beneficiaries including him or herself who wishes to disclaim the power but yet preserve the possibility of another trustee exercising the power would seek the appointment of a disinterested co-trustee to exercise the power and then disclaim the power for him or herself. The subsection thus makes the disclaimer effective only as to the disclaiming fiduciary unless the disclaimer states otherwise. If the disclaimer does attempt to bind other fiduciaries, be they co-fiduciaries or successor fiduciaries, the effect of the disclaimer will depend on local law.

As with any action by a fiduciary, a disclaimer of fiduciary powers must be compatible with the fiduciary's duties.

§ 2-1112. Delivery or Filing.

(a) In this section, "beneficiary designation" means an instrument, other than an instrument creating a trust, naming the beneficiary of:

(1) an annuity or insurance policy;

(2) an account with a designation for payment on death;

(3) a security registered in beneficiary form;

(4) a pension, profit-sharing, retirement, or other employment-related benefit plan; or

(5) any other nonprobate transfer at death.

(b) Subject to subsections (c) through (l), delivery of a disclaimer may be effected by personal delivery, first-class mail, or any other method likely to result in its receipt.

(c) In the case of an interest created under the law of intestate succession or an interest created by will, other than an interest in a testamentary trust:

(1) a disclaimer must be delivered to the personal representative of the decedent's estate; or

(2) if no personal representative is then serving, it must be filed with a court having jurisdiction to appoint the personal representative.

(d) In the case of an interest in a testamentary trust:

(1) a disclaimer must be delivered to the trustee then serving, or if no trustee is then serving, to the personal representative of the decedent's estate; or

(2) if no personal representative is then serving, it must be filed with a court having jurisdiction to enforce the trust.

(e) In the case of an interest in an inter vivos trust:

(1) a disclaimer must be delivered to the trustee then serving;

(2) if no trustee is then serving, it must be filed with a court having jurisdiction to enforce the trust; or

(3) if the disclaimer is made before the time the instrument creating the trust becomes irrevocable, it must be delivered to the settlor of a revocable trust or the transferor of the interest.

(f) In the case of an interest created by a beneficiary designation which is disclaimed before the designation becomes irrevocable, the disclaimer must be delivered to the person making the beneficiary designation.

(g) In the case of an interest created by a beneficiary designation which is disclaimed after the designation becomes irrevocable:

(1) the disclaimer of an interest in personal property must be delivered to the person obligated to distribute the interest; and

(2) the disclaimer of an interest in real property must be recorded in [the office of the county recorder of deeds] of the [county] where the real property that is the subject of the disclaimer is

located.

(h) In the case of a disclaimer by a surviving holder of jointly held property, the disclaimer must be delivered to the person to whom the disclaimed interest passes.

(i) In the case of a disclaimer by an object or taker in default of exercise of a power of appointment at any time after the power was created:

(1) the disclaimer must be delivered to the holder of the power or to the fiduciary acting under the instrument that created the power; or

(2) if no fiduciary is then serving, it must be filed with a court having authority to appoint the fiduciary.

(j) In the case of a disclaimer by an appointee of a nonfiduciary power of appointment:

(1) the disclaimer must be delivered to the holder, the personal representative of the holder's estate or to the fiduciary under the instrument that created the power; or

(2) if no fiduciary is then serving, it must be filed with a court having authority to appoint the fiduciary.

(k) In the case of a disclaimer by a fiduciary of a power over a trust or estate, the disclaimer must be delivered as provided in subsection (c), (d), or (e), as if the power disclaimed were an interest in property.

(l) In the case of a disclaimer of a power by an agent, the disclaimer must be delivered to the principal or the principal's representative.

Comment

The rules set forth in Section 2-1112 are designed to provide notice of the disclaimer. For example, a disclaimer of an interest in a decedent's estate must be delivered to the personal representative of the estate. A disclaimer is required to be filed in court only in very limited circumstances.

Historical Note. This Comment was revised in 2010 to account for the amendment of subsections (f) and (g)(1) and the addition of subsection (g)(2), amendments that were necessitated by the aproval of the Uniform Real Property Transfer on Death Act, which is codified in this Code at Article VI, Part 4.

Former (1993) Version

§ 2-801(b) [Time of Disclaimer.] The following rules govern the time when a disclaimer must be filed or delivered:

(1) If the property or interest has devolved to the disclaimant under a testamentary instrument or by the laws of intestacy, the disclaimer must be filed, if of a present interest, not later than [nine] months after the death of the deceased owner or deceased donee of a power of appointment and, if of a future interest, not later than [nine] months after the event determining that the taker of the property or interest is finally ascertained and his [or her] interest is indefeasibly vested. The disclaimer must be filed in the [probate] court of the county in which proceedings for the administration of the estate of the deceased owner or deceased donee of the power have been commenced. A copy of the disclaimer must be delivered in person or mailed by registered or certified mail, return receipt requested, to any personal representative or other fiduciary of the decedent or donee of the power.

(2) If a property or interest has devolved to the disclaimant under a nontestamentary instrument or contract, the disclaimer must be delivered or filed, if of a present interest, not later than [nine] months after the effective date of the nontestamentary instrument or contract and, if of a future interest, not later than [nine] months after the event determining that the taker of the property or interest is finally ascertained and his [or her] interest is indefeasibly vested. If the person entitled to disclaim does not know of the existence of the interest, the disclaimer must be delivered or filed not later than [nine] months after the person learns of the existence of the interest. The effective date of a revocable instrument or contract is the date on which the maker no longer has power to revoke it or to transfer to himself [or herself] or another the entire legal and equitable ownership of the interest. The disclaimer or a copy thereof must be delivered in person or mailed by registered or certified mail, return receipt requested, to the person who has legal title to or possession of the interest disclaimed.

(3) A surviving joint tenant [or tenant by the entireties] may disclaim as a separate interest any property or interest therein devolving to him [or her] by right of survivorship. A surviving joint tenant [or tenant by the entireties] may disclaim the entire interest in any property or interest therein that is the subject of a joint tenancy [or tenancy by the entireties] devolving to him [or her], if the joint tenancy [or tenancy by the entireties] was created by act of a deceased joint tenant [or tenant by the entireties], the survivor did not join in creating the joint tenancy [or tenancy by the entireties], and has not accepted a benefit under it.

(4) If real property or an interest therein is disclaimed, a copy of the disclaimer may be recorded in the office of the [Recorder of Deeds] of the county in which the property or interest disclaimed is located.*

* If Torrens system is in effect, add provisions to comply with local law.

§ 2-1113. When Disclaimer Barred or Limited.

(a) A disclaimer is barred by a written waiver of the right to disclaim.

(b) A disclaimer of an interest in property is barred if any of the following events occur before the disclaimer becomes effective:

(1) the disclaimant accepts the interest sought to be disclaimed;

(2) the disclaimant voluntarily assigns, conveys, encumbers, pledges, or transfers the interest sought to be disclaimed or contracts to do so; or

(3) a judicial sale of the interest sought to be disclaimed occurs.

(c) A disclaimer, in whole or part, of the future exercise of a power held in a fiduciary capacity is not barred by its previous exercise.

(d) A disclaimer, in whole or part, of the future exercise of a power not held in a fiduciary capacity is not barred by its previous exercise unless the power is exercisable in favor of the disclaimant.

(e) A disclaimer is barred or limited if so provided by law other than this [part].

(f) A disclaimer of a power over property which is barred by this section is ineffective. A disclaimer of an interest in property which is barred by this section takes effect as a transfer of the interest disclaimed to the persons who would have taken the interest under this [part] had the disclaimer not been barred.

Comment

The 1978 Act required that an effective disclaimer be made within nine months of the event giving rise to the right to disclaim (e.g., nine months from the death of the decedent or donee of a power or the vesting of a future interest). The nine month period corresponded in some situations with the Internal Revenue Code provisions governing qualified tax disclaimers. Under the common law an effective disclaimer had to be made only within a "reasonable" time.

This Act specifically rejects a time requirement for making a disclaimer. Recognizing that disclaimers are used for purposes other than tax planning, a disclaimer can be made effectively under the Act so long as the disclaimant is not barred from disclaiming the property or interest or has not waived the right to disclaim. Persons seeking to make tax qualified disclaimers will continue to have to conform to the requirements of the Internal Revenue Code.

The events resulting in a bar to the right to disclaim set forth in this section are similar to those found in the 1978 Acts and former Section 2-801. Subsection (a) provides that a written waiver of the right to disclaim is effective to bar a disclaimer. Such a waiver might be sought, for example, by a creditor who wishes to make sure that property acquired in the future will be available to satisfy the debt.

Whether particular actions by the disclaimant amount to accepting the interest sought to be disclaimed within the meaning of subsection (b)(1) will necessarily be determined by the courts based upon the particular facts. (*See Leipham v. Adams*, 77 Wash.App. 827, 894 P.2d 576 (1995); *Matter of Will of Hall*, 318 S.C. 188, 456 S.E.2d 439 (Ct.App. 1995); *Jordan v. Trower*, 208 Ga.App. 552, 431 S.E.2d 160 (1993); *Matter of Gates*, 189 A.D.2d 427, 595 N.Y.S.2d 194 (3d Dept. 1993); "What Constitutes or Establishes Beneficiary's Acceptance or Renunciation of Devise or Bequest," 93 ALR2d 8).

The addition in this Act of the word "voluntary" to the list of actions barring a disclaimer which also appears in the earlier Acts reflects the numerous cases holding that only actions by the disclaimant taken after the right to disclaim has arisen will act as a bar. (*See Troy v. Hart*, 116 Md.App. 468, 697 A.2d 113 (1997), *Estate of Opatz*, 554 N.W.2d 813 (N.D. 1996), *Frances Slocum Bank v. Martin*, 666 N.E.2d 411 (Ind.App. 1996), *Brown v. Momar, Inc.*, 201 Ga.App. 542, 411 S.E.2d 718 (1991), *Tompkins State Bank v. Niles*, 127 Ill.2d 209, 130 Ill.Dec. 207, 537 N.E.2d 274 (1989).) An existing lien, therefore, will not prevent a disclaimer, although the disclaimant's actions before the right to disclaim arises may work an estoppel. *See Hale v. Bardouh*, 975 S.W.2d 419 (Tex.Ct.App. 1998). With regard to joint property, the event giving rise to the right to disclaim is the death of a joint holder, not the creation of the joint interest and any benefit received during the deceased joint tenant's life is ignored.

The reference to judicial sale in subsection (b)(3) continues a provision from the earlier Acts and ensures that title gained from a judicial sale by a personal representative will not be clouded by a possible disclaimer.

Subsection (c) rephrases the rules of Section 2-1111 governing the effect of disclaimers of powers.

Subsection (d) is applicable to powers which can be disclaimed under Section 2-1109. It bars the disclaimer of a general power of appointment once it has been exercised. A general power of appointment allows the holder to take the property subject to the power for him or herself, whether outright or by using it to pay his or her creditors (for estate and gift tax purposes, a general power is one that allows the holder to appoint to himself, his estate, his creditors, or the creditors of his estate). The power is presently exercisable if the holder need not wait to some time or for some event to occur before exercising the power. If the holder has exercised such a power, it can no longer be disclaimed.

Subsection (e), unlike the 1978 Act, specifies that "other law" may bar the right to disclaim. Some states, including Minnesota (M.S.A. § 525.532 (c)(6)), Massachusetts (Mass. Gen. Law c. 191A, § 8), and Florida (Fla. Stat. § 732.801(6)), bar a disclaimer by an insolvent disclaimant. In others a disclaimer by an insolvent debtor is treated as a fraudulent "transfer". *See Stein v. Brown*, 18 Ohio St.3d 305 (1985);

Pennington v. Bigham, 512 So.2d 1344 (Ala. 1987). A number of states refuse to recognize a disclaimer used to qualify the disclaimant for Medicaid or other public assistance. These decisions often rely on the definition of "transfer" in the federal Medical Assistance Handbook which includes a "waiver" of the right to receive an inheritance (*see* 42 U.S.C.A. § 1396p(e)(1)). *See Hinschberger v. Griggs County Social Services*, 499 N.W.2d 876 (N.D. 1993); *Department of Income Maintenance v. Watts*, 211 Conn. 323 (1989), *Matter of Keuning*, 190 A.D.2d 1033, 593 N.Y.S.2d 653 (4th Dept. 1993), and *Matter of Molloy*, 214 A.D.2d 171, 631 N.Y.S.2d 910 (2nd Dept. 1995), *Troy v. Hart*, 116 Md.App. 468, 697 A.2d 113 (1997), *Tannler v. Wisconsin Dept. of Health & Social Services*, 211 Wis. 2d 179, 564 N.W.2d 735 (1997); *but see*, *Estate of Kirk*, 591 N.W.2d 630 (Iowa, 1999)(valid disclaimer by executor of surviving spouse who was Medicaid beneficiary prevents recovery by Medicaid authorities). It is also likely that state policies will begin to address the question of disclaimers of real property on which an environmental hazard is located in order to avoid saddling the state, as title holder of last resort, with the resulting liability, although the need for fiduciaries to disclaim property subject to environmental liability has probably been diminished by the 1996 amendments to CERCLA by the Asset Conservation Act of 1996 (PL 104-208). These larger policy issues are not addressed in this Act and must, therefore, continue to be addressed by the states. On the federal level, the United States Supreme Court has held that a valid disclaimer does not defeat a federal tax lien levied under IRC § 6321, *Dyre, Jr. v. United States*, 528 U.S. 49, 120 S.Ct. 474 (1999).

Subsection (f) provides a rule stating what happens if an attempt is made to disclaim a power or property interest whose disclaimer is barred by this section. A disclaimer of a power is ineffective, but the attempted disclaimer of the property interest, although invalid as a disclaimer, will operate as a transfer of the disclaimed property interest to the person or persons who would have taken the interest had the disclaimer not been barred. This provision removes the ambiguity that would otherwise be caused by an ineffective refusal to accept property. Whoever has control of the property will know to whom to deliver it and the person attempting the disclaimer will bear any transfer tax consequences.

Former (1993) Version

§ 2-801(e) [Waiver and Bar.] The right to disclaim property or an interest therein is barred by (i) an assignment, conveyance, encumbrance, pledge, or transfer of the property or interest, or a contract therefor, (ii) a written waiver of the right to disclaim, (iii) an acceptance of the property or interest or a benefit under it or (iv) a sale of the property or interest under judicial sale made before the disclaimer is made.

---

§ 2-1114. Tax Qualified Disclaimer. Notwithstanding any other provision of this [part], if as a result of a disclaimer or transfer the disclaimed or transferred interest is treated pursuant to the provisions of Title 26 of the United States Code, as now or hereafter amended, or any successor statute thereto, and the regulations promulgated thereunder, as never having been transferred to the disclaimant, then the disclaimer or transfer is effective as a disclaimer under this [part].

Legislative Note: States with constitutions that prohibit a dynamic reference to federal law ("as now or hereafter amended, or any successor statute thereto") may wish to refer instead to Title 26 of the United States Code as it exists on a specified date. See, e.g., Ariz. Rev. Stat. sec. 14-10014; Or. Rev. Stat. sec. 105.645.

Comment

This section coordinates the Act with the requirements of a qualified disclaimer for transfer tax purposes under IRC § 2518. Any disclaimer which is qualified for estate and gift tax purposes is a valid disclaimer under this Act even if its does not otherwise meet the Act's more specific requirements.

§ 2-1115. Recording of Disclaimer. If an instrument transferring an interest in or power over property subject to a disclaimer is required or permitted by law to be filed, recorded, or registered, the disclaimer may be so filed, recorded, or registered. Except as otherwise provided in Section 2-1112(g)(2), failure to file, record, or register the disclaimer does not affect its validity as between the disclaimant and persons to whom the property interest or power passes by reason of the disclaimer.

Comment

This section permits the recordation of a disclaimer of an interest in property ownership of or title to which is the subject of a recording system. This section expands on the corresponding provision of previous Uniform Acts which referred to permissive recording of a disclaimer of an interest in real property. While local practice may vary, disclaimants should realize that in order to establish the chain of title to real property, and to ward off creditors and bona fide purchasers, the disclaimer may have to be recorded. This section does not change the law of the state governing notice. The reference to Section 2-1112(g)(2) concerns the disclaimer of an interest in real property created by a "beneficiary designation: as that term is defined in Section 2-1112(a). Such a disclaimer must be recorded.

2010 Technical Amendment. The cross-reference to Section 2-1112 was added in 2010. This addition was necessitated by the approval of the Uniform Transfer on Death Real Property Act, which is codified in this Code at Article VI, Part 4.

§ 2-1116. Application to Existing Relationships. Except as otherwise provided in Section 2-1113, an interest in or power over property existing on the effective date of this [part] as to which the time for delivering or filing a disclaimer under law superseded by this [part] has not expired may be disclaimed after the effective date of this [part].

Comment

This section deals with the application of the Act to existing interests and powers. It insures that disclaimers barred by the running of a time period under prior law will not be revived by the Act. For example, assume prior law, like the prior Acts and former Section 2-801, allows the disclaimer of present interests within nine months of their creation and the disclaimer of future interests nine months after they are indefeasibly vested. Under T's will, X receives an outright devise of a sum of money and also has a contingent remainder in a trust created under the will. The Act is effective in the jurisdiction governing the administration of T's estate 10 months after T's death. X cannot disclaim the general devise, irrespective of the application of Section 2-1113 of the Act, because the nine months allowed under prior law have run. The contingent remainder, however, may be disclaimed so long as it is not barred under Section 2-1113 without regard to the nine month period of prior law.

§ 2-1117. Relation to Electronic Signatures in Global and National Commerce Act. This [part] modifies, limits, and supercedes the federal Electronic Signatures in Global and National Commerce Act (15 U.S.C. Section 7001, et seq.) but does not modify, limit, or supercede Section 101(c) of that act (15 U.S.C. Section 7001(c)) or authorize electronic delivery of any of the notices described in Section 103(b) of that act (15 U.S.C. Section 7003(b)).

ARTICLE III
PROBATE OF WILLS AND ADMINISTRATION

PART 1
GENERAL PROVISIONS

PART 2
VENUE FOR PROBATE AND ADMINISTRATION; PRIORITY TO ADMINISTER; DEMAND FOR NOTICE

PART 3
INFORMAL PROBATE AND APPOINTMENT PROCEEDINGS; SUCCESSION WITHOUT ADMINISTRATION

Subpart 1. Informal Probate and Appointment Proceedings

Subpart 2. Succession Without Administration

PART 4
FORMAL TESTACY AND APPOINTMENT PROCEEDINGS

PART 5
SUPERVISED ADMINISTRATION

PART 6
PERSONAL REPRESENTATIVE; APPOINTMENT, CONTROL AND TERMINATION OF AUTHORITY

PART 7
DUTIES AND POWERS OF PERSONAL REPRESENTATIVES

PART 8
CREDITORS' CLAIMS

PART 9
SPECIAL PROVISIONS RELATING TO DISTRIBUTION

PART 9A
UNIFORM ESTATE TAX APPORTIONMENT ACT

PART 10
CLOSING ESTATES

PART 11
COMPROMISE OF CONTROVERSIES

PART 12
COLLECTION OF PERSONAL PROPERTY BY AFFIDAVIT AND SUMMARY ADMINISTRATION PROCEDURE FOR SMALL ESTATES

§ 3-1203. Small Estates; Summary Administration Procedure.

§ 3-1204. Small Estates; Closing by Sworn Statement of Personal Representative.

General Comment

The provisions of this article describe the Flexible System of Administration of Decedents' Estates. Designed to be applicable to both intestate and testate estates and to provide persons interested in decedents' estates with as little or as much by way of procedural and adjudicative safeguards as may be suitable under varying circumstances, this system is the heart of the Uniform Probate Code.

The organization and detail of the system here described may be expressed in varying ways and some states may see fit to reframe parts of this article to better accommodate local institutions. Variations in language from state to state can be tolerated without loss of the essential purposes of procedural uniformity and flexibility, if the following essential characteristics are carefully protected in the redrafting process:

(1) Post-mortem probate of a will must occur to make a will effective and appointment of a personal representative by a public official after the decedent's death is required in order to create the duties and powers attending the office of personal representative. Neither are compelled, however, but are left to be obtained by persons having an interest in the consequence of probate or appointment. Estates descend at death to successors identified by any probated will, or to heirs if no will is probated, subject to rights which may be implemented through administration.

(2) Two methods of securing probate of wills which include a non-adjudicative determination (informal probate) on the one hand, and a judicial determination after notice to all interested persons (formal probate) on the other, are provided.

(3) Two methods of securing appointment of a personal representative which include appointment without notice and without final adjudication of matters relevant to priority for appointment (informal appointment), on the one hand, and appointment by judicial order after notice to interested persons (formal appointment) on the other, are provided.

(4) A five day waiting period from death preventing informal probate or informal appointment of any but a special administrator is required.

(5) Probate of a will by informal or formal proceedings or an adjudication of intestacy may occur without any attendant requirement of appointment of a personal representative.

(6) One judicial, in rem, proceeding encompassing formal probate of any wills (or a determination after notice that the decedent left no will), appointment of a personal representative and complete settlement of an estate under continuing supervision of the court (supervised administration) is provided for testators and persons interested in a decedent's estate, whether testate or intestate, who desire to use it.

(7) Unless supervised administration is sought and ordered, persons interested in estates (including personal representatives, whether appointed informally or after notice) may use an "in and out" relationship to the court so that any question or assumption relating to the estate, including the status of an estate as testate or intestate, matters relating to one or more claims, disputed titles, accounts of personal representatives, and distribution, may be resolved or established by adjudication after notice without necessarily subjecting the estate to the necessity of judicial orders in regard to other or further questions or assumptions.

(8) The status of a decedent in regard to whether he left a valid will or died intestate must be resolved by adjudication after notice in proceedings commenced within three years after his death. If not so resolved, any will probated informally becomes final, and if there is no such probate, the status of the decedent as intestate is finally determined, by a statute of limitations which bars probate and appointment unless requested within three years after death.

(9) Personal representatives appointed informally or after notice, and whether supervised or not, have statutory powers enabling them to collect, protect, sell, distribute and otherwise handle all steps in administration without further order of the court, except that supervised personal representatives may be subjected to special restrictions on power as endorsed on their letters.

(10) Purchasers from personal representatives

and from distributees of personal representatives are protected so that adjudications regarding the testacy status of a decedent or any other question going to the propriety of a sale are not required in order to protect purchasers.

(11) Provisions protecting a personal representative who distributes without adjudication are included to make nonadjudicated settlements feasible.

(12) Statutes of limitation bar creditors of the decedent who fail to present claims within four months after legal advertising of the administration and unsecured claims not previously barred by non-claim statutes are barred after three years from the decedent's death.

Overall, the system accepts the premise that the court's role in regard to probate and administration, and its relationship to personal representatives who derive their power from public appointment, is wholly passive until some interested person invokes its power to secure resolution of a matter. The state, through the court, should provide remedies which are suitable and efficient to protect any and all rights regarding succession, but should refrain from intruding into family affairs unless relief is requested, and limit its relief to that sought.

PART 1
GENERAL PROVISIONS

§ 3-101. Devolution of Estate at Death; Restrictions. The power of a person to leave property by will, and the rights of creditors, devisees, and heirs to his property are subject to the restrictions and limitations contained in this [code] to facilitate the prompt settlement of estates. Upon the death of a person, his real and personal property devolves to the persons to whom it is devised by his last will or to those indicated as substitutes for them in cases involving lapse, renunciation, or other circumstances affecting the devolution of testate estate, or in the absence of testamentary disposition, to his heirs, or to those indicated as substitutes for them in cases involving renunciation or other circumstances affecting devolution of intestate estates, subject to homestead allowance, exempt property and family allowance, to rights of creditors, elective share of the surviving spouse, and to administration.

ALTERNATIVE SECTION FOR COMMUNITY PROPERTY STATES

[**§ 3-101A. Devolution of Estate at Death; Restrictions.** The power of a person to leave property by will, and the rights of creditors, devisees, and heirs to the decedent's property are subject to the restrictions and limitations contained in this [code] to facilitate the prompt settlement of estates. Upon death, the decedent's separate property devolves to the persons to whom it is devised by the decedent's will, or to those indicated as substitutes for them in cases involving lapse, renunciation or other circumstances affecting the devolution of testate estates, or in the absence of testamentary disposition to the decedent's heirs, or to those indicated as substitutes for them in cases involving renunciation or other circumstances affecting the devolution of intestate estates. The decedent's share of community property devolves to the persons to whom it is devised by the decedent's will, or in the absence of testamentary disposition, to the decedent's heirs, but the community property which is under the management and control of the decedent is subject to the decedent's debts and administration, and that portion of the community property which is not under the management and control of the decedent but which is necessary to carry out the provisions of the decedent's will is subject to administration; but the devolution of all the above described property is subject to rights to homestead allowance, exempt property and family allowances, to renunciation, to rights of creditors, [elective share of the surviving spouse] and to administration.]

§ 3-102. Necessity of Order of Probate For Will. Except as provided in Section 3-1201, to be effective to prove the transfer of any property or to nominate an executor, a will must be declared to be valid by an order of informal probate by the Registrar, or an adjudication of probate by the court.

§ 3-103. Necessity of Appointment For Administration. Except as otherwise provided in [Article] IV, to acquire the powers and undertake the duties and liabilities of a personal representative of a decedent, a person must be appointed by order of the court or Registrar, qualify and be issued letters. Administration of an estate is commenced by the issuance of letters.

§ 3-104. Claims Against Decedent; Necessity of Administration. No proceeding to enforce a claim against the estate of a decedent or his successors may be revived or commenced before the appointment of a personal representative. After the appointment and until distribution, all proceedings and actions to enforce a claim against the estate are governed by the procedure prescribed by this [article]. After distribution a creditor whose claim has not been barred may recover from the distributees as provided in Section 3-1004 or from a former personal representative individually liable as provided in Section 3-1005. This section has no application to a proceeding by a secured creditor of the decedent to enforce his right to his security except as to any deficiency judgment which might be sought therein.

§ 3-105. Proceedings Affecting Devolution and Administration; Jurisdiction of Subject Matter. Persons interested in decedents' estates may apply to the Registrar for determination in the informal proceedings provided in this [article], and may petition the court for orders in formal proceedings within the court's jurisdiction including but not limited to those described in this [article]. The court has exclusive jurisdiction of formal proceedings to determine how decedents' estates subject to the laws of this state are to be administered, expended and distributed. The court has concurrent jurisdiction of any other action or proceeding concerning a succession or to which an estate, through a personal representative, may be a party, including actions to determine title to property alleged to belong to the estate, and of any action or proceeding in which property distributed by a personal representative or its value is sought to be subjected to rights of creditors or successors of the decedent.

§ 3-106. Proceedings Within the Exclusive Jurisdiction of Court; Service; Jurisdiction Over Persons. In proceedings within the exclusive jurisdiction of the court where notice is required by this [code] or by rule, and in proceedings to construe probated wills or determine heirs which concern estates that have not been and cannot now be open for administration, interested persons may be bound by the orders of the court in respect to property in or subject to the laws of this state by notice in conformity with Section 1-401. An order is binding as to all who are given notice of the proceeding though less than all interested persons are notified.

§ 3-107. Scope of Proceedings; Proceedings Independent; Exception. Unless supervised administration as described in Part 5 is involved,

(1) each proceeding before the court or Registrar is independent of any other proceeding involving the same estate;

(2) petitions for formal orders of the court may combine various requests for relief in a single proceeding if the orders sought may be finally granted without delay. Except as required for proceedings which are particularly described by other sections of this [article], no petition is defective because it fails to embrace all matters which might then be the subject of a final order;

(3) proceedings for probate of wills or adjudications of no will may be combined with proceedings

for appointment of personal representatives; and

(4) a proceeding for appointment of a personal representative is concluded by an order making or declining the appointment.

§ 3-108. Probate, Testacy and Appointment Proceedings; Ultimate Time Limit.

(a) No informal probate or appointment proceeding or formal testacy or appointment proceeding, other than a proceeding to probate a will previously probated at the testator's domicile and appointment proceedings relating to an estate in which there has been a prior appointment, may be commenced more than three years after the decedent's death, except:

(1) if a previous proceeding was dismissed because of doubt about the fact of the decedent's death, appropriate probate, appointment, or testacy proceedings may be maintained at any time thereafter upon a finding that the decedent's death occurred before the initiation of the previous proceeding and the applicant or petitioner has not delayed unduly in initiating the subsequent proceeding;

(2) appropriate probate, appointment, or testacy proceedings may be maintained in relation to the estate of an absent, disappeared or missing person for whose estate a conservator has been appointed, at any time within three years after the conservator becomes able to establish the death of the protected person;

(3) a proceeding to contest an informally probated will and to secure appointment of the person with legal priority for appointment in the event the contest is successful, may be commenced within the later of twelve months from the informal probate or three years from the decedent's death;

(4) an informal appointment or a formal testacy or appointment proceeding may be commenced thereafter if no proceedings concerning the succession or estate administration has occurred within the three year period after decedent's death, but the personal representative has no right to possess estate assets as provided in Section 3-709 beyond that necessary to confirm title thereto in the successors to the estate and claims other than expenses of administration may not be presented against the estate; and

(5) a formal testacy proceeding may be commenced at any time after three years from the decedent's death for the purpose of establishing an instrument to direct or control the ownership of property passing or distributable after the decedent's death from one other than the decedent when the property is to be appointed by the terms of the decedent's will or is to pass or be distributed as a part of the decedent's estate or its transfer is otherwise to be controlled by the terms of the decedent's will.

(b) These limitations do not apply to proceedings to construe probated wills or determine heirs of an intestate.

(c) In cases under subsection (a)(1) or (2), the date on which a testacy or appointment proceeding is properly commenced shall be deemed to be the date of the decedent's death for purposes of other limitations provisions of this [code] which relate to the date of death.

§ 3-109. Statutes of Limitation on Decedent's Cause of Action. No statute of limitation running on a cause of action belonging to a decedent which had not been barred as of the date of his death, shall apply to bar a cause of action surviving the decedent's death sooner than four months after death. A cause of action which, but for this section, would have been barred less than four months after death, is barred after four months unless tolled.

PART 2
VENUE FOR PROBATE AND ADMINISTRATION; PRIORITY TO ADMINISTER; DEMAND FOR NOTICE

§ 3-201. Venue for First and Subsequent Estate Proceedings; Location of Property.

(a) Venue for the first informal or formal testacy or appointment proceedings after a decedent's death is:

(1) in the [county] where the decedent had his domicile at the time of his death; or

(2) if the decedent was not domiciled in this state, in any [county] where property of the decedent was located at the time of his death.

(b) Venue for all subsequent proceedings within the exclusive jurisdiction of the court is in the place where the initial proceeding occurred, unless the initial proceeding has been transferred as provided in Section 1-303 or subsection (c).

(c) If the first proceeding was informal, on application of an interested person and after notice to the proponent in the first proceeding, the court, upon finding that venue is elsewhere, may transfer the proceeding and the file to the other court.

(d) For the purpose of aiding determinations concerning location of assets which may be relevant in cases involving non-domiciliaries, a debt, other than one evidenced by investment or commercial paper or other instrument in favor of a non-domiciliary is located where the debtor resides or, if the debtor is a person other than an individual, at the place where it has its principal office. Commercial paper, investment paper and other instruments are located where the instrument is. An interest in property held in trust is located where the trustee may be sued.

§ 3-202. Appointment or Testacy Proceedings; Conflicting Claim of Domicile in Another State. If conflicting claims as to the domicile of a decedent are made in a formal testacy or appointment proceeding commenced in this state, and in a testacy or appointment proceeding after notice pending at the same time in another state, the court of this state must stay, dismiss, or permit suitable amendment in, the proceeding here unless it is determined that the local proceeding was commenced before the proceeding elsewhere. The determination of domicile in the proceeding first commenced must be accepted as determinative in the proceeding in this state.

§ 3-203. Priority Among Persons Seeking Appointment as Personal Representative.

(a) Whether the proceedings are formal or informal, persons who are not disqualified have priority for appointment in the following order:

(1) the person with priority as determined by a probated will including a person nominated by a power conferred in a will;

(2) the surviving spouse of the decedent who is a devisee of the decedent;

(3) other devisees of the decedent;

(4) the surviving spouse of the decedent;

(5) other heirs of the decedent;

(6) 45 days after the death of the decedent, any creditor.

(b) An objection to an appointment can be made only in formal proceedings. In case of objection the priorities stated in subsection (a) apply except that

(1) if the estate appears to be more than adequate to meet exemptions and costs of administration but inadequate to discharge anticipated unsecured claims, the court, on petition of creditors, may appoint any qualified person;

(2) in case of objection to appointment of a person other than one whose priority is determined

by will by an heir or devisee appearing to have a substantial interest in the estate, the court may appoint a person who is acceptable to heirs and devisees whose interests in the estate appear to be worth in total more than half of the probable distributable value, or, in default of this accord any suitable person.

(c) A person entitled to letters under paragraphs (2) through (5) of subsection (a) above, and a person aged [18] and over who would be entitled to letters but for his age, may nominate a qualified person to act as personal representative. Any person aged [18] and over may renounce his right to nominate or to an appointment by appropriate writing filed with the court. When two or more persons share a priority, those of them who do not renounce must concur in nominating another to act for them, or in applying for appointment.

(d) Conservators of the estates of protected persons, or if there is no conservator, any guardian except a guardian ad litem of a minor or incapacitated person, may exercise the same right to nominate, to object to another's appointment, or to participate in determining the preference of a majority in interest of the heirs and devisees that the protected person or ward would have if qualified for appointment.

(e) Appointment of one who does not have priority, including priority resulting from renunciation or nomination determined pursuant to this section, may be made only in formal proceedings. Before appointing one without priority, the court must determine that those having priority, although given notice of the proceedings, have failed to request appointment or to nominate another for appointment, and that administration is necessary.

(f) No person is qualified to serve as a personal representative who is:

(1) under the age of [21];

(2) a person whom the court finds unsuitable in formal proceedings.

(g) A personal representative appointed by a court of the decedent's domicile has priority over all other persons except where the decedent's will nominates different persons to be personal representative in this state and in the state of domicile. The domiciliary personal representative may nominate another, who shall have the same priority as the domiciliary personal representative.

(h) This section governs priority for appointment of a successor personal representative but does not apply to the selection of a special administrator.

§ 3-204. Demand for Notice of Order or Filing Concerning Decedent's Estate. Any person desiring notice of any order or filing pertaining to a decedent's estate in which he has a financial or property interest, may file a demand for notice with the court at any time after the death of the decedent stating the name of the decedent, the nature of his interest in the estate, and the demandant's address or that of his attorney. The clerk shall mail a copy of the demand to the personal representative if one has been appointed. After filing of a demand, no order or filing to which the demand relates shall be made or accepted without notice as prescribed in Section 1-401 to the demandant or his attorney. The validity of an order which is issued or filing which is accepted without compliance with this requirement shall not be affected by the error, but the petitioner receiving the order or the person making the filing may be liable for any damage caused by the absence of notice. The requirement of notice arising from a demand under this provision may be waived in writing by the demandant and shall cease upon the termination of his interest in the estate.

PART 3
INFORMAL PROBATE AND APPOINTMENT PROCEEDINGS;
SUCCESSION WITHOUT ADMINISTRATION

SUBPART 1. INFORMAL PROBATE AND APPOINTMENT PROCEEDINGS

§ 3-301. Informal Probate or Appointment Proceedings; Application; Contents.

(a) Applications for informal probate or informal appointment shall be directed to the Registrar, and verified by the applicant to be accurate and complete to the best of his knowledge and belief as to the following information:

(1) Every application for informal probate of a will or for informal appointment of a personal representative, other than a special or successor representative, shall contain the following:

(A) a statement of the interest of the applicant;

(B) the name, and date of death of the decedent, his age, and the county and state of his domicile at the time of death, and the names and addresses of the spouse, children, heirs and devisees and the ages of any who are minors so far as known or ascertainable with reasonable diligence by the applicant;

(C) if the decedent was not domiciled in the state at the time of his death, a statement showing venue;

(D) a statement identifying and indicating the address of any personal representative of the decedent appointed in this state or elsewhere whose appointment has not been terminated;

(E) a statement indicating whether the applicant has received a demand for notice, or is aware of any demand for notice of any probate or appointment proceeding concerning the decedent that may have been filed in this state or elsewhere; and

(F) that the time limit for informal probate or appointment as provided in this [article] has not expired either because three years or less have passed since the decedent's death, or, if more than three years from death have passed, circumstances as described by Section 3-108 authorizing tardy probate or appointment have occurred.

(2) An application for informal probate of a will shall state the following in addition to the statements required by paragraph (1):

(A) that the original of the decedent's last will is in the possession of the court, or accompanies the application, or that an authenticated copy of a will probated in another jurisdiction accompanies the application;

(B) that the applicant, to the best of his knowledge, believes the will to have been validly executed;

(C) that after the exercise of reasonable diligence, the applicant is unaware of any instrument revoking the will, and that the applicant believes that the instrument which is the subject of the application is the decedent's last will.

(3) An application for informal appointment of a personal representative to administer an estate under a will shall describe the will by date of execution and state the time and place of probate or the pending application or petition for probate. The application for appointment shall adopt the statements in the application or petition for probate and state the name, address and priority for appointment of the person whose appointment is sought.

(4) An application for informal appointment of an administrator in intestacy shall state in addition to the statements required by paragraph (1):

(A) that after the exercise of reasonable diligence, the applicant is unaware of any unrevoked testamentary instrument relating to property having a situs in this state under Section 1-301, or, a statement why any such instrument of which he may be aware is not being probated;

(B) the priority of the person whose appointment is sought and the names of any other persons having a prior or equal right to the appointment under Section 3-203.

(5) An application for appointment of a personal representative to succeed a personal representative appointed under a different testacy status shall refer to the order in the most recent testacy proceeding, state the name and address of the person whose appointment is sought and of the person whose appointment will be terminated if the application is granted, and describe the priority of the applicant.

(6) An application for appointment of a personal representative to succeed a personal representative who has tendered a resignation as provided in 3-610(c), or whose appointment has been terminated by death or removal, shall adopt the statements in the application or petition which led to the appointment of the person being succeeded except as specifically changed or corrected, state the name and address of the person who seeks appointment as successor, and describe the priority of the applicant.

(b) By verifying an application for informal probate, or informal appointment, the applicant submits personally to the jurisdiction of the court in any proceeding for relief from fraud relating to the application, or for perjury, that may be instituted against him.

§ 3-302. Informal Probate; Duty of Registrar; Effect of Informal Probate. Upon receipt of an application requesting informal probate of a will, the Registrar, upon making the findings required by Section 3-303 shall issue a written statement of informal probate if at least 120 hours have elapsed since the decedent's death. Informal probate is conclusive as to all persons until superseded by an order in a formal testacy proceeding. No defect in the application or procedure relating thereto which leads to informal probate of a will renders the probate void.

§ 3-303. Informal Probate; Proof and Findings Required.
(a) In an informal proceeding for original probate of a will, the Registrar shall determine whether:
(1) the application is complete;
(2) the applicant has made oath or affirmation that the statements contained in the application are true to the best of his knowledge and belief;
(3) the applicant appears from the application to be an interested person as defined in Section 1-201(23);
(4) on the basis of the statements in the application, venue is proper;
(5) an original, duly executed and apparently unrevoked will is in the Registrar's possession;
(6) any notice required by Section 3-204 has been given and that the application is not within Section 3-304; and
(7) it appears from the application that the time limit for original probate has not expired.

(b) The application shall be denied if it indicates that a personal representative has been appointed in another [county] of this state or except as provided in subsection (d) below, if it appears that this or another will of the decedent has been the subject of a previous probate order.

(c) A will which appears to have the required signatures and which contains an attestation clause showing that requirements of execution under Section 2-502, 2-503 or 2-506 have been met shall be probated without further proof. In other cases, the Registrar may assume execution if the will appears to have been properly executed, or he may accept a sworn statement or affidavit of any person having knowledge of the circumstances of execution, whether or not the person was a witness to the will.

(d) Informal probate of a will which has been previously probated elsewhere may be granted at any time upon written application by any interested person, together with deposit of an authenticated copy of the will and of the statement probating it from the office or court where it was first probated.

(e) A will from a place which does not provide for probate of a will after death and which is not eligible for probate under subsection (a) above, may be probated in this state upon receipt by the

Registrar of a duly authenticated copy of the will and a duly authenticated certificate of its legal custodian that the copy filed is a true copy and that the will has become operative under the law of the other place.

§ 3-304. Informal Probate; Unavailable in Certain Cases.
Applications for informal probate which relate to one or more of a known series of testamentary instruments (other than a will and one or more codicils thereto), the latest of which does not expressly revoke the earlier, shall be declined.

§ 3-305. Informal Probate; Registrar Not Satisfied.
If the Registrar is not satisfied that a will is entitled to be probated in informal proceedings because of failure to meet the requirements of Sections 3-303 and 3-304 or any other reason, he may decline the application. A declination of informal probate is not an adjudication and does not preclude formal probate proceedings.

§ 3-306. Informal Probate; Notice Requirements.
[(a)]* The moving party must give notice as described by Section 1-401 of his application for informal probate to any person demanding it pursuant to Section 3-204, and to any personal representative of the decedent whose appointment has not been terminated. No other notice of informal probate is required.

[(b) If an informal probate is granted, within 30 days thereafter the applicant shall give written information of the probate to the heirs and devisees. The information shall include the name and address of the applicant, the name and location of the court granting the informal probate, and the date of the probate. The information shall be delivered or sent by ordinary mail to each of the heirs and devisees whose address is reasonably available to the applicant. No duty to give information is incurred if a personal representative is appointed who is required to give the written information required by Section 3-705. An applicant's failure to give information as required by this section is a breach of his duty to the heirs and devisees but does not affect the validity of the probate.]

*This paragraph becomes subsection (a) if optional subsection (b) is accepted.

§ 3-307. Informal Appointment Proceedings; Delay in Order; Duty of Registrar; Effect of Appointment.
(a) Upon receipt of an application for informal appointment of a personal representative other than a special administrator as provided in Section 3-614, if at least 120 hours have elapsed since the decedent's death, the Registrar, after making the findings required by Section 3-308, shall appoint the applicant subject to qualification and acceptance; provided, that if the decedent was a non-resident, the Registrar shall delay the order of appointment until 30 days have elapsed since death unless the personal representative appointed at the decedent's domicile is the applicant, or unless the decedent's will directs that his estate be subject to the laws of this state.

(b) The status of personal representative and the powers and duties pertaining to the office are fully established by informal appointment. An appointment, and the office of personal representative created thereby, is subject to termination as provided in Sections 3-608 through 3-612, but is not subject to retroactive vacation.

§ 3-308. Informal Appointment Proceedings; Proof and Findings Required.
(a) In informal appointment proceedings, the Registrar must determine whether:

(1) the application for informal appointment of a personal representative is complete;

(2) the applicant has made oath or affirmation that the statements contained in the application are true to the best of his knowledge and belief;

(3) the applicant appears from the application to be an interested person as defined in Section 1-201(23);

(4) on the basis of the statements in the application, venue is proper;

(5) any will to which the requested appointment relates has been formally or informally probated; but this requirement does not apply to the appointment of a special administrator;

(6) any notice required by Section 3-204 has been given;

(7) from the statements in the application, the person whose appointment is sought has priority entitling him to the appointment.

(b) Unless Section 3-612 controls, the application must be denied if it indicates that a personal representative who has not filed a written statement of resignation as provided in Section 3-610(c) has been appointed in this or another [county] of this state, that (unless the applicant is the domiciliary personal representative or his nominee) the decedent was not domiciled in this state and that a personal representative whose appointment has not been terminated has been appointed by a court in the state of domicile, or that other requirements of this section have not been met.

§ 3-309. Informal Appointment Proceedings; Registrar Not Satisfied. If the Registrar is not satisfied that a requested informal appointment of a personal representative should be made because of failure to meet the requirements of Sections 3-307 and 3-308, or for any other reason, he may decline the application. A declination of informal appointment is not an adjudication and does not preclude appointment in formal proceedings.

§ 3-310. Informal Appointment Proceedings; Notice Requirements. The moving party must give notice as described by Section 1-401 of his intention to seek an appointment informally: (1) to any person demanding it pursuant to Section 3-204; and (2) to any person having a prior or equal right to appointment not waived in writing and filed with the court. No other notice of an informal appointment proceeding is required.

§ 3-311. Informal Appointment Unavailable in Certain Cases. If an application for informal appointment indicates the existence of a possible unrevoked testamentary instrument which may relate to property subject to the laws of this state, and which is not filed for probate in this court, the Registrar shall decline the application.

SUBPART 2. SUCCESSION WITHOUT ADMINISTRATION

Prefatory Note

This subpart to the Uniform Probate Code is an alternative to other methods of administering a decedent's estate. The Uniform Probate Code otherwise provides procedures for informal administration, formal administration and supervised administration. This subpart adds another alternative to the system of flexible administration provided by the Uniform Probate Code and permits the heirs of an intestate or residuary devisees of a testator to accept the estate assets without administration by assuming responsibility for discharging those obligations that normally would be discharged by the personal representative.

The concept of succession without administration is drawn from the civil law and is a variation of the method which is followed largely on the Continent in Europe, in Louisiana and in Quebec.

This subpart contains cross- references to the procedures in the Uniform Probate Code and particularly implements the policies and concepts reflected in Sections 1-102, 3-101 and 3-901....

§ 3-312. Universal Succession; In General. The heirs of an intestate or the residuary devisees under a will, excluding minors and incapacitated, protected, or unascertained persons, may become universal successors to the decedent's estate by assuming personal liability for (i) taxes, (ii) debts of the decedent, (iii) claims against the decedent or the estate, and (iv) distributions due other heirs, devisees, and persons entitled to property of the decedent as provided in Sections 3-313 through 3-322.

§ 3-313. Universal Succession; Application; Contents.

(a) An application to become universal successors by the heirs of an intestate or the residuary devisees under a will must be directed to the Registrar, signed by each applicant, and verified to be accurate and complete to the best of the applicant's knowledge and belief as follows:

(1) An application by heirs of an intestate must contain the statements required by Section 3-301(a)(1) and (4)(A) and state that the applicants constitute all the heirs other than minors and incapacitated, protected, or unascertained persons.

(2) An application by residuary devisees under a will must be combined with a petition for informal probate if the will has not been admitted to probate in this state and must contain the statements required by Section 3-301(a)(1) and (2). If the will has been probated in this state, an application by residuary devisees must contain the statements required by Section 3-301(a)(2)(C). An application by residuary devisees must state that the applicants constitute the residuary devisees of the decedent other than any minors and incapacitated, protected, or unascertained persons. If the estate is partially intestate, all of the heirs other than minors and incapacitated, protected, or unascertained persons must join as applicants.

(b) The application must state whether letters of administration are outstanding, whether a petition for appointment of a personal representative of the decedent is pending in any court of this state, and that the applicants waive their right to seek appointment of a personal representative.

(c) The application may describe in general terms the assets of the estate and must state that the applicants accept responsibility for the estate and assume personal liability for (i) taxes, (ii) debts of the decedent, (iii) claims against the decedent or the estate and (iv) distributions due other heirs, devisees, and persons entitled to property of the decedent as provided in Sections 3-316 through 3-322.

§ 3-314. Universal Succession; Proof and Findings Required.

(a) The Registrar shall grant the application if:

(1) the application is complete in accordance with Section 3-313;

(2) all necessary persons have joined and have verified that the statements contained therein are true, to the best knowledge and belief of each;

(3) venue is proper;

(4) any notice required by Section 3-204 has been given or waived;

(5) the time limit for original probate or appointment proceedings has not expired and the applicants claim under a will;

(6) the application requests informal probate of a will, the application and findings conform with Sections 3-301(a)(2) and 3-303(a), (c), (d), and (e) so the will is admitted to probate; and

(7) none of the applicants is a minor or an incapacitated or protected person.

(b) The Registrar shall deny the application if letters of administration are outstanding.

(c) Except as provided in Section 3-322, the Registrar shall deny the application if any creditor, heir, or devisee who is qualified by Section 3-605 to demand bond files an objection.

§ 3-315. Universal Succession; Duty of Registrar; Effect of Statement of Universal Succession. Upon receipt of an application under Section 3-313, if at least 120 hours have elapsed since the decedent's death, the Registrar, upon granting the application, shall issue a written statement of universal succession describing the estate as set forth in the application and stating that the applicants (i) are the universal successors to the assets of the estate as provided in Section 3-312, (ii) have assumed liability for the obligations of the decedent, and (iii) have acquired the powers and liabilities of universal successors. The statement of universal succession is evidence of the universal successors' title to the assets of the estate. Upon its issuance, the powers and liabilities of universal successors provided in Sections 3-316 through 3-322 attach and are assumed by the applicants.

§ 3-316. Universal Succession; Universal Successors' Powers.
Upon the [Registrar's] issuance of a statement of universal succession:

(1) Universal successors have full power of ownership to deal with the assets of the estate subject to the limitations and liabilities in this [subpart]. The universal successors shall proceed expeditiously to settle and distribute the estate without adjudication but if necessary may invoke the jurisdiction of the court to resolve questions concerning the estate.

(2) Universal successors have the same powers as distributees from a personal representative under Sections 3-908 and 3-909 and third persons with whom they deal are protected as provided in Section 3-910.

(3) For purposes of collecting assets in another state whose law does not provide for universal succession, universal successors have the same standing and power as personal representatives or distributees in this state.

§ 3-317. Universal Succession; Universal Successors' Liability to Creditors, Other Heirs, Devisees and Persons Entitled to Decedent's Property; Liability of Other Persons Entitled to Property.

(a) In the proportions and subject to the limits expressed in Section 3-321, universal successors assume all liabilities of the decedent that were not discharged by reason of death and liability for all taxes, claims against the decedent or the estate, and charges properly incurred after death for the preservation of the estate, to the extent those items, if duly presented, would be valid claims against the decedent's estate.

(b) In the proportions and subject to the limits expressed in Section 3-321, universal successors are personally liable to other heirs, devisees, and persons entitled to property of the decedent for the assets or amounts that would be due those heirs, were the estate administered, but no allowance having priority over devisees may be claimed for attorney's fees or charges for preservation of the estate in excess of reasonable amounts properly incurred.

(c) Universal successors are entitled to their interests in the estate as heirs or devisees subject to priority and abatement pursuant to Section 3-902 and to agreement pursuant to Section 3-912.

(d) Other heirs, devisees, and persons to whom assets have been distributed have the same powers and liabilities as distributees under Sections 3-908, 3-909, and 3-910.

(e) Absent breach of fiduciary obligations or express undertaking, a fiduciary's liability is limited to the assets received by the fiduciary.

§ 3-318. Universal Succession; Universal Successors' Submission to Jurisdiction; When Heirs or Devisees May Not Seek Administration.

(a) Upon issuance of the statement of universal succession, the universal successors become subject to the personal jurisdiction of the courts of this state in any proceeding that may be instituted relating to the estate or to any liability assumed by them.

(b) Any heir or devisee who voluntarily joins in an application under Section 3-313 may not subsequently seek appointment of a personal representative.

§ 3-319. Universal Succession; Duty of Universal Successors; Information to Heirs and Devisees. Not later than 30 days after issuance of the statement of universal succession, each universal successor shall inform the heirs and devisees who did not join in the application of the succession without administration. The information must be delivered or be sent by ordinary mail to each of the heirs and devisees whose address is reasonably available to the universal successors. The information must include the names and addresses of the universal successors, indicate that it is being sent to persons who have or may have some interest in the estate, and describe the court where the application and statement of universal succession has been filed. The failure of a universal successor to give this information is a breach of duty to the persons concerned but does not affect the validity of the approval of succession without administration or the powers or liabilities of the universal successors. A universal successor may inform other persons of the succession without administration by delivery or by ordinary first class mail.

§ 3-320. Universal Succession; Universal Successors' Liability For Restitution to Estate. If a personal representative is subsequently appointed, universal successors are personally liable for restitution of any property of the estate to which they are not entitled as heirs or devisees of the decedent and their liability is the same as a distributee under Section 3-909, subject to the provisions of Sections 3-317 and 3-321 and the limitations of Section 3-1006.

§ 3-321. Universal Succession; Liability of Universal Successors for Claims, Expenses, Intestate Shares and Devises. The liability of universal successors is subject to any defenses that would have been available to the decedent. Other than liability arising from fraud, conversion, or other wrongful conduct of a universal successor, the personal liability of each universal successor to any creditor, claimant, other heir, devisee, or person entitled to decedent's property may not exceed the proportion of the claim that the universal successor's share bears to the share of all heirs and residuary devisees.

§ 3-322. Universal Succession; Remedies of Creditors, Other Heirs, Devisees or Persons Entitled to Decedent's Property. In addition to remedies otherwise provided by law, any creditor, heir, devisee, or person entitled to decedent's property qualified under Section 3-605, may demand bond of universal successors. If the demand for bond precedes the granting of an application for universal succession, it must be treated as an objection under Section 3-314(c) unless it is withdrawn, the claim satisfied, or the applicants post bond in an amount sufficient to protect the demandant. If the demand for bond follows the granting of an application for universal succession, the universal successors, within 10 days after notice of the demand, upon satisfying the claim or posting bond sufficient to protect the demandant, may disqualify the demandant from seeking administration of the estate.

PART 4
FORMAL TESTACY AND APPOINTMENT PROCEEDINGS

§ 3-401. Formal Testacy Proceedings; Nature; When Commenced. A formal testacy proceeding is litigation to determine whether a decedent left a valid will. A formal testacy proceeding may be commenced by an interested person filing a petition as described in Section 3-402(a) in which he requests that the court, after notice and hearing, enter an order probating a will, or a petition to set aside an informal probate of a will or to prevent informal probate of a will which is the subject of a pending application, or a petition in accordance with Section 3-402(b) for an order that the decedent died intestate.

A petition may seek formal probate of a will without regard to whether the same or a conflicting will has been informally probated. A formal testacy proceeding may, but need not, involve a request for appointment of a personal representative.

During the pendency of a formal testacy proceeding, the Registrar shall not act upon any application for informal probate of any will of the decedent or any application for informal appointment of a personal representative of the decedent.

Unless a petition in a formal testacy proceeding also requests confirmation of the previous informal appointment, a previously appointed personal representative, after receipt of notice of the commencement of a formal probate proceeding, must refrain from exercising his power to make any further distribution of the estate during the pendency of the formal proceeding. A petitioner who seeks the appointment of a different personal representative in a formal proceeding also may request an order restraining the acting personal representative from exercising any of the powers of his office and requesting the appointment of a special administrator. In the absence of a request, or if the request is denied, the commencement of a formal proceeding has no effect on the powers and duties of a previously appointed personal representative other than those relating to distribution.

§ 3-402. Formal Testacy or Appointment Proceedings; Petition; Contents.

(a) Petitions for formal probate of a will, or for adjudication of intestacy with or without request for appointment of a personal representative, must be directed to the court, request a judicial order after notice and hearing and contain further statements as indicated in this section. A petition for formal probate of a will

(1) requests an order as to the testacy of the decedent in relation to a particular instrument which may or may not have been informally probated and determining the heirs,

(2) contains the statements required for informal applications as stated in the six subparagraphs under Section 3-301(a)(1), the statements required by subparagraphs (B) and (C) of Section 3-301(a)(2), and

(3) states whether the original of the last will of the decedent is in the possession of the court or accompanies the petition.

If the original will is neither in the possession of the court nor accompanies the petition and no authenticated copy of a will probated in another jurisdiction accompanies the petition, the petition also must state the contents of the will, and indicate that it is lost, destroyed, or otherwise unavailable.

(b) A petition for adjudication of intestacy and appointment of an administrator in intestacy must request a judicial finding and order that the decedent left no will and determining the heirs, contain the statements required by paragraphs (1) and (4) of Section 3-301(a) and indicate whether supervised administration is sought. A petition may request an order determining intestacy and heirs without requesting the appointment of an administrator, in which case, the statements required by subparagraph (B) of Section 3-301(a)(4) above may be omitted.

§ 3-403. Formal Testacy Proceedings; Notice of Hearing on Petition.

(a) Upon commencement of a formal testacy proceeding, the court shall fix a time and place of hearing. Notice shall be given in the manner prescribed by Section 1-401 by the petitioner to the persons herein enumerated and to any additional person who has filed a demand for notice under Section 3-204 of this [code].

Notice shall be given to the following persons: the surviving spouse, children, and other heirs of the decedent, the devisees and executors named in any will that is being, or has been, probated, or offered for informal or formal probate in the [county,] or that is known by the petitioner to have been probated, or offered for informal or formal probate elsewhere, and any personal representative of the decedent whose appointment has not been terminated. Notice may be given to other persons. In addition, the petitioner shall give notice by publication to all unknown persons and to all known persons whose addresses are unknown who have any interest in the matters being litigated.

(b) If it appears by the petition or otherwise that the fact of the death of the alleged decedent may be in doubt, or on the written demand of any interested person, a copy of the notice of the hearing on said petition shall be sent by registered mail to the alleged decedent at his last known address. The court shall direct the petitioner to report the results of, or make and report back concerning, a reasonably diligent search for the alleged decedent in any manner that may seem advisable, including any or all of the following methods:

(1) by inserting in one or more suitable periodicals a notice requesting information from any person having knowledge of the whereabouts of the alleged decedent;

(2) by notifying law enforcement officials and public welfare agencies in appropriate locations of the disappearance of the alleged decedent;

(3) by engaging the services of an investigator.

The costs of any search so directed shall be paid by the petitioner if there is no administration or by the estate of the decedent in case there is administration.

§ 3-404. Formal Testacy Proceedings; Written Objections to Probate. Any party to a formal proceeding who opposes the probate of a will for any reason shall state in his pleadings his objections to probate of the will.

§ 3-405. Formal Testacy Proceedings; Uncontested Cases; Hearings and Proof. If a petition in a testacy proceeding is unopposed, the court may order probate or intestacy on the strength of the pleadings if satisfied that the conditions of Section 3-409 have been met, or conduct a hearing in open court and require proof of the matters necessary to support the order sought. If evidence concerning execution of the will is necessary, the affidavit or testimony of one of any attesting witnesses to the instrument is sufficient. If the affidavit or testimony of an attesting witness is not available, execution of the will may be proved by other evidence or affidavit.

§ 3-406. Formal Testacy Proceedings; Contested Cases. In a contested case in which the proper execution of a will is at issue, the following rules apply:

(1) If the will is self-proved pursuant to Section 2-504, the will satisfies the requirements for execution without the testimony of any attesting witness, upon filing the will and the acknowledgment and affidavits annexed or attached to it, unless there is evidence of fraud or forgery affecting the acknowledgment or affidavit.

(2) If the will is notarized pursuant to Section 2-502(a)(3)(B), but not self-proved, there is a rebuttable presumption that the will satisfies the requirements for execution upon filing the will.

(3) If the will is witnessed pursuant to Section 2-502(a)(3)(A), but not notarized or self-proved, the testimony of at least one of the attesting witnesses is required to establish proper execution if the witness is within this state, competent, and able to testify. Proper execution may be established by other evidence, including an affidavit of an attesting witness. An attestation clause that is signed by the attesting witnesses raises a rebuttable presumption that the events recited in the clause occurred.

Comment

2008 Revisions. This section, which applies in a contested case in which the proper execution of a will is at issue, was substantially revised and clarified in 2008.

Self-Proved Wills: Paragraph (1) provides that a will that is self-proved pursuant to Section 2-504 satisfies the requirements for execution without the testimony of any attesting witness, upon filing the will and the acknowledgment and affidavits annexed or attached to it, unless there is evidence of fraud or forgery affecting the acknowledgment or affidavit. Paragraph (1) does not preclude evidence of undue influence, lack of testamentary capacity, revocation, or any relevant evidence that the testator was unaware of the contents of the document.

Notarized Wills: Paragraph (2) provides that if the will is notarized pursuant to Section 2-502(a)(3)(B), but not self-proved, there is a rebuttable presumption that the will satisfies the requirements for execution upon filing the will.

Witnessed Wills: Paragraph (3) provides that if the will is witnessed pursuant to Section 2-502(a)(3)(A), but not notarized or self-proved, the testimony of at least one of the attesting witnesses is required to establish proper execution if the witness is within this state, competent, and able to testify. Proper execution may be established by other evidence, including an affidavit of an attesting witness. An attestation clause that is signed by the attesting witnesses raises a rebuttable presumption that the events recited in the clause occurred. For further explanation of the effect of an attestation clause, see Restatement (Third) of Property: Wills and Other Donative Transfers § 3.1 cmt. q (1999).

Historical Note. This Comment was revised in 2008.

§ 3-407. Formal Testacy Proceedings; Burdens in Contested Cases. In contested cases, petitioners who seek to establish intestacy have the burden of establishing prima facie proof of death, venue, and heirship. Proponents of a will have the burden of establishing prima facie proof of due execution in all cases, and, if they are also petitioners, prima facie proof of death and venue. Contestants of a will have the burden of establishing lack of testamentary intent or capacity, undue influence, fraud, duress, mistake or revocation. Parties have the ultimate burden of persuasion as to matters with respect to which they have the initial burden of proof. If a will is opposed by the petition for probate of a later will revoking the former, it shall be determined first whether the later will is entitled to probate, and if a will is opposed by a petition for a declaration of intestacy, it shall be determined first whether the will is entitled to probate.

§ 3-408. Formal Testacy Proceedings; Will Construction; Effect of Final Order in Another Jurisdiction. A final order of a court of another state determining testacy, the validity or construction of a will, made in a proceeding involving notice to and an opportunity for contest by all interested persons must be accepted as determinative by the courts of this state if it includes, or is based upon, a finding that the decedent was domiciled at his death in the state where the order was made.

§ 3-409. Formal Testacy Proceedings; Order; Foreign Will. After the time required for any notice has expired, upon proof of notice, and after any hearing that may be necessary, if the court finds that the testator is dead, venue is proper and that the proceeding was commenced within the limitation prescribed by Section 3-108, it shall determine the decedent's domicile at death, his heirs and his state of testacy. Any will found to be valid and unrevoked shall be formally probated. Termination of any previous informal appointment of a personal representative, which may be appropriate in view of the relief requested and findings, is governed by Section 3-612. The petition shall be dismissed or appropriate amendment allowed if the court is not satisfied that the alleged decedent is dead. A will from a place which does not provide for probate of a will after death, may be proved for probate in this state by a duly authenticated certificate of its legal custodian that the copy introduced is a true copy and that the will has become effective under the law of the other place.

§ 3-410. Formal Testacy Proceedings; Probate of More Than One Instrument. If two or more instruments are offered for probate before a final order is entered in a formal testacy proceeding, more than one instrument may be probated if neither expressly revokes the other or contains provisions which work a total revocation by implication. If more than one instrument is probated, the order shall indicate what provisions control in respect to the nomination of an executor, if any. The order may, but need not, indicate how many provisions of a particular instrument are affected by the other instrument. After a final order in a testacy proceeding has been entered, no petition for probate of any other instrument of the decedent may be entertained, except incident to a petition to vacate or modify a previous probate order and subject to the time limits of Section 3-412.

§ 3-411. Formal Testacy Proceedings; Partial Intestacy. If it becomes evident in the course of a formal testacy proceeding that, though one or more instruments are entitled to be probated, the decedent's estate is or may be partially intestate, the court shall enter an order to that effect.

§ 3-412. Formal Testacy Proceedings; Effect of Order; Vacation. Subject to appeal and subject to vacation as provided in this section and in Section 3-413, a formal testacy order under Sections 3-409 to 3-411, including an order that the decedent left no valid will and determining heirs, is final as to all persons with respect to all issues concerning the decedent's estate that the court considered or might have considered incident to its rendition relevant to the question of whether the decedent left a valid will, and to the determination of heirs, except that:

(1) The court shall entertain a petition for modification or vacation of its order and probate of another will of the decedent if it is shown that the proponents of the later-offered will: (i) were unaware of its existence at the time of the earlier proceeding; or (ii) were unaware of the earlier proceeding and were given no notice thereof, except by publication.

(2) If intestacy of all or part of the estate has been ordered, the determination of heirs of the decedent may be reconsidered if it is shown that one or more persons were omitted from the determination and if it is also shown that the persons were unaware of their relationship to the decedent, were unaware of his death, or were given no notice of any proceeding concerning his estate, except by publication.

(3) A petition for vacation under paragraph (1) or (2) must be filed prior to the earlier of the following time limits:

(A) if a personal representative has been appointed for the estate, the time of entry of any order approving final distribution of the estate, or, if the estate is closed by statement, six months after the filing of the closing statement;

(B) whether or not a personal representative has been appointed for the estate of the decedent, the time prescribed by Section 3-108 when it is no longer possible to initiate an original proceeding to probate a will of the decedent; or

(C) twelve months after the entry of the order sought to be vacated.

(4) The order originally rendered in the testacy proceeding may be modified or vacated, if appropriate under the circumstances, by the order of probate of the later-offered will or the order redetermining heirs.

(5) The finding of the fact of death is conclusive as to the alleged decedent only if notice of the hearing on the petition in the formal testacy proceeding was sent by registered or certified mail addressed to the alleged decedent at his last known address and the court finds that a search under Section 3-403(b) was made.

If the alleged decedent is not dead, even if notice was sent and search was made, he may recover estate assets in the hands of the personal representative. In addition to any remedies available to the alleged decedent by reason of any fraud or intentional wrongdoing, the alleged decedent may recover any estate or its proceeds from distributees that is in their hands, or the value of distributions received by them, to the extent that any recovery from distributees is equitable in view of all of the circumstances.

§ 3-413. Formal Testacy Proceedings; Vacation of Order For Other Cause. For good cause shown, an order in a formal testacy proceeding may be modified or vacated within the time allowed for appeal.

§ 3-414. Formal Proceedings Concerning Appointment of Personal Representative.

(a) A formal proceeding for adjudication regarding the priority or qualification of one who is an applicant for appointment as personal representative, or of one who previously has been appointed personal representative in informal proceedings, if an issue concerning the testacy of the decedent is or may be involved, is governed by Section 3-402, as well as by this section. In other cases, the petition shall contain or adopt the statements required by Section 3-301(1) and describe the question relating to priority or qualification of the personal representative which is to be resolved. If the proceeding precedes any appointment of a personal representative, it shall stay any pending informal appointment proceedings as well as any commenced thereafter. If the proceeding is commenced after appointment, the previously appointed personal representative, after receipt of notice thereof, shall refrain from exercising any power of administration except as necessary to preserve the estate or unless the court orders otherwise.

(b) After notice to interested persons, including all persons interested in the administration of the estate as successors under the applicable assumption concerning testacy, any previously appointed personal representative and any person having or claiming priority for appointment as personal representative, the court shall determine who is entitled to appointment under Section 3-203, make a proper appointment and, if appropriate, terminate any prior appointment found to have been improper as provided in cases of removal under Section 3-611.

PART 5
SUPERVISED ADMINISTRATION

§ 3-501. Supervised Administration; Nature of Proceeding. Supervised administration is a single in rem proceeding to secure complete administration and settlement of a decedent's estate under the continuing authority of the court which extends until entry of an order approving distribution of the estate and discharging the personal representative or other order terminating the proceeding. A supervised personal representative is responsible to the court, as well as to the interested parties, and is subject to directions concerning the estate made by the court on its own motion or on the motion of any interested party. Except as otherwise provided in this [part], or as otherwise ordered by the court, a supervised personal representative has the same duties and powers as a personal representative who is not supervised.

§ 3-502. Supervised Administration; Petition; Order. A petition for supervised administration may be filed by any interested person or by a personal representative at any time or the prayer for supervised administration may be joined with a petition in a testacy or appointment proceeding. If the testacy of the decedent and the priority and qualification of any personal representative have not been adjudicated previously, the petition for supervised administration shall include the matters required of a petition in a formal testacy proceeding and the notice requirements and procedures applicable to a formal testacy proceeding apply. If not previously adjudicated, the court shall adjudicate the testacy of the decedent and questions relating to the priority and qualifications of the personal representative in any case involving a request for supervised administration, even though the request for supervised administration may be denied. After notice to interested persons, the court shall order supervised administration of a decedent's estate:

(1) if the decedent's will directs supervised administration, it shall be ordered unless the court finds that circumstances bearing on the need for supervised administration have changed since the execution of the will and that there is no necessity for supervised administration;

(2) if the decedent's will directs unsupervised administration, supervised administration shall be ordered only upon a finding that it is necessary for protection of persons interested in the estate; or

(3) in other cases if the court finds that supervised administration is necessary under the circumstances.

§ 3-503. Supervised Administration; Effect on Other Proceedings.

(a) The pendency of a proceeding for supervised administration of a decedent's estate stays action on any informal application then pending or thereafter filed.

(b) If a will has been previously probated in informal proceedings, the effect of the filing of a petition for supervised administration is as provided for formal testacy proceedings by Section 3-401.

(c) After he has received notice of the filing of a petition for supervised administration, a personal representative who has been appointed previously shall not exercise his power to distribute any estate. The filing of the petition does not affect his other powers and duties unless the court restricts the exercise of any of them pending full hearing on the petition.

§ 3-504. Supervised Administration; Powers of Personal Representative. Unless restricted by the court, a supervised personal representative has, without interim orders approving exercise of a power, all powers of personal representatives under this [code], but he shall not exercise his power to make any distribution of the estate without prior order of the court. Any other restriction on the power of a personal representative which may be ordered by the court must be endorsed on his letters of appointment and, unless so endorsed, is ineffective as to persons dealing in good faith with the personal representative.

§ 3-505. Supervised Administration; Interim Orders; Distribution and Closing Orders. Unless otherwise ordered by the court, supervised administration is terminated by order in accordance with time restrictions, notices and contents of orders prescribed for proceedings under Section 3-1001. Interim orders approving or directing partial distributions or granting other relief may be issued by the court at any time during the pendency of a supervised administration on the application of the personal representative or any interested person.

PART 6
PERSONAL REPRESENTATIVE; APPOINTMENT, CONTROL AND TERMINATION OF AUTHORITY

§ 3-601. Qualification. Prior to receiving letters, a personal representative shall qualify by filing with the appointing court any required bond and a statement of acceptance of the duties of the office.

§ 3-602. Acceptance of Appointment; Consent to Jurisdiction. By accepting appointment, a personal representative submits personally to the jurisdiction of the court in any proceeding relating to the estate that may be instituted by any interested person. Notice of any proceeding shall be delivered to

the personal representative, or mailed to him by ordinary first class mail at his address as listed in the application or petition for appointment or as thereafter reported to the court and to his address as then known to the petitioner.

§ 3-603. Bond Not Required Without Court Order, Exceptions.

No bond is required of a personal representative appointed in informal proceedings, except (i) upon the appointment of a special administrator; (ii) when an executor or other personal representative is appointed to administer an estate under a will containing an express requirement of bond or (iii) when bond is required under Section 3-605. Bond may be required by court order at the time of appointment of a personal representative appointed in any formal proceeding except that bond is not required of a personal representative appointed in formal proceedings if the will relieves the personal representative of bond, unless bond has been requested by an interested party and the court is satisfied that it is desirable. Bond required by any will may be dispensed with in formal proceedings upon determination by the court that it is not necessary. No bond is required of any personal representative who, pursuant to statute, has deposited cash or collateral with an agency of this state to secure performance of his duties.

§ 3-604. Bond Amount; Security; Procedure; Reduction.

If bond is required and the provisions of the will or order do not specify the amount, unless stated in his application or petition, the person qualifying shall file a statement under oath with the Registrar indicating his best estimate of the value of the personal estate of the decedent and of the income expected from the personal and real estate during the next year, and he shall execute and file a bond with the Registrar, or give other suitable security, in an amount not less than the estimate. The Registrar shall determine that the bond is duly executed by a corporate surety, or one or more individual sureties whose performance is secured by pledge of personal property, mortgage on real property or other adequate security. The Registrar may permit the amount of the bond to be reduced by the value of assets of the estate deposited with a domestic financial institution (as defined in Section 6-101) in a manner that prevents their unauthorized disposition. On petition of the personal representative or another interested person the court may excuse a requirement of bond, increase or reduce the amount of the bond, release sureties, or permit the substitution of another bond with the same or different sureties.

§ 3-605. Demand for Bond by Interested Person.

Any person apparently having an interest in the estate worth in excess of [$5,000], or any creditor having a claim in excess of [$5,000], may make a written demand that a personal representative give bond. The demand must be filed with the Registrar and a copy mailed to the personal representative, if appointment and qualification have occurred. Thereupon, bond is required, but the requirement ceases if the person demanding bond ceases to be interested in the estate, or if bond is excused as provided in Section 3-603 or 3-604. After he has received notice and until the filing of the bond or cessation of the requirement of bond, the personal representative shall refrain from exercising any powers of his office except as necessary to preserve the estate. Failure of the personal representative to meet a requirement of bond by giving suitable bond within 30 days after receipt of notice is cause for his removal and appointment of a successor personal representative.

§ 3-606. Terms and Conditions of Bonds.

(a) The following requirements and provisions apply to any bond required by this [part]:

(1) Bonds shall name the [state] as obligee for the benefit of the persons interested in the estate and shall be conditioned upon the faithful discharge by the fiduciary of all duties according to law.

(2) Unless otherwise provided by the terms of the approved bond, sureties are jointly and severally liable with the personal representative and with each other. The address of sureties shall be stated in the bond.

(3) By executing an approved bond of a personal representative, the surety consents to the jurisdiction of the probate court which issued letters to the primary obligor in any proceedings pertaining to the fiduciary duties of the personal representative and naming the surety as a party. Notice of any proceeding shall be delivered to the surety or mailed to him by registered or certified mail at his address as listed with the court where the bond is filed and to his address as then known to the petitioner.

(4) On petition of a successor personal representative, any other personal representative of the same decedent, or any interested person, a proceeding in the court may be initiated against a surety for breach of the obligation of the bond of the personal representative.

(5) The bond of the personal representative is not void after the first recovery but may be proceeded against from time to time until the whole penalty is exhausted.

(b) No action or proceeding may be commenced against the surety on any matter as to which an action or proceeding against the primary obligor is barred by adjudication or limitation.

§ 3-607. Order Restraining Personal Representative.

(a) On petition of any person who appears to have an interest in the estate, the court by temporary order may restrain a personal representative from performing specified acts of administration, disbursement, or distribution, or exercise of any powers or discharge of any duties of his office, or make any other order to secure proper performance of his duty, if it appears to the court that the personal representative otherwise may take some action which would jeopardize unreasonably the interest of the applicant or of some other interested person. Persons with whom the personal representative may transact business may be made parties.

(b) The matter shall be set for hearing within 10 days unless the parties otherwise agree. Notice as the court directs shall be given to the personal representative and his attorney of record, if any, and to any other parties named defendant in the petition.

§ 3-608. Termination of Appointment; General.
Termination of appointment of a personal representative occurs as indicated in Sections 3-609 to 3-612, inclusive. Termination ends the right and power pertaining to the office of personal representative as conferred by this [code] or any will, except that a personal representative, at any time prior to distribution or until restrained or enjoined by court order, may perform acts necessary to protect the estate and may deliver the assets to a successor representative. Termination does not discharge a personal representative from liability for transactions or omissions occurring before termination, or relieve him of the duty to preserve assets subject to his control, to account therefor and to deliver the assets. Termination does not affect the jurisdiction of the court over the personal representative, but terminates his authority to represent the estate in any pending or future proceeding.

§ 3-609. Termination of Appointment; Death or Disability.
The death of a personal representative or the appointment of a conservator for the estate of a personal representative, terminates his appointment. Until appointment and qualification of a successor or special representative to replace the deceased or protected representative, the representative of the estate of the deceased or protected personal representative, if any, has the duty to protect the estate possessed and being administered by his decedent or ward at the time his appointment terminates, has the power to perform acts necessary for protection and shall account for and deliver the estate assets to a successor or special personal

representative upon his appointment and qualification.

§ 3-610. Termination of Appointment; Voluntary.

(a) An appointment of a personal representative terminates as provided in Section 3-1003, one year after the filing of a closing statement.

(b) An order closing an estate as provided in Section 3-1001 or 3-1002 terminates an appointment of a personal representative.

(c) A personal representative may resign his position by filing a written statement of resignation with the Registrar after he has given at least 15 days written notice to the persons known to be interested in the estate. If no one applies or petitions for appointment of a successor representative within the time indicated in the notice, the filed statement of resignation is ineffective as a termination of appointment and in any event is effective only upon the appointment and qualification of a successor representative and delivery of the assets to him.

§ 3-611. Termination of Appointment by Removal; Cause; Procedure.

(a) A person interested in the estate may petition for removal of a personal representative for cause at any time. Upon filing of the petition, the court shall fix a time and place for hearing. Notice shall be given by the petitioner to the personal representative, and to other persons as the court may order. Except as otherwise ordered as provided in Section 3-607, after receipt of notice of removal proceedings, the personal representative shall not act except to account, to correct maladministration or preserve the estate. If removal is ordered, the court also shall direct by order the disposition of the assets remaining in the name of, or under the control of, the personal representative being removed.

(b) Cause for removal exists when removal would be in the best interests of the estate, or if it is shown that a personal representative or the person seeking his appointment intentionally misrepresented material facts in the proceedings leading to his appointment, or that the personal representative has disregarded an order of the court, has become incapable of discharging the duties of his office, or has mismanaged the estate or failed to perform any duty pertaining to the office. Unless the decedent's will directs otherwise, a personal representative appointed at the decedent's domicile, incident to securing appointment of himself or his nominee as ancillary personal representative, may obtain removal of another who was appointed personal representative in this state to administer local assets.

§ 3-612. Termination of Appointment; Change of Testacy Status.
Except as otherwise ordered in formal proceedings, the probate of a will subsequent to the appointment of a personal representative in intestacy or under a will which is superseded by formal probate of another will, or the vacation of an informal probate of a will subsequent to the appointment of the personal representative thereunder, does not terminate the appointment of the personal representative although his powers may be reduced as provided in Section 3-401. Termination occurs upon appointment in informal or formal appointment proceedings of a person entitled to appointment under the later assumption concerning testacy. If no request for new appointment is made within 30 days after expiration of time for appeal from the order in formal testacy proceedings, or from the informal probate, changing the assumption concerning testacy, the previously appointed personal representative upon request may be appointed personal representative under the subsequently probated will, or as in intestacy as the case may be.

§ 3-613. Successor Personal Representative.
Parts 3 and 4 of this [article] govern proceedings for appointment of a personal representative to succeed one whose appointment has been terminated.

After appointment and qualification, a successor personal representative may be substituted in all actions and proceedings to which the former personal representative was a party, and no notice, process or claim which was given or served upon the former personal representative need be given to or served upon the successor in order to preserve any position or right the person giving the notice or filing the claim may thereby have obtained or preserved with reference to the former personal representative. Except as otherwise ordered by the ourt, the successor personal representative has the powers and duties in respect to the continued administration which the former personal representative would have had if his appointment had not been terminated.

§ 3-614. Special Administrator; Appointment. A special administrator may be appointed:

(1) informally by the Registrar on the application of any interested person when necessary to protect the estate of a decedent prior to the appointment of a general personal representative or if a prior appointment has been terminated as provided in Section 3-609;

(2) in a formal proceeding by order of the court on the petition of any interested person and finding, after notice and hearing, that appointment is necessary to preserve the estate or to secure its proper administration including its administration in circumstances where a general personal representative cannot or should not act. If it appears to the court that an emergency exists, appointment may be ordered without notice.

§ 3-615. Special Administrator; Who May Be Appointed.

(a) If a special administrator is to be appointed pending the probate of a will which is the subject of a pending application or petition for probate, the person named executor in the will shall be appointed if available, and qualified.

(b) In other cases, any proper person may be appointed special administrator.

§ 3-616. Special Administrator; Appointed Informally; Powers and Duties. A special administrator appointed by the Registrar in informal proceedings pursuant to Section 3-614(1) has the duty to collect and manage the assets of the estate, to preserve them, to account therefor and to deliver them to the general personal representative upon his qualification. The special administrator has the power of a personal representative under the [code] necessary to perform his duties.

§ 3-617. Special Administrator; Formal Proceedings; Power and Duties. A special administrator appointed by order of the court in any formal proceeding has the power of a general personal representative except as limited in the appointment and duties as prescribed in the order. The appointment may be for a specified time, to perform particular acts or on other terms as the court may direct.

§ 3-618. Termination of Appointment; Special Administrator. The appointment of a special administrator terminates in accordance with the provisions of the order of appointment or on the appointment of a general personal representative. In other cases, the appointment of a special administrator is subject to termination as provided in Sections 3-608 through 3-611.

PART 7
DUTIES AND POWERS OF PERSONAL REPRESENTATIVES

§ 3-701. Time of Accrual of Duties and Powers. The duties and powers of a personal representative commence upon his appointment. The powers of a personal representative relate back in time to give acts by the person appointed which are beneficial to the estate occurring prior to appointment the same effect as those occurring thereafter. Prior to appointment, a person named executor in a will may carry out written instructions of the decedent relating to his body, funeral and burial arrangements. A personal representative may ratify and accept acts on behalf of the estate done by others where the acts would have been proper for a personal representative.

§ 3-702. Priority Among Different Letters. A person to whom general letters are issued first has exclusive authority under the letters until his appointment is terminated or modified. If, through error, general letters are afterwards issued to another, the first appointed representative may recover any property of the estate in the hands of the representative subsequently appointed, but the acts of the latter done in good faith before notice of the first letters are not void for want of validity of appointment.

§ 3-703. General Duties; Relation and Liability to Persons Interested In Estate; Standing to Sue.
(a) A personal representative is a fiduciary who shall observe the standards of care applicable to trustees. A personal representative is under a duty to settle and distribute the estate of the decedent in accordance with the terms of any probated and effective will and this [code], and as expeditiously and efficiently as is consistent with the best interests of the estate. He shall use the authority conferred upon him by this [code], the terms of the will, if any, and any order in proceedings to which he is party for the best interests of successors to the estate.

(b) A personal representative may not be surcharged for acts of administration or distribution if the conduct in question was authorized at the time. Subject to other obligations of administration, an informally probated will is authority to administer and distribute the estate according to its terms. An order of appointment of a personal representative, whether issued in informal or formal proceedings, is authority to distribute apparently intestate assets to the heirs of the decedent if, at the time of distribution, the personal representative is not aware of a pending testacy proceeding, a proceeding to vacate an order entered in an earlier testacy proceeding, a formal proceeding questioning his appointment or fitness to continue, or a supervised administration proceeding. This section does not affect the duty of the personal representative to administer and distribute the estate in accordance with the rights of claimants whose claims have been allowed, the surviving spouse, any minor and dependent children and any pretermitted child of the decedent as described elsewhere in this [code].

(c) Except as to proceedings which do not survive the death of the decedent, a personal representative of a decedent domiciled in this state at his death has the same standing to sue and be sued in the courts of this state and the courts of any other jurisdiction as his decedent had immediately prior to death.

§ 3-704. Personal Representative to Proceed Without Court Order; Exception. A personal representative shall proceed expeditiously with the settlement and distribution of a decedent's estate and, except as otherwise specified or ordered in regard to a supervised personal representative, do so without adjudication, order, or direction of the court, but he may invoke the jurisdiction of the court, in proceedings authorized by this [code], to resolve questions concerning the estate or its administration.

§ 3-705. Duty of Personal Representative; Information to Heirs and Devisees. Not later than 30 days after his appointment every personal representative, except any special administrator, shall give information of his appointment to the heirs and devisees, including, if there has been no formal testacy proceeding and if the personal representative was appointed on the assumption that the decedent died intestate, the devisees in any will mentioned in the application for appointment of a personal representative. The information shall be delivered or sent by ordinary mail to each of the heirs and devisees whose address is reasonably available to the personal representative. The duty does not extend to require information to persons who have been adjudicated in a prior formal testacy proceeding to have no interest in the estate. The information shall include the name and address of the personal representative, indicate that it is being sent to persons who have or may have some interest in the estate being administered, indicate whether bond has been filed, and describe the court where papers relating to the estate are on file. The information shall state that the estate is being administered by the personal representative under the [State] Probate Code without supervision by the court but that recipients are entitled to information regarding the administration from the personal representative and can petition the court in any matter relating to the estate, including distribution of assets and expenses of administration. The personal representative's failure to give this information is a breach of his duty to the persons concerned but does not affect the validity of his appointment, his powers or other duties. A personal representative may inform other persons of his appointment by delivery or ordinary first class mail.

§ 3-706. Duty of Personal Representative; Inventory and Appraisement. Within three months after his appointment, a personal representative, who is not a special administrator or a successor to another representative who has previously discharged this duty, shall prepare and file or mail an inventory of property owned by the decedent at the time of his death, listing it with reasonable detail, and indicating as to each listed item, its fair market value as of the date of the decedent's death, and the type and amount of any encumbrance that may exist with reference to any item.

The personal representative shall send a copy of the inventory to interested persons who request it. He may also file the original of the inventory with the court.

§ 3-707. Employment of Appraisers. The personal representative may employ a qualified and disinterested appraiser to assist him in ascertaining the fair market value as of the date of the decedent's death of any asset the value of which may be subject to reasonable doubt. Different persons may be employed to appraise different kinds of assets included in the estate. The names and addresses of any appraiser shall be indicated on the inventory with the item or items he appraised.

§ 3-708. Duty of Personal Representative; Supplementary Inventory. If any property not included in the original inventory comes to the knowledge of a personal representative or if the personal representative learns that the value or description indicated in the original inventory for any item is erroneous or misleading, he shall make a supplementary inventory or appraisement showing the market value as of the date of the decedent's death of the new item or the revised market value or descriptions, and the appraisers or other data relied upon, if any, and file it with the court if the original inventory was filed, or furnish copies thereof or information thereof to persons interested in the new information.

§ 3-709. Duty of Personal Representative; Possession of Estate. Except as otherwise provided by a decedent's will, every personal representative has a right to, and shall take possession or control of, the decedent's property, except that any real property or tangible personal property may be left with or surrendered to the person presumptively entitled thereto unless or until, in the judgment of the personal representative, possession of the property by him will be necessary for purposes of administration. The request by a personal representative for delivery of any property possessed by an heir or devisee is conclusive evidence, in any action against the heir or devisee for possession thereof, that the possession of the property by the personal representative is necessary for purposes of administration. The personal representative shall pay taxes on, and take all steps reasonably necessary for the management, protection and preservation of, the estate in his possession. He may maintain an action to recover possession of property or to determine the title thereto.

§ 3-710. Power to Avoid Transfers. The property liable for the payment of unsecured debts of a decedent includes all property transferred by him by any means which is in law void or voidable as against his creditors, and subject to prior liens, the right to recover this property, so far as necessary for the payment of unsecured debts of the decedent, is exclusively in the personal representative.

§ 3-711. Powers of Personal Representatives; In General.
   [(a)] Until termination of his appointment a personal representative has the same power over the title to property of the estate that an absolute owner would have, in trust however, for the benefit of the creditors and others interested in the estate. This power may be exercised without notice, hearing, or order of court.
   [(b) A personal representative has access to and authority over a digital asset of the decedent to the extent provided by [the Revised Uniform Fiduciary Access to Digital Assets Act] or by order of court.]

§ 3-712. Improper Exercise of Power; Breach of Fiduciary Duty. If the exercise of power concerning the estate is improper, the personal representative is liable to interested persons for damage or loss resulting from breach of his fiduciary duty to the same extent as a trustee of an express trust. The rights of purchasers and others dealing with a personal representative shall be determined as provided in Sections 3-713 and 3-714.

§ 3-713. Sale, Encumbrance or Transaction Involving Conflict of Interest; Voidable; Exceptions. Any sale or encumbrance to the personal representative, his spouse, agent or attorney, or any corporation or trust in which he has a substantial beneficial interest, or any transaction which is affected by a substantial conflict of interest on the part of the personal representative, is voidable by any person interested in the estate except one who has consented after fair disclosure, unless
   (1) the will or a contract entered into by the decedent expressly authorized the transaction; or
   (2) the transaction is approved by the court after notice to interested persons.

§ 3-714. Persons Dealing with Personal Representative; Protection. A person who in good faith either assists a personal representative or deals with him for value is protected as if the personal representative properly exercised his power. The fact that a person knowingly deals with a personal representative does not alone require the person to inquire into the existence of a power or the propriety of its exercise. Except for restrictions on powers of supervised personal representatives which are endorsed on letters as provided in Section 3-504, no provision in any will or order of court purporting to limit the power of a personal representative is effective except as to persons with actual knowledge thereof. A person is not bound to see to the proper application of estate assets paid or delivered to a personal representative. The protection here expressed extends to instances in which some procedural irregularity or jurisdictional defect occurred in proceedings leading to the issuance of letters, including a case in which the alleged decedent is found to be alive. The protection here expressed is not by substitution for that provided by comparable provisions of the laws relating to commercial transactions and laws simplifying transfers of securities by fiduciaries.

§ 3-715. Transactions Authorized for Personal Representatives; Exceptions. Except as restricted or otherwise provided by the will or by an order in a formal proceeding and subject to the priorities stated in Section 3-902, a personal representative, acting reasonably for the benefit of the interested persons, may properly:

(1) retain assets owned by the decedent pending distribution or liquidation including those in which the representative is personally interested or which are otherwise improper for trust investment;

(2) receive assets from fiduciaries, or other sources;

(3) perform, compromise or refuse performance of the decedent's contracts that continue as obligations of the estate, as he may determine under the circumstances. In performing enforceable contracts by the decedent to convey or lease land, the personal representative, among other possible courses of action, may:

(A) execute and deliver a deed of conveyance for cash payment of all sums remaining due or the purchaser's note for the sum remaining due secured by a mortgage or deed of trust on the land; or

(B) deliver a deed in escrow with directions that the proceeds, when paid in accordance with the escrow agreement, be paid to the successors of the decedent, as designated in the escrow agreement;

(4) satisfy written charitable pledges of the decedent irrespective of whether the pledges constituted binding obligations of the decedent or were properly presented as claims, if in the judgment of the personal representative the decedent would have wanted the pledges completed under the circumstances;

(5) if funds are not needed to meet debts and expenses currently payable and are not immediately distributable, deposit or invest liquid assets of the estate, including moneys received from the sale of other assets, in federally insured interest-bearing accounts, readily marketable secured loan arrangements or other prudent investments which would be reasonable for use by trustees generally;

(6) acquire or dispose of an asset, including land in this or another state, for cash or on credit, at public or private sale; and manage, develop, improve, exchange, partition, change the character of, or abandon an estate asset;

(7) make ordinary or extraordinary repairs or alterations in buildings or other structures, demolish any improvements, raze existing or erect new party walls or buildings;

(8) subdivide, develop or dedicate land to public use; make or obtain the vacation of plats and adjust boundaries; or adjust differences in valuation on exchange or partition by giving or receiving considerations; or dedicate easements to public use without consideration;

(9) enter for any purpose into a lease as lessor or lessee, with or without option to purchase or renew, for a term within or extending beyond the period of administration;

(10) enter into a lease or arrangement for exploration and removal of minerals or other natural resources or enter into a pooling or unitization agreement;

(11) abandon property when, in the opinion of the personal representative, it is valueless, or is so encumbered, or is in condition that it is of no benefit to the estate;

(12) vote stocks or other securities in person or by general or limited proxy;

(13) pay calls, assessments, and other sums chargeable or accruing against or on account of securities, unless barred by the provisions relating to claims;

(14) hold a security in the name of a nominee or in other form without disclosure of the interest of the estate but the personal representative is liable for any act of the nominee in connection with the security so held;

(15) insure the assets of the estate against damage, loss and liability and himself against liability as to third persons;

(16) borrow money with or without security to be repaid from the estate assets or otherwise; and advance money for the protection of the estate;

(17) effect a fair and reasonable compromise with any debtor or obligor, or extend, renew or in any manner modify the terms of any obligation owing to the estate. If the personal representative holds a mortgage, pledge or other lien upon property of another person, he may, in lieu of foreclosure, accept a conveyance or transfer of encumbered assets from the owner thereof in satisfaction of the indebtedness secured by lien;

(18) pay taxes, assessments, compensation of the personal representative, and other expenses incident to the administration of the estate;

(19) sell or exercise stock subscription or conversion rights; consent, directly or through a committee or other agent, to the reorganization, consolidation, merger, dissolution, or liquidation of a corporation or other business enterprise;

(20) allocate items of income or expense to either estate income or principal, as permitted or provided by law;

(21) employ persons, including attorneys, auditors, investment advisors, or agents, even if they are associated with the personal representative, to advise or assist the personal representative in the performance of his administrative duties; act without independent investigation upon their recommendations; and instead of acting personally, employ one or more agents to perform any act of administration, whether or not discretionary;

(22) prosecute or defend claims, or proceedings in any jurisdiction for the protection of the estate and of the personal representative in the performance of his duties;

(23) sell, mortgage, or lease any real or personal property of the estate or any interest therein for cash, credit, or for part cash and part credit, and with or without security for unpaid balances;

(24) continue any unincorporated business or venture in which the decedent was engaged at the time of his death (i) in the same business form for a period of not more than 4 months from the date of appointment of a general personal representative if continuation is a reasonable means of preserving the value of the business including good will, (ii) in the same business form for any additional period of time that may be approved by order of the court in a formal proceeding to which the persons interested in the estate are parties; or (iii) throughout the period of administration if the business is incorporated by the personal representative and if none of the probable distributees of the business who are competent adults object to its incorporation and retention in the estate;

(25) incorporate any business or venture in which the decedent was engaged at the time of his death;

(26) provide for exoneration of the personal representative from personal liability in any contract entered into on behalf of the estate;

(27) satisfy and settle claims and distribute the estate as provided in this [code].

§ 3-716. Powers and Duties of Successor Personal Representative. A successor personal representative has the same power and duty as the original personal representative to complete the administration and distribution of the estate, as expeditiously as possible, but he shall not exercise any power expressly made personal to the executor named in the will.

§ 3-717. Co-representatives; When Joint Action Required. If two or more persons are appointed co-representatives and unless the will provides otherwise, the concurrence of all is required on all acts connected with the administration and distribution of the estate. This restriction does not apply when any co-representative receives and receipts for property due the estate, when the concurrence of all cannot readily be obtained in the time reasonably available for emergency action necessary to preserve the estate, or when a co-representative has been delegated to act for the others. Persons dealing with a co-representative if actually unaware that another has been appointed to serve with him or if advised by the personal representative with whom they deal that he has authority to act alone for any of the reasons mentioned herein, are as fully protected as if the person with whom they dealt had been the sole personal representative.

§ 3-718. Powers of Surviving Personal Representative. Unless the terms of the will otherwise provide, every power exercisable by personal co-representatives may be exercised by the one or more remaining after the appointment of one or more is terminated, and if one of two or more nominated as co-executors is not appointed, those appointed may exercise all the powers incident to the office.

§ 3-719. Compensation of Personal Representative. A personal representative is entitled to reasonable compensation for his services. If a will provides for compensation of the personal representative and there is no contract with the decedent regarding compensation, he may renounce the provision before qualifying and be entitled to reasonable compensation. A personal representative also may renounce his right to all or any part of the compensation. A written renunciation of fee may be filed with the court.

§ 3-720. Expenses in Estate Litigation. If any personal representative or person nominated as personal representative defends or prosecutes any proceeding in good faith, whether successful or not he is entitled to receive from the estate his necessary expenses and disbursements including reasonable attorneys' fees incurred.

§ 3-721. Proceedings for Review of Employment of Agents and Compensation of Personal Representatives and Employees of Estate. After notice to all interested persons or on petition of an interested person or on appropriate motion if administration is supervised, the propriety of employment of any person by a personal representative including any attorney, auditor, investment advisor or other specialized agent or assistant, the reasonableness of the compensation of any person so employed, or the reasonableness of the compensation determined by the personal representative for his own services, may be reviewed by the court. Any person who has received excessive compensation from an estate for services rendered may be ordered to make appropriate refunds.

PART 8
CREDITORS' CLAIMS

General Comment

The need for uniformity of law regarding creditors' claims against estates is especially strong. Commercial and consumer credit depends upon efficient collection procedures. The cost of credit is pushed up by the cost of credit life insurance which becomes a practical necessity for lenders unwilling to bear the expense of understanding or using the cumbersome and provincial collection procedures found in 50 codes of probate.

The sections which follow facilitate collection of claims against decedents in several ways. First, a simple written statement mailed to the personal representative is a sufficient "claim." Allowance of claims is handled by the personal representative and is assumed if a claimant is not advised of disallowance. Also, a personal representative may pay any just claims without presentation and at any time, if he is willing to assume risks which will be minimal in many cases. The period of uncertainty regarding possible claims is only four months from first publication. This should expedite settlement and distribution of estates.

§ 3-801. Notice to Creditors.

(a) Unless notice has already been given under this section, a personal representative upon appointment [may] [shall] publish a notice to creditors once a week for three successive weeks in a newspaper of general circulation in the [county] announcing the appointment and the personal representative's address and notifying creditors of the estate to present their claims within four months after the date of the first publication of the notice or be forever barred.

(b) A personal representative may give written notice by mail or other delivery to a creditor, notifying the creditor to present his [or her] claim within four months after the published notice, if given as provided in subsection (a), or within 60 days after the mailing or other delivery of the notice, whichever is later, or be forever barred. Written notice must be the notice described in subsection (a) above or a similar notice.

(c) The personal representative is not liable to a creditor or to a successor of the decedent for giving or failing to give notice under this section.

§ 3-802. Statutes of Limitations.

(a) Unless an estate is insolvent, the personal representative, with the consent of all successors whose interests would be affected, may waive any defense of limitations available to the estate. If the defense is not waived, no claim barred by a statute of limitations at the time of the decedent's death may be allowed or paid.

(b) The running of a statute of limitations measured from an event other than death or the giving of notice to creditors is suspended for four months after the decedent's death, but resumes thereafter as to claims not barred by other sections.

(c) For purposes of a statute of limitations, the presentation of a claim pursuant to Section 3-804 is equivalent to commencement of a proceeding on the claim.

§ 3-803. Limitations on Presentation of Claims.

(a) All claims against a decedent's estate which arose before the death of the decedent, including claims of the state and any political subdivision thereof, whether due or to become due, absolute or contingent, liquidated or unliquidated, founded on contract, tort, or other legal basis, if not barred earlier by another statute of limitations or non-claim statute, are barred against the estate, the personal representative, the heirs and devisees, and nonprobate transferees of the decedent, unless presented within the earlier of the following:

(1) one year after the decedent's death; or

(2) the time provided by Section 3-801(b) for creditors who are given actual notice, and within the time provided in Section 3-801(a) for all creditors barred by publication.

(b) A claim described in subsection (a) which is barred by the non-claim statute of the decedent's domicile before the giving of notice to creditors in this state is barred in this state.

(c) All claims against a decedent's estate which arise at or after the death of the decedent, including claims of the state and any subdivision thereof, whether due or to become due, absolute or contingent, liquidated or unliquidated, founded on contract, tort, or other legal basis, are barred against the estate, the personal representative, and the heirs and devisees of the decedent, unless presented as follows:

(1) a claim based on a contract with the personal representative, within four months after performance by the personal representative is due; or

(2) any other claim, within the later of four months after it arises, or the time specified in subsection (a)(1).

(d) Nothing in this section affects or prevents:

(1) any proceeding to enforce any mortgage, pledge, or other lien upon property of the estate;

(2) to the limits of the insurance protection only, any proceeding to establish liability of the decedent or the personal representative for which he is protected by liability insurance; or

(3) collection of compensation for services rendered and reimbursement for expenses advanced by the personal representative or by the attorney or accountant for the personal representative of the estate.

§ 3-804. Manner of Presentation of Claims. Claims against a decedent's estate may be presented as follows:

(1) The claimant may deliver or mail to the personal representative a written statement of the claim indicating its basis, the name and address of the claimant, and the amount claimed, or may file a written statement of the claim, in the form prescribed by rule, with the clerk of the court. The claim is deemed presented on the first to occur of receipt of the written statement of claim by the personal representative, or the filing of the claim with the court. If a claim is not yet due, the date when it will become due shall be stated. If the claim is contingent or unliquidated, the nature of the uncertainty shall be stated. If the claim is secured, the security shall be described. Failure to describe correctly the security, the nature of any uncertainty, and the due date of a claim not yet due does not invalidate the presentation made.

(2) The claimant may commence a proceeding against the personal representative in any court where the personal representative may be subjected to jurisdiction, to obtain payment of his claim against the estate, but the commencement of the proceeding must occur within the time limited for presenting the claim. No presentation of claim is required in regard to matters claimed in proceedings against the decedent which were pending at the time of his death.

(3) If a claim is presented under paragraph (1), no proceeding thereon may be commenced more than 60 days after the personal representative has mailed a notice of disallowance; but, in the case of a claim which is not presently due or which is contingent or unliquidated, the personal representative may consent to an extension of the 60-day period, or to avoid injustice the court, on petition, may order an extension of the 60-day period, but in no event shall the extension run beyond the applicable statute of limitations.

§ 3-805. Classification of Claims.

(a) If the applicable assets of the estate are insufficient to pay all claims in full, the personal representative shall make payment in the following order:

(1) costs and expenses of administration;

(2) reasonable funeral expenses;

(3) debts and taxes with preference under federal law;

(4) reasonable and necessary medical and hospital expenses of the last illness of the decedent, including compensation of persons attending him;

(5) debts and taxes with preference under other laws of this state;

(6) all other claims.

(b) No preference shall be given in the payment of any claim over any other claim of the same class, and a claim due and payable shall not be entitled to a preference over claims not due.

§ 3-806. Allowance of Claims.

(a) As to claims presented in the manner described in Section 3-804 within the time limit prescribed in 3-803, the personal representative may mail a notice to any claimant stating that the claim has been disallowed. If, after allowing or disallowing a claim, the personal representative changes his decision concerning the claim, he shall notify the claimant. The personal representative may not change a disallowance of a claim after the time for the claimant to file a petition for allowance or to commence a proceeding on the claim has run and the claim has been barred. Every claim which is disallowed in whole or in part by the personal representative is barred so far as not allowed unless the claimant files a petition for allowance in the court or commences a proceeding against the personal representative not later than 60 days after the mailing of the notice of disallowance or partial allowance if the notice warns the claimant of the impending bar. Failure of the personal representative to mail notice to a claimant of action on his claim for 60 days after the time for original presentation of the claim has expired has the effect of a notice of allowance.

(b) After allowing or disallowing a claim the personal representative may change the allowance or disallowance as hereafter provided. The personal representative may prior to payment change the allowance to a disallowance in whole or in part, but not after allowance by a court order or judgment or an order directing payment of the claim. He shall notify the claimant of the change to disallowance, and the disallowed claim is then subject to bar as provided in subsection (a). The personal representative may change a disallowance to an allowance, in whole or in part, until it is barred under subsection (a); after it is barred, it may be allowed and paid only if the estate is solvent and all successors whose interests would be affected consent.

(c) Upon the petition of the personal representative or a claimant in a proceeding for the purpose, the court may allow in whole or in part any claim or claims presented to the personal representative or filed with the clerk of the court in due time and not barred by subsection (a). Notice in this proceeding shall be given to the claimant, the personal representative and those other persons interested in the estate as the court may direct by order entered at the time the proceeding is commenced.

(d) A judgment in a proceeding in another court against a personal representative to enforce a claim against a decedent's estate is an allowance of the claim.

(e) Unless otherwise provided in any judgment in another court entered against the personal representative, allowed claims bear interest at the legal rate for the period commencing 60 days after the time for original presentation of the claim has expired unless based on a contract making a provision for interest, in which case they bear interest in accordance with that provision.

§ 3-807. Payment of Claims.

(a) Upon the expiration of the earlier of the time limitations provided in Section 3-803 for the presentation of claims, the personal representative shall proceed to pay the claims allowed against the estate in the order of priority prescribed, after making provision for homestead, family and support allowances, for claims already presented that have not yet been allowed or whose allowance has been appealed, and for unbarred claims that may yet be presented, including costs and expenses of administration. By petition to the court in a proceeding for the purpose, or by appropriate motion if the administration is supervised, a claimant whose claim has been allowed but not paid may secure an order directing the personal representative to pay the claim to the extent funds of the estate are available to pay it.

(b) The personal representative at any time may pay any just claim that has not been barred, with or without formal presentation, but is personally liable to any other claimant whose claim is allowed and who is injured by its payment if:

(1) payment was made before the expiration of the time limit stated in subsection (a) and the personal representative failed to require the payee to give adequate security for the refund of any of the payment necessary to pay other claimants; or

(2) payment was made, due to negligence or willful fault of the personal representative, in such manner as to deprive the injured claimant of priority.

§ 3-808. Individual Liability of Personal Representative.

(a) Unless otherwise provided in the contract, a personal representative is not individually liable on a contract properly entered into in his fiduciary capacity in the course of administration of the estate unless he fails to reveal his representative capacity and identify the estate in the contract.

(b) A personal representative is individually liable for obligations arising from ownership or control of the estate or for torts committed in the course of administration of the estate only if he is personally at fault.

(c) Claims based on contracts entered into by a personal representative in his fiduciary capacity, on obligations arising from ownership or control of the estate or on torts committed in the course of estate administration may be asserted against the estate by proceeding against the personal representative in his fiduciary capacity, whether or not the personal representative is individually liable therefor.

(d) Issues of liability as between the estate and the personal representative individually may be determined in a proceeding for accounting, surcharge or indemnification or other appropriate proceeding.

§ 3-809. Secured Claims.

Payment of a secured claim is upon the basis of the amount allowed if the creditor surrenders his security; otherwise payment is upon the basis of one of the following:

(1) if the creditor exhausts his security before receiving payment, [unless precluded by other law] upon the amount of the claim allowed less the fair value of the security; or

(2) if the creditor does not have the right to exhaust his security or has not done so, upon the amount of the claim allowed less the value of the security determined by converting it into money according to the terms of the agreement pursuant to which the security was delivered to the creditor, or by the creditor and personal representative by agreement, arbitration, compromise or litigation.

§ 3-810. Claims Not Due and Contingent or Unliquidated Claims.

(a) If a claim which will become due at a future time or a contingent or unliquidated claim becomes due or certain before the distribution of the estate, and if the claim has been allowed or established by a proceeding, it is paid in the same manner as presently due and absolute claims of the same class.

(b) In other cases the personal representative or, on petition of the personal representative or the claimant in a special proceeding for the purpose, the court may provide for payment as follows:

(1) if the claimant consents, he may be paid the present or agreed value of the claim, taking any uncertainty into account;

(2) arrangement for future payment, or possible payment, on the happening of the contingency or on liquidation may be made by creating a trust, giving a mortgage, obtaining a bond or security from a distributee, or otherwise.

§ 3-811. Counterclaims.

In allowing a claim the personal representative may deduct any counterclaim which the estate has against the claimant. In determining a claim against an estate a court shall reduce the amount allowed by the amount of any counterclaims and, if the counterclaims exceed the claim, render a judgment against the claimant in the amount of the excess. A counterclaim, liquidated or unliquidated, may arise from a transaction other than that upon which the claim is based. A counterclaim may give rise to relief exceeding in amount or different in kind from that sought in the claim.

§ 3-812. Execution and Levies Prohibited.

No execution may issue upon nor may any levy be made against any property of the estate under any judgment against a decedent or a personal representative, but this section shall not be construed to prevent the enforcement of mortgages, pledges or liens upon real or personal property in an appropriate proceeding.

§ 3-813. Compromise of Claims. When a claim against the estate has been presented in any manner, the personal representative may, if it appears for the best interest of the estate, compromise the claim, whether due or not due, absolute or contingent, liquidated or unliquidated.

§ 3-814. Encumbered Assets. If any assets of the estate are encumbered by mortgage, pledge, lien, or other security interest, the personal representative may pay the encumbrance or any part thereof, renew or extend any obligation secured by the encumbrance or convey or transfer the assets to the creditor in satisfaction of his lien, in whole or in part, whether or not the holder of the encumbrance has presented a claim, if it appears to be for the best interest of the estate. Payment of an encumbrance does not increase the share of the distributee entitled to the encumbered assets unless the distributee is entitled to exoneration.

§ 3-815. Administration in More than One State; Duty of Personal Representative.
(a) All assets of estates being administered in this state are subject to all claims, allowances and charges existing or established against the personal representative wherever appointed.

(b) If the estate either in this state or as a whole is insufficient to cover all family exemptions and allowances determined by the law of the decedent's domicile, prior charges and claims, after satisfaction of the exemptions, allowances and charges, each claimant whose claim has been allowed either in this state or elsewhere in administrations of which the personal representative is aware, is entitled to receive payment of an equal proportion of his claim. If a preference or security in regard to a claim is allowed in another jurisdiction but not in this state, the creditor so benefitted is to receive dividends from local assets only upon the balance of his claim after deducting the amount of the benefit.

(c) In case the family exemptions and allowances, prior charges and claims of the entire estate exceed the total value of the portions of the estate being administered separately and this state is not the state of the decedent's last domicile, the claims allowed in this state shall be paid their proportion if local assets are adequate for the purpose, and the balance of local assets shall be transferred to the domiciliary personal representative. If local assets are not sufficient to pay all claims allowed in this state the amount to which they are entitled, local assets shall be marshalled so that each claim allowed in this state is paid its proportion as far as possible, after taking into account all dividends on claims allowed in this state from assets in other jurisdictions.

§ 3-816. Final Distribution to Domiciliary Representative. The estate of a non-resident decedent being administered by a personal representative appointed in this state shall, if there is a personal representative of the decedent's domicile willing to receive it, be distributed to the domiciliary personal representative for the benefit of the successors of the decedent unless (i) by virtue of the decedent's will, if any, and applicable choice of law rules, the successors are identified pursuant to the local law of this state without reference to the local law of the decedent's domicile; (ii) the personal representative of this state, after reasonable inquiry, is unaware of the existence or identity of a domiciliary personal representative; or (iii) the court orders otherwise in a proceeding for a closing order under Section 3-1001 or incident to the closing of a supervised administration. In other cases, distribution of the estate of a decedent shall be made in accordance with the other [parts] of this [article].

PART 9
SPECIAL PROVISIONS RELATING TO DISTRIBUTION

§ 3-901. Successors' Rights if No Administration. In the absence of administration, the heirs and devisees are entitled to the estate in accordance with the terms of a probated will or the laws of intestate succession. Devisees may establish title by the probated will to devised property. Persons entitled to property by homestead allowance, exemption or intestacy may establish title thereto by proof of the decedent's ownership, his death, and their relationship to the decedent. Successors take subject to all charges incident to administration, including the claims of creditors and allowances of surviving spouse and dependent children, and subject to the rights of others resulting from abatement, retainer, advancement, and ademption.

§ 3-902. Distribution; Order in Which Assets Appropriated; Abatement.

(a) Except as provided in subsection (b) and except as provided in connection with the share of the surviving spouse who elects to take an elective share, shares of distributees abate, without any preference or priority as between real and personal property, in the following order: (i) property not disposed of by the will; (ii) residuary devises; (iii) general devises; (iv) specific devises. For purposes of abatement, a general devise charged on any specific property or fund is a specific devise to the extent of the value of the property on which it is charged, and upon the failure or insufficiency of the property on which it is charged, a general devise to the extent of the failure or insufficiency. Abatement within each classification is in proportion to the amounts of property each of the beneficiaries would have received if full distribution of the property had been made in accordance with the terms of the will.

[handwritten margin note: demonstrative devise]

(b) If the will expresses an order of abatement, or if the testamentary plan or the express or implied purpose of the devise would be defeated by the order of abatement stated in subsection (a), the shares of the distributees abate as may be found necessary to give effect to the intention of the testator.

Alternative A

(c) If the subject of a preferred devise is sold or used incident to administration, abatement shall be achieved by appropriate adjustments in, or contribution from, other interests in the remaining assets.

Alternative B

(c) If an estate of a decedent consists partly of separate property and partly of community property, the debts and expenses of administration shall be apportioned and charged against the different kinds of property in proportion to the relative value thereof.

(d) If the subject of a preferred devise is sold or used incident to administration, abatement shall be achieved by appropriate adjustments in, or contribution from, other interests in the remaining assets.

End of Alternatives

Comment

Alternative A is for common law states. Alternative B is for community property states.

A testator may determine the order in which the assets of his estate are applied to the payment of his debts. If he does not, then the provisions of this section express rules which may be regarded as approximating what testators generally want. The statutory order of abatement is designed to aid in resolving doubts concerning the intention of a particular testator, rather than to defeat his purpose. Hence, subsection (b) directs that consideration be given to the purpose of a testator. This may be revealed in many ways. Thus, it is commonly held that, even in the absence of statute, general legacies to a wife, or to persons with respect to which the testator is in loco parentis, are to be preferred to other legacies in the same class because this accords with the probable purpose of the legacies.

In Alternative B, subsection (c) is suggested for inclusion in a community property state. Its inclusion causes subsection (c) as drafted for common law states to be redesignated subsection (d). As is the case with other insertions suggested in the Code for community property states, the specific language of this draft is to be taken as illustrative.

§ 3-903. Right of Retainer. The amount of a non-contingent indebtedness of a successor to the estate if due, or its present value if not due, shall be offset against the successor's interest; but the successor has the benefit of any defense which would be available to him in a direct proceeding for recovery of the debt.

§ 3-904. Interest on General Pecuniary Devise. General pecuniary devises bear interest at the legal rate beginning one year after the first appointment of a personal representative until payment, unless a contrary intent is indicated by the will.

§ 3-905. Penalty Clause for Contest. A provision in a will purporting to penalize any interested person for contesting the will or instituting other proceedings relating to the estate is unenforceable if probable cause exists for instituting proceedings.

Restatement (Third) of Property: Wills and Other Donative Transfers (2003)

§ 8.5 No-Contest Clauses. A provision in a donative document purporting to rescind a donative transfer to, or a fiduciary appointment of, any person who institutes a proceeding challenging the validity of all or part of the donative document is enforceable unless probable cause existed for instituting the proceeding.

. . . .

Comment c. Probable cause. Probable cause exists when, at the time of instituting the proceeding, there was evidence that would lead a reasonable person, properly informed and advised, to conclude that there was a substantial likelihood that the challenge would be successful. A factor that bears on the existence of probable cause is whether the beneficiary relied upon the advice of independent legal counsel sought in good faith after a full disclosure of the facts. The mere fact that the person mounting the challenge was represented by counsel is not controlling, however, since the institution of a legal proceeding challenging a donative transfer normally involves representation by legal counsel.

---

§ 3-906. Distribution in Kind; Valuation; Method.

(a) Unless a contrary intention is indicated by the will, the distributable assets of a decedent's estate shall be distributed in kind to the extent possible through application of the following provisions:

(1) A specific devisee is entitled to distribution of the thing devised to him, and a spouse or child who has selected particular assets of an estate as provided in Section 2-403 shall receive the items selected.

(2) Any homestead or family allowance or devise of a stated sum of money may be satisfied in kind provided

(A) the person entitled to the payment has not demanded payment in cash;

(B) the property distributed in kind is valued at fair market value as of the date of its distribution, and

(C) no residuary devisee has requested that the asset in question remain a part of the residue of the estate.

(3) For the purpose of valuation under paragraph (2) securities regularly traded on recognized exchanges, if distributed in kind, are valued at the price for the last sale of like securities traded on the

business day prior to distribution, or if there was no sale on that day, at the median between amounts bid and offered at the close of that day. Assets consisting of sums owed the decedent or the estate by solvent debtors as to which there is no known dispute or defense are valued at the sum due with accrued interest or discounted to the date of distribution. For assets which do not have readily ascertainable values, a valuation as of a date not more than 30 days prior to the date of distribution, if otherwise reasonable, controls. For purposes of facilitating distribution, the personal representative may ascertain the value of the assets as of the time of the proposed distribution in any reasonable way, including the employment of qualified appraisers, even if the assets may have been previously appraised.

(4) The residuary estate shall be distributed in any equitable manner.

(b) After the probable charges against the estate are known, the personal representative may mail or deliver a proposal for distribution to all persons who have a right to object to the proposed distribution. The right of any distributee to object to the proposed distribution on the basis of the kind or value of asset he is to receive, if not waived earlier in writing, terminates if he fails to object in writing received by the personal representative within 30 days after mailing or delivery of the proposal.

§ 3-907. Distribution in Kind; Evidence.

If distribution in kind is made, the personal representative shall execute an instrument or deed of distribution assigning, transferring or releasing the assets to the distributee as evidence of the distributee's title to the property.

§ 3-908. Distribution; Right or Title of Distributee.

Proof that a distributee has received an instrument or deed of distribution of assets in kind, or payment in distribution, from a personal representative, is conclusive evidence that the distributee has succeeded to the interest of the estate in the distributed assets, as against all persons interested in the estate, except that the personal representative may recover the assets or their value if the distribution was improper.

§ 3-909. Improper Distribution; Liability of Distributee.

Unless the distribution or payment no longer can be questioned because of adjudication, estoppel, or limitation, a distributee of property improperly distributed or paid, or a claimant who was improperly paid, is liable to return the property improperly received and its income since distribution if he has the property. If he does not have the property, then he is liable to return the value as of the date of disposition of the property improperly received and its income and gain received by him.

§ 3-910. Purchasers from Distributees Protected.

If property distributed in kind or a security interest therein is acquired for value by a purchaser from or lender to a distributee who has received an instrument or deed of distribution from the personal representative, or is so acquired by a purchaser from or lender to a transferee from such distributee, the purchaser or lender takes title free of rights of any interested person in the estate and incurs no personal liability to the estate, or to any interested person, whether or not the distribution was proper or supported by court order or the authority of the personal representative was terminated before execution of the instrument or deed. This section protects a purchaser from or lender to a distributee who, as personal representative, has executed a deed of distribution to himself, as well as a purchaser from or lender to any other distributee or his transferee. To be protected under this provision, a purchaser or lender need not inquire whether a personal representative acted properly in making the distribution in kind, even if the personal representative and the distributee are the same person, or whether the authority of the personal representative had terminated before the distribution. Any recorded instrument described in this section on which a state documentary fee is noted pursuant to [insert appropriate reference] shall be prima facie evidence that such transfer was made for value.

§ 3-911. Partition for Purpose of Distribution. When two or more heirs or devisees are entitled to distribution of undivided interests in any real or personal property of the estate, the personal representative or one or more of the heirs or devisees may petition the court prior to the formal or informal closing of the estate, to make partition. After notice to the interested heirs or devisees, the court shall partition the property in the same manner as provided by the law for civil actions of partition. The court may direct the personal representative to sell any property which cannot be partitioned without prejudice to the owners and which cannot conveniently be allotted to any one party.

§ 3-912. Private Agreements Among Successors to Decedent Binding on Personal Representative. Subject to the rights of creditors and taxing authorities, competent successors may agree among themselves to alter the interests, shares, or amounts to which they are entitled under the will of the decedent, or under the laws of intestacy, in any way that they provide in a written contract executed by all who are affected by its provisions. The personal representative shall abide by the terms of the agreement subject to his obligation to administer the estate for the benefit of creditors, to pay all taxes and costs of administration, and to carry out the responsibilities of his office for the benefit of any successors of the decedent who are not parties. Personal representatives of decedents' estates are not required to see to the performance of trusts if the trustee thereof is another person who is willing to accept the trust. Accordingly, trustees of a testamentary trust are successors for the purposes of this section. Nothing herein relieves trustees of any duties owed to beneficiaries of trusts.

§ 3-913. Distributions to Trustee.

(a) Before distributing to a trustee, the personal representative may require that the trust be registered if the state in which it is to be administered provides for registration and that the trustee inform the beneficiaries as provided in [Section 813 of the Uniform Trust Code].

(b) If the trust instrument does not excuse the trustee from giving bond, the personal representative may petition the appropriate Court to require that the trustee post bond if he apprehends that distribution might jeopardize the interests of persons who are not able to protect themselves, and he may withhold distribution until the Court has acted.

(c) No inference of negligence on the part of the personal representative shall be drawn from his failure to exercise the authority conferred by subsections (a) and (b).

[§ 3-914. Disposition of Unclaimed Assets.

(a) If an heir, devisee or claimant cannot be found, the personal representative shall distribute the share of the missing person to his conservator, if any, otherwise to the [state treasurer] to become a part of the [state escheat fund].

(b) The money received by [state treasurer] shall be paid to the person entitled on proof of his right thereto or, if the [state treasurer] refuses or fails to pay, the person may petition the court which appointed the personal representative, whereupon the court upon notice to the [state treasurer] may determine the person entitled to the money and order the [treasurer] to pay it to him. No interest is allowed thereon and the heir, devisee or claimant shall pay all costs and expenses incident to the proceeding. If no petition is made to the [court] within 8 years after payment to the [state treasurer], the right of recovery is barred.]

§ 3-915. Distribution to Person Under Disability.

(a) A personal representative may discharge his obligation to distribute to any person under legal disability by distributing in a manner expressly provided in the will.

(b) Unless contrary to an express provision in the will, the personal representative may discharge his obligation to distribute to a minor or person under other disability as authorized by Section 5-104 or any other statute. If the personal representative knows that a conservator has been appointed or that a proceeding for appointment of a conservator is pending, the personal representative is authorized to distribute only to the conservator.

(c) If the heir or devisee is under disability other than minority, the personal representative is authorized to distribute to:

(1) an attorney in fact who has authority under a power of attorney to receive property for that person; or

(2) the spouse, parent or other close relative with whom the person under disability resides if the distribution is of amounts not exceeding [$10,000] a year, or property not exceeding [$50,000] in value, unless the court authorizes a larger amount or greater value.

Persons receiving money or property for the disabled person are obligated to apply the money or property to the support of that person, but may not pay themselves except by way of reimbursement for out-of-pocket expenses for goods and services necessary for the support of the disabled person. Excess sums must be preserved for future support of the disabled person. The personal representative is not responsible for the proper application of money or property distributed pursuant to this subsection.

§ 3-916. [Reserved].

PART 9A
UNIFORM ESTATE TAX APPORTIONMENT ACT (2003)

§ 3-9A-101. Short Title. This [part] may be cited as the Uniform Estate Tax Apportionment Act.

§ 3-9A-102. Definitions. In this [part]:

(1) "Apportionable estate" means the value of the gross estate as finally determined for purposes of the estate tax to be apportioned reduced by:

(A) any claim or expense allowable as a deduction for purposes of the tax;

(B) the value of any interest in property that, for purposes of the tax, qualifies for a marital or charitable deduction or otherwise is deductible or is exempt; and

(C) any amount added to the decedent's gross estate because of a gift tax on transfers made before death.

(2) "Estate tax" means a federal, state, or foreign tax imposed because of the death of an individual and interest and penalties associated with the tax. The term does not include an inheritance tax, income tax, or generation-skipping transfer tax other than a generation-skipping transfer tax incurred on a direct skip taking effect at death.

(3) "Gross estate" means, with respect to an estate tax, all interests in property subject to the tax.

(4) "Person" means an individual, corporation, business trust, estate, trust, partnership, limited liability company, association, joint venture, public corporation, government, governmental subdivision, agency, or instrumentality, or any other legal or commercial entity.

(5) "Ratable" means apportioned or allocated pro rata according to the relative values of interests

to which the term is to be applied. "Ratably" has a corresponding meaning.

(6) "Time-limited interest" means an interest in property which terminates on a lapse of time or on the occurrence or nonoccurrence of an event or which is subject to the exercise of discretion that could transfer a beneficial interest to another person. The term does not include a cotenancy unless the cotenancy itself is a time-limited interest.

(7) "Value" means, with respect to an interest in property, fair market value as finally determined for purposes of the estate tax that is to be apportioned, reduced by any outstanding debt secured by the interest without reduction for taxes paid or required to be paid or for any special valuation adjustment.

§ 3-9A-103. Apportionment by Will or Other Dispositive Instrument.

(a) Except as otherwise provided in subsection (c), the following rules apply:

(1) To the extent that a provision of a decedent's will expressly and unambiguously directs the apportionment of an estate tax, the tax must be apportioned accordingly.

(2) Any portion of an estate tax not apportioned pursuant to paragraph (1) must be apportioned in accordance with any provision of a revocable trust of which the decedent was the settlor which expressly and unambiguously directs the apportionment of an estate tax. If conflicting apportionment provisions appear in two or more revocable trust instruments, the provision in the most recently dated instrument prevails. For purposes of this paragraph:

(A) a trust is revocable if it was revocable immediately after the trust instrument was executed, even if the trust subsequently becomes irrevocable; and

(B) the date of an amendment to a revocable trust instrument is the date of the amended instrument only if the amendment contains an apportionment provision.

(3) If any portion of an estate tax is not apportioned pursuant to paragraph (1) or (2), and a provision in any other dispositive instrument expressly and unambiguously directs that any interest in the property disposed of by the instrument is or is not to be applied to the payment of the estate tax attributable to the interest disposed of by the instrument, the provision controls the apportionment of the tax to that interest.

(b) Subject to subsection (c), and unless the decedent expressly and unambiguously directs the contrary, the following rules apply:

(1) If an apportionment provision directs that a person receiving an interest in property under an instrument is to be exonerated from the responsibility to pay an estate tax that would otherwise be apportioned to the interest,

(A) the tax attributable to the exonerated interest must be apportioned among the other persons receiving interests passing under the instrument, or

(B) if the values of the other interests are less than the tax attributable to the exonerated interest, the deficiency must be apportioned ratably among the other persons receiving interests in the apportionable estate that are not exonerated from apportionment of the tax.

(2) If an apportionment provision directs that an estate tax is to be apportioned to an interest in property a portion of which qualifies for a marital or charitable deduction, the estate tax must first be apportioned ratably among the holders of the portion that does not qualify for a marital or charitable deduction and then apportioned ratably among the holders of the deductible portion to the extent that the value of the nondeductible portion is insufficient.

(3) Except as otherwise provided in paragraph (4), if an apportionment provision directs that an estate tax be apportioned to property in which one or more time-limited interests exist, other than interests in specified property under Section 3-9A-107, the tax must be apportioned to the principal of that property, regardless of the deductibility of some of the interests in that property.

(4) If an apportionment provision directs that an estate tax is to be apportioned to the holders of interests in property in which one or more time-limited interests exist and a charity has an interest that otherwise qualifies for an estate tax charitable deduction, the tax must first be apportioned, to the extent feasible, to interests in property that have not been distributed to the persons entitled to receive the interests.

(c) A provision that apportions an estate tax is ineffective to the extent that it increases the tax apportioned to a person having an interest in the gross estate over which the decedent had no power to transfer immediately before the decedent executed the instrument in which the apportionment direction was made. For purposes of this subsection, a testamentary power of appointment is a power to transfer the property that is subject to the power.

§ 3-9A-104. Statutory Apportionment of Estate Taxes.

To the extent that apportionment of an estate tax is not controlled by an instrument described in Section 3-9A-103 and except as otherwise provided in Sections 3-9A-106 and 3-9A-107, the following rules apply:

(1) Subject to paragraphs (2), (3),and (4), the estate tax is apportioned ratably to each person that has an interest in the apportionable estate.

(2) A generation-skipping transfer tax incurred on a direct skip taking effect at death is charged to the person to which the interest in property is transferred.

(3) If property is included in the decedent's gross estate because of Section 2044 of the Internal Revenue Code of 1986 or any similar estate tax provision, the difference between the total estate tax for which the decedent's estate is liable and the amount of estate tax for which the decedent's estate would have been liable if the property had not been included in the decedent's gross estate is apportioned ratably among the holders of interests in the property. The balance of the tax, if any, is apportioned ratably to each other person having an interest in the apportionable estate.

(4) Except as otherwise provided in Section 3-9A-103(b)(4) and except as to property to which Section 3-9A-107 applies, an estate tax apportioned to persons holding interests in property subject to a time-limited interest must be apportioned, without further apportionment, to the principal of that property.

§ 3-9A-105. Credits and Deferrals.

Except as otherwise provided in Sections 3-9A-106 and 3-9A-107, the following rules apply to credits and deferrals of estate taxes:

(1) A credit resulting from the payment of gift taxes or from estate taxes paid on property previously taxed inures ratably to the benefit of all persons to which the estate tax is apportioned.

(2) A credit for state or foreign estate taxes inures ratably to the benefit of all persons to which the estate tax is apportioned, except that the amount of a credit for a state or foreign tax paid by a beneficiary of the property on which the state or foreign tax was imposed, directly or by a charge against the property, inures to the benefit of the beneficiary.

(3) If payment of a portion of an estate tax is deferred because of the inclusion in the gross estate of a particular interest in property, the benefit of the deferral inures ratably to the persons to which the estate tax attributable to the interest is apportioned. The burden of any interest charges incurred on a deferral of taxes and the benefit of any tax deduction associated with the accrual or payment of the interest charge is allocated ratably among the persons receiving an interest in the property.

§ 3-9A-106. Insulated Property: Advancement of Tax.

(a) In this section:

(1) "Advanced fraction" means a fraction that has as its numerator the amount of the advanced tax and as its denominator the value of the interests in insulated property to which that tax is

attributable.

(2) "Advanced tax" means the aggregate amount of estate tax attributable to interests in insulated property which is required to be advanced by uninsulated holders under subsection (c).

(3) "Insulated property" means property subject to a time-limited interest which is included in the apportionable estate but is unavailable for payment of an estate tax because of impossibility or impracticability.

(4) "Uninsulated holder" means a person who has an interest in uninsulated property.

(5) "Uninsulated property" means property included in the apportionable estate other than insulated property.

(b) If an estate tax is to be advanced pursuant to subsection (c) by persons holding interests in uninsulated property subject to a time-limited interest other than property to which Section 3-9A-107 applies, the tax must be advanced, without further apportionment, from the principal of the uninsulated property.

(c) Subject to Section 3-9A-109(b) and (d), an estate tax attributable to interests in insulated property must be advanced ratably by uninsulated holders. If the value of an interest in uninsulated property is less than the amount of estate taxes otherwise required to be advanced by the holder of that interest, the deficiency must be advanced ratably by the persons holding interests in properties that are excluded from the apportionable estate under Section 3-9A-102(1)(B) as if those interests were in uninsulated property.

(d) A court having jurisdiction to determine the apportionment of an estate tax may require a beneficiary of an interest in insulated property to pay all or part of the estate tax otherwise apportioned to the interest if the court finds that it would be substantially more equitable for that beneficiary to bear the tax liability personally than for that part of the tax to be advanced by uninsulated holders.

(e) When a distribution of insulated property is made, each uninsulated holder may recover from the distributee a ratable portion of the advanced fraction of the property distributed. To the extent that undistributed insulated property ceases to be insulated, each uninsulated holder may recover from the property a ratable portion of the advanced fraction of the total undistributed property.

(f) Upon a distribution of insulated property for which, pursuant to subsection (d), the distributee becomes obligated to make a payment to uninsulated holders, a court may award an uninsulated holder a recordable lien on the distributee's property to secure the distributee's obligation to that uninsulated holder.

§ 3-9A-107. Apportionment and Recapture of Special Elective Benefits.

(a) In this section:

(1) "Special elective benefit" means a reduction in an estate tax obtained by an election for:

(A) a reduced valuation of specified property that is included in the gross estate;

(B) a deduction from the gross estate, other than a marital or charitable deduction, allowed for specified property; or

(C) an exclusion from the gross estate of specified property.

(2) "Specified property" means property for which an election has been made for a special elective benefit.

(b) If an election is made for one or more special elective benefits, an initial apportionment of a hypothetical estate tax must be computed as if no election for any of those benefits had been made. The aggregate reduction in estate tax resulting from all elections made must be allocated among holders of interests in the specified property in the proportion that the amount of deduction, reduced valuation, or exclusion attributable to each holder's interest bears to the aggregate amount of deductions, reduced valuations, and exclusions obtained by the decedent's estate from the elections. If the estate tax initially apportioned to the holder of an interest in specified property is reduced to zero, any excess amount of reduction reduces ratably the estate tax apportioned to other persons that receive interests in the apportionable estate.

(c) An additional estate tax imposed to recapture all or part of a special elective benefit must be charged to the persons that are liable for the additional tax under the law providing for the recapture.

§ 3-9A-108. Securing Payment of Estate Tax from Property in Possession of Fiduciary.

(a) A fiduciary may defer a distribution of property until the fiduciary is satisfied that adequate provision for payment of the estate tax has been made.

(b) A fiduciary may withhold from a distributee an amount equal to the amount of estate tax apportioned to an interest of the distributee.

(c) As a condition to a distribution, a fiduciary may require the distributee to provide a bond or other security for the portion of the estate tax apportioned to the distributee.

§ 3-9A-109. Collection of Estate Tax by Fiduciary.

(a) A fiduciary responsible for payment of an estate tax may collect from any person the tax apportioned to and the tax required to be advanced by the person.

(b) Except as otherwise provided in Section 3-9A-106, any estate tax due from a person that cannot be collected from the person may be collected by the fiduciary from other persons in the following order of priority:

(1) any person having an interest in the apportionable estate which is not exonerated from the tax;

(2) any other person having an interest in the apportionable estate;

(3) any person having an interest in the gross estate.

(c) A domiciliary fiduciary may recover from an ancillary personal representative the estate tax apportioned to the property controlled by the ancillary personal representative.

(d) The total tax collected from a person pursuant to this [part] may not exceed the value of the person's interest.

§ 3-9A-110. Right of Reimbursement.

(a) A person required under Section 3-9A-109 to pay an estate tax greater than the amount due from the person under Section 3-9A-103 or 3-9A-104 has a right to reimbursement from another person to the extent that the other person has not paid the tax required by Section 3-9A-103 or 3-9A-104 and a right to reimbursement ratably from other persons to the extent that each has not contributed a portion of the amount collected under Section 3-9A-109(b).

(b) A fiduciary may enforce the right of reimbursement under subsection (a) on behalf of the person that is entitled to the reimbursement and shall take reasonable steps to do so if requested by the person.

§ 3-9A-111. Action to Determine or Enforce Part. A fiduciary, transferee, or beneficiary of the gross estate may maintain an action for declaratory judgment to have a court determine and enforce this [part].

§ 3-9A-112. [Reserved.]

§ 3-9A-113. [Reserved.]

§ 3-9A-114. Delayed Application.

(a) Sections 3-9A-103 through 3-9A-107 do not apply to the estate of a decedent who dies on or within [three] years after [the effective date of this [part]], nor to the estate of a decedent who dies more than [three] years after [the effective date of this [part]] if the decedent continuously lacked testamentary capacity from the expiration of the [three-year] period until the date of death.

(b) For the estate of a decedent who dies on or after [the effective date of this [part]] to which Sections 3-9A-103 through 3-9A-107 do not apply, estate taxes must be apportioned pursuant to the law in effect immediately before [the effective date of this [part]].

§ 3-9A-115. Effective Date. This [part] takes effect ....

PART 10
CLOSING ESTATES

§ 3-1001. Formal Proceedings Terminating Administration; Testate or Intestate; Order of General Protection.

(a) A personal representative or any interested person may petition for an order of complete settlement of the estate. The personal representative may petition at any time, and any other interested person may petition after one year from the appointment of the original personal representative except that no petition under this section may be entertained until the time for presenting claims which arose prior to the death of the decedent has expired. The petition may request the court to determine testacy, if not previously determined, to consider the final account or compel or approve an accounting and distribution, to construe any will or determine heirs and adjudicate the final settlement and distribution of the estate. After notice to all interested persons and hearing the court may enter an order or orders, on appropriate conditions, determining the persons entitled to distribution of the estate, and, as circumstances require, approving settlement and directing or approving distribution of the estate and discharging the personal representative from further claim or demand of any interested person.

(b) If one or more heirs or devisees were omitted as parties in, or were not given notice of, a previous formal testacy proceeding, the court, on proper petition for an order of complete settlement of the estate under this section, and after notice to the omitted or unnotified persons and other interested parties determined to be interested on the assumption that the previous order concerning testacy is conclusive as to those given notice of the earlier proceeding, may determine testacy as it affects the omitted persons and confirm or alter the previous order of testacy as it affects all interested persons as appropriate in the light of the new proofs. In the absence of objection by an omitted or unnotified person, evidence received in the original testacy proceeding shall constitute prima facie proof of due execution of any will previously admitted to probate, or of the fact that the decedent left no valid will if the prior proceedings determined this fact.

§ 3-1002. Formal Proceedings Terminating Testate Administration; Order Construing Will Without Adjudicating Testacy. A personal representative administering an estate under an informally probated will or any devisee under an informally probated will may petition for an order of settlement of the estate which will not adjudicate the testacy status of the decedent. The personal representative may petition at any time, and a devisee may petition after one year, from the appointment of the original personal representative, except that no petition under this section may be entertained until the time for presenting claims which arose prior to the death of the decedent has expired. The petition

may request the court to consider the final account or compel or approve an accounting and distribution, to construe the will and adjudicate final settlement and distribution of the estate. After notice to all devisees and the personal representative and hearing, the court may enter an order or orders, on appropriate conditions, determining the persons entitled to distribution of the estate under the will, and, as circumstances require, approving settlement and directing or approving distribution of the estate and discharging the personal representative from further claim or demand of any devisee who is a party to the proceeding and those he represents. If it appears that a part of the estate is intestate, the proceedings shall be dismissed or amendments made to meet the provisions of Section 3-1001.

§ 3-1003. Closing Estates; By Sworn Statement of Personal Representative.

(a) Unless prohibited by order of the court and except for estates being administered in supervised administration proceedings, a personal representative may close an estate by filing with the court no earlier than six months after the date of original appointment of a general personal representative for the estate, a verified statement stating that the personal representative, or a previous personal representative, has:

(1) determined that the time limited for presentation of creditors' claims has expired.

(2) fully administered the estate of the decedent by making payment, settlement, or other disposition of all claims that were presented, expenses of administration and estate, inheritance and other death taxes, except as specified in the statement, and that the assets of the estate have been distributed to the persons entitled. If any claims remain undischarged, the statement must state whether the personal representative has distributed the estate subject to possible liability with the agreement of the distributees or state in detail other arrangements that have been made to accommodate outstanding liabilities; and

(3) sent a copy of the statement to all distributees of the estate and to all creditors or other claimants of whom the personal representative is aware whose claims are neither paid nor barred and has furnished a full account in writing of the personal representative's administration to the distributees whose interests are affected thereby.

(b) If no proceedings involving the personal representative are pending in the court one year after the closing statement is filed, the appointment of the personal representative terminates.

§ 3-1004. Liability of Distributees to Claimants.

After assets of an estate have been distributed and subject to Section 3-1006, an undischarged claim not barred may be prosecuted in a proceeding against one or more distributees. No distributee shall be liable to claimants for amounts received as exempt property, homestead or family allowances, or for amounts in excess of the value of his distribution as of the time of distribution. As between distributees, each shall bear the cost of satisfaction of unbarred claims as if the claim had been satisfied in the course of administration. Any distributee who shall have failed to notify other distributees of the demand made upon him by the claimant in sufficient time to permit them to join in any proceeding in which the claim was asserted against him loses his right of contribution against other distributees.

§ 3-1005. Limitations on Proceedings Against Personal Representatives.

Unless previously barred by adjudication and except as provided in the closing statement, the rights of successors and of creditors whose claims have not otherwise been barred against the personal representative for breach of fiduciary duty are barred unless a proceeding to assert the same is commenced within six months after the filing of the closing statement. The rights thus barred do not include rights to recover from a personal representative for fraud, misrepresentation, or inadequate disclosure related to the settlement of the decedent's estate.

§ 3-1006. Limitations on Actions and Proceedings Against Distributees. Unless previously adjudicated in a formal testacy proceeding or in a proceeding settling the accounts of a personal representative or otherwise barred, the claim of a claimant to recover from a distributee who is liable to pay the claim, and the right of an heir or devisee, or of a successor personal representative acting in their behalf, to recover property improperly distributed or its value from any distributee is forever barred at the later of three years after the decedent's death or one year after the time of its distribution, but all claims of creditors of the decedent, are barred one year after the decedent's death. This section does not bar an action to recover property or value received as a result of fraud.

§ 3-1007. Certificate Discharging Liens Securing Fiduciary Performance. After his appointment has terminated, the personal representative, his sureties, or any successor of either, upon the filing of a verified application showing, so far as is known by the applicant, that no action concerning the estate is pending in any court, is entitled to receive a certificate from the Registrar that the personal representative appears to have fully administered the estate in question. The certificate evidences discharge of any lien on any property given to secure the obligation of the personal representative in lieu of bond or any surety, but does not preclude action against the personal representative or the surety.

§ 3-1008. Subsequent Administration. If other property of the estate is discovered after an estate has been settled and the personal representative discharged or after one year after a closing statement has been filed, the court upon petition of any interested person and upon notice as it directs may appoint the same or a successor personal representative to administer the subsequently discovered estate. If a new appointment is made, unless the court orders otherwise, the provisions of this [code] apply as appropriate; but no claim previously barred may be asserted in the subsequent administration.

PART 11
COMPROMISE OF CONTROVERSIES

§ 3-1101. Effect of Approval of Agreements Involving Trusts, Inalienable Interests, or Interests of Third Persons. A compromise of any controversy as to admission to probate of any instrument offered for formal probate as the will of a decedent, the construction, validity, or effect of any governing instrument, the rights or interests in the estate of the decedent, of any successor, or the administration of the estate, if approved in a formal proceeding in the court for that purpose, is binding on all the parties thereto including those unborn, unascertained or who could not be located. An approved compromise is binding even though it may affect a trust or an inalienable interest. A compromise does not impair the rights of creditors or of taxing authorities who are not parties to it.

§ 3-1102. Procedure for Securing Court Approval of Compromise. The procedure for securing court approval of a compromise is as follows:

(1) The terms of the compromise shall be set forth in an agreement in writing which shall be executed by all competent persons and parents acting for any minor child having beneficial interests or having claims which will or may be affected by the compromise. Execution is not required by any person whose identity cannot be ascertained or whose whereabouts is unknown and cannot reasonably be ascertained.

(2) Any interested person, including the personal representative, if any, or a trustee, then may submit the agreement to the court for its approval and for execution by the personal representative, the trustee of every affected testamentary trust, and other fiduciaries and representatives.

(3) After notice to all interested persons or their representatives, including the personal representative of any estate and all affected trustees of trusts, the court, if it finds that the contest or controversy is in good faith and that the effect of the agreement upon the interests of persons represented by fiduciaries or other representatives is just and reasonable, shall make an order approving the agreement and directing all fiduciaries subject to its jurisdiction to execute the agreement. Minor children represented only by their parents may be bound only if their parents join with other competent persons in execution of the compromise. Upon the making of the order and the execution of the agreement, all further disposition of the estate is in accordance with the terms of the agreement.

PART 12

COLLECTION OF PERSONAL PROPERTY BY AFFIDAVIT AND SUMMARY ADMINISTRATION PROCEDURE FOR SMALL ESTATES

General Comment

The four sections which follow include two designed to facilitate transfer of small estates without use of a personal representative, and two designed to simplify the duties of a personal representative, who is appointed to handle a small estate.

The Flexible System of Administration described by earlier portions of Article III lends itself well to situations involving small estates. Letters may be obtained quickly without notice or judicial involvement. Immediately, the personal representative is in a position to distribute to successors whose deeds or transfers will protect purchasers. This route accommodates the need for quick and inexpensive transfers of land of small value as well as other assets. Consequently, it was unnecessary to frame complex provisions extending the affidavit procedures to land.

Indeed, transfers via letters of administration may prove to be less troublesome than use of the affidavit procedure. Still, it seemed desirable to provide a quick collection mechanism which avoids all necessity to visit the probate court. For one thing, unpredictable local variations in probate practice may produce situations where the alternative procedure will be very useful. For another, the provision of alternatives is in line with the overall philosophy of Article III to provide maximum flexibility.

Figures gleaned from a 1970 authoritative report of a major survey of probated estates in Cleveland, Ohio, demonstrate that more than one-half of all estates in probate had a gross value of less than $15,000. *See,* M. Susman, J. Cates & D. Smith, The Family and Inheritance (1970). This means that the principal measure of the relevance of any legislation dealing with probate procedures is to be found in its impact on very small and moderate sized estates. Here is the area where probate affects most people.

§ 3-1201. Collection of Personal Property by Affidavit.

(a) Thirty days after the death of a decedent, any person indebted to the decedent or having possession of tangible personal property or an instrument evidencing a debt, obligation, stock or chose in action belonging to the decedent shall make payment of the indebtedness or deliver the tangible personal property or an instrument evidencing a debt, obligation, stock or chose in action to a person claiming to be the successor of the decedent upon being presented an affidavit made by or on behalf of the successor stating that:

(1) the value of the entire estate, wherever located, less liens and encumbrances, does not exceed $25,000;

(2) 30 days have elapsed since the death of the decedent;

(3) no application or petition for the appointment of a personal representative is pending or has been granted in any jurisdiction; and

(4) the claiming successor is entitled to payment or delivery of the property.

(b) A transfer agent of any security shall change the registered ownership on the books of a corporation from the decedent to the successor or successors upon the presentation of an affidavit as provided in subsection (a).

§ 3-1202. Effect of Affidavit.

The person paying, delivering, transferring, or issuing personal property or the evidence thereof pursuant to affidavit is discharged and released to the same extent as if he dealt with a personal representative of the decedent. He is not required to see to the application of the personal property or evidence thereof or to inquire into the truth of any statement in the affidavit. If any person to whom an affidavit is delivered refuses to pay, deliver, transfer, or issue any personal property or evidence thereof, it may be recovered or its payment, delivery, transfer, or issuance compelled upon proof of their right in a proceeding brought for the purpose by or on behalf of the persons entitled thereto. Any person to whom payment, delivery, transfer or issuance is made is answerable and accountable therefor to any personal representative of the estate or to any other person having a superior right.

§ 3-1203. Small Estates; Summary Administration Procedure.

If it appears from the inventory and appraisal that the value of the entire estate, less liens and encumbrances, does not exceed homestead allowance, exempt property, family allowance, costs and expenses of administration, reasonable funeral expenses, and reasonable and necessary medical and hospital expenses of the last illness of the decedent, the personal representative, without giving notice to creditors, may immediately disburse and distribute the estate to the persons entitled thereto and file a closing statement as provided in Section 3-1204.

§ 3-1204. Small Estates; Closing by Sworn Statement of Personal Representative.

(a) Unless prohibited by order of the court and except for estates being administered by supervised personal representatives, a personal representative may close an estate administered under the summary procedures of Section 3-1203 by filing with the court, at any time after disbursement and distribution of the estate, a verified statement stating that:

(1) to the best knowledge of the personal representative, the value of the entire estate, less liens and encumbrances, did not exceed homestead allowance, exempt property, family allowance, costs and expenses of administration, reasonable funeral expenses, and reasonable, necessary medical and hospital expenses of the last illness of the decedent;

(2) the personal representative has fully administered the estate by disbursing and distributing it to the persons entitled thereto; and

(3) the personal representative has sent a copy of the closing statement to all distributees of the estate and to all creditors or other claimants of whom he is aware whose claims are neither paid nor barred and has furnished a full account in writing of his administration to the distributees whose interests are affected.

(b) If no actions or proceedings involving the personal representative are pending in the court one year after the closing statement is filed, the appointment of the personal representative terminates.

(c) A closing statement filed under this section has the same effect as one filed under Section 3-1003.

ARTICLE IV
FOREIGN PERSONAL REPRESENTATIVES;
ANCILLARY ADMINISTRATION

PART 1
DEFINITIONS

PART 2
POWERS OF FOREIGN PERSONAL REPRESENTATIVES

PART 3
JURISDICTION OVER FOREIGN REPRESENTATIVES

PART 4
JUDGMENTS AND PERSONAL REPRESENTATIVE

General Comment

This Article concerns the law applicable in estate problems which involve more than a single state. It covers the powers and responsibilities in the adopting state of personal representatives appointed in other states.

Some provisions of the Code covering local appointment of personal representatives for non-residents appear in Article III. These include the following: Sections 3-201 (venue), 3-202 (resolution of conflicting claims regarding domicile), 3-203 (priority as personal representative of representative previously appointed at domicile), 3-307(a) (30 days delay required before appointment of a local representative for a non-resident), 3-803(a) (claims barred by non-claim at domicile before local administration commenced are barred locally) and 3-815 (duty of personal representative in regard to claims where estate is being administered in more than one state). See also Sections 3-308, 3-611(a) and 3-816. Also, see Section 4-207.

The recognition provisions contained in Article IV and the various provisions of Article III which relate to administration of estates of non-residents are designed to coerce respect for domiciliary procedures and administrative acts to the extent possible.

The first part of Article IV contains some definitions of particular relevance to estates located in two or more states.

The second part of Article IV deals with the powers of foreign personal representatives in a jurisdiction adopting the Uniform Probate Code. There are different types of power which may be exercised. First, a foreign personal representative has the power under Section 4-201 to receive payments of debts owed to the decedent or to accept delivery of property belonging to the decedent. The foreign personal representative provides an affidavit indicating the date of death of the non-resident decedent, that no local administration has been commenced and that the foreign personal representative is entitled to payment or delivery. Payment under this provision can be made any time more than 60 days after the death of the decedent. When made in good faith the payment operates as a discharge of the debtor. A protection for local creditors of the decedent is provided in Section 4-203, under which local debtors of the non-resident decedent can be notified of the claims which local creditors have against the estate. This notification will prevent payment under this provision.

A second type of power is provided in Sections 4-204 to 4-206. Under these provisions a foreign personal representative can file with the appropriate court a copy of his appointment and official bond if he has one. Upon so filing, the foreign personal representative has all of the powers of a personal representative appointed by the local court. This would be all of the powers provided for in an unsupervised administration as provided in Article III of the Code.

The third type of power which may be obtained by a foreign personal representative is conferred by the priority the domiciliary personal representative enjoys in respect to local appointment. This is covered by Section 3-203. Also, see Section 3.611(b).

Part 3 provides for power in the local court over foreign personal representatives who act locally. If a local or ancillary administration has been started, provisions in Article III subject the appointee to the power of the court. See Section 3-602. In Part 3 of this article, it is provided that a foreign personal representative submits himself to the jurisdiction of the local court by filing a copy of his appointment to get the powers provided in Section 4-205 or by doing any act which would give the state jurisdiction over him as an individual. In addition, the collection of funds as provided in Section 4-201 gives the court quasi-in-rem jurisdiction over the foreign personal representative to the extent of the funds collected.

Finally, Section 4-303 provides that the foreign personal representative is subject to the jurisdiction of the local court "to the same extent that his decedent was subject to jurisdiction immediately prior to death." This is similar to the typical non-resident motorist provision that provides for jurisdiction over the personal representative of a deceased non-resident motorist, see Note, 44 Iowa L.Rev. 384 (1959). It is, however, a much broader provision. Section 4-304 provides for the mechanical steps to be taken in serving the foreign personal representatives.

Part 4 of the article deals with the res judicata effect to be given adjudications for or against a foreign personal representative. Any such adjudication is to be conclusive on a local personal representative "unless it resulted from fraud or collusion ... to the prejudice of the estate." This provision must be read with Section 3-408 which deals with certain out-of-state findings concerning a decedent's estate.

PART 1
DEFINITIONS

§ 4-101. Definitions. In this [article]

(1) "local administration" means administration by a personal representative appointed in this state pursuant to appointment proceedings described in [Article] III.

(2) "local personal representative" includes any personal representative appointed in this state pursuant to appointment proceedings described in [Article] III and excludes foreign personal representatives who acquire the power of a local personal representative pursuant to Section 4-205.

(3) "resident creditor" means a person domiciled in, or doing business in this state, who is, or could be, a claimant against an estate of a non-resident decedent.

PART 2
POWERS OF FOREIGN PERSONAL REPRESENTATIVES

§ 4-201. Payment of Debt and Delivery of Property to Domiciliary Foreign Personal Representative Without Local Administration. At any time after the expiration of 60 days from the death of a nonresident decedent, any person indebted to the estate of the nonresident decedent or having possession or control of personal property, or of an instrument evidencing a debt, obligation, stock or chose in action belonging to the estate of the non-resident decedent may pay the debt, deliver the personal property, or the instrument evidencing the debt, obligation, stock or chose in action, to the domiciliary foreign personal representative of the nonresident decedent upon being presented with proof of his appointment and an affidavit made by or on behalf of the representative stating:

 (1) the date of the death of the nonresident decedent,

 (2) that no local administration, or application or petition therefor, is pending in this state,

 (3) that the domiciliary foreign personal representative is entitled to payment or delivery.

§ 4-202. Payment or Delivery Discharges. Payment or delivery made in good faith on the basis of the proof of authority and affidavit releases the debtor or person having possession of the personal property to the same extent as if payment or delivery had been made to a local personal representative.

§ 4-203. Resident Creditor Notice. Payment or delivery under Section 4-201 may not be made if a resident creditor of the nonresident decedent has notified the debtor of the nonresident decedent or the person having possession of the personal property belonging to the nonresident decedent that the debt should not be paid nor the property delivered to the domiciliary foreign personal representative.

§ 4-204. Proof of Authority-Bond. If no local administration or application or petition therefor is pending in this state, a domiciliary foreign personal representative may file with a court in this state in a [county] in which property belonging to the decedent is located, authenticated copies of his appointment and of any official bond he has given.

§ 4-205. Powers. A domiciliary foreign personal representative who has complied with Section 4-204 may exercise as to assets in this state all powers of a local personal representative and may maintain actions and proceedings in this state subject to any conditions imposed upon nonresident parties generally.

§ 4-206. Power of Representatives in Transition. The power of a domiciliary foreign personal representative under Section 4-201 or 4-205 shall be exercised only if there is no administration or application therefor pending in this state. An application or petition for local administration of the estate terminates the power of the foreign personal representative to act under Section 4-205, but the local court may allow the foreign personal representative to exercise limited powers to preserve the estate. No person who, before receiving actual notice of a pending local administration, has changed his position in reliance upon the powers of a foreign personal representative shall be prejudiced by reason of the application or petition for, or grant of, local administration. The local personal representative is subject to all duties and obligations which have accrued by virtue of the exercise of the powers by the foreign personal representative and may be substituted for him in any action or proceedings in this state.

§ 4-207. Ancillary and Other Local Administrations; Provisions Governing. In respect to a nonresident decedent, the provisions of Article III of this [code] govern:

(1) proceedings, if any, in a court of this state for probate of the will, appointment, removal, supervision, and discharge of the local personal representative, and any other order concerning the estate; and

(2) the status, powers, duties and liabilities of any local personal representative and the rights of claimants, purchasers, distributees and others in regard to a local administration.

PART 3
JURISDICTION OVER FOREIGN REPRESENTATIVES

§ 4-301. Jurisdiction by Act of Foreign Personal Representative. A foreign personal representative submits personally to the jurisdiction of the courts of this state in any proceeding relating to the estate by (i) filing authenticated copies of his appointment as provided in Section 4-204, (ii) receiving payment of money or taking delivery of personal property under Section 4-201, or (iii) doing any act as a personal representative in this state which would have given the state jurisdiction over him as an individual. Jurisdiction under clause (ii) is limited to the money or value of personal property collected.

§ 4-302. Jurisdiction by Act of Decedent. In addition to jurisdiction conferred by Section 4-301, a foreign personal representative is subject to the jurisdiction of the courts of this state to the same extent that his decedent was subject to jurisdiction immediately prior to death.

§ 4-303. Service on Foreign Personal Representative.

(a) Service of process may be made upon the foreign personal representative by registered or certified mail, addressed to his last reasonably ascertainable address, requesting a return receipt signed by addressee only. Notice by ordinary first class mail is sufficient if registered or certified mail service to the addressee is unavailable. Service may be made upon a foreign personal representative in the manner in which service could have been made under other laws of this state on either the foreign personal representative or his decedent immediately prior to death.

(b) If service is made upon a foreign personal representative as provided in subsection (a), he shall be allowed at least [30] days within which to appear or respond.

PART 4
JUDGMENTS AND PERSONAL REPRESENTATIVE

§ 4-401. Effect of Adjudication For or Against Personal Representative. An adjudication rendered in any jurisdiction in favor of or against any personal representative of the estate is as binding on the local personal representative as if he were a party to the adjudication.

ARTICLE V
UNIFORM GUARDIANSHIP AND PROTECTIVE PROCEEDINGS ACT (1997/1998)

PART 1
GENERAL PROVISIONS

PART 2
GUARDIANSHIP OF MINOR

PART 3
GUARDIANSHIP OF INCAPACITATED PERSON

PART 4
PROTECTION OF PROPERTY OF PROTECTED PERSONS

The following free-standing Acts are associated with Article V:

Uniform Guardianship and Protective
Proceedings Act (1997/1998)

Approval of the 1997 Act necessitated technical amendments elsewhere in the UPC, consisting of correction of definitions and cross-references. The following sections were amended: 1-201, 3-303, 3-308, and 3-915.

In addition, UGPPA (1997/1998) Sections 103 (Supplemental General Principles of Law Applicable) and 109 (Practice in Court) are not incorporated into the UPC because they duplicate provisions in UPC Article 1. To preserve comparable numbering of sections between UPGGA (1997/1998) and the UPC, UPC Sections 5-103 and 5-109 are titled "Reserved."

Uniform Adult Guardianship and Protective
Proceedings Jurisdiction Act (2007)

Article 5A has also been adopted as the free-standing Uniform Adult Guardianship and Protective Proceedings Jurisdiction Act (2007). Because this article also dealt with jurisdiction and related issues, upon the addition of Article 5A to this Code, conforming amendments to this article were necessary. See Sections 5-106, 5-107, 5-432, 5-433, and 5-434.

Uniform Power of Attorney Act (2006)

Article 5B has also been adopted as the free-standing Uniform Power of Attorney Act (2006).

PART 1
GENERAL PROVISIONS

§ 5-101. Short Title. This [article] may be cited as the Uniform Guardianship and Protective Proceedings Act.

§ 5-102. Definitions. In this [article]:

(1) "Conservator" means a person who is appointed by a court to manage the estate of a protected person. The term includes a limited conservator.

(2) "Court" means the [designate appropriate court].

(3) "Guardian" means a person who has qualified as a guardian of a minor or incapacitated person pursuant to appointment by a parent or spouse, or by the court. The term includes a limited, emergency, and temporary substitute guardian but not a guardian ad litem.

(4) "Incapacitated person" means an individual who, for reasons other than being a minor, is unable to receive and evaluate information or make or communicate decisions to such an extent that the individual lacks the ability to meet essential requirements for physical health, safety, or self-care, even with appropriate technological assistance.

(5) "Legal representative" includes the lawyer for the respondent, a representative payee, a guardian or conservator acting for a respondent in this state or elsewhere, a trustee or custodian of a trust or custodianship of which the respondent is a beneficiary, and an agent designated under a power of attorney, whether for health care or property, in which the respondent is identified as the principal.

(6) "Minor" means an unemancipated individual who has not attained [18] years of age.

(7) "Parent" means a parent whose parental rights have not been terminated.

(8) "Protected person" means a minor or other individual for whom a conservator has been

appointed or other protective order has been made.

(9) "Respondent" means an individual for whom the appointment of a guardian or conservator or other protective order is sought.

(10) "Ward" means an individual for whom a guardian has been appointed.

§ 5-103. [Reserved.]

§ 5-104. Facility of Transfer

(a) Unless a person required to transfer money or personal property to a minor knows that a conservator has been appointed or that a proceeding for appointment of a conservator of the estate of the minor is pending, the person may do so, as to an amount or value not exceeding [$10,000] a year, by transferring it to:

(1) a person who has the care and custody of the minor and with whom the minor resides;

(2) a guardian of the minor;

(3) a custodian under the Uniform Transfers To Minors Act or custodial trustee under the Uniform Custodial Trust Act; or

(4) a financial institution as a deposit in an interest-bearing account or certificate in the sole name of the minor and giving notice of the deposit to the minor.

(b) A person who transfers money or property in compliance with this section is not responsible for its proper application.

(c) A guardian or other person who receives money or property for a minor under subsection (a)(1) or (2) may only apply it to the support, care, education, health, and welfare of the minor, and may not derive a personal financial benefit except for reimbursement for necessary expenses. Any excess must be preserved for the future support, care, education, health, and welfare of the minor, and any balance must be transferred to the minor upon emancipation or attaining majority.

§ 5-105. Delegation of Power by Parent or Guardian. A parent or guardian of a minor or incapacitated person, by a power of attorney, may delegate to another person, for a period not exceeding six months, any power regarding care, custody, or property of the minor or ward, except the power to consent to marriage or adoption.

§ 5-106. Subject-Matter Jurisdiction.

(a) Except to the extent the guardianship is subject to the [insert citation to Uniform Child Custody Jurisdiction and Enforcement Act], the court of this state has jurisdiction over guardianship for minors domiciled or present in this state. The court of this state has jurisdiction over protective proceedings for minors domiciled in or having property in this state.

(b) The court of this state has jurisdiction over guardianship and protective proceedings for an adult individual as provided in the [insert citation to Uniform Adult Guardianship and Protective Proceedings Jurisdiction Act].

§ 5-107. Transfer of Jurisdiction

(a) Except as otherwise provided in subsection (b), the following rules apply:

(1) After the appointment of a guardian or conservator or entry of another protective order, the court making the appointment or entering the order may transfer the proceeding to a court in another [county] in this state or to another state if the court is satisfied that a transfer will serve the best interest of the ward or protected person.

(2) If a guardianship or protective proceeding is pending in another state or a foreign country and

a petition for guardianship or protective proceeding is filed in a court in this state, the court in this state shall notify the original court and, after consultation with the original court, assume or decline jurisdiction, whichever is in the best interest of the ward or protected person.

(3) A guardian, conservator, or like fiduciary appointed in another state may petition the court for appointment as a guardian or conservator in this state if venue in this state is or will be established. The appointment may be made upon proof of appointment in the other state and presentation of a certified copy of the portion of the court record in the other state specified by the court in this state. Notice of hearing on the petition, together with a copy of the petition, must be given to the ward or protected person, if the ward or protected person has attained 14 years of age, and to the persons who would be entitled to notice if the regular procedures for appointment of a guardian or conservator under this [article] were applicable. The court shall make the appointment in this state unless it concludes that the appointment would not be in the best interest of the ward or protected person. On the filing of an acceptance of office and any required bond, the court shall issue appropriate letters of guardianship or conservatorship. No later than 14 days after an appointment, the guardian or conservator shall send or deliver a copy of the order of appointment to the ward or protected person, if the ward or protected person has attained 14 years of age, and to all persons given notice of the hearing on the petition.

(b) This section does not apply to a guardianship or protective proceeding for an adult individual that is subject to the transfer provisions of [insert citation to Article 3 of the Uniform Adult Guardianship and Protective Proceedings Jurisdiction Act (2007)].

§ 5-108. Venue

(a) Venue for a guardianship proceeding for a minor is in the [county] of this state in which the minor resides or is present at the time the proceeding is commenced.

(b) Venue for a guardianship proceeding for an incapacitated person is in the [county] of this state in which the respondent resides and, if the respondent has been admitted to an institution by order of a court of competent jurisdiction, in the [county] in which the court is located. Venue for the appointment of an emergency or a temporary substitute guardian of an incapacitated person is also in the [county] in which the respondent is present.

(c) Venue for a protective proceeding is in the [county] of this state in which the respondent resides, whether or not a guardian has been appointed in another place or, if the respondent does not reside in this state, in any [county] of this state in which property of the respondent is located.

(d) If a proceeding under this [article] is brought in more than one [county] in this state, the court of the [county] in which the proceeding is first brought has the exclusive right to proceed unless that court determines that venue is properly in another court or that the interests of justice otherwise require that the proceeding be transferred.

§ 5-109. [Reserved.]

§ 5-110. Letters of Office. Upon the guardian's filing of an acceptance of office, the court shall issue appropriate letters of guardianship. Upon the conservator's filing of an acceptance of office and any required bond, the court shall issue appropriate letters of conservatorship. Letters of guardianship must indicate whether the guardian was appointed by the court, a parent, or the spouse. Any limitation on the powers of a guardian or conservator or of the assets subject to a conservatorship must be endorsed on the guardian's or conservator's letters.

§ 5-111. Effect of Acceptance of Appointment. By accepting appointment, a guardian or conservator submits personally to the jurisdiction of the court in any proceeding relating to the guardianship or conservatorship. The petitioner shall send or deliver notice of any proceeding to the guardian or conservator at the guardian's or conservator's address shown in the court records and at any other address then known to the petitioner.

§ 5-112. Termination of or Change in Guardian's or Conservator's Appointment

(a) The appointment of a guardian or conservator terminates upon the death, resignation, or removal of the guardian or conservator or upon termination of the guardianship or conservatorship. A resignation of a guardian or conservator is effective when approved by the court. [A parental or spousal appointment as guardian under an informally probated will terminates if the will is later denied probate in a formal proceeding.] Termination of the appointment of a guardian or conservator does not affect the liability of either for previous acts or the obligation to account for money and other assets of the ward or protected person.

(b) A ward, protected person, or person interested in the welfare of a ward or protected person may petition for removal of a guardian or conservator on the ground that removal would be in the best interest of the ward or protected person or for other good cause. A guardian or conservator may petition for permission to resign. A petition for removal or permission to resign may include a request for appointment of a successor guardian or conservator.

(c) The court may appoint an additional guardian or conservator at any time, to serve immediately or upon some other designated event, and may appoint a successor guardian or conservator in the event of a vacancy or make the appointment in contemplation of a vacancy, to serve if a vacancy occurs. An additional or successor guardian or conservator may file an acceptance of appointment at any time after the appointment, but not later than 30 days after the occurrence of the vacancy or other designated event. The additional or successor guardian or conservator becomes eligible to act on the occurrence of the vacancy or designated event, or the filing of the acceptance of appointment, whichever last occurs. A successor guardian or conservator succeeds to the predecessor's powers, and a successor conservator succeeds to the predecessor's title to the protected person's assets.

§ 5-113. Notice

(a) Except as otherwise ordered by the court for good cause, if notice of a hearing on a petition is required, other than a notice for which specific requirements are otherwise provided, the petitioner shall give notice of the time and place of the hearing to the person to be notified. Notice must be given in compliance with [insert the applicable rule of civil procedure], at least 14 days before the hearing.

(b) Proof of notice must be made before or at the hearing and filed in the proceeding.

(c) A notice under this [article] must be given in plain language.

§ 5-114. Waiver of Notice. A person may waive notice by a writing signed by the person or the person's attorney and filed in the proceeding. However, a respondent, ward, or protected person may not waive notice.

§ 5-115. Guardian Ad Litem. At any stage of a proceeding, a court may appoint a guardian ad litem if the court determines that representation of the interest otherwise would be inadequate. If not precluded by a conflict of interest, a guardian ad litem may be appointed to represent several individuals or interests. The court shall state on the record the duties of the guardian ad litem and its reasons for the appointment.

§ 5-116. Request for Notice; Interested Persons. An interested person not otherwise entitled to notice who desires to be notified before any order is made in a guardianship proceeding, including a proceeding after the appointment of a guardian, or in a protective proceeding, may file a request for notice with the clerk of the court in which the proceeding is pending. The clerk shall send or deliver a copy of the request to the guardian and to the conservator if one has been appointed. A request is not effective unless it contains a statement showing the interest of the person making it and the address of that person or a lawyer to whom notice is to be given. The request is effective only as to proceedings conducted after its filing. A governmental agency paying or planning to pay benefits to the respondent or protected person is an interested person in a protective proceeding.

§ 5-117. Multiple Appointments or Nominations. If a respondent or other person makes more than one written appointment or nomination of a guardian or a conservator, the most recent controls.

PART 2
GUARDIANSHIP OF MINOR

§ 5-201. Appointment and Status of Guardian. A person becomes a guardian of a minor by parental appointment or upon appointment by the court. The guardianship continues until terminated, without regard to the location of the guardian or minor ward.

§ 5-202. Parental Appointment of Guardian

(a) A guardian may be appointed by will or other signed writing by a parent for any minor child the parent has or may have in the future. The appointment may specify the desired limitations on the powers to be given to the guardian. The appointing parent may revoke or amend the appointment before confirmation by the court.

(b) Upon petition of an appointing parent and a finding that the appointing parent will likely become unable to care for the child within [two] years, and after notice as provided in Section 5-205(a), the court, before the appointment becomes effective, may confirm the parent's selection of a guardian and terminate the rights of others to object.

(c) Subject to Section 5-203, the appointment of a guardian becomes effective upon the appointing parent's death, an adjudication that the parent is an incapacitated person, or a written determination by a physician who has examined the parent that the parent is no longer able to care for the child, whichever first occurs.

(d) The guardian becomes eligible to act upon the filing of an acceptance of appointment, which must be filed within 30 days after the guardian's appointment becomes effective. The guardian shall:

(1) file the acceptance of appointment and a copy of the will with the court of the [county] in which the will was or could be probated or, in the case of another appointing instrument, file the acceptance of appointment and the appointing instrument with the court of the [county] in which the minor resides or is present; and

(2) give written notice of the acceptance of appointment to the appointing parent, if living, the minor, if the minor has attained 14 years of age, and a person other than the parent having care and custody of the minor.

(e) Unless the appointment was previously confirmed by the court, the notice given under subsection (d)(2) must include a statement of the right of those notified to terminate the appointment by filing a written objection in the court as provided in Section 5-203.

(f) Unless the appointment was previously confirmed by the court, within 30 days after filing the notice and the appointing instrument, a guardian shall petition the court for confirmation of the appointment, giving notice in the manner provided in Section 5-205(a).

(g) The appointment of a guardian by a parent does not supersede the parental rights of either parent. If both parents are dead or have been adjudged incapacitated persons, an appointment by the last parent who died or was adjudged incapacitated has priority. An appointment by a parent which is effected by filing the guardian's acceptance under a will probated in the state of the testator's domicile is effective in this state.

(h) The powers of a guardian who timely complies with the requirements of subsections (d) and (f) relate back to give acts by the guardian which are of benefit to the minor and occurred on or after the date the appointment became effective the same effect as those that occurred after the filing of the acceptance of the appointment.

(i) The authority of a guardian appointed under this section terminates upon the first to occur of the appointment of a guardian by the court or the giving of written notice to the guardian of the filing of an objection pursuant to Section 5-203.

§ 5-203. Objection by Minor or Others to Parental Appointment.

Until the court has confirmed an appointee under Section 5-202, a minor who is the subject of an appointment by a parent and who has attained 14 years of age, the other parent, or a person other than a parent or guardian having care or custody of the minor may prevent or terminate the appointment at any time by filing a written objection in the court in which the appointing instrument is filed and giving notice of the objection to the guardian and any other persons entitled to notice of the acceptance of the appointment. An objection may be withdrawn, and if withdrawn is of no effect. The objection does not preclude judicial appointment of the person selected by the parent. The court may treat the filing of an objection as a petition for the appointment of an emergency or a temporary guardian under Section 5-204, and proceed accordingly.

§ 5-204. Judicial Appointment of Guardian: Conditions for Appointment

(a) A minor or a person interested in the welfare of a minor may petition for appointment of a guardian.

(b) The court may appoint a guardian for a minor if the court finds the appointment is in the minor's best interest, and:

   (1) the parents consent;

   (2) all parental rights have been terminated; or

   (3) the parents are unwilling or unable to exercise their parental rights.

(c) If a guardian is appointed by a parent pursuant to Section 5-202 and the appointment has not been prevented or terminated under Section 5-203, that appointee has priority for appointment. However, the court may proceed with another appointment upon a finding that the appointee under Section 5-202 has failed to accept the appointment within 30 days after notice of the guardianship proceeding.

(d) If necessary and on petition or motion and whether or not the conditions of subsection (b) have been established, the court may appoint a temporary guardian for a minor upon a showing that an immediate need exists and that the appointment would be in the best interest of the minor. Notice in the manner provided in Section 5-113 must be given to the parents and to a minor who has attained 14 years of age. Except as otherwise ordered by the court, the temporary guardian has the authority of an unlimited guardian, but the duration of the temporary guardianship may not exceed six months. Within five days after the appointment, the temporary guardian shall send or deliver a copy of the order to all individuals who would be entitled to notice of hearing under Section 5-205.

(e) If the court finds that following the procedures of this [part] will likely result in substantial harm to a minor's health or safety and that no other person appears to have authority to act in the circumstances, the court, on appropriate petition, may appoint an emergency guardian for the minor. The duration of the guardian's authority may not exceed [30] days and the guardian may exercise only the powers specified in the order. Reasonable notice of the time and place of a hearing on the petition for appointment of an emergency guardian must be given to the minor, if the minor has attained 14 years of age, to each living parent of the minor, and a person having care or custody of the minor, if other than a parent. The court may dispense with the notice if it finds from affidavit or testimony that the minor will be substantially harmed before a hearing can be held on the petition. If the guardian is appointed without notice, notice of the appointment must be given within 48 hours after the appointment and a hearing on the appropriateness of the appointment held within [five] days after the appointment.

§ 5-205. Judicial Appointment of Guardian: Procedure

(a) After a petition for appointment of a guardian is filed, the court shall schedule a hearing, and the petitioner shall give notice of the time and place of the hearing, together with a copy of the petition, to:

(1) the minor, if the minor has attained 14 years of age and is not the petitioner;

(2) any person alleged to have had the primary care and custody of the minor during the 60 days before the filing of the petition;

(3) each living parent of the minor or, if there is none, the adult nearest in kinship that can be found;

(4) any person nominated as guardian by the minor if the minor has attained 14 years of age;

(5) any appointee of a parent whose appointment has not been prevented or terminated under Section 5-203; and

(6) any guardian or conservator currently acting for the minor in this state or elsewhere.

(b) The court, upon hearing, shall make the appointment if it finds that a qualified person seeks appointment, venue is proper, the required notices have been given, the conditions of Section 5-204(b) have been met, and the best interest of the minor will be served by the appointment. In other cases, the court may dismiss the proceeding or make any other disposition of the matter that will serve the best interest of the minor.

(c) If the court determines at any stage of the proceeding, before or after appointment, that the interests of the minor are or may be inadequately represented, it may appoint a lawyer to represent the minor, giving consideration to the choice of the minor if the minor has attained 14 years of age.

§ 5-206. Judicial Appointment of Guardian: Priority of Minor's Nominee; Limited Guardianship

(a) The court shall appoint as guardian a person whose appointment will be in the best interest of the minor. The court shall appoint a person nominated by the minor, if the minor has attained 14 years of age, unless the court finds the appointment will be contrary to the best interest of the minor.

(b) In the interest of developing self-reliance of a ward or for other good cause, the court, at the time of appointment or later, on its own motion or on motion of the minor ward or other interested person, may limit the powers of a guardian otherwise granted by this [part] and thereby create a limited guardianship. Following the same procedure, the court may grant additional powers or withdraw powers previously granted.

§ 5-207. Duties of Guardian

(a) Except as otherwise limited by the court, a guardian of a minor ward has the duties and responsibilities of a parent regarding the ward's support, care, education, health, and welfare. A guardian shall act at all times in the ward's best interest and exercise reasonable care, diligence, and prudence.

(b) A guardian shall:

(1) become or remain personally acquainted with the ward and maintain sufficient contact with the ward to know of the ward's capacities, limitations, needs, opportunities, and physical and mental health;

(2) take reasonable care of the ward's personal effects and bring a protective proceeding if necessary to protect other property of the ward;

(3) expend money of the ward which has been received by the guardian for the ward's current needs for support, care, education, health, and welfare;

(4) conserve any excess money of the ward for the ward's future needs, but if a conservator has been appointed for the estate of the ward, the guardian shall pay the money at least quarterly to the conservator to be conserved for the ward's future needs;

(5) report the condition of the ward and account for money and other assets in the guardian's possession or subject to the guardian's control, as ordered by the court on application of any person interested in the ward's welfare or as required by court rule; and

(6) inform the court of any change in the ward's custodial dwelling or address.

§ 5-208. Powers of Guardian

(a) Except as otherwise limited by the court, a guardian of a minor ward has the powers of a parent regarding the ward's support, care, education, health, and welfare.

(b) A guardian may:

(1) apply for and receive money for the support of the ward otherwise payable to the ward's parent, guardian, or custodian under the terms of any statutory system of benefits or insurance or any private contract, devise, trust, conservatorship, or custodianship;

(2) if otherwise consistent with the terms of any order by a court of competent jurisdiction relating to custody of the ward, take custody of the ward and establish the ward's place of custodial dwelling, but may only establish or move the ward's custodial dwelling outside the state upon express authorization of the court;

(3) if a conservator for the estate of a ward has not been appointed with existing authority, commence a proceeding, including an administrative proceeding, or take other appropriate action to compel a person to support the ward or to pay money for the benefit of the ward;

(4) consent to medical or other care, treatment, or service for the ward;

(5) consent to the marriage of the ward; and

(6) if reasonable under all of the circumstances, delegate to the ward certain responsibilities for decisions affecting the ward's well-being.

(c) The court may specifically authorize the guardian to consent to the adoption of the ward.

§ 5-209. Rights and Immunities of Guardian

(a) A guardian is entitled to reasonable compensation for services as guardian and to reimbursement for room, board, and clothing provided by the guardian to the ward, but only as approved by the court. If a conservator, other than the guardian or a person who is affiliated with the guardian, has been appointed for the estate of the ward, reasonable compensation and reimbursement to the guardian may be approved and paid by the conservator without order of the court.

(b) A guardian need not use the guardian's personal funds for the ward's expenses. A guardian is not liable to a third person for acts of the ward solely by reason of the guardianship. A guardian is not liable for injury to the ward resulting from the negligence or act of a third person providing medical or other care, treatment, or service for the ward except to the extent that a parent would be liable under the circumstances.

§ 5-210. Termination of Guardianship; Other Proceedings After Appointment

(a) A guardianship of a minor terminates upon the minor's death, adoption, emancipation or attainment of majority or as ordered by the court.

(b) A ward or a person interested in the welfare of a ward may petition for any order that is in the best interest of the ward. The petitioner shall give notice of the hearing on the petition to the ward, if the ward has attained 14 years of age and is not the petitioner, the guardian, and any other person as ordered by the court.

PART 3
GUARDIANSHIP OF INCAPACITATED PERSONS

§ 5-301. Appointment and Status of Guardian. A person becomes a guardian of an incapacitated person by a parental or spousal appointment or upon appointment by the court. The guardianship continues until terminated, without regard to the location of the guardian or ward.

§ 5-302. Appointment of Guardian by Will or Other Writing

(a) A parent, by will or other signed writing, may appoint a guardian for an unmarried child who the parent believes is an incapacitated person, specify desired limitations on the powers to be given to the guardian, and revoke or amend the appointment before confirmation by the court.

(b) An individual, by will or other signed writing, may appoint a guardian for the individual's spouse who the appointing spouse believes is an incapacitated person, specify desired limitations on the powers to be given to the guardian, and revoke or amend the appointment before confirmation by the court.

(c) The incapacitated person, the person having care or custody of the incapacitated person if other than the appointing parent or spouse, or the adult nearest in kinship to the incapacitated person may file a written objection to an appointment, unless the court has confirmed the appointment under subsection (d). The filing of the written objection terminates the appointment. An objection may be withdrawn and, if withdrawn, is of no effect. The objection does not preclude judicial appointment of the person selected by the parent or spouse. Notice of the objection must be given to the guardian and any other person entitled to notice of the acceptance of the appointment. The court may treat the filing of an objection as a petition for the appointment of an emergency guardian under Section 5-312 or for the appointment of a limited or unlimited guardian under Section 5-304 and proceed accordingly.

(d) Upon petition of the appointing parent or spouse, and a finding that the appointing parent or spouse will likely become unable to care for the incapacitated person within [two] years, and after notice as provided in this section, the court, before the appointment becomes effective, may confirm the appointing parent's or spouse's selection of a guardian and terminate the rights of others to object.

§ 5-303. Appointment of Guardian by Will or Other Writing: Effectiveness; Acceptance; Confirmation

(a) The appointment of a guardian under Section 5-302 becomes effective upon the death of the appointing parent or spouse, the adjudication of incapacity of the appointing parent or spouse, or a written determination by a physician who has examined the appointing parent or spouse that the appointing parent or spouse is no longer able to care for the incapacitated person, whichever first occurs.

(b) A guardian appointed under Section 5-302 becomes eligible to act upon the filing of an acceptance of appointment, which must be filed within 30 days after the guardian's appointment becomes effective. The guardian shall:

(1) file the notice of acceptance of appointment and a copy of the will with the court of the [county] in which the will was or could be probated or, in the case of another appointing instrument, file the acceptance of appointment and the appointing instrument with the court in the [county] in which the incapacitated person resides or is present; and

(2) give written notice of the acceptance of appointment to the appointing parent or spouse if living, the incapacitated person, a person having care or custody of the incapacitated person other than the appointing parent or spouse, and the adult nearest in kinship.

(c) Unless the appointment was previously confirmed by the court, the notice given under subsection (b)(2) must include a statement of the right of those notified to terminate the appointment by filing a written objection as provided in Section 5-302.

(d) An appointment effected by filing the guardian's acceptance under a will probated in the state of the testator's domicile is effective in this state.

(e) Unless the appointment was previously confirmed by the court, within 30 days after filing the notice and the appointing instrument, a guardian appointed under Section 5-302 shall file a petition in the court for confirmation of the appointment. Notice of the filing must be given in the manner provided in Section 5-309.

(f) The authority of a guardian appointed under Section 5-302 terminates upon the appointment of a guardian by the court or the giving of written notice to the guardian of the filing of an objection pursuant to Section 5-302, whichever first occurs.

(g) The appointment of a guardian under this section is not a determination of incapacity.

(h) The powers of a guardian who timely complies with the requirements of subsections (b) and (e) relate back to give acts by the guardian which are of benefit to the incapacitated person and occurred on or after the date the appointment became effective the same effect as those that occurred after the filing of the acceptance of appointment.

§ 5-304. Judicial Appointment of Guardian: Petition

(a) An individual or a person interested in the individual's welfare may petition for a determination of incapacity, in whole or in part, and for the appointment of a limited or unlimited guardian for the individual.

(b) The petition must set forth the petitioner's name, residence, current address if different, relationship to the respondent, and interest in the appointment and, to the extent known, state or contain the following with respect to the respondent and the relief requested:

(1) the respondent's name, age, principal residence, current street address, and, if different, the address of the dwelling in which it is proposed that the respondent will reside if the appointment is made;

(2) the name and address of the respondent's:

(A) spouse, or if the respondent has none, an adult with whom the respondent has resided for more than six months before the filing of the petition; and

(B) adult children or, if the respondent has none, the respondent's parents and adult brothers and sisters, or if the respondent has none, at least one of the adults nearest in kinship to the respondent who can be found;

(3) the name and address of any person responsible for care or custody of the respondent;

(4) the name and address of any legal representative of the respondent;

(5) the name and address of any person nominated as guardian by the respondent;

(6) the name and address of any proposed guardian and the reason why the proposed guardian should be selected;

(7) the reason why guardianship is necessary, including a brief description of the nature and extent of the respondent's alleged incapacity;

(8) if an unlimited guardianship is requested, the reason why limited guardianship is inappropriate and, if a limited guardianship is requested, the powers to be granted to the limited guardian; and

(9) a general statement of the respondent's property with an estimate of its value, including any insurance or pension, and the source and amount of any other anticipated income or receipts.

§ 5-305. Judicial Appointment of Guardian: Preliminaries to Hearing

(a) Upon receipt of a petition to establish a guardianship, the court shall set a date and time for hearing the petition and appoint a [visitor]. The duties and reporting requirements of the [visitor] are limited to the relief requested in the petition. The [visitor] must be an individual having training or experience in the type of incapacity alleged.

Alternative A

(b) The court shall appoint a lawyer to represent the respondent in the proceeding if:

(1) requested by the respondent;

(2) recommended by the [visitor]; or

(3) the court determines that the respondent needs representation.

Alternative B

(b) Unless the respondent is represented by a lawyer, the court shall appoint a lawyer to represent the respondent in the proceeding, regardless of the respondent's ability to pay.

End of Alternatives

(c) The [visitor] shall interview the respondent in person and, to the extent that the respondent is able to understand:

(1) explain to the respondent the substance of the petition, the nature, purpose, and effect of the proceeding, the respondent's rights at the hearing, and the general powers and duties of a guardian;

(2) determine the respondent's views about the proposed guardian, the proposed guardian's powers and duties, and the scope and duration of the proposed guardianship;

(3) inform the respondent of the right to employ and consult with a lawyer at the respondent's own expense and the right to request a court-appointed lawyer; and

(4) inform the respondent that all costs and expenses of the proceeding, including respondent's attorney's fees, will be paid from the respondent's estate.

(d) In addition to the duties imposed by subsection (c), the [visitor] shall:

(1) interview the petitioner and the proposed guardian;

(2) visit the respondent's present dwelling and any dwelling in which the respondent will live if the appointment is made;

(3) obtain information from any physician or other person who is known to have treated, advised, or assessed the respondent's relevant physical or mental condition; and

(4) make any other investigation the court directs.

(e) The [visitor] shall promptly file a report in writing with the court, which must include:

(1) a recommendation as to whether a lawyer should be appointed to represent the respondent;

(2) a summary of daily functions the respondent can manage without assistance, could manage

with the assistance of supportive services or benefits, including use of appropriate technological assistance, and cannot manage;

(3) recommendations regarding the appropriateness of guardianship, including as to whether less restrictive means of intervention are available, the type of guardianship, and, if a limited guardianship, the powers to be granted to the limited guardian;

(4) a statement of the qualifications of the proposed guardian, together with a statement as to whether the respondent approves or disapproves of the proposed guardian, and the powers and duties proposed or the scope of the guardianship;

(5) a statement as to whether the proposed dwelling meets the respondent's individual needs;

(6) a recommendation as to whether a professional evaluation or further evaluation is necessary; and

(7) any other matters the court directs.

Legislative Note: Those states that enact Alternative B of subsection (b) which requires appointment of counsel for the respondent in all proceedings for appointment of a guardian should not enact subsection (e)(1).

§ 5-306. Judicial Appointment of Guardian: Professional Evaluation. At or before a hearing under this [part], the court may order a professional evaluation of the respondent and shall order the evaluation if the respondent so demands. If the court orders the evaluation, the respondent must be examined by a physician, psychologist, or other individual appointed by the court who is qualified to evaluate the respondent's alleged impairment. The examiner shall promptly file a written report with the court. Unless otherwise directed by the court, the report must contain:

(1) a description of the nature, type, and extent of the respondent's specific cognitive and functional limitations;

(2) an evaluation of the respondent's mental and physical condition and, if appropriate, educational potential, adaptive behavior, and social skills;

(3) a prognosis for improvement and a recommendation as to the appropriate treatment or habilitation plan; and

(4) the date of any assessment or examination upon which the report is based.

§ 5-307. Confidentiality of Records. The written report of a [visitor] and any professional evaluation are confidential and must be sealed upon filing, but are available to:

(1) the court;

(2) the respondent without limitation as to use;

(3) the petitioner, the [visitor], and the petitioner's and respondent's lawyers, for purposes of the proceeding; and

(4) other persons for such purposes as the court may order for good cause.

§ 5-308. Judicial Appointment of Guardian: Presence and Rights at Hearing

(a) Unless excused by the court for good cause, the proposed guardian shall attend the hearing. The respondent shall attend and participate in the hearing, unless excused by the court for good cause. The respondent may present evidence and subpoena witnesses and documents; examine witnesses, including any court-appointed physician, psychologist, or other individual qualified to evaluate the alleged impairment, and the [visitor]; and otherwise participate in the hearing. The hearing may be held in a location convenient to the respondent and may be closed upon the request of the respondent and a showing of good cause.

(b) Any person may request permission to participate in the proceeding. The court may grant the request, with or without hearing, upon determining that the best interest of the respondent will be served. The court may attach appropriate conditions to the participation.

§ 5-309. Notice

(a) A copy of a petition for guardianship and notice of the hearing on the petition must be served personally on the respondent. The notice must include a statement that the respondent must be physically present unless excused by the court, inform the respondent of the respondent's rights at the hearing, and include a description of the nature, purpose, and consequences of an appointment. A failure to serve the respondent with a notice substantially complying with this subsection precludes the court from granting the petition.

(b) In a proceeding to establish a guardianship, notice of the hearing must be given to the persons listed in the petition. Failure to give notice under this subsection does not preclude the appointment of a guardian or the making of a protective order.

(c) Notice of the hearing on a petition for an order after appointment of a guardian, together with a copy of the petition, must be given to the ward, the guardian, and any other person the court directs.

(d) A guardian shall give notice of the filing of the guardian's report, together with a copy of the report, to the ward and any other person the court directs. The notice must be delivered or sent within 14 days after the filing of the report.

§ 5-310. Who May Be Guardian: Priorities

(a) Subject to subsection (c), the court in appointing a guardian shall consider persons otherwise qualified in the following order of priority:

(1) a guardian, other than a temporary or emergency guardian, currently acting for the respondent in this state or elsewhere;

(2) a person nominated as guardian by the respondent, including the respondent's most recent nomination made in a durable power of attorney, if at the time of the nomination the respondent had sufficient capacity to express a preference;

(3) an agent appointed by the respondent under [a durable power of attorney for health care] [the Uniform Health-Care Decisions Act];

(4) the spouse of the respondent or a person nominated by will or other signed writing of a deceased spouse;

(5) an adult child of the respondent;

(6) a parent of the respondent, or an individual nominated by will or other signed writing of a deceased parent; and

(7) an adult with whom the respondent has resided for more than six months before the filing of the petition.

(b) With respect to persons having equal priority, the court shall select the one it considers best qualified. The court, acting in the best interest of the respondent, may decline to appoint a person having priority and appoint a person having a lower priority or no priority.

(c) An owner, operator, or employee of [a long-term-care institution] at which the respondent is receiving care may not be appointed as guardian unless related to the respondent by blood, marriage, or adoption.

§ 5-311. Findings; Order of Appointment

(a) The court may:

(1) appoint a limited or unlimited guardian for a respondent only if it finds by clear and

convincing evidence that:

> (A) the respondent is an incapacitated person; and

> (B) the respondent's identified needs cannot be met by less restrictive means, including use of appropriate technological assistance; or

> (2) with appropriate findings, treat the petition as one for a protective order under Section 5-401, enter any other appropriate order, or dismiss the proceeding.

(b) The court, whenever feasible, shall grant to a guardian only those powers necessitated by the ward's limitations and demonstrated needs and make appointive and other orders that will encourage the development of the ward's maximum self-reliance and independence.

(c) Within 14 days after an appointment, a guardian shall send or deliver to the ward and to all other persons given notice of the hearing on the petition a copy of the order of appointment, together with a notice of the right to request termination or modification.

§ 5-312. Emergency Guardian

(a) If the court finds that compliance with the procedures of this [part] will likely result in substantial harm to the respondent's health, safety, or welfare, and that no other person appears to have authority and willingness to act in the circumstances, the court, on petition by a person interested in the respondent's welfare, may appoint an emergency guardian whose authority may not exceed [60] days and who may exercise only the powers specified in the order. Immediately upon receipt of the petition for an emergency guardianship, the court shall appoint a lawyer to represent the respondent in the proceeding. Except as otherwise provided in subsection (b), reasonable notice of the time and place of a hearing on the petition must be given to the respondent and any other persons as the court directs.

(b) An emergency guardian may be appointed without notice to the respondent and the respondent's lawyer only if the court finds from affidavit or testimony that the respondent will be substantially harmed before a hearing on the appointment can be held. If the court appoints an emergency guardian without notice to the respondent, the respondent must be given notice of the appointment within 48 hours after the appointment. The court shall hold a hearing on the appropriateness of the appointment within [five] days after the appointment.

(c) Appointment of an emergency guardian, with or without notice, is not a determination of the respondent's incapacity.

(d) The court may remove an emergency guardian at any time. An emergency guardian shall make any report the court requires. In other respects, the provisions of this [article] concerning guardians apply to an emergency guardian.

§ 5-313. Temporary Substitute Guardian

(a) If the court finds that a guardian is not effectively performing the guardian's duties and that the welfare of the ward requires immediate action, it may appoint a temporary substitute guardian for the ward for a specified period not exceeding six months. Except as otherwise ordered by the court, a temporary substitute guardian so appointed has the powers set forth in the previous order of appointment. The authority of any unlimited or limited guardian previously appointed by the court is suspended as long as a temporary substitute guardian has authority. If an appointment is made without previous notice to the ward or the affected guardian, the court, within five days after the appointment, shall inform the ward or guardian of the appointment.

(b) The court may remove a temporary substitute guardian at any time. A temporary substitute guardian shall make any report the court requires. In other respects, the provisions of this [article] concerning guardians apply to a temporary substitute guardian.

§ 5-314. Duties of Guardian

(a) Except as otherwise limited by the court, a guardian shall make decisions regarding the ward's support, care, education, health, and welfare. A guardian shall exercise authority only as necessitated by the ward's limitations and, to the extent possible, shall encourage the ward to participate in decisions, act on the ward's own behalf, and develop or regain the capacity to manage the ward's personal affairs. A guardian, in making decisions, shall consider the expressed desires and personal values of the ward to the extent known to the guardian. A guardian at all times shall act in the ward's best interest and exercise reasonable care, diligence, and prudence.

(b) A guardian shall:

(1) become or remain personally acquainted with the ward and maintain sufficient contact with the ward to know of the ward's capacities, limitations, needs, opportunities, and physical and mental health;

(2) take reasonable care of the ward's personal effects and bring protective proceedings if necessary to protect the property of the ward;

(3) expend money of the ward that has been received by the guardian for the ward's current needs for support, care, education, health, and welfare;

(4) conserve any excess money of the ward for the ward's future needs, but if a conservator has been appointed for the estate of the ward, the guardian shall pay the money to the conservator, at least quarterly, to be conserved for the ward's future needs;

(5) immediately notify the court if the ward's condition has changed so that the ward is capable of exercising rights previously removed; and

(6) inform the court of any change in the ward's custodial dwelling or address.

§ 5-315. Powers of Guardian

(a) Except as otherwise limited by the court, a guardian may:

(1) apply for and receive money payable to the ward or the ward's guardian or custodian for the support of the ward under the terms of any statutory system of benefits or insurance or any private contract, devise, trust, conservatorship, or custodianship;

(2) if otherwise consistent with the terms of any order by a court of competent jurisdiction relating to custody of the ward, take custody of the ward and establish the ward's place of custodial dwelling, but may only establish or move the ward's place of dwelling outside this state upon express authorization of the court;

(3) if a conservator for the estate of the ward has not been appointed with existing authority, commence a proceeding, including an administrative proceeding, or take other appropriate action to compel a person to support the ward or to pay money for the benefit of the ward;

(4) consent to medical or other care, treatment, or service for the ward;

(5) consent to the marriage [or divorce] of the ward; and

(6) if reasonable under all of the circumstances, delegate to the ward certain responsibilities for decisions affecting the ward's well-being.

(b) The court may specifically authorize the guardian to consent to the adoption of the ward.

§ 5-316. Rights and Immunities of Guardian; Limitations

(a) A guardian is entitled to reasonable compensation for services as guardian and to reimbursement for room, board, and clothing provided to the ward, but only as approved by order of the court. If a conservator, other than the guardian or one who is affiliated with the guardian, has been appointed for the estate of the ward, reasonable compensation and reimbursement to the guardian may be approved and paid by the conservator without order of the court.

(b) A guardian need not use the guardian's personal funds for the ward's expenses. A guardian is not liable to a third person for acts of the ward solely by reason of the relationship. A guardian who exercises reasonable care in choosing a third person providing medical or other care, treatment, or service for the ward is not liable for injury to the ward resulting from the wrongful conduct of the third party.

(c) A guardian, without authorization of the court, may not revoke a power of attorney for health care [made pursuant to the Uniform Health-Care Decisions Act (1993)] of which the ward is the principal. If a power of attorney for health care [made pursuant to the Uniform Health-Care Decisions Act (1993)] is in effect, absent an order of the court to the contrary, a health-care decision of the agent takes precedence over that of a guardian.

(d) A guardian may not initiate the commitment of a ward to a [mental health-care] institution except in accordance with the state's procedure for involuntary civil commitment.

§ 5-317. Reports; Monitoring of Guardianship

(a) Within 30 days after appointment, a guardian shall report to the court in writing on the condition of the ward and account for money and other assets in the guardian's possession or subject to the guardian's control. A guardian shall report at least annually thereafter and whenever ordered by the court. A report must state or contain:

(1) the current mental, physical, and social condition of the ward;

(2) the living arrangements for all addresses of the ward during the reporting period;

(3) the medical, educational, vocational, and other services provided to the ward and the guardian's opinion as to the adequacy of the ward's care;

(4) a summary of the guardian's visits with the ward and activities on the ward's behalf and the extent to which the ward has participated in decision-making;

(5) if the ward is institutionalized, whether the guardian considers the current plan for care, treatment, or habilitation to be in the ward's best interest;

(6) plans for future care; and

(7) a recommendation as to the need for continued guardianship and any recommended changes in the scope of the guardianship.

(b) The court may appoint a [visitor] to review a report, interview the ward or guardian, and make any other investigation the court directs.

(c) The court shall establish a system for monitoring guardianships, including the filing and review of annual reports.

§ 5-318. Termination or Modification of Guardianship

(a) A guardianship terminates upon the death of the ward or upon order of the court.

(b) On petition of a ward, a guardian, or another person interested in the ward's welfare, the court may terminate a guardianship if the ward no longer needs the assistance or protection of a guardian. The court may modify the type of appointment or powers granted to the guardian if the extent of protection or assistance previously granted is currently excessive or insufficient or the ward's capacity to provide for support, care, education, health, and welfare has so changed as to warrant that action.

(c) Except as otherwise ordered by the court for good cause, the court, before terminating a guardianship, shall follow the same procedures to safeguard the rights of the ward as apply to a petition for guardianship. Upon presentation by the petitioner of evidence establishing a prima facie case for termination, the court shall order the termination unless it is proven that continuation of the guardianship is in the best interest of the ward.

PART 4
PROTECTION OF PROPERTY OF PROTECTED PERSON

§ 5-401. Protective Proceeding. Upon petition and after notice and hearing, the court may appoint a limited or unlimited conservator or make any other protective order provided in this [part] in relation to the estate and affairs of:

(1) a minor, if the court determines that the minor owns money or property requiring management or protection that cannot otherwise be provided or has or may have business affairs that may be put at risk or prevented because of the minor's age, or that money is needed for support and education and that protection is necessary or desirable to obtain or provide money; or

(2) any individual, including a minor, if the court determines that, for reasons other than age:

(A) by clear and convincing evidence, the individual is unable to manage property and business affairs because of an impairment in the ability to receive and evaluate information or make decisions, even with the use of appropriate technological assistance, or because the individual is missing, detained, or unable to return to the United States; and

(B) by a preponderance of evidence, the individual has property that will be wasted or dissipated unless management is provided or money is needed for the support, care, education, health, and welfare of the individual or of individuals who are entitled to the individual's support and that protection is necessary or desirable to obtain or provide money.

§ 5-402. Jurisdiction Over Business Affairs of Protected Person. After the service of notice in a proceeding seeking a conservatorship or other protective order and until termination of the proceeding, the court in which the petition is filed has:

(1) exclusive jurisdiction to determine the need for a conservatorship or other protective order;

(2) exclusive jurisdiction to determine how the estate of the protected person which is subject to the laws of this state must be managed, expended, or distributed to or for the use of the protected person, individuals who are in fact dependent upon the protected person, or other claimants; and

(3) concurrent jurisdiction to determine the validity of claims against the person or estate of the protected person and questions of title concerning assets of the estate.

§ 5-403. Original Petition for Appointment or Protective Order

(a) The following may petition for the appointment of a conservator or for any other appropriate protective order:

(1) the person to be protected;

(2) an individual interested in the estate, affairs, or welfare of the person to be protected, including a parent, guardian, or custodian; or

(3) a person who would be adversely affected by lack of effective management of the property and business affairs of the person to be protected.

(b) A petition under subsection (a) must set forth the petitioner's name, residence, current address if different, relationship to the respondent, and interest in the appointment or other protective order, and, to the extent known, state or contain the following with respect to the respondent and the relief requested:

(1) the respondent's name, age, principal residence, current street address, and, if different, the address of the dwelling where it is proposed that the respondent will reside if the appointment is made;

(2) if the petition alleges impairment in the respondent's ability to receive and evaluate information, a brief description of the nature and extent of the respondent's alleged impairment;

(3) if the petition alleges that the respondent is missing, detained, or unable to return to the United States, a statement of the relevant circumstances, including the time and nature of the disappearance or detention and a description of any search or inquiry concerning the respondent's whereabouts;

(4) the name and address of the respondent's:

(A) spouse or, if the respondent has none, an adult with whom the respondent has resided for more than six months before the filing of the petition; and

(B) adult children or, if the respondent has none, the respondent's parents and adult brothers and sisters or, if the respondent has none, at least one of the adults nearest in kinship to the respondent who can be found;

(5) the name and address of the person responsible for care or custody of the respondent;

(6) the name and address of any legal representative of the respondent;

(7) a general statement of the respondent's property with an estimate of its value, including any insurance or pension, and the source and amount of other anticipated income or receipts; and

(8) the reason why a conservatorship or other protective order is in the best interest of the respondent.

(c) If a conservatorship is requested, the petition must also set forth to the extent known:

(1) the name and address of any proposed conservator and the reason why the proposed conservator should be selected;

(2) the name and address of any person nominated as conservator by the respondent if the respondent has attained 14 years of age; and

(3) the type of conservatorship requested and, if an unlimited conservatorship, the reason why limited conservatorship is inappropriate or, if a limited conservatorship, the property to be placed under the conservator's control and any limitation on the conservator's powers and duties.

§ 5-404. Notice

(a) A copy of the petition and the notice of hearing on a petition for conservatorship or other protective order must be served personally on the respondent, but if the respondent's whereabouts is unknown or personal service cannot be made, service on the respondent must be made by [substituted service] [or] [publication]. The notice must include a statement that the respondent must be physically present unless excused by the court, inform the respondent of the respondent's rights at the hearing, and, if the appointment of a conservator is requested, include a description of the nature, purpose, and consequences of an appointment. A failure to serve the respondent with a notice substantially complying with this subsection precludes the court from granting the petition.

(b) In a proceeding to establish a conservatorship or for another protective order, notice of the hearing must be given to the persons listed in the petition. Failure to give notice under this subsection does not preclude the appointment of a conservator or the making of another protective order.

(c) Notice of the hearing on a petition for an order after appointment of a conservator or making of another protective order, together with a copy of the petition, must be given to the protected person, if the protected person has attained 14 years of age and is not missing, detained, or unable to return to the United States, any conservator of the protected person's estate, and any other person as ordered by the court.

(d) A conservator shall give notice of the filing of the conservator's inventory, report, or plan of conservatorship, together with a copy of the inventory, report, or plan of conservatorship to the protected person and any other person the court directs. The notice must be delivered or sent within

14 days after the filing of the inventory, report, or plan of conservatorship.

§ 5-405. Original Petition: Minors; Preliminaries to Hearing

(a) Upon the filing of a petition to establish a conservatorship or for another protective order for the reason that the respondent is a minor, the court shall set a date for hearing. If the court determines at any stage of the proceeding that the interests of the minor are or may be inadequately represented, it may appoint a lawyer to represent the minor, giving consideration to the choice of the minor if the minor has attained 14 years of age.

(b) While a petition to establish a conservatorship or for another protective order is pending, after preliminary hearing and without notice to others, the court may make orders to preserve and apply the property of the minor as may be required for the support of the minor or individuals who are in fact dependent upon the minor. The court may appoint a [master] to assist in that task.

§ 5-406. Original Petition: Preliminaries to Hearing

(a) Upon the filing of a petition for a conservatorship or other protective order for a respondent for reasons other than being a minor, the court shall set a date for hearing. The court shall appoint a [visitor] unless the petition does not request the appointment of a conservator and the respondent is represented by a lawyer. The duties and reporting requirements of the [visitor] are limited to the relief requested in the petition. The [visitor] must be an individual having training or experience in the type of incapacity alleged.

Alternative A

(b) The court shall appoint a lawyer to represent the respondent in the proceeding if:

(1) requested by the respondent;

(2) recommended by the [visitor]; or

(3) the court determines that the respondent needs representation.

Alternative B

(b) Unless the respondent is represented by a lawyer, the court shall appoint a lawyer to represent the respondent in the proceeding, regardless of the respondent's ability to pay.

End of Alternatives

(c) The [visitor] shall interview the respondent in person and, to the extent that the respondent is able to understand:

(1) explain to the respondent the substance of the petition and the nature, purpose, and effect of the proceeding;

(2) if the appointment of a conservator is requested, inform the respondent of the general powers and duties of a conservator and determine the respondent's views regarding the proposed conservator, the proposed conservator's powers and duties, and the scope and duration of the proposed conservatorship;

(3) inform the respondent of the respondent's rights, including the right to employ and consult with a lawyer at the respondent's own expense, and the right to request a court-appointed lawyer; and

(4) inform the respondent that all costs and expenses of the proceeding, including respondent's attorney's fees, will be paid from the respondent's estate.

(d) In addition to the duties imposed by subsection (c), the [visitor] shall:

(1) interview the petitioner and the proposed conservator, if any; and

(2) make any other investigation the court directs.

(e) The [visitor] shall promptly file a report with the court, which must include:

(1) a recommendation as to whether a lawyer should be appointed to represent the respondent;

(2) recommendations regarding the appropriateness of a conservatorship, including whether less

restrictive means of intervention are available, the type of conservatorship, and, if a limited conservatorship, the powers and duties to be granted the limited conservator, and the assets over which the conservator should be granted authority;

(3) a statement of the qualifications of the proposed conservator, together with a statement as to whether the respondent approves or disapproves of the proposed conservator, and a statement of the powers and duties proposed or the scope of the conservatorship;

(4) a recommendation as to whether a professional evaluation or further evaluation is necessary; and

(5) any other matters the court directs.

(f) The court may also appoint a physician, psychologist, or other individual qualified to evaluate the alleged impairment to conduct an examination of the respondent.

(g) While a petition to establish a conservatorship or for another protective order is pending, after preliminary hearing and without notice to others, the court may issue orders to preserve and apply the property of the respondent as may be required for the support of the respondent or individuals who are in fact dependent upon the respondent. The court may appoint a [master] to assist in that task.

Legislative Note: Those states that enact Alternative B of subsection (b) which requires appointment of counsel for the respondent in all protective proceedings should not enact subsection (e)(1).

§ 5-407. **Confidentiality of Records.** The written report of a [visitor] and any professional evaluation are confidential and must be sealed upon filing, but are available to:

(1) the court;

(2) the respondent without limitation as to use;

(3) the petitioner, the [visitor], and the petitioner's and respondent's lawyers, for purposes of the proceeding; and

(4) other persons for such purposes as the court may order for good cause.

§ 5-408. **Original Petition: Procedure at Hearing**

(a) Unless excused by the court for good cause, a proposed conservator shall attend the hearing. The respondent shall attend and participate in the hearing, unless excused by the court for good cause. The respondent may present evidence and subpoena witnesses and documents, examine witnesses, including any court-appointed physician, psychologist, or other individual qualified to evaluate the alleged impairment, and the [visitor], and otherwise participate in the hearing. The hearing may be held in a location convenient to the respondent and may be closed upon request of the respondent and a showing of good cause.

(b) Any person may request permission to participate in the proceeding. The court may grant the request, with or without hearing, upon determining that the best interest of the respondent will be served. The court may attach appropriate conditions to the participation.

§ 5-409. **Original Petition: Orders**

(a) If a proceeding is brought for the reason that the respondent is a minor, after a hearing on the petition, upon finding that the appointment of a conservator or other protective order is in the best interest of the minor, the court shall make an appointment or other appropriate protective order.

(b) If a proceeding is brought for reasons other than that the respondent is a minor, after a hearing on the petition, upon finding that a basis exists for a conservatorship or other protective order, the court shall make the least restrictive order consistent with its findings. The court shall make orders necessitated by the protected person's limitations and demonstrated needs, including appointive and other orders that will encourage the development of maximum self-reliance and independence of the protected person.

(c) Within 14 days after an appointment, the conservator shall deliver or send a copy of the order of appointment, together with a statement of the right to seek termination or modification, to the protected person, if the protected person has attained 14 years of age and is not missing, detained, or unable to return to the United States, and to all other persons given notice of the petition.

(d) The appointment of a conservator or the entry of another protective order is not a determination of incapacity of the protected person.

§ 5-410. Powers of Court

(a) After hearing and upon determining that a basis for a conservatorship or other protective order exists, the court has the following powers, which may be exercised directly or through a conservator:

(1) with respect to a minor for reasons of age, all the powers over the estate and business affairs of the minor which may be necessary for the best interest of the minor and members of the minor's immediate family; and

(2) with respect to an adult, or to a minor for reasons other than age, for the benefit of the protected person and individuals who are in fact dependent on the protected person for support, all the powers over the estate and business affairs of the protected person which the person could exercise if the person were an adult, present, and not under conservatorship or other protective order.

(b) Subject to Section 5-110 requiring endorsement of limitations on the letters of office, the court may limit at any time the powers of a conservator otherwise conferred and may remove or modify any limitation.

§ 5-411. Required Court Approval

(a) After notice to interested persons and upon express authorization of the court, a conservator may:

(1) make gifts, except as otherwise provided in Section 5-427(b);

(2) convey, release, or disclaim contingent and expectant interests in property, including marital property rights and any right of survivorship incident to joint tenancy or tenancy by the entireties;

(3) exercise or release a power of appointment;

(4) create a revocable or irrevocable trust of property of the estate, whether or not the trust extends beyond the duration of the conservatorship, or revoke or amend a trust revocable by the protected person;

(5) exercise rights to elect options and change beneficiaries under insurance policies and annuities or surrender the policies and annuities for their cash value;

(6) exercise any right to an elective share in the estate of the protected person's deceased spouse and to renounce or disclaim any interest by testate or intestate succession or by transfer inter vivos; and

(7) make, amend, or revoke the protected person's will.

(b) A conservator, in making, amending, or revoking the protected person's will, shall comply with [the state's statute for executing wills].

(c) The court, in exercising or in approving a conservator's exercise of the powers listed in subsection (a), shall consider primarily the decision that the protected person would have made, to the extent that the decision can be ascertained. The court shall also consider:

(1) the financial needs of the protected person and the needs of individuals who are in fact dependent on the protected person for support and the interest of creditors;

(2) possible reduction of income, estate, inheritance, or other tax liabilities;

(3) eligibility for governmental assistance;

(4) the protected person's previous pattern of giving or level of support;

(5) the existing estate plan;

(6) the protected person's life expectancy and the probability that the conservatorship will terminate before the protected person's death; and

(7) any other factors the court considers relevant.

(d) Without authorization of the court, a conservator may not revoke or amend a durable power of attorney of which the protected person is the principal. If a durable power of attorney is in effect, absent a court order to the contrary, a decision of the agent takes precedence over that of a conservator.

§ 5-412. Protective Arrangements and Single Transactions

(a) If a basis is established for a protective order with respect to an individual, the court, without appointing a conservator, may:

(1) authorize, direct, or ratify any transaction necessary or desirable to achieve any arrangement for security, service, or care meeting the foreseeable needs of the protected person, including:

(A) payment, delivery, deposit, or retention of funds or property;

(B) sale, mortgage, lease, or other transfer of property;

(C) purchase of an annuity;

(D) making a contract for life care, deposit contract, or contract for training and education; or

(E) addition to or establishment of a suitable trust[, including a trust created under the Uniform Custodial Trust Act (1987)]; and

(2) authorize, direct, or ratify any other contract, trust, will, or transaction relating to the protected person's property and business affairs, including a settlement of a claim, upon determining that it is in the best interest of the protected person.

(b) In deciding whether to approve a protective arrangement or other transaction under this section, the court shall consider the factors described in Section 5-411(c).

(c) The court may appoint a [master] to assist in the accomplishment of any protective arrangement or other transaction authorized under this section. The [master] has the authority conferred by the order and shall serve until discharged by order after report to the court.

§ 5-413. Who May Be Conservator: Priorities

(a) Except as otherwise provided in subsection (d), the court, in appointing a conservator, shall consider persons otherwise qualified in the following order of priority:

(1) a conservator, guardian of the estate, or other like fiduciary appointed or recognized by an appropriate court of any other jurisdiction in which the protected person resides;

(2) a person nominated as conservator by the respondent, including the respondent's most recent nomination made in a durable power of attorney, if the respondent has attained 14 years of age and at the time of the nomination had sufficient capacity to express a preference;

(3) an agent appointed by the respondent to manage the respondent's property under a durable power of attorney;

(4) the spouse of the respondent;

(5) an adult child of the respondent;

(6) a parent of the respondent; and

(7) an adult with whom the respondent has resided for more than six months before the filing of the petition.

(b) A person having priority under subsection (a)(1), (4), (5), or (6) may designate in writing a substitute to serve instead and thereby transfer the priority to the substitute.

(c) With respect to persons having equal priority, the court shall select the one it considers best qualified. The court, acting in the best interest of the protected person, may decline to appoint a person having priority and appoint a person having a lower priority or no priority.

(d) An owner, operator, or employee of [a long-term care institution] at which the respondent is receiving care may not be appointed as conservator unless related to the respondent by blood, marriage, or adoption.

§ 5-414. Petition for Order Subsequent to Appointment

(a) A protected person or a person interested in the welfare of a protected person may file a petition in the appointing court for an order:

(1) requiring bond or collateral or additional bond or collateral, or reducing bond;

(2) requiring an accounting for the administration of the protected person's estate;

(3) directing distribution;

(4) removing the conservator and appointing a temporary or successor conservator;

(5) modifying the type of appointment or powers granted to the conservator if the extent of protection or management previously granted is currently excessive or insufficient or the protected person's ability to manage the estate and business affairs has so changed as to warrant the action; or

(6) granting other appropriate relief.

(b) A conservator may petition the appointing court for instructions concerning fiduciary responsibility.

(c) Upon notice and hearing the petition, the court may give appropriate instructions and make any appropriate order.

§ 5-415. Bond.
The court may require a conservator to furnish a bond conditioned upon faithful discharge of all duties of the conservatorship according to law, with sureties as it may specify. Unless otherwise directed by the court, the bond must be in the amount of the aggregate capital value of the property of the estate in the conservator's control, plus one year's estimated income, and minus the value of assets deposited under arrangements requiring an order of the court for their removal and the value of any real property that the fiduciary, by express limitation, lacks power to sell or convey without court authorization. The court, in place of sureties on a bond, may accept collateral for the performance of the bond, including a pledge of securities or a mortgage of real property.

§ 5-416. Terms and Requirements of Bond

(a) The following rules apply to any bond required:

(1) Except as otherwise provided by the terms of the bond, sureties and the conservator are jointly and severally liable.

(2) By executing the bond of a conservator, a surety submits to the jurisdiction of the court that issued letters to the primary obligor in any proceeding pertaining to the fiduciary duties of the conservator in which the surety is named as a party. Notice of any proceeding must be sent or delivered to the surety at the address shown in the court records at the place where the bond is filed and to any other address then known to the petitioner.

(3) On petition of a successor conservator or any interested person, a proceeding may be brought against a surety for breach of the obligation of the bond of the conservator.

(4) The bond of the conservator may be proceeded against until liability under the bond is exhausted.

(b) A proceeding may not be brought against a surety on any matter as to which an action or proceeding against the primary obligor is barred.

§ 5-417. **Compensation and Expenses.** If not otherwise compensated for services rendered, a guardian, conservator, lawyer for the respondent, lawyer whose services resulted in a protective order or in an order beneficial to a protected person's estate, or any other person appointed by the court is entitled to reasonable compensation from the estate. Compensation may be paid and expenses reimbursed without court order. If the court determines that the compensation is excessive or the expenses are inappropriate, the excessive or inappropriate amount must be repaid to the estate.

§ 5-418. General Duties of Conservator; Plan

(a) A conservator, in relation to powers conferred by this [part] or implicit in the title acquired by virtue of the proceeding, is a fiduciary and shall observe the standards of care applicable to a trustee.

(b) A conservator may exercise authority only as necessitated by the limitations of the protected person, and to the extent possible, shall encourage the person to participate in decisions, act in the person's own behalf, and develop or regain the ability to manage the person's estate and business affairs.

(c) Within 60 days after appointment, a conservator shall file with the appointing court a plan for protecting, managing, expending, and distributing the assets of the protected person's estate. The plan must be based on the actual needs of the person and take into consideration the best interest of the person. The conservator shall include in the plan steps to develop or restore the person's ability to manage the person's property, an estimate of the duration of the conservatorship, and projections of expenses and resources.

(d) In investing an estate, selecting assets of the estate for distribution, and invoking powers of revocation or withdrawal available for the use and benefit of the protected person and exercisable by the conservator, a conservator shall take into account any estate plan of the person known to the conservator and may examine the will and any other donative, nominative, or other appointive instrument of the person.

§ 5-419. Inventory; Records

(a) Within 60 days after appointment, a conservator shall prepare and file with the appointing court a detailed inventory of the estate subject to the conservatorship, together with an oath or affirmation that the inventory is believed to be complete and accurate as far as information permits.

(b) A conservator shall keep records of the administration of the estate and make them available for examination on reasonable request of an interested person.

§ 5-420. Reports; Appointment of [Visitor]; Monitoring

(a) A conservator shall report to the court for administration of the estate annually unless the court otherwise directs, upon resignation or removal, upon termination of the conservatorship, and at other times as the court directs. An order, after notice and hearing, allowing an intermediate report of a conservator adjudicates liabilities concerning the matters adequately disclosed in the accounting. An order, after notice and hearing, allowing a final report adjudicates all previously unsettled liabilities relating to the conservatorship.

(b) A report must state or contain:

(1) a list of the assets of the estate under the conservator's control and a list of the receipts, disbursements, and distributions during the period for which the report is made;

(2) a list of the services provided to the protected person; and

(3) any recommended changes in the plan for the conservatorship as well as a recommendation

as to the continued need for conservatorship and any recommended changes in the scope of the conservatorship.

(c) The court may appoint a [visitor] to review a report or plan, interview the protected person or conservator, and make any other investigation the court directs. In connection with a report, the court may order a conservator to submit the assets of the estate to an appropriate examination to be made in a manner the court directs.

(d) The court shall establish a system for monitoring conservatorships, including the filing and review of conservators' reports and plans.

§ 5-421. Title by Appointment

(a) The appointment of a conservator vests title in the conservator as trustee to all property of the protected person, or to the part thereof specified in the order, held at the time of appointment or thereafter acquired. An order vesting title in the conservator to only a part of the property of the protected person creates a conservatorship limited to assets specified in the order.

(b) Letters of conservatorship are evidence of vesting title of the protected person's assets in the conservator. An order terminating a conservatorship transfers title to assets remaining subject to the conservatorship, including any described in the order, to the formerly protected person or the person's successors.

(c) Subject to the requirements of other statutes governing the filing or recordation of documents of title to land or other property, letters of conservatorship and orders terminating conservatorships may be filed or recorded to give notice of title as between the conservator and the protected person.

§ 5-422. Protected Person's Interest Inalienable

(a) Except as otherwise provided in subsections (c) and (d), the interest of a protected person in property vested in a conservator is not transferable or assignable by the protected person. An attempted transfer or assignment by the protected person, although ineffective to affect property rights, may give rise to a claim against the protected person for restitution or damages which, subject to presentation and allowance, may be satisfied as provided in Section 5-429.

(b) Property vested in a conservator by appointment and the interest of the protected person in that property are not subject to levy, garnishment, or similar process for claims against the protected person unless allowed under Section 5-429.

(c) A person without knowledge of the conservatorship who in good faith and for security or substantially equivalent value receives delivery from a protected person of tangible personal property of a type normally transferred by delivery of possession, is protected as if the protected person or transferee had valid title.

(d) A third party who deals with the protected person with respect to property vested in a conservator is entitled to any protection provided in other law.

§ 5-423. Sale, Encumbrance, or Other Transaction Involving Conflict of Interest.

Any transaction involving the conservatorship estate which is affected by a substantial conflict between the conservator's fiduciary and personal interests is voidable unless the transaction is expressly authorized by the court after notice to interested persons. A transaction affected by a substantial conflict between personal and fiduciary interests includes any sale, encumbrance, or other transaction involving the conservatorship estate entered into by the conservator, the spouse, descendant, agent, or lawyer of a conservator, or a corporation or other enterprise in which the conservator has a substantial beneficial interest.

§ 5-424. Protection of Person Dealing with Conservator

(a) A person who assists or deals with a conservator in good faith and for value in any transaction other than one requiring a court order under Section 5-410 or 5-411 is protected as though the conservator properly exercised the power. That a person knowingly deals with a conservator does not alone require the person to inquire into the existence of a power or the propriety of its exercise, but restrictions on powers of conservators which are endorsed on letters as provided in Section 5-110 are effective as to third persons. A person who pays or delivers assets to a conservator is not responsible for their proper application.

(b) Protection provided by this section extends to any procedural irregularity or jurisdictional defect that occurred in proceedings leading to the issuance of letters and is not a substitute for protection provided to persons assisting or dealing with a conservator by comparable provisions in other law relating to commercial transactions or to simplifying transfers of securities by fiduciaries.

§ 5-425. Powers of Conservator in Administration

(a) Except as otherwise qualified or limited by the court in its order of appointment and endorsed on the letters, a conservator has all of the powers granted in this section and any additional powers granted by law to a trustee in this state.

(b) A conservator, acting reasonably and in an effort to accomplish the purpose of the appointment, and without further court authorization or confirmation, may:

(1) collect, hold, and retain assets of the estate, including assets in which the conservator has a personal interest and real property in another state, until the conservator considers that disposition of an asset should be made;

(2) receive additions to the estate;

(3) continue or participate in the operation of any business or other enterprise;

(4) acquire an undivided interest in an asset of the estate in which the conservator, in any fiduciary capacity, holds an undivided interest;

(5) invest assets of the estate as though the conservator were a trustee;

(6) deposit money of the estate in a financial institution, including one operated by the conservator;

(7) acquire or dispose of an asset of the estate, including real property in another state, for cash or on credit, at public or private sale, and manage, develop, improve, exchange, partition, change the character of, or abandon an asset of the estate;

(8) make ordinary or extraordinary repairs or alterations in buildings or other structures, demolish any improvements, and raze existing or erect new party walls or buildings;

(9) subdivide, develop, or dedicate land to public use, make or obtain the vacation of plats and adjust boundaries, adjust differences in valuation or exchange or partition by giving or receiving considerations, and dedicate easements to public use without consideration;

(10) enter for any purpose into a lease as lessor or lessee, with or without option to purchase or renew, for a term within or extending beyond the term of the conservatorship;

(11) enter into a lease or arrangement for exploration and removal of minerals or other natural resources or enter into a pooling or unitization agreement;

(12) grant an option involving disposition of an asset of the estate and take an option for the acquisition of any asset;

(13) vote a security, in person or by general or limited proxy;

(14) pay calls, assessments, and any other sums chargeable or accruing against or on account of securities;

(15) sell or exercise stock subscription or conversion rights;

(16) consent, directly or through a committee or other agent, to the reorganization, consolidation, merger, dissolution, or liquidation of a corporation or other business enterprise;

(17) hold a security in the name of a nominee or in other form without disclosure of the conservatorship so that title to the security may pass by delivery;

(18) insure the assets of the estate against damage or loss and the conservator against liability with respect to a third person;

(19) borrow money, with or without security, to be repaid from the estate or otherwise and advance money for the protection of the estate or the protected person and for all expenses, losses, and liability sustained in the administration of the estate or because of the holding or ownership of any assets, for which the conservator has a lien on the estate as against the protected person for advances so made;

(20) pay or contest any claim, settle a claim by or against the estate or the protected person by compromise, arbitration, or otherwise, and release, in whole or in part, any claim belonging to the estate to the extent the claim is uncollectible;

(21) pay taxes, assessments, compensation of the conservator and any guardian, and other expenses incurred in the collection, care, administration, and protection of the estate;

(22) allocate items of income or expense to income or principal of the estate, as provided by other law, including creation of reserves out of income for depreciation, obsolescence, or amortization or for depletion of minerals or other natural resources;

(23) pay any sum distributable to a protected person or individual who is in fact dependent on the protected person by paying the sum to the distributee or by paying the sum for the use of the distributee:

(A) to the guardian of the distributee;

(B) to a distributee's custodian under [the Uniform Transfers to Minors Act (1983/1986)] or custodial trustee under [the Uniform Custodial Trust Act (1987)]; or

(C) if there is no guardian, custodian, or custodial trustee, to a relative or other person having physical custody of the distributee;

(24) prosecute or defend actions, claims, or proceedings in any jurisdiction for the protection of assets of the estate and of the conservator in the performance of fiduciary duties; and

(25) execute and deliver all instruments that will accomplish or facilitate the exercise of the powers vested in the conservator.

§ 5-426. Delegation

(a) A conservator may not delegate to an agent or another conservator the entire administration of the estate, but a conservator may otherwise delegate the performance of functions that a prudent trustee of comparable skills may delegate under similar circumstances.

(b) The conservator shall exercise reasonable care, skill, and caution in:

(1) selecting an agent;

(2) establishing the scope and terms of a delegation, consistent with the purposes and terms of the conservatorship;

(3) periodically reviewing an agent's overall performance and compliance with the terms of the delegation; and

(4) redressing an action or decision of an agent which would constitute a breach of trust if performed by the conservator.

(c) A conservator who complies with subsections (a) and (b) is not liable to the protected person or to the estate for the decisions or actions of the agent to whom a function was delegated.

(d) In performing a delegated function, an agent shall exercise reasonable care to comply with the terms of the delegation.

(e) By accepting a delegation from a conservator subject to the law of this state, an agent submits to the jurisdiction of the courts of this state.

§ 5-427. Principles of Distribution by Conservator

(a) Unless otherwise specified in the order of appointment and endorsed on the letters of appointment or contrary to the plan filed pursuant to Section 5-418, a conservator may expend or distribute income or principal of the estate of the protected person without further court authorization or confirmation for the support, care, education, health, and welfare of the protected person and individuals who are in fact dependent on the protected person, including the payment of child or spousal support, in accordance with the following rules:

(1) A conservator shall consider recommendations relating to the appropriate standard of support, care, education, health, and welfare for the protected person or an individual who is in fact dependent on the protected person made by a guardian, if any, and, if the protected person is a minor, the conservator shall consider recommendations made by a parent.

(2) A conservator may not be surcharged for money paid to persons furnishing support, care, education, or benefit to a protected person, or an individual who is in fact dependent on the protected person, in accordance with the recommendations of a parent or guardian of the protected person unless the conservator knows that the parent or guardian derives personal financial benefit therefrom, including relief from any personal duty of support, or the recommendations are not in the best interest of the protected person.

(3) In making distributions under this subsection, the conservator shall consider:

(A) the size of the estate, the estimated duration of the conservatorship, and the likelihood that the protected person, at some future time, may be fully self-sufficient and able to manage business affairs and the estate;

(B) the accustomed standard of living of the protected person and individuals who are in fact dependent on the protected person; and

(C) other money or sources used for the support of the protected person.

(4) Money expended under this subsection may be paid by the conservator to any person, including the protected person, as reimbursement for expenditures that the conservator might have made, or in advance for services to be rendered to the protected person if it is reasonable to expect the services will be performed and advance payments are customary or reasonably necessary under the circumstances.

(b) If an estate is ample to provide for the distributions authorized by subsection (a), a conservator for a protected person other than a minor may make gifts that the protected person might have been expected to make, in amounts that do not exceed in the aggregate for any calendar year 20 percent of the income of the estate in that year.

§ 5-428. Death of Protected Person

[(a)] If a protected person dies, the conservator shall deliver to the court for safekeeping any will of the protected person which may have come into the conservator's possession, inform the personal representative or beneficiary named in the will of the delivery, and retain the estate for delivery to the personal representative of the decedent or to another person entitled to it.

[(b) If a personal representative has not been appointed within 40 days after the death of a protected person and an application or petition for appointment is not before the court, the conservator may apply to exercise the powers and duties of a personal representative in order to administer and distribute the decedent's estate. Upon application for an order conferring upon the conservator the powers of a personal representative, after notice given by the conservator to any person nominated as personal representative by any will of which the applicant is aware, the court may grant the application upon determining that there is no objection and endorse the letters of conservatorship to note that the formerly protected person is deceased and that the conservator has acquired all of the powers and duties of a personal representative.

(c) The issuance of an order under this section has the effect of an order of appointment of a personal representative [as provided in Section 3-308 and [Parts] 6 through 10 of [Article] III]. However, the estate in the name of the conservator, after administration, may be distributed to the decedent's successors without retransfer to the conservator as personal representative.]

§ 5-429. Presentation and Allowance of Claims

(a) A conservator may pay, or secure by encumbering assets of the estate, claims against the estate or against the protected person arising before or during the conservatorship upon their presentation and allowance in accordance with the priorities stated in subsection (d). A claimant may present a claim by:

(1) sending or delivering to the conservator a written statement of the claim, indicating its basis, the name and address of the claimant, and the amount claimed; or

(2) filing a written statement of the claim, in a form acceptable to the court, with the clerk of court and sending or delivering a copy of the statement to the conservator.

(b) A claim is deemed presented on receipt of the written statement of claim by the conservator or the filing of the claim with the court, whichever first occurs. A presented claim is allowed if it is not disallowed by written statement sent or delivered by the conservator to the claimant within 60 days after its presentation. The conservator before payment may change an allowance to a disallowance in whole or in part, but not after allowance under a court order or judgment or an order directing payment of the claim. The presentation of a claim tolls the running of any statute of limitations relating to the claim until 30 days after its disallowance.

(c) A claimant whose claim has not been paid may petition the court for determination of the claim at any time before it is barred by a statute of limitations and, upon due proof, procure an order for its allowance, payment, or security by encumbering assets of the estate. If a proceeding is pending against a protected person at the time of appointment of a conservator or is initiated against the protected person thereafter, the moving party shall give to the conservator notice of any proceeding that could result in creating a claim against the estate.

(d) If it appears that the estate is likely to be exhausted before all existing claims are paid, the conservator shall distribute the estate in money or in kind in payment of claims in the following order:

(1) costs and expenses of administration;

(2) claims of the federal or state government having priority under other law;

(3) claims incurred by the conservator for support, care, education, health, and welfare previously provided to the protected person or individuals who are in fact dependent on the protected person;

(4) claims arising before the conservatorship; and

(5) all other claims.

(e) Preference may not be given in the payment of a claim over any other claim of the same class, and a claim due and payable may not be preferred over a claim not due.

(f) If assets of the conservatorship are adequate to meet all existing claims, the court, acting in the best interest of the protected person, may order the conservator to grant a security interest in the conservatorship estate for the payment of any or all claims at a future date.

§ 5-430. Personal Liability of Conservator

(a) Except as otherwise agreed, a conservator is not personally liable on a contract properly entered into in a fiduciary capacity in the course of administration of the estate unless the conservator fails to reveal in the contract the representative capacity and identify the estate.

(b) A conservator is personally liable for obligations arising from ownership or control of property of the estate or for other acts or omissions occurring in the course of administration of the estate only if personally at fault.

(c) Claims based on contracts entered into by a conservator in a fiduciary capacity, obligations arising from ownership or control of the estate, and claims based on torts committed in the course of administration of the estate may be asserted against the estate by proceeding against the conservator in a fiduciary capacity, whether or not the conservator is personally liable therefor.

(d) A question of liability between the estate and the conservator personally may be determined in a proceeding for accounting, surcharge, or indemnification, or in another appropriate proceeding or action.

[(e) A conservator is not personally liable for any environmental condition on or injury resulting from any environmental condition on land solely by reason of an acquisition of title under Section 5-421.]

§ 5-431. Termination of Proceedings

(a) A conservatorship terminates upon the death of the protected person or upon order of the court. Unless created for reasons other than that the protected person is a minor, a conservatorship created for a minor also terminates when the protected person attains majority or is emancipated.

(b) Upon the death of a protected person, the conservator shall conclude the administration of the estate by distribution to the person's successors. The conservator shall file a final report and petition for discharge within [30] days after distribution.

(c) On petition of a protected person, a conservator, or another person interested in a protected person's welfare, the court may terminate the conservatorship if the protected person no longer needs the assistance or protection of a conservator. Termination of the conservatorship does not affect a conservator's liability for previous acts or the obligation to account for funds and assets of the protected person.

(d) Except as otherwise ordered by the court for good cause, before terminating a conservatorship, the court shall follow the same procedures to safeguard the rights of the protected person that apply to a petition for conservatorship. Upon the establishment of a prima facie case for termination, the court shall order termination unless it is proved that continuation of the conservatorship is in the best interest of the protected person.

(e) Upon termination of a conservatorship and whether or not formally distributed by the conservator, title to assets of the estate passes to the formerly protected person or the person's successors. The order of termination must provide for expenses of administration and direct the conservator to execute appropriate instruments to evidence the transfer of title or confirm a distribution previously made and to file a final report and a petition for discharge upon approval of the final report.

(f) The court shall enter a final order of discharge upon the approval of the final report and satisfaction by the conservator of any other conditions placed by the court on the conservator's discharge.

§ 5-432. Registration of Guardianship Orders.
If a guardian has been appointed in another state and a petition for the appointment of a guardian is not pending in this state, the guardian appointed in

the other state, after giving notice to the appointing court of an intent to register, may register the guardianship order in this state by filing as a foreign judgment in a court, in any appropriate [county] of this state, certified copies of the order and letters of office.

§ 5-433. Registration of Protective Orders. If a conservator has been appointed in another state and a petition for a protective order is not pending in this state, the conservator appointed in the other state, after giving notice to the appointing court of an intent to register, may register the protective order in this state by filing as a foreign judgment in a court of this state, in any [county] in which property belonging to the protected person is located, certified copies of the order and letters of office and of any bond.

§ 5-434. Effect of Registration.

(a) Upon registration of a guardianship or protective order from another state, the guardian or conservator may exercise in this state all powers authorized in the order of appointment except as prohibited under the laws of this state, including maintaining actions and proceedings in this state and, if the guardian or conservator is not a resident of this state, subject to any conditions imposed upon nonresident parties.

(b) A court of this state may grant any relief available under this [article] and other law of this state to enforce a registered order.

ARTICLE 5A
UNIFORM ADULT GUARDIANSHIP AND PROTECTIVE PROCEEDINGS JURISDICTION ACT (2007)

PART 1
GENERAL PROVISIONS

PART 2
JURISDICTION

PART 3
TRANSFER OF GUARDIANSHIP OR CONSERVATORSHIP

PART 4
REGISTRATION AND RECOGNITION OF ORDERS FROM OTHER STATES

Prefatory Note

The Uniform Guardianship and Protective Proceedings Act (UGPPA), which was last revised in 1997 and which is codified at Article V, is a comprehensive act addressing all aspects of guardianships and protective proceedings for both minors and adults. The Uniform Adult Guardianship and Protective Proceedings Jurisdiction Act (UAGPPJA) has a much narrower scope, dealing only with jurisdiction and related issues in adult proceedings. Drafting of the UAGPPJA began in 2005. The Act had its first reading at the Uniform Law Commission's 2006 Annual Meeting, and was approved at the 2007 Annual Meeting.

States may enact the UAGPPJA either separately or as part of the broader UGPPA or the even broader Uniform Probate Code (UPC), of which the UGPPA and UAGPPJA form a part.

The Problem of Multiple Jurisdiction. Because the United States has 50 plus guardianship systems, problems of determining jurisdiction are frequent. Questions of which state has jurisdiction to appoint a guardian or conservator can arise between an American state and another country. But more frequently, problems arise because the individual has contacts with more than one American state.

In nearly all American states, a guardian may be appointed by a court in a state in which the individual is domiciled or is physically present. In nearly all American states, a conservator may be appointed by a court in a state in which the individual is domiciled or has property. Contested cases in which courts in more than one state have jurisdiction are becoming more frequent. Sometimes these cases arise because the adult is physically located in a state other than the adult's domicile. Sometimes the case arises because of uncertainty as to the adult's domicile, particularly if the adult owns a second home in another state. There is a need for an effective mechanism for resolving multi-jurisdictional disputes. Part 2 of this article is intended to provide such a mechanism.

The Problem of Transfer. Oftentimes, problems arise even absent a dispute. Even if everyone is agreed that an already existing guardianship or conservatorship should be moved to another state, few states have streamlined procedures for transferring a proceeding to another state or for accepting such a transfer. In most states, all of the procedures for an original appointment must be repeated, a time consuming and expensive prospect. Part 3 of this article is designed to provide an expedited process for making such transfers, thereby avoiding the need to relitigate incapacity and whether the guardian or conservator appointed in the first state was an appropriate selection.

The Problem of Out-of-State Recognition. The Full Faith and Credit Clause of the United States Constitution requires that court orders in one state be honored in another state. But there are exceptions to the full faith and credit doctrine, of which guardianship and protective proceedings is one. Sometimes, guardianship or protective proceedings must be initiated in a second state because of the refusal of financial institutions, care facilities, and the

courts to recognize a guardianship or protective order issued in another state. Part 4 of this article creates a registration procedure. Following registration of the guardianship or protective order in the second state, the guardian may exercise in the second state all powers authorized in the original state's order of appointment except for powers that cannot be legally exercised in the second state.

The Proposed Uniform Law and the Child Custody Analogy. Similar problems of jurisdiction existed for many years in the United States in connection with child custody determinations. If one parent lived in one state and the other parent lived in another state, frequently courts in more than one state had jurisdiction to issue custody orders. But the Uniform Law Conference has approved two uniform acts that have effectively minimized the problem of multiple court jurisdiction in child custody matters; the Uniform Child Custody Jurisdiction Act (UCCJA), approved in 1968, succeeded by the Uniform Child Custody Jurisdiction and Enforcement Act (UCCJEA), approved in 1997. The drafters of the UAGPPJA have elected to model Part 2 and portions of Part 1 of their Act after these child custody analogues. However, the UAGPPJA applies only to adult proceedings. The UAGPPJA is limited to adults in part because most jurisdictional issues involving guardianships for minors are subsumed by the UCCJEA.

The Objectives and Key Concepts of the Proposed UAGPPJA. The UAGPPJA is organized into five articles, the first four of which are codified into Article 5A of the UPC. Part 1 contains definitions and provisions designed to facilitate cooperation between courts in different states. Part 2 is the heart of the Act, specifying which court has jurisdiction to appoint a guardian or conservator or issue another type of protective order and contains definitions applicable only to that part. Its principal objective is to assure that an appointment or order is made or issued in only one state except in cases of emergency or in situations where the individual owns property located in multiple states. Part 3 specifies a procedure for transferring a guardianship or conservatorship proceedings from one state to another state. Part 4 deals with enforcement of guardianship and protective orders in other states. The final article of UAGPPJA, not codified into this article of the UPC, contains an effective date provision, a place to list provisions of existing law to be repealed or amended, and boilerplate provisions common to all uniform acts.

Key Definitions (Section 5A-201). To determine which court has primary jurisdiction under the UAGPPJA, the key factors are to determine the individual's "home state" and "significant-connection state." A "home state" (Section 5A-201(a)(2)) is the state in which the individual was physically present, including any period of temporary absence, for at least six consecutive months immediately before the filing of a petition for a protective order or appointment of a guardian. If the respondent was not physically present in a single state for the six months immediately preceding the filing of the petition, the home state is the place where the respondent was last physically present for at least six months as long a such presence ended within the six months prior to the filing of the petition. Section 5A-201(a)(2). Stated another way, the ability of the home state to appoint a guardian or enter a protective order for an individual continues for up to six months following the individual's physical relocation to another state.

A "significant-connection state," which is a potentially broader concept, means the state in which the individual has a significant connection other than mere physical presence, and where substantial evidence concerning the individual is available. Section 5A-201(a)(3). Factors that may be considered in deciding whether a particular respondent has a significant connection include:

- the location of the respondent's family and others required to be notified of the guardianship or protective proceeding;
- the length of time the respondent was at any time physically present in the state and the duration of any absences;
- the location of the respondent's property; and
- the extent to which the respondent has other ties to the state such as voting registration, filing of state or local tax returns, vehicle registration, driver's license, social relationships, and receipt of services. Section 5A-201(b).

A respondent in a guardianship or protective proceeding may have multiple significant-connection states but will have only one home state.

Jurisdiction (Part 2). Section 5A-203 is the principal provision governing jurisdiction, creating a three-level priority; the home state, followed by a significant-connection state, followed by other jurisdictions:

Home State: The home state has primary jurisdiction to appoint a guardian or conservator or issue another type of protective order.

Significant-connection State: A significant-connection state has jurisdiction to appoint a guardian or conservator or issue another type of protective order if on the date the petition was filed:

- the respondent does not have a home state or the home state has declined jurisdiction on the basis that the significant-connection state is a more appropriate forum; or
- the respondent has a home state, a petition for an appointment or order is not pending in a court of that state or another significant-connection state, and, before the court makes the appointment or issues the order (1) a petition for an appointment or order is not filed in the respondent's home state; (2) an objection to the court's jurisdiction is not filed by a person required to be notified of the proceeding; and (3) the court in this state concludes that it is an appropriate forum under the factors set forth in Section 5A-206.

Another State: A court in another state has jurisdiction if the home state and all significant-connection states have declined jurisdiction because the court in the other state is a more appropriate forum, or the respondent does not have a home state or significant-connection state.

Section 5A-204 addresses special cases. Regardless of whether it has jurisdiction under the general principles stated in Section 5A-203, a court in the state where the respondent is currently physically present has jurisdiction to appoint a guardian in an emergency, and a court in a state where a respondent's real or tangible personal property is located has jurisdiction to appoint a conservator or issue another type of protective order with respect to that property. In addition, a court not otherwise having jurisdiction under Section 5A-203 has jurisdiction to consider a petition to accept the transfer of an already existing guardianship or conservatorship from another state as provided in Part 3.

The remainder of Part 2 elaborates on these core concepts. Section 5A-205 provides that once a guardian or conservator is appointed or other protective order is issued, the court's jurisdiction continues until the proceeding is terminated or transferred or the appointment or order expires by its own terms. Section 5A-206 authorizes a court to decline jurisdiction if it determines that the court of another state is a more appropriate forum, and specifies the factors to be taken into account in making this determination. Section 207 authorizes a court to decline jurisdiction or fashion another appropriate remedy if jurisdiction was acquired because of unjustifiable conduct. Section 5A-208 prescribes additional notice requirements if a proceeding is brought in a state other than the respondent's home state. Section 5A-209 specifies a procedure for resolving jurisdictional issues if petitions are pending in more than one state. The UAGPPJA also includes provisions regarding communication between courts in different states, requests for assistance made by a court to a court of another state, and the taking of testimony in another state. Sections 5A-104 to 5A-106.

Transfer to Another State (Part 3). Part 3 specifies a procedure for transferring an already existing guardianship or conservatorship to another state. To make the transfer, court orders are necessary from both the court transferring the case and from the court accepting the case. The transferring court must find that the incapacitated or protected person is physically present in or is reasonably expected to move permanently to the other state, that adequate arrangements have been made for the person or the person's property in the other state, and that the court is satisfied the case will be accepted by the court in the other state. To assure continuity, the court in the transferring state cannot dismiss the local proceeding until the order from the state accepting the case is filed with the transferring court. To expedite the transfer process, the court in the accepting state must give deference to the transferring court's finding of incapacity and selection of the guardian or conservator. Much of Part 3 is based on the pioneering work of the National Probate Court Standards, a 1993 joint project of the National College of Probate Judges and the National Center for State Courts.

Out of State Enforcement (Part 4). To facilitate enforcement of guardianship and protective orders in other states, Part 4 authorizes a guardian or conservator to register these orders in other states. Upon registration, the guardian or conservator may exercise in the registration state all powers authorized in the order except as prohibited by the laws of the registration state.

International Application (Section 5A-103). Section 5A-103 addresses application of the Act to guardianship and protective orders issued in other countries. A foreign order is not enforceable pursuant to the registration procedures under Part 4, but a court in the United State may otherwise apply the Act as if the foreign country were an American state.

The Problem of Differing Terminology. States differ on terminology for the person appointed by the court to handle the personal and financial affairs of a minor or incapacitated adult. Under the UGPPA and in a majority of American states, a "guardian" is appointed to make decisions regarding the person of an "incapacitated person;" a "conservator" is appointed in a "protective proceeding" to manage the property of a "protected person." But in many states, only a "guardian" is appointed, either a guardian of the person or guardian of the estate, and in a few states, the terms guardian and conservator are used but with different meanings. The UAGPPJA adopts the terminology used in the UGPPA and in a majority of the states. An enacting state that uses a different term than "guardian" or "conservator" for the person appointed by the court or that defines either of these terms differently than does the UGPPA may, but is not encouraged to, substitute its own term or definition. Use of common terms and definitions by states enacting the Act will facilitate resolution of cases involving multiple jurisdictions.

The Drafting Committee was assisted by numerous officially designated advisors and observers, representing an array of organizations. In addition to the American Bar Association advisors listed above, important contributions were made by Sally Hurme of AARP, Terry W. Hammond of the National Guardianship Association, Kathleen T. Whitehead and Shirley B. Whitenack of the National Academy of Elder Law Attorneys, Catherine Anne Seal of the Colorado Bar Association, Kay Farley of the National Center for State Courts, and Robert G. Spector, the Reporter for the Joint Editorial Board for Uniform Family Laws and the Reporter for the Uniform Child Custody Jurisdiction and Enforcement Act (1997).

PART 1
GENERAL PROVISIONS

General Comment

Part 1 contains definitions and general provisions used throughout the Article. Definitions applicable only to Part 2 are found in Section 5A-201. Section 5A-101 is the title, Section 5A-102 contains the definitions, and Sections 5A-103 through 5A-106, the general provisions. Section 5A-103 provides that a court of an enacting state may treat a foreign country as a state for the purpose of applying all portions of the Article other than Part 4, Section 5A-104 addresses communication between courts, Section 5A-105 requests by a court to a court in another state for assistance, and Section 5A-106 the taking of testimony in other states. These Part 1 provisions relating to court communication and assistance are essential tools to assure the effectiveness of the provisions of Part 2 determining jurisdiction and in facilitating transfer of a proceeding to another state as authorized in Part 3.

§ 5A-101. Short Title. This [article] may be cited as the Uniform Adult Guardianship and Protective Proceedings Jurisdiction Act (2007).

§ 5A-102. Definitions. In this [article]:

(1) "Adult" means an individual who has attained [18] years of age.

(2) "Conservator" means a person appointed by the court to administer the property of an adult as provided in [Article] V.

(3) "Guardian" means a person appointed by the court to make decisions regarding the person of an adult as provided in [Article] V.

(4) "Guardianship order" means an order appointing a guardian.

(5) "Guardianship proceeding" means a judicial proceeding in which an order for the appointment of a guardian is sought or has been issued.

(6) "Incapacitated person" means an adult for whom a guardian has been appointed.

(7) "Party" means the respondent, petitioner, guardian, conservator, or any other person allowed by the court to participate in a guardianship or protective proceeding.

(8) "Protected person" means an adult for whom a protective order has been issued.

(9) "Protective order" means an order appointing a conservator or other order related to management of an adult's property.

(10) "Protective proceeding" means a judicial proceeding in which a protective order is sought or has been issued.

(11) "Respondent" means an adult for whom a protective order or the appointment of a guardian is sought.

§ 5A-103. International Application of [Article]. A court of this state may treat a foreign country as if it were a state for the purpose of applying this [part] and [parts] 2 and 3.

§ 5A-104. Communication Between Courts.

[(a)] A court of this state may communicate with a court in another state concerning a proceeding arising under this [article]. The court may allow the parties to participate in the communication. [Except as otherwise provided in subsection (b), the court shall make a record of the communication. The record may be limited to the fact that the communication occurred.

(b) Courts may communicate concerning schedules, calendars, court records, and other administrative matters without making a record.]

§ 5A-105. Cooperation Between Courts.

(a) In a guardianship or protective proceeding in this state, a court of this state may request the appropriate court of another state to do any of the following:

(1) hold an evidentiary hearing;

(2) order a person in that state to produce evidence or give testimony pursuant to procedures of that state;

(3) order that an evaluation or assessment be made of the respondent;

(4) order any appropriate investigation of a person involved in a proceeding;

(5) forward to the court of this state a certified copy of the transcript or other record of a hearing under paragraph (1) or any other proceeding, any evidence otherwise produced under paragraph (2), and any evaluation or assessment prepared in compliance with an order under paragraph (3) or (4);

(6) issue any order necessary to assure the appearance in the proceeding of a person whose presence is necessary for the court to make a determination, including the respondent or the incapacitated or protected person;

(7) issue an order authorizing the release of medical, financial, criminal, or other relevant information in that state, including protected health information as defined in 45 C.F.R. Section 160.103 [, as amended].

(b) If a court of another state in which a guardianship or protective proceeding is pending requests assistance of the kind provided in subsection (a), a court of this state has jurisdiction for the limited purpose of granting the request or making reasonable efforts to comply with the request.

§ 5A-106. Taking Testimony in Another State.

(a) In a guardianship or protective proceeding, in addition to other procedures that may be available, testimony of a witness who is located in another state may be offered by deposition or other means allowable in this state for testimony taken in another state. The court on its own motion may order that the testimony of a witness be taken in another state and may prescribe the manner in which and the terms upon which the testimony is to be taken.

(b) In a guardianship or protective proceeding, a court in this state may permit a witness located in another state to be deposed or to testify by telephone or audiovisual or other electronic means. A court of this state shall cooperate with the court of the other state in designating an appropriate location for the deposition or testimony.

[(c) Documentary evidence transmitted from another state to a court of this state by technological means that do not produce an original writing may not be excluded from evidence on an objection based on the best evidence rule.]

PART 2
JURISDICTION

General Comment

The jurisdictional rules in Part 2 will determine which state's courts may appoint a guardian or conservator or issue another type of protective order. Section 5A-201 contains definitions of "emergency," "home state," and "significant-connection state," terms used only in Part 2 that are key to understanding the jurisdictional rules under the Article. Section 5A-202 provides that Part 2 is the exclusive jurisdictional basis for a court of the enacting state to appoint a guardian or issue a protective order for an adult. Consequently, Part 2 is applicable even if all of the respondent's significant contacts are in-state. Section 5A-203 is the principal provision governing jurisdiction, creating a three-level priority; the home state, followed by a significant-connection state, followed by other jurisdictions. But there are circumstances under Section 5A-203 where a significant-connection state may have jurisdiction even if the respondent also has a home state, or a state that is neither a home or significant-connection state may be able to assume jurisdiction even though the particular respondent has both a home state and one or more significant-connection states. One of these situations is if a state declines to exercise jurisdiction under Section 5A-206 because a court of that state concludes that a court of another state is a more appropriate forum. Another is Section 5A-207, which authorizes a court to decline jurisdiction or fashion another appropriate remedy if jurisdiction was acquired because of unjustifiable conduct. Section 5A-205 provides that once an appointment is made or order issued, the court's jurisdiction continues until the proceeding is terminated or the appointment or order expires by its own terms.

Section 5A-204 addresses special cases. Regardless of whether it has jurisdiction under the general principles state in Section 5A-203, a court in the state where the individual is currently physically present has jurisdiction to appoint a guardian in an emergency, and a court in a state where an individual's real or tangible personal property is located has jurisdiction to appoint a conservator or issue another type of protective order with respect to that property. In addition, a court not otherwise having jurisdiction under Section 5A-203 has jurisdiction to consider a petition to accept the transfer of an already existing guardianship or conservatorship from another state as provided in Part 3.

The remainder of Part 2 addresses procedural issues. Section 5A-208 prescribes additional notice requirements if a proceeding is brought in a state other than the respondent's home state. Section 5A-209 specifies a procedure for resolving jurisdictional issues if petitions are pending in more than one state.

§ 5A-201. Definitions; Significant Connection Factors.

(a) In this [part]:

(1) "Emergency" means a circumstance that likely will result in substantial harm to a respondent's health, safety, or welfare, and for which the appointment of a guardian is necessary because no other person has authority and is willing to act on the respondent's behalf;

(2) "Home state" means the state in which the respondent was physically present, including any period of temporary absence, for at least six consecutive months immediately before the filing of a petition for a protective order or the appointment of a guardian; or if none, the state in which the respondent was physically present, including any period of temporary absence, for at least six consecutive months ending within the six months prior to the filing of the petition.

(3) "Significant-connection state" means a state, other than the home state, with which a respondent has a significant connection other than mere physical presence and in which substantial evidence concerning the respondent is available.

(b) In determining under Sections 5A-203 and Section 5A-301(e) whether a respondent has a significant connection with a particular state, the court shall consider:

(1) the location of the respondent's family and other persons required to be notified of the guardianship or protective proceeding;

(2) the length of time the respondent at any time was physically present in the state and the duration of any absence;

(3) the location of the respondent's property; and

(4) the extent to which the respondent has ties to the state such as voting registration, state or local tax return filing, vehicle registration, driver's license, social relationship, and receipt of services.

§ 5A-202. Exclusive Basis.
This [part] provides the exclusive jurisdictional basis for a court of this state to appoint a guardian or issue a protective order for an adult.

§ 5A-203. Jurisdiction.
A court of this state has jurisdiction to appoint a guardian or issue a protective order for a respondent if:

(1) this state is the respondent's home state;

(2) on the date the petition is filed, this state is a significant-connection state and:

(A) the respondent does not have a home state or a court of the respondent's home state has declined to exercise jurisdiction because this state is a more appropriate forum; or

(B) the respondent has a home state, a petition for an appointment or order is not pending in a court of that state or another significant-connection state, and, before the court makes the appointment or issues the order:

(i) a petition for an appointment or order is not filed in the respondent's home state;

(ii) an objection to the court's jurisdiction is not filed by a person required to be notified of the proceeding; and;

(iii) the court in this state concludes that it is an appropriate forum under the factors set forth in Section 5A-206;

(3) this state does not have jurisdiction under either paragraph (1) or (2), the respondent's home state and all significant-connection states have declined to exercise jurisdiction because this state is the more appropriate forum, and jurisdiction in this state is consistent with the constitutions of this state and the United States; or

(4) the requirements for special jurisdiction under Section 5A-204 are met.

§ 5A-204. Special Jurisdiction.

(a) A court of this state lacking jurisdiction under Section 5A-203 has special jurisdiction to do any of the following:

(1) appoint a guardian in an emergency for a term not exceeding [90] days for a respondent who is physically present in this state;

(2) issue a protective order with respect to real or tangible personal property located in this state;

(3) appoint a guardian or conservator for an incapacitated or protected person for whom a provisional order to transfer the proceeding from another state has been issued under procedures similar to Section 5A-301.

(b) If a petition for the appointment of a guardian in an emergency is brought in this state and this state was not the respondent's home state on the date the petition was filed, the court shall dismiss the proceeding at the request of the court of the home state, if any, whether dismissal is requested before or after the emergency appointment.

§ 5A-205. Exclusive and Continuing Jurisdiction.
Except as otherwise provided in Section 5A-204, a court that has appointed a guardian or issued a protective order consistent with this [article] has exclusive and continuing jurisdiction over the proceeding until it is terminated by the court or the appointment or order expires by its own terms.

§ 5A-206. Appropriate Forum.

(a) A court of this state having jurisdiction under Section 5A-203 to appoint a guardian or issue a protective order may decline to exercise its jurisdiction if it determines at any time that a court of another state is a more appropriate forum.

(b) If a court of this state declines to exercise its jurisdiction under subsection (a), it shall either dismiss or stay the proceeding. The court may impose any condition the court considers just and proper, including the condition that a petition for the appointment of a guardian or issuance of a protective order be filed promptly in another state.

(c) In determining whether it is an appropriate forum, the court shall consider all relevant factors, including:

(1) any expressed preference of the respondent;

(2) whether abuse, neglect, or exploitation of the respondent has occurred or is likely to occur and which state could best protect the respondent from the abuse, neglect, or exploitation;

(3) the length of time the respondent was physically present in or was a legal resident of this or another state;

(4) the distance of the respondent from the court in each state;

(5) the financial circumstances of the respondent's estate;

(6) the nature and location of the evidence;

(7) the ability of the court in each state to decide the issue expeditiously and the procedures necessary to present evidence;

(8) the familiarity of the court of each state with the facts and issues in the proceeding; and

(9) if an appointment were made, the court's ability to monitor the conduct of the guardian or conservator.

§ 5A-207. Jurisdiction Declined by Reason of Conduct.

(a) If at any time a court of this state determines that it acquired jurisdiction to appoint a guardian or issue a protective order because of unjustifiable conduct, the court may:

(1) decline to exercise jurisdiction;

(2) exercise jurisdiction for the limited purpose of fashioning an appropriate remedy to ensure the health, safety, and welfare of the respondent or the protection of the respondent's property or prevent a repetition of the unjustifiable conduct, including staying the proceeding until a petition for the appointment of a guardian or issuance of a protective order is filed in a court of another state having jurisdiction; or

(3) continue to exercise jurisdiction after considering:

(A) the extent to which the respondent and all persons required to be notified of the proceedings have acquiesced in the exercise of the court's jurisdiction;

(B) whether it is a more appropriate forum than the court of any other state under the factors set forth in Section 5A-206(c); and

(C) whether the court of any other state would have jurisdiction under factual circumstances in substantial conformity with the jurisdictional standards of Section 5A-203.

(b) If a court of this state determines that it acquired jurisdiction to appoint a guardian or issue a protective order because a party seeking to invoke its jurisdiction engaged in unjustifiable conduct, it may assess against that party necessary and reasonable expenses, including attorney's fees, investigative fees, court costs, communication expenses, witness fees and expenses, and travel expenses. The court may not assess fees, costs, or expenses of any kind against this state or a governmental subdivision, agency, or instrumentality of this state unless authorized by law other than this [article].

§ 5A-208. Notice of Proceeding.

If a petition for the appointment of a guardian or issuance of a protective order is brought in this state and this state was not the respondent's home state on the date the petition was filed, in addition to complying with the notice requirements of this state, notice of the petition must be given to those persons who would be entitled to notice of the petition if a proceeding were brought in the respondent's home state. The notice must be given in the same manner as notice is required to be given in this state.

§ 5A-209. Proceedings in More than One State.

Except for a petition for the appointment of a guardian in an emergency or issuance of a protective order limited to property located in this state under Section 5A-204(a)(1) or (2), if a petition for the appointment of a guardian or issuance of a protective order is filed in this state and in another state and neither petition has been dismissed or withdrawn, the following rules apply:

(1) If the court in this state has jurisdiction under Section 5A-203, it may proceed with the case unless a court in another state acquires jurisdiction under provisions similar to Section 5A-203 before the appointment or issuance of the order.

(2) If the court in this state does not have jurisdiction under Section 5A-203, whether at the time the petition is filed or at any time before the appointment or issuance of the order, the court shall stay the proceeding and communicate with the court in the other state. If the court in the other state has jurisdiction, the court in this state shall dismiss the petition unless the court in the other state determines that the court in this state is a more appropriate forum.

PART 3
TRANSFER OF GUARDIANSHIP OR CONSERVATORSHIP

General Comment

While this part consists of two separate sections, they are part of one integrated procedure. Part 3 authorizes a guardian or conservator to petition the court to transfer the guardianship or conservatorship proceeding to a court of another state. Such a transfer is often appropriate when the incapacitated or protected person has moved or has been placed in a facility in another state, making it impossible for the original court to adequately monitor the proceeding. Part 3 authorizes a transfer of a guardianship, a conservatorship, or both. There is no requirement that both categories of proceeding be administered in the same state.

Section 5A-301 addresses procedures in the transferring state. Section 5A-302 addresses procedures in the accepting state.

A transfer begins with the filing of a petition by the guardian or conservator as provided in Section 5A-301(a). Notice of this petition must be given to the persons who would be entitled to notice were the petition a petition for an original appointment. Section 5A-301(b). A hearing on the petition is required only if requested or on the court's own motion. Section 5A-301(c). Assuming the court in the transferring state is satisfied that the grounds for transfer stated in Section 5A-301(d) (guardianship) or 5A-301(e) (conservatorship) have been met, one of which is that the court is satisfied that the court in the other state will accept the case, the court must issue a provisional order approving the transfer. The transferring court will not issue a final order dismissing the case until, as provided in Section 5A-301(f), it receives a copy of the provisional order from the accepting court accepting the transferred proceeding.

Following issuance of the provisional order by the transferring court, a petition must be filed in the accepting court as provided in Section 5A-302(a). Notice of that petition must be given to those who would be entitled to notice of an original petition for appointment in both the transferring state and in the accepting state. Section 5A-302(b). A hearing must be held only if requested or on the court's own motion. Section 5A-302(c). The court must issue a provisional order accepting the case unless it is established that the transfer would be contrary to the incapacitated or protected person's interests or the guardian or conservator is ineligible for appointment in the accepting state. Section 5A-302(d). The term "interests" as opposed to "best interests" was chosen because of the strong autonomy values in modern guardianship law. Should the court decline the transfer petition, it may consider a separately brought petition for the appointment of a guardian or issuance of a protective order only if the court has a basis for jurisdiction under Sections 5A-203 or 5A-204 other than by reason of the provisional order of transfer. Section 5A-302(h).

The final steps are largely ministerial. Pursuant to Section 5A-301(f), the provisional order from the accepting court must be filed in the transferring court. The transferring court will then issue a final order terminating the proceeding, subject to local requirements such as filing of a final report or account and the release of any bond. Pursuant to Section 5A-302(e), the final order terminating the proceeding in the transferring court must then be filed in the accepting court, which will then convert its provisional order accepting the case into a final order appointing the petitioning guardian or conservator as guardian or conservator in the accepting state.

Because guardianship and conservatorship law and practice will likely differ between the two states, the court in the accepting state must within 90 days after issuance of a final order determine whether the guardianship or conservatorship needs to be modified to conform to the law of the accepting state. Section 5A-302(f). The number "90" is placed in brackets to encourage states to coordinate this time limit with the time limits for other required filings such as guardianship or conservatorship plans. This initial period in the accepting state is also an appropriate time to change the guardian or conservator if there is a more appropriate person to act as guardian or conservator in the accepting state. The drafters specifically did not try to design the procedures in Part 3 for the difficult problems that can arise in connection with a transfer when the guardian or conservator is ineligible to act in the second state, a circumstance that can occur when a financial institution is acting as conservator or a government agency is acting as guardian. Rather, the procedures in Part 3 are designed for the typical case where the guardian or conservator is legally eligible to act in the second state. Should that particular guardian or conservator not be the best person to act in the accepting state, a change of guardian or conservator

can be initiated once the transfer has been secured.

The transfer procedure in this part responds to numerous problems that have arisen in connection with attempted transfers under the existing law of most states. Sometimes a court will dismiss a case on the assumption a proceeding will be brought in another state, but such proceeding is never filed. Sometimes a court will refuse to dismiss a case until the court in the other state accepts the matter, but the court in the other state refuses to consider the petition until the already existing guardianship or conservatorship has been terminated. Oftentimes the court will conclude that it is without jurisdiction to make an appointment until the respondent is physically present in the state, a problem which Section 5A-204(a)(3) addresses by granting a court special jurisdiction to consider a petition to accept a proceeding from another state. But the most serious problem is the need to prove the case in the second state from scratch, including proving the respondent's incapacity and the choice of guardian or conservator. Part 3 eliminates this problem. Section 5A-302(g) requires that the court accepting the case recognize a guardianship or conservatorship order from the other state, including the determination of the incapacitated or protected person's incapacity and the appointment of the guardian or conservator, if otherwise eligible to act in the accepting state.

§ 5A-301. Transfer of Guardianship or Conservatorship to Another State.

(a) A guardian or conservator appointed in this state may petition the court to transfer the guardianship or conservatorship to another state.

(b) Notice of a petition under subsection (a) must be given to the persons that would be entitled to notice of a petition in this state for the appointment of a guardian or conservator.

(c) On the court's own motion or on request of the guardian or conservator, the incapacitated or protected person, or other person required to be notified of the petition, the court shall hold a hearing on a petition filed pursuant to subsection (a).

(d) The court shall issue an order provisionally granting a petition to transfer a guardianship and shall direct the guardian to petition for guardianship in the other state if the court is satisfied that the guardianship will be accepted by the court in the other state and the court finds that:

(1) the incapacitated person is physically present in or is reasonably expected to move permanently to the other state;

(2) an objection to the transfer has not been made or, if an objection has been made, the objector has not established that the transfer would be contrary to the interests of the incapacitated person; and

(3) plans for care and services for the incapacitated person in the other state are reasonable and sufficient.

(e) The court shall issue a provisional order granting a petition to transfer a conservatorship and shall direct the conservator to petition for conservatorship in the other state if the court is satisfied that the conservatorship will be accepted by the court of the other state and the court finds that:

(1) the protected person is physically present in or is reasonably expected to move permanently to the other state, or the protected person has a significant connection to the other state considering the factors in Section 5A-201(b);

(2) an objection to the transfer has not been made or, if an objection has been made, the objector has not established that the transfer would be contrary to the interests of the protected person; and

(3) adequate arrangements will be made for management of the protected person's property.

(f) The court shall issue a final order confirming the transfer and terminating the guardianship or conservatorship upon its receipt of:

(1) a provisional order accepting the proceeding from the court to which the proceeding is to be transferred which is issued under provisions similar to Section 5A-302; and

(2) the documents required to terminate a guardianship or conservatorship in this state.

§ 5A-302. Accepting Guardianship or Conservatorship Transferred from Another State.

(a) To confirm transfer of a guardianship or conservatorship transferred to this state under provisions similar to Section 5A-301, the guardian or conservator must petition the court in this state to accept the guardianship or conservatorship. The petition must include a certified copy of the other state's provisional order of transfer.

(b) Notice of a petition under subsection (a) must be given to those persons that would be entitled to notice if the petition were a petition for the appointment of a guardian or issuance of a protective order in both the transferring state and this state. The notice must be given in the same manner as notice is required to be given in this state.

(c) On the court's own motion or on request of the guardian or conservator, the incapacitated or protected person, or other person required to be notified of the proceeding, the court shall hold a hearing on a petition filed pursuant to subsection (a).

(d) The court shall issue an order provisionally granting a petition filed under subsection (a) unless:

(1) an objection is made and the objector establishes that transfer of the proceeding would be contrary to the interests of the incapacitated or protected person; or

(2) the guardian or conservator is ineligible for appointment in this state.

(e) The court shall issue a final order accepting the proceeding and appointing the guardian or conservator as guardian or conservator in this state upon its receipt from the court from which the proceeding is being transferred of a final order issued under provisions similar to Section 5A-301 transferring the proceeding to this state.

(f) Not later than [90] days after issuance of a final order accepting transfer of a guardianship or conservatorship, the court shall determine whether the guardianship or conservatorship needs to be modified to conform to the law of this state.

(g) In granting a petition under this section, the court shall recognize a guardianship or conservatorship order from the other state, including the determination of the incapacitated or protected person's incapacity and the appointment of the guardian or conservator.

(h) The denial by a court of this state of a petition to accept a guardianship or conservatorship transferred from another state does not affect the ability of the guardian or conservator to seek appointment as guardian or conservator in this state under [insert statutory references to this state's ordinary procedures law for the appointment of guardian or conservator] if the court has jurisdiction to make an appointment other than by reason of the provisional order of transfer.

PART 4
REGISTRATION AND RECOGNITION OF ORDERS FROM OTHER STATES

General Comment

Part 4 is designed to facilitate the enforcement of guardianship and protective orders in other states. This part does not make distinctions among the types of orders that can be enforced. This part is applicable whether the guardianship or conservatorship is full or limited. While some states have expedited procedures for sales of real estate by conservators appointed in other states, few states have enacted statutes dealing with enforcement of guardianship orders, such as when a care facility questions the authority of a guardian appointed in another state. Sometimes, these sorts of refusals necessitate that the proceeding be transferred to the other state or that an entirely new petition be filed, problems that could often be avoided if guardianship and protective orders were entitled to recognition in other states.

Part 4 provides for such recognition. The key concept is registration. Section 5A- 401 provides for registration of guardianship orders, and Section 5A-402 for registration of protective orders. Following registration of the order in the appropriate county of the other state, and after giving notice to the appointing court of the intent to register the order in the other state, Section 5A-403 authorizes the guardian or conservator to thereafter exercise all powers authorized in the order of appointment except as prohibited under the laws of the registering state.

The drafters of the Act concluded that the registration of certified copies provides sufficient protection and that it was not necessary to mandate the filing of authenticated copies.

§ **5A-401. Registration of Guardianship Orders.** If a guardian has been appointed in another state and a petition for the appointment of a guardian is not pending in this state, the guardian appointed in the other state, after giving notice to the appointing court of an intent to register, may register the guardianship order in this state by filing as a foreign judgment in a court, in any appropriate [county] of this state, certified copies of the order and letters of office.

§ **5A-402. Registration of Protective Orders.** If a conservator has been appointed in another state and a petition for a protective order is not pending in this state, the conservator appointed in the other state, after giving notice to the appointing court of an intent to register, may register the protective order in this state by filing as a foreign judgment in a court of this state, in any [county] in which property belonging to the protected person is located, certified copies of the order and letters of office and of any bond.

§ **5A-403. Effect of Registration.**

(a) Upon registration of a guardianship or protective order from another state, the guardian or conservator may exercise in this state all powers authorized in the order of appointment except as prohibited under the laws of this state, including maintaining actions and proceedings in this state and, if the guardian or conservator is not a resident of this state, subject to any conditions imposed upon nonresident parties.

(b) A court of this state may grant any relief available under this [article] and other law of this state to enforce a registered order.

ARTICLE 5B
UNIFORM POWER OF ATTORNEY ACT (2006)

PART 1
GENERAL PROVISIONS

PART 2
AUTHORITY

§ 5B-213. Personal and Family Maintenance.

§ 5B-214. Benefits From Governmental Programs or Civil or Military Service.

§ 5B-215. Retirement Plans.

§ 5B-216. Taxes.

§ 5B-217. Gifts.

PART 3
STATUTORY FORMS

§ 5B-301. Statutory Form Power of Attorney.

§ 5B-302. Agent's Certification.

Prefatory Note

The catalyst for the Uniform Power of Attorney Act (2006) (the "Act") was a national review of state power of attorney legislation. The review revealed growing divergence among states' statutory treatment of powers of attorney. The original Uniform Durable Power of Attorney Act ("Original Act"), last amended in 1987, was at one time followed by all but a few jurisdictions. Despite initial uniformity, the review found that a majority of states had enacted non-uniform provisions to deal with specific matters upon which the Original Act is silent. The topics about which there was increasing divergence included: 1) the authority of multiple agents; 2) the authority of a later-appointed fiduciary or guardian; 3) the impact of dissolution or annulment of the principal's marriage to the agent; 4) activation of contingent powers; 5) the authority to make gifts; and 6) standards for agent conduct and liability. Other topics about which states had legislated, although not necessarily in a divergent manner, included: successor agents, execution requirements, portability, sanctions for dishonor of a power of attorney, and restrictions on authority that has the potential to dissipate a principal's property or alter a principal's estate plan.

A national survey was then conducted by the Joint Editorial Board for Uniform Trust and Estate Acts (JEB) to ascertain whether there was actual divergence of opinion about default rules for powers of attorney or only the lack of a detailed uniform model. The survey was distributed to probate and elder law sections of all state bar associations, to the fellows of the American College of Trust and Estate Counsel, the leadership of the ABA Section of Real Property, Probate and Trust Law and the National Academy of Elder Law Attorneys, as well as to special interest list serves of the ABA Commission on Law and Aging.

Forty-four jurisdictions were represented in the 371 surveys returned.

The survey responses demonstrated a consensus of opinion in excess of seventy percent that a power of attorney statute should:

(1) provide for confirmation that contingent powers are activated;

(2) revoke a spouse-agent's authority upon the dissolution or annulment of the   marriage to the principal;

(3) include a portability provision;

(4) require gift making authority to be expressly stated in the grant of authority;

(5) provide a default standard for fiduciary duties;

(6) permit the principal to alter the default fiduciary standard;

(7) require notice by an agent when the agent is no longer willing or able to act;

(8) include safeguards against abuse by the agent;

(9) include remedies and sanctions for abuse by the agent;

(10) protect the reliance of other persons on a power of attorney; and

(11) include remedies and sanctions for refusal of other persons to honor a power of attorney.

Informed by the review and the survey results, the Conference's drafting process also incorporated input from the American College of Trust and Estate Counsel, the ABA Section of Real Property, Probate and Trust Law, the ABA Commission on Law and Aging, the Joint Editorial Board for Uniform Trust and Estate Acts, the National Conference of Lawyers and Corporate Fiduciaries, the American Bankers Association, AARP, other professional groups, as well as numerous individual lawyers and corporate counsel. As a result of this process, the Act codifies both state legislative trends and collective best practices, and strikes a balance between the need for flexibility and acceptance of an agent's authority and the need to prevent and redress financial abuse.

While the Act contains safeguards for the protection of an incapacitated principal, the Act is primarily a set of default rules that preserve a principal's freedom to choose both the extent of an agent's authority and the principles to govern the agent's conduct. Among the Act's features that enhance drafting flexibility are the statutory definitions of powers in Part 2, which can be incorporated by reference in an individually drafted power of attorney or selected for inclusion on the optional statutory form provided in Part 3. The statutory definitions of enumerated powers are an updated version of those in the Uniform Statutory Form Power of Attorney Act (1988), which the Act supersedes. The national review found that eighteen jurisdictions had adopted some type of statutory form power of attorney. The decision to include a statutory form power of attorney in the Act was based on this trend and the proliferation of power of attorney forms currently available to the public.

Sections 5B-119 and 5B-120 of the Act address the problem of persons refusing to accept an agent's authority. Section 5B-119 provides protection from liability for persons that in good faith accept an acknowledged power of attorney. Section 5B-120 sanctions refusal to accept an acknowledged power of attorney unless the refusal meets limited statutory exceptions. An alternate Section 5B-120 is provided for states that may wish to limit sanctions to refusal of an acknowledged statutory form power of attorney.

In exchange for mandated acceptance of an agent's authority, the Act does not require persons that deal with an agent to investigate the agent or the agent's actions. Instead, safeguards against abuse are provided through heightened requirements for granting authority that could dissipate the principal's property or alter the principal's estate plan (Section 5B-201(a)), provisions that set out the agent's duties and liabilities (Sections 5B-114 and 5B-117) and by specification of the categories of persons that have standing to request judicial review of the agent's conduct (Section 5B-116). The following provides a brief overview of the entire Act.

Overview of the Uniform Power of Attorney Act

The Act consists of 4 articles, of which the first three are codified into this Code as Article 5B, Parts 1, 2, and 3. The basic substance of the Act is located in Parts 1 and 2. Part 3 contains the optional statutory form. Article 4, not codified into this Code, consists primarily of general boilerplate provisions common to all uniform acts.

Part 1 – General Provisions and Definitions – Section 5B-102 lists definitions which are useful in interpretation of the Act. Of particular note is the definition of "incapacity" which replaces the term "disability" used in the Original Act. The definition of "incapacity" is consistent with the standard for appointment of a conservator under Section 401 of the Uniform Guardianship and Protective Proceedings Act (1997) (Section 5-401 of this Code). Another significant change in terminology from the Original Act is the use of "agent" in place of the term "attorney in fact." The term "agent" was also used in the Uniform Statutory Form Power of Attorney Act (1988) and is intended to clarify confusion in the lay public about the meaning of "attorney in fact." Section 5B-103 provides that the Act is to apply broadly to all powers of attorney, but excepts from the Act powers of attorney for health care and certain specialized powers such as those coupled with an interest or dealing with proxy voting.

Another innovation is the default rule in Section 5B-104 that a power of attorney is durable unless it contains express language indicating otherwise. This change from the Original Act reflects the view that most principals prefer their powers of attorney to be durable as a hedge against the need for guardianship. While the Original Act was silent on execution requirements for a power of attorney, Section 5B-105 requires the principal's signature and provides that an acknowledged signature is presumed genuine. Section 5B-106 recognizes military powers of attorney and powers of attorney properly executed in other states or countries, or which were properly executed in the state of enactment prior to the Act's effective date. Section 5B-107 states a choice of law rule for determining the law that governs the meaning and effect of a power of attorney.

Section 5B-108 addresses the relationship of the agent to a later court-appointed fiduciary. The Original Act conferred upon a conservator or other later-appointed fiduciary the same power to revoke or amend the power of attorney as the principal would have had prior to incapacity. In contrast, the Act reserves this power to the court and states that the agent's authority continues until limited, suspended, or terminated by the court. This approach reflects greater deference for the previously expressed preferences of the principal and is consistent with the state legislative trend that has departed from the Original Act.

The default rule for when a power of attorney becomes effective is stated in Section 5B-109. Unless the principal specifies that it is to become effective upon a future date, event, or contingency, the authority of an agent under a power of attorney becomes effective when the power is executed. Section 5B-109 permits the principal to designate who may determine when contingent powers are triggered. If the trigger for contingent powers is the principal's incapacity, Section 5B-109 provides that the person designated to make that determination has the authority to act as the principal's personal representative under the Health Insurance Portability and Accountability Act (HIPAA) for purposes of accessing the principal's health-care information and communicating with the principal's health-care provider. This provision does not, however, confer on the designated person the authority to make health-care decisions for the principal. If the trigger for contingent powers is incapacity but the principal has not designated anyone to make the determination, or the person authorized is unable or unwilling to make the determination, the determination may be made by a physician or licensed psychologist, who must find that the principal's ability to manage property or business affairs is impaired, or by an attorney at law, judge, or appropriate governmental official, who must find that the principal is missing, detained, or unable to return to the United States.

The bases for termination of a power of attorney are covered in Section 5B-110. In response to concerns expressed in the JEB survey, the Act provides as the default rule that authority granted to a principal's spouse is revoked upon the commencement of proceedings for legal separation, marital dissolution or annulment.

Sections 5B-111 through 5B-118 address matters related to the agent, including default rules for coagents and successor agents (Section 5B-111), reimbursement and compensation (Section 5B-112), an agent's acceptance of appointment (Section 5B-113), and the agent's duties (Section 5B-114). Section 5B-115 provides that a principal may lower the standard of liability for agent conduct subject to a minimum level of accountability for actions taken dishonestly, with an improper motive, or with reckless indifference to the purposes of the power of attorney or the best interest of the principal. Section 5B-116

sets out a comprehensive list of persons that may petition the court to review the agent's conduct and Section 5B-117 addresses agent liability. An agent may resign by following the notice procedures described in Section 5B-118.

Sections 5B-119 and 5B-120 are included in the Act to address the frequently reported problem of persons refusing to accept a power of attorney. Section 5B-119 protects persons that in good faith accept an acknowledged power of attorney without actual knowledge that the power of attorney is revoked, terminated, or invalid or that the agent is exceeding or improperly exercising the agent's powers. Subject to statutory exceptions, alternative Sections 5B-120 impose liability for refusal to accept a power of attorney. Alternative A sanctions refusal of an acknowledged power of attorney and Alternative B sanctions only refusal of an acknowledged statutory form power of attorney.

Sections 5B-121 through 5B-123 address the relationship of the Act to other law. Section 5B-121 clarifies that the Act is supplemented by the principles of common law and equity to the extent those principles are not displaced by a specific provision of the Act, and Section 5B-122 further clarifies that the Act is not intended to supersede any law applicable to financial institutions or other entities. With respect to remedies, Section 5B-123 provides that the remedies under the Act are not exclusive and do not abrogate any other cause of action or remedy that may be available under the law of the enacting jurisdiction.

Part 2 – Authority – The Act offers the drafting attorney enhanced flexibility whether drafting an individually tailored power of attorney or using the statutory form. Like the Uniform Statutory Form Power of Attorney Act, Sections 5B-204 through 5B-217 of the Act set forth detailed descriptions of authority relating to subjects such as "real property," "retirement plans," and "taxes," which a principal, pursuant to Section 5B-202, may incorporate in full into the power of attorney either by a reference to the short descriptive term for the subject used in the Act or to the section number. Section 5B-202 further states that a principal may modify in a power of attorney any authority incorporated by reference. The definitions in Part 2 also provide meaning for authority with respect to subjects enumerated on the optional statutory form in Part 3. Section 5B-203 applies to all incorporated authority and grants of general authority, providing further detail on how the authority is to be construed.

Part 2 also addresses concerns about authority that might be used to dissipate the principal's property or alter the principal's estate plan. Section 5B-201(a) lists specific categories of authority that cannot be implied from a grant of general authority, but which may be granted only through express language in the power of attorney. Section 5B-201(b) contains a default rule prohibiting an agent that is not an ancestor, spouse, or descendant of the principal from creating in the agent or in a person to whom the agent owes a legal obligation of support an interest in the principal's property, whether by gift, right of survivorship, beneficiary designation, disclaimer, or otherwise.

Part 3 – Statutory Forms – The optional form in

Article 3 is designed for use by lawyers as well as lay persons. It contains, in plain language, instructions to the principal and agent. Step-by-step prompts are given for designation of the agent and successor agents, and grant of general and specific authority. In the section of the form addressing general authority, the principal must initial the subjects over which the principal wishes to delegate general authority to the agent. In the section of the form addressing specific authority, the Section 5B-201(a) categories of specific authority are listed, preceded by a warning to the principal about the potential consequences of granting such authority to an agent. The principal is instructed to initial only the specific categories of actions that the principal intends to authorize. Part 3 also contains a sample agent certification form.

PART 1
GENERAL PROVISIONS

General Comment

The Uniform Power of Attorney Act (2006) replaces the Uniform Durable Power of Attorney Act (1979/1987), formerly codified at Article V, Part 5 of this Code, and the Uniform Statutory Form Power of Attorney Act (1988), which was not codified in this Code. The primary purpose of the Uniform Durable Power of Attorney Act (1979/1987) was to provide individuals with an inexpensive, non-judicial method of surrogate property management in the event of later incapacity. Two key concepts were introduced by the Uniform Durable Power of Attorney Act: (1) creation of a durable agency—one that survives, or is triggered by, the principal's incapacity, and (2) validation of post-mortem exercise of powers by an agent who acts in good faith and without actual knowledge of the principal's death. The success of the Uniform Durable Power of Attorney Act (1979/1987) is evidenced by the widespread use of durable powers in every jurisdiction, not only for incapacity planning, but also for convenience while the principal retains capacity. However, the limitations of the Uniform Durable Power of Attorney Act (1979/1987) are evidence by the number of states that have supplemented and revised their statutes to address myriad issues upon which the Uniform Durable Power of Attorney Act (1979/1987) is silent. These issues include parameters for the creation and use of powers of attorney as well as guidelines for the principal, the agent, and the person who is asked to

accept the agent's authority. The general provisions and definitions of Article 1 in the Uniform Power of Attorney Act (2006) (Article 5B, Part 1 of this Code) address those issues

In addition to providing greater detail than the Uniform Durable Power of Attorney Act (1979/1987), this Act changes two presumptions in the earlier act: (1) that a power of attorney is not durable unless it contains language to make it durable; and (2) that a later court-appointed fiduciary for the principal has the power to revoke or amend a previously executed power of attorney. Section 5B-104 of this part reverses the non-durability presumption by stating that a power of attorney is durable unless it expressly provides that it is terminated by the incapacity of the principal. Section 5B-108 gives deference to the principal's choice of agent by providing that if a court appoints a fiduciary to manage some or all of the principal's property, the agent's authority continues unless limited, suspended, or terminated by the court.

Although the Act is primarily a default statute, Part 1 also contains rules that govern all powers of attorney subject to the Act. Examples of these rules include imposition of certain minimum fiduciary duties on an agent who has accepted appointment (Section 5B-114(a)), recognition of persons who have standing to request judicial construction of the power of attorney or review of the agent's conduct (Section

5B-116), and protections for persons who accept an acknowledged power of attorney without actual knowledge that the power of attorney or the agent's authority is void, invalid, or terminated, or that the agent is exceeding or improperly exercising the power (Section 5B-119). In contrast with the rules of general application in Part 1, the default provisions are clearly indicated by signals such as "unless the power of attorney otherwise provides,"or "except as otherwise provided in the power of attorney." These signals alert the draftsperson to options for enlarging or limiting the Act's default terms. For example, default provisions in Part 1 state that, unless the power of attorney otherwise provides, the power of attorney is effective immediately (Section 5B-109), coagents may exercise their authority independently (Section 5B-111), and an agent is entitled to reimbursement of expenses reasonably incurred and to reasonable compensation (Section 5B-112).

§ 5B-101. Short Title. This [article] may be cited as the Uniform Power of Attorney Act (2006).

§ 5B-102. Definitions. In this [article]:

(1) "Agent" means a person granted authority to act for a principal under a power of attorney, whether denominated an agent, attorney-in-fact, or otherwise. The term includes an original agent, coagent, successor agent, and a person to which an agent's authority is delegated.

(2) "Durable," with respect to a power of attorney, means not terminated by the principal's incapacity.

(3) "Electronic" means relating to technology having electrical, digital, magnetic, wireless, optical, electromagnetic, or similar capabilities.

(4) "Good faith" means honesty in fact.

(5) "Incapacity" means inability of an individual to manage property or business affairs because the individual:

(A) has an impairment in the ability to receive and evaluate information or make or communicate decisions even with the use of technological assistance; or

(B) is:

(i) missing;

(ii) detained, including incarcerated in a penal system; or

(iii) outside the United States and unable to return.

(6) "Person" means an individual, corporation, business trust, estate, trust, partnership, limited liability company, association, joint venture, public corporation, government or governmental subdivision, agency, or instrumentality, or any other legal or commercial entity.

(7) "Power of attorney" means a writing or other record that grants authority to an agent to act in the place of the principal, whether or not the term power of attorney is used.

(8) "Presently exercisable general power of appointment," with respect to property or a property interest subject to a power of appointment, means power exercisable at the time in question to vest absolute ownership in the principal individually, the principal's estate, the principal's creditors, or the creditors of the principal's estate. The term includes a power of appointment not exercisable until the occurrence of a specified event, the satisfaction of an ascertainable standard, or the passage of a specified period only after the occurrence of the specified event, the satisfaction of the ascertainable standard, or the passage of the specified period. The term does not include a power exercisable in a fiduciary capacity or only by will.

(9) "Principal" means an individual who grants authority to an agent in a power of attorney.

(10) "Property" means anything that may be the subject of ownership, whether real or personal, or legal or equitable, or any interest or right therein.

(11) "Stocks and bonds" means stocks, bonds, mutual funds, and all other types of securities and financial instruments, whether held directly, indirectly, or in any other manner. The term does not

include commodity futures contracts and call or put options on stocks or stock indexes.

§ **5B-103. Applicability.** This [article] applies to all powers of attorney except:

(1) a power to the extent it is coupled with an interest in the subject of the power, including a power given to or for the benefit of a creditor in connection with a credit transaction;

(2) a power to make health-care decisions;

(3) a proxy or other delegation to exercise voting rights or management rights with respect to an entity; and

(4) a power created on a form prescribed by a government or governmental subdivision, agency, or instrumentality for a governmental purpose.

§ **5B-104. Power of Attorney Is Durable.** A power of attorney created under this [article] is durable unless it expressly provides that it is terminated by the incapacity of the principal.

§ **5B-105. Execution of Power of Attorney.** A power of attorney must be signed by the principal or in the principal's conscious presence by another individual directed by the principal to sign the principal's name on the power of attorney. A signature on a power of attorney is presumed to be genuine if the principal acknowledges the signature before a notary public or other individual authorized by law to take acknowledgments.

§ **5B-106. Validity of Power of Attorney.**

(a) A power of attorney executed in this state on or after [the effective date of this [article]] is valid if its execution complies with Section 5B-105.

(b) A power of attorney executed in this state before [the effective date of this [article]] is valid if its execution complied with the law of this state as it existed at the time of execution.

(c) A power of attorney executed other than in this state is valid in this state if, when the power of attorney was executed, the execution complied with:

(1) the law of the jurisdiction that determines the meaning and effect of the power of attorney pursuant to Section 5B-107; or

(2) the requirements for a military power of attorney pursuant to 10 U.S.C. Section 1044b [, as amended].

(d) Except as otherwise provided by statute other than this [article], a photocopy or electronically transmitted copy of an original power of attorney has the same effect as the original.

§ **5B-107. Meaning and Effect of Power of Attorney.** The meaning and effect of a power of attorney is determined by the law of the jurisdiction indicated in the power of attorney and, in the absence of an indication of jurisdiction, by the law of the jurisdiction in which the power of attorney was executed.

§ **5B-108. Nomination of [Conservator or Guardian]; Relation of Agent to Court-appointed Fiduciary.**

(a) In a power of attorney, a principal may nominate a [conservator or guardian] of the principal's estate or [guardian] of the principal's person for consideration by the court if protective proceedings for the principal's estate or person are begun after the principal executes the power of attorney. [Except for good cause shown or disqualification, the court shall make its appointment in accordance with the principal's most recent nomination.]

(b) If, after a principal executes a power of attorney, a court appoints a [conservator or guardian] of the principal's estate or other fiduciary charged with the management of some or all of the principal's property, the agent is accountable to the fiduciary as well as to the principal. [The power of attorney is not terminated and the agent's authority continues unless limited, suspended, or terminated by the court.]

§ 5B-109. When Power of Attorney Effective.

(a) A power of attorney is effective when executed unless the principal provides in the power of attorney that it becomes effective at a future date or upon the occurrence of a future event or contingency.

(b) If a power of attorney becomes effective upon the occurrence of a future event or contingency, the principal, in the power of attorney, may authorize one or more persons to determine in a writing or other record that the event or contingency has occurred.

(c) If a power of attorney becomes effective upon the principal's incapacity and the principal has not authorized a person to determine whether the principal is incapacitated, or the person authorized is unable or unwilling to make the determination, the power of attorney becomes effective upon a determination in a writing or other record by:

(1) a physician [or licensed psychologist] that the principal is incapacitated within the meaning of Section 5B-102(5)(A); or

(2) an attorney at law, a judge, or an appropriate governmental official that the principal is incapacitated within the meaning of Section 5B-102(5)(B).

(d) A person authorized by the principal in the power of attorney to determine that the principal is incapacitated may act as the principal's personal representative pursuant to the Health Insurance Portability and Accountability Act, Sections 1171 through 1179 of the Social Security Act, 42 U.S.C. Section 1320d, [as amended,] and applicable regulations, to obtain access to the principal's health-care information and communicate with the principal's health-care provider.

§ 5B-110. Termination of Power of Attorney or Agent's Authority.

(a) A power of attorney terminates when:
(1) the principal dies;
(2) the principal becomes incapacitated, if the power of attorney is not durable;
(3) the principal revokes the power of attorney;
(4) the power of attorney provides that it terminates;
(5) the purpose of the power of attorney is accomplished; or
(6) the principal revokes the agent's authority or the agent dies, becomes incapacitated, or resigns, and the power of attorney does not provide for another agent to act under the power of attorney.

(b) An agent's authority terminates when:
(1) the principal revokes the authority;
(2) the agent dies, becomes incapacitated, or resigns;
(3) an action is filed for the [dissolution] or annulment of the agent's marriage to the principal or their legal separation, unless the power of attorney otherwise provides; or
(4) the power of attorney terminates.

(c) Unless the power of attorney otherwise provides, an agent's authority is exercisable until the authority terminates under subsection (b), notwithstanding a lapse of time since the execution of the power of attorney.

(d) Termination of an agent's authority or of a power of attorney is not effective as to the agent or another person that, without actual knowledge of the termination, acts in good faith under the power of attorney. An act so performed, unless otherwise invalid or unenforceable, binds the principal and the principal's successors in interest.

(e) Incapacity of the principal of a power of attorney that is not durable does not revoke or terminate the power of attorney as to an agent or other person that, without actual knowledge of the incapacity, acts in good faith under the power of attorney. An act so performed, unless otherwise invalid or unenforceable, binds the principal and the principal's successors in interest.

(f) The execution of a power of attorney does not revoke a power of attorney previously executed by the principal unless the subsequent power of attorney provides that the previous power of attorney is revoked or that all other powers of attorney are revoked.

§ 5B-111. Coagents and Successor Agents.

(a) A principal may designate two or more persons to act as coagents. Unless the power of attorney otherwise provides, each coagent may exercise its authority independently.

(b) A principal may designate one or more successor agents to act if an agent resigns, dies, becomes incapacitated, is not qualified to serve, or declines to serve. A principal may grant authority to designate one or more successor agents to an agent or other person designated by name, office, or function. Unless the power of attorney otherwise provides, a successor agent:

(1) has the same authority as that granted to the original agent; and

(2) may not act until all predecessor agents have resigned, died, become incapacitated, are no longer qualified to serve, or have declined to serve.

(c) Except as otherwise provided in the power of attorney and subsection (d), an agent that does not participate in or conceal a breach of fiduciary duty committed by another agent, including a predecessor agent, is not liable for the actions of the other agent.

(d) An agent that has actual knowledge of a breach or imminent breach of fiduciary duty by another agent shall notify the principal and, if the principal is incapacitated, take any action reasonably appropriate in the circumstances to safeguard the principal's best interest. An agent that fails to notify the principal or take action as required by this subsection is liable for the reasonably foreseeable damages that could have been avoided if the agent had notified the principal or taken such action.

§ 5B-112. Reimbursement and Compensation of Agent.

Unless the power of attorney otherwise provides, an agent is entitled to reimbursement of expenses reasonably incurred on behalf of the principal and to compensation that is reasonable under the circumstances.

§ 5B-113. Agent's Acceptance.

Except as otherwise provided in the power of attorney, a person accepts appointment as an agent under a power of attorney by exercising authority or performing duties as an agent or by any other assertion or conduct indicating acceptance.

§ 5B-114. Agent's Duties.

(a) Notwithstanding provisions in the power of attorney, an agent that has accepted appointment shall:

(1) act in accordance with the principal's reasonable expectations to the extent actually known by the agent and, otherwise, in the principal's best interest;

(2) act in good faith; and

(3) act only within the scope of authority granted in the power of attorney.

(b) Except as otherwise provided in the power of attorney, an agent that has accepted appointment shall:

(1) act loyally for the principal's benefit;

(2) act so as not to create a conflict of interest that impairs the agent's ability to act impartially

in the principal's best interest;

(3) act with the care, competence, and diligence ordinarily exercised by agents in similar circumstances;

(4) keep a record of all receipts, disbursements, and transactions made on behalf of the principal;

(5) cooperate with a person that has authority to make health-care decisions for the principal to carry out the principal's reasonable expectations to the extent actually known by the agent and, otherwise, act in the principal's best interest; and

(6) attempt to preserve the principal's estate plan, to the extent actually known by the agent, if preserving the plan is consistent with the principal's best interest based on all relevant factors, including:

(A) the value and nature of the principal's property;

(B) the principal's foreseeable obligations and need for maintenance;

(C) minimization of taxes, including income, estate, inheritance, generation-skipping transfer, and gift taxes; and

(D) eligibility for a benefit, a program, or assistance under a statute or regulation.

(c) An agent that acts in good faith is not liable to any beneficiary of the principal's estate plan for failure to preserve the plan.

(d) An agent that acts with care, competence, and diligence for the best interest of the principal is not liable solely because the agent also benefits from the act or has an individual or conflicting interest in relation to the property or affairs of the principal.

(e) If an agent is selected by the principal because of special skills or expertise possessed by the agent or in reliance on the agent's representation that the agent has special skills or expertise, the special skills or expertise must be considered in determining whether the agent has acted with care, competence, and diligence under the circumstances.

(f) Absent a breach of duty to the principal, an agent is not liable if the value of the principal's property declines.

(g) An agent that exercises authority to delegate to another person the authority granted by the principal or that engages another person on behalf of the principal is not liable for an act, error of judgment, or default of that person if the agent exercises care, competence, and diligence in selecting and monitoring the person.

(h) Except as otherwise provided in the power of attorney, an agent is not required to disclose receipts, disbursements, or transactions conducted on behalf of the principal unless ordered by a court or requested by the principal, a guardian, a conservator, another fiduciary acting for the principal, a governmental agency having authority to protect the welfare of the principal, or, upon the death of the principal, by the personal representative or successor in interest of the principal's estate. If so requested, within 30 days the agent shall comply with the request or provide a writing or other record substantiating why additional time is needed and shall comply with the request within an additional 30 days.

§ 5B-115. Exoneration of Agent. A provision in a power of attorney relieving an agent of liability for breach of duty is binding on the principal and the principal's successors in interest except to the extent the provision:

(1) relieves the agent of liability for breach of duty committed dishonestly, with an improper motive, or with reckless indifference to the purposes of the power of attorney or the best interest of the principal; or

(2) was inserted as a result of an abuse of a confidential or fiduciary relationship with the principal.

§ 5B-116. Judicial Relief.

(a) The following persons may petition a court to construe a power of attorney or review the agent's conduct, and grant appropriate relief:

(1) the principal or the agent;

(2) a guardian, conservator, or other fiduciary acting for the principal;

(3) a person authorized to make health-care decisions for the principal;

(4) the principal's spouse, parent, or descendant;

(5) an individual who would qualify as a presumptive heir of the principal;

(6) a person named as a beneficiary to receive any property, benefit, or contractual right on the principal's death or as a beneficiary of a trust created by or for the principal that has a financial interest in the principal's estate;

(7) a governmental agency having regulatory authority to protect the welfare of the principal;

(8) the principal's caregiver or another person that demonstrates sufficient interest in the principal's welfare; and

(9) a person asked to accept the power of attorney.

(b) Upon motion by the principal, the court shall dismiss a petition filed under this section, unless the court finds that the principal lacks capacity to revoke the agent's authority or the power of attorney.

§ 5B-117. Agent's Liability.

An agent that violates this [article] is liable to the principal or the principal's successors in interest for the amount required to:

(1) restore the value of the principal's property to what it would have been had the violation not occurred; and

(2) reimburse the principal or the principal's successors in interest for the attorney's fees and costs paid on the agent's behalf.

§ 5B-118. Agent's Resignation; Notice.

Unless the power of attorney provides a different method for an agent's resignation, an agent may resign by giving notice to the principal and, if the principal is incapacitated:

(1) to the [conservator or guardian], if one has been appointed for the principal, and a coagent or successor agent; or

(2) if there is no person described in paragraph (1), to:

(A) the principal's caregiver;

(B) another person reasonably believed by the agent to have sufficient interest in the principal's welfare; or

(C) a governmental agency having authority to protect the welfare of the principal.

§ 5B-119. Acceptance of and Reliance upon Acknowledged Power of Attorney.

(a) For purposes of this section and Section 5B-120, "acknowledged" means purportedly verified before a notary public or other individual authorized to take acknowledgements.

(b) A person that in good faith accepts an acknowledged power of attorney without actual knowledge that the signature is not genuine may rely upon the presumption under Section 5B-105 that the signature is genuine.

(c) A person that in good faith accepts an acknowledged power of attorney without actual knowledge that the power of attorney is void, invalid, or terminated, that the purported agent's authority is void, invalid, or terminated, or that the agent is exceeding or improperly exercising the agent's authority may rely upon the power of attorney as if the power of attorney were genuine, valid and still in effect, the agent's authority were genuine, valid and still in effect, and the agent had not exceeded and had properly exercised the authority.

(d) A person that is asked to accept an acknowledged power of attorney may request, and rely upon, without further investigation:

(1) an agent's certification under penalty of perjury of any factual matter concerning the principal, agent, or power of attorney;

(2) an English translation of the power of attorney if the power of attorney contains, in whole or in part, language other than English; and

(3) an opinion of counsel as to any matter of law concerning the power of attorney if the person making the request provides in a writing or other record the reason for the request.

(e) An English translation or an opinion of counsel requested under this section must be provided at the principal's expense unless the request is made more than seven business days after the power of attorney is presented for acceptance.

(f) For purposes of this section and Section 5B-120, a person that conducts activities through employees is without actual knowledge of a fact relating to a power of attorney, a principal, or an agent if the employee conducting the transaction involving the power of attorney is without actual knowledge of the fact.

Alternative A
§ 5B-120. Liability for Refusal to Accept Acknowledged Power of Attorney.

(a) Except as otherwise provided in subsection (b):

(1) a person shall either accept an acknowledged power of attorney or request a certification, a translation, or an opinion of counsel under Section 5B-119(d) no later than seven business days after presentation of the power of attorney for acceptance;

(2) if a person requests a certification, a translation, or an opinion of counsel under Section 119(d), the person shall accept the power of attorney no later than five business days after receipt of the certification, translation, or opinion of counsel; and

(3) a person may not require an additional or different form of power of attorney for authority granted in the power of attorney presented.

(b) A person is not required to accept an acknowledged power of attorney if:

(1) the person is not otherwise required to engage in a transaction with the principal in the same circumstances;

(2) engaging in a transaction with the agent or the principal in the same circumstances would be inconsistent with federal law;

(3) the person has actual knowledge of the termination of the agent's authority or of the power of attorney before exercise of the power;

(4) a request for a certification, a translation, or an opinion of counsel under Section 5B-119(d) is refused;

(5) the person in good faith believes that the power is not valid or that the agent does not have the authority to perform the act requested, whether or not a certification, a translation, or an opinion of counsel under Section 5B-119(d) has been requested or provided; or

(6) the person makes, or has actual knowledge that another person has made, a report to the [local adult protective services office] stating a good faith belief that the principal may be subject to physical or financial abuse, neglect, exploitation, or abandonment by the agent or a person acting for or with the agent.

(c) A person that refuses in violation of this section to accept an acknowledged power of attorney is subject to:

(1) a court order mandating acceptance of the power of attorney; and

(2) liability for reasonable attorney's fees and costs incurred in any action or proceeding that confirms the validity of the power of attorney or mandates acceptance of the power of attorney.

Alternative B

§ 5B-120. Liability for Refusal to Accept Acknowledged Statutory Form Power of Attorney.

(a) In this section, "statutory form power of attorney" means a power of attorney substantially in the form provided in Section 5B-301 or that meets the requirements for a military power of attorney pursuant to 10 U.S.C. Section 1044b [, as amended].

(b) Except as otherwise provided in subsection (c):

(1) a person shall either accept an acknowledged statutory form power of attorney or request a certification, a translation, or an opinion of counsel under Section 5B-119(d) no later than seven business days after presentation of the power of attorney for acceptance;

(2) if a person requests a certification, a translation, or an opinion of counsel under Section 5B-119(d), the person shall accept the statutory form power of attorney no later than five business days after receipt of the certification, translation, or opinion of counsel; and

(3) a person may not require an additional or different form of power of attorney for authority granted in the statutory form power of attorney presented.

(c) A person is not required to accept an acknowledged statutory form power of attorney if:

(1) the person is not otherwise required to engage in a transaction with the principal in the same circumstances;

(2) engaging in a transaction with the agent or the principal in the same circumstances would be inconsistent with federal law;

(3) the person has actual knowledge of the termination of the agent's authority or of the power of attorney before exercise of the power;

(4) a request for a certification, a translation, or an opinion of counsel under Section 5B-119(d) is refused;

(5) the person in good faith believes that the power is not valid or that the agent does not have the authority to perform the act requested, whether or not a certification, a translation, or an opinion of counsel under Section 5B-119(d) has been requested or provided; or

(6) the person makes, or has actual knowledge that another person has made, a report to the [local adult protective services office] stating a good faith belief that the principal may be subject to physical or financial abuse, neglect, exploitation, or abandonment by the agent or a person acting for or with the agent.

(d) A person that refuses in violation of this section to accept an acknowledged statutory form power of attorney is subject to:

(1) a court order mandating acceptance of the power of attorney; and

(2) liability for reasonable attorney's fees and costs incurred in any action or proceeding that confirms the validity of the power of attorney or mandates acceptance of the power of attorney.

Legislative Note: Section 5B-120 enumerates the bases for legitimate refusals of a power of attorney as well as sanctions for refusals that violate the Act. Alternatives A and B are identical except that Alternative B applies only to acknowledged statutory form powers of attorney while Alternative A applies to all acknowledged powers of attorney.

Under both alternatives, the phrase "local adult protective services office" is bracketed to indicate where an enacting jurisdiction should insert the appropriate designation for the governmental agency with regulatory authority to protect the welfare of the principal.

End of Alternatives

§ 5B-121. Principles of Law and Equity. Unless displaced by a provision of this [article], the principles of law and equity supplement this [article].

§ 5B-122. Laws Applicable to Financial Institutions and Entities. This [article] does not supersede any other law applicable to financial institutions or other entities, and the other law controls if inconsistent with this [article].

§ 5B-123. Remedies under Other Law. The remedies under this [article] are not exclusive and do not abrogate any right or remedy under the law of this state other than this [article].

PART 2
AUTHORITY

General Comment

Part 2 is based in part on the predecessor Uniform Statutory Form Power of Attorney Act, approved in 1988. It provides the default statutory construction for authority granted in a power of attorney. Sections 5B-204 through 5B-217 describe authority with respect to various subject matters. These descriptions may be incorporated by reference in the optional statutory form (Section 5B-301) or in an individually drafted power of attorney. Incorporation is accomplished either by referring to the descriptive term for the subject or by providing a citation to the section in which the authority is described (Section 5B-202). A principal may also modify any authority incorporated by reference (section 5B-202(c)). Section 5B-203 supplements Sections 5B-204 through 5B-217 by providing general terms of construction that apply to all grant of authority under those sections unless otherwise indicated in the power of attorney.

Most of the language in Sections 5B-204 through 5B-216 of Part 2 comes directly from the Uniform Statutory Form Power of Attorney Act (1988). The language has been revised where necessary to reflect modern custom and practice. Where significant changes have been made, they are noted in a comment to the relevant section. In general, there are two important differences between the statutory treatment of authority in this Act and in the Uniform Statutory Form Power of Attorney Act (1988). First, this Act includes a section that provides a default rule for the parameters of gift making authority (Section 5B-217). Second, this Act identifies specific acts that may be authorized only by an express grant in the power of attorney (Section 5B-201(a)). Express authorization for the acts listed in Section 5B-201(a) is required because of the risk those acts pose to the principal's property and estate plan. The purpose of Section 5B-201(a) is to make clear that authority for these acts may not be inferred from a grant of general authority.

§ 5B-201. Authority That Requires Specific Grant; Grant of General Authority.

(a) An agent under a power of attorney may do the following on behalf of the principal or with the principal's property only if the power of attorney expressly grants the agent the authority and exercise of the authority is not otherwise prohibited by another agreement or instrument to which the authority or property is subject:

    (1) create, amend, revoke, or terminate an inter vivos trust;

    (2) make a gift;

    (3) create or change rights of survivorship;

    (4) create or change a beneficiary designation;

    (5) delegate authority granted under the power of attorney;

    (6) waive the principal's right to be a beneficiary of a joint and survivor annuity, including a

survivor benefit under a retirement plan;

    (7) exercise fiduciary powers that the principal has authority to delegate; [or]

    (8) exercise authority over the content of electronic communications, as defined in 18 U.S.C. Section 2501(12)[, as amended,] sent or received by the principal[; or

    (9) disclaim property, including a power of appointment].

    (b) Notwithstanding a grant of authority to do an act described in subsection (a), unless the power of attorney otherwise provides, an agent that is not an ancestor, spouse, or descendant of the principal, may not exercise authority under a power of attorney to create in the agent, or in an individual to whom the agent owes a legal obligation of support, an interest in the principal's property, whether by gift, right of survivorship, beneficiary designation, disclaimer, or otherwise.

    (c) Subject to subsections (a), (b), (d), and (e), if a power of attorney grants to an agent authority to do all acts that a principal could do, the agent has the general authority described in Sections 5B-204 through 5B-216.

    (d) Unless the power of attorney otherwise provides, a grant of authority to make a gift is subject to Section 5B-217.

    (e) Subject to subsections (a), (b), and (d), if the subjects over which authority is granted in a power of attorney are similar or overlap, the broadest authority controls.

    (f) Authority granted in a power of attorney is exercisable with respect to property that the principal has when the power of attorney is executed or acquires later, whether or not the property is located in this state and whether or not the authority is exercised or the power of attorney is executed in this state.

    (g) An act performed by an agent pursuant to a power of attorney has the same effect and inures to the benefit of and binds the principal and the principal's successors in interest as if the principal had performed the act.

§ 5B-202. Incorporation of Authority.

    (a) An agent has authority described in this [article] if the power of attorney refers to general authority with respect to the descriptive term for the subjects stated in Sections 5B-204 through 5B-217 or cites the section in which the authority is described.

    (b) A reference in a power of attorney to general authority with respect to the descriptive term for a subject in Sections 5B-204 through 5B-217 or a citation to a section of Sections 5B-204 through 5B-217 incorporates the entire section as if it were set out in full in the power of attorney.

    (c) A principal may modify authority incorporated by reference.

§ 5B-203. Construction of Authority Generally. Except as otherwise provided in the power of attorney, by executing a power of attorney that incorporates by reference a subject described in Sections 5B-204 through 5B-217 or that grants to an agent authority to do all acts that a principal could do pursuant to Section 5B-201(c), a principal authorizes the agent, with respect to that subject, to:

    (1) demand, receive, and obtain by litigation or otherwise, money or another thing of value to which the principal is, may become, or claims to be entitled, and conserve, invest, disburse, or use anything so received or obtained for the purposes intended;

    (2) contract in any manner with any person, on terms agreeable to the agent, to accomplish a purpose of a transaction and perform, rescind, cancel, terminate, reform, restate, release, or modify the contract or another contract made by or on behalf of the principal;

    (3) execute, acknowledge, seal, deliver, file, or record any instrument or communication the agent considers desirable to accomplish a purpose of a transaction, including creating at any time a schedule

listing some or all of the principal's property and attaching it to the power of attorney;

(4) initiate, participate in, submit to alternative dispute resolution, settle, oppose, or propose or accept a compromise with respect to a claim existing in favor of or against the principal or intervene in litigation relating to the claim;

(5) seek on the principal's behalf the assistance of a court or other governmental agency to carry out an act authorized in the power of attorney;

(6) engage, compensate, and discharge an attorney, accountant, discretionary investment manager, expert witness, or other advisor;

(7) prepare, execute, and file a record, report, or other document to safeguard or promote the principal's interest under a statute or regulation;

(8) communicate with any representative or employee of a government or governmental subdivision, agency, or instrumentality, on behalf of the principal;

(9) access communications intended for, and communicate on behalf of the principal, whether by mail, electronic transmission, telephone, or other means; and

(10) do any lawful act with respect to the subject and all property related to the subject.

§ 5B-204. Real Property. Unless the power of attorney otherwise provides, language in a power of attorney granting general authority with respect to real property authorizes the agent to:

(1) demand, buy, lease, receive, accept as a gift or as security for an extension of credit, or otherwise acquire or reject an interest in real property or a right incident to real property;

(2) sell; exchange; convey with or without covenants, representations, or warranties; quitclaim; release; surrender; retain title for security; encumber; partition; consent to partitioning; subject to an easement or covenant; subdivide; apply for zoning or other governmental permits; plat or consent to platting; develop; grant an option concerning; lease; sublease; contribute to an entity in exchange for an interest in that entity; or otherwise grant or dispose of an interest in real property or a right incident to real property;

(3) pledge or mortgage an interest in real property or right incident to real property as security to borrow money or pay, renew, or extend the time of payment of a debt of the principal or a debt guaranteed by the principal;

(4) release, assign, satisfy, or enforce by litigation or otherwise a mortgage, deed of trust, conditional sale contract, encumbrance, lien, or other claim to real property which exists or is asserted;

(5) manage or conserve an interest in real property or a right incident to real property owned or claimed to be owned by the principal, including:

(A) insuring against liability or casualty or other loss;

(B) obtaining or regaining possession of or protecting the interest or right by litigation or otherwise;

(C) paying, assessing, compromising, or contesting taxes or assessments or applying for and receiving refunds in connection with them; and

(D) purchasing supplies, hiring assistance or labor, and making repairs or alterations to the real property;

(6) use, develop, alter, replace, remove, erect, or install structures or other improvements upon real property in or incident to which the principal has, or claims to have, an interest or right;

(7) participate in a reorganization with respect to real property or an entity that owns an interest in or right incident to real property and receive, and hold, and act with respect to stocks and bonds or other property received in a plan of reorganization, including:

(A) selling or otherwise disposing of them;

(B) exercising or selling an option, right of conversion, or similar right with respect to them; and

(C) exercising any voting rights in person or by proxy;

(8) change the form of title of an interest in or right incident to real property; and

(9) dedicate to public use, with or without consideration, easements or other real property in which the principal has, or claims to have, an interest.

§ 5B-205. Tangible Personal Property. Unless the power of attorney otherwise provides, language in a power of attorney granting general authority with respect to tangible personal property authorizes the agent to:

(1) demand, buy, receive, accept as a gift or as security for an extension of credit, or otherwise acquire or reject ownership or possession of tangible personal property or an interest in tangible personal property;

(2) sell; exchange; convey with or without covenants, representations, or warranties; quitclaim; release; surrender; create a security interest in; grant options concerning; lease; sublease; or, otherwise dispose of tangible personal property or an interest in tangible personal property;

(3) grant a security interest in tangible personal property or an interest in tangible personal property as security to borrow money or pay, renew, or extend the time of payment of a debt of the principal or a debt guaranteed by the principal;

(4) release, assign, satisfy, or enforce by litigation or otherwise, a security interest, lien, or other claim on behalf of the principal, with respect to tangible personal property or an interest in tangible personal property;

(5) manage or conserve tangible personal property or an interest in tangible personal property on behalf of the principal, including:

(A) insuring against liability or casualty or other loss;

(B) obtaining or regaining possession of or protecting the property or interest, by litigation or otherwise;

(C) paying, assessing, compromising, or contesting taxes or assessments or applying for and receiving refunds in connection with taxes or assessments;

(D) moving the property from place to place;

(E) storing the property for hire or on a gratuitous bailment; and

(F) using and making repairs, alterations, or improvements to the property; and

(6) change the form of title of an interest in tangible personal property.

§ 5B-206. Stocks and Bonds. Unless the power of attorney otherwise provides, language in a power of attorney granting general authority with respect to stocks and bonds authorizes the agent to:

(1) buy, sell, and exchange stocks and bonds;

(2) establish, continue, modify, or terminate an account with respect to stocks and bonds;

(3) pledge stocks and bonds as security to borrow, pay, renew, or extend the time of payment of a debt of the principal;

(4) receive certificates and other evidences of ownership with respect to stocks and bonds; and

(5) exercise voting rights with respect to stocks and bonds in person or by proxy, enter into voting trusts, and consent to limitations on the right to vote.

§ 5B-207. Commodities and Options. Unless the power of attorney otherwise provides, language in a power of attorney granting general authority with respect to commodities and options authorizes the agent to:

(1) buy, sell, exchange, assign, settle, and exercise commodity futures contracts and call or put options on stocks or stock indexes traded on a regulated option exchange; and

(2) establish, continue, modify, and terminate option accounts.

§ 5B-208. Banks and Other Financial Institutions. Unless the power of attorney otherwise provides, language in a power of attorney granting general authority with respect to banks and other financial institutions authorizes the agent to:

(1) continue, modify, and terminate an account or other banking arrangement made by or on behalf of the principal;

(2) establish, modify, and terminate an account or other banking arrangement with a bank, trust company, savings and loan association, credit union, thrift company, brokerage firm, or other financial institution selected by the agent;

(3) contract for services available from a financial institution, including renting a safe deposit box or space in a vault;

(4) withdraw, by check, order, electronic funds transfer, or otherwise, money or property of the principal deposited with or left in the custody of a financial institution;

(5) receive statements of account, vouchers, notices, and similar documents from a financial institution and act with respect to them;

(6) enter a safe deposit box or vault and withdraw or add to the contents;

(7) borrow money and pledge as security personal property of the principal necessary to borrow money or pay, renew, or extend the time of payment of a debt of the principal or a debt guaranteed by the principal;

(8) make, assign, draw, endorse, discount, guarantee, and negotiate promissory notes, checks, drafts, and other negotiable or nonnegotiable paper of the principal or payable to the principal or the principal's order, transfer money, receive the cash or other proceeds of those transactions, and accept a draft drawn by a person upon the principal and pay it when due;

(9) receive for the principal and act upon a sight draft, warehouse receipt, or other document of title whether tangible or electronic, or other negotiable or nonnegotiable instrument;

(10) apply for, receive, and use letters of credit, credit and debit cards, electronic transaction authorizations, and traveler's checks from a financial institution and give an indemnity or other agreement in connection with letters of credit; and

(11) consent to an extension of the time of payment with respect to commercial paper or a financial transaction with a financial institution.

§ 5B-209. Operation of Entity or Business. Subject to the terms of a document or an agreement governing an entity or an entity ownership interest, and unless the power of attorney otherwise provides, language in a power of attorney granting general authority with respect to operation of an entity or business authorizes the agent to:

(1) operate, buy, sell, enlarge, reduce, or terminate an ownership interest;

(2) perform a duty or discharge a liability and exercise in person or by proxy a right, power, privilege, or option that the principal has, may have, or claims to have;

(3) enforce the terms of an ownership agreement;

(4) initiate, participate in, submit to alternative dispute resolution, settle, oppose, or propose or accept a compromise with respect to litigation to which the principal is a party because of an ownership interest;

(5) exercise in person or by proxy, or enforce by litigation or otherwise, a right, power, privilege, or option the principal has or claims to have as the holder of stocks and bonds;

(6) initiate, participate in, submit to alternative dispute resolution, settle, oppose, or propose or accept a compromise with respect to litigation to which the principal is a party concerning stocks and

bonds;

(7) with respect to an entity or business owned solely by the principal:

(A) continue, modify, renegotiate, extend, and terminate a contract made by or on behalf of the principal with respect to the entity or business before execution of the power of attorney;

(B) determine:

(i) the location of its operation;

(ii) the nature and extent of its business;

(iii) the methods of manufacturing, selling, merchandising, financing, accounting, and advertising employed in its operation;

(iv) the amount and types of insurance carried; and

(v) the mode of engaging, compensating, and dealing with its employees and accountants, attorneys, or other advisors;

(C) change the name or form of organization under which the entity or business is operated and enter into an ownership agreement with other persons to take over all or part of the operation of the entity or business; and

(D) demand and receive money due or claimed by the principal or on the principal's behalf in the operation of the entity or business and control and disburse the money in the operation of the entity or business;

(8) put additional capital into an entity or business in which the principal has an interest;

(9) join in a plan of reorganization, consolidation, conversion, domestication, or merger of the entity or business;

(10) sell or liquidate all or part of an entity or business;

(11) establish the value of an entity or business under a buy-out agreement to which the principal is a party;

(12) prepare, sign, file, and deliver reports, compilations of information, returns, or other papers with respect to an entity or business and make related payments; and

(13) pay, compromise, or contest taxes, assessments, fines, or penalties and perform any other act to protect the principal from illegal or unnecessary taxation, assessments, fines, or penalties, with respect to an entity or business, including attempts to recover, in any manner permitted by law, money paid before or after the execution of the power of attorney.

§ 5B-210. Insurance and Annuities. Unless the power of attorney otherwise provides, language in a power of attorney granting general authority with respect to insurance and annuities authorizes the agent to:

(1) continue, pay the premium or make a contribution on, modify, exchange, rescind, release, or terminate a contract procured by or on behalf of the principal which insures or provides an annuity to either the principal or another person, whether or not the principal is a beneficiary under the contract;

(2) procure new, different, and additional contracts of insurance and annuities for the principal and the principal's spouse, children, and other dependents, and select the amount, type of insurance or annuity, and mode of payment;

(3) pay the premium or make a contribution on, modify, exchange, rescind, release, or terminate a contract of insurance or annuity procured by the agent;

(4) apply for and receive a loan secured by a contract of insurance or annuity;

(5) surrender and receive the cash surrender value on a contract of insurance or annuity;

(6) exercise an election;

(7) exercise investment powers available under a contract of insurance or annuity;

(8) change the manner of paying premiums on a contract of insurance or annuity;

(9) change or convert the type of insurance or annuity with respect to which the principal has or claims to have authority described in this section;

(10) apply for and procure a benefit or assistance under a statute or regulation to guarantee or pay premiums of a contract of insurance on the life of the principal;

(11) collect, sell, assign, hypothecate, borrow against, or pledge the interest of the principal in a contract of insurance or annuity;

(12) select the form and timing of the payment of proceeds from a contract of insurance or annuity; and

(13) pay, from proceeds or otherwise, compromise or contest, and apply for refunds in connection with, a tax or assessment levied by a taxing authority with respect to a contract of insurance or annuity or its proceeds or liability accruing by reason of the tax or assessment.

§ 5B-211. Estates, Trusts, and Other Beneficial Interests.

(a) In this section, "estate, trust, or other beneficial interest" means a trust, probate estate, guardianship, conservatorship, escrow, or custodianship or a fund from which the principal is, may become, or claims to be, entitled to a share or payment.

(b) Unless the power of attorney otherwise provides, language in a power of attorney granting general authority with respect to estates, trusts, and other beneficial interests authorizes the agent to:

(1) accept, receive, receipt for, sell, assign, pledge, or exchange a share in or payment from an estate, trust, or other beneficial interest;

(2) demand or obtain money or another thing of value to which the principal is, may become, or claims to be, entitled by reason of an estate, trust, or other beneficial interest, by litigation or otherwise;

(3) exercise for the benefit of the principal a presently exercisable general power of appointment held by the principal;

(4) initiate, participate in, submit to alternative dispute resolution, settle, oppose, or propose or accept a compromise with respect to litigation to ascertain the meaning, validity, or effect of a deed, will, declaration of trust, or other instrument or transaction affecting the interest of the principal;

(5) initiate, participate in, submit to alternative dispute resolution, settle, oppose, or propose or accept a compromise with respect to litigation to remove, substitute, or surcharge a fiduciary;

(6) conserve, invest, disburse, or use anything received for an authorized purpose; [and]

(7) transfer an interest of the principal in real property, stocks and bonds, accounts with financial institutions or securities intermediaries, insurance, annuities, and other property to the trustee of a revocable trust created by the principal as settlor [; and

(8) reject, renounce, disclaim, release, or consent to a reduction in or modification of a share in or payment from an estate, trust, or other beneficial interest].

§ 5B-212. Claims and Litigation. Unless the power of attorney otherwise provides, language in a power of attorney granting general authority with respect to claims and litigation authorizes the agent to:

(1) assert and maintain before a court or administrative agency a claim, claim for relief, cause of action, counterclaim, offset, recoupment, or defense, including an action to recover property or other thing of value, recover damages sustained by the principal, eliminate or modify tax liability, or seek an injunction, specific performance, or other relief;

(2) bring an action to determine adverse claims or intervene or otherwise participate in litigation;

(3) seek an attachment, garnishment, order of arrest, or other preliminary, provisional, or

intermediate relief and use an available procedure to effect or satisfy a judgment, order, or decree;

(4) make or accept a tender, offer of judgment, or admission of facts, submit a controversy on an agreed statement of facts, consent to examination, and bind the principal in litigation;

(5) submit to alternative dispute resolution, settle, and propose or accept a compromise;

(6) waive the issuance and service of process upon the principal, accept service of process, appear for the principal, designate persons upon which process directed to the principal may be served, execute and file or deliver stipulations on the principal's behalf, verify pleadings, seek appellate review, procure and give surety and indemnity bonds, contract and pay for the preparation and printing of records and briefs, receive, execute, and file or deliver a consent, waiver, release, confession of judgment, satisfaction of judgment, notice, agreement, or other instrument in connection with the prosecution, settlement, or defense of a claim or litigation;

(7) act for the principal with respect to bankruptcy or insolvency, whether voluntary or involuntary, concerning the principal or some other person, or with respect to a reorganization, receivership, or application for the appointment of a receiver or trustee which affects an interest of the principal in property or other thing of value;

(8) pay a judgment, award, or order against the principal or a settlement made in connection with a claim or litigation; and

(9) receive money or other thing of value paid in settlement of or as proceeds of a claim or litigation.

§ 5B-213. Personal and Family Maintenance.

(a) Unless the power of attorney otherwise provides, language in a power of attorney granting general authority with respect to personal and family maintenance authorizes the agent to:

(1) perform the acts necessary to maintain the customary standard of living of the principal, the principal's spouse, and the following individuals, whether living when the power of attorney is executed or later born:

(A) the principal's children;

(B) other individuals legally entitled to be supported by the principal; and

(C) the individuals whom the principal has customarily supported or indicated the intent to support;

(2) make periodic payments of child support and other family maintenance required by a court or governmental agency or an agreement to which the principal is a party;

(3) provide living quarters for the individuals described in paragraph (1) by:

(A) purchase, lease, or other contract; or

(B) paying the operating costs, including interest, amortization payments, repairs, improvements, and taxes, for premises owned by the principal or occupied by those individuals;

(4) provide normal domestic help, usual vacations and travel expenses, and funds for shelter, clothing, food, appropriate education, including postsecondary and vocational education, and other current living costs for the individuals described in paragraph (1);

(5) pay expenses for necessary health care and custodial care on behalf of the individuals described in paragraph (1);

(6) act as the principal's personal representative pursuant to the Health Insurance Portability and Accountability Act, Sections 1171 through 1179 of the Social Security Act, 42 U.S.C. Section 1320d, [as amended,] and applicable regulations, in making decisions related to the past, present, or future payment for the provision of health care consented to by the principal or anyone authorized under the law of this state to consent to health care on behalf of the principal;

(7) continue any provision made by the principal for automobiles or other means of

transportation, including registering, licensing, insuring, and replacing them, for the individuals described in paragraph (1);

(8) maintain credit and debit accounts for the convenience of the individuals described in paragraph (1) and open new accounts; and

(9) continue payments incidental to the membership or affiliation of the principal in a religious institution, club, society, order, or other organization or to continue contributions to those organizations.

(b) Authority with respect to personal and family maintenance is neither dependent upon, nor limited by, authority that an agent may or may not have with respect to gifts under this [article].

§ 5B-214. Benefits from Governmental Programs or Civil or Military Service.

(a) In this section, "benefits from governmental programs or civil or military service" means any benefit, program or assistance provided under a statute or regulation including Social Security, Medicare, and Medicaid.

(b) Unless the power of attorney otherwise provides, language in a power of attorney granting general authority with respect to benefits from governmental programs or civil or military service authorizes the agent to:

(1) execute vouchers in the name of the principal for allowances and reimbursements payable by the United States or a foreign government or by a state or subdivision of a state to the principal, including allowances and reimbursements for transportation of the individuals described in Section 5B-213(a)(1), and for shipment of their household effects;

(2) take possession and order the removal and shipment of property of the principal from a post, warehouse, depot, dock, or other place of storage or safekeeping, either governmental or private, and execute and deliver a release, voucher, receipt, bill of lading, shipping ticket, certificate, or other instrument for that purpose;

(3) enroll in, apply for, select, reject, change, amend, or discontinue, on the principal's behalf, a benefit or program;

(4) prepare, file, and maintain a claim of the principal for a benefit or assistance, financial or otherwise, to which the principal may be entitled under a statute or regulation;

(5) initiate, participate in, submit to alternative dispute resolution, settle, oppose, or propose or accept a compromise with respect to litigation concerning any benefit or assistance the principal may be entitled to receive under a statute or regulation; and

(6) receive the financial proceeds of a claim described in paragraph (4) and conserve, invest, disburse, or use for a lawful purpose anything so received.

§ 5B-215. Retirement Plans.

(a) In this section, "retirement plan" means a plan or account created by an employer, the principal, or another individual to provide retirement benefits or deferred compensation of which the principal is a participant, beneficiary, or owner, including a plan or account under the following sections of the Internal Revenue Code:

(1) an individual retirement account under Internal Revenue Code Section 408, 26 U.S.C. Section 408 [, as amended];

(2) a Roth individual retirement account under Internal Revenue Code Section 408A, 26 U.S.C. Section 408A [, as amended];

(3) a deemed individual retirement account under Internal Revenue Code Section 408(q), 26 U.S.C. Section 408(q) [, as amended];

(4) an annuity or mutual fund custodial account under Internal Revenue Code Section 403(b),

26 U.S.C. Section 403(b) [, as amended];

(5) a pension, profit-sharing, stock bonus, or other retirement plan qualified under Internal Revenue Code Section 401(a), 26 U.S.C. Section 401(a) [, as amended];

(6) a plan under Internal Revenue Code Section 457(b), 26 U.S.C. Section 457(b) [, as amended]; and

(7) a nonqualified deferred compensation plan under Internal Revenue Code Section 409A, 26 U.S.C. Section 409A [, as amended].

(b) Unless the power of attorney otherwise provides, language in a power of attorney granting general authority with respect to retirement plans authorizes the agent to:

(1) select the form and timing of payments under a retirement plan and withdraw benefits from a plan;

(2) make a rollover, including a direct trustee-to-trustee rollover, of benefits from one retirement plan to another;

(3) establish a retirement plan in the principal's name;

(4) make contributions to a retirement plan;

(5) exercise investment powers available under a retirement plan; and

(6) borrow from, sell assets to, or purchase assets from a retirement plan.

§ 5B-216. Taxes. Unless the power of attorney otherwise provides, language in a power of attorney granting general authority with respect to taxes authorizes the agent to:

(1) prepare, sign, and file federal, state, local, and foreign income, gift, payroll, property, Federal Insurance Contributions Act, and other tax returns, claims for refunds, requests for extension of time, petitions regarding tax matters, and any other tax-related documents, including receipts, offers, waivers, consents, including consents and agreements under Internal Revenue Code Section 2032A, 26 U.S.C. Section 2032A, [as amended,] closing agreements, and any power of attorney required by the Internal Revenue Service or other taxing authority with respect to a tax year upon which the statute of limitations has not run and the following 25 tax years;

(2) pay taxes due, collect refunds, post bonds, receive confidential information, and contest deficiencies determined by the Internal Revenue Service or other taxing authority;

(3) exercise any election available to the principal under federal, state, local, or foreign tax law; and

(4) act for the principal in all tax matters for all periods before the Internal Revenue Service, or other taxing authority.

§ 5B-217. Gifts.

(a) In this section, a gift "for the benefit of" a person includes a gift to a trust, an account under the Uniform Transfers to Minors Act, and a tuition savings account or prepaid tuition plan as defined under Internal Revenue Code Section 529, 26 U.S.C. Section 529 [, as amended].

(b) Unless the power of attorney otherwise provides, language in a power of attorney granting general authority with respect to gifts authorizes the agent only to:

(1) make outright to, or for the benefit of, a person, a gift of any of the principal's property, including by the exercise of a presently exercisable general power of appointment held by the principal, in an amount per donee not to exceed the annual dollar limits of the federal gift tax exclusion under Internal Revenue Code Section 2503(b), 26 U.S.C. Section 2503(b), [as amended,] without regard to whether the federal gift tax exclusion applies to the gift, or if the principal's spouse agrees to consent to a split gift pursuant to Internal Revenue Code Section 2513, 26 U.S.C. 2513, [as amended,] in an amount per donee not to exceed twice the annual federal gift tax exclusion limit; and

(2) consent, pursuant to Internal Revenue Code Section 2513, 26 U.S.C. Section 2513, [as

amended,] to the splitting of a gift made by the principal's spouse in an amount per donee not to exceed the aggregate annual gift tax exclusions for both spouses.

(c) An agent may make a gift of the principal's property only as the agent determines is consistent with the principal's objectives if actually known by the agent and, if unknown, as the agent determines is consistent with the principal's best interest based on all relevant factors, including:

    (1) the value and nature of the principal's property;

    (2) the principal's foreseeable obligations and need for maintenance;

    (3) minimization of taxes, including income, estate, inheritance, generation-skipping transfer, and gift taxes;

    (4) eligibility for a benefit, a program, or assistance under a statute or regulation; and

    (5) the principal's personal history of making or joining in making gifts.

PART 3
STATUTORY FORMS

General Comment

Part 3 provides a concise, optional statutory form for creating a power of attorney under this Act (Section 5B-301). With the proliferation of power of attorney forms in the public domain, the advantage of a statutorily-sanctioned form is the promotion of uniformity in power of attorney practice. In states such as Illinois and New York, where state-sanctioned statutory forms have existed for many years, the statutory form is widely used by both lawyers and lay persons. The familiarity and common understanding achieved with the use of one statutory form also facilitates acceptance of powers of attorney. In the twenty years preceding this Act, the number of states with statutory forms has increased from only a few to eighteen.

In addition to the statutory form power of attorney, Part 3 provides an optional form for agent certification of facts pertaining to a power of attorney (Section 5B-302). Pursuant to Section 5B-119, a person may request an agent to certify any factual matter concerning the principal, agent, or power of attorney. The form in Section 5B-302 is intended to facilitate agent compliance with these requests. The form lists factual matters about which persons commonly request certification (*e.g.*, the principal is alive and has not revoked the power of attorney or the agent's authority), and provides a designated space for certification of additional factual statements. Both the statutory form power of attorney and the agent certification form may be tailored to accommodate individual circumstances and objectives.

§ **5B-301. Statutory Form Power of Attorney.** A document substantially in the following form may be used to create a statutory form power of attorney that has the meaning and effect prescribed by this [article].

[INSERT NAME OF JURISDICTION]
STATUTORY FORM POWER OF ATTORNEY

IMPORTANT INFORMATION

This power of attorney authorizes another person (your agent) to make decisions concerning your property for you (the principal). Your agent will be able to make decisions and act with respect to your property (including your money) whether or not you are able to act for yourself. The meaning of authority over subjects listed on this form is explained in the Uniform Power of Attorney Act [insert citation].

This power of attorney does not authorize the agent to make health-care decisions for you.

You should select someone you trust to serve as your agent. Unless you specify otherwise, generally the agent's authority will continue until you die or revoke the power of attorney or the agent resigns or is unable to act for you.

Your agent is entitled to reasonable compensation unless you state otherwise in the Special Instructions.

This form provides for designation of one agent. If you wish to name more than one agent you may name a coagent in the Special Instructions. Coagents are not required to act together unless you include that requirement in the Special Instructions.

If your agent is unable or unwilling to act for you, your power of attorney will end unless you have named a successor agent. You may also name a second successor agent.

This power of attorney becomes effective immediately unless you state otherwise in the Special Instructions.

If you have questions about the power of attorney or the authority you are granting to your agent, you should seek legal advice before signing this form.

DESIGNATION OF AGENT

I _____ name the following
(Name of Principal)
person as my agent:

Name of Agent: _____

Agent's Address: _____

Agent's Telephone Number: _____

DESIGNATION OF SUCCESSOR AGENT(S) (OPTIONAL)

If my agent is unable or unwilling to act for me, I name as my successor agent:

Name of Successor Agent: _____

Successor Agent's Address: _____

Successor Agent's Telephone Number: _____

If my successor agent is unable or unwilling to act for me, I name as my second successor agent:

Name of Second Successor Agent: _____

Second Successor Agent's Address: _____

Second Successor Agent's Telephone Number: _____

GRANT OF GENERAL AUTHORITY

I grant my agent and any successor agent general authority to act for me with respect to the following subjects as defined in the Uniform Power of Attorney Act [insert citation]:

(INITIAL each subject you want to include in the agent's general authority. If you wish to grant general authority over all of the subjects you may initial "All Preceding Subjects" instead of initialing each subject.)

(___) Real Property
(___) Tangible Personal Property
(___) Stocks and Bonds
(___) Commodities and Options
(___) Banks and Other Financial Institutions
(___) Operation of Entity or Business
(___) Insurance and Annuities
(___) Estates, Trusts, and Other Beneficial Interests
(___) Claims and Litigation
(___) Personal and Family Maintenance
(___) Benefits from Governmental Programs or Civil or Military Service
(___) Retirement Plans
(___) Taxes
(___) All Preceding Subjects

GRANT OF SPECIFIC AUTHORITY (OPTIONAL)

My agent MAY NOT do any of the following specific acts for me UNLESS I have INITIALED the specific authority listed below:

(CAUTION: Granting any of the following will give your agent the authority to take actions that could significantly reduce your property or change how your property is distributed at your death. INITIAL ONLY the specific authority you WANT to give your agent.)

(___) Create, amend, revoke, or terminate an inter vivos trust
(___) Make a gift, subject to the limitations of the Uniform Power of Attorney Act [insert citation to Section 217 of the act] and any special instructions in this power of attorney
(___) Create or change rights of survivorship
(___) Create or change a beneficiary designation
(___) Authorize another person to exercise the authority granted under this power of attorney
(___) Waive the principal's right to be a beneficiary of a joint and survivor annuity, including a survivor benefit under a retirement plan
(___) Exercise fiduciary powers that the principal has authority to delegate
(___) Access the content of electronic communications

[(___) Disclaim or refuse an interest in property, including a power of appointment]

LIMITATION ON AGENT'S AUTHORITY

An agent that is not my ancestor, spouse, or descendant MAY NOT use my property to benefit the agent or a person to whom the agent owes an obligation of support unless I have included that authority in the Special Instructions.

SPECIAL INSTRUCTIONS (OPTIONAL)

You may give special instructions on the following lines:

_____

_____

_____

_____

_____

_____

_____

EFFECTIVE DATE

This power of attorney is effective immediately unless I have stated otherwise in the Special Instructions.

NOMINATION OF [CONSERVATOR OR GUARDIAN] (OPTIONAL)

If it becomes necessary for a court to appoint a [conservator or guardian] of my estate or [guardian] of my person, I nominate the following person(s) for appointment:

Name of Nominee for [conservator or guardian] of my estate:

_____

Nominee's Address: _____

Nominee's Telephone Number: _____

Name of Nominee for [guardian] of my person: _____

Nominee's Address: _____

Nominee's Telephone Number: _____

RELIANCE ON THIS POWER OF ATTORNEY

Any person, including my agent, may rely upon the validity of this power of attorney or a copy of it unless that person knows it has terminated or is invalid.

SIGNATURE AND ACKNOWLEDGMENT

_____   _____
Your Signature   Date

_____
Your Name Printed

_____

_____
Your Address

_____
Your Telephone Number

State of _____

[County] of _____

This document was acknowledged before me on _____,

                                                (Date)

by _____.
              (Name of Principal)

_____   (Seal, if any)
Signature of Notary
My commission expires: _____

[This document prepared by:

_____

_____]

IMPORTANT INFORMATION FOR AGENT

Agent's Duties

When you accept the authority granted under this power of attorney, a special legal relationship is created between you and the principal. This relationship imposes upon you legal duties that continue until you resign or the power of attorney is terminated or revoked. You must:

(1) do what you know the principal reasonably expects you to do with the principal's property or, if you do not know the principal's expectations, act in the principal's best interest;
(2) act in good faith;
(3) do nothing beyond the authority granted in this power of attorney; and
(4) disclose your identity as an agent whenever you act for the principal by writing or printing the name of the principal and signing your own name as "agent" in the following manner:

(Principal's Name) by (Your Signature) as Agent

Unless the Special Instructions in this power of attorney state otherwise, you must also:

(1) act loyally for the principal's benefit;
(2) avoid conflicts that would impair your ability to act in the principal's best interest;
(3) act with care, competence, and diligence;
(4) keep a record of all receipts, disbursements, and transactions made on behalf of the principal;
(5) cooperate with any person that has authority to make health-care decisions for the principal to do what you know the principal reasonably expects or, if you do not know the principal's expectations, to act in the principal's best interest; and
(6) attempt to preserve the principal's estate plan if you know the plan and preserving the plan is consistent with the principal's best interest.

Termination of Agent's Authority
You must stop acting on behalf of the principal if you learn of any event that terminates this power of attorney or your authority under this power of attorney. Events that terminate a power of attorney or your authority to act under a power of attorney include:

(1) death of the principal;
(2) the principal's revocation of the power of attorney or your authority;
(3) the occurrence of a termination event stated in the power of attorney;
(4) the purpose of the power of attorney is fully accomplished; or
(5) if you are married to the principal, a legal action is filed with a court to end your marriage, or for your legal separation, unless the Special Instructions in this power of attorney state that such an action will not terminate your authority.

Liability of Agent
The meaning of the authority granted to you is defined in the Uniform Power of Attorney Act [insert citation]. If you violate the Uniform Power of Attorney Act [insert citation] or act outside the authority granted, you may be liable for any damages caused by your violation.

If there is anything about this document or your duties that you do not understand, you should seek legal advice.

§ 5B-302. Agent's Certification. The following optional form may be used by an agent to certify facts concerning a power of attorney.

AGENT'S CERTIFICATION AS TO THE VALIDITY OF POWER OF ATTORNEY AND AGENT'S AUTHORITY

State of _____

[County] of _____]

I, _____ (Name of Agent), [certify] under penalty of perjury that _____ (Name of Principal) granted me authority as an agent or successor agent in a power of attorney dated _____.

I further [certify] that to my knowledge:

(1) the Principal is alive and has not revoked the Power of Attorney or my authority to act under the Power of Attorney and the Power of Attorney and my authority to act under the Power of Attorney have not terminated;

(2) if the Power of Attorney was drafted to become effective upon the happening of an event or contingency, the event or contingency has occurred;

(3) if I was named as a successor agent, the prior agent is no longer able or willing to serve; and

(4) _____
_____
_____
_____

(Insert other relevant statements)

SIGNATURE AND ACKNOWLEDGMENT

_____   _____
Agent's Signature   Date

_____
Agent's Name Printed

_____

_____
Agent's Address

_____
Agent's Telephone Number

This document was acknowledged before me on _____,
                                                                              (Date)

by _____.
            (Name of Agent)

_____   (Seal, if any)
Signature of Notary
My commission expires: _____

[This document prepared by: _____
_____]

ARTICLE VI
NONPROBATE TRANSFERS ON DEATH

PART 1
PROVISIONS RELATING TO EFFECT OF DEATH

PART 2
UNIFORM MULTIPLE-PERSON ACCOUNTS ACT (1989/1998)

SUBPART 1
DEFINITIONS AND GENERAL PROVISIONS

SUBPART 2
OWNERSHIP AS BETWEEN PARTIES AND OTHERS

SUBPART 3
PROTECTION OF FINANCIAL INSTITUTIONS

PART 3
UNIFORM TOD SECURITY REGISTRATION ACT (1989/1998)

PART 4
UNIFORM REAL PROPERTY TRANSFER ON DEATH ACT (2009)

Prefatory Note

The 1989 amendment of Uniform Probate Code Article VI (nonprobate transfers) replaced former Article VI with a revised article. Part 1 (provisions relating to effect of death) of the revised article was amended and relocated from former Part 2. Part 2 (Uniform Multiple-Person Accounts Act (1989/1998)) of the revised article was amended and relocated from former Part 1. Part 3 (Uniform TOD Security Registration Act (1989/1998)) of the revised article was added. This reorganization allowed for general provisions at the beginning of the article, and permitted parts to be divided into subparts that group related provisions together. This reorganization also facilitated the addition of the Uniform Real Property Transfer on Death Act (2009) as Part 4.

Multiple-Person Accounts. The 1989 amendment of Part 2 (Uniform Multiple-Person Accounts Act (1989/1998)) of the revised article simplified drafting and terminology. It consolidated treatment of POD accounts and trust accounts so that the same rules apply to both, since both types of account operate identically and serve the same function of passing property to a beneficiary at the death of the account owner. The amendment likewise eliminated references to "joint" accounts, since the statute treats joint tenancy accounts and tenancy in common accounts the same for all purposes other than survivorship. Other terminological and drafting simplifications and standardizations were made throughout the statute. Treatment of existing accounts is included.

The 1989 amendment made a few substantive changes in rules previously established in the multiple-person account statute. The changes included recognition of checks issued by an account owner before death and presented for payment after death, revision of the creditor rights procedure to enable a survivor or beneficiary to spread the burden among survivors and beneficiaries of other accounts of the decedent and to provide a uniform one-year limitation period for creditors, and a provision that a financial institution must have received notice at the appropriate office and have had a reasonable time to act before it is charged with knowledge that any change in account circumstances has occurred. A provision was also added that on the death of a married person, beneficial ownership of the decedent's share in a survivorship account passes to the surviving spouse who is an account party in preference to other surviving account parties.

The 1989 amendment included a number of important improvements designed to make multiple-person accounts more useful. An agency designation is authorized to enable an account owner to add another person to the account as a convenience in making withdrawals without creating any ownership or survivorship interest in the person identified as an agent. Optional statutory forms for multiple-person accounts are provided for the convenience and protection of financial institutions. Payment to a minor who is an account beneficiary is authorized pursuant to the Uniform Transfers to Minors Act (1983/1986). A provision is added to make clear that marital funds deposited in an account retain any community property incidents, and the law governing tenancy by the entireties is preserved where applicable.

The drafting committee believes that the 1989 amendment of the multiple-person account statute is a substantial improvement in an already successful law. This part of the Uniform Probate Code is one of the most broadly accepted, having been adopted either as part of the code or independently by over half the states. This amendment draws on useful improvements made by various states that have enacted the statute, and should make the statute even more attractive.

Uniform TOD Security Registration Act. The purpose of Part 3 (Uniform TOD Security Registration Act) of the revised article is to allow the owner of securities to register the title in transfer-on-death (TOD) form. Mutual fund shares and accounts maintained by brokers and others to reflect a customer's holdings of securities (so-called "street accounts") are also covered. The legislation enables an issuer, transfer agent, broker, or other such intermediary to transfer the securities directly to the designated transferee on the owner's death. Thus, TOD registration achieves for securities a certain parity with existing TOD and pay-on-death (POD) facilities for bank deposits and other assets passing at death outside the probate process.

The TOD registration under this part is designed to give the owner of securities who wishes to arrange for a nonprobate transfer at death an alternative to the frequently troublesome joint tenancy form of title. Because joint tenancy registration of securities normally entails a sharing of lifetime entitlement and control, it works satisfactorily only so long as the co-owners cooperate. Difficulties arise when co-owners fall into disagreement, or when one becomes afflicted or insolvent.

Use of the TOD registration form encouraged by this legislation has no effect on the registered owner's full control of the affected security during his or her lifetime. A TOD designation and any beneficiary interest arising under the designation ends whenever the registered asset is transferred, or whenever the owner otherwise complies with the issuer's conditions for changing the title form of the investment. The part recognizes, in Section 6-302, that co-owners with right of survivorship may be registered as owners together with a TOD beneficiary designated to take if the registration remains unchanged until the beneficiary survives the joint owners. In such a case, the survivor of the joint owners has full control of the asset and may change the registration form as he or she sees fit after the other's death.

Implementation of the part is wholly optional with issuers. The drafting committee received the benefit of considerable advice and assistance from representatives of the mutual fund and stock transfer industries during the course of its three years of preparatory work. Accordingly, it is believed that this part takes full account of the practical requirements for efficient transfer within the securities industry.

Section 6-303 invites application of the legislation to locally owned securities though the statute may not have been locally enacted, so long as the part or similar legislation is in force in a jurisdiction of the issuer or transfer agent. Thus, if the principal jurisdictions in which securities issuers and transfer agents are sited enact the measure, its benefits will become generally available to persons domiciled in states that do not at once enact the statute.

The 1989 legislation was drafted as a separate part, hence not interpolated as an expansion of the former UPC Article VI, Part 1, treating bank accounts ("multiple-party accounts"). Securities merit a distinct statutory regime, because a different principle has governed concurrent ownership of securities. By virtue either of statute or of account terms (contract), multiple-party bank accounts allow any one cotenant to consume or transfer account balances. See R. Brown, The Law of Personal Property § 65, at 217 (2d ed. 1955); Langbein, The Nonprobate Revolution and the Future of the Law of Succession, 97 Harv.L.Rev. 1108, 1112 (1984). The rule for securities, however, has been the rule that applies to real property: all cotenants must act together in transferring the securities. This difference in the legal regime reflects differences in function among the types of assets. Multiple-party bank accounts typically arise as convenience accounts, to facilitate frequent small transactions, often on an agency basis (as when spouses or relatives share an account). Securities resemble real estate in that the values are typically large and the transactions relatively infrequent, which is why the legal regime requires the concurrence of all concurrent owners for transfers affecting such assets.

This distinction between bank accounts and securities has begun to crumble. Banks are offering certificates of deposit of large value under the same account forms that were devised for low-value convenience accounts. Meanwhile, brokerage houses with their so-called cash management accounts and mutual funds with their money market accounts have rendered securities subject to small recurrent transactions. Even the line between real estate and bank accounts is becoming indistinct, as the "home equity line of credit" creates a check-writing conduit to real estate values.

Nevertheless, even though new forms of contract have rendered the boundaries between securities and bank accounts less firm, the distinction seems intuitively correct for statutory default rules. True co-owners of securities, like owners of realty, should act together in transferring the asset.

The joint bank account and the Totten trust originated in ambiguous lifetime ownership forms, which required former UPC Section 6-103 or comparable state legislation to clarify that an inter vivos transfer was not intended. In the securities field, by contrast, we start with unambiguous lifetime ownership rules. The sole purpose of the present statute is to facilitate a nonprobate TOD mechanism as an option for those owners.

For a comprehensive discussion of the issues entailed in this legislation, see Wellman, Transfer-on-Death Securities Registration: A New Title Form, 21 Ga.L.Rev. 789 (1987).

Uniform Real Property Transfer on Death Act (2009). One of the main innovations in the property law of the twentieth century has been the development of asset-specific will substitutes for the transfer of property at death. By these mechanisms, an owner may designate beneficiaries to receive the property at the owner's death without waiting for probate and without the beneficiary designation needing to comply with the witnessing requirements of wills. Examples of specific assets that today routinely pass outside of probate include the proceeds of life insurance policies and pension plans, securities registered in transfer on death (TOD) form, and funds held in pay on death (POD) bank accounts.

Today, nonprobate transfers are widely accepted. The trend has largely focused on assets that are personal property, such as the assets described in the preceding paragraph. However, long-standing uniform law speaks more broadly. Section 6-101 of the Uniform Probate Code (UPC) provides: "A provision for a nonprobate transfer on death in an insurance policy, contract of employment, bond, mortgage, promissory note, certificated or uncertificated security, account agreement, custodial agreement, deposit agreement, compensation plan, pension plan, property agreement, or other written instrument of a similar nature is nontestamentary."

A small but growing number of jurisdictions have implemented the principle of UPC Section 6-101 by enacting statutes providing an asset-specific mechanism for the nonprobate transfer of land. This is done by permitting owners of interests in real property to execute and record a transfer on death (TOD) deed. By this deed, the owner identifies the beneficiary or beneficiaries who will succeed to the property at the owner's death. During the owner's lifetime, the beneficiaries have no interest in the property, and the owner retains full power to transfer or encumber the property or to revoke the TOD deed.

PART 1

PROVISIONS RELATING TO EFFECT OF DEATH

§ 6-101. Nonprobate Transfers on Death. A provision for a nonprobate transfer on death in an insurance policy, contract of employment, bond, mortgage, promissory note, certificated or uncertificated security, account agreement, custodial agreement, deposit agreement, compensation plan, pension plan, individual retirement plan, employee benefit plan, trust, conveyance, deed of gift, marital property agreement, or other written instrument of a similar nature is nontestamentary. This subsection includes a written provision that:

(1) money or other benefits due to, controlled by, or owned by a decedent before death must be paid after the decedent's death to a person whom the decedent designates either in the instrument or in a separate writing, including a will, executed either before or at the same time as the instrument, or later;

(2) money due or to become due under the instrument ceases to be payable in the event of death of the promisee or the promisor before payment or demand; or

(3) any property controlled by or owned by the decedent before death which is the subject of the instrument passes to a person the decedent designates either in the instrument or in a separate writing, including a will, executed either before or at the same time as the instrument, or later.

Comment

This section is a revised version of former Section 6-201 of the original Uniform Probate Code, which authorized a variety of contractual arrangements that had sometimes been treated as testamentary in prior law. For example, most courts treated as testamentary a provision in a promissory note that if the payee died before making payment, the note should be paid to another named person; or a provision in a land contract that if the seller died before completing payment, the balance should be canceled and the property should belong to the vendee. These provisions often occurred in family arrangements. The result of holding such provisions testamentary was usually to invalidate them because not executed in accordance with the statute of wills. On the other hand, the same courts for years upheld beneficiary designations in life insurance contracts. The drafters of the original Uniform Probate Code declared in the Comment that they were unable to identify policy reasons for continuing to treat these varied arrangements as testamentary. The drafters said that the benign experience with such familiar will substitutes as the revocable inter vivos trust, the multiple-party bank account, and United States government bonds payable on death to named beneficiaries all demonstrated that the evils envisioned if the statute of wills were not rigidly enforced simply do not materialize. The Comment also observed that because these provisions often are part of a business transaction and are evidenced by a writing, the danger of fraud is largely eliminated.

Because the modes of transfer authorized by an instrument under this section are declared to be nontestamentary, the instrument does not have to be executed in compliance with the formalities for wills prescribed under Section 2-502; nor does the instrument have to be probated, nor does the personal representative have any power or duty with respect to the assets.

The sole purpose of this section is to prevent the transfers authorized here from being treated as testamentary. This section does not invalidate other arrangements by negative implication. Thus, this section does not speak to the phenomenon of the oral trust to hold property at death for named persons, an arrangement already generally enforceable under trust law.

The reference to a "marital property agreement" in the introductory portion of subsection (a) of Section 6-101 includes an agreement made during marriage as well as a premarital contract.

The term "or other written instrument of a similar nature" in the introductory portion of subsection (a) replaces the former language "or any other written instrument effective as a contract, gift, conveyance or trust" in the original Section 6-201. The Supreme Court of Washington read that language to relieve against the delivery requirement of the law of deeds, a result that was not intended. Estate of O'Brien v. Woodhouse, 109 Wash.2d 913, 749 P.2d 154 (1988). The point was correctly decided in First National Bank in Minot v. Bloom, 264 N.W.2d 208, 212

(N.D.1978), in which the Supreme Court of North Dakota held that "nothing in [former Section 6-201] of the Uniform Probate Code ... eliminates the necessity of delivery of a deed to effectuate a conveyance from one living person to another."

Restatement (Third) of Property: Wills and Other Donative Transfers (2003)

§ 7.1 Will Substitute—Definition and Validity

(a) A will substitute is an arrangement respecting property or contractual rights that is established during the donor's life, under which (1) the right to possession or enjoyment of the property or to a contractual payment shifts outside of probate to the donee at the donor's death; and (2) substantial lifetime rights of dominion, control, possession, or enjoyment are retained by the donor.

(b) To be valid, a will substitute need not be executed in compliance with the statutory formalities required for a will.

---

§ 6-102. Liability of Nonprobate Transferees for Creditor Claims and Statutory Allowances.

(a) In this section, "nonprobate transfer" means a valid transfer effective at death, other than a transfer of a survivorship interest in a joint tenancy of real estate, by a transferor whose last domicile was in this state to the extent that the transferor immediately before death had power, acting alone, to prevent the transfer by revocation or withdrawal and instead to use the property for the benefit of the transferor or apply it to discharge claims against the transferor's probate estate.

(b) Except as otherwise provided by statute, a transferee of a nonprobate transfer is subject to liability to any probate estate of the decedent for allowed claims against decedent's probate estate and statutory allowances to the decedent's spouse and children to the extent the estate is insufficient to satisfy those claims and allowances. The liability of a nonprobate transferee may not exceed the value of nonprobate transfers received or controlled by that transferee.

(c) Nonprobate transferees are liable for the insufficiency described in subsection (b) in the following order of priority:

(1) a transferee designated in the decedent's will or any other governing instrument, as provided in the instrument;

(2) the trustee of a trust serving as the principal nonprobate instrument in the decedent's estate plan as shown by its designation as devisee of the decedent's residuary estate or by other facts or circumstances, to the extent of the value of the nonprobate transfer received or controlled;

(3) other nonprobate transferees, in proportion to the values received.

(d) Unless otherwise provided by the trust instrument, interests of beneficiaries in all trusts incurring liabilities under this section abate as necessary to satisfy the liability, as if all of the trust instruments were a single will and the interests were devises under it.

(e) A provision made in one instrument may direct the apportionment of the liability among the nonprobate transferees taking under that or any other governing instrument. If a provision in one instrument conflicts with a provision in another, the later one prevails.

(f) Upon due notice to a nonprobate transferee, the liability imposed by this section is enforceable in proceedings in this state, whether or not the transferee is located in this state.

(g) A proceeding under this section may not be commenced unless the personal representative of the decedent's estate has received a written demand for the proceeding from the surviving spouse or a child, to the extent that statutory allowances are affected, or a creditor. If the personal representative declines or fails to commence a proceeding after demand, a person making demand may commence the proceeding in the name of the decedent's estate, at the expense of the person making the demand and not of the estate. A personal representative who declines in good faith to commence a requested proceeding incurs no personal liability for declining.

(h) A proceeding under this section must be commenced within one year after the decedent's death, but a proceeding on behalf of a creditor whose claim was allowed after proceedings challenging disallowance of the claim may be commenced within 60 days after final allowance of the claim.

(i) Unless a written notice asserting that a decedent's probate estate is nonexistent or insufficient to pay allowed claims and statutory allowances has been received from the decedent's personal representative, the following rules apply:

(1) Payment or delivery of assets by a financial institution, registrar, or other obligor, to a nonprobate transferee in accordance with the terms of the governing instrument controlling the transfer releases the obligor from all claims for amounts paid or assets delivered.

(2) A trustee receiving or controlling a nonprobate transfer is released from liability under this section with respect to any assets distributed to the trust's beneficiaries. Each beneficiary to the extent of the distribution received becomes liable for the amount of the trustee's liability attributable to assets received by the beneficiary.

Comment

1. Added to the Code in 1998, this section clarifies that the recipients of nonprobate transfers can be required to contribute to pay allowed claims and statutory allowances to the extent the probate estate is inadequate. The maximum liability for a single nonprobate transferee is the value of the transfer. Values are determined under subsection (b) as of the time when the benefits are "received or controlled by that transferee." This would be the date of the decedent's death for nonprobate transfers made by means of a revocable trust, and date of receipt for other nonprobate transfers. Two or more transferees are severally liable for the portion of the liability based on the value of the transfers received by each.

This section replaces Section 6-107 of the original Code, and its 1989 sequel, Section 6-215. To the extent a deceased party's probate estate was insufficient, these sections made a deceased party's interest in multiple-name accounts in financial institutions passing outside probate liable for the deceased party's statutory allowances and creditor claims. Assets passing at death by revocable trust or TOD asset registration agreements were not covered by these sections. Also, Section 6-201(b) of the original Code and its 1989 sequel, Section 6-101(b), provided merely that the section did not limit any other rights that might exist. Neither section created any rights.

If there are no probate assets, a creditor or other person seeking to use this Section 6-102 would first need to secure appointment of a personal representative to invoke Code procedures for establishing a creditor's claim as "allowed." The use of probate proceedings as a prerequisite to gaining rights for creditors against nonprobate transferees has

been a feature of UPC Article VI since originally approved in 1969. It works well in practice. The Article III procedures for opening estates, satisfying probate exemptions, and presenting claims are very efficient.

2. Section 6-102 replaces Section 6-215 with coverage designed to extend the principle of Section 6-215 to transfers at death by revocable trust, TOD security registration agreements and similar death benefits not insulated from decedents' creditors or statutory allowances by other legislation. The initial clause of subsection (b), "Except as otherwise provided by statute," is designed to prevent a conflict with and to clarify that this section does not supersede existing legislation protecting death benefits in life insurance, retirement plans or IRAs from claims by creditors.

If a state's insurance laws do not exempt or protect a particular insurance death benefit, the insured's creditors would not be able to establish a "nonprobate transfer" under subsection (a) except to the extent of any cash surrender value generated by premiums paid by the insured that the insured could have obtained immediately before death. Note, also, that subsection (i)(1) would protect a life insurance company that paid a death benefit before receiving written notice from the decedent's personal representative.

3. The definition of "nonprobate transfer" in subsection (a) includes revocable transfers by a decedent; it does not include a transfer at death incident to a decedent's exercise or non-exercise of a presently exercisable general power of appointment created by another person. The drafters decided against including such powers even though presently

exercisable general powers of appointment are subject to the Code's augmented estate provisions dealing with protection of a surviving spouse from disinheritance. Spousal protection against disinheritance by the other spouse supports the institution of marriage; creditors are better able to fend for themselves than financially disadvantaged surviving spouses. In addition, a presently exercisable general power of appointment created by another person is commonly viewed as a provision in the trust creator's instrument designed to provide flexibility in the estate plan rather than as a gift to the donee.

4. The required ability to revoke or otherwise prevent a nonprobate transfer at death that is vital to application of subsection (a) is described as a "power," a word intended by the drafters to signify legal authority rather than capacity or practical ability. This corresponds to the definition in Section 2-201(6).

5. The exclusion of "a survivorship interest in a joint tenancy of real estate" from the definition of "nonprobate transfer" in subsection (a) is contrary to the law of some states (e.g., South Dakota) that allow an insolvent decedent's creditors to reach the share the decedent could have received prior to death by unilateral severance of the joint tenancy. The law in most other states is to the contrary. By excluding real estate joint tenancies, stability of title and ease of title examination is preserved. Moreover, real estate joint tenancies have served for generations to keep the share of a couple's real estate owned by the first to die out of probate and away from estate creditors. This familiar arrangement need not be disturbed incident to expanding the ability of decedents' creditors to reach newly recognized nonprobate transfers at death.

No view is expressed as to whether a survivorship interest in personal or intangible property registered in two or more names as joint tenants with right of survivorship would come within Section 6-102(a). The outcome might depend on who originated the registration and whether severance by any co-owner acting alone was possible immediately preceding a co-owner's death.

6. A feature of replaced Section 6-215 that was clarified by a 1991 technical amendment protected a survivor beneficiary of a joint account from liability to the probate estate of a deceased co-depositor for funds in the account owned by the survivor prior to decedent's death. Subsection (a) continues this protection by use of the language "valid transfer effective at death ... by a transferor ... [who] had power, acting alone, to prevent the transfer by revocation or withdrawal and instead use the property

for the benefit of the transferor...." Section 6-211 and related sections of the Code make it clear that parties to a joint and survivor account separately own values in the account in proportion to net contributions. Hence, a surviving joint account depositor who had contributed to the balance on deposit prior to the death of the other party is subject to the remedies described in this section only to the extent of new account values gained through survival of the decedent.

7. Transferees of nonprobate transfers subject to the possible liability described in subsection (b) include trustees of revocable trusts to the extent assets transferred to the trust before death were subject to the decedent's sole power to revoke. Such assets would be valued as of the date of death. While the trustee of an irrevocable trust, or of a trust that may be revoked only by the settlor and another person would ordinarily not be subject to this section, this section could apply if the trust is named as a beneficiary of a nonprobate transfer, such as of securities registered in TOD form. Under subsection (b), such a transfer would involve a possibility of trust liability based on the value of the TOD transfer as of the time of its receipt. Liability under this section incurred by a trustee is a trust liability for which the trustee does not incur personal liability except as provided by Section 3-808(b).

8. Trusts and non-trust recipients of nonprobate transfers incur liability in the order prescribed in subsection (c). Note that either a revocable or an irrevocable trust might be designated devisee of a pour-over provision that would make the trust the "principal non-probate instrument in the decedent's estate plan" and, consequently, make it liable under subsection (c)(2) ahead of other nonprobate transferees to the extent of values acquired by a transfer at death as described in subsection (a). Note, too, that nothing would pass to the receptacle trust by the pour-over devise if all probate estate assets are used to discharge statutory allowances and claims. However, the fact that the trust was designated to receive a pour-over devise signals that the trust probably includes the equivalent of a residuary clause measuring benefits by available assets and signaling probable intention of the settlor that residuary benefits should abate to pay the settlor's debts prior to other trust gifts.

9. The abatement order among classes of beneficiaries of trusts specified by subsection (d) applies to all trusts subject to liability to the extent of nonprobate transfers received or administered

whether or not the trust instrument is the principal nonprobate instrument in the decedent's estate plan. The drafters decided against a cross-reference to the Code's abatement provision, Section 3-902, in part because that section deals with intestate and partially intestate estates as well as estates governed by wills. Note, too, that trusts for successive beneficiaries also will be governed by income and principal accounting rules that will serve to resolve some abatement issues.

10. Subsection (e) recognizes that a number of separate instruments and transactions, executed at different times and with or without internal references linking them to other documents, may constitute the paperwork describing succession to a decedent's assets by probate and nonprobate methods. By authorizing control of abatement among gifts made by various transfers at death by the last executed instrument, the subsection permits a simple, last-minute override of earlier directions concerning a decedent's wishes regarding priorities among successors. Thus, a will or trust amendment can correct or avoid liquidity and abatement problems discovered prior to death. The expression "block buster will" was coined by estate planners in the mid 70's to refer to interest in legislation enabling a later will to override death benefits by any nonprobate transfer device. This subsection meets some of the goals of advocates of this legislation.

11. Subsection (f) builds on the principle employed in the Code's augmented estate provisions (UPC Sections 2-201 through 2-214) in relation to nonprobate transfers made to persons in other states, possibly by transactions governed by laws of other states. The underlying principle is that the law of a decedent's last domicile should be controlling as to rules of public policy that override the decedent's power to devise the estate to anyone the decedent chooses. The principle is implemented by subjecting donee recipients of the decedent to liability under the decedent's domiciliary law, with the belief that judgments recovered in that state following appropriate due process notice to defendants in other states will be accorded full faith and credit by courts in other states should collection proceedings be necessary.

12. The first and third sentences of subsection (g) are identical to sentences from former Section 6-215, which this section replaces. The second sentence is new. It reflects sensitivity for the dilemma confronting a probate fiduciary who, acting as required of a fiduciary, concludes that the costs and risks associated with a possible recovery from a nonprobate transferee outweigh the probable advantages to the estate and its claimants. A creditor whose claim has been allowed but remains unsatisfied and whose demand for a proceeding has been turned down by the estate fiduciary may proceed at personal risk in efforts to enforce the estate claim against the nonprobate beneficiary. This is so because the last two sentences of subsection (g) shift the risk of unrecoverable costs from the decedent's estate to the claimant who undertakes collection efforts on behalf of the decedent's estate. Any recovery of costs should be used to reimburse the claimant who bore the risk of loss for the proceeding. A personal representative tempted to decline a demand for a proceeding should note that the "good faith" standard of this subsection must be determined in light of the fiduciary responsibility imposed by Section 3-703.

13. Subsection (h) meshes with time limits in the Code's sections governing allowance and disallowance of claims. See Sections 3-804 and 3-806.

14. Subsection (i)(1) is designed to protect issuers of TOD security registrations who make payments or delivery to designated death beneficiaries before receiving notice from the decedent's probate estate of a probable insolvency. These entities are not "transferees" subject to liability under subsection (b), but they might incur legal or other costs if the beneficiaries request payment in spite of warning notices from estate fiduciaries.

Subsection (i)(2) is designed to enable trustees handling nonprobate transfers to distribute trust assets in accordance with trust terms if a warning of probable estate insolvency has not been received. Beneficiaries receiving distributions from a trustee take subject to personal liability in the amount and priority of the trustee based on the value distributed.

PART 2
UNIFORM MULTIPLE-PERSON ACCOUNTS ACT (1989/1998)

SUBPART 1
DEFINITIONS AND GENERAL PROVISIONS

§ 6-201. Definitions. In this [part]:

(1) "Account" means a contract of deposit between a depositor and a financial institution, and includes a checking account, savings account, certificate of deposit, and share account.

(2) "Agent" means a person authorized to make account transactions for a party.

(3) "Beneficiary" means a person named as one to whom sums on deposit in an account are payable on request after death of all parties or for whom a party is named as trustee.

(4) "Financial institution" means an organization authorized to do business under state or federal laws relating to financial institutions, and includes a bank, trust company, savings bank, building and loan association, savings and loan company or association, and credit union.

(5) "Multiple-party account" means an account payable on request to one or more of two or more parties, whether or not a right of survivorship is mentioned.

(6) "Party" means a person who, by the terms of an account, has a present right, subject to request, to payment from the account other than as a beneficiary or agent.

(7) "Payment" of sums on deposit includes withdrawal, payment to a party or third person pursuant to check or other request, and a pledge of sums on deposit by a party, or a set-off, reduction, or other disposition of all or part of an account pursuant to a pledge.

(8) "POD designation" means the designation of (i) a beneficiary in an account payable on request to one party during the party's lifetime and on the party's death to one or more beneficiaries, or to one or more parties during their lifetimes and on death of all of them to one or more beneficiaries, or (ii) a beneficiary in an account in the name of one or more parties as trustee for one or more beneficiaries if the relationship is established by the terms of the account and there is no subject of the trust other than the sums on deposit in the account, whether or not payment to the beneficiary is mentioned.

(9) "Receive," as it relates to notice to a financial institution, means receipt in the office or branch office of the financial institution in which the account is established, but if the terms of the account require notice at a particular place, in the place required.

(10) "Request" means a request for payment complying with all terms of the account, including special requirements concerning necessary signatures and regulations of the financial institution; but, for purposes of this [part], if terms of the account condition payment on advance notice, a request for payment is treated as immediately effective and a notice of intent to withdraw is treated as a request for payment.

(11) "Sums on deposit" means the balance payable on an account, including interest and dividends earned, whether or not included in the current balance, and any deposit life insurance proceeds added to the account by reason of death of a party.

(12) "Terms of the account" includes the deposit agreement and other terms and conditions, including the form, of the contract of deposit.

Comment

This and the sections that follow are designed to reduce certain questions concerning many forms of multiple-person accounts (including the so-called Totten trust account). A "payable on death" designation and an "agency" designation are also authorized for both single-party and multiple-party accounts. The POD designation is a more direct means of achieving the same purpose as a Totten trust account; this part therefore discourages creation of a Totten trust account and treats existing Totten trust accounts as POD designations.

An agent (paragraph (2)) may not be a party. The agency designation must be signed by all parties, and the agent is the agent of all parties. See Section 6-205 (designation of agent).

A "beneficiary" of a party (paragraph (3)) may be either a POD beneficiary or the beneficiary of a Totten trust; the two types of designations in an account serve the same function and are treated the same under this part. See paragraph (8) ("POD designation" defined). The definition of "beneficiary" refers to a "person," who may be an individual, corporation, organization, or other legal entity. Section 1-201(34). Thus a church, trust company, family corporation, or other entity, as well as any individual, may be designated as a beneficiary.

The term "multiple-party account" (paragraph (5)) is used in this part in a broad sense to include any account having more than one owner with a present interest in the account. Thus an account may be a "multiple-party account" within the meaning of this part regardless of whether the terms of the account refer to it as "joint tenancy" or as "tenancy in common," regardless of whether the parties named are coupled by "or" or "and," and regardless of whether any reference is made to survivorship rights, whether expressly or by abbreviation such as JTWROS or JT TEN. Survivorship rights in a multiple-party account are determined by the terms of the account and by statute, and survivorship is not a necessary incident of a multiple-party account. See Section 6-212 (rights at death).

Under paragraph (6), a "party" is a person with a present right to payment from an account. Therefore, present owners of a multiple-party account are parties, as is the present owner of an account with a POD designation. The beneficiary of an account with a POD designation is not a party, but is entitled to payment only on the death of all parties. The trustee of a Totten trust is a party but the beneficiary is not. An agent with the right of withdrawal on behalf of a party is not itself a party. A person claiming on behalf of a party such as a guardian or conservator, or claiming the interest of a party such as a creditor, is not itself a party, and the right of such a person to payment is governed by general law other than this part.

Various signature requirements may be involved in order to meet the payment requirements of the account. A "request" (paragraph (10)) involves compliance with these requirements. A party is one to whom an account is presently payable without regard to whose signature may be required for a "request."

§ 6-202. Limitation on Scope of Part.
This [part] does not apply to:

(1) an account established for a partnership, joint venture, or other organization for a business purpose,

(2) an account controlled by one or more persons as an agent or trustee for a corporation, unincorporated association, or charitable or civic organization, or

(3) a fiduciary or trust account in which the relationship is established other than by the terms of the account.

Comment

This part applies to accounts in this state. Section 1-301(4).

The reference to a fiduciary or trust account in paragraph (3) includes a regular trust account under a testamentary trust or a trust agreement that has significance apart from the account, and a fiduciary account arising from a fiduciary relation such as attorney-client.

§ 6-203. Types of Account; Existing Accounts.

(a) An account may be for a single party or multiple parties. A multiple-party account may be with or without a right of survivorship between the parties. Subject to Section 6-212(c), either a single-party account or a multiple-party account may have a POD designation, an agency designation, or both.

(b) An account established before, on, or after the effective date of this [part], whether in the form prescribed in Section 6-204 or in any other form, is either a single-party account or a multiple-party account, with or without right of survivorship, and with or without a POD designation or an agency designation, within the meaning of this [part], and is governed by this [part].

Comment

In the case of an account established before (or after) the effective date of this part that is not in substantially the form provided in Section 6-204, the account is governed by the provisions of this part applicable to the type of account that most nearly conforms to the depositor's intent. See Section 6-204 (forms).

Thus, a tenancy in common account established before or after the effective date of this part would be classified as a "multiple-party account" for purposes of this part. See Section 6-201(5) ("multiple-party account" defined). On death of a party there would not be a right of survivorship since the tenancy in common title would be treated as a multiple-party account without right of survivorship. See Section 6-212(c). It should be noted that a POD designation may not be made in a multiple-party account without right of survivorship. See Sections 6-201(8) ("POD designation" defined), 6-204 (forms), and 6-212 (rights at death).

Under this section, a Totten trust account established before, on, or after the effective date of this part is governed by the provisions of this part applicable to an account with a POD designation. See Section 6-201(8) ("POD designation" defined) and the Comment to Section 6-201.

§ 6-204. Forms.

(a) A contract of deposit that contains provisions in substantially the following form establishes the type of account provided, and the account is governed by the provisions of this [part] applicable to an account of that type:

UNIFORM SINGLE- OR MULTIPLE-PARTY ACCOUNT FORM

PARTIES [Name One or More Parties]:

_____   _____

OWNERSHIP [Select One And Initial]:

_____ SINGLE-PARTY ACCOUNT

_____ MULTIPLE-PARTY ACCOUNT

Parties own account in proportion to net contributions unless there is clear and convincing evidence of a different intent.

RIGHTS AT DEATH [Select One And Initial]:

_____ SINGLE-PARTY ACCOUNT

At death of party, ownership passes as part of party's estate.

_____ SINGLE-PARTY ACCOUNT WITH POD (PAY ON DEATH) DESIGNATION [Name One Or More Beneficiaries]:

_____   _____

At death of party, ownership passes to POD beneficiaries and is not part of party's estate.

_____ MULTIPLE-PARTY ACCOUNT WITH RIGHT OF SURVIVORSHIP

At death of party, ownership passes to surviving parties.

_____ MULTIPLE-PARTY ACCOUNT WITH RIGHT OF SURVIVORSHIP AND POD (PAY ON DEATH) DESIGNATION

[handwritten left margin: when one person dies, that person's $ goes to other acct owners - when last person dies the $ in acct goes to POD designation - avoid probate]

[Name One Or More Beneficiaries]:

_____	_____

At death of last surviving party, ownership passes to POD beneficiaries and is not part of last surviving party's estate.

_____ MULTIPLE-PARTY ACCOUNT WITHOUT RIGHT OF SURVIVORSHIP

At death of party, deceased party's ownership passes as part of deceased party's estate.

[handwritten: rarely used]	*[handwritten: = goes to probate]*

AGENCY (POWER OF ATTORNEY) DESIGNATION [Optional]

Agents may make account transactions for parties but have no ownership or rights at death unless named as POD beneficiaries.

[To Add Agency Designation To Account, Name One Or More Agents]:

_____	_____

[Select One And Initial]:

_____ AGENCY DESIGNATION SURVIVES DISABILITY OR INCAPACITY OF PARTIES

_____ AGENCY DESIGNATION TERMINATES ON DISABILITY OR INCAPACITY OF PARTIES

[handwritten: — usually person in family in next generation]

(b) A contract of deposit that does not contain provisions in substantially the form provided in subsection (a) is governed by the provisions of this [part] applicable to the type of account that most nearly conforms to the depositor's intent.

Comment

This section provides short forms for single-and multiple-party accounts which, if used, bring the accounts within the terms of this part. A financial institution that uses the statutory form language in its accounts is protected in acting in reliance on the form of the account. See also Section 6-226 (discharge).

The forms provided in this section enable a person establishing a multiple-party account to state expressly in the account whether there are to be survivorship rights between the parties. The account forms permit greater flexibility than traditional account designations. It should be noted that no separate form is provided for a Totten trust account, since the POD designation serves the same function.

An account that is not substantially in the form provided in this section is nonetheless governed by this part. See Section 6-203 (types of account; existing accounts).

§ 6-205. Designation of Agent.

(a) By a writing signed by all parties, the parties may designate as agent of all parties on an account a person other than a party.

(b) Unless the terms of an agency designation provide that the authority of the agent terminates on disability or incapacity of a party, the agent's authority survives disability and incapacity. The agent may act for a disabled or incapacitated party until the authority of the agent is terminated.

(c) Death of the sole party or last surviving party terminates the authority of an agent.

Comment

An agent has no beneficial interest in the account. See Section 6-211 (ownership during lifetime). The agency relationship is governed by the general law of agency of the state, except to the extent this part provides express rules, including the rule that the agency survives the disability or incapacity of a party.

A financial institution may make payments at the direction of an agent notwithstanding disability, incapacity, or death of the party, subject to receipt of a stop notice. Section 6-226 (discharge); see also Section 6-224 (payment to designated agent).

The rule of subsection (b) applies to agency designations on all types of accounts, including nonsurvivorship as well as survivorship forms of multiple-party accounts.

§ 6-206. Applicability of Part. The provisions of [Subpart] 2 concerning beneficial ownership as between parties or as between parties and beneficiaries apply only to controversies between those persons and their creditors and other successors, and do not apply to the right of those persons to payment as determined by the terms of the account. [Subpart] 3 governs the liability and set-off rights of financial institutions that make payments pursuant to it.

SUBPART 2
OWNERSHIP AS BETWEEN PARTIES AND OTHERS

§ 6-211. Ownership During Lifetime.

(a) In this section, "net contribution" of a party means the sum of all deposits to an account made by or for the party, less all payments from the account made to or for the party which have not been paid to or applied to the use of another party and a proportionate share of any charges deducted from the account, plus a proportionate share of any interest or dividends earned, whether or not included in the current balance. The term includes deposit life insurance proceeds added to the account by reason of death of the party whose net contribution is in question.

(b) During the lifetime of all parties, sums deposited into an account belong to the parties in proportion to the net contribution of each, unless there is clear and convincing evidence of a different intent. As between parties married to each other, in the absence of proof otherwise, the net contribution of each is presumed to be an equal amount.

(c) A beneficiary in an account having a POD designation has no right to sums on deposit during the lifetime of any party.

(d) An agent in an account with an agency designation has no beneficial right to sums on deposit.

Comment

This section reflects the assumption that a person who deposits funds in an account normally does not intend to make an irrevocable gift of all or any part of the funds represented by the deposit. Rather, the person usually intends no present change of beneficial ownership. The section permits parties to accounts to be as definite, or as indefinite, as they wish in respect to the matter of how beneficial ownership should be apportioned between them.

The assumption that no present change of beneficial ownership is intended may be disproved by showing that a gift was intended. For example, under subsection (c) it is presumed that the beneficiary of a POD designation has no present ownership interest during lifetime. However, it is possible that in the case of a POD designation in trust form an irrevocable gift was intended.

It is important to note that the section is limited to ownership of an account while parties are alive.

Section 6-212 prescribes what happens to beneficial ownership on the death of a party.

The section does not undertake to describe the situation between parties if one party withdraws more than that party is then entitled to as against the other party. Sections 6-221 and 6-226 protect a financial institution in that circumstance without reference to whether a withdrawing party may be entitled to less than that party withdraws as against another party. Rights between parties in this situation are governed by general law other than this part.

"Net contribution" as defined by subsection (a) has no application to the financial institution-depositor relationship. Rather, it is relevant only to controversies that may arise between parties to a multiple-party account.

The last sentence of subsection (b) provides a clear rule concerning the amount of "net contribution" in a case where the actual amount cannot be established as between spouses. This part otherwise contains no provision dealing with a failure of proof. The omission is deliberate. The theory of these sections is that the basic relationship of the parties is that of individual ownership of values attributable to their respective deposits and withdrawals, and not equal and undivided ownership that would be an incident of joint tenancy.

In a state that recognizes tenancy by the entireties for personal property, this section would not change the rule that parties who are married to each other own their combined net contributions to an account as tenants by the entireties. See Section 6-216 (community property and tenancy by the entireties).

§ 6-212. Rights at Death.

(a) Except as otherwise provided in this [part], on death of a party sums on deposit in a multiple-party account belong to the surviving party or parties. If two or more parties survive and one is the surviving spouse of the decedent, the amount to which the decedent, immediately before death, was beneficially entitled under Section 6-211 belongs to the surviving spouse. If two or more parties survive and none is the surviving spouse of the decedent, the amount to which the decedent, immediately before death, was beneficially entitled under Section 6-211 belongs to the surviving parties in equal shares, and augments the proportion to which each survivor, immediately before the decedent's death, was beneficially entitled under Section 6-211, and the right of survivorship continues between the surviving parties.

(b) In an account with a POD designation:

(1) On death of one of two or more parties, the rights in sums on deposit are governed by subsection (a).

(2) On death of the sole party or the last survivor of two or more parties, sums on deposit belong to the surviving beneficiary or beneficiaries. If two or more beneficiaries survive, sums on deposit belong to them in equal and undivided shares, and there is no right of survivorship in the event of death of a beneficiary thereafter. If no beneficiary survives, sums on deposit belong to the estate of the last surviving party.

(c) Sums on deposit in a single-party account without a POD designation, or in a multiple-party account that, by the terms of the account, is without right of survivorship, are not affected by death of a party, but the amount to which the decedent, immediately before death, was beneficially entitled under Section 6-211 is transferred as part of the decedent's estate. A POD designation in a multiple-party account without right of survivorship is ineffective. For purposes of this section, designation of an account as a tenancy in common establishes that the account is without right of survivorship.

(d) The ownership right of a surviving party or beneficiary, or of the decedent's estate, in sums on deposit is subject to requests for payment made by a party before the party's death, whether paid by the financial institution before or after death, or unpaid. The surviving party or beneficiary, or the decedent's estate, is liable to the payee of an unpaid request for payment. The liability is limited to a proportionate share of the amount transferred under this section, to the extent necessary to discharge the request for payment.

Comment

The effect of subsection (a) is to make an account payable to one or more of two or more parties a survivorship arrangement unless a nonsurvivorship arrangement is specified in the terms of the account. This rule applies to community property as well as other forms of marital property. See Section 6-216 (community property and tenancy by the entireties).

The section also applies to various forms of multiple-party accounts that may be in use at the effective date of the legislation. See Sections 6-203 (type of account; existing accounts) and 6-204 (forms).

By technical amendment effective August 5, 1991, the word "part" was substituted for "section" in the first sentence of subsection (a). The amendment clarified the original purpose of the drafters and Commissioners to permit a court to implement the intentions of parties to a joint account governed by Section 6-204(b) if it finds that the account was opened solely for the convenience of a party who supplied all funds reflected by the account and intended no present gift or death benefit for the other party. In short, the account characteristics described in this section must be determined by reference to the form of the account and the impact of Sections 6-203 and 6-204 on the admissibility of extrinsic evidence tending to confirm or contradict intention as signalled by the form.

Subsection (b) applies to both POD and Totten trust beneficiaries. See Section 6-201(8) ("POD designation" defined). It accepts the New York view that an account opened by "A" in A's name as "trustee for B" usually is intended by A to be an informal will of any balance remaining on deposit at A's death.

§ 6-213. Alteration of Rights.

(a) Rights at death of a party under Section 6-212 are determined by the terms of the account at the death of the party. A party may alter the terms of the account by a notice signed by the party and given to the financial institution to change the terms of the account or to stop or vary payment under the terms of the account. To be effective, the notice must be received by the financial institution during the party's lifetime.

(b) A right of survivorship arising from the express terms of the account, Section 6-212, or a POD designation, may not be altered by will.

Comment

Under this section, rights of parties and beneficiaries are determined by the type of account at the time of death. It is to be noted that only a "party" may give notice blocking the provisions of Section 6-212 (rights at death). "Party" is defined by Section 6-201(6). Thus if there is an account with a POD designation in the name of A and B with C as beneficiary, C cannot change the right of survivorship because C has no present right to payment and hence is not a party.

1995 Technical Amendment. By technical amendment in 1995, subsection (a) was amended to substitute "terms of the account" (as defined in Section 6-201(12)) for the language "type of account." The purpose of this amendment is to reject any implication that to fall within this section an alteration of an account must affect the "type" of account, not merely its "terms."

Restatement (Third) of Property: Wills and Other Donative Transfers (2003)

§ 7.2, *Comment e. Revocation or amendment of a will substitute by later will.* A revocable trust may be revoked or amended by a later will. See Restatement Third, Trusts § 63, Comment h; Uniform Trust Code § 602(c). At least one state has by statute authorized the revocation by a later will of will substitutes except real property joint tenancies, life insurance, retirement plans, and a few other will substitutes. A few judicial decisions have upheld the effort to revoke certain will substitutes by a later will. See Reporter's Note. It is generally agreed that Totten trusts may be revoked by will (see Restatement Third, Trusts § 26, Comment c), but under Revised UPC § 6-213(b) POD accounts, including Totten trusts, cannot be changed by will.

Insurance contracts, multiple party accounts, pension accounts, and other will substitutes commonly require the account owner to follow a particular procedure for altering or amending the beneficiary designation, such as completing a form supplied by the financial intermediary or other payor. Such a term governs as a matter of the contract between the account owner and the financial intermediary or payor. It sometimes happens that the account owner misunderstands this requirement and attempts to revoke the beneficiary designation by will. The courts are divided about whether to enforce the account term, thereby defeating the account owner's later contrary expression of donative intent.

In such cases, when the financial intermediary or other payor has paid the beneficiary of record on the account in good faith before learning of the later inconsistent designation in the will, the account term is effective to protect the financial intermediary or payor from liability to the beneficiary designated in the will. In such circumstances, that intended beneficiary is remitted to an action in restitution against the account-designated beneficiary who received the payment. See Restatement of Restitution § 126.

When the financial intermediary or payor receives notice of the inconsistent beneficiary designation contained in the subsequent will before paying the beneficiary of record on the account, the financial intermediary or payor should pay the proceeds as directed under the will, notwithstanding the failure of the account owner to comply with the account term specifying account-specific procedures for revocation or alteration. If the financial intermediary or payor is uncertain about the priority or effectiveness of the attempted revocation or alteration by will, the financial intermediary or payor may discharge its responsibilities by interpleading and/or paying the proceeds into court.

When a designation by will supersedes a designation contained in the instrument of account, the proceeds remain separate from probate property and pass in accordance with the provisions of the nonprobate account, unless the language of the later will expresses an intent that the account proceeds are to become part of the probate estate.

The principles set forth in this comment also apply to circumstances in which the account owner attempts to modify the beneficiary designation by a subsequent instrument other than a validly executed will. Because such an instrument does not comply with the formalities required for a will to assure that the document represents the owner's donative intent (see § 3.1), the proponent of such an instrument bears the burden of proving by clear and convincing evidence that the instrument reflects the account owner's donative intent.

The party alleging revocation bears the burden of proving that an asserted revocation actually referred to the will substitute in question. Thus, a mere residuary clause in a later will or a comparable provision in a later revocable inter vivos trust does not revoke an earlier beneficiary designation in a will substitute.

§ 6-214. Accounts and Transfers Nontestamentary. Except as provided in [Part] 2 of [Article] II (elective share of surviving spouse) or as a consequence of, and to the extent directed by, Section 6-215, a transfer resulting from the application of Section 6-212 is effective by reason of the terms of the account involved and this [part] and is not testamentary or subject to [Articles] I through IV (estate administration).

Comment

The purpose of classifying the transactions contemplated by this part as nontestamentary is to bolster the explicit statement that their validity as effective modes of transfers on death is not to be determined by the requirements for wills. The section is consistent with Part 1 of Article VI (provisions relating to effect of death).

§ 6-215. [Reserved].

Comment

Former Section 6-215 became unnecessary with the approval in 1998 of Section 6-102. The former section, titled "Rights of Creditors and Others," imposed potential liability on survivor beneficiaries of multiple person bank accounts for the debts of a deceased party and statutory allowances owed by the decedent's estate. Section 6-102 is more comprehensive, subjecting other types of nonprobate transfers to creditor claims and statutory allowances.

§ 6-216. Community Property and Tenancy by the Entireties.

(a) A deposit of community property in an account does not alter the community character of the property or community rights in the property, but a right of survivorship between parties married to each other arising from the express terms of the account or Section 6-212 may not be altered by will.

(b) This [part] does not affect the law governing tenancy by the entireties.

Comment

Section 6-216 does not affect or limit the right of the financial institution to make payments pursuant to Subpart 3 (protection of financial institutions) and the deposit agreement. See Section 6-206 (applicability of part). For this reason, Section 6-216 does not affect the definiteness and certainty that the financial institution must have in order to be induced to make payments from the account and, at the same time, the section preserves the rights of the parties, creditors, and successors that arise out of the nature of the funds in the account—community or separate, or tenancy by the entireties.

SUBPART 3
PROTECTION OF FINANCIAL INSTITUTIONS

§ 6-221. Authority of Financial Institution. A financial institution may enter into a contract of deposit for a multiple-party account to the same extent it may enter into a contract of deposit for a single-party account, and may provide for a POD designation and an agency designation in either a single-party account or a multiple-party account. A financial institution need not inquire as to the source of a deposit to an account or as to the proposed application of a payment from an account.

Comment

The provisions of this subpart relate only to protection of a financial institution that makes payment as provided in the subpart. Nothing in this subpart affects the beneficial rights of persons to sums on deposit or paid out. Ownership as between parties, and others, is governed by Subpart 2. See Section 6-206 (applicability of part).

§ 6-222. Payment on Multiple-Party Account. A financial institution, on request, may pay sums on deposit in a multiple-party account to:

(1) one or more of the parties, whether or not another party is disabled, incapacitated, or deceased when payment is requested and whether or not the party making the request survives another party; or

(2) the personal representative, if any, or, if there is none, the heirs or devisees of a deceased party if proof of death is presented to the financial institution showing that the deceased party was the survivor of all other persons named on the account either as a party or beneficiary, unless the account is without right of survivorship under Section 6-212.

Comment

A financial institution that makes payment on proper request under this section is protected unless the financial institution has received written notice not to. Section 6-226 (discharge). Paragraph (1) applies to both a multiple-party account with right of survivorship and a multiple-party account without right of survivorship (including an account in tenancy in common form). Paragraph (2) is limited to a multiple-party account with right of survivorship; payment to the personal representative or heirs or devisees of a deceased party to an account without right of survivorship is governed by the general law of the state relating to the authority of such persons to collect assets alleged to belong to a decedent.

§ 6-223. Payment on POD Designation. A financial institution, on request, may pay sums on deposit in an account with a POD designation to:

(1) one or more of the parties, whether or not another party is disabled, incapacitated, or deceased when the payment is requested and whether or not a party survives another party;

(2) the beneficiary or beneficiaries, if proof of death is presented to the financial institution showing that the beneficiary or beneficiaries survived all persons named as parties; or

(3) the personal representative, if any, or, if there is none, the heirs or devisees of a deceased party,

if proof of death is presented to the financial institution showing that the deceased party was the survivor of all other persons named on the account either as a party or beneficiary.

Comment

A financial institution that makes payment on proper request under this section is protected unless the financial institution has received written notice not to. Section 6-226 (discharge). Payment to the personal representative or heirs or devisees of a deceased beneficiary who would be entitled to payment under paragraph (2) is governed by the general law of the state relating to the authority of such persons to collect assets alleged to belong to a decedent.

§ 6-224. Payment to Designated Agent. A financial institution, on request of an agent under an agency designation for an account, may pay to the agent sums on deposit in the account, whether or not a party is disabled, incapacitated, or deceased when the request is made or received, and whether or not the authority of the agent terminates on the disability or incapacity of a party.

Comment

This section is intended to protect a financial institution that makes a payment pursuant to an account with an agency designation even though the agency may have terminated at the time of the payment due to disability, incapacity, or death of the principal. The protection does not apply if the financial institution has received notice under Section 6-226 not to make payment or that the agency has terminated. This section applies whether or not the agency survives the party's disability or incapacity under Section 6-205 (designation of agent).

§ 6-225. Payment to Minor. If a financial institution is required or permitted to make payment pursuant to this [part] to a minor designated as a beneficiary, payment may be made pursuant to the Uniform Transfers to Minors Act (1983/1986).

Comment

Section 6-225 is intended to avoid the need for a guardianship or other protective proceeding in situations where the Uniform Transfers to Minors Act (1983/1986) may be used.

§ 6-226. Discharge.

(a) Payment made pursuant to this [part] in accordance with the terms of the account discharges the financial institution from all claims for amounts so paid, whether or not the payment is consistent with the beneficial ownership of the account as between parties, beneficiaries, or their successors. Payment may be made whether or not a party, beneficiary, or agent is disabled, incapacitated, or deceased when payment is requested, received, or made.

(b) Protection under this section does not extend to payments made after a financial institution has received written notice from a party, or from the personal representative, surviving spouse, or heir or devisee of a deceased party, to the effect that payments in accordance with the terms of the account, including one having an agency designation, should not be permitted, and the financial institution has had a reasonable opportunity to act on it when the payment is made. Unless the notice is withdrawn by the person giving it, the successor of any deceased party must concur in a request for payment if the financial institution is to be protected under this section. Unless a financial institution has been served with process in an action or proceeding, no other notice or other information shown to have been available to the financial institution affects its right to protection under this section.

(c) A financial institution that receives written notice pursuant to this section or otherwise has reason to believe that a dispute exists as to the rights of the parties may refuse, without liability, to make payments in accordance with the terms of the account.

(d) Protection of a financial institution under this section does not affect the rights of parties in disputes between themselves or their successors concerning the beneficial ownership of sums on deposit in accounts or payments made from accounts.

Comment

The provision of subsection (a) protecting a financial institution for payments made after the death, disability, or incapacity of a party is a specific elaboration of the general protective provisions of this section and is drawn from Uniform Commercial Code Section 4-405.

Knowledge of disability, incapacity, or death of a party does not affect payment on request of an agent, whether or not the agent's authority survives disability or incapacity. See Section 6-224 (payment to designated agent). But under subsection (b), the financial institution may not make payments on request of an agent after it has received written notice not to, whether because the agency has terminated or otherwise.

1995 Technical Amendment. By technical amendment in 1995, the defined expression "terms of the account" was substituted for "type of account" in the first sentence of subsection (a). This amendment, made in association with a similar technical amendment to Section 6-213, was not intended to change the meaning of this section. Rather, it was made to negate a possible interpretation of the words "type of account" that is more restrictive than that intended by the drafters.

§ 6-227. Set-Off. Without qualifying any other statutory right to set-off or lien and subject to any contractual provision, if a party is indebted to a financial institution, the financial institution has a right to set-off against the account. The amount of the account subject to set-off is the proportion to which the party is, or immediately before death was, beneficially entitled under Section 6-211 or, in the absence of proof of that proportion, an equal share with all parties.

PART 3
UNIFORM TOD SECURITY REGISTRATION ACT (1989/1998)

§ 6-301. Definitions. In this [part]:

(1) "Beneficiary form" means a registration of a security which indicates the present owner of the security and the intention of the owner regarding the person who will become the owner of the security upon the death of the owner.

(2) "Register," including its derivatives, means to issue a certificate showing the ownership of a certificated security or, in the case of an uncertificated security, to initiate or transfer an account showing ownership of securities.

(3) "Registering entity" means a person who originates or transfers a security title by registration, and includes a broker maintaining security accounts for customers and a transfer agent or other person acting for or as an issuer of securities.

(4) "Security" means a share, participation, or other interest in property, in a business, or in an obligation of an enterprise or other issuer, and includes a certificated security, an uncertificated security, and a security account.

(5) "Security account" means (i) a reinvestment account associated with a security, a securities account with a broker, a cash balance in a brokerage account, cash, interest, earnings, or dividends earned or declared on a security in an account, a reinvestment account, or a brokerage account, whether or not credited to the account before the owner's death, or (ii) a cash balance or other property held for or due to the owner of a security as a replacement for or product of an account security, whether or not credited to the account before the owner's death.

Comment

The definition of "security" is derived from UCC Section 8-102 and includes shares of mutual funds and other investment companies. The defined term "security account" is not intended to include securities held in the name of a bank or similar institution as nominee for the benefit of a trust.

"Survive" is not defined. No effort is made in this part to define survival as it is for purposes of intestate succession in UPC Section 2-104 which requires survival by an heir of the ancestor for 120 hours. For purposes of this part, survive is used in its common law sense of outliving another for any time interval no matter how brief. The drafting committee sought to avoid imposition of a new and unfamiliar meaning of the term on intermediaries familiar with the meaning of "survive" in joint tenancy registrations.

§ 6-302. Registration in Beneficiary Form; Sole or Joint Tenancy Ownership. Only individuals whose registration of a security shows sole ownership by one individual or multiple ownership by two or more with right of survivorship, rather than as tenants in common, may obtain registration in beneficiary form. Multiple owners of a security registered in beneficiary form hold as joint tenants with right of survivorship, as tenants by the entireties, or as owners of community property held in survivorship form, and not as tenants in common.

Comment

This section is designed to prevent co-owners from designating any death beneficiary other than one who is to take only upon survival of all co-owners. It coerces co-owning registrants to signal whether they hold as joint tenants with right of survivorship (JT TEN), as tenants by the entireties (T ENT), or as owners of community property. Also, it imposes survivorship on co-owners holding in a beneficiary form that fails to specify a survivorship form of holding. Tenancy in common and community property otherwise than in a survivorship setting is negated for registration in beneficiary form because persons desiring to signal independent death beneficiaries for each individual's fractional interest in a co-owned security normally will split their holding into separate registrations of the number of units previously constituting their fractional share. Once divided, each can name his or her own choice of death beneficiary.

The term "individuals," as used in this section, limits those who may register as owner or co-owner of a security in beneficiary form to natural persons. However, the section does not restrict individuals using this ownership form as to their choice of death beneficiary. The definition of "beneficiary form" in Section 6-301 indicates that any "person" may be designated beneficiary in a registration in beneficiary form. "Person" is defined so that a church, trust company, family corporation, or other entity, as well as any individual, may be designated as a beneficiary. Section 1-201(34).

§ 6-303. Registration in Beneficiary Form; Applicable Law. A security may be registered in beneficiary form if the form is authorized by this or a similar statute of the state of organization of the issuer or registering entity, the location of the registering entity's principal office, the office of its transfer agent or its office making the registration, or by this or a similar statute of the law of the state listed as the owner's address at the time of registration. A registration governed by the law of a jurisdiction in which this or similar legislation is not in force or was not in force when a registration in beneficiary form was made is nevertheless presumed to be valid and authorized as a matter of contract law.

Comment

This section encourages registrations in beneficiary form to be made whenever a state with which either of the parties to a registration has contact has enacted this or a similar statute. Thus, a registration in beneficiary form of X Company shares might rely on an enactment of this Part in X Company's state of incorporation, or in the state of incorporation of X Company's transfer agent. Or, an enactment by the state of the issuer's principal office, the transfer agent's principal office, or of the issuer's office making the registration also would validate the registration. An enactment of the state of the registering owner's address at time of registration also might be used for validation purposes.

The last sentence of this section is designed, as is UPC Section 6-101, to establish a statutory presumption that a general principle of law is available to achieve a result like that made possible by this part.

§ 6-304. Origination of Registration in Beneficiary Form.

A security, whether evidenced by certificate or account, is registered in beneficiary form when the registration includes a designation of a beneficiary to take the ownership at the death of the owner or the deaths of all multiple owners.

Comment

As noted above in commentary to Section 6-302, this part places no restriction on who may be designated beneficiary in a registration in beneficiary form.

§ 6-305. Form of Registration in Beneficiary Form.

Registration in beneficiary form may be shown by the words "transfer on death" or the abbreviation "TOD," or by the words "pay on death" or the abbreviation "POD," after the name of the registered owner and before the name of a beneficiary.

Comment

The abbreviation POD is included for use without regard for whether the subject is a money claim against an issuer, such as its own note or bond for money loaned, or is a claim to securities evidenced by conventional title documentation. The use of POD in a registration in beneficiary form of shares in an investment company should not be taken as a signal that the investment is to be sold or redeemed on the owner's death so that the sums realized may be "paid" to the death beneficiary. Rather, only a transfer on death, not a liquidation on death, is indicated. The committee would have used only the abbreviation TOD except for the familiarity, rooted in experience with certificates of deposit and other deposit accounts in banks, with the abbreviation POD as signalling a valid nonprobate death benefit or transfer on death.

§ 6-306. Effect of Registration in Beneficiary Form.

The designation of a TOD beneficiary on a registration in beneficiary form has no effect on ownership until the owner's death. A registration of a security in beneficiary form may be canceled or changed at any time by the sole owner or all then surviving owners without the consent of the beneficiary.

Comment

This section simply affirms the right of a sole owner, or the right of all multiple owners, to end a TOD beneficiary registration without the assent of the beneficiary. The section says nothing about how a TOD beneficiary designation may be canceled, meaning that the registering entity's terms and conditions, if any, may be relevant. See Section 6-310. If the terms and conditions have nothing on the point, cancellation of a beneficiary designation presumably would be effected by a reregistration showing a different beneficiary or omitting reference to a TOD beneficiary.

§ 6-307. Ownership on Death of Owner.

On death of a sole owner or the last to die of all multiple owners, ownership of securities registered in beneficiary form passes to the beneficiary or beneficiaries who survive all owners. On proof of death of all owners and compliance with any applicable requirements of the registering entity, a security registered in beneficiary form may be reregistered in the name of the beneficiary or beneficiaries who survived the death of all owners. Until division of the security after the death of all owners, multiple beneficiaries surviving the death of all owners hold their interests as tenants in common. If no beneficiary survives the death of all owners, the security belongs to the estate of the deceased sole owner or the estate of the last to die of all multiple owners.

Comment

Even though multiple owners holding in the beneficiary form here authorized hold with right of survivorship, no survivorship rights attend the positions of multiple beneficiaries who become entitled to securities by reason of having survived the sole owner or the last to die of multiple owners. Issuers (and registering entities) who decide to accept registrations in beneficiary form involving more than one primary beneficiary also should provide by rule whether fractional shares will be registered in the names of surviving beneficiaries where the number of shares held by the deceased owner does not divide without remnant among the survivors. If fractional shares are not desired, the issuer may wish to provide for sale of odd shares and division of proceeds, for an uneven distribution with the first or last named to receive the odd share, or for other resolution. Section 6-308 deals with whether intermediaries have any obligation to offer beneficiary registrations of any sort; Section 6-310 enables issuers to adopt terms and conditions controlling the details of applications for registrations they decide to accept and procedures for implementing such registrations after an owner's death.

The reference to surviving, multiple TOD beneficiaries as tenants in common is not intended to suggest that a registration form specifying unequal shares, such as "TOD A (20%), B (30%), C (50%)," would be improper. Though not included in the beneficiary forms described for illustrative purposes in Section 6-310, the part enables a registering entity to accept and implement a TOD beneficiary designation like the one just suggested. If offered, such a registration form should be implemented by registering entity terms and conditions providing for disposition of the share of a beneficiary who predeceases the owner when two or more of a group of multiple beneficiaries survive the owner. For example, the terms might direct the share of the predeceased beneficiary to the survivors in the proportion that their original shares bore to each other. Unless unequal shares are specified in a registration in beneficiary form designating multiple beneficiaries, the shares of the beneficiaries would, of course, be equal.

The statement that a security registered in beneficiary form is in the deceased owner's estate when no beneficiary survives the owner is not intended to prevent application of any anti-lapse statute that might direct a nonprobate transfer on death to the surviving issue of a beneficiary who failed to survive the owner. Rather, the statement is intended only to indicate that the registering entity involved should transfer or reregister the security as directed by the decedent's personal representative.

See the Comment to Section 6-301 regarding the meaning of "survive" for purposes of this part.

§ 6-308. Protection of Registering Entity.

(a) A registering entity is not required to offer or to accept a request for security registration in beneficiary form. If a registration in beneficiary form is offered by a registering entity, the owner requesting registration in beneficiary form assents to the protections given to the registering entity by this [part].

(b) By accepting a request for registration of a security in beneficiary form, the registering entity agrees that the registration will be implemented on death of the deceased owner as provided in this [part].

(c) A registering entity is discharged from all claims to a security by the estate, creditors, heirs, or devisees of a deceased owner if it registers a transfer of the security in accordance with Section 6-307 and does so in good faith reliance (i) on the registration, (ii) on this [part], and (iii) on information provided to it by affidavit of the personal representative of the deceased owner, or by the surviving beneficiary or by the surviving beneficiary's representatives, or other information available to the registering entity. The protections of this [part] do not extend to a reregistration or payment made after a registering entity has received written notice from any claimant to any interest in the security objecting to implementation of a registration in beneficiary form. No other notice or other information available to the registering entity affects its right to protection under this [part].

(d) The protection provided by this [part] to the registering entity of a security does not affect the rights of beneficiaries in disputes between themselves and other claimants to ownership of the security transferred or its value or proceeds.

Comment

It is to be noted that the "request" for a registration in beneficiary form may be in any form chosen by a registering entity. This part does not prescribe a particular form and does not impose record-keeping requirements. Registering entities' business practices, including any industry standards or rules of transfer agent associations, will control.

"Good faith" as used in this section is intended to mean "honesty in fact and the observance of reasonable commercial standards of fair dealing," as specified in Revised U.C.C. § 1-201(b)(20).

The protections described in this section are generally in harmony with those provided in the Uniform Commercial Code. U.C.C. Section 8-404(c), as revised in 1994, provides that an issuer is generally not liable to third parties for registering transfer of a security pursuant to an effective indorsement or instruction. U.C.C. Section 8-107(b) provides that an indorsement or instruction is effective if it is made by the appropriate person, and under Section 8-107(a)(4) the term "appropriate person" includes a deceased person's "successor taking under other law." The beneficiary under Uniform Probate Code Section 6-307 is such a successor, so that the issuer registering transfer as contemplated by that section pursuant to

the beneficiary's indorsement or instruction is generally protected. See also official comment 2 to U.C.C. Section 8-107 ("If the registration of a security or securities account contains a designation of a death beneficiary under the Uniform Transfer on Death Security Registration Act or comparable legislation, the designated beneficiary would, under that law, have power to transfer upon the person's death and so would be the appropriate person.")

Under subsection (c) of this section, the protections of this part do not apply to a registration made after the registering entity receives "written notice" of objection from a claimant. The protections of the Uniform Commercial Code may, however, continue to apply notwithstanding such a notice, because the exceptions to U.C.C. Section 8-404(c) generally require substantially more than written notice—for example, an injunction or other legal process enjoining the issuer from registering the transfer. See U.C.C. Section 8-404(a)(3). Under the statute as revised in 1994, an issuer receiving mere notice from a third party no longer has a duty to inquire into the third party's claim. See official comment 3 to U.C.C. Section 8-404.

§ 6-309. Nontestamentary Transfer on Death. A transfer on death resulting from a registration in beneficiary form is effective by reason of the contract regarding the registration between the owner and the registering entity and this [part] and is not testamentary.

Comment

This section is comparable to UPC Section 6-214.

Incident to the addition of Section 6-102 in 1998, former subsection (b) was deleted and the text of former subsection (a) became the entire text of the section. Section 6-102 makes the decedent's nonprobate transferees liable for statutory allowances

and allowed claims against the decedent's estate to the extent the decedent's probate estate is inadequate. Former subsection (b) provided:

This part does not limit the rights of creditors of security owners against beneficiaries and other transferees under other laws of this state.

§ 6-310. Terms, Conditions, and Forms for Registration.

(a) A registering entity offering to accept registrations in beneficiary form may establish the terms and conditions under which it will receive requests (i) for registrations in beneficiary form, and (ii) for implementation of registrations in beneficiary form, including requests for cancellation of previously registered TOD beneficiary designations and requests for reregistration to effect a change of beneficiary. The terms and conditions so established may provide for proving death, avoiding or resolving any problems concerning fractional shares, designating primary and contingent beneficiaries, and substituting a named beneficiary's descendants to take in the place of the named beneficiary in the event of the beneficiary's death. Substitution may be indicated by appending to the name of the primary beneficiary the letters LDPS, standing for "lineal descendants per stirpes." This designation substitutes a deceased beneficiary's descendants who survive the owner for a beneficiary who fails to so survive, the descendants to be identified and to share in accordance with the law of the beneficiary's domicile at the owner's death governing inheritance by descendants of an intestate. Other forms of identifying beneficiaries who are to take on one or more contingencies, and rules for providing proofs and assurances needed to satisfy reasonable concerns by registering entities regarding conditions and identities relevant to accurate implementation of registrations in beneficiary form, may be contained in a registering entity's terms and conditions.

(b) The following are illustrations of registrations in beneficiary form which a registering entity may authorize:

(1) Sole owner-sole beneficiary: John S. Brown TOD (or POD) John S. Brown Jr.

(2) Multiple owners-sole beneficiary: John S. Brown Mary B. Brown JT TEN TOD John S. Brown Jr.

(3) Multiple owners-primary and secondary (substituted) beneficiaries: John S. Brown Mary B. Brown JT TEN TOD John S. Brown Jr. SUB BENE Peter Q. Brown or John S. Brown Mary B. Brown JT TEN TOD John S. Brown Jr. LDPS.

Comment

Use of "and" or "or" between the names of persons registered as co-owners is unnecessary under this part and should be discouraged. If used, the two words should have the same meaning insofar as concerns a title form; i.e., that of "and" to indicate that both named persons own the asset.

Descendants of a named beneficiary who take by virtue of a "LDPS" designation appended to a beneficiary's name take as TOD beneficiaries rather than as intestate successors. If no descendant of a predeceased primary beneficiary survives the owner, the security passes as a part of the owner's estate as provided in Section 6-307.

§ 6-311. Application of Part. This [part] applies to registrations of securities in beneficiary form made before or after [effective date], by decedents dying on or after [effective date].]

Comment

Section 6-311 is an optional provision that may be particularly useful in a state that has previously enacted the Uniform Probate Code, since the general effective date and transitional provisions of UPC Section 8-101 are not expressly adapted for the addition of this part. A state newly enacting the Uniform Probate Code, including this part, may find that general Section 8-101 is adequate for this purpose and addition of optional Section 6-311 unnecessary.

PART 4
UNIFORM REAL PROPERTY TRANSFER ON DEATH ACT (2009)

§ 6-401. Short Title. This [part] may be cited as the Uniform Real Property Transfer on Death Act.

§ 6-402. Definitions. In this [part]:

(1) "Beneficiary" means a person that receives property under a transfer on death deed.

(2) "Designated beneficiary" means a person designated to receive property in a transfer on death deed.

(3) "Joint owner" means an individual who owns property concurrently with one or more other individuals with a right of survivorship. The term includes a joint tenant[,][and] [owner of community property with a right of survivorship[,][and tenant by the entirety]. The term does not include a tenant

in common [or owner of community property without a right of survivorship].

(4) "Person" means an individual, corporation, business trust, estate, trust, partnership, limited liability company, association, joint venture, public corporation, government or governmental subdivision, agency, or instrumentality, or any other legal or commercial entity.

(5) "Property" means an interest in real property located in this state which is transferable on the death of the owner.

(6) "Transfer on death deed" means a deed authorized under this [part].

(7) "Transferor" means an individual who makes a transfer on death deed.

Comment

Paragraph (1) defines a beneficiary as a person that receives property under a transfer on death deed. This links the definition of a "beneficiary" to the definition of a "person." A beneficiary can be any person, including the trustee of a revocable trust.

Paragraph (2) defines a designated beneficiary as a person designated to receive property in a transfer on death deed. This links the definition of a "designated beneficiary" to the definition of a "person." A designated beneficiary can be any person, including a revocable trust.

The distinction between a "beneficiary" and a "designated beneficiary" is easily illustrated. Section 6-413 provides that, on the transferor's death, the property that is the subject of a transfer on death deed is transferred to the designated beneficiaries who survive the transferor. If X and Y are the designated beneficiaries but only Y survives the transferor, then Y is a beneficiary and X is not. A further illustration comes into play if Section 6-413 is made subject to the state's antilapse statute. If X fails to survive the transferor but has a descendant, Z, who survives the transferor, the antilapse statute may create a substitute gift in favor of Z. In such a case, the designated beneficiaries are X and Y, but the beneficiaries are Y and Z.

Paragraph (3) provides a definition of a "joint owner" as an individual who owns property with one or more other individuals with a right of survivorship. The term is used in Sections 6-411 and 6-413.

Paragraph (4) is the standard Uniform Law Commission definition of a "person."

The effect of paragraph (5) is that this part applies to all interests in real property located in this state that are transferable at the death of the owner.

Paragraph (6) provides that a "transfer on death deed" is a deed authorized under this part. In some states with existing transfer on death deed legislation, the legislation has instead used the term "beneficiary deed." The term "transfer on death deed" is preferred, to be consistent with the transfer on death registration of securities. See Article VI, Part 3, containing the Uniform TOD Security Registration Act.

Paragraph (7) limits the definition of a "transferor" to an individual. The term "transferor" does not include a corporation, business trust, estate, trust, partnership, limited liability company, association, joint venture, public corporation, government or governmental subdivision, agency, or instrumentality, or any legal or commercial entity other than an individual. The term also does not include an agent or other representative. If a transfer on death deed is made by an agent on behalf of a principal or by a conservator, guardian, or judge on behalf of a ward, the principal or ward is the transferor. By way of analogy, see Uniform Trust Code (2000/2005) Section 103(15) (defining "settlor") and the accompanying Comment (excluding an individual "acting as the agent for the person who will be funding the trust"). The power of an agent to make or revoke a transfer on death deed on behalf of a principal is determined by other law, such as the Uniform Power of Attorney Act (2006) (UPC Article 5B), as indicated in the Comments to Sections 6-409 and 6-411.

§ 6-403. Applicability.

This [part] applies to a transfer on death deed made before, on, or after [the effective date of this [part]] by a transferor dying on or after [the effective date of this [part]].

Comment

This section provides that this part applies to a transfer on death deed made before, on, or after the effective date of this part by a transferor dying on or after the effective date of this part. This section is consistent with the provisions governing transfer on death registration of securities. Those provisions "appl[y] to registrations of securities in beneficiary form made before or after [effective date], by decedents dying on or after [effective date]." See Section 6-311.

§ 6-404. Nonexclusivity. This [part] does not affect any method of transferring property otherwise permitted under the law of this state.

Comment

This section provides that this part is nonexclusive. This part does not affect any method of transferring property otherwise permitted under state law.

One such method is a present transfer with a retained legal life estate. Consider the following examples:

Example 1. A conveys Blackacre to B while reserving A's right to remain in possession until A's death. By this conveyance, A has made a present transfer of a future interest to B. The transfer is irrevocable. The future interest will ripen into possession at A's death, even if B fails to survive A.

Example 2. A executes, acknowledges, and records a transfer on death deed for Blackacre, naming B as the designated beneficiary. During A's lifetime, no interest passes to B, and A may revoke the deed. If unrevoked, the deed will transfer possession to B at A's death only if B survives A.

As illustrated in these examples, the two methods of transfer have different effects and are governed by different rules.

§ 6-405. Transfer on Death Deed Authorized. An individual may transfer property to one or more beneficiaries effective at the transferor's death by a transfer on death deed.

Comment

This section authorizes a transfer on death deed and makes it clear that the transfer is not an inter vivos transfer. The transfer occurs at the transferor's death.

The transferor is an individual, but the singular includes the plural. Multiple individuals can readily act together to transfer property by a transfer on death deed, as in the common case of a husband and wife who own the property as joint tenants or as tenants by the entirety. On the effect of a transfer on death deed made by joint owners, see Section 6-413(c) and the accompanying Comment.

The transferor may select any form of ownership, concurrent or successive, absolute or conditional, contingent or vested, valid under state law. Among many other things, this permits the transferor to reserve interests for his estate (e.g., mineral interests); to specify the nature and extent of the beneficiary's interest; and to designate one or more primary beneficiaries and one or more alternate beneficiaries to take in the event the primary beneficiaries fail to survive the transferor. This freedom to specify the form and terms of the transferee's interest comports with the fundamental principle of American law recognized by the Restatement (Third) of Property (Wills and Other Donative Transfers) § 10.1 that the donor's intention should be "given effect to the maximum extent allowed by law." As the Restatement explains in Comment c to § 10.1, "American law curtails freedom of disposition only to the extent that the donor attempts to make a disposition or achieve a purpose that is prohibited or restricted by an overriding rule of law."

Notwithstanding this freedom of disposition, transferors are encouraged as a practical matter to avoid formulating dispositions that would complicate title. Dispositions containing conditions or class gifts, for example, may require a court proceeding to sort out the beneficiaries' interests. Other estate planning mechanisms, such as trusts, may be more appropriate in such cases.

§ 6-406. Transfer on Death Deed Revocable. A transfer on death deed is revocable even if the deed or another instrument contains a contrary provision.

Comment

A fundamental feature of a transfer on death deed under this part is that the transferor retains the power to revoke the deed. Section 6-406 is framed as a mandatory rule, for two reasons. First, the rule prevents an off-record instrument from affecting the revocability of a transfer on death deed. Second, the rule protects the transferor who may wish later to revoke the deed.

If the transferor promises to make the deed irrevocable or not to revoke the deed, the promisee may have a remedy under other law if the promise is broken. The deed remains revocable despite the promise.

§ 6-407. Transfer on Death Deed Nontestamentary. A transfer on death deed is nontestamentary.

Comment

This section is consistent with Section 6-101(a), which provides: "A provision for a nonprobate transfer on death in an insurance policy, contract of employment, bond, mortgage, promissory note, certificated or uncertificated security, account agreement, custodial agreement, deposit agreement, compensation plan, pension plan, individual retirement plan, employee benefit plan, trust, conveyance, deed of gift, marital property agreement, or other written instrument of a similar nature is nontestamentary."

As the Comment to Section 6-101 explains, because the mode of transfer is declared to be nontestamentary, the instrument of transfer is not a will and does not have to be executed in compliance with the formalities for wills, nor does the instrument need to be probated.

Whether a document that is ineffective as a transfer on death deed (e.g., because it has not been recorded before the transferor's death) should be given effect as a testamentary instrument will depend on the applicable facts and on the wills law of the jurisdiction. Section 2-503 provides in pertinent part: "Although a document ... was not executed in compliance with Section 2-502, the document ... is treated as if it had been executed in compliance with that section if the proponent of the document ... establishes by clear and convincing evidence that the decedent intended the document ... to constitute ... (iii) an addition to or alteration of the [decedent's] will ...."

§ 6-408. Capacity of Transferor. The capacity required to make or revoke a transfer on death deed is the same as the capacity required to make a will.

Comment

This section provides that the capacity required to make or revoke a transfer on death deed, which is a revocable will substitute, is the same as the capacity required to make a will. It is appropriate that a will and a transfer on death deed require the same level of capacity, for both mechanisms are revocable and ambulatory, the latter term meaning that they do not operate before the grantor's death. This approach is consistent with the Restatement (Third) of Property (Wills and Other Donative Transfers) § 8.1(b), which applies the standard of testamentary capacity, and not the standard of capacity for inter vivos gifts, to revocable will substitutes: "If the donative transfer is in the form of a will, a revocable will substitute, or a revocable gift, the testator or donor must be capable of knowing and understanding in a general way the nature and extent of his or her property, the natural objects of his or her bounty, and the disposition that he or she is making of that property, and must also be capable of relating these elements to one another and forming an orderly desire regarding the disposition of the property." This section is also consistent with Uniform Trust Code Section 601: "The capacity required to create, amend, revoke, or add property to a revocable trust, or to direct the actions of the trustee of a revocable trust, is the same as that required to make a will."

A transfer on death deed is not affected if the transferor subsequently loses capacity. On the ability of an agent under a power of attorney to make or revoke a transfer on death deed, see the Comments to   Sections 6-409 and 6-411.

§ 6-409. Requirements. A transfer on death deed:

(1) except as otherwise provided in paragraph (2), must contain the essential elements and formalities of a properly recordable inter vivos deed;

(2) must state that the transfer to the designated beneficiary is to occur at the transferor's death; and

(3) must be recorded before the transferor's death in the public records in [the office of the county recorder of deeds] of the [county] where the property is located.

Comment

Paragraph (1) requires a transfer on death deed to contain the same essential elements and formalities, other than a present intention to convey, as are required for a properly recordable inter vivos deed under state law. "Essential elements" is a term with a long usage in the law of deeds of real property. The essential elements of a deed vary from one state to another but commonly include the names of the grantor and grantee, a clause transferring title, a description of the property transferred, and the grantor's signature. In all states, the essential elements of a properly recordable deed include the requirement that the deed be acknowledged by the grantor before a notary public or other individual authorized by law to take acknowledgments. See Thompson on Real Property § 92.04(c) (observing that a "certificate of acknowledgment or attestation is universally required to qualify an instrument for recordation"). In the context of transfer on death deeds, the requirement of acknowledgment fulfills at least four functions. First, it cautions a transferor that he or she is performing an act with legal consequences. Such caution is important where, as here, the transferor does not experience the wrench of delivery because the transfer occurs at death. Second, acknowledgment helps to prevent fraud. Third, acknowledgment facilitates the recording of the deed. Fourth, acknowledgment enables the rule in Section 6-411 that a later acknowledged deed prevails over an earlier acknowledged deed.

Paragraph (2) emphasizes an important distinction between an inter vivos transfer and a transfer on death. An inter vivos transfer reflects an intention to transfer, at the time of the conveyance, an interest in property, either a present interest or a future interest. In contrast, a transfer on death reflects an intention that the transfer occur at the transferor's death. Under no circumstances should a transfer on death be given effect inter vivos; to do so would violate the transferor's intention that the transfer occur at the transferor's death.

Paragraph (3) requires a transfer on death deed to be recorded before the transferor's death in the county (or other appropriate administrative division of a state, such as a parish) where the land is located. If the property described in the deed is in more than one county, the deed is effective only with respect to the property in the county or counties where the deed is recorded. The requirement of recordation before death helps to prevent fraud by ensuring that all steps necessary to the effective transfer on death deed are completed during the transferor's lifetime. The requirement of recordation before death also enables all parties to rely on the recording system.

An individual's agent may execute a transfer on death deed on the individual's behalf to the extent permitted by other law, such as the Uniform Power of Attorney Act (2006). This part does not define, but instead relies on other law to determine, the authority of an agent.

§ 6-410. Notice, Delivery, Acceptance, Consideration Not Required. A transfer on death deed is effective without:

(1) notice or delivery to or acceptance by the designated beneficiary during the transferor's life; or

(2) consideration.

Comment

This section makes it clear that a transfer on death deed is effective without notice or delivery to or acceptance by the beneficiary during the transferor's lifetime (paragraph (1)) and without consideration

(paragraph (2)).

Paragraph (1) is consistent with the fundamental distinction under this part between a transfer on death deed and an inter vivos deed. Under the former, but not under the latter, the transfer occurs at the transferor's death. Therefore, there is no requirement of notice, delivery, or acceptance during the transferor's life. This does not mean that the beneficiary is required to accept the property. The beneficiary may disclaim the property, as explained in Section 6-414 and the accompanying Comment.

Paragraph (2) is consistent with the law of donative transfers. A deed need not be supported by consideration.

§ 6-411. Revocation by Instrument Authorized; Revocation by Act Not Permitted.

(a) Subject to subsection (b), an instrument is effective to revoke a recorded transfer on death deed, or any part of it, only if the instrument:

(1) is one of the following:

(A) a transfer on death deed that revokes the deed or part of the deed expressly or by inconsistency;

(B) an instrument of revocation that expressly revokes the deed or part of the deed; or

(C) an inter vivos deed that expressly revokes the transfer on death deed or part of the deed; and

(2) is acknowledged by the transferor after the acknowledgment of the deed being revoked and recorded before the transferor's death in the public records in [the office of the county recorder of deeds] of the [county] where the deed is recorded.

(b) If a transfer on death deed is made by more than one transferor:

(1) revocation by a transferor does not affect the deed as to the interest of another transferor; and

(2) a deed of joint owners is revoked only if it is revoked by all of the living joint owners.

(c) After a transfer on death deed is recorded, it may not be revoked by a revocatory act on the deed.

(d) This section does not limit the effect of an inter vivos transfer of the property.

Comment

This section concerns revocation by instrument and revocation by act. On revocation by change of circumstances, such as by divorce or homicide, see Section 6-413 and the accompanying Comment.

Subsection (a) provides the exclusive methods of revoking, in whole or in part, a recorded transfer on death deed by a subsequent instrument. Revocation by an instrument not specified, such as the transferor's will, is not permitted.

The rule that a transfer on death deed may not be revoked by the transferor's subsequent will is a departure from the Restatement (Third) of Property (Wills and Other Donative Transfers) § 7.2 comment e (see also the corresponding Reporter's Note), which encourages the revocability of will substitutes by will. However, there is a sound reason for the departure in the specific case of a transfer on death deed. A transfer on death deed operates on real property, for which certainty of title is essential. This certainty would be difficult, and in many cases impossible, to achieve if an off-record instrument, such as the grantor's will, could revoke a recorded transfer on death deed. The rule in this part against revocation by will is also consistent with the rule governing multiple-party bank accounts. See Section 6-213(b)

("A right of survivorship arising from the express terms of the account, Section 6-212, or a POD designation, may not be altered by will.")

A recorded transfer on death deed may be revoked by instrument only by (1) a subsequently acknowledged transfer on death deed, (2) a subsequently acknowledged instrument of revocation, such as the form in Section 6-417, or (3) a subsequently acknowledged inter vivos deed containing an express revocation clause. Consider the following examples:

Example 1. T executes, acknowledges, and records a transfer on death deed for Blackacre. Later, T executes, acknowledges, and records a second transfer on death deed for Blackacre, containing an express revocation clause revoking "all my prior transfer on death deeds concerning this property." The second deed revokes the first deed. The revocation occurs when the second deed is recorded. (For the result if the second deed had not contained the express revocation clause, see Example 5.)

Example 2. T executes, acknowledges, and records two transfer on death deeds for Blackacre. Both deeds expressly revoke "all my prior transfer on death deeds concerning this property." The dates of acknowledgment determine which deed revoked the other. The first deed is acknowledged November 1; the second deed is acknowledged December 15. The second deed is the later acknowledged, so it revokes the first deed. The revocation occurs when the second deed is recorded.

Example 3. T executes and acknowledges a transfer on death deed for Blackacre. T later executes and acknowledges a revocation form. Both instruments are recorded. Because the revocation form is acknowledged later than the deed, the form revokes the deed. The revocation occurs when the form is recorded.

Example 4. T executes and acknowledges a transfer on death deed for Blackacre. T later executes and acknowledges an inter vivos deed conveying Blackacre and expressly revoking the transfer on death deed. Both instruments are recorded. Because the inter vivos deed contains an express revocation provision and is acknowledged later than the transfer on death deed, the inter vivos deed revokes the transfer on death deed. The revocation occurs when the inter vivos deed is recorded. (For the result if the inter vivos deed had not contained an express revocation clause, see the discussion below on "ademption by extinction.")

The same rules apply whether the revocation is total or partial. In the previous examples, suppose instead that the initial transfer on death deed provides for the transfer of two parcels, Blackacre and Whiteacre, and that the subsequent instrument revokes the transfer on death deed as to Blackacre. The subsequent instrument revokes the transfer on death deed in part.

If the property described in the original deed is in more than one county, the revocation is effective only with respect to the property in the county or counties where the revoking deed or instrument is recorded.

Subsection (a)(1)(A) speaks of revocation "expressly or by inconsistency." This provision references the well-established law of revocation by inconsistency of wills. Consider the following examples:

Example 5. T executes, acknowledges, and records a transfer on death deed for Blackacre naming X as the designated beneficiary. Later, T executes, acknowledges, and records a transfer on death deed

for the same property, Blackacre, containing no express revocation of the earlier deed but naming Y as the designated beneficiary. Later, T dies. The recording of the deed in favor of Y revokes the deed in favor of X by inconsistency. At T's death, Y is the owner of Blackacre.

Example 6. T, the owner of Blackacre in fee simple absolute, executes, acknowledges, and records a transfer on death deed for Blackacre naming X as the designated beneficiary. Later, T executes, acknowledges, and records a transfer on death deed containing no express revocation of the earlier deed but naming Y as the designated beneficiary of a life estate (or a mineral interest) in Blackacre. Later, T dies. The recording of the deed in favor of Y partially revokes the deed in favor of X by inconsistency. At T's death, Y is the owner of a life estate (or a mineral interest) in Blackacre, and X is the owner of the remainder.

The question is sometimes raised whether a recorded inter vivos deed *without an express revocation clause* operates as a revocation of an earlier transfer on death deed. The answer highlights the important distinction between "revocation" and "ademption by extinction." See Atkinson on Wills § 134. Revocation means that the instrument is rendered void. Ademption by extinction means that the transfer of the property cannot occur because the property is not owned by the transferor at death. The doctrines are different.

In some instances, revocation and ademption have the same practical effect: the designated beneficiary of the property receives nothing. Nothing in this section changes that fact, as indicated in subsection (d). However, there are other instances where the doctrines have differing effects. Consider the following illustration, drawn from the law of wills.

Example 7. T executes a will devising Blackacre to A. Later, T becomes legally incompetent, and G is appointed as T's conservator. G, acting within the scope of his authority, sells Blackacre to B for $100,000. Later, T dies.

The law of wills provides that the devise to A is adeemed rather than revoked. This means that A is not entitled to Blackacre but is entitled to a pecuniary devise in the amount of $100,000. See Section 2-606(b). See also Atkinson on Wills § 134; *Wasserman v. Cohen*, 606 N.E.2d 901, 903 (Mass. 1993). The result is designed to effectuate *T*'s presumed intention.

The Joint Editorial Board for Uniform Trust and Estate Acts has begun a conversation on whether this Code's provisions on ademption should be extended to nonprobate transfers, thus harmonizing the treatment of wills and will substitutes on this aspect of the law. This part accepts the well recognized distinction between revocation and ademption in order to leave the door open for such future harmonization, which would effectuate the presumed intention of nonprobate grantors.

Subsection (b) supplies rules governing revocation by instrument in the event of a transfer on death deed made by multiple owners. Subsection (b)(1) provides that revocation by a transferor does not affect a transfer on death deed as to the interest of another transferor. Subsection (b)(2) provides that a transfer on death deed of joint owners is revoked only if it is revoked by all of the living joint owners. This rule is consistent with §6-306, which provides in pertinent part: "A registration of a security in beneficiary form may be canceled or changed at any time by the sole owner or all then surviving owners without the consent of the beneficiary." Subsection (b)(2) applies only to a deed of joint owners. A joint tenant who severs the joint tenancy, thereby destroying the right of survivorship, is no longer a joint owner.

Subsection (c) provides that a recorded transfer on death deed may not be revoked by a revocatory act performed on the deed. Such an act includes burning, tearing, canceling, obliterating, or destroying the deed or any part of it.

This part does not define, but instead looks to other law to determine, the authority of an agent. An individual's agent may revoke a transfer on death deed on the individual's behalf to the extent permitted by other law, such as the Uniform Power of Attorney Act (2006).

§ 6-412. Effect of Transfer on Death Deed During Transferor's Life.

During a transferor's life, a transfer on death deed does not:

(1) affect an interest or right of the transferor or any other owner, including the right to transfer or encumber the property;

(2) affect an interest or right of a transferee, even if the transferee has actual or constructive notice of the deed;

(3) affect an interest or right of a secured or unsecured creditor or future creditor of the transferor, even if the creditor has actual or constructive notice of the deed;

(4) affect the transferor's or designated beneficiary's eligibility for any form of public assistance;

(5) create a legal or equitable interest in favor of the designated beneficiary; or

(6) subject the property to claims or process of a creditor of the designated beneficiary.

Comment

A fundamental feature of a transfer on death deed under this part is that it does not operate until the transferor's death. The transfer occurs at the transferor's death, not before.

Paragraph (1): A transfer on death deed, during the transferor's lifetime, does not affect the interests or property rights of the transferor or any other owners. Therefore, the deed does not, among many other things: affect the transferor's right to transfer or encumber the property inter vivos; sever a joint tenancy or a joint tenant's right of survivorship; trigger a due-on-sale clause in the transferor's mortgage; trigger the imposition of real estate transfer tax; or affect the transferor's homestead or real estate tax exemptions, if any.

Paragraph (2): A transfer on death deed does not affect transferees, whether or not they have notice of the deed. Like a will, the transfer on death deed is ambulatory. It has no effect on inter vivos transfers.

Paragraph (3): A transfer on death deed, during the transferor's lifetime, does not affect pre-existing or future creditors, secured or unsecured, whether or not they have an interest in the property or notice of the deed.

Paragraph (4): A transfer on death deed, during the transferor's lifetime, does not affect the transferor's or designated beneficiary's eligibility for any form of public assistance, including Medicaid. On this point, the drafting committee of this part specifically disapproves of the contrary approach of Colo. Rev. Stat. § 15-15-403.

Paragraph (5): During the transferor's lifetime, a

transfer on death deed does not create a legal or equitable interest in the designated beneficiary. The beneficiary does not have an interest that can be assigned or encumbered. Note, however, that this rule would not preclude the doctrine of after-acquired title. A warranty deed from a designated beneficiary to a third party would operate to pass the beneficiary's title to the third party after the transferor's death.

Paragraph (6): A transfer on death deed, during the transferor's lifetime, does not make the property subject to claims or process of the designated beneficiary's creditors. The deed has no more effect than a will.

If a transferor combines an inter vivos transfer of an interest in property (such as a mineral interest) with a transfer on death of the remainder interest, the inter vivos transfer may have present effect even though the transfer on death does not occur until the transferor's death.

§ 6-413. Effect of Transfer on Death Deed at Transferor's Death.

(a) Except as otherwise provided in the transfer on death deed[,][or] in this section[,][or in [cite state statutes on antilapse, revocation by divorce or homicide, survival and simultaneous death, and elective share, if applicable to nonprobate transfers]], on the death of the transferor, the following rules apply to property that is the subject of a transfer on death deed and owned by the transferor at death:

(1) Subject to paragraph (2), the interest in the property is transferred to the designated beneficiary in accordance with the deed.

(2) The interest of a designated beneficiary is contingent on the designated beneficiary surviving the transferor. The interest of a designated beneficiary that fails to survive the transferor lapses.

(3) Subject to paragraph (4), concurrent interests are transferred to the beneficiaries in equal and undivided shares with no right of survivorship.

(4) If the transferor has identified two or more designated beneficiaries to receive concurrent interests in the property, the share of one which lapses or fails for any reason is transferred to the other, or to the others in proportion to the interest of each in the remaining part of the property held concurrently.

(b) Subject to [cite state recording act], a beneficiary takes the property subject to all conveyances, encumbrances, assignments, contracts, mortgages, liens, and other interests to which the property is subject at the transferor's death. For purposes of this subsection and [cite state recording act], the recording of the transfer on death deed is deemed to have occurred at the transferor's death.

(c) If a transferor is a joint owner and is:

(1) survived by one or more other joint owners, the property that is the subject of a transfer on death deed belongs to the surviving joint owner or owners with right of survivorship; or

(2) the last surviving joint owner, the transfer on death deed is effective.

(d) A transfer on death deed transfers property without covenant or warranty of title even if the deed contains a contrary provision.

Comment

Subsection (a) states four default rules, except as otherwise provided by the transfer on death deed, by this section, or by other provisions of state law governing nonprobate transfers.

The four default rules established by subsection (a) are these. First, the property that is the subject of an effective transfer on death deed and owned by the transferor at death is transferred at the transferor's death to the designated beneficiaries as provided in the deed. The rule implements the transferor's intention as described in the deed. Consider the following example:

Example 1. A executes, acknowledges, and records a transfer on death deed for Blackacre naming X as the primary beneficiary and Y as the alternate beneficiary if X fails to survive A. Both X and Y survive A. Blackacre is transferred to X at A's death in accordance with the provisions of the deed.

This default rule implements the fundamental principle that the provisions of the deed control the disposition of the property, unless otherwise provided by state law.

The drafting committee of this part approves of the result in *In re Estate of Roloff*, 143 P.3d 406 (Kan. Ct. App. 2006) (holding that crops should be transferred with the land under a transfer on death deed because this result would be reached on the same facts with any other deed).

The bracketed language at the beginning of subsection (a) enables a state to make the default rules subject to other statutes, such as an antilapse statute or a statute providing for revocation on divorce. Consider the following examples:

Example 2. A executes, acknowledges, and records a transfer on death deed for Blackacre naming X as the primary beneficiary and Y as the alternate beneficiary if X fails to survive A. In fact, X and Y fail to survive A, who is survived only by X's child, Z. Assume that the state's antilapse statute applies to transfer on death deeds and creates a substitute gift in Z. (For such a statute, see Section 2-706.) Blackacre is transferred to Z at A's death in accordance with the provisions of the deed as modified by the antilapse statute.

Example 3. A executes, acknowledges, and records a transfer on death deed for Blackacre naming her spouse, X, as the primary beneficiary and Y as the alternate beneficiary if X fails to survive A. Later, A and X divorce. Assume that the state's statute on revocation by divorce applies to transfer on death deeds and revokes the designation in favor of X, with the effect that the provisions of the transfer on death deed are given effect as if X had disclaimed. (For such a statute, see Section 2-804.) Assume further that the effect of the putative disclaimer is that X is treated as having failed to survive A. (See Section 2-1106(a)(3)(B).) Blackacre is transferred to Y at A's death in accordance with the provisions of the deed as modified by the revocation on divorce and disclaimer statutes.

Note that the property must be owned by the transferor at death. Property no longer owned by the transferor at death cannot be transferred by a transfer on death deed, just as it cannot be transferred by a will. This is the principle of ademption by extinction, discussed in the Comment to Section 6-411.

In almost every instance, the transferor will own the property not only at death but also when the transfer on death deed is executed, but the latter is not imperative. Consider the following example. H and W, a married couple, hold Blackacre as tenants by the entirety. H executes, acknowledges, and records a transfer on death deed for Blackacre in favor of X. W later dies, at which point H owns Blackacre in fee simple absolute. Later, H dies. Under the law of some states, there may be a question whether the transfer on death deed is effective, given that H executed it when Blackacre was owned, not by H and W, but by the marital entity. The correct answer is that the transfer on death deed is effective at H's death because Blackacre is owned by H at H's death. See, e.g., *Mitchell v. Wilmington Trust Co.*, 449 A.2d 1055 (Del. Ch. 1982) (mortgage granted by one tenant by the entirety is not void upon execution but remains inchoate during the lives of both spouses, and becomes a valid lien if the spouse who executed the mortgage survives the other spouse or if the spouses get divorced).

The second default rule established by subsection (a) is that the interest of a designated beneficiary is contingent on surviving the transferor. This default rule treats wills and will substitutes alike. The interest of a designated beneficiary who fails to survive the transferor lapses.

The third default rule established by subsection (a) is that concurrent beneficiaries receive equal and undivided interests with no right of survivorship among them. This default rule is consistent with the general presumption in favor of tenancy in common. See Powell on Real Property § 51.02. The rule is also consistent with Section 6-212 governing multiple-party accounts and Section 6-307 governing the transfer on death registration of securities.

The fourth and last default rule established by subsection (a) is that, in the event of the lapse or failure of an interest to be held concurrently, the share that lapses or fails passes proportionately to the surviving concurrent beneficiaries. Consider the following example:

Example 4. A executes, acknowledges, and records a transfer on death deed for Blackacre naming X, Y, and Z as the designated beneficiaries. X and Y survive A, but Z fails to survive A. The transfer on death deed is effective and, in the absence of an antilapse statute, transfers Blackacre to X and Y. This default rule is consistent with the transferor's probable intention in the absence of an antilapse statute and also with Section 2-604(b) on the lapse of a residuary devise.

Subsection (b) concerns the effect of transactions during the transferor's life. The subsection states an intermediate rule between two extremes. One extreme would provide that transactions during the transferor's life affect the beneficiary only if the transactions are recorded before the transferor's death. This would unfairly disadvantage the transferor's creditors and inter vivos transferees. The other extreme would provide that transactions during the transferor's life always supersede the beneficiary's interest, even if the recording act would provide otherwise. Between these two positions is the rule of subsection (b).

Subsection (b) provides that the beneficiary's interest is subject to *all* conveyances, encumbrances, assignments, contracts, mortgages, liens, and other interests to which the property is subject at the transferor's death. "Liens" includes liens arising by operation of law, such as state Medicaid liens.

The only exception to this rule arises when the state recording act so provides. The state recording act will so provide only when two conditions are met: (1) the inter vivos conveyance or encumbrance is unrecorded throughout the transferor's life (the legal fiction in this subsection protects persons who transact with the transferor and record any time before the transferor's death); and (2) the beneficiary is protected by the recording act. These two conditions will be met only in rare instances. Most beneficiaries of transfer on death deeds are gratuitous, whereas state recording acts typically protect only purchasers for value. See Powell on Real Property § 82.02.

Subsection (c) provides that the survivorship right of a joint owner takes precedence over the transfer on death deed. This rule is consistent with the law of joint tenancy and wills: the right of survivorship takes precedence over a provision in a joint tenant's will.

Subsection (d) states the mandatory rule that a transfer on death deed transfers the property without covenant or warranty of title. The rule is mandatory for two reasons: first, to prevent mishaps by uninformed grantors; and second, to recognize that a transfer on death deed is a will substitute. The rule of this section is consistent with the longstanding law of wills. As stated by Sir Edward Coke, "an express warranty cannot be created by will." Coke on Littleton 386a.

§ 6-414. Disclaimer. A beneficiary may disclaim all or part of the beneficiary's interest as provided by [cite state statute or the Uniform Disclaimer of Property Interests Act (1999/2006) (UPC Article II, Part 11)].

Comment

A beneficiary of a transfer on death deed may disclaim the property interest the deed attempts to transfer. While this section relies on other law, such as the Uniform Disclaimer of Property Interests Act (1999/2006), to govern the disclaimer, two general principles should be noted.

First, there is no need under the law of disclaimers to execute a disclaimer in advance. During the transferor's life, a designated beneficiary has no interest in the property. See Section 6-412. Nothing passes to the designated beneficiary while the transferor is alive, hence there is no need to execute a disclaimer during that time.

Second, an effective disclaimer executed after the testator's death "relates back" to the moment of the attempted transfer, here the death of the transferor. Because the disclaimer "relates back," the beneficiary is regarded as never having had an interest in the disclaimed property. The Uniform Disclaimer of Property Interests Act (1999/2006) reaches this result, without using the language of relation back. See Section 2-1106(b)(1): "The disclaimer takes effect as of the time the instrument creating the interest becomes irrevocable ...." As the Comment to Section 2-1106 explains, "This Act continues the effect of the relation back doctrine, not by using the specific words, but by directly stating what the relation back doctrine has been interpreted to mean."

§ 6-415. Liability for Creditor Claims and Statutory Allowances.
Alternative A

A beneficiary of a transfer on death deed is liable for an allowed claim against the transferor's probate estate and statutory allowances to a surviving spouse and children to the extent provided in

Section 6-102.

Alternative B

(a) To the extent the transferor's probate estate is insufficient to satisfy an allowed claim against the estate or a statutory allowance to a surviving spouse or child, the estate may enforce the liability against property transferred at the transferor's death by a transfer on death deed.

(b) If more than one property is transferred by one or more transfer on death deeds, the liability under subsection (a) is apportioned among the properties in proportion to their net values at the transferor's death.

(c) A proceeding to enforce the liability under this section must be commenced not later than [18 months] after the transferor's death.

End of Alternatives

Comment

Alternative A defers to Section 6-102 to establish the liability of a beneficiary of a transfer on death deed for creditor claims and statutory allowances.

Section 6-102 was added in 1998 to establish the principle that recipients of nonprobate transfers can be required to contribute to pay allowed claims and statutory allowances to the extent the probate estate is insufficient. The fundamental rule of liability is contained in Section 6-102(b): "Except as otherwise provided by statute, a transferee of a nonprobate transfer is subject to liability to any probate estate of the decedent for allowed claims against the decedent's probate estate and statutory allowances to the decedent's spouse and children to the extent the estate is insufficient to satisfy those claims and allowances. The liability of a nonprobate transferee may not exceed the value of nonprobate transfers received or controlled by that transferee." The other provisions of Section 6-102 implement this liability rule.

For states not favoring the comprehensive approach of Section 6-102(b) or the equivalent, Alternative B provides an *in rem* liability rule applying to transfer on death deeds. The property transferred

under a transfer on death deed is liable to the transferor's probate estate for properly allowed claims and statutory allowances to the extent the estate is insufficient.

One of the functions of probate is creditor protection. Section 6-102, referenced in Alternative A, attempts to provide comprehensive creditor protection within the realm of nonprobate transfers. In addition, this part in Alternative B provides more creditor protection than is typically available under current law. For many transferors, the transfer on death deed will be used in lieu of joint tenancy with right of survivorship. Under the usual law of joint tenancy, the unsecured creditors of a deceased joint tenant have no recourse against the property or against the other joint tenant. Instead, the property passes automatically to the survivor, free of the decedent's debts. See Comment 5 to Section 6-102. If the debts cannot be paid from the probate estate, the creditor is out of luck. Under Alternative B, in contrast, the property transferred under a transfer on death deed is liable to the probate estate for properly allowed claims and statutory allowances to the extent the estate is insufficient.

[§ 6-416. Optional Form of Transfer on Death Deed. The following form may be used to create a transfer on death deed. The other sections of this [part] govern the effect of this or any other instrument used to create a transfer on death deed:

(front of form)
REVOCABLE TRANSFER ON DEATH DEED

NOTICE TO OWNER
You should carefully read all information on the other side of this form. You May Want to Consult a Lawyer Before Using This Form.

This form must be recorded before your death, or it will not be effective.

IDENTIFYING INFORMATION
Owner or Owners Making This Deed:

_____   _____
Printed name   Mailing address

_____   _____
Printed name   Mailing address

Legal description of the property:

_____

PRIMARY BENEFICIARY
I designate the following beneficiary if the beneficiary survives me.

_____   _____
Printed name   Mailing address, if available

ALTERNATE BENEFICIARY – Optional
If my primary beneficiary does not survive me, I designate the following alternate beneficiary if that beneficiary survives me.

_____   _____
Printed name   Mailing address, if available

TRANSFER ON DEATH
At my death, I transfer my interest in the described property to the beneficiaries as designated above.

Before my death, I have the right to revoke this deed.

SIGNATURE OF OWNER OR OWNERS MAKING THIS DEED

_____ [(SEAL)] _____
Signature   Date

_____ [(SEAL)] _____
Signature   Date

ACKNOWLEDGMENT
(insert acknowledgment for deed here)

(back of form)

COMMON QUESTIONS ABOUT THE USE OF THIS FORM

What does the Transfer on Death (TOD) deed do? When you die, this deed transfers the described property, subject to any liens or mortgages (or other encumbrances) on the property at your death. Probate is not required. The TOD deed has no effect until you die. You can revoke it at any time. You are also free to transfer the property to someone else during your lifetime. If you do not own any interest in the property when you die, this deed will have no effect.

How do I make a TOD deed? Complete this form. Have it acknowledged before a notary public or other individual authorized by law to take acknowledgments. Record the form in each [county] where any part of the property is located. The form has no effect unless it is acknowledged and recorded before your death.

Is the "legal description" of the property necessary? Yes.

How do I find the "legal description" of the property? This information may be on the deed you received when you became an owner of the property. This information may also be available in [the office of the county recorder of deeds] for the [county] where the property is located. If you are not absolutely sure, consult a lawyer.

Can I change my mind before I record the TOD deed? Yes. If you have not yet recorded the deed and want to change your mind, simply tear up or otherwise destroy the deed.

How do I "record" the TOD deed? Take the completed and acknowledged form to [the office of the county recorder of deeds] of the [county] where the property is located. Follow the instructions given by the [county recorder] to make the form part of the official property records. If the property is in more than one [county], you should record the deed in each [county].

Can I later revoke the TOD deed if I change my mind? Yes. You can revoke the TOD deed. No one, including the beneficiaries, can prevent you from revoking the deed.

How do I revoke the TOD deed after it is recorded? There are three ways to revoke a recorded TOD deed: (1) Complete and acknowledge a revocation form, and record it in each [county] where the property is located. (2) Complete and acknowledge a new TOD deed that disposes of the same property, and record it in each [county] where the property is located. (3) Transfer the property to someone else during your lifetime by a recorded deed that expressly revokes the TOD deed. You may not revoke the TOD deed by will.

I am being pressured to complete this form. What should I do? Do not complete this form under pressure. Seek help from a trusted family member, friend, or lawyer.

Do I need to tell the beneficiaries about the TOD deed? No, but it is recommended. Secrecy can cause later complications and might make it easier for others to commit fraud.

I have other questions about this form. What should I do? This form is designed to fit some but not all situations. If you have other questions, you are encouraged to consult a lawyer.]

Comment

The form in this section is optional. The section is based on Section 4 of the Uniform Health-Care Decisions Act.

The transfer on death deed is likely to be used by consumers for whom the preparation of a tailored inter vivos revocable trust is too costly. The form in this section is designed to be understandable and consumer friendly.

For examples of statutory forms containing answers to questions likely to be asked by consumers, see the Illinois statutory forms for powers of attorney. 755 Ill. Comp. Stat. 45/3-3 (power of attorney for property); 755 Ill. Comp. Stat. 45/4-10 (power of attorney for health care).

[**§ 6-417. Optional Form of Revocation.** The following form may be used to create an instrument of revocation under this [part]. The other sections of this [part] govern the effect of this or any other instrument used to revoke a transfer on death deed.

(front of form)

REVOCATION OF TRANSFER ON DEATH DEED

NOTICE TO OWNER

This revocation must be recorded before you die or it will not be effective. This revocation is effective only as to the interests in the property of owners who sign this revocation.

IDENTIFYING INFORMATION

Owner or Owners of Property Making This Revocation:

_____   _____
Printed name   Mailing address

_____   _____
Printed name   Mailing address

Legal description of the property:

_____

REVOCATION

I revoke all my previous transfers of this property by transfer on death deed.

SIGNATURE OF OWNER OR OWNERS MAKING THIS REVOCATION

_____ [(SEAL)] _____
Signature   Date

_____ [(SEAL)] _____
Signature   Date

ACKNOWLEDGMENT
(insert acknowledgment here)

(back of form)
COMMON QUESTIONS ABOUT THE USE OF THIS FORM

How do I use this form to revoke a Transfer on Death (TOD) deed? Complete this form. Have it acknowledged before a notary public or other individual authorized to take acknowledgments. Record the form in the public records in [the office of the county recorder of deeds] of each [county] where the property is located. The form must be acknowledged and recorded before your death or it has no effect.

How do I find the "legal description" of the property? This information may be on the TOD deed. It may also be available in [the office of the county recorder of deeds] for the [county] where the property is located. If you are not absolutely sure, consult a lawyer.

How do I "record" the form? Take the completed and acknowledged form to [the office of the county recorder of deeds] of the [county] where the property is located. Follow the instructions given by the [county recorder] to make the form part of the official property records. If the property is located in more than one [county], you should record the form in each of those [counties].

I am being pressured to complete this form. What should I do? Do not complete this form under pressure. Seek help from a trusted family member, friend, or lawyer.

I have other questions about this form. What should I do? This form is designed to fit some but not all situations. If you have other questions, consult a lawyer.]

Comment

The form in this section is optional. The section is based on Section 4 of the Uniform Health-Care Decisions Act.

The aim of the form in this section is to be understandable and consumer friendly.

ARTICLE VII
TRUST ADMINISTRATION

Historical Note

Article VII of the Uniform Probate Code addressed selected issues of trust administration, including trust registration, the jurisdiction of the courts concerning trusts, and the duties and liabilities of trustees. Article VII of the UPC was superseded by the Uniform Trust Code, approved in 2000, and was withdrawn in 2010 following the widespread enactment of the UTC.

ARTICLE VIII
EFFECTIVE DATE AND REPEALER

§ 8-101. Time of Taking Effect; Provisions for Transition.

§ 8-102. Specific Repealer and Amendments.

———

§ 8-101. Time of Taking Effect; Provisions for Transition.

(a) This [code] takes effect on January 1, 20__ .

(b) Except as provided elsewhere in this [code], on the effective date of this [code]:

(1) the [code] applies to governing instruments executed by decedents dying thereafter;

(2) the [code] applies to any proceedings in court then pending or thereafter commenced regardless of the time of the death of decedent except to the extent that in the opinion of the court the former procedure should be made applicable in a particular case in the interest of justice or because of infeasibility of application of the procedure of this [code];

(3) every personal representative or other fiduciary holding an appointment under this [code] on that date, continues to hold the appointment but has only the powers conferred by this [code] and is subject to the duties imposed with respect to any act occurring or done thereafter;

(4) an act done before the effective date in any proceeding and any accrued right is not impaired by this [code]. If a right is acquired, extinguished or barred upon the expiration of a prescribed period of time which has commenced to run by the provisions of any statute before the effective date, the provisions shall remain in force with respect to that right;

(5) any rule of construction or presumption provided in this [code] applies to governing instruments executed before the effective date unless there is a clear indication of a contrary intent.

(6) a person holding office as judge of the court on the effective date of this [code] may continue the office of judge of this court and may be selected for additional terms after the effective date of this [code] even though he does not meet the qualifications of a judge as provided in [Article] I.

Legislative Note: *States that have previously enacted the Uniform Probate Code and are enacting an amendment or amendments to the Code are encouraged to include the following effective date provision in their enacting legislation. The purpose of this effective date provision, which is patterned after Section 8-101 of the original UPC, is to assure that the amendment or amendments will apply to instruments executed prior to the effective date, to court proceedings pending on the effective date, and to acts occurring prior to the effective date, to the same limited extent and in the same situations as the effective date provision of the original UPC.*

Time of Taking Effect; Provisions for Transition.

(a) This [act] takes effect on January 1, 20__.

(b) On the effective date of this [act]:

(1) the [act] applies to governing instruments executed by decedents dying thereafter;

(2) the [act] applies to any proceedings in court then pending or thereafter commenced regardless of the time of the death of decedent except to the extent that in the opinion of the court the former procedure should be made applicable in a particular case in the interest of justice or because of infeasibility of application of the procedure of this code;

(3) an act done before the effective date of this [act] in any proceeding and any accrued right is not impaired by this [act]. If a right is acquired, extinguished, or barred upon the expiration of a prescribed period of time which has commenced to run by the provisions of any statute before the effective date of this [act], the provisions shall remain in force with respect to that right; and

(4) any rule of construction or presumption provided in this [act] applies to governing instruments executed

before the effective date unless there is a clear indication of a contrary intent.

§ 8-102. Specific Repealer and Amendments.

(a) The following [acts] and parts of [acts] are repealed:

(1)

(2)

(3)

(b) The following [acts] and parts of [acts] are amended:

(1)

(2)

(3)

UNITED KINGDOM INHERITANCE (PROVISION FOR FAMILY AND DEPENDANTS) ACT 1975, with Subsequent Amendments

United Kingdom Inheritance Act 1975 is reproduced under the terms of Crown Copyright Policy Guidance issued by HMSO.

§ 1 Application for financial provision from deceased's estate.

(1) Where after the commencement of this Act a person dies domiciled in England and Wales and is survived by any of the following persons: —

(a) the spouse or civil partner of the deceased;

(b) a former spouse or former civil partner of the deceased, but not one who has formed a subsequent marriage or civil partnership;

(ba) any person (not being a person included in paragraph (a) or (b) above) to whom subsection (1A) or (1B) below applies;

(c) a child of the deceased;

(d) any person (not being a child of the deceased) who in relation to any marriage or civil partnership to which the deceased was at any time a party, or otherwise in relation to any family in which the deceased at any time stood in the role of a parent, was treated by the deceased as a child of the family;

(e) any person (not being a person included in the foregoing paragraphs of this subsection) who immediately before the death of the deceased was being maintained, either wholly or partly, by the deceased;

that person may apply to the court for an order under section 2 of this Act on the ground that the disposition of the deceased's estate effected by his will or the law relating to intestacy, or the combination of his will and that law, is not such as to make reasonable financial provision for the applicant.

(1A) This subsection applies to a person if the deceased died on or after 1st January 1996 and, during the whole of the period of two years ending immediately before the date when the deceased died, the person was living —

(a) in the same household as the deceased, and

(b) as the husband or wife of the deceased.

(1B) This subsection applies to a person if for the whole of the period of two years ending immediately before the date when the deceased died the person was living —

(a) in the same household as the deceased, and

(b) as the civil partner of the deceased.

(2) In this Act "reasonable financial provision" —

(a) in the case of an application made by virtue of subsection (1)(a) above by the husband or wife of the deceased (except where the marriage with the deceased was the subject of a decree of judicial separation and at the date of death the decree was in force and the separation was continuing), means such financial provision as it would be reasonable in all the circumstances of the case for a husband or wife to receive, whether or not that provision is required for his or her maintenance;

(aa) in the case of an application made by virtue of subsection (1)(a) above by the civil partner of the deceased (except where, at the date of death, a separation order under Chapter 2 of Part 2 of the Civil Partnership Act 2004 was in force in relation to the civil partnership and the separation was continuing), means such financial provision as it would be reasonable in all the circumstances of the case for a civil partner to receive, whether or not that provision is required for his or her maintenance;

(b) in the case of any other application made by virtue of subsection (1) above, means such financial provision as it would be reasonable in all the circumstances of the case for the applicant to receive for his maintenance.

(2A) The reference in subsection (1)(d) above to a family in which the deceased stood in the role of a parent includes a family of which the deceased was the only member (apart from the applicant).

(3) For the purposes of subsection (1)(e) above, a person is to be treated as being maintained by the deceased (either wholly or partly, as the case may be) only if the deceased was making a substantial contribution in money or money's worth towards the reasonable needs of that person, other than a contribution made for full valuable consideration pursuant to an arrangement of a commercial nature.

§ 2 Powers of court to make orders.

(1) Subject to the provisions of this Act, where an application is made for an order under this section, the court may, if it is satisfied that the disposition of the deceased's estate effected by his will or the law relating to intestacy, or the combination of his will and that law, is not such as to make reasonable financial provision for the applicant, make any one or more of the following orders: —

(a) an order for the making to the applicant out of the net estate of the deceased of such periodical payments and for such term as may be specified in the order;

(b) an order for the payment to the applicant out of that estate of a lump sum of such amount as may be so specified;

(c) an order for the transfer to the applicant of such property comprised in that estate as may be so specified;

(d) an order for the settlement for the benefit of the applicant of such property comprised in that estate as may be so specified;

(e) an order for the acquisition out of property comprised in that estate of such property as may be so specified and for the transfer of the property so acquired to the applicant or for the settlement thereof for his benefit;

(f) an order varying any ante-nuptial or post-nuptial settlement (including such a settlement made by will) made on the parties to a marriage to which the deceased was one of the parties, the variation being for the benefit of the surviving party to that marriage, or any child of that marriage, or any person who was treated by the deceased as a child of the family in relation to that marriage;

(g) an order varying any settlement made —

(i) during the subsistence of a civil partnership formed by the deceased, or

(ii) in anticipation of the formation of a civil partnership by the deceased,

on the civil partners (including such a settlement made by will), the variation being for the benefit of the surviving civil partner, or any child of both the civil partners, or any person who was treated by the deceased as a child of the family in relation to that civil partnership;

(h) an order varying for the applicant's benefit the trusts on which the deceased's estate is held (whether arising under the will, or the law relating to intestacy, or both).

(2) An order under subsection (1)(a) above providing for the making out of the net estate of the deceased of periodical payments may provide for—

(a) payments of such amount as may be specified in the order,

(b) payments equal to the whole of the income of the net estate or of such portion thereof as may be so specified,

(c) payments equal to the whole of the income of such part of the net estate as the court may direct to be set aside or appropriated for the making out of the income thereof of payments under this section,

or may provide for the amount of the payments or any of them to be determined in any other way the court thinks fit.

(3) Where an order under subsection (1)(a) above provides for the making of payments of an amount specified in the order, the order may direct that such part of the net estate as may be so specified shall be set aside or appropriated for the making out of the income thereof of those payments; but no larger part of the net estate shall be so set aside or appropriated than is sufficient, at the date of the order, to produce by the income thereof the amount required for the making of those payments.

(3A) In assessing for the purposes of an order under this section the extent (if any) to which the net estate is reduced by any debts or liabilities (including any inheritance tax paid or payable out of the estate), the court may assume that the order has already been made.

(4) An order under this section may contain such consequential and supplemental provisions as the court thinks necessary or expedient for the purpose of giving effect to the order or for the purpose of securing that the order operates fairly as between one beneficiary of the estate of the deceased and another and may, in particular, but without prejudice to the generality of this subsection—

(a) order any person who holds any property which forms part of the net estate of the deceased to make such payment or transfer such property as may be specified in the order;

(b) vary the disposition of the deceased's estate effected by the will or the law relating to intestacy, or by both the will and the law relating to intestacy, in such manner as the court thinks fair and reasonable having regard to the provisions of the order and all the circumstances of the case;

(c) confer on the trustees of any property which is the subject of an order under this section such powers as appear to the court to be necessary or expedient.

§ 3 Matters to which court is to have regard in exercising powers under § 2.

(1) Where an application is made for an order under section 2 of this Act, the court shall, in determining whether the disposition of the deceased's estate effected by his will or the law relating to intestacy, or the combination of his will and that law, is such as to make reasonable financial provision for the applicant and, if the court considers that reasonable financial provision has not been made, in determining whether and in what manner it shall exercise its powers under that section, have regard to the following matters, that is to say—

(a) the financial resources and financial needs which the applicant has or is likely to have in the foreseeable future;

(b) the financial resources and financial needs which any other applicant for an order under section 2 of this Act has or is likely to have in the foreseeable future;

(c) the financial resources and financial needs which any beneficiary of the estate of the deceased has or is likely to have in the foreseeable future;

(d) any obligations and responsibilities which the deceased had towards any applicant for an order under the said section 2 or towards any beneficiary of the estate of the deceased;

(e) the size and nature of the net estate of the deceased;

(f) any physical or mental disability of any applicant for an order under the said section 2 or any beneficiary of the estate of the deceased;

(g) any other matter, including the conduct of the applicant or any other person, which in the circumstances of the case the court may consider relevant.

(2) This subsection applies, without prejudice to the generality of paragraph (g) of subsection (1) above, where an application for an order under section 2 of this Act is made by virtue of section 1(1)(a) or (b) of this Act.

The court shall, in addition to the matters specifically mentioned in paragraphs (a) to (f) of that subsection, have regard to: –

(a) the age of the applicant and the duration of the marriage or civil partnership;

(b) the contribution made by the applicant to the welfare of the family of the deceased, including any contribution made by looking after the home or caring for the family.

In the case of an application by the wife or husband of the deceased, the court shall also, unless at the date of death a decree of judicial separation was in force and the separation was continuing, have regard to the provision which the applicant might reasonably have expected to receive if on the day on which the deceased died the marriage, instead of being terminated by death, had been terminated by a decree of divorce; but nothing requires the court to treat such provision as setting an upper or lower limit on the provision which may be made by an order under section 2.

In the case of an application by the civil partner of the deceased, the court shall also, unless at the date of the death a separation order under Chapter 2 of Part 2 of the Civil Partnership Act 2004 was in force and the separation was continuing, have regard to the provision which the application might reasonably have expected to receive if on the day on which the deceased died the civil partnership, instead of being terminated by death, had been terminated by a dissolution order; but nothing requires the court to treat such provision as setting an upper or lower limit on the provision which may be made by an order under section 2.

(2A) Without prejudice to the generality of paragraph (g) of subsection (1) above, where an application for an order under section 2 of this Act is made by virtue of section 1(1)(ba) of this Act, the court shall, in addition to the matters specifically mentioned in paragraphs (a) to (f) of that subsection, have regard to –

(a) the age of the applicant and the length of the period during which the applicant lived as the husband or wife or civil partner of the deceased and in the same household as the deceased;

(b) the contribution made by the applicant to the welfare of the family of the deceased, including any contribution made by looking after the home or caring for the family.

(3) Without prejudice to the generality of paragraph (g) of subsection (1) above, where an application for an order under section 2 of this Act is made by virtue of section 1(1)(c) or 1(1)(d) of this Act, the court shall, in addition to the matters specifically mentioned in paragraphs (a) to (f) of that subsection, have regard to the manner in which the applicant was being or in which he might expect to be educated or trained, and where the application is made by virtue of section 1(1)(d) the court shall also have regard –

(a) to whether the deceased maintained the applicant and, if so, to the length of time for which and basis n which the deceased did so, and to the extent of the contribution made by way of maintenance;

(b) to whether and, if so, to what extent the deceased assumed responsibility for the maintenance of the applicant;

(c) to the liability of any other person to maintain the applicant.

(4) Without prejudice to the generality of paragraph (g) of subsection (1) above, where an application for an order under section 2 of this Act is made by virtue of section 1(1)(e) of this Act, the court shall, in addition to the matters specifically mentioned in paragraphs (a) to (f) of that subsection, have regard —

(a) to the length of time for which and basis on which the deceased maintained the applicant, and to the extent of the contribution made by way of maintenance;

(b) to whether and, if so, to what extent the deceased assumed responsibility for the maintenance of the applicant.

(5) In considering the matters to which the court is required to have regard under this section, the court shall take into account the facts as known to the court at the date of the hearing.

(6) In considering the financial resources of any person for the purposes of this section the court shall take into account his earning capacity and in considering the financial needs of any person for the purposes of this section the court shall take into account his financial obligations and responsibilities.

§ 4 Time-limit for applications. An application for an order under section 2 of this Act shall not, except with the permission of the court, be made after the end of the period of six months from the date on which representation with respect to the estate of the deceased is first taken out (but nothing prevents the making of an application before such representation is first taken out).

§ 5 Interim orders.

(1) Where on an application for an order under section 2 of this Act it appears to the court—

(a) that the applicant is in immediate need of financial assistance, but it is not yet possible to determine what order (if any) should be made under that section; and

(b) that property forming part of the net estate of the deceased is or can be made available to meet the need of the applicant;

the court may order that, subject to such conditions or restrictions, if any, as the court may impose and to any further order of the court, there shall be paid to the applicant out of the net estate of the deceased such sum or sums and (if more than one) at such intervals as the court thinks reasonable; and the court may order that, subject to the provisions of this Act, such payments are to be made until such date as the court may specify, not being later than the date on which the court either makes an order under the said section 2 or decides not to exercise its powers under that section.

(2) Subsections (2), (3) and (4) of section 2 of this Act shall apply in relation to an order under this section as they apply in relation to an order under that section.

(3) In determining what order, if any, should be made under this section the court shall, so far as the urgency of the case admits, have regard to the same matters as those to which the court is required to have regard under section 3 of this Act.

(4) An order made under section 2 of this Act may provide that any sum paid to the applicant by virtue of this section shall be treated to such an extent and in such manner as may be provided by that order as having been paid on account of any payment provided for by that order.

§ 6 Variation, discharge etc. of orders for periodical payments.

(1) Subject to the provisions of this Act, where the court has made an order under section 2(1)(a) of this Act (in this section referred to as "the original order") for the making of periodical payments to any person (in this section referred to as "the original recipient"), the court, on an application under this section, shall have power by order to vary or discharge the original order or to suspend any provision of it temporarily and to revive the operation of any provision so suspended.

(2) Without prejudice to the generality of subsection (1) above, an order made on an application for the variation of the original order may—

(a) provide for the making out of any relevant property of such periodical payments and for such term as may be specified in the order to any person who has applied, or would but for section 4 of this Act be entitled to apply, for an order under section 2 of this Act (whether or not, in the case of any application, an order was made in favour of the applicant);

(b) provide for the payment out of any relevant property of a lump sum of such amount as may be so specified to the original recipient or to any such person as is mentioned in paragraph (a) above;

(c) provide for the transfer of the relevant property, or such part thereof as may be so specified, to the original recipient or to any such person as is so mentioned.

(3) Where the original order provides that any periodical payments payable thereunder to the original recipient are to cease on the occurrence of an event specified in the order (other than the formation of a subsequent marriage or civil partnership by a former spouse or former civil partner) or on the expiration of a period so specified, then, if, before the end of the period of six months from the date of the occurrence of that event or of th e expiration of that period, an application is made for an order under this section, the court shall have power to make any order which it would have had power to make if the application had been made before the date (whether in favour of the original recipient or any such person as is mentioned in subsection (2)(a) above and whether having effect from that date or from such later date as the court may specify).

(4) Any reference in this section to the original order shall include a reference to an order made under this section and any reference in this section to the original recipient shall include a reference to any person to whom periodical payments are required to be made by virtue of an order under this section.

(5) An application under this section may be made by any of the following persons, that is to say—

(a) any person who by virtue of section 1(1) of this Act has applied, or would but for section 4 of this Act be entitled to apply, for an order under section 2 of this Act,

(b) the personal representatives of the deceased,

(c) the trustees of any relevant property, and

(d) any beneficiary of the estate of the deceased.

(6) An order under this section may only affect —

(a) property the income of which is at the date of the order applicable wholly or in part for the making of periodical payments to any person who has applied for an order under this Act, or

(b) in the case of an application under subsection (3) above in respect of payments which have ceased to be payable on the occurrence of an event or the expiration of a period, property the income of which was so applicable immediately before the occurrence of that event or the expiration of that period, as the case may be,

and any such property as is mentioned in paragraph (a) or (b) above is in subsections (2) and (5) above referred to as "relevant property".

(7) In exercising the powers conferred by this section the court shall have regard to all the circumstances of the case, including any change in any of the matters to which the court was required to have regard when making the order to which the application relates.

(8) Where the court makes an order under this section, it may give such consequential directions as it thinks necessary or expedient having regard to the provisions of the order.

(9) No such order as is mentioned in sections 2(1)(d), (e) or (f), 9, 10 or 11 of this Act shall be made on an application under this section.

(10) For the avoidance of doubt it is hereby declared that, in relation to an order which provides for the making of periodical payments which are to cease on the occurrence of an event specified in the order (other than the formation of a subsequent marriage or civil partnership by a former spouse or former civil partner) or on the expiration of a period so specified, the power to vary an order includes power to provide for the making of periodical payments after the expiration that period or the occurrence of that event.

§ 7 Payment of lump sums by instalments.

(1) An order under section 2(1)(b) or 6(2)(b) of this Act for the payment of a lump sum may provide for the payment of that sum by instalments of such amount as may be specified in the order.

(2) Where an order is made by virtue of subsection (1) above, the court shall have power, on an application made by the person to whom the lump sum is payable, by the personal representatives of the deceased or by the trustees of the property out of which the lump sum is payable, to vary that order by varying the number of instalments payable, the amount of any instalment and the date on which any instalment becomes payable.

§ 8 Property treated as part of "net estate".

(1) Where a deceased person has in accordance with the provisions of any enactment nominated any person to receive any sum of money or other property on his death and that nomination is in force at the time of his death, that sum of money, after deducting therefrom any capital transfer tax payable in respect thereof, or that other property, to the extent of the value thereof at the date of the death of the deceased after deducting therefrom any capital transfer tax so payable, shall be treated for the purposes of this Act as part of the net estate of the deceased; but this subsection shall not render any person liable for having paid that sum or transferred that other property to the person named in the nomination in accordance with the directions given in the nomination.

(2) Where any sum of money or other property is received by any person as a donatio mortis causa made by a deceased person, that sum of money, after deducting therefrom any capital transfer tax payable thereon, or that other property, to the extent of the value thereof at the date of the death of the deceased after deducting therefrom any capital transfer tax so payable, shall be treated for the purposes of this Act as part of the net estate of the deceased; but this subsection shall not render any person liable for having paid that sum or transferred that other property in order to give effect to that donatio mortis causa.

(3) The amount of capital transfer tax to be deducted for the purposes of this section shall not exceed the amount of that tax which has been borne by the person nominated by the deceased or, as the case may be, the person who has received a sum of money or other property as a donatio mortis causa.

§ 9 Property held on a joint tenancy.

(1) Where a deceased person was immediately before his death beneficially entitled to a joint tenancy of any property, then, if, before the end of the period of six months from the date on which representation with respect to the estate of the deceased was first taken out, an application is made for an order under section 2 of this Act, the court for the purpose of facilitating the making of financial provision for the applicant under this Act may order that the deceased's severable share of

that property, at the value thereof immediately before his death, shall, to such extent as appears to the court to be just in all the circumstances of the case, be treated for the purposes of this Act as part of the net estate of the deceased.

(1A) Where an order is made under subsection (1) the value of the deceased's severable share of the property concerned is taken for the purposes of this Act to be the value that the share would have had at the date of the hearing of the application for an order under section 2 had the share been severed immediately before the deceased's death, unless the court orders that the share is to be valued at a different date.

(2) In determining the extent to which any severable share is to be treated as part of the net estate of the deceased by virtue of an order under subsection (1) above, the court shall have regard to any capital transfer tax payable in respect of that severable share.

(3) Where an order is made under subsection (1) above, the provisions of this section shall not render any person liable for anything done by him before the order was made.

(4) For the avoidance of doubt it is hereby declared that for the purposes of this section there may be a joint tenancy of a chose in action.

§ 10 Dispositions intended to defeat applications for financial provision.

(1) Where an application is made to the court for an order under section 2 of this Act, the applicant may, in the proceedings on that application, apply to the court for an order under subsection (2) below.

(2) Where on an application under subsection (1) above the court is satisfied —

(a) that, less than six years before the date of the death of the deceased, the deceased with the intention of defeating an application for financial provision under this Act made a disposition, and

(b) that full valuable consideration for that disposition was not given by the person to whom or for the benefit of whom the disposition was made (in this section referred to as "the donee") or by any other person, and

(c) that the exercise of the powers conferred by this section would facilitate the making of financial provision for the applicant under this Act,

then, subject to the provisions of this section and of sections 12 and 13 of this Act, the court may order the donee (whether or not at the date of the order he holds any interest in the property disposed of to him or for his benefit by the deceased) to provide, for the purpose of the making of that financial provision, such sum of money or other property as may be specified in the order.

(3) Where an order is made under subsection (2) above as respects any disposition made by the deceased which consisted of the payment of money to or for the benefit of the donee, the amount of any sum of money or the value of any property ordered to be provided under that subsection shall not exceed the amount of the payment made by the deceased after deducting therefrom any capital transfer tax borne by the donee in respect of that payment.

(4) Where an order is made under subsection (2) above as respects any disposition made by the deceased which consisted of the transfer of property (other than a sum of money) to or for the benefit of the donee, the amount of any sum of money or the value of any property ordered to be provided under that subsection shall not exceed the value at the date of the death of the deceased of the property disposed of by him to or for the benefit of the donee (or if that property has been disposed of by the person to whom it was transferred by the deceased, the value at the date of that disposal thereof) after deducting therefrom any capital transfer tax borne by the donee in respect of the transfer of that property by the deceased.

(5) Where an application (in this subsection referred to as "the original application") is made for an order under subsection (2) above in relation to any disposition, then, if on an application under

this subsection by the donee or by any applicant for an order under section 2 of this Act the court is satisfied —

(a) that, less than six years before the date of the death of the deceased, the deceased with the intention of defeating an application for financial provision under this Act made a disposition other than the disposition which is the subject of the original application, and

(b) that full valuable consideration for that other disposition was not given by the person to whom or for the benefit of whom that other disposition was made or by any other person,

the court may exercise in relation to the person to whom or for the benefit of whom that other disposition was made the powers which the court would have had under subsection (2) above if the original application had been made in respect of that other disposition and the court had been satisfied as to the matters set out in paragraphs (a), (b) and (c) of that subsection; and where any application is made under this subsection, any reference in this section (except in subsection (2)(b) to the donee shall include a reference to the person to whom or for the benefit of whom that other disposition was made.

(6) In determining whether and in what manner to exercise its powers under this section, the court shall have regard to the circumstances in which any disposition was made and any valuable consideration which was given therefor, the relationship, if any, of the donee to the deceased, the conduct and financial resources of the donee and all the other circumstances of the case.

(7) In this section "disposition" does not include —

(a) any provision in a will, any such nomination as is mentioned in section 8(1) of this Act or any donatio mortis causa, or

(b) any appointment of property made, otherwise than by will, in the exercise of a special power of appointment,

but, subject to these exceptions, includes any payment of money (including the payment of a premium under a policy of assurance) and any conveyance, assurance, appointment or gift of property of any description, whether made by an instrument or otherwise.

(8) The provisions of this section do not apply to any disposition made before the commencement of this [part].

§ 11 Contracts to leave property by will.

(1) Where an application is made to a court for an order under section 2 of this Act, the applicant may, in the proceedings on that application, apply to the court for an order under this section.

(2) Where on an application under subsection (1) above the court is satisfied —

(a) that the deceased made a contract by which he agreed to leave by his will a sum of money or other property to any person or by which he agreed that a sum of money or other property would be paid or transferred to any person out of his estate, and

(b) that the deceased made that contract with the intention of defeating an application for financial provision under this Act, and

(c) that when the contract was made full valuable consideration for that contract was not given or promised by the person with whom or for the benefit of whom the contract was made (in this section referred to as "the donee") or by any other person, and

(d) that the exercise of the powers conferred by this section would facilitate the making of financial provision for the applicant under this Act,

then, subject to the provisions of this section and of sections 12 and 13 of this Act, the court may make any one or more of the following orders, that is to say —

(i) if any money has been paid or any other property has been transferred to or for the benefit of the donee in accordance with the contract, an order directing the donee to provide, for the purpose of the making of that financial provision, such sum of money or other property as may be specified in the order;

(ii) if the money or all the money has not been paid or the property or all the property has not been transferred in accordance with the contract, an order directing the personal representatives not to make any payment or transfer any property, or not to make any further payment or transfer any further property, as the case may be, in accordance therewith or directing the personal representatives only to make such payment or transfer such property as may be specified in the order.

(3) Notwithstanding anything in subsection (2) above, the court may exercise its powers thereunder in relation to any contract made by the deceased only to the extent that the court considers that the amount of any sum of money paid or to be paid or the value of any property transferred or to be transferred in accordance with the contract exceeds the value of any valuable consideration given or to be given for that contract, and for this purpose the court shall have regard to the value of property at the date of the hearing.

(4) In determining whether and in what manner to exercise its powers under this section, the court shall have regard to the circumstances in which the contract was made, the relationship, if any, of the donee to the deceased, the conduct and financial resources of the donee and all the other circumstances of the case.

(5) Where an order has been made under subsection (2) above in relation to any contract, the rights of any person to enforce that contract or to recover damages or to obtain other relief for the breach thereof shall be subject to any adjustment made by the court under section 12(3) of this Act and shall survive to such extent only as is consistent with giving effect to the terms of that order.

(6) The provisions of this section do not apply to a contract made before the commencement of this Act.

§ 12 Provisions supplementary to §§ 10 and 11.

(1) Where the exercise of any of the powers conferred by section 10 or 11 of this Act is conditional on the court being satisfied that a disposition or contract was made by a deceased person with the intention of defeating an application for financial provision under this Act, that condition shall be fulfilled if the court is of the opinion that, on a balance of probabilities, the intention of the deceased (though not necessarily his sole intention) in making the disposition or contract was to prevent an order for financial provision being made under this Act or to reduce the amount of the provision which might otherwise be granted by an order thereunder.

(2) Where an application is made under section 11 of this Act with respect to any contract made by the deceased and no valuable consideration was given or promised by any person for that contract then, notwithstanding anything in subsection (1) above, it shall be presumed, unless the contrary is shown, that the deceased made that contract with the intention of defeating an application for financial provision under this Act.

(3) Where the court makes an order under section 10 or 11 of this Act it may give such consequential directions as it thinks fit (including directions requiring the making of any payment or the transfer of any property) for giving effect to the order or for securing a fair adjustment of the rights of the persons affected thereby.

(4) Any power conferred on the court by the said section 10 or 11 to order the donee, in relation to any disposition or contract, to provide any sum of money or other property shall be exercisable in like manner in relation to the personal representative of the donee, and —

(a) any reference in section 10(4) to the disposal of property by the donee shall include a reference to disposal by the personal representative of the donee, and

(b) any reference in section 10(5) to an application by the donee under that subsection shall

include a reference to an application by the personal representative of the donee;
but the court shall not have power under the said section 10 or 11 to make an order in respect of any property forming part of the estate of the donee which has been distributed by the personal representative; and the personal representative shall not be liable for having distributed any such property before he has notice of the making of an application under the said section 10 or 11 on the ground that he ought to have taken into account the possibility that such an application would be made.

§ 13 Provisions as to trustees in relation to §§ 10 and 11.

(1) Where an application is made for —

(a) an order under section 10 of this Act in respect of a disposition made by the deceased to any person as a trustee, or

(b) an order under section 11 of this Act in respect of any payment made or property transferred, in accordance with a contract made by the deceased, to any person as a trustee,

the powers of the court under the said section 10 or 11 to order that trustee to provide a sum of money or other property shall be subject to the following limitation (in addition, in a case of an application under section 10, to any provision regarding the deduction of capital transfer tax) namely, that the amount of any sum of money or the value of any property ordered to be provided—

(i) in the case of an application in respect of a disposition which consisted of the payment of money or an application in respect of the payment of money in accordance with a contract, shall not exceed the aggregate of so much of that money as is at the date of the order in the hands of the trustee and the value at that date of any property which represents that money or is derived therefrom and is at that date in the hands of the trustee;

(ii) in the case of an application in respect of a disposition which consisted of the transfer of property (other than a sum of money) or an application in respect of the transfer of property (other than a sum of money) in accordance with a contract, shall not exceed the aggregate of the value at the date of the order of so much of that property as is at that date in the hands of the trustee and the value at that date of any property which represents the first-mentioned property or is derived therefrom and is at that date in the hands of the trustee.

(2) Where any such application is made in respect of a disposition made to any person as a trustee or in respect of any payment made or property transferred in pursuance of a contract to any person as a trustee, the trustee shall not be liable for having distributed any money or other property on the ground that he ought to have taken into account the possibility that such an application would be made.

(3) Where any such application is made in respect of a disposition made to any person as a trustee or in respect of any payment made or property transferred in accordance with a contract to any person as a trustee, any reference in the said section 10 or 11 to the donee shall be construed as including a reference to the trustee or trustees for the time being of the trust in question and any reference in subsection (1) or (2) above to a trustee shall be construed in the same way.

§ 19 Effect, duration and form of orders.

(1) Where an order is made under section 2 of this Act then for all purposes, including the purposes of the enactments relating to capital transfer tax, the will or the law relating to intestacy, or both the will and the law relating to intestacy, as the case may be, shall have effect and be deemed to have had effect as from the deceased's death subject to the provisions of the order.

(2) Any order made under section 2 or 5 of this Act in favour of —

(a) an applicant who was the former spouse or former civil partner of the deceased, or

(b) an applicant who was the husband or wife of the deceased in a case where the marriage with the deceased was the subject of a decree of judicial separation and at the date of death the decree was in force and the separation was continuing, or

(c) an applicant who was the civil partner of the deceased where, at the date of death, a separation order under Chapter 2 of Part 2 of the Civil Partnership Act 2004 was in force in relation to their civil partnership and the separation was continuing,

shall, in so far as it provides for the making of periodical payments, cease to have effect on the formation by the applicant of a subsequent marriage or civil partnership, except in relation to any arrears due under the order on the date of the formation of the subsequent marriage or civil partnership.

(3) A copy of every order made under this Act other than an order made under section 15(1) or 15ZA(1) of this Act shall be sent to the principal registry of the Family Division for entry and filing, and a memorandum of the order shall be endorsed on, or permanently annexed to, the probate or letters of administration under which the estate is being administered.

§ 20 Provisions as to personal representatives.

(1) The provisions of this Act shall not render the personal representative of a deceased person liable for having distributed any part of the estate of the deceased, after the end of the period of six months from the date on which representation with respect to the estate of the deceased is first taken out, on the ground that he ought to have taken into account the possibility—

(a) that the court might permit the making of an application for an order under section 2 of this Act after the end of that period, or

(b) that, where an order has been made under the said section 2, the court might exercise in relation thereto the powers conferred on it by section 6 of this Act, but this subsection shall not prejudice any power to recover, by reason of the making of an order under this Act, any part of the estate so distributed.

(2) Where the personal representative of a deceased person pays any sum directed by an order under section 5 of this Act to be paid out of the deceased's net estate, he shall not be under any liability by reason of that estate not being sufficient to make the payment, unless at the time of making the payment he has reasonable cause to believe that the estate is not sufficient.

(3) Where a deceased person entered into a contract by which he agreed to leave by his will any sum of money or other property to any person or by which he agreed that a sum of money or other property would be paid or transferred to any person out of his estate, then, if the personal representative of the deceased has reason to believe that the deceased entered into the contract with the intention of defeating an application for financial provision under this Act, he may, notwithstanding anything in that contract, postpone the payment of that sum of money or the transfer of that property until the expiration of the period of six months from the date on which representation with respect to the estate of the deceased is first taken out or, if during that period an application is made for an order under section 2 of this Act, until the determination of the proceedings on that application.

PART TWO: TRUST STATUTES

Uniform Trust Code (2000, with Subsequent Amendments)

Uniform Directed Trust Act (2017)

Uniform Trust Decanting Act (2015, with Subsequent Amendments)

Uniform Principal and Income Act (1997, with Subsequent Amendments)

Uniform Prudent Investor Act (1994)

Uniform Custodial Trust Act (1987)

UNIFORM TRUST CODE (2000)
(With Subsequent Amendments)

Table of Sections

ARTICLE 1
GENERAL PROVISIONS AND DEFINITIONS

ARTICLE 2
JUDICIAL PROCEEDINGS

ARTICLE 3
REPRESENTATION

ARTICLE 4
CREATION, VALIDITY, MODIFICATION,
AND TERMINATION OF TRUST

ARTICLE 5
CREDITOR'S CLAIMS; SPENDTHRIFT AND DISCRETIONARY TRUSTS

ARTICLE 6
REVOCABLE TRUSTS

ARTICLE 7
OFFICE OF TRUSTEE

ARTICLE 8
DUTIES AND POWERS OF TRUSTEE

ARTICLE 9
UNIFORM PRUDENT INVESTOR ACT

ARTICLE 10
LIABILITY OF TRUSTEES AND RIGHTS OF PERSONS DEALING WITH TRUSTEE

ARTICLE 11
MISCELLANEOUS PROVISIONS

Prefatory Note

The Uniform Trust Code (2000) is the first national codification of the law of trusts. The primary stimulus to the Commissioners' drafting of the Uniform Trust Code is the greater use of trusts in recent years, both in family estate planning and in commercial transactions, both in the United States and internationally. This greater use of the trust, and consequent rise in the number of day-to-day questions involving trusts, has led to a recognition that the trust law in many states is thin. It has also led to a recognition that the existing Uniform Acts relating to trusts, while numerous, are fragmentary. The Uniform Trust Code will provide states with precise, comprehensive, and easily accessible guidance on trust law questions. On issues on which states diverge or on which the law is unclear or unknown, the Code will for the first time provide a uniform rule. The Code also contains a number of innovative provisions.

Default Rule: Most of the Uniform Trust Code consists of default rules that apply only if the terms of the trust fail to address or insufficiently cover a particular issue. Pursuant to § 105, a drafter is free to override a substantial majority of the Code's provisions. The exceptions are scheduled in § 105(b).

Innovative Provisions: Much of the Uniform Trust Code is a codification of the common law of trusts. But the Code does contain a number of innovative provisions. Among the more significant are specification of the rules of trust law that are not subject to override in the trust's terms (§ 105), the inclusion of a comprehensive article on representation of beneficiaries (Article 3), rules on trust modification and termination that will enhance flexibility (§§ 410-417), and the inclusion of an article collecting the special rules pertaining to revocable trusts (Article 6).

Models for Drafting: While the Uniform Trust Code is the first comprehensive Uniform Act on the subject of trusts, comprehensive trust statutes are already in effect in several states. Notable examples include the statutes in California, Georgia, Indiana, Texas, and Washington, all of which were referred to in the drafting process. Most influential was the 1986 California statute, found at Division 9 of the California Probate Code (§§ 15000 *et seq.*), which was used by the drafting committee as its initial model.

Existing Uniform Laws on Trust Law Subjects: Certain older Uniform Acts are incorporated into the Uniform Trust Code. Others, addressing more specialized topics, will continue to be available for enactment in free-standing form.

The following Uniform Acts are incorporated into or otherwise superseded by the Uniform Trust Code:

Uniform Probate Code Article VII - Originally approved in 1969, Article VII has been enacted in about 15 jurisdictions. Article VII, although titled "Trust Administration," is a modest statute, addressing only a limited number of topics. Article VII is superseded by the Uniform Trust Code. Its provisions on jurisdiction are incorporated into Article 2 of the Code, and its provision on trustee liability to persons other than beneficiaries are replaced by § 1010.

Uniform Prudent Investor Act (1994) - This Act has been enacted in 35 jurisdictions. This Act, and variant forms enacted in a number of other states, has displaced the older "prudent man" standard, bringing trust law into line with modern investment practice. States that have enacted the Uniform Prudent Investor Act are encouraged to recodify it as part of their enactment of the Uniform Trust Code. A place for this is provided in Article 9.

Uniform Trustee Powers Act (1964) This Act has

been enacted in 16 states. The Act contains a list of specific trustee powers and deals with other selected issues, particularly relations of a trustee with persons other than beneficiaries. The Uniform Trustee Powers Act is outdated and is entirely superseded by the Uniform Trust Code, principally at §§ 815, 816 and 1012. States enacting the Uniform Trust Code should repeal their existing trustee powers legislation.

Uniform Trusts Act (1937) - This largely overlooked Act of similar name was enacted in only six states, none within the past several decades. Despite a title suggesting comprehensive coverage of its topic, this Act, like Article VII of the UPC, addresses only a limited number of topics. These include the duty of loyalty, the registration and voting of securities, and trustee liability to persons other than beneficiaries. States enacting the Uniform Trust Code should repeal this earlier namesake.

The following Uniform Acts are not affected by enactment of the Uniform Trust Code and do not need to be amended or repealed:

Uniform Common Trust Fund Act - Originally approved in 1938, this Act has been enacted in 34 jurisdictions. The Uniform Trust Code does not address the subject of common trust funds. In recent years, many banks have replaced their common trust funds with mutual funds that may also be available to non-trust customers. The Code addresses investment in mutual funds at § 802(f).

Uniform Custodial Trust Act (1987) - This Act has been enacted in 14 jurisdictions. This Act allows standard trust provisions to be automatically incorporated into the terms of a trust simply by referring to the Act. This Act is not displaced by the Uniform Trust Code but complements it.

Uniform Management of Institutional Funds Act (1972) - This Act has been enacted in 47 jurisdictions. It governs the administration of endowment funds held by charitable, religious, and other eleemosynary institutions. The Uniform Management of Institutional Funds Act establishes a standard of prudence for use of appreciation on assets, provides specific authority for the making of investments, authorizes the delegation of this authority, and specifies a procedure, through either donor consent or court approval, for removing restrictions on the use of donated funds.

Uniform Principal and Income Act (1997) - The 1997 Uniform Principal and Income Act is a major revision of the widely enacted Uniform Act of the same name approved in 1962. Because this Act addresses issues with respect both to decedent's estates and trusts, a jurisdiction enacting the revised Uniform Principal and Income Act may wish to include it either as part of this Code or as part of its probate laws.

Uniform Probate Code - Originally approved in 1969, and enacted in close to complete form in about 20 states but influential in virtually all, the UPC overlaps with trust topics in several areas. One area of overlap, already mentioned, is UPC Article VII. Another area of overlap concerns representation of beneficiaries. UPC § 1-403 provides principles of representation for achieving binding judicial settlements of matters involving both estates and trusts. The Uniform Trust Code refines these representation principles, and extends them to nonjudicial settlement agreements and to optional notices and consents. *See* Unif. Trust Code, § 111 and Article 3. A final area of overlap between the UPC and trust law concerns rules of construction. The UPC, in Article II, Part 7, extends certain of the rules on the construction of wills to trusts and other nonprobate instruments. The Uniform Trust Code similarly extends to trusts the rules on the construction of wills. Unlike the UPC, however, the Trust Code does not prescribe the exact rules. Instead, § 112 of the Uniform Trust Code is an optional provision applying to trusts whatever rules the enacting jurisdiction already has in place on the construction of wills.

Uniform Statutory Rule Against Perpetuities - Originally approved in 1986, this Act has been enacted in 27 jurisdictions. The Act reforms the durational limit on when property interests, including interests created under trusts, must vest or fail. The Uniform Trust Code does not limit the duration of trusts or alter the time when interests must otherwise vest, but leaves this issue to other state law. The Code may be enacted without change regardless of the status of the perpetuities law in the enacting jurisdiction.

Uniform Supervision of Trustees for Charitable Purposes Act (1954) - This Act, which has been enacted in four states, is limited to mechanisms for monitoring the actions of charitable trustees. Unlike the Uniform Trust Code, the Supervision of Trustees for Charitable Purposes Act does not address the substantive law of charitable trusts.

Uniform Testamentary Additions to Trusts Act - This Act is available in two versions: the 1960 Act, with 24 enactments; and the 1991 Act, with 20 enactments through 1999. As its name suggests, this Act validates pourover devises to trusts. Because it validates provisions in wills, it is incorporated into the Uniform Probate Code, not into the Uniform Trust Code.

Role of Restatement of Trusts: The Restatement (Second) of Trusts was approved by the American Law Institute in 1957. Work on the Restatement Third began in the late 1980s. The portion of Restatement Third relating to the prudent investor rule and other investment topics was completed and approved in 1990. A tentative draft of the portion of Restatement Third relating to the rules on the creation and validity of trusts was approved in 1996, and the portion relating to the office of trustee, trust purposes, spendthrift provisions and the rights of creditors was approved in 1999. The Uniform Trust Code was drafted in close coordination with the writing of the Restatement Third.

Overview of Uniform Trust Code

The Uniform Trust Code consists of 11 articles. The substance of the Code is focused in the first 10 articles; Article 11 is primarily an effective date provision.

Article 1 — General Provisions and Definitions - In addition to definitions, this article addresses miscellaneous but important topics. The Uniform Trust Code is primarily default law. A settlor, subject to certain limitations, is free to draft trust terms departing from the provisions of this Code. The settlor, if minimum contacts are present, may in addition designate the trust's principal place of administration; the trustee, if certain standards are met, may transfer the principal place of administration to another state or country. To encourage nonjudicial resolution of disputes, the Uniform Trust Code provides more certainty for when such settlements are binding. While the Code does not prescribe the exact rules to be applied to the construction of trusts, it does extend to trusts whatever rules the enacting jurisdiction has on the construction of wills. The Uniform Trust Code,

although comprehensive, does not legislate on every issue. Its provisions are supplemented by the common law of trusts and principles of equity.

Article 2 — Judicial Proceedings - This article addresses selected issues involving judicial proceedings concerning trusts, particularly trusts having contacts with more than one state or country. The courts in the trust's principal place of administration have jurisdiction over both the trustee and the beneficiaries as to any matter relating to the trust. Optional provisions on subject-matter jurisdiction and venue are provided. The minimal coverage of this article was deliberate. The drafting committee concluded that most issues related to jurisdiction and procedure are not appropriate to a Trust Code, but are best left to other bodies of law.

Article 3 — Representation - This article deals with the representation of beneficiaries and other interested persons, both by fiduciaries (personal representatives, guardians and conservators), and through what is known as virtual representation. The representation principles of the article apply to settlement of disputes, whether by a court or nonjudicially. They apply for the giving of required notices. They apply for the giving of consents to certain actions. The article also authorizes a court to appoint a representative if the court concludes that representation of a person might otherwise be inadequate. The court may appoint a representative to represent and approve a settlement on behalf of a minor, incapacitated, or unborn person or person whose identity or location is unknown and not reasonably ascertainable.

Article 4 — Creation, Validity, Modification and Termination of Trust - This article specifies the requirements for creating, modifying and terminating trusts. Most of the requirements relating to creation of trusts (§§ 401 through 409) track traditional doctrine, including requirements of intent, capacity, property, and valid trust purpose. The Uniform Trust Code articulates a three-part classification system for trusts: noncharitable, charitable, and honorary. Noncharitable trusts, the most common type, require an ascertainable beneficiary and a valid purpose. Charitable trusts, on the other hand, by their very nature are created to benefit the public at large. The so called honorary or purposes trust, although unenforceable at common law, is valid and enforceable under this Code despite the absence of an ascertainable beneficiary. The most common example is a trust for the care of an animal.

Sections 410 through 417 provide a series of

interrelated rules on when a trust may be terminated or modified other than by its express terms. The overall objective of these sections is to enhance flexibility consistent with the principle that preserving the settlor's intent is paramount. Termination or modification may be allowed upon beneficiary consent if the court concludes that the trust or a particular provision no longer serves a material purpose or if the settlor concurs; by the court in response to unanticipated circumstances or to remedy ineffective administrative terms; or by the court or trustee if the trust is of insufficient size to justify continued administration under its existing terms. Trusts may be reformed to correct a mistake of law or fact, or modified to achieve the settlor's tax objectives. Trusts may be combined or divided. Charitable trusts may be modified or terminated under cy pres to better achieve the settlor's charitable purposes.

Article 5 — Creditor's Claims; Spendthrift and Discretionary Trusts - This article addresses the validity of a spendthrift provision and other issues relating to the rights of creditors to reach the trust to collect a debt. To the extent a trust is protected by a spendthrift provision, a beneficiary's creditor may not reach the beneficiary's interest until distribution is made by the trustee. To the extent not protected by a spendthrift provision, a creditor can reach the beneficiary's interest, subject to the court's power to limit the award. Certain categories of claims are exempt from a spendthrift restriction, including certain governmental claims and claims for child support or alimony. Other issues addressed in this article include creditor claims against discretionary trusts; creditor claims against a settlor, whether the trust is revocable or irrevocable; and the rights of creditors when a trustee fails to make a required distribution within a reasonable time.

Article 6 — Revocable Trusts - This short article deals with issues of significance not totally settled under current law. The basic policy of this article and of the Uniform Trust Code in general is to treat the revocable trust as the functional equivalent of a will. The article specifies a standard of capacity, provides that a trust is presumed revocable unless its terms provide otherwise, prescribes the procedure for revocation or amendment of a revocable trust, addresses the rights of beneficiaries during the settlor's lifetime, and provides a statute of limitations on contests.

Article 7 — Office of Trustee - This article contains a series of default rules dealing with the office of trustee, all of which may be modified in the terms of the trust. Rules are provided on acceptance of office and bonding. The role of the cotrustee is addressed, including the extent that one cotrustee may delegate to another, and the extent to which one cotrustee can be held liable for actions of another trustee. Also covered are changes in trusteeship, including the circumstances when a vacancy must be filled, the procedure for resignation, the grounds for removal, and the process for appointing a successor trustee. Finally, standards are provided for trustee compensation and reimbursement for expenses.

Article 8 — Duties and Powers of Trustee - This article states the fundamental duties of a trustee and enumerates the trustee's powers. The duties listed are not new, although some of the particulars have changed over the years. This article was drafted where possible to conform to the Uniform Prudent Investor Act. The Uniform Prudent Investor Act prescribes a trustee's responsibilities with respect to the management and investment of trust property. This article also addresses a trustee's duties regarding distributions to beneficiaries.

Article 9 — Uniform Prudent Investor Act - This article provides a place for a jurisdiction to enact, reenact or codify its version of the Uniform Prudent Investor Act. States adopting the Uniform Trust Code which have previously enacted the Uniform Prudent Investor Act are encouraged to reenact their version of the Prudent Investor Act in this article.

Article 10 — Liability of Trustees and Rights of Persons Dealing With Trustees - §§ 1001 through 1009 list the remedies for breach of trust, describe how money damages are to be determined, provide a statute of limitations on claims against a trustee, and specify other defenses, including consent of a beneficiary and recognition of and limitations on the effect of an exculpatory clause. Sections 1010 through 1013 address trustee relations with persons other than beneficiaries. The objective is to encourage third parties to engage in commercial transactions with trustees to the same extent as if the property were not held in trust.

Article 11 — Miscellaneous Provisions - The Uniform Trust Code is intended to have the widest possible application, consistent with constitutional limitations. The Code applies not only to trusts created on or after the effective date, but also to trusts in existence on the date of enactment.

The drafting committee was assisted by numerous officially designated advisors and observers, representing an array of organizations. In addition to the American Bar Association advisors listed above, advisors and observers who attended a majority of the drafting committee meetings include Edward C. Halbach, Jr., Reporter, Restatement (Third) of Trust Law; Kent H. McMahan, American College of Trust and Estate Counsel; Alex Misheff, American Bankers Association; and Lawrence W. Waggoner, Reporter, Restatement (Third) of Property: Wills and Other Donative Transfers. Significant input was also received from the Joint Editorial Board for Uniform Trusts and Estates Acts and the Committee on State Laws of the American College of Trust and Estate Counsel.

ARTICLE 1
GENERAL PROVISIONS AND DEFINITIONS

General Comment

The Uniform Trust Code is primarily a default statute. Most of the Code's provisions can be overridden in the terms of the trust. The provisions not subject to override are scheduled in § 105(b). These include the duty of a trustee to act in good faith and with regard to the purposes of the trust, public policy exceptions to enforcement of spendthrift provisions, the requirements for creating a trust, and the authority of the court to modify or terminate a trust on specified grounds.

The remainder of the article specifies the scope of the Code (§ 102), provides definitions (§ 103), and collects provisions of importance not amenable to codification elsewhere in the Uniform Trust Code. Sections 106 and 107 focus on the sources of law that will govern a trust. Section 106 clarifies that despite the Code's comprehensive scope, not all aspects of the law of trusts have been codified. The Uniform Trust Code is supplemented by the common law of trusts and principles of equity. Section 107 addresses selection of the jurisdiction or jurisdictions whose laws will govern the trust. A settlor, absent overriding public policy concerns, is free to select the law that will determine the meaning and effect of a trust's terms.

Changing a trust's principal place of administration is sometimes desirable, particularly to lower a trust's state income tax. Such transfers are authorized in § 108. The trustee, following notice to the "qualified beneficiaries," defined in § 103(13), may without approval of court transfer the principal place of administration to another state or country if a qualified beneficiary does not object and if the transfer is consistent with the trustee's duty to administer the trust at a place appropriate to its purposes, its administration, and the interests of the beneficiaries. The settlor, if minimum contacts are present, may also designate the trust's principal place of administration.

Sections 104 and 109 through 111 address procedural issues. Section 104 specifies when persons, particularly persons who work in organizations, are deemed to have acquired knowledge of a fact. Section 109 specifies the methods for giving notice and excludes from the Code's notice requirements persons whose identity or location is unknown and not reasonably ascertainable. Section 110 allows beneficiaries with remote interests to request notice of actions, such as notice of a trustee resignation, which are normally given only to the qualified beneficiaries.

Section 111 ratifies the use of nonjudicial settlement agreements. While the judicial settlement procedures may be used in all court proceedings relating to the trust, the nonjudicial settlement procedures will not always be available. The terms of the trust may direct that the procedures not be used, or settlors may negate or modify them by specifying their own methods for obtaining consents. Also, a nonjudicial settlement may include only terms and conditions a court could properly approve.

The Uniform Trust Code does not prescribe the rules of construction to be applied to trusts created under the Code. The Code instead recognizes that enacting jurisdictions are likely to take a diversity of approaches, just as they have with respect to the rules of construction applicable to wills. Section 112 accommodates this variation by providing that the state's specific rules on construction of wills, whatever they may be, also apply to the construction of trusts.

§ 101. Short Title. This [Act] may be cited as the Uniform Trust Code.

§ 102. Scope. This [Code] applies to express trusts, charitable or noncharitable, and trusts created pursuant to a statute, judgment, or decree that requires the trust to be administered in the manner of an express trust.

Comment

The Uniform Trust Code, while comprehensive, applies only to express trusts. Excluded from the Code's coverage are resulting and constructive trusts, which are not express trusts but remedial devices imposed by law. For the requirements for creating an express trust and the methods by which express trusts are created, see §§ 401-402. The Code does not attempt to distinguish express trusts from other legal relationships with respect to property, such as agencies and contracts for the benefit of third parties. For the distinctions, see Restatement (Third) of Trusts §§ 2, 5 (Tentative Draft No. 1, approved 1996); Restatement (Second) of Trusts §§ 2, 5-16C (1959).

The Uniform Trust Code is directed primarily at trusts that arise in an estate planning or other donative context, but express trusts can arise in other contexts. For example, a trust created pursuant to a divorce action would be included, even though such a trust is not donative but is created pursuant to a bargained-for exchange. Commercial trusts come in numerous forms, including trusts created pursuant to

a state business trust act and trusts created to administer specified funds, such as to pay a pension or to manage pooled investments. Commercial trusts are often subject to special-purpose legislation and case law, which in some respects displace the usual rules stated in this Code. *See* John H. Langbein, *The Secret Life of the Trust: The Trust as an Instrument of Commerce,* 107 Yale L.J. 165 (1997).

Express trusts also may be created by means of court judgment or decree. Examples include trusts created to hold the proceeds of personal injury recoveries and trusts created to hold the assets of a protected person in a conservatorship proceeding. *See, e.g.,* Unif. Probate Code § 5-411(a)(4).

§ 103. Definitions. In this [Code]:

(1) "Action," with respect to an act of a trustee, includes a failure to act.

(2) "Ascertainable standard" means a standard relating to an individual's health, education, support, or maintenance within the meaning of Section 2041(b)(1)(A) or 2514(c)(1) of the Internal Revenue Code of 1986, as in effect on [the effective date of this [Code] [amendment] [, or as later amended].

(3) "Beneficiary" means a person that:

    (A) has a present or future beneficial interest in a trust, vested or contingent; or

    (B) in a capacity other than that of trustee, holds a power of appointment over trust property.

(4) "Charitable trust" means a trust, or portion of a trust, created for a charitable purpose described in Section 405(a).

(5) "[Conservator]" means a person appointed by the court to administer the estate of a minor or adult individual.

(6) "Environmental law" means a federal, state, or local law, rule, regulation, or ordinance relating to protection of the environment.

(7) "[Guardian]" means a person appointed by the court [, a parent, or a spouse] to make decisions regarding the support, care, education, health, and welfare of a minor or adult individual. The term does not include a guardian ad litem.

(8) "Interests of the beneficiaries" means the beneficial interests provided in the terms of the trust.

(9) "Jurisdiction," with respect to a geographic area, includes a State or country.

(10) "Person" means an individual, corporation, business trust, estate, trust, partnership, limited liability company, association, joint venture, government; governmental subdivision, agency, or instrumentality; public corporation, or any other legal or commercial entity.

(11) "Power of withdrawal" means a presently exercisable general power of appointment other than a power: (A) exercisable by a trustee and limited by an ascertainable standard; or (B) exercisable by another person only upon consent of the trustee or a person holding an adverse interest.

(12) "Property" means anything that may be the subject of ownership, whether real or personal, legal or equitable, or any interest therein.

(13) "Qualified beneficiary" means a beneficiary who, on the date the beneficiary's qualification is determined:

    (A) is a distributee or permissible distributee of trust income or principal;

    (B) would be a distributee or permissible distributee of trust income or principal if the interests of the distributees described in subparagraph (A) terminated on that date without causing the trust to terminate; or

(C) would be a distributee or permissible distributee of trust income or principal if the trust terminated on that date.

(14) "Revocable," as applied to a trust, means revocable by the settlor without the consent of the trustee or a person holding an adverse interest.

(15) "Settlor" means a person, including a testator, who creates, or contributes property to, a trust. If more than one person creates or contributes property to a trust, each person is a settlor of the portion of the trust property attributable to that person's contribution except to the extent another person has the power to revoke or withdraw that portion.

(16) "Spendthrift provision" means a term of a trust which restrains both voluntary and involuntary transfer of a beneficiary's interest.

(17) "State" means a State of the United States, the District of Columbia, Puerto Rico, the United States Virgin Islands, or any territory or insular possession subject to the jurisdiction of the United States. The term includes an Indian tribe or band recognized by federal law or formally acknowledged by a State.

(18) "Terms of a trust" means:

(A) Except as otherwise provided in subparagraph (B), the manifestation of the settlor's intent regarding a trust's provisions as:

(i) expressed in the trust instrument; or

(ii) established by other evidence that would be admissible in a judicial proceeding; or

(B) the trust's provisions, as established, determined, or amended by:

(i) a trustee or other person in accordance with applicable law;

(ii) a court order; [or]

(iii) a nonjudicial settlement agreement under Section 111.

(19) "Trust instrument" means an instrument executed by the settlor that contains terms of the trust, including any amendments thereto.

(20) "Trustee" includes an original, additional, and successor trustee, and a cotrustee.

Comment

A definition of "action" (paragraph (1)) is included for drafting convenience, to avoid having to clarify in the numerous places in the Uniform Trust Code where reference is made to an "action" by the trustee that the term includes a failure to act.

The definition of "ascertainable standard" (paragraph (2)) was added to the Code by a 2004 amendment. The term was previously used only in and defined in § 814. Other 2004 amendments add the term to §§ 103(11) and 504, necessitating the need to move the definition to the list of defined terms in § 103 and make it applicable to the entire Code.

"Beneficiary" (paragraph (3)) refers only to a beneficiary of a trust as defined in the Uniform Trust Code. In addition to living and ascertained individuals, beneficiaries may be unborn or unascertained. Pursuant to § 402(b), a trust is valid only if a beneficiary can be ascertained now or in the future. The term "beneficiary" includes not only beneficiaries who received their interests under the terms of the trust but also beneficiaries who received their interests by other means, including by assignment, exercise of a power of appointment, resulting trust upon the failure of an interest, gap in a disposition, operation of an antilapse statute upon the predecease of a named beneficiary, or upon termination of the trust. The fact that a person incidentally benefits from the trust does not mean that the person is a beneficiary. For example, neither a trustee nor persons hired by the trustee become beneficiaries merely because they receive compensation from the trust. *See* Restatement (Third) of Trusts § 48 cmt. c (Tentative Draft No. 2, approved 1999); Restatement (Second) of Trusts § 126 cmt. c (1959).

While the holder of a power of appointment is not

considered a trust beneficiary under the common law of trusts, holders of powers are classified as beneficiaries under the Uniform Trust Code. Holders of powers are included on the assumption that their interests are significant enough that they should be afforded the rights of beneficiaries. A power of appointment as used in state trust law and this Code is as defined in state property law and not federal tax law although there is considerable overlap between the two definitions.

A power of appointment is authority to designate the recipients of beneficial interests in property. *See* Restatement (Second) of Property: Donative Transfers §11.1 (1986). A power is either general or nongeneral and either presently exercisable or not presently exercisable. A general power of appointment is a power exercisable in favor of the holder of the power, the power holder's creditors, the power holder's estate, or the creditors of the power holder's estate. *See* Restatement (Second) of Property: Donative Transfers §11.4 (1986). All other powers are nongeneral. A power is presently exercisable if the power holder can currently create an interest, present or future, in an object of the power. A power of appointment is not presently exercisable if exercisable only by the power holder's will or if its exercise is not effective for a specified period of time or until occurrence of some event. *See* Restatement (Second) of Property: Donative Transfers §11.5 (1986). Powers of appointment may be held in either a fiduciary or nonfiduciary capacity. The definition of "beneficiary" excludes powers held by a trustee but not powers held by others in a fiduciary capacity.

While all categories of powers of appointment are included within the definition of "beneficiary," the Uniform Trust Code elsewhere makes distinctions among types of powers. Under § 302, the holder of a testamentary general power of appointment may represent and bind persons whose interests are subject to the power. A "power of withdrawal" (paragraph (11)) is defined as a presently exercisable general power of appointment other than a power exercisable by a trustee and limited by an ascertainable standard, or a power which is exercisable by another person only upon consent of the trustee or a person holding an adverse interest. The exception for a power exercisable by a trustee that is limited by an ascertainable standard was added in 2004. For a discussion of this amendment, see the comment on the 2004 Amendment to § 504, which made a related change.

The definition of "beneficiary" includes only those who hold beneficial interests in the trust. Because a charitable trust is not created to benefit ascertainable beneficiaries but to benefit the community at large (*see* § 405(a)), persons receiving distributions from a charitable trust are not beneficiaries as that term is defined in this Code. However, pursuant to § 110(b), also granted rights of a qualified beneficiary under the Code are charitable organizations expressly designated to receive distributions under the terms of a charitable trust, but only if their beneficial interests are sufficient to satisfy the definition of qualified beneficiary for a noncharitable trust.

The Uniform Trust Code leaves certain issues concerning beneficiaries to the common law. Any person with capacity to take and hold legal title to intended trust property has capacity to be a beneficiary. *See* Restatement (Third) of Trusts § 43 (Tentative Draft No. 2, approved 1999); Restatement (Second) of Trusts §§ 116-119 (1959). Except as limited by public policy, the extent of a beneficiary's interest is determined solely by the settlor's intent. *See* Restatement (Third) of Trusts § 49 (Tentative Draft No. 2, approved 1999); Restatement (Second) of Trusts §§ 127-128 (1959). While most beneficial interests terminate upon a beneficiary's death, the interest of a beneficiary may devolve by will or intestate succession the same as a corresponding legal interest. *See* Restatement (Third) of Trusts § 55(1) (Tentative Draft No. 2, approved 1999); Restatement (Second) of Trusts §§ 140, 142 (1959).

Under the Uniform Trust Code, when a trust has both charitable and noncharitable beneficiaries only the charitable portion qualifies as a "charitable trust" (paragraph (4)). The great majority of the Code's provisions apply to both charitable and noncharitable trusts without distinction. The distinctions between the two types of trusts are found in the requirements relating to trust creation and modification. Pursuant to §§ 405 and 413, a charitable trust must have a charitable purpose and charitable trusts may be modified or terminated under the doctrine of cy pres. Also, § 411 allows a noncharitable trust to in certain instances be terminated by its beneficiaries while charitable trusts do not have beneficiaries in the usual sense. To the extent of these distinctions, a split-interest trust is subject to two sets of provisions, one applicable to the charitable interests, the other the noncharitable.

For discussion of the definition of "conservator" (paragraph (5)), see the definition of "guardian" (paragraph (7)).

To encourage trustees to accept and administer

trusts containing real property, the Uniform Trust Code contains several provisions designed to limit exposure to possible liability for violation of "environmental law" (paragraph (6)). Section 701(c)(2) authorizes a nominated trustee to investigate trust property to determine potential liability for violation of environmental law or other law without accepting the trusteeship. Section 816(13) grants a trustee comprehensive and detailed powers to deal with property involving environmental risks. Section 1010(b) immunizes a trustee from personal liability for violation of environmental law arising from the ownership and control of trust property.

Under the Uniform Trust Code, a "guardian" (paragraph (7)) makes decisions with respect to personal care; a "conservator" (paragraph (5)) manages property. The terminology used is that employed in Article V of the Uniform Probate Code, and in its free-standing Uniform Guardianship and Protective Proceedings Act. Enacting jurisdictions not using these terms in the defined sense should substitute their own terminology. For this reason, both terms have been placed in brackets. The definition of "guardian" accommodates those jurisdictions which allow appointment of a guardian by a parent or spouse in addition to appointment by a court. Enacting jurisdictions which allow appointment of a guardian solely by a court should delete the bracketed language "a parent, or a spouse."

The phrase "interests of the beneficiaries" (paragraph (8)) is used with some frequency in the Uniform Trust Code. The definition clarifies that the interests are as provided in the terms of the trust and not as determined by the beneficiaries. Absent authority to do so in the terms of the trust, § 108 prohibits a trustee from changing a trust's principal place of administration if the transfer would violate the trustee's duty to administer the trust at a place appropriate to the interests of the beneficiaries. Section 706(b) conditions certain of the grounds for removing a trustee on the court's finding that removal of the trustee will best serve the interests of the beneficiaries. Section 801 requires the trustee to administer the trust in the interests of the beneficiaries, and § 802 makes clear that a trustee may not place its own interests above those of the beneficiaries. Section 808(d) requires the holder of a power to direct who is subject to a fiduciary obligation to act with regard to the interests of the beneficiaries. Section 1002(b) may impose greater liability on a cotrustee who commits a breach of trust with reckless indifference to the interests of the

beneficiaries. Section 1008 invalidates an exculpatory term to the extent it relieves a trustee of liability for breach of trust committed with reckless indifference to the interests of the beneficiaries.

"Jurisdiction" (paragraph (9)), when used with reference to a geographic area, includes a state or country but is not necessarily so limited. Its precise scope will depend on the context in which it is used. "Jurisdiction" is used in §§ 107 and 403 to refer to the place whose law will govern the trust. The term is used in § 108 to refer to the trust's principal place of administration. The term is used in § 816 to refer to the place where the trustee may appoint an ancillary trustee and to the place in whose courts the trustee can bring and defend legal proceedings.

The definition of "property" (paragraph (12)) is intended to be as expansive as possible and to encompass anything that may be the subject of ownership. Included are choses in action, claims, and interests created by beneficiary designations under policies of insurance, financial instruments, and deferred compensation and other retirement arrangements, whether revocable or irrevocable. Any such property interest is sufficient to support creation of a trust. *See* § 401 comment.

Due to the difficulty of identifying beneficiaries whose interests are remote and contingent, and because such beneficiaries are not likely to have much interest in the day-to-day affairs of the trust, the Uniform Trust Code uses the concept of "qualified beneficiary" (paragraph (13)) to limit the class of beneficiaries to whom certain notices must be given or consents received. The definition of qualified beneficiaries is used in § 705 to define the class to whom notice must be given of a trustee resignation. The term is used in § 813 to define the class to be kept informed of the trust's administration. Section 417 requires that notice be given to the qualified beneficiaries before a trust may be combined or divided. Actions which may be accomplished by the consent of the qualified beneficiaries include the appointment of a successor trustee as provided in § 704. Prior to transferring a trust's principal place of administration, § 108(d) requires that the trustee give at least 60 days notice to the qualified beneficiaries.

The qualified beneficiaries consist of the beneficiaries currently eligible to receive a distribution from the trust together with those who might be termed the first-line remaindermen. These are the beneficiaries who would become eligible to receive distributions were the event triggering the termination of a beneficiary's interest or of the trust itself to occur on the date in question. Such a terminating event will typically be the death or deaths of the beneficiaries currently eligible to receive the income. Should a qualified beneficiary be a minor, incapacitated, or unknown, or a beneficiary whose identity or location is not reasonably ascertainable, the representation and virtual representation principles of Article 3 may be employed, including the possible appointment by the court of a representative to represent the beneficiary's interest.

The qualified beneficiaries who take upon termination of the beneficiary's interest or of the trust can include takers in default of the exercise of a power of appointment. The term can also include the persons entitled to receive the trust property pursuant to the exercise of a power of appointment. Because the exercise of a testamentary power of appointment is not effective until the testator's death and probate of the will, the qualified beneficiaries do not include appointees under the will of a living person. Nor would the term include the objects of an unexercised inter vivos power.

Charitable trusts and trusts for a valid noncharitable purpose do not have beneficiaries in the usual sense. However, certain persons, while not technically beneficiaries, do have an interest in seeing that the trust is enforced. Section 110 expands the definition of qualified beneficiaries to encompass this wider group. Section 110(b) grants the rights of qualified beneficiaries to charitable organizations expressly designated under the terms of a charitable trust and whose beneficial interests are sufficient to satisfy the definition of qualified beneficiary for a noncharitable trust. Section 110(c) also grants the rights of qualified beneficiaries to a person appointed by the terms of the trust or by the court to enforce a trust created for an animal or other noncharitable purpose. Section 110(d) is an optional provision granting the rights of a qualified beneficiary with respect to a charitable trust to the attorney general of the enacting jurisdiction.

The definition of "revocable" (paragraph (14)) clarifies that revocable trusts include only trusts whose revocation is substantially within the settlor's control. The fact that the settlor becomes incapacitated does not convert a revocable trust into an irrevocable trust. The trust remains revocable until the settlor's death or the power of revocation is released. The consequences of classifying a trust as revocable are many. The Uniform Trust Code contains provisions relating to liability of a revocable trust for payment of the settlor's debts (§ 505), the

standard of capacity for creating a revocable trust (§ 601), the procedure for revocation (§ 602), the subjecting of the beneficiaries' rights to the settlor's control (§ 603), the period for contesting a revocable trust (§ 604), the power of the settlor of a revocable trust to direct the actions of a trustee (§ 808(a)), notice to the qualified beneficiaries upon the settlor's death (§ 813(b)), and the liability of a trustee of a revocable trust for the obligations of a partnership of which the trustee is a general partner (§ 1011(d)).

Because under § 603(b) the holder of a power of withdrawal has the rights of a settlor of a revocable trust, the definition of "power of withdrawal" (paragraph (11)), and "revocable" (paragraph (14)) are similar. Both exclude individuals who can exercise their power only with the consent of the trustee or person having an adverse interest although the definition of "power of withdrawal" excludes powers subject to an ascertainable standard, a limitation which is not present in the definition of "revocable.".

The definition of "settlor" (paragraph (15)) refers to the person who creates, or contributes property to, a trust, whether by will, self-declaration, transfer of property to another person as trustee, or exercise of a power of appointment. For the requirements for creating a trust, see § 401. Determining the identity of the "settlor" is usually not an issue. The same person will both sign the trust instrument and fund the trust. Ascertaining the identity of the settlor becomes more difficult when more than one person signs the trust instrument or funds the trust. The fact that a person is designated as the "settlor" by the terms of the trust is not necessarily determinative. For example, the person who executes the trust instrument may be acting as the agent for the person who will be funding the trust. In that case, the person funding the trust, and not the person signing the trust instrument, will be the settlor. Should more than one person contribute to a trust, all of the contributors will ordinarily be treated as settlors in proportion to their respective contributions, regardless of which one signed the trust instrument. *See* § 602(b).

In the case of a revocable trust employed as a will substitute, gifts to the trust's creator are sometimes made by placing the gifted property directly into the trust. To recognize that such a donor is not intended to be treated as a settlor, the definition of "settlor" excludes a contributor to a trust that is revocable by another person or over which another person has a power of withdrawal. Thus, a parent who contributes to a child's revocable trust would not be treated as one of the trust's settlors. The definition of settlor would treat the child as the sole settlor of the trust to the extent of the child's proportionate contribution. Pursuant to § 603(b), the child's power of withdrawal over the trust would also result in the child being treated as the settlor with respect to the portion of the trust attributable to the parent's contribution.

Ascertaining the identity of the settlor is important for a variety of reasons. It is important for determining rights in revocable trusts. *See* §§ 505(a)(1), (3) (creditor claims against settlor of revocable trust), 602 (revocation or modification of revocable trust), and 604 (limitation on contest of revocable trust). It is also important for determining rights of creditors in irrevocable trusts. *See* § 505(a)(2) (creditors of settlor can reach maximum amount trustee can distribute to settlor). While the settlor of an irrevocable trust traditionally has no continuing rights over the trust except for the right under § 411 to terminate the trust with the beneficiaries' consent, the Uniform Trust Code also authorizes the settlor of an irrevocable trust to petition for removal of the trustee and to enforce or modify a charitable trust. *See* §§ 405(c) (standing to enforce charitable trust), 413 (doctrine of cy pres), and 706 (removal of trustee).

"Spendthrift provision" (paragraph (16)) means a term of a trust which restrains the transfer of a beneficiary's interest, whether by a voluntary act of the beneficiary or by an action of a beneficiary's creditor or assignee, which at least as far as the beneficiary is concerned, would be involuntary. A spendthrift provision is valid under the Uniform Trust Code only if it restrains both voluntary and involuntary transfer. For a discussion of this requirement and the effect of a spendthrift provision in general, see § 502. The insertion of a spendthrift provision in the terms of the trust may also constitute a material purpose sufficient to prevent termination of the trust by agreement of the beneficiaries under § 411, although the Code does not presume this result.

"Terms of a trust" (paragraph (18)) is a defined term used frequently in the Uniform Trust Code. While the wording of a written trust instrument is almost always the most important determinant of a trust's terms, the definition is not so limited. Oral statements, the situation of the beneficiaries, the purposes of the trust, the circumstances under which the trust is to be administered, and, to the extent the settlor was otherwise silent, rules of construction, all may have a bearing on determining a trust's meaning. *See* Restatement (Third) of Trusts § 4 cmt. a (Tentative Draft No. 1, approved 1996); Restatement

(Second) of Trusts § 4 cmt. a (1959). If a trust established by order of court is to be administered as an express trust, the terms of the trust are determined from the court order as interpreted in light of the general rules governing interpretation of judgments. *See* Restatement (Third) of Trusts § 4 cmt. f (Tentative Draft No. 1, approved 1996).

A manifestation of a settlor's intention does not constitute evidence of a trust's terms if it would be inadmissible in a judicial proceeding in which the trust's terms are in question. *See* Restatement (Third) of Trusts § 4 cmt. b (Tentative Draft No. 1, approved 1996); Restatement (Second) of Trusts § 4 cmt. b (1959). *See also* Restatement (Third) Property: Donative Transfers §§ 10.2, 11.1-11.3 (Tentative Draft No. 1, approved 1995). For example, in many states a trust of real property is unenforceable unless evidenced by a writing, although § 407 of this Code does not so require, leaving this issue to be covered by separate statute if the enacting jurisdiction so elects. Evidence otherwise relevant to determining the terms of a trust may also be excluded under other principles of law, such as the parol evidence rule.

"Trust instrument" (paragraph (19)) is a subset of the definition of "terms of a trust" (paragraph (18)), referring to only such terms as are found in an instrument executed by the settlor. Section 403 provides that a trust is validly created if created in compliance with the law of the place where the trust instrument was executed. Pursuant to § 604(a)(2), the contest period for a revocable trust can be shortened by providing the potential contestant with a copy of the trust instrument plus other information. Section 813(b)(1) requires that the trustee upon request furnish a beneficiary with a copy of the trust instrument. To allow a trustee to administer a trust with some dispatch without concern about liability if the terms of a trust instrument are contradicted by evidence outside of the instrument, § 1006 protects a trustee from liability to the extent a breach of trust resulted from reasonable reliance on those terms. Section 1013 allows a trustee to substitute a certification of trust in lieu of providing a third person with a copy of the trust instrument. Section 1106(a)(4) provides that unless there is a clear indication of a contrary intent, rules of construction and presumptions provided in the Uniform Trust Code apply to trust instruments executed before the effective date of the Code.

The definition of "trustee" (paragraph (20)) includes not only the original trustee but also an additional and successor trustee as well as a cotrustee.

Because the definition of trustee includes trustees of all types, any trustee, whether original or succeeding, single or cotrustee, has the powers of a trustee and is subject to the duties imposed on trustees under the Uniform Trust Code. Any natural person, including a settlor or beneficiary, has capacity to act as trustee if the person has capacity to hold title to property free of trust. *See* Restatement (Third) of Trusts § 32 (Tentative Draft No. 2, approved 1999); Restatement (Second) of Trusts § 89 (1959). State banking statutes normally impose additional requirements before a corporation can act as trustee.

2004 Amendment. Section 103(2) adds a definition of "ascertainable standard." The term was formerly used only in § 814. Other 2004 amendments add the term to §§ 103(11) and 504. The amendment moves into this section the definition previously found in § 814, thereby making it apply generally throughout the Code. Adding this definition required the renumbering of all subsequent definitions in the Section and corrections to cross-references to this Section throughout the Code and comments.

Section 103(11), the definition of "power of withdrawal," is amended to exclude a possible inference that the term includes a discretionary power in a trustee to make distributions for the trustee's own benefit which is limited by an ascertainable standard. For an explanation of the reason for this amendment, see the comment to the 2004 amendment to § 504, which addresses a related issue.

Clarifying language is added to § 103(13), the definition of "qualified beneficiary," to make clear that the second category in the definition refers to termination of an interest not associated with termination of the trust.

2018 Amendment. Section 103(18) was amended in 2018 to conform to the more detailed definition of "terms of trust" used in the Uniform Directed Trust Act. The revised definition acknowledges the possibility that the terms of a trust may change over time at the direction of a court, by nonjudicial settlement agreement, or in accordance with applicable law, such as by a decanting under the Uniform Trust Decanting Act (2015), or by a third party, such as under the Uniform Directed Trust Act (2017).

§ 104. Knowledge.

(a) Subject to subsection (b), a person has knowledge of a fact if the person:

(1) has actual knowledge of it;

(2) has received a notice or notification of it; or

(3) from all the facts and circumstances known to the person at the time in question, has reason to know it.

(b) An organization that conducts activities through employees has notice or knowledge of a fact involving a trust only from the time the information was received by an employee having responsibility to act for the trust, or would have been brought to the employee's attention if the organization had exercised reasonable diligence. An organization exercises reasonable diligence if it maintains reasonable routines for communicating significant information to the employee having responsibility to act for the trust and there is reasonable compliance with the routines. Reasonable diligence does not require an employee of the organization to communicate information unless the communication is part of the individual's regular duties or the individual knows a matter involving the trust would be materially affected by the information.

Comment

This section specifies when a person is deemed to know a fact. Subsection (a) states the general rule. Subsection (b) provides a special rule dealing with notice to organizations. Pursuant to subsection (a), a fact is known to a person if the person had actual knowledge of the fact, received notification of it, or had reason to know of the fact's existence based on all of the circumstances and other facts known to the person at the time. Under subsection (b), notice to an organization is not necessarily achieved by giving notice to a branch office. Nor does the organization necessarily acquire knowledge at the moment the notice arrives in the organization's mailroom. Rather, the organization has notice or knowledge of a fact only when the information is received by an employee having responsibility to act for the trust, or would have been brought to the employee's attention had the organization exercised reasonable diligence.

"Know" is used in its defined sense in §§ 109 (methods and waiver of notice), 305 (appointment of representative), 604(b) (limitation on contest of revocable trust), 812 (collecting trust property), 1009 (nonliability of trustee upon beneficiary's consent,

release, or ratification), and 1012 (protection of person dealing with trustee). But as to certain actions, a person is charged with knowledge of facts the person would have discovered upon reasonable inquiry. *See* § 1005 (limitation of action against trustee following report of trustee).

This section is based on Uniform Commercial Code § 1-202 (2000 Annual Meeting Draft).

§ 105. Default and Mandatory Rules.

(a) Except as otherwise provided in the terms of the trust, this [Code] governs the duties and powers of a trustee, relations among trustees, and the rights and interests of a beneficiary.

(b) The terms of a trust prevail over any provision of this [Code] except:

(1) the requirements for creating a trust;

(2) [subject to [Uniform Directed Trust Act Sections 9, 11, and 12],] the duty of a trustee to act in good faith and in accordance with the terms and purposes of the trust and the interests of the beneficiaries;

(3) the requirement that a trust and its terms be for the benefit of its beneficiaries, and that the trust have a purpose that is lawful, not contrary to public policy, and possible to achieve;

(4) the power of the court to modify or terminate a trust under Sections 410 through 416;

(5) the effect of a spendthrift provision and the rights of certain creditors and assignees to reach a trust as provided in [Article] 5;

(6) the power of the court under Section 702 to require, dispense with, or modify or terminate a bond;

(7) the power of the court under Section 708(b) to adjust a trustee's compensation specified in the terms of the trust which is unreasonably low or high;

[(8) the duty under Section 813(b)(2) and (3) to notify qualified beneficiaries of an irrevocable trust who have attained 25 years of age of the existence of the trust, of the identity of the trustee, and of their right to request trustee's reports;]

[(9) the duty under Section 813(a) to respond to the request of a [qualified] beneficiary of an irrevocable trust for trustee's reports and other information reasonably related to the administration of a trust;]

(10) the effect of an exculpatory term under Section 1008;

(11) the rights under Sections 1010 through 1013 of a person other than a trustee or beneficiary;

(12) periods of limitation for commencing a judicial proceeding; [and]

(13) the power of the court to take such action and exercise such jurisdiction as may be necessary in the interests of justice [; and

(14) the subject-matter jurisdiction of the court and venue for commencing a proceeding as provided in Sections 203 and 204].

Legislative Note: *A state that has enacted the Uniform Directed Trust Act should add the introductory phrase "subject to [Uniform Directed Trust Act Sections 9, 11, and 12]" at the beginning of subsection (b)(2), for the reasons given in the 2018 Amendment to the comment below.*

Comment

Subsection (a) emphasizes that the Uniform Trust Code is primarily a default statute. While this Code provides numerous procedural rules on which a settlor may wish to rely, the settlor is generally free to override these rules and to prescribe the conditions under which the trust is to be administered. With only limited exceptions, the duties and powers of a trustee, relations among trustees, and the rights and interests of a beneficiary are as specified in the terms of the trust.

Subsection (b) lists the items not subject to override in the terms of the trust. Because subsection (b) refers specifically to other sections of the Code, enacting jurisdictions modifying these other sections may also need to modify subsection (b).

Subsection (b)(1) confirms that the requirements for a trust's creation, such as the necessary level of capacity and the requirement that a trust have a legal purpose, are controlled by statute and common law, not by the settlor. For the requirements for creating a trust, see §§ 401-409. Subsection (b)(12) makes clear that the settlor may not reduce any otherwise applicable period of limitations for commencing a judicial proceeding. *See* §§ 604 (period of limitations for contesting validity of revocable trust), and 1005 (period of limitation on action for breach of trust). Similarly, a settlor may not so negate the responsibilities of a trustee that the trustee would no longer be acting in a fiduciary capacity. Subsection (b)(2) provides that the terms may not eliminate a trustee's duty to act in good faith and in accordance with the purposes of the trust and the interests of the beneficiaries. For this duty, see §§ 801 and 814(a). Subsection (b)(3) provides that the terms may not eliminate the requirement that a trust and its terms must be for the benefit of the beneficiaries. Subsection (b)(3) also provides that the terms may not eliminate the requirement that the trust have a purpose that is lawful, not contrary to public policy, and possible to achieve. Subsections (b)(2)-(3) are echoed in §§ 404 (trust and its terms must be for benefit of beneficiaries; trust must have a purpose that is lawful, not contrary to public policy, and possible to achieve), 801 (trustee must administer trust in good faith, in accordance with its terms and purposes and the interests of the beneficiaries), 802(a) (trustee must administer trust solely in the interests of the beneficiaries), 814 (trustee must exercise discretionary power in good faith and in accordance with its terms and purposes and the interests of the beneficiaries), and 1008 (exculpatory term unenforceable to extent it relieves trustee of liability for breach of trust committed in bad faith or with reckless indifference to the purposes of the trust and the interests of the beneficiaries).

The terms of a trust may not deny a court authority to take such action as necessary in the interests of justice, including requiring that a trustee furnish bond. Subsection (b)(6), (13). Additionally, should the jurisdiction adopting this Code enact the optional provisions on subject-matter jurisdiction and venue, subsection (b)(14) similarly provides that such provisions cannot be altered in the terms of the trust. The power of the court to modify or terminate a trust under §§ 410 through 416 is not subject to variation in the terms of the trust. Subsection (b)(4). However, all of these Code sections involve situations which the settlor could have addressed had the settlor had sufficient foresight. These include situations where the purpose of the trust has been achieved, a mistake was made in the trust's creation, or circumstances have arisen that were not anticipated by the settlor.

Section 813 imposes a general obligation to keep the beneficiaries informed as well as several specific notice requirements. Subsections (b)(8) and (b)(9), which were placed in brackets and made optional provisions by a 2004 amendment, specify limits on the settlor's ability to waive these information requirements. With respect to beneficiaries age 25 or older, a settlor may dispense with all of the requirements of § 813 except for the duties to inform the beneficiaries of the existence of the trust, of the identity of the trustee, and to provide a beneficiary upon request with such reports as the trustee may have prepared. Among the specific requirements that a settlor may waive include the duty to provide a beneficiary upon request with a copy of the trust instrument (§ 813(b)(1)), and the requirement that the trustee provide annual reports to the qualified beneficiaries (§ 813(c)). The furnishing of a copy of the entire trust instrument and preparation of annual reports may be required in a particular case, however, if such information is requested by a beneficiary and is reasonably related to the trust's administration.

Responding to the desire of some settlors that younger beneficiaries not know of the trust's bounty until they have reached an age of maturity and self-sufficiency, subsection (b)(8) allows a settlor to provide that the trustee need not even inform beneficiaries under age 25 of the existence of the trust. However, pursuant to subsection (b)(9), if the younger beneficiary learns of the trust and requests information, the trustee must respond. More generally, subsection (b)(9) prohibits a settlor from overriding the right provided to a beneficiary in § 813(a) to request from the trustee of an irrevocable trust copies of trustee reports and other information reasonably related to the trust's administration.

During the drafting of the Uniform Trust Code, the drafting committee discussed and rejected a proposal that the ability of the settlor to waive required notice be based on the nature of the beneficiaries' interest and not on the beneficiaries' age. Advocates of this alternative approach concluded that a settlor should be able to waive required notices to the remainder beneficiaries, regardless of their age. Enacting jurisdictions preferring this alternative should substitute the language "adult and current or permissible distributees of trust income or principal" for the reference to "qualified beneficiaries" in subsection (b)(8). They should also delete the reference to beneficiaries "who have attained the age of 25 years."

Waiver by a settlor of the trustee's duty to keep the beneficiaries informed of the trust's administration does not otherwise affect the trustee's duties. The trustee remains accountable to the beneficiaries for the trustee's actions.

Neither subsection (b)(8) nor (b)(9) apply to revocable trusts. The settlor of a revocable trust may waive all reporting to the beneficiaries, even in the event the settlor loses capacity. If the settlor is silent about the subject, reporting to the beneficiaries will be required upon the settlor's loss of capacity. *See* § 603.

In conformity with traditional doctrine, the Uniform Trust Code limits the ability of a settlor to exculpate a trustee from liability for breach of trust. The limits are specified in § 1008. Subsection (b)(10) of this section provides a cross-reference. Similarly, subsection (b)(7) provides a cross-reference to § 708(b), which limits the binding effect of a provision specifying the trustee's compensation.

Finally, subsection (b)(11) clarifies that a settlor is not free to limit the rights of third persons, such as purchasers of trust property. Subsection (b)(5) clarifies that a settlor may not restrict the rights of a beneficiary's creditors except to the extent a spendthrift restriction is allowed as provided in Article 5.

2001 Amendment. By amendment in 2001, subsections (b)(3), (8) and (9) were revised. The language in subsection (b)(3) "that the trust have a purpose that is lawful, not contrary to public policy, and possible to achieve" is new. This addition clarifies that the settlor may not waive this common law requirement, which is codified in the Code at § 404.

Subsections (b)(8) and (9) formerly provided:

(8) the duty to notify the qualified beneficiaries of an irrevocable trust who have attained 25 years of age of the existence of the trust, and of their right to request trustee's reports and other information reasonably related to the administration of the trust;

(9) the duty to respond to the request of a beneficiary of an irrevocable trust for trustee's reports and other information reasonably related to the administration of a trust.

The amendment clarifies that the information requirements not subject to waiver are requirements specified in § 813 of the Code.

2003 Amendment. By amendment in 2003, subsection (b)(8) was revised. Under the previous provision, as amended in 2001, the presence of two "excepts" n the same sentence, the first in the introductory language to subsection (b) and the second at the beginning of subsection (b)(8), has caused considerable confusion. The revision eliminates the second "except" in (b)(8) without changing the meaning of the provision.

2004 Amendment. Sections 105(b)(8) and 105(b)(9) address the extent to which a settlor may waive trustee notices and other disclosures to beneficiaries that would otherwise be required under the Code. These subsections have generated more discussion in jurisdictions considering enactment of the UTC than have any other provisions of the Code. A majority of the enacting jurisdictions have modified these provisions but not in a consistent way. This lack of agreement and resulting variety of approaches is expected to continue as additional states enact the Code.

Placing these sections in brackets signals that uniformity is not expected. States may elect to enact these provisions without change, delete these provisions, or enact them with modifications. In § 105(b)(9), an internal bracket has been added to make clear that an enacting jurisdiction may limit to the qualified beneficiaries the obligation to respond to a beneficiary's request for information.

The placing of these provisions in brackets does not mean that the Drafting Committee recommends that an enacting jurisdiction delete §§ 105(b)(8) and 105(b)(9). The Committee continues to believe that § 105(b)(8) and (b)(9), enacted as is, represent the best balance of competing policy considerations. Rather, the provisions were placed in brackets out of a recognition that there is a lack of consensus on the extent to which a settlor ought to be able to waive reporting to beneficiaries, and that there is little chance that the states will enact §§ 105(b)(8) and (b)(9) with any uniformity.

The policy debate is succinctly stated in Joseph Kartiganer & Raymond H. Young, *The UTC: Help for Beneficiaries and Their Attorneys*, Prob. & Prop., Mar./April 2003, at 18, 20:

> The beneficiaries' rights to information and reports are among the most important provisions in the UTC. They also are among the provisions that have attracted the most attention. The UTC provisions reflect a compromise position between opposing viewpoints.
>
> Objections raised to beneficiaries' rights to information include the wishes of some settlors who believe that knowledge of trust benefits would not be good for younger beneficiaries, encouraging them to take up a life of ease rather than work and be productive citizens. Sometimes trustees themselves desire secrecy and freedom from interference by beneficiaries.
>
> The policy arguments on the other side are: that the essence of the trust relationship is accounting to the beneficiaries; that it is wise administration to account and inform beneficiaries, to avoid the greater danger of the beneficiary learning of a breach or possible breach long after the event; and that there are practical difficulties with secrecy (for example, the trustee must tell a child that he or she is not eligible for financial aid at college because the trust will pay, and must determine whether to accumulate income at high income tax rates or pay it out for inclusion in the beneficiary's own return). Furthermore, there is the practical advantage of a one-year statute of limitations when the beneficiary is informed of the trust transactions and advised of the bar if no claim is made within the year. UTC §§ 1005. In the absence of notice, the trustee is exposed to liability until five years after the trustee ceases to serve, the interests of

beneficiaries end, or the trust terminates. UTC §§ 1005(c)

2005 Amendment. Subsection (b)(2) is revised to make the language consistent with the corresponding duties in §§ 801 and 814(a), which require that a trustee act in good faith and in accordance with the terms and purposes of the trust and the interests of the beneficiaries. Previously, subsection (b)(2) provided that the settlor could not waive the duty of a trustee to act in good faith and in accordance with the purposes of the trust. The amendment adds that also cannot waive the obligation to act in accordance with the terms of the trust and the interests of the beneficiaries.

The purpose of the amendment is to make the language consistent, not to change the substance of the section. Absent some other restriction, a settlor is always free to specify the trust's terms to which the trustee must comply. Also, "interests of the beneficiaries" is a defined term in § 103(8) meaning the beneficial interests as provided in the terms of the trust, which the settlor is also free to specify.

2018 Amendment. Following the promulgation of the Uniform Directed Trust Act (UDTA) in 2017, subsection (b)(2) was revised to include bracketed language that makes subsection (b)(2) subject to the UDTA. With respect to a directed trust as that term is defined by the UDTA, fiduciary responsibility is allocated among trust directors and directed trustees according to their functions under the terms of the trust. Under the UDTA, the mandatory minimum duties described in subsection (b)(2) are assigned to a trust director rather than a directed trustee, and the UDTA prescribes a mandatory minimum fiduciary duty for the directed trustee that supersedes subsection (b)(2). The UDTA also allows a similar division and assignment of fiduciary responsibility among cotrustees. A corresponding legislative note was also added.

§ 106. Common Law of Trusts; Principles of Equity.
The common law of trusts and principles of equity supplement this [Code], except to the extent modified by this [Code] or another statute of this State.

Comment

The Uniform Trust Code codifies those portions of the law of express trusts that are most amenable to codification. The Code is supplemented by the common law of trusts, including principles of equity. To determine the common law and principles of

equity in a particular state, a court should look first to prior case law in the state and then to more general sources, such the Restatement of Trusts, Restatement (Third) of Property: Wills and Other Donative Transfers, and the Restatement of Restitution. The common law of trusts is not static but includes the contemporary and evolving rules of decision developed by the courts in exercise of their power to adapt the law to new situations and changing conditions. It also includes the traditional and broad equitable jurisdiction of the court, which the Code in no way restricts.

The statutory text of the Uniform Trust Code is also supplemented by these comments, which, like the comments to any Uniform Act, may be relied on as a guide for interpretation. *See Acierno v. Worthy*

Bros. Pipeline Corp. 656 A.2d 1085, 1090 (Del. 1995) (interpreting Uniform Commercial Code); *Yale University v. Blumenthal*, 621 A.2d 1304, 1307 (Conn. 1993) (interpreting Uniform Management of Institutional Funds Act); 2 Norman Singer, Statutory Construction § 52.05 (6th ed. 2000); Jack Davies, Legislative Law and Process in a Nutshell § 55-4 (2d ed. 1986).

Comment Amended in 2005.

§ 107. Governing Law. The meaning and effect of the terms of a trust are determined by:

(1) the law of the jurisdiction designated in the terms unless the designation of that jurisdiction's law is contrary to a strong public policy of the jurisdiction having the most significant relationship to the matter at issue; or

(2) in the absence of a controlling designation in the terms of the trust, the law of the jurisdiction having the most significant relationship to the matter at issue.

Comment

This section provides rules for determining the law that will govern the meaning and effect of particular trust terms. The law to apply to determine whether a trust has been validly created is determined under § 403.

Paragraph (1) allows a settlor to select the law that will govern the meaning and effect of the terms of the trust. The jurisdiction selected need not have any other connection to the trust. The settlor is free to select the governing law regardless of where the trust property may be physically located, whether it consists of real or personal property, and whether the trust was created by will or during the settlor's lifetime. This section does not attempt to specify the strong public policies sufficient to invalidate a settlor's choice of governing law. These public policies will vary depending upon the locale and may change over time.

Paragraph (2) provides a rule for trusts without governing law provisions – the meaning and effect of the trust's terms are to be determined by the law of the jurisdiction having the most significant relationship to the matter at issue. Factors to consider in determining the governing law include the place of the trust's creation, the location of the trust property, and the domicile of the settlor, the trustee, and the beneficiaries. *See* Restatement (Second) of Conflict of Laws §§ 270 cmt. c & 272 cmt. d (1971). Other more general factors that may be pertinent in particular cases include the relevant policies of the forum, the

relevant policies of other interested jurisdictions and degree of their interest, the protection of justified expectations and certainty, and predictability and uniformity of result. *See* Restatement (Second) of Conflict of Laws § 6 (1971). Usually, the law of the trust's principal place of administration will govern administrative matters and the law of the place having the most significant relationship to the trust's creation will govern the dispositive provisions.

This section is consistent with and was partially patterned on the Hague Convention on the Law Applicable to Trusts and on their Recognition, signed on July 1, 1985. Like this section, the Hague Convention allows the settlor to designate the governing law. Hague Convention art. 6. Absent a designation, the Convention provides that the trust is to be governed by the law of the place having the closest connection to the trust. Hague Convention art. 7. The Convention also lists particular public policies for which the forum may decide to override the choice of law that would otherwise apply. These policies are protection of minors and incapable parties, personal and proprietary effects of marriage, succession rights, transfer of title and security interests in property, protection of creditors in matters of insolvency, and, more generally, protection of third parties acting in good faith. Hague Convention art. 15.

For the authority of a settlor to designate a trust's principal place of administration, see § 108(a).

§ 108. Principal Place of Administration.

(a) Without precluding other means for establishing a sufficient connection with the designated jurisdiction, terms of a trust designating the principal place of administration are valid and controlling if:

(1) a trustee's principal place of business is located in or a trustee is a resident of the designated jurisdiction; or

(2) all or part of the administration occurs in the designated jurisdiction.

(b) A trustee is under a continuing duty to administer the trust at a place appropriate to its purposes, its administration, and the interests of the beneficiaries.

(c) Without precluding the right of the court to order, approve, or disapprove a transfer, the trustee, in furtherance of the duty prescribed by subsection (b), may transfer the trust's principal place of administration to another State or to a jurisdiction outside of the United States.

(d) The trustee shall notify the qualified beneficiaries of a proposed transfer of a trust's principal place of administration not less than 60 days before initiating the transfer. The notice of proposed transfer must include:

(1) the name of the jurisdiction to which the principal place of administration is to be transferred;

(2) the address and telephone number at the new location at which the trustee can be contacted;

(3) an explanation of the reasons for the proposed transfer;

(4) the date on which the proposed transfer is anticipated to occur; and

(5) the date, not less than 60 days after the giving of the notice, by which the qualified beneficiary must notify the trustee of an objection to the proposed transfer.

(e) The authority of a trustee under this section to transfer a trust's principal place of administration terminates if a qualified beneficiary notifies the trustee of an objection to the proposed transfer on or before the date specified in the notice.

(f) In connection with a transfer of the trust's principal place of administration, the trustee may transfer some or all of the trust property to a successor trustee designated in the terms of the trust or appointed pursuant to Section 704.

Comment

This section prescribes rules relating to a trust's principal place of administration. Locating a trust's principal place of administration will ordinarily determine which court has primary if not exclusive jurisdiction over the trust. It may also be important for other matters, such as payment of state income tax or determining the jurisdiction whose laws will govern the trust. *See* § 107 comment.

Because of the difficult and variable situations sometimes involved, the Uniform Trust Code does not attempt to further define principal place of administration. A trust's principal place of administration ordinarily will be the place where the trustee is located. Determining the principal place of administration becomes more difficult, however, when cotrustees are located in different states or when a single institutional trustee has trust operations in more than one state. In such cases, other factors may become relevant, including the place where the trust records are kept or trust assets

held, or in the case of an institutional trustee, the place where the trust officer responsible for supervising the account is located.

A concept akin to principal place of administration is used by the Office of the Comptroller of the Currency. Reserves that national banks are required to deposit with state authorities is based on the location of the office where trust assets are primarily administered. *See* 12 C.F.R. § 9.14(b).

Under the Uniform Trust Code, the fixing of a trust's principal place of administration will determine where the trustee and beneficiaries have consented to suit (§ 202), and the rules for locating venue within a particular state (§ 204). It may also be considered by a court in another jurisdiction in determining whether it has jurisdiction, and if so, whether it is a convenient forum.

A settlor expecting to name a trustee or cotrustees with significant contacts in more than one state may eliminate possible uncertainty about the location of the trust's principal place of administration by specifying the jurisdiction in the terms of the trust. Under subsection (a), a designation in the terms of the trust is controlling if (1) a trustee is a resident of or has its principal place of business in the designated jurisdiction, or (2) all or part of the administration occurs in the designated jurisdiction. Designating the principal place of administration should be distinguished from designating the law to determine the meaning and effect of the trust's terms, as authorized by § 107. A settlor is free to designate one jurisdiction as the principal place of administration and another to govern the meaning and effect of the trust's provisions.

Subsection (b) provides that a trustee is under a continuing duty to administer the trust at a place appropriate to its purposes, its administration, and the interests of the beneficiaries. "Interests of the beneficiaries," defined in § 103(8), means the beneficial interests provided in the terms of the trust. Ordinarily, absent a substantial change or circumstances, the trustee may assume that the original place of administration is also the appropriate place of administration. The duty to administer the trust at an appropriate place may also dictate that the trustee not move the trust.

Subsections (c)-(f) provide a procedure for changing the principal place of administration to another state or country. Such changes are often beneficial. A change may be desirable to secure a lower state income tax rate, or because of relocation of the trustee or beneficiaries, the appointment of a new trustee, or a change in the location of the trust investments. The procedure for transfer specified in this section applies only in the absence of a contrary provision in the terms of the trust. *See* § 105. To facilitate transfer in the typical case, where all concur

that a transfer is either desirable or is at least not harmful, a transfer can be accomplished without court approval unless a qualified beneficiary objects. To allow the qualified beneficiaries sufficient time to review a proposed transfer, the trustee must give the qualified beneficiaries at least 60 days prior notice of the transfer. Notice must be given not only to qualified beneficiaries as defined in § 103(13) but also to those granted the rights of qualified beneficiaries under § 110. To assure that those receiving notice have sufficient information upon which to make a decision, minimum contents of the notice are specified. If a qualified beneficiary objects, a trustee wishing to proceed with the transfer must seek court approval.

In connection with a transfer of the principal place of administration, the trustee may transfer some or all of the trust property to a new trustee located outside of the state. The appointment of a new trustee may also be essential if the current trustee is ineligible to administer the trust in the new place. Subsection (f) clarifies that the appointment of the new trustee must comply with the provisions on appointment of successor trustees as provided in the terms of the trust or under § 704. Absent an order of succession in the terms of the trust, § 704(c) provides the procedure for appointment of a successor trustee of a noncharitable trust, and § 704(d) the procedure for appointment of a successor trustee of a charitable trust.

While transfer of the principal place of administration will normally change the governing law with respect to administrative matters, a transfer does not normally alter the controlling law with respect to the validity of the trust and the construction of its dispositive provisions. *See* 5A Austin W. Scott & William F. Fratcher, The Law of Trusts § 615 (4th ed. 1989).

§ 109. Methods and Waiver of Notice.

(a) Notice to a person under this [Code] or the sending of a document to a person under this [Code] must be accomplished in a manner reasonably suitable under the circumstances and likely to result in receipt of the notice or document. Permissible methods of notice or for sending a document include first-class mail, personal delivery, delivery to the person's last known place of residence or place of business, or a properly directed electronic message.

(b) Notice otherwise required under this [Code] or a document otherwise required to be sent under this [Code] need not be provided to a person whose identity or location is unknown to and not reasonably ascertainable by the trustee.

(c) Notice under this [Code] or the sending of a document under this [Code] may be waived by the person to be notified or sent the document.

(d) Notice of a judicial proceeding must be given as provided in the applicable rules of civil procedure.

Comment

Subsection (a) clarifies that notices under the Uniform Trust Code may be given by any method likely to result in its receipt by the person to be notified. The specific methods listed in the subsection are illustrative, not exhaustive. Subsection (b) relieves a trustee of responsibility for what would otherwise be an impossible task, the giving of notice to a person whose identity or location is unknown and not reasonably ascertainable by the trustee. The section does not define when a notice is deemed to have been sent or delivered or person deemed to be unknown or not reasonably ascertainable, the drafters preferring to leave this issue to the enacting jurisdiction's rules of civil procedure.

Under the Uniform Trust Code, certain actions can be taken upon unanimous consent of the beneficiaries or qualified beneficiaries. *See* §§ 411 (termination of noncharitable irrevocable trust), 704 (appointment of successor trustee). Subsection (b) of this section only authorizes waiver of notice. A consent required from a beneficiary in order to achieve unanimity is not waived because the beneficiary is missing. But the fact a beneficiary cannot be located may be a sufficient basis for a substitute consent to be given by another person on the beneficiary's behalf under the representation principles of Article 3.

To facilitate administration, subsection (c) allows waiver of notice by the person to be notified or sent the document. Among the notices and documents to which this subsection can be applied are notice of a proposed transfer of principal place of administration (§ 108(d)) or of a trustee's report (§ 813(c)). This subsection also applies to notice to qualified beneficiaries of a proposed trust combination or division (§ 417), of a temporary assumption of duties without accepting trusteeship (§ 701(c)(1)), and of a trustee's resignation (§ 705(a)(1)).

Notices under the Uniform Trust Code are nonjudicial. Pursuant to subsection (d), notice of a judicial proceeding must be given as provided in the applicable rules of civil procedure.

§ 110. Others Treated as Qualified Beneficiaries.

(a) Whenever notice to qualified beneficiaries of a trust is required under this [Code], the trustee must also give notice to any other beneficiary who has sent the trustee a request for notice.

(b) A charitable organization expressly designated to receive distributions under the terms of a charitable trust has the rights of a qualified beneficiary under this [Code] if the charitable organization, on the date the charitable organization's qualification is being determined:

(A) is a distributee or permissible distributee of trust income or principal;

(B) would be a distributee or permissible distributee of trust income or principal upon the termination of the interests of other distributees or permissible distributees then receiving or eligible to receive distributions; or

(C) would be a distributee or permissible distributee of trust income or principal if the trust terminated on that date.

(c) A person appointed to enforce a trust created for the care of an animal or another noncharitable purpose as provided in Section 408 or 409 has the rights of a qualified beneficiary under this [Code].

[(d) The [attorney general of this State] has the rights of a qualified beneficiary with respect to a charitable trust having its principal place of administration in this State.]

Comment

Under the Uniform Trust Code, certain notices need be given only to the "qualified" beneficiaries. For the definition of "qualified beneficiary," see § 103(13). Among these notices are notice of a transfer of the trust's principal place of administration (§ 108(d)), notice of a trust division or combination (§ 417), notice of a trustee resignation (§ 705(a)(1)), and notice of a trustee's annual report (§ 813(c)). Subsection (a) of this section authorizes other beneficiaries to receive one or more of these notices by filing a request for notice with the trustee.

Under the Code, certain actions, such as the appointment of a successor trustee, can be accomplished by the consent of the qualified beneficiaries. *See, e.g.,* § 704 (filling vacancy in trusteeship). Subsection (a) only addresses notice, not required consent. A person who requests notice under subsection (a) does not thereby acquire a right to participate in actions that can be taken only upon consent of the qualified beneficiaries.

Charitable trusts do not have beneficiaries in the usual sense. However, certain persons, while not technically beneficiaries, do have an interest in seeing that the trust is enforced. In the case of a charitable trust, this includes the state's attorney general and charitable organizations expressly designated to receive distributions under the terms of the trust. Under subsection (b), charitable organizations expressly designated in the terms of the trust to receive distributions and who would qualify as a qualified beneficiary were the trust noncharitable, are granted the rights of qualified beneficiaries under the Code. Because the charitable organization must be expressly named in the terms of the trust and must be designated to receive distributions, excluded are organizations that might receive distributions in the trustee's discretion but that are not named in the trust's terms. Requiring that the organization have an interest similar to that of a beneficiary of a private trust also denies the rights of a qualified beneficiary to organizations holding remote remainder interests. For further discussion of the definition of "qualified beneficiary," see § 103 comment.

Subsection (c) similarly grants the rights of qualified beneficiaries to persons appointed by the terms of the trust or by the court to enforce a trust created for an animal or other trust with a valid purpose but no ascertainable beneficiary. For the requirements for creating such trusts, see §§ 408 and 409.

"Attorney general" is placed in brackets in subsection (d) to accommodate jurisdictions which grant enforcement authority over charitable trusts to another designated official. Because states take various approaches to enforcement of charitable trusts, by a 2004 amendment subsection (d) was placed in brackets in its entirety. For a discussion, see 2004 Amendment below.

Subsection (d) does not limit other means by which

the attorney general or other designated official can enforce a charitable trust.

2001 Amendment. By amendment in 2001, "charitable organization expressly designated to receive distributions" was substituted for "charitable organization expressly entitled to receive benefits" in subsection (b). The amendment conforms the language of this section to terminology used elsewhere in the Code.

2004 Amendment. Subsection (b) is amended to better conform this provision to the Drafting Committee's intent. Charitable trusts do not have beneficiaries in the usual sense. Yet, such trusts are often created to benefit named charitable organizations. Under this amendment, which is based on the definition of qualified beneficiary in § 103, a designated charitable organization has the rights of a qualified beneficiary only if it holds an interest similar to that of a qualified beneficiary in a noncharitable trust. The effect of the amendment is to exclude charitable organizations that might receive distributions in the trustee's discretion even though not expressly mentioned in the trust's terms. Also denied the rights of qualified beneficiaries are charitable organizations that hold only remote remainder interests. The previous version of subsection (b) had a similar intent but the language could be read more broadly.

The placing of subsection (d) in brackets recognizes that the role of the attorney general in the enforcement of charitable trusts varies greatly in the states. In some states, the legislature may prefer that the attorney general be granted the rights of a qualified beneficiary. In other states, the attorney general may play a lesser role in enforcement. The expectation is that states considering enactment will adapt this provision to the particular role that the attorney general plays in the enforcement of charitable trusts in their state. Some states may prefer to delete this provision. Other states might provide that the attorney general has the rights of a qualified beneficiary only for trusts in which no charitable organization has been designated to receive distributions. Yet other states may prefer to enact the provision without change.

§ 111. Nonjudicial Settlement Agreements.

(a) For purposes of this section, "interested persons" means persons whose consent would be required in order to achieve a binding settlement were the settlement to be approved by the court.

(b) Except as otherwise provided in subsection (c), interested persons may enter into a binding nonjudicial settlement agreement with respect to any matter involving a trust.

(c) A nonjudicial settlement agreement is valid only to the extent it does not violate a material purpose of the trust and includes terms and conditions that could be properly approved by the court under this [Code] or other applicable law.

(d) Matters that may be resolved by a nonjudicial settlement agreement include:

(1) the interpretation or construction of the terms of the trust;

(2) the approval of a trustee's report or accounting;

(3) direction to a trustee to refrain from performing a particular act or the grant to a trustee of any necessary or desirable power;

(4) the resignation or appointment of a trustee and the determination of a trustee's compensation;

(5) transfer of a trust's principal place of administration; and

(6) liability of a trustee for an action relating to the trust.

(e) Any interested person may request the court to approve a nonjudicial settlement agreement, to determine whether the representation as provided in [Article] 3 was adequate, and to determine whether the agreement contains terms and conditions the court could have properly approved.

Comment

While the Uniform Trust Code recognizes that a court may intervene in the administration of a trust to the extent its jurisdiction is invoked by interested persons or otherwise provided by law (*see* § 201(a)), resolution of disputes by nonjudicial means is encouraged. This section facilitates the making of such agreements by giving them the same effect as if approved by the court. To achieve such certainty, however, subsection (c) requires that the nonjudicial settlement must contain terms and conditions that a court could properly approve. Under this section, a nonjudicial settlement cannot be used to produce a result not authorized by law, such as to terminate a trust in an impermissible manner.

Trusts ordinarily have beneficiaries who are minors, incapacitated, unborn or unascertained. Because such beneficiaries cannot signify their consent to an agreement, binding settlements can ordinarily be achieved only through the application of doctrines such as virtual representation or appointment of a guardian ad litem, doctrines traditionally available only in the case of judicial settlements. The effect of this section and the Uniform Trust Code more generally is to allow for such binding representation even if the agreement is not submitted for approval to a court. For the rules on representation, including appointments of representatives by the court to approve particular settlements, see Article 3.

Subsection (d) is a nonexclusive list of matters to which a nonjudicial settlement may pertain. The fact that the trustee and beneficiaries may resolve a matter nonjudicially does not mean that beneficiary approval is required. For example, a trustee may resign pursuant to § 705 solely by giving notice to the qualified beneficiaries, to a living settlor, and any cotrustees. But a nonjudicial settlement between the trustee and beneficiaries will frequently prove helpful in working out the terms of the resignation.

Because of the great variety of matters to which a nonjudicial settlement may be applied, this section does not attempt to precisely define the "interested persons" whose consent is required to obtain a binding settlement as provided in subsection (a). However, the consent of the trustee would ordinarily be required to obtain a binding settlement with respect to matters involving a trustee's administration, such as approval of a trustee's report or resignation.

[§ 112. Rules of Construction. The rules of construction that apply in this State to the interpretation of and disposition of property by will also apply as appropriate to the interpretation of the terms of a trust and the disposition of the trust property.]

Comment

This section is patterned after Restatement (Third) of Trusts § 25(2) and comment e (Tentative Draft No. 1, approved 1996), although this section, unlike the Restatement, also applies to irrevocable trusts. The revocable trust is used primarily as a will substitute, with its key provision being the determination of the persons to receive the trust property upon the settlor's death. Given this functional equivalence between the revocable trust and a will, the rules for interpreting the disposition of property at death should be the same whether the individual has chosen a will or revocable trust as the individual's primary estate planning instrument. Over the years, the legislatures of the states and the courts have developed a series of rules of construction reflecting the legislative or judicial understanding of how the average testator would wish to dispose of property in cases where the will is silent or insufficiently clear. Few legislatures have yet to extend these rules of construction to revocable trusts, and even fewer to irrevocable trusts, although a number of courts have done so as a matter of judicial construction. *See* Restatement (Third) of Trusts § 25, Reporter's Notes to cmt. d & e (Tentative Draft No. 1, approved 1996).

Because of the wide variation among the states on the rules of construction applicable to wills, this Code does not attempt to prescribe the exact rules to be applied to trusts but instead adopts the philosophy of the Restatement that the rules applicable to trusts ought to be the same, whatever those rules might be.

Rules of construction are not the same as constructional preferences. A constructional preference is general in nature, providing general guidance for resolving a wide variety of ambiguities. An example is a preference for a construction that results in a complete disposition and avoid illegality. Rules of construction, on the other hand, are specific in nature, providing guidance for resolving specific situations or construing specific terms. Unlike a constructional preference, a rule of construction, when applicable, can lead to only one result. *See* Restatement (Third) of Property: Donative Transfers § 11.3 & cmt. b (Tentative Draft No. 1, approved 1995).

Rules of construction attribute intention to individual donors based on assumptions of common intention. Rules of construction are found both in enacted statutes and in judicial decisions. Rules of construction can involve the meaning to be given to particular language in the document, such as the meaning to be given to "heirs" or "issue." Rules of construction also address situations the donor failed to anticipate. These include the failure to anticipate the predecease of a beneficiary or to specify the source from which expenses are to be paid. Rules of construction can also concern assumptions as to how a donor would have revised donative documents in light of certain events occurring after execution. These include rules dealing with the effect of a divorce and whether a specific devisee will receive a substitute gift if the subject matter of the devise is disposed of during the testator's lifetime.

Instead of enacting this section, a jurisdiction enacting this Code may wish to enact detailed rules on the construction of trusts, either in addition to its rules on the construction of wills or as part of one comprehensive statute applicable to both wills and trusts. For this reason and to encourage this alternative, the section has been made optional. For possible models, see Uniform Probate Code, Article 2, Parts 7 and 8, which was added to the UPC in 1990, and California Probate Code §§ 21101-21630, enacted in 1994.

[§ 113. Insurable Interest of Trustee.

(a) In this section, "settlor" means a person that executes a trust instrument. The term includes a person for which a fiduciary or agent is acting.

(b) A trustee of a trust has an insurable interest in the life of an individual insured under a life insurance policy that is owned by the trustee of the trust acting in a fiduciary capacity or that designates the trust itself as the owner if, on the date the policy is issued:

(1) the insured is:

(A) a settlor of the trust; or

(B) an individual in whom the settlor of the trust has, or would have had if living at the time the policy was issued, an insurable interest; and

(2) the life insurance proceeds are primarily for the benefit of one or more trust beneficiaries that have[:

(A)] an insurable interest in the life of the insured [; or

(B) a substantial interest engendered by love and affection in the continuation of the life of the insured and, if not already included under subparagraph (A), who are:

(i) related within the third degree or closer, as measured by the civil law system of determining degrees of relation, either by blood or law, to the insured; or

(ii) stepchildren of the insured].]

Comment

This section was added in 2010.

Every state requires, either as a matter of statutory or common law, that a purchaser of life insurance on another individual have an insurable interest in the life of the insured. See generally Robert H. Jerry, II & Douglas R. Richmond, Understanding Insurance Law, §§ 40, 43 (LexisNexis Publishing, 4th ed., 2007), at 273-77, 293-98. The definition of insurable interest became a matter of widespread concern among trust and estate planners after *Chawla ex rel Giesinger v. Transamerica Occidental Life Insurance Co.*, 2005 WL 405405 (E.D. Va. 2005), aff'd in part, vac'd in part, 440 F.3d 639 (4th Cir. 2006), where a Virginia federal district court applying Maryland law held that a trust did not have an insurable interest in the life of the insured who was the settlor and the creator of the trust. This portion of the district court's decision was subsequently vacated by the Fourth Circuit when holding that the district court's decision should be affirmed on other grounds, but the appellate decision did not question or criticize the district court's insurable interest analysis. The Maryland legislature subsequently enacted a statute in the state's insurance code clarifying the circumstances when a trustee or trust has an insurable interest in another's life, and several other states have enacted various forms of statutory clarification designed to address the "*Chawla* problem." During this process, the American College of Trust and Estate Counsel, among others, expressed the opinion that it would be best if a uniform approach could be fashioned in resolving the matter.

Consequently, the Uniform Law Commission, after studying the issue, decided to clarify the issue with respect to the Uniform Trust Code (UTC) and established a drafting committee for that purpose. The drafting committee, consisting of knowledgeable Conference members, was assisted by representatives from the American Bar Association, the American College of Trust and Estate Counsel, and the American Council of Life Insurers, consumer advocates, and other interested parties. This amendment resulted from their efforts and is designed to be inserted at the end of Article 1 of the UTC as Section 113. In keeping with the charge to the committee, the purpose of the amendment is to clarify when, for purposes of the Code, a trustee has an insurable interest in an individual whose life is to be the subject of an insurance policy to fund the trust. Clarification of this area of law that was subjected to uncertainty by the *Chawla* decision will provide a reliable basis upon which trust and estate planning practitioners may draft trust instruments that involve the eventual payment of expected death benefits.

It should be noted that the entire amendment is placed in brackets to indicate that each state should consider whether it is needed or its adoption would be appropriate. In some states *Chawla* may not present serious problems under pre-existing insurable interest law because it may be clear that a trustee already has an appropriate insurable interest for estate planning purposes. In other states, *Chawla* would present problems but, as indicated above, the state may have already addressed the issue so that the amendment may not be needed. Currently there are at least ten states that have enacted legislation on the subject (Delaware, Florida, Illinois, Georgia, Maine, Maryland, Minnesota, South Dakota, Virginia, and Washington). In those states, that do need to respond to *Chawla* (plus those that may want to revisit the matter) the amendment offers a reasonable solution that has the support of many in the estate planning field, as well as the life insurance industry.

With regard to the language of the amendment, subsection (a) provides that the term "settlor" is limited to a person who *executes* the trust instrument. This is narrower than the UTC definition of "settlor," which, in addition to the person who executes the trust instrument, would include a person who merely contributes property to the trust. See Section 103(15). As explained in the comment to Section 103(15), the broader definition serves a useful purpose in connection with the UTC generally; however, none of those situations relates to the issue of whose life should properly be the subject of a life insurance policy that is used to fund a trust. Moreover, to use the broader definition would needlessly complicate the issue of whose life should be the subject of insurance because it would be rare, if ever, that a life insurance policy used to fund a trust for estate planning purposes would be on the life of someone other than the settlor signing the trust or someone in whose life that settlor would have an insurable interest. Because there are situations in which a trust instrument will be executed by a fiduciary or agent for the creator of the trust, subsection (a) also makes clear that in such circumstances the fiduciary or agent is deemed to be the equivalent of the settlor.

Subsection (b) carries forward the widely approved rule that the time at which insurable interest in a life insurance policy is determined is that date the policy is issued, otherwise understood as the inception of the policy. Thus, if on the date the policy is issue the trustee has an insurable interest in the individual whose life is insured, the policy is not subject to be declared void for lack of such an interest. Under the reasoning that an individual has an unlimited insurable interest in his or her own life, subsection (b) provides that a trustee has an insurable interest in the settlor's own life. If an individual, as settlor, has created a trust to hold a life insurance policy on his or her own life, has funded that trust with the policy or with money to pay its premiums, and has selected the trustee of the trust, it follows that the trustee should have the same insurable interest that the settlor has in his or her own life. Similarly, recognizing that an individual may purchase insurance on the life of anyone in whom that individual has an insurable interest up to, generally speaking, the amount of that interest, subsection (b) provides that the trustee has an insurable interest in an individual in whom the settlor has, or would have had if living at the time the policy was issued, an insurable interest.

Moreover, paragraph (1) of subsection (b) addresses the *Chawla* issue by referring to the jurisdiction's insurance code or other law regarding insurable interest as a separate, independent source of law for determining whether a trustee has an insurable interest in the life of an individual on whose life the trust has purchased insurance. This means that the trustee would be entitled to apply for and purchase an insurance policy not only on the life of a settlor but also on the life of any other individual in whom the settlor has an insurable interest, e.g., the spouse or children of the settlor, in the enacting jurisdiction. Exactly whose lives may be insured depends on the law of the enacting jurisdiction. In short, the amendment does not change the enacting jurisdiction's pre-existing law of insurable interest.

Paragraph (2) of subsection (b) addresses a somewhat different issue, although it also references the insurable interest law of the enacting jurisdiction.

It is designed to ensure that irrevocable life insurance trusts (ILITs) are created to serve *bona fide* estate planning purposes by restricting who may be a beneficiary of insurance proceeds from a policy used to fund an ILIT. It establishes the requirement that the proceeds of such a life insurance policy used to fund the trust be payable primarily to certain types of trust beneficiaries. As to the latter, paragraph (2) contains bracketed language designed to provide states with a choice with regard to who those beneficiaries might be.

One choice may be exercised by deleting all the brackets, and all the language contained within the brackets, in paragraph (2) of subsection (b). By doing so, the class of beneficiaries for whom the insurance proceeds must primarily benefit is limited to those who, in the enacting jurisdiction, have an insurable interest in the life of the settlor. Depending on the law of the jurisdiction, this could mean that only those individuals traditionally recognized as having an insurable interest, such as spouses and their children, would qualify, or it could mean that additional family members, such as siblings, grandchildren, grandparents, and perhaps other, have an insurable interest in the life of the settlor. In some other jurisdictions, the law may not be clear on this point. In these jurisdictions, estate planners generally may be concerned that strictly tying the class of beneficiaries to the state's insurable interest law might unduly restrict their ability to provide appropriate legal services to their clients. To help alleviate this concern, an alternative is offered to clarify the law in these jurisdictions. To exercise this choice, the enacting jurisdiction need only remove the brackets while retaining the language contained therein, thereby adopting the language as part of the amendment.

Removing the brackets and retaining the bracketed language in paragraph (2) of subsection (b) clarifies and broadens to a limited extent the class of individuals for whom the insurance must primarily benefit. By including anyone who is related to the settlor or other insured by blood or law within the third degree, the amendment makes clear that not only parents and their children would fall in the required beneficiary category, but also that siblings, grandparents, grandchildren, great-grandparents, great-grandchildren, aunts, uncles, nephews, and nieces would also qualify. Lineal consanguinity, to use the more technical term for relation by blood, is the relationship between individuals when one directly descends from the other. Each generation in this direct line constitutes a degree. Collateral consanguinity refers to the relationship between individuals who descend from a common ancestor but not from each other. The civil law method of calculating degree of collateral consanguinity, which is used in most states, counts the number of generations from one individual, e.g., the insured, up to the common ancestor and then down to the other individual. See Restatement (Third) of Property: Wills and Other Donative Transfers § 2.4 cmt. *k* (1999).

The following table identifies the relatives of an insured within three degrees of lineal and collateral consanguinity using the civil law method, with each row representing a generation.

			Great-grand-parents (3)
		Grand-parents (2)	
	Parents (1)	Aunts and Uncles (2)	
Insured	Sisters and Brothers (2)		
Children (1)	Nieces and Nephews (3)		
Grand-children (2)			
Great-grand-children (3)			

The reference in subparagraph (B)(i) to relation by "law"–if that term is interpreted to have the same legal meaning as the term "affinity"–may extend the category of beneficiaries that must be primarily benefited to in-laws. If that is the case, degrees of relationship by law or affinity should be computed in the same manner as degrees of relationship by consanguinity. See State v. Hooper, 140 Kan. 481, 37 P.2d 52 (1934) (explaining, for example, that a husband has the same relation, by affinity, to his wife's blood relatives as she has to them by consanguinity, and vice versa). This would mean that a son- or daughter-in-law of the insured would be related in the first degree and a brother- or sister-in-law of the insured would be related in the second degree. A father- or mother-in-law would be related to the insured in the first degree, whereas an aunt- or uncle-in-law would be related to the insured in the third degree. See State v. Allen, 304 N.W.2d 203, at 207 (Iowa 1981) (listing authorities on who to compute degrees of relation).

At the very least, the term "law" should be interpreted to include the relation between spouses and the relation between an adoptive parent and adopted child, if they were not already included under subparagraph (A). Additionally, in case there is any doubt as to whether an adopted grandchild, i.e., a child adopted by an insured's child, is sufficiently related to the insured, as a biological grandchild might be, to have an insurable interest under subparagraph (A), the reference in (B)(i) may ensure that the adopted grandchild falls within the required category of beneficiaries. This is because the adopted grandchild arguably would, at the very least, be related by affinity to the insured in the second degree, just as a biological child of the insured's child would be related by blood in the second degree to the insured. In other words, the adopted grandchild would be treated in the same manner as a biological child for purposes of the amendment.

Stepchildren, who may not otherwise have an insurable interest in the life of the settlor or other insured under subparagraph (A) or who may not be included under subparagraph (B)(i), depending on the interpretation given to the term "law," are specifically included in subparagraph (B)(ii) to ensure that they occupy the same status as any other child of the settlor, biological or adopted.

The reason for the modifying language "if not already included under subparagraph (A)" found in subparagraph (B) of paragraph (2) of subsection (b) is to make it clear that there is no negative implication with regard to anyone related within the third degree to the insured and who would be included by virtue of the adopting jurisdiction's insurable interest law referred to in subparagraph (A). In other words, some of the people, but not all, included under subparagraph (A) will be related to the person whose life is insured within the third degree and the modifying language is designed to make it clear that subparagraph (B)(i) merely adds any others so related. The same reasoning applies to stepchildren. The adopting jurisdiction may already include them under its insurable interest law referred to in subparagraph (A). If not, however, subparagraph (B)(ii) makes sure they are included in the category of people for whom the insurance policy proceeds must primarily benefit.

Although estate planners expressed concern were a jurisdiction to delete subparagraph (B) because they felt doing so would unduly limit their ability to serve their clients' needs, there was a general consensus that including those identified in subparagraph (B) should suffice for the great majority of estate plans. Thus, estate planners strongly support the adoption of the language in subparagraph (B).

It should also be noted that, regardless of the decision relating to the choices presented by the bracketed language in paragraph (2) of subsection (b), the test concerning whether the beneficiaries designated in paragraph (2) are the primary beneficiaries of the policy proceeds takes place at the inception of the life insurance policy, i.e., when the policy is issued. The fact that there may be contingent trust beneficiaries or that the proceeds would be payable to different beneficiaries based on subsequent events or conditions is not relevant to the determination. One need only identify those trust beneficiaries that would receive the policy proceeds were the insured life to expire immediately after the policy is issued and the trust were to terminate at the same time. Among these beneficiaries, the proceeds must be payable primarily to those specified in subparagraph (2) of subsection (b). If that is so, the condition is satisfied and may not be challenged thereafter or on the basis that subsequent events might change who would receive the proceeds.

As for the term "primarily," it will often be the case that one is able to calculate that more than fifty percent of the policy proceeds will be payable to the required class of beneficiaries under paragraph (2), but this may not always be the situation. For example, if the purpose of the trust is to provide a lifetime benefit to a spouse or funds for children to obtain an education, the amount may be indeterminate. This, however, does not mean that the policy proceeds are not primarily for the benefit of those individuals if upon the inception of the policy they are the people who will immediately and mainly benefit from the trust, even though there are others not designated in paragraph (2) who may also benefit concurrently or benefit subsequently upon the satisfaction of some condition in the future. In short, the term is intended to be applied in a common sense manner than in a hyper-technical manner that would require that a precise dollar amount be payable to certain beneficiaries.

Finally, the amendment is drafted as it would appear in the UTC were it to be part of the Code when the latter is enacted or as it would appear as an amendment to a previously enacted version of the Code. In either case, since Section 1106 of the UTC, as originally drafted, already deals with the applicability of the UTC to trusts existing at the time of enactment, there may be no need to address that issue in this amendment. However, if an issue should arise regarding which trusts *and* life insurance policies are subject to the amendment, the following language may be helpful in resolving that issue:

> This section applies to any trust existing before, on, or after the effective date of this section, regardless of the effective date of the governing instrument under which the trust was created, but only as to a life insurance policy that is in force and for which an insured is alive on or after the effective date of this section.

ARTICLE 2
JUDICIAL PROCEEDINGS

General Comment

This article addresses selected issues involving judicial proceedings concerning trusts, particularly trusts with contacts in more than one state or country. This article is not intended to provide comprehensive coverage of court jurisdiction or procedure with respect to trusts. These issues are better addressed elsewhere, for example in the state's rules of civil procedure or as provided by court rule.

Section 201 makes clear that the jurisdiction of the court is available as invoked by interested persons or as otherwise provided by law. Proceedings involving the administration of a trust normally will be brought in the court at the trust's principal place of administration. Section 202 provides that the trustee and beneficiaries are deemed to have consented to the jurisdiction of the court at the principal place of administration as to any matter relating to the trust. Sections 203 and 204 are optional, bracketed provisions relating to subject-matter jurisdiction and venue.

§ 201. Role of Court in Administration of Trust.

(a) The court may intervene in the administration of a trust to the extent its jurisdiction is invoked by an interested person or as provided by law.

(b) A trust is not subject to continuing judicial supervision unless ordered by the court.

(c) A judicial proceeding involving a trust may relate to any matter involving the trust's administration, including a request for instructions and an action to declare rights.

Comment

While the Uniform Trust Code encourages the resolution of disputes without resort to the courts by providing such options as the nonjudicial settlement authorized by § 111, the court is always available to the extent its jurisdiction is invoked by interested persons. The jurisdiction of the court with respect to trust matters is inherent and historical and also includes the ability to act on its own initiative, to appoint a special master to investigate the facts of a case, and to provide a trustee with instructions even in the absence of an actual dispute.

Contrary to the trust statutes in some states, the Uniform Trust Code does not create a system of routine or mandatory court supervision. While subsection (b) authorizes a court to direct that a particular trust be subject to continuing court supervision, the court's intervention will normally be confined to the particular matter brought before it.

Subsection (c) makes clear that the court's jurisdiction may be invoked even absent an actual dispute. Traditionally, courts in equity have heard petitions for instructions and have issued declaratory judgments if there is a reasonable doubt as to the extent of the trustee's powers or duties. The court will not ordinarily instruct trustees on how to exercise discretion, however. *See* Restatement (Second) of Trusts §§ 187, 259 (1959). This section does not limit the court's equity jurisdiction. Beyond mentioning petitions for instructions and actions to declare rights, subsection (c) does not attempt to list the types of judicial proceedings involving trust administration that might be brought by a trustee or beneficiary. Such an effort is made in California Probate Code § 17200. Excluding matters not germane to the Uniform Trust Code, the California statute lists the following as items relating to the "internal affairs" of a trust: determining questions of construction; determining the existence or nonexistence of any immunity, power, privilege, duty, or right; determining the validity of a trust provision; ascertaining beneficiaries and determining to whom property will pass upon final or partial termination of the trust; settling accounts and passing upon the acts of a trustee, including the exercise of discretionary powers; instructing the trustee; compelling the trustee to report information about the trust or account to the beneficiary; granting powers to the trustee; fixing or allowing payment of the trustee's compensation or reviewing the reasonableness of the compensation; appointing or removing a trustee; accepting the resignation of a trustee; compelling redress of a breach of trust by any available remedy; approving or directing the modification or termination of a trust; approving or directing the combination or division of trusts; and authorizing or directing transfer of a trust or trust property to or from another jurisdiction.

§ 202. Jurisdiction over Trustee and Beneficiary.

(a) By accepting the trusteeship of a trust having its principal place of administration in this State or by moving the principal place of administration to this State, the trustee submits personally to the jurisdiction of the courts of this State regarding any matter involving the trust.

(b) With respect to their interests in the trust, the beneficiaries of a trust having its principal place of administration in this State are subject to the jurisdiction of the courts of this State regarding any matter involving the trust. By accepting a distribution from such a trust, the recipient submits personally to the jurisdiction of the courts of this State regarding any matter involving the trust.

(c) This section does not preclude other methods of obtaining jurisdiction over a trustee, beneficiary, or other person receiving property from the trust.

Comment

This section clarifies that the courts of the principal place of administration have jurisdiction to enter orders relating to the trust that will be binding on both the trustee and beneficiaries. Consent to jurisdiction does not dispense with any required notice, however. With respect to jurisdiction over a beneficiary, the Comment to Uniform Probate Code § 7-103, upon which portions of this section are based, is instructive:

It also seems reasonable to require beneficiaries to go to the seat of the trust when litigation has been instituted there concerning a trust in which they claim beneficial interests, much as the rights of shareholders of a corporation can be determined at a corporate seat. The settlor has indicated a principal place of administration by its selection of a trustee or otherwise, and it is reasonable to subject rights under the trust to the jurisdiction of the Court where the trust is properly administered.

The jurisdiction conferred over the trustee and beneficiaries by this section does not preclude jurisdiction by courts elsewhere on some other basis. Furthermore, the fact that the courts in a new state acquire jurisdiction under this section following a change in a trust's principal place of administration does not necessarily mean that the courts of the former principal place of administration lose jurisdiction, particularly as to matters involving events occurring prior to the transfer.

The jurisdiction conferred by this section is limited. Pursuant to subsection (b), until a distribution is made, jurisdiction over a beneficiary is limited to the beneficiary's interests in the trust. Personal jurisdiction over a beneficiary is conferred only upon the making of a distribution. Subsection (b) also gives the court jurisdiction over other recipients of distributions. This would include individuals who receive distributions in the mistaken belief they are beneficiaries.

For a discussion of jurisdictional issues concerning trusts, see 5A Austin W. Scott & William F. Fratcher, The Law of Trusts §§ 556-573 (4th ed. 1989).

[§ 203. Subject-matter Jurisdiction.

(a) The [designate] court has exclusive jurisdiction of proceedings in this State brought by a trustee or beneficiary concerning the administration of a trust.

(b) The [designate] court has concurrent jurisdiction with other courts of this State of other proceedings involving a trust.]

Comment

This section provides a means for distinguishing the jurisdiction of the court having primary jurisdiction for trust matters, whether denominated the probate court, chancery court, or by some other name, from other courts in a state that may on occasion resolve disputes concerning trusts. The section has been placed in brackets because the enacting jurisdiction may already address subject-matter jurisdiction by other statute or court rule. The topic also need not be addressed in states having unified court systems. For an explanation of types of proceedings which may be brought concerning the administration of a trust, see the Comment to § 201.

[§ 204. Venue.

(a) Except as otherwise provided in subsection (b), venue for a judicial proceeding involving a trust is in the [county] of this State in which the trust's principal place of administration is or will be located and, if the trust is created by will and the estate is not yet closed, in the [county] in which the decedent's estate is being administered.

(b) If a trust has no trustee, venue for a judicial proceeding for the appointment of a trustee is in a [county] of this State in which a beneficiary resides, in a [county] in which any trust property is located, and if the trust is created by will, in the [county] in which the decedent's estate was or is being administered.]

Comment

This optional, bracketed section is made available for jurisdictions that conclude that venue for a judicial proceeding involving a trust is not adequately addressed in local rules of civil procedure. For jurisdictions enacting this section, general rules governing venue continue to apply in cases not covered by this section. This includes most proceedings where jurisdiction over a trust, trust property, or parties to a trust is based on a factor other than the trust's principal place of administration. The general rules governing venue also apply when the principal place of administration of a trust is in another locale, but jurisdiction is proper in the enacting state.

ARTICLE 3
REPRESENTATION

General Comment

This article deals with representation of beneficiaries, both representation by fiduciaries (personal representatives, trustees, guardians, and conservators), and what is known as virtual representation. Representation is a topic not adequately addressed under the trust law of most states. Representation is addressed in the Restatement (First) of Property §§ 180-186 (1936), but the coverage of this article is more complete.

Section 301 is the introductory section, laying out the scope of the article. The representation principles of this article have numerous applications under this Code. The representation principles of the article apply for purposes of settlement of disputes, whether by a court or nonjudicially. They apply for the giving of required notices. They apply for the giving of consents to certain actions.

Sections 302-305 cover the different types of representation. Section 302 deals with representation by the holder of a general testamentary power of appointment. (Revocable trusts and presently exercisable general powers of appointment are covered by § 603, which grant the settlor or holder of the power all rights of the beneficiaries or persons whose interests are subject to the power). Section 303 deals with representation by a fiduciary, whether of an estate, trust, conservatorship, or guardianship. The section also allows a parent without a conflict of interest to represent and bind a minor or unborn child. Section 304 is the virtual representation provision. It provides for representation of and the giving of a binding consent by another person having a substantially identical interest with respect to the particular issue. Section 305 authorizes the court to appoint a representative to represent the interests of unrepresented persons or persons for whom the court concludes the other available representation might be inadequate.

The provisions of this article are subject to modification in the terms of the trust. *See* § 105. Settlors are free to specify their own methods for providing substituted notice and obtaining substituted consent.

§ 301. Representation: Basic Effect.

(a) Notice to a person who may represent and bind another person under this [article] has the same effect as if notice were given directly to the other person.

(b) The consent of a person who may represent and bind another person under this [article] is binding on the person represented unless the person represented objects to the representation before the consent would otherwise have become effective.

(c) Except as otherwise provided in Sections [411 and] 602, a person who under this [article] may represent a settlor who lacks capacity may receive notice and give a binding consent on the settlor's behalf.

[(d) A settlor may not represent and bind a beneficiary under this [article] with respect to the termination or modification of a trust under Section 411(a).]

Comment

This section is general and introductory, laying out the scope of the article.

Subsection (a) validates substitute notice to a person who may represent and bind another person as provided in the succeeding sections of this article. Notice to the substitute has the same effect as if given directly to the other person. Subsection (a) does not apply to notice of a judicial proceeding. Pursuant to § 109(d), notice of a judicial proceeding must be given as provided in the applicable rules of civil procedure, which may require that notice not only be given to the representative but also to the person represented. For a model statute for the giving of notice in such cases, see Unif. Probate Code § 1-403(3). Subsection (a) may be used to facilitate the giving of notice to the qualified beneficiaries of a proposed transfer of principal place of administration (§ 108(d)), of a proposed trust combination or division (§ 417), of a temporary assumption of duties without accepting trusteeship (§ 701(c)(1)), of a trustee's resignation (§ 705(a)(1)), and of a trustee's report (§ 813(c)).

Subsection (b) deals with the effect of a consent, whether by actual or virtual representation. Subsection (b) may be used to facilitate consent of the beneficiaries to modification or termination of a trust, with or without the consent of the settlor (§ 411), agreement of the qualified beneficiaries on appointment of a successor trustee of a noncharitable trust (§ 704(c)(2)), and a beneficiary's consent to or release or affirmance of the actions of trustee (§ 1009). A consent by a representative bars a later objection by the person represented, but a consent is not binding if the person represented raises an objection prior to the date the consent would otherwise become effective. The possibility that a beneficiary might object to a consent given on the beneficiary's behalf will not be germane in many cases because the person represented will be unborn or unascertained. However, the representation principles of this article will sometimes apply to adult and competent beneficiaries. For example, while the

trustee of a revocable trust entitled to a pourover devise has authority under § 303 to approve the personal representative's account on behalf of the trust beneficiaries, such consent would not be binding on a trust beneficiary who registers an objection. Subsection (b) implements cases such as *Barber v. Barber*, 837 P.2d 714 (Alaska 1992), which held that the a refusal to allow an objection by an adult competent remainder beneficiary violated due process.

Subsection (c) implements the policy of §§ 411 and 602 requiring express authority in the power of attorney or approval of court before the settlor's agent, conservator or guardian may consent on behalf of the settlor to the termination or revocation of the settlor's revocable trust.

2004 Amendment. For an explanation of the new subsection (d) and of the bracketed language in subsection (c), see the comment to the amendment to § 411.

§ 302. Representation by Holder of General Testamentary Power of Appointment.

§ 302. Representation by Holder of General Testamentary Power of Appointment. To the extent there is no conflict of interest between the holder of a general testamentary power of appointment and the persons represented with respect to the particular question or dispute, the holder may represent and bind persons whose interests, as permissible appointees, takers in default, or otherwise, are subject to the power.

Comment

This section specifies the circumstances under which a holder of a general testamentary power of appointment may receive notices on behalf of and otherwise represent and bind persons whose interests are subject to the power, whether as permissible appointees, takers in default, or otherwise. Such representation is allowed except to the extent there is a conflict of interest with respect to the particular matter or dispute. Typically, the holder of a general

testamentary power of appointment is also a life income beneficiary of the trust, oftentimes of a trust intended to qualify for the federal estate tax marital deduction. *See* I.R.C. § 2056(b)(5). Without the exception for conflict of interest, the holder of the power could act in a way that could enhance the holder's income interests to the detriment of the appointees or takers in default, whoever they may be.

§ 303. Representation by Fiduciaries and Parents.

§ 303. Representation by Fiduciaries and Parents. To the extent there is no conflict of interest between the representative and the person represented or among those being represented with respect to a particular question or dispute:

(1) a [conservator] may represent and bind the estate that the [conservator] controls;

(2) a [guardian] may represent and bind the ward if a [conservator] of the ward's estate has not been appointed;

(3) an agent having authority to act with respect to the particular question or dispute may represent and bind the principal;

(4) a trustee may represent and bind the beneficiaries of the trust;

(5) a personal representative of a decedent's estate may represent and bind persons interested in the

estate; and

(6) a parent may represent and bind the parent's minor or unborn child if a [conservator] or [guardian] for the child has not been appointed.

Comment

This section allows for representation of persons by their fiduciaries (conservators, guardians, agents, trustees, and personal representatives), a principle that has long been part of the law. Paragraph (6), which allows parents to represent their children, is more recent, having originated in 1969 upon approval of the Uniform Probate Code. This section is not limited to representation of beneficiaries. It also applies to representation of the settlor. Representation is not available if the fiduciary or parent is in a conflict position with respect to the particular matter or dispute, however. A typical conflict would be where the fiduciary or parent seeking to represent the beneficiary is either the trustee or holds an adverse beneficial interest.

Paragraph (2) authorizes a guardian to bind and represent a ward if a conservator of the ward's estate has not been appointed. Granting a guardian authority to represent the ward with respect to interests in the trust can avoid the need to seek appointment of a conservator. This grant of authority to act with respect to the ward's trust interest may broaden the authority of a guardian in some states although not in states that have adopted the § 1-403 of the Uniform Probate Code, from which this section was derived. Under the Uniform Trust Code, a "conservator" is appointed by the court to manage the ward's property, a "guardian" to make decisions with respect to the ward's personal affairs. *See* § 103.

Paragraph (3) authorizes an agent to represent a principal only to the extent the agent has authority to act with respect to the particular question or dispute. Pursuant to Sections 411 and 602, an agent may represent a settlor with respect to the amendment, revocation or termination of the trust only to the extent this authority is expressly granted either in the trust or the power. Otherwise, depending on the particular question or dispute, a general grant of authority in the power may be sufficient to confer the necessary authority.

§ 304. Representation by Person Having Substantially Identical Interest. Unless otherwise represented, a minor, incapacitated, or unborn individual, or a person whose identity or location is unknown and not reasonably ascertainable, may be represented by and bound by another having a substantially identical interest with respect to the particular question or dispute, but only to the extent there is no conflict of interest between the representative and the person represented.

Comment

This section authorizes a person with a substantially identically interest with respect to a particular question or dispute to represent and bind an otherwise unrepresented minor, incapacitated or unborn individual, or person whose location is unknown and not reasonably ascertainable. This section is derived from § 1-403(2)(iii) of the Uniform Probate Code, but with several modifications. Unlike the UPC, this section does not expressly require that the representation be adequate, the drafters preferring to leave this issue to the courts. Furthermore, this section extends the doctrine of virtual representation to representation of minors and incapacitated individuals. Finally, this section does not apply to the extent there is a conflict of interest between the representative and the person represented.

Restatement (First) of Property §§ 181 and 185 (1936) provide that virtual representation is inapplicable if the interest represented was not sufficiently protected. Representation is deemed sufficiently protective as long as it does not appear that the representative acted in hostility to the interest of the person represented. Restatement (First) of Property § 185 (1936). Evidence of inactivity or lack of skill is material only to the extent it establishes such hostility. Restatement (First) of Property § 185 cmt. b (1936).

Typically, the interests of the representative and the person represented will be identical. A common example would be a trust providing for distribution to the settlor's children as a class, with an adult child being able to represent the interests of children who are either minors or unborn. Exact identity of interests is not required, only substantial identity with respect to the particular question or dispute. Whether such identity is present may depend on the nature of the interest. For example, a presumptive remaindermen may be able to represent alternative remaindermen with respect to approval of a trustee's report but not with respect to interpretation of the remainder provision or termination of the trust. Even if the beneficial interests of the representative and person represented are identical, representation is not allowed in the event of conflict of interest. The representative may have interests outside of the trust that are adverse to the interest of the person represented, such as a prior relationship with the trustee or other beneficiaries. *See* Restatement (First) of Property § 185 cmt. d (1936).

§ 305. Appointment of Representative.

(a) If the court determines that an interest is not represented under this [article], or that the otherwise available representation might be inadequate, the court may appoint a [representative] to receive notice, give consent, and otherwise represent, bind, and act on behalf of a minor, incapacitated, or unborn individual, or a person whose identity or location is unknown. A [representative] may be appointed to represent several persons or interests.

(b) A [representative] may act on behalf of the individual represented with respect to any matter arising under this [Code], whether or not a judicial proceeding concerning the trust is pending.

(c) In making decisions, a [representative] may consider general benefit accruing to the living members of the individual's family.

Comment

This section is derived from § 1-403(4) of the Uniform Probate Code. However, this section substitutes "representative" for "guardian ad litem" to signal that a representative under this Code serves a different role. Unlike a guardian ad litem, under this section a representative can be appointed to act with respect to a nonjudicial settlement or to receive a notice on a beneficiary's behalf. Furthermore, in making decisions, a representative may consider general benefit accruing to living members of the family. "Representative" is placed in brackets in case the enacting jurisdiction prefers a different term. The court may appoint a representative to act for a person even if the person could be represented under another section of this article.

ARTICLE 4
CREATION, VALIDITY, MODIFICATION, AND TERMINATION OF TRUST

General Comment

Sections 401 through 409, which specify the requirements for the creation of a trust, largely codify traditional doctrine. Section 401 specifies the methods by which trusts are created, that is, by transfer of property, self-declaration, or exercise of a power of appointment. Whatever method may have been employed, other requirements, including intention, capacity and, for certain types of trusts, an ascertainable beneficiary, also must be satisfied before a trust is created. These requirements are listed in § 402. Section 403 addresses the validity in the enacting jurisdiction of trusts created in other jurisdictions. A trust not created by will is validly created if its creation complied with the law of specified jurisdictions in which the settlor or trustee had a significant contact. Section 404 forbids trusts for illegal or impossible purposes, and requires that a trust and its terms must be for the benefit of its beneficiaries. Section 405 recites the permitted purposes of a charitable trust. Section 406 lists some of the grounds for contesting a trust. Section 407 validates oral trusts. The remaining sections address what are often referred to as "honorary" trusts, although such trusts are valid and enforceable under this Code. Section 408 covers a trust for the care of an animal; Section 409 allows creation of a trust for another noncharitable purpose such as maintenance of a cemetery lot.

Sections 410 through 417 provide a series of interrelated rules on when a trust may be terminated or modified other than by its express terms. The overall objective of these sections is to enhance flexibility consistent with the principle that preserving the settlor's intent is paramount. Termination or modification may be allowed upon beneficiary consent if the court concludes that the trust or a particular provision no longer achieves a material purpose or if the settlor concurs (§ 411), by the court in response to unanticipated circumstances or due to ineffective administrative terms (§ 412), or by the court or trustee if continued administration under the trust's existing terms would be uneconomical (§ 414). A trust may be reformed to correct a mistake of law or fact (§ 415), or modified to achieve the settlor's tax objectives (§ 416). Trusts may be combined or divided (§ 417). A trustee or beneficiary has standing to petition the court with respect to a proposed termination or modification (§ 410).

Section 413 codifies and at the same time modifies the doctrine of cy pres, at least as applied in most states. The Uniform Trust Code authorizes the court to apply cy pres not only if the original means becomes impossible or unlawful but also if the means become impracticable or wasteful. Section 413 also creates a presumption of general charitable intent. Upon failure of the settlor's original plan, the court cannot divert the trust property to a noncharity unless the terms of the trust expressly so provide. Furthermore, absent a contrary provision in the terms of the trust, limits are placed on when a gift over to a noncharity can take effect upon failure or impracticality of the original charitable purpose. The gift over is effective only if, when the provision takes effect, the trust property is to revert to the settlor and the settlor is still living, or fewer than 21 years have elapsed since the date of the trust's creation.

The requirements for a trust's creation, such as the necessary level of capacity and the requirement that a trust have a legal purpose, are controlled by statute and common law, not by the settlor. See § 105(b)(1), (3). Nor may the settlor negate the court's ability to modify or terminate a trust as provided in §§ 410 through 416. See § 105(b)(4). However, a settlor is free to restrict or modify the trustee's power to terminate an uneconomic trust as provided in §§ 414, and the trustee's power to combine and divide trusts as provided in § 417.

§ 401. Methods of Creating Trust. A trust may be created by:

(1) transfer of property to another person as trustee during the settlor's lifetime or by will or other disposition taking effect upon the settlor's death;

(2) declaration by the owner of property that the owner holds identifiable property as trustee; or

(3) exercise of a power of appointment in favor of a trustee.

Comment

This section is based on Restatement (Third) of Trusts § 10 (Tentative Draft No. 1, approved 1996), and Restatement (Second) of Trusts § 17 (1959). Under the methods specified for creating a trust in this section, a trust is not created until it receives property. For what constitutes an adequate property interest, see Restatement (Third) of Trusts §§ 40-41 (Tentative Draft No. 2, approved 1999); Restatement (Second) of Trusts §§ 74-86 (1959). The property interest necessary to fund and create a trust need not be substantial. A revocable designation of the trustee as beneficiary of a life insurance policy or employee benefit plan has long been understood to be a property interest sufficient to create a trust. *See* § 103(12) ("property" defined). Furthermore, the property interest need not be transferred contemporaneously with the signing of the trust instrument. A trust instrument signed during the settlor's lifetime is not rendered invalid simply because the trust was not created until property was transferred to the trustee at a much later date, including by contract after the settlor's death. A pourover devise to a previously unfunded trust is also valid and may constitute the property interest creating the trust. *See* Unif. Testamentary Additions to Trusts Act § 1 (1991), *codified at* Uniform Probate Code § 2-511 (pourover devise to trust valid regardless of existence, size, or character of trust corpus). *See also* Restatement (Third) of Trusts § 19 (Tentative Draft No. 1, approved 1996).

While this section refers to transfer of property to a trustee, a trust can be created even though for a period of time no trustee is in office. *See* Restatement (Third) of Trusts § 2 cmt. g (Tentative Draft No. 1, approved 1996); Restatement (Second) of Trusts § 2 cmt. i (1959). A trust can also be created without notice to or acceptance by a trustee or beneficiary. *See* Restatement (Third) of Trusts § 14 (Tentative Draft No. 1, approved 1996); Restatement (Second) of Trusts §§ 35-36 (1959).

The methods specified in this section are not exclusive. Section 102 recognizes that trusts can also be created by special statute or court order. *See also* Restatement (Third) of Trusts § 1 cmt. a (Tentative Draft No. 1, approved 1996); Unif. Probate Code § 2-212 (elective share of incapacitated surviving spouse to be held in trust on terms specified in statute); Unif. Probate Code § 5-411(a)(4) (conservator may create trust with court approval); Restatement (Second) of Trusts § 17 cmt. i (1959)

(trusts created by statutory right to bring wrongful death action).

A trust can also be created by a promise that creates enforceable rights in a person who immediately or later holds these rights as trustee. *See* Restatement (Third) of Trusts §10(e) (Tentative Draft No. 1, approved 1996). A trust thus created is valid notwithstanding that the trustee may resign or die before the promise is fulfilled. Unless expressly made personal, the promise can be enforced by a successor trustee. For examples of trusts created by means of promises enforceable by the trustee, see Restatement (Third) of Trusts § 10 cmt. g (Tentative Draft No. 1, approved 1996); Restatement (Second) of Trusts §§ 14 cmt. h, 26 cmt. n (1959).

A trust created by self-declaration is best created by reregistering each of the assets that comprise the trust into the settlor's name as trustee. However, such reregistration is not necessary to create the trust. *See, e.g., In re Estate of Heggstad,* 20 Cal. Rptr. 2d 433 (Ct. App. 1993); Restatement (Third) of Trusts § 10 cmt. e (Tentative Draft No. 1, approved 1996); Restatement (Second) of Trusts § 17 cmt. a (1959). A declaration of trust can be funded merely by attaching a schedule listing the assets that are to be subject to the trust without executing separate instruments of transfer. But such practice can make it difficult to later confirm title with third party transferees and for this reason is not recommended.

While a trust created by will may come into existence immediately at the testator's death and not necessarily only upon the later transfer of title from the personal representative, § 701 makes clear that the nominated trustee does not have a duty to act until there is an acceptance of the trusteeship, express or implied. To avoid an implied acceptance, a nominated testamentary trustee who is monitoring the actions of the personal representative but who has not yet made a final decision on acceptance should inform the beneficiaries that the nominated trustee has assumed only a limited role. The failure so to inform the beneficiaries could result in liability if misleading conduct by the nominated trustee causes harm to the trust beneficiaries. *See* Restatement (Third) of Trusts § 35 cmt. b (Tentative Draft No. 2, approved 1999).

While this section confirms the familiar principle that a trust may be created by means of the exercise of a power of appointment (paragraph (3)), this Code does not legislate comprehensively on the subject of powers of appointment but addresses only selected issues. *See* §§ 302 (representation by holder of general testamentary power of appointment); 505(b) (creditor claims against holder of power of withdrawal); and 603(b) (rights of holder of power of withdrawal). For the law on powers of appointment generally, see Restatement (Second) of Property: Donative Transfers §§ 11.1-24.4 (1986); Restatement (Third) of Property: Wills and Other Donative Transfers (in progress).

§ 402. Requirements for Creation.

   (a) A trust is created only if:

      (1) the settlor has capacity to create a trust;

      (2) the settlor indicates an intention to create the trust;

      (3) the trust has a definite beneficiary or is:

         (A) a charitable trust;

         (B) a trust for the care of an animal, as provided in Section 408; or

         (C) a trust for a noncharitable purpose, as provided in Section 409;

      (4) the trustee has duties to perform; and

      (5) the same person is not the sole trustee and sole beneficiary.

   (b) A beneficiary is definite if the beneficiary can be ascertained now or in the future, subject to any applicable rule against perpetuities.

   (c) A power in a trustee to select a beneficiary from an indefinite class is valid. If the power is not exercised within a reasonable time, the power fails and the property subject to the power passes to the persons who would have taken the property had the power not been conferred.

Comment

Subsection (a) codifies the basic requirements for the creation of a trust. To create a valid trust, the settlor must indicate an intention to create a trust. *See* Restatement (Third) of Trusts § 13 (Tentative Draft No. 1, approved 1996); Restatement (Second) of Trusts § 23 (1959). But only such manifestations of intent as are admissible as proof in a judicial proceeding may be considered. *See* § 103(17) ("terms of a trust" defined).

To create a trust, a settlor must have the requisite mental capacity. To create a revocable or testamentary trust, the settlor must have the capacity to make a will. To create an irrevocable trust, the settlor must have capacity during lifetime to transfer the property free of trust. *See* § 601 (capacity of settlor to create revocable trust), and *see generally* Restatement (Third) of Trusts § 11 (Tentative Draft No. 1, approved 1996); Restatement (Second) of Trusts §§ 18-22 (1959); and Restatement (Third) of Property: Wills and Other Donative Transfers §8.1 (Tentative Draft No. 3, 2001).

Subsection (a)(3) requires that a trust, other than a charitable trust, a trust for the care of an animal, or a trust for another valid noncharitable purpose, have a definite beneficiary. While some beneficiaries will be definitely ascertained as of the trust's creation, subsection (b) recognizes that others may be ascertained in the future as long as this occurs within the applicable perpetuities period. The definite beneficiary requirement does not prevent a settlor from making a disposition in favor of a class of persons. Class designations are valid as long as the membership of the class will be finally determined within the applicable perpetuities period. For background on the definite beneficiary requirement, see Restatement (Third) of Trusts §§ 44-46 (Tentative Draft No. 2, approved 1999); Restatement (Second) of Trusts §§ 112-122 (1959).

Subsection (a)(4) recites standard doctrine that a trust is created only if the trustee has duties to perform. *See* Restatement (Third) of Trusts § 2 (Tentative Draft No. 1, approved 1996); Restatement (Second) of Trusts § 2 (1959). Trustee duties are usually active, but a validating duty may also be passive, implying only that the trustee has an obligation not to interfere with the beneficiary's enjoyment of the trust property. Such passive trusts, while valid under this Code, may be terminable under the enacting jurisdiction's Statute of Uses. *See* Restatement (Third) of Trusts § 6 (Tentative Draft No. 1, approved 1996); Restatement (Second) of Trusts §§ 67-72 (1959).

Subsection (a)(5) addresses the doctrine of merger, which, as traditionally stated, provides that a trust is not created if the settlor is the sole trustee and sole beneficiary of *all* beneficial interests. The doctrine of merger has been inappropriately applied by the courts in some jurisdictions to invalidate self-declarations of trust in which the settlor is the sole life beneficiary but other persons are designated as beneficiaries of the remainder. The doctrine of merger is properly applicable only if all beneficial interests, both life interests and remainders, are vested in the same person, whether in the settlor or someone else. An example of a trust to which the doctrine of merger would apply is a trust of which the settlor is sole trustee, sole beneficiary for life, and with the remainder payable to the settlor's probate estate. On the doctrine of merger generally, see Restatement (Third) of Trusts § 69 (Tentative Draft No. 3, 2001); Restatement (Second) of Trusts § 341 (1959).

Subsection (c) allows a settlor to empower the trustee to select the beneficiaries even if the class from whom the selection may be made cannot be ascertained. Such a provision would fail under traditional doctrine; it is an imperative power with no designated beneficiary capable of enforcement. Such a provision is valid, however, under both this Code and the Restatement, if there is at least one person who can meet the description. If the trustee does not exercise the power within a reasonable time, the power fails and the property will pass by resulting trust. *See* Restatement (Third) of Trusts § 46 (Tentative Draft No. 2, approved 1999). *See also* Restatement (Second) of Trusts § 122 (1959); Restatement (Second) of Property: Donative Transfers § 12.1 cmt. e (1986).

§ 403. Trusts Created in Other Jurisdictions.

A trust not created by will is validly created if its creation complies with the law of the jurisdiction in which the trust instrument was executed, or the law of the jurisdiction in which, at the time of creation:

(1) the settlor was domiciled, had a place of abode, or was a national;

(2) a trustee was domiciled or had a place of business; or

(3) any trust property was located.

Comment

The validity of a trust created by will is ordinarily determined by the law of the decedent's domicile. No such certainty exists with respect to determining the law governing the validity of inter vivos trusts. Generally, at common law a trust was created if it complied with the law of the state having the most significant contacts to the trust. Contacts for making this determination include the domicile of the trustee, the domicile of the settlor at the time of trust creation, the location of the trust property, the place where the trust instrument was executed, and the domicile of the beneficiary. *See* 5A Austin Wakeman Scott & William Franklin Fratcher, The Law of Trusts §§ 597, 599 (4th ed. 1987). Furthermore, if the trust has contacts with two or more states, one of which would validate the trust's creation and the other of which would deny the trust's validity, the tendency is to select the law upholding the validity of the trust. *See* 5A Austin Wakeman Scott & William Franklin Fratcher, The Law of Trusts § 600 (4th ed. 1987).

Section 403 extends the common law rule by validating a trust if its creation complies with the law of any of a variety of states in which the settlor or trustee had significant contacts. Pursuant to § 403, a trust not created by will is validly created if its creation complies with the law of the jurisdiction in which the trust instrument was executed, or the law of the jurisdiction in which, at the time of creation the settlor was domiciled, had a place of abode, or was a national; the trustee was domiciled or had a place of business; or any trust property was located.

Section 403 is comparable to § 2-506 of the Uniform Probate Code, which validates wills executed in compliance with the law of a variety of places in which the testator had a significant contact. Unlike the UPC, however, § 403 is not limited to execution of the instrument but applies to the entire process of a trust's creation, including compliance with the requirement that there be trust property. In addition, unlike the UPC, § 403 validates a trust valid under the law of the domicile or place of business of the designated trustee, or if valid under the law of the place where any of the trust property is located.

The section does not supercede local law requirements for the transfer of real property, such that title can be transferred only by recorded deed.

§ 404. Trust Purposes. A trust may be created only to the extent its purposes are lawful, not contrary to public policy, and possible to achieve. A trust and its terms must be for the benefit of its beneficiaries.

Comment

For an explication of the requirement that a trust must not have a purpose that is unlawful or against public policy, see Restatement (Third) of Trusts §§ 27-30 (Tentative Draft No. 2, approved 1999); Restatement (Second) of Trusts §§ 59-65 (1959). A trust with a purpose that is unlawful or against public policy is invalid. Depending on when the violation occurred, the trust may be invalid at its inception or it may become invalid at a later date. The invalidity may also affect only particular provisions. Generally, a trust has a purpose which is illegal if (1) its performance involves the commission of a criminal or tortious act by the trustee; (2) the settlor's purpose in creating the trust was to defraud creditors or others; or (3) the consideration for the creation of the trust was illegal. *See* Restatement (Third) of Trusts § 28 cmt. a (Tentative Draft No. 2, approved 1999); Restatement (Second) of Trusts § 60 cmt. a (1959). Purposes violative of public policy include those that tend to encourage criminal or tortious conduct, that interfere with freedom to marry or encourage divorce, that limit religious freedom, or which are frivolous or capricious. *See* Restatement (Third) of Trusts § 29 cmt. d-h (Tentative Draft No. 2, 1999); Restatement (Second) of Trusts § 62 (1959).　Pursuant to § 402(a), a trust must have an identifiable beneficiary unless the trust is of a type that does not have beneficiaries in the usual sense, such as a charitable trust or, as provided in §§ 408 and 409, trusts for the care of an animal or other valid noncharitable purpose. The general purpose of trusts having identifiable beneficiaries is to benefit those beneficiaries in accordance with their interests as defined in the trust's terms. The requirement of this section that a trust and its terms be for the benefit of its beneficiaries, which is derived from Restatement (Third) of Trusts § 27(2) (Tentative Draft No. 2, approved 1999), implements this general purpose. While a settlor has considerable latitude in specifying how a particular trust purpose is to be pursued, the administrative and other nondispositive trust terms must reasonably relate to this purpose and not divert the trust property to achieve a trust purpose that is invalid, such as one which is frivolous or capricious. *See* Restatement (Third) of Trusts § 27 cmt. b (Tentative Draft No. 2, approved 1999).

Section 412(b), which allows the court to modify administrative terms that are impracticable, wasteful, or impair the trust's administration, is a specific application of the requirement that a trust and its terms be for the benefit of the beneficiaries. The fact that a settlor suggests or directs an unlawful or other inappropriate means for performing a trust does not invalidate the trust if the trust has a substantial purpose that can be achieved by other methods. *See* Restatement (Third) of Trusts § 28 cmt. e (Tentative Draft No. 2, approved 1999).

§ 405. Charitable Purposes; Enforcement.

(a) A charitable trust may be created for the relief of poverty, the advancement of education or religion, the promotion of health, governmental or municipal purposes, or other purposes the achievement of which is beneficial to the community.

(b) If the terms of a charitable trust do not indicate a particular charitable purpose or beneficiary, the court may select one or more charitable purposes or beneficiaries. The selection must be consistent with the settlor's intention to the extent it can be ascertained.

(c) The settlor of a charitable trust, among others, may maintain a proceeding to enforce the trust.

Comment

The required purposes of a charitable trust specified in subsection (a) restate the well-established categories of charitable purposes listed in Restatement (Third) of Trusts § 28 (Tentative Draft No. 3, approved 2001), and Restatement (Second) of Trusts § 368 (1959), which ultimately derive from the Statute of Charitable Uses, 43 Eliz. I, c.4 (1601). The directive to the courts to validate purposes the achievement of which are beneficial to the community has proved to be remarkably adaptable

445

[handwritten: Adds valid trust charity purpose to it! to clients]

over the centuries. The drafters concluded that it should not be disturbed.

Charitable trusts are subject to the restriction in § 404 that a trust purpose must be legal and not contrary to public policy. This would include trusts that involve invidious discrimination. *See* Restatement (Third) of Trusts § 28 cmt. f (Tentative Draft No. 3, approved 2001).

Under subsection (b), a trust that states a general charitable purpose does not fail if the settlor neglected to specify a particular charitable purpose or organization to receive distributions. The court may instead validate the trust by specifying particular charitable purposes or recipients, or delegate to the trustee the framing of an appropriate scheme. *See* Restatement (Second) of Trusts § 397 cmt. d (1959). Subsection (b) of this section is a corollary to § 413, which states the doctrine of cy pres. Under § 413(a), a trust failing to state a general charitable purpose does not fail upon failure of the particular means specified in the terms of the trust. The court must instead apply the trust property in a manner consistent with the settlor's charitable purposes to the extent they can be ascertained.

Subsection (b) does not apply to the long-established estate planning technique of delegating to the trustee the selection of the charitable purposes or recipients. In that case, judicial intervention to supply particular terms is not necessary to validate the creation of the trust. The necessary terms instead will be supplied by the trustee. *See* Restatement (Second) of Trusts § 396 (1959). Judicial intervention under subsection (b) will become necessary only if the trustee fails to make a selection. *See* Restatement (Second) of Trusts § 397 cmt. d (1959). Pursuant to § 110(b), the charitable organizations selected by the trustee would not have the rights of qualified beneficiaries under this Code because they are not expressly designated to receive distributions under the terms of the trust. Contrary to Restatement (Second) of Trusts § 391 (1959), subsection (c) grants a settlor standing to maintain an action to enforce a charitable trust. The grant of standing to the settlor does not negate the right of the state attorney general or persons with special interests to enforce either the trust or their interests. For the law on the enforcement of charitable trusts, see Susan N. Gary, *Regulating the Management of Charities: Trust Law, Corporate Law, and Tax Law*, 21 U. Hawaii L. Rev. 593 (1999).

§ 406. Creation of Trust Induced by Fraud, Duress, or Undue Influence. A trust is void to the extent its creation was induced by fraud, duress, or undue influence.

Comment

This section is a specific application of Restatement (Third) of Trusts § 12 (Tentative Draft No. 1, approved 1996), and Restatement (Second) of Trusts § 333 (1959), which provide that a trust can be set aside or reformed on the same grounds as those which apply to a transfer of property not in trust, among which include undue influence, duress, and fraud, and mistake. This section addresses undue influence, duress, and fraud. For reformation of a trust on grounds of mistake, see § 415. See also Restatement (Third) of Property: Wills and Other Donative Transfers § 8.3 (Tentative Draft No. 3, approved 2001), which closely tracks the language above. Similar to a will, the invalidity of a trust on grounds of undue influence, duress, or fraud may be in whole or in part.

 ## § 407. Evidence of Oral Trust. Except as required by a statute other than this [Code], a trust need not be evidenced by a trust instrument, but the creation of an oral trust and its terms may be established only by clear and convincing evidence.

Comment

While it is always advisable for a settlor to reduce a trust to writing, the Uniform Trust Code follows established law in recognizing oral trusts. Such trusts are viewed with caution, however. The requirement of this section that an oral trust can be established only by clear and convincing evidence is a higher standard than is in effect in many states. *See* Restatement (Third) of Trusts § 20 Reporter's Notes (Tentative Draft No. 1, approved 1996).

Absent some specific statutory provision, such as a provision requiring that transfers of real property be in writing, a trust need not be evidenced by a writing.

States with statutes of frauds or other provisions requiring that the creation of certain trusts must be evidenced by a writing may wish specifically to cite such provisions.

For the Statute of Frauds generally, see Restatement (Second) of Trusts §§ 40-52 (1959). For a description of what the writing must contain, assuming that a writing is required, see Restatement (Third) of Trusts § 22 (Tentative Draft No. 1, approved 1996); Restatement (Second) of Trusts § 46-49 (1959). For a discussion of when the writing must be signed, see Restatement (Third) of Trusts § 23 (Tentative Draft No. 1, approved 1996); Restatement (Second) of Trusts § 41-42 (1959). For the law of oral trusts, see Restatement (Third) of Trusts § 20 (Tentative Draft No. 1, approved 1996); Restatement (Second) of Trusts §§ 43-45 (1959).

§ 408. Trust for Care of Animal.

(a) A trust may be created to provide for the care of an animal alive during the settlor's lifetime. The trust terminates upon the death of the animal or, if the trust was created to provide for the care of more than one animal alive during the settlor's lifetime, upon the death of the last surviving animal.

(b) A trust authorized by this section may be enforced by a person appointed in the terms of the trust or, if no person is so appointed, by a person appointed by the court. A person having an interest in the welfare of the animal may request the court to appoint a person to enforce the trust or to remove a person appointed.

(c) Property of a trust authorized by this section may be applied only to its intended use, except to the extent the court determines that the value of the trust property exceeds the amount required for the intended use. Except as otherwise provided in the terms of the trust, property not required for the intended use must be distributed to the settlor, if then living, otherwise to the settlor's successors in interest.

[handwritten: - No Authorized Responsibility to Pet]

Comment

[handwritten: - Can't be Excessive]

This section and the next section of the Code validate so called honorary trusts. Unlike honorary trusts created pursuant to the common law of trusts, which are arguably no more than powers of appointment, the trusts created by this and the next section are valid and enforceable. For a discussion of the common law doctrine, see Restatement (Third) of Trusts § 47 (Tentative Draft No. 2, approved 1999); Restatement (Second) of Trusts § 124 (1959).

This section addresses a particular type of honorary trust, the trust for the care of an animal. Section 409 specifies the requirements for trusts without ascertainable beneficiaries that are created for other noncharitable purposes. A trust for the care of an animal may last for the life of the animal. While the animal will ordinarily be alive on the date the trust is created, an animal may be added as a beneficiary after that date as long as the addition is made prior to the settlor's death. Animals in gestation but not yet born at the time of the trust's creation may also be covered by its terms. A trust authorized by this section may be created to benefit one designated animal or several designated animals.

Subsection (b) addresses enforcement. Noncharitable trusts ordinarily may be enforced by their beneficiaries. Charitable trusts may be enforced by the state's attorney general or by a person deemed to have a special interest. See Restatement (Second) of Trusts § 391 (1959). But at common law, a trust for the care of an animal or a trust without an ascertainable beneficiary created for a noncharitable purpose was unenforceable because there was no person authorized to enforce the trustee's obligations.

Sections 408 and 409 close this gap. The intended use of a trust authorized by either section may be enforced by a person designated in the terms of the trust or, if none, by a person appointed by the court. In either case, § 110(b) grants to the person appointed the rights of a qualified beneficiary for the purpose of receiving notices and providing consents. If the trust is created for the care of an animal, a person with an interest in the welfare of the animal has standing to petition for an appointment. The person appointed by the court to enforce the trust should also be a person who has exhibited an interest in the animal's welfare. The concept of granting standing to a person with a demonstrated interest in the animal's welfare is derived from the Uniform Guardianship and Protective Proceedings Act, which allows a person interested in the welfare of a ward or protected person to file petitions on behalf of the ward or protected person. *See, e.g.,* Unif. Probate Code §§ 5-210(b), 5-414(a).

Subsection (c) addresses the problem of excess funds. If the court determines that the trust property exceeds the amount needed for the intended purpose and that the terms of the trust do not direct the disposition, a resulting trust is ordinarily created in the settlor or settlor's successors in interest. *See* Restatement (Third) of Trusts § 47 (Tentative Draft No. 2, approved 1999); Restatement (Second) of Trusts § 124 (1959). Successors in interest include the beneficiaries under the settlor's will, if the settlor has a will, or in the absence of an effective will provision, the settlor's heirs. The settlor may also anticipate the problem of excess funds by directing their disposition in the terms of the trust. The disposition of excess funds is within the settlor's control. *See* § 105(a). While a trust for an animal is usually not created until the settlor's death, subsection (a) allows such a trust to be created during the settlor's lifetime. Accordingly, if the settlor is still living, subsection (c) provides for distribution of excess funds to the settlor, and not to the settlor's successors in interest.

Should the means chosen not be particularly efficient, a trust created for the care of an animal can also be terminated by the trustee or court under § 414. Termination of a trust under that section, however, requires that the trustee or court develop an alternative means for carrying out the trust purposes. *See* § 414(c).

This section and the next section are suggested by § 2-907 of the Uniform Probate Code, but much of this and the following section is new.

Under the Uniform Directed Trust Act (UDTA), approved by the Uniform Law Commission in 2017, a person named by the terms of a trust to enforce the trust qualifies as a "trust director" in a state that adopts the UDTA. See Official Comment to UDTA Section 6, stating in relevant part:

> *Pet and other noncharitable purpose trust enforcers.* Statutes in every state validate a trust for a pet animal and certain other noncharitable purposes. Following Uniform Probate Code § 2-907(c)(4) (1993) and Uniform Trust Code §§ 408(b) and 409(2) (2000), most of these statutes authorize enforcement of the trust by a person named in the terms of the trust. In a state that enacts this act, such a person would be a trust director.

Historical Note. The previous paragraph of this comment was added in 2018 following the approval of the Uniform Directed Trust Act.

§ 409. Noncharitable Trust Without Ascertainable Beneficiary. Except as otherwise provided in Section 408 or by another statute, the following rules apply:

(1) A trust may be created for a noncharitable purpose without a definite or definitely ascertainable beneficiary or for a noncharitable but otherwise valid purpose to be selected by the trustee. The trust may not be enforced for more than [21] years.

(2) A trust authorized by this section may be enforced by a person appointed in the terms of the trust or, if no person is so appointed, by a person appointed by the court.

(3) Property of a trust authorized by this section may be applied only to its intended use, except to the extent the court determines that the value of the trust property exceeds the amount required for the intended use. Except as otherwise provided in the terms of the trust, property not required for the intended use must be distributed to the settlor, if then living, otherwise to the settlor's successors in interest.

Comment

This section authorizes two types of trusts without ascertainable beneficiaries; trusts for general but noncharitable purposes, and trusts for a specific noncharitable purpose other than the care of an animal, on which see § 408. Examples of trusts for general noncharitable purposes include a bequest of money to be distributed to such objects of benevolence as the trustee might select. Unless such attempted disposition was interpreted as charitable, at common law the disposition was honorary only and did not create a trust. Under this section, however, the disposition is enforceable as a trust for a period of up to 21 years, although that number is placed in brackets to indicate that states may wish to select a different time limit.

The most common example of a trust for a specific noncharitable purpose is a trust for the care of a cemetery plot. The lead-in language to the section recognizes that some special purpose trusts, particularly those for care of cemetery plots, are subject to other statutes. Such legislation will typically endeavor to facilitate perpetual care as opposed to care limited to 21 years as under this section.

For the requirement that a trust, particularly the type of trust authorized by this section, must have a purpose that is not capricious, see § 404 comment. For examples of the types of trusts authorized by this section, see Restatement (Third) of Trusts § 47 (Tentative Draft No. 2, approved 1999), and Restatement (Second) of Trusts § 62 cmt. w & § 124 (1959). The case law on capricious purposes is collected in 2 Austin W. Scott & William F. Fratcher, The Law of Trusts § 124.7 (4th ed. 1987).

This section is similar to § 408, although less detailed. Much of the Comment to § 408 also applies to this section.

Under the Uniform Directed Trust Act (UDTA), approved by the Uniform Law Commission in 2017,

a person named by the terms of a trust to enforce the trust qualifies as a "trust director" in a state that adopts the UDTA. See Official Comment to UDTA Section 6, stating in relevant part:

Pet and other noncharitable purpose trust enforcers. Statutes in every state validate a trust for a pet animal and certain other noncharitable purposes. Following Uniform Probate Code § 2-907(c)(4) (1993) and Uniform Trust Code §§ 408(b) and 409(2) (2000), most of these statutes authorize enforcement of the trust by a person named in the terms of the trust. In a state that enacts this act, such a person would be a trust director.

Historical Note. The previous paragraph of this comment was added in 2018 following the approval of the Uniform Directed Trust Act.

§ 410. Modification or Termination of Trust; Proceedings for Approval or Disapproval.

(a) In addition to the methods of termination prescribed by Sections 411 through 414, a trust terminates to the extent the trust is revoked or expires pursuant to its terms, no purpose of the trust remains to be achieved, or the purposes of the trust have become unlawful, contrary to public policy, or impossible to achieve.

(b) A proceeding to approve or disapprove a proposed modification or termination under Sections 411 through 416, or trust combination or division under Section 417, may be commenced by a trustee or beneficiary, [and a proceeding to approve or disapprove a proposed modification or termination under Section 411 may be commenced by the settlor.] The settlor of a charitable trust may maintain a proceeding to modify the trust under Section 413.

Comment

Subsection (a) lists the grounds on which trusts typically terminate. For a similar formulation, see Restatement (Third) of Trusts § 61 (Tentative Draft No. 3, approved 2001). Terminations under subsection (a) may be in either in whole or in part. Other types of terminations, all of which require action by a court, trustee, or beneficiaries, are covered in §§ 411-414, which also address trust modification. Of these sections, all but § 411 apply to charitable trusts and all but § 413 apply to noncharitable trusts.

Withdrawal of the trust property is not an event terminating a trust. The trust remains in existence although the trustee has no duties to perform unless and until property is later contributed to the trust.

Subsection (b) specifies the persons who have standing to seek court approval or disapproval of proposed trust modifications, terminations, combinations, or divisions. An approval or

disapproval may be sought for an action that does not require court permission, including a petition questioning the trustee's distribution upon termination of a trust under $50,000 (§ 414), and a petition to approve or disapprove a proposed trust division or consolidation (§ 417). Subsection (b) makes the settlor an interested person with respect to a judicial proceeding brought by the beneficiaries under § 411 to terminate or modify a trust. Contrary to Restatement (Second) of Trusts § 391 (1959), subsection (b) grants a settlor standing to petition the court under § 413 to apply cy pres to modify the settlor's charitable trust.

2004 Amendment. For an explanation of why a portion of subsection (b) has been placed in brackets, see the comment to the 2004 Amendment to § 411.

§ 411. Modification or Termination of Noncharitable Irrevocable Trust by Consent.

[(a) [A noncharitable irrevocable trust may be modified or terminated upon consent of the settlor and all beneficiaries, even if the modification or termination is inconsistent with a material purpose of the trust.] [If, upon petition, the court finds that the settlor and all beneficiaries consent to the modification or termination of a noncharitable irrevocable trust, the court shall approve the modification or termination even if the modification or termination is inconsistent with a material purpose of the trust.] A settlor's power to consent to a trust's modification or termination may be exercised by an agent under a power of attorney only to the extent expressly authorized by the power of attorney or the terms of the trust; by the settlor's [conservator] with the approval of the court supervising the [conservatorship] if an agent is not so authorized; or by the settlor's [guardian] with the approval of the court supervising the [guardianship] if an agent is not so authorized and a conservator has not been appointed. [This subsection does not apply to irrevocable trusts created before or to revocable trusts that become irrevocable before [the effective date of this [Code]] [amendment].]]

(b) A noncharitable irrevocable trust may be terminated upon consent of all of the beneficiaries if the court concludes that continuance of the trust is not necessary to achieve any material purpose of the trust. A noncharitable irrevocable trust may be modified upon consent of all of the beneficiaries if the court concludes that modification is not inconsistent with a material purpose of the trust.

[(c) A spendthrift provision in the terms of the trust is not presumed to constitute a material purpose of the trust.]

(d) Upon termination of a trust under subsection (a) or (b), the trustee shall distribute the trust property as agreed by the beneficiaries.

(e) If not all of the beneficiaries consent to a proposed modification or termination of the trust under subsection (a) or (b), the modification or termination may be approved by the court if the court is satisfied that:

(1) if all of the beneficiaries had consented, the trust could have been modified or terminated under this section; and

(2) the interests of a beneficiary who does not consent will be adequately protected.

Comment

This section describes the circumstances in which termination or modification of a noncharitable irrevocable trust may be compelled by the beneficiaries, with or without the concurrence of the settlor. For provisions governing modification or termination of trusts without the need to seek beneficiary consent, see §§ 412 (modification or termination due to unanticipated circumstances or inability to administer trust effectively), 414 (termination or modification of uneconomic noncharitable trust), and 416 (modification to achieve settlor's tax objectives). If the trust is revocable by the settlor, the method of revocation specified in § 602 applies.

Subsection (a), which was placed in brackets pursuant to a 2004 amendment, states the test for termination or modification by the beneficiaries with the concurrence of the settlor. For an explanation of why subsection (a) has been placed in brackets see the

2004 comment at the end of this section.

Subsection (b) states the test for termination or modification by unanimous consent of the beneficiaries without the concurrence of the settlor. The rules on trust termination in Subsections (a)-(b) carries forward the *Claflin* rule, first stated in the famous case of *Claflin v. Claflin*, 20 N.E. 454 (Mass. 1889). Subsection (c) addresses the effect of a spendthrift provision. Subsection (d) directs how the trust property is to be distributed following a termination under either subsection (a) or (b). Subsection (e) creates a procedure for judicial approval of a proposed termination or modification when the consent of less than all of the beneficiaries is available.

Under this section, a trust may be modified or terminated over a trustee's objection. However, pursuant to § 410, the trustee has standing to object

450

to a proposed termination or modification.

The settlor's right to join the beneficiaries in terminating or modifying a trust under this section does not rise to the level of a taxable power. *See* Treas. Reg. § 20.2038-1(a)(2). No gift tax consequences result from a termination as long as the beneficiaries agree to distribute the trust property in accordance with the value of their proportionate interests.

The provisions of Article 3 on representation, virtual representation and the appointment and approval of representatives appointed by the court apply to the determination of whether all beneficiaries have signified consent under this section. The authority to consent on behalf of another person, however, does not include authority to consent over the other person's objection. *See* § 301(b). Regarding the persons who may consent on behalf of a beneficiary, see §§ 302 through 305. A consent given by a representative is invalid to the extent there is a conflict of interest between the representative and the person represented. Given this limitation, virtual representation of a beneficiary's interest by another beneficiary pursuant to § 304 will rarely be available in a trust termination case, although it should be routinely available in cases involving trust modification, such as a grant to the trustee of additional powers. If virtual or other form of representation is unavailable, § 305 of the Code permits the court to appoint a representative who may give the necessary consent to the proposed modification or termination on behalf of the minor, incapacitated, unborn, or unascertained beneficiary. The ability to use virtual and other forms of representation to consent on a beneficiary's behalf to a trust termination or modification has not traditionally been part of the law, although there are some notable exceptions. *Compare* Restatement (Second) § 337(1) (1959) (beneficiary must not be under incapacity), *with Hatch v. Riggs National Bank*, 361 F.2d 559 (D.C. Cir. 1966) (guardian ad litem authorized to consent on beneficiary's behalf).

Subsection (a) also addresses the authority of an agent, conservator, or guardian to act on a settlor's behalf. Consistent with § 602 on revocation or modification of a revocable trust, the section assumes that a settlor, in granting an agent general authority, did not intend for the agent to have authority to consent to the termination or modification of a trust, authority that could be exercised to radically alter the settlor's estate plan. In order for an agent to validly consent to a termination or modification of the settlor's revocable trust, such authority must be expressly conveyed either in the power or in the terms of the trust.

Subsection (a), however, does not impose restrictions on consent by a conservator or guardian, other than prohibiting such action if the settlor is represented by an agent. The section instead leaves the issue of a conservator's or guardian's authority to local law. Many conservatorship statutes recognize that termination or modification of the settlor's trust is a sufficiently important transaction that a conservator should first obtain the approval of the court supervising the conservatorship. *See, e.g.*, Unif. Probate Code § 5-411(a)(4). Because the Uniform Trust Code uses the term "conservator" to refer to the person appointed by the court to manage an individual's property (*see* § 103(4)), a guardian may act on behalf of a settlor under this section only if a conservator has not been appointed.

Subsection (a) is similar to Restatement (Third) of Trusts § 65(2) (Tentative Draft No. 3, approved 2001), and Restatement (Second) of Trusts § 338(2) (1959), both of which permit termination upon joint action of the settlor and beneficiaries. Unlike termination by the beneficiaries alone under subsection (b), termination with the concurrence of the settlor does not require a finding that the trust no longer serves a material purpose. No finding of failure of material purpose is required because all parties with a possible interest in the trust's continuation, both the settlor and beneficiaries, agree there is no further need for the trust. Restatement Third goes further than subsection (b) of this section and Restatement Second, however, in also allowing the beneficiaries to compel termination of a trust that still serves a material purpose if the reasons for termination outweigh the continuing material purpose.

Subsection (b), similar to Restatement Third but not Restatement Second, allows modification by beneficiary action. The beneficiaries may modify any term of the trust if the modification is not inconsistent with a material purpose of the trust. Restatement Third, though, goes further than this Code in also allowing the beneficiaries to use trust modification as a basis for removing the trustee if removal would not be inconsistent with a material purpose of the trust. Under the Code, however, § 706 is the exclusive provision on removal of trustees. Section 706(b)(4) recognizes that a request for removal upon unanimous agreement of the qualified beneficiaries is a factor for the court to consider, but before removing the trustee the court must also find that such action best serves the interests of all the beneficiaries, that removal is not inconsistent with a material purpose of the trust, and that a suitable cotrustee or successor trustee is available. *Compare* § 706(b)(4), *with* Restatement (Third) § 65 cmt. f (Tentative Draft No. 3, approved 2001).

The requirement that the trust no longer serve a material purpose before it can be terminated by the beneficiaries does not mean that the trust has no remaining function. In order to be material, the purpose remaining to be performed must be of some significance:

> Material purposes are not readily to be inferred. A finding of such a purpose generally requires some showing of a particular concern or objective on the part of the settlor, such as concern with regard to the beneficiary's management skills, judgment, or level of maturity. Thus, a court may look for some circumstantial or other evidence indicating that the trust arrangement represented to the settlor more than a method of allocating the benefits of property among multiple beneficiaries, or a means of offering to the beneficiaries (but not imposing on them) a particular advantage. Sometimes, of course, the very nature or design of a trust suggests its protective nature or some other material purpose.

Restatement (Third) of Trusts § 65 cmt. d (Tentative Draft No. 3, approved 2001).

Subsection (c) of this section deals with the effect of a spendthrift provision on the right of a beneficiary to concur in a trust termination or modification. By a 2004 amendment, subsection (c) has been placed in brackets and thereby made optional. Spendthrift terms have sometimes been construed to constitute a material purpose without inquiry into the intention of the particular settlor. For examples, see Restatement (Second) of Trusts § 337 (1959); George G. Bogert & George T. Bogert, The Law of Trusts and Trustees § 1008 (Rev. 2d ed. 1983); and 4 Austin W. Scott & William F. Fratcher, The Law of Trusts § 337 (4th ed. 1989). This result is troublesome because spendthrift provisions are often added to instruments with little thought. Subsection (c), similar to Restatement (Third) of Trusts § 65 cmt. e (Tentative Draft No. 3, approved 2001), does not negate the possibility that continuation of a trust to assure spendthrift protection might have been a material purpose of the particular settlor. The

question of whether that was the intent of a particular settlor is instead a matter of fact to be determined on the totality of the circumstances.

Subsection (d) recognizes that the beneficiaries' power to compel termination of the trust includes the right to direct how the trust property is to be distributed. While subsection (a) requires the settlor's consent to terminate an irrevocable trust, the settlor does not control the subsequent distribution of the trust property. Once termination has been approved, how the trust property is to be distributed is solely for the beneficiaries to decide.

Subsection (e), similar to Restatement (Third) of Trusts § 65 cmt. c (Tentative Draft No. 3, approved 2001), and Restatement (Second) of Trusts §§ 338(2) & 340(2) (1959), addresses situations in which a termination or modification is requested by less than all the beneficiaries, either because a beneficiary objects, the consent of a beneficiary cannot be obtained, or representation is either unavailable or its application uncertain. Subsection (e) allows the court to fashion an appropriate order protecting the interests of the nonconsenting beneficiaries while at the same time permitting the remainder of the trust property to be distributed without restriction. The order of protection for the nonconsenting beneficiaries might include partial continuation of the trust, the purchase of an annuity, or the valuation and cashout of the interest.

2003 Amendment. The amendment, which adds the language "modification or" to subsection (a), fixes an inadvertent omission. It was the intent of the drafting committee that an agent with authority or a conservator or guardian with the approval of the court be able to participate not only in a decision to terminate a trust but also in a decision to modify it.

2004 Amendments.

Section 411(a), Section 301(d), and Conforming Changes to Sections 301(c) and 410(b). Section 411(a) was amended in 2004 on the recommendation of the Estate and Gift Taxation Committee of the American College of Trust and Estate Counsel. Enacting jurisdictions now have several options all of which are indicated by brackets:

• delete subsection (a), meaning that the state's prior law would control on this issue.

• require court approval of the modification or termination.

• make the provision prospective and applicable only to irrevocable trusts created on or after the effective date or to revocable trusts that become irrevocable on or after the effective date of the provision.

    • enact subsection (a) in its original form.

    Section 411(a), as originally drafted did not require that a court approve a joint decision of the settlor and beneficiaries to terminate or modify an irrevocable trust. The ACTEC Committee was concerned that:

    • Section 411(a), without amendment, could potentially result in the taxation for federal estate tax purposes of irrevocable trusts created in states which previously required that a court approve a settlor/beneficiary termination or modification; and

    • Because of the ability of a settlor under § 301 to represent and bind a beneficiary with respect to a termination or modification of an irrevocable trust, § 411(a) might result in inclusion of the trust in the settlor's gross estate. New § 301(d) eliminates the possibility of such representation.

    The Drafting Committee recommends that all jurisdictions enact the amendment to § 301(d). The Drafting Committee recommends that jurisdictions conform § 411(a) to prior law on whether or not court approval is necessary for the settlor and beneficiaries to jointly terminate or modify an irrevocable trust. If prior law is in doubt, the enacting jurisdiction may wish to make § 411(a) prospective only. The enacting jurisdiction may also elect to delete § 411(a).

    States electing to delete § 411(a) should also delete the cross-references to § 411 found in §§ 301(c) and 410(b). These cross-references have therefore been placed in brackets. States electing to delete § 411(a) should also not enact § 301(d), which for this reason has similarly been placed in brackets.

Section 411(c)

    Section 411(c), which by the 2004 amendment was placed in brackets and therefore made optional, provides that a spendthrift provision is not presumed to constitute a material purpose of the trust. Several states that have enacted the Code have not agreed with the provision and have either deleted it or have reversed the presumption. Given these developments, the Drafting Committee concluded that uniformity could not be achieved. The Joint Editorial Board for Uniform Trusts and Estates Acts, however, is of the view that the better approach is to enact subsection (c) in its original form for the reasons stated in the comment to this Section.

§ 412. Modification or Termination Because of Unanticipated Circumstances or Inability to Administer Trust Effectively.

    (a) The court may modify the administrative or dispositive terms of a trust or terminate the trust if, because of circumstances not anticipated by the settlor, modification or termination will further the purposes of the trust. To the extent practicable, the modification must be made in accordance with the settlor's probable intention.

    (b) The court may modify the administrative terms of a trust if continuation of the trust on its existing terms would be impracticable or wasteful or impair the trust's administration.

    (c) Upon termination of a trust under this section, the trustee shall distribute the trust property in a manner consistent with the purposes of the trust.

Comment

    This section broadens the court's ability to apply equitable deviation to terminate or modify a trust. Subsection (a) allows a court to modify the dispositive provisions of the trust as well as its administrative terms. For example, modification of the dispositive provisions to increase support of a beneficiary might be appropriate if the beneficiary has become unable to provide for support due to poor health or serious injury. Subsection (a) is similar to Restatement (Third) of Trusts § 66(1) (Tentative Draft No. 3, approved 2001), except that this section, unlike the Restatement, does not impose a duty on the trustee to petition the court if the trustee is aware of circumstances justifying judicial modification. The purpose of the "equitable deviation" authorized by subsection (a) is not to disregard the settlor's intent but to modify inopportune details to effectuate better the settlor's broader purposes. Among other things, equitable deviation may be used to modify administrative or dispositive terms due to the failure to anticipate economic change or the incapacity of a beneficiary. For numerous illustrations, see Restatement (Third) of Trusts § 66 cmt. b (Tentative Draft No. 3, approved 2001). While it is necessary that there be circumstances not anticipated by the settlor before the court may grant relief under subsection (a), the circumstances may have been in existence when the trust was created. This section

Equitable Deviation

Change in circumstances
Unanticipated by settlor
makes necessary

453

Jpc: devectn Furths Trust
purpose

thus complements § 415, which allows for reformation of a trust based on mistake of fact or law at the creation of the trust.

Subsection (b) broadens the court's ability to modify the administrative terms of a trust. The standard under subsection (b) is similar to the standard for applying cy pres to a charitable trust. *See* § 413(a). Just as a charitable trust may be modified if its particular charitable purpose becomes impracticable or wasteful, so can the administrative terms of any trust, charitable or noncharitable. Subsections (a) and (b) are not mutually exclusive. Many situations justifying modification of administrative terms under subsection (a) will also justify modification under subsection (b). Subsection (b) is also an application of the requirement in § 404 that a trust and its terms must be for the benefit of its beneficiaries. *See also* Restatement (Third) of Trusts § 27(2) & cmt. b (Tentative Draft No. 2, approved 1999). Although the settlor is granted considerable latitude in defining the purposes of the trust, the principle that a trust have a purpose which is for the benefit of its beneficiaries precludes unreasonable restrictions on the use of trust property. An owner's freedom to be capricious about the use of the owner's own property ends when the property is impressed with a trust for the benefit of others. *See* Restatement

(Second) of Trusts § 124 cmt. g (1959). Thus, attempts to impose unreasonable restrictions on the use of trust property will fail. *See* Restatement (Third) of Trusts § 27 Reporter's Notes to cmt. b (Tentative Draft No. 2, approved 1999). Subsection (b), unlike subsection (a), does not have a direct precedent in the common law, but various states have insisted on such a measure by statute. *See, e.g.,* Mo. Rev. Stat. §456.590.1.

Upon termination of a trust under this section, subsection (c) requires that the trust be distributed in a manner consistent with the purposes of the trust. As under the doctrine of cy pres, effectuating a distribution consistent with the purposes of the trust requires an examination of what the settlor would have intended had the settlor been aware of the unanticipated circumstances. Typically, such terminating distributions will be made to the qualified beneficiaries, often in proportion to the actuarial value of their interests, although the section does not so prescribe. For the definition of qualified beneficiary, see § 103(13).

Modification under this section, because it does not require beneficiary action, is not precluded by a spendthrift provision.

§ 413. Cy Pres.

(a) Except as otherwise provided in subsection (b), if a particular charitable purpose becomes unlawful, impracticable, impossible to achieve, or wasteful:

    (1) the trust does not fail, in whole or in part;

    (2) the trust property does not revert to the settlor or the settlor's successors in interest; and

    (3) the court may apply cy pres to modify or terminate the trust by directing that the trust property be applied or distributed, in whole or in part, in a manner consistent with the settlor's charitable purposes.

(b) A provision in the terms of a charitable trust that would result in distribution of the trust property to a noncharitable beneficiary prevails over the power of the court under subsection (a) to apply cy pres to modify or terminate the trust only if, when the provision takes effect:

    (1) the trust property is to revert to the settlor and the settlor is still living; or

    (2) fewer than 21 years have elapsed since the date of the trust's creation.

Comment

Subsection (a) codifies the court's inherent authority to apply cy pres. The power may be applied to modify an administrative or dispositive term. The court may order the trust terminated and distributed to other charitable entities. Partial termination may also be ordered if the trust property is more than sufficient to satisfy the trust's current purposes.

Subsection (a), which is similar to Restatement (Third) of Trusts § 67, modifies the doctrine of cy pres by presuming that the settlor had a general charitable intent when a particular charitable purpose becomes impossible or impracticable to achieve. Traditional doctrine did not supply that presumption, leaving it to the courts to determine whether the

General Intent = general cause — Cy pres's cool

Specific Intent = specific charity

UTC: presumes General

settlor had a general charitable intent. If such an intent is found, the trust property is applied to other charitable purposes. If not, the charitable trust fails. *See* Restatement (Second) of Trusts § 399 (1959). In the great majority of cases the settlor would prefer that the property be used for other charitable purposes. Courts are usually able to find a general charitable purpose to which to apply the property, no matter how vaguely such purpose may have been expressed by the settlor. Under subsection (a), if the particular purpose for which the trust was created becomes impracticable, unlawful, impossible to achieve, or wasteful, the trust does not fail. The court instead must either modify the terms of the trust or distribute the property of the trust in a manner consistent with the settlor's charitable purposes.

The settlor, with one exception, may mandate that the trust property pass to a noncharitable beneficiary upon failure of a particular charitable purpose. Responding to concerns about the clogging of title and other administrative problems caused by remote default provisions upon failure of a charitable purpose, subsection (b) invalidates a gift over to a noncharitable beneficiary upon failure of a particular charitable purpose unless the trust property is to revert to a living settlor or fewer than 21 years have elapsed since the trust's creation. Subsection (b) will not apply to a charitable lead trust, under which a charity receives payments for a term certain with a remainder to a noncharity. In the case of a charitable lead trust, the settlor's particular charitable purpose does not fail upon completion of the specified trust term and distribution of the remainder to the noncharity. Upon completion of the specified trust term, the settlor's particular charitable purpose has instead been fulfilled. For a discussion of the reasons for a provision such as subsection (b), see Ronald Chester, *Cy Pres of Gift Over: The Search for Coherence*

in Judicial Reform of Failed Charitable Trusts, 23 Suffolk U. L. Rev. 41 (1989).

The doctrine of cy pres is applied not only to trusts, but also to other types of charitable dispositions, including those to charitable corporations. This section does not control dispositions made in nontrust form. However, in formulating rules for such dispositions, the courts often refer to the principles governing charitable trusts, which would include this Code. See Restatement of Charitable Nonprofit Organizations § 3.02, Comment f (Tentative Draft No. 1, 2016), recognizing and approving the application of cy pres "not only to charitable trusts, but also to charities that [are] corporations and to gifts made for specific charitable purposes to charities that [are] corporations whether expressly in trust or in nontrust form." Under longstanding and prevailing law, it would be incorrect to say, as the court did in dictum in Williams v. City of Kuttawa, 466 S.W.3d 505, 511 (Ky. App. 2015), that the "application of the cy pres doctrine is inappropriate" merely "because no trust exists."

For the definition of charitable purpose, see § 405(a). Pursuant to §§ 405(c) and 410(b), a petition requesting a court to enforce a charitable trust or to apply cy pres may be maintained by a settlor. Such actions can also be maintained by a cotrustee, the state attorney general, or by a person having a special interest in the charitable disposition. *See* Restatement (Second) of Trusts § 391 (1959).

Historical Note. The penultimate paragraph of this Comment was amended in 2017 to cite the Restatement of Charitable Nonprofit Organizations and to disapprove of dictum in Williams v. City of Kuttawa.

§ 414. Modification or Termination of Uneconomic Trust.

(a) After notice to the qualified beneficiaries, the trustee of a trust consisting of trust property having a total value less than [$50,000] may terminate the trust if the trustee concludes that the value of the trust property is insufficient to justify the cost of administration.

(b) The court may modify or terminate a trust or remove the trustee and appoint a different trustee if it determines that the value of the trust property is insufficient to justify the cost of administration.

(c) Upon termination of a trust under this section, the trustee shall distribute the trust property in a manner consistent with the purposes of the trust.

(d) This section does not apply to an easement for conservation or preservation.

Comment

Subsection (a) assumes that a trust with a value of $50,000 or less is sufficiently likely to be inefficient to administer that a trustee should be able to terminate it without the expense of a judicial termination proceeding. The amount has been placed in brackets to signal to enacting jurisdictions that they may wish to designate a higher or lower figure. Because subsection (a) is a default rule, a settlor is free to set a higher or lower figure or to specify different procedures or to prohibit termination without a court order. *See* § 105 and Article 4 General Comment.

Subsection (b) allows the court to modify or terminate a trust if the costs of administration would otherwise be excessive in relation to the size of the trust. The court may terminate a trust under this section even if the settlor has forbidden it. *See* § 105(b)(4). Judicial termination under this subsection may be used whether or not the trust is larger or smaller than $50,000.

When considering whether to terminate a trust under either subsection (a) or (b), the trustee or court should consider the purposes of the trust. Termination under this section is not always wise. Even if administrative costs may seem excessive in relation to the size of the trust, protection of the assets from beneficiary mismanagement may indicate that the trust be continued. The court may be able to reduce the costs of administering the trust by appointing a new trustee.

Upon termination of a trust under this section, subsection (c) requires that the trust property be distributed in a manner consistent with the purposes of the trust. In addition to outright distribution to the beneficiaries, § 816(21) authorizes payment to be made by a variety of alternate payees. Distribution under this section will typically be made to the qualified beneficiaries in proportion to the actuarial value of their interests.

Even though not accompanied by the usual trappings of a trust, the creation and transfer of an easement for conservation or preservation will frequently create a charitable trust. The organization to whom the easement was conveyed will be deemed to be acting as trustee of what will ostensibly appear to be a contractual or property arrangement. Because of the fiduciary obligation imposed, the termination or substantial modification of the easement by the "trustee" could constitute a breach of trust. The drafters of the Uniform Trust Code concluded that easements for conservation or preservation are sufficiently different from the typical cash and securities found in small trusts that they should be excluded from this section, and subsection (d) so provides. Most creators of such easements, it was surmised, would prefer that the easement be continued unchanged even if the easement, and hence the trust, has a relatively low market value. For the law of conservation easements, see Restatement (Third) of Property: Servitudes §1.6 (2000).

While this section is not directed principally at honorary trusts, it may be so applied. *See* §§ 408, 409.

Because termination of a trust under this section is initiated by the trustee or ordered by the court, termination is not precluded by a spendthrift provision.

§ 415. Reformation to Correct Mistakes.

§ 415. Reformation to Correct Mistakes. The court may reform the terms of a trust, even if unambiguous, to conform the terms to the settlors's intention if it is proved by clear and convincing evidence what the settlor's intention was and that the terms of the trust were affected by a mistake of fact or law, whether in expression or inducement.

Comment

Reformation of inter vivos instruments to correct a mistake of law or fact is a long-established remedy. Restatement (Third) of Property: Donative Transfers § 12.1 (Tentative Draft No. 1, approved 1995), which this section copies, clarifies that this doctrine also applies to wills.

This section applies whether the mistake is one of expression or one of inducement. A mistake of expression occurs when the terms of the trust misstate the settlor's intention, fail to include a term that was intended to be included, or include a term that was not intended to be included. A mistake in the inducement occurs when the terms of the trust accurately reflect what the settlors intended to be included or excluded but this intention was based on a mistake of fact or law. *See* Restatement (Third) of Property: Donative Transfers § 12.1 cmt. i (Tentative Draft No. 1, approved 1995). Mistakes of expression are frequently caused by scriveners' errors while mistakes of inducement often trace to errors of the settlors.

Reformation is different from resolving an ambiguity. Resolving an ambiguity involves the interpretation of language already in the instrument. Reformation, on the other hand, may involve the addition of language not originally in the instrument, or the deletion of language originally included by mistake, if necessary to conform the instrument to the settlor's intent.

Because reformation may involve the addition of language to the instrument, or the deletion of language that may appear clear on its face, reliance on extrinsic evidence is essential. To guard against the possibility of unreliable or contrived evidence in such circumstance, the higher standard of clear and convincing proof is required. *See* Restatement (Third) of Property: Donative Transfers § 12.1 cmt. e (Tentative Draft No. 1, approved 1995).

In determining the settlor's original intent, the court may consider evidence relevant to the settlor's intention even though it contradicts an apparent plain meaning of the text. The objective of the plain meaning rule, to protect against fraudulent testimony, is satisfied by the requirement of clear and convincing proof. *See* Restatement (Third) of Property: Donative Transfers § 12.1 cmt. d & Reporter's Notes (Tentative Draft No. 1, approved 1995). *See also* John H. Langbein & Lawrence W. Waggoner, *Reformation of Wills on the Ground of Mistake: Change of Direction in American Law?*, 130 U. Pa. L. Rev. 521 (1982).

For further discussion of the rule of this section and its application to illustrative cases, see Restatement (Third) of Property: Donative Transfers § 12.1 cmts. & Reporter's Notes (Tentative Draft No. 1, approved 1995).

2011 Amendment. This section was revised by technical amendment in 2011. The amendment better conforms the language of the section to the language of the Restatement (Third) of Property provision on which the section is based.

Restatement (Third) of Property: Wills and Other Donative Transfers (2003)

§ 12.1 Reforming Donative Documents to Correct Mistakes. A donative document, though unambiguous, may be reformed to conform the text to the donor's intention if it is established by clear and convincing evidence (1) that a mistake of fact or law, whether in expression or inducement, affected specific terms of the document; and (2) what the donor's intention was. In determining whether these elements have been established by clear and convincing evidence, direct evidence of intention contradicting the plain meaning of the text as well as other evidence of intention may be considered.

---

§ 416. Modification to Achieve Settlor's Tax Objectives. To achieve the settlor's tax objectives, the court may modify the terms of a trust in a manner that is not contrary to the settlor's probable intention. The court may provide that the modification has retroactive effect.

Comment

This section is copied from Restatement (Third) of Property: Donative Transfers § 12.2 (Tentative Draft No. 1, approved 1995). "Modification" under this section is to be distinguished from the "reformation" authorized by § 415. Reformation under § 415 is available when the terms of a trust fail to reflect the donor's original, particularized intention. The mistaken terms are then reformed to conform to this specific intent. The modification authorized here allows the terms of the trust to be changed to meet the settlor's tax-saving objective as long as the resulting terms, particularly the dispositive provisions, are not inconsistent with the settlor's probable intent. The modification allowed by this subsection is similar in concept to the cy pres doctrine for charitable trusts (*see* § 413), and the deviation doctrine for unanticipated circumstances (*see* § 412).

Whether a modification made by the court under this section will be recognized under federal tax law is a matter of federal law. Absent specific statutory or regulatory authority, binding recognition is normally given only to modifications made prior to the taxing event, for example, the death of the testator or settlor in the case of the federal estate tax. *See* Rev. Rul. 73-142, 1973-1 C.B. 405. Among the specific modifications authorized by the Internal Revenue Code or Service include the revision of split-interest trusts to qualify for the charitable deduction, modification of a trust for a noncitizen spouse to become eligible as a qualified domestic trust, and the splitting of a trust to utilize better the exemption from generation-skipping tax.

For further discussion of the rule of this section and the relevant case law, see Restatement (Third) of

Property: Donative Transfers § 12.2 cmts. & Reporter's Notes (Tentative Draft No. 1, approved 1995).

Restatement (Third) of Property: Wills and Other Donative Transfers (2003)

§ 12.2 Modifying Donative Documents to Achieve Donor's Tax Objectives. A donative document may be modified, in a manner that does not violate the donor's probable intention, to achieve the donor's tax objectives.

---

§ 417. Combination and Division of Trusts. After notice to the qualified beneficiaries, a trustee may combine two or more trusts into a single trust or divide a trust into two or more separate trusts, if the result does not impair rights of any beneficiary or adversely affect achievement of the purposes of the trust.

Comment

This section, which authorizes the combination or division of trusts, is subject to contrary provision in the terms of the trust. *See* § 105 and Article 4 General Comment. Many trust instruments and standardized estate planning forms include comprehensive provisions governing combination and division of trusts. Except for the requirement that the qualified beneficiaries receive advance notice of a proposed combination or division, this section is similar to Restatement (Third) of Trusts § 68 (Tentative Draft No. 3, approved 2001).

This section allows a trustee to combine two or more trusts even though their terms are not identical. Typically the trusts to be combined will have been created by different members of the same family and will vary on only insignificant details, such as the presence of different perpetuities savings periods. The more the dispositive provisions of the trusts to be combined differ from each other the more likely it is that a combination would impair some beneficiary's interest, hence the less likely that the combination can be approved. Combining trusts may prompt more efficient trust administration and is sometimes an alternative to terminating an uneconomic trust as authorized by § 414. Administrative economies promoted by combining trusts include a potential reduction in trustees' fees, particularly if the trustee charges a minimum fee per trust, the ability to file one trust income tax return instead of multiple returns, and the ability to invest a larger pool of capital more effectively. Particularly if the terms of the trust are identical, available administrative economies may suggest that the trustee has a responsibility to pursue a combination. *See* § 805 (duty to incur only reasonable costs).

Division of trusts is often beneficial and, in certain circumstances, almost routine. Division of trusts is frequently undertaken due to a desire to obtain maximum advantage of exemptions available under the federal generation-skipping tax. While the terms of the trusts which result from such a division are identical, the division will permit differing investment objectives to be pursued and allow for discretionary distributions to be made from one trust and not the other. Given the substantial tax benefits often involved, a failure by the trustee to pursue a division might in certain cases be a breach of fiduciary duty. The opposite could also be true if the division is undertaken to increase fees or to fit within the small trust termination provision. *See* § 414.

This section authorizes a trustee to divide a trust even if the trusts that result are dissimilar. Conflicts among beneficiaries, including differing investment objectives, often invite such a division, although as in the case with a proposed combination of trusts, the more the terms of the divided trusts diverge from the original plan, the less likely it is that the settlor's purposes would be achieved and that the division could be approved.

This section does not require that a combination or division be approved either by the court or by the beneficiaries. Prudence may dictate, however, that court approval under § 410 be sought and beneficiary consent obtained whenever the terms of the trusts to be combined or the trusts that will result from a division differ substantially one from the other. For the provisions relating to beneficiary consent or ratification of a transaction, or release of trustee from liability, see § 1009.

While the consent of the beneficiaries is not

necessary before a trustee may combine or divide trusts under this section, advance notice to the qualified beneficiaries of the proposed combination or division is required. This is consistent with § 813, which requires that the trustee keep the beneficiaries reasonably informed of trust administration, including the giving of advance notice to the qualified beneficiaries of several specified actions that may have a major impact on their interests.

Numerous states have enacted statutes authorizing division of trusts, either by trustee action or upon court order. For a list of these statutes, see Restatement (Third) Property: Donative Transfers § 12.2 Statutory Note (Tentative Draft No. 1, approved 1995). Combination or division has also been authorized by the courts in the absence of authorizing statute. *See, e.g., In re Will of Marcus*, 552 N.Y.S. 2d 546 (Surr. Ct.1990) (combination); *In re Heller Inter Vivos Trust*, 613 N.Y.S. 2d 809 (Surr. Ct. 1994) (division); and *BankBoston v. Marlow*, 701 N.E. 2d 304 (Mass. 1998) (division).

For a provision authorizing a trustee, in distributing the assets of the divided trust, to make non-pro-rata distributions, see § 816(22).

ARTICLE 5
CREDITOR'S CLAIMS; SPENDTHRIFT AND DISCRETIONARY TRUSTS

General Comment

This article addresses the validity of a spendthrift provision and the rights of creditors, both of the settlors and beneficiaries, to reach a trust to collect a debt. Sections 501 and 502 state the general rules. Section 501 applies if the trust does not contain a spendthrift provision or the spendthrift provision, if any, does not apply to the beneficiary's interest. Section 502 states the effect of a spendthrift provision. Unless a claim is being made by an exception creditor, a spendthrift provision bars a beneficiary's creditor from reaching the beneficiary's interest until distribution is made by the trustee. An exception creditor, however, can reach the beneficiary's interest subject to the court's power to limit the relief. Section 503 lists the categories of exception creditors whose claims are not subject to a spendthrift restriction. Sections 504 through 507 address special categories in which the rights of a beneficiary's creditors are the same whether or not the trust contains a spendthrift provision. Section 504 deals with discretionary trusts and trusts for which distributions are subject to a standard. Section 505 covers creditor claims against a settlors, whether the trust is revocable or irrevocable, and if revocable, whether the claim is made during the settlor's lifetime or incident to the settlor's death. Section 506 provides a creditor with a remedy if a trustee fails to make a mandated distribution within a reasonable time. Section 507 clarifies that although the trustee holds legal title to trust property, that property is not subject to the trustee's personal debts.

The provisions of this article relating to the validity and effect of a spendthrift provision and the rights of certain creditors and assignees to reach the trust may not be modified by the terms of the trust. *See* § 105(b)(5).

This article does not supersede state exemption statutes nor an enacting jurisdiction's Uniform Fraudulent Transfers Act which, when applicable, invalidates any type of gratuitous transfer, including transfers into trust.

Comment Amended in 2004.

§ 501. Rights of Beneficiary's Creditor or Assignee. To the extent a beneficiary's interest is not subject to a spendthrift provision, the court may authorize a creditor or assignee of the beneficiary to reach the beneficiary's interest by attachment of present or future distributions to or for the benefit of the beneficiary or other means. The court may limit the award to such relief as is appropriate under the circumstances.

Comment

This section applies only if the trust does not contain a spendthrift provision or the spendthrift provision does not apply to a particular beneficiary's interest. A settlor may subject to spendthrift protection the interests of certain beneficiaries but not others. A settlor may also subject only a portion of the trust to spendthrift protection such as an interest in the income but not principal. For the effect of the provision on creditor claims, see Section 503.

Absent a valid spendthrift provision, a creditor may ordinarily reach the interest of a beneficiary the same as any other of the beneficiary's assets. This does not necessarily mean that the creditor can collect all distributions made to the beneficiary. The interest may be too indefinite or contingent for the creditor to reach or the interest may qualify for an exemption under the state's general creditor exemption statutes. See Restatement (Third) of Trusts § 56 (2003); Restatement (Second) of Trusts §§ 147-149, 162 (1959). Other creditor law of the state may limit the creditor to a specified percentage of a distribution. *See, e.g.,* Cal. Prob. Code § 15306.5. This section does not prescribe the procedures ("other means") for reaching a beneficiary's interest or of priority among claimants, leaving those issues to the enacting state's laws on creditor rights. The section does clarify, however, that an order obtained against the trustee, whatever state procedure may have been used, may extend to future distributions whether made directly to the beneficiary or to others for the beneficiary's benefit. By allowing an order to extend to future payments, the need for the creditor periodically to return to court will be reduced.

Because proceedings to satisfy a claim are equitable in nature, the second sentence of this section ratifies the court's discretion to limit the award as appropriate under the circumstances. In exercising its discretion to limit relief, the court may appropriately consider the circumstances of a beneficiary and the beneficiary's family. *See* Restatement (Third) of Trusts § 56 cmt. e (Tentative Draft No. 2, approved 1999).

2005 Amendment. A 2005 amendment changes "protected by" to "subject to" in the first sentence of the section. No substantive change is intended. The amendment was made to negate an implication that this section allowed an exception creditor to reach a beneficiary's interest even though the trust contained a spendthrift provision. The list of exception creditors and their remedies are contained in § 503. Clarifying changes are also made in the comments and unnecessary language on creditor remedies omitted.

§ 502. Spendthrift Provision.

(a) A spendthrift provision is valid only if it restrains both voluntary and involuntary transfer of a beneficiary's interest.

(b) A term of a trust providing that the interest of a beneficiary is held subject to a "spendthrift trust," or words of similar import, is sufficient to restrain both voluntary and involuntary transfer of the beneficiary's interest.

(c) A beneficiary may not transfer an interest in a trust in violation of a valid spendthrift provision and, except as otherwise provided in this [article], a creditor or assignee of the beneficiary may not reach the interest or a distribution by the trustee before its receipt by the beneficiary.

Comment

Under this section, a settlor has the power to restrain the transfer of a beneficiary's interest, regardless of whether the beneficiary has an interest in income, in principal, or in both. Unless one of the exceptions under this article applies, a creditor of the beneficiary is prohibited from attaching a protected interest and may only attempt to collect directly from the beneficiary after payment is made. This section is similar to Restatement (Third) of Trusts § 58 (Tentative Draft No. 2, approved 1999), and Restatement (Second) of Trusts §§ 152-153 (1959). For the definition of spendthrift provision, see § 103(15).

For a spendthrift provision to be effective under this Code, it must prohibit both the voluntary and involuntary transfer of the beneficiary's interest, that is, a settlor may not allow a beneficiary to assign while prohibiting a beneficiary's creditor from collecting, and vice versa. *See* Restatement (Third) of Trusts § 58 cmt. b (Tentative Draft No. 2, approved 1999). *See also* Restatement (Second) of Trusts § 152(2) (1959). A spendthrift provision valid under this Code will also be recognized as valid in a federal bankruptcy proceeding. *See* 11 U.S.C. § 541(c)(2).

Subsection (b), which is derived from Texas Property Code § 112.035(b), allows a settlor to provide maximum spendthrift protection simply by stating in the instrument that all interests are held subject to a "spendthrift trust" or words of similar effect.

A disclaimer, because it is a refusal to accept ownership of an interest and not a transfer of an interest already owned, is not affected by the presence or absence of a spendthrift provision. Most disclaimer statutes expressly provide that the validity of a disclaimer is not affected by a spendthrift protection. *See, e.g.,* Unif. Probate Code § 2-801(a). Releases and exercises of powers of appointment are also not affected because they are not transfers of property. *See* Restatement (Third) of Trusts § 58 cmt. c (Tentative Draft No. 2, approved 1999).

A spendthrift provision is ineffective against a beneficial interest retained by the settlor. *See* Restatement (Third) of Trusts §58(2) (Tentative Draft No. 2, approved 1999. This is a necessary corollary to § 505(a)(2), which allows a creditor or assignee of the settlor to reach the maximum amount that can be distributed to or for the settlor's benefit. This right to reach the trust applies whether or not the trust contains a spendthrift provision.

A valid spendthrift provision makes it impossible for a beneficiary to make a legally binding transfer, but the trustee may choose to honor the beneficiary's purported assignment. The trustee may recommence distributions to the beneficiary at anytime. The beneficiary, not having made a binding transfer, can withdraw the beneficiary's direction but only as to future payments. *See* Restatement (Third) of Trusts § 58 cmt. d (Tentative Draft No. 2, approved 1999); Restatement (Second) of Trusts § 152 cmt. i (1959).

§ 503. Exceptions to Spendthrift Provision.

(a) In this section, "child" includes any person for whom an order or judgment for child support has been entered in this or another State.

(b) A spendthrift provision is unenforceable against:

(1) a beneficiary's child, spouse, or former spouse who has a judgment or court order against the beneficiary for support or maintenance;

(2) a judgment creditor who has provided services for the protection of a beneficiary's interest in the trust; and

(3) a claim of this State or the United States to the extent a statute of this State or federal law so provides.

(c) A claimant against whom a spendthrift provision cannot be enforced may obtain from a court an order attaching present or future distributions to or for the benefit of the beneficiary. The court may limit the award to such relief as is appropriate under the circumstances.

Comment

This section exempts the claims of certain categories of creditors from the effects of a spendthrift restriction and specifies the remedies such exemption creditors may take to satisfy their claims.

The exception in subsection (b)(1) for judgments or orders to support a beneficiary's child or current or former spouse is in accord with Restatement (Third) of Trusts § 59(a) (Tentative Draft No. 2, approved 1999), Restatement (Second) of Trusts § 157(a) (1959), and numerous state statutes. It is also consistent with federal bankruptcy law, which exempts such support orders from discharge. The effect of this exception is to permit the claimant for unpaid support to attach present or future distributions that would otherwise be made to the beneficiary. Distributions subject to attachment include distributions required by the express terms of the trust, such as mandatory payments of income, and distributions the trustee has otherwise decided to make, such as through the exercise of discretion. Subsection (b)(1), unlike § 504, does not authorize the spousal or child claimant to compel a distribution from the trust. Section 504 authorizes a spouse or child claimant to compel a distribution to the extent the trustee has abused a discretion or failed to comply with a standard for distribution.

Subsection (b)(1) refers both to "support" and "maintenance" in order to accommodate differences among the states in terminology employed. No difference in meaning between the two terms is intended.

The definition of "child" in subsection (a) accommodates the differing approaches States take to defining the class of individuals eligible for child support, including such issues as whether support can be awarded to stepchildren. However the state making the award chooses to define "child" will be recognized under this Code, whether the order sought to be enforced was entered in the same or different State. For the definition of "state," which includes Puerto Rico and other American possessions, see § 103(17).

The definition of "child" in subsection (a) is not exclusive. The definition clarifies that a "child" includes an individual awarded child support in any state. The definition does not expressly include but neither does it exclude persons awarded child support in some other country or political subdivision, such as a Canadian province.

The exception in subsection (b)(2) for a judgment creditor who has provided services for the protection of a beneficiary's interest in the trust is in accord with Restatement (Third) of Trusts § 59(b) (Tentative Draft No. 2, approved 1999), and Restatement (Second) of Trusts § 157(c) (1959). This exception allows a beneficiary of modest means to overcome an obstacle preventing the beneficiary's obtaining services essential to the protection or enforcement of the beneficiary's rights under the trust. *See* Restatement (Third) of Trusts § 59 cmt. d (Tentative Draft No. 2, approved 1999).

Subsection (b)(3), which is similar to Restatement (Third) of Trusts § 59 cmt. a (Tentative Draft No. 2, approved 1999), exempts certain governmental claims from a spendthrift restriction. Federal preemption guarantees that certain federal claims, such as claims by the Internal Revenue Service, may bypass a spendthrift provision no matter what this Code might say. The case law and relevant Internal Revenue Code provisions on the exception for federal tax claims are collected in George G. Bogert & George T. Bogert, The Law of Trusts and Trustees § 224 (Rev. 2d ed. 1992); and 2A Austin W. Scott & William F. Fratcher, The Law of Trusts § 157.4 (4th ed. 1987). Regarding claims by state governments, this subsection recognizes that states take a variety of approaches with respect to collection, depending on whether the claim is for unpaid taxes, for care provided at an institution, or for other charges. Acknowledging this diversity, subsection (c) does not prescribe a rule, but refers to other statutes of the state on whether particular claims are subject to or exempted from spendthrift provisions.

Unlike Restatement (Third) of Trusts § 59(2) (Tentative Draft No. 2, approved 1999), and Restatement (Second) of Trusts § 157(b) (1959), this Code does not create an exception to the spendthrift restriction for creditors who have furnished necessary services or supplies to the beneficiary. Most of these cases involve claims by governmental entities, which the drafters concluded are better handled by the enactment of special legislation as authorized by subsection (b)(3). The drafters also declined to create an exception for tort claimants. For a discussion of the exception for tort claims, which has not generally been recognized, see Restatement (Third) of Trusts § 59 Reporter's Notes to cmt. a (Tentative Draft No. 2, approved 1999). For a discussion of other exceptions to a spendthrift restriction, recognized in some states, see George G. Bogert & George T. Bogert, The Law of Trusts and Trustees § 224 (Rev. 2d ed. 1992); and 2A Austin W. Scott & William F. Fratcher, The Law of Trusts §§ 157-157.5 (4th ed. 1987).

Subsection (c) provides that the only remedy available to an exception creditor is attachment of present or future distributions. Depending on other creditor law of the state, additional remedies may be available should a beneficiary's interest not be subject to a spendthrift provision. Section 501. which applies in such situations, provides that the creditor may reach the beneficiary's interest under that section by attachment or "other means." Subsection (c), similar to § 501, clarifies that the court has the authority to limit the creditor's relief as appropriate under the circumstances.

2005 Amendment. The amendment rewrote ths section. The section previously provided:

Section 503. Exceptions to Spendthrift Provision.

(a) In this section, "child" includes any person for whom an order or judgment for child support has been entered in this or another State.

(b) Even if a trust contains a spendthrift provision, a beneficiary's child, spouse, or former spouse who has a judgment or court order against the beneficiary for support or maintenance, or a judgment creditor who has provided services for the protection of a beneficiary's interest in the trust, may obtain from a court an order attaching present or future distributions to or for the benefit of the beneficiary.

(c) A spendthrift provision is unenforceable against a claim of this State or the United States to the extent a statute of this State or federal law so provides.

§ 504. Discretionary Trusts; Effect of Standard.

(a) In this section, "child" includes any person for whom an order or judgment for child support has been entered in this or another State.

(b) Except as otherwise provided in subsection (c), whether or not a trust contains a spendthrift provision, a creditor of a beneficiary may not compel a distribution that is subject to the trustee's discretion, even if:

    (1) the discretion is expressed in the form of a standard of distribution; or

    (2) the trustee has abused the discretion.

(c) To the extent a trustee has not complied with a standard of distribution or has abused a discretion:

    (1) a distribution may be ordered by the court to satisfy a judgment or court order against the beneficiary for support or maintenance of the beneficiary's child, spouse, or former spouse; and

    (2) the court shall direct the trustee to pay to the child, spouse, or former spouse such amount as is equitable under the circumstances but not more than the amount the trustee would have been

required to distribute to or for the benefit of the beneficiary had the trustee complied with the standard or not abused the discretion.

(d) This section does not limit the right of a beneficiary to maintain a judicial proceeding against a trustee for an abuse of discretion or failure to comply with a standard for distribution.

(e) If the trustee's or cotrustee's discretion to make distributions for the trustee's or cotrustee's own benefit is limited by an ascertainable standard, a creditor may not reach or compel distribution of the beneficial interest except to the extent the interest would be subject to the creditor's claim were the beneficiary not acting as trustee or cotrustee.

Comment

This section addresses the ability of a beneficiary's creditor to reach the beneficiary's discretionary trust interest, whether or not the exercise of the trustee's discretion is subject to a standard. This section, similar to the Restatement, eliminates the distinction between discretionary and support trusts, unifying the rules for all trusts fitting within either of the former categories. *See* Restatement (Third) of Trusts § 60 Reporter's Notes to cmt. a (Tentative Draft No. 2, approved 1999). By eliminating this distinction, the rights of a creditor are the same whether the distribution standard is discretionary, subject to a standard, or both. Other than for a claim by a child, spouse or former spouse, a beneficiary's creditor may not reach the beneficiary's interest. Eliminating this distinction affects only the rights of creditors. The affect [sic] of this change is limited to the rights of creditors. It does not affect the rights of a beneficiary to compel a distribution. Whether the trustee has a duty in a given situation to make a distribution depends on factors such as the breadth of the discretion granted and whether the terms of the trust include a support or other standard. *See* § 814 comment.

For a discussion of the definition of "child" in subsection (a), see § 503 Comment.

Subsection (b), which establishes the general rule, forbids a creditor from compelling a distribution from the trust, even if the trustee has failed to comply with the standard of distribution or has abused a discretion. Under subsection (d), the power to force a distribution due to an abuse of discretion or failure to comply with a standard belongs solely to the beneficiary. Under § 814(a), a trustee must always exercise a discretionary power in good faith and with regard to the purposes of the trust and the interests of the beneficiaries.

Subsection (c) creates an exception for support claims of a child, spouse, or former spouse who has a judgment or order against a beneficiary for support or maintenance. While a creditor of a beneficiary generally may not assert that a trustee has abused a discretion or failed to comply with a standard of distribution, such a claim may be asserted by the beneficiary's child, spouse, or former spouse enforcing a judgment or court order against the beneficiary for unpaid support or maintenance. The court must direct the trustee to pay the child, spouse or former spouse such amount as is equitable under the circumstances but not in excess of the amount the trustee was otherwise required to distribute to or for the benefit of the beneficiary. Before fixing this amount, the court having jurisdiction over the trust should consider that in setting the respective support award, the family court has already considered the respective needs and assets of the family. The Uniform Trust Code does not prescribe a particular procedural method for enforcing a judgment or order against the trust, leaving that matter to local collection law.

Subsection (e), which was added by a 2004 amendment, is discussed below.

2004 Amendment
Section 504(e), 103(11)

Trusts are frequently drafted in which a trustee is also a beneficiary. A common example is what is often referred to as a bypass trust, under which the settlor's spouse will frequently be named as both trustee and beneficiary. An amount equal to the exemption from federal estate tax will be placed in the bypass trust, and the trustee, who will often be the settlor's spouse, will be given discretion to make distributions to the beneficiaries, a class which will usually include the spouse/trustee. To prevent the inclusion of the trust in the spouse-trustee's gross estate, the spouse's discretion to make distributions for the spouse's own benefit will be limited by an ascertainable standard relating to health, education, maintenance, or support.

The UTC, as previously drafted, did not specifically address the issue of whether a creditor of a beneficiary may reach the interest of a beneficiary who is also a trustee. However, Restatement (Third) of Trusts § 60, comment g, which was approved by the American law Institute in 1999, provides that the beneficial interest of a beneficiary/trustee may be reached by the beneficiary/trustee's creditors. Because the UTC is supplemented by the common law (see UTC § 106), this Restatement rule might also apply in states enacting the UTC. The drafting committee has concluded that adoption of the Restatement rule would unduly disrupt standard estate planning and should be limited. Consequently, § 504 is amended to provide that the provisions of this section, which generally prohibit a creditor of a beneficiary from reaching a beneficiary's discretionary interest, apply even if the beneficiary is also a trustee or cotrustee. The beneficiary-trustee is protected from creditor claims to the extent the beneficiary-trustee's discretion is protected by an ascertainable standard as defined in the relevant Internal Revenue Code sections. The result is that the beneficiary's trustee's interest is protected to the extent it is also exempt from federal estate tax. The amendment thereby achieves its main purpose, which is to protect the trustee-beneficiary of a bypass trust from creditor claims.

The protection conferred by this subsection, however, is no greater than if the beneficiary had not been named trustee. If an exception creditor can reach the beneficiary's interest under some other provision, the interest is not insulated from creditor claims by the fact the beneficiary is or becomes a trustee.

In addition, the definition of "power of withdrawal" in § 103 is amended to clarify that a power of withdrawal does not include a power exercisable by the trustee that is limited by an ascertainable standard. The purpose of this amendment is to preclude a claim that the power of a trustee-beneficiary to make discretionary distributions for the trustee-beneficiary's own benefit results in an enforceable claim of the trustee-beneficiary's creditors to reach the trustee-beneficiary's interest as provided in § 505(b). Similar to the amendment to § 504, the amendment to "power of withdrawal" is being made because of concerns that Restatement (Third) of Trusts § 60, comment g, otherwise might allow a beneficiary-trustee's creditors to reach the trustee's beneficial interest.

The Code does not specifically address the extent to which a creditor of a trustee/beneficiary may reach a beneficial interest of a beneficiary/trustee that is not limited by an ascertainable standard.

For the definition of "ascertainable standard," see § 103(2).

Restatement (Third) of Trusts (2003)

§ 60. Transfer Or Attachment Of Discretionary Interests. Subject to the rules stated in §§ 58 and 59 (on spendthrift trusts), if the terms of a trust provide for a beneficiary to receive distributions in the trustee's discretion, a transferee or creditor of the beneficiary is entitled to receive or attach any distributions the trustee makes or is required to make in the exercise of that discretion after the trustee has knowledge of the transfer or attachment. The amounts a creditor can reach may be limited to provide for the beneficiary's needs (Comment c), or the amounts may be increased where the beneficiary either is the settlor (Comment f) or holds the discretionary power to determine his or her own distributions (Comment g).

Restatement (Second) of Trusts (1959)

§ 154. Trusts For Support. Except as stated in §§ 156 ["Where the Settlor Is a Beneficiary"] and 157 ["Particular Classes of Claimants"], if by the terms of a trust it is provided that the trustee shall pay or apply only so much of the income and principal or either as is necessary for the education or support of the beneficiary, the beneficiary cannot transfer his interest and his creditors cannot reach it.

§ 155. Discretionary Trusts.

(1) Except as stated in § 156 ["Where the Settlor Is a Beneficiary"], if by the terms of a trust it is provided that the trustee shall pay to or apply for a beneficiary only so much of the income and principal or either as the trustee in his uncontrolled discretion shall see fit to pay or apply, a transferee or creditor of the beneficiary cannot compel the trustee to pay any part of the income or principal.

(2) Unless a valid restraint on alienation has been imposed in accordance with the rules stated in §§ 152 and 153, if the trustee pays to or applies for the beneficiary any part of the income or principal with knowledge of the transfer or after he has been served with process in a proceeding by a creditor to reach it, he is liable to such transferee or creditor.

§ 505. Creditor's Claim Against Settlor.

(a) Whether or not the terms of a trust contain a spendthrift provision, the following rules apply:

(1) During the lifetime of the settlor, the property of a revocable trust is subject to claims of the settlor's creditors.

(2) With respect to an irrevocable trust, a creditor or assignee of the settlor may reach the maximum amount that can be distributed to or for the settlor's benefit. If a trust has more than one settlor, the amount the creditor or assignee of a particular settlor may reach may not exceed the settlor's interest in the portion of the trust attributable to that settlor's contribution.

(3) After the death of a settlor, and subject to the settlor's right to direct the source from which liabilities will be paid, the property of a trust that was revocable at the settlor's death is subject to claims of the settlor's creditors, costs of administration of the settlor's estate, the expenses of the settlor's funeral and disposal of remains, and [statutory allowances] to a surviving spouse and children to the extent the settlor's probate estate is inadequate to satisfy those claims, costs, expenses, and [allowances].

(b) For purposes of this section:

(1) during the period the power may be exercised, the holder of a power of withdrawal is treated in the same manner as the settlor of a revocable trust to the extent of the property subject to the power; and

(2) upon the lapse, release, or waiver of the power, the holder is treated as the settlor of the trust only to the extent the value of the property affected by the lapse, release, or waiver exceeds the greater of the amount specified in Section 2041(b)(2) or 2514(e) of the Internal Revenue Code of 1986, or Section 2503(b) of the Internal Revenue Code of 1986, in each case as in effect on [the effective date of this [Code]] [, or as later amended].

Comment

Subsection (a)(1) states what is now a well accepted conclusion, that a revocable trust is subject to the claims of the settlor's creditors while the settlor is living. *See* Restatement (Third) of Trusts § 25 cmt. e (Tentative Draft No. 1, approved 1996). Such claims were not allowed at common law, however. *See* Restatement (Second) of Trusts § 330 cmt. o (1959). Because a settlor usually also retains a beneficial interest that a creditor may reach under subsection (a)(2), the common law rule, were it retained in this Code, would be of little significance. *See* Restatement (Second) of Trusts § 156(2) (1959).

Subsection (a)(2), which is based on Restatement (Third) of Trusts § 58(2) & cmt. e (Tentative Draft No. 2, approved 1999), and Restatement (Second) of Trusts § 156 (1959), follows traditional doctrine in providing that a settlor who is also a beneficiary may not use the trust as a shield against the settlor's creditors. The drafters of the Uniform Trust Code concluded that traditional doctrine reflects sound policy. Consequently, the drafters rejected the approach taken in states like Alaska and Delaware, both of which allow a settlor to retain a beneficial interest immune from creditor claims. *See* Henry J.

Lischer, Jr., *Domestic Asset Protection Trusts: Pallbearers to Liability*, 35 Real Prop. Prob. & Tr. J. 479 (2000); John E. Sullivan, III, *Gutting the Rule Against Self-Settled Trusts: How the Delaware Trust Law Competes with Offshore Trusts*, 23 Del. J. Corp. L. 423 (1998). Under the Code, whether the trust contains a spendthrift provision or not, a creditor of the settlor may reach the maximum amount that the trustee could have paid to the settlors-beneficiary. If the trustee has discretion to distribute the entire income and principal to the settlors, the effect of this subsection is to place the settlor's creditors in the same position as if the trust had not been created. For the definition of "settlor," see § 103(14).

This section does not address possible rights against a settlor who was insolvent at the time of the trust's creation or was rendered insolvent by the transfer of property to the trust. This subject is instead left to the state's law on fraudulent transfers. A transfer to the trust by an insolvent settlor might also constitute a voidable preference under federal bankruptcy law.

Subsection (a)(3) recognizes that a revocable trust is usually employed as a will substitute. As such, the trust assets, following the death of the settlor, should be subject to the settlor's debts and other charges. However, in accordance with traditional doctrine, the assets of the settlor's probate estate must normally first be exhausted before the assets of the revocable trust can be reached. This section does not attempt to address the procedural issues raised by the need first to exhaust the decedent's probate estate before reaching the assets of the revocable trust. Nor does this section address the priority of creditor claims or liability of the decedent's other nonprobate assets for the decedent's debts and other charges. Subsection (a)(3), however, does ratify the typical pourover will, revocable trust plan. As long as the rights of the creditor or family member claiming a statutory allowance are not impaired, the settlor is free to shift liability from the probate estate to the revocable trust. Regarding other issues associated with potential liability of nonprobate assets for unpaid claims, see § 6-102 of the Uniform Probate Code, which was added to that Code in 1998.

Subsection (b)(1) treats a power of withdrawal as the equivalent of a power of revocation because the two powers are functionally identical. This is also the approach taken in Restatement (Third) of Trusts § 56 cmt. b (Tentative Draft No. 2, approved 1999). If the power is unlimited, the property subject to the power will be fully subject to the claims of the power holder's creditors, the same as the power holder's other assets. If the power holder retains the power until death, the property subject to the power may be liable for claims and statutory allowances to the extent the power holder's probate estate is insufficient to satisfy those claims and allowances. For powers

limited either in time or amount, such as a right to withdraw a $10,000 annual exclusion contribution within 30 days, this subsection would limit the creditor to the $10,000 contribution and require the creditor to take action prior to the expiration of the 30-day period.

Upon the lapse, release, or waiver of a power of withdrawal, the property formerly subject to the power will normally be subject to the claims of the power holder's creditors and assignees the same as if the power holder were the settlor of a now irrevocable trust. Pursuant to subsection (a)(2), a creditor or assignee of the power holder generally may reach the power holder's entire beneficial interest in the trust, whether or not distribution is subject to the trustee's discretion. However, following the lead of Arizona Revised Statutes § 14-7705(g) and Texas Property Code § 112.035(e), subsection (b)(2) creates an exception for trust property which was subject to a Crummey or five and five power. Upon the lapse, release, or waiver of a power of withdrawal, the holder is treated as the settlor of the trust only to the extent the value of the property subject to the power at the time of the lapse, release, or waiver exceeded the greater of the amounts specified in IRC §§ 2041(b)(2) or 2514(e) [greater of 5% or $5,000], or IRC § 2503(b) [$10,000 in 2001].

The Uniform Trust Code does not address creditor issues with respect to property subject to a special power of appointment or a testamentary general power of appointment. For creditor rights against such interests, see Restatement (Property) Second: Donative Transfers §§ 13.1-13.7 (1986).

§ 506. Overdue Distribution.

(a) In this section, "mandatory distribution" means a distribution of income or principal which the trustee is required to make to a beneficiary under the terms of the trust, including a distribution upon termination of the trust. The term does not include a distribution subject to the exercise of the trustee's discretion even if (1) the discretion is expressed in the form of a standard of distribution, or (2) the terms of the trust authorizing a distribution couple language of discretion with language of direction.

(b) Whether or not a trust contains a spendthrift provision, a creditor or assignee of a beneficiary may reach a mandatory distribution of income or principal, including a distribution upon termination of the trust, if the trustee has not made the distribution to the beneficiary within a reasonable time after the designated distribution date.

Comment

The effect of a spendthrift provision is generally to insulate totally a beneficiary's interest until a

distribution is made and received by the beneficiary. *See* § 502. But this section, along with several other sections in this article, recognizes exceptions to this general rule. Whether a trust contains a spendthrift provision or not, a trustee should not be able to avoid creditor claims against a beneficiary by refusing to make a distribution required to be made by the express terms of the trust. On the other hand, a spendthrift provision would become largely a nullity were a beneficiary's creditors able to attach all required payments as soon as they became due. This section reflects a compromise between these two competing principles. A creditor can reach a mandatory distribution, including a distribution upon termination, if the trustee has failed to make the payment within a reasonable time after the designated distribution date. Following this reasonable period, payments mandated by the express terms of the trust are in effect being held by the trustee as agent for the beneficiary and should be treated as part of the beneficiary's personal assets.

This section is similar to Restatement (Third) of Trusts § 58 cmt. d (Tent. Draft No. 2, approved1999).

2001 Amendment. By amendment in 2001, "designated distribution date" was substituted for "required distribution date" in subsection (b). The amendment conforms the language of this section to terminology used elsewhere in the Code.

2005 Amendment. The amendment adds a clarifying definition of "mandatory distribution" in subsection (a), which is based on an Ohio proposal.

The amendment:

tracks the traditional understanding that a mandatory distribution includes a provision requiring that a beneficiary be paid the income of a trust or receive principal upon termination;

correlates the definition of "mandatory distribution" in this section to the broad definition of discretionary trust used in § 504. Under both §§ 504 and 506, a trust is discretionary even if the discretion is expressed in the form of a standard, such as a provision directing a trustee to pay for a beneficiary's support;

addresses the situation where the terms of the trust couple language of discretion with language of direction. An example of such a provision is "my trustees shall, in their absolute discretion, distribute such amounts as are necessary for the beneficiary's support." Despite the presence of the imperative "shall," the provision is discretionary, not mandatory. For a more elaborate example of such a discretionary "shall" provision, see Marsman. Nasca, 573 N.E.2d 1025 (Mass. Ct. App. 1991);

is clarifying. No change of substance is intended by this amendment. Ths amendment merely clarifies that a mandatory distribution is to be understood in its traditional sense such as a provision requiring that the beneficiary receive an income or receive principal upon termination of the trust.

§ 507. Personal Obligations of Trustee.
Trust property is not subject to personal obligations of the trustee, even if the trustee becomes insolvent or bankrupt.

Comment

Because the beneficiaries of the trust hold the beneficial interest in the trust property and the trustee holds only legal title without the benefits of ownership, the creditors of the trustee have only a personal claim against the trustee. *See* Restatement (Third) § 5 cmt. k (Tentative Draft No.1, approved 1996); Restatement (Second) of Trusts § 12 cmt. a (1959). Similarly, a personal creditor of the trustee who attaches trust property to satisfy the debt does not acquire title as a bona fide purchaser even if the creditor is unaware of the trust. *See* Restatement (Second) of Trusts § 308 (1959). The protection afforded by this section is consistent with that provided by the Bankruptcy Code. Property in which the trustee holds legal title as trustee is not part of the trustee's bankruptcy estate. 11 U.S.C. § 541(d).

The exemption of the trust property from the personal obligations of the trustee is the most significant feature of Anglo-American trust law by comparison with the devices available in civil law countries. A principal objective of the Hague Convention on the Law Applicable to Trusts and on their Recognition is to protect the Anglo-American trust with respect to transactions in civil law countries. *See* Hague Convention art. 11. *See also* Henry Hansmann & Ugo Mattei, *The Functions of Trust Law: A Comparative Legal and Economic Analysis*, 73 N.Y.U. L. Rev. 434 (1998); John H. Langbein, *The Secret Life of the Trust: The Trust as an Instrument of Commerce*, 107 Yale L.J. 165, 179-80 (1997).

ARTICLE 6
REVOCABLE TRUSTS

General Comment

This article deals with issues of significance not totally settled under prior law. Because of the widespread use in recent years of the revocable trust as an alternative to a will, this short article is one of the more important articles of the Code. This article and the other articles of the Code treat the revocable trust as the functional equivalent of a will. Section 601 provides that the capacity standard for wills applies in determining whether the settlor had capacity to create a revocable trust. Section 602, after providing that a trust is presumed revocable unless stated otherwise, prescribes the procedure for revocation or amendment, whether the trust contains one or several settlors. Section 603 provides that while a trust is revocable and the settlor has capacity, the rights of the beneficiaries are subject to the settlor's control. Section 604 prescribes a statute of limitations on contest of revocable trusts.

Sections 601 and 604, because they address requirements relating to creation and contest of trusts, are not subject to alteration or restriction in the terms of the trust. *See* § 105. §§ 602 and 603, by contrast, are not so limited and are fully subject to the settlor's control.

§ 601. Capacity of Settlor of Revocable Trust. The capacity required to create, amend, revoke, or add property to a revocable trust, or to direct the actions of the trustee of a revocable trust, is the same as that required to make a will.

Comment

This section is patterned after Restatement (Third) of Trusts § 11(1) (Tentative Draft No. 1, approved 1996). The revocable trust is used primarily as a will substitute, with its key provision being the determination of the persons to receive the trust property upon the settlor's death. To solidify the use of the revocable trust as a device for transferring property at death, the settlor usually also executes a pourover will. The use of a pourover will assures that property not transferred to the trust during life will be combined with the property the settlors did manage to convey. Given this primary use of the revocable trust as a device for disposing of property at death, the capacity standard for wills rather than that for lifetime gifts should apply. The application of the capacity standard for wills does not mean that the revocable trust must be executed with the formalities of a will. There are no execution requirements under this Code for a trust not created by will, and a trust not containing real property may be created by an oral statement. *See* § 407 and comment.

The Uniform Trust Code does not explicitly spell out the standard of capacity necessary to create other types of trusts, although § 402 does require that the settlor have capacity. This section includes a capacity standard for creation of a revocable trust because of the uncertainty in the case law and the importance of the issue in modern estate planning. No such uncertainty exists with respect to the capacity standard for other types of trusts. To create a testamentary trust, the settlor must have the capacity to make a will. To create an irrevocable trust, the settlor must have the capacity that would be needed to transfer the property free of trust. *See generally* Restatement (Third) of Trusts § 11 (Tentative Draft No. 1, approved 1996); Restatement (Third) of Property: Wills and Other Donative Transfers § 8.1 (Tentative Draft No. 3, approved 2001).

§ 602. Revocation or Amendment of Revocable Trust.

(a) Unless the terms of a trust expressly provide that the trust is irrevocable, the settlor may revoke or amend the trust. This subsection does not apply to a trust created under an instrument executed before [the effective date of this [Code]].

(b) If a revocable trust is created or funded by more than one settlor:

    (1) to the extent the trust consists of community property, the trust may be revoked by either spouse acting alone but may be amended only by joint action of both spouses;

(2) to the extent the trust consists of property other than community property, each settlor may revoke or amend the trust with regard the portion of the trust property attributable to that settlor's contribution; and

(3) upon the revocation or amendment of the trust by fewer than all of the settlors, the trustee shall promptly notify the other settlors of the revocation or amendment.

(c) The settlor may revoke or amend a revocable trust:

(1) by substantial compliance with a method provided in the terms of the trust; or

(2) if the terms of the trust do not provide a method or the method provided in the terms is not expressly made exclusive, by:

(A) a later will or codicil that expressly refers to the trust or specifically devises property that would otherwise have passed according to the terms of the trust; or

(B) any other method manifesting clear and convincing evidence of the settlor's intent.

(d) Upon revocation of a revocable trust, the trustee shall deliver the trust property as the settlor directs.

(e) A settlor's powers with respect to revocation, amendment, or distribution of trust property may be exercised by an agent under a power of attorney only to the extent expressly authorized by the terms of the trust or the power.

(f) A [conservator] of the settlor or, if no [conservator] has been appointed, a [guardian] of the settlor may exercise a settlor's powers with respect to revocation, amendment, or distribution of trust property only with the approval of the court supervising the [conservatorship] or [guardianship].

(g) A trustee who does not know that a trust has been revoked or amended is not liable to the settlor or settlor's successors in interest for distributions made and other actions taken on the assumption that the trust had not been amended or revoked.

Comment

Subsection (a), which provides that a settlor may revoke or modify a trust unless the terms of the trust expressly state that the trust is irrevocable, changes the common law. Most states follow the rule that a trust is presumed irrevocable absent evidence of contrary intent. *See* Restatement (Second) of Trusts § 330 (1959). California, Iowa, Montana, Oklahoma, and Texas presume that a trust is revocable. The Uniform Trust Code endorses this minority approach, but only for trusts created after its effective date. This Code presumes revocability when the instrument is silent because the instrument was likely drafted by a nonprofessional, who intended the trust as a will substitute. The most recent revision of the Restatement of Trusts similarly reverses the former approach. A trust is presumed revocable if the settlor has retained a beneficial interest. *See* Restatement (Third) of Trusts § 63 cmt. c (Tentative Draft No. 3, approved 2001). Because professional drafters habitually spell out whether or not a trust is revocable, subsection (a) will have limited application.

A power of revocation includes the power to amend. An unrestricted power to amend may also include the power to revoke a trust. *See* Restatement (Third) of Trusts § 63 cmt. g (Tentative Draft No. 3, approved 2001); Restatement (Second) of Trusts § 331 cmt. g & h (1959).

Subsection (b), which is similar to Restatement (Third) of Trusts § 63 cmt. k (Tentative Draft No. 3, approved 2001), provides default rules for revocation or amendment of a trust having several settlors. The settlor's authority to revoke or modify the trust depends on whether the trust contains community property. To the extent the trust contains community property, the trust may be revoked by either spouse acting alone but may be amended only by joint action of both spouses. The purpose of this provision, and the reason for the use of joint trusts in community property states, is to preserve the community character of property transferred to the trust. While community property does not prevail in a majority of states, contributions of community property to trusts created in noncommunity property states does occur. This is due to the mobility of settlors, and the fact that community property retains its community character when a couple move from a community to a noncommunity state. For this reason, subsection (b), and its provision on contributions of community property, should be enacted in all states, whether community or noncommunity.

With respect to separate property contributed to the trust, or all property of the trust if none of the trust property consists of community property, subsection (b) provides that each settlor may revoke or amend the trust as to the portion of the trust contributed by that settlor. The inclusion of a rule for contributions of separate property does not mean that the drafters of this Code concluded that the use of joint trusts should be encouraged. The rule is included because of the widespread use of joint trusts in noncommunity property states in recent years. Due to the desire to preserve the community character of trust property, joint trusts are a necessity in community property states. Unless community property will be contributed to the trust, no similarly important reason exists for the creation of a joint trust in a noncommunity property state. Joint trusts are often poorly drafted, confusing the dispositive provisions of the respective settlors. Their use can also lead to unintended tax consequences. *See* Melinda S. Merk, *Joint Revocable Trusts for Married Couples Domiciled in Common-Law Property States*, 32 Real Prop. Prob. & Tr. J. 345 (1997).

Subsection (b) does not address the many technical issues that can arise in determining the settlors' proportionate contribution to a joint trust. Most problematic are contributions of jointly-owned property. In the case of joint tenancies in real estate, each spouse would presumably be treated as having made an equal contribution because of the right to sever the interest and convert it into a tenancy in common. This is in contrast to joint accounts in financial institutions, ownership of which in most states is based not on fractional interest but on actual dollar contribution. *See, e.g.,* Unif. Probate Code § 6-211. Most difficult may be determining a contribution rule for entireties property. In *Holdener v. Fieser*, 971 S.W. 2d 946 (Mo. Ct. App. 1998), the court held that a surviving spouse could revoke the trust with respect to the entire interest but did not express a view as to revocation rights while both spouses were living

Subsection (b)(3) requires that the other settlor or settlors be notified if a joint trust is revoked by less than all of the settlors. Notifying the other settlor or settlors of the revocation or amendment will place them in a better position to protect their interests. If the revocation or amendment by less than all of the settlors breaches an implied agreement not to revoke

or amend the trust, those harmed by the action can sue for breach of contract. If the trustee fails to notify the other settlor or settlors of the revocation or amendment, the parties aggrieved by the trustee's failure can sue the trustee for breach of trust.

Subsection (c), which is similar to Restatement (Third) of Trusts § 63 cmt. h & i (Tentative Draft No. 3, approved 2001), specifies the method of revocation and amendment. Revocation of a trust differs fundamentally from revocation of a will. Revocation of a will, because a will is not effective until death, cannot affect an existing fiduciary relationship. With a trust, however, because a revocation will terminate an already existing fiduciary relationship, there is a need to protect a trustee who might act without knowledge that the trust has been revoked. There is also a need to protect trustees against the risk that they will misperceive the settlor's intent and mistakenly assume that an informal document or communication constitutes a revocation when that was not in fact the settlor's intent. To protect trustees against these risks, drafters habitually insert provisions providing that a revocable trust may be revoked only by delivery to the trustee of a formal revoking document. Some courts require strict compliance with the stated formalities. Other courts, recognizing that the formalities were inserted primarily for the trustee's and not the settlor's benefit, will accept other methods of revocation as long as the settlor's intent is clear. *See* Restatement (Third) of Trusts § 63 Reporter's Notes to cmt. h-j (Tentative Draft No. 3, approved 2001).

This Code tries to effectuate the settlor's intent to the maximum extent possible while at the same time protecting a trustee against inadvertent liability. While notice to the trustee of a revocation is good practice, this section does not make the giving of such notice a prerequisite to a trust's revocation. To protect a trustee who has not been notified of a revocation or amendment, subsection (g) provides that a trustee who does not know that a trust has been revoked or amended is not liable to the settlor or settlor's successors in interest for distributions made and other actions taken on the assumption that the trust, as unamended, was still in effect. However, to honor the settlor's intent, subsection (c) generally honors a settlor's clear expression of intent even if inconsistent with stated formalities in the terms of the trust.

Under subsection (c), the settlor may revoke or amend a revocable trust by substantial compliance with the method specified in the terms of the trust or by a later will or codicil or any other method manifesting clear and convincing evidence of the settlor's intent. Only if the method specified in the terms of the trust is made exclusive is use of the other methods prohibited. Even then, a failure to comply with a technical requirement, such as required notarization, may be excused as long as compliance with the method specified in the terms of the trust is otherwise substantial.

While revocation of a trust will ordinarily continue to be accomplished by signing and delivering a written document to the trustee, other methods, such as a physical act or an oral statement coupled with a withdrawal of the property, might also demonstrate the necessary intent. These less formal methods, because they provide less reliable indicia of intent, will often be insufficient, however. The method specified in the terms of the trust is a reliable safe harbor and should be followed whenever possible.

Revocation or amendment by will is mentioned in subsection (c) not to encourage the practice but to make clear that it is not precluded by omission. *See* Restatement (Third) of Property: Will and Other Donative Transfers § 7.2 cmt. e (Tentative Draft No. 3, approved 2001), which validates revocation or amendment of will substitutes by later will. Situations do arise, particularly in death-bed cases, where revocation by will may be the only practicable method. In such cases, a will, a solemn document executed with a high level of formality, may be the most reliable method for expressing intent. A revocation in a will ordinarily becomes effective only upon probate of the will following the testator's death. For the cases, see Restatement (Third) of Trusts § 63 Reporter's Notes to cmt. h-i (Tentative Draft No. 3, approved 2001).

A residuary clause in a will disposing of the estate differently than the trust is alone insufficient to revoke or amend a trust. The provision in the will must either be express or the will must dispose of specific assets contrary to the terms of the trust. The substantial body of law on revocation of Totten trusts by will offers helpful guidance. The authority is collected in William H. Danne, Jr., *Revocation of Tentative ("Totten") Trust of Savings Bank Account by Inter Vivos Declaration or Will*, 46 A.L.R. 3d 487 (1972).

Subsection (c) does not require that a trustee concur in the revocation or amendment of a trust. Such a concurrence would be necessary only if required by the terms of the trust. If the trustee concludes that an amendment unacceptably changes

the trustee's duties, the trustee may resign as provided in § 705.

Subsection (d), providing that upon revocation the trust property is to be distributed as the settlor directs, codifies a provision commonly included in revocable trust instruments.

A settlor's power to revoke is not terminated by the settlor's incapacity. The power to revoke may instead be exercised by an agent under a power of attorney as authorized in subsection (e), by a conservator or guardian as authorized in subsection (f), or by the settlor personally if the settlor regains capacity.

Subsection (e), which is similar to Restatement (Third) of Trusts § 63 cmt. l (Tentative Draft No. 3, approved 2001), authorizes an agent under a power of attorney to revoke or modify a revocable trust only to the extent the terms of the trust or power of attorney expressly so permit. An express provision is required because most settlors usually intend that the revocable trust, and not the power of attorney, to function as the settlor's principal property management device. The power of attorney is usually intended as a backup for assets not transferred to the revocable trust or to address specific topics, such as the power to sign tax returns or apply for government benefits, which may be beyond the authority of a trustee or are not customarily granted to a trustee.

Subsection (f) addresses the authority of a conservator or guardian to revoke or amend a revocable trust. Under the Uniform Trust Code, a "conservator" is appointed by the court to manage the ward's party, a "guardian" to make decisions with respect to the ward's personal affairs. *See* § 103. Consequently, subsection (f) authorizes a guardian to exercise a settlor's power to revoke or amend a trust only if a conservator has not been appointed.

Many state conservatorship statutes authorize a conservator to exercise the settlor's power of revocation with the prior approval of the court supervising the conservatorship. *See, e.g.,* Unif. Probate Code § 411(a)(4). Subsection (f) ratifies this practice. Under the Code, a conservator may exercise a settlor's power of revocation, amendment, or right to withdraw trust property upon approval of the court supervising the conservatorship. Because a settlor often creates a revocable trust for the very purpose of avoiding conservatorship, this power should be exercised by the court reluctantly. Settlors concerned about revocation by a conservator may wish to deny a conservator a power to revoke. However, while such a provision in the terms of the trust is entitled to considerable weight, the court may override the restriction if it concludes that the action is necessary in the interests of justice. See § 105(b)(13).

Steps a conservator can take to stem possible abuse is not limited to petitioning to revoke the trust. The conservator could petition for removal of the trustee under § 706. The conservator, acting on the settlor-beneficiary's behalf, could also bring an action to enforce the trust according to its terms. Pursuant to § 303, a conservator may act on behalf of the beneficiary whose estate the conservator controls whenever a consent or other action by the beneficiary is required or may be given under the Code.

If a conservator has not been appointed, subsection (f) authorizes a guardian to exercise a settlor's power to revoke or amend the trust upon approval of the court supervising the guardianship. The court supervising the guardianship will need to determine whether it can grant a guardian authority to revoke a revocable trust under local law or whether it will be necessary to appoint a conservator for that purpose.

2001 Amendment. By amendment in 2001, revocation by "executing a later will or codicil" in subsection (c)(2)(A) was changed to revocation by a "later will or codicil" to avoid an implication that the trust is revoked immediately upon execution of the will or codicil and not at the testator's death.

Restatement (Third) of Trusts (2003)

§ 63, *Comment c. Presumptions regarding revocability.* Where the settlor has failed expressly to provide whether a trust is subject to revocation or amendment, if the settlor has retained no interest in the trust ..., it is rebuttably presumed that the settlor has no power to revoke or amend the trust. If, however, the settlor has failed expressly to provide whether the trust is revocable or amendable but has retained an interest in the trust (other than by resulting trust), the presumption is that the trust is revocable and amendable by the settlor.

Restatement (Third) of Property: Wills and Other Donative Transfers (2003)

§ 7.2, *Comment e. Revocation or amendment of a will substitute by later will.* A revocable trust may be revoked or amended by a later will. See Restatement Third, Trusts § 63, Comment *h*; Uniform Trust Code § 602(c). At least one state has by statute authorized the revocation by a later will of will substitutes except real property joint tenancies, life insurance, retirement plans, and a few other will substitutes. A few judicial decisions have upheld the effort to revoke certain will substitutes by a later will. See Reporter's Note. It is generally agreed that Totten trusts may be revoked by will (see Restatement Third, Trusts § 26, Comment *c*), but under the Revised UPC POD accounts, including Totten trusts, cannot be changed by will (see Revised UPC § 6-213(b)).

Insurance contracts, multiple party accounts, pension accounts, and other will substitutes commonly require the account owner to follow a particular procedure for altering or amending the beneficiary designation, such as completing a form supplied by the financial intermediary or other payor. Such a term governs as a matter of the contract between the account owner and the financial intermediary or payor. It sometimes happens that the account owner misunderstands this requirement and attempts to revoke the beneficiary designation by will. The courts are divided about whether to enforce the account term, thereby defeating the account owner's later contrary expression of donative intent.

In such cases, when the financial intermediary or other payor has paid the beneficiary of record on the account in good faith before learning of the later inconsistent designation in the will, the account term is effective to protect the financial intermediary or payor from liability to the beneficiary designated in the will. In such circumstances, that intended beneficiary is remitted to an action in restitution against the account-designated beneficiary who received the payment. See Restatement of Restitution § 126.

When the financial intermediary or payor receives notice of the inconsistent beneficiary designation contained in the subsequent will before paying the beneficiary of record on the account, the financial intermediary or payor should pay the proceeds as directed under the will notwithstanding the failure of the account owner to comply with the account term specifying account-specific procedures for revocation or alteration. If the financial intermediary or payor is uncertain about the priority or effectiveness of the attempted revocation or alteration by will, the financial intermediary or payor may discharge its responsibilities by interpleading and/or paying the proceeds into court.

When a designation by will supersedes a designation contained in the instrument of account, the proceeds remain separate from probate property and pass in accordance with the provisions of the nonprobate account, unless the language of the later will expresses an intent that the account proceeds are to become part of the probate estate.

The principles set forth in this comment also apply to circumstances in which the account owner attempts to modify the beneficiary designation by a subsequent instrument other than a validly executed will. Because such an instrument does not comply with the formalities required for a will to assure that the document represents the owner's donative intent (see § 3.1), the proponent of such an instrument bears the burden of proving by clear and convincing evidence that the instrument reflects the account owner's donative intent. See § 3.3; see also § 7.2, Comment d.

The party alleging revocation bears the burden of proving that an asserted revocation actually referred to the will substitute in question. Thus, a mere residuary clause in a later will or a comparable provision in a later revocable inter vivos trust does not revoke an earlier beneficiary designation in a will substitute.

§ 603. Settlor's Powers; Powers of Withdrawal.

(a) To the extent a trust is revocable by a settlor, a trustee may follow a direction of the settlor that is contrary to the terms of the trust. To the extent a trust is revocable by a settlor in conjunction with a person other than a trustee or person holding an adverse interest, the trustee may follow a direction from the settlor and the other person holding the power to revoke even if the direction is contrary to the terms of the trust.

(b) To the extent a trust is revocable [and the settlor has capacity to revoke the trust], rights of the beneficiaries are subject to the control of, and the duties of the trustee are owed exclusively to, the settlor.

(c) During the period the power may be exercised, the holder of a power of withdrawal has the rights of a settlor of a revocable trust under this section to the extent of the property subject to the power.

Comment

This section recognizes that the settlor of a revocable trust is in control of the trust and should have the right to enforce the trust.

Pursuant to this section, the duty under § 813 to inform and report to beneficiaries is owed to the settlor of a revocable trust as long as the settlor has capacity. In the case of a trust having several settlors, subsection (c) clarifies that this duty extends to all settlors having capacity. Should fewer than all settlors revoke or modify their portion of the trust, the trustee must notify the other settlor or settlors of the action. *See* § 602 Comment.

If the settlor loses capacity, subsection (b) no longer applies, with the consequence that the rights of the beneficiaries are no longer subject to the settlor's control. The beneficiaries are entitled to request information concerning the trust and the trustee must provide the beneficiaries with annual trustee reports and whatever other information may be required under § 813. However, because this section may be freely overridden in the terms of the trust, a settlor is free to deny the beneficiaries these rights, even to the point of directing the trustee not to inform them of the existence of the trust. Also, should an incapacitated settlor later regain capacity, the beneficiaries' rights will again be subject to the settlor's control.

Typically, the settlor of a revocable trust will also be the sole or primary beneficiary of the trust, and the settlor has control over whether to take action against a trustee for breach of trust. Upon the settlor's incapacity, any right of action the settlor-trustee may have against the trustee for breach of trust occurring while the settlor had capacity will pass to the settlor's agent or conservator, who would succeed to the settlor's right to have property restored to the trust. Following the death or incapacity of the settlor, the beneficiaries would have a right to maintain an action against a trustee for breach of trust. However, with respect to actions occurring prior to the settlor's death or incapacity, an action by the beneficiaries could be barred by the settlor's consent or by other events such as approval of the action by a successor trustee. For the requirements of a consent, see § 1009.

Subsection (c) makes clear that a holder of a power

of withdrawal has the same powers over the trust as the settlor of a revocable trust. Equal treatment is warranted due to the holder's equivalent power to control the trust. For the definition of power of withdrawal, see § 103(11).

2001 Amendment. By a 2001 amendment, former subsection (b) was deleted. Former subsection (b) provided: "While a trust is revocable and the settlor does not have capacity to revoke the trust, rights of the beneficiaries are held by the beneficiaries." No substantive change was intended by this amendment. Former subsection (b) was superfluous. Rights of the beneficiaries are always held by the beneficiaries unless taken away by some other provision. Current subsection (b) grants these rights to the settlor of a revocable trust while the settlor has capacity. Upon a settlor's loss of capacity, these rights are held by the beneficiaries with or without former subsection (b).

2003 Amendment. The purpose of former subsection (b), which was deleted in 2003, was to make certain that upon revocation of amendment of a joint trust by fewer than all of its settlors, that the trustee would notify the nonparticipating settlor or settlors. The subsection, which provided that "If a revocable trust has more than one settlor, the duties of the trustee are owed to all of the settlors having capacity to revoke the trust," imposed additional duties upon a trustee and unnecessarily raised interpretative questions as to its scope. The drafter's original intent is restored, and in a much clearer form, by repealing former subsection (b), and by amending § 602 to add a subsection (b)(3) that states explicitly what former subsection (b) was trying to achieve.

2004 Amendment. The amendment places in brackets and makes optional the language in subsection (b) dealing with the settlor's capacity.

Section 603 generally provides that while a trust is revocable, all rights that the trusts's beneficiaries would otherwise possess are subject to the control of the settlor. This section, however, negates the settlor's control if the settlor is incapacitated. In such case, the beneficiaries are entitled to assert all rights provided to them under the Code, including the right to information concerning the trust.

Two issues have arisen concerning this incapacity limitation. First, because determining when a settlor is incapacitated is not always clear, concern has been expressed that it will often be difficult in a particular case to determine whether the settlor has become incapacitated and the settlor's control of the beneficiary's rights have ceased. Second, concern has

been expressed that this section prescribes a different rule for revocable trusts than for wills and that the rules for both should instead be the same. In the case of a will, the devisees have no right to know of the dispositions made in their favor until the testator's death, whether or not the testator is incapacitated. Under § 603, however, the remainder beneficiary's right to know commences on the settlor's incapacity.

Concluding that uniformity among the states on this issue is not essential, the drafting committee has decided to place the reference to the settlor's incapacity in § 603(b) in brackets. Enacting jurisdictions are free to strike the incapacity limitation or to provide a more precise definition of when a settlor is incapacitated, as has been done in the Missouri enactment (Mo. Stat. Ann. § 456.6-603). For further discussion, see David J. Feder & Robert H. Sitkoff, Revocable Trusts and Incapacity Planning: More than Just a Will Substitute, 24 Elder L. J. 1 (2016).

2018 Amendment. With the 2017 approval of the Uniform Directed Trust Act (UDTA), most of former Section 808 of the Uniform Trust Code, titled "Powers to Direct," was removed as superseded by the UDTA. However, former Section 808(a), which addresses directions from the settlor of a revocable trust to a trustee, was retained and relocated to Section 603 as a new subsection (a). With that change, former subsections (a) and (b) were redesignated as subsections (b) and (c), respectively. The comment to former Section 808(a) explained:

> Subsection (a) is an application of Section 603(a) [now redesignated (b)], which provides that a revocable trust is subject to the settlor's exclusive control as long as the settlor has capacity. Because of the settlor's degree of control, subsection (a) of this section authorizes a trustee to rely on a direction from the settlor even if it is contrary to the terms of the trust. The direction of the settlor might be regarded as an amendment of the trust. Subsection (a) has limited application upon a settlor's incapacity. An agent, conservator, or guardian has authority to give the trustee instructions contrary to the terms of the trust only if the agent, conservator, or guardian succeeds to the settlor's powers with respect to revocation, amendment, or distribution as provided in Section 602(e).

New Section 603(a) is consistent with the

definition of "revocable" in Section 103(14), which reads: "'Revocable,' as applied to a trust, means revocable by the settlor without the consent of the trustee or a person holding an adverse interest.' Under this definition, a trust is revocable if the settlor may revoke it without the consent of the trustee or person holding an adverse interest. The second sentence of new subsection (a) allows the trustee of such a trust to follow a direction of the settlor and other person holding a power to revoke even if contrary to the terms of the trust.

A further clarifying amendment to UTC Section 603 changed the phrase "While a trust is revocable..." in what had been subsection (a) and is now subsection (b) to "To the extent a trust is revocable...." No substantive change was intended. The revised language more clearly recognizes that a trust may be revocable in part and irrevocable in part or that a trust may have more than one settlor. In such a trust, a settlor's powers enumerated in this section apply only to the extent the trust is revocable by that settlor.

§ 604. Limitation on Action Contesting Validity of Revocable Trust; Distribution of Trust Property.

(a) A person may commence a judicial proceeding to contest the validity of a trust that was revocable at the settlor's death within the earlier of:

(1) [three] years after the settlor's death; or

(2) [120] days after the trustee sent the person a copy of the trust instrument and a notice informing the person of the trust's existence, of the trustee's name and address, and of the time allowed for commencing a proceeding.

(b) Upon the death of the settlor of a trust that was revocable at the settlor's death, the trustee may proceed to distribute the trust property in accordance with the terms of the trust. The trustee is not subject to liability for doing so unless:

(1) the trustee knows of a pending judicial proceeding contesting the validity of the trust; or

(2) a potential contestant has notified the trustee of a possible judicial proceeding to contest the trust and a judicial proceeding is commenced within 60 days after the contestant sent the notification.

(c) A beneficiary of a trust that is determined to have been invalid is liable to return any distribution received.

Comment

This section provides finality to the question of when a contest of a revocable trust may be brought. The section is designed to allow an adequate time in which to bring a contest while at the same time permitting the expeditious distribution of the trust property following the settlor's death.

A trust can be contested on a variety of grounds. For example, the contestant may allege that no trust was created due to lack of intent to create a trust or lack of capacity (*see* § 402), that undue influence, duress, or fraud was involved in the trust's creation (*see* § 406), or that the trust had been revoked or modified (*see* § 602). A "contest" is an action to invalidate all or part of the terms of the trust or of property transfers to the trustee. An action against a beneficiary or other person for intentional interference with an inheritance or gift, not being a

contest, is not subject to this section. For the law on intentional interference, see Restatement (Second) of Torts § 774B (1979). Nor does this section preclude an action to determine the validity of a trust that is brought during the settlor's lifetime, such as a petition for a declaratory judgment, if such action is authorized by other law. *See* § 106 (Uniform Trust Code supplemented by common law of trusts and principles of equity).

This section applies only to a revocable trust that becomes irrevocable by reason of the settlor's death. A trust that became irrevocable by reason of the settlor's lifetime release of the power to revoke is outside its scope. A revocable trust does not become irrevocable upon a settlor's loss of capacity. Pursuant to § 602, the power to revoke may be exercised by the settlor's agent, conservator, or guardian, or personally by the settlor if the settlor regains capacity.

Subsection (a) specifies a time limit on when a contest can be brought. A contest is barred upon the first to occur of two possible events. The maximum possible time for bringing a contest is three years from the settlor's death. This should provide potential contestants with ample time in which to determine whether they have an interest that will be affected by the trust, even if formal notice of the trust is lacking. The three-year period is derived from §§ 3-108 of the Uniform Probate Code. Three years is the maximum limit under the UPC for contesting a nonprobated will. Enacting jurisdictions prescribing shorter or longer time limits for contest of a nonprobated will should substitute their own time limit. To facilitate this process, the "three-year" period has been placed in brackets.

A trustee who wishes to shorten the contest period may do so by giving notice. Drawing from California Probate Code § 16061.7, subsection (a)(2) bars a contest by a potential contestant 120 days after the date the trustee sent that person a copy of the trust instrument and informed the person of the trust's existence, of the trustee's name and address, and of the time allowed for commencing a contest. The reference to "120" days is placed in brackets to suggest to the enacting jurisdiction that it substitute its statutory time period for contesting a will following notice of probate. The 120 day period in subsection (a)(2) is subordinate to the three-year bar in subsection (a)(1). A contest is automatically barred three years after the settlor's death even if notice is sent by the trustee less than 120 days prior to the end of that period.

Because only a small minority of trusts are actually contested, trustees should not be restrained from making distributions because of concern about possible liability should a contest later be filed.

Absent a protective statute, a trustee is ordinarily absolutely liable for misdelivery of the trust assets, even if the trustee reasonably believed that the distribution was proper. *See* Restatement (Second) of Trusts § 226 (1959). Subsection (b) addresses liability concerns by allowing the trustee, upon the settlor's death, to proceed expeditiously to distribute the trust property. The trustee may distribute the trust property in accordance with the terms of the trust until and unless the trustee receives notice of a pending judicial proceeding contesting the validity of the trust, or until notified by a potential contestant of a possible contest, followed by its filing within 60 days.

Even though a distribution in compliance with subsection (b) discharges the trustee from potential liability, subsection (c) makes the beneficiaries of what later turns out to have been an invalid trust liable to return any distribution received. Issues as to whether the distribution must be returned with interest, or with income earned or profit made are not addressed in this section but are left to the law of restitution.

For purposes of notices under this section, the substitute representation principles of Article 3 are applicable. The notice by the trustee under subsection (a)(2) or by a potential contestant under subsection (b)(2) must be given in a manner reasonably suitable under the circumstances and likely to result in its receipt. *See* § 109(a).

This section does not address possible liability for the debts of the deceased settlor or a trustee's possible liability to creditors for distributing trust assets. For possible liability of the trust, see § 505(a)(3) and Comment. Whether a trustee can be held personally liable for creditor claims following distribution of trust assets is addressed in Uniform Probate Code § 6-102, which was added to that Code in 1998.

ARTICLE 7
OFFICE OF TRUSTEE

General Comment

This article contains a series of default rules dealing with the office of trustee. Sections 701 and 702 address the process for getting a trustee into office, including the procedures for indicating an acceptance and whether bond will be required. Section 703 addresses cotrustees, permitting the cotrustees to act by majority action and specifying the extent to which one trustee may delegate to another. §§ 704 through 707 address changes in the office of trustee, specifying the circumstances when a vacancy must be filled, the procedure for resignation, the grounds for removal, and the process for appointing a successor. Sections 708 and 709 prescribe the standards for determining trustee compensation and reimbursement for expenses advanced.

Except for the court's authority to order bond, all of the provisions of this article are subject to modification in the terms of the trust. *See* § 105.

§ 701. Accepting or Declining Trusteeship.

(a) Except as otherwise provided in subsection (c), a person designated as trustee accepts the trusteeship:

(1) by substantially complying with a method of acceptance provided in the terms of the trust; or

(2) if the terms of the trust do not provide a method or the method provided in the terms is not expressly made exclusive, by accepting delivery of the trust property, exercising powers or performing duties as trustee, or otherwise indicating acceptance of the trusteeship.

(b) A person designated as trustee who has not yet accepted the trusteeship may reject the trusteeship. A designated trustee who does not accept the trusteeship within a reasonable time after knowing of the designation is deemed to have rejected the trusteeship.

(c) A person designated as trustee, without accepting the trusteeship, may:

(1) act to preserve the trust property if, within a reasonable time after acting, the person sends a rejection of the trusteeship to the settlor or, if the settlor is dead or lacks capacity, to a qualified beneficiary; and

(2) inspect or investigate trust property to determine potential liability under environmental or other law or for any other purpose.

Comment

This section, which specifies the requirements for a valid acceptance of the trusteeship, implicates many of the same issues that arise in determining whether a trust has been revoked. Consequently, the two provisions track each other closely. *Compare* § 701(a), *with* § 602(c) (procedure for revoking or modifying trust). Procedures specified in the terms of the trust are recognized, but only substantial, not literal compliance is required. A failure to meet technical requirements, such as notarization of the trustee's signature, does not result in a failure to accept. Ordinarily, the trustee will indicate acceptance by signing the trust instrument or signing a separate written instrument. However, this section validates any other method demonstrating the necessary intent, such as by knowingly exercising trustee powers, unless the terms of the trust make the specified method exclusive. This section also does not preclude an acceptance by estoppel. For general background on issues relating to trustee acceptance and rejection, see Restatement (Third) of Trusts § 35 (Tentative Draft No. 2, approved 1999); Restatement (Second) of Trusts § 102 (1959). Consistent with § 201(b), which emphasizes that continuing judicial supervision of a trust is the rare exception, not the rule, the Uniform Trust Code does not require that a trustee qualify in court.

To avoid the inaction that can result if the person designated as trustee fails to communicate a decision either to accept or to reject the trusteeship, subsection (b) provides that a failure to accept within a reasonable time constitutes a rejection of the trusteeship. What will constitute a reasonable time depends on the facts and circumstances of the particular case. A major consideration is possible harm that might occur if a vacancy in a trusteeship is not filled in a timely manner. A trustee's rejection normally precludes a later acceptance but does not cause the trust to fail. *See* Restatement (Third) of Trusts § 35 cmt. c (Tentative Draft No. 2, approved 1999). Regarding the filling of a vacancy in the event of a rejection, see § 704.

A person designated as trustee who decides not to accept the trusteeship need not provide a formal rejection, but a clear and early communication is recommended. The appropriate recipient of the rejection depends upon the circumstances. Ordinarily, it would be appropriate to communicate the rejection to the person who informed the designee of the proposed trusteeship. If judicial proceedings involving the trust are pending, the rejection could be filed with the court. In the case of a person named as trustee of a revocable trust, it would be appropriate to communicate the rejection to the settlor. In any event, it would be best to inform a beneficiary with a significant interest in the trust because that beneficiary might be more motivated than others to seek appointment of a new trustee.

Subsection (c)(1) makes clear that a nominated trustee may act expeditiously to protect the trust property without being considered to have accepted the trusteeship. However, upon conclusion of the intervention, the nominated trustee must send a rejection of office to the settlor, if living and competent, otherwise to a qualified beneficiary.

Because of the potential liability that can inhere in trusteeship, subsection (c)(2) allows a person designated as trustee to inspect the trust property without accepting the trusteeship. The condition of real property is a particular concern, including possible tort liability for the condition of the premises or liability for violation of state or federal environmental laws such as CERCLA, 42 U.S.C. § 9607. For a provision limiting a trustee's personal liability for obligations arising from ownership or control of trust property, see § 1010(b).

§ 702. Trustee's Bond.

(a) A trustee shall give bond to secure performance of the trustee's duties only if the court finds that a bond is needed to protect the interests of the beneficiaries or is required by the terms of the trust and the court has not dispensed with the requirement.

(b) The court may specify the amount of a bond, its liabilities, and whether sureties are necessary. The court may modify or terminate a bond at any time.

[(c) A regulated financial-service institution qualified to do trust business in this State need not give bond, even if required by the terms of the trust.]

Comment

This provision is consistent with the Restatement Third and with the bonding provisions of the Uniform Probate Code. *See* Restatement (Third) of Trusts § 34(3) & cmt. a (Tentative Draft No. 2, approved 1999); Unif. Probate Code §§ 3-604 (personal representatives), 5-415 (conservators), and 7-304 (trustees). Because a bond is required only if the terms of the trust require bond or a bond is found by the court to be necessary to protect the interests of beneficiaries, bond should rarely be required under this Code.

Despite the ability of the court pursuant to § 105(b)(6) to override a term of the trust waiving bond, the court should order bond in such cases only for good reasons. Similarly, the court should rarely dispense with bond if the settlor directed that the trustee give bond.

This section does not attempt to detail all of the technical bonding requirements that the court may impose. Typical requirements are listed in the Uniform Probate Code sections cited above. The amount of a bond otherwise required may be reduced by the value of trust property deposited in a manner that prevents its unauthorized disposition, and by the value of real property which the trustee, by express limitation of power, lacks power to convey without court authorization. Also, the court may excuse or otherwise modify a requirement of a bond, reduce or increase the amount of a bond, release a surety, or permit the substitution of another bond with the same or different sureties.

Subsection (c) clarifies that a regulated financial-service institution need not provide bond for individual trusts. Such institutions must meet detailed financial responsibility requirements in order to do trust business in the state, thereby obviating the need to post bonds in individual trusts. Subsection (c) is placed in brackets because the enacting jurisdiction may have already dealt with the subject in separate legislation, such as in its statutes on regulation of financial institutions. Instead of the phrase "regulated financial-service institution," enacting jurisdictions may wish to substitute their own term for institutions qualified to engage in trust business in the state.

§ 703. Cotrustees.

(a) Cotrustees who are unable to reach a unanimous decision may act by majority decision.

(b) If a vacancy occurs in a cotrusteeship, the remaining cotrustees may act for the trust.

(c) [Subject to [Uniform Directed Trust Act § 12], a] [A] cotrustee must participate in the performance of a trustee's function unless the cotrustee is unavailable to perform the function because of absence, illness, disqualification under other law, or other temporary incapacity or the cotrustee has properly delegated the performance of the function to another trustee.

(d) If a cotrustee is unavailable to perform duties because of absence, illness, disqualification under other law, or other temporary incapacity, and prompt action is necessary to achieve the purposes of the trust or to avoid injury to the trust property, the remaining cotrustee or a majority of the remaining cotrustees may act for the trust.

(e) A trustee may not delegate to a cotrustee the performance of a function the settlor reasonably expected the trustees to perform jointly. Unless a delegation was irrevocable, a trustee may revoke a delegation previously made.

(f) Except as otherwise provided in subsection (g), a trustee who does not join in an action of another trustee is not liable for the action.

(g) [Subject to [Uniform Directed Trust Act § 12], each] [Each] trustee shall exercise reasonable care to:

(1) prevent a cotrustee from committing a serious breach of trust; and

(2) compel a cotrustee to redress a serious breach of trust.

(h) A dissenting trustee who joins in an action at the direction of the majority of the trustees and who notified any cotrustee of the dissent at or before the time of the action is not liable for the action unless the action is a serious breach of trust.

Legislative Note: *A state that has enacted the Uniform Directed Trust Act should add the introductory phrase "Subject to [Uniform Directed Trust Act Section 12]" at the beginning of paragraphs (c) and (g).*

Comment

This section contains most but not all of the Code's provisions on cotrustees. Other provisions relevant to cotrustees include §§ 704 (vacancy in trusteeship need not be filled if cotrustee remains in office), 705 (notice of resignation must be given to cotrustee), 706 (lack of cooperation among cotrustees as ground for removal), 707 (obligations of resigning or removed trustee), 813 (reporting requirements upon vacancy in trusteeship), and 1013 (authority of cotrustees to authenticate documents).

Cotrustees are appointed for a variety of reasons. Having multiple decision-makers serves as a safeguard against eccentricity or misconduct. Cotrustees are often appointed to gain the advantage of differing skills, perhaps a financial institution for its permanence and professional skills, and a family member to maintain a personal connection with the beneficiaries. On other occasions, cotrustees are appointed to make certain that all family lines are represented in the trust's management.

Cotrusteeship should not be called for without careful reflection. Division of responsibility among cotrustees is often confused, the accountability of any individual trustee is uncertain, obtaining consent of all trustees can be burdensome, and unless an odd number of trustees is named deadlocks requiring court resolution can occur. Potential problems can be reduced by addressing division of responsibilities in the terms of the trust. Like the other sections of this article, this section is freely subject to modification in the terms of the trust. *See* § 105.

Much of this section is based on comparable

provisions of the Restatement of Trusts, although with extensive modifications. Reference should also be made to ERISA § 405 (29 U.S.C. § 1105), which in recent years has been the statutory base for the most significant case law on the powers and duties of cotrustees.

Subsection (a) is in accord with Restatement (Third) of Trusts § 39 (Tentative Draft No. 2, approved 1999), which rejects the common law rule, followed in earlier Restatements, requiring unanimity among the trustees of a private trust. *See* Restatement (Second) of Trusts § 194 (1959). This section is consistent with the prior Restatement rule applicable to charitable trusts, which allowed for action by a majority of trustees. *See* Restatement (Second) of Trusts § 383 (1959).

Under subsection (b), a majority of the remaining trustees may act for the trust when a vacancy occurs in a cotrusteeship. Section 704 provides that a vacancy in a cotrusteeship need be filled only if there is no trustee remaining in office.

Pursuant to subsection (c), a cotrustee must participate in the performance of a trustee function unless the cotrustee has properly delegated performance to another cotrustee, or the cotrustee is unable to participate due to temporary incapacity or disqualification under other law. Other laws under which a cotrustee might be disqualified include federal securities law and the ERISA prohibited transactions rules. Subsection (d) authorizes a cotrustee to assume some or all of the functions of another trustee who is unavailable to perform duties as provided in subsection (c).

Subsection (e) addresses the extent to which a trustee may delegate the performance of functions to a cotrustee. The standard differs from the standard for delegation to an agent as provided in § 807 because the two situations are different. Section 807, which is identical to § 9 of the Uniform Prudent Investor Act, recognizes that many trustees are not professionals. Consequently, trustees should be encouraged to delegate functions they are not competent to perform. Subsection (e) is premised on the assumption that the settlor selected cotrustees for a specific reason and that this reason ought to control the scope of a permitted delegation to a cotrustee. Subsection (e) prohibits a trustee from delegating to another trustee functions the settlor reasonably expected the trustees to perform jointly. The exact extent to which a trustee may delegate functions to another trustee in a particular case will vary depending on the reasons the settlor decided to appoint cotrustees. The better practice is to address the division of functions in the terms of the trust, as allowed by § 105. Subsection (e) is based on language derived from Restatement (Second) of Trusts § 171 (1959). This section of the Restatement Second, which applied to delegations to both agents and cotrustees, was superseded, as to delegation to agents, by Restatement (Third) of Trusts: Prudent Investor Rule § 171 (1992).

By permitting the trustees to act by a majority, this section contemplates that there may be a trustee or trustees who might dissent. Trustees who dissent from the acts of a cotrustee are in general protected from liability. Subsection (f) protects trustees who refused to join in the action. Subsection (h) protects a dissenting trustee who joined the action at the direction of the majority, such as to satisfy a demand of the other side to a transaction, if the trustee expressed the dissent to a cotrustee at or before the time of the action in question. However, the protections provided by subsections (f) and (h) no longer apply if the action constitutes a serious breach of trust. In that event, subsection (g) may impose liability against a dissenting trustee for failing to take reasonable steps to rectify the improper conduct. The responsibility to take action against a breaching cotrustee codifies the substance of §§ 184 and 224 of the Restatement (Second) of Trusts (1959).

2018 Amendment. Optional language was added to subsections (c) and (g) in 2018 to reconcile this section with Uniform Directed Trust Act Section 12, which was approved by the Uniform Law Commission in 2017.

§ 704. Vacancy in Trusteeship; Appointment of Successor.

(a) A vacancy in a trusteeship occurs if:

    (1) a person designated as trustee rejects the trusteeship;

    (2) a person designated as trustee cannot be identified or does not exist;

    (3) a trustee resigns;

    (4) a trustee is disqualified or removed;

    (5) a trustee dies; or

(6) a [guardian] or [conservator] is appointed for an individual serving as trustee.

(b) If one or more cotrustees remain in office, a vacancy in a trusteeship need not be filled. A vacancy in a trusteeship must be filled if the trust has no remaining trustee.

(c) A vacancy in a trusteeship of a noncharitable trust that is required to be filled must be filled in the following order of priority:

(1) by a person designated in the terms of the trust to act as successor trustee;

(2) by a person appointed by unanimous agreement of the qualified beneficiaries; or

(3) by a person appointed by the court.

(d) A vacancy in a trusteeship of a charitable trust that is required to be filled must be filled in the following order of priority:

(1) by a person designated in the terms of the trust to act as successor trustee;

(2) by a person selected by the charitable organizations expressly designated to receive distributions under the terms of the trust [if the [attorney general] concurs in the selection]; or

(3) by a person appointed by the court.

(e) Whether or not a vacancy in a trusteeship exists or is required to be filled, the court may appoint an additional trustee or special fiduciary whenever the court considers the appointment necessary for the administration of the trust.

Comment

This section lists the ways in which a trusteeship becomes vacant and the rules on filling the vacancy. *See also* §§ 701 (accepting or declining trusteeship), 705 (resignation), and 706 (removal). Good drafting practice suggests that the terms of the trust deal expressly with the problem of vacancies, naming successors and specifying the procedure for filling vacancies. This section applies only if the terms of the trust fail to specify a procedure.

The disqualification of a trustee referred to in subsection (a)(4) would include a financial institution whose right to engage in trust business has been revoked or removed. Such disqualification might also occur if the trust's principal place of administration is transferred to a jurisdiction in which the trustee, whether an individual or institution, is not qualified to act.

Subsection (b) provides that a vacancy in the cotrusteeship must be filled only if the trust has no remaining trustee. If a vacancy in the cotrusteeship is not filled, § 703 authorizes the remaining cotrustees to continue to administer the trust. However, as provided in subsection (d), the court, exercising its inherent equity authority, may always appoint additional trustees if the appointment would promote better administration of the trust. *See* Restatement (Third) of Trusts § 34 cmt. e (Tentative Draft No. 2, approved 1999); Restatement (Second) of Trusts § 108 cmt. e (1959).

Subsection (c) provides a procedure for filling a vacancy in the trusteeship of a noncharitable trust.

Absent an effective provision in the terms of the trust, subsection (c)(2) permits a vacancy in the trusteeship to be filled, without the need for court approval, by a person selected by unanimous agreement of the qualified beneficiaries. An effective provision in the terms of the trust for the designation of a successor trustee includes a procedure under which the successor trustee is selected by a person designated in those terms. Pursuant to § 705(a)(1), the qualified beneficiaries may also receive the trustee's resignation. If a trustee resigns following notice as provided in § 705, the trust may be transferred to a successor appointed pursuant to subsection (c)(2) of this section, all without court involvement. A nonqualified beneficiary who is displeased with the choice of the qualified beneficiaries may petition the court for removal of the trustee under § 706.

If the qualified beneficiaries fail to make an appointment, subsection (c)(3) authorizes the court to fill the vacancy. In making the appointment, the court should consider the objectives and probable intention of the settlor, the promotion of the proper administration of the trust, and the interests and wishes of the beneficiaries. *See* Restatement (Third) of Trusts § 34 cmt. f (Tentative Draft No. 2, approved 1999); Restatement (Second) of Trusts § 108 cmt. d (1959).

Subsection (d) specifies a procedure for filling a vacancy in the trusteeship of a charitable trust. Absent an effective designation in the terms of the trust, a successor trustee may be selected by the charitable organizations expressly designated to receive distributions in the terms of the trust bur only if the attorney general concurs in the selection. If the attorney general does not concur in the selection, however, or if the trust does not designate a charitable organization to receive distributions, the vacancy may be filled only by the court. For the reason why the reference to the Attorney General is placed in brackets see 2004 Amendment below.

In the case of a revocable trust, the appointment of a successor will normally be made directly by the settlors. As to the duties of a successor trustee with respect to the actions of a predecessor, see § 812.

2001 Amendment. Subsection (d), which creates a procedure for the filling of a vacancy in the trusteeship of a charitable trust, was added by a 2001 amendment.

2004 Amendment. The amendment to § 704(d)(2) is a conforming amendment to the amendment to § 110(d). Section 110(d) provides that the attorney general has the rights of a qualified beneficiary with respect to charitable trusts having a principal place of administration in the state. If the enacting jurisdiction elects to delete or modify § 110(d), then the enacting jurisdiction may wish to also modify subsection 704(d)(2) of this Section, which requires that the attorney general concur in the selection of a successor trustee nominated by a designated charitable organization.

§ 705. Resignation of Trustee.

(a) A trustee may resign:

(1) upon at least 30 days' notice to the qualified beneficiaries, the settlors, if living, and all cotrustees; or

(2) with the approval of the court.

(b) In approving a resignation, the court may issue orders and impose conditions reasonably necessary for the protection of the trust property.

(c) Any liability of a resigning trustee or of any sureties on the trustee's bond for acts or omissions of the trustee is not discharged or affected by the trustee's resignation.

Comment

This section rejects the common law rule that a trustee may resign only with permission of the court, and goes further than the Restatements, which allow a trustee to resign with the consent of the beneficiaries. *See* Restatement (Third) of Trusts § 36 (Tentative Draft No.2, approved 1999); Restatement (Second) of Trusts § 106 (1959). Concluding that the default rule ought to approximate standard drafting practice, the drafting committee provided in subsection (a) that a trustee may resign by giving notice to the qualified beneficiaries, a living settlor, and any cotrustee. A resigning trustee may also follow the traditional method and resign with approval of the court.

Restatement (Third) of Trusts § 36 cmt. d (Tentative Draft No. 2, approved 1999), and Restatement (Second) of Trusts § 106 cmt. b (1959), provide, similar to subsection (c), that a resignation does not release the resigning trustee from potential liabilities for acts or omissions while in office. The act of resignation can give rise to liability if the trustee resigns for the purpose of facilitating a breach of trust by a cotrustee. *See Ream v. Frey,* 107 F.3d 147 (3rd Cir. 1997).

Regarding the residual responsibilities of a resigning trustee until the trust property is delivered to a successor trustee, see § 707.

In the case of a revocable trust, because the rights of the qualified beneficiaries are subject to the settlor's control (*see* § 603), resignation of the trustee is accomplished by giving notice to the settlors instead of the beneficiaries.

2001 Amendment. By a 2001 amendment, subsection (a)(1) was amended to require that notice of a trustee's resignation be given to a living settlors. Previously, notice to a living settlors was required for a revocable but not irrevocable trust. Notice to the settlors of a revocable trust was required because the rights of the qualified beneficiaries, including the right to receive a trustee's resignation, are subject to the settlor's exclusive control. *See* § 603.

§ 706. Removal of Trustee.

(a) The settlors, a cotrustee, or a beneficiary may request the court to remove a trustee, or a trustee may be removed by the court on its own initiative.

(b) The court may remove a trustee if:

(1) the trustee has committed a serious breach of trust;

(2) lack of cooperation among cotrustees substantially impairs the administration of the trust;

(3) because of unfitness, unwillingness, or persistent failure of the trustee to administer the trust effectively, the court determines that removal of the trustee best serves the interests of the beneficiaries; or

(4) there has been a substantial change of circumstances or removal is requested by all of the qualified beneficiaries, the court finds that removal of the trustee best serves the interests of all of the beneficiaries and is not inconsistent with a material purpose of the trust, and a suitable cotrustee or successor trustee is available.

(c) Pending a final decision on a request to remove a trustee, or in lieu of or in addition to removing a trustee, the court may order such appropriate relief under Section 1001(b) as may be necessary to protect the trust property or the interests of the beneficiaries.

Comment

Subsection (a), contrary to the common law, grants the settlors of an irrevocable trust the right to petition for removal of a trustee. The right to petition for removal does not give the settlors of an irrevocable trust any other rights, such as the right to an annual report or to receive other information concerning administration of the trust. The right of a beneficiary to petition for removal does not apply to a revocable trust while the settlors has capacity. Pursuant to § 603(a), while a trust is revocable and the settlors has capacity, the rights of the beneficiaries are subject to the settlor's exclusive control.

Trustee removal may be regulated by the terms of the trust. *See* § 105. In fashioning a removal provision for an irrevocable trust, the drafter should be cognizant of the danger that the trust may be included in the settlor's federal gross estate if the settlors retains the power to be appointed as trustee or to appoint someone who is not independent. *See* Rev. Rul. 95-58, 1995-2 C.B. 191.

Subsection (b) lists the grounds for removal of the trustee. The grounds for removal are similar to those found in Restatement (Third) of Trusts § 37 cmt. e (Tentative Draft No. 2, approved 1999). A trustee may be removed for untoward action, such as for a serious breach of trust, but the section is not so limited. A trustee may also be removed under a variety of circumstances in which the court concludes that the trustee is not best serving the interests of the beneficiaries. The term "interests of the beneficiaries" means the beneficial interests as provided in the terms of the trust, not as defined by

the beneficiaries. *See* § 103(7). Removal for conduct detrimental to the interests of the beneficiaries is a well-established standard for removal of a trustee. *See* Restatement (Third) of Trusts § 37 cmt. d (Tentative Draft No. 2, approved 1999); Restatement (Second) of Trusts § 107 cmt. a (1959).

Subsection (b)(1), consistent with Restatement (Third) of Trusts § 37 cmt. e & g (Tentative Draft No, 2, approved 1999), makes clear that not every breach of trust justifies removal of the trustee. The breach must be "serious." A serious breach of trust may consist of a single act that causes significant harm or involves flagrant misconduct. A serious breach of trust may also consist of a series of smaller breaches, none of which individually justify removal when considered alone, but which do so when considered together. A particularly appropriate circumstance justifying removal of the trustee is a serious breach of the trustee's duty to keep the beneficiaries reasonably informed of the administration of the trust or to comply with a beneficiary's request for information as required by § 813. Failure to comply with this duty may make it impossible for the beneficiaries to protect their interests. It may also mask more serious violations by the trustee.

The lack of cooperation among trustees justifying removal under subsection (b)(2) need not involve a breach of trust. The key factor is whether the administration of the trust is significantly impaired by the trustees' failure to agree. Removal is particularly appropriate if the naming of an even number of trustees, combined with their failure to agree, has resulted in deadlock requiring court resolution. The court may remove one or more or all of the trustees. If a cotrustee remains in office following the removal, under § 704 appointment of a successor trustee is not required.

Subsection (b)(2) deals only with lack of cooperation among cotrustees, not with friction between the trustee and beneficiaries. Friction between the trustee and beneficiaries is ordinarily not a basis for removal. However, removal might be justified if a communications breakdown is caused by the trustee or appears to be incurable. *See* Restatement (Third) of Trusts § 37 cmt. e (Tentative Draft No. 2, approved 1999).

Subsection (b)(3) authorizes removal for a variety of grounds, including unfitness, unwillingness, or persistent failure to administer the trust effectively. Removal in any of these cases is allowed only if it best serves the interests of the beneficiaries. For the definition of "interests of the beneficiaries," see § 103(8). "Unfitness" may include not only mental incapacity but also lack of basic ability to administer the trust. Before removing a trustee for unfitness the court should consider the extent to which the problem might be cured by a delegation of functions the trustee is personally incapable of performing. "Unwillingness" includes not only cases where the trustee refuses to act but also a pattern of indifference to some or all of the beneficiaries. *See* Restatement (Third) of Trusts § 37 cmt. e (Tentative Draft No. 2, approved 1999). A "persistent failure to administer the trust effectively" might include a long-term pattern of mediocre performance, such as consistently poor investment results when compared to comparable trusts.

It has traditionally been more difficult to remove a trustee named by the settlor than a trustee named by the court, particularly if the settlor at the time of the appointment was aware of the trustee's failings. *See* Restatement (Third) of Trusts § 37 cmt. f (Tentative Draft No.2, approved 1999); Restatement (Second) of Trusts § 107 cmt. f-g (1959). Because of the discretion normally granted to a trustee, the settlor's confidence in the judgment of the particular person whom the settlor selected to act as trustee is entitled to considerable weight. This deference to the settlor's choice can weaken or dissolve if a substantial change in the trustee's circumstances occurs. To honor a settlor's reasonable expectations, subsection (b)(4) lists a substantial change of circumstances as a possible basis for removal of the trustee. Changed circumstances justifying removal of a trustee might include a substantial change in the character of the service or location of the trustee. A corporate reorganization of an institutional trustee is not itself a change of circumstances if it does not affect the service provided the individual trust account. Before removing a trustee on account of changed circumstances, the court must also conclude that removal is not inconsistent with a material purpose of the trust, that it will best serve the interests of the beneficiaries, and that a suitable cotrustee or successor trustee is available.

Subsection (b)(4) also contains a specific but more limited application of § 411. Section 411 allows the beneficiaries by unanimous agreement to compel modification of a trust if the court concludes that the particular modification is not inconsistent with a material purpose of the trust. Subsection (b)(4) of this section similarly allows the qualified beneficiaries to request removal of the trustee if the designation of the trustee was not a material purpose of the trust. Before removing the trustee the court must also find that removal will best serve the interests of the beneficiaries and that a suitable cotrustee or successor trustee is available.

Subsection (c) authorizes the court to intervene pending a final decision on a request to remove a trustee. Among the relief that the court may order under § 1001(b) is an injunction prohibiting the trustee from performing certain acts and the appointment of a special fiduciary to perform some or all of the trustee's functions. Pursuant to § 1004, the court may also award attorney's fees as justice and equity may require.

§ 707. Delivery of Property by Former Trustee.

(a) Unless a cotrustee remains in office or the court otherwise orders, and until the trust property is delivered to a successor trustee or other person entitled to it, a trustee who has resigned or been removed has the duties of a trustee and the powers necessary to protect the trust property.

(b) A trustee who has resigned or been removed shall proceed expeditiously to deliver the trust property within the trustee's possession to the cotrustee, successor trustee, or other person entitled to it.

Comment

This section addresses the continuing authority and duty of a resigning or removed trustee. Subject to the power of the court to make other arrangements or unless a cotrustee remains in office, a resigning or removed trustee has continuing authority until the trust property is delivered to a successor. If a cotrustee remains in office, there is no reason to grant a resigning or removed trustee any continuing authority, and none is granted under this section. In addition, if a cotrustee remains in office, the former trustee need not submit a final trustee's report. *See* § 813(c).

There is ample authority in the Uniform Trust Code for the appointment of a special fiduciary, an appointment which can avoid the need for a resigning or removed trustee to exercise residual powers until a successor can take office. *See* §§ 704(e) (court may appoint additional trustee or special fiduciary whenever court considers appointment necessary for administration of trust), 705(b) (in approving

resignation, court may impose conditions necessary for protection of trust property), 706(c) (pending decision on petition for removal, court may order appropriate relief), and 1001(b)(5) (to remedy breach of trust, court may appoint special fiduciary as necessary to protect trust property or interests of beneficiary).

If the former trustee has died, the Uniform Trust Code does not require that the trustee's personal representative windup the deceased trustee's administration. Nor is a trustee's conservator or guardian required to complete the former trustee's administration if the trustee's authority terminated due to an adjudication of incapacity. However, to limit the former trustee's liability, the personal representative, conservator or guardian may submit a trustee's report on the former trustee's behalf as authorized by § 813(c). Otherwise, the former trustee remains liable for actions taken during the trustee's term of office until liability is otherwise barred.

§ 708. Compensation of Trustee.

(a) If the terms of a trust do not specify the trustee's compensation, a trustee is entitled to compensation that is reasonable under the circumstances.

(b) If the terms of a trust specify the trustee's compensation, the trustee is entitled to be compensated as specified, but the court may allow more or less compensation if:

(1) the duties of the trustee are substantially different from those contemplated when the trust was created; or

(2) the compensation specified by the terms of the trust would be unreasonably low or high.

Comment

Subsection (a) establishes a standard of reasonable compensation. Relevant factors in determining this compensation, as specified in the Restatement, include the custom of the community; the trustee's skill, experience, and facilities; the time devoted to trust duties; the amount and character of the trust property; the degree of difficulty, responsibility and risk assumed in administering the trust, including in making discretionary distributions; the nature and costs of services rendered by others; and the quality of the trustee's performance. *See* Restatement (Third) of Trusts § 38 cmt. c (Tentative Draft No. 2, approved 1999); Restatement (Second) of Trusts § 242 cmt. b (1959).

In setting compensation, the services actually performed and responsibilities assumed by the trustee should be closely examined. A downward adjustment of fees may be appropriate if a trustee has delegated significant duties to agents, such as the delegation of

investment authority to outside managers. *See* § 807 (delegation by trustee). On the other hand, a trustee with special skills, such as those of a real estate agent, may be entitled to extra compensation for performing services that would ordinarily be delegated. *See* Restatement (Third) of Trusts § 38 cmt. d (Tentative Draft No. 2, approved 1999); Restatement (Second) of Trusts § 242 cmt. d (1959).

Because "trustee" as defined in § 103(20) includes not only an individual trustee but also cotrustees, each trustee, including a cotrustee, is entitled to reasonable compensation under the circumstances. The fact that a trust has more than one trustee does not mean that the trustees together are entitled to more compensation than had either acted alone. Nor does the appointment of more than one trustee mean that the trustees are eligible to receive the compensation in equal shares. The total amount of the compensation to be paid and how it will be divided depend on the totality of the circumstances. Factors to be considered include the settlor's reasons for naming more than one trustee and the level of responsibility assumed and exact services performed by each trustee. Often the fees of cotrustees will be in the aggregate higher than the fees for a single trustee because of the duty of each trustee to participate in administration and not delegate to a cotrustee duties the settlor expected the trustees to perform jointly. *See* Restatement (Third) of Trusts § 38 cmt. i (Tentative Draft No. 2, approved 1999). The trust may benefit in such cases from the enhanced quality of decision-making resulting from the collective deliberations of the trustees.

Financial institution trustees normally base their fees on published fee schedules. Published fee schedules are subject to the same standard of reasonableness under the Uniform Trust Code as are other methods for computing fees. The courts have generally upheld published fee schedules but this is not automatic. Among the more litigated topics is the issue of termination fees. Termination fees are charged upon termination of the trust and sometimes upon transfer of the trust to a successor trustee. Factors relevant to whether the fee is appropriate include the actual work performed; whether a termination fee was authorized in the terms of the trust; whether the fee schedule specified the circumstances in which a termination fee would be charged; whether the trustee's overall fees for administering the trust from the date of the trust's creation, including the termination fee, were reasonable; and the general practice in the community regarding termination fees. Because significantly less work is normally involved, termination fees are less appropriate upon transfer to a successor trustee than upon termination of the trust. For representative cases, see *Cleveland Trust Co. v. Wilmington Trust Co.*, 258 A.2d 58 (Del. 1969); *In re Trusts Under Will of Dwan*, 371 N.W. 2d 641 (Minn. Ct. App. 1985); *Mercer v. Merchants National Bank*, 298 A.2d 736 (N.H. 1972); *In re Estate of Payson*, 562 N.Y.S. 2d 329 (Surr. Ct. 1990); *In re Indenture Agreement of Lawson*, 607 A. 2d 803 (Pa. Super. Ct. 1992); *In re Estate of Ischy*, 415 A.2d 37 (Pa. 1980); *Memphis Memorial Park v. Planters National Bank*, 1986 Tenn. App. LEXIS 2978 (May 7, 1986); *In re Trust of Sensenbrenner*, 252 N.W. 2d 47 (Wis. 1977).

This Code does not take a specific position on whether dual fees may be charged when a trustee hires its own law firm to represent the trust. The trend is to authorize dual compensation as long as the overall fees are reasonable. For a discussion, see Ronald C. Link, *Developments Regarding the Professional Responsibility of the Estate Administration Lawyer: The Effect of the Model Rules of Professional Conduct*, 26 Real Prop. Prob. & Tr. J. 1, 22-38 (1991)

Subsection (b) permits the terms of the trust to override the reasonable compensation standard, subject to the court's inherent equity power to make adjustments downward or upward in appropriate circumstances. Compensation provisions should be drafted with care. Common questions include whether a provision in the terms of the trust setting the amount of the trustee's compensation is binding on a successor trustee, whether a dispositive provision for the trustee in the terms of the trust is in addition to or in lieu of the trustee's regular compensation, and whether a dispositive provision for the trustee is conditional on the person performing services as trustee. *See* Restatement (Third) of Trusts § 38 cmt. e (Tentative Draft No.2, approved 1999); Restatement (Second) of Trusts § 242 cmt. f (1959).

Compensation may be set by agreement. A trustee may enter into an agreement with the beneficiaries for lesser or increased compensation, although an agreement increasing compensation is not binding on a nonconsenting beneficiary. *See* § 111(d) (matters that may be the resolved by nonjudicial settlement). *See also* Restatement (Third) of Trusts § 38 cmt. f (Tentative Draft No. 2, approved 1999); Restatement (Second) of Trusts § 242 cmt. i (1959). A trustee may also agree to waive compensation and should do so prior to rendering significant services if concerned about possible gift and income taxation of the compensation accrued prior to the waiver. *See* Rev. Rul. 66-167, 1966-1 C.B. 20. *See also* Restatement (Third) of Trusts § 38 cmt. g (Tentative Draft No. 2, approved 1999); Restatement (Second) of Trusts § 242 cmt. j (1959).

Section 816(15) grants the trustee authority to fix and pay its compensation without the necessity of prior court review, subject to the right of a beneficiary to object to the compensation in a later judicial proceeding. Allowing the trustee to pay its compensation without prior court approval promotes efficient trust administration but does place a significant burden on a beneficiary who believes the compensation is unreasonable. To provide a beneficiary with time to take action, and because of the importance of trustee's fees to the beneficiaries' interests, § 813(b)(4) requires a trustee to provide the qualified beneficiaries with advance notice of any change in the method or rate of the trustee's compensation. Failure to provide such advance notice constitutes a breach of trust, which, if sufficiently serious, would justify the trustee's removal under § 706.

Under §§ 501-502 of the Uniform Principal and

Income Act (1997), one-half of a trustee's regular compensation is charged to income and the other half to principal. Chargeable to principal are fees for acceptance, distribution, or termination of the trust, and fees charged on disbursements made to prepare property for sale.

§ 709. Reimbursement of Expenses.

(a) A trustee is entitled to be reimbursed out of the trust property, with interest as appropriate, for:

(1) expenses that were properly incurred in the administration of the trust; and

(2) to the extent necessary to prevent unjust enrichment of the trust, expenses that were not properly incurred in the administration of the trust.

(b) An advance by the trustee of money for the protection of the trust gives rise to a lien against trust property to secure reimbursement with reasonable interest.

Comment

A trustee has the authority to expend trust funds as necessary in the administration of the trust, including expenses incurred in the hiring of agents. *See* §§ 807 (delegation by trustee) and 816(15) (trustee to pay expenses of administration from trust).

Subsection (a)(1) clarifies that a trustee is entitled to reimbursement from the trust for incurring expenses within the trustee's authority. The trustee may also withhold appropriate reimbursement for expenses before making distributions to the beneficiaries. *See* Restatement (Third) of Trusts § 38 cmt. b (Tentative Draft No. 2, approved 1999); Restatement (Second) of Trusts § 244 cmt. b (1959). A trustee is ordinarily not entitled to reimbursement for incurring unauthorized expenses. Such expenses are normally the personal responsibility of the trustee.

As provided in subsection (a)(2), a trustee is entitled to reimbursement for unauthorized expenses only if the unauthorized expenditures benefitted the trust The purpose of this provision, which is derived from Restatement (Second) of Trusts § 245 (1959), is not to ratify the unauthorized conduct of the trustee, but to prevent unjust enrichment of the trust. Given

this purpose, a court, on appropriate grounds, may delay or even deny reimbursement for expenses which benefitted the trust. Appropriate grounds include: (1) whether the trustee acted in bad faith in incurring the expense; (2) whether the trustee knew that the expense was inappropriate; (3) whether the trustee reasonably believed the expense was necessary for the preservation of the trust estate; (4) whether the expense has resulted in a benefit; and (5) whether indemnity can be allowed without defeating or impairing the purposes of the trust. *See* Restatement (Second) of Trusts § 245 cmt. g (1959).

Subsection (b) implements § 802(h)(5), which creates an exception to the duty of loyalty for advances by the trustee for the protection of the trust if the transaction is fair to the beneficiaries.

Reimbursement under this section may include attorney's fees and expenses incurred by the trustee in defending an action. However, a trustee is not ordinarily entitled to attorney's fees and expenses if it is determined that the trustee breached the trust. *See* 3A Austin W. Scott & William F. Fratcher, The Law of Trusts § 245 (4th ed. 1988).

ARTICLE 8
DUTIES AND POWERS OF TRUSTEE

General Comment

This article states the fundamental duties of a trustee and lists the trustee's powers. The duties listed are not new, but how the particular duties are formulated and applied has changed over the years. This article was drafted where possible to conform with the 1994 Uniform Prudent Investor Act, which has been enacted in approximately two thirds of the states. The Uniform Prudent Investor Act prescribes a trustee's responsibilities with respect to the management and investment of trust property. The Uniform Trust Code also addresses a trustee's duties with respect to distribution to beneficiaries.

Because of the widespread adoption of the Uniform Prudent Investor Act, it was decided not to disassemble and fully integrate the Prudent Investor Act into the Uniform Trust Code. Instead, states enacting the Uniform Trust Code are encouraged to recodify their version of the Prudent Investor Act by reenacting it as Article 9 of this Code rather than leaving it elsewhere in their statutes. Where the Uniform Trust Code and Uniform Prudent Investor Act overlap, states should enact the provisions of this article and not enact the duplicative provisions of the Prudent Investor Act. Sections of this article which overlap with the Prudent Investor Act are §§ 802 (duty of loyalty), 803 (impartiality), 805 (costs of administration), 806 (trustee's skills), and 807 (delegation). For more complete instructions on how to enact the Uniform Prudent Investor Act as part of this Code, see the General Comment to Article 9.

All of the provisions of this article may be overridden in the terms of the trust except for certain aspects of the trustee's duty to keep the beneficiaries informed of administration (*see* § 105(b)(8)-(9)), and the trustee's fundamental obligation to act in good faith, in accordance with the purposes of the trust, and for the benefit of the beneficiaries (*see* § 105(b)(2)-(3)).

§ 801. Duty to Administer Trust. Upon acceptance of a trusteeship, the trustee shall administer the trust in good faith, in accordance with its terms and purposes and the interests of the beneficiaries, and in accordance with this [Code].

Comment

This section confirms that a primary duty of a trustee is to follow the terms and purposes of the trust and to do so in good faith. Only if the terms of a trust are silent or for some reason invalid on a particular issue does this Code govern the trustee's duties. This section also confirms that a trustee does not have a duty to act until the trustee has accepted the trusteeship. For the procedure for accepting a trusteeship, see § 701.

In administering the trust, the trustee must not only comply with this section but also with the other duties specified in this article, particularly the obligation not to place the interests of others above those of the beneficiaries (§ 802), the duty to act with prudence (§ 804), and the duty to keep the qualified beneficiaries reasonably informed about the administration of the trust (§ 813).

While a trustee generally must administer a trust in accordance with its terms and purposes, the purposes and particular terms of the trust can on occasion conflict. If such a conflict occurs because of circumstances not anticipated by the settlors, it may be appropriate for the trustee to petition under § 412 to modify or terminate the trust. Pursuant to § 404, the trustee is not required to perform a duty prescribed by the terms of the trust if performance would be impossible, illegal or contrary to public policy.

For background on the trustee's duty to administer the trust, see Restatement (Second) of Trusts §§ 164-169 (1959).

§ 802. Duty of Loyalty.

(a) A trustee shall administer the trust solely in the interests of the beneficiaries.

(b) Subject to the rights of persons dealing with or assisting the trustee as provided in Section 1012, a sale, encumbrance, or other transaction involving the investment or management of trust property entered into by the trustee for the trustee's own personal account or which is otherwise affected by a conflict between the trustee's fiduciary and personal interests is voidable by a beneficiary affected by the transaction unless:

(1) the transaction was authorized by the terms of the trust;

(2) the transaction was approved by the court;

(3) the beneficiary did not commence a judicial proceeding within the time allowed by Section 1005;

(4) the beneficiary consented to the trustee's conduct, ratified the transaction, or released the trustee in compliance with Section 1009; or

(5) the transaction involves a contract entered into or claim acquired by the trustee before the person became or contemplated becoming trustee.

(c) A sale, encumbrance, or other transaction involving the investment or management of trust property is presumed to be affected by a conflict between personal and fiduciary interests if it is entered into by the trustee with:

(1) the trustee's spouse;

(2) the trustee's descendants, siblings, parents, or their spouses;

(3) an agent or attorney of the trustee; or

(4) a corporation or other person or enterprise in which the trustee, or a person that owns a significant interest in the trustee, has an interest that might affect the trustee's best judgment.

(d) A transaction between a trustee and a beneficiary that does not concern trust property but that occurs during the existence of the trust or while the trustee retains significant influence over the beneficiary and from which the trustee obtains an advantage is voidable by the beneficiary unless the trustee establishes that the transaction was fair to the beneficiary.

(e) A transaction not concerning trust property in which the trustee engages in the trustee's individual capacity involves a conflict between personal and fiduciary interests if the transaction concerns an opportunity properly belonging to the trust.

(f) An investment by a trustee in securities of an investment company or investment trust to which the trustee, or its affiliate, provides services in a capacity other than as trustee is not presumed to be affected by a conflict between personal and fiduciary interests if the investment otherwise complies with the prudent investor rule of [Article] 9. In addition to its compensation for acting as trustee, the trustee may be compensated by the investment company or investment trust for providing those services out of fees charged to the trust. If the trustee receives compensation from the investment company or investment trust for providing investment advisory or investment management services, the trustee at least annually shall notify the persons entitled under Section 813 to receive a copy of the trustee's annual report of the rate and method by which that compensation was determined.

(g) In voting shares of stock or in exercising powers of control over similar interests in other forms of enterprise, the trustee shall act in the best interests of the beneficiaries. If the trust is the sole owner of a corporation or other form of enterprise, the trustee shall elect or appoint directors or other managers who will manage the corporation or enterprise in the best interests of the beneficiaries.

(h) This section does not preclude the following transactions, if fair to the beneficiaries:

(1) an agreement between a trustee and a beneficiary relating to the appointment or compensation of the trustee;

(2) payment of reasonable compensation to the trustee;

(3) a transaction between a trust and another trust, decedent's estate, or [conservatorship] of which the trustee is a fiduciary or in which a beneficiary has an interest;

(4) a deposit of trust money in a regulated financial-service institution operated by the trustee; or

(5) an advance by the trustee of money for the protection of the trust.

(i) The court may appoint a special fiduciary to make a decision with respect to any proposed transaction that might violate this section if entered into by the trustee.

Comment

This section addresses the duty of loyalty, perhaps the most fundamental duty of the trustee. Subsection (a) states the general principle, which is copied from Restatement (Second) of Trusts § 170(1) (1959). A trustee owes a duty of loyalty to the beneficiaries, a principle which is sometimes expressed as the obligation of the trustee not to place the trustee's own interests over those of the beneficiaries. Most but not all violations of the duty of loyalty concern transactions involving the trust property, but breaches of the duty can take other forms. For a discussion of the different types of violations, see George G. Bogert & George T. Bogert, The Law of Trusts and Trustees § 543 (Rev. 2d ed. 1993); and 2A Austin W. Scott & William F. Fratcher, The Law of Trusts §§ 170-170.24 (4th ed. 1987). The "interests of the beneficiaries" to which the trustee must be loyal are the beneficial interests as provided in the terms of the trust. *See* § 103(7).

The duty of loyalty applies to both charitable and noncharitable trusts, even though the beneficiaries of charitable trusts are indefinite. In the case of a charitable trust, the trustee must administer the trust solely in the interests of effectuating the trust's charitable purposes. *See* Restatement (Second) of Trusts § 379 cmt. a (1959).

Duty of loyalty issues often arise in connection with the settlor's designation of the trustee. For example, it is not uncommon that the trustee will also be a beneficiary. Or the settlor will name a friend or family member who is an officer of a company in which the settlor owns stock. In such cases, settlors should be advised to consider addressing in the terms of the trust how such conflicts are to be handled. Section 105 authorizes a settlor to override an otherwise applicable duty of loyalty in the terms of the trust. Sometimes the override is implied. The grant to a trustee of authority to make a discretionary distribution to a class of beneficiaries that includes the trustee implicitly authorizes the trustee to make distributions for the trustee's own benefit.

Subsection (b) states the general rule with respect to transactions involving trust property that are affected by a conflict of interest. A transaction affected by a conflict between the trustee's fiduciary and personal interests is voidable by a beneficiary who is affected by the transaction. Subsection (b) carries out the "no further inquiry" rule by making transactions involving trust property entered into by a trustee for the trustee's own personal account voidable without further proof. Such transactions are irrebuttably presumed to be affected by a conflict between personal and fiduciary interests. It is immaterial whether the trustee acts in good faith or pays a fair consideration. *See* Restatement (Second) of Trusts § 170 cmt. b (1959).

The rule is less severe with respect to transactions involving trust property entered into with persons who have close business or personal ties with the trustee. Under subsection (c), a transaction between a trustee and certain relatives and business associates is presumptively voidable, not void. Also presumptively voidable are transactions with corporations or other enterprises in which the trustee, or a person who owns a significant interest in the trustee, has an interest that might affect the trustee's best judgment. The presumption is rebutted if the trustee establishes that the transaction was not affected by a conflict between personal and fiduciary interests. Among the factors tending to rebut the presumption are whether the consideration was fair and whether the other terms of the transaction are similar to those that would be transacted with an independent party.

Even where the presumption under subsection (c) does not apply, a transaction may still be voided by a beneficiary if the beneficiary proves that a conflict between personal and fiduciary interests existed and that the transaction was affected by the conflict. The right of a beneficiary to void a transaction affected by a conflict of interest is optional. If the transaction proves profitable to the trust and unprofitable to the trustee, the beneficiary will likely allow the transaction to stand. For a comparable provision regulating fiduciary investments by national banks, see 12 C.F.R. § 9.12(a).

As provided in subsection (b), no breach of the duty of loyalty occurs if the transaction was authorized by the terms of the trust or approved by the court, or if the beneficiary failed to commence a judicial proceeding within the time allowed or chose to ratify the transaction, either prior to or subsequent to its occurrence. In determining whether a beneficiary has consented to a transaction, the principles of representation from Article 3 may be applied.

Subsection (b)(5), which is derived from § 3-713(1) of the Uniform Probate Code, allows a trustee to implement a contract or pursue a claim that the trustee entered into or acquired before the person became or contemplated becoming trustee. While this subsection allows the transaction to proceed without automatically being voidable by a beneficiary, the transaction is not necessarily free from scrutiny. In implementing the contract or pursuing the claim, the trustee must still complete the transaction in a way that avoids a conflict between the trustee's fiduciary and personal interests. Because avoiding such a conflict will frequently be difficult, the trustee should consider petitioning the court to appoint a special fiduciary, as authorized by subsection (i), to work out the details and complete the transaction.

Subsection (d) creates a presumption that a transaction between a trustee and a beneficiary not involving trust property is an abuse by the trustee of a confidential relationship with the beneficiary. This subsection has limited scope. If the trust has terminated, there must be proof that the trustee's influence with the beneficiary remained. Furthermore, whether or not the trust has terminated, there must be proof that the trustee obtained an advantage from the relationship. The fact the trustee profited is insufficient to show an abuse if a third party would have similarly profited in an arm's length transaction. Subsection (d) is based on Cal. Prob. Code §16004(c). *See also* 2A Austin W. Scott & William F. Fratcher § 170.25 (4th ed. 1987), which states the same principle in a slightly different form: "Where he deals directly with the beneficiaries, the transaction may stand, but only if the trustee makes full disclosure and takes no advantage of his position and the transaction is in all respects fair and reasonable."

Subsection (e), which allows a beneficiary to void a transaction entered into by the trustee that involved an opportunity belonging to the trust, is based on Restatement (Second) of Trusts § 170 cmt. k (1959). While normally associated with corporations and with their directors and officers, what is usually referred to as the corporate opportunity doctrine also applies to other types of fiduciary. The doctrine prohibits the trustee's pursuit of certain business activities, such as entering into a business in direct competition with a business owned by the trust, or

the purchasing of an investment that the facts suggest the trustee was expected to purchase for the trust. For discussion of the corporate opportunity doctrine, see Kenneth B. Davis, Jr., *Corporate Opportunity and Comparative Advantage*, 84 Iowa L. Rev. 211 (1999); and Richard A. Epstein, *Contract and Trust in Corporate Law: The Case of Corporate Opportunity*, 21 Del. J. Corp. L. 5 (1996). *See also* Principles of Corporate Governance: Analysis and Recommendations § 5.05 (American Law Inst. 1994).

Subsection (f) creates an exception to the no further inquiry rule for trustee investment in mutual funds. This exception applies even though the mutual fund company pays the financial-service institution trustee a fee for providing investment advice and other services, such as custody, transfer agent, and distribution, that would otherwise be provided by agents of the fund. Mutual funds offer several advantages for fiduciary investing. By comparison with common trust funds, mutual fund shares may be distributed in-kind when trust interests terminate, avoiding liquidation and the associated recognition of gain for tax purposes. Mutual funds commonly offer daily pricing, which gives trustees and beneficiaries better information about performance. Because mutual funds can combine fiduciary and nonfiduciary accounts, they can achieve larger size, which can enhance diversification and produce economies of scale that can lower investment costs.

Mutual fund investment also has a number of potential disadvantages. It adds another layer of expense to the trust, and it causes the trustee to lose control over the nature and timing of transactions in the fund. Trustee investment in mutual funds sponsored by the trustee, its affiliate, or from which the trustee receives extra fees has given rise to litigation implicating the trustee's duty of loyalty, the duty to invest with prudence, and the right to receive only reasonable compensation. Because financial institution trustees ordinarily provide advisory services to and receive compensation from the very funds in which they invest trust assets, the contention is made that investing the assets of individual trusts in these funds is imprudent and motivated by the effort to generate additional fee income. Because the financial institution trustee often will also charge its regular fee for administering the trust, the contention is made that the financial institution trustee's total compensation, both direct and indirect, is excessive.

Subsection (f) attempts to retain the advantages of mutual funds while at the same time making clear that such investments are subject to traditional fiduciary responsibilities. Nearly all of the states have enacted statutes authorizing trustees to invest in funds from which the trustee might derive additional compensation. Portions of subsection (f) are based on these statutes. Subsection (f) makes clear that such dual investment-fee arrangements are not automatically presumed to involve a conflict between the trustee's personal and fiduciary interests, but subsection (f) does not otherwise waive or lessen a trustee's fiduciary obligations. The trustee, in deciding whether to invest in a mutual fund, must not place its own interests ahead of those of the beneficiaries. The investment decision must also comply with the enacting jurisdiction's prudent investor rule. To obtain the protection afforded by subsection (f), the trustee must disclose at least annually to the beneficiaries entitled to receive a copy of the trustee's annual report the rate and method by which the additional compensation was determined. Furthermore, the selection of a mutual fund, and the resulting delegation of certain of the trustee's functions, may be taken into account under § 708 in setting the trustee's regular compensation. *See also* Unif. Prudent Investor Act §§ 7 & 9 & comments; Restatement (Third) of Trusts: Prudent Investor Rule § 227 cmt. m (1992).

Subsection (f) applies whether the services to the fund are provided directly by the trustee or by an affiliate. While the term "affiliate" is not used in subsection (c), the individuals and entities listed there are examples of affiliates. The term is also used in the regulations under ERISA. An "affiliate" of a fiduciary includes (1) any person who directly or indirectly, through one or more intermediaries, controls, is controlled by, or is under common control with the fiduciary; (2) any officer, director, partner, employee, or relative of the fiduciary, and any corporation or partnership of which the fiduciary is an officer, director or partner. *See* 29 C.F.R. § 2510.3-21(e).

Subsection (g) addresses an overlap between trust and corporate law. It is based on Restatement of Trusts (Second) § 193 cmt. a (1959), which provides that "[i]t is the duty of the trustee in voting shares of stock to use proper care to promote the interest of the beneficiary," and that the fiduciary responsibility of a trustee in voting a control block "is heavier than where he holds only a small fraction of the shares." Similarly, the Department of Labor construes ERISA's duty of loyalty to make share voting a fiduciary function. *See* 29 C.F.R. §2509.94-2. When the trust owns the entirety of the shares of a

corporation, the corporate assets are in effect trust assets that the trustee determines to hold in corporate form. The trustee may not use the corporate form to escape the fiduciary duties of trust law. Thus, for example, a trustee whose duty of impartiality would require the trustee to make current distributions for the support of current beneficiaries may not evade that duty by holding assets in corporate form and pleading the discretion of corporate directors to determine dividend policy. Rather, the trustee must vote for corporate directors who will follow a dividend policy consistent with the trustee's trust-law duty of impartiality.

Subsection (h) contains several exceptions to the general duty of loyalty, which apply if the transaction was fair to the beneficiaries. Subsection (h)(1)-(2) clarify that a trustee is free to contract about the terms of appointment and rate of compensation. Consistent with Restatement (Second) of Trusts § 170 cmt. r (1959), subsection (h)(3) authorizes a trustee to engage in a transaction involving another trust of which the trustee is also trustee, a transaction with a decedent's estate or a conservatorship estate of which the trustee is personal representative or conservator, or a transaction with another trust or other fiduciary relationship in which a beneficiary of the trust has an interest. The authority of a trustee to deposit funds in a financial institution operated by the trustee, as provided in subsection (h)(4), is recognized as an exception to the duty of loyalty in a number of state statutes although deemed to be a breach of trust in Restatement (Second) of Trusts § 170 cmt. m (1959). The power to deposit funds in its own institution does not negate the trustee's responsibility to invest prudently, including the obligation to earn a reasonable rate of interest on deposits. Subsection (h)(5) authorizes a trustee to advance money for the protection of the trust. Such advances usually are of small amounts and are made in emergencies or as a matter of convenience. Pursuant to § 709(b), the trustee has a lien against the trust property for any advances made.

2003 Amendment. The amendment revises subsection (f) to clarify that compensation received from a mutual fund for providing services to the fund is in addition to the trustee's regular compensation. It also clarifies that the trustee obligation to notify certain of the beneficiaries of compensation received from the fund applies only to compensation received for providing investment management or advisory services. The amendment conforms subsection (f) to the drafters' original intent.

Subsection (f) formerly provided:

(f) An investment by a trustee in securities of an investment company or investment trust to which the trustee, or its affiliate, provides services in a capacity other than as trustee is not presumed to be affected by a conflict between personal and fiduciary interests if the investment complies with the prudent investor rule of [Article] 9. The trustee may be compensated by the investment company or investment trust for providing those services out of fees charged to the trust if the trustee at least annually notifies the persons entitled under § 813 to receive a copy of the trustee's annual report of the rate and method by which the compensation was determined.

2004 Amendment. Section 802(f) creates an exception to the prohibition on self-dealing for certain investments in mutual funds in which the trustee, or its affiliate, provides services in a capacity other than that as trustee. As originally drafted, § 802(f) provided that the exception applied only if the investment complied with the Uniform Prudent Investor Act and the trustee notified the qualified beneficiaries of the additional compensation received for providing the services. However, the Uniform Prudent Investor Act itself contains its own duty of loyalty provision (§ 5), thereby arguably limiting or undoing this exception to the UTC's loyalty provision. The amendment, by providing that the investment does not violate the duty of loyalty under the UTC if it "otherwise" complies with the Uniform Prudent Investor Act, is intended to negate the implication that the investment must also comply with the Uniform Prudent Investor Act's own duty of loyalty provision.

§ 803. Impartiality. If a trust has two or more beneficiaries, the trustee shall act impartially in investing, managing, and distributing the trust property, giving due regard to the beneficiaries' respective interests.

Comment

The duty of impartiality is an important aspect of the duty of loyalty. This section is identical to § 6 of the Uniform Prudent Investor Act, except that this section also applies to all aspects of trust administration and to decisions by a trustee with respect to distributions. The Prudent Investor Act is limited to duties with respect to the investment and management of trust property. The differing beneficial interests for which the trustee must act impartially include those of the current beneficiaries versus those of beneficiaries holding interests in the remainder; and among those currently eligible to receive distributions. In fulfilling the duty to act impartially, the trustee should be particularly sensitive to allocation of receipts and disbursements between income and principal and should consider, in an appropriate case, a reallocation of income to the principal account and vice versa, if allowable under local law. For an example of such authority, see Uniform Principal and Income Act § 104 (1997).

The duty to act impartially does not mean that the trustee must treat the beneficiaries equally. Rather, the trustee must treat the beneficiaries equitably in light of the purposes and terms of the trust. A settlors who prefers that the trustee, when making decisions, generally favor the interests of one beneficiary over those of others should provide appropriate guidance in the terms of the trust. *See* Restatement (Second) of § 183 cmt. a (1959).

§ 804. Prudent Administration. A trustee shall administer the trust as a prudent person would, by considering the purposes, terms, distributional requirements, and other circumstances of the trust. In satisfying this standard, the trustee shall exercise reasonable care, skill, and caution.

Comment

The duty to administer a trust with prudence is a fundamental duty of the trustee. This duty does not depend on whether the trustee receives compensation. The duty may be altered by the terms of the trust. *See* § 105. This section is similar to § 2(a) of the Uniform Prudent Investor Act and Restatement (Third) of Trusts: Prudent Investor Rule § 227 (1992).

The language of this section diverges from the language of the previous Restatement. The prior

Restatement can be read as applying the same standard - "man of ordinary prudence would exercise in dealing with his own property" - regardless of the type or purposes of the trust. *See* Restatement (Second) of Trusts § 174 cmt. a (1959). This section appropriately bases the standard on the purposes and other circumstances of the particular trust.

A settlor who wishes to modify the standard of care specified in this section is free to do so, but there is a limit. Section 1008 prohibits a settlor from exculpating a trustee from liability for breach of trust committed in bad faith or with reckless indifference to the purposes of the trust or to the interests of the beneficiaries.

§ 805. Costs of Administration. In administering a trust, the trustee may incur only costs that are reasonable in relation to the trust property, the purposes of the trust, and the skills of the trustee.

Comment

This section is similar to § 7 of the Uniform Prudent Investor Act and is consistent with the rules concerning costs in Restatement (Third) of Trusts: Prudent Investor Rule § 227(c)(3) (1992). For related rules concerning compensation and reimbursement of trustees, see §§ 708 and 709. The duty not to incur unreasonable costs applies when a trustee decides whether and how to delegate to agents, as well as to other aspects of trust administration. In deciding whether and how to delegate, the trustee must be alert to balancing projected benefits against the likely costs. To protect the beneficiary against excessive costs, the trustee should also be alert to adjusting compensation for functions which the trustee has delegated to others. The obligation to incur only necessary or appropriate costs of administration has long been part of the law of trusts. *See* Restatement (Second) of Trusts § 188 (1959).

§ 806. Trustee's Skills. A trustee who has special skills or expertise, or is named trustee in reliance upon the trustee's representation that the trustee has special skills or expertise, shall use those special skills or expertise.

Comment

This section is similar to § 7-302 of the Uniform Probate Code, Restatement (Second) of Trusts § 174 (1959), and § 2(f) of the Uniform Prudent Investor Act.

§ 807. Delegation by Trustee.

(a) A trustee may delegate duties and powers that a prudent trustee of comparable skills could properly delegate under the circumstances. The trustee shall exercise reasonable care, skill, and caution in:

(1) selecting an agent;

(2) establishing the scope and terms of the delegation, consistent with the purposes and terms of the trust; and

(3) periodically reviewing the agent's actions in order to monitor the agent's performance and compliance with the terms of the delegation.

(b) In performing a delegated function, an agent owes a duty to the trust to exercise reasonable care to comply with the terms of the delegation.

(c) A trustee who complies with subsection (a) is not liable to the beneficiaries or to the trust for an action of the agent to whom the function was delegated.

(d) By accepting a delegation of powers or duties from the trustee of a trust that is subject to the law of this State, an agent submits to the jurisdiction of the courts of this State.

Comment

This section permits trustees to delegate various aspects of trust administration to agents, subject to the standards of the section. The language is derived from § 9 of the Uniform Prudent Investor Act. *See also* John H. Langbein, *Reversing the Nondelegation Rule of Trust-Investment Law*, 59 Mo. L. Rev. 105 (1994) (discussing prior law).

This section encourages and protects the trustee in making delegations appropriate to the facts and circumstances of the particular trust. Whether a particular function is delegable is based on whether it is a function that a prudent trustee might delegate under similar circumstances. For example, delegating some administrative and reporting duties might be prudent for a family trustee but unnecessary for a corporate trustee.

This section applies only to delegation to agents, not to delegation to a cotrustee. For the provision regulating delegation to a cotrustee, see § 703(e).

§ 808. [Reserved]

Legislative Note: A state that has enacted the Uniform Directed Trust Act (UDTA) should repeal Section 808 and revise certain other provision of the UTC as indicated in the legislative notes to the UDTA.

Comment

2018 Amendment. Former UTC Section 808 was largely superseded by the Uniform Directed Trust Act (UDTA) in 2017. The UDTA addresses the subject of trust director and directed trustees more comprehensively. Former subsection (a), addressing directions from the settlor of a revocable trust to the trustee, was revised for clarity and relocated to UTC Section 603 with other rules governing revocable trusts. Former subsections (b)-(d) were deleted.

Former UTC Section 808 provided as follows:

(a) While a trust is revocable, the trustee may follow a direction of the settlor that is contrary to the terms of the trust.

(b) If the terms of a trust confer upon a person other than the settlor of a revocable trust power to direct certain actions of the trustee, the trustee shall act in accordance with an exercise of the power unless the attempted exercise is manifestly contrary to the terms of the trust or the trustee knows the attempted exercise would constitute a serious breach of a fiduciary duty that the person holding the power owes to the beneficiaries of the trust.

(c) The terms of a trust may confer upon a trustee or other person a power to direct the modification or termination of the trust.

(d) A person, other than a beneficiary, who holds a power to direct is presumptively a fiduciary who, as such, is required to act in good faith with regard to the purposes of the trust and the interests of the beneficiaries. The holder of a power to direct is liable for any loss that results from breach of a fiduciary duty.

§ 809. Control and Protection of Trust Property. A trustee shall take reasonable steps to take control of and protect the trust property.

Comment

This section codifies the substance of §§ 175 and 176 of the Restatement (Second) of Trusts (1959). The duty to take control of and safeguard trust property is an aspect of the trustee's duty of prudent administration as provided in § 804. *See also* §§ 816(1) (power to collect trust property), 816(11) (power to insure trust property), and 816(12) (power to abandon trust property). The duty to take control normally means that the trustee must take physical possession of tangible personal property and securities belonging to the trust, and must secure payment of any choses in action. *See* Restatement (Second) of Trusts § 175 cmt. a, c & d (1959). This section, like the other sections in this article, is subject to alteration by the terms of the trust. *See* § 105. For example, the settlors may provide that the spouse may occupy the settlor's former residence rent free, in which event the spouse's occupancy would prevent the trustee from taking possession.

§ 810. Recordkeeping and Identification of Trust Property.

(a) A trustee shall keep adequate records of the administration of the trust.

(b) A trustee shall keep trust property separate from the trustee's own property.

(c) Except as otherwise provided in subsection (d), a trustee shall cause the trust property to be designated so that the interest of the trust, to the extent feasible, appears in records maintained by a party other than a trustee or beneficiary.

(d) If the trustee maintains records clearly indicating the respective interests, a trustee may invest as a whole the property of two or more separate trusts.

Comment

The duty to keep adequate records stated in subsection (a) is implicit in the duty to act with prudence (§ 804) and the duty to report to beneficiaries (§ 813). For an application, see *Green v. Lombard*, 343 A. 2d 905, 911 (Md. Ct. Spec. App. 1975). *See also* Restatement (Second) of Trusts §§ 172, 174 (1959).

The duty to earmark trust assets and the duty of a trustee not to mingle the assets of the trust with the trustee's own are closely related. Subsection (b), which addresses the duty not to mingle, is derived from § 179 of the Restatement (Second) of Trusts (1959). Subsection (c) makes the requirement that assets be earmarked more precise than that articulated in Restatement (Second) § 179 by requiring that the interest of the trust must appear in the records of a third party, such as a bank, brokerage firm, or transfer agent. Because of the serious risk of mistake or misappropriation even if disclosure is made to the beneficiaries, showing the interest of the trust solely in the trustee's own internal records is insufficient. Section 816(7)(B), which allows a trustee to hold securities in nominee form, is not inconsistent with this requirement. While securities held in nominee form are not specifically registered in the name of the trustee, they are properly earmarked because the trustee's holdings are indicated in the records maintained by an independent party, such as in an account at a brokerage firm.

Earmarking is not practical for all types of assets. With respect to assets not subject to registration, such as tangible personal property and bearer bonds, arranging for the trust's ownership interest to be reflected on the records of a third-party custodian would not be feasible. For this reason, subsection (c) waives separate recordkeeping for these types of assets. Under subsection (b), however, the duty of the trustee not to mingle these or any other trust assets with the trustee's own remains absolute.

Subsection (d), following the lead of a number of state statutes, allows a trustee to use the property of two or more trusts to make joint investments, even though under traditional principles a joint investment would violate the duty to earmark. A joint investment frequently is more economical than attempting to invest the funds of each trust separately. Also, the risk of misappropriation or mistake is less when the trust property is invested jointly with the property of another trust than when pooled with the property of the trustee or other person.

§ 811. Enforcement and Defense of Claims.

A trustee shall take reasonable steps to enforce claims of the trust and to defend claims against the trust.

Comment

This section codifies the substance of §§ 177 and 178 of the Restatement (Second) of Trusts (1959). It may not be reasonable to enforce a claim depending upon the likelihood of recovery and the cost of suit and enforcement. It might also be reasonable to settle an action or suffer a default rather than to defend an action. *See also* § 816(14) (power to pay, contest, settle, or release claims).

§ 812. Collecting Trust Property.

A trustee shall take reasonable steps to compel a former trustee or other person to deliver trust property to the trustee, and to redress a breach of trust known to the trustee to have been committed by a former trustee.

Comment

This section is a specific application of § 811 on the duty to enforce claims, which includes a claim for trust property held by a former trustee or others, and a claim against a predecessor trustee for breach of trust. The duty imposed by this section is not absolute. Pursuit of a claim is not required if the amount of the claim, costs of suit and enforcement, and likelihood of recovery, make such action uneconomic. Unlike Restatement (Second) of Trusts § 223 (1959), this section only requires a successor trustee to redress breaches of trust "known" to have been committed by the predecessor. For the

definition of "know," see § 104. Limiting the successor's obligation to known breaches is a common feature of state trust statutes. *See, e.g.,* Mo. Rev. Stat. § 456.187.2.

As authorized by § 1009, the beneficiaries may relieve the trustee from potential liability for failing to pursue a claim against a predecessor trustee or other person holding trust property. The obligation to pursue a predecessor trustee can also be addressed in the terms of the trust. *See* § 105.

§ 813. Duty to Inform and Report.

(a) A trustee shall keep the qualified beneficiaries of the trust reasonably informed about the administration of the trust and of the material facts necessary for them to protect their interests. Unless unreasonable under the circumstances, a trustee shall promptly respond to a beneficiary's request for information related to the administration of the trust.

(b) A trustee: ·

(1) upon request of a beneficiary, shall promptly furnish to the beneficiary a copy of the trust instrument;

(2) within 60 days after accepting a trusteeship, shall notify the qualified beneficiaries of the acceptance and of the trustee's name, address, and telephone number;

(3) within 60 days after the date the trustee acquires knowledge of the creation of an irrevocable trust, or the date the trustee acquires knowledge that a formerly revocable trust has become irrevocable, whether by the death of the settlors or otherwise, shall notify the qualified beneficiaries of the trust's existence, of the identity of the settlors or settlors, of the right to request a copy of the trust instrument, and of the right to a trustee's report as provided in subsection (c); and

(4) shall notify the qualified beneficiaries in advance of any change in the method or rate of the trustee's compensation.

(c) A trustee shall send to the distributees or permissible distributees of trust income or principal, and to other qualified or nonqualified beneficiaries who request it, at least annually and at the termination of the trust, a report of the trust property, liabilities, receipts, and disbursements, including the source and amount of the trustee's compensation, a listing of the trust assets and, if feasible, their respective market values. Upon a vacancy in a trusteeship, unless a cotrustee remains in office, a report must be sent to the qualified beneficiaries by the former trustee. A personal representative, [conservator], or [guardian] may send the qualified beneficiaries a report on behalf of a deceased or incapacitated trustee.

(d) A beneficiary may waive the right to a trustee's report or other information otherwise required to be furnished under this section. A beneficiary, with respect to future reports and other information, may withdraw a waiver previously given.

(e) Subsections (b)(2) and (3) do not apply to a trustee who accepts a trusteeship before [the effective date of this [Code]], to an irrevocable trust created before [the effective date of this [Code]], or to a revocable trust that becomes irrevocable before [the effective date of this [Code]].

Comment

The duty to keep the beneficiaries reasonably   informed of the administration of the trust is a fundamental duty of a trustee. This duty, which is stated in subsection (a), is derived from § 7-303(a) of the Uniform Probate Code, which was approved in 1969 and which has been enacted in about a third of the states. This provision of the UPC has also been enacted in states that have not otherwise enacted the Uniform Probate Code. *See, e.g.,* Cal. Prob. Code. §§ 16060-16061. Unlike the cited provision of the UPC, subsection (a) of this section limits the duty to keep the beneficiaries informed to the qualified beneficiaries. For the definition of qualified beneficiary, see § 103(13). The result of this limitation is that the information need not be furnished to beneficiaries with remote remainder interests unless they have made a request to the trustee.

For the extent to which a settlors may waive the requirements of this section in the terms of the trust, see § 105(b)(8)-(9).

Subsection (a) requires that the trustee keep the qualified beneficiaries of the trust reasonably informed about the administration of the trust and of the material facts necessary for them to protect their interests. This may include a duty to communicate to a qualified beneficiary information about the administration of the trust that is reasonably necessary to enable the beneficiary to enforce the beneficiary's rights and to prevent or redress a breach of trust. *See* Restatement (Second) of Trusts § 173 cmt. c (1959). With respect to the permissible distributees, the duty articulated in subsection (a) would ordinarily be satisfied by providing the beneficiary with a copy of the annual report mandated by subsection (c). Otherwise, the trustee is not ordinarily under a duty to furnish information to a beneficiary in the absence of a specific request for the information. *See* Restatement (Second) of Trusts § 173 cmt. d (1959). However, special circumstances may require that the trustee take affirmative steps to provide additional information. For example, if the trustee is dealing with the beneficiary on the trustee's own account, the trustee must communicate material facts relating to the transaction that the trustee knows or should know. *See* Restatement (Second) of Trusts § 173 cmt. d (1959). Furthermore, to enable the beneficiaries to take action to protect their interests, the trustee may be required to provide advance notice of transactions involving real estate, closely-held business interests, and other assets that are difficult to value or to replace. *See In re Green Charitable Trust,* 431 N.W. 2d 492 (Mich. Ct. App. 1988); *Allard v.*

Pacific National Bank, 663 P.2d 104 (Wash. 1983). The trustee is justified in not providing such advance disclosure if disclosure is forbidden by other law, as under federal securities laws, or if disclosure would be seriously detrimental to the interests of the beneficiaries, for example, when disclosure would cause the loss of the only serious buyer.

Subsection (a) also requires that the trustee promptly respond to the request of any beneficiary, whether qualified or not, for information related to the administration of the trust. Performance is excused only if compliance is unreasonable under the circumstances. Within the bounds of the reasonableness limit, this provision allows the beneficiary to determine what information is relevant to protect the beneficiary's interest. Should a beneficiary so request, subsection (b)(1) also requires the trustee to furnish the beneficiary with a complete copy of the trust instrument and not merely with those portions the trustee deems relevant to the beneficiary's interest. For a case reaching the same result, see *Fletcher v. Fletcher,* 480 S.E. 2d 488 (Va. Ct. App. 1997). Subsection (b)(1) is to more expansive § 7-303(b) of the Uniform Probate Code, which provides that "[u]pon reasonable request, the trustee shall provide the beneficiary with a copy of the terms of the trust which describe or affect his interest. . . ."

The drafters of this Code decided to leave open for further consideration by the courts the extent to which a trustee may claim attorney-client privilege against a beneficiary seeking discovery of attorney-client communications between the trustee and the trustee's attorney. The courts are split because of the important values that are in tension on this question. "The [attorney-client] privilege recognizes that sound legal advice or advocacy serves public ends and that such advice or advocacy depends upon the lawyer's being fully informed by the client." *Upjohn Co. v. United States,* 449 U.S. 383 (1981). On the other hand, subsection (a) of this section requires that a trustee keep the qualified beneficiaries reasonably informed about the administration of the trust and of the material facts necessary for them to protect their interests, which could include facts that the trustee has revealed only to the trustee's attorney. There is authority for the view that the trustee is estopped from pleading attorney-client privilege in such circumstances. In the leading case, *Riggs National Bank v. Zimmer,* 355 A.2d 709, 713 (Del. Ch. 1976), the court reasoned that the beneficiary, not the trustee, is the attorney's client: "As a representative for the beneficiaries of the trust which he is administering, the trustee is not the real client . . . ." This beneficiary-as-client theory has been criticized on the ground that it conflicts with the trustee's fiduciary duty to implement the intentions of the settlor, which are sometimes in tension with the wishes of one or more beneficiaries. *See* Louis H. Hamel, Jr., *Trustee's Privileged Counsel: A Rebuttal*, 21 ACTEC Notes 156 (1995); Charles F. Gibbs & Cindy D. Hanson, *The Fiduciary Exception to a Trustee's Attorney/Client Privilege*, 21 ACTEC Notes 236 (1995). Prominent decisions in California and Texas have refused to follow Delaware in recognizing an exception for the beneficiary against the trustee's attorney-client privilege. *Wells Fargo Bank v. Superior Court (Boltwood)*, 990 P.2d 591 (Cal. 2000); *Huie v. De Shazo*, 922 S.W.2d 920 (Tex. 1996). The beneficiary-as-client theory continues to be applied to ERISA trusts. *See, e.g., United States v. Mett*, 178 F.3d 1058, 1062-64 (9th Cir. 1999). However, in a pension trust the beneficiaries are the settlors of their own trust because the trust is funded with their own earnings. Accordingly, in ERISA attorney-client cases "[t]here are no competing interests such as other stockholders or the intentions of the Settlor." Gibbs & Hanson, 21 ACTEC Notes at 238. For further discussion of the attorney-client privilege and whether there is a duty to disclose to the beneficiaries, see ACTEC Commentaries on the Model Rules of Professional Conduct, Commentary on MRPC 1.2 (3d ed. 1999); Rust E. Reid et al., *Privilege and Confidentiality Issues When a Lawyer Represents a Fiduciary*, 30 Real Prop. Prob. & Tr. J. 541 (1996).

To enable beneficiaries to protect their interests effectively, it is essential that they know the identity of the trustee. Subsection (b)(2) requires that a trustee inform the qualified beneficiaries within 60 days of the trustee's acceptance of office and of the trustee's name, address and telephone number. Similar to the obligation imposed on a personal representative following admission of the will to probate, subsection (b)(3) requires the trustee of a revocable trust to inform the qualified beneficiaries of the trust's existence within 60 days after the settlor's death. These two duties can overlap. If the death of the settlors happens also to be the occasion for the appointment of a successor trustee, the new trustee of the formerly revocable trust would need to inform the qualified beneficiaries both of the trustee's acceptance and of the trust's existence.

Subsection (b)(4) deals with the sensitive issue of changes, usually increases, in trustee compensation. Changes can include changes in a periodic base fee, rate of percentage compensation, hourly rate, termination fee, or transaction charge. Regarding the standard for setting trustee compensation, see § 708 and Comment.

Subsection (c) requires the trustee to furnish the current beneficiaries and other beneficiaries who request it with a copy of a trustee's report at least annually and upon termination of the trust. Unless a cotrustee remains in office, the former trustee also must provide a report to all of the qualified beneficiaries upon the trustee's resignation or removal. If the vacancy occurred because of the former trustee's death or adjudication of incapacity, a report may, but need not be provided by the former trustee's personal representative, conservator, or guardian.

The Uniform Trust Code employs the term "report" instead of "accounting" in order to negate any inference that the report must be prepared in any particular format or with a high degree of formality. The reporting requirement might even be satisfied by providing the beneficiaries with copies of the trust's income tax returns and monthly brokerage account statements if the information on those returns and statements is complete and sufficiently clear. The key factor is not the format chosen but whether the report provides the beneficiaries with the information necessary to protect their interests. For model account forms, together with practical advice on how to prepare reports, see Robert Whitman, Fiduciary Accounting Guide (2d ed. 1998).

Subsection (d) allows trustee reports and other required information to be waived by a beneficiary. A beneficiary may also withdraw a consent. However, a waiver of a trustee's report or other information does not relieve the trustee from accountability and potential liability for matters that the report or other information would have disclosed.

Subsection (e), which was added to the Code in 2004, is discussed in 2004 Amendment below.

2004 Amendment. Subsection (b)(2) and (b)(3) require that certain notices be sent by the trustee to the qualified beneficiaries within 60 days of the trustee's acceptance of office, or within 60 days after the creation of an irrevocable trust or the date a revocable trust becomes irrevocable. Subsection (e) is added to make clear the drafting committee's intent that these requirements are not to be retroactively applied to trustee acceptances of office occurring prior to the effective date of the Code and to trusts which have become irrevocable prior to the effective   date.

§ 814. Discretionary Powers; Tax Savings.

(a) Notwithstanding the breadth of discretion granted to a trustee in the terms of the trust, including the use of such terms as "absolute", "sole", or "uncontrolled", the trustee shall exercise a discretionary power in good faith and in accordance with the terms and purposes of the trust and the interests of the beneficiaries.

(b) Subject to subsection (d), and unless the terms of the trust expressly indicate that a rule in this subsection does not apply:

(1) a person other than a settlor who is a beneficiary and trustee of a trust that confers on the trustee a power to make discretionary distributions to or for the trustee's personal benefit may exercise the power only in accordance with an ascertainable standard; and

(2) a trustee may not exercise a power to make discretionary distributions to satisfy a legal obligation of support that the trustee personally owes another person.

(c) A power whose exercise is limited or prohibited by subsection (b) may be exercised by a majority of the remaining trustees whose exercise of the power is not so limited or prohibited. If the power of all trustees is so limited or prohibited, the court may appoint a special fiduciary with authority to exercise the power.

(d) Subsection (b) does not apply to:

(1) a power held by the settlor's spouse who is the trustee of a trust for which a marital deduction, as defined in Section 2056(b)(5) or 2523(e) of the Internal Revenue Code of 1986, as in effect on [the effective date of this [Code]] [, or as later amended], was previously allowed;

(2) any trust during any period that the trust may be revoked or amended by its settlors; or

(3) a trust if contributions to the trust qualify for the annual exclusion under Section 2503(c) of the Internal Revenue Code of 1986, as in effect on [the effective date of this [Code]] [, or as later amended].

Comment

Despite the breadth of discretion purportedly granted by the wording of a trust, no grant of discretion to a trustee, whether with respect to management or distribution, is ever absolute. A grant of discretion establishes a range within which the trustee may act. The greater the grant of discretion, the broader the range. Pursuant to subsection (a), a trustee's action must always be in good faith, with regard to the purposes of the trust, and in accordance with the trustee's other duties, including the obligation to exercise reasonable skill, care and caution. *See* §§ 801 (duty to administer trust), 804 (duty to act with prudence). The standard stated in subsection (a) applies only to powers which are to be exercised in a fiduciary as opposed to a nonfiduciary capacity. Regarding the standards for exercising discretion and construing particular language of discretion, see Restatement (Third) of Trusts § 50 (Tentative Draft No. 2, approved 1999); Restatement (Second) of Trusts § 187 (1959). *See also* Edward C. Halbach, Jr., *Problems of Discretion in Discretionary*

Trusts, 61 Colum. L. Rev. 1425 (1961). An abuse by the trustee of the discretion granted in the terms of the trust is a breach of trust that can result in surcharge. *See* § 1001(b) (remedies for breach of trust).

Subsections (b) through (d) rewrite the terms of a trust that might otherwise result in adverse estate and gift tax consequences to a beneficiary-trustee. This Code does not generally address the subject of tax curative provisions. These are provisions that automatically rewrite the terms of trusts that might otherwise fail to qualify for probable intended tax benefits. Such provisions, because they apply to all trusts using or failing to use specified language, are often overbroad, applying not only to trusts intended to qualify for tax benefits but also to smaller trust situations where taxes are not a concern. Enacting tax-curative provisions also requires special diligence by state legislatures to make certain that these provisions are periodically amended to account for the frequent changes in federal tax law. Furthermore, many failures to draft with sufficient care may be correctable by including a tax savings clause in the terms of the trust or by seeking modification of the trust using one or more of the methods authorized by §§ 411-417. Notwithstanding these reasons, the unintended inclusion of the trust in the beneficiary-trustee's gross estate is a frequent enough occurrence that the drafters concluded that it is a topic that this Code should address. It is also a topic on which numerous states have enacted corrective statutes.

A tax curative provision differs from a statute such as § 416 of this Code, which allows a court to modify a trust to achieve an intended tax benefit. Absent Congressional or regulatory authority authorizing the specific modification, a lower court decree in state court modifying a trust is controlling for federal estate tax purposes only if the decree was issued before the taxing event, which in the case of the estate tax would be the decedent's death. *See* Rev. Rul. 73-142, 1973-1 C.B. 405. There is specific federal authority authorizing modification of trusts for a number of reasons (*see* Comment to § 416) but not on the specific issues addressed in this section. Subsections (b) through (d), by interpreting the original language of the trust instrument in a way that qualifies for intended tax benefits, obviates the need to seek a later modification of the trust.

Subsection (b)(1) states the main rule. Unless the terms of the trust expressly indicate that the rule in this subsection is not to apply, the power to make discretionary distributions to a beneficiary-trustee is automatically limited by the requisite ascertainable standard necessary to avoid inclusion of the trust in the trustee's gross estate or result in a taxable gift upon the trustee's release or exercise of the power. Trusts of which the trustee-beneficiary is also a settlors are not subject to this subsection. In such a case, limiting the discretion of a settlors-trustee to an ascertainable standard would not be sufficient to avoid inclusion of the trust in the settlor's gross estate. *See generally* John J. Regan, Rebecca C. Morgan & David M. English, Tax, Estate and Financial Planning for the Elderly § 17.07[2][h]. Furthermore, the inadvertent inclusion of a trust in a settlor-trustee's gross estate is a far less frequent and better understood occurrence than is the inadvertent inclusion of the trust in the estate of a nonsettlor trustee-beneficiary.

Subsection (b)(2) addresses a common trap, the trustee who is not a beneficiary but who has power to make discretionary distributions to those to whom the trustee owes a legal obligation of support.

Discretion to make distributions to those to whom the trustee owes a legal obligation of support, such as to the trustee's minor children, results in inclusion of the trust in the trustee's gross estate even if the power is limited by an ascertainable standard. The applicable regulation provides that the ascertainable standard exception applies only to distributions for the benefit of the decedent, not to distributions to those to whom the decedent owes a legal obligation of support. *See* Treas. Reg. § 20.2041-1(c)(2).

Subsection (c) deals with cotrustees and adopts the common planning technique of granting the broader discretion only to the independent trustee. Cotrustees who are beneficiaries of the trust or who have a legal obligation to support a beneficiary may exercise the power only as limited by subsection (b). If all trustees are so limited, the court may appoint a special fiduciary to make a decision as to whether a broader exercise is appropriate.

Subsection (d) excludes certain trusts from the operation of this section. Trusts qualifying for the marital deduction will be includable in the surviving spouse's gross estate regardless of whether this section applies. Consequently, if the spouse is acting as trustee, there is no need to limit the power of the spouse-trustee to make discretionary distributions for the spouse's benefit. Similar reasoning applies to the revocable trust, which, because of the settlor's power to revoke, is automatically includable in the settlor's gross estate even if the settlor is not named as a beneficiary.

QTIP marital trusts are subject to this section, however. QTIP trusts qualify for the marital deduction only if so elected on the federal estate tax return. Excluding a QTIP for which an election has been made from the operation of this section would allow the terms of the trust to be modified after the settlor's death. By not making the QTIP election, an otherwise unascertainable standard would be limited. By making the QTIP election, the trustee's discretion would not be curtailed. This ability to modify a trust depending on elections made on the federal estate tax return could itself constitute a taxable power of appointment resulting in inclusion of the trust in the surviving spouse's gross estate.

The exclusion of the § 2503(c) minors trust is necessary to avoid loss of gift tax benefits. While preventing a trustee from distributing trust funds in discharge of a legal obligation of support would keep the trust out of the trustee's gross estate, such a restriction might result in loss of the gift tax annual exclusion for contributions to the trust, even if the trustee were otherwise granted unlimited discretion. *See* Rev. Rul. 69-345, 1969-1 C.B. 226.

2004 Amendment. The amendment substitutes

"ascertainable standard" which is now a defined term in § 103(2) for the former and identical definition in this section. No substantive change is intended.

§ 815. General Powers of Trustee.

(a) A trustee, without authorization by the court, may exercise:

(1) powers conferred by the terms of the trust; and

(2) except as limited by the terms of the trust:

(A) all powers over the trust property which an unmarried competent owner has over individually owned property;

(B) any other powers appropriate to achieve the proper investment, management, and distribution of the trust property; and

(C) any other powers conferred by this [Code].

(b) The exercise of a power is subject to the fiduciary duties prescribed by this [article].

Comment

This section is intended to grant trustees the broadest possible powers, but to be exercised always in accordance with the duties of the trustee and any limitations stated in the terms of the trust. This broad authority is denoted by granting the trustee the powers of an unmarried competent owner of individually owned property, unlimited by restrictions that might be placed on it by marriage, disability, or cotenancy.

The powers conferred elsewhere in this Code that are subsumed under this section include all of the specific powers listed in § 816 as well as other powers described elsewhere in this Code. *See* §§ 108(c) (transfer of principal place of administration), 414(a) (termination of uneconomic trust with value less than $50,000), 417 (combination and division of trusts),

703(e) (delegation to cotrustee), 802(h) (exception to duty of loyalty), 807 (delegation to agent of powers and duties), 810(d) (joint investments), and Article 9 (Uniform Prudent Investor Act). The powers conferred by this Code may be exercised without court approval. If court approval of the exercise of a power is desired, a petition for court approval should be filed.

A power differs from a duty. A duty imposes an obligation or a mandatory prohibition. A power, on the other hand, is a discretion, the exercise of which is not obligatory. The existence of a power, however created or granted, does not speak to the question of whether it is prudent under the circumstances to exercise the power.

§ 816. Specific Powers of Trustee.
Without limiting the authority conferred by Section 815, a trustee may:

(1) collect trust property and accept or reject additions to the trust property from a settlor or any other person;

(2) acquire or sell property, for cash or on credit, at public or private sale;

(3) exchange, partition, or otherwise change the character of trust property;

(4) deposit trust money in an account in a regulated financial-service institution;

(5) borrow money, with or without security, and mortgage or pledge trust property for a period within or extending beyond the duration of the trust;

(6) with respect to an interest in a proprietorship, partnership, limited liability company, business trust, corporation, or other form of business or enterprise, continue the business or other enterprise and take any action that may be taken by shareholders, members, or property owners, including merging, dissolving, or otherwise changing the form of business organization or contributing additional capital;

(7) with respect to stocks or other securities, exercise the rights of an absolute owner, including the right to:

(A) vote, or give proxies to vote, with or without power of substitution, or enter into or continue a voting trust agreement;

(B) hold a security in the name of a nominee or in other form without disclosure of the trust so that title may pass by delivery;

(C) pay calls, assessments, and other sums chargeable or accruing against the securities, and sell or exercise stock subscription or conversion rights; and

(D) deposit the securities with a depositary or other regulated financial-service institution;

(8) with respect to an interest in real property, construct, or make ordinary or extraordinary repairs to, alterations to, or improvements in, buildings or other structures, demolish improvements, raze existing or erect new party walls or buildings, subdivide or develop land, dedicate land to public use or grant public or private easements, and make or vacate plats and adjust boundaries;

(9) enter into a lease for any purpose as lessor or lessee, including a lease or other arrangement for exploration and removal of natural resources, with or without the option to purchase or renew, for a period within or extending beyond the duration of the trust;

(10) grant an option involving a sale, lease, or other disposition of trust property or acquire an option for the acquisition of property, including an option exercisable beyond the duration of the trust, and exercise an option so acquired;

(11) insure the property of the trust against damage or loss and insure the trustee, the trustee's agents, and beneficiaries against liability arising from the administration of the trust;

(12) abandon or decline to administer property of no value or of insufficient value to justify its collection or continued administration;

(13) with respect to possible liability for violation of environmental law:

(A) inspect or investigate property the trustee holds or has been asked to hold, or property owned or operated by an organization in which the trustee holds or has been asked to hold an interest, for the purpose of determining the application of environmental law with respect to the property;

(B) take action to prevent, abate, or otherwise remedy any actual or potential violation of any environmental law affecting property held directly or indirectly by the trustee, whether taken before or after the assertion of a claim or the initiation of governmental enforcement;

(C) decline to accept property into trust or disclaim any power with respect to property that is or may be burdened with liability for violation of environmental law;

(D) compromise claims against the trust which may be asserted for an alleged violation of environmental law; and

(E) pay the expense of any inspection, review, abatement, or remedial action to comply with environmental law;

(14) pay or contest any claim, settle a claim by or against the trust, and release, in whole or in part, a claim belonging to the trust;

(15) pay taxes, assessments, compensation of the trustee and of employees and agents of the trust, and other expenses incurred in the administration of the trust;

(16) exercise elections with respect to federal, state, and local taxes;

(17) select a mode of payment under any employee benefit or retirement plan, annuity, or life insurance payable to the trustee, exercise rights thereunder, including exercise of the right to indemnification for expenses and against liabilities, and take appropriate action to collect the proceeds;

(18) make loans out of trust property, including loans to a beneficiary on terms and conditions the trustee considers to be fair and reasonable under the circumstances, and the trustee has a lien on future distributions for repayment of those loans;

(19) pledge trust property to guarantee loans made by others to the beneficiary;

(20) appoint a trustee to act in another jurisdiction with respect to trust property located in the other jurisdiction, confer upon the appointed trustee all of the powers and duties of the appointing trustee, require that the appointed trustee furnish security, and remove any trustee so appointed;

(21) pay an amount distributable to a beneficiary who is under a legal disability or who the trustee reasonably believes is incapacitated, by paying it directly to the beneficiary or applying it for the beneficiary's benefit, or by:

(A) paying it to the beneficiary's [conservator] or, if the beneficiary does not have a [conservator], the beneficiary's [guardian];

(B) paying it to the beneficiary's custodian under [the Uniform Transfers to Minors Act] or custodial trustee under [the Uniform Custodial Trust Act], and, for that purpose, creating a custodianship or custodial trust;

(C) if the trustee does not know of a [conservator], [guardian], custodian, or custodial trustee, paying it to an adult relative or other person having legal or physical care or custody of the beneficiary, to be expended on the beneficiary's behalf; or

(D) managing it as a separate fund on the beneficiary's behalf, subject to the beneficiary's continuing right to withdraw the distribution;

(22) on distribution of trust property or the division or termination of a trust, make distributions in divided or undivided interests, allocate particular assets in proportionate or disproportionate shares, value the trust property for those purposes, and adjust for resulting differences in valuation;

(23) resolve a dispute concerning the interpretation of the trust or its administration by mediation, arbitration, or other procedure for alternative dispute resolution;

(24) prosecute or defend an action, claim, or judicial proceeding in any jurisdiction to protect trust property and the trustee in the performance of the trustee's duties;

(25) sign and deliver contracts and other instruments that are useful to achieve or facilitate the exercise of the trustee's powers; and

(26) on termination of the trust, exercise the powers appropriate to wind up the administration of the trust and distribute the trust property to the persons entitled to it.

Comment

This section enumerates specific powers commonly included in trust instruments and in trustee powers legislation. All the powers listed are subject to alteration in the terms of the trust. *See* § 105. The powers listed are also subsumed under the general authority granted in § 815(a)(2) to exercise all powers over the trust property which an unmarried competent owner has over individually owned property, and any other powers appropriate to achieve the proper management, investment, and distribution of the trust property. The powers listed add little of substance not already granted by § 815 and powers conferred elsewhere in the Code, which are listed in the comment to § 815. While the committee drafting this Code discussed dropping the list of specific powers, it concluded that the demand of third parties to see language expressly authorizing specific transactions justified retention of a detailed list.

As provided in § 815(b), the exercise of a power is subject to fiduciary duties except as modified in the terms of the trust. The fact that the trustee has a power does not imply a duty that the power must be exercised.

Many of the powers listed in this section are similar to the powers listed in § 3 of the Uniform Trustees' Powers Act (1964). Several are new, however, and other powers drawn from that Act have been updated. The powers enumerated in this section may be divided into categories. Certain powers, such as the powers to acquire or sell property, borrow money, and deal with real estate, securities, and business interests, are powers that any individual can exercise. Other powers, such as the power to collect trust property, are by their very nature only applicable to trustees. Other specific powers, particularly those listed in other sections of the Uniform Trust Code, modify a trustee duty that would otherwise apply. *See, e.g.*, §§ 802(h) (exceptions to duty of loyalty), and 810(d) (joint investments as exception to earmarking requirement).

Paragraph (1) authorizes a trustee to collect trust property and collect or decline additions to the trust property. The power to collect trust property is an incident of the trustee's duty to administer the trust as provided in § 801. The trustee has a duty to enforce claims as provided in § 811, the successful prosecution of which can result in collection of trust property. Pursuant to § 812, the trustee also has a duty to collect trust property from a former trustee or other person holding trust property. For an application of the power to reject additions to the trust property, see § 816(13) (power to decline property with possible environmental liability).

Paragraph (2) authorizes a trustee to sell trust property, for cash or on credit, at public or private sale. Under the Restatement, a power of sale is implied unless limited in the terms of the trust. Restatement (Third) of Trusts: Prudent Investor Rule § 190 (1992). In arranging a sale, a trustee must comply with the duty to act prudently as provided in § 804. This duty may dictate that the sale be made with security.

Paragraph (4) authorizes a trustee to deposit funds in an account in a regulated financial-service institution. This includes the right of a financial institution trustee to deposit funds in its own banking department as authorized by § 802(h)(4).

Paragraph (5) authorizes a trustee to borrow money. Under the Restatement, the sole limitation on such borrowing is the general obligation to invest prudently. *See* Restatement (Third) of Trusts: Prudent Investor Rule § 191 (1992). Language clarifying that the loan may extend beyond the duration of the trust was added to negate an older view that the trustee only had power to encumber the trust property for the period that the trust was in existence.

Paragraph (6) authorizes the trustee to continue, contribute additional capital to, or change the form of a business. Any such decision by the trustee must be made in light of the standards of prudent investment stated in Article 9.

Paragraph (7), regarding powers with respect to securities, codifies and amplifies the principles of Restatement (Second) of Trusts § 193 (1959).

Paragraph (9), authorizing the leasing of property, negates the older view, reflected in Restatement (Second) of Trusts § 189 cmt. c (1959), that a trustee could not lease property beyond the duration of the trust. Whether a longer term lease is appropriate is judged by the standards of prudence applicable to all investments.

Paragraph (10), authorizing a trustee to grant options with respect to sales, leases or other dispositions of property, negates the older view, reflected in Restatement (Second) of Trusts § 190 cmt. k (1959), that a trustee could not grant another person an option to purchase trust property. Like any other investment decision, whether the granting of an option is appropriate is a question of prudence under the standards of Article 9.

Paragraph (11), authorizing a trustee to purchase insurance, empowers a trustee to implement the duty to protect trust property. *See* § 809. The trustee may also insure beneficiaries, agents, and the trustee against liability, including liability for breach of trust.

Paragraph (13) is one of several provisions in the Uniform Trust Code designed to address trustee concerns about possible liability for violations of environmental law. This paragraph collects all the powers relating to environmental concerns in one place even though some of the powers, such as the powers to pay expenses, compromise claims, and decline property, overlap with other paragraphs of this section (decline property, paragraph (1); compromise claims, paragraph (14); pay expenses, paragraph (15)). Numerous states have legislated on the subject of environmental liability of fiduciaries. For a representative state statute, see Tex. Prop. Code Ann. § 113.025. *See also* §§ 701(c)(2) (designated trustee may inspect property to determine potential violation of environmental or other law or for any purpose), and 1010(b) (trustee not personally liable for violation of environmental law arising from ownership or control of trust property).

Paragraph (14) authorizes a trustee to pay, contest, settle, or release claims. § 811 requires that a trustee need take only "reasonable" steps to enforce claims, meaning that a trustee may release a claim not only when it is uncollectible, but also when collection would be uneconomic. *See* Restatement (Second) of Trusts § 192 (1959) (power to compromise, arbitrate and abandon claims).

Paragraph (15), among other things, authorizes a trustee to pay compensation to the trustee and agents without prior approval of court. Regarding the standard for setting trustee compensation, see § 708. *See also* § 709 (repayment of trustee expenditures). While prior court approval is not required, § 813(b)(4) requires the trustee to inform the qualified beneficiaries in advance of a change in the method or rate of compensation.

Paragraph (16) authorizes a trustee to make elections with respect to taxes. The Uniform Trust Code leaves to other law the issue of whether the trustee, in making such elections, must make compensating adjustments in the beneficiaries' interests.

Paragraph (17) authorizes a trustee to take action with respect to employee benefit or retirement plans, or annuities or life insurance payable to the trustee. Typically, these will be beneficiary designations which the settlors has made payable to the trustee, but this Code also allows the trustee to acquire ownership of annuities or life insurance.

Paragraphs (18) and (19) allow a trustee to make loans to a beneficiary or to guarantee loans of a beneficiary upon such terms and conditions as the trustee considers fair and reasonable. The determination of what is fair and reasonable must be made in light of the fiduciary duties of the trustee and the purposes of the trust. Frequently, a trustee will make loans to a beneficiary which might be considered less than prudent in an ordinary commercial sense although of great benefit to the beneficiary and which help carry out the trust purposes. If the trustee requires security for the loan to the beneficiary, adequate security under this paragraph may consist of a charge on the beneficiary's interest in the trust. *See* Restatement (Second) of Trusts § 255 (1959). However, the interest of a beneficiary subject to a spendthrift restraint may not be pledged as security for a loan. *See* § 502.

Paragraph (20) authorizes the appointment of ancillary trustees in jurisdictions in which the regularly appointed trustee is unable or unwilling to act. Normally, an ancillary trustee will be appointed only when there is a need to manage real estate located in another jurisdiction. This paragraph allows the regularly appointed trustee to select the ancillary trustee and to confer on the ancillary trustee such powers and duties as may be necessary. The appointment of ancillary trustees is a topic which a settlors may wish to address in the terms of the trust.

Paragraph (21) authorizes a trustee to make payments to another person for the use or benefit of a beneficiary who is under a legal disability or who the trustee reasonably believes is incapacitated. Although an adult relative or other person receiving funds is required to spend it on the beneficiary's behalf, it is preferable that the trustee make the distribution to a person having more formal fiduciary responsibilities. For this reason, payment may be made to an adult relative only if the trustee does not know of a conservator, guardian, custodian, or custodial trustee capable of acting for the beneficiary.

Paragraph (22) authorizes a trustee to make non-pro-rata distributions and allocate particular assets in proportionate or disproportionate shares. This power provides needed flexibility and lessens the risk that a non-pro-rata distribution will be treated as a taxable sale.

Paragraph (23) authorizes a trustee to resolve disputes through mediation, arbitration or other methods of alternative dispute resolution. The drafters of this Code encourage the use of such alternate methods for resolving disputes. Arbitration is a form of nonjudicial settlement agreement authorized by § 111. In representing beneficiaries and others in connection with arbitration or in approving settlements obtained through mediation or other methods of ADR, the representation principles of Article 3 may be applied. Settlors wishing to encourage use of alternate dispute resolution may draft to provide it. For sample language, see American Arbitration Association, Arbitration Rules for Wills and Trusts (1995).

Paragraph (24) authorizes a trustee to prosecute or defend an action. As to the propriety of reimbursement for attorney's fees and other expenses of an action or judicial proceeding, see § 709 and Comment. *See also* § 811 (duty to defend actions).

Paragraph (26), which is similar to § 344 of the Restatement (Second) of Trusts (1959), clarifies that even though the trust has terminated, the trustee retains the powers needed to wind up the administration of the trust and distribute the remaining trust property.

§ 817. Distribution upon Termination.

(a) Upon termination or partial termination of a trust, the trustee may send to the beneficiaries a proposal for distribution. The right of any beneficiary to object to the proposed distribution terminates if the beneficiary does not notify the trustee of an objection within 30 days after the proposal was sent but only if the proposal informed the beneficiary of the right to object and of the time allowed for objection.

(b) Upon the occurrence of an event terminating or partially terminating a trust, the trustee shall proceed expeditiously to distribute the trust property to the persons entitled to it, subject to the right of the trustee to retain a reasonable reserve for the payment of debts, expenses, and taxes.

(c) A release by a beneficiary of a trustee from liability for breach of trust is invalid to the extent:

(1) it was induced by improper conduct of the trustee; or

(2) the beneficiary, at the time of the release, did not know of the beneficiary's rights or of the material facts relating to the breach.

Comment

This section contains several independent provisions governing distribution upon termination. Other provisions of the Uniform Trust Code relevant to distribution upon termination include § 816(26) (powers upon termination to windup administration and distribution), and 1005 (limitation of action against trustee).

Subsection (a) is based on § 3-906(b) of the Uniform Probate Code. It addresses the dilemma that sometimes arises when the trustee is reluctant to make distribution until the beneficiary approves but the beneficiary is reluctant to approve until the assets are in hand. The procedure made available under subsection (a) facilitates the making of non-pro-rata distributions. However, whenever practicable it is normally better practice to obtain the advance written consent of the beneficiaries to a proposed plan of distribution. Similar to other notices under the Code, the right of a beneficiary to object may be barred by delivery of the proposal to another person if that other person may represent and bind the beneficiary as provided in Article 3.

The failure of a beneficiary to object to a plan of distribution pursuant to subsection (a) is not a release as provided in subsection (c) or § 1009. A release requires an affirmative act by a beneficiary and is not accomplished upon a mere failure to object. Furthermore, a failure of a beneficiary to object does not preclude the beneficiary from bringing an action with respect to matters not disclosed in the proposal for distribution.

Subsection (b) recognizes that upon an event terminating or partially terminating a trust, expeditious distribution should be encouraged to the extent reasonable under the circumstances. However, a trustee is entitled to retain a reasonable reserve for payment of debts, expenses, and taxes. Sometimes these reserves must be quite large, for example, upon the death of the beneficiary of a QTIP trust that is subject to federal estate tax in the beneficiary's estate. Not infrequently, a substantial reserve must be retained until the estate tax audit is concluded several years after the beneficiary's death.

Subsection (c) is an application of § 1009. Section 1009 addresses the validity of any type of release that a beneficiary might give. Subsection (c) is more limited, dealing only with releases given upon termination of the trust. Factors affecting the validity of a release include adequacy of disclosure, whether the beneficiary had a legal incapacity and was not represented under Article 3, and whether the trustee engaged in any improper conduct. *See* Restatement (Second) of Trusts § 216 (1959).

Comment Amended in 2005.

ARTICLE 9
UNIFORM PRUDENT INVESTOR ACT

General Comment

Because of the widespread adoption of the Uniform Prudent Investor Act, no effort has been made to disassemble and integrate the Uniform Prudent Investor Act into the Uniform Trust Code. States adopting the Uniform Trust Code that have previously enacted the Prudent Investor Act are encouraged to reenact their version of the Prudent Investor Act as Article 9 of the Uniform Trust Code. Reenacting the Uniform Prudent Investor Act as a unit will preserve uniformity with states that have enacted the Uniform Prudent Investor Act in free-standing form.

The Uniform Prudent Investor Act prescribes a series of duties relevant to the *investment* and *management* of trust property. The Uniform Trust Code, Article 8 contains duties and powers of a trustee relevant to the *investment, administration,* and *distribution* of trust property. There is therefore significant overlap between Article 8 and the Prudent Investor Act. Where the Uniform Prudent Investor Act and Uniform Trust Code are duplicative, enacting jurisdictions are encouraged to enact the Uniform Prudent Investor Act in this article but *without* the provisions already addressed in Article 8 of the Uniform Trust Code. The duplicative provisions of the Uniform Prudent Investor Act and Article 8 of this Code are as follows:

	Prudent Investor Act	Article 8
Special Skills	2(f)	806
Loyalty	5	802
Impartiality	6	803
Investment costs	7	805
Delegation	9	807

Deleting these duplicative provisions leaves the following sections of the Uniform Prudent Investor Act for enactment in this article:

Section 1	Prudent Investor Rule
Section 2 (a)-(e)	Standard of Care; Portfolio Strategy; Risk and Return Objectives
Section 3	Diversification
Section 4	Duties at Inception of Trusteeship
Section 8	Reviewing Compliance
Section 10	Language Invoking Standard of [Act]

ARTICLE 10
LIABILITY OF TRUSTEES AND RIGHTS OF PERSONS DEALING WITH TRUSTEE

General Comment

Sections 1001 through 1009 identify the remedies for breach of trust, describe how money damages are to be determined, and specify potential defenses. Section 1001 lists the remedies for breach of trust and specifies when a breach of trust occurs. A breach of trust occurs when the trustee breaches one of the duties contained in Article 8 or elsewhere in the Code. The remedies for breach of trust in § 1001 are broad and flexible. Section 1002 provides how money damages for breach of trust are to be determined. The standard for determining money damages rests on two principles: (1) the trust should be restored to the position it would have been in had the harm not occurred; and (2) the trustee should not be permitted to profit from the trustee's own wrong. Section 1003 holds a trustee accountable for profits made from the trust even in the absence of a breach of trust. Section 1004 reaffirms the court's power in equity to award costs and attorney's fees as justice requires.

Sections 1005 through 1009 deal with potential defenses. Section 1005 provides a statute of limitations on actions against a trustee. Section 1006 protects a trustee who acts in reasonable reliance on the terms of a written trust instrument. Section 1007 protects a trustee who has exercised reasonable care to ascertain the happening of events that might affect distribution, such as a beneficiary's marriage or death. Section 1008 describes the effect and limits on the use of an exculpatory clause. Section 1009 deals with the standards for recognizing beneficiary approval of acts of the trustee that might otherwise constitute a breach of trust.

Sections 1010 through 1013 address trustee relations with persons other than beneficiaries. The emphasis is on encouraging third parties to engage in commercial transactions to the same extent as if the property were not held in trust. Section 1010 negates personal liability on contracts entered into by the trustee if the fiduciary capacity was properly disclosed. The trustee is also relieved from liability for torts committed in the course of administration unless the trustee was personally at fault. Section 1011 negates personal liability for contracts entered into by partnerships in which the trustee is a general partner as long as the fiduciary capacity was disclosed in the contract or partnership certificate. Section 1012 protects persons other than beneficiaries who deal with a trustee in good faith and without knowledge that the trustee is exceeding or improperly exercising a power. Section 1013 permits a third party to rely on a certification of trust, thereby reducing the need for a third party to request a copy of the complete trust instrument.

Much of this article is not subject to override in the terms of the trust. The settlors may not limit the rights of persons other than beneficiaries as provided in §§ 1010 through 1013, nor interfere with the court's ability to take such action to remedy a breach of trust as my be necessary in the interests of justice. *See* § 105.

§ 1001. Remedies for Breach of Trust.

(a) A violation by a trustee of a duty the trustee owes to a beneficiary is a breach of trust.

(b) To remedy a breach of trust that has occurred or may occur, the court may:

(1) compel the trustee to perform the trustee's duties;

(2) enjoin the trustee from committing a breach of trust;

(3) compel the trustee to redress a breach of trust by paying money, restoring property, or other means;

(4) order a trustee to account;

(5) appoint a special fiduciary to take possession of the trust property and administer the trust;

(6) suspend the trustee;

(7) remove the trustee as provided in Section 706;

(8) reduce or deny compensation to the trustee;

(9) subject to Section 1012, void an act of the trustee, impose a lien or a constructive trust on trust property, or trace trust property wrongfully disposed of and recover the property or its proceeds; or

(10) order any other appropriate relief.

Comment

This section codifies the remedies available to rectify or to prevent a breach of trust for violation of a duty owed to a beneficiary. The duties that a trust might breach include those contained in Article 8 in addition to those specified elsewhere in the Code.

This section identifies the available remedies but does not attempt to cover the refinements and exceptions developed in case law. The availability of a remedy in a particular circumstance will be determined not only by this Code but also by the common law of trusts and principles of equity. *See* § 106.

Beneficiaries and cotrustees have standing to bring a petition to remedy a breach of trust. Following a successor trustee's acceptance of office, a successor trustee has standing to sue a predecessor for breach of trust. *See* Restatement (Second) of Trusts § 200 (1959). A person who may represent a beneficiary's interest under Article 3 would have standing to bring a petition on behalf of the person represented. In the case of a charitable trust, those with standing include the state attorney general, a charitable organization expressly designated to receive distributions under the terms of the trust, and other persons with a special interest. *See* § 110 & Restatement (Second) of Trusts § 391 (1959). A person appointed to enforce a trust for an animal or a trust for a noncharitable purpose would have standing to sue for a breach of trust. *See* §§ 110(b), 408, 409.

Traditionally, remedies for breach of trust at law were limited to suits to enforce unconditional obligations to pay money or deliver chattels. *See* Restatement (Second) of Trusts § 198 (1959). Otherwise, remedies for breach of trust were exclusively equitable, and as such, punitive damages were not available and findings of fact were made by the judge and not a jury. *See* Restatement (Second) of Trusts § 197 (1959). The Uniform Trust Code does not preclude the possibility that a particular enacting jurisdiction might not follow these norms.

The remedies identified in this section are derived from Restatement (Second) of Trusts § 199 (1959). The reference to payment of money in subsection (b)(3) includes liability that might be characterized as damages, restitution, or surcharge. For the measure of liability, see § 1002. Subsection (b)(5) makes explicit the court's authority to appoint a special fiduciary, also sometimes referred to as a receiver. *See* Restatement (Second) of Trusts § 199(d) (1959). The authority of the court to appoint a special fiduciary is not limited to actions alleging breach of trust but is available whenever the court, exercising its equitable jurisdiction, concludes that an appointment would promote administration of the trust. *See* § 704(d) (special fiduciary may be appointed whenever court considers such appointment necessary for administration).

Subsection (b)(8), which allows the court to reduce or deny compensation, is in accord with Restatement (Second) of Trusts § 243 (1959). For the factors to consider in setting a trustee's compensation absent breach of trust, see § 708 and Comment. In deciding whether to reduce or deny a trustee compensation, the court may wish to consider (1) whether the trustee acted in good faith; (2) whether the breach of trust was intentional; (3) the nature of the breach and the extent of the loss; (4) whether the trustee has restored the loss; and (5) the value of the trustee's services to the trust. *See* Restatement (Second) of Trusts § 243 cmt. c (1959).

The authority under subsection (b)(9) to set aside wrongful acts of the trustee is a corollary of the power to enjoin a threatened breach as provided in subsection (b)(2). However, in setting aside the wrongful acts of the trustee the court may not impair the rights of bona fide purchasers protected under § 1012. *See* Restatement (Second) of Trusts § 284 (1959).

§ 1002. Damages for Breach of Trust.

(a) A trustee who commits a breach of trust is liable to the beneficiaries affected for the greater of:

(1) the amount required to restore the value of the trust property and trust distributions to what they would have been had the breach not occurred; or

(2) the profit the trustee made by reason of the breach.

(b) Except as otherwise provided in this subsection, if more than one trustee is liable to the beneficiaries for a breach of trust, a trustee is entitled to contribution from the other trustee or trustees. A trustee is not entitled to contribution if the trustee was substantially more at fault than another trustee or if the trustee committed the breach of trust in bad faith or with reckless indifference to the purposes of the trust or the interests of the beneficiaries. A trustee who received a benefit from the breach of trust is not entitled to contribution from another trustee to the extent of the benefit received.

Comment

Subsection (a) is based on Restatement (Third) of Trusts: Prudent Investor Rule § 205 (1992). If a trustee commits a breach of trust, the beneficiaries may either affirm the transaction or, if a loss has occurred, hold the trustee liable for the amount necessary to compensate fully for the consequences of the breach. This may include recovery of lost income, capital gain, or appreciation that would have resulted from proper administration. Even if a loss has not occurred, the trustee may not benefit from the improper action and is accountable for any profit the trustee made by reason of the breach.

For extensive commentary on the determination of damages, traditionally known as trustee surcharge, with numerous specific applications, see Restatement (Third) of Trusts: Prudent Investor Rule §§ 205-213 (1992). For the use of benchmark portfolios to determine damages, see Restatement (Third) of Trusts: Prudent Investor Rule Reporter's Notes to §§ 205 & 208-211 (1992). On the authority of a court of equity to reduce or excuse damages for breach of trust, see Restatement (Second) of Trusts § 205 cmt. g (1959).

For purposes of this Section and § 1003, "profit" does not include the trustee's compensation. A trustee who has committed a breach of trust is entitled to reasonable compensation for administering the trust unless the court reduces or denies the trustee compensation pursuant to § 1001(b)(8).

Subsection (b) is based on Restatement (Second) of Trusts § 258 (1959). Cotrustees are jointly and severally liable for a breach of trust if there was joint participation in the breach. Joint and several liability also is imposed on a nonparticipating cotrustee who,

as provided in § 703(g), failed to exercise reasonable care (1) to prevent a cotrustee from committing a serious breach of trust, or (2) to compel a cotrustee to redress a serious breach of trust. Joint and several liability normally carries with it a right in any trustee to seek contribution from a cotrustee to the extent the trustee has paid more than the trustee's proportionate share of the liability. Subsection (b), consistent with Restatement (Second) of Trusts § 258 (1959), creates an exception. A trustee who was substantially more at fault or committed the breach of trust in bad faith or with reckless indifference to the purposes of the trust or the interests of the beneficiaries is not entitled to contribution from the other trustees.

Determining degrees of comparative fault is a question of fact. The fact that one trustee was more culpable or more active than another does not necessarily establish that this trustee was substantially more at fault. Nor is a trustee substantially less at fault because the trustee did not actively participate in the breach. *See* Restatement (Second) of Trusts § 258 cmt. e (195). Among the factors to consider: (1) Did the trustee fraudulently induce the other trustee to join in the breach? (2) Did the trustee commit the breach intentionally while the other trustee was at most negligent? (3) Did the trustee, because of greater experience or expertise, control the actions of the other trustee? (4) Did the trustee alone commit the breach with liability imposed on the other trustee only because of an improper delegation or failure to properly monitor the actions of the cotrustee? *See* Restatement (Second) of Trusts § 258 cmt. d (1959).

§ 1003. Damages in Absence of Breach.

(a) A trustee is accountable to an affected beneficiary for any profit made by the trustee arising from the administration of the trust, even absent a breach of trust.

(b) Absent a breach of trust, a trustee is not liable to a beneficiary for a loss or depreciation in the value of trust property or for not having made a profit.

Comment

The principle on which a trustee's duty of loyalty is premised is that a trustee should not be allowed to use the trust as a means for personal profit other than for routine compensation earned. While most instances of personal profit involve situations where the trustee has breached the duty of loyalty, not all cases of personal profit involve a breach of trust. Subsection (a), which holds a trustee accountable for any profit made, even absent a breach of trust, is based on Restatement (Second) of Trusts § 203 (1959). A typical example of a profit is receipt by the trustee of a commission or bonus from a third party for actions relating to the trust's administration. *See* Restatement (Second) of Trusts § 203 cmt. a (1959).

A trustee is not an insurer. Similar to Restatement (Second) of Trusts § 204 (1959), subsection (b) provides that absent a breach of trust a trustee is not liable for a loss or depreciation in the value of the trust property or for failure to make a profit.

§ 1004. Attorney's Fees and Costs. In a judicial proceeding involving the administration of a trust, the court, as justice and equity may require, may award costs and expenses, including reasonable attorney's fees, to any party, to be paid by another party or from the trust that is the subject of the controversy.

Comment

This section, which is based on Massachusetts General Laws chapter 215, § 45, codifies the court's historic authority to award costs and fees, including reasonable attorney's fees, in judicial proceedings grounded in equity. The court may award a party its own fees and costs from the trust. The court may also charge a party's costs and fees against another party to the litigation. Generally, litigation expenses were at common law chargeable against another party only in the case of egregious conduct such as bad faith or fraud. With respect to a party's own fees, § 709 authorizes a trustee to recover expenditures properly incurred in the administration of the trust. The court may award a beneficiary litigation costs if the litigation is deemed beneficial to the trust. Sometimes, litigation brought by a beneficiary involves an allegation that the trustee has committed a breach of trust. On other occasions, the suit by the beneficiary is brought because of the trustee's failure to take action against a third party, such as to recover property properly belonging to the trust. For the authority of a beneficiary to bring an action when the trustee fails to take action against a third party, see Restatement (Second) of Trusts §§ 281-282 (1959). For the case law on the award of attorney's fees and other litigation costs, see 3 Austin W. Scott & William F. Fratcher, The Law of Trusts §§ 188.4 (4th ed. 1988).

§ 1005. Limitation of Action Against Trustee.

(a) A beneficiary may not commence a proceeding against a trustee for breach of trust more than one year after the date the beneficiary or a representative of the beneficiary was sent a report that adequately disclosed the existence of a potential claim for breach of trust and informed the beneficiary of the time allowed for commencing a proceeding.

(b) A report adequately discloses the existence of a potential claim for breach of trust if it provides sufficient information so that the beneficiary or representative knows of the potential claim or should have inquired into its existence.

(c) If subsection (a) does not apply, a judicial proceeding by a beneficiary against a trustee for breach of trust must be commenced within five years after the first to occur of:

(1) the removal, resignation, or death of the trustee;

(2) the termination of the beneficiary's interest in the trust; or

(3) the termination of the trust.

Comment

The one-year and five-year limitations periods under this section are not the only means for barring an action by a beneficiary. A beneficiary may be foreclosed by consent, release, or ratification as provided in § 1009. Claims may also be barred by principles such as estoppel and laches arising in equity under the common law of trusts. *See* § 106.

The representative referred to in subsection (a) is the person who may represent and bind a beneficiary as provided in Article 3. During the time that a trust is revocable and the settlor has capacity, the person holding the power to revoke is the one who must receive the report. *See* § 603(a) (rights of settlor of revocable trust).

This section addresses only the issue of when the clock will start to run for purposes of the statute of limitations. If the trustee wishes to foreclose possible claims immediately, a consent to the report or other information may be obtained pursuant to § 1009. For the provisions relating to the duty to report to beneficiaries, see § 813.

Subsection (a) applies only if the trustee has furnished a report. The one-year statute of limitations does not begin to run against a beneficiary who has waived the furnishing of a report as provided in § 813(d).

Subsection (c) is intended to provide some ultimate repose for actions against a trustee. It applies to cases in which the trustee has failed to report to the beneficiaries or the report did not meet the disclosure requirements of subsection (b). It also applies to beneficiaries who did not receive notice of the report, whether personally or through representation. While the five-year limitations period will normally begin to run on termination of the trust, it can also begin earlier. If a trustee leaves office prior to the termination of the trust, the limitations period for actions against that particular trustee begins to run on the date the trustee leaves office. If a beneficiary receives a final distribution prior to the date the trust terminates, the limitations period for actions by that particular beneficiary begins to run on the date of final distribution.

If a trusteeship terminates by reason of death, a claim against the trustee's estate for breach of fiduciary duty would, like other claims against the trustee's estate, be barred by a probate creditor's claim statute even though the statutory period prescribed by this section has not yet expired.

This section does not specifically provide that the statutes of limitations under this section are tolled for fraud or other misdeeds, the drafters preferring to leave the resolution of this question to other law of the state.

§ 1006. Reliance on Trust Instrument.

A trustee who acts in reasonable reliance on the terms of the trust as expressed in the trust instrument is not liable to a beneficiary for a breach of trust to the extent the breach resulted from the reliance.

Comment

It sometimes happens that the intended terms of the trust differ from the apparent meaning of the trust instrument. This can occur because the court, in determining the terms of the trust, is allowed to consider evidence extrinsic to the trust instrument. *See* § 103(18) (definition of "terms of a trust"). Furthermore, if a trust is reformed on account of mistake of fact or law, as authorized by § 415, provisions of a trust instrument can be deleted or contradicted and provisions not in the trust instrument may be added. The concept of the "terms of a trust," both as defined in this Code and as used in the doctrine of reformation, is intended to effectuate the principle that a trust should be administered and distributed in accordance with the settlor's intent. However, a trustee should also be able to administer a trust with some dispatch and without concern that a reasonable reliance on the terms of the trust instrument is misplaced. This section protects a trustee who so relies on a trust instrument but only to the extent the breach of trust resulted from such reliance. This section is similar to § 1(b) of the Uniform Prudent Investor Act, which protects a trustee from liability to the extent that the trustee acted in reasonable reliance on the provisions of the trust.

This section protects a trustee only if the trustee's reliance is reasonable. For example, a trustee's reliance on the trust instrument would not be justified if the trustee is aware of a prior court decree or binding nonjudicial settlement agreement clarifying or changing the terms of the trust.

§ 1007. Event Affecting Administration or Distribution. If the happening of an event, including marriage, divorce, performance of educational requirements, or death, affects the administration or distribution of a trust, a trustee who has exercised reasonable care to ascertain the happening of the event is not liable for a loss resulting from the trustee's lack of knowledge.

Comment

This section, which is based on Washington Revised Code § 11.98.100, is designed to encourage trustees to administer trusts expeditiously and without undue concern about liability for failure to ascertain external facts, often of a personal nature, that might affect administration or distribution of the trust. The common law, contrary to this section, imposed absolute liability against a trustee for misdelivery regardless of the trustee's level of care. *See* Restatement (Second) of Trusts § 226 (1959). The events listed in this section are not exclusive. A trustee who has exercised reasonable care to ascertain the occurrence of other events, such as the attainment by a beneficiary of a certain age, is also protected from liability.

§ 1008. Exculpation of Trustee.

(a) A term of a trust relieving a trustee of liability for breach of trust is unenforceable to the extent that it:

(1) relieves the trustee of liability for breach of trust committed in bad faith or with reckless indifference to the purposes of the trust or the interests of the beneficiaries; or

(2) was inserted as the result of an abuse by the trustee of a fiduciary or confidential relationship to the settlor.

(b) An exculpatory term drafted or caused to be drafted by the trustee is invalid as an abuse of a fiduciary or confidential relationship unless the trustee proves that the exculpatory term is fair under the circumstances and that its existence and contents were adequately communicated to the settlor.

Comment

Even if the terms of the trust attempt to completely exculpate a trustee for the trustee's acts, the trustee must always comply with a certain minimum standard. As provided in subsection (a), a trustee must always act in good faith with regard to the purposes of the trust and the interests of the beneficiaries. Subsection (a) is consistent with the standards expressed in §§ 105 and 814(a), which, similar to this section, place limits on the power of a settlor to negate trustee duties. This section is also similar to § 222 of the Restatement (Second) of Trusts (1959), except that this Code, unlike the Restatement, allows a settlor to exculpate a trustee for a profit that the trustee made from the trust.

Subsection (b) disapproves of cases such as *Marsman v. Nasca*, 573 N.E.2d 1025 (Mass. App. Ct. 1991), which held that an exculpatory clause in a trust instrument drafted by the trustee was valid because the beneficiary could not prove that the clause was inserted as a result of an abuse of a fiduciary relationship. For a later case where sufficient proof of abuse was present, see *Rutanan v. Ballard*, 678 N.E.2d 133 (Mass. 1997). Subsection (b) responds to the danger that the insertion of such a clause by the fiduciary or its agent may have been undisclosed or inadequately understood by the settlor. To overcome the presumption of abuse in subsection (b), the trustee must establish that the clause was fair and that its existence and contents were adequately communicated to the settlor. In determining whether the clause was fair, the court may wish to examine: (1) the extent of the prior relationship between the settlor and trustee; (2) whether the settlor received independent advice; (3) the sophistication of the settlor with respect to business and fiduciary matters; (4) the trustee's reasons for inserting the clause; and (5) the scope of the particular provision inserted. *See* Restatement (Second) of Trusts § 222 cmt. d (1959).

The requirements of subsection (b) are satisfied if the settlor was represented by independent counsel. If the settlor was represented by independent counsel, the settlor's attorney is considered the drafter of the instrument even if the attorney used the trustee's form. Because the settlor's attorney is an agent of the settlor, disclosure of an exculpatory term to the settlor's attorney is disclosure to the settlor.

§ 1009. Beneficiary's Consent, Release, or Ratification. A trustee is not liable to a beneficiary for breach of trust if the beneficiary consented to the conduct constituting the breach, released the trustee from liability for the breach, or ratified the transaction constituting the breach, unless:

(1) the consent, release, or ratification of the beneficiary was induced by improper conduct of the trustee; or

(2) at the time of the consent, release, or ratification, the beneficiary did not know of the beneficiary's rights or of the material facts relating to the breach.

Comment

This section is based on §§ 216 through 218 of the Restatement (Second) of Trusts (1959). A consent, release, or affirmance under this section may occur either before or after the approved conduct. This section requires an affirmative act by the beneficiary. A failure to object is not sufficient. *See* Restatement (Second) of Trusts § 216 cmt. a (1959). A consent is binding on a consenting beneficiary although other beneficiaries have not consented. *See* Restatement (Second) of Trusts § 216 cmt. g (1959). To constitute a valid consent, the beneficiary must know of the beneficiary's rights and of the material facts relating to the breach. *See* Restatement (Second) of Trusts § 216 cmt. k (1959). If the beneficiary's approval involves a self-dealing transaction, the approval is binding only if the transaction was fair and reasonable. *See* Restatement (Second) of Trusts

§§ 170(2), 216(3) & cmt. n (1959).

An approval by the settlor of a revocable trust or by the holder of a presently exercisable power of withdrawal binds all the beneficiaries. *See* § 603. A beneficiary is also bound to the extent an approval is given by a person authorized to represent the beneficiary as provided in Article 3.

2001 Amendment. By a 2001 amendment, the limitation of this section to beneficiaries "having capacity" was deleted. This limitation was included by mistake. As indicated in the second paragraph of the comment, the drafting committee did not intend to prohibit the use of the representation provisions of Article 3, several of which address representation of and the giving of a binding consent on behalf of an incapacitated beneficiary.

§ 1010. Limitation on Personal Liability of Trustee.

(a) Except as otherwise provided in the contract, a trustee is not personally liable on a contract properly entered into in the trustee's fiduciary capacity in the course of administering the trust if the trustee in the contract disclosed the fiduciary capacity.

(b) A trustee is personally liable for torts committed in the course of administering a trust, or for obligations arising from ownership or control of trust property, including liability for violation of environmental law, only if the trustee is personally at fault.

(c) A claim based on a contract entered into by a trustee in the trustee's fiduciary capacity, on an obligation arising from ownership or control of trust property, or on a tort committed in the course of administering a trust, may be asserted in a judicial proceeding against the trustee in the trustee's fiduciary capacity, whether or not the trustee is personally liable for the claim.

Comment

This section is based on § 7-306 of the Uniform Probate Code. However, unlike the Uniform Probate Code, which requires that the contract both disclose the representative capacity and identify the trust, subsection (a) protects a trustee who reveals the fiduciary relationship either by indicating a signature as trustee or by simply referring to the trust. The protection afforded the trustee by this section applies

only to contracts that are properly entered into in the trustee's fiduciary capacity, meaning that the trustee is exercising an available power and is not violating a duty. This section does not excuse any liability the trustee may have for breach of trust.

Subsection (b) addresses trustee liability arising from ownership or control of trust property and for torts occurring incident to the administration of the trust. Liability in such situations is imposed on the trustee personally only if the trustee was personally at fault, either intentionally or negligently. This is contrary to Restatement (Second) of Trusts § 264 (1959), which imposes liability on a trustee regardless of fault, including liability for acts of agents under respondeat superior. Responding to a particular concern of trustees, subsection (b) specifically protects a trustee from personal liability for violations of environmental law such as CERCLA (42 U.S.C. § 9607) or its state law counterparts, unless the trustee

was personally at fault. *See also* §§ 701(c)(2) (nominated trustee may investigate trust property to determine potential violation of environmental law without having accepted trusteeship), 816(13) (trustee powers with respect to possible liability for violation of environmental law).

Subsection (c) alters the common law rule that a trustee could not be sued in a representative capacity if the trust estate was not liable.

[§ 1011. Interest as General Partner.

(a) Except as otherwise provided in subsection (c) or unless personal liability is imposed in the contract, a trustee who holds an interest as a general partner in a general or limited partnership is not personally liable on a contract entered into by the partnership after the trust's acquisition of the interest if the fiduciary capacity was disclosed in the contract or in a statement previously filed pursuant to the [Uniform Partnership Act or Uniform Limited Partnership Act].

(b) Except as otherwise provided in subsection (c), a trustee who holds an interest as a general partner is not personally liable for torts committed by the partnership or for obligations arising from ownership or control of the interest unless the trustee is personally at fault.

(c) The immunity provided by this section does not apply if an interest in the partnership is held by the trustee in a capacity other than that of trustee or is held by the trustee's spouse or one or more of the trustee's descendants, siblings, or parents, or the spouse of any of them.

(d) If the trustee of a revocable trust holds an interest as a general partner, the settlors is personally liable for contracts and other obligations of the partnership as if the settlors were a general partner.]

Comment

Section 1010 protects a trustee from personal liability on contracts that the trustee enters into on behalf of the trust. Section 1010 also absolves a trustee from liability for torts committed in administering the trust unless the trustee was personally at fault. It does not protect a trustee from personal liability for contracts entered into or torts committed by a general or limited partnership of which the trustee was a general partner. That is the purpose of this section, which is modeled after Ohio Revised Code § 1339.65. Subsection (a) protects the trustee from personal liability for such partnership obligations whether the trustee signed the contract or it was signed by another general partner. Subsection (b) protects a trustee from personal liability for torts committed by the partnership unless the trustee was personally at fault. Protection from the partnership's contractual obligations is available under subsection (a) only if the other party is on notice of the fiduciary relationship, either in the contract itself or in the partnership certificate on file.

Special protection is not needed for other business

interests that the trustee may own, such as an interest as a limited partner, a membership interest in an LLC, or an interest as a corporate shareholder. In these cases the nature of the entity or the interest owned by the trustee carries with it its own limitation on liability.

Certain exceptions apply. The section is not intended to be used as a device for individuals or their families to shield assets from creditor claims. Consequently, subsection (c) excludes from the protections provided by this section trustees who own an interest in the partnership in another capacity or if an interest is owned by the trustee's spouse or the trustee's descendants, siblings, parents, or the spouse of any of them.

Nor can a revocable trust be used as a device for avoiding claims against the partnership. Subsection (d) imposes personal liability on the settlors for partnership contracts and other obligations of the partnership the same as if the settlors were a general partner.

This section has been placed in brackets to alert

enacting jurisdictions to consider modifying the section to conform it to the state's specific laws on

partnerships and other forms of unincorporated businesses.

§ 1012. Protection of Person Dealing with Trustee.

(a) A person other than a beneficiary who in good faith assists a trustee, or who in good faith and for value deals with a trustee, without knowledge that the trustee is exceeding or improperly exercising the trustee's powers is protected from liability as if the trustee properly exercised the power.

(b) A person other than a beneficiary who in good faith deals with a trustee is not required to inquire into the extent of the trustee's powers or the propriety of their exercise.

(c) A person who in good faith delivers assets to a trustee need not ensure their proper application.

(d) A person other than a beneficiary who in good faith assists a former trustee, or who in good faith and for value deals with a former trustee, without knowledge that the trusteeship has terminated is protected from liability as if the former trustee were still a trustee.

(e) Comparable protective provisions of other laws relating to commercial transactions or transfer of securities by fiduciaries prevail over the protection provided by this section.

Comment

This section is derived from § 7 of the Uniform Trustee Powers Act.

Subsection (a) protects two different classes; persons other than beneficiaries who assist a trustee with a transaction, and persons other than beneficiaries who deal with the trustee for value. As long as the assistance was provided or the transaction was entered into in good faith and without knowledge, third persons in either category are protected in the transaction even if the trustee was exceeding or improperly exercising the power. For the definition of "know," see § 104. This Code does not define "good faith" for purposes of this and the next section. Defining good faith with reference to the definition used in the state's commercial statutes would be consistent with the purpose of this section, which is to treat commercial transactions with trustees similar to other commercial transactions.

Subsection (b) confirms that a third party who is acting in good faith is not charged with a duty to inquire into the extent of a trustee's powers or the propriety of their exercise. The third party may assume that the trustee has the necessary power. Consequently, there is no need to request or examine a copy of the trust instrument. A third party who wishes assurance that the trustee has the necessary authority instead should request a certification of trust as provided in § 1013. Subsection (b), and the comparable provisions enacted in numerous states, are intended to negate the rule, followed by some

courts, that a third party is charged with constructive notice of the trust instrument and its contents. The cases are collected in George G. Bogert & George T. Bogert, The Law of Trusts and Trustees § 897 (Rev. 2d ed. 1995); and 4 Austin W. Scott & William F. Fratcher, The Law of Trusts § 297 (4th ed. 1989).

Subsection (c) protects any person, including a beneficiary, who in good faith delivers property to a trustee. The standard of protection in the Restatement is phrased differently although the result is similar. Under Restatement (Second) of Trusts § 321 (1959), the person delivering property to a trustee is liable if at the time of the delivery the person had notice that the trustee was misapplying or intending to misapply the property.

Subsection (d) extends the protections afforded by the section to assistance provided to or dealings for value with a former trustee. The third party is protected the same as if the former trustee still held the office.

Subsection (e) clarifies that a statute relating to commercial transactions controls whenever both it and this section could apply to a transaction. Consequently, the protections provided by this section are superseded by comparable protective provisions of these other laws. The principal statutes in question are the various articles of the Uniform Commercial Code, including Article 8 on the transfer of securities, as well as the Uniform Simplification of Fiduciary Securities Transfer Act.

§ 1013. Certification of Trust.

(a) Instead of furnishing a copy of the trust instrument to a person other than a beneficiary, the trustee may furnish to the person a certification of trust containing the following information:

(1) that the trust exists and the date the trust instrument was executed;

(2) the identity of the settlors;

(3) the identity and address of the currently acting trustee;

(4) the powers of the trustee;

(5) the revocability or irrevocability of the trust and the identity of any person holding a power to revoke the trust;

(6) the authority of cotrustees to sign or otherwise authenticate and whether all or less than all are required in order to exercise powers of the trustee;

(7) the trust's taxpayer identification number; and

(8) the manner of taking title to trust property.

(b) A certification of trust may be signed or otherwise authenticated by any trustee.

(c) A certification of trust must state that the trust has not been revoked, modified, or amended in any manner that would cause the representations contained in the certification of trust to be incorrect.

(d) A certification of trust need not contain the dispositive terms of a trust.

(e) A recipient of a certification of trust may require the trustee to furnish copies of those excerpts from the original trust instrument and later amendments which designate the trustee and confer upon the trustee the power to act in the pending transaction.

(f) A person who acts in reliance upon a certification of trust without knowledge that the representations contained therein are incorrect is not liable to any person for so acting and may assume without inquiry the existence of the facts contained in the certification. Knowledge of the terms of the trust may not be inferred solely from the fact that a copy of all or part of the trust instrument is held by the person relying upon the certification.

(g) A person who in good faith enters into a transaction in reliance upon a certification of trust may enforce the transaction against the trust property as if the representations contained in the certification were correct.

(h) A person making a demand for the trust instrument in addition to a certification of trust or excerpts is liable for damages if the court determines that the person did not act in good faith in demanding the trust instrument.

(i) This section does not limit the right of a person to obtain a copy of the trust instrument in a judicial proceeding concerning the trust.

Comment

This section, derived from California Probate Code § 18100.5, is designed to protect the privacy of a trust instrument by discouraging requests from persons other than beneficiaries for complete copies of the instrument in order to verify a trustee's authority. Even absent this section, such requests are usually unnecessary. Pursuant to § 1012(b), a third person proceeding in good faith is not required to inquire into the extent of the trustee's powers or the propriety of their exercise. This section adds another layer of protection.

Third persons frequently insist on receiving a copy of the complete trust instrument solely to verify a specific and narrow authority of the trustee to engage in a particular transaction. While a testamentary trust, because it is created under a will, is a matter of public record, an inter vivos trust instrument is private. Such privacy is compromised, however, if the trust instrument must be distributed to third persons. A certification of trust is a document signed by a currently acting trustee that may include excerpts from the trust instrument necessary to facilitate the particular transaction. A certification provides the third party with an assurance of authority without having to disclose the trust's dispositive provisions. Nor is there a need for third persons who may already have a copy of the instrument to pry into its provisions. Persons acting in reliance on a certification may assume the truth of the certification even if they have a complete copy of the trust instrument in their possession.

Subsections (a) through (c) specify the required contents of a certification. Subsection (d) clarifies that the certification need not include the trust's dispositive terms. A certification, however, normally will contain the administrative terms of the trust relevant to the transaction. Subsection (e) provides that the third party may make this a condition of acceptance. Subsections (f) and (g) protect a third party who relies on the certification. The third party may assume that the certification is true, and is not charged with constructive knowledge of the terms of the trust instrument even if the third party has a copy.

To encourage compliance with this section, a person demanding a trust instrument after already being offered a certification may be liable under subsection (h) for damages if the refusal to accept the certification is determined not to have been in good faith. A person acting in good faith would include a person required to examine a complete copy of the trust instrument pursuant to due diligence standards or as required by other law. Examples of such due diligence and legal requirements include (1) in connection with transactions to be executed in the capital markets where documentary standards have been established in connection with underwriting concerns; (2) to satisfy documentary requirements established by state or local government or regulatory agency; (3) to satisfy documentary requirements established by a state or local government or regulatory agency; and (4) where the insurance rates or premiums or other expenses of the party would be higher absent the availability of the documentation.

The Uniform Trust Code leaves to other law the issue of how damages for a bad faith refusal are to be computed and whether attorney's fees might be recoverable. For a discussion of the meaning of "good faith," see § 1012 Comment.

ARTICLE 11
MISCELLANEOUS PROVISIONS

§ 1101. Uniformity of Application and Construction. In applying and construing this Uniform Act, consideration must be given to the need to promote uniformity of the law with respect to its subject matter among States that enact it.

§ 1102. Electronic Records and Signatures. The provisions of this [Code] governing the legal effect, validity, or enforceability of electronic records or electronic signatures, and of contracts formed or performed with the use of such records or signatures, conform to the requirements of Section 102 of the Electronic Signatures in Global and National Commerce Act (15 U.S.C. § 7002) and supersede, modify, and limit the requirements of the Electronic Signatures in Global and National Commerce Act.

Comment

This section, which is being inserted in all Uniform Acts approved in 2000 or later, preempts the federal Electronic Signatures in Global and National Commerce Act. Section 102(a)(2)(B) of that Act provides that the federal law can be preempted by a later statute of the state that specifically refers to the federal law. The effect of this section, when enacted as part of this Code, is to leave to state law the procedures for obtaining and validating an electronic signature. The Uniform Trust Code does not require that any document be in paper form, allowing all documents under this Code to be transmitted in electronic form. A properly directed electronic message is a valid method of notice under the Code as long as it is reasonably suitable under the circumstances and likely to result in receipt of the notice or document. *See* § 109(a).

§ 1103. Severability Clause. If any provision of this [Code] or its application to any person or circumstances is held invalid, the invalidity does not affect other provisions or applications of this [Code] which can be given effect without the invalid provision or application, and to this end the provisions of this [Code] are severable.

§ 1104. Effective Date. This [Code] takes effect on _____.

§ 1105. Repeals. The following Acts are repealed:
    (1) Uniform Trustee Powers Act ;
    (2) Uniform Probate Code, Article VII;
    (3) Uniform Trusts Act (1937); and
    (4) Uniform Prudent Investor Act.

Comment

For the reasons why the above Uniform Acts should be repealed upon enactment of the Uniform Trust Code, see the Prefatory Note. Enacting jurisdictions that have not enacted one or more of the specified Uniform Acts should repeal their comparable legislation. Because of the comprehensive scope of the Uniform Trust Code, many states will have trust provisions not based on any Uniform Act that will need to be repealed upon enactment of this Code. This section does not attempt to list the types of conforming amendments, whether in the enacting state's probate code or elsewhere, that need to be made upon enactment of this Code.

§ 1106. Application to Existing Relationships.

(a) Except as otherwise provided in this [Code], on [the effective date of this [Code]]:

(1) this [Code] applies to all trusts created before, on, or after [its effective date];

(2) this [Code] applies to all judicial proceedings concerning trusts commenced on or after [its effective date];

(3) this [Code] applies to judicial proceedings concerning trusts commenced before [its effective date] unless the court finds that application of a particular provision of this [Code] would substantially interfere with the effective conduct of the judicial proceedings or prejudice the rights of the parties, in which case the particular provision of this [Code] does not apply and the superseded law applies;

(4) any rule of construction or presumption provided in this [Code] applies to trust instruments executed before [the effective date of the [Code]] unless there is a clear indication of a contrary intent in the terms of the trust; and

(5) an act done before [the effective date of the [Code]] is not affected by this [Code].

(b) If a right is acquired, extinguished, or barred upon the expiration of a prescribed period that has commenced to run under any other statute before [the effective date of the [Code]], that statute continues to apply to the right even if it has been repealed or superseded.

Comment

The Uniform Trust Code is intended to have the widest possible effect within constitutional limitations. Specifically, the Code applies to all trusts whenever created, to judicial proceedings concerning trusts commenced on or after its effective date, and unless the court otherwise orders, to judicial proceedings in progress on the effective date. In addition, any rules of construction or presumption provided in the Code apply to preexisting trusts unless there is a clear indication of a contrary intent in the trust's terms. By applying the Code to preexisting trusts, the need to know two bodies of law will quickly lessen.

This Code cannot be fully retroactive, however. Constitutional limitations preclude retroactive application of rules of construction to alter property rights under trusts that became irrevocable prior to the effective date. Also, rights already barred by a statute of limitation or rule under former law are not revived by a possibly longer statute or more liberal rule under this Code. Nor is an act done before the effective date of the Code affected by the Code's enactment.

The Uniform Trust Code contains an additional effective date provision. Pursuant to § 602(a), prior law will determine whether a trust executed prior to the effective date of the Code is presumed to be revocable or irrevocable.

For a comparable uniform law effective date provision, see Unif. Probate Code § 8-101.

UNIFORM DIRECTED TRUST ACT
(2017)

Table of Sections

Prefatory Note

Background. The Uniform Directed Trust Act addresses an increasingly common arrangement in contemporary estate planning and asset management known as a "directed trust." In a directed trust, the terms of the trust grant a person other than a trustee a power over some aspect of the trust's administration. There is no consistent vocabulary to describe the person other than a trustee that holds a power in a directed trust. Several terms are common in practice, including "trust protector," "trust adviser," and "trust director." There is much uncertainty in existing law about the fiduciary status of a nontrustee that has a power over a trust and about the fiduciary duty of a trustee, sometimes called an "administrative trustee" or "directed trustee," with regard to actions taken or directed by the nontrustee. Existing uniform trusts and estates acts address the issue inadequately. Existing nonuniform state laws are in disarray.

Under the Uniform Directed Trust Act, a power over a trust held by a nontrustee is called a "power of direction." The holder of a power of direction is called a "trust director." A trustee that is subject to a power of direction is called a "directed trustee." The main contribution of the act is to address the many complications created by giving a power of direction to a trust director, including the fiduciary duty of a trust director and the fiduciary duty of a directed trustee.

Enabling Settlor Autonomy Consistent with Fiduciary Minimums. By validating terms of a trust that grant a trust director a power of direction, the Uniform Directed Trust Act promotes settlor autonomy in accordance with the principle of freedom of disposition. At the same time, the act imposes a mandatory minimum of fiduciary duty on both a directed trustee and a trust director in accordance with the traditional principle that a trust is a fiduciary relationship. *See, e.g.,* Restatement (Third) of Trusts § 96 cmt. c (2012) ("[F]or reasons of policy trust fiduciary law imposes limitations on the types and degree of misconduct for which the trustee can be excused from liability.").

Structure of the Act. The heart of the Uniform

Directed Trust Act appears in Sections 6 through 11, which address the powers and duties of a trust director and a directed trustee. Sections 6 through 8 address the kinds of powers that the terms of a trust can grant to a trust director and the default and mandatory fiduciary duties of the director. Section 9 addresses the fiduciary duty of a directed trustee. Sections 10 and 11 further elaborate the duties of a trust director and directed trustee, prescribing specific rules for information sharing and monitoring among trust directors and trustees. Section 12 addresses cotrusteeship, enabling a settlor to apply the fiduciary standards of conduct for a directed trust under this act to a cotrusteeship. The remaining sections address a variety of important technical issues in this act's relationship to existing law and in the administration of a directed trust, including rules of construction for recurring matters that might be overlooked in the drafting of a directed trust.

Fiduciary Duty in a Directed Trust. Under the Uniform Directed Trust Act, a trust director has the same default and mandatory fiduciary duties as a trustee in a like position and under similar circumstances (Section 8). In complying with a trust director's exercise of a power of direction, a directed trustee is liable only for the trustee's own "willful misconduct" (Section 9). The logic behind these rules is that in a directed trust the trust director functions much like a trustee in an undirected trust. Accordingly, the trust director should have the same

duties as a trustee in the exercise or nonexercise of the director's power of direction, and the fiduciary duty of the directed trustee is reduced with respect to the director's power of direction.

In preserving some minimal fiduciary duty in a directed trustee, the drafting committee was influenced by the prominent directed trust statute in Delaware, which provides likewise. *See* Del. Code Ann. tit. 12, § 3313 (2017). The popularity of directed trusts in Delaware establishes that a directed trust statute that preserves in a directed trustee a duty to avoid "willful misconduct" is workable in practice. The drafting committee therefore declined the suggestion that the Uniform Directed Trust Act should eliminate the fiduciary duty of a directed trustee completely.

In summary, under the Uniform Directed Trust Act a beneficiary's main recourse for misconduct by a trust director is an action against the director for breach of the director's fiduciary duty to the beneficiary. The beneficiary also has recourse against a directed trustee, but only to the extent of the trustee's own willful misconduct. Compared with a non-directed trust in which a trustee holds all power over the trust, a directed trust subject to this act provides for more aggregate fiduciary duties owed to a beneficiary. All of the usual duties of trusteeship are preserved in the trust director, and in addition the directed trustee has a duty to avoid willful misconduct.

§ 1. Short Title. This [act] may be cited as the Uniform Directed Trust Act.

Comment

This act governs an arrangement commonly known as a "directed trust." In a directed trust, the terms of the trust grant a person other than a trustee a power over some aspect of the trust's administration. Under this act, such a power is called a "power of direction," the person that holds the power is called a "trust director," a trustee that is subject to the power is

called a "directed trustee," and the trust is a "directed trust" (see Sections 2(5), (9), (3), and (2) respectively). This act applies to any arrangement that exhibits the functional features of a directed trust within the meaning of this act, even if the terms of the trust use other terminology, such as "trust protector," "trust advisor," or "administrative trustee."

§ 2. Definitions. In this [act]:

(1) "Breach of trust" includes a violation by a trust director or trustee of a duty imposed on that director or trustee by the terms of the trust, this [act], or law of this state other than this [act] pertaining to trusts.

(2) "Directed trust" means a trust for which the terms of the trust grant a power of direction.

(3) "Directed trustee" means a trustee that is subject to a trust director's power of direction.

(4) "Person" means an individual, estate, business or nonprofit entity, public corporation, government or governmental subdivision, agency, or instrumentality, or other legal entity.

(5) "Power of direction" means a power over a trust granted to a person by the terms of the trust to the extent the power is exercisable while the person is not serving as a trustee. The term includes a power over the investment, management, or distribution of trust property or other matters of trust administration. The term excludes the powers described in Section 5(b).

(6) "Settlor" means a person, including a testator, that creates, or contributes property to, a trust. If more than one person creates or contributes property to a trust, each person is a settlor of the portion of the trust property attributable to that person's contribution except to the extent another person has the power to revoke or withdraw that portion.

(7) "State" means a state of the United States, the District of Columbia, Puerto Rico, the United States Virgin Islands, or any other territory or possession subject to the jurisdiction of the United States.

(8) "Terms of a trust" means:

(A) except as otherwise provided in subparagraph (B), the manifestation of the settlor's intent regarding a trust's provisions as:

(i) expressed in the trust instrument; or

(ii) established by other evidence that would be admissible in a judicial proceeding; or

(B) the trust's provisions as established, determined, or amended by:

(i) a trustee or trust director in accordance with applicable law; [or]

(ii) court order[; or

(iii) a nonjudicial settlement agreement under [Uniform Trust Code Section 111]].

(9) "Trust director" means a person that is granted a power of direction by the terms of a trust to the extent the power is exercisable while the person is not serving as a trustee. The person is a trust director whether or not the terms of the trust refer to the person as a trust director and whether or not the person is a beneficiary or settlor of the trust.

(10) "Trustee" includes an original, additional, and successor trustee, and a cotrustee.

Legislative Note: *A state that has enacted Uniform Trust Code (Last Revised or Amended in 2010) Section 103(18), defining "terms of a trust," or Uniform Trust Decanting Act (2015) Section 2(28), defining "terms of the trust," should update those definitions to conform to paragraph (8). A state that has enacted Uniform Trust Code Section 103(15) and (20) could replace paragraphs (6) and (10) of this section with cross-references to those provisions. A state that has not enacted Uniform Trust Code Section 111 should replace the bracketed language of paragraph (8)(B)(iii) with a cross reference to the state's statute governing nonjudicial settlement or should omit paragraph (8)(B)(iii) if the state does not have such a statute.*

Comment

(1) *Breach of trust.* The definition of "breach of trust" in paragraph (1) makes clear that the term includes a breach by a trust director or a trustee of a duty imposed on that director or trustee by the terms of the trust, this act, or other law pertaining to trusts. Historically, the term has been used to reference a breach of duty by a trustee, as under Uniform Trust Code § 1001(a) (2000) and Restatement (Third) of Trusts § 93 (2012). By expanding the meaning of the term to include a breach of duty by a trust director, this paragraph resolves any doubt about whether such conduct is also a "breach of trust."

In defining a breach of trust to include a breach of a duty imposed by this act, it is important to recognize that some of the duties imposed by this act are default rules that may be varied by the terms of the trust. The drafting committee contemplated that a trust director or a trustee would not be in breach of trust for conduct that was authorized by the terms of a trust to the extent that those terms are permissible under this act or other applicable law.

(2) *Directed trust.* Under paragraph (2), a "directed trust" is a trust for which the terms of the trust grant a power of direction. A "power of direction" is defined by paragraph (5).

(3) *Directed trustee.* The definition of "directed

trustee" in paragraph (3) refers only to a trustee that is subject to direction by a trust director. A trustee that is subject to direction by a cotrustee is not for that reason a directed trustee, as paragraphs (5) and (9) exclude a person from being a trust director while that person is serving as trustee. The term "directed trustee" thus includes many but not all trustees that in practice are sometimes called "administrative trustees." Relations between multiple trustees are governed by the law of cotrusteeship as modified by Section 12.

(4) Person. The definition of "person" in paragraph (4) follows the current Uniform Law Commission definition.

(5) Power of direction. The definition of "power of direction" in paragraph (5) is expansive. It includes any "power over a trust" to the extent the power is exercisable at a time the power holder is not serving as a trustee. A power of direction may be structured as a power to direct the trustee in the exercise of the trustee's powers—for example, a power to direct the trustee in the investment or management of the trust property. A power of direction may also be structured as a power to act independently—for example, by amending the terms of a trust or releasing a trustee from liability.

The definition includes a power only to the extent the power is exercisable at a time the power holder is not serving as a trustee. The purpose of this limitation is to exclude a person serving as trustee from the definition of a trust director, even though as trustee the person will inevitably have a "power over a trust." A trust director, in other words, is someone other than a trustee. The contribution of this act is to address the complications created by giving a person other than a trustee—that is, a trust director—a power over a trust. A power over a trust held by a trustee is governed by existing trust fiduciary law.

The restriction in the definition to powers held by a person that is "not serving as a trustee" is also designed to be consistent with the definition of "trustee" in paragraph (10). Under paragraph (10), the term "trustee" includes an original, additional, and successor trustee. The definition of power of direction thus clarifies that a person that qualifies as a trustee under paragraph (10) by virtue of having served as an original trustee in the past or having been named as a successor trustee in the future may nevertheless be a "trust director" at a time when the person is not serving as a trustee. An original trustee that has ceased serving as a trustee but continues to hold a power over investments, for example, is a trust

director under paragraph (5) even though the person also qualifies as a trustee under paragraph (10).

The definition confirms that a power of direction may include a power over "matters of trust administration" as well as a power over "investment, management, or distribution of trust property." These examples are meant to illustrate the potential scope of a power of direction rather than to limit it. In using the term "administration," the drafting committee intended a meaning at least as broad as that found in the context of determining a trust's "principal place of administration," such as under Section 3(b). The drafting committee also intended the terms "investment, management, or distribution" to have a meaning at least as broad as that found in Uniform Trust Code § 815(a)(2)(b) (2000), which specifies a trustee's default powers. The comment to Section 6 provides examples of the kinds of specific powers that the drafting committee contemplated would fall within the definition of a power of direction.

(6) Settlor. The definition of "settlor" in paragraph (6) follows Uniform Trust Code § 103(15) (2004).

(7) State. The definition of "state" in paragraph (7) follows the current Uniform Law Commission definition.

(8) Terms of a trust. The definition of "terms of a trust" in paragraph (8) updates the comparable definition in Uniform Trust Code § 103(18) (2004) to take notice of court orders and nonjudicial settlement agreements, both of which are of growing practical significance and are sometimes used to vary the terms of a trust from a settlor's original intent. The definition also takes notice of a power in a trustee or a trust director to modify the terms of a trust.

The expanded definition of "terms of a trust" in this paragraph is consistent with the Restatement, which recognizes the possibility that the terms of a trust may later be varied from the settlor's initial expression. *See* Restatement (Third) of Trusts § 76 cmt. b(1) (2007) ("References ... to the terms of the trust ... also refer to trust terms as reformed or modified by court decree, and as modified by the settlor or others or by consent of all beneficiaries.") (internal cross-references omitted).

(9) Trust director. The definition of a "trust director" in paragraph (9) refers to a person other than a serving trustee that is granted a power of direction by the terms of a trust. Such a person is a trust director even if the terms of the trust or the parties call the person a "trust adviser" or "trust protector" or

otherwise purport to disclaim trust director status. A person may be a trust director even if the person is a beneficiary or settlor of the trust, though certain powers of a beneficiary and a settlor are excluded from the application of this act by Section 5.

A serving trustee cannot be a "trust director" for the same reasons that under paragraph (5) a power over a trust cannot be a "power of direction" while the person that holds the power is serving as a trustee. Relations between multiple trustees are governed by the law of cotrusteeship as modified by Section 12.

(10) Trustee. Following Uniform Trust Code § 103(20) (2004), paragraph (10) provides that the term "trustee" includes an original, additional, and successor trustee, and a cotrustee.

This act governs an arrangement commonly known as a "directed trust." In a directed trust, the terms of the trust grant a person other than a trustee a power over some aspect of the trust's administration. Under this act, such a power is called a "power of direction," the person that holds the power is called a "trust director," a trustee that is subject to the power is called a "directed trustee," and the trust is a "directed trust" (see Sections 2(5), (9), (3), and (2) respectively). This act applies to any arrangement that exhibits the functional features of a directed trust within the meaning of this act, even if the terms of the trust use other terminology, such as "trust protector," "trust advisor," or "administrative trustee."

§ 3. Application; Principal Place of Administration.

(a) This [act] applies to a trust, whenever created, that has its principal place of administration in this state, subject to the following rules:

(1) If the trust was created before [the effective date of this [act]], this [act] applies only to a decision or action occurring on or after [the effective date of this [act]].

(2) If the principal place of administration of the trust is changed to this state on or after [the effective date of this [act]], this [act] applies only to a decision or action occurring on or after the date of the change.

(b) Without precluding other means to establish a sufficient connection with the designated jurisdiction in a directed trust, terms of the trust which designate the principal place of administration of the trust are valid and controlling if:

(1) a trustee's principal place of business is located in or a trustee is a resident of the designated jurisdiction;

(2) a trust director's principal place of business is located in or a trust director is a resident of the designated jurisdiction; or

(3) all or part of the administration occurs in the designated jurisdiction.

Legislative Note: *A state that has enacted Uniform Trust Code (Last Revised or Amended in 2010) Section 108(a) could omit subsection (b) and instead add subsection (b)(2) to Section 108 if the state also adds to the state's Uniform Trust Code the definitions of power of direction and trust director from Section 2(5) and (9).*

Comment

Subsection (a). Subsection (a) addresses two matters. First, because powers and duties in a directed trust are matters of trust administration, see Restatement (Second) of Conflict of Laws § 271 cmt. a (1971), this subsection follows the prevailing conflict of laws rule by linking application of this act to the trust's principal place of administration. As with other matters of administration, the parties are protected against inconsistent court orders by the common law principle of "primary supervision." *See* id. § 267 cmt. e.

Second, this subsection applies this act to all trusts administered in an enacting state regardless of whether the trust was in existence on the effective date of this act. However, under subsections (a)(1) and (2), this act applies only with respect to a decision or action occurring on or after the effective date or, if the trust's principal place of administration was changed to the enacting state after the effective date, only with respect to a decision or action occurring on or after that change. Because some of the standards of conduct prescribed by this act depart from Uniform

Trust Code § 808 (2000) and Restatement (Third) of Trusts § 75 (2007), the drafting committee reasoned that the act should apply prospectively, following the model of Uniform Prudent Investor Act § 11 (1994).

Subsection (b). Subsection (b), which derives from Uniform Trust Code § 108(a) (2000), establishes a safe harbor for a settlor's designation of the principal place of administration for a directed trust. Such a designation is valid if (1) a trustee is located in the designated jurisdiction, (2) a trust director is located in the designated jurisdiction, or (3) at least some of the trust administration occurs in the designated jurisdiction. Subsections (b)(1) and (b)(3) reproduce without change the safe harbor prescribed by Uniform Trust Code § 108(a) (2000). Subsection (b)(2) expands the safe harbor of Section 108(a) to add the presence of a trust director as a sufficient connection with the designated jurisdiction.

Other than the expansion in subsection (b)(2) of the Uniform Trust Code's safe harbor for a settlor's designation of a trust's principal place of administration, the drafting committee did not undertake to prescribe rules for ascertaining a trust's principal place of administration. In this respect, the drafting committee followed the Uniform Trust Code in "not attempt[ing] to further define principal place of administration." Uniform Trust Code § 108 cmt. Accordingly, for a directed trust in an enacting state, just as for all trusts in a Uniform Trust Code state, if the safe harbor of subsection (b) does not apply, the question of a trust's principal place of administration will be governed by the state's then-existing law on principal place of administration. *See, e.g.,* Restatement (Second) of Conflict of Laws §§ 271-72, 279 (1971).

§ 4. Common Law and Principles of Equity.
The common law and principles of equity supplement this [act], except to the extent modified by this [act] or law of this state other than this [act].

Comment

This section confirms that the common law and principles of equity remain applicable to a directed trust except to the extent modified by this act or other law. For example, other than the safe harbor under Section 3(b) for a term of a trust that designates the trust's principal place of administration, the law of an enacting state by which principal place of administration is determined would continue to apply to a directed trust. Provisions such as this one are familiar from other uniform acts. *See, e.g.,*

Uniform Powers of Appointment Act § 104 (2013); Uniform Trust Code § 106 (2000). The drafting committee contemplated that, by ordinary principles of statutory interpretation, other statutes pertaining to trusts such as the Uniform Trust Code (2000), Uniform Trust Decanting Act (2015), Uniform Principal and Income Act (1997), and Uniform Prudent Investor Act (1994), would continue to apply to a directed trust except as modified by this act.

§ 5. Exclusions.
(a) In this section, "power of appointment" means a power that enables a person acting in a nonfiduciary capacity to designate a recipient of an ownership interest in or another power of appointment over trust property.

(b) This [act] does not apply to a:

(1) power of appointment;

(2) power to appoint or remove a trustee or trust director;

(3) power of a settlor over a trust to the extent the settlor has a power to revoke the trust;

(4) power of a beneficiary over a trust to the extent the exercise or nonexercise of the power affects the beneficial interest of:

(A) the beneficiary; or

(B) another beneficiary represented by the beneficiary[under Uniform Trust Code Sections 301 through 305] with respect to the exercise or nonexercise of the power; or

(5) power over a trust if:

(A) the terms of the trust provide that the power is held in a nonfiduciary capacity; and

(B) the power must be held in a nonfiduciary capacity to achieve the settlor's tax objectives under the United States Internal Revenue Code of 1986[, as amended][, and regulations issued thereunder][, as amended].

(c) Unless the terms of a trust provide otherwise, a power granted to a person to designate a recipient of an ownership interest in or power of appointment over trust property which is exercisable while the person is not serving as a trustee is a power of appointment and not a power of direction.

Legislative Note: *A state that has not enacted Uniform Trust Code (Last Revised or Amended in 2010) Sections 301 through 305 should replace the bracketed language in subsection (b)(4)(B) with a cross reference to the state's statute governing virtual representation or should omit the bracketed language if the state does not have such a statute.*

A state that does not permit the phrase "as amended" when incorporating federal statutes or permit reference to "regulations issued thereunder" should delete the bracketed language in subsection (b)(5)(B).

Comment

This section excludes five categories of powers that the drafting committee concluded should not be covered by this act for reasons of policy, coverage by other law, or both. Questions regarding a power that falls within one of these exclusions, such as the duty of the holder of the power and the duty of a trustee or other person subject to the power, are governed by law other than this act.

(1) Power of appointment. Subsection (b)(1) excludes a "power of appointment," which is defined by subsection (a) to mean "a power that enables a person acting in a nonfiduciary capacity to designate a recipient of an ownership interest in or another power of appointment over trust property." This definition of "power of appointment" is based on the definition in Uniform Powers of Appointment Act § 102(13) (2013). The definition is consistent with what Restatement (Third) of Property: Wills and Other Donative Transfers § 17.1 cmt. g (2011), refers to as a "discretionary" power of appointment, that is, one in which "the donee may exercise the power arbitrarily as long as the exercise is within the scope of the power."

Accordingly, if the terms of a trust purport to grant a person not serving as trustee a nonfiduciary power to direct distributions of trust property, under this act that power will be construed as a power of appointment governed by law other than this act, such as the Uniform Powers of Appointment Act (2013) and Restatement (Third) of Property: Wills and Other Donative Transfers §§ 17.1–23.1 (2011).

The exclusion prescribed by subsection (b)(1) applies only to a nonfiduciary power of appointment. It does not apply to a fiduciary power of distribution. Thus, if the terms of a trust grant a person a fiduciary power to direct a distribution of trust property, and

the power is exercisable while the person is not serving as trustee, then the power is a power of direction subject to this act.

To resolve doubt about whether a power over distribution is a power of appointment or a power of direction, subsection (c) prescribes a rule of construction under which a power over distribution is a power of appointment, and so is not held in a fiduciary capacity, unless the terms of the trust provide that the power is held in a fiduciary capacity.

A power in a serving trustee to designate a recipient of an ownership interest in or a power of appointment over trust property can never be a power of direction, because a serving trustee can never be a trust director (see Sections 2(5) and (9)). Whether a power over distribution granted to a serving trustee is held in a fiduciary capacity (making it a fiduciary distributive power) or is instead a nonfiduciary power of appointment is governed by law other than this act, such as under Restatement (Third) of Trusts § 50 cmt. a (2003).

(2) Power to appoint or remove. Subsection (b)(2) excludes "a power to appoint or remove a trustee or trust director." This exclusion addresses the compelling suggestion to the drafting committee that granting a person a power to appoint or remove a trustee is a common drafting practice that arose separately from the phenomenon of directed trusts. Under prevailing law, the only limit on the exercise of a power to appoint or remove a trustee is that it "must conform to any valid requirements or limitations imposed by the trust terms." Restatement (Third) of Trusts § 37 cmt. c (2003). If the terms of the trust do not impose any requirements or limitations on the power to remove, then "it is unnecessary for the holder to show cause" before

exercising the power. Austin Wakeman Scott, William Franklin Fratcher & Mark L. Ascher, Scott and Ascher on Trusts § 11.10.2 (5th ed. 2006).

(3) Revocable trust. Subsection (b)(3) excludes a power of a settlor over a trust to the extent the settlor has a power to revoke the trust. The drafting committee intended that this exception would apply only to that portion of a trust over which the settlor has a power to revoke, that is, "to the extent" of the settlor's power to revoke.

Because the settlor of a revocable trust may at any time revoke the trust and take back the trust property, under modern law, including Uniform Trust Code § 603(a) (2004), the trustee's duties run to the settlor rather than to the beneficiaries. The trustee must "comply with a direction of the settlor even though the direction is contrary to the terms of the trust or the trustee's normal fiduciary duties." Restatement (Third) of Trusts § 74(1)(a)(i) (2007).

Without the exclusion of this subsection, the definitions contained in paragraphs (3), (5), and (9) of Section 2 could have been read to transform a settlor's power over a revocable trust into fiduciary powers of a trust director, thus subjecting the settlor to the fiduciary duties of a trust director under Section 8 and the trustee to the modified fiduciary duties of a directed trustee under Sections 9 through 11.

To the extent that a conservator or agent of the settlor may exercise the settlor's power to revoke, as under Uniform Trust Code § 602(e)–(f) (2001), subsection (b)(3) of this section would apply to the conservator or agent. A nonfiduciary power in a person other than the settlor to withdraw the trust property is a power of appointment that would fall within subsection (b)(1).

(4) Power of a beneficiary. Paragraph (4) excludes a power of a beneficiary to the extent that the exercise or nonexercise of the power affects (A) the beneficial interest of the beneficiary, or (B) the beneficial interest of another beneficiary who is represented by the beneficiary under virtual representation law.

Subparagraph (A) follows from traditional law, under which "[a] power that is for the sole benefit of the person holding the power is not a fiduciary power." Restatement (Third) of Trusts § 75 cmt. d (2007). Thus, for example, a power in a beneficiary to release a trustee from a claim by the beneficiary is excluded from this act. To the extent the power affects another person, however, then it is not for the sole benefit of the person holding the power. Hence, a power over a trust held by a beneficiary may be a

power of direction subject to this act if it affects the beneficial interest of another beneficiary. For example, a power in a beneficiary to release the trustee from a claim by another beneficiary is not excluded by this paragraph unless the power to bind the other beneficiary arises by reason of virtual representation.

The same rules apply if the beneficiary's power is jointly held. Thus, for example, if the terms of a trust provide that a trustee may be released from liability by a majority of the beneficiaries, and a majority of the beneficiaries grants such a release, then those beneficiaries would be acting as trust directors to the extent the release bound other beneficiaries by reason of the power other than by virtual representation. This act would therefore reverse the result in Vena v. Vena, 899 N.E.2d 522 (Ill. App. 2008), in which the court refused to enforce a provision for release of a trustee by a majority of the beneficiaries on the grounds that the minority beneficiaries did not have recourse against the majority for an abusive release. Under this act, the minority beneficiaries would have recourse against the majority for breach of their fiduciary duty as trust directors.

The carve-out for virtual representation in subparagraph (B) reflects the drafting committee's intent not to impose the fiduciary rules of this act on top of the law of virtual representation, which contains its own limits and safeguards. Without the exclusion of this subsection, the definitions contained in paragraphs (5) and (9) of Section 2 could have been read to transform a beneficiary who represented another beneficiary by virtual representation into a trust director.

By way of illustration, under Uniform Trust Code § 304 (2000), a beneficiary who suffers from an incapacitating case of Alzheimer's disease may sometimes be represented by another beneficiary in litigation against a trustee for breach of trust. In such a case, paragraph (4) of this section prevents the beneficiary who represents the beneficiary with Alzheimer's from being a trust director. Instead, the safeguards provided by the law of virtual representation will apply. Under § 304, for example, the representative beneficiary and the beneficiary with Alzheimer's disease must have "a substantially identical interest with respect to the particular question or dispute," and have "no conflict of interest" with each other.

(5) The settlor's tax objectives. Subsection (b)(5) excludes a power if (A) the terms of the trust provide that the power is held in a nonfiduciary capacity, and

(B) the power must be held in a nonfiduciary capacity to achieve the settlor's tax objectives under federal tax law. This exclusion is responsive to multiple suggestions to the drafting committee that certain powers held by a person other than a trustee must be nonfiduciary to achieve the settlor's federal tax objectives.

For example, to ensure that a trust is a grantor trust for federal income tax purposes, a common practice is to include in the trust instrument a provision that allows the settlor or another person to substitute assets of the trust for assets of an equivalent value, exercisable in a nonfiduciary capacity. If the power to substitute assets is exercisable in a fiduciary capacity, the power will not cause the trust to be a grantor trust. Without the exception of subsection (b)(5), therefore, this common drafting practice might no longer ensure grantor trust status in a state that enacts this Act, and the tax status of existing trusts with such a provision would be thrown into disarray.

In light of the evolving nature of tax planning, the frequency of amendments to the tax law, and the potential for disagreement about which powers must be nonfiduciary to achieve the settlor's federal tax objectives, the drafting committee reasoned that a standard referring broadly to a settlor's tax objectives was preferable to a prescribed list of sections of the tax code.

The drafting committee deliberately opted to reference tax objectives only under federal law, thereby excluding tax objectives under state law. The concern was that some states levy a tax on income in a trust if the trust has a fiduciary in the state. If this exclusion reached state tax law, then in such a state a trust director could argue that the director is not a fiduciary, because the settlor would not have wanted the trust to pay income tax. The consequence would be to negate fiduciary status for virtually all trust directors in those states. The purpose of this exception is to protect normal and customary estate planning techniques, not to allow circumvention of the central policy choice encoded in Section 8 that a trust director is generally subject to the same default and mandatory fiduciary duties as a similarly situated trustee.

§ 6. Powers of Trust Director.

(a) Subject to Section 7, the terms of a trust may grant a power of direction to a trust director.

(b) Unless the terms of a trust provide otherwise:

(1) a trust director may exercise any further power appropriate to the exercise or nonexercise of a power of direction granted to the director under subsection (a); and

(2) trust directors with joint powers must act by majority decision.

Comment

Validating a trust director. Subsection (a) validates a provision for a trust director in the terms of a trust. This subsection does not provide any powers to a trust director by default. Nor does it specify the scope of a power of direction. The existence and scope of a power of direction must instead be specified by the terms of a trust. A trust director may be named by the terms of the trust, by a procedure prescribed by the terms of the trust, or in accordance with Section 16(6).

Breadth of subsection (a). Without limiting the definition of a "power of direction" in Section 2(5), the drafting committee specifically contemplated that subsection (a) would validate terms of a trust that grant a power to a trust director to:

- direct investments, including a power to:
  - acquire, dispose of, exchange, or retain an investment;
  - make or take loans;
  - vote proxies for securities held in trust;
  - adopt a particular valuation of trust property or determine the frequency or methodology of valuation;
  - adjust between principal and income or convert to a unitrust;
  - manage a business held in the trust; or
  - select a custodian for trust assets;
- modify, reform, terminate, or decant a trust;
- direct a trustee's or another director's delegation of the trustee's or other director's powers;
- change the principal place of administration, situs, or governing law of the trust;
- ascertain the happening of an event that affects the administration of the trust;
- determine the capacity of a trustee, settlor, director, or beneficiary of the trust;
- determine the compensation to be paid to a trustee or trust director;

- prosecute, defend, or join an action, claim, or judicial proceeding relating to the trust;
- grant permission before a trustee or another director may exercise a power of the trustee or other director; or
- release a trustee or another trust director from liability for an action proposed or previously taken by the trustee or other director.

This subsection does not, however, override the background law that regulates the formation of a trust, such as the requirements that a trust be lawful, not contrary to public policy, and possible to achieve. *See, e.g.,* Uniform Trust Code § 404 (2000); Restatement (Third) of Trusts §§ 29–30 (2003).

Pet and other noncharitable purpose trust enforcers. Statutes in every state validate a trust for a pet animal and certain other noncharitable purposes. Following Uniform Probate Code § 2-907(c)(4) (1993) and Uniform Trust Code §§ 408(b) and 409(2) (2000), most of these statutes authorize enforcement of the trust by a person named in the terms of the trust. In a state that enacts this act, such a person would be a trust director.

Exclusions. Like the other provisions of this act, this section does not apply to matters that are excluded by Section 5. Thus, because Sections 5(b)(1)-(2) exclude a "power of appointment," and a "power to appoint or remove a trustee or trust director," subsection 6(a) does not authorize the granting of such powers. Instead, such a power is governed by law other than this act.

Subsection (b). Subsection (b) prescribes two rules of construction that apply unless the terms of a trust provide otherwise.

(1) Further appropriate powers. Subsection (b)(1) prescribes a default rule under which a trust director may exercise any "further" power that is "appropriate" to the director's exercise of the director's express powers granted by the terms of the trust under subsection (a). The term "appropriate" is drawn from Uniform Trust Code § 815(a)(2)(B) (2000). Appropriateness should be judged in relation to the purpose for which the power was granted and the function being carried out by the director. Examples of further powers that might be appropriate include a power to: (1) incur reasonable costs and direct indemnification for those costs; (2) make a report or accounting to a beneficiary or other interested party; (3) direct a trustee to issue a certification of trust under Uniform Trust Code § 1013 (2000); (4) prosecute, defend, or join an action, claim, or judicial proceeding relating to a trust; or (5) employ a

professional to assist or advise the director in the exercise or nonexercise of the director's powers.

Delegation by trust director. In some circumstances, it may be appropriate under subsection (b)(1) for a trust director to exercise a further power to delegate the director's powers, much as it may sometimes be appropriate for a trustee to delegate its powers. Under Section 8, a trust director is subject to the same fiduciary duty regarding delegation as a trustee in a like position and under similar circumstances. In most states, therefore, a trust director would be required to exercise reasonable care, skill, and caution in selecting, instructing, and monitoring an agent, and a director that did so would not be liable for the action of the agent. In accordance with prevailing law governing delegation by a trustee, see, e.g., Uniform Trust Code § 807 (2000); Uniform Prudent Investor Act § 9 (1994); Restatement (Third) of Trusts § 80 (2007), the drafting committee contemplated that in performing a function delegated by a trust director, the agent would owe a duty to exercise reasonable care.

Trust director's standing to sue. Subsection (b)(1) addresses the situation that arose in Schwartz v. Wellin, No. 2:13-CV-3595-DCN, 2014 WL 1572767 (D.S.C. Apr. 17, 2014). The court held that a trust director, which the terms of the trust referred to as a "trust protector," lacked standing to bring a lawsuit under Rule 17(a)(1) of the Federal Rules of Civil Procedure, because the director was neither a real party in interest nor a party that could pursue a claim if not a real party in interest.

In some circumstances, subsection (b)(1) may produce a different outcome. Rule 17(a)(1) allows a party to participate in litigation even if the party is not a real party in interest if the party is "authorized by statute." Subsection (b)(1) supplies the requisite statutory authorization if participating in a lawsuit would be "appropriate" to a director's exercise or nonexercise of a power granted by the terms of the trust under subsection (a). It would normally be "appropriate," for example, for a trust director to bring an action against a directed trustee if the trustee refused to comply with a director's exercise of a power of direction. The requisite statutory authorization might also come from subsection (a) if the terms of the trust expressly confer a power of litigation on a director.

(2) Majority decision. Subsection (b)(2) provides a default rule of majority action for multiple trust directors with "joint powers," such as a three-person committee with a power of direction over investment

or distribution. Majority action is the prevailing default for cotrustees. *See* Uniform Trust Code § 703(a) (2000); Restatement (Third) of Trusts § 39 (2003). In the event of a deadlock among trust directors with joint powers, by analogy to a deadlock among cotrustees, a court could "direct exercise of the [joint] power or take other action to break the deadlock." Restatement (Third) of Trusts § 39 cmt. e

(2003).

The duty and liability of a trust director is governed by Section 8, which applies the fiduciary duty of trusteeship to a trust director. Thus, under Section 8(a)(1)(B), a trust director that holds a power of direction jointly with a trustee or another trust director would be subject to the fiduciary duty of a cotrustee.

§ 7. Limitations on Trust Director. A trust director is subject to the same rules as a trustee in a like position and under similar circumstances in the exercise or nonexercise of a power of direction or further power under Section 6(b)(1) regarding:

(1) a payback provision in the terms of a trust necessary to comply with the reimbursement requirements of Medicaid law in Section 1917 of the Social Security Act, 42 U.S.C. Section 1396p(d)(4)(A)[, as amended][, and regulations issued thereunder][, as amended]; and

(2) a charitable interest in the trust, including notice regarding the interest to [the Attorney General].

Legislative Note: A state that does not permit the phrase "as amended" when incorporating federal statutes or that does not permit reference to "regulations issued thereunder" should delete the bracketed language in paragraph (1) accordingly.

In paragraph (2), "Attorney General" is in brackets to accommodate a state that grants enforcement authority over a charitable interest in a trust to another public official.

Comment

This section applies to a trust director the same rules that apply to a trustee in two specific situations in which many states have particular regulatory interests. The first, in paragraph (1), concerns a payback provision necessary to comply with the reimbursement requirements of Medicaid law in a trust for a beneficiary with a disability. The second, in paragraph (2), concerns a charitable interest in a trust.

In both circumstances, this section imposes all the same rules that would apply to a trustee in a like position and under similar circumstances. For example, many states require a trustee to give notice to the Attorney General before taking certain actions with respect to a charitable interest in a trust. Some states also disempower a trustee from taking certain actions with respect to a payback provision in a trust meant to comply with the reimbursement

requirements of Medicaid law.

The drafting committee referenced "rules" rather than "duties" in order to make clear that this section absorbs every provision of state law in the areas specified by paragraphs (1) and (2), regardless of whether the law in these areas is classified as a duty, a limit on a trustee's powers, a regulation, or otherwise. In referencing rules, rather than duties, this section stands in contrast to Section 8(a) and the other sections of this act that apply a trustee's duties to a trust director. Section 8(a) and these other sections absorb only duties of a fiduciary nature, whereas this section absorbs all rules, whether fiduciary, regulatory, or otherwise. Also unlike Section 8(a), this section applies only to two limited subject areas, rather than to the whole range of a director's possible conduct.

§ 8. Duty and Liability of Trust Director.

(a) Subject to subsection (b), with respect to a power of direction or further power under Section 6(b)(1):

(1) a trust director has the same fiduciary duty and liability in the exercise or nonexercise of the power:

(A) if the power is held individually, as a sole trustee in a like position and under similar circumstances; or

(B) if the power is held jointly with a trustee or another trust director, as a cotrustee in a like position and under similar circumstances; and

(2) the terms of the trust may vary the director's duty or liability to the same extent the terms of the trust could vary the duty or liability of a trustee in a like position and under similar circumstances.

(b) Unless the terms of a trust provide otherwise, if a trust director is licensed, certified, or otherwise authorized or permitted by law other than this [act] to provide health care in the ordinary course of the director's business or practice of a profession, to the extent the director acts in that capacity, the director has no duty or liability under this [act].

(c) The terms of a trust may impose a duty or liability on a trust director in addition to the duties and liabilities under this section.

Comment

Duty and liability of a trust director. This section addresses the duty and liability of a trust director. It should be read in conjunction with Section 10, which governs information sharing among directed trustees and trust directors, and Section 11, which eliminates certain duties to monitor, inform, or give advice. The drafting committee contemplated that this section, along with Sections 10 and 11, would prescribe the mandatory minimum fiduciary duties of a trust director, displacing any contrary mandatory minimum such as under Uniform Trust Code § 105 (2005).

Subsection (a). Subsection (a) imposes the same fiduciary duties on a trust director that would apply to a trustee in a like position and under similar circumstances. A trust director with a power to make or direct investments, for example, has the same duties that would apply to a trustee with the same power, including a duty to act prudently, in the sole interest of the beneficiaries, and impartially with due regard for the respective interests of the beneficiaries. *See, e.g.,* Restatement (Third) of Trusts §§ 77-79, 90-92 (2007). The theory behind subsection (a) is that if a trust director has a power of direction, the director is the most appropriate person to bear the duty associated with the exercise or nonexercise of that power. Put differently, in a directed trust, a trust director functions much like a trustee in a non-directed trust, and thus should have the same duties as a trustee.

Accordingly, subsection (a)(1) sets the default duties of a trust director by absorbing the default duties that would ordinarily apply to a trustee in a like position and under similar circumstances. Subsection (a)(2) sets the mandatory minimum duties of a trust director by absorbing the mandatory minimum duties that the terms of a trust cannot vary

for a trustee in a like position and under similar circumstances. The default and mandatory rules applicable to a trustee include those prescribed by the other provisions of this act.

In making a trust director a fiduciary, subsection (a) follows the great majority of the existing state directed trust statutes. Subsection (a) is more specific than many state statutes, however, as the existing statutes tend to say only that a trust director is a "fiduciary," without specifying which kind of fiduciary or which fiduciary duties apply. Subsection (a) provides greater clarity by specifically absorbing the fiduciary duty of a similarly situated trustee.

Absorption of existing trust fiduciary law. Subsection (a) operates by absorbing existing state law rather than by inventing a new body of law. Absorbing existing state law in this manner offers several advantages. First, it avoids the need to spell out the entirety of trust fiduciary law. That is, it avoids the need to replicate something like Article 8 of the Uniform Trust Code for trust directors. Second, absorbing the trust fiduciary law of each enacting state accommodates diversity across the states in the particulars of a trustee's default and mandatory fiduciary duties, such as the duties to diversify and to give information to the beneficiaries, both of which have become increasingly differentiated across the states. Third, absorption allows for changes to the law of a trustee's fiduciary duties to be absorbed automatically into the duties of a trust director without need for periodic conforming revisions to this act.

Varied circumstances of trust directors. In applying the law of trustee fiduciary duties to a trust director, a court must make use of the flexibility built into fiduciary law. Courts have long applied the duties of loyalty and prudence across a wide array of circumstances, including many different kinds of trusts as well as other fiduciary relationships, such as corporations and agencies. Fiduciary principles are thus amenable to application in a context-specific manner that is sensitive to the particular circumstances and structure of each directed trust. In assessing the actions of a director that holds a power to modify a trust, for example, a court should apply the standards of loyalty and prudence in a manner that is appropriate to the particular context, including the trust's terms and purposes and the director's particular powers.

The trust director's duty of disclosure. Under subsection (a), a trust director is subject to the same duties of disclosure as a trustee in a like position and under similar circumstances. For example, if a trust director intends to direct a nonroutine transaction, to change "investment ... strategies," or to take "significant actions ... involving hard-to-value assets or special sensitivity to beneficiaries," the director is under a duty of affirmative advance disclosure, just like a trustee. Restatement (Third) of Trusts § 82 cmt. d (2007). A trust director's disclosure duties are limited, however, by Section 11, which eliminates certain duties to monitor, inform, or give advice.

Sole versus joint powers. Under subsection (a), a trust director has the same fiduciary duties as a sole trustee when a power of direction is held individually and the same fiduciary duties as a cotrustee when a power of direction is held jointly. A trust director that individually holds a power to amend the trust, for example, does not have the duties of a cotrustee to monitor the actions of the trustee concerning investments or the actions of another trust director concerning the determination of a beneficiary's capacity.

Subject to Section 11, a trust director that holds a power of direction jointly with a trustee or another trust director, by contrast, has the duties of a cotrustee regarding the actions of that trustee or other trust director that are within the scope of the jointly held power. Thus, a trust director that jointly exercises a power to direct investments with other trust directors has the same fiduciary duties as a cotrustee regarding its own actions and the actions of the other directors with respect to the power. Under subsection (a)(2), a settlor may vary the duty and liability of a trust director that holds a power of direction jointly to the same extent the settlor could vary the duty and liability of a cotrustee under Section 12 or otherwise.

Springing powers without a duty to monitor. The drafting committee contemplated that a settlor could construct a trust director's power to be springing such that the director would not be under a continuous obligation to monitor the administration of the trust. For example, a settlor could grant a trust director a power to direct a distribution, but only if the director was requested to do so by a beneficiary. A director holding such a power would not be under a duty to act unless requested to do so by a beneficiary. Moreover, because under subsection (a)(2) a settlor can vary the fiduciary duties of a trust director to the same extent that the settlor could vary the fiduciary duties of a trustee, under Uniform Trust Code § 105(b)(2) (2004) the terms of a trust could waive all of the director's otherwise applicable duties other than the duty "to act in good faith and in accordance with the terms and purposes of the trust and the interests of the beneficiaries." A director with a power to direct a distribution upon a beneficiary's request, for example, would be subject to this mandatory duty when it responds to a beneficiary's request.

Extended discretion. Under subsection (a), if the terms of a trust give a trust director extended discretion, such as "sole," "absolute," or "uncontrolled" discretion, those terms would have the same effect on the duty and liability of the director as they would have for a trustee. Under prevailing law, a trustee with extended discretion may not "act in bad faith or for some purpose or motive other than to accomplish the purposes of the discretionary power." Restatement (Third) of Trusts § 50 cmt. c (2003); *see also* Uniform Trust Code § 814(a) (2004).

Exculpation or exoneration. A trust director is likewise subject to the same rules as a trustee with regard to an exculpation or exoneration clause. Under prevailing law, such as Uniform Trust Code § 1008 (2000) and Restatement (Third) of Trusts § 96 (2012), an exculpation or exoneration clause cannot protect a trustee against liability for acting in bad faith or with reckless indifference. Under subsection (a)(2) of this section, the same rules would apply to an exculpation or exoneration clause for a trust director. Thus, if the terms of a trust provide that a director can never be liable to a beneficiary, then the trust director would have the same liability as a trustee would have under a similar exculpatory clause.

Directed director. The terms of a trust may provide that a trust director has a power over a trust that requires another director to comply with the director's exercise or nonexercise of the power. In other words, a director may have the power to direct another director. In such a trust, subsection (a)(1) would absorb for the directed director the same fiduciary duties that would apply to a directed trustee. A directed director would thus be subject to the willful misconduct standard that Section 9 applies to a directed trustee. Under subsection (a)(2), the terms of a trust may vary the duty of a directed director to the same extent they could vary the duty of a directed trustee.

Subsection (b)—health-care professionals. Subsection (b) refers to a trust director who is "licensed, certified, or otherwise authorized or permitted by law ... to provide health care in the ordinary course of the director's business or practice of a profession." This phrasing is based on the definition of "health-care provider" in Uniform Health-Care Decisions Act § 1(8) (1993). To the extent that a trust director acts in the director's business or practice of a profession to provide health care, the director is relieved from duty and liability under this act unless the terms of the trust provide otherwise.

This subsection addresses the concern that a health-care professional might refuse appointment as a trust director if such service would expose the professional to fiduciary duty under this act. For example, the terms of a trust might call for a health-care professional to determine the capacity or sobriety of a beneficiary or the capacity of a settlor. In making such a determination, under subsection (b) the health-care professional would not be subject to duty or liability under this act.

Although the professional would not be subject to duty or liability under this act, the professional would remain subject to any rules and regulations otherwise applicable to the professional, such as the rules of medical ethics. The professional would also be subject to the other provisions of this act that do not create a duty or liability, such as the rules of construction prescribed by Sections 6(b) and 16. Moreover, a trustee subject to a direction by a health-care professional under subsection (b) of this section is still subject to the duties under Section 9 to take reasonable action to comply with the professional's direction and to avoid willful misconduct in doing so.

Subsection (c)—no ceiling on duties. Subsection (c) confirms that the duties under this section are defaults and minimums, not ceilings. The terms of a trust may impose further duties in addition to those prescribed by this section.

§ 9. Duty and Liability of Directed Trustee.

(a) Subject to subsection (b), a directed trustee shall take reasonable action to comply with a trust director's exercise or nonexercise of a power of direction or further power under Section 6(b)(1), and the trustee is not liable for the action.

(b) A directed trustee must not comply with a trust director's exercise or nonexercise of a power of direction or further power under Section 6(b)(1) to the extent that by complying the trustee would engage in willful misconduct.

(c) An exercise of a power of direction under which a trust director may release a trustee or another trust director from liability for breach of trust is not effective if:

(1) the breach involved the trustee's or other director's willful misconduct;

(2) the release was induced by improper conduct of the trustee or other director in procuring the release; or

(3) at the time of the release, the director did not know the material facts relating to the breach.

(d) A directed trustee that has reasonable doubt about its duty under this section may petition the [court] for instructions.

(e) The terms of a trust may impose a duty or liability on a directed trustee in addition to the duties and liabilities under this section.

Legislative Note: *A state that has enacted the Uniform Trust Code (Last Revised or Amended in 2010) should move Section 808(a) into Section 603, delete Section 808(b) through (d), and add "subject to [insert cite to Uniform Directed Trust Act Sections 9, 11, and 12]," to the beginning of subsection (b)(2) of Section 105. Section 105(b)(2) prescribes the mandatory minimum fiduciary duty of a trustee, which is superseded with respect to a directed trustee by the willful misconduct mandatory minimum of this section.*

The term "court" in subsection (d) of this section should be revised as needed to refer to the appropriate court having jurisdiction over trust matters.

Comment

Duties of a directed trustee. This section addresses the duty and liability of a directed trustee. It should be read in conjunction with Section 10, which governs information sharing among directed trustees and trust directors, and Section 11, which eliminates certain duties to monitor, inform, or advise. The drafting committee contemplated that this section, along with Sections 10 and 11, would prescribe the mandatory minimum fiduciary duties of a directed trustee, displacing any contrary mandatory minimum such as under Uniform Trust Code § 105 (2005).

Subsection (a)–duty to take reasonable action; nonliability other than under subsection (b). Subject to subsection (b), subsection (a) requires a directed trustee to take reasonable action to comply with a trust director's exercise or nonexercise of the director's power of direction or further power under Section 6(b)(1) and provides that the trustee is not liable for so acting.

The duty of a trustee in subsection (a) to take reasonable action depends on context. A power of direction under which a trust director may give a trustee an express direction will require the trustee to comply by following the direction. A power that requires a trustee to obtain permission from a trust director before acting imposes a duty on the trustee to obtain the required permission. A power that allows a director to amend the trust imposes a duty on the trustee to take reasonable action to facilitate the amendment and then comply with its terms. The duty prescribed by subsection (a) is to take reasonable action to comply with whatever the terms of the trust require of a trustee in connection with a trust director's exercise or nonexercise of the director's power of direction or further power under Section 6(b)(1).

A trustee's duty to take reasonable action is limited by the scope of the trust director's power of direction. A directed trustee should not comply with a direction that is outside of the director's power of direction and beyond the director's further powers under Section 6(b)(1). To do so would violate the trustee's duty under subsection (a) and the trustee's background duty to act in accordance with the terms of the trust. *See, e.g.,* Uniform Trust Code § 105(b)(2) (amended 2005) (making mandatory "the duty of a trustee to act ... in accordance with the terms ... of the trust");

Restatement (Third) of Trusts § 76 (2007) ("The trustee has a duty to administer the trust ... in accordance with the terms of the trust."). For example, an attempt by a director to exercise a power of direction in a form contrary to that required by the terms of the trust, such as an oral direction if the terms of the trust require a writing, is not within the trust director's power.

Subsection (a) requires a trustee to act reasonably as it carries out the acts necessary to comply with a trust director's exercise or nonexercise of the director's powers. If a trust director with a power to direct investments directs the trustee to purchase a particular security, for example, the trustee must take care to ensure that the security is purchased within a reasonable time and at reasonable cost and must refrain from self-dealing and conflicts of interest in doing so.

The duty to take reasonable action under subsection (a) does not, however, impose a duty to ensure that the substance of the direction is reasonable. To the contrary, subject to subsection (b), a trustee that takes reasonable action to comply with a power of direction is not liable for so acting even if the substance of the direction is unreasonable. In other words, subject to the willful misconduct rule of subsection (b), a trustee is liable only for its own breach of trust in executing a direction, and not for the director's breach of trust in giving the direction. Returning to the example of a direction to purchase a security, the trustee is not required to assess whether the purchase of the security would be prudent in relation to the trust's investment portfolio; the trustee is only required to execute the purchase reasonably.

Powers jointly held with a trust director. A trustee may hold a power of direction jointly with a trust director. For example, the terms of a trust may confer a power to determine the capacity of a beneficiary upon a committee of people, and the committee may include both the trustee and the beneficiary's son, who is a trust director. When a trustee holds a power jointly with a trust director, the trustee continues to have the normal duties of a trustee regarding its own exercise or nonexercise of the joint power. Subsection (a), in other words, does not relieve the trustee from the trustee's normal duties as to powers that belong directly to the trustee, including powers held jointly with a trust director. In deciding how to vote as a member of the committee to determine the beneficiary's capacity, for example, the trustee would be subject to the same duties as if it held its power jointly with another trustee instead of with another trust director.

A trustee's participation in joint decisionmaking with a trust director, however, must be distinguished from the trustee's execution of those joint decisions. Although the trustee is subject to the normal fiduciary duties of trusteeship in making a decision jointly with a trust director, the trustee is subject to the reduced duty of subsections (a) and (b) in executing the decision. Returning to the example of a committee including a trustee with power to determine a beneficiary's capacity, the trustee has its normal fiduciary duties in deciding how to cast its vote about whether the beneficiary lacks capacity. But the trustee has only the duties prescribed by subsections (a) and (b) when the trustee takes action to comply with the decision of the committee.

Powers to veto or approve. The terms of a trust may give a trust director a power to veto or approve the actions of a trustee. A trustee, for example, may have the power to invest trust property, subject to the power of a trust director to review and override the trustee's decision. A trustee that operates under this kind of veto or approval power has the normal duties of a trustee regarding the trustee's exercise of its own powers, but has only the duties of a directed trustee regarding the trust director's exercise of its power to veto or approve. Thus, the trustee would be subject to the normal duty of prudence in deciding which investments to propose to a director, but then would be subject only to the willful misconduct rule of subsection (b) in choosing whether to comply with the director's veto or disapproval of the proposed investments.

Subsection (b)—willful misconduct. Subsection (b) provides an exception to the duty of compliance prescribed by subsection (a). Under subsection (b), a trustee must not comply with a trust director's exercise or nonexercise of a power of direction or a further power under Section 6(b)(1) to the extent that by complying the trustee would engage in "willful misconduct."

The willful misconduct standard in subsection (b) is to be distinguished from the duty to take reasonable action in subsection (a). The reasonable action rule of subsection (a) applies to the manner by which a trustee complies with a power of direction. The willful misconduct standard of subsection (b)

applies to the decision of whether to comply with a power of direction.

The willful misconduct standard in subsection (b) is a mandatory minimum. The terms of a trust may not reduce a trustee's duty below the standard of willful misconduct. Terms of a trust that attempt to give a trustee no duty or to indicate that a trustee is not a fiduciary or is an "excluded fiduciary" or other such language are not enforceable under subsection (b). Instead, such provisions should be construed to provide for the willful misconduct standard of subsection (b).

The drafting committee settled upon the "willful misconduct" standard after a review of the existing directed trust statutes. Roughly speaking, the existing statutes fall into two groups. In one group, which constitutes a majority, are the statutes that provide that a directed trustee has no duty or liability for complying with an exercise of a power of direction. This group includes Alaska, New Hampshire, Nevada, and South Dakota.

The policy rationale for these no duty statutes is that duty should follow power. If a director has the exclusive authority to exercise a power of direction, then the director should be the exclusive bearer of fiduciary duty in the exercise or nonexercise of the power. Placing the exclusive duty on a director does not diminish the total duty owed to a beneficiary, because a settlor of a directed trust could have chosen to make the trust director the sole trustee instead. Thus, on greater-includes-the-lesser reasoning, a settlor who could have named a trust director to serve instead as a trustee should also be able to give the trust director the duties of the trustee. Under the no duty statutes, a beneficiary's only recourse for misconduct by the trust director is an action against the director for breach of the director's fiduciary duty to the beneficiary.

In the other group of statutes, which includes Delaware, Illinois, Texas, and Virginia, a directed trustee is not liable for complying with a direction of a trust director unless by so doing the directed trustee would personally engage in "willful" or "intentional" misconduct. The policy rationale for these statutes is that, because a trustee stands at the center of a trust, the trustee must bear at least some duty even if the trustee is acting under the direction of a director. Although the settlor could have made the trust director the sole trustee, the settlor did not actually do so—and under traditional understandings of trust law, a trustee must always be accountable to a beneficiary in some way. *See, e.g.*, Restatement (Third) of Trusts § 96 cmt. c (2012) ("Notwithstanding the breadth of language in a trust provision relieving a trustee from liability for breach of trust, for reasons of policy trust fiduciary law imposes limitations on the types and degree of misconduct for which the trustee can be excused from liability.").

The states in the second group also recognize, however, that to facilitate the settlor's intent that the trust director rather than the directed trustee be the primary or even sole decisionmaker, it is appropriate to reduce the trustee's duty below the usual level with respect to a matter subject to a power of direction. Accordingly, under these statutes a beneficiary's main recourse for misconduct by the trust director is an action against the director for breach of the director's fiduciary duty to the beneficiary. The beneficiary also has recourse against the trustee, but only if the trustee's compliance with the director's exercise or nonexercise of the director's powers amounted to "willful misconduct" by the trustee. Relative to a non-directed trust, this second approach has the effect of increasing the total fiduciary duties owed to a beneficiary. All of the usual duties of trusteeship are preserved in the trust director, but in addition the directed trustee has a duty to avoid willful misconduct.

After extensive deliberation and debate, the drafting committee opted to follow the second group of statutes on the grounds that this model is more consistent with traditional fiduciary policy. The popularity of directed trusts in Delaware, which also adopts the willful misconduct standard, establishes that a directed trust regime that preserves a willful misconduct safeguard is workable and that a total elimination of duty in a directed trustee is unnecessary to satisfy the needs of directed trust practice.

The willful misconduct standard prescribed by this subsection changes the policy of Uniform Trust Code § 808 (2000), which is similar in substance to Restatement (Third) of Trusts § 75 (2007). Section 808(b) provides:

> If the terms of a trust confer upon a person other than the settlor of a revocable trust power to direct certain actions of the trustee, the trustee shall act in accordance with an exercise of the power unless the attempted exercise is manifestly contrary to the terms of the trust or the trustee knows the attempted exercise would constitute a serious breach of a fiduciary duty that the person holding the power owes to the beneficiaries of the trust.

In deciding to adopt a different standard, the drafting committee was deeply influenced by the fact that a growing number of states that had previously adopted Section 808 have since abandoned or modified it to follow one of the two other models discussed above. The drafting committee was also strongly influenced by the fact that a review of every existing specialized state statute on directed trusts showed that no state that has legislated specifically on the issue of directed trustee fiduciary duties has chosen to follow Section 808.

Subsection (c)–release by trust director. The terms of a trust may empower a trust director to release a trustee or another trust director from liability for breach of trust. If the director grants such a release, the trustee or other director is not liable to the extent of the release. The terms of a trust may authorize such a release to be given at any time, whether before or after the trustee or other director acts. The precise scope of a power of release and the manner of its exercise depend on the terms of the trust.

Although a settlor has wide latitude in designing a power of direction, subsection (c) prescribes three mandatory safeguards that limit a director's power to release a trustee or other director from liability. First, consistent with the policy of subsection (b), a trustee or other director cannot be released for a breach that involves the trustee's or the other director's own willful misconduct. Second, consistent with prevailing law governing a release of a trustee by a beneficiary, a release by a trust director is not enforceable if it was procured by the improper conduct of the trustee or other director. Third, again consistent with prevailing law governing a release of a trustee by a beneficiary, a release by a trust director is not enforceable if at the time of the release the director did not know the material facts relating to the breach. The drafting committee based the second and third of these safeguards on Uniform Trust Code § 1009 (2001), which is similar in substance to Restatement (Third) of Trusts § 97 (2012).

Subsection (d)–petition for instructions. Subsection (d) confirms that, in accordance with existing law, a directed trustee that has reasonable doubt about its duty under this section may petition the court for instructions. *See, e.g.,* Restatement (Third) of Trusts § 71 (2007) ("A trustee or beneficiary may apply to an appropriate court for instructions regarding the administration or distribution of the trust if there is reasonable doubt about the powers or duties of the trusteeship or about the proper interpretation of the trust provisions."). The safe harbor of this subsection is permissive rather than mandatory. Though a trustee may satisfy its duties by petitioning for instructions, this subsection does not require a trustee to petition.

Subsection (e)–no ceiling on duties. Subsection (e) confirms that the duties prescribed by this section are defaults and minimums, not ceilings. The terms of a trust may impose further duties in addition to those prescribed by this section.

§ 10. Duty to Provide Information to Trust Director or Trustee.

(a) Subject to Section 11, a trustee shall provide information to a trust director to the extent the information is reasonably related both to:

(1) the powers or duties of the trustee; and

(2) the powers or duties of the director.

(b) Subject to Section 11, a trust director shall provide information to a trustee or another trust director to the extent the information is reasonably related both to:

(1) the powers or duties of the director; and

(2) the powers or duties of the trustee or other director.

(c) A trustee that acts in reliance on information provided by a trust director is not liable for a breach of trust to the extent the breach resulted from the reliance, unless by so acting the trustee engages in willful misconduct.

(d) A trust director that acts in reliance on information provided by a trustee or another trust director is not liable for a breach of trust to the extent the breach resulted from the reliance, unless by so acting the trust director engages in willful misconduct.

Comment

Subsections (a) and (b)–Duty to provide information. This section imposes duties on trustees and trust directors to provide information to each other. Subsection (a) imposes this duty on a directed trustee, and subsection (b) imposes this duty on a trust director. The drafting committee contemplated that the duties created by this section would provide trustees and trust directors with sufficient information to fulfill their obligations under trust law as well as other law, including banking, securities, and tax law.

Disclosure to beneficiaries. This section governs disclosure of information to trustees and trust directors. The duty of a trust director to disclose information to a beneficiary is governed by Section 8, which prescribes the fiduciary duties of a trust director, subject to Section 11. The duty of a trustee to disclose information to a beneficiary is governed by the background law of an enacting state under Section 4 as modified by Section 11, which limits a directed trustee's duty to inform a beneficiary about the actions of a trust director.

Reasonableness. This section relies heavily on the concept of reasonableness. Information must be disclosed only if it is reasonably related both to the powers or duties of the person making the disclosure and to the powers or duties of the person receiving the disclosure. The information must be reasonably related to the powers or duties of the person making the disclosure, because otherwise that person cannot be expected to possess the information. The information must also be reasonably related to the powers or duties of the person receiving the disclosure, because otherwise that person would not need the information. Examples of matters that might require disclosure under this section include asset valuations, modifications to the terms of a trust, changes to investment policy or strategy, distributions, changes in accounting procedure or valuations, and removal or appointment of trustees and trust directors.

Both an affirmative and a responsive duty to inform. This section imposes an affirmative duty to provide information (even in the absence of a request for that information) as well as a responsive duty to reply to requests for information. For example, if a trust director exercises a power to modify the terms of a trust, the director would have an affirmative duty to inform the trustees and other trust directors whose powers or duties are reasonably related to the amendment whether or not the trustees or other trust directors inquired about it. Similarly, the director would have a responsive duty to provide information about the amendment upon a request by a trustee or another trust director whose powers or duties were reasonably related to the amendment.

Interaction with Section 11. The duties of a trustee (in subsection (a)) and of a trust director (in subsection (b)) to disclose information are subject to the limitations of Section 11. Thus, although a trustee has a duty under this section to disclose information that is related to both the powers or duties of the trustee and the powers or duties of the director, a trustee does not have a duty to inform or give advice to the trust director concerning instances in which the trustee would have exercised the director's powers differently. The same is true for a trust director.

Shelton v. Tamposi. In Shelton v. Tamposi, 62 A.3d 741 (N.H. 2013), the terms of the trust left distribution in the hands of the trustee, but shifted power over investment to a trust director (the "investment director"). As a result, the trustee could not liquidate investments to raise the cash necessary to fund a distribution to one of the beneficiaries. Under subsection (b), the trust director would have been under a duty to give the trustee information about the effects of the director's investment program on the trust's cash position, and the trustee would have been under a duty to give the director information about the cash requirements of the trustee's distribution program. Moreover, in making and implementing the investment program, under Section 8(a) the trust director would be subject to the same duties as a similarly situated trustee, just as the trustee would be subject to the duties of a trustee in making and implementing the distribution program.

Subsections (c) and (d)—Subsection (c) provides a safe harbor for a trustee that acts in reliance on information provided by a trust director. Subsection (d) provides a similar safe harbor for a trust director for information provided by a trustee or other trust director. Under both subsections, the safe harbor only applies if the trustee or trust director that acts in reliance on the information is not engaged in willful misconduct. For example, subsection (c) protects a trustee if the trustee acts in reliance on a trust director's valuation of an asset, unless by accepting the valuation the trustee would engage in willful misconduct. As in Section 9, the rationale for the safe harbor and willful misconduct limit is to implement the settlor's division of labor subject to a mandatory fiduciary minimum.

No ceiling on duties to share information. This section imposes a mandatory floor, rather than a ceiling, on a directed trustee's and a trust director's duty to share information. The terms of a trust may specify more extensive duties of information sharing among directed trustees and trust directors.

§ 11. No Duty to Monitor, Inform, or Advise.

(a) Unless the terms of a trust provide otherwise:

(1) a trustee does not have a duty to:

(A) monitor a trust director; or

(B) inform or give advice to a settlor, beneficiary, trustee, or trust director concerning an instance in which the trustee might have acted differently than the director; and

(2) by taking an action described in paragraph (1), a trustee does not assume the duty excluded by paragraph (1).

(b) Unless the terms of a trust provide otherwise:

(1) a trust director does not have a duty to:

(A) monitor a trustee or another trust director; or

(B) inform or give advice to a settlor, beneficiary, trustee, or another trust director concerning an instance in which the director might have acted differently than a trustee or another trust director; and

(2) by taking an action described in paragraph (1), a trust director does not assume the duty excluded by paragraph (1).

Comment

Following existing statutes. Subsection (a) provides that a trustee does not have a duty to monitor a trust director or inform or give advice to a settlor, beneficiary, trustee, or trust director concerning instances in which the trustee might have acted differently than the director. Many existing state statutes are to similar effect, though the language in this section is simpler and more direct. Subsection (b) applies the same rule to a trust director regarding the actions of a trustee or another trust director.

The existing statutes on which this section is based were meant to reverse the result in Rollins v. Branch Banking & Trust Company of Virginia, 56 Va. Cir. 147 (2002), in which the court considered the liability of a trustee that was subject to direction in investment. The court declined to hold the trustee liable for the investment director's failure to direct diversification of the trust's investments, but the court nevertheless held the trustee liable for failing to advise the beneficiaries about the risks of the investment director's actions.

Survival of trustee's and trust director's general duty of disclosure. Although this section confirms that a directed trustee has no duty to monitor a trust director or inform or give advice to others concerning instances in which the trustee might have acted differently than the director, this section does not relieve a trustee of its ordinary duties to disclose, report, or account under otherwise applicable law such as under Uniform Trust Code § 813 (2004) or Restatement (Third) of Trusts § 82 (2007). The same is true for a trust director, on whom Section 8(a) imposes the fiduciary duties of a trustee.

For example, if a trust director has a power to direct investments, this section would relieve a directed trustee of any duty to advise a beneficiary

about the risks of the director's decision to concentrate the investment portfolio. The trustee would remain under a duty, however, to make periodic reports or accountings to the beneficiary and to answer reasonable inquiries by the beneficiary about the administration of the trust to the extent required by otherwise applicable law. The trustee would also remain under the duty imposed by Section 10 to provide a trust director with information reasonably related to its powers and duties.

No assumption of duty. In addition to waiving a directed trustee's duty to monitor, inform, or give advice as under subsection (a)(1), many state statutes go further and also provide that if a trustee for some reason chooses to monitor, inform, or give advice, these activities will be deemed to be "administrative actions." *See, e.g.,* Del. Code Ann. tit. 12, § 3313(e) (2017). The purpose of these provisions is to ensure that if a directed trustee chooses for some reason to monitor, inform, or give advice, the trustee does not assume a continuing obligation to do so or concede a prior duty to have done so. This section dispenses with the opacity of an administrative classification and achieves the intended result more directly. Subsection (a)(2) provides that if a trustee monitors, informs, or gives advice about the actions of a trust director, the trustee does not thereby assume a duty to do so. Subsection (b)(2) applies the same rule for a trust director.

§ 12. Application to Cotrustee.

§ 12. Application to Cotrustee. The terms of a trust may relieve a cotrustee from duty and liability with respect to another cotrustee's exercise or nonexercise of a power of the other cotrustee to the same extent that in a directed trust a directed trustee is relieved from duty and liability with respect to a trust director's power of direction under Sections 9 through 11.

Legislative Note: *A state that has enacted Uniform Trust Code (Last Revised or Amended in 2010) Section 703(c) or (g) should revise those sections to make them subject to this section. In the alternative, the state could insert this section as a new subsection in Section 703, and make subsections (c) and (g) subject to that new subsection if the state also adds to its Uniform Trust Code the definitions of "directed trustee," "power of direction," and "trust director" from Section 2(3), (5), and (9).*

Comment

Traditional law. Under traditional law, each cotrustee "has a duty to use reasonable care to prevent a cotrustee from committing a breach of trust and, if a breach of trust occurs, to obtain redress." Restatement (Third) of Trusts § 81(2) (2007). This rule applies even if the settlor limits the role or function of one of the cotrustees. "Even in matters

for which a trustee is relieved of responsibility, ... if the trustee knows that a co-trustee is committing or attempting to commit a breach of trust, the trustee has a duty to take reasonable steps to prevent the fiduciary misconduct." *Id.* cmt. b. Moreover, "even in the absence of any duty to intervene or grounds for suspicion, a trustee is entitled to request and receive reasonable information regarding an aspect of trust administration in which the trustee is not required to participate." *Id*. These rules for cotrusteeship contrast with the less demanding fiduciary standards for a directed trusteeship under Sections 9, 10, and 11 of this act.

Settlor autonomy. This section allows a settlor to choose either fiduciary regime for a cotrusteeship—the traditional rules of cotrusteeship or the more permissive rules of a directed trusteeship. There seems little reason to prohibit a settlor from applying the fiduciary rules of this act to a cotrusteeship given that the settlor could choose the more permissive rules of a directed trusteeship by labeling one of the cotrustees as a trust director and another as a directed trustee. The rationale for permitting the terms of a trust to reduce the duty of a cotrustee that is subject to direction by another trustee is the same as the rationale for permitting the terms of a trust to reduce the duty of a directed trustee. In both instances, a trustee must act according to directions from another person and therefore the other person, not the trustee, should bear the full fiduciary responsibility for the action.

Accordingly, if the terms of a trust so provide, a cotrustee may have only the duty required by the reasonable action and willful misconduct standards specified in Section 9, and be subject to the narrower rules governing information sharing and monitoring specified in Sections 10 and 11, with respect to another cotrustee's exercise or nonexercise of a power of that other cotrustee. If the terms of a trust indicate that a directed cotrustee is to have no duty or is not a fiduciary, then the effect will be to reduce the cotrustee's duties to those prescribed by Sections 9 through 11, just as would be the effect of similar language for a directed trustee.

Mechanics of choosing directed trustee duties. Under this section the default rule is that, if a settlor names cotrustees, the traditional law of cotrusteeship applies. The fiduciary duties of directed trusteeship will only apply to a cotrustee if the terms of the trust manifest such an intent. Whether this section applies to a given trust is thus a question of construction. This section does not impose a requirement of express reference to this section or to this act. Moreover, under Section 3(a), this section applies to a trust

created before the effective date of this act, but only as to a decision or action on or after that date.

For example, a familiar drafting strategy is to name cotrustees but also to provide that in the event of disagreement about a particular matter the decision of a specified trustee controls and the other cotrustee has no liability in that event. Under traditional law, notwithstanding this provision, the other cotrustee would be liable if it did not take reasonable steps to prevent a breach by the controlling cotrustee. Under this section, on a prospective basis the other cotrustee would be liable only for its own willful misconduct akin to a directed trustee.

Cotrustees as directed trustees and trust directors. The terms of a trust can place a cotrustee in a position of either giving direction, like a trust director, or taking direction, like a directed trustee. This section only applies to a cotrustee that takes direction. This section does not address the duties of a cotrustee that is not directed. Nor does this section address the duties of a cotrustee that gives direction. Under Section 8, the background law of an enacting state that applies to a directing cotrustee also applies to a similarly situated trustee. The drafting committee intended that the language "with respect to another cotrustee's exercise or nonexercise of a power of the other cotrustee" would refer only to a power of another cotrustee and not a power held jointly with the directed cotrustee, because a cotrustee cannot be thought of as taking direction from another cotrustee if the two cotrustees exercise a power jointly.

No third-party effects. Although this section changes the degree to which the terms of a trust may reduce a cotrustee's duty and liability, it does not alter the rules that affect the rights of third parties who contract with or otherwise interact with a cotrustee. The principal difference between cotrusteeship and directed trusteeship is that in a cotrusteeship every cotrustee has title to the trust property, whereas in a directed trusteeship, title to trust property belongs only to the trustee, and not to the trust director. The placement of title can have important consequences for dealings with third parties and for tax, property, and other bodies of law outside of trust law. This section does not change the rights of third parties who deal with a cotrustee in the cotrustee's capacity as such.

§ 13. Limitation of Action Against Trust Director.

(a) An action against a trust director for breach of trust must be commenced within the same limitation period as[under Uniform Trust Code Section 1005] for an action for breach of trust against a trustee in a like position and under similar circumstances.

(b) A report or accounting has the same effect on the limitation period for an action against a trust director for breach of trust that the report or accounting would have[under Uniform Trust Code Section 1005] in an action for breach of trust against a trustee in a like position and under similar circumstances.

Legislative Note: A state that has enacted Uniform Trust Code (Last Revised or Amended in 2010) Section 1005 should update the bracketed language to refer to that enactment. A state that has enacted a statute other than Uniform Trust Code Section 1005 to govern limitation of an action against a trustee should replace the bracketed language with a cross reference to that statute. A state that has not enacted a statutory limitation should delete the bracketed language.

Comment

This section absorbs for a trust director the law of an enacting state governing limitations on an action against a trustee. A limitation applies to a trust director as it would to a trustee in a like position and under similar circumstances. Whether the law is default or mandatory as applied to a trust director, for example, is determined by whether it is default or mandatory as applied to a trustee.

Subsection (a) extends to a trust director the same limits on liability that a trustee enjoys under the law of an enacting state by way of a statutory limitations period, such as under Uniform Trust Code § 1005(c) (2000). The limitations period absorbed by subsection (a) applies to all claims against a trust director for breach of trust, whether by a beneficiary, a trustee, another trust director, or some other party.

Subsection (b) extends to a trust director the same limitation period that a trustee enjoys under the law of an enacting state arising from the making of a report or accounting, such as under Uniform Trust Code § 1005(a)–(b) (2000). The rule of subsection (b) applies regardless of whether the report or accounting was made by the trust director. A trust director may therefore be protected by a report or accounting made by a trustee or another trust director even though the director did not make the report or accounting, so long as the report or accounting fairly discloses the relevant facts of the director's conduct.

Laches, which strictly speaking is an equitable defense rather than a limitations period, would apply to an action against a trust director under Section 14.

§ 14. Defenses in Action Against Trust Director. In an action against a trust director for breach of trust, the director may assert the same defenses a trustee in a like position and under similar circumstances could assert in an action for breach of trust against the trustee.

Comment

Absorption. This section makes available to a trust director the same defenses that are available to a trustee in a like position and under similar circumstances in an action for breach of trust. A trust director can assert any defense that would be available to a trustee in a comparable action for breach of trust under existing state law, including:

- laches or estoppel (see Restatement (Third) of Trusts § 98 (2012));
- consent, release, or ratification by a beneficiary (see Uniform Trust Code § 1009 (2001); Restatement (Third) of Trusts § 97(b)–(c) (2012));
- reasonable reliance on the terms of a trust (see Uniform Trust Code § 1006 (2000); Uniform Prudent Investor Act § 1(b) (1994)); and

- reasonable care in ascertaining the happening of an event affecting administration or distribution (see Uniform Trust Code § 1007 (2000); Restatement (Third) of Trusts § 76 cmt. f (2007)).

Exculpation or exoneration. The comments to Section 8 address the effect of an exculpation or exoneration clause on the duty and liability of a trust director.

Attorney's fees and indemnification. Attorney's fees and indemnification for a trust director are governed by Section 6(b)(1), which establishes a default rule that allows a trust director to exercise "any further power appropriate to the exercise or nonexercise of a power of direction granted to the director." By default, therefore, a trust director has a power to incur attorney's fees and other expenses and to direct indemnification for them if doing so would be "appropriate" to the exercise of the director's express powers.

§ 15. Jurisdiction over Trust Director.

(a) By accepting appointment as a trust director of a trust subject to this [act], the director submits to personal jurisdiction of the courts of this state regarding any matter related to a power or duty of the director.

(b) This section does not preclude other methods of obtaining jurisdiction over a trust director.

Comment

Under subsection (a), by accepting appointment as a trust director of a trust subject to this act, the director submits to personal jurisdiction of the courts of this state with respect to "any matter related to a power or duty of the director." This subsection does not apply to a person that has not accepted appointment as a trust director (the question of whether a person has accepted appointment is governed by Section 16(1)). The drafting committee contemplated that a purported director could contest acceptance, and therefore jurisdiction, in the normal course of a judicial proceeding in which the matter arose, as under Fed. R. Civ. P. § 12(b)(2).

Jurisdiction over a person that has accepted appointment as trust director is mandatory. The terms of a trust or an agreement among the trust director and other parties cannot negate personal jurisdiction over a trust director under this section. However, this section does not preclude a court from declining to exercise jurisdiction under the doctrine of forum non conveniens.

Subsection (b) confirms that subsection (a) does not prescribe the exclusive method of obtaining jurisdiction over a trust director.

§ 16. Office of Trust Director.
Unless the terms of a trust provide otherwise, the rules applicable to a trustee apply to a trust director regarding the following matters:

(1) acceptance[under Uniform Trust Code Section 701];

(2) giving of bond to secure performance[under Uniform Trust Code Section 702];

(3) reasonable compensation[under Uniform Trust Code Section 708];

(4) resignation[under Uniform Trust Code Section 705];

(5) removal[under Uniform Trust Code Section 706]; and

(6) vacancy and appointment of successor[under Uniform Trust Code Section 704].

Legislative Note: A state that has enacted the Uniform Trust Code (Last Revised or Amended in 2010) provisions cited in this section should update the bracketed language to refer to the appropriate provisions of that enactment. A state that has enacted relevant statutory provisions other than the provisions of the Uniform Trust Code cited in this section should replace the bracketed language with cross references to those provisions, except that a state that allows statutory commissions rather than reasonable compensation for a trustee is advised for the reasons given in the comments below to apply a rule of reasonable compensation to a trust director. A state that has not enacted relevant statutory provisions should delete the bracketed language.

Comment

This section applies the law of trusteeship to a trust directorship with regard to seven subjects. Whether the law is default or mandatory as applied to a trust director depends on whether it is default or mandatory as applied to a trustee.

Paragraph (1)–acceptance. This paragraph absorbs an enacting state's law governing acceptance of a trusteeship, such as under Uniform Trust Code § 701(a)–(b) (2000) or Restatement (Third) of Trusts § 35 (2003), for application to acceptance of a trust directorship. However, whereas a trustee is expected to participate actively in the administration of the trust, and is therefore usually capable of signaling acceptance by conduct, some trust directors, such as a director with a power to determine the settlor's competence, may not take any action for long stretches of time, if ever. This delay in action may complicate acceptance by conduct.

Paragraph (2)–bond. This paragraph absorbs an enacting state's law governing bond to secure performance by a trustee, such as under Uniform Trust Code § 702(a)-(b) (2000) and Restatement (Third) of Trusts § 34(3) (2003), for application to bond by a trust director. The drafting committee assumed that bond would seldom be required for a trust director, as in the usual case the director would not have custody of the trust property.

Paragraph (3)–reasonable compensation. This paragraph absorbs an enacting state's law governing reasonable compensation of a trustee, such as under Uniform Trust Code § 708 (2000) and Restatement (Third) of Trusts § 38 cmt. i (2003), for application to compensation of a trust director. The drafting committee contemplated that, just as in total "the reasonable fees for multiple trustees may be higher than for a single trustee," Restatement (Third) of Trusts § 38 cmt. i (2003), so too the total reasonable fees for a trust with a directed trustee and a trust director may be higher than for a single trustee.

Reasonable compensation for a trust director will vary based on the nature of the director's powers, and in some circumstances may well be zero. A state that provides a statutory commission for a trustee should therefore refrain from using the commission for a trust director and should instead use a rule of reasonable compensation. Statutory trustee commissions will often overcompensate a trust director, especially a director that does not participate actively on an ongoing basis in the administration of the trust. The problem will be especially serious in a trust with multiple such directors.

Moreover, the reasonable compensation of a directed trustee is likely to be less than that for a trustee that is not directed. An apt analogy is to a trustee that hires others to "render services expected or normally to be performed by the trustee." Restatement (Third) of Trusts § 38 cmt. c(1) (2003); *see also* Uniform Prudent Investor Act § 9 cmt. (1994) ("If, for example, the trustee's regular compensation

schedule presupposes that the trustee will conduct the investment management function, it should ordinarily follow that the trustee will lower its fee when delegating the investment function to an outside manager.").

Paragraph (4)–resignation. This paragraph absorbs an enacting state's law governing resignation by a trustee, such as under Uniform Trust Code § 705 (2001) and Restatement (Third) of Trusts § 36 (2003), for application to resignation by a trust director.

Paragraph (5)–removal. This subsection absorbs an enacting state's law governing removal of a trustee, such as under Uniform Trust Code § 706 (2000) and Restatement (Third) of Trusts § 37 cmt. e (2003), for application to removal of a trust director.

Paragraph (6)–vacancy. This section absorbs an enacting state's law applicable to a vacancy in a trusteeship for application to a vacancy in a trust directorship. For example, under Uniform Trust Code § 704 (2004), "a vacancy in a trusteeship need not be filled" if "one or more cotrustees remain in office." So too, if three of five trust directors with a joint power to determine the settlor's capacity remain in office, the court "need not" fill the vacancies, though the vacancies should be filled if doing so would be more consistent with the settlor's plan. Likewise, if the sole trust director with power over investment of the trust property ceases to serve, in most circumstances the vacancy should be filled, and this is true even if other directors with unrelated powers remain in office. An apt analogy is to a trust with several cotrustees, each of whom has controlling authority over different aspects of the trust's administration. If any of those trustees ceases to serve, in many circumstances a court should appoint a successor even though other cotrustees remain in office.

Costs and indemnification. The power of a trust director to incur reasonable costs and to direct indemnification for expenses would in most cases be covered by Section 6(b)(1).

§ 17. Uniformity of Application and Construction.
In applying and construing this uniform act, consideration must be given to the need to promote uniformity of the law with respect to its subject matter among states that enact it.

§ 18. Relation to Electronic Signatures in Global and National Commerce Act.
This [act] modifies, limits, or supersedes the Electronic Signatures in Global and National Commerce Act, 15 U.S.C. Section 7001 et seq., but does not modify, limit, or supersede Section 101(c) of that act, 15 U.S.C.

Section 7001(c), or authorize electronic delivery of any of the notices described in Section 103(b) of that act, 15 U.S.C. Section 7003(b).

§ 19. Repeals; Conforming Amendments.
    (a) . . . .
    (b) . . . .
    (c) . . . .

§ 20. Effective Date. This [act] takes effect . . . .

UNIFORM TRUST DECANTING ACT
(2015, with Subsequent Amendments)

Table of Sections

Prefatory Note

The Uniform Trust Decanting Act is promulgated in the midst of a rising tide of state decanting statutes. These statutes represent one of several recent innovations in trust law that seek to make trusts more flexible so that the settlor's material purposes can best be carried out under current circumstances. A decanting statute provides flexibility by statutorily expanding discretion already granted to the trustee to permit the trustee to modify the trust either directly or by distributing its assets to another trust. While some trusts expressly grant the trustee or another person a power to modify or decant the trust, a statutory provision can better describe the power granted, impose limits on the power to protect the beneficiaries and the settlor's intent, protect against inadvertent tax consequences, provide procedural rules for exercising the power and provide for appropriate remedies. While decanting may be permitted in some situations under common law in some states, in many states it is unclear whether common law decanting is permitted, and if it is, the circumstances in which it is permitted and the parameters within which it may be exercised.

Need for Uniformity. Trusts may be governed by the laws of different states for purposes of validity, meaning and effect, and administration. The place of administration of a trust may move from state to state. It often may be difficult to determine the state in which a trust is administered if a trust has co-trustees domiciled in different states or has a corporate trustee that performs different trust functions in different states. As a result it may sometimes be unclear whether a particular state's decanting statute applies to a trust and sometimes more than one state's decanting statute may apply to a trust. A uniform statute can eliminate conflicts between different state statutes. It can also protect a trustee who decants under one state's statute when more than one state's statute might apply and protect a trustee who reasonably relies on a prior decanting.

Currently there is limited guidance on the income, gift, and generation-skipping transfer ("GST") tax implications of decanting. A uniform statute also may provide common ground for the promulgation of tax guidance.

What Trusts May Be Decanted. Generally, the Uniform Trust Decanting Act permits decanting of an irrevocable, express trust in which the terms of the trust grant the trustee or another fiduciary the discretionary power to make principal distributions. See Section 3 and Section 2(3) (defining "authorized fiduciary"). The act does not apply to revocable trusts unless they are revocable by the settlor only with the consent of the trustee or an adverse party. Section 3(a). The act does not apply to wholly charitable trusts. Section 3(b). With one exception, if no fiduciary has discretion to distribute principal, the act does not apply unless the court appoints a special fiduciary and authorizes the special fiduciary to exercise the decanting power. See Section 9(1)(2). The exception is that a fiduciary who is responsible for making trust distributions may decant a trust to create a special-needs trust even if the fiduciary does not have discretion over principal if the decanting will further the purposes of the first trust.

Who May Decant. As discussed below, the decanting power is a fiduciary power, and thus must be entrusted to one of the fiduciaries of the first trust. The act entrusts the "authorized fiduciary" with the decanting power. The "authorized fiduciary"

generally is the fiduciary who has discretion to distribute principal, although a more expansive definition is needed in the case of a special-needs trust. Generally, the authorized fiduciary will be the trustee. Where there is a divided trusteeship that gives the power to make or direct principal distributions to another fiduciary, such as a distribution director, such other fiduciary will be the authorized fiduciary.

Discretion Over Principal. Except in the case of special-needs trusts, the decanting power is granted only to an authorized fiduciary who by definition must have the discretion to distribute principal. The extent of the decanting authority depends upon the extent of the discretion granted to the trustee to distribute principal. When the authorized fiduciary has "limited distribution discretion" that is constrained by an ascertainable or reasonably definite standard, the interests of each beneficiary in the second trust must be substantially similar to such beneficiary's interests in the first trust. Thus when the authorized fiduciary has limited distributive discretion, an exercise of the decanting power generally can modify administrative, but not dispositive, trust provisions. When the authorized fiduciary has "expanded distributive discretion," the authorized fiduciary may exercise the decanting power to modify beneficial interests, subject to restrictions to protect interests that are current, noncontingent rights or vested remainder interests, to protect qualification for tax benefits and to protect charitable interests.

Sometimes a trust may have two or more authorized fiduciaries, some of whom have limited distributive discretion and some of whom have expanded distributive discretion. The authorized fiduciaries with limited distributive discretion may exercise the decanting power under Section 12 and the authorized fiduciaries with expanded distributive discretion may exercise the decanting power under Section 11.

Fiduciary Power. The Uniform Trust Decanting Act does not impose any duty on the authorized fiduciary to exercise the decanting power, but if the authorized fiduciary does exercise that power, the power must be exercised in accordance with the fiduciary duties of the authorized fiduciary. See Section 4. A fiduciary must administer a trust in good faith, in accordance with its terms (subject to the decanting power) and purposes, and in the interests of the beneficiaries. An exercise of decanting power must be in accordance with the purposes of the first trust. The purpose of decanting is not to disregard the settlor's intent but to modify the trust to better effectuate the settlor's broader purposes or the settlor's probable intent if the settlor had anticipated the circumstances at the time of decanting.

As a fiduciary power, the decanting power may be exercised without consent or approval of the beneficiaries or the court, except in the case of a few specific modifications that may benefit the fiduciary personally. Nonetheless, qualified beneficiaries are entitled to notice and may petition the court if they believe the authorized fiduciary has breached its fiduciary duty. Further, the authorized fiduciary, another fiduciary, a beneficiary, the settlor or, in the case of a trust with a charitable interest, the Attorney General or other official who may enforce the charitable interest, may petition the court for instructions, appointment of a special fiduciary who may exercise the decanting power, approval of an exercise of decanting power, a determination that the authorized fiduciary breached its fiduciary duties, a determination that the savings provisions in Section 22 apply or a determination that the attempted decanting is invalid.

Decanting Procedure. Initially, the power to decant was often considered a derivative of the power to make a discretionary distribution to a beneficiary. Under this construct the decanting power was exercised by making a distribution from one trust to another, and a second trust, separate and distinct from the first trust, was required.

The Uniform Trust Decanting Act views the decanting power as a power to modify the first trust, either by changing the terms of the first trust or by distributing property from the first trust to a second trust. While the act generally modulates the extent of the authorized fiduciary's power to decant according to the degree of discretion granted to the authorized fiduciary over principal, the power to decant is distinct from the power to distribute.

Thus the authorized fiduciary may exercise the decanting power by modifying the first trust, in which case the "second trust" is merely the modified first trust. The decanting instrument can, when appropriate, merely identify the specific provisions in the first trust that are to be modified and set forth the modified provisions, much like an amendment to a revocable trust. If the decanting power is exercised by modifying the terms of the first trust, the trustee could either treat the second trust as a new trust or treat the second trust as a continuation of the first

trust. If the second trust is treated as a continuation of the first trust, there should be no need to transfer or retitle the trust property. Further, subject to future tax guidance, if the second trust is a continuation of the first trust, there may be no need to treat the first trust as having terminated for income tax purposes and no need to obtain a new tax identification number.

Innovations. The Uniform Trust Decanting Act contains a number of innovations, in addition to borrowing concepts from existing state decanting statutes.

The act, like some state statutes, intentionally applies broadly to trusts that have their principal place of administration in the state, trusts that are governed by the law of the state for administration and trusts that are governed by the law of the state for purposes of construction or determining meaning or effect. See Section 5. By casting a wide net for applicability, questions about whether a state's uniform statute applies to a particular trust may be minimized.

Further, the act permits a trustee to reasonably rely on a prior decanting under the law of the enacting state or a different state. See Section 6.

The Uniform Trust Decanting Act also addresses in detail the extent to which charitable interests may be modified by decanting. The act does not permit decanting of wholly charitable trusts. See Section 3. With respect to charitable interests within trusts, the act protects any charitable deduction that may have been taken. See Section 19(b)(2). The act also balances protecting the settlor's charitable intent with the need to permit decanting of trusts that include contingent charitable interests. If the first trust contains a charitable interest, the second trust cannot diminish the charitable interest, change an identified charitable organization or change the charitable purpose. To ensure that these protections are respected, the Attorney General must receive notice of any decanting of a trust with a charitable interest. Further, the Act prohibits changing the governing law of trusts containing determinable charitable interests without court approval if the Attorney General objects. See Section 14.

The act also delineates the role of the court in greater detail than in existing state statutes. See Section 9. While decanting generally does not require court approval, the authorized fiduciary may wish to seek instructions or approval from the court to confirm that the decanting is not an abuse of discretion. A fiduciary may also wish to seek court instructions as to the effect of a prior decanting, particularly if the prior decanting may be in some way flawed. A few state statutes permit a special fiduciary to be appointed to exercise decanting power where the statute does not permit the acting trustee to decant. The act borrows the concept of a special fiduciary but does not restrict its use to cases in which the acting trustee is not permitted to decant.

The Uniform Trust Decanting Act provides a remedy for an imperfect attempted decanting, to avoid the uncertainty that would exist if an attempted decanting is later discovered to have failed to fully comply with the decanting statute. Section 22 of the act essentially reads out of the second-trust instrument any impermissible provision and reads into the second-trust instrument any required provision. This gives authorized fiduciaries exercising decanting power greater comfort that their intent will be implemented and not subject to challenge for an inadvertent misstep or technicality.

The act borrows from some of the state statutes a provision that deals with the disposition of later discovered property. See Section 26. This provision ensures that if property was not retitled at the time of the decanting, it will be owned by the trust that most likely was intended to receive it. The act also includes a provision that recognizes that the liabilities of the first trust pass with the trust property to the second trust. See Section 27.

Overview of the Act. Sections 1 through 6 of the act deal with the scope and application of the act, fiduciary duty and definitions. Section 1 names the act. Section 2 contains definitions. Definitions of terms used only in one Section are found within that Section. Section 3 addresses the types of trusts to which the act applies (or does not apply) and Section 5 describes the connections to the adopting state that are sufficient for a trust to utilize the act. Section 4 addresses fiduciary duty in exercising or not exercising the decanting power. Section 6 addresses reliance on prior decantings, including decantings performed under other states' laws.

Sections 7 through 10 of the act deal with the procedures for exercising the decanting power. Section 7 sets forth the notice requirements for decanting. Section 8 is an optional provision dealing with representation of beneficiaries, including the representation of certain charitable interests by the state's Attorney General or other appropriate official. Section 9 describes the authority of the court with respect to decanting. Section 10 describes the formalities for decanting.

Sections 11 through 23 contain the heart of the decanting power and describe what modifications can be made by decanting. Section 11 delineates the decanting power when the authorized fiduciary has expanded distributive discretion and Section 12 delineates the decanting power when the authorized fiduciary has limited distributive discretion.

Section 13 contains special rules to facilitate decanting into a special-needs trust for a beneficiary with a disability. The Uniform Trust Decanting Act permits a trust to be decanted to modify the interest of the beneficiary with a disability even if the trustee does not have expanded distributive discretion. When a trust has a beneficiary with a disability, it may not be in the beneficiary's interest to make mandatory distributions to the beneficiary. Further, it may be in the beneficiary's interest to restructure the trust as a special-needs trust so that the trust does not adversely affect the beneficiary's qualification for governmental benefits. This carries out the settlor's probable intent if the settlor had known of the beneficiary's disability.

Section 14 provides special rules to protect charitable interests.

Sections 15 through 20 generally provide limitations on the exercise of the decanting power. Section 15 addresses how express restrictions contained within the first-trust instrument may limit the decanting power. Sections 16, 17, and 18 impose limitations on an authorized fiduciary exercising the decanting power in ways that might be considered self-dealing. Section 16 restricts decanting to increase the authorized fiduciary's compensation. Section 17 restricts decanting to increase the authorized fiduciary's protection from liability. Section 18 restricts the modification or elimination of a provision permitting a person to remove or replace the authorized fiduciary. Section 19 imposes limitations on the decanting power that may be necessary to avoid disqualifying a trust for a particular tax benefit. Section 20 addresses limits on the duration of a trust, such as the rule against perpetuities.

Section 21 makes clear that even though the extent of the authorized fiduciary's power to decant is generally determined based upon the degree of discretion over principal distributions, the authorized fiduciary may exercise the decanting power even if the authorized fiduciary would not have made a discretionary distribution at such time.

Section 22 contains the remediation provision that is intended to salvage imperfect decantings. Section 23 authorizes under certain circumstances decanting of trusts for the care of a nonhuman animal.

Sections 24 through 32 contain miscellaneous provisions. These provisions include Section 25, which recognizes that when a trust has been decanted it may no longer be obvious who is the settlor for different purposes and addresses who should be treated as the settlor for different purposes. Section 26 provides a default rule for determining whether the first trust or second trust owns later-discovered property. Section 27 makes clear that liabilities of the first trust are also liabilities of the second trust to the extent it received property from the first trust.

§ 1. Short Title. This [act] may be cited as the Uniform Trust Decanting Act.

§ 2. Definitions. In this [act]:

(1) "Appointive property" means the property or property interest subject to a power of appointment.

(2) "Ascertainable standard" means a standard relating to an individual's health, education, support, or maintenance within the meaning of 26 U.S.C. Section 2041(b)(1)(A)[, as amended,] or 26 U.S.C. Section 2514(c)(1)[, as amended,] and any applicable regulations.

(3) "Authorized fiduciary" means:

(A) a trustee or other fiduciary, other than a settlor, that has discretion to distribute or direct a trustee to distribute part or all of the principal of the first trust to one or more current beneficiaries;

(B) a special fiduciary appointed under Section 9; or

(C) a special-needs fiduciary under Section 13.

(4) "Beneficiary" means a person that:

(A) has a present or future, vested or contingent, beneficial interest in a trust;

(B) holds a power of appointment over trust property; or

(C) is an identified charitable organization that will or may receive distributions under the terms of the trust.

(5) "Charitable interest" means an interest in a trust which:

(A) is held by an identified charitable organization and makes the organization a qualified beneficiary;

(B) benefits only charitable organizations and, if the interest were held by an identified charitable organization, would make the organization a qualified beneficiary; or

(C) is held solely for charitable purposes and, if the interest were held by an identified charitable organization, would make the organization a qualified beneficiary.

(6) "Charitable organization" means:

(A) a person, other than an individual, organized and operated exclusively for charitable purposes; or

(B) a government or governmental subdivision, agency, or instrumentality, to the extent it holds funds exclusively for a charitable purpose.

(7) "Charitable purpose" means the relief of poverty, the advancement of education or religion, the promotion of health, a municipal or other governmental purpose, or another purpose the achievement of which is beneficial to the community.

(8) "Court" means the court in this state having jurisdiction in matters relating to trusts.

(9) "Current beneficiary" means a beneficiary that on the date the beneficiary's qualification is determined is a distributee or permissible distributee of trust income or principal. The term includes the holder of a presently exercisable general power of appointment but does not include a person that is a beneficiary only because the person holds any other power of appointment.

(10) "Decanting power" or "the decanting power" means the power of an authorized fiduciary under this [act] to distribute property of a first trust to one or more second trusts or to modify the terms of

the first trust.

(11) "Expanded distributive discretion" means a discretionary power of distribution that is not limited to an ascertainable standard or a reasonably definite standard.

(12) "First trust" means a trust over which an authorized fiduciary may exercise the decanting power.

(13) "First-trust instrument" means the trust instrument for a first trust.

(14) "General power of appointment" means a power of appointment exercisable in favor of a powerholder, the powerholder's estate, a creditor of the powerholder, or a creditor of the powerholder's estate.

(15) "Jurisdiction", with respect to a geographic area, includes a state or country.

(16) "Person" means an individual, estate, business or nonprofit entity, public corporation, government or governmental subdivision, agency, or instrumentality, or other legal entity.

(17) "Power of appointment" means a power that enables a powerholder acting in a nonfiduciary capacity to designate a recipient of an ownership interest in or another power of appointment over the appointive property. The term does not include a power of attorney.

(18) "Powerholder" means a person in which a donor creates a power of appointment.

(19) "Presently exercisable power of appointment" means a power of appointment exercisable by the powerholder at the relevant time. The term:

(A) includes a power of appointment exercisable only after the occurrence of a specified event, the satisfaction of an ascertainable standard, or the passage of a specified time only after:

(i) the occurrence of the specified event;

(ii) the satisfaction of the ascertainable standard; or

(iii) the passage of the specified time; and

(B) does not include a power exercisable only at the powerholder's death.

(20) "Qualified beneficiary" means a beneficiary that on the date the beneficiary's qualification is determined:

(A) is a distributee or permissible distributee of trust income or principal;

(B) would be a distributee or permissible distributee of trust income or principal if the interests of the distributees described in subparagraph (A) terminated on that date without causing the trust to terminate; or

(C) would be a distributee or permissible distributee of trust income or principal if the trust terminated on that date.

(21) "Reasonably definite standard" means a clearly measurable standard under which a holder of a power of distribution is legally accountable within the meaning of 26 U.S.C. Section 674(b)(5)(A)[, as amended,] and any applicable regulations.

(22) "Record" means information that is inscribed on a tangible medium or that is stored in an electronic or other medium and is retrievable in perceivable form.

(23) "Second trust" means:

(A) a first trust after modification under this [act]; or

(B) a trust to which a distribution of property from a first trust is or may be made under this [act].

(24) "Second-trust instrument" means the trust instrument for a second trust.

(25) "Settlor", except as otherwise provided in Section 25, means a person, including a testator, that creates or contributes property to a trust. If more than one person creates or contributes property to a trust, each person is a settlor of the portion of the trust property attributable to the person's contribution except to the extent another person has power to revoke or withdraw that portion.

(26) "Sign" means, with present intent to authenticate or adopt a record:

(A) to execute or adopt a tangible symbol; or

(B) to attach to or logically associate with the record an electronic symbol, sound, or process.

(27) "State" means a state of the United States, the District of Columbia, Puerto Rico, the United States Virgin Islands, or any territory or insular possession subject to the jurisdiction of the United States.

(28) "Terms of the trust" means:

(A) Except as otherwise provided in subparagraph (B), the manifestation of the settlor's intent regarding a trust's provisions as:

(i) expressed in the trust instrument; or

(ii) established by other evidence that would be admissible in a judicial proceeding; or

(B) the trust's provisions as established, determined, or amended by:

(i) a trustee or other person in accordamce with applicable law;

(ii) a court order[; or]

(iii) a nonjudicial settlement agreement under [Uniform Trust Code Section 111]].

(29) "Trust instrument" means a record executed by the settlor to create a trust or by any person to create a second trust which contains some or all of the terms of the trust, including any amendments.

Legislative Note: *A number of definitions in this section are identical to the definitions in the Uniform Trust Code. A state that has adopted the Uniform Trust Code and is adopting this act as part of the Trust Code can omit these definitions. If a state that has adopted the Uniform Trust Code is adopting this act but is not incorporating it into the Uniform Trust Code, the legislation could either repeat the definitions in this act or substitute where appropriate: "_____" has the meaning in Section _____ of the Uniform Trust Code.*

In states in which the constitution, or other law, does not permit the phrase "as amended" when federal statutes are incorporated into state law, the phrase should be deleted in paragraphs (2) and (21).

In Section 2(8) the definition of "court" should be revised as needed to refer to the appropriate court having jurisdiction over trust matters.

A state that has not enacted Uniform Trust Code Section 111 should replace the bracketed language of paragraph (28)(B)(iii) with a cross reference to the state's statute governing nonjudicial settlement or should omit paragraph (28)(B)(iii) if the state does not have such a statute.

Comment

Appointive Property. The definition of "appointive property" is identical to the definition in Section 102(2) of the Uniform Powers of Appointment Act.

Ascertainable Standard. The definition of "ascertainable standard" is similar to the definition found in Section 103(2) of the Uniform Trust Code, but also includes the regulations to the cited sections of the Internal Revenue Code.

A power that is limited to health, education, support or maintenance is limited to an ascertainable standard. Treas. Reg. § 25.2514-1(c)(2). Other powers limited to an ascertainable standard include "support in reasonable comfort," "maintenance in health and reasonable comfort," "support in the beneficiary's accustomed manner of living," "education, including college and professional education" and "medical, dental, hospital and nursing expenses and expenses of invalidism." A power to make distributions for comfort, welfare, happiness or best interests is not limited to an ascertainable standard. In determining whether a power is limited by an ascertainable standard, it is immaterial whether the beneficiary is required to exhaust other income or resources before the power can be exercised.

The entire context of the document should be considered in determining whether the standard is ascertainable. For example, if the trust instrument provides that the determination of the trustee is conclusive with respect to the exercise of the standard, the power is not ascertainable.

A power to make distributions "as the trustee deems advisable" or in the trustee's "sole and absolute discretion" without further limitation is not subject to an ascertainable standard.

The term is also construed by case law regarding Internal Revenue Code Sections 2036 and 2038.

Authorized Fiduciary. The definition of "authorized fiduciary" includes only a person acting in a fiduciary capacity. Only a fiduciary, subject to fiduciary duties, should have the power to decant. A distribution director who is not a fiduciary should not have the power to decant.

The definition excludes a settlor acting as a trustee. If a settlor is a trustee of an irrevocable trust, gift and estate tax problems could result if the settlor had a decanting power. The definition does not exclude a beneficiary who is acting as a trustee (an "interested trustee") because the act only permits a trustee with expanded distributive discretion to decant in a manner that would change beneficial interests. Typically trusts will not give an interested trustee unascertainable discretion over discretionary distributions because such discretion would create gift and estate tax issues. In the unusual event that a trust does give an interested trustee unascertainable discretion, the trustee will incur the tax effects of holding a general power of appointment whether or not the trustee also has a decanting power.

If the discretion to distribute or to direct the trustee to distribute is held jointly by two or more trustees or other fiduciaries, the "authorized fiduciary" is such trustees or other fiduciaries collectively. If the authorized fiduciary is comprised of two or more fiduciaries, the trust instrument or state law will generally provide whether they must act unanimously or whether they may act by majority or some other percentage vote. For example, Section 703(a) of the Uniform Trust Code provides that trustees who are unable to reach unanimous decision may act by majority decision.

The term also includes a special fiduciary appointed by the court under Section 9, who may exercise the decanting power.

The term also includes a special-needs fiduciary under Section 13 even if such fiduciary does not have discretion to distribute principal of the first trust.

Beneficiary. The definition of "beneficiary" in Section 2(4)(A) and (B) is substantially similar to the definition found in Section 103(3) of the Uniform Trust Code. Section 2(4)(C) adds as a beneficiary a charitable organization identified to receive distributions from a trust. Cf. Uniform Trust Code § 110(a) and § 405(a). Thus an identified charitable organization has the rights of a beneficiary under this act. Absent Section 2(4)(C) such charities would not be considered beneficiaries. Because a charitable interest is not created to benefit ascertainable charitable organizations but to benefit the community at large, persons receiving distributions from a charitable interest are not beneficiaries as that term is defined in the Uniform Trust Code. See Uniform

Trust Code § 103, Comment.

In addition to living and ascertained individuals, beneficiaries may be unborn or unascertained. The term "beneficiary" includes not only beneficiaries who received their interests under the terms of the trust but also beneficiaries who received their interests by other means, including by assignment, exercise of a power of appointment, resulting trust upon the failure of an interest, gap in a disposition, operation of an antilapse statute upon the predecease of a named beneficiary, or upon termination of the trust. A potential appointee of a power of appointment is not a beneficiary unless a presently exercisable power of appointment has been exercised in favor of such appointee. A person who merely incidentally benefits from the trust is not a beneficiary. See Restatement Third of Trusts § 48.

While the holder of a power of appointment is not considered a trust beneficiary under the common law of trusts, powerholders are classified as beneficiaries under the Uniform Trust Code. Powerholders are included on the principle that their interests are significant enough that they should be afforded the rights of beneficiaries. A power of appointment as used in state trust law and the Uniform Trust Code is as defined in state property law and not federal tax law although there is considerable overlap between the two definitions.

Charitable Interest. The term "charitable interest" includes an interest held by a charitable organization that makes the charitable organization a qualified beneficiary. Section 2(5). See Section 2(4)(C) defining the term "beneficiary" to include an identified charitable organization that may or will receive distributions under the terms of a trust. See Section 2(20) defining a qualified beneficiary.

For example, a trust might provide for a certain amount to be distributed annually to Gentoos Need You, a charitable organization, and permit the trustee to make discretionary distributions of principal to the settlor's descendants. Upon the death of the settlor's last surviving child, $100,000 is to be paid to Gentoos Need You and the remainder to trusts for the settlor's grandchildren. The annuity interest and the remainder interest held by Gentoos Need You are both charitable interests because they are held by an identified charitable organization and make the organization a qualified beneficiary.

The term "charitable interest" also includes an interest that can benefit only charitable organizations and that, if held by an identified charitable organization, would make the charitable organization a qualified beneficiary. Section 2(5)(B). For example, if the trustee is to distribute $50,000 from the trust each year for ten years to one or more charitable organizations selected by the trustee that protect Antarctica and its wildlife, the trustee also has discretion to distribute income and principal to individual beneficiaries, and at the end of ten years the trustee is to distribute the remainder to the settlor's descendants, the $50,000 annuity is a charitable interest because it may be distributed only to charitable organizations.

As another example, if the trustee may make discretionary principal distributions to the settlor's spouse, and upon the spouse's death is to distribute one-half of the principal to charitable organizations that protect the Arctic and its wildlife, and the other one-half to the settlor's descendants, there is a charitable interest in one-half of the remainder.

The term "charitable interest" also includes an interest devoted solely to charitable purposes, even if the charitable purposes may be carried out directly by the trust rather than through distributions to charitable organizations. Section 2(5)(C). The act, however, does not apply to a wholly charitable trust. See Section 3(b).

The term does not include contingent, successor charitable interests that are not equivalent to the interests held by qualified beneficiaries. For example, if a trust permits distributions to Child A, and upon Child A's death the trust distributes to Child A's descendants, or if none, to the settlor's descendants, or if none, to the Manatee Preservation Fund, a charitable organization, and Child A or the settlor has one or more descendants living, the interest of the Manatee Preservation Fund does not make it a qualified beneficiary and therefore its interest is not a charitable interest.

Charitable Organization. The definition of "charitable organization" is based on the definition of "institution" in the Uniform Prudent Management of Institutional Funds Act (Section 2(4)), except that it excludes trusts.

Charitable Purpose. The definition of "charitable purpose" is similar to the definition in Section 405 of the Uniform Trust Code. The definition of "charitable purpose" follows that of Section 28 of the Restatement Third of Trusts and Section 2(1) of the Uniform Prudent Management of Institutional Funds Act. This definition derives from common law and ultimately the English Statute of Charitable Uses, enacted in 1601. A charitable purpose is a nonprofit purpose (and not a purpose for private benefit) that

benefits an indefinite class of the public.

The definition includes purposes "beneficial to the community" because that concept is part of the traditional definition of charitable purposes. The definition means purposes considered charitable and not merely beneficial. Many activities and organizations, such as social welfare organizations, cooperative associations, and business entities, benefit the community. Nonetheless, these organizations and the activities they carry on are not charitable within the meaning of the act because their earnings inure to the benefit of private persons such as members or shareholders. *Attorney General v. Weymouth Agricultural & Industrial Society*, 400 Mass. 475, 479, 509 N.E.2d 1193, 1195 (1987). The definition of charitable has long been limited to those beneficial purposes that fit within one of the other categories of charitable, for example educational, relating to the relief of poverty, or providing some general good such as improvement of the environment. By using the standard definition, the act intends to include the case law that has developed around the term "charitable" in trust law. See the comment to Section 2(2) of the Model Protection of Charitable Assets Act.

Court. The term "court" means the court having jurisdiction in matters related to trusts. The definition should be revised by the enacting state as appropriate.

Current Beneficiary. The term "current beneficiary" means a beneficiary who is currently a distributee or permissible distributee of income or principal. A current beneficiary is a qualified beneficiary described in Section 2(20)(A). A mere holder of a power of appointment is not a current beneficiary unless the power is a presently exercisable general power of appointment. The term does not include the objects of an unexercised inter vivos power of appointment.

Decanting Power or The Decanting Power. The term "decanting power" or "the decanting power" means the power granted in this act to the authorized fiduciary (see Section 2(3)) to distribute all or part of the property of the first trust to a second trust or, alternatively, to modify the terms of the first trust to create the second trust. The term does not include any similar power that may be granted under the terms of the trust instrument or pursuant to common law.

If the terms of the first trust are modified, it is not necessary to treat the second trust as a newly created, separate trust, thus avoiding the need to transfer title of the property of the first trust to the second trust.

If all of the property of the first trust is distributed pursuant to an exercise of the decanting power to a separate second trust, then the first trust would terminate. The termination of the first trust may impose certain duties on the trustee such as providing reports to the beneficiaries and filing final income tax returns.

Expanded Distributive Discretion. "Expanded distributive discretion" is any discretion that is not limited to an ascertainable standard (see Section 2(2)) as used in Internal Revenue Code Section 2514(c)(1) or to a reasonably definite standard (see Section 2(21)) as used in Internal Revenue Code Section 674(b)(5)(A). The tax terms are used here, one from gift tax rules and one from income tax rules, because the definitions of these tax terms are generally clearer than the definitions of nontax terms sometimes used to describe different types of trustee discretion.

First Trust. The terms "first trust" and "second trust" (Section 2(23)) are relative to the particular exercise of the decanting power. Thus when the decanting power is exercised over Trust A to make a distribution to Trust B, Trust A is the first trust and Trust B is the second trust with respect to such exercise of the decanting power. If the decanting power is later exercised over Trust B to make a distribution to Trust C, then Trust B would be the first trust and Trust C the second trust with respect to such exercise of the decanting power.

First-Trust Instrument. See Section 2(12) for the definition of "first trust" and Section 2(29) for the definition of "trust instrument."

General Power of Appointment. The definition of "general power of appointment" is identical to the definition in Section 102(6) of the Uniform Powers of Appointment Act.

Jurisdiction. The definition of "jurisdiction" is virtually identical to the definition in Section 103(9) of the Uniform Trust Code.

Person. The definition of "person" is identical to the definition of "person" in Section 102(12) of the Uniform Powers of Appointment Act. With one exception, this is the standard definition approved by the Uniform Law Commission. The exception is that the word "trust" has been added to the definition of "person." Trust law in the United States is moving in the direction of viewing the trust as an entity, see Restatement Third of Trusts introductory note to Chapter 21, but does not yet do so. This definition differs slightly in wording, but not in substance, from the definition of "person" used in Section 103(10) of

the Uniform Trust Code. The Uniform Trust Code defines "person" as "an individual, corporation, business trust, estate, trust, partnership, limited liability company, association, joint venture, government; governmental subdivision, agency, or instrumentality; public corporation, or any other legal or commercial entity."

Power of Appointment. The definition of "power of appointment" is identical to the definition in Section 102(13) of the Uniform Powers of Appointment Act.

Powerholder. The definition of "powerholder" is identical to the definition in Section 102(14) of the Uniform Powers of Appointment Act.

Presently Exercisable Power of Appointment. The definition of "presently exercisable power of appointment" is substantially similar to the definition in Section 102(15) of the Uniform Powers of Appointment Act.

Qualified Beneficiary. The definition of "qualified beneficiary" is substantially the same as the definition in Section 103(13) of the Uniform Trust Code. Note, however, that the expanded definition of "beneficiary" in Section 2(4) includes charitable organizations identified to receive distributions in charitable trusts. Such charitable organizations would be entitled to notice of an exercise of the decanting power under Section 7.

The qualified beneficiaries consist of the current beneficiaries (see Section 2(9)) and the presumptive remainder beneficiaries (see Section 11(a)(2)).

The holder of a presently exercisable general power of appointment is a qualified beneficiary. A person who would have a presently exercisable general power of appointment if the trust terminated on that date or if the interests of the current beneficiaries terminated on that date without causing the trust to terminate is also a qualified beneficiary. The term does not include the holder of a testamentary general power of appointment or the holder of a nongeneral limited power of appointment. Nor does the term include the objects of an unexercised inter vivos power of appointment.

When a trust has distributees or permissible distributees of trust income or principal who are in more than one generation of the descendants of a person and the trust continues after the deaths of the members of the most senior generation who are included among such distributees, Section 2(20)(B) should be construed to include the distributees or permissible distributees after the interests of the most senior generation of such distributees terminate and subparagraph (C) would not ordinarily be applicable if there are any current beneficiaries who are not members of the most senior generation. Assume a trust permits discretionary distributions to any of A's descendants, and only terminates if A has no living descendants, in which case it is distributed to B, and A's now living descendants are Child 1, Child 2, Grandchild 1A and Grandchild 1B. The presumptive remainder beneficiaries are Grandchild 1A and Grandchild 1B pursuant to Section 2(20)(B), and Section 2(20)(C) should not apply to cause B to be a presumptive remainder beneficiary. On the other hand, if A's then living descendants were limited to Child 1 and Child 2, then B would be the presumptive remainder beneficiary under Section 2(20)(C), because there is no presumptive remainder beneficiary under Section 2(20)(B).

Reasonably Definite Standard. "Reasonably definite standard" is defined in Treasury Regulations Section 1.674(b)-1(b)(5). "Reasonably definite standard" includes an ascertainable standard but may also include standards that would not be considered ascertainable standards. A power to distribute principal for the education, support, maintenance, or health of the beneficiary; for the beneficiary's reasonable support and comfort; or to enable the beneficiary to maintain the beneficiary's accustomed standard of living; or to meet an emergency; would be a reasonably definite standard. A power to distribute principal for the pleasure, desire, or happiness of a beneficiary is not a reasonably definite standard. A power to make distributions "as the trustee deems advisable" or in the trustee's "sole and absolute discretion" without further limitation is not a reasonably definite standard. A reasonably definite standard need not require consideration of the needs and circumstances of the beneficiary.

The entire context of a provision of a trust instrument granting a power should be considered in determining whether there is a reasonably definite standard. For example, if a trust instrument provides that the determination of the trustee shall be conclusive with respect to the exercise or nonexercise of a power, the power is not limited by a reasonably definite standard. The fact, however, that the governing instrument is phrased in discretionary terms is not in itself an indication that no reasonably definite standard exists.

Internal Revenue Code Section 674(d) uses the term "reasonably definite external standard." The term "reasonably definite external standard" appears to have the same meaning as "reasonably definite standard." See Treas. Reg. § 1.674(d)-1.

The term is also construed by case law regarding Internal Revenue Code Sections 2036 and 2038.

Record. The definition of "record" is identical to the definition in Section 102(16) of the Uniform Powers of Appointment Act. This is a standard definition approved by the Uniform Law Commission.

Second Trust. The definition of "second trust" includes (1) an irrevocable trust already in existence, whether created by the settlor of the first trust or a different settlor, (2) a "restatement" of the first trust which could be executed by the authorized fiduciary or another person as the nominal grantor, (3) the first trust as modified to create the second trust, or (4) a new trust executed by the authorized fiduciary or another person as the nominal settlor for the purpose of decanting. A decanting that is implemented by "restating" or modifying the first trust presumably would not require the issuance of a new tax identification number or the retitling of property or a final income tax return for the trust. A decanting that distributes the property of the first trust to another trust presumably would require that the property be retitled. Further, if the first trust was terminated by reason of the decanting, a final income tax return for the first trust would be required.

Second-Trust Instrument. See Section 2(23) for the definition of "second trust" and Section 2(29) for the definition of "trust instrument."

Settlor. The definition of "settlor" generally follows the definition in Section 103(15) of the Uniform Trust Code, but is modified by Section 25 of this act to address the issue of who is the settlor of the second trust after the exercise of the decanting power. When more than one person signs the trust instrument or funds a trust, generally the person funding the trust will be the settlor. See comments to Section 103 of the Uniform Trust Code. Should more than one person contribute to a trust, all of the contributors will ordinarily be treated as settlors in proportion to their respective contributions, regardless of which one signed the trust instrument. *Id.* A "settlor" includes a testator who creates a testamentary trust.

Sign. The definition of "sign" is the same definition used in Section 2(8) of the Uniform Premarital and Marital Agreements Act.

State. The definition of "state" is virtually identical to the definition in Section 103(17) of the Uniform Trust Code except that it omits the sentence including certain Indian tribes or bands.

Terms of the Trust. The definition of "terms of the trust" is similar to the definition in Section 103(18) of the Uniform Trust Code, including the manifestation of the settlor's intent regarding a trust's provisions as expressed in the trust instrument as may be established by other evidence admissible in a judicial proceeding. The definition in Section 2(28) expands on the definition in the Uniform Trust Code by providing that the terms of the trust may also be established by court order or nonjudicial settlement agreement.

Trust Instrument. The definition of "trust instrument" is substantially similar to the definition in Section 103(19) of the Uniform Trust Code, except that it expressly includes any second trust and clarifies that the trust instrument may only contain some of the terms of the trust. The Uniform Trust Code definition is expanded to make clear that where the second trust is a trust created by the trustee for the purpose of decanting, such instrument is considered to be an "instrument" even though the trustee is not considered to be the settlor of the

second trust for all purposes. See Section 25. Other terms of the trust may be established by other evidence that would be admissible in a judicial proceeding, or by court order or nonjudicial settlement agreement. See Section 2(28). If the second trust is created for purposes of decanting, the second-trust instrument may be executed by the authorized fiduciary or another person as the nominal settlor.

2018 Amendment. Section 2(28) was amended in 2018 to conform to the clearer and more expansive definition of "terms of trust" used in the Uniform Directed Trust Act. The revised definition acknowledges the possibility that the terms of a trust may change over time at the direction of a court, by nonjudicial settlement agreement, or in accordance with applicable law, such as by a decanting under this Act, or by a third party, such as under the Uniform Directed Trust Act (2017).

§ 3. Scope.

(a) Except as otherwise provided in subsections (b) and (c), this [act] applies to an express trust that is irrevocable or revocable by the settlor only with the consent of the trustee or a person holding an adverse interest.

(b) This [act] does not apply to a trust held solely for charitable purposes.

(c) Subject to Section 15, a trust instrument may restrict or prohibit exercise of the decanting power.

(d) This [act] does not limit the power of a trustee, powerholder, or other person to distribute or appoint property in further trust or to modify a trust under the trust instrument, law of this state other than this [act], common law, a court order, or a nonjudicial settlement agreement.

(e) This [act] does not affect the ability of a settlor to provide in a trust instrument for the distribution of the trust property or appointment in further trust of the trust property or for modification of the trust instrument.

Comment

The Uniform Trust Decanting Act applies to all express trusts that are irrevocable or that are revocable by the settlor only with the consent of the trustee or a person holding an adverse interest. The act does not apply to a trust revocable by the settlor without the consent of the trustee or a person holding an adverse interest, even if the settlor is incapacitated and thus unable to exercise the power to amend or revoke. Thus the act does not apply to a revocable trust as that term is defined in Section 103(14) of the Uniform Trust Code.

Section 5-411(a)(4) of the Uniform Guardianship and Protective Proceedings Act allows a conservator to amend (and revoke) the terms of a protected person's revocable trust. Section 201(a)(1) of the

Uniform Power of Attorney Act allows a settlor to grant a power to amend or revoke to an agent. Accordingly, while the settlor is alive, there are uniform rules for modifying a revocable trust. States that have not adopted these uniform rules may have other provisions for modification of a revocable trust when the settlor is incapacitated.

The act does not permit decanting a trust held solely for charitable purposes (a "wholly charitable trust"). Section 3(b). A private foundation structured as a trust would be a wholly charitable trust that could not be decanted pursuant to the act.

A wholly charitable trust is subject to different public policy concerns than a private trust. Private trusts have identifiable beneficiaries who may enforce their interests in the trust. Charitable trusts have as beneficiaries the community as a whole or charitable organizations, and enforcement may be left to the state's Attorney General or another official. Further, charitable trusts often have particular charitable purposes, and conditions or restrictions on the use of the trust assets. Settlors of wholly charitable trusts often have particularly strong interests in seeing that these purposes, conditions and restrictions are not changed. Special legal doctrines, such as *cy pres*, are available when it becomes unlawful, impossible, or impracticable to carry out the purposes of a wholly charitable trust.

If an irrevocable trust that has noncharitable beneficiaries will in the future be used to fund a wholly charitable trust, the decanting power may be exercised over the irrevocable trust, subject to Section 14, but the decanting may not change the terms of the wholly charitable trust.

To the extent a conservation easement or other restricted gift is considered to be an express trust, such an interest would be a wholly charitable trust that could not be decanted pursuant to the act.

While a split interest trust such as a charitable remainder trust or charitable lead trust would not be a wholly charitable trust, in almost all cases the trustee of such a trust would not have discretion to distribute principal to a current beneficiary and therefore there would not be an authorized fiduciary (see Section 2(3)) who would have authority to exercise the decanting power under Section 11 or Section 12.

If an authorized fiduciary has discretion to distribute principal of a trust that is not a wholly charitable trust but that contains a charitable interest (see Section 2(5)), the charitable interest may not be diminished, the charitable purpose set forth in the first trust may not be changed and any conditions or restrictions on the charitable interest may not be changed. See subsection 14(c).

The Uniform Trust Decanting Act is not the exclusive way to decant a trust and is not the exclusive way to modify a trust. The terms of the trust instrument may grant a fiduciary or other person the power to modify the trust. This act does not supplant any authority granted under such a trust provision. Any such authority granted under the trust instrument does not affect the application of this act unless the trust instrument imposes an express restriction on the exercise of the decanting power under this act or other state statute authorizing a fiduciary to decant. See Section 15(b).

A decanting statute of another state may apply to a trust and, even if this act could also apply to the trust, this act does not supplant the right of a trustee to decant under the statute of such other state. Thus in some situations a fiduciary may have the option of decanting under this act or the decanting statute of another state.

Common law in some states may permit a trustee to decant. This act does not supplant any right to decant under common law. Thus in some cases a fiduciary may have the option of decanting under this act or under common law.

Section 111 of the Uniform Trust Code and statutes in many states permit certain matters regarding a trust to be resolved by a nonjudicial settlement agreement among the interested persons. Those statutes generally permit certain beneficiaries of a trust to approve an exercise of a power by a trustee and thus would permit certain beneficiaries to approve an exercise of the decanting power. In some cases the modification made by an exercise of the decanting power could also have been made by a virtual representation agreement, and in those cases an exercise of the decanting power sometimes might be combined with a nonjudicial settlement agreement. Generally, the nonjudicial settlement agreement would prevent any subsequent challenges to the decanting. The tax consequences of having the beneficiaries consent to the nonjudicial settlement agreement should be considered.

§ 4. Fiduciary Duty.

(a) In exercising the decanting power, an authorized fiduciary shall act in accordance with its fiduciary duties, including the duty to act in accordance with the purposes of the first trust.

(b) This [act] does not create or imply a duty to exercise the decanting power or to inform beneficiaries about the applicability of this [act].

(c) Except as otherwise provided in a first-trust instrument, for purposes of this [act] [and Sections 801 and 802(a) of the Uniform Trust Code], the terms of the first trust are deemed to include the decanting power.

Legislative Note: Section 801 of the Uniform Trust Code provides that the trustee shall administer a trust in accordance with its terms. Section 802(a) of the Uniform Trust Code provides that a trustee shall administer a trust solely in the interests of the beneficiaries. If a state has adopted the Uniform Trust Code, the bracketed language in subsection (c) should be included to make clear that the terms of the trust include the decanting power and that the "interests of the beneficiaries" takes into account the decanting power.

Comment

Except as noted below, in exercising the decanting power, the authorized fiduciary is subject to the same fiduciary duties as in exercising any other discretionary power. For example, Section 801 of the Uniform Trust Code provides that the trustee shall administer the trust in good faith, in accordance with its terms and purposes and the interests of the beneficiaries. Section 814(a) of the Uniform Trust Code provides that a trustee shall exercise a discretionary power in good faith and in accordance with the terms and purposes of the trust and the interests of the beneficiaries. Section 76 of the Restatement Third of Trusts provides that a trustee has a duty to administer the trust diligently and in good faith, in accordance with the terms of the trust and applicable law.

An exercise of the decanting power must be in accordance with the purposes of the first trust. The purpose of decanting is not to disregard the settlor's intent but to modify the trust to better effectuate the settlor's broader purposes or the settlor's probable intent if the settlor had anticipated the circumstances in place at the time of the decanting. The settlor's purposes generally include efficient administration of the trust. The settlor's purposes may also include achieving certain tax objectives or generally minimizing overall tax liabilities. The settlor's purposes often include avoiding fruitless, needless dissipation of the trust assets should a beneficiary develop dependencies such as substance abuse or gambling, have creditor problems, or otherwise be unfit to prudently manage assets that might be distributed from the trust.

The exercise of the decanting power need not be in accord with the literal terms of the first-trust instrument because decanting by definition is a modification of the terms of the first trust. Therefore subsection 4(c) provides that the terms of the first trust shall be deemed to include the decanting power for purposes of determining the fiduciary duties of the authorized fiduciary. Nonetheless, the other terms of the first trust may provide insight into the purposes of the first trust and the settlor's probable intent under current circumstances.

Section 802 of the Uniform Trust Code and Section 78 of the Restatement Third of Trusts impose a duty of loyalty on the trustee. Thus in exercising a decanting power the trustee cannot place the trustee's own interests over those of the beneficiaries. For example, an authorized fiduciary may breach its fiduciary duties if the authorized fiduciary decants to permit self-dealing. While Sections 16, 17 and 18 expressly prohibit making certain changes that benefit the authorized fiduciary and are not likely to be in the beneficiaries' interests, these sections do not include all of the changes that may be breaches of the authorized fiduciary's fiduciary duties.

Section 803 of the Uniform Trust Code and Section 79 of the Restatement Third of Trusts impose a duty to treat the beneficiaries impartially. The duty to act impartially does not mean that the trustee must treat the beneficiaries equally. Rather the trustee must treat the beneficiaries equitably in light of the purposes and terms of the trust.

Section 804 of the Uniform Trust Code imposes a duty to administer the trust as a prudent person would and to exercise reasonable care, skill and caution. *See also* Restatement Third of Trusts: Prudent Investor Rule § 90 (2007).

Decanting may be appropriate in many situations in which judicial modification would be appropriate such as (1) when modification, because of circumstances not anticipated by the settlor, would further the purposes of the trust (see Uniform Trust Code § 412(a) and Restatement Third of Trusts § 66); (2) when continuation of the trust on its existing terms would be impracticable or wasteful or impair the trust's administration (see Uniform Trust Code § 412(b)); (3) to replace the trustee if the value of the trust is insufficient to justify the costs of administration with the current trustee (see Uniform Trust Code § 414(b)); (4) to correct mistakes (see Uniform Trust Code § 415); (5) to achieve the settlor's tax objectives (see Uniform Trust Code § 416); and (6) to combine or divide trusts (see Uniform Trust Code § 417 and Restatement Third of Trusts § 68).

The Uniform Trust Decanting Act does not

impose a duty on the authorized fiduciary to decant. To impose a duty on the authorized fiduciary to consider whether any possible decanting could improve the administration of the trust or further the trust purposes would create unfair risks and burdens for fiduciaries and also might, in some situations, present impartiality issues. A trustee cannot possibly consider all the possible ways in which a trust could be improved by decanting. While this act does not create a presumption in favor of the terms of the first trust, an authorized fiduciary generally should not be penalized for not modifying the terms of the trust.

There may be, however, circumstances in which the authorized fiduciary or trustee has a duty under general trust law to seek a deviation from the terms of the trust even if the authorized fiduciary or trustee does not have a duty to exercise a decanting power. Subsection 66(2) of the Restatement Third of Trusts provides:

> (2) If a trustee knows or should know of circumstances that justify judicial action under Subsection (1) with respect to an administrative provision, and of the potential of those circumstances to cause substantial harm to the trust or its beneficiaries, the trustee has a duty to petition the court for appropriate modification of or deviation from the terms of the trust.

While subsection 66(2) is literally limited to deviations involving administrative provisions, Comment e to subsection 66(2) extends the trustee's duty to distribution provisions when the trustee is actually aware that a purpose of the settlor would be jeopardized by adhering to the existing provision regarding distributions.

The Reporter's Note to Comment e to subsection 66(2) of the Restatement Third of Trusts notes that the situations that might result in a duty to seek a deviation if the trustee has actual knowledge of the circumstances include extraordinary needs of the life beneficiary or irresponsibility of a potential distributee. See Illustration 2 in the Comments on subsection 66(1) of the Restatement Third of Trusts and the last paragraph of the Reporter's Note to Comment b to Section 66 of the Restatement Third of Trusts. In the Reporter's Notes to Comment b of Section 66 of the Restatement Third of Trusts, the Reporter notes that there may be a duty to seek deviation when there would be substantial distributions to beneficiaries who are legally competent to manage funds but practically at serious risk of squandering those distributions due, for example, to substance addiction or gambling. Although the Uniform Trust Decanting Act does not impose a duty to decant, an exercise of the decanting power would usually be an appropriate exercise of the authorized fiduciary's discretion in such circumstances. *See also* Restatement Third of Trusts § 87.

Where the trustee has a duty to seek a deviation and the appropriate deviation could be achieved by an exercise of the decanting power, the trustee could fulfill such duty by an exercise of the decanting power rather than seeking a judicial deviation.

§ 5. Application; Governing Law.

This [act] applies to a trust created before, on, or after [the effective date of this [act]] which:

(1) has its principal place of administration in this state, including a trust whose principal place of administration has been changed to this state; or

(2) provides by its trust instrument that it is governed by the law of this state or is governed by the law of this state for the purpose of:

(A) administration, including administration of a trust whose governing law for purposes of administration has been changed to the law of this state;

(B) construction of terms of the trust; or

(C) determining the meaning or effect of terms of the trust.

Comment

Because the authorized fiduciary by decanting is exercising a power over the first trust, the requirements in Section 5 apply to the first trust. It is irrelevant whether the second trust is governed by the law of the state or administered in the state.

The laws of different states may govern a trust for purposes of determining its validity, for purposes of construing the trust and for purposes of administration of the trust. The determination of the state law that governs for these purposes is also dependent upon whether the trust property consists of movables or land and whether the trust was created by a will or by an inter vivos instrument. See Restatement Second of Conflict of Laws §§ 267-279; Uniform Trust Code § 107; see also Uniform Probate Code § 2-703.

To provide greater certainty about whether the act applies to a trust, Section 5(2) provides that the act applies to a trust that by its terms provides that it is governed by the law of the enacting state, without further inquiry as to whether the law of the enacting state actually applies. The act also applies where the law of the enacting state in fact governs administration of the trust, construction of the terms of the trust, or determination of the meaning or effect of terms of the trust, whether or not the trust instrument expressly so states.

Decanting is considered an administrative power because it deals with the powers of the trustee. *See* Comment a to the Restatement Second Conflict of Laws § 271 (testamentary trusts) and Comment a to § 272 (inter vivos trusts). Decanting, however, can alter the beneficial interests of a trust. In order to avoid having different rules for the application of the act depending upon whether the exercise of the decanting power changes administrative provision or beneficial interests, and the difficulty of drawing a distinct line between modifications that are administrative in nature and modifications that

change beneficial interests, the act is intended to have broad application.

This act applies if the law of the state governs for purposes of any one or more of administration, meaning or effect. "Meaning and effect" are the terms used in the Uniform Trust Code (see Section 107). "Construction" is the term used in the Restatement Second of Conflicts.

This act also applies if the trust instrument states that the law of the state governs for purposes of any one or more of administration, meaning or effect without the necessity of establishing that the law of the state in fact governs for such purpose.

Alternatively, it is sufficient if the trust has its principal place of administration in the state. See Section 108 of the Uniform Trust Code with respect to the principal place of administration of a trust. While a change of principal place of administration will usually change the law governing the administration of the trust, that is not the result under all circumstances. To avoid the difficulties of determining whether the law governing administration has changed when the principal place of administration has changed, the act applies to any trust with a principal place of administration in the state, regardless of what state law governs its administration and meaning and effect.

§ 6. Reasonable Reliance.
A trustee or other person that reasonably relies on the validity of a distribution of part or all of the property of a trust to another trust, or a modification of a trust, under this [act], law of this state other than this [act], or the law of another jurisdiction is not liable to any person for any action or failure to act as a result of the reliance.

Comment

A trustee should be able to administer a trust with some dispatch and without concern that reliance on a prior decanting is misplaced. This section allows a trustee, other fiduciary or other person to reasonably rely on the validity of a prior decanting, whether that decanting was performed under the act or under other law of the state or another jurisdiction. Thus this section relieves a trustee or other fiduciary from any duty it might otherwise have to determine definitively the validity of a prior decanting.

The person's reliance on the validity of a prior decanting must be reasonable. Thus a fiduciary must still review the facts of the prior decanting, whether it appears to be in compliance with the statute or other law under which the decanting was performed, and whether the law under which the decanting was performed appears to be applicable to the trust. If the

second trust contains provisions that clearly are prohibited by the applicable decanting law, or fails to contain provisions that are clearly required by the applicable decanting law, reliance would not be reasonable.

When trusts have changed jurisdictions, it may be difficult to determine what law governs the administration of the trust. When trusts have multiple trustees, or a trustee conducts different trust functions in different places, it may be difficult to determine where the trust is administered. Thus it may be difficult in some cases to confirm with certainty which state decanting law applied to a prior attempted decanting. In some instances more than one state's decanting law may appear to apply, creating further uncertainty if the prior attempted decanting did not comply with all of the potentially applicable statutes. Section 6 protects a trustee or other person who makes a reasonable determination about which state decanting law applied to a prior decanting.

Ordinarily, a trustee or other person relying on a prior decanting need not independently verify compliance with every procedural rule of the decanting law. For example, ordinarily, the person relying on the prior decanting need not verify that every person required by the statute to receive notice in fact received notice. If such person knew, however, that the decanting law required notice and that no notice was given, reliance would not be reasonable.

This section does not validate any or all attempted decantings. Even if a trustee or other person may reasonably rely on a prior decanting, an interested person may still have the ability to challenge the decanting as invalid.

There may be times when the trustee or other person has sufficient questions about a prior attempted decanting that additional action is required to determine whether the prior attempted decanting was valid, in whole or in part, and to clarify the operating terms of the trust. In some cases the authorized fiduciary might use a new, properly implemented decanting to clarify the terms of the trust prospectively. In other cases a nonjudicial settlement agreement between the trustee and interested parties might be used to conform the effective terms of the trust. In some cases the trustee or other person might petition the court to determine the effective terms of the trust.

§ 7. Notice; Exercise of Decanting Power.

(a) In this section, a notice period begins on the day notice is given under subsection (c) and ends [59] days after the day notice is given.

(b) Except as otherwise provided in this [act], an authorized fiduciary may exercise the decanting power without the consent of any person and without court approval.

(c) Except as otherwise provided in subsection (f), an authorized fiduciary shall give notice in a record of the intended exercise of the decanting power not later than [60] days before the exercise to:

(1) each settlor of the first trust, if living or then in existence;

(2) each qualified beneficiary of the first trust;

(3) each holder of a presently exercisable power of appointment over any part or all of the first trust;

(4) each person that currently has the right to remove or replace the authorized fiduciary;

(5) each other fiduciary of the first trust;

(6) each fiduciary of the second trust; and

(7) [the Attorney General], if Section 14(b) applies.

(d) [An authorized fiduciary is not required to give notice under subsection (c) to a qualified beneficiary who is a minor and has no representative or] [An authorized fiduciary is not required to give notice under subsection (c)] to a person that is not known to the fiduciary or is known to the fiduciary but cannot be located by the fiduciary after reasonable diligence.

(e) A notice under subsection (c) must:

(1) specify the manner in which the authorized fiduciary intends to exercise the decanting power;

(2) specify the proposed effective date for exercise of the power;

(3) include a copy of the first-trust instrument; and

(4) include a copy of all second-trust instruments.

(f) The decanting power may be exercised before expiration of the notice period under subsection (a) if all persons entitled to receive notice waive the period in a signed record.

(g) The receipt of notice, waiver of the notice period, or expiration of the notice period does not affect the right of a person to file an application under Section 9 asserting that:

(1) an attempted exercise of the decanting power is ineffective because it did not comply with this [act] or was an abuse of discretion or breach of fiduciary duty; or

(2) Section 22 applies to the exercise of the decanting power.

(h) An exercise of the decanting power is not ineffective because of the failure to give notice to one or more persons under subsection (c) if the authorized fiduciary acted with reasonable care to comply with subsection (c).

Legislative Note: Subsection (a) might apply a different rule than the state's general rule governing computation of days.

In subsection (c)(7), "Attorney General" is placed in brackets to accommodate a jurisdiction that grants enforcement authority over charitable interests in trusts to another designated official. The bracketed text in subsection (d) should be included when state law does not in all cases provide a representative for a minor beneficiary, so that notice is not required to be given to the minor personally.

Comment

Generally a trustee is not required to provide notice to beneficiaries prior to exercising a discretionary power. This section is not intended to change the law in this regard except with respect to exercises of the decanting power. Because qualified beneficiaries are entitled to know the terms of the trust, they should receive notice of any change in the terms of the trust. Requiring prior notice seems reasonable, in light of the significant trust modifications that can be made by decanting, and practical, in that it helps determine if any settlor, fiduciary or beneficiary has an objection to or may challenge the decanting. Any person entitled to notice under subsection 7(c) may petition the court under Section 9 for a determination of whether the proposed or attempted exercise of the decanting power is an abuse of discretion or does not otherwise comply with the act.

If a qualified beneficiary is a minor, incapacitated, or unknown, or a beneficiary whose identity or location is not reasonably ascertainable, the representation principles of applicable state law may be employed. Under state law, an emancipated minor presumably may represent himself or herself.

Notice must be given to (a) each settlor of the first trust (see Section 2(25)); (b) all qualified beneficiaries (see Section 2(20)); (c) each holder of a presently exercisable power of appointment, whether or not such holder is a qualified beneficiary; (d) any person who may remove or replace the authorized fiduciary; (e) all other fiduciaries of the first trust; (f) all fiduciaries of the second trust or trusts; and (g) the Attorney General (or other official with enforcement authority over charitable interests) if there is a determinable charitable interest (see Section 14(a)(1)). If the authorized fiduciary is comprised of more than one fiduciary, notice should be given to any person

who may remove or replace any of such fiduciaries. The term "replace" refers to the power to both remove and designate a successor for the authorized fiduciary, and does not refer to the power merely to designate a successor when a vacancy occurs.

Other notice provisions under state law may also apply to a decanting. Under Section 813(a) of the Uniform Trust Code, a trustee shall keep the qualified beneficiaries of the trust reasonably informed about the administration of the trust and of the material facts necessary for them to protect their interests. An exercise of the decanting power is a material fact. If the second trust is newly created for purposes of decanting, state law may require notice of the creation of the trust to certain beneficiaries. For example, Section 813 of the Uniform Trust Code requires a trustee, within 60 days after accepting a trusteeship, to notify the qualified beneficiaries of the acceptance and of the trustee's name, address, and telephone number. In addition, if the exercise of the decanting power results in a distribution of property, the distribution would be considered a disbursement that should be reported on the accounting of the first trust. If the exercise of the decanting power results in the termination of the first trust, state law or the trust instrument may require a final accounting.

Subsection (c)(7) entitles the Attorney General to notice of an exercise of the decanting power with respect to a trust containing a determinable charitable interest. See Section 14(a)(1).

Subsection (d) provides that notice need not be given to a person who is not known to the fiduciary or who is known to the fiduciary but cannot be located by the fiduciary after reasonable diligence. An analogous term, "reasonable care," is used in Section 1007 of the Uniform Trust Code. Section 1007 provides that a trustee who has exercised reasonable care to ascertain the happening of an event that affects the administration of a trust is not liable for a loss resulting from the trustee's lack of knowledge.

Although the act does not limit the amount of time that may pass between the giving of notice and the exercise of the decanting power, if the exercise of the power does not occur within a reasonable period of time from the proposed effective date set forth in the notice, a new notice should be given with a new notice period. Further, the authorized fiduciary's duties to keep beneficiaries and interested persons informed about the trust may require the authorized fiduciary to inform such persons if the decanting is not completed as proposed or when the decanting has been completed.

If after notice is given and before the decanting power is exercised, relevant facts change in a manner that entitles an additional person to receive notice, unless such additional person can be represented by another person who has already received notice, notice should be provided to such additional person. A new notice period should begin to run, unless such additional person waives the notice period.

Subsection (e) describes the items that must be included in the notice. Subparagraph (1) requires that the notice specify the manner in which the authorized fiduciary intends to exercise the decanting power. Depending upon the circumstances, the authorized fiduciary might describe the modifications being made, provide a comparison of the first trust and the second trust or, where the second trust is extensively different than the first trust, refer the notice recipient to the trust instruments. As a best practice, it is desirable to tell each notice recipient in which capacity he or she is receiving the notice. For example, a notice might state: "You are receiving this notice because you are the settlor of Trust XYZ" or "You are receiving this notice because you are a qualified beneficiary of Trust XYZ." In the case of notice to an Attorney General, it is a best practice to indicate where in the instruments the determinable charitable interest may be found and whether the second trust will be administered under the law of a different state (see Section 14(e)).

Although under Section 7(h) an exercise of the decanting power will not be ineffective because of the failure to provide the required notice to one or more persons, provided that the authorized fiduciary acted with reasonable care, the act does not override the court's ability to address breaches of fiduciary duty and to fashion appropriate remedies.

[§ 8. Representation.

(a) Notice to a person with authority to represent and bind another person under a first-trust instrument or [this state's trust code] has the same effect as notice given directly to the person represented.

(b) Consent of or waiver by a person with authority to represent and bind another person under a first-trust instrument or [this state's trust code] is binding on the person represented unless the person represented objects to the representation before the consent or waiver otherwise would become effective.

(c) A person with authority to represent and bind another person under a first-trust instrument or [this state's trust code] may file an application under Section 9 on behalf of the person represented.

(d) A settlor may not represent or bind a beneficiary under this [act].]

Legislative Note: State law generally specifies when a beneficiary who is a minor or otherwise incapacitated may be represented by another party. State law also may specify when an incapacitated settlor may be represented by another party. These provisions with respect to trusts may be contained in the state's trust code. For example, Article 3 of the Uniform Trust Code provides rules for representation. If state law does not already provide for representation of an incapacitated beneficiary or settlor, representation provisions should be included in the act.

If this act is inserted into the state's Uniform Trust Code, Section 8 may be omitted.

Comment

Subsection (a) provides that the first-trust instrument or general rules in the state's trust code or other law determine who may receive notice of an exercise of the decanting power on behalf of a minor beneficiary or an incapacitated beneficiary, settlor, holder of a presently exercisable power of appointment or person with the right to remove or replace the authorized fiduciary. It is similar to Section 301(a) of the Uniform Trust Code except that it expressly recognizes that if the first-trust instrument authorizes certain persons to receive notice on behalf of incapacitated beneficiaries or other persons, such rules should also apply for purposes of notice under Section 7.

Subsection (b) provides that the first-trust instrument or general rules in the state's trust code or other law determine who may waive the notice period under Section 7 or consent to certain modifications under Section 16 and Section 18. It is similar to Section 301(b) of the Uniform Trust Code except that it expressly recognizes that if the first-trust instrument authorizes certain persons to consent on behalf of minor or incapacitated persons, such rules

should also apply for purposes of waiving the notice period under Section 7 or consenting to modifications under Section 16 or Section 18.

Subsection (c) makes clear that a person who represents another may file a court petition under Section 9 on behalf of the person represented. This includes the Attorney General or other official with enforcement authority over charitable interests. See Section 2(5) for the definition of "charitable interest."

Subsection (d) prohibits a settlor from representing a beneficiary. Subsection (d) is similar to optional subsection (d) of Section 301 of the Uniform Trust Code, which was added to the Uniform Trust Code because of a concern that allowing a settlor to represent a beneficiary could cause the trust to be included in the settlor's estate.

§ 9. Court Involvement.

(a) On application of an authorized fiduciary, a person entitled to notice under Section 7(c), a beneficiary, or with respect to a charitable interest the [Attorney General] or other person that has standing to enforce the charitable interest, the court may:

(1) provide instructions to the authorized fiduciary regarding whether a proposed exercise of the decanting power is permitted under this [act] and consistent with the fiduciary duties of the authorized fiduciary;

(2) appoint a special fiduciary and authorize the special fiduciary to determine whether the decanting power should be exercised under this [act] and to exercise the decanting power;

(3) approve an exercise of the decanting power;

(4) determine that a proposed or attempted exercise of the decanting power is ineffective because:

(A) after applying Section 22, the proposed or attempted exercise does not or did not comply with this [act]; or

(B) the proposed or attempted exercise would be or was an abuse of the fiduciary's discretion or a breach of fiduciary duty;

(5) determine the extent to which Section 22 applies to a prior exercise of the decanting power;

(6) provide instructions to the trustee regarding the application of Section 22 to a prior exercise of the decanting power; or

(7) order other relief to carry out the purposes of this [act].

(b) On application of an authorized fiduciary, the court may approve:

(1) an increase in the fiduciary's compensation under Section 16; or

(2) a modification under Section 18 of a provision granting a person the right to remove or replace the fiduciary.

Legislative Note: In a state with a limited-jurisdiction court, it may be necessary to grant the power to the court to order remedial action for an ineffective attempted decanting.

In subsection (a), "Attorney General" is placed in brackets to accommodate a jurisdiction that grants enforcement authority over charitable trusts to another designated official.

Comment

Decanting by definition is an exercise of fiduciary   discretion and is not an alternative basis for a court modification of the trust.

The decanting power, however, is a very broad discretionary power. Therefore, Section 9 provides that the authorized fiduciary, any person who would be entitled to notice of the exercise of the decanting power, any beneficiary or the Attorney General or other official who has enforcement authority over a charitable interest in the first trust, may petition the court for certain purposes with respect to a prior decanting or a proposed decanting. The persons who receive notice under Section 7 and who could petition the court include the settlor, the holder of a presently exercisable power of appointment over the first trust, each person who has a right to remove or replace the authorized fiduciary and each fiduciary of the first and second trusts.

A successor beneficiary, even though such beneficiary is not entitled to notice under Section 7, could petition the court under Section 9. Even though the Attorney General is entitled to notice under Section 7 only if there is a *determinable* charitable interest, the Attorney General may petition the court under Section 9 with respect to any charitable interest.

Any such person may request instructions with respect to whether a proposed decanting complies with the act and is consistent with the fiduciary duties of the authorized fiduciary. Section 9(a)(1). The authorized fiduciary need not have provided notice of a proposed decanting or even be the person proposing the decanting in order for the court to provide instructions. Such an instruction, however, would not create in the authorized fiduciary a duty to decant.

While generally the authorized fiduciary should decide whether or not to exercise the decanting power, and may seek instructions from the court when in doubt as to whether the proposed exercise is permitted and consistent with the authorized fiduciary's fiduciary duties, there may be times when the exercise of the decanting power is appropriate but the authorized fiduciary cannot or should not be the person to exercise the power. Under such circumstances the court may appoint a special fiduciary to determine if the decanting power should be exercised and, if so, to exercise the power. Section 9(a)(2). The terms of the appointment may limit the special fiduciary's power to determine whether a proposed exercise is appropriate or may grant the special fiduciary broader power to determine the scope of a decanting. The term of appointment may also limit the period of time during which the special

fiduciary may act. For example, assume a trust permits discretionary principal distributions to the settlor's descendants subject to an ascertainable standard if a beneficiary is acting as trustee and subject to expanded discretion if a disinterested person is acting as trustee. If a beneficiary is acting as trustee and believes that an exercise of the decanting power under Section 11 may be appropriate, the trustee could request that the court appoint a disinterested person as special fiduciary to determine whether the decanting power should be exercised and, if so, to exercise the power. As another example, if the authorized fiduciary is a beneficiary of the first trust and it is appropriate to create a special-needs trust for another beneficiary, but the decanting might incidentally increase the authorized fiduciary's interest in the trust, it may be advisable for the authorized fiduciary to request under subsection (a)(2) the appointment of a special fiduciary to decide whether to exercise the decanting power.

The special fiduciary essentially temporarily steps into the office of the trustee or other fiduciary who has the power to make trust distributions (the "distribution fiduciary"). If the special fiduciary, if acting as the distribution fiduciary, would have expanded distributive discretion, the court may authorize the special fiduciary to exercise the decanting power under Section 11. If the special fiduciary, if acting as the distribution fiduciary, would have limited distributive discretion, the court may authorize the special fiduciary to exercise the decanting power under Section 12. If the distribution fiduciary has no discretion to distribute principal, then the special fiduciary could not exercise the decanting power under Section 11 or 12, but could exercise the decanting power under Section 13.

For example, assume A is acting as trustee of a trust that is required to distribute income to A and upon A's death distributes to A's descendants. A special fiduciary cannot exercise the decanting power under Section 11 or Section 12 because the special fiduciary, if acting as trustee, has no distributive discretion over principal.

Now assume that the trust also provides that if a person who is not a beneficiary is acting as trustee, such trustee may make discretionary distributions of principal to A for A's health care. A special fiduciary who is not a beneficiary could be appointed and granted the authority to exercise the decanting power under Section 12.

Alternatively, assume that the trust provides that if a person who is not a beneficiary is acting as trustee, such trustee may make discretionary distributions of principal to A for A's best interests. A special fiduciary who is not a beneficiary could be appointed and granted the authority to exercise the decanting power under Section 11.

Any person described in Section 9(a) may request that the court approve an exercise of the decanting power. Such approval should be granted if the decanting complies with this act and is not an abuse of the trustee's discretion.

A petition to the court may also request that the court determine whether an attempted decanting is ineffective because it did not comply with the act. The court may also determine whether the remedial provisions of Section 22 apply to an attempted decanting and how such remedial provisions modify the second-trust instrument. If a trust has been administered after an attempted decanting under the assumed terms of the second-trust instrument, but after applying Section 22 should have been administered on different terms, the court may also instruct the fiduciary on the corrective action that should be taken.

For example, if an attempted decanting eliminated a noncontingent right to mandatory income distributions, and several years after the attempted decanting the income beneficiary of the first trust petitioned the court to apply Section 22 to the attempted decanting, the court might declare that the second trust must grant the income beneficiary such beneficiary's mandatory income interest and might order a makeup distribution to the income beneficiary for the period the income was not paid.

In addition, certain changes in a decanting require either approval by certain persons or court approval. Under Section 16, certain increases in the compensation of the authorized fiduciary require either the consent of all qualified beneficiaries or court approval. Under Section 18, modification of a power to remove or replace an authorized fiduciary requires the consent of the person holding such power (and, in some cases, consent of the qualified beneficiaries) or court approval.

The court may, but need not, take any of the actions described in Section 9.

§ 10. Formalities. An exercise of the decanting power must be made in a record signed by an authorized fiduciary. The signed record must, directly or by reference to the notice required by Section 7, identify the first trust and the second trust or trusts and state the property of the first trust being distributed to each second trust and the property, if any, that remains in the first trust.

Comment

Once the authorized fiduciary has provided the requisite notice of a proposed decanting under Section 7 and the notice period has either passed or been waived as provided in Section 7(f), then on or about the proposed effective date for the exercise of the decanting power the authorized fiduciary may effectuate the decanting by a signed record. The notice (a) includes copies of the first-trust instrument and the second-trust instrument, (b) specifies the manner in which the decanting power would be exercised, including which property of the first trust is being distributed to each of the second trusts and which property, if any, remains in the first trust, and (c) specifies the proposed effective date for the decanting. In the case of an exercise of the decanting power that is structured as a modification of the first trust, the signed record required by Section 10 may be the same instrument setting forth the terms of the modified trust. Where the decanting is structured as a distribution to a separate second trust, generally the signed record required by Section 10 will be a separate instrument from the second-trust instrument.

The decanting power can be exercised by either an actual distribution of property to one or more second trusts or by modifying the terms of the first trust to create the second trust with or without an actual distribution of property. If the decanting power is exercised by modifying the terms of the first trust, the trustee could either treat the second trust created by such modification as a new trust, in which case the property of the first trust would need to be transferred to the second trust, or alternatively treat the second trust as a continuation of the first trust, in which case the property of the first trust would not need to be retitled.

Other actions may be required to formally complete the transfer of property from the first trust to the second trust, such as retitling accounts, executing deeds, and signing assignments.

§ 11. Decanting Power under Expanded Distributive Discretion.

(a) In this section:

(1) "Noncontingent right" means a right that is not subject to the exercise of discretion or the occurrence of a specified event that is not certain to occur. The term does not include a right held by a beneficiary if any person has discretion to distribute property subject to the right to any person other than the beneficiary or the beneficiary's estate.

(2) "Presumptive remainder beneficiary" means a qualified beneficiary other than a current beneficiary.

(3) "Successor beneficiary" means a beneficiary that is not a qualified beneficiary on the date the beneficiary's qualification is determined. The term does not include a person that is a beneficiary only because the person holds a nongeneral power of appointment.

(4) "Vested interest" means:

(A) a right to a mandatory distribution that is a noncontingent right as of the date of the exercise of the decanting power;

(B) a current and noncontingent right, annually or more frequently, to a mandatory distribution of income, a specified dollar amount, or a percentage of value of some or all of the trust property;

(C) a current and noncontingent right, annually or more frequently, to withdraw income, a specified dollar amount, or a percentage of value of some or all of the trust property;

(D) a presently exercisable general power of appointment; or

(E) a right to receive an ascertainable part of the trust property on the trust's termination which is not subject to the exercise of discretion or to the occurrence of a specified event that is not certain to occur.

(b) Subject to subsection (c) and Section 14, an authorized fiduciary that has expanded distributive discretion over the principal of a first trust for the benefit of one or more current beneficiaries may exercise the decanting power over the principal of the first trust.

(c) Subject to Section 13, in an exercise of the decanting power under this section, a second trust may not:

(1) include as a current beneficiary a person that is not a current beneficiary of the first trust, except as otherwise provided in subsection (d);

(2) include as a presumptive remainder beneficiary or successor beneficiary a person that is not a current beneficiary, presumptive remainder beneficiary, or successor beneficiary of the first trust, except as otherwise provided in subsection (d); or

(3) reduce or eliminate a vested interest.

(d) Subject to subsection (c)(3) and Section 14, in an exercise of the decanting power under this section, a second trust may be a trust created or administered under the law of any jurisdiction and may:

(1) retain a power of appointment granted in the first trust;

(2) omit a power of appointment granted in the first trust, other than a presently exercisable general power of appointment;

(3) create or modify a power of appointment if the powerholder is a current beneficiary of the first trust and the authorized fiduciary has expanded distributive discretion to distribute principal to the beneficiary; and

(4) create or modify a power of appointment if the powerholder is a presumptive remainder beneficiary or successor beneficiary of the first trust, but the exercise of the power may take effect only after the powerholder becomes, or would have become if then living, a current beneficiary.

(e) A power of appointment described in subsection (d)(1) through (4) may be general or

571

nongeneral. The class of permissible appointees in favor of which the power may be exercised may be broader than or different from the beneficiaries of the first trust.

(f) If an authorized fiduciary has expanded distributive discretion over part but not all of the principal of a first trust, the fiduciary may exercise the decanting power under this section over that part of the principal over which the authorized fiduciary has expanded distributive discretion.

Comment

Noncontingent Right. The term "noncontingent right" describes interests that are certain to occur. A right is not noncontingent if it is subject to the occurrence of a specified event that is not certain to occur. For example, if A's children who survive A are to receive trust assets upon A's death, the rights of A's children are not noncontingent, because each must survive A to take and they may not survive A. The rights of A's children are not noncontingent regardless of whether the requirement of survival is expressed as a condition precedent or a condition subsequent. Thus the result is the same if the gift upon A's death is to A's children in equal shares, but if any child predeceases A such child's share shall be distributed to such child's descendants in shares per stirpes.

A right also is not a noncontingent right if it is subject to the exercise of discretion. Thus if a trustee has discretion to make distributions to A and A's descendants for their support and health care, the interests of A and A's descendants are not noncontingent. The result is the same even if the trust directs the trustee to make distributions to A and A's descendants for their support and health care because the timing and amount of the distributions are subject to the trustee's discretion.

A right also is not noncontingent if a person has discretion to distribute the property subject to the interest to any person other than the beneficiary or the beneficiary's estate. Thus if a trust provides that all income shall be distributed annually to A, but gives the trustee discretion to distribute principal to B for B's support and medical care, A's right is not noncontingent.

A current mandatory right to receive income, an annuity or a unitrust payment where the trustee has no discretion to make distributions to others is a noncontingent right.

Presumptive Remainder Beneficiary. "Presumptive remainder beneficiary" means a qualified beneficiary (see Section 2(20)) other than a current beneficiary (see Section 2(9)). The presumptive remainder beneficiaries might be termed the first-line remainder beneficiaries. These are the beneficiaries who would become eligible to receive distributions were the event triggering the termination of a current beneficiary's interest or of the trust itself to occur on the date in question. Such a terminating event will often be the death or deaths of the current beneficiaries. A person who would have a presently exercisable general power of appointment if the trust terminated on that date or if the interests of the current beneficiaries terminated on that date without causing the trust to terminate is a presumptive remainder beneficiary.

Presumptive remainder beneficiaries can include takers in default of the exercise of a power of appointment. The term may sometimes include the persons entitled to receive the trust property pursuant to the irrevocable exercise of an inter vivos power of appointment. Because the exercise of a testamentary power of appointment is not effective until the testator's death, the qualified beneficiaries do not include appointees under the will of a living person. Nor would the term include the objects of an unexercised inter vivos power.

Successor Beneficiary. The term "successor beneficiary" means a beneficiary who has a future beneficial interest in a trust, vested or contingent, including a person who may become a beneficiary in the future by reason of inclusion in a class, other than a beneficiary who is a qualified beneficiary. Thus it includes beneficiaries who might be termed "second line" or more remote remainder beneficiaries. It also includes unborn or unascertained beneficiaries who are beneficiaries by reason of being members of a class. It does not include, however, a person who is merely a holder of a power of appointment but not otherwise a beneficiary.

Vested Interest. "Vested interest" includes a right to a mandatory distribution that is a noncontingent right as of the date of the exercise of the decanting power. Section 11(a)(4)(A). For example, if the trustee is required to distribute the trust principal to A when A attains age 30 if A is then living, and A has attained age 30 but the trustee has not yet made the distribution, A's right to receive the trust principal is a right to a mandatory distribution that is a noncontingent right. If A is age 29, however, A's right is not a noncontingent right because A must survive to age 30.

The right to a mandatory distribution does not include a right to a distribution pursuant to a standard or a right to a distribution in the discretion of a fiduciary. Thus a right to receive distributions for "support and health care," or for "best interests" would not be a mandatory distribution right for purposes of Section 11.

"Vested interest" also includes a current and noncontingent right, annually or more frequently, to a mandatory distribution of income, a specified dollar amount or a percentage of value of some or all of the trust properties. Section 11(a)(4)(B). Thus if A is currently entitled to all trust income payable annually, and the trustee has no discretion to not pay the income to A and no discretion to distribute principal to anyone other than A, A's right to income is a vested interest. A's right to income is a vested interest even if the trustee has discretion to distribute principal to A. The result is the same if instead of an income right, A has the right to receive a specified dollar amount or a percentage of value of trust assets. A's right is a vested interest even if the right will cease upon some future event, such as A's death or a particular date, so long as the future event is not an exercise of fiduciary discretion. A specified dollar amount includes a dollar amount that is dependent upon factors other than fiduciary discretion or specific events not certain to occur, such as the inflation rate. A "vested interest" includes a current right to a unitrust distribution based on the value of certain or all trust assets.

A fiduciary's power to make equitable adjustments to income or principal, whether granted under the trust instrument or state law, does not make an income interest not mandatory or not noncontingent. A fiduciary's power to exclude certain assets in determining a unitrust distribution to attain an equitable result, whether granted under the trust instrument or state law, does not make a unitrust interest not mandatory or not noncontingent. For example, a beneficiary's current right to receive an annual distribution equal to 4% of the value of the trust principal is a vested interest even if the fiduciary has a right to exclude from the value of trust principal non-income producing assets.

Even if all conditions to such right have been met, the decanting may eliminate current mandatory rights to income, annuity or unitrust distributions that have come into effect with respect to a beneficiary if the authorized fiduciary has discretion to make principal distributions to another beneficiary. For example, if the first trust provides for mandatory income distributions to A, but permits the authorized fiduciary to make discretionary principal distributions to A, B or C for their best interests, the decanting may eliminate A's mandatory income interest. In such case the first trust indirectly gave the authorized fiduciary the ability to reduce or eliminate A's income interest by making discretionary principal distributions to B or C.

A right to receive mandatory payments less frequently than annually is not a vested interest. For example, a right to receive 5% of the trust value every fifth year is not a vested interest, except with respect to any amounts currently payable. As another example, a right to receive distributions of one-third of the trust principal at ages 30, 35 and 40 is not a vested interest if the beneficiary has not attained age 30. If the beneficiary is age 30 but the trustee has not yet distributed the one-third payable at age 30, the beneficiary's right to that one-third is a vested interest, but the beneficiary's right to receive distributions at ages 35 and 40 is not a vested interest.

"Vested interest" also includes a current and noncontingent right, annually or more frequently, to withdraw income, a specified dollar amount, or a percentage of value of some or all of the trust property. Section 11(a)(4)(C). Thus, for example, it makes no difference whether the trustee is required to distribute income annually or whether the beneficiary may withdraw income annually. As another example, if B has a current right to withdraw annually the greater of $5,000 or 5% of the trust value each year, B's right is a vested interest. If B's right to withdraw did not begin until B attained age 25 and B has not attained age 25, B's right would not be a vested interest.

"Vested interest" also includes a presently exercisable general power of appointment. A power of appointment is presently exercisable if it is exercisable at the time in question. Typically, a presently exercisable power of appointment is exercisable at the time in question during the powerholder's life and also at the powerholder's death, e.g., by the powerholder's will. Thus, a power of appointment that is exercisable "by deed or will" is a presently exercisable power.

A power to withdraw from a trust is a power of appointment. See Restatement Third of Trusts § 56 comment b. Thus if a beneficiary has already attained an age at which the beneficiary can withdraw all or a portion of the trust, the second trust may not modify or eliminate that right of withdrawal. If a Crummey withdrawal power is still in effect with respect to a prior contribution to the trust, the second trust cannot modify or eliminate the Crummey withdrawal right.

For example, if the trustee may make discretionary distributions to C and C's descendants, C has a right to withdraw one-half of trust principal after attaining age 28, and C has attained age 28, C's right is a vested interest under Section 11(a)(4)(D) even if the trustee has power to distribute trust principal to anyone other than C.

"Vested interest" also includes a right to receive an ascertainable part of the trust property on the trust's termination which is not subject to the exercise of discretion or to the occurrence of a specified event that is not certain to occur. Thus if the trustee is to distribute income to F, and upon F's death is to distribute the principal to G or G's estate, G's interest is a vested interest. G would not have a vested interest if the trustee had discretion to distribute principal to F or if G was required to survive F to take the remainder interest. Thus the right of a person to receive the trust property upon the termination of such trust if such person is then living would not be a vested interest. Any interest with a condition is not a vested interest, regardless of whether the condition is a condition precedent or condition subsequent. For example, A does not have a vested interest if upon termination the trust property passes to A or A's estate, provided that A is then married or was married at the time of A's prior death.

Expanded Distributive Discretion Decanting. Under Section 11 an authorized fiduciary who has expanded distributive discretion to distribute all or part of the principal of a trust to one or more of the current beneficiaries may exercise the decanting power over the principal subject to such expanded distributive discretion.

"Expanded distributive discretion" is defined in Section 2(11). When a trustee is granted expanded distributive discretion, that is an indication that the settlor intended to rely on the trustee's judgment and discretion in making distributions. The settlor's faith in the trustee's judgment supports the assumption that the settlor would trust the trustee's judgment in making modifications to the trust instrument in light of changed circumstances including the beneficiary's circumstances and changes in tax and other laws.

The decanting power, like most discretionary distribution powers, can be exercised over all or part of the first trust. If it is exercised over only part of the

first trust, the second trust would need to be a separate trust and could not be a continuation of the first trust. If the decanting power is exercised to more than one second trusts, then the second trusts (or at least all but one of the second trusts) would need to be separate trusts and could not be a continuation of the first trust.

If the authorized fiduciary has expanded discretion over only part of the first trust, the authorized fiduciary may exercise the decanting power under this section only over such part. See Section 11(f). With respect to the remainder of the trust, the authorized fiduciary may have the ability to decant under Section 12 or Section 13.

The second trust may contain any terms permissible for a trust subject only to the restrictions found in the act. Thus subject to subsections (c) and (f) of Section 11 and the other restrictions in Sections 14 through 20 and subject to the fiduciary duty in Section 4(a), the second trust may (1) eliminate (but not add) one or more current beneficiaries; (2) make a current beneficiary a presumptive remainder beneficiary or a successor beneficiary; (3) eliminate (but not add) one or more presumptive remainder and successor beneficiaries; (4) make a presumptive remainder beneficiary a successor beneficiary, or vice versa; (5) alter or eliminate rights that are not vested interests; (6) change the standard for distributions; (7) add or eliminate a spendthrift provision; (8) extend the duration of a trust (subject to Section 20); (9) change the jurisdiction of the trust and the law governing the administration of the trust (subject to Section 14(e)); (10) eliminate, modify or add powers of appointment; (11) change the trustee or trustee succession provisions; (12) change the powers of the trustee; (13) change administrative provisions of the trust; (14) add investment advisors, trust protectors or other fiduciaries; (15) divide a trust into more than one trust; and (16) consolidate trusts. The foregoing list merely provides examples and is not exhaustive.

The second trust, however, cannot make a remainder beneficiary a current beneficiary. This prohibition on accelerating a remainder interest is included to avoid any argument under Internal Revenue Code Section 674 that the mere existence of a power to make a remainder beneficiary a current beneficiary causes the trust to be a grantor trust, whether or not the decanting power is ever exercised in such manner.

Section 11(c)(3) prohibits the second trust from reducing or eliminating a vested interest. A vested interest is not reduced, however, just because other changes made as a result of a decanting may have incidental effects on the interest. For example, a modification of the fiduciary's investment powers or the manner of determining the fiduciary's compensation may have incidental effects on a beneficiary's interest, but such modifications do not reduce a vested interest.

The restrictions in Section 11(c)(3) do not apply to a decanting under Section 13. Section 13(c)(2).

Subsections (d) and (e) permit the second trust to retain or omit a power of appointment included in the first trust, or to create powers of appointment in one or more current beneficiaries of the first trust. For example, if the first trust permits the authorized fiduciary to make discretionary distributions of income or principal to the settlor's child A, and upon A's death the remainder is allocated for the settlor's descendants per stirpes, to be held in further trust for each such descendant, the second trust could grant A a lifetime and/or testamentary power, general or nongeneral. The second trust could grant A a lifetime power to appoint to A's descendants, spouse and charitable organizations and a testamentary power to appoint to A's estate or to the creditors of A's estate. The second trust also could provide that each descendant of the settlor for whom a trust is established at A's death will have an inter vivos or a testamentary, general or limited, power of appointment. The second trust could even give A's now living children, D and E, powers of appointment that they may exercise in their Wills, but that will only take effect upon A's death or, if later, their deaths.

Subsection (e) makes clear that persons who are not otherwise beneficiaries of the first trust may be permissible appointees of a power of appointment granted to a current beneficiary.

Sometimes state law may provide more than one method for making the same modification to a trust. For example, a combination of trusts or a division of a trust that would be permitted under Section 417 of the Uniform Trust Code may also be accomplished under this act through decanting. When a desired modification could be accomplished by decanting or by another method, the trustee may select either method.

§ 12. Decanting Power under Limited Distributive Discretion.

(a) In this section, "limited distributive discretion" means a discretionary power of distribution that is limited to an ascertainable standard or a reasonably definite standard.

(b) An authorized fiduciary that has limited distributive discretion over the principal of the first trust for benefit of one or more current beneficiaries may exercise the decanting power over the principal of the first trust.

(c) Under this section and subject to Section 14, a second trust may be created or administered under the law of any jurisdiction. Under this section, the second trusts, in the aggregate, must grant each beneficiary of the first trust beneficial interests which are substantially similar to the beneficial interests of the beneficiary in the first trust.

(d) A power to make a distribution under a second trust for the benefit of a beneficiary who is an individual is substantially similar to a power under the first trust to make a distribution directly to the beneficiary. A distribution is for the benefit of a beneficiary if:

(1) the distribution is applied for the benefit of the beneficiary;

(2) the beneficiary is under a legal disability or the trustee reasonably believes the beneficiary is incapacitated, and the distribution is made as permitted under [this state's trust code]; or

(3) the distribution is made as permitted under the terms of the first-trust instrument and the second-trust instrument for the benefit of the beneficiary.

(e) If an authorized fiduciary has limited distributive discretion over part but not all of the principal of a first trust, the fiduciary may exercise the decanting power under this section over that part of the principal over which the authorized fiduciary has limited distributive discretion.

Comment

Limited Distributive Discretion. "Limited distributive discretion" means a discretionary power of distribution that is limited to an ascertainable standard or a reasonably definite standard. Section

12(a). "Ascertainable standard" is defined in Section 2(2). "Reasonably definite standard" is defined in Section 2(21). "Limited distributive discretion" and "expanded distributive discretion" (see Section 2(11)) are mutually exclusive terms. An authorized fiduciary who has expanded distributive discretion over principal may decant under Section 11. An authorized fiduciary who has limited distributive discretion over principal may decant under Section 12. An authorized fiduciary who has no distributive discretion over principal, even if the authorized fiduciary has distributive discretion over income, may not decant under the act except as provided in Section 13.

Substantially Similar Beneficial Interests. When the authorized fiduciary has limited distributive discretion over principal, the authorized fiduciary may exercise the decanting power to effect modifications in administrative provisions, including trustee succession provisions, but may not materially change the dispositive provisions of the trust. This section requires the beneficial provisions of the second trust to be substantially the same as in the first trust, because the settlor did not choose to give the authorized fiduciary expanded discretion. Thus, for example, if a trust provides for principal distributions subject to an ascertainable standard to the settlor's child, and upon the child's death the remainder is to be distributed to Charitable Organization A, the decanting power cannot be exercised in a manner that substantially changes the interests of the child or of Charitable Organization A. Nonetheless, the settlor did entrust the authorized fiduciary with some discretion over principal distributions indicating some confidence in the trustee's judgment, justifying a limited decanting power in these situations.

"Substantially similar" means that there is no material change in a beneficiary's beneficial interests except as provided in subsection (d). A distribution standard that was more restrictive or more expansive would not be substantially similar. Thus if the first trust permitted distributions for support, health care and education, the beneficial interests would not be substantially similar if the second trust permitted distributions only for support and health care. If the first trust, however, permitted distributions for education without elaboration with respect to what was included within the term, the second trust might define education to include college, graduate school and vocational schools if otherwise consistent with applicable law.

If the first trust requires that a trust be distributed at age 35, a second trust that permits the beneficiary to withdraw any part or all of the trust at any time after age 35 would be substantially similar. A second trust that delayed the distribution to age 40 would not be substantially similar.

Changes to a fiduciary's administrative powers or investment powers, changes in a fiduciary, or changes in jurisdiction or the state law governing the administration of the trust, are not material changes in a beneficiary's beneficial interests, even though such changes may have incidental effects on the beneficial interests. For example, changing the trustee from one person to another could impact how the trustee exercises discretionary distribution authority, but is not a material change because the trustee's discretion is subject to the same standard and the trustee is subject to fiduciary duties.

Section 12(d), which permits distributions to be made for the benefit of the beneficiary instead of directly to such beneficiary, in part reflects existing law and in part expands existing law. Section 816(21) of the Uniform Trust Code permits a trustee to pay an amount distributable to a beneficiary who is under a legal disability or who the trustee reasonably believes is incapacitated by paying it directly to the beneficiary, applying it for the beneficiary's benefit, paying it to certain other persons on behalf of such beneficiary, or managing it as a separate fund on the beneficiary's behalf subject to the beneficiary's continuing right to withdraw the distribution. Section 12(d)(1) permits an amount distributable to a beneficiary to be applied for the beneficiary's benefit, but does not require that the beneficiary be under a legal disability or incapacitated. Section 12(d)(2) permits an amount distributable to a beneficiary who is under a legal disability or whom the trustee reasonably believes is incapacitated to be paid as permitted under the state's trust code. Under the Uniform Trust Code, as noted above, the trustee may pay such amount to certain other persons such as a conservator or guardian on behalf of the beneficiary. Section 12(d)(3) recognizes that the first-trust instrument may contain certain provisions authorizing the trustee to pay amounts distributable to beneficiaries to certain persons on their behalf or in certain ways. If the second-trust instrument also contains the same provisions, they are another permissible way to make distributions to a beneficiary because they were authorized by the settlor.

For example, if a trust requires that all income be distributed to A and permits the trustee to distribute principal to A for A's support, the trustee may decant the trust to require that all trust income be held in an accumulated income fund under the trust agreement, which permits A to withdraw the accumulated income fund at any time and permits the trustee to use the accumulated income fund to directly pay A's expenses. This might be helpful, for example, if A was incapacitated, incarcerated or uninterested in managing the funds herself or himself.

Section 12 is intended to permit a severance of a trust if the beneficial interests in the second trust, in the aggregate, are substantially similar to the beneficial interests in the first trust. For this purpose, an equal vertical division of a trust in which multiple beneficiaries have equal discretionary interests would usually be considered to be substantially similar. For example, if a testamentary trust created by A provides for discretionary distributions of income and principal to A's children for support, education and health care and A has three living children (B, C and D), the authorized fiduciary may exercise the decanting power under Section 12 to sever the trust into three equal trusts, one for each of B, C and D. The beneficial interest of each child in the second trusts is different because before the severance each child could conceivably receive discretionary distributions of more than one-third of the first trust and after the severance each child may only receive distributions from such child's second trust (one-third of the first trust). A child's interest would usually be considered substantially similar, however, because the loss of the possibility of receiving distributions of more than one-third of the first trust is offset by the fact that after the severance the other children may not receive discretionary distributions from such child's second trust. A child's interest after severance might not be considered substantially similar, however, if the first-trust instrument made clear that B's health care needs should be given priority and it seemed likely that B's health care needs would exceed one-third of the principal of the first trust.

§ 13. Trust for Beneficiary with Disability.

(a) In this section:

(1) "Beneficiary with a disability" means a beneficiary of a first trust who the special-needs fiduciary believes may qualify for governmental benefits based on disability, whether or not the beneficiary currently receives those benefits or is an individual who has been adjudicated [incompetent].

(2) "Governmental benefits" means financial aid or services from a state, federal, or other public agency.

(3) "Special-needs fiduciary" means, with respect to a trust that has a beneficiary with a disability:

(A) a trustee or other fiduciary, other than a settlor, that has discretion to distribute part or all of the principal of a first trust to one or more current beneficiaries;

(B) if no trustee or fiduciary has discretion under subparagraph (A), a trustee or other fiduciary, other than a settlor, that has discretion to distribute part or all of the income of the first trust to one or more current beneficiaries; or

(C) if no trustee or fiduciary has discretion under subparagraphs (A) and (B), a trustee or other fiduciary, other than a settlor, that is required to distribute part or all of the income or principal of the first trust to one or more current beneficiaries.

(4) "Special-needs trust" means a trust the trustee believes would not be considered a resource for purposes of determining whether a beneficiary with a disability is eligible for governmental benefits.

(b) A special-needs fiduciary may exercise the decanting power under Section 11 over the principal of a first trust as if the fiduciary had authority to distribute principal to a beneficiary with a disability subject to expanded distributive discretion if:

(1) a second trust is a special-needs trust that benefits the beneficiary with a disability; and

(2) the special-needs fiduciary determines that exercise of the decanting power will further the purposes of the first trust.

(c) In an exercise of the decanting power under this section, the following rules apply:

(1) Notwithstanding Section 11(c)(2), the interest in the second trust of a beneficiary with a disability may:

577

(A) be a pooled trust as defined by Medicaid law for the benefit of the beneficiary with a disability under 42 U.S.C. Section 1396p(d)(4)(C)[, as amended]; or

(B) contain payback provisions complying with reimbursement requirements of Medicaid law under 42 U.S.C. Section 1396p(d)(4)(A)[, as amended].

(2) Section 11(c)(3) does not apply to the interests of the beneficiary with a disability.

(3) Except as affected by any change to the interests of the beneficiary with a disability, the second trust, or if there are two or more second trusts, the second trusts in the aggregate, must grant each other beneficiary of the first trust beneficial interests in the second trusts which are substantially similar to the beneficiary's beneficial interests in the first trust.

Legislative Note: *In subsection (a)(1), substitute for "incompetent" the appropriate term for a judicial determination of disability or incompetency.*

In states in which the constitution, or other law, does not permit the phrase "as amended" when federal statutes are incorporated into state law, the phrase should be deleted in subsection (c)(1).

Comment

Section 13 permits an authorized fiduciary to exercise the decanting power over a trust that has a beneficiary with a disability to create a special-needs trust that governmental benefits programs may not consider a "resource" for purposes of the eligibility of the beneficiary with a disability for those benefits. Many governmental benefit programs restrict eligibility for those programs to only persons of limited resources. These resources may include any assets from which the beneficiary with a disability has the right to compel a distribution or a withdrawal. Special-needs trusts are drafted so as to limit the distribution rights of the beneficiary with a disability and thus better permit the beneficiary with a disability to qualify for governmental benefits. Under Section 13 the authorized fiduciary may modify the dispositive provisions for the beneficiary with a disability even if the authorized fiduciary has no discretion to make distributions or only discretion over income.

Beneficiary with a Disability. "Beneficiary with a disability" means a beneficiary who the special-needs fiduciary believes may qualify for governmental benefits based on disability. Section 13(a)(1). The beneficiary need not be adjudicated incompetent or totally incapacitated. The beneficiary need not be currently receiving governmental benefits based on disability. Nor need it be certain that the beneficiary would qualify for such benefits but for the terms of the first trust. The special-needs fiduciary need only have a reasonable belief that the decanting may permit the beneficiary to qualify for such benefits. The governmental benefits must be ones, however, that are based on disability and not merely on

financial need. Thus a decanting intended to permit a beneficiary with no disability to qualify for a needs-based college scholarship is not permitted under Section 13.

Governmental Benefits. "Governmental benefits" means financial aid or services from a state, federal or other public agency. Section 13(a)(2). It does not include benefits from a private entity.

Special-Needs Fiduciary. Because the term "authorized fiduciary" is limited to a fiduciary who has the power to make discretionary distributions of principal and Section 13 is intended to permit a fiduciary to decant even if the fiduciary does not have discretion over principal, Section 13 uses the separate term "special-needs fiduciary" to identify the fiduciary who has the power to decant. If there is no fiduciary who has discretion over principal, the special-needs fiduciary is the fiduciary with discretion over income, or if none, the fiduciary who is directed to make distributions. Section 13(a)(3).

Special-Needs Trust. "Special-needs trust" means a trust the trustee believes would not be considered a resource for purposes of determining whether a beneficiary with a disability is eligible for governmental benefits based on disability. Section 13(a)(4).

Furtherance of Purposes of Trust. The exercise of the decanting power must be in furtherance of the purposes of the first trust. Section 13(b)(2). Thus the decanting must effectuate better the settlor's broader purposes. In most cases, if the first trust did not anticipate the beneficiary's disability and the settlor's broader purpose was to provide for the beneficiary's support, a decanting that would permit the beneficiary with a disability to qualify for governmental benefits while still being eligible to receive discretionary distributions from the trust would further the purposes of the trust.

For example, assume the first trust was created and funded by A, requires all income to be distributed to the beneficiary after age 21, permits the trustee to distribute principal to the beneficiary pursuant to an ascertainable standard for the beneficiary's support, permits the beneficiary to withdraw the trust principal at age 30, grants the beneficiary a testamentary general power of appointment, and upon the beneficiary's death distributes any unappointed property per stirpes to A's descendants then living. If the beneficiary is age 25 and is disabled, the authorized fiduciary may exercise the decanting power to distribute the principal of the first trust to a trust that provides only for distributions to the beneficiary in the trustee's absolute discretion and upon the beneficiary's death distributes the remaining trust assets per stirpes to A's descendants then living. The exercise of the decanting power may eliminate the beneficiary's right to income, the beneficiary's prospective right to withdraw the trust at age 30 and the beneficiary's power of appointment. The second trust may not, however, change the remainder beneficiaries. Section 13(c)(3).

The result is the same if the beneficiary is age 31 and thus has a right to withdraw the trust assets, because Section 13(c)(2) provides that Section 11(c)(3) does not apply to the interest of the beneficiary with a disability.

If in the above example the trustee had no discretion to distribute principal, but was either required to distribute income or had discretion to distribute income for A's support, the authorized fiduciary could still decant to a special-needs trust. The trustee would be considered the special-needs fiduciary under Section 13(a)(3).

The decanting, however, must further the purposes of the first trust. Section 13(b)(2). For example, if a trust was created solely for the purpose of funding college education for the settlor's grandchildren, the authorized fiduciary may not decant to pay for the support of a grandchild who is a beneficiary with a disability. Conceivably, however, a trust for the education at all levels of the settlor's grandchildren might be decanted to a trust that permits distributions to a grandchild who is a beneficiary with a disability for such grandchild's occupational therapy and vocational training.

Pooled or Payback Trust. The second trust may be a pooled trust or a payback trust. Section 13(c)(1). For example, assume a trust was funded by the beneficiary, directly or indirectly, and provides for distributions of income to the beneficiary until age 30 and then provides for the remainder of the trust to be distributed to the beneficiary. The beneficiary is age 28. The authorized fiduciary may exercise the decanting power, and the second trust may be a "pooled trust" or a payback trust. Section 13(c)(1). The act does not require that the second trust be a "pooled trust" or a payback trust, but other state law may impose such a requirement.

Other Beneficial Interests Must Be Substantially Similar. Subsection (c)(3) generally requires that any beneficial interests of beneficiaries other than the beneficiary with a disability be substantially similar to their interests in the first trust except to the extent they are affected by changes to the interest of the beneficiary with a disability. The beneficiary's disability justifies permitting a modification of the interest of the beneficiary with a disability even when the trustee has limited or no discretion, but does not justify otherwise changing the interests of other beneficiaries. The modifications to the interest of the beneficiary with a disability, however, might affect the amount or timing of the other beneficiaries' interests.

Thus if the first trust has more than one current beneficiary, one of whom is a beneficiary with a disability, the special-needs fiduciary may decant under Section 11 as if the special-needs fiduciary had expanded discretion to distribute principal to the beneficiary with a disability, but may not alter the interest of the other beneficiaries except to the extent they are affected by the changes to the interest of the beneficiary with a disability. For example, assume the first trust was created and funded by A, continues for the rule against perpetuities period, requires that income be distributed per stirpes to A's descendants, and permits discretionary distributions of principal to A's descendants pursuant to an ascertainable standard. The exercise of the decanting power might, for example, distribute part of the principal of the first trust to a special-needs trust solely for the benefit of the beneficiary with a disability (the "Special-Needs Trust") and distribute the remaining principal to a trust solely for the benefit of the nondisabled beneficiaries (the "Non-Special-Needs Trust"), the terms of which are otherwise identical to the terms of the first trust. The Special-Needs Trust might give the trustee absolute discretion to make distributions to the beneficiary with a disability. Upon the death of the beneficiary with a disability, however, the remaining assets of the Special-Needs Trust must be distributed to the Non-Special-Needs Trust, because the decanting cannot change the interests of the non-disabled beneficiaries, except to the extent they are affected by the changes to the interest of the beneficiary with a disability. The non-disabled beneficiaries' remainder interests may be affected, for example, because the trustee of the Special-Needs Trust may make distributions to the beneficiary with a disability in the trustee's absolute discretion and is not limited by an ascertainable standard. The Non-Special-Needs Trust must have the same terms as the first trust, except that it may modify or eliminate the interest of the beneficiary with a disability. So, for example, the Non-Special-Needs Trust might provide that no distributions would be made to the beneficiary with a disability unless the Special-Needs Trust was exhausted.

§ 14. Protection of Charitable Interest.

(a) In this section:

(1) "Determinable charitable interest" means a charitable interest that is a right to a mandatory distribution currently, periodically, on the occurrence of a specified event, or after the passage of a specified time and which is unconditional or will be held solely for charitable purposes.

(2) "Unconditional" means not subject to the occurrence of a specified event that is not certain to occur, other than a requirement in a trust instrument that a charitable organization be in existence or qualify under a particular provision of the United States Internal Revenue Code of 1986[, as amended,] on the date of the distribution, if the charitable organization meets the requirement on the date of determination.

(b) If a first trust contains a determinable charitable interest, [the Attorney General] has the rights of a qualified beneficiary and may represent and bind the charitable interest.

(c) If a first trust contains a charitable interest, the second trust or trusts may not:

(1) diminish the charitable interest;

(2) diminish the interest of an identified charitable organization that holds the charitable interest;

(3) alter any charitable purpose stated in the first-trust instrument; or

(4) alter any condition or restriction related to the charitable interest.

(d) If there are two or more second trusts, the second trusts shall be treated as one trust for purposes of determining whether the exercise of the decanting power diminishes the charitable interest or diminishes the interest of an identified charitable organization for purposes of subsection (c).

(e) If a first trust contains a determinable charitable interest, the second trust or trusts that include a charitable interest pursuant to subsection (c) must be administered under the law of this state unless:

(1) [the Attorney General], after receiving notice under Section 7, fails to object in a signed record delivered to the authorized fiduciary within the notice period;

(2) [the Attorney General] consents in a signed record to the second trust or trusts being administered under the law of another jurisdiction; or

(3) the court approves the exercise of the decanting power.

(f) This [act] does not limit the powers and duties of the [Attorney General] under law of this state other than this [act].

Legislative Note: *In states in which the constitution, or other law, does not permit the phrase "as amended" when federal statutes are incorporated into state law, the phrase should be deleted in subsection (a)(2).*

In subsections (b), (e), and (f), "Attorney General" is placed in brackets to accommodate a jurisdiction that grants enforcement authority over charitable trusts to another designated official.

Comment

The Uniform Trust Decanting Act does not permit the decanting of a trust held solely for charitable purposes (a "wholly charitable trust"). See Section 3(b). While a split interest trust such as a charitable remainder trust or a charitable lead trust is not a wholly charitable trust, in almost all cases the trustee of such a trust would not have discretion to distribute principal to a current beneficiary and therefore there would be no authorized fiduciary (see Section 2(3)) who would have authority to exercise the decanting power under Section 11 or Section 12.

Other trusts that could be decanted under Sections 11, 12 or 13, however, may contain charitable interests. Section 14 imposes special protections for charitable interests. When a charitable interest is a "determinable charitable interest," Section 14 gives the Attorney General (or other official with enforcement authority over charitable interests) the rights of a qualified beneficiary and restricts the ability to decant to change the law governing the trust's administration. Generally, a determinable charitable interest is a charitable interest not subject to fiduciary discretion or any significant contingencies.

Determinable Charitable Interest. An interest must meet three requirements to be a determinable charitable interest. Section 14(a)(1). First, the interest must be a charitable interest. See Section 2(5). Determinable charitable interests are a subset of charitable interests. Thus a remote contingent interest cannot be a determinable charitable interest.

Second, a determinable interest must be a right to a mandatory distribution. A mandatory distribution is a right that is not subject to the exercise of discretion. The mandatory distribution may be a right to income, principal or both. A mandatory distribution may be a right to a current distribution, for example, where a charitable organization is entitled to a certain portion of trust principal on a date that has already occurred and the distribution has not yet been made. A mandatory distribution also includes a right to periodic distributions of income, a specific dollar amount or a percentage of value of some or all of the trust property. A mandatory distribution also includes a right to receive an ascertainable part of the trust property currently or on the occurrence of a specified event or after the passage of a specified time.

This requirement would be met, for example, if a trust required the trustee to distribute to charitable organizations or for charitable purposes one-half of the trust's net income annually or, alternatively, one percent of the value of the trust's assets annually. It would also be met if the trustee was required to distribute ten percent of the trust principal to charitable organizations or for charitable purposes ten

years after the settlor's death or alternatively upon the death of the settlor's surviving spouse. This requirement would not be met if the charitable distribution was subject to the trustee's discretion.

A mandatory distribution would also include a right of withdrawal held by a charitable organization.

The third and final requirement for a determinable charitable interest is that the charitable interest either must be unconditional or must in all events be held for charitable purposes. Unconditional generally means not subject to the occurrence of a specified event that may not occur. For example, assume the trustee is to distribute $100,000 annually to the Ornithology Institute, a charitable organization, but only if it uses the funds to search for the ivory billed woodpecker, and if it does not so use the funds, to Resurrect Extinct Species, a charitable organization, but only if it uses the funds to recreate the ivory billed woodpecker from genetic material, and if it does not so use the funds, to Woods for Woodpeckers, a charitable organization. The individual interests of Ornithology Institute, Resurrect Extinct Species, and Woods for Woodpeckers are each conditional. The charitable interest to receive $100,000 annually, in the aggregate, meets the third requirement because in all events it will be held for charitable purposes for one of the three charitable organizations.

A charitable interest is conditional (i.e., not an unconditional interest) if the trustee has discretion to make or not make the distribution. For example, if the trustee has discretion to make distributions of income to Manors for Meerkats, a charitable organization, the charitable interest is not unconditional. The charitable interest would not be a determinable charitable interest unless it would in all events be held for charitable purposes. For example, if the trustee was required to distribute all income annually to Manors for Meerkats or to such other charitable organization as the trustee selected for the benefit of wildlife of the Kalahari Desert, the charitable interest is determinable even though the interest of Manors for Meerkats is not unconditional.

A charitable interest, however, would not be conditional merely because the trustee's exercise of discretion in favor of other beneficiaries could affect the charitable interest. For example, if the trustee is required to distribute $200,000 annually to Lonely George Research Fund and has discretion to distribute principal to the settlor's children, the charitable interest is unconditional because so long as there are sufficient funds in the trust the charitable distribution must be made. As another example, assume the trustee had discretion to distribute income and principal to the settlor's children, and upon the death of the surviving child the remainder was to be distributed to Gone with the Wolves, a charitable organization. The interest of Gone with the Wolves is a determinable charitable interest, even though it may be reduced, or even eliminated, by the trustee's exercise of discretion in favor of the settlor's children.

An interest held by a charitable organization is not conditional merely because it is subject to the requirement that the organization be in existence at the time the distribution is to be made. Further, an interest held by a charitable organization is not conditional merely because the organization must qualify as a charitable organization under a particular provision of the Internal Revenue Code, if the organization so qualifies on the date of determination.

For example, assume a trust provides for distributions for the education of the settlor's children and upon the youngest living child attaining age 28 distributes to Whale Whisperers, if it is then in existence and contributions to it qualify for a federal income tax charitable deduction. The interest of Whale Whisperers is unconditional if at the time of the determination Whale Whisperers is in existence and contributions to it qualify for the federal income tax deduction.

Attorney General Rights. Subsection (b) provides that if the first trust contains a determinable charitable interest, the Attorney General (or other official with enforcement authority over charitable interests) may represent the interest and has all the rights of a qualified beneficiary. The Attorney General is entitled to notice under Section 7(c)(7). The Attorney General may petition the court under Section 9, consent to a change in the compensation of an authorized fiduciary under Section 16 or consent to a change in the identity of the person who may remove or replace the authorized fiduciary under Section 18.

If the decanting changes the jurisdiction of a trust containing a determinable charitable interest, the Attorney General may block the decanting by objecting, even without petitioning the court, unless the court approves the decanting. Section 14(e).

If the determinable charitable interest is held by an identified charitable organization, the organization is a qualified beneficiary, has the rights of a qualified beneficiary and may represent and bind itself. In such a case, either the Attorney General or the

organization could consent to a change in the compensation of an authorized fiduciary under Section 16 or consent to a change in the identity of the person who may remove or replace the authorized fiduciary under Section 18. If one of the Attorney General or the organization consented, but the other affirmatively objected, the other could petition the court under Section 9 for a determination.

Preservation of Charitable Interests. Although Section 14(b) gives the Attorney General the rights of a qualified beneficiary only when a charitable interest is determinable, Section 14(c) applies to all charitable interests whether or not determinable. If the first trust contains a charitable interest, whether or not determinable, the second trust may not diminish such interest. Section 14(c)(1). If the interest is held by an identified charitable organization, the second trust may not change the organization. Section 14(c)(2). If the first-trust instrument sets forth a particular charitable purpose, the second trust may not change the charitable purpose. Section 14(c)(3). If the first trust imposes certain conditions or restrictions on the charitable gift, the second trust cannot change the conditions or restrictions. Section 14(c)(4).

If a charitable trust indicates a particular charitable purpose, the exercise of the decanting power may not change the charitable purpose. Section 14(c)(3). Thus if the first trust provides that upon A's death the remainder will be paid to Companion Animals for the benefit and protection of dogs, the second trust may not change the purpose of the charitable gift to the benefit of cats. As another example, if the first trust provides that upon A's death the remainder will be distributed to such charities as the trustee selects for the purpose of preserving habitat for blue footed boobies, the second trust cannot change the charitable purpose to the protection of polar bears.

If an authorized fiduciary has limited discretion to distribute principal and exercises the decanting power under Section 12, Section 12(c) requires that the second trusts must grant each beneficiary of the first trust, including charitable organizations, beneficial interests that are substantially similar to such beneficiary's interests in the first trust. If the first trust contains a charitable interest that is not held by an identified charitable organization, Section 12(c) does not apply but Section 14(c) requires that the second trust may not diminish the charitable interest and that any stated charitable purpose must remain the same.

For example, assume a trust permits discretionary income and principal distributions to the settlor's children for their support and health care, requires that the trustee distribute $25,000 each year to one or more charitable organizations selected by the trustee for the purpose of caring for stray, neglected and abused large dogs, gives the trustee discretion to make additional distributions to charitable organizations for the same purpose, and upon the death of the settlor's last surviving child the principal is to be distributed to charitable organizations selected by the trustee for the same purpose. The trustee has limited discretion to distribute principal and therefore may decant under Section 12, but not Section 11. The exercise of the decanting power may change administrative provisions and trustee provisions, but may not alter the beneficial interests of the children. Because the charitable interests are not held by an identified charitable organization, they are not subject to Section 12(c). Section 14(c), however, requires that the second trust not diminish the charitable interests to the $25,000 annual distributions, to receive discretionary distributions and to the remainder interest. In addition, Section 14(c) requires that the charitable purpose remain the same. Thus the second trust could not change the charitable purpose to supporting dog parks for small dogs.

If the trust was as described above except that the trustee had discretion to make distributions to the children for their best interests, the trustee could exercise the decanting power under Section 11. Thus the trustee could eliminate or reduce the interest of one or more of the settlor's children. The decanting could not, however, diminish the charitable interests because Section 14(c) requires that the charitable interest not be diminished. The trustee could not, for example, grant a power of appointment to a child because such a power would diminish the charitable interests.

If a trust gave the trustee expanded discretion to make distributions to the settlor's children for best interests, and upon the death of the surviving child provided for the remaining assets to be distributed to Howl at the Moon, a charitable organization for the peaceful co-existence of wolves and humans, the authorized fiduciary could not exercise the decanting power to provide that each child would receive an equal share of the trust assets when the youngest child attained age 25, because that would diminish the charitable interest. The authorized fiduciary also could not exercise the decanting power to change the charitable remainder beneficiary from Howl at the Moon to another charitable organization. By contrast, the authorized fiduciary could exercise the decanting power to provide that when the youngest child attained age 25 the trust would be distributed to Howl at the Moon, because that would enhance the charitable interest.

Subsection (c)(4) prohibits altering any condition or restriction related to the charitable interest. For example, if the first trust requires that the trustee consult with certain persons before making distributions or provide reports to certain persons, or gives enforcement rights to certain persons to ensure the charitable purpose is fulfilled, the second trust may not change such provisions.

Some state Attorneys General (or other officials charged with protecting charitable interests) may be concerned that trusts with charitable interests will be moved out of their jurisdiction by decanting. Section 14(e) addresses this concern by requiring that the second trust be administered under the law of the enacting state unless the court approved the decanting or the Attorney General either approved the decanting or, after receiving notice, failed to object within the notice period.

Subsection (f) makes clear that the Uniform Trust Decanting Act does not limit the powers and duties of the Attorney General under other law of the state, whether statutory or common law. For example, other law of the state may give the Attorney General the right to sue for breach of fiduciary duties with respect to charitable interests.

§ 15. Trust Limitation on Decanting.

(a) An authorized fiduciary may not exercise the decanting power to the extent the first-trust instrument expressly prohibits exercise of:

(1) the decanting power; or

(2) a power granted by state law to the fiduciary to distribute part or all of the principal of the trust to another trust or to modify the trust.

(b) Exercise of the decanting power is subject to any restriction in the first-trust instrument that expressly applies to exercise of:

(1) the decanting power; or

(2) a power granted by state law to a fiduciary to distribute part or all of the principal of the trust to another trust or to modify the trust.

(c) A general prohibition of the amendment or revocation of a first trust, a spendthrift clause, or a clause restraining the voluntary or involuntary transfer of a beneficiary's interest does not preclude exercise of the decanting power.

(d) Subject to subsections (a) and (b), an authorized fiduciary may exercise the decanting power under this [act] even if the first-trust instrument permits the authorized fiduciary or another person to modify the first-trust instrument or to distribute part or all of the principal of the first trust to another trust.

(e) If a first-trust instrument contains an express prohibition described in subsection (a) or an express restriction described in subsection (b), the provision must be included in the second-trust instrument.

Comment

A trust instrument may expressly preclude the exercise of a decanting power under the act or any similar state statute with respect to the entire trust or with respect to one or more provisions of the trust. See Section 15(a). The exercise of a decanting power, however, is not prohibited by a statement that the trust is irrevocable or unamendable, or by a spendthrift provision. See Section 15(c). In order to preclude the exercise of the decanting power, the first-trust instrument must expressly refer to the act or to a power granted by state law to the fiduciary to distribute part or all of the principal of the trust to another trust or to modify the trust. For example, assume a first-trust instrument states: "There shall always be a trustee who is an attorney or accountant." That sentence alone would not prohibit the exercise of the decanting power to eliminate that requirement. If the first-trust instrument, however, also stated that "this provision may not be modified by the exercise of any decanting power," then the exercise of the decanting power to modify that provision would be prohibited by Section 15(a).

Any restriction in the first-trust instrument that expressly applies to decanting is honored. Thus, for example, a restriction in the first-trust instrument that

requires court approval of any decanting that accelerates the distribution of trust assets would be enforced. As another example, a restriction requiring approval of any decanting by a particular third party would also be enforced.

An irrevocable trust may provide in the trust instrument a mechanism for modifying the trust, for example, by granting a trust protector the power to modify the trust. The fact that a trust instrument provides such a mechanism for modification does not preclude the application of this act. Any requirements or restrictions contained in the trust instrument for such modification mechanism do not apply to an exercise of a decanting power under this act unless such requirements or restrictions expressly apply to an exercise of a decanting power under this act or a similar state statute.

If the first-trust instrument contains a restriction on decanting, the provision must be included in the second-trust instrument. Section 15(e). This provision is intended to prevent serial decanting in which the first decanting removes the restriction on changing a particular provision in the first-trust instrument, and the second decanting then changes such provision.

§ 16. Change in Compensation.

(a) If a first-trust instrument specifies an authorized fiduciary's compensation, the fiduciary may not exercise the decanting power to increase the fiduciary's compensation above the specified compensation unless:

(1) all qualified beneficiaries of the second trust consent to the increase in a signed record; or

(2) the increase is approved by the court.

(b) If a first-trust instrument does not specify an authorized fiduciary's compensation, the fiduciary may not exercise the decanting power to increase the fiduciary's compensation above the compensation permitted by [this state's trust code] unless:

(1) all qualified beneficiaries of the second trust consent to the increase in a signed record; or

(2) the increase is approved by the court.

(c) A change in an authorized fiduciary's compensation which is incidental to other changes made by the exercise of the decanting power is not an increase in the fiduciary's compensation for purposes of subsections (a) and (b).

Comment

An exercise of the decanting power generally is an action taken by the authorized fiduciary that does not require beneficiary consent or court approval. The purpose of requiring beneficiary consent or court approval to a change in the compensation of the authorized fiduciary is to place a check on an authorized fiduciary increasing its own compensation by decanting. In this context it does not seem necessary to require the consent of all beneficiaries. Obtaining the consent of qualified beneficiaries, who would generally be immediately impacted by a change in compensation, should be sufficient.

If the first-trust instrument specifies the authorized fiduciary's compensation, the decanting may not increase the fiduciary's compensation without either the consent of all qualified beneficiaries of the second trust or court approval. Section 16(a). This subsection applies whether the increase in compensation would result from omitting the provision in the trust instrument specifying compensation, modifying such provision or replacing such provision with a different provision. If it is unclear whether a change in method of calculating compensation would result in an increase, either court approval or consent of all qualified beneficiaries should be obtained.

If the first-trust instrument does not specify the authorized fiduciary's compensation, the decanting may not increase the compensation above the compensation permitted in the trust code of the enacting state without either the consent of all qualified beneficiaries or court approval. Section 16(b).

Section 16 expressly does not prohibit an increase in compensation arising incidentally because of other changes made by the exercise of the decanting power. For example, any increase in the compensation of the authorized fiduciary because the second trust may last longer than the first trust is incidental. Also incidental are any increases in compensation that may arise because the second trust may have a greater value in the future than the first trust would have had, for example, because property is retained in the trust longer or smaller distributions are made. Other incidental increases in the compensation of the authorized fiduciary may occur because of changes in investments, changes in the law governing the administration of the trust, changes in the identity of the authorized fiduciary, or changes in the duties of the authorized fiduciary.

In many cases the consideration of a proposed decanting or the implementation of a decanting is fairly seen as an exercise of a discretionary fiduciary power that does not warrant any additional compensation for the authorized fiduciary. In some cases, however, the authorized fiduciary may be required to spend an extraordinary amount of time in evaluating a potential exercise of the decanting power, particularly when an exercise of the power is suggested by a beneficiary, or in exercising the decanting power. In such cases, and regardless of whether the authorized fiduciary ultimately exercises the decanting power, the authorized fiduciary may be entitled to additional compensation under the trust instrument or under state law. See Section 708 of the Uniform Trust Code. In the absence of explicit authority on the appropriate amount of any such compensation, such compensation should be reasonable considering the relevant factors, including the time devoted to the decanting and the degree of difficulty. *See* Restatement Third of Trusts Section 38 comment c. The authorized fiduciary may also be entitled to have reasonable expenses related to evaluating a potential exercise of the decanting power or in exercising the decanting power paid from the first trust. See Section 709 of the Uniform Trust Code.

§ 17. Relief from Liability and Indemnification.

(a)Except as otherwise provided in this section, a second-trust instrument may not relieve an authorized fiduciary from liability for breach of trust to a greater extent than the first-trust instrument.

(b) A second-trust instrument may provide for indemnification of an authorized fiduciary of the first trust or another person acting in a fiduciary capacity under the first trust for any liability or claim that would have been payable from the first trust if the decanting power had not been exercised.

(c) A second-trust instrument may not reduce fiduciary liability in the aggregate.

(d) Subject to subsection (c), a second-trust instrument may divide and reallocate fiduciary powers among fiduciaries, including one or more trustees, distribution advisors, investment advisors, trust protectors, or other persons, and relieve a fiduciary from liability for an act or failure to act of another fiduciary as permitted by law of this state other than this [act].

Comment

An authorized fiduciary should not be permitted to decant in order to insert in the second-trust instrument a provision directly exculpating the authorized fiduciary or indemnifying the authorized fiduciary except to the extent such provision was contained in the first-trust instrument or applicable law would have provided such exculpation or indemnification. Nonetheless, decanting may appropriately reduce the authorized fiduciary's liability indirectly. For example, if the second trust is subject to the law of a different state, the law governing the second trust may provide additional protection to the authorized fiduciary.

The terms of the second trust may reduce an authorized fiduciary's liability indirectly, for example, by modifying the rules for approving accounts or expressly permitting the retention of certain property. While such provisions may not violate Section 16, they could under certain circumstances violate the authorized fiduciary's general fiduciary duties. For example, while it may be appropriate in the second trust to expressly permit the retention of a residence used by a current beneficiary of the trust, it may not be appropriate to permit the retention of all of the current trust property without any liability.

Subsection (b) recognizes that the trustee of the first trust may be unwilling to distribute the assets of the first trust to the second trust unless the trustee is indemnified for any liability or claim that may become payable from the first trust after its assets are distributed. Subsection (b) is consistent with Section 27, which provides that decanting does not relieve the trust property from any liability that otherwise attaches to the trust property. The indemnification described in subsection (b) may be contained in the second-trust instrument or may be contained in the record exercising the decanting power.

An authorized fiduciary can decant to a trust that divides the trustee responsibilities (i.e., jobs) among various parties, but cannot eliminate the fiduciary duties that accompany those jobs. To the extent that the second trust assigns a fiduciary responsibility and the fiduciary duty that accompanies such responsibility to a particular fiduciary, the other fiduciaries may be relieved from liability for the actions of that particular fiduciary. For example, an investment advisor can be appointed and the authorized fiduciary can be relieved of fiduciary liability for the investment decisions to the extent permitted by the law of the enacting state so long as the investment advisor is acting in a fiduciary capacity and has fiduciary liability for the investment decisions. Section 17(c), (d).

§ 18. Removal or Replacement of Authorized Fiduciary.
An authorized fiduciary may not exercise the decanting power to modify a provision in a first-trust instrument granting another person power to remove or replace the fiduciary unless:

(1) the person holding the power consents to the modification in a signed record and the modification applies only to the person;

(2) the person holding the power and the qualified beneficiaries of the second trust consent to the modification in a signed record and the modification grants a substantially similar power to another person; or

(3) the court approves the modification and the modification grants a substantially similar power to another person.

Comment

Section 18 authorizes a modification of a trustee removal provision only with either court approval or the consent of the person currently holding the right to remove or replace the trustee. The power to remove a fiduciary is a power to remove the fiduciary without the fiduciary's consent regardless of whether the remover has the power to designate the successor fiduciary. The power to replace a fiduciary is the power to remove the fiduciary and to designate the successor for the fiduciary without the consent of the fiduciary.

Unless the qualified beneficiaries also consent to such change, the person currently holding the right to remove the authorized fiduciary may only consent to the modification of the right with respect to himself or herself and cannot consent to the modification of such right with respect to any successor remover. Section 18(1). For example, if a trust provides that the authorized fiduciary may be removed by X (the "current remover"), so long as X is living and not incapacitated, and after X is deceased or incapacitated, by Y, X may consent to a modification that would permit the authorized fiduciary to be removed only by the joint agreement of X and Z and only with 90 days' prior notice, but such modification would not affect Y's power of removal after X is deceased or incapacitated unless Y also consents to the modification or unless the qualified beneficiaries consent to such change.

Alternatively, the removal power may be modified by the current remover and the qualified beneficiaries if the modification grants a substantially similar removal right to another person. Section 18(2). In the previous example, X (the current remover) and the qualified beneficiaries could consent to a modification that would permit the authorized fiduciary to be removed by Z, or if Z were not willing and able to act, by W. Y, the successor remover named in the first-trust instrument, would not need to consent to such modification if X and the qualified beneficiaries consent to it.

Alternatively, the power to remove or replace the authorized fiduciary may be modified if the court approves the modification and the modification grants a substantially similar power to another person. Section 18(3).

In the case of a modification with the consent of the qualified beneficiaries or with court approval, the modification must grant a substantially similar power to another person. A power to remove a fiduciary only for cause would not be substantially similar to a power to remove a fiduciary for any reason. A power to remove a fiduciary only after the fiduciary has attained age 75 or served for ten years is not substantially similar to a power to remove the fiduciary at any time. A power to replace a fiduciary is not substantially similar unless it contains substantially the same restrictions on who may serve as the replacement fiduciary. For example, a power to remove a fiduciary and replace the fiduciary with any person would not be substantially similar to a power to remove the fiduciary and replace the fiduciary with a person who is not related or subordinate to the settlor.

In exercising the decanting power to designate a different person to remove and replace the trustee, the authorized trustee should be alert to the tax consequences if the person so designated is not independent for tax purposes.

§ 19. Tax-Related Limitations.

(a) In this section:

(1) "Grantor trust" means a trust as to which a settlor of a first trust is considered the owner under 26 U.S.C. Sections 671 through 677[, as amended,] or 26 U.S.C. Section 679[, as amended].

(2) "Internal Revenue Code" means the United States Internal Revenue Code of 1986[, as amended].

(3) "Nongrantor trust" means a trust that is not a grantor trust.

(4) "Qualified benefits property" means property subject to the minimum distribution requirements of 26 U.S.C. Section 401(a)(9)[, as amended,], and any applicable regulations, or to any similar requirements that refer to 26 U.S.C. Section 401(a)(9) or the regulations.

(b) An exercise of the decanting power is subject to the following limitations:

(1) If a first trust contains property that qualified, or would have qualified but for provisions of this [act] other than this section, for a marital deduction for purposes of the gift or estate tax under

the Internal Revenue Code or a state gift, estate, or inheritance tax, the second-trust instrument must not include or omit any term that, if included in or omitted from the trust instrument for the trust to which the property was transferred, would have prevented the transfer from qualifying for the deduction, or would have reduced the amount of the deduction, under the same provisions of the Internal Revenue Code or state law under which the transfer qualified.

(2) If the first trust contains property that qualified, or would have qualified but for provisions of this [act] other than this section, for a charitable deduction for purposes of the income, gift, or estate tax under the Internal Revenue Code or a state income, gift, estate, or inheritance tax, the second-trust instrument must not include or omit any term that, if included in or omitted from the trust instrument for the trust to which the property was transferred, would have prevented the transfer from qualifying for the deduction, or would have reduced the amount of the deduction, under the same provisions of the Internal Revenue Code or state law under which the transfer qualified.

(3) If the first trust contains property that qualified, or would have qualified but for provisions of this [act] other than this section, for the exclusion from the gift tax described in 26 U.S.C. Section 2503(b)[, as amended], the second-trust instrument must not include or omit a term that, if included in or omitted from the trust instrument for the trust to which the property was transferred, would have prevented the transfer from qualifying under 26 U.S.C. Section 2503(b)[, as amended]. If the first trust contains property that qualified, or would have qualified but for provisions of this [act] other than this section, for the exclusion from the gift tax described in 26 U.S.C. Section 2503(b)[, as amended,] by application of 26 U.S.C. Section 2503(c)[,as amended], the second-trust instrument must not include or omit a term that, if included or omitted from the trust instrument for the trust to which the property was transferred, would have prevented the transfer from qualifying under 26 U.S.C. Section 2503(c)[, as amended].

(4) If the property of the first trust includes shares of stock in an S corporation, as defined in 26 U.S.C. Section 1361[, as amended,] and the first trust is, or but for provisions of this [act] other than this section would be, a permitted shareholder under any provision of 26 U.S.C. Section 1361[, as amended], an authorized fiduciary may exercise the power with respect to part or all of the S-corporation stock only if any second trust receiving the stock is a permitted shareholder under 26 U.S.C. Section 1361(c)(2)[, as amended]. If the property of the first trust includes shares of stock in an S corporation and the first trust is, or but for provisions of this [act] other than this section would be, a qualified subchapter-S trust within the meaning of 26 U.S.C. Section 1361(d)[, as amended], the second-trust instrument must not include or omit a term that prevents the second trust from qualifying as a qualified subchapter-S trust.

(5) If the first trust contains property that qualified, or would have qualified but for provisions of this [act] other than this section, for a zero inclusion ratio for purposes of the generation-skipping transfer tax under 26 U.S.C. Section 2642(c)[, as amended,] the second-trust instrument must not include or omit a term that, if included in or omitted from the first-trust instrument, would have prevented the transfer to the first trust from qualifying for a zero inclusion ratio under 26 U.S.C. Section 2642(c)[, as amended].

(6) If the first trust is directly or indirectly the beneficiary of qualified benefits property, the second-trust instrument may not include or omit any term that, if included in or omitted from the first-trust instrument, would have increased the minimum distributions required with respect to the qualified benefits property under 26 U.S.C. Section 401(a)(9)[, as amended,] and any applicable regulations, or any similar requirements that refer to 26 U.S.C. Section 401(a)(9)[, as amended] or the regulations. If an attempted exercise of the decanting power violates the preceding sentence, the trustee is deemed to have held the qualified benefits property and any reinvested distributions of the property as a separate share from the date of the exercise of the power and Section 22 applies to the

separate share.

(7) If the first trust qualifies as a grantor trust because of the application of 26 U.S.C. Section 672(f)(2)(A)[, as amended,] the second trust may not include or omit a term that, if included in or omitted from the first-trust instrument, would have prevented the first trust from qualifying under 26 U.S.C. Section 672(f)(2)(A)[, as amended].

(8) In this paragraph, "tax benefit" means a federal or state tax deduction, exemption, exclusion, or other benefit not otherwise listed in this section, except for a benefit arising from being a grantor trust. Subject to paragraph (9), a second-trust instrument may not include or omit a term that, if included in or omitted from the first-trust instrument, would have prevented qualification for a tax benefit if:

(A) the first-trust instrument expressly indicates an intent to qualify for the benefit or the first-trust instrument clearly is designed to enable the first trust to qualify for the benefit; and

(B) the transfer of property held by the first trust or the first trust qualified, or but for provisions of this [act] other than this section, would have qualified for the tax benefit.

(9) Subject to paragraph (4):

(A) except as otherwise provided in paragraph (7), the second trust may be a nongrantor trust, even if the first trust is a grantor trust; and

(B) except as otherwise provided in paragraph (10), the second trust may be a grantor trust, even if the first trust is a nongrantor trust.

(10) An authorized fiduciary may not exercise the decanting power if a settlor objects in a signed record delivered to the fiduciary within the notice period and:

(A) the first trust and a second trust are both grantor trusts, in whole or in part, the first trust grants the settlor or another person the power to cause the second trust to cease to be a grantor trust, and the second trust does not grant an equivalent power to the settlor or other person; or

(B) the first trust is a nongrantor trust and a second trust is a grantor trust, in whole or in part, with respect to the settlor, unless:

(i) the settlor has the power at all times to cause the second trust to cease to be a grantor trust; or

(ii) the first-trust instrument contains a provision granting the settlor or another person a power that would cause the first trust to cease to be a grantor trust and the second-trust instrument contains the same provision.

Legislative Note: *In states in which the constitution, or other law, does not permit the phrase "as amended" when federal statutes are incorporated into state law, the phrase should be deleted in subsection (a)(1), (2) and (4) and subsection (b)(3) through (7).*

Comment

Certain tax benefits granted under the Internal Revenue Code (the "Code") or state law are dependent upon a trust containing specific provisions. For example, a qualified terminable interest property ("QTIP") marital trust or general power of appointment marital trust requires that the surviving spouse be entitled for life to all income, and a general power of appointment marital trust also requires that the surviving spouse have a general power of appointment exercisable alone and in all events. If a trustee had the power to decant the trust in a manner that deprived the surviving spouse of the requisite income interest, or in the case of a general power of appointment marital trust, the requisite general power of appointment, then arguably the trust would not qualify for the marital deduction from the inception of the trust. Similarly, it is important to ensure that charitable lead trusts and charitable remainder trusts cannot be modified in a way that arguably would prevent them from qualifying for the charitable deduction or that would reduce the amount of that deduction at their inception.

Grantor Trust. For purposes of this section, a grantor trust means a trust as to which a settlor of the first trust is considered the owner for income tax purposes under the Internal Revenue Code. Section 19(a)(1). The term does not include a trust over which someone other than the settlor (e.g., a beneficiary) is treated as the owner under Code section 678. A "nongrantor trust" is a trust that is not a grantor trust. Section 19(a)(3).

Marital Deduction. Subsection (b)(1) protects the marital deduction. For example, for property to qualify as qualified terminable interest property, the surviving spouse must have a qualifying income interest for life and a QTIP election must be made. Code § 2056(b)(7)(B)(i). The surviving spouse has a qualifying income interest for life if the surviving spouse is entitled to all the income from the property payable annually or at more frequent intervals and no person has a power to appoint any part of the property to any person other than the surviving spouse. Code § 2056(b)(7)(B)(ii). If the first trust is a trust with respect to which a QTIP election was made, subsection (b)(1) prohibits decanting the property to a trust that does not give the surviving spouse a qualifying income interest for life. For example, if the trustee had expanded discretion to distribute principal to the surviving spouse, the trustee could not decant to give the surviving spouse a lifetime power of appointment in favor of descendants. In addition, both Section 11(c)(3) and Section 19(b)(1) would prohibit the trustee from decanting in a manner that would alter the surviving spouse's income interest.

As another example, assume the first trust qualified for the marital deduction under Code Section 2056(b)(5) because the surviving spouse is entitled for life to all the income, the surviving spouse has a testamentary power of appointment in favor of her estate, and no person has any power to appoint other than to the surviving spouse, and the trustee also has a power to make discretionary distributions to the surviving spouse subject to expanded discretion. Subsection (b)(1) prohibits decanting to a second trust that does not give the surviving spouse a right to all income or that gives any person a power to appoint to anyone other than the surviving spouse. Subsection (b)(1) also requires that the second trust qualify for the marital deduction under the same section of the Code, Section 2056(b)(5). It is not sufficient that the second trust qualify for the marital deduction under another section of the Code. Although Code Section 2056(b)(5) requires that the

trust give the surviving spouse a power to appoint to either herself or her estate, the second trust could give the surviving spouse a lifetime power to appoint to herself instead of a testamentary power in favor of her estate, or could expand her testamentary power to include persons other than her estate as potential appointees, because the second trust would still qualify for the marital deduction under Code Section 2056(b)(5). If the first trust, however, gave the surviving spouse a lifetime general power of appointment, the authorized fiduciary could not decant in a manner that eliminated such power of appointment. Section 11(c)(3).

Charitable Deduction. Section 19(b)(2) protects the charitable deduction. The act does not apply to wholly charitable trusts. Section 3(b). While a split interest trust such as a charitable remainder trust or charitable lead trust would not be a wholly charitable trust, in almost all cases the trustee of such a trust would not have discretion to distribute principal to a current beneficiary and therefore there would not be an authorized fiduciary (see Section 2(3)) who would have authority to exercise the decanting power under Section 11 or Section 12. In the rare case in which a split interest charitable trust could be decanted, Section 19(b)(2) requires that the second trust qualify for the charitable deduction under the same provision of the Internal Revenue Code or state law.

Subject to the provisions of Section 14, Section 19(b)(2) does not prohibit the modification or omission of a future gift to a charitable organization even if such gift, if made, would result in a future charitable deduction.

Gift Tax Annual Exclusion. Code Section 2503(b) grants a gift tax annual exclusion for gifts of a "present interest." Present interests are often created in trusts by granting the beneficiary a Crummey right of withdrawal over contributions to the trust. If a trustee could decant in a manner that prematurely terminated a beneficiary's existing Crummey right of withdrawal over a prior contribution to the trust, then arguably the contribution would not qualify for the gift tax annual exclusion. The restriction in Section 11(c)(3) prohibiting the modification or elimination of a presently exercisable power of appointment also protects the annual exclusion for a prior gift to a Crummey trust.

Code Section 2503(c) provides another method for qualifying gifts to a trust for the gift tax annual exclusion. Code Section 2503(c) permits a gift tax annual exclusion for a gift to a trust for an individual under age 21 provided that the property and its income may be expended for the benefit of the donee before attaining age 21, to the extent not so expended passes to the donee upon attaining age 21, and, in the event of the donee's death, is payable to the estate of the donee or pursuant to a general power of appointment.

Assume, for example that the first trust permitted distributions of income and principal subject to expanded discretion to A, provided that the trust property should be distributed to A at age 21 and directed that the trust be distributed to A's estate if A died prior to age 21. A is age 19. The authorized fiduciary could decant to a second trust that, instead of distributing the property to A at age 21, provided A a right to withdraw the trust property for 60 days and that, instead of distributing the property to A's estate, gave A a general testamentary power of appointment. Such a decanting is permitted because the second trust would still qualify under Code Section 2503(c). The authorized fiduciary could not decant to a trust that did not permit it to withdraw the assets until age 30 or that neither gave A a testamentary general power of appointment nor directed distribution of the property to A's estate.

S Corporation Stock. Under Code Section 1361, only certain types of trusts are permitted to own S corporation stock. If the first trust owns S corporation stock, the second trust must also qualify to own S corporation stock under Code Section 1361(c)(2). If the first trust qualifies because it is an electing small business trust (an "ESBT"), the second trust may either be an ESBT or qualify to hold S corporation stock because it is a grantor trust or a qualified subchapter S trust (a "QSST"). Similarly, if the first trust owns S corporation stock and is a grantor trust, the second trust may qualify to hold S corporation stock by being a grantor trust, an ESBT or a QSST.

Subsection (b)(4) imposes a more stringent rule if the first trust is a QSST. In order for a trust to qualify as a QSST, (a) the terms of the trust must require that during the life of the current income beneficiary there shall be only one income beneficiary and (b) all of the income must be distributed to such beneficiary. Code § 1361(d)(3). Thus it may be important that a trust intended to qualify as a QSST not be permitted to be decanted into a trust that would not qualify as a QSST. If the first trust owns S corporation stock and qualifies as an S corporation shareholder because it is a QSST, subsection (b)(4) requires that the second trust also be a QSST. If the first trust is a QSST, it is not sufficient that the

second trust qualify to hold S corporation stock under another provision of the Code. If the authorized fiduciary had the power to modify a trust intended to qualify as a QSST to a trust that did not so qualify, the trust would not be a QSST from its inception.

GST "Annual Exclusion" Gifts. Code Section 2642(c) grants a zero inclusion ratio, essentially a "GST annual exclusion," to gifts that qualify for the gift tax annual exclusion but imposes two additional requirements for gifts to trusts. First, the trust must be only for a single individual and second, if the individual dies before the termination of the trust, the property of the trust must be included in the gross estate of such individual. Thus while gifts to trusts for multiple beneficiaries could qualify for the gift tax annual exclusion through the use of Crummey withdrawal rights, such gifts generally would not qualify for the GST annual exclusion. The Code Section 2642(c) restriction requiring a trust be for a single individual for such individual's life could be violated through decanting if the decanting permitted a remainder beneficiary to receive distributions prior to the individual's death. Section 19(b)(5) prohibits such a modification. The requirement that the trust be included in the gross estate of the individual could perhaps be violated by decanting to a trust that was not includible in the beneficiary's gross estate. Section 19(b)(5) prohibits such a decanting.

Qualified Benefits. Complicated rules determine when the life expectancy of a trust beneficiary can be considered in determining the required minimum distribution rules when a trust is the beneficiary of a qualified retirement plan or IRA. These rules are found in Code Section 401(a)(9) and the corresponding regulations, and in other Code sections that refer to Section 401(a)(9). For example, with IRAs, Code Section 408(a)(6) states: "Under regulations prescribed by the Secretary, rules similar to the rules of section 401(a)(9) and the incidental death benefit requirements of section 401(a) shall apply to the distribution of the entire interest of an individual for whose benefit the trust is maintained." Under the rules in Code Section 401(a)(9), only trusts with certain provisions and restrictions permit the life expectancy of the beneficiary to be used to determine required minimum distributions. If a trustee could decant to a trust that would not meet these requirements, then arguably the old trust would not qualify from the inception to use the life expectancy of the beneficiary.

Subsection (b)(6) applies not only to any trust that

is currently the beneficiary of an individual retirement account ("IRA") or qualified benefit, but also to any successor trust. The need to apply subsection (b)(6) to successor trusts is demonstrated by the following example. Assume Trust A is the beneficiary of Parent's $100,000 IRA. Child is the current beneficiary of Trust A and upon Child's death the assets of Trust A will be distributed to Trusts X and Y for Child's children. Trust A is not a "conduit trust," but qualified to take IRA distributions over Child's life expectancy because Trust A, and Trusts X and Y, have only individuals as beneficiaries and all future beneficiaries must be younger than Child. If Trusts X and Y permitted the exercise of a decanting power in any way that could result in the addition of charities or individuals older than Child as beneficiaries or permissible appointees, Trust A would not have qualified to take IRA distributions over Child C's life expectancy. Therefore, the restrictions on decanting must apply to Trusts X and Y, as well as to Trust A. Trusts X and Y are indirect beneficiaries of the qualified benefit property.

If an attempted decanting violates subsection (b)(6), the qualified benefit property is deemed to be held as a separate share as of the date of the exercise of the decanting power. Holding the qualified benefit property as a separate share permits the remedial rules of Section 22 to apply only with respect to the qualified benefit property and its proceeds.

Foreign Grantor Trusts. Generally, the grantor trust rules apply only to a "grantor" who is a citizen or resident of the United States or a domestic corporation. An exception to this rule applies if (a) the foreign grantor has the power to revest title to the trust property in the grantor and such power is exercisable (1) solely by the grantor without the approval or consent of any other person or (2) with the consent of a related or subordinate party who is subservient to the grantor, or (b) distributions may be made only to the grantor and the grantor's spouse during the life of the grantor. If a foreign trust qualifies as a grantor trust because of Code Section 672(f)(2)(A), subsection (b)(7) provides that the decanting power cannot be exercised to a second trust that does not meet the requirements of Code Section 672(f)(2)(A).

Catch-all. Subsection (b)(8) is a catch-all provision intended to preserve any tax benefits not specifically listed in Section 19 for which the first trust qualified if the first-trust instrument expressly indicates an intent to qualify for the tax benefit or is clearly designed to qualify for the tax benefit. Note that subsection (b)(8) does not address any tax benefits for which the trust may qualify in the future. For example, assume that the first trust was a credit shelter trust that was not subject to federal estate tax at the death of the first to die of a married couple because of the decedent's federal exclusion. Assume that an independent person may make discretionary distributions to the surviving spouse and descendants pursuant to expanded discretion. Also assume that the credit shelter trust was designed so that it would not be included in the surviving spouse's estate. The authorized fiduciary could decant and the second trust could grant the surviving spouse a general power of appointment that would cause inclusion in the surviving spouse's estate. Although the credit shelter trust was designed to be excluded from the surviving spouse's estate, such tax benefit is one that would occur, if at all, in the future at the surviving spouse's death; it is not a tax benefit claimed in the past. Therefore subsection (b)(8) does not prohibit such a modification. If the settlor's purposes include saving taxes, and causing inclusion in the spouse's estate may save more taxes by causing a basis adjustment at the surviving spouse's death even though the trust assets would then be included in the surviving spouse's estate, then such a decanting may be appropriate and is not prohibited by subsection (b)(8).

Grantor Trusts. Subsection (b)(9) expressly permits an exercise of the decanting power to change the income tax status of the trust from a grantor trust to a nongrantor trust or vice versa. Although, absent subsection (b)(9), grantor trust status generally might be viewed as a tax benefit of the first trust, grantor trust status is treated differently under the act because the grantor does not necessarily intend that the grantor trust status be maintained until the grantor's death and because other desirable modifications of the trust may result in a loss of grantor trust status.

An exercise of the decanting power may cause a nongrantor trust to become a grantor trust either as a primary purpose of the exercise of the decanting power or as an incidental consequence of other changes made by the decanting. Subsection (b)(9)(B). It would be fundamentally unfair, however, to permit a decanting to impose on the settlor liability for the second trust's income taxes if the settlor objected to such liability. Therefore subsection (b)(10)(B) permits the settlor to block the decanting by objection during the notice period unless the settlor has the power to cause the second trust to cease to be a grantor trust.

The settlor receives prior notice of the exercise of the decanting power under Section 7(c)(1).

Where the first trust is a grantor trust, often the settlor or another person has the power to cause the trust to cease to be a grantor trust. This power permits the settlor or someone acting on the settlor's behalf to relieve the settlor of the income tax liability for the trust. If the second trust is a grantor trust and does not contain the same provisions permitting the grantor trust treatment to be "turned off," the settlor may block the proposed decanting by objecting during the notice period. Subsection (b)(10)(A).

If a portion of a trust is a grantor trust and the remaining portion is a nongrantor trust, subsection (b)(10) applies to the portion that is a grantor trust.

§ 20. Duration of Second Trust.

(a) Subject to subsection (b), a second trust may have a duration that is the same as or different from the duration of the first trust.

(b) To the extent that property of a second trust is attributable to property of the first trust, the property of the second trust is subject to any rules governing maximum perpetuity, accumulation, or suspension of the power of alienation which apply to property of the first trust.

Comment

To implement the public policy of the state law applicable to the first trust, subsection (b) requires that any maximum perpetuity, accumulation, or suspension-of-the-power-of-alienation period (collectively referred to as a "perpetuities rule") applicable to the first trust apply to the second trust to the extent its assets are attributed to the first trust. This rule is also supported by pragmatic considerations. An exercise of a decanting power could inadvertently violate a perpetuities rule applicable to the first trust if the second trust does not comply with the same perpetuities rule. Even in states that have abolished the maximum perpetuity rule, the state may still impose another perpetuities rule (e.g., a suspension-of-the-power-of-alienation rule), the first trust may still be subject to a rule against perpetuities under prior law or the first trust may be subject to a rule against perpetuities under the law of a different state. Further, if a trust is grandfathered from generation-skipping transfer ("GST") tax or has an inclusion ratio less than one, decanting to a trust that does not comply with the same rule against perpetuities period (or a federal rule against perpetuities period) may have adverse GST consequences.

Thus if the first trust was created in a state with a traditional rule against perpetuities, the authorized fiduciary may not exercise the decanting power to change the governing law to a state with no rule against perpetuities and to eliminate the rule against perpetuities applicable to the first trust.

Where the maximum term of the first trust is measured by reference to lives in being on the date the first trust became irrevocable, Section 20 does not preclude the second trust from using an expanded class of measuring lives so long as the expanded class were in being on the date the first trust became irrevocable. For example, assume the first trust is subject to State A's trust duration rule, which is a traditional rule against perpetuities that requires that an interest in a trust vest within twenty-one years of the last to die of lives in being when the trust became irrevocable. The first trust contains a perpetuities savings clause that requires the trust to terminate twenty-one years after the death of the survivor of the settlor's descendants living when the first trust was created. The second trust may replace the perpetuities savings clause with a provision that requires the trust to terminate twenty-one years after the death of the survivor of the descendants of any grandparent of the settlor who were living when the first trust was created.

As another example, assume the first trust is subject to State A's trust duration rule, which is a traditional rule against perpetuities, but which permits a trust to opt out of the rule against perpetuities. The first trust does not opt out of the rule against perpetuities. The second trust may opt out of the rule against perpetuities if the first trust could have done so.

If the first trust and the state law applicable to the first trust permitted the springing of the "Delaware Tax Trap" of Code Section 2041(a)(3), the second trust may also permit the springing of the Delaware Tax Trap.

The second trust may terminate earlier than the trust duration rule applicable to the first trust would require. Assume Trust A and Trust B are both subject to State Z's trust duration rule, which is a traditional rule against perpetuities. Both trusts were created by the same settlor and contain a perpetuities savings clause that requires the termination of the trust twenty-one years after the death of the survivor of the settlor's descendants living on the date the trust was created. Trust A was created on June 6, 1966. Trust B was created May 5, 1955. Trust A may be decanted into Trust B because Trust B will terminate prior to the rule against perpetuities applicable to Trust A. Trust B may be decanted into Trust A if Trust A is modified to provide, or the decanting instrument provides, that the portion of Trust A attributable to the addition of the assets of Trust B must vest within the rule against perpetuities period applicable to Trust B. The trustee could segregate the assets Trust A receives from the decanting of Trust B. Alternatively, the trustee could determine the fractional share of the total assets attributable to Trust B, based upon values at the time of decanting, and such fractional share of Trust A will be subject to the rule against perpetuities period applicable to Trust B.

If the authorized fiduciary attempts to decant Trust B into Trust A without providing either in Trust A or the decanting instrument that the portion of the trust attributable to Trust B must vest within the rule against perpetuities period applicable to Trust B, the decanting may still be valid. First, the statutes of State Z may contain a rule against perpetuities savings clause that will cause the trust to vest or terminate within the applicable rule against perpetuities period. Second, if there is no statutory savings clause, Section 22 of this act may apply to read into Trust A an appropriate savings clause with respect to the portion of the trust attributable to Trust B.

Section 20 does not address whether, if the decanting changes the place of administration for the trust or the law governing the trust, and the new jurisdiction has a more restrictive trust duration rule, the new jurisdiction may impose its maximum perpetuity, accumulation or suspension-of-the-power-of-alienation period on the second trust. The new jurisdiction may do so if the rule of the first jurisdiction is contrary to a strong public policy of the new jurisdiction. Thus if the first jurisdiction has no rule against perpetuities, and the second jurisdiction has a traditional rule against perpetuities, the second jurisdiction may but need not determine that its rule expresses a strong public policy against perpetual trusts.

Subsection (a) provides that, except as provided by subsection (b), the second trust may have a term that is the same as or different from the term of the first trust. Thus the term of the second trust may be longer than or shorter than the term of the first trust.

§ 21. Need to Distribute Not Required. An authorized fiduciary may exercise the decanting power whether or not under the first trust's discretionary distribution standard the fiduciary would have made or could have been compelled to make a discretionary distribution of principal at the time of the exercise.

Comment

Although the decanting power under Sections 11 and 12 is premised on the authorized fiduciary's power to distribute principal of the first trust to one or more current beneficiaries, the authorized fiduciary may exercise the decanting power even if the authorized fiduciary would not have made a distribution of principal to a current beneficiary under the distribution standard of the first trust. For example, assume a trust permits the trustee to distribute income and principal to S for S's support and health care, considering S's other resources, and that given S's other resources the trustee would not currently make a distribution to S. The trustee may still exercise the decanting power under Section 12.

Section 21, however, does not authorize an exercise of the decanting power under Sections 11 and 12 if the authorized fiduciary does not currently have a power to distribute principal. For example, if a trust permits income to be distributed to A, but does not permit principal distributions until A is age 25 or has a child, and A is age 21 and has no child, the trustee may not decant the trust under Section 11 or Section 12.

§ 22. Saving Provision.

(a) If exercise of the decanting power would be effective under this [act] except that the second-trust instrument in part does not comply with this [act], the exercise of the power is effective and the following rules apply with respect to the principal of the second trust attributable to the exercise of the power:

(1) A provision in the second-trust instrument which is not permitted under this [act] is void to the extent necessary to comply with this [act].

(2) A provision required by this [act] to be in the second-trust instrument which is not contained in the instrument is deemed to be included in the instrument to the extent necessary to comply with this [act].

(b) If a trustee or other fiduciary of a second trust determines that subsection (a) applies to a prior exercise of the decanting power, the fiduciary shall take corrective action consistent with the fiduciary's duties.

Comment

In order to provide as much certainty as possible to the trustee and the beneficiaries with respect to the operative terms of a trust, an exercise of a decanting power should not be wholly invalid because the second-trust instrument in part violates this act. Section 22(a) modifies the second-trust instrument to delete impermissible provisions in the second-trust instrument and to insert required provisions in the second-trust instrument. For example, if the second trust sets forth an impermissible rule against perpetuities period (see Section 20), the other modifications made by the decanting should be effective.

The remedial rules of Section 22 apply only to the least extent required to comply with this act. Thus if a provision in the second-trust instrument would be permissible with respect to some of the trust property but is impermissible with respect to other trust property, such provision will be void only as to the trust property with respect to which it is impermissible. Further, any modification to a provision of the second-trust instrument that is required by Section 22 should be the modification that implements the intended modifications to the greatest extent permitted under the act. Thus the authorized fiduciary's intent is relevant in determining how to apply the provisions of Section 22.

For example, assume a trust holds $500,000 of marketable assets and is the beneficiary of Grantor's $100,000 IRA. Grantor's Child is the sole current beneficiary of the trust. The trust is qualified to use Child's life expectancy in determining the distribution period for the IRA because the trust restricts all future beneficiaries, including appointees under any power of appointment and takers in default, to individuals younger than Child. The authorized fiduciary attempts to decant the trust to permit Child to appoint to her spouse. This is in violation of Section 19(b)(6) because if Child could appoint the IRA to a spouse who is older than Child, Trust would not have qualified to take IRA distributions over Child's life expectancy. Section 19(b)(6) causes the qualified benefit property and any reinvested distributions of the qualified benefit property to be treated as a separate share. Section 22 will void the power to appoint to a spouse only with respect to the qualified benefit property and any reinvested distributions of the qualified benefit property, and only if the spouse is (or could be) older than Child, because that is the least intrusive remediation required to comply with Section 19(b)(6).

As another example, assume the authorized fiduciary attempts to decant a trust to permit Child to appoint to her sibling. If Child's sibling is older than Child, this is in violation of Section 19(b)(6) because if Child could appoint the IRA to her older sibling, the trust would not have qualified to take IRA distributions over Child's life expectancy. Section 19(b)(6) causes the qualified benefit property and any reinvested distributions of the qualified benefit property to be treated as a separate share. Section 22 will void the power to appoint to a sibling only with respect to the qualified benefit property and any reinvested distributions of the qualified benefit property, which are treated as a separate share, and only if the sibling is older than Child, because that is the least intrusive remediation required to comply with Section 19(b)(6).

As yet another example, assume the authorized fiduciary attempts to decant Trust to change (1) the successor fiduciaries, (2) the manner in which the first trust instrument directed that the authorized fiduciary be compensated, which will increase the authorized fiduciary's compensation, and (3) the identity of the person who can remove the authorized fiduciary (the "Remover"). The authorized fiduciary obtains the written consent of the qualified beneficiaries of the second trust, but does not obtain consent of the Remover or approval by the court. The changes to the successor fiduciaries will be effective. The change to the authorized fiduciary's compensation will also be effective because the requirement in Section 16(a) or Section 16(b) was met. The change to the identity of the Remover will not be effective because the Remover named in the first trust instrument did not consent. See Section 18.

Section 22(b) provides that if the savings provision in Section 22(a) applies, the trustee or other fiduciary shall take corrective action consistent with the fiduciary's duties. When Section 22(a) applies, the copy of the second-trust instrument provided to qualified beneficiaries and other parties under Section 7 would not accurately state the terms of the

second trust. A trustee or other fiduciary may have a duty to notify certain persons of the accurate terms of the second trust. See, for example, Section 813(a) of the Uniform Trust Code imposing a duty on the trustee to keep the qualified beneficiaries reasonably informed about the administration of the trust and the material facts necessary for them to protect their interests.

Additional corrective action may be required, especially if distributions were made or not made in reliance on the assumed terms of the second-trust instrument and such terms are altered by Section 22(a).

Where a fiduciary is uncertain about whether corrective action should be taken, the fiduciary may apply to the court for instructions under Section 9.

§ 23. Trust for Care of an Animal.

(a) In this section:

(1) "Animal trust" means a trust or an interest in a trust created to provide for the care of one or more animals.

(2) "Protector" means a person appointed in an animal trust to enforce the trust on behalf of the animal or, if no such person is appointed in the trust, a person appointed by the court for that purpose.

(b) The decanting power may be exercised over an animal trust that has a protector to the extent the trust could be decanted under this [act] if each animal that benefits from the trust were an individual, if the protector consents in a signed record to the exercise of the power.

(c) A protector for an animal has the rights under this [act] of a qualified beneficiary.

(d) Notwithstanding any other provision of this [act], if a first trust is an animal trust, in an exercise of the decanting power, the second trust must provide that trust property may be applied only to its intended purpose for the period the first trust benefitted the animal.

Comment

Section 408 of the Uniform Trust Code permits a trust to be created for one or more animals who are alive during the settlor's lifetime. "Animal" is not defined in the Uniform Trust Code and thus is not defined in this act. It should be construed in its common usage as referring to a multicell living organism that feeds on organic matter, and that typically is motile at some point in its life and has sensory organs. It thus includes, for example, mammals, birds, reptiles, fish and insects. In this section, the term "animal" should be construed to mean nonhuman animals. The term includes, without limitation, pets and domesticated animals.

The Uniform Trust Code provides that an animal trust may be enforced by a person appointed in the terms of the trust or, if no such person is appointed,

by a person appointed by the court. Subsection (a)(2) incorporates that concept in the definition of "protector."

One impediment to applying decanting to an animal trust is that animal trusts often do not technically have a beneficiary because the definition of "beneficiary" is restricted to a person who has a particular interest in the trust. The definition of the term "person" does not include a nonhuman animal. This impediment is resolved by treating the animal as if it were a person so that the animal trust does have a beneficiary for purposes of the decanting power. The extent of the decanting power would then depend upon the amount of discretion that the authorized fiduciary has to make distributions for the animal and to any other person. If the trustee has expanded discretion, then the decanting power could be exercised under Section 11. If the trustee only has limited discretion to make distributions to the animal, then the decanting power can be exercised under Section 12.

The second impediment to exercising a decanting power over an animal trust is identifying a person who can receive notice of the decanting on behalf of the animal and bring a court action with respect to the decanting if appropriate. This impediment is resolved because an animal trust will usually have a person who is designated to enforce the trust on behalf of the animal. Section 408(b) of the Uniform Trust Code provides that such a trust may be enforced by a person appointed in the terms of the trust or, if no person is so appointed, by a person appointed by the court. Thus if an animal trust did not designate a person to enforce the trust on behalf of the animal, the trustee could request that the court appoint such a person and then proceed with any exercise of the decanting power.

Section 408 of the Uniform Trust Code provides that the property of an animal trust may be applied only to its intended use, except to the extent the court determines that the value of the trust property exceeds the amount required for the intended use. Although Section 23 permits the decanting of an animal trust, it mirrors the requirement of the Uniform Trust Code that the property of the animal trust may be applied only to its intended use for the period of time the first trust was intended to benefit the animals (usually the lives of the animals). Therefore, the authorized fiduciary cannot, by decanting, reduce the value of the animal trust; such a power is reserved only to the court. Further, the authorized fiduciary cannot divert assets of the animal trust to other beneficiaries of the trust.

Assume that Trust was established for the support of Double Trouble, a husky, after the death of Double Trouble's human companion. Trust directs that the Trust shall continue to maintain Double Trouble in her Alaskan house, which is owned by the Trust, under the care of Joan, a retired musher, and permits distributions of income and principal to maintain the house and for Double Trouble's best interests so long as Double Trouble is living. Upon the death of Double Trouble, Trust is distributed to the Husky Rescue Society, a charitable organization. Double Trouble is aging and the veterinarian advises a move to a warmer climate. The assets of the Trust are diminishing, and may not be sufficient to maintain the Alaskan house and pay for Double Trouble's care. Joan is aging too, and would prefer to care for Double Trouble in Joan's house in Hawaii. The authorized trustee may, with the consent of the protector, modify Trust to permit the sale of the Alaskan house and to permit Joan to care for Double Trouble in her Hawaii home. Notice of the decanting must be provided to the protector, the Husky Rescue Society and to the Attorney General (or other official with enforcement authority over charitable interests). The second trust, however, may not add Joan as a beneficiary because such a modification would not be permitted under Section 11. Nor may the decanting provide that one year after the move to Hawaii, one-half of the principal will be distributed to the Husky Rescue Society, because Section 23(d) requires that the trust property be applied only for its intended purpose (the care of Double Trouble) for the period the first trust benefitted the animal (the life of Double Trouble).

Under the Uniform Directed Trust Act (UDTA), approved by the Uniform Law Commission in 2017, a person named by the terms of a trust to enforce the trust qualifies as a "trust director" in a state that adopts the UDTA. See Official Comment to UDTA Section 6, stating in relevant part:

> *Pet and other noncharitable trust enforcers.* Statutes in every state validate a trust for a pet animal and certa other noncharitable purposes. Following Uniform Probate Code § 2-907(c)(4) (1993) and Uniform Trust Code §§ 408(b) and 409(2) (2000), most of these statutes authorize enforcement of the trust by a person named in the terms of the trust. In a state that enacts this act, such a person would be a trust director.

Historical Note. The previous paragraph of this comment was added in 2018 following the approval of the Uniform Directed Trust Act.

§ 24. Terms of Second Trust. A reference in [this state's trust code] to a trust instrument or terms of the trust includes a second-trust instrument and the terms of the second trust.

Legislative Note: Conforming amendments may be required to this state's trust code.

§ 25. Settlor.

(a) For purposes of law of this state other than this [act] and subject to subsection (b), a settlor of a first trust is deemed to be the settlor of the second trust with respect to the portion of the principal of the first trust subject to the exercise of the decanting power.

(b) In determining settlor intent with respect to a second trust, the intent of a settlor of the first trust, a settlor of the second trust, and the authorized fiduciary may be considered.

Legislative Note: *Conforming amendments may be required to this state's trust code.*

Comment

"Settlor" is defined in Section 2(25) as the person who creates or contributes property of the trust, except as provided in Section 25. The comments to Section 102 and Section 103 of the Uniform Trust Code generally consider the person who funded a trust as the settlor and would not treat as the settlor a nominal grantor, meaning a person who signs the trust instrument to create the trust but who does not contribute the property to the trust (except perhaps for nominal funding).

When a new trust instrument is created for purposes of serving as the second trust for a decanting, the second-trust instrument may be signed by the trustee of the first trust, a beneficiary, the settlor of the first trust, an attorney for the settlor, the trustee or a beneficiary of the first trust, or some other person. Under these circumstances, the creator of the second trust generally will not be the settlor of the second trust unless such person funded the first trust or is the authorized fiduciary exercising the decanting power.

For most purposes, when a trust is decanted the settlor of the first trust should be considered the settlor of the second trust to the extent of the decanting. If the second trust is a pre-existing trust funded by a different settlor, then the original settlor of the second trust would continue to be considered the settlor over the portion of the trust property attributable to that person's contribution and the original settlor of the first trust would be considered the settlor of the portion of the second trust property attributable to the decanting. This general rule of Section 25(a) would apply, for example, for purposes of determining who holds the rights granted to the settlor or who must consent when the settlor's consent is required for an action and for tax purposes. For example, under the Uniform Trust Code this rule would apply for purposes of Section 113 (Insurable Interest), Section 301(d) (limiting the ability of a settlor to represent a beneficiary), Section 405(a) (enforcement of a charitable trust), Section 411 (modification of a trust with the settlor's intent), Section 505 (Creditor's Claims), Section 706(a) (request to remove a trustee), and Section 814 (limiting certain discretionary powers).

For purposes of determining the settlor's intent or purpose in creating a trust, or whether the settlor did not anticipate certain circumstances, it may sometimes be appropriate to consider the intent of the original settlor of the second trust. For example, if a decanting distribution is made to a pre-existing trust with property of its own, the intent of the original settlor of the second trust may be more relevant in construing, modifying or reforming the second-trust instrument after the decanting distribution. In such a case, the decanting distribution adopts the language of the second-trust instrument, which is most appropriately construed with respect to the intent of the creator of such trust. When a decanting distribution is made to a second trust created by the authorized fiduciary for the purposes of decanting, or when the decanting is a modification of the first trust, the intent of the authorized fiduciary may be most relevant in later construing the terms of the second trust, or at least the terms modified by the decanting. The intent of the settlor of the first trust may still be relevant, however, because the decanting would have been made to better carry out the purposes of the first trust. Further, to the extent the second trust does not modify the terms of the first trust, the intent of the settlor of the first trust would be relevant in construing such terms.

Section 25(b) would apply, under the Uniform Trust Code, with respect to Section 412 (Modification or Termination Because of Unanticipated Circumstances), Section 415 (Reformation to Correct Mistakes) and Section 416 (Modification to Achieve Settlor's Tax Objectives). For example, under Section 412 of the Uniform Trust Code, a court may make certain trust modifications if because of "circumstances not anticipated by the settlor, modification or termination will further the purposes of the trust." The modification, to the extent practicable, is to be made in "accordance with the settlor's probable intention." Thus where the authorized fiduciary of the first trust, or some other person, has created the second trust, the intent of the maker of the second trust may be relevant in determining, with respect to the second trust, what circumstances were not anticipated by the settlor and what would be the settlor's probable intent.

Section 25(b) may also apply in other contexts for determining the purposes and material purposes of the trust. The material purposes of the trust may, for example, be relevant in determining whether a nonjudicial settlement agreement is valid. Settlor intent is relevant in determining a trust's purposes and material purposes.

§ 26. Later-Discovered Property.

(a) Except as otherwise provided in subsection (c), if exercise of the decanting power was intended to distribute all the principal of the first trust to one or more second trusts, later-discovered property belonging to the first trust and property paid to or acquired by the first trust after the exercise of the power is part of the trust estate of the second trust or trusts.

(b) Except as otherwise provided in subsection (c), if exercise of the decanting power was intended to distribute less than all the principal of the first trust to one or more second trusts, later-discovered property belonging to the first trust or property paid to or acquired by the first trust after exercise of the power remains part of the trust estate of the first trust.

(c) An authorized fiduciary may provide in an exercise of the decanting power or by the terms of a second trust for disposition of later-discovered property belonging to the first trust or property paid to or acquired by the first trust after exercise of the power.

Comment

If the decanting power is exercised by modifying the terms of the first trust, the trustee could either treat the second trust created by such modification as a new trust, in which case the property of the first trust would need to be transferred to the second trust, or alternatively treat the second trust as a continuation of the first trust, in which case the property of the first trust would not need to be retitled. When the second trust is a continuation of the first trust, any property owned by the first trust is still owned by the trust after the decanting, even if the authorized fiduciary is not aware of such property at the time of the decanting.

When the decanting power is exercised by distributing property of the first trust to a separate second trust, regardless of whether the terms of such second trust are set forth in an entirely separate trust instrument or a modification of the first-trust instrument, the property of the first trust need to be transferred to the second trust(s). Inevitably, there will be cases where the trustee fails to transfer all of the property to the second trust. The trustee can protect against this possibility by, in the exercise of the decanting power, making a global assignment of all trust property to the second trust. When the property of the first trust is being divided among more than one second trusts or not all of the property of the first trust is being decanted, it is more complicated, but still possible, to specify in the exercise of the decanting power how later-discovered property should be allocated.

Section 26(c) explicitly permits an authorized fiduciary to provide, in an exercise of the decanting power or by the terms of a second trust, for disposition of later-discovered property belonging to the first trust or property paid to or acquired by the first trust after exercise of the decanting power. For example, if an authorized fiduciary exercises the decanting power over a trust to create a special-needs trust for the settlor's child J and to create a separate trust for the settlor's other children, the exercise of the decanting power might state that the trust for J will be funded with marketable securities and cash with a value of $1,000,000 and that all other property, including later-discovered property, will be distributed to and owned by the trust for the other children. Assume the trust for J is then funded with $1,000,000 of marketable securities and all other property then known to the trustee is assigned to the trust for the other children. If subsequently other trust assets are discovered, it would be clear that they belong to the trust for the other children and not the trust for J.

The trustee in transferring title to the first trust's property pursuant to a decanting may also take the precaution of executing a global assignment of all property not otherwise expressly transferred to the appropriate second trusts.

Section 26(a) and (b) specify default rules when later-discovered property and property paid to or acquired by the first trust after the exercise of the decanting power is not expressly allocated to a particular trust by the exercise, by the second-trust instrument or by an assignment.

Subsection (a) provides that if the decanting intended to distribute all of the principal of the first trust to one or more second trusts, then the property is part of the second trust or trusts. When there is more than one second trusts, the exercise of the decanting power might specify their respective interests in the property of the first trust or if it does not, the second trusts may need to reach agreement about their respective ownership interests.

Subsection (b) provides that if the decanting was not intended to distribute all of the principal of the first trust to one or more second trusts, such property remains part of the first trust.

§ 27. Obligations. A debt, liability, or other obligation enforceable against property of a first trust is enforceable to the same extent against the property when held by the second trust after exercise of the decanting power.

Comment

It would be inequitable to permit a second trust to evade liabilities incurred by the trustee of the first trust to the extent the creditor would have been entitled to satisfaction out of the trust property. Section 27 provides that a debt, liability or other obligation of the first trust against property of a first trust is enforceable to the same extent against such property when held by the second trust. Section 27 may apply to contractual claims, obligations arising from ownership or control of trust property and to torts committed in the course of administering a trust. *Cf.* Uniform Trust Code § 1010(c).

The Restatement Second of Trusts provides various situations in which a person to whom the trustee has incurred a liability in the course of the administration of a trust can by a proceeding in equity reach trust property and apply it to the satisfaction of such person's claim. See Restatement Second of Trusts § 267. Section 268 of the Restatement Second of Trusts provides that the creditor can reach trust property to the extent the creditor cannot obtain satisfaction of the claim out of the trustee's individual property to the extent the trustee is entitled to exoneration out of the trust estate. Section 269 of the Restatement Second of Trusts provides that a creditor who cannot obtain satisfaction out of the trustee's individual property can by a proceeding in equity reach trust property to the extent the trust estate has benefitted. Section 270 of the Restatement Second of Trusts permits the creditor to reach trust property if by the terms of the trust the settlor manifested an intention to confer such a power on the creditor. Section 271 of the Restatement Second of Trusts permits a creditor to reach trust property on a contractual claim if the contract provides that the trustee shall not be personally liable upon the contract and the contract was properly made by the trustee in the administration of the trust. Section 271A of the Restatement Second of Trusts permits a creditor to obtain satisfaction out of the trust estate if it is equitable to permit him to do so.

For example, assume Chicago Bank makes a loan to the trustee of First Trust, secured by First Trust's holdings of Fuchsia Corp. stock. The loan provides that trustee is not personally liable. The trustee decants First Trust and distributes all of its assets to Second Trust. Chicago Bank may enforce the loan against the property of Second Trust, including the Fuchsia Corp. stock, to the same extent it could have enforced the loan against the property of First Trust. If Second Trust also owns property not attributed to the decanting, Section 27 does not expose such property to Chicago Bank's claim.

Assume instead that the trustee of First Trust decanted and distributed all of the Fuchsia Corp. stock to Second Trust, and distributed all of the other assets of First Trust to Third Trust. Chicago Bank may enforce the loan against the Fuchsia Corp. stock held by Second Trust to the same extent it could have enforced the loan against the Fuchsia Corp. stock when it was held by First Trust. If prior to the decanting Chicago Bank could have enforced the loan against the property of First Trust other than the Fuchsia Corp. stock to the extent the value of the

Fuchsia Corp. stock was insufficient to satisfy the loan, after the decanting Chicago Bank may enforce the loan, to the extent the Fuchsia Corp. stock is insufficient to satisfy the loan, against the other property of Second Trust and Third Trust to the extent it was attributable to the property of First Trust.

Section 27 only applies to a debt, liability or other obligation that is in existence and enforceable against the property of the first trust at the time of the decanting.

Section 27 is not intended to impede an authorized fiduciary from exercising the decanting power in a manner that may protect the property of the second trust from debts, liabilities or obligations of the settlor or a beneficiary to a greater extent than the property of the first trust would have been protected from such debts, liabilities or obligations. For example, a decanting may add a spendthrift provision to a trust. As another example, a decanting under Section 11 could postpone or eliminate a prospective withdrawal right of a beneficiary or eliminate a general power of appointment that is not presently exercisable.

§ 28. Uniformity of Application and Construction. In applying and construing this uniform act, consideration must be given to the need to promote uniformity of the law with respect to its subject matter among states that enact it.

§ 29. Relation to Electronic Signatures in Global and National Commerce Act. This [act] modifies, limits, or supersedes the Electronic Signatures in Global and National Commerce Act, 15 U.S.C. Section 7001 et seq., but does not modify, limit, or supersede Section 101(c) of that act, 15 U.S.C. Section 7001(c), or authorize electronic delivery of any of the notices described in Section 103(b) of that act, 15 U.S.C. Section 7003(b).

[**§ 30. Severability.** If any provision of this [act] or its application to any person or circumstance is held invalid, the invalidity does not affect other provisions or applications of this [act] which can be given effect without the invalid provision or application, and to this end the provisions of this [act] are severable.]

Legislative Note: *Include this section only if this state lacks a general severability statute or a decision by the highest court of this state stating a general rule of severability.*

§ 31. Repeals; Conforming Amendments.
    (a) . . . .
    (b) . . . .
    (c) . . . .

§ 32. Effective Date. This [act] takes effect . . . .

UNIFORM PRINCIPAL AND INCOME ACT (1997)

(with Subsequent Amendments)

Table of Sections

[Article] 5. Allocation of Disbursements During Administration of Trust

[Article] 6. Miscellaneous Provisions

Prefatory Note

This revision of the 1931 Uniform Principal and Income Act and the 1962 Revised Uniform Principal and Income Act has two purposes.

One purpose is to revise the 1931 and the 1962 Acts. Revision is needed to support the now widespread use of the revocable living trust as a will substitute, to change the rules in those Acts that experience has shown need to be changed, and to establish new rules to cover situations not provided for in the old Acts, including rules that apply to financial instruments invented since 1962.

The other purpose is to provide a means for implementing the transition to an investment regime based on principles embodied in the Uniform Prudent Investor Act, especially the principle of investing for total return rather than a certain level of "income" as traditionally perceived in terms of interest, dividends, and rents.

Revision of the 1931 and 1962 Acts

The prior Acts and this revision of those Acts deal with four questions affecting the rights of beneficiaries:

(1) How is income earned during the probate of an estate to be distributed to trusts and to persons who receive outright bequests of specific property, pecuniary gifts, and the residue?

(2) When an income interest in a trust begins (i.e., when a person who creates the trust dies or when she transfers property to a trust during life), what property is principal that will eventually go to the remainder beneficiaries and what is income?

(3) When an income interest ends, who gets the income that has been received but not distributed, or that is due but not yet collected, or that has accrued but is not yet due?

(4) After an income interest begins and before it ends, how should its receipts and disbursements be allocated to or between principal and income?

Changes in the traditional sections are of three types: new rules that deal with situations not covered by the prior Acts, clarification of provisions in the 1962 Act, and changes to rules in the prior Acts.

New rules. Issues addressed by some of the more significant new rules include:

(1) The application of the probate administration rules to revocable living trusts after the settlor's death and to other terminating trusts. Articles 2 and 3.

(2) The payment of interest or some other amount on the delayed payment of an outright pecuniary gift that is made pursuant to a trust agreement instead of a will when the agreement or state law does not provide for such a payment. Section 201(3).

(3) The allocation of net income from partnership interests acquired by the trustee other than from a decedent (the old Acts deal only with partnership interests acquired from a decedent). Section 401.

(4) An "unincorporated entity" concept has been introduced to deal with businesses operated by a trustee, including farming and livestock operations,

and investment activities in rental real estate, natural resources, timber, and derivatives. Section 403.

(5) The allocation of receipts from discount obligations such as zero-coupon bonds. Section 406(b).

(6) The allocation of net income from harvesting and selling timber between principal and income. Section 412.

(7) The allocation between principal and income of receipts from derivatives, options, and asset-backed securities. Sections 414 and 415.

(8) Disbursements made because of environmental laws. Section 502(a)(7).

(9) Income tax obligations resulting from the ownership of S corporation stock and interests in partnerships. Section 505.

(10) The power to make adjustments between principal and income to correct inequities caused by tax elections or peculiarities in the way the fiduciary income tax rules apply. Section 506.

Clarifications and changes in existing rules. A number of matters provided for in the prior Acts have been changed or clarified in this revision, including the following:

(1) An income beneficiary's estate will be entitled to receive only net income actually received by a trust before the beneficiary's death and not items of accrued income. Section 303.

(2) Income from a partnership is based on actual distributions from the partnership, in the same manner as corporate distributions. Section 401.

(3) Distributions from corporations and partnerships that exceed 20% of the entity's gross assets will be principal whether or not intended by the entity to be a partial liquidation. Section 401(d)(2).

(4) Deferred compensation is dealt with in greater detail in a separate section. Section 409.

(5) The 1962 Act rule for "property subject to depletion," (patents, copyrights, royalties, and the like), which provides that a trustee may allocate up to 5% of the asset's inventory value to income and the balance to principal, has been replaced by a rule that allocates 90% of the amounts received to principal and the balance to income. Section 410.

(6) The percentage used to allocate amounts received from oil and gas has been changed - 90% of those receipts are allocated to principal and the balance to income. Section 411.

(7) The unproductive property rule has been eliminated for trusts other than marital deduction trusts. Section 413.

(8) Charging depreciation against income is no longer mandatory, and is left to the discretion of the trustee. Section 503.

Coordination with the Uniform Prudent Investor Act

The law of trust investment has been modernized. See Uniform Prudent Investor Act (1994); Restatement (Third) of Trusts: Prudent Investor Rule (1992) (hereinafter Restatement of Trusts 3d: Prudent Investor Rule). Now it is time to update the principal and income allocation rules so the two bodies of doctrine can work well together. This revision deals conservatively with the tension between modern investment theory and traditional income allocation. The starting point is to use the traditional system. If prudent investing of all the assets in a trust viewed as a portfolio and traditional allocation effectuate the intent of the settlors, then nothing need be done. The Act, however, helps the trustee who has made a prudent, modern portfolio-based investment decision that has the initial effect of skewing return from all the assets under management, viewed as a portfolio, as between income and principal beneficiaries. The Act gives that trustee a power to reallocate the portfolio return suitably. To leave a trustee constrained by the traditional system would inhibit the trustee's ability to fully implement modern portfolio theory.

As to modern investing see, e.g., the Preface to, terms of, and Comments to the Uniform Prudent Investor Act (1994); the discussion and reporter's note by Edward C. Halbach, Jr. in Restatement of Trusts 3d: Prudent Investor Rule; John H. Langbein, The Uniform Prudent Investor Act and the Future of Trust Investing, 81 Iowa L. Rev. 641 (1996); Bevis Longstreth, Modern Investment Management and the Prudent Man Rule (1986); John H. Langbein & Richard A. Posner, The Revolution in Trust Investment Law, 62 A.B.A.J. 887 (1976); and Jeffrey N. Gordon, The Puzzling Persistence of the Constrained Prudent Man Rule, 62 N.Y.U. L. Rev. 52 (1987). See also R.A. Brearly, An Introduction to Risk and Return from Common Stocks (2d ed. 1983); Jonathan R. Macey, An Introduction to Modern Financial Theory (1991). As to the need for principal and income reform see, e.g., Joel C. Dobris, Real Return, Modern Portfolio Theory and College, University and Foundation Decisions on Annual Spending From Endowments: A Visit to the World of Spending Rules, 28 Real Prop., Prob., & Tr. J. 49 (1993); Joel C. Dobris, The Probate World at the End of the Century: Is a New Principal and Income Act in Your Future?, 28 Real Prop., Prob., & Tr. J. 393 (1993); and Kenneth L. Hirsch, Inflation and the Law of Trusts, 18 Real Prop., Prob., & Tr. J. 601 (1983).

See also, Jerold I. Horn, The Prudent Investor Rule - Impact on Drafting and Administration of Trusts, 20 ACTEC Notes 26 (Summer 1994).

[ARTICLE] 1
DEFINITIONS AND FIDUCIARY DUTIES

§ 101. Short Title. This [Act] may be cited as the Uniform Principal and Income Act (1997).

§ 102. Definitions. In this [Act]:

(1) "Accounting period" means a calendar year unless another 12-month period is selected by a fiduciary. The term includes a portion of a calendar year or other 12-month period that begins when an income interest begins or ends when an income interest ends.

(2) "Beneficiary" includes, in the case of a decedent's estate, an heir [, legatee,] and devisee and, in the case of a trust, an income beneficiary and a remainder beneficiary.

(3) "Fiduciary" means a personal representative or a trustee. The term includes an executor, administrator, successor personal representative, special administrator, and a person performing substantially the same function.

(4) "Income" means money or property that a fiduciary receives as current return from a principal asset. The term includes a portion of receipts from a sale, exchange, or liquidation of a principal asset, to the extent provided in [Article] 4.

(5) "Income beneficiary" means a person to whom net income of a trust is or may be payable.

(6) "Income interest" means the right of an income beneficiary to receive all or part of net income, whether the terms of the trust require it to be distributed or authorize it to be distributed in the trustee's discretion.

(7) "Mandatory income interest" means the right of an income beneficiary to receive net income that the terms of the trust require the fiduciary to distribute.

(8) "Net income" means the total receipts allocated to income during an accounting period minus the disbursements made from income during the period, plus or minus transfers under this [Act] to or from income during the period.

(9) "Person" means an individual, corporation, business trust, estate, trust, partnership, limited liability company, association, joint venture, government; governmental subdivision, agency, or instrumentality; public corporation, or any other legal or commercial entity.

(10) "Principal" means property held in trust for distribution to a remainder beneficiary when the trust terminates.

(11) "Remainder beneficiary" means a person entitled to receive principal when an income interest ends.

(12) "Terms of a trust" means the manifestation of the intent of a settlors or decedent with respect to the trust, expressed in a manner that admits of its proof in a judicial proceeding, whether by written or spoken words or by conduct.

(13) "Trustee" includes an original, additional, or successor trustee, whether or not appointed or confirmed by a court.

Comment

"Income beneficiary." The definitions of income beneficiary (Section 102(5)) and income interest (Section 102(6)) cover both mandatory and discretionary beneficiaries and interests. There are no definitions for "discretionary income beneficiary" or "discretionary income interest" because those terms are not used in the Act.

Inventory value. There is no definition for inventory value in this Act because the provisions in which that term was used in the 1962 Act have either been eliminated (in the case of the underproductive property provision) or changed in a way that eliminates the need for the term (in the case of bonds and other money obligations, property subject to depletion, and the method for determining entitlement to income distributed from a probate estate).

"**Net income.**" The reference to "transfers under this Act to or from income" means transfers made under Sections 104(a), 412(b), 502(b), 503(b), 504(a), and 506.

"**Terms of a trust.**" This term was chosen in preference to "terms of the trust instrument" (the phrase used in the 1962 Act) to make it clear that the Act applies to oral trusts as well as those whose terms are expressed in written documents. The definition is based on the Restatement (Second) of Trusts § 4 (1959) and the Restatement (Third) of Trusts § 4 (Tent. Draft No. 1, 1996). Constructional preferences or rules would also apply, if necessary, to determine the terms of the trust.

Former (1962) Version

§ 1. [Definitions.] As used in this Act:

(1) "income beneficiary" means the person to whom income is presently payable or for whom it is accumulated for distribution as income;

(2) "inventory value" means the cost of property purchased by the trustee and the market value of other property at the time it became subject to the trust, but in the case of a testamentary trust the trustee may use any value finally determined for the purposes of an estate or inheritance tax;

(3) "remainderman" means the person entitled to principal, including income which has been accumulated and added to principal;

(4) "trustee" means an original trustee and any successor or added trustee.

---

§ 103. Fiduciary Duties; General Principles.

(a) In allocating receipts and disbursements to or between principal and income, and with respect to any matter within the scope of [Articles] 2 and 3, a fiduciary:

(1) shall administer a trust or estate in accordance with the terms of the trust or the will, even if there is a different provision in this [Act];

(2) may administer a trust or estate by the exercise of a discretionary power of administration given to the fiduciary by the terms of the trust or the will, even if the exercise of the power produces a result different from a result required or permitted by this [Act];

(3) shall administer a trust or estate in accordance with this [Act] if the terms of the trust or the will do not contain a different provision or do not give the fiduciary a discretionary power of administration; and

(4) shall add a receipt or charge a disbursement to principal to the extent that the terms of the trust and this [Act] do not provide a rule for allocating the receipt or disbursement to or between principal and income.

(b) In exercising the power to adjust under Section 104(a) or a discretionary power of administration regarding a matter within the scope of this [Act], whether granted by the terms of a trust, a will, or this [Act], a fiduciary shall administer a trust or estate impartially, based on what is fair and reasonable to all of the beneficiaries, except to the extent that the terms of the trust or the will clearly manifest an intention that the fiduciary shall or may favor one or more of the beneficiaries. A determination in accordance with this [Act] is presumed to be fair and reasonable to all of the beneficiaries.

Comment

Prior Act. The rule in Section 2(a) of the 1962 Act is restated in Section 103(a), without changing its substance, to emphasize that the Act contains only default rules and that provisions in the terms of the trust are paramount. However, Section 2(a) of the 1962 Act applies only to the allocation of receipts and disbursements to or between principal and income. In this Act, the first sentence of Section 103(a) states that it also applies to matters within the scope of Articles 2 and 3. Section 103(a)(2) incorporates the rule in Section 2(b) of the 1962 Act that a discretionary allocation made by the trustee that is contrary to a rule in the Act should not give rise to an inference of imprudence or partiality by the trustee.

The Act deletes the language that appears at the end of 1962 Act Section 2(a)(3) - "and in view of the manner in which men of ordinary prudence, discretion and judgment would act in the management of their affairs" - because persons of ordinary prudence, discretion and judgment, acting in the management of their own affairs do not normally think in terms of the interests of successive beneficiaries. If there is an analogy to an individual's decision-making process, it is probably the individual's decision to spend or to save, but this is not a useful guideline for trust administration. No case has been found in which a court has relied on the "prudent man" rule of the 1962 Act.

Fiduciary discretion. The general rule is that if a discretionary power is conferred upon a trustee, the exercise of that power is not subject to control by a court except to prevent an abuse of discretion. Restatement (Second) of Trusts § 187. The situations in which a court will control the exercise of a trustee's discretion are discussed in the comments to § 187. See also id. § 233 Comment *p*.

Questions for which there is no provision. Section 103(a)(4) allocates receipts and disbursements to principal when there is no provision for a different allocation in the terms of the trust, the will, or the Act. This may occur because money is received from a financial instrument not available at the present time (inflation-indexed bonds might have fallen into this category had they been announced after this Act was approved by the Commissioners on Uniform State Laws) or because a transaction is of a type or occurs in a manner not anticipated by the Drafting Committee for this Act or the drafter of the trust instrument.

Allocating to principal a disbursement for which there is no provision in the Act or the terms of the trust preserves the income beneficiary's level of income in the year it is allocated to principal, but thereafter will reduce the amount of income produced by the principal. Allocating to principal a receipt for which there is no provision will increase the income received by the income beneficiary in subsequent years, and will eventually, upon

termination of the trust, also favor the remainder beneficiary. Allocating these items to principal implements the rule that requires a trustee to administer the trust impartially, based on what is fair and reasonable to both income and remainder beneficiaries. However, if the trustee decides that an adjustment between principal and income is needed to enable the trustee to comply with Section 103(b), after considering the return from the portfolio as a whole, the trustee may make an appropriate adjustment under Section 104(a).

Duty of impartiality. Whenever there are two or more beneficiaries, a trustee is under a duty to deal impartially with them. Restatement of Trusts 3d: Prudent Investor Rule § 183 (1992). This rule applies whether the beneficiaries' interests in the trust are concurrent or successive. If the terms of the trust give the trustee discretion to favor one beneficiary over another, a court will not control the exercise of such discretion except to prevent the trustee from abusing it. Id. § 183, Comment *a*. "The precise meaning of the trustee's duty of impartiality and the balancing of competing interests and objectives inevitably are matters of judgment and interpretation. Thus, the duty and balancing are affected by the purposes, terms, distribution requirements, and other circumstances of the trust, not only at the outset but as they may change from time to time." Id. § 232, Comment *c*.

The terms of a trust may provide that the trustee, or an accountant engaged by the trustee, or a committee of persons who may be family members or business associates, shall have the power to determine what is income and what is principal. If the terms of a trust provide that this Act specifically or principal and income legislation in general does not apply to the trust but fail to provide a rule to deal with a matter provided for in this Act, the trustee has an implied grant of discretion to decide the question. Section 103(b) provides that the rule of impartiality applies in the exercise of such a discretionary power to the extent that the terms of the trust do not provide that one or more of the beneficiaries are to be favored. The fact that a person is named an income beneficiary or a remainder beneficiary is not by itself an indication of partiality for that beneficiary.

§ 104. Trustee's Power to Adjust.

(a) A trustee may adjust between principal and income to the extent the trustee considers necessary if the trustee invests and manages trust assets as a prudent investor, the terms of the trust describe the amount that may or must be distributed to a beneficiary by referring to the trust's income, and the trustee determines, after applying the rules in Section 103(a), that the trustee is unable to comply with Section 103(b).

(b) In deciding whether and to what extent to exercise the power conferred by subsection (a), a trustee shall consider all factors relevant to the trust and its beneficiaries, including the following factors to the extent they are relevant:

(1) the nature, purpose, and expected duration of the trust;

(2) the intent of the settlors;

(3) the identity and circumstances of the beneficiaries;

(4) the needs for liquidity, regularity of income, and preservation and appreciation of capital;

(5) the assets held in the trust; the extent to which they consist of financial assets, interests in closely held enterprises, tangible and intangible personal property, or real property; the extent to which an asset is used by a beneficiary; and whether an asset was purchased by the trustee or received from the settlors;

(6) the net amount allocated to income under the other sections of this [Act] and the increase or decrease in the value of the principal assets, which the trustee may estimate as to assets for which market values are not readily available;

(7) whether and to what extent the terms of the trust give the trustee the power to invade principal or accumulate income or prohibit the trustee from invading principal or accumulating income, and the extent to which the trustee has exercised a power from time to time to invade principal or accumulate income;

(8) the actual and anticipated effect of economic conditions on principal and income and effects of inflation and deflation; and

(9) the anticipated tax consequences of an adjustment.

(c) A trustee may not make an adjustment:

(1) that diminishes the income interest in a trust that requires all of the income to be paid at least annually to a surviving spouse and for which an estate tax or gift tax marital deduction would be allowed, in whole or in part, if the trustee did not have the power to make the adjustment;

(2) that reduces the actuarial value of the income interest in a trust to which a person transfers property with the intent to qualify for a gift tax exclusion;

(3) that changes the amount payable to a beneficiary as a fixed annuity or a fixed fraction of the value of the trust assets;

(4) from any amount that is permanently set aside for charitable purposes under a will or the terms of a trust unless both income and principal are so set aside;

(5) if possessing or exercising the power to make an adjustment causes an individual to be treated as the owner of all or part of the trust for income tax purposes, and the individual would not be treated as the owner if the trustee did not possess the power to make an adjustment;

(6) if possessing or exercising the power to make an adjustment causes all or part of the trust assets to be included for estate tax purposes in the estate of an individual who has the power to remove a trustee or appoint a trustee, or both, and the assets would not be included in the estate of the individual if the trustee did not possess the power to make an adjustment;

(7) if the trustee is a beneficiary of the trust; or

(8) if the trustee is not a beneficiary, but the adjustment would benefit the trustee directly or indirectly.

(d) If subsection (c)(5), (6), (7), or (8) applies to a trustee and there is more than one trustee, a cotrustee to whom the provision does not apply may make the adjustment unless the exercise of the power by the remaining trustee or trustees is not permitted by the terms of the trust.

(e) A trustee may release the entire power conferred by subsection (a) or may release only the power to adjust from income to principal or the power to adjust from principal to income if the trustee is uncertain about whether possessing or exercising the power will cause a result described in subsection (c)(1) through (6) or (c)(8) or if the trustee determines that possessing or exercising the power will or may deprive the trust of a tax benefit or impose a tax burden not described in subsection (c). The release may be permanent or for a specified period, including a period measured by the life of an individual.

(f) Terms of a trust that limit the power of a trustee to make an adjustment between principal and income do not affect the application of this section unless it is clear from the terms of the trust that the terms are intended to deny the trustee the power of adjustment conferred by subsection (a).

Comment

Purpose and Scope of Provision. The purpose of Section 104 is to enable a trustee to select investments using the standards of a prudent investor without having to realize a particular portion of the portfolio's total return in the form of traditional trust accounting income such as interest, dividends, and rents. Section 104(a) authorizes a trustee to make adjustments between principal and income if three conditions are met: (1) the trustee must be managing the trust assets under the prudent investor rule; (2) the terms of the trust must express the income beneficiary's distribution rights in terms of the right to receive "income" in the sense of traditional trust accounting income; and (3) the trustee must determine, after applying the rules in Section 103(a), that he is unable to comply with Section 103(b). In deciding whether and to what extent to exercise the

power to adjust, the trustee is required to consider the factors described in Section 104(b), but the trustee may not make an adjustment in circumstances described in Section 104(c).

Section 104 does not empower a trustee to increase or decrease the degree of beneficial enjoyment to which a beneficiary is entitled under the terms of the trust; rather, it authorizes the trustee to make adjustments between principal and income that may be necessary if the income component of a portfolio's total return is too small or too large because of investment decisions made by the trustee under the prudent investor rule. The paramount consideration in applying Section 104(a) is the requirement in Section 103(b) that "a fiduciary must administer a trust or estate impartially, based on what is fair and reasonable to all of the beneficiaries, except to the extent that the terms of the trust or the will clearly manifest an intention that the fiduciary shall or may favor one or more of the beneficiaries." The power to adjust is subject to control by the court to prevent an abuse of discretion. Restatement (Second) of Trusts § 187 (1959). See also id. §§ 183, 232, 233, Comment *p* (1959).

Section 104 will be important for trusts that are irrevocable when a State adopts the prudent investor rule by statute or judicial approval of the rule in Restatement of Trusts 3d: Prudent Investor Rule. Wills and trust instruments executed after the rule is adopted can be drafted to describe a beneficiary's distribution rights in terms that do not depend upon the amount of trust accounting income, but to the extent that drafters of trust documents continue to describe an income beneficiary's distribution rights by referring to trust accounting income, Section 104 will be an important tool in trust administration.

Three conditions to the exercise of the power to adjust. The first of the three conditions that must be met before a trustee can exercise the power to adjust - that the trustee invest and manage trust assets as a prudent investor - is expressed in this Act by language derived from the Uniform Prudent Investor Act, but the condition will be met whether the prudent investor rule applies because the Uniform Act or other prudent investor legislation has been enacted, the prudent investor rule has been approved by the courts, or the terms of the trust require it. Even if a State's legislature or courts have not formally adopted the rule, the Restatement establishes the prudent investor rule as an authoritative interpretation of the common law prudent man rule, referring to the prudent investor rule as a "modest reformulation of the Harvard College dictum and the basic rule of prior Restatements." Restatement of Trusts 3d: Prudent Investor Rule, Introduction, at 5. As a result, there is a basis for concluding that the first condition is satisfied in virtually all States except those in which a trustee is permitted to invest only in assets set forth in a statutory "legal list."

The second condition will be met when the terms of the trust require all of the "income" to be distributed at regular intervals; or when the terms of the trust require a trustee to distribute all of the income, but permit the trustee to decide how much to distribute to each member of a class of beneficiaries; or when the terms of a trust provide that the beneficiary shall receive the greater of the trust accounting income and a fixed dollar amount (an annuity), or of trust accounting income and a fractional share of the value of the trust assets (a unitrust amount). If the trust authorizes the trustee in its discretion to distribute the trust's income to the beneficiary or to accumulate some or all of the income, the condition will be met because the terms of the trust do not permit the trustee to distribute more than the trust accounting income.

To meet the third condition, the trustee must first meet the requirements of Section 103(a), i.e., she must apply the terms of the trust, decide whether to exercise the discretionary powers given to the trustee under the terms of the trust, and must apply the provisions of the Act if the terms of the trust do not contain a different provision or give the trustee discretion. Second, the trustee must determine the extent to which the terms of the trust clearly manifest an intention by the settlor that the trustee may or must favor one or more of the beneficiaries. To the extent that the terms of the trust do not require partiality, the trustee must conclude that she is unable to comply with the duty to administer the trust impartially. To the extent that the terms of the trust do require or permit the trustee to favor the income beneficiary or the remainder beneficiary, the trustee must conclude that she is unable to achieve the degree of partiality required or permitted. If the trustee comes to either conclusion - that she is unable to administer the trust impartially or that she is unable to achieve the degree of partiality required or permitted - she may exercise the power to adjust under Section 104(a).

Impartiality and productivity of income. The duty of impartiality between income and remainder beneficiaries is linked to the trustee's duty to make the portfolio productive of trust accounting income whenever the distribution requirements are expressed in terms of distributing the trust's "income." The 1962 Act implies that the duty to produce income applies on an asset by asset basis because the right of an income beneficiary to receive "delayed income" from the sale proceeds of underproductive property under Section 12 of that Act arises if "any part of principal ... has not produced an average net income of at least 1% per year of its inventory value for more than a year ... ." Under the prudent investor rule, "[t]o whatever extent a requirement of income productivity exists, ... the requirement applies not investment by investment but to the portfolio as a whole." Restatement of Trusts 3d: Prudent Investor Rule § 227, Comment *i*, at 34. The power to adjust under Section 104(a) is also to be exercised by considering net income from the portfolio as a whole and not investment by investment. Section 413(b) of this Act eliminates the underproductive property rule in all cases other than trusts for which a marital deduction is allowed, and it applies to a marital deduction trust if the trust's assets "consist substantially of property that does not provide the surviving spouse with sufficient income from or use of the trust assets ..." - in other words, the section applies by reference to the portfolio as a whole.

While the purpose of the power to adjust in Section 104(a) is to eliminate the need for a trustee who operates under the prudent investor rule to be concerned about the income component of the portfolio's total return, the trustee must still determine the extent to which a distribution must be made to an income beneficiary and the adequacy of the portfolio's liquidity as a whole to make that distribution.

For a discussion of investment considerations involving specific investments and techniques under the prudent investor rule, see Restatement of Trusts 3d: Prudent Investor Rule § 227, Comments k-p.

Factors to consider in exercising the power to adjust. Section 104(b) requires a trustee to consider factors relevant to the trust and its beneficiaries in deciding whether and to what extent the power to adjust should be exercised. Section 2(c) of the Uniform Prudent Investor Act sets forth circumstances that a trustee is to consider in investing and managing trust assets. The circumstances in Section 2(c) of the Uniform Prudent Investor Act are the source of the factors in paragraphs (3) through (6) and (8) of Section 104(b) (modified where necessary to adapt them to the purposes of this Act) so that, to the extent possible, comparable factors will apply to investment decisions and decisions involving the power to adjust. If a trustee who is operating under the prudent investor rule decides that the portfolio should be composed of financial assets whose total return will result primarily from capital appreciation rather than dividends, interest, and rents, the trustee can decide at the same time the extent to which an adjustment from principal to income may be necessary under Section 104. On the other hand, if a trustee decides that the risk and return objectives for the trust are best achieved by a portfolio whose total return includes interest and dividend income that is sufficient to provide the income beneficiary with the beneficial interest to which the beneficiary is entitled under the terms of the trust, the trustee can decide that it is unnecessary to exercise the power to adjust.

Assets received from the settlors. Section 3 of the

Uniform Prudent Investor Act provides that "[a] trustee shall diversify the investments of the trust unless the trustee reasonably determines that, because of special circumstances, the purposes of the trust are better served without diversifying." The special circumstances may include the wish to retain a family business, the benefit derived from deferring liquidation of the asset in order to defer payment of income taxes, or the anticipated capital appreciation from retaining an asset such as undeveloped real estate for a long period. To the extent the trustee retains assets received from the settlors because of special circumstances that overcome the duty to diversify, the trustee may take these circumstances into account in determining whether and to what extent the power to adjust should be exercised to change the results produced by other provisions of this Act that apply to the retained assets. See Section 104(b)(5); Uniform Prudent Investor Act § 3, Comment, 7B U.L.A. 18, at 25-26 (Supp. 1997); Restatement of Trusts 3d: Prudent Investor Rule § 229 and Comments a-e.

Limitations on the power to adjust. The purpose of subsections (c)(1) through (4) is to preserve tax benefits that may have been an important purpose for creating the trust. Subsections (c)(5), (6), and (8) deny the power to adjust in the circumstances described in those subsections in order to prevent adverse tax consequences, and subsection (c)(7) denies the power to adjust to any beneficiary, whether or not possession of the power may have adverse tax consequences.

Under subsection (c)(1), a trustee cannot make an adjustment that diminishes the income interest in a trust that requires all of the income to be paid at least annually to a surviving spouse and for which an estate tax or gift tax marital deduction is allowed; but this subsection does not prevent the trustee from making an adjustment that increases the amount of income paid from a marital deduction trust to the surviving spouse. Subsection (c)(1) applies to a trust that qualifies for the marital deduction because the surviving spouse has a general power of appointment over the trust, but it applies to a qualified terminable interest property (QTIP) trust only if and to the extent that the fiduciary makes the election required to obtain the tax deduction. Subsection (c)(1) does not apply to a so-called "estate" trust. This type of trust qualifies for the marital deduction because the terms of the trust require the principal and undistributed income to be paid to the surviving spouse's estate when the spouse dies; it is not necessary for the terms of an estate trust to require the income to be distributed annually. Reg. § 20.2056(c)-2(b)(1)(iii).

Subsection (c)(3) applies to annuity trusts and unitrusts with no charitable beneficiaries as well as to trusts with charitable income or remainder beneficiaries; its purpose is to make it clear that a beneficiary's right to receive a fixed annuity or a fixed fraction of the value of a trust's assets is not subject to adjustment under Section 104(a). Subsection (c)(3) does not apply to any additional amount to which the beneficiary may be entitled that is expressed in terms of a right to receive income from the trust. For example, if a beneficiary is to receive a fixed annuity or the trust's income, whichever is greater, subsection (c)(3) does not prevent a trustee from making an adjustment under Section 104(a) in determining the amount of the trust's income.

If subsection (c)(5), (6), (7), or (8), prevents a trustee from exercising the power to adjust, subsection (d) permits a cotrustee who is not subject to the provision to exercise the power unless the terms of the trust do not permit the cotrustee to do so.

Release of the power to adjust. Section 104(e) permits a trustee to release all or part of the power to adjust in circumstances in which the possession or exercise of the power might deprive the trust of a tax benefit or impose a tax burden. For example, if possessing the power would diminish the actuarial value of the income interest in a trust for which the income beneficiary's estate may be eligible to claim a credit for property previously taxed if the beneficiary dies within ten years after the death of the person creating the trust, the trustee is permitted under subsection (e) to release just the power to adjust from income to principal.

Trust terms that limit a power to adjust. Section 104(f) applies to trust provisions that limit a trustee's power to adjust. Since the power is intended to enable trustees to employ the prudent investor rule without being constrained by traditional principal and income rules, an instrument executed before the adoption of this Act whose terms describe the amount that may or must be distributed to a beneficiary by referring to the trust's income or that prohibit the invasion of principal or that prohibit equitable adjustments in general should not be construed as forbidding the use of the power to adjust under Section 104(a) if the need for adjustment arises because the trustee is operating under the prudent investor rule. Instruments containing such provisions

that are executed after the adoption of this Act should specifically refer to the power to adjust if the settlors intends to forbid its use. See generally, Joel C. Dobris, Limits on the Doctrine of Equitable Adjustment in Sophisticated Postmortem Tax Planning, 66 Iowa L. Rev. 273 (1981).

Examples. The following examples illustrate the application of Section 104:

Example (1) - T is the successor trustee of a trust that provides income to A for life, remainder to B. T has received from the prior trustee a portfolio of financial assets invested 20% in stocks and 80% in bonds. Following the prudent investor rule, T determines that a strategy of investing the portfolio 50% in stocks and 50% in bonds has risk and return objectives that are reasonably suited to the trust, but T also determines that adopting this approach will cause the trust to receive a smaller amount of dividend and interest income. After considering the factors in Section 104(b), T may transfer cash from principal to income to the extent T considers it necessary to increase the amount distributed to the income beneficiary.

Example (2) - T is the trustee of a trust that requires the income to be paid to the settlor's son C for life, remainder to C's daughter D. In a period of very high inflation, T purchases bonds that pay double-digit interest and determines that a portion of the interest, which is allocated to income under Section 406 of this Act, is a return of capital. In consideration of the loss of value of principal due to inflation and other factors that T considers relevant, T may transfer part of the interest to principal.

Example (3) - T is the trustee of a trust that requires the income to be paid to the settlor's sister E for life, remainder to charity F. E is a retired schoolteacher who is single and has no children. E's income from her social security, pension, and savings exceeds the amount required to provide for her accustomed standard of living. The terms of the trust permit T to invade principal to provide for E's health and to support her in her accustomed manner of living, but do not otherwise indicate that T should favor E or F. Applying the prudent investor rule, T determines that the trust assets should be invested entirely in growth stocks that produce very little dividend income. Even though it is not necessary to invade principal to maintain E's accustomed standard of living, she is entitled to receive from the trust the degree of beneficial enjoyment normally accorded a person who is the sole income beneficiary of a trust, and T may transfer cash from principal to income to provide her with that degree of enjoyment.

Example (4) - T is the trustee of a trust that is governed by the law of State X. The trust became irrevocable before State X adopted the prudent investor rule. The terms of the trust require all of the income to be paid to G for life, remainder to H, and also give T the power to invade principal for the benefit of G for "dire emergencies only." The terms of the trust limit the aggregate amount that T can distribute to G from principal during G's life to 6% of the trust's value at its inception. The trust's portfolio is invested initially 50% in stocks and 50% in bonds, but after State X adopts the prudent investor rule T determines that, to achieve suitable risk and return objectives for the trust, the assets should be invested 90% in stocks and 10% in bonds. This change increases the total return from the portfolio and decreases the dividend and interest income. Thereafter, even though G does not experience a dire emergency, T may exercise the power to adjust under Section 104(a) to the extent that T determines that the adjustment is from only the capital appreciation resulting from the change in the portfolio's asset allocation. If T is unable to determine the extent to which capital appreciation resulted from the change in asset allocation or is unable to maintain adequate records to determine the extent to which principal distributions to G for dire emergencies do not exceed the 6% limitation, T may not exercise the power to adjust. See Joel C. Dobris, Limits on the Doctrine of Equitable Adjustment in Sophisticated Postmortem Tax Planning, 66 Iowa L. Rev. 273 (1981).

Example (5) - T is the trustee of a trust for the settlor's child. The trust owns a diversified portfolio of marketable financial assets with a value of $600,000, and is also the sole beneficiary of the settlor's IRA, which holds a diversified portfolio of marketable financial assets with a value of $900,000. The trust receives a distribution from the IRA that is the minimum amount required to be distributed under the Internal Revenue Code, and T allocates 10% of the distribution to income under Section 409(c) of this Act. The total return on the IRA's assets exceeds the amount distributed to the trust, and the value of the IRA at the end of the year is more than its value at the beginning of the year. Relevant factors that T may consider in determining whether to exercise the power to adjust and the extent to which an adjustment should be made to comply with Section 103(b) include the total return from all of the trust's assets, those owned directly as well as its interest in the IRA, the extent to which the trust will be subject to income tax on the portion of the IRA distribution that is allocated to principal, and the extent to which the income beneficiary will be subject to income tax on the amount that T distributes to the income beneficiary.

Example (6) - T is the trustee of a trust whose portfolio includes a large parcel of undeveloped real estate. T pays real property taxes on the undeveloped parcel from income each year pursuant to Section 501(3). After considering the return from the trust's portfolio as a whole and other relevant factors described in Section 104(b), T may exercise the power to adjust under Section 104(a) to transfer cash from principal to income in order to distribute to the income beneficiary an amount that T considers necessary to comply with Section 103(b).

Example (7) - T is the trustee of a trust whose portfolio includes an interest in a mutual fund that is sponsored by T. As the manager of the mutual fund, T charges the fund a management fee that reduces the amount available to distribute to the trust by $2,000. If the fee had been paid directly by the trust, one-half of the fee would have been paid from income under Section 501(1) and the other one-half would have been paid from principal under Section 502(a)(1). After considering the total return from the portfolio as a whole and other relevant factors described in Section 104(b), T may exercise its power to adjust under Section 104(a) by transferring $1,000, or half of the trust's proportionate share of the fee, from principal to income.

§ 105. Judicial Control of Discretionary Power.

(a) The court may not order a fiduciary to change a decision to exercise or not to exercise a discretionary power conferred by this [Act] unless it determines that the decision was an abuse of the fiduciary's discretion. A fiduciary's decision is not an abuse of discretion merely because the court would have exercised the power in a different manner or would not have exercised the power.

(b) The decisions to which subsection (a) applies include:

(1) a decision under Section 104(a) as to whether and to what extent an amount should be transferred from principal to income or from income to principal.

(2) a decision regarding the factors that are relevant to the trust and its beneficiaries, the extent to which the factors are relevant, and the weight, if any, to be given to those factors, in deciding whether and to what extent to exercise the discretionary power conferred by Section 104(a).

(c) If the court determines that a fiduciary has abused the fiduciary's discretion, the court may place the income and remainder beneficiaries in the positions they would have occupied if the discretion had not been abused, according to the following rules:

(1) To the extent that the abuse of discretion has resulted in no distribution to a beneficiary or in a distribution that is too small, the court shall order the fiduciary to distribute from the trust to the beneficiary an amount that the court determines will restore the beneficiary, in whole or in part, to the beneficiary's appropriate position.

(2) To the extent that the abuse of discretion has resulted in a distribution to a beneficiary which is too large, the court shall place the beneficiaries, the trust, or both, in whole or in part, in their appropriate positions by ordering the fiduciary to withhold an amount from one or more future distributions to the beneficiary who received the distribution that was too large or ordering that beneficiary to return some or all of the distribution to the trust.

(3) To the extent that the court is unable, after applying paragraphs (1) and (2), to place the beneficiaries, the trust, or both, in the positions they would have occupied if the discretion had not been abused, the court may order the fiduciary to pay an appropriate amount from its own funds to one or more of the beneficiaries or the trust or both.

(d) Upon [petition] by the fiduciary, the court having jurisdiction over a trust or estate shall determine whether a proposed exercise or nonexercise by the fiduciary of a discretionary power conferred by this [Act] will result in an abuse of the fiduciary's discretion. If the petition describes the proposed exercise or nonexercise of the power and contains sufficient information to inform the beneficiaries of the reasons for the proposal, the facts upon which the fiduciary relies, and an explanation of how the income and remainder beneficiaries will be affected by the proposed exercise or nonexercise of the power, a beneficiary who challenges the proposed exercise or nonexercise has the burden of establishing that it will result in an abuse of discretion.

Comment

General. All of the discretionary powers in the 1997 Act are subject to the normal rules that govern a fiduciary's exercise of discretion. Section 105 codifies those rules for purposes of the Act so that they will be readily apparent and accessible to fiduciaries, beneficiaries, their counsel and the courts if and when questions concerning such powers arise.

Section 105 also makes clear that the normal rules governing the exercise of a fiduciary's powers apply to the discretionary power to adjust conferred upon a trustee by Section 104(a). Discretionary provisions authorizing trustees to determine what is income and what is principal have been used in governing instruments for years; Section 2 of the 1931 Uniform Principal and Income Act recognized that practice by providing that "the person establishing the principal may himself direct the manner of ascertainment of income and principal...or grant discretion to the trustee or other person to do so...." Section 103(a)(2) also recognizes the power of a settlor to grant such discretion to the trustee. Section 105 applies to a discretionary power granted by the terms of a trust or a will as well as the power to adjust in Section 104(a).

Power to Adjust. The exercise of the power to adjust is governed by a trustee's duty of impartiality, which requires the trustee to strike an appropriate balance between the interests of the income and remainder beneficiaries. Section 103(b) expresses this duty by requiring the trustee to "administer a trust or estate impartially, based on what is fair and reasonable to all of the beneficiaries, except to the extent that the terms of the trust or the will clearly manifest an intention that the fiduciary shall or may favor one or more of the beneficiaries." Because this involves the exercise of judgment in circumstances rarely capable of perfect resolution, trustees are not expected to achieve perfection; they are, however, required to make conscious decisions in good faith and with proper motives.

In seeking the proper balance between the interests

of the beneficiaries in matters involving principal and income, a trustee's traditional approach has been to determine the settlor's objectives from the terms of the trust, gather the information needed to ascertain the financial circumstances of the beneficiaries, determine the extent to which the settlor's objectives can be achieved with the resources available in the trust, and then allocate the trust's assets between stocks and fixed-income securities in a way that will produce a particular level or range of income for the income beneficiary. The key element in this process has been to determine the appropriate level or range of income for the income beneficiary, and that will continue to be the key element in deciding whether and to what extent to exercise the discretionary power conferred by Section 104(a). If it becomes necessary for a court to determine whether an abuse of the discretionary power to adjust between principal and income has occurred, the criteria should be the same as those that courts have used in the past to determine whether a trustee has abused its discretion in allocating the trust's assets between stocks and fixed-income securities.

A fiduciary has broad latitude in choosing the methods and criteria to use in deciding whether and to what extent to exercise the power to adjust in order to achieve impartiality between income beneficiaries and remainder beneficiaries or the degree of partiality for one or the other that is provided for by the terms of the trust or the will. For example, in deciding what the appropriate level or range of income should be for the income beneficiary and whether to exercise the power, a trustee may use the methods employed prior to the adoption of the 1997 Act in deciding how to allocate trust assets between stocks and fixed-income securities; or may consider the amount that would be distributed each year based on a percentage of the portfolio's value at the beginning or end of an accounting period, or the average portfolio value for several accounting periods, in a manner similar to a unitrust, and may select a percentage that the trustee believes is appropriate for this purpose and use the same percentage or different percentages in subsequent years. The trustee may also use hypothetical portfolios of marketable securities to determine an appropriate level or range of income within which a distribution might fall.

An adjustment may be made prospectively at the beginning of an accounting period, based on a projected return or range of returns for a trust's portfolio, or retrospectively after the fiduciary knows the total realized or unrealized return for the period;

and instead of an annual adjustment, the trustee may distribute a fixed dollar amount for several years, in a manner similar to an annuity, and may change the fixed dollar amount periodically. No inference of abuse is to be drawn if a fiduciary uses different methods or criteria for the same trust from time to time, or uses different methods or criteria for different trusts for the same accounting period.

While a trustee must consider the portfolio as a whole in deciding whether and to what extent to exercise the power to adjust, a trustee may apply different criteria in considering the portion of the portfolio that is composed of marketable securities and the portion whose market value cannot be determined readily, and may take into account a beneficiary's use or possession of a trust asset.

Under the prudent investor rule, a trustee is to incur costs that are appropriate and reasonable in relation to the assets and the purposes of the trust, and the same consideration applies in determining whether and to what extent to exercise the power to adjust. In making investment decisions under the prudent investor rule, the trustee will have considered the purposes, terms, distribution requirements, and other circumstances of the trust for the purpose of adopting an overall investment strategy having risk and return objectives reasonably suited to the trust. A trustee is not required to duplicate that work for principal and income purposes, and in many cases the decision about whether and to what extent to exercise the power to adjust may be made at the same time as the investment decisions. To help achieve the objective of reasonable investment costs, a trustee may also adopt policies that apply to all trusts or to individual trusts or classes of trusts, based on their size or other criteria, stating whether and under what circumstances the power to adjust will be exercised and the method of making adjustments; no inference of abuse is to be drawn if a trustee adopts such policies.

General rule. The first sentence of Section 105(a) is from Restatement (Second) of Trusts § 187 and Restatement (Third) of Trusts (Tentative Draft No. 2, 1999) § 50(1). The second sentence of Section 105(a) derives from Comment *e* to § 187 of the Second Restatement and Comment *b* to § 50 of the Third Restatement.

The reference in Section 105(a) to a fiduciary's decision to exercise or not to exercise a discretionary power underscores a fundamental precept, which is that a fiduciary has a duty to make a conscious decision about exercising or not exercising a discretionary power. Comment *b* to § 50 of the Third Restatement states:

> [A] court will intervene where the exercise of a power is left to the judgment of a trustee who improperly fails to exercise that judgment. Thus, even where a trustee has discretion whether or not to make any payments to a particular beneficiary, the court will interpose if the trustee, arbitrarily or without knowledge of or inquiry into relevant circumstances, fails to exercise the discretion.

Section 105(b) makes clear that the rule of subsection (a) applies not only to the power conferred by Section 104(a) but also to the evaluation process required by Section 104(b) in deciding whether and to what extent to exercise the power to adjust. Under Section 104(b), a trustee is to consider all of the factors that are relevant to the trust and its beneficiaries, including, to the extent the trustee determines they are relevant, the nine factors enumerated in Section 104(b). Section 104(b) derives from Section 2(c) of the Uniform Prudent Investor Act, which lists eight circumstances that a trustee shall consider, to the extent they are relevant, in investing and managing assets. The trustee's decisions about what factors are relevant for purposes of Section 104(b) and the weight to be accorded each of the relevant factors are part of the discretionary decision-making process. As such, these decisions are not subject to change for the purpose of changing the trustee's ultimate decision unless the court determines that there has been an abuse of discretion in determining the relevancy and weight of these factors.

Remedy. The exercise or nonexercise of a discretionary power under the Act normally affects the amount or timing of a distribution to the income or remainder beneficiaries. The primary remedy under Section 105(c) for abuse of discretion is the restoration of the beneficiaries and the trust to the positions they would have occupied if the abuse had not occurred. It draws on a basic principle of restitution that if a person pays money to someone who is not intended to receive it (and in a case to which this Act applies, not intended by the settlor to receive it in the absence of an abuse of discretion by the trustee), that person is entitled to restitution on the ground that the payee would be unjustly enriched if he were permitted to retain the payment. See Restatement of Restitution § 22 (1937). The objective is to accomplish the restoration initially by making adjustments between the beneficiaries and the trust to the extent possible; to the extent that restoration is not possible by such adjustments, a court may order the trustee to pay an amount to one or more of the beneficiaries, the trust, or both the beneficiaries and the trust. If the court determines that it is not possible in the circumstances to restore them to the their appropriate positions, the court may provide other remedies appropriate to the circumstances. The approach of Section 105(c) is supported by Comment *b* to § 50 of the Third Restatement of Trusts:

> When judicial intervention is required, a court may direct the trustee to make or refrain from making certain payments; issue instructions to clarify the standards or guidelines applicable to the exercise of the power; or rescind the trustee's payment decisions, usually directing the trustee to recover amounts improperly distributed and holding the trustee liable for failure or inability to do so....

Advance determinations. Section 105(d) employs the familiar remedy of the trustee's petition to the court for instructions. It requires the court to determine, upon a petition by the fiduciary, whether a proposed exercise or nonexercise of a discretionary power by the fiduciary of a power conferred by the Act would be an abuse of discretion under the general rule of Section 105(a). If the petition contains the information prescribed in the second sentence of subsection (d), the proposed action or inaction is presumed not to result in an abuse, and a beneficiary who challenges the proposal must establish that it will.

Subsection (d) is intended to provide a fiduciary the opportunity to obtain an assurance of finality in a judicial proceeding before proceeding with a proposed exercise or nonexercise of a discretionary power. Its purpose is not, however, to have the court instruct the fiduciary how to exercise the discretion.

A fiduciary may also obtain the consent of the beneficiaries to a proposed act or an omission to act, and a beneficiary cannot hold the fiduciary liable for that act or omission unless:

(a) the beneficiary was under an incapacity at the time of such consent or of such act or omission; or

(b) the beneficiary, when he gave his consent, did not know of his rights and of the material facts which the trustee knew or should have known and which the trustee did not reasonably believe that the beneficiary knew; or

(c) the consent of the beneficiary was induced by improper conduct of the trustee.

Restatement (Second) of Trusts § 216.

If there are many beneficiaries, including some who are incapacitated or unascertained, the fiduciary may prefer the greater assurance of finality provided by a judicial proceeding that will bind all persons who have an interest in the trust.

[ARTICLE] 2
DECEDENT'S ESTATE OR
TERMINATING INCOME INTEREST

§ 201. Determination and Distribution of Net Income. After a decedent dies, in the case of an estate, or after an income interest in a trust ends, the following rules apply:

(1) A fiduciary of an estate or of a terminating income interest shall determine the amount of net income and net principal receipts received from property specifically given to a beneficiary under the rules in [Articles] 3 through 5 which apply to trustees and the rules in paragraph (5). The fiduciary shall distribute the net income and net principal receipts to the beneficiary who is to receive the specific property.

(2) A fiduciary shall determine the remaining net income of a decedent's estate or a terminating income interest under the rules in [Articles] 3 through 5 which apply to trustees and by:

(A) including in net income all income from property used to discharge liabilities;

(B) paying from income or principal, in the fiduciary's discretion, fees of attorneys, accountants, and fiduciaries; court costs and other expenses of administration; and interest on death taxes, but the fiduciary may pay those expenses from income of property passing to a trust for which the fiduciary claims an estate tax marital or charitable deduction only to the extent that the payment of those expenses from income will not cause the reduction or loss of the deduction; and

(C) paying from principal all other disbursements made or incurred in connection with the settlement of a decedent's estate or the winding up of a terminating income interest, including debts, funeral expenses, disposition of remains, family allowances, and death taxes and related penalties that are apportioned to the estate or terminating income interest by the will, the terms of the trust, or applicable law.

(3) A fiduciary shall distribute to a beneficiary who receives a pecuniary amount outright the interest or any other amount provided by the will, the terms of the trust, or applicable law from net income determined under paragraph (2) or from principal to the extent that net income is insufficient. If a beneficiary is to receive a pecuniary amount outright from a trust after an income interest ends and no interest or other amount is provided for by the terms of the trust or applicable law, the fiduciary shall distribute the interest or other amount to which the beneficiary would be entitled under applicable law if the pecuniary amount were required to be paid under a will.

(4) A fiduciary shall distribute the net income remaining after distributions required by paragraph (3) in the manner described in Section 202 to all other beneficiaries, including a beneficiary who receives a pecuniary amount in trust, even if the beneficiary holds an unqualified power to withdraw assets from the trust or other presently exercisable general power of appointment over the trust.

(5) A fiduciary may not reduce principal or income receipts from property described in paragraph (1) because of a payment described in Section 501 or 502 to the extent that the will, the terms of the trust, or applicable law requires the fiduciary to make the payment from assets other than the property or to the extent that the fiduciary recovers or expects to recover the payment from a third party. The net income and principal receipts from the property are determined by including all of the amounts the fiduciary receives or pays with respect to the property, whether those amounts accrued or became due before, on, or after the date of a decedent's death or an income interest's terminating event, and by making a reasonable provision for amounts that the fiduciary believes the estate or terminating income interest may become obligated to pay after the property is distributed.

Comment

Terminating income interests and successive income interests. A trust that provides for a single income beneficiary and an outright distribution of the remainder ends when the income interest ends. A more complex trust may have a number of income interests, either concurrent or successive, and the trust will not necessarily end when one of the income interests ends. For that reason, the Act speaks in terms of income interests ending and beginning rather than trusts ending and beginning. When an income interest in a trust ends, the trustee's powers continue during the winding up period required to complete its administration. A terminating income interest is one that has ended but whose administration is not complete.

If two or more people are given the right to receive specified percentages or fractions of the income from a trust concurrently and one of the concurrent interests ends, e.g., when a beneficiary dies, the beneficiary's income interest ends but the trust does not. Similarly, when a trust with only one income beneficiary ends upon the beneficiary's death, the trust instrument may provide that part or all of the trust assets shall continue in trust for another income beneficiary. While it is common to think and speak of this (and even to characterize it in a trust instrument) as a "new" trust, it is a continuation of the original trust for a remainder beneficiary who has an income interest in the trust assets instead of the right to receive them outright. For purposes of this Act, this is a successive income interest in the same trust. The fact that a trust may or may not end when an income interest ends is not significant for purposes of this Act.

If the assets that are subject to a terminating income interest pass to another trust because the income beneficiary exercises a general power of appointment over the trust assets, the recipient trust would be a new trust; and if they pass to another trust because the beneficiary exercises a nongeneral power of appointment over the trust assets, the recipient trust might be a new trust in some States (see 5A Austin W. Scott & William F. Fratcher, The Law of Trusts § 640, at 483 (4th ed. 1989)); but for purposes of this Act a new trust created in these circumstances is also a successive income interest.

Gift of a pecuniary amount. Section 201(3) and (4) provide different rules for an outright gift of a pecuniary amount and a gift in trust of a pecuniary amount; this is the same approach used in Section 5(b)(2) of the 1962 Act.

Interest on pecuniary amounts. Section 201(3) provides that the beneficiary of an outright pecuniary amount is to receive the interest or other amount provided by applicable law if there is no provision in the will or the terms of the trust. Many States have no applicable law that provides for interest or some other amount to be paid on an outright pecuniary gift under an inter vivos trust; this section provides that in such a case the interest or other amount to be paid shall be the same as the interest or other amount required to be paid on testamentary pecuniary gifts. This provision is intended to accord gifts under inter vivos instruments the same treatment as testamentary gifts. The various state authorities that provide for the amount that a beneficiary of an outright pecuniary amount is entitled to receive are collected in Richard B. Covey, Marital Deduction and Credit Shelter Dispositions and the Use of Formula Provisions, App. B (Supp. 1997).

Administration expenses and interest on death taxes. Under Section 201(2)(B) a fiduciary may pay administration expenses and interest on death taxes from either income or principal. An advantage of permitting the fiduciary to choose the source of the payment is that, if the fiduciary's decision is consistent with the decision to deduct these expenses for income tax purposes or estate tax purposes, it eliminates the need to adjust between principal and income that may arise when, for example, an expense that is paid from principal is deducted for income tax purposes or an expense that is paid from income is deducted for estate tax purposes.

The United States Supreme Court has considered the question of whether an estate tax marital deduction or charitable deduction should be reduced when administration expenses are paid from income produced by property passing in trust for a surviving spouse or for charity and deducted for income tax purposes. The Court rejected the IRS position that administration expenses properly paid from income under the terms of the trust or state law must reduce the amount of a marital or charitable transfer, and held that the value of the transferred property is not reduced for estate tax purposes unless the administration expenses are material in light of the income the trust corpus could have been expected to generate. *Commissioner v. Estate of Otis C. Hubert*, 117 S.Ct. 1124 (1997). The provision in Section 201(2)(B) permits a fiduciary to pay and deduct administration expenses from income only to the extent that it will not cause the reduction or loss of an estate tax marital or charitable contributions deduction, which means that the limit on the amount payable from income will be established eventually by Treasury Regulations.

Interest on estate taxes. The IRS agrees that interest on estate and inheritance taxes may be deducted for income tax purposes without having to reduce the estate tax deduction for amounts passing to a charity or surviving spouse, whether the interest is paid from principal or income. Rev. Rul. 93-48, 93-2 C.B. 270. For estates of persons who died before 1998, a fiduciary may not want to deduct for income tax purposes interest on estate tax that is deferred under Section 6166 or 6163 because deducting that interest for estate tax purposes may produce more beneficial results, especially if the estate has little or no income or the income tax bracket is significantly lower than the estate tax bracket. For estates of persons who die after 1997, no estate tax or income tax deduction will be allowed for interest paid on estate tax that is deferred under Section 6166. However, interest on estate tax deferred under Section 6163 will continue to be deductible for both purposes, and interest on estate tax deficiencies will continue to be deductible for estate tax purposes if an election under Section 6166 is not in effect.

Under the 1962 Act, Section 13(c)(5) charges interest on estate and inheritance taxes to principal. The 1931 Act has no provision. Section 501(3) of this Act provides that, except to the extent provided in Section 201(2)(B) or (C), all interest must be paid from income.

§ 202. Distribution to Residuary and Remainder Beneficiaries.

(a) Each beneficiary described in Section 201(4) is entitled to receive a portion of the net income equal to the beneficiary's fractional interest in undistributed principal assets, using values as of the distribution date. If a fiduciary makes more than one distribution of assets to beneficiaries to whom this section applies, each beneficiary, including one who does not receive part of the distribution, is entitled, as of each distribution date, to the net income the fiduciary has received after the date of death or terminating event or earlier distribution date but has not distributed as of the current distribution date.

(b) In determining a beneficiary's share of net income, the following rules apply:

(1) The beneficiary is entitled to receive a portion of the net income equal to the beneficiary's fractional interest in the undistributed principal assets immediately before the distribution date, including assets that later may be sold to meet principal obligations.

(2) The beneficiary's fractional interest in the undistributed principal assets must be calculated without regard to property specifically given to a beneficiary and property required to pay pecuniary amounts not in trust.

(3) The beneficiary's fractional interest in the undistributed principal assets must be calculated on the basis of the aggregate value of those assets as of the distribution date without reducing the value by any unpaid principal obligation.

(4) The distribution date for purposes of this section may be the date as of which the fiduciary calculates the value of the assets if that date is reasonably near the date on which assets are actually distributed.

(c) If a fiduciary does not distribute all of the collected but undistributed net income to each person as of a distribution date, the fiduciary shall maintain appropriate records showing the interest of each beneficiary in that net income.

(d) A trustee may apply the rules in this section, to the extent that the trustee considers it appropriate, to net gain or loss realized after the date of death or terminating event or earlier distribution date from the disposition of a principal asset if this section applies to the income from the asset.

Comment

Relationship to prior Acts. Section 202 retains the concept in Section 5(b)(2) of the 1962 Act that the residuary legatees of estates are to receive net income earned during the period of administration on the basis of their proportionate interests in the undistributed assets when distributions are made. It changes the basis for determining their proportionate interests by using asset values as of a date reasonably near the time of distribution instead of inventory values; it extends the application of these rules to distributions from terminating trusts; and it extends these rules to gain or loss realized from the disposition of assets during administration, an omission in the 1962 Act that has been noted by several commentators. See, e.g., Richard B. Covey, Marital Deduction and Credit Shelter Dispositions and the Use of Formula Provisions 80 (1984 & Supp. 1997); Thomas H. Cantrill, Fractional or Percentage Residuary Bequests: Allocation of Postmortem Income, Gain and Unrealized Appreciation, 10 Prob. Notes 322, 327 (1985).

[ARTICLE] 3
APPORTIONMENT AT BEGINNING
AND END OF INCOME INTEREST

§ 301. When Right to Income Begins and Ends.

(a) An income beneficiary is entitled to net income from the date on which the income interest begins. An income interest begins on the date specified in the terms of the trust or, if no date is specified, on the date an asset becomes subject to a trust or successive income interest.

(b) An asset becomes subject to a trust:

(1) on the date it is transferred to the trust in the case of an asset that is transferred to a trust during the transferor's life;

(2) on the date of a testator's death in the case of an asset that becomes subject to a trust by reason of a will, even if there is an intervening period of administration of the testator's estate; or

(3) on the date of an individual's death in the case of an asset that is transferred to a fiduciary by a third party because of the individual's death.

(c) An asset becomes subject to a successive income interest on the day after the preceding income interest ends, as determined under subsection (d), even if there is an intervening period of administration to wind up the preceding income interest.

(d) An income interest ends on the day before an income beneficiary dies or another terminating event occurs, or on the last day of a period during which there is no beneficiary to whom a trustee may distribute income.

Comment

Period during which there is no beneficiary. The purpose of the second part of subsection (d) is to provide that, at the end of a period during which there is no beneficiary to whom a trustee may distribute income, the trustee must apply the same apportionment rules that apply when a mandatory income interest ends. This provision would apply, for example, if a settlor creates a trust for grandchildren before any grandchildren are born. When the first grandchild is born, the period preceding the date of birth is treated as having ended, followed by a successive income interest, and the apportionment rules in Sections 302 and 303 apply accordingly if the terms of the trust do not contain different provisions.

Former (1962) Version

§ 4. [When Right to Income Arises; Apportionment of Income.]

(a) An income beneficiary is entitled to income from the date specified in the trust instrument, or, if none is specified, from the date an asset becomes subject to the trust. In the case of an asset becoming subject to a trust by reason of a will, it becomes subject to the trust as of the date of the death of the testator even though there is an intervening period of administration of the testator's estate.

(b) In the administration of a decedent's estate or an asset becoming subject to a trust by reason of a will

(1) receipts due but not paid at the date of death of the testator are principal;

(2) receipts in the form of periodic payments (other than corporate distributions to stockholders), including rent, interest, or annuities, not due at the date of the death of the testator shall be treated as accruing from day to day. That portion of the receipt accruing before the date of death is principal, and the balance is income.

(c) In all other cases, any receipt from an income producing asset is income even though the receipt was earned or accrued in whole or in part before the date when the asset became subject to the trust.

(d) On termination of an income interest, the income beneficiary whose interest is terminated, or his estate, is entitled to

---

(1) income undistributed on the date of termination;

(2) income due but not paid to the trustee on the date of termination;

(3) income in the form of periodic payments (other than corporate distributions to stockholders), including rent, interest or annuities, not due on the date of termination, accrued from day to day.

(e) Corporate distributions to stockholders shall be treated as due on the day fixed by the corporation for determination of stockholders of record entitled to distribution or, if no date is fixed, on the date of declaration of the distribution by the corporation.

§ 302. Apportionment of Receipts and Disbursements When Decedent Dies or Income Interest Begins.

(a) A trustee shall allocate an income receipt or disbursement other than one to which Section 201(1) applies to principal if its due date occurs before a decedent dies in the case of an estate or before an income interest begins in the case of a trust or successive income interest.

(b) A trustee shall allocate an income receipt or disbursement to income if its due date occurs on or after the date on which a decedent dies or an income interest begins and it is a periodic due date. An income receipt or disbursement must be treated as accruing from day to day if its due date is not periodic or it has no due date. The portion of the receipt or disbursement accruing before the date on which a decedent dies or an income interest begins must be allocated to principal and the balance must be allocated to income.

(c) An item of income or an obligation is due on the date the payer is required to make a payment. If a payment date is not stated, there is no due date for the purposes of this [Act]. Distributions to shareholders or other owners from an entity to which Section 401 applies are deemed to be due on the date fixed by the entity for determining who is entitled to receive the distribution or, if no date is fixed, on the declaration date for the distribution. A due date is periodic for receipts or disbursements that must be paid at regular intervals under a lease or an obligation to pay interest or if an entity customarily makes distributions at regular intervals.

Comment

Prior Acts. Professor Bogert stated that "Section 4 of the [1962] Act makes a change with respect to the apportionment of the income of trust property not due until after the trust began but which accrued in part before the commencement of the trust. It treats such income as to be credited entirely to the income account in the case of a living trust, but to be apportioned between capital and income in the case of a testamentary trust. The [1931] Act apportions such income in the case of both types of trusts, except in the case of corporate dividends." George G. Bogert, The Revised Uniform Principal and Income Act, 38 Notre Dame Law. 50, 52 (1962). The 1962 Act also provides that an asset passing to an inter vivos trust by a bequest in the settlor's will is governed by the rule that applies to a testamentary trust, so that different rules apply to assets passing to an inter vivos trust depending upon whether they were transferred to the trust during the settlor's life or by his will.

Having several different rules that apply to similar transactions is confusing. In order to simplify administration, Section 302 applies the same rule to inter vivos trusts (revocable and irrevocable), testamentary trusts, and assets that become subject to an inter vivos trust by a testamentary bequest.

Periodic payments. Under Section 302, a periodic payment is principal if it is due but unpaid before a decedent dies or before an asset becomes subject to a trust, but the next payment is allocated entirely to income and is not apportioned. Thus, periodic receipts such as rents, dividends, interest, and annuities, and disbursements such as the interest portion of a mortgage payment, are not apportioned. This is the original common law rule. Edwin A. Howes, Jr., The American Law Relating to Income and Principal 70 (1905). In trusts in which a surviving spouse is dependent upon a regular flow of cash from the decedent's securities portfolio, this rule will help to maintain payments to the spouse at the same level as before the settlor's death. Under the 1962 Act, the pre-death portion of the first periodic payment due after death is apportioned to principal in the case of a testamentary trust or securities bequeathed by will to an inter vivos trust.

Nonperiodic payments. Under the second sentence of Section 302(b), interest on an obligation that does not provide a due date for the interest payment, such as interest on an income tax refund, would be apportioned to principal to the extent it accrues before a person dies or an income interest begins unless the obligation is specifically given to a devisee or remainder beneficiary, in which case all of the accrued interest passes under Section 201(1) to the person who receives the obligation. The same rule applies to interest on an obligation that has a due date but does not provide for periodic payments. If there is no stated interest on the obligation, such as a zero coupon bond, and the proceeds from the obligation are received more than one year after it is purchased or acquired by the trustee, the entire amount received is principal under Section 406.

Former (1962) Version

§ 5. [Income Earned During Administration of a Decedent's Estate.]

(a) Unless the will otherwise provides and subject to subsection (b), all expenses incurred in connection with the settlement of a decedent's estate, including debts, funeral expenses, estate taxes, interest and penalties concerning taxes, family allowances, fees of attorneys and personal representatives, and court costs shall be charged against the principal of the estate.

(b) Unless the will otherwise provides, income from the assets of a decedent's estate after the death of the testator and before distribution, including income from property used to discharge liabilities, shall be determined in accordance with the rules applicable to a trustee under this Act and distributed as follows:

(1) to specific legatees and devisees, the income from the property bequeathed or devised to them respectively, less taxes, ordinary repairs, and other expenses of management and operation of the property, and an appropriate portion of interest accrued since the death of the testator and of taxes imposed on income (excluding taxes on capital gains) which accrue during the period of administration;

(2) to all other legatees and devisees, except legatees of pecuniary bequests not in trust, the balance of the income, less the balance of taxes, ordinary repairs, and other expenses of management and operation of all property from which the estate is entitled to income, interest accrued since the death of the testator, and taxes imposed on income (excluding taxes on capital gains) which accrue during the period of administration, in proportion to their respective interests in the undistributed assets of the estate computed at times of distribution on the basis of inventory value.

(c) Income received by a trustee under subsection (b) shall be treated as income of the trust.

---

§ 303. Apportionment When Income Interest Ends.

(a) In this section, "undistributed income" means net income received before the date on which an income interest ends. The term does not include an item of income or expense that is due or accrued or net income that has been added or is required to be added to principal under the terms of the trust.

(b) When a mandatory income interest ends, the trustee shall pay to a mandatory income beneficiary who survives that date, or the estate of a deceased mandatory income beneficiary whose death causes the interest to end, the beneficiary's share of the undistributed income that is not disposed of under the terms of the trust unless the beneficiary has an unqualified power to revoke more than five percent of the trust immediately before the income interest ends. In the latter case, the undistributed income from the portion of the trust that may be revoked must be added to principal.

(c) When a trustee's obligation to pay a fixed annuity or a fixed fraction of the value of the trust's assets ends, the trustee shall prorate the final payment if and to the extent required by applicable law to accomplish a purpose of the trust or its settlors relating to income, gift, estate, or other tax requirements.

Comment

Prior Acts. Both the 1931 Act (Section 4) and the 1962 Act (Section 4(d)) provide that a deceased income beneficiary's estate is entitled to the undistributed income. The Drafting Committee concluded that this is probably not what most settlors would want, and that, with respect to undistributed income, most settlors would favor the income beneficiary first, the remainder beneficiaries second, and the income beneficiary's heirs last, if at all. However, it decided not to eliminate this provision to avoid causing disputes about whether the trustee should have distributed collected cash before the income beneficiary died.

Accrued periodic payments. Under the prior Acts, an income beneficiary or his estate is entitled to receive a portion of any payments, other than dividends, that are due or that have accrued when the income interest terminates. The last sentence of subsection (a) changes that rule by providing that such items are not included in undistributed income. The items affected include periodic payments of interest, rent, and dividends, as well as items of income that accrue over a longer period of time; the rule also applies to expenses that are due or accrued.

Example - accrued periodic payments. The rules in Section 302 and Section 303 work in the following manner: Assume that a periodic payment of rent that is due on July 20 has not been paid when an income interest ends on July 30; the successive income interest begins on July 31, and the rent payment that was due on July 20 is paid on August 3. Under Section 302(a), the July 20 payment is added to the principal of the successive income interest when received. Under Section 302(b), the entire periodic payment of rent that is due on August 20 is income when received by the successive income interest.

Under Section 303, neither the income beneficiary of the terminated income interest nor the beneficiary's estate is entitled to any part of either the July 20 or the August 20 payments because neither one was received before the income interest ended on July 30. The same principles apply to expenses of the trust.

Beneficiary with an unqualified power to revoke. The requirement in subsection (b) to pay undistributed income to a mandatory income beneficiary or her estate does not apply to the extent the beneficiary has an unqualified power to revoke more than five percent of the trust immediately before the income interest ends. Without this exception, subsection (b) would apply to a revocable living trust whose settlors is the mandatory income beneficiary during her lifetime, even if her will provides that all of the assets in the probate estate are to be distributed to the trust.

If a trust permits the beneficiary to withdraw all or a part of the trust principal after attaining a specified age and the beneficiary attains that age but fails to withdraw all of the principal that she is permitted to withdraw, a trustee is not required to pay her or her estate the undistributed income attributable to the portion of the principal that she left in the trust. The assumption underlying this rule is that the beneficiary has either provided for the disposition of the trust assets (including the undistributed income) by exercising a power of appointment that she has been given or has not withdrawn the assets because she is willing to have the principal and undistributed income be distributed under the terms of the trust. If the beneficiary has the power to withdraw 25% of the trust principal, the trustee must pay to her or her estate the undistributed income from the 75% that she cannot withdraw.

[ARTICLE] 4
ALLOCATION OF RECEIPTS DURING ADMINISTRATION OF TRUST

Former (1962) Version

§ 3. [Income; Principal; Charges.]

(a) Income is the return in money or property derived from the use of principal, including return received as

(1) rent of real or personal property, including sums received for cancellation or renewal of a lease;

(2) interest on money lent, including sums received as consideration for the privilege of prepayment of principal except as provided in section 7 on bond premium and bond discount;

(3) income earned during administration of a decedent's estate as provided in section 5;

(4) corporate distributions as provided in section 6;

(5) accrued increment on bonds or other obligations issued at discount as provided in section 7;

(6) receipts from business and farming operations as provided in section 8;

(7) receipts from disposition of natural resources as provided in sections 9 and 10;

(8) receipts from other principal subject to depletion as provided in section 11;

(9) receipts from disposition of underproductive property as provided in section 12.

(b) Principal is the property which has been set aside by the owner or the person legally empowered so that it is held in trust eventually to be delivered to a remainderman while the return or use of the principal is in the meantime taken or received by or held for accumulation for an income beneficiary. Principal includes

(1) consideration received by the trustee on the sale or other transfer of principal or on repayment of a loan or as a refund or replacement or change in the form of principal;

(2) proceeds of property taken on eminent domain proceedings;

(3) proceeds of insurance upon property forming part of the principal except proceeds of insurance upon a separate interest of an income beneficiary;

(4) stock dividends, receipts on liquidation of a corporation, and other corporate distributions as provided in section 6;

(5) receipts from the disposition of corporate securities as provided in section 7;

(6) royalties and other receipts from disposition of natural resources as provided in sections 9 and 10;

(7) receipts from other principal subject to depletion as provided in section 11;

(8) any profit resulting from any change in the form of principal except as provided in section 12 on underproductive property;

(9) receipts from disposition of underproductive property as provided in section 12;

(10) any allowances for depreciation established under sections 8 and 13(a)(2).

(c) After determining income and principal in accordance with the terms of the trust instrument or of this Act, the trustee shall charge to income or principal expenses and other charges as provided in section 13.

[PART 1
RECEIPTS FROM ENTITIES]

§ 401. Character of Receipts.

(a) In this section, "entity" means a corporation, partnership, limited liability company, regulated investment company, real estate investment trust, common trust fund, or any other organization in which a trustee has an interest other than a trust or estate to which Section 402 applies, a business or activity to which Section 403 applies, or an asset-backed security to which Section 415 applies.

(b) Except as otherwise provided in this section, a trustee shall allocate to income money received from an entity.

(c) A trustee shall allocate the following receipts from an entity to principal:

(1) property other than money;

(2) money received in one distribution or a series of related distributions in exchange for part or all of a trust's interest in the entity;

(3) money received in total or partial liquidation of the entity; and

(4) money received from an entity that is a regulated investment company or a real estate investment trust if the money distributed is a capital gain dividend for federal income tax purposes.

(d) Money is received in partial liquidation:

(1) to the extent that the entity, at or near the time of a distribution, indicates that it is a distribution in partial liquidation; or

(2) if the total amount of money and property received in a distribution or series of related distributions is greater than 20 percent of the entity's gross assets, as shown by the entity's year-end financial statements immediately preceding the initial receipt.

(e) Money is not received in partial liquidation, nor may it be taken into account under subsection (d)(2), to the extent that it does not exceed the amount of income tax that a trustee or beneficiary must pay on taxable income of the entity that distributes the money.

(f) A trustee may rely upon a statement made by an entity about the source or character of a distribution if the statement is made at or near the time of distribution by the entity's board of directors or other person or group of persons authorized to exercise powers to pay money or transfer property comparable to those of a corporation's board of directors.

Comment

Entities to which Section 401 applies. The reference to partnerships in Section 401(a) is intended to include all forms of partnerships, including limited partnerships, limited liability partnerships, and variants that have slightly different names and characteristics from State to State. The section does not apply, however, to receipts from an interest in property that a trust owns as a tenant in common with one or more co-owners, nor would it apply to an interest in a joint venture if, under applicable law, the trust's interest is regarded as that of a tenant in common.

Capital gain dividends. Under the Internal Revenue Code and the Income Tax Regulations, a "capital gain dividend" from a mutual fund or real estate investment trust is the excess of the fund's or

trust's net long-term capital gain over its net short-term capital loss. As a result, a capital gain dividend does not include any net short-term capital gain, and cash received by a trust because of a net short-term capital gain is income under this Act.

Reinvested dividends. If a trustee elects (or continues an election made by its predecessor) to reinvest dividends in shares of stock of a distributing corporation or fund, whether evidenced by new certificates or entries on the books of the distributing entity, the new shares would be principal, but the trustee may determine, after considering the return from the portfolio as a whole, whether an adjustment under Section 104 is necessary as a result.

Distribution of property. The 1962 Act describes a number of types of property that would be principal if distributed by a corporation. This becomes unwieldy in a section that applies to both corporations and all other entities. By stating that principal includes the distribution of any property other than money, Section 401 embraces all of the items enumerated in Section 6 of the 1962 Act as well as any other form of nonmonetary distribution not specifically mentioned in that Act.

Partial liquidations. Under subsection (d)(1), any distribution designated by the entity as a partial liquidating distribution is principal regardless of the percentage of total assets that it represents. If a distribution exceeds 20% of the entity's gross assets, the entire distribution is a partial liquidation under subsection (d)(2) whether or not the entity describes it as a partial liquidation. In determining whether a distribution is greater than 20% of the gross assets, the portion of the distribution that does not exceed the amount of income tax that the trustee or a beneficiary must pay on the entity's taxable income is ignored.

Other large distributions. A cash distribution may be quite large (for example, more than 10% but not more than 20% of the entity's gross assets) and have characteristics that suggest it should be treated as principal rather than income. For example, an entity may have received cash from a source other than the conduct of its normal business operations because it sold an investment asset; or because it sold a business asset other than one held for sale to customers in the normal course of its business and did not replace it; or it borrowed a large sum of money and secured the repayment of the loan with a substantial asset; or a principal source of its cash was from assets such as mineral interests, 90% of which would have been allocated to principal if the trust had owned the assets directly. In such a case the trustee, after considering the total return from the portfolio as a whole and the income component of that return, may decide to exercise the power under Section 104(a) to make an adjustment between income and principal, subject to the limitations in Section 104(c).

Former (1962) Version

§ 6. [Corporate Distributions.]

(a) Corporate distributions of shares of the distributing corporation, including distributions in the form of a stock split or stock dividend, are principal. A right to subscribe to shares or other securities issued by the distributing corporation accruing to stockholders on account of their stock ownership and the proceeds of any sale of the right are principal.

(b) Except to the extent that the corporation indicates that some part of a corporate distribution is a settlement of preferred or guaranteed dividends accrued since the trustee became a stockholder or is in lieu of an ordinary cash dividend, a corporate distribution is principal if the distribution is pursuant to

    (1) a call of shares;

    (2) a merger, consolidation, reorganization, or other plan by which assets of the corporation are acquired by another corporation; or

    (3) a total or partial liquidation of the corporation, including any distribution which the corporation indicates is a distribution in total or partial liquidation or any distribution of assets, other than cash, pursuant to a court decree or final administrative order by a government agency ordering distribution of the particular assets.

(c) Distributions made from ordinary income by a regulated investment company or by a trust qualifying and electing to be taxed under federal law as a real estate investment trust are income. All other distributions made by the company or trust, including distributions from capital gains, depreciation, or depletion, whether in the form of cash or an option to take new stock or cash or an option to purchase additional shares, are principal.

(d) Except as provided in subsections (a), (b), and (c), all corporate distributions are income, including cash dividends, distributions of or rights to subscribe to shares or securities or obligations of corporations other than the distributing corporation, and the proceeds of the rights or property distributions. Except as provided in subsections (b) and (c), if the distributing corporation gives a stockholder an option to receive a distribution either in cash or in its own shares, the distribution chosen is income.

(e) The trustee may rely upon any statement of the distributing corporation as to any fact relevant under any provision of this Act concerning the source or character of dividends or distributions of corporate assets.

---

§ 7. [Bond Premium and Discount.]

(a) Bonds or other obligations for the payment of money are principal at their inventory value, except as provided in subsection (b) for discount bonds. No provision shall be made for amortization of bond premiums or for accumulation for discount. The proceeds of sale, redemption, or other disposition of the bonds or obligations are principal.

(b) The increment in value of a bond or other obligation for the payment of money payable at a future time in accordance with a fixed schedule of appreciation in excess of the price at which it was issued is distributable as income. The increment in value is distributable to the beneficiary who was the income beneficiary at the time of increment from the first principal cash available or, if none is available, when realized by sale, redemption, or other disposition. Whenever unrealized increment is distributed as income but out of principal, the principal shall be reimbursed for the increment when realized.

---

§ 402. Distribution from Trust or Estate. A trustee shall allocate to income an amount received as a distribution of income from a trust or an estate in which the trust has an interest other than a purchased interest, and shall allocate to principal an amount received as a distribution of principal from such a trust or estate. If a trustee purchases an interest in a trust that is an investment entity, or a decedent or donor transfers an interest in such a trust to a trustee, Section 401 or 415 applies to a receipt from the trust.

Comment

Terms of the distributing trust or estate. Under Section 103(a), a trustee is to allocate receipts in accordance with the terms of the recipient trust or, if there is no provision, in accordance with this Act. However, in determining whether a distribution from another trust or an estate is income or principal, the trustee should also determine what the terms of the distributing trust or estate say about the distribution - for example, whether they direct that the distribution, even though made from the income of the distributing trust or estate, is to be added to principal of the recipient trust. Such a provision should override the terms of this Act, but if the terms of the recipient trust contain a provision requiring such a distribution to be allocated to income, the trustee may have to obtain a judicial resolution of the conflict between the terms of the two documents.

Investment trusts. An investment entity to which the second sentence of this section applies includes a mutual fund, a common trust fund, a business trust or other entity organized as a trust for the purpose of receiving capital contributed by investors, investing that capital, and managing investment assets, including asset-backed security arrangements to which Section 415 applies. See John H. Langbein, The Secret Life of the Trust: The Trust as an Instrument of Commerce, 107 Yale L.J. 165 (1997).

§ 403. Business and Other Activities Conducted by Trustee.

(a) If a trustee who conducts a business or other activity determines that it is in the best interest of all the beneficiaries to account separately for the business or activity instead of accounting for it as part of the trust's general accounting records, the trustee may maintain separate accounting records for its transactions, whether or not its assets are segregated from other trust assets.

(b) A trustee who accounts separately for a business or other activity may determine the extent to which its net cash receipts must be retained for working capital, the acquisition or replacement of fixed assets, and other reasonably foreseeable needs of the business or activity, and the extent to which the remaining net cash receipts are accounted for as principal or income in the trust's general accounting records. If a trustee sells assets of the business or other activity, other than in the ordinary course of the business or activity, the trustee shall account for the net amount received as principal in the trust's general accounting records to the extent the trustee determines that the amount received is no longer required in the conduct of the business.

(c) Activities for which a trustee may maintain separate accounting records include:

(1) retail, manufacturing, service, and other traditional business activities;

(2) farming;

(3) raising and selling livestock and other animals;

(4) management of rental properties;

(5) extraction of minerals and other natural resources;

(6) timber operations; and

(7) activities to which Section 414 applies.

Comment

Purpose and scope. The provisions in Section 403 are intended to give greater flexibility to a trustee who operates a business or other activity in proprietorship form rather than in a wholly-owned corporation (or, where permitted by state law, a single-member limited liability company), and to facilitate the trustee's ability to decide the extent to which the net receipts from the activity should be allocated to income, just as the board of directors of a corporation owned entirely by the trust would decide the amount of the annual dividend to be paid to the trust. It permits a trustee to account for farming or livestock operations, rental properties, oil and gas properties, timber operations, and activities in derivatives and options as though they were held by a separate entity. It is not intended, however, to permit a trustee to account separately for a traditional securities portfolio to avoid the provisions of this Act that apply to such securities.

Section 403 permits the trustee to account separately for each business or activity for which the trustee determines separate accounting is appropriate. A trustee with a computerized accounting system may account for these activities in a "subtrust"; an individual trustee may continue to use the business and record-keeping methods employed by the decedent or transferor who may have conducted the business under an assumed name. The intent of this section is to give the trustee broad authority to select business record-keeping methods that best suit the activity in which the trustee is engaged.

If a fiduciary liquidates a sole proprietorship or other activity to which Section 403 applies, the proceeds would be added to principal, even though derived from the liquidation of accounts receivable, because the proceeds would no longer be needed in the conduct of the business. If the liquidation occurs during probate or during an income interest's winding up period, none of the proceeds would be income for purposes of Section 201.

Separate accounts. A trustee may or may not maintain separate bank accounts for business activities that are accounted for under Section 403. A professional trustee may decide not to maintain separate bank accounts, but an individual trustee, especially one who has continued a decedent's business practices, may continue the same banking arrangements that were used during the decedent's lifetime. In either case, the trustee is authorized to decide to what extent cash is to be retained as part of the business assets and to what extent it is to be transferred to the trust's general accounts, either as income or principal.

Former (1962) Version

§ 8. [Business and Farming Operations.]

(a) If a trustee uses any part of the principal in the continuance of a business of which the settlor was a sole proprietor or a partner, the net profits of the business, computed in accordance with generally accepted accounting principles for a comparable business, are income. If a loss results in any fiscal or calendar year, the loss falls on principal and shall not be carried into any other fiscal or calendar year for purposes of calculating net income.

(b) Generally accepted accounting principles shall be used to determine income from an agricultural or farming operation, including the raising of animals or the operation of a nursery.

[PART 2
RECEIPTS NOT NORMALLY APPORTIONED]

§ 404. Principal Receipts. A trustee shall allocate to principal:

(1) to the extent not allocated to income under this [Act], assets received from a transferor during the transferor's lifetime, a decedent's estate, a trust with a terminating income interest, or a payer under a contract naming the trust or its trustee as beneficiary;

(2) money or other property received from the sale, exchange, liquidation, or change in form of a principal asset, including realized profit, subject to this [article];

(3) amounts recovered from third parties to reimburse the trust because of disbursements described in Section 502(a)(7) or for other reasons to the extent not based on the loss of income;

(4) proceeds of property taken by eminent domain, but a separate award made for the loss of income with respect to an accounting period during which a current income beneficiary had a mandatory income interest is income;

(5) net income received in an accounting period during which there is no beneficiary to whom a trustee may or must distribute income; and

(6) other receipts as provided in [Part 3].

Comment

Eminent domain awards. Even though the award in an eminent domain proceeding may include an amount for the loss of future rent on a lease, if that amount is not separately stated the entire award is principal. The rule is the same in the 1931 and 1962 Acts.

§ 405. Rental Property. To the extent that a trustee accounts for receipts from rental property pursuant to this section, the trustee shall allocate to income an amount received as rent of real or personal property, including an amount received for cancellation or renewal of a lease. An amount received as a refundable deposit, including a security deposit or a deposit that is to be applied as rent for future periods, must be added to principal and held subject to the terms of the lease and is not available for distribution to a beneficiary until the trustee's contractual obligations have been satisfied with respect to that amount.

Comment

Application of Section 403. This section applies to the extent that the trustee does not account separately under Section 403 for the management of rental properties owned by the trust.

Receipts that are capital in nature. A portion of the payment under a lease may be a reimbursement of principal expenditures for improvements to the leased property that is characterized as rent for purposes of invoking contractual or statutory remedies for nonpayment. If the trustee is accounting for rental income under Section 405, a transfer from income to reimburse principal may be appropriate under Section 504 to the extent that some of the "rent" is really a reimbursement for improvements. This set of facts could also be a relevant factor for a trustee to consider under Section 104(b) in deciding whether and to what extent to make an adjustment between principal and income under Section 104(a) after considering the return from the portfolio as a whole.

§ 406. Obligation to Pay Money.

(a) An amount received as interest, whether determined at a fixed, variable, or floating rate, on an obligation to pay money to the trustee, including an amount received as consideration for prepaying principal, must be allocated to income without any provision for amortization of premium.

(b) A trustee shall allocate to principal an amount received from the sale, redemption, or other

633

disposition of an obligation to pay money to the trustee more than one year after it is purchased or acquired by the trustee, including an obligation whose purchase price or value when it is acquired is less than its value at maturity. If the obligation matures within one year after it is purchased or acquired by the trustee, an amount received in excess of its purchase price or its value when acquired by the trust must be allocated to income.

(c) This section does not apply to an obligation to which Section 409, 410, 411, 412, 414, or 415 applies.

Comment

Variable or floating interest rates. The reference in subsection (a) to variable or floating interest rate obligations is intended to clarify that, even though an obligation's interest rate may change from time to time based upon changes in an index or other market indicator, an obligation to pay money containing a variable or floating rate provision is subject to this section and is not to be treated as a derivative financial instrument under Section 414.

Discount obligations. Subsection (b) applies to all obligations acquired at a discount, including short-term obligations such as U.S. Treasury Bills, long-term obligations such as U.S. Savings Bonds, zero-coupon bonds, and discount bonds that pay interest during part, but not all, of the period before maturity. Under subsection (b), the entire increase in value of these obligations is principal when the trustee receives the proceeds from the disposition unless the obligation, when acquired, has a maturity of less than one year. In order to have one rule that applies to all

discount obligations, the Act eliminates the provision in the 1962 Act for the payment from principal of an amount equal to the increase in the value of U.S. Series E bonds. The provision for bonds that mature within one year after acquisition by the trustee is derived from the Illinois act. 760 ILCS 15/8 (1996).

Subsection (b) also applies to inflation-indexed bonds - any increase in principal due to inflation after issuance is principal upon redemption if the bond matures more than one year after the trustee acquires it; if it matures within one year, all of the increase, including any attributable to an inflation adjustment, is income.

Effect of Section 104. In deciding whether and to what extent to exercise the power to adjust between principal and income granted by Section 104(a), a relevant factor for the trustee to consider is the effect on the portfolio as a whole of having a portion of the assets invested in bonds that do not pay interest currently.

§ 407. Insurance Policies and Similar Contracts.

(a) Except as otherwise provided in subsection (b), a trustee shall allocate to principal the proceeds of a life insurance policy or other contract in which the trust or its trustee is named as beneficiary, including a contract that insures the trust or its trustee against loss for damage to, destruction of, or loss of title to a trust asset. The trustee shall allocate dividends on an insurance policy to income if the premiums on the policy are paid from income, and to principal if the premiums are paid from principal.

(b) A trustee shall allocate to income proceeds of a contract that insures the trustee against loss of occupancy or other use by an income beneficiary, loss of income, or, subject to Section 403, loss of profits from a business.

(c) This section does not apply to a contract to which Section 409 applies.

[PART 3
RECEIPTS NORMALLY APPORTIONED]

§ 408. Insubstantial Allocations Not Required.
If a trustee determines that an allocation between principal and income required by Section 409, 410, 411, 412, or 415 is insubstantial, the trustee may allocate the entire amount to principal unless one of the circumstances described in Section 104(c)

applies to the allocation. This power may be exercised by a cotrustee in the circumstances described in Section 104(d) and may be released for the reasons and in the manner described in Section 104(e). An allocation is presumed to be insubstantial if:

(1) the amount of the allocation would increase or decrease net income in an accounting period, as determined before the allocation, by less than 10 percent; or

(2) the value of the asset producing the receipt for which the allocation would be made is less than 10 percent of the total value of the trust's assets at the beginning of the accounting period.

Comment

This section is intended to relieve a trustee from making relatively small allocations while preserving the trustee's right to do so if an allocation is large in terms of absolute dollars.

For example, assume that a trust's assets, which include a working interest in an oil well, have a value of $1,000,000; the net income from the assets other than the working interest is $40,000; and the net receipts from the working interest are $400. The trustee may allocate all of the net receipts from the working interest to principal instead of allocating 10%, or $40, to income under Section 411. If the net receipts from the working interest are $35,000, so that the amount allocated to income under Section 411 would be $3,500, the trustee may decide that this amount is sufficiently significant to the income

beneficiary that the allocation provided for by Section 411 should be made, even though the trustee is still permitted under Section 408 to allocate all of the net receipts to principal because the $3,500 would increase the net income of $40,000, as determined before making an allocation under Section 411, by less than 10%. Section 408 will also relieve a trustee from having to allocate net receipts from the sale of trees in a small wood lot between principal and income.

While the allocation to principal of small amounts under this section should not be a cause for concern for tax purposes, allocations are not permitted under this section in circumstances described in Section 104(c) to eliminate claims that the power in this section has adverse tax consequences.

§ 409. Deferred Compensation, Annuities, and Similar Payments.

(a) In this section:

(1) "Payment" means a payment that a trustee may receive over a fixed number of years or during the life of one or more individuals because of services rendered or property transferred to the payer in exchange for future payments. The term includes a payment made in money or property from the payer's general assets or from a separate fund created by the payer. For purposes of subsections (d), (e), (f), and (g), the term also includes any payment from a separate fund, regardless of the reason for the payment.

(2) "Separate fund" includes a private or commercial annuity, an individual retirement account, and a pension, profit-sharing, stock-bonus, or stock-ownership plan.

(b) To the extent that a payment is characterized as interest, a dividend, or a payment made in lieu of interest or a dividend, a trustee shall allocate the payment to income. The trustee shall allocate to principal the balance of the payment and any other payment received in the same accounting period that is not characterized as interest, a dividend, or an equivalent payment.

(c) If no part of a payment is characterized as interest, a dividend, or an equivalent payment, and all or part of the payment is required to be made, a trustee shall allocate to income 10 percent of the part that is required to be made during the accounting period and the balance to principal. If no part of a payment is required to be made or the payment received is the entire amount to which the trustee is entitled, the trustee shall allocate the entire payment to principal. For purposes of this subsection, a payment is not "required to be made" to the extent that it is made because the trustee exercises a right of withdrawal.

(d) Except as otherwise provided in subsection (e), subsections (f) and (g) apply, and subsections (b) and (c) do not apply, in determining the allocation of a payment made from a separate fund to:

(1) a trust to which an election to qualify for a marital deduction under Section 2056(b)(7) of the Internal Revenue Code of 1986 [, as amended,] [, 26 U.S.C. Section 2056(b)(7)] [, as amended] has been made; or

(2) a trust that qualifies for the marital deduction under Section 2056(b)(5) of the Internal Revenue Code of 1986 [, as amended] [, 26 U.S.C. Section 2056(b)(7)] [, as amended].

(e) Subsections (d), (f), and (g) do not apply if and to the extent that the series of payments would, without the application of subsection (d), qualify for the marital deduction under Section 2056(b)(7)(C) of the Internal Revenue Code of 1986 [, as amended] [, 26 U.S.C. Section 2056(b)(7)] [, as amended].

(f) A trustee shall determine the internal income of each separate fund for the accounting period as if the separate fund were a trust subject to this [act]. Upon request of the surviving spouse, the trustee shall demand that the person administering the separate fund distribute the internal income to the trust. The trustee shall allocate a payment from the separate fund to income to the extent of the internal income of the separate fund and distribute that amount to the surviving spouse. The trustee shall allocate the balance to principal. Upon request of the surviving spouse, the trustee shall allocate principal to income to the extent the internal income of the separate fund exceeds payments made from the separate fund to the trust during the accounting period.

(g) If a trustee cannot determine the internal income of a separate fund but can determine the value of the separate fund, the internal income of the separate fund is deemed to equal [insert number at least three percent and not more than five percent] of the fund's value, according to the most recent statement of value preceding the beginning of the accounting period. If the trustee can determine neither the internal income of the separate fund nor the fund's value, the internal income of the fund is deemed to equal the product of the interest rate and the present value of the expected future payments, as determined under Section 7520 of the Internal Revenue Code of 1986 [, as amended,] [, 26 U.S.C. Section 7520] [, as amended] for the month preceding the accounting period for which the computation is made.

(h) This section does not apply to a payment to which Section 410 applies.

Comment

Scope. Section 409 applies to amounts received under contractual arrangements that provide for payments to a third party beneficiary as a result of services rendered or property transferred to the payer. While the right to receive such payments is a liquidating asset of the kind described in Section 410 (i.e., "an asset whose value will diminish or terminate because the asset is expected to produce receipts for a period of limited duration"), these payment rights are covered separately in Section 409 because of their special characteristics.

Section 409 applies to receipts from all forms of annuities and deferred compensation arrangements, whether the payment will be received by the trust in a lump sum or in installments over a period of years. It applies to bonuses that may be received over two or three years and payments that may last for much longer periods, including payments from an individual retirement account (IRA), deferred compensation plan (whether qualified or not qualified for special federal income tax treatment), and insurance renewal commissions. It applies to a retirement plan to which the settlors has made contributions, just as it applies to an annuity policy that the settlors may have purchased individually, and it applies to variable annuities, deferred annuities, annuities issued by commercial insurance companies, and "private annuities" arising from the sale of property to another individual or entity in exchange for payments that are to be made for the life of one or more individuals. The section applies whether the payments begin when the payment right becomes subject to the trust or are deferred until a future date, and it applies whether payments are made in cash or in kind, such as employer stock (in-kind payments usually will be made in a single distribution that will be allocated to principal under the second sentence of subsection (c)).

The 1962 Act. Under Section 12 of the 1962 Act, receipts from "rights to receive payments on a contract for deferred compensation" are allocated to income each year in an amount "not in excess of 5% per year" of the property's inventory value. While "not in excess of 5%" suggests that the annual allocation may range from zero to 5% of the inventory value, in practice the rule is usually treated as prescribing a 5% allocation. The inventory value is usually the present value of all the future payments, and since the inventory value is determined as of the date on which the payment right becomes subject to the trust, the inventory value, and thus the amount of the annual income allocation, depends significantly on the applicable interest rate on the decedent's date of death. That rate may be much higher or lower than the average long-term interest rate. The amount determined under the 5% formula tends to become fixed and remain unchanged even though the amount received by the trust increases or decreases.

Allocations Under Section 409(b). Section 409(b) applies to plans whose terms characterize payments made under the plan as dividends, interest, or payments in lieu of dividends or interest. For example, some deferred compensation plans that hold debt obligations or stock of the plan's sponsor in an account for future delivery to the person rendering the services provide for the annual payment to that person of dividends received on the stock or interest received on the debt obligations. Other plans provide that the account of the person rendering the services shall be credited with "phantom" shares of stock and require an annual payment that is equivalent to the dividends that would be received on that number of shares if they were actually issued; or a plan may entitle the person rendering the services to receive a fixed dollar amount in the future and provide for the annual payment of interest on the deferred amount during the period prior to its payment. Under Section 409(b), payments of dividends, interest or payments in lieu of dividends or interest under plans of this type are allocated to income; all other payments received under these plans are allocated to principal.

Section 409(b) does not apply to an IRA or an arrangement with payment provisions similar to an IRA. IRAs and similar arrangements are subject to the provisions in Section 409(c).

Allocations Under Section 409(c). The focus of Section 409, for purposes of allocating payments received by a trust to or between principal and income, is on the payment right rather than on assets that may be held in a fund from which the payments are made. Thus, if an IRA holds a portfolio of marketable stocks and bonds, the amount received by the IRA as dividends and interest is not taken into account in determining the principal and income allocation except to the extent that the Internal Revenue Service may require them to be taken into account when the payment is received by a trust that qualifies for the estate tax marital deduction (a situation that is provided for in Section 409(d)). An IRA is subject to federal income tax rules that require payments to begin by a particular date and be made over a specific number of years or a period measured by the lives of one or more persons. The payment right of a trust that is named as a beneficiary of an IRA is not a right to receive particular items that are paid to the IRA, but is instead the right to receive an amount determined by dividing the value of the IRA by the remaining number of years in the payment period. This payment right is similar to the right to receive a unitrust amount, which is normally expressed as an amount equal to a percentage of the value of the unitrust assets without regard to dividends or interest that may be received by the unitrust.

An amount received from an IRA or a plan with a payment provision similar to that of an IRA is allocated under Section 409(c), which differentiates between payments that are required to be made and all other payments. To the extent that a payment is required to be made (either under federal income tax rules or, in the case of a plan that is not subject to those rules, under the terms of the plan), 10% of the amount received is allocated to income and the balance is allocated to principal. All other payments are allocated to principal because they represent a change in the form of a principal asset; Section 409 follows the rule in Section 404(2), which provides that money or property received from a change in the form of a principal asset be allocated to principal.

Section 409(c) produces an allocation to income that is similar to the allocation under the 1962 Act formula if the annual payments are the same throughout the payment period, and it is simpler to administer. The amount allocated to income under Section 409 is not dependent upon the interest rate that is used for valuation purposes when the decedent dies, and if the payments received by the trust increase or decrease from year to year because the fund from which the payment is made increases or decreases in value, the amount allocated to income will also increase or decrease.

Marital deduction requirements. When an IRA or

other retirement arrangement (a "plan") is payable to a marital deduction trust, the IRS treats the plan as a separate property interest that itself must qualify for the marital deduction. IRS Revenue Ruling 2006-26 said that, as written, Section 409 does not cause a trust to qualify for the IRS' safe harbors. Revenue Ruling 2006-26 was limited in scope to certain situations involving IRAs and defined contribution retirement plans. Without necessarily agreeing with the IRS' position in that ruling, the revision to this section is designed to satisfy the IRS' safe harbor and to address concerns that might be raised for similar assets. No IRS pronouncements have addressed the scope of Code § 2056(b)(7)(C).

Subsection (e) requires the trustee to demand certain distributions if the surviving spouse so requests. The safe harbor of Revenue Ruling 2006-26 requires that the surviving spouse be separately entitled to demand the fund's income (without regard to the income from the trust's other assets) and the income from the other assets (without regard to the fund's income). In any event, the surviving spouse is not required to demand that the trustee distribute all of the fund's income from the fund or from other trust assets. Treas. Reg. § 20.2056(b)-5(f)(8).

Subsection (e) also recognizes that the trustee might not control the payments that the trustee receives and provides a remedy to the surviving spouse if the distributions under subsection (d)(1) are insufficient.

Subsection (f) addresses situations where, due to lack of information provided by the fund's administrator, the trustee is unable to determine the fund's actual income. The bracketed language is the range approved for unitrust payments by Treas. Reg. § 1.643(b)-1. In determining the value for purposes of applying the unitrust percentage, the trustee would seek to obtain the value of the assets as of the most recent statement of value immediately preceding the beginning of the year. For example, suppose a trust's accounting period is January 1 through December 31. If a retirement plan administrator furnishes information annually each September 30 and declines to provide information as of December 31, then the trustee may rely on the September 30 value to determine the distribution for the following year. For funds whose values are not readily available, subsection (f) relies on Code section 7520 valuation methods because many funds described in Section 409 are annuities, and one consistent set of valuation principles should apply whether or not the fund is, in fact, an annuity.

Application of Section 104. Section 104(a) of this Act gives a trustee who is acting under the prudent investor rule the power to adjust from principal to income if, considering the portfolio as a whole and not just receipts from deferred compensation, the trustee determines that an adjustment is necessary. See Example (5) in the Comment following Section 104.

§ 410. Liquidating Asset.

(a) In this section, "liquidating asset" means an asset whose value will diminish or terminate because the asset is expected to produce receipts for a period of limited duration. The term includes a leasehold, patent, copyright, royalty right, and right to receive payments during a period of more than one year under an arrangement that does not provide for the payment of interest on the unpaid balance. The term does not include a payment subject to Section 409, resources subject to Section 411, timber subject to Section 412, an activity subject to Section 414, an asset subject to Section 415, or any asset for which the trustee establishes a reserve for depreciation under Section 503.

(b) A trustee shall allocate to income 10 percent of the receipts from a liquidating asset and the balance to principal.

Comment

Prior Acts. Section 11 of the 1962 Act allocates receipts from "property subject to depletion" to income in an amount "not in excess of 5%" of the asset's inventory value. The 1931 Act has a similar 5% rule that applies when the trustee is under a duty to change the form of the investment. The 5% rule imposes on a trust the obligation to pay a fixed annuity to the income beneficiary until the asset is exhausted. Under both the 1931 and 1962 Acts the balance of each year's receipts is added to principal. A fixed payment can produce unfair results. The remainder beneficiary receives all of the receipts from unexpected growth in the asset, e.g., if royalties on a patent or copyright increase significantly. Conversely, if the receipts diminish more rapidly than expected, most of the amount received by the trust will be allocated to income and little to principal. Moreover, if the annual payments remain the same for the life of the asset, the amount allocated to principal will usually be less than the original inventory value. For these reasons, Section 410 abandons the annuity approach under the 5% rule.

Lottery payments. The reference in subsection (a) to rights to receive payments under an arrangement that does not provide for the payment of interest includes state lottery prizes and similar fixed amounts payable over time that are not deferred compensation arrangements covered by Section 409.

Former (1962) Version

§ 11. [Other Property Subject to Depletion.] Except as provided in sections 9 and 10, if the principal consists of property subject to depletion, including leaseholds, patents, copyrights, royalty rights, and rights to receive payments on a contract for deferred compensation, receipts from the property, not in excess of 5% per year of its inventory value, are income, and the balance is principal.

---

§ 411. Minerals, Water, and Other Natural Resources.

(a) To the extent that a trustee accounts for receipts from an interest in minerals or other natural resources pursuant to this section, the trustee shall allocate them as follows:

(1) If received as nominal delay rental or nominal annual rent on a lease, a receipt must be allocated to income.

(2) If received from a production payment, a receipt must be allocated to income if and to the extent that the agreement creating the production payment provides a factor for interest or its equivalent. The balance must be allocated to principal.

(3) If an amount received as a royalty, shut-in-well payment, take-or-pay payment, bonus, or delay rental is more than nominal, 90 percent must be allocated to principal and the balance to income.

(4) If an amount is received from a working interest or any other interest not provided for in paragraph (1), (2), or (3), 90 percent of the net amount received must be allocated to principal and the balance to income.

(b) An amount received on account of an interest in water that is renewable must be allocated to income. If the water is not renewable, 90 percent of the amount must be allocated to principal and the balance to income.

(c) This [Act] applies whether or not a decedent or donor was extracting minerals, water, or other natural resources before the interest became subject to the trust.

(d) If a trust owns an interest in minerals, water, or other natural resources on [the effective date of this [Act]], the trustee may allocate receipts from the interest as provided in this [Act] or in the manner used by the trustee before [the effective date of this [Act]]. If the trust acquires an interest in minerals, water, or other natural resources after [the effective date of this [Act]], the trustee shall allocate receipts from the interest as provided in this [Act].

Comment

Prior Acts. The 1962 Act allocates to principal as a depletion allowance, 27-1/2% of the gross receipts, but not more than 50% of the net receipts after paying expenses. The Internal Revenue Code no longer provides for a 27-1/2% depletion allowance, although the major oil-producing States have retained the 27-1/2% provision in their principal and income acts (Texas amended its Act in 1993, but did not change the depletion provision). Section 9 of the 1931 Act allocates all of the net proceeds received as consideration for the "permanent severance of natural resources from the lands" to principal.

Section 411 allocates 90% of the net receipts to principal and 10% to income. A depletion provision that is tied to past or present Code provisions is undesirable because it causes a large portion of the oil and gas receipts to be paid out as income. As wells are depleted, the amount received by the income beneficiary falls drastically. Allocating a larger portion of the receipts to principal enables the trustee to acquire other income producing assets that will continue to produce income when the mineral reserves are exhausted.

Application of Sections 403 and 408. This section applies to the extent that the trustee does not account separately for receipts from minerals and other natural resources under Section 403 or allocate all of the receipts to principal under Section 408.

Open mine doctrine. The purpose of Section 411(c) is to abolish the "open mine doctrine" as it may apply to the rights of an income beneficiary and a remainder beneficiary in receipts from the production of minerals from land owned or leased by a trust. Instead, such receipts are to be allocated to or between principal and income in accordance with the provisions of this Act. For a discussion of the open mine doctrine, see generally 3A Austin W. Scott & William F. Fratcher, The Law of Trusts § 239.3 (4th ed. 1988), and *Nutter v. Stockton*, 626 P.2d 861 (Okla. 1981).

Effective date provision. Section 9(b) of the 1962 Act provides that the natural resources provision does not apply to property interests held by the trust on the effective date of the Act, which reflects concerns about the constitutionality of applying a retroactive administrative provision to interests in real estate, based on the opinion in the Oklahoma case of *Franklin v. Margay Oil Corporation*, 153 P.2d 486, 501

(Okla. 1944). Section 411(d) permits a trustee to use either the method provided for in this Act or the method used before the Act takes effect. Lawyers in jurisdictions other than Oklahoma may conclude that retroactivity is not a problem as to property situated in their States, and this provision permits trustees to decide, based on advice from counsel in States whose law may be different from that of Oklahoma, whether they may apply this provision retroactively if they conclude that to do so is in the best interests of the beneficiaries.

If the property is in a State other than the State where the trust is administered, the trustee must be aware that the law of the property's situs may control this question. The outcome turns on a variety of questions: whether the terms of the trust specify that the law of a State other than the situs of the property shall govern the administration of the trust, and whether the courts will follow the terms of the trust; whether the trust's asset is the land itself or a leasehold interest in the land (as it frequently is with oil and gas property); whether a leasehold interest or its proceeds should be classified as real property or personal property, and if as personal property, whether applicable state law treats it as a movable or an immovable for conflict of laws purposes. See 5A Austin W. Scott & William F. Fratcher, The Law of Trusts §§ 648, at 531, 533-534; § 657, at 600 (4th ed. 1989).

Former (1962) Version

§ 9. [Disposition of Natural Resources.]

(a) If any part of the principal consists of a right to receive royalties, overriding or limited royalties, working interests, production payments, net profit interests, or other interests in minerals or other natural resources in, on or under land, the receipts from taking the natural resources from the land shall be allocated as follows:

(1) If received as rent on a lease or extension payments on a lease, the receipts are income.

(2) If received from a production payment, the receipts are income to the extent of any factor for interest or its equivalent provided in the governing instrument. There shall be allocated to principal the fraction of the balance of the receipts which the unrecovered cost of the production payments bears to the balance owed on the production payment, exclusive of any factor for interest or its equivalent. The receipts not allocated to principal are income.

(3) If received as a royalty, overriding or limited royalty, or bonus, or from a working, net profit, or any other interest in minerals or other natural resources, receipts not provided for in the preceding paragraphs of this section shall be apportioned on a yearly basis in accordance with this paragraph whether or not any natural resource was being taken from the land at the time the trust was established. Twenty-seven and one-half per cent of the gross receipts (but not to exceed 50% of the net receipts remaining after payment of all expenses, direct and indirect, computed without allowance for depletion) shall be added to principal as an allowance for depletion. The balance of the gross receipts, after payment therefrom of all expenses, direct and indirect, is income.

(b) If a trustee, on the effective date of this Act, held an item of depletable property of a type specified in this section he shall allocate receipts from the property in the manner used before the effective date of this Act, but as to all depletable property acquired after the effective date of this Act by an existing or new trust, the method of allocation provided herein shall be used.

(c) This section does not apply to timber, water, soil, sod, dirt, turf, or mosses.

§ 412. Timber.

(a) To the extent that a trustee accounts for receipts from the sale of timber and related products pursuant to this section, the trustee shall allocate the net receipts:

(1) to income to the extent that the amount of timber removed from the land does not exceed the rate of growth of the timber during the accounting periods in which a beneficiary has a mandatory income interest;

(2) to principal to the extent that the amount of timber removed from the land exceeds the rate of growth of the timber or the net receipts are from the sale of standing timber;

(3) to or between income and principal if the net receipts are from the lease of timberland or from a contract to cut timber from land owned by a trust, by determining the amount of timber removed from the land under the lease or contract and applying the rules in paragraphs (1) and (2); or

(4) to principal to the extent that advance payments, bonuses, and other payments are not allocated pursuant to paragraph (1), (2), or (3).

(b) In determining net receipts to be allocated pursuant to subsection (a), a trustee shall deduct and transfer to principal a reasonable amount for depletion.

(c) This [Act] applies whether or not a decedent or transferor was harvesting timber from the property before it become subject to the trust.

(d) If a trust owns an interest in timberland on [the effective date of this [Act]], the trustee may allocate net receipts from the sale of timber and related products as provided in this [Act] or in the manner used by the trustee before [the effective date of this [Act]]. If the trust acquires an interest in timberland after [the effective date of this [Act]], the trustee shall allocate net receipts from the sale of timber and related products as provided in this [Act].

Comment

Scope of section. The rules in Section 412 are intended to apply to net receipts from the sale of trees and by-products from harvesting and processing trees without regard to the kind of trees that are cut or whether the trees are cut before or after a particular number of years of growth. The rules apply to the sale of trees that are expected to produce lumber for building purposes, trees sold as pulpwood, and Christmas and other ornamental trees. Subsection (a) applies to net receipts from property owned by the trustee and property leased by the trustee. The Act is not intended to prevent a tenant in possession of the property from using wood that he cuts on the property for personal, noncommercial purposes, such as a Christmas tree, firewood, mending old fences or building new fences, or making repairs to structures on the property.

Under subsection (a), the amount of net receipts allocated to income depends upon whether the amount of timber removed is more or less than the rate of growth. The method of determining the amount of timber removed and the rate of growth is up to the trustee, based on methods customarily used for the kind of timber involved.

Application of Sections 403 and 408. This section applies to the extent that the trustee does not account separately for net receipts from the sale of timber and related products under Section 403 or allocate all of the receipts to principal under Section 408. The option to account for net receipts separately under Section 403 takes into consideration the possibility that timber harvesting operations may have been conducted before the timber property became subject to the trust, and that it may make sense to continue using accounting methods previously established for the property. It also permits a trustee to use customary accounting practices for timber operations even if no harvesting occurred on the property before it became subject to the trust.

Former (1962) Version

§ 10. [Timber.] If any part of the principal consists of land from which merchantable timber may be removed, the receipts from taking the timber from the land shall be allocated in accordance with section 2(a)(3).

---

§ 413. Property Not Productive of Income.

(a) If a marital deduction is allowed for all or part of a trust whose assets consist substantially of property that does not provide the surviving spouse with sufficient income from or use of the trust assets, and if the amounts that the trustee transfers from principal to income under Section 104 and distributes to the spouse from principal pursuant to the terms of the trust are insufficient to provide the spouse with the beneficial enjoyment required to obtain the marital deduction, the spouse may require the trustee to make property productive of income, convert property within a reasonable time, or exercise the power conferred by Section 104(a). The trustee may decide which action or combination of actions to take.

(b) In cases not governed by subsection (a), proceeds from the sale or other disposition of an asset are principal without regard to the amount of income the asset produces during any accounting period.

Comment

Prior Acts' Conflict with Uniform Prudent Investor Act. Section 2(b) of the Uniform Prudent Investor Act provides that "[a] trustee's investment and management decisions respecting individual assets must be evaluated not in isolation but in the context of the trust portfolio as a whole ... ." The underproductive property provisions in Section 12 of the 1962 Act and Section 11 of the 1931 Act give the income beneficiary a right to receive a portion of the proceeds from the sale of underproductive property as "delayed income." In each Act the provision applies on an asset by asset basis and not by taking into consideration the trust portfolio as a whole, which conflicts with the basic precept in Section 2(b) of the Prudent Investor Act. Moreover, in determining the amount of delayed income, the prior Acts do not permit a trustee to take into account the extent to which the trustee may have distributed principal to the income beneficiary, under principal invasion provisions in the terms of the trust, to compensate for insufficient income from the unproductive asset. Under Section 104(b)(7) of this Act, a trustee must consider prior distributions of principal to the income beneficiary in deciding whether and to what extent to exercise the power to adjust conferred by Section 104(a).

Duty to make property productive of income. In order to implement the Uniform Prudent Investor Act, this Act abolishes the right to receive delayed income from the sale proceeds of an asset that produces little or no income, but it does not alter existing state law regarding the income beneficiary's right to compel the trustee to make property productive of income. As the law continues to develop in this area, the duty to make property productive of current income in a particular situation should be determined by taking into consideration the performance of the portfolio as a whole and the extent to which a trustee makes principal distributions to the income beneficiary under the terms of the trust and adjustments between principal and income under Section 104 of this Act.

Trusts for which the value of the right to receive income is important for tax reasons may be affected by Reg. § 1.7520-3(b)(2)(v) *Example (1)*, § 20.7520-3(b)(2)(v) *Examples (1)* and *(2)*, and § 25.7520-3(b)(2)(v) *Examples (1)* and *(2)*, which provide that if the income beneficiary does not have the right to compel the trustee to make the property productive, the income interest is considered unproductive and may not be valued actuarially under those sections.

Marital deduction trusts. Subsection (a) draws on language in Reg. § 20.2056(b)-5(f)(4) and (5) to enable a trust for a surviving spouse to qualify for a marital deduction if applicable state law is unclear about the surviving spouse's right to compel the trustee to make property productive of income. The trustee should also consider the application of Section 104 of this Act and the provisions of Restatement of Trusts 3d: Prudent Investor Rule § 240, at 186, app. § 240, at 252 (1992). Example (6) in the Comment to Section 104 describes a situation involving the payment from income of carrying charges on unproductive real estate in which Section 104 may apply.

Once the two conditions have occurred - insufficient beneficial enjoyment from the property and the spouse's demand that the trustee take action under this section - the trustee must act; but instead of the formulaic approach of the 1962 Act, which is triggered only if the trustee sells the property, this Act permits the trustee to decide whether to make the property productive of income, convert it, transfer funds from principal to income, or to take some combination of those actions. The trustee may rely on the power conferred by Section 104(a) to adjust from principal to income if the trustee decides that it is not feasible or appropriate to make the property productive of income or to convert the property. Given the purpose of Section 413, the power under Section 104(a) would be exercised to transfer principal to income and not to transfer income to principal.

Section 413 does not apply to a so-called "estate" trust, which will qualify for the marital deduction, even though the income may be accumulated for a term of years or for the life of the surviving spouse, if the terms of the trust require the principal and undistributed income to be paid to the surviving spouse's estate when the spouse dies. Reg. § 20.2056(c)-2(b)(1)(iii).

Former (1962) Version

§ 12. [Underproductive Property.]

(a) Except as otherwise provided in this section, a portion of the net proceeds of sale of any part of principal which has not produced an average net income of at least 1% per year of its inventory value for more than a year (including as income the value of any beneficial use of the property by the income beneficiary) shall be treated as delayed income to which the income beneficiary is entitled as provided in this section. The net proceeds of sale are the gross proceeds received, including the value of any property received in substitution for the property disposed of, less the expenses, including capital gains tax, if any, incurred in disposition and less any carrying charge paid while the property was underproductive.

(b) The sum allocated as delayed income is the difference between the net proceeds and the amount which, had it been invested at simple interest at [4%] per year while the property was underproductive, would have produced the net proceeds. This sum, plus any carrying charges and expenses previously charged against income while the property was underproductive, less any income received by the income beneficiary from the property and less the value of any beneficial use of the property by the income beneficiary, is income, and the balance is principal.

(c) An income beneficiary or his estate is entitled to delayed income under this section as if it accrued from day to day during the time he was a beneficiary.

(d) If principal subject to this section is disposed of by conversion into property which cannot be apportioned easily, including land or mortgages (for example, realty acquired by or in lieu of foreclosure), the income beneficiary is entitled to the net income from any property or obligation into which the original principal is converted while the substituted property or obligation is held. If within 5 years after the conversion the substituted property has not been further converted into easily apportionable property, no allocation as provided in this section shall be made.

---

§ 414. Derivatives and Options.

(a) In this section, "derivative" means a contract or financial instrument or a combination of contracts and financial instruments which gives a trust the right or obligation to participate in some or all changes in the price of a tangible or intangible asset or group of assets, or changes in a rate, an index of prices or rates, or other market indicator for an asset or a group of assets.

(b) To the extent that a trustee does not account under Section 403 for transactions in derivatives, the trustee shall allocate to principal receipts from and disbursements made in connection with those transactions.

(c) If a trustee grants an option to buy property from the trust, whether or not the trust owns the property when the option is granted, grants an option that permits another person to sell property to the trust, or acquires an option to buy property for the trust or an option to sell an asset owned by the trust, and the trustee or other owner of the asset is required to deliver the asset if the option is exercised, an amount received for granting the option must be allocated to principal. An amount paid to acquire the option must be paid from principal. A gain or loss realized upon the exercise of an option, including an option granted to a settlor of the trust for services rendered, must be allocated to principal.

Comment

Scope and application. It is difficult to predict how frequently and to what extent trustees will invest directly in derivative financial instruments rather than participating indirectly through investment entities that may utilize these instruments in varying degrees. If the trust participates in derivatives indirectly through an entity, an amount received from the entity will be allocated under Section 401 and not Section 414. If a trustee invests directly in derivatives to a significant extent, the expectation is that receipts and disbursements related to derivatives will be accounted for under Section 403; if a trustee chooses not to account under Section 403, Section 414(b) provides the default rule. Certain types of option transactions in which trustees may engage are dealt with in subsection (c) to distinguish those transactions from ones involving options that are embedded in derivative financial instruments.

Definition of "derivative." "Derivative" is a difficult term to define because new derivatives are invented daily as dealers tailor their terms to achieve specific financial objectives for particular clients. Since derivatives are typically contract-based, a derivative can probably be devised for almost any set of objectives if another party can be found who is willing to assume the obligations required to meet those objectives.

The most comprehensive definition of derivative is in the Exposure Draft of a Proposed Statement of Financial Accounting Standards titled "Accounting for Derivative and Similar Financial Instruments and for Hedging Activities," which was released by the Financial Accounting Standards Board (FASB) on June 20, 1996 (No. 162-B). The definition in Section 414(a) is derived in part from the FASB definition. The purpose of the definition in subsection (a) is to implement the substantive rule in subsection (b) that provides for all receipts and disbursements to be

allocated to principal to the extent the trustee elects not to account for transactions in derivatives under Section 403. As a result, it is much shorter than the FASB definition, which serves much more ambitious objectives.

A derivative is frequently described as including futures, forwards, swaps and options, terms that also require definition, and the definition in this Act avoids these terms. FASB used the same approach, explaining in paragraph 65 of the Exposure Draft:

> The definition of *derivative financial instrument* in this Statement includes those financial instruments generally considered to be derivatives, such as forwards, futures, swaps, options, and similar instruments. The Board considered defining a derivative financial instrument by merely referencing those commonly understood instruments, similar to paragraph 5 of Statement 119, which says that "... a derivative financial instrument is a futures, forward, swap, or option contract, or other financial instrument with similar characteristics." However, the continued development of financial markets and innovative financial instruments could ultimately render a definition based on examples inadequate and obsolete. The Board, therefore, decided to base the definition of a derivative financial instrument on a description of the common characteristics of those instruments in order to accommodate the accounting for newly developed derivatives. (Footnote omitted.)

Marking to market. A gain or loss that occurs because the trustee marks securities to market or to another value during an accounting period is not a transaction in a derivative financial instrument that is income or principal under the Act - only cash receipts and disbursements, and the receipt of property in exchange for a principal asset, affect a trust's principal and income accounts.

Receipt of property other than cash. If a trustee receives property other than cash upon the settlement of a derivatives transaction, that property would be principal under Section 404(2).

Options. Options to which subsection (c) applies include an option to purchase real estate owned by the trustee and a put option purchased by a trustee to guard against a drop in value of a large block of marketable stock that must be liquidated to pay estate taxes. Subsection (c) would also apply to a continuing and regular practice of selling call options on securities owned by the trust if the terms of the option require delivery of the securities. It does not apply if the consideration received or given for the option is something other than cash or property, such as cross-options granted in a buy-sell agreement between owners of an entity.

§ 415. Asset-Backed Securities.

(a) In this section, "asset-backed security" means an asset whose value is based upon the right it gives the owner to receive distributions from the proceeds of financial assets that provide collateral for the security. The term includes an asset that gives the owner the right to receive from the collateral financial assets only the interest or other current return or only the proceeds other than interest or current return. The term does not include an asset to which Section 401 or 409 applies.

(b) If a trust receives a payment from interest or other current return and from other proceeds of the collateral financial assets, the trustee shall allocate to income the portion of the payment which the payer identifies as being from interest or other current return and shall allocate the balance of the payment to principal.

(c) If a trust receives one or more payments in exchange for the trust's entire interest in an asset-backed security in one accounting period, the trustee shall allocate the payments to principal. If a payment is one of a series of payments that will result in the liquidation of the trust's interest in the security over more than one accounting period, the trustee shall allocate 10 percent of the payment to income and the balance to principal.

Comment

Scope of section. Typical asset-backed securities include arrangements in which debt obligations such as real estate mortgages, credit card receivables and auto loans are acquired by an investment trust and interests in the trust are sold to investors. The source for payments to an investor is the money received from principal and interest payments on the underlying debt. An asset-backed security includes an "interest only" or a "principal only" security that permits the investor to receive only the interest payments received from the bonds, mortgages or other assets that are the collateral for the asset-backed security, or only the principal payments made on those collateral assets. An asset-backed security also includes a security that permits the investor to participate in either the capital appreciation of an underlying security or in the interest or dividend return from such a security, such as the "Primes" and "Scores" issued by Americus Trust. An asset-backed security does not include an interest in a corporation, partnership, or an investment trust described in the Comment to Section 402, whose assets consist significantly or entirely of investment assets. Receipts from an instrument that do not come within the scope of this section or any other section of the Act would be allocated entirely to principal under the rule in Section 103(a)(4), and the trustee may then consider whether and to what extent to exercise the power to adjust in Section 104, taking into account the return from the portfolio as whole and other relevant factors.

[ARTICLE] 5
ALLOCATION OF DISBURSEMENTS DURING ADMINISTRATION OF TRUST

§ 501. Disbursements from Income. A trustee shall make the following disbursements from income to the extent that they are not disbursements to which Section 201(2)(B) or (C) applies:

(1) one-half of the regular compensation of the trustee and of any person providing investment advisory or custodial services to the trustee;

(2) one-half of all expenses for accountings, judicial proceedings, or other matters that involve both the income and remainder interests;

(3) all of the other ordinary expenses incurred in connection with the administration, management, or preservation of trust property and the distribution of income, including interest, ordinary repairs, regularly recurring taxes assessed against principal, and expenses of a proceeding or other matter that concerns primarily the income interest; and

(4) recurring premiums on insurance covering the loss of a principal asset or the loss of income from or use of the asset.

Comment

Trustee fees. The regular compensation of a trustee or the trustee's agent includes compensation based on a percentage of either principal or income or both.

Insurance premiums. The reference in paragraph (4) to "recurring" premiums is intended to distinguish premiums paid annually for fire insurance from premiums on title insurance, each of which covers the loss of a principal asset. Title insurance premiums would be a principal disbursement under Section 502(a)(5).

Regularly recurring taxes. The reference to "regularly recurring taxes assessed against principal" includes all taxes regularly imposed on real property and tangible and intangible personal property.

Former (1962) Version

§ 13. [Charges Against Income and Principal.]

(a) The following charges shall be made against income:

(1) ordinary expenses incurred in connection with the administration, management, or preservation of the trust property, including regularly recurring taxes assessed against any portion of the principal, water rates, premiums on insurance taken upon the interests of the income beneficiary, remainderman, or trustee, interest paid by the trustee, and ordinary repairs;

(2) a reasonable allowance for depreciation on property subject to depreciation under generally accepted accounting principles, but no allowance shall be made for depreciation of that portion of any real property used by a beneficiary as a residence or for depreciation of any property held by the trustee on the effective date of this Act for which the trustee is not then making an allowance for depreciation;

(3) one-half of court costs, attorney's fees, and other fees on periodic judicial accounting, unless the court directs otherwise;

(4) court costs, attorney's fees, and other fees on other accountings or judicial proceedings if the matter primarily concerns the income interest, unless the court directs otherwise;

(5) one-half of the trustee's regular compensation, whether based on a percentage of principal or income, and all expenses reasonably incurred for current management of principal and application of income;

(6) any tax levied upon receipts defined as income under this Act or the trust instrument and payable by the trustee.

(b) If charges against income are of unusual amount, the trustee may by means of reserves or other reasonable means charge them over a reasonable period of time and withhold from distribution sufficient sums to regularize distributions.

. . . .

§ 502. Disbursements from Principal.

(a) A trustee shall make the following disbursements from principal:

(1) the remaining one-half of the disbursements described in Section 501(1) and (2);

(2) all of the trustee's compensation calculated on principal as a fee for acceptance, distribution, or termination, and disbursements made to prepare property for sale;

(3) payments on the principal of a trust debt;

(4) expenses of a proceeding that concerns primarily principal, including a proceeding to construe the trust or to protect the trust or its property;

(5) premiums paid on a policy of insurance not described in Section 501(4) of which the trust is the owner and beneficiary;

(6) estate, inheritance, and other transfer taxes, including penalties, apportioned to the trust; and

(7) disbursements related to environmental matters, including reclamation, assessing environmental conditions, remedying and removing environmental contamination, monitoring remedial activities and the release of substances, preventing future releases of substances, collecting amounts from persons liable or potentially liable for the costs of those activities, penalties imposed under environmental laws or regulations and other payments made to comply with those laws or regulations, statutory or common law claims by third parties, and defending claims based on environmental matters.

(b) If a principal asset is encumbered with an obligation that requires income from that asset to be paid directly to the creditor, the trustee shall transfer from principal to income an amount equal to the income paid to the creditor in reduction of the principal balance of the obligation.

Comment

Environmental expenses. All environmental expenses are payable from principal, subject to the power of the trustee to transfer funds to principal from income under Section 504. However, the Drafting Committee decided that it was not necessary to broaden this provision to cover other expenditures made under compulsion of governmental authority. See generally the annotation at 43 A.L.R.4th 1012 (Duty as Between Life Tenant and Remainderman with Respect to Cost of Improvements or Repairs Made Under Compulsion of Governmental Authority).

Environmental expenses paid by a trust are to be paid from principal under Section 502(a)(7) on the assumption that they will usually be extraordinary in nature. Environmental expenses might be paid from income if the trustee is carrying on a business that uses or sells toxic substances, in which case environmental cleanup costs would be a normal cost of doing business and would be accounted for under Section 403. In accounting under that Section, environmental costs will be a factor in determining

how much of the net receipts from the business is trust income. Paying all other environmental expenses from principal is consistent with this Act's approach regarding receipts - when a receipt is not clearly a current return on a principal asset, it should be added to principal because over time both the income and remainder beneficiaries benefit from this treatment. Here, allocating payments required by environmental laws to principal imposes the detriment of those payments over time on both the income and remainder beneficiaries.

Under Sections 504(a) and 504(b)(5), a trustee who makes or expects to make a principal disbursement for an environmental expense described in Section 502(a)(7) is authorized to transfer an appropriate amount from income to principal to reimburse principal for disbursements made or to provide a reserve for future principal disbursements.

The first part of Section 502(a)(7) is based upon the definition of an "environmental remediation trust" in Treas. Reg. § 301.7701-4(e)(as amended in 1996). This is not because the Act applies to an environmental remediation trust, but because the definition is a useful and thoroughly vetted description of the kinds of expenses that a trustee owning contaminated property might incur. Expenses incurred to comply with environmental laws include the cost of environmental consultants, administrative proceedings and burdens of every kind imposed as the result of an administrative or judicial proceeding, even though the burden is not formally characterized as a penalty.

Title proceedings. Disbursements that are made to protect a trust's property, referred to in Section 502(a)(4), include an "action to assure title" that is mentioned in Section 13(c)(2) of the 1962 Act.

Insurance premiums. Insurance premiums referred to in Section 502(a)(5) include title insurance premiums. They also include premiums on life insurance policies owned by the trust, which represent the trust's periodic investment in the insurance policy. There is no provision in the 1962 Act for life insurance premiums.

Taxes. Generation-skipping transfer taxes are payable from principal under subsection (a)(6).

Former (1962) Version

§ 13. [Charges Against Income and Principal.]

. . . .

(c) The following charges shall be made against principal:

(1) trustee's compensation not chargeable to income under subsections (a)(4) and (a)(5), special compensation of trustees, expenses reasonably incurred in connection with principal, court costs and attorney's fees primarily concerning matters of principal, and trustee's compensation computed on principal as an acceptance, distribution, or termination fee;

(2) charges not provided for in subsection (a), including the cost of investing and reinvesting principal, the payments on principal of an indebtedness (including a mortgage amortized by periodic payments of principal), expenses for preparation of property for rental or sale, and, unless the court directs otherwise, expenses incurred in maintaining or defending any action to construe the trust or protect it or the property or assure the title of any trust property;

(3) extraordinary repairs or expenses incurred in making a capital improvement to principal, including special assessments, but, a trustee may establish an allowance for depreciation out of income to the extent permitted by subsection (a)(2) and by section 8;

(4) any tax levied upon profit, gain, or other receipts allocated to principal notwithstanding denomination of the tax as an income tax by the taxing authority;

(5) if an estate or inheritance tax is levied in respect of a trust in which both an income beneficiary and a remainderman have an interest, any amount apportioned to the trust, including interest and penalties, even though the income beneficiary also has rights in the principal.

(d) Regularly recurring charges payable from income shall be apportioned to the same extent and in the same manner that income is apportioned under section 4.

---

§ 503. Transfers from Income to Principal for Depreciation.

(a) In this section, "depreciation" means a reduction in value due to wear, tear, decay, corrosion, or gradual obsolescence of a fixed asset having a useful life of more than one year.

(b) A trustee may transfer to principal a reasonable amount of the net cash receipts from a principal asset that is subject to depreciation, but may not transfer any amount for depreciation:

(1) of that portion of real property used or available for use by a beneficiary as a residence or of tangible personal property held or made available for the personal use or enjoyment of a beneficiary;

(2) during the administration of a decedent's estate; or

(3) under this section if the trustee is accounting under Section 403 for the business or activity in which the asset is used.

(c) An amount transferred to principal need not be held as a separate fund.

Comment

Prior Acts. The 1931 Act has no provision for depreciation. Section 13(a)(2) of the 1962 Act provides that a charge shall be made against income for "... a reasonable allowance for depreciation on property subject to depreciation under generally accepted accounting principles ... ." That provision has been resisted by many trustees, who do not provide for any depreciation for a variety of reasons. One reason relied upon is that a charge for depreciation is not needed to protect the remainder beneficiaries if the value of the land is increasing; another is that generally accepted accounting principles may not require depreciation to be taken if the property is not part of a business. The Drafting Committee concluded that the decision to provide for depreciation should be discretionary with the trustee. The power to transfer funds from income to principal that is granted by this section is a discretionary power of administration referred to in Section 103(b), and in exercising the power a trustee must comply with Section 103(b).

One purpose served by transferring cash from income to principal for depreciation is to provide funds to pay the principal of an indebtedness secured by the depreciable property. Section 504(b)(4) permits the trustee to transfer additional cash from income to principal for this purpose to the extent that the amount transferred from income to principal for depreciation is less than the amount of the principal payments.

§ 504. Transfers from Income to Reimburse Principal.

(a) If a trustee makes or expects to make a principal disbursement described in this section, the trustee may transfer an appropriate amount from income to principal in one or more accounting periods to reimburse principal or to provide a reserve for future principal disbursements.

(b) Principal disbursements to which subsection (a) applies include the following, but only to the extent that the trustee has not been and does not expect to be reimbursed by a third party:

(1) an amount chargeable to income but paid from principal because it is unusually large, including extraordinary repairs;

(2) a capital improvement to a principal asset, whether in the form of changes to an existing asset or the construction of a new asset, including special assessments;

(3) disbursements made to prepare property for rental, including tenant allowances, leasehold improvements, and broker's commissions;

(4) periodic payments on an obligation secured by a principal asset to the extent that the amount transferred from income to principal for depreciation is less than the periodic payments; and

(5) disbursements described in Section 502(a)(7).

(c) If the asset whose ownership gives rise to the disbursements becomes subject to a successive income interest after an income interest ends, a trustee may continue to transfer amounts from income to principal as provided in subsection (a).

Comment

Prior Acts. The sources of Section 504 are Section 13(b) of the 1962 Act, which permits a trustee to "regularize distributions," if charges against income are unusually large, by using "reserves or other reasonable means" to withhold sums from income distributions; Section 13(c)(3) of the 1962 Act, which authorizes a trustee to establish an allowance for depreciation out of income if principal is used for extraordinary repairs, capital improvements and special assessments; and Section 12(3) of the 1931 Act, which permits the trustee to spread income expenses of unusual amount "throughout a series of years." Section 504 contains a more detailed enumeration of the circumstances in which this authority may be used, and includes in subsection (b)(4) the express authority to use income to make principal payments on a mortgage if the depreciation charge against income is less than the principal payments on the mortgage.

§ 505. Income Taxes.

(a) A tax required to be paid by a trustee based on receipts allocated to income must be paid from income.

(b) A tax required to be paid by a trustee based on receipts allocated to principal must be paid from principal, even if the tax is called an income tax by the taxing authority.

(c) A tax required to be paid by a trustee on the trust's share of an entity's taxable income must be paid:

(1) from income to the extent that receipts from the entity are allocated only to income;

(2) from principal to the extent that receipts from the entity are allocated only to principal; and

(3) proportionately from principal and income to the extent that receipts from the entity are allocated to both income and principal; and

(4) from principal to the extent that the tax exceeds the total receipts from the entity.

(d) After applying subsections (a) through (c), the trustee shall adjust income or principal receipts to the extent that the trust's taxes are reduced because the trust receives a deduction for payments made to a beneficiary.

Comment

Taxes on Undistributed Entity Taxable Income. When a trust owns an interest in a pass-through entity, such as a partnership or S corporation, it must report its share of the entity's taxable income regardless of how much the entity distributes to the trust. Whether the entity distributes more or less than the trust's tax on its share of the entity's taxable income, the trust must pay the taxes and allocate them between income and principal.

Subsection (c) requires the trust to pay the taxes on its share of an entity's taxable income from income or principal receipts to the extent that receipts from the entity are allocable to each. This assures the trust a source of cash to pay some or all of the taxes on its share of the entity's taxable income. Subsection 505(d) recognizes that, except in the case of an Electing Small Business Trust (ESBT), a trust normally receives a deduction for amounts distributed to a beneficiary. Accordingly, subsection 505(d) requires the trust to increase receipts payable to a beneficiary as determined under subsection (c) to the extent the trust's taxes are reduced by distributing those receipts to the beneficiary.

Because the trust's taxes and amounts distributed to a beneficiary are interrelated, the trust may be required to apply a formula to determine the correct amount payable to a beneficiary. This formula should take into account that each time a distribution is made to a beneficiary, the trust taxes are reduced and amounts distributable to a beneficiary are increased. The formula assures that after deducting distributions to a beneficiary, the trust has enough to satisfy its taxes on its share of the entity's taxable income as reduced by distributions to beneficiaries.

Example (1) – Trust T receives a Schedule K-1 from Partnership P reflecting taxable income of $1 million. Partnership P distributes $100,000 to T, which allocates the receipts to income. Both Trust T and income Beneficiary B are in the 35 percent tax bracket. Trust T's tax on $1 million of taxable income is $350,000. Under Subsection (c) T's tax must be paid from income receipts because receipts from the entity are allocated only to income. Therefore, T must apply the entire $100,000 of income receipts to pay its tax. In this case, Beneficiary B receives nothing.

Example (2) - Trust T receives a Schedule K-1 from Partnership P reflecting taxable income of $1 million. Partnership P distributes $500,000 to T, which allocates the receipts to income. Both Trust T and income Beneficiary B are in the 35 percent tax bracket. Trust T's tax on $1 million of taxable income is $350,000. Under Subsection (c), T's tax must be paid from income receipts because receipts from P are allocated only to income. Therefore, T uses $350,000 of the $500,000 to pay its taxes and distributes the remaining $150,000 to B. The $150,000 payment to B reduces T's taxes by $52,500, which it must pay to B. But the $52,500 further reduces T's taxes by $18,375, which it also must pay to B. In fact, each time T makes a distribution to B, its taxes are further reduced, causing another payment to be due B.

Alternatively, T can apply the following algebraic formula to determine the amount payable to B:

$$D = (C\text{-}R^*K)/(1\text{-}R)$$

D = Distribution to income beneficiary
C = Cash paid by the entity to the trust
R = tax rate on income
K = entity's K-1 taxable income

Applying the formula to Example (2) above, Trust T must pay $230,769 to B so that after deducting the payment, T has exactly enough to pay its tax on the remaining taxable income from P.

Taxable Income per K-1	1,000,000
Payment to beneficiary	230,769[1]
Trust Taxable Income	$ 769,231
35 percent tax	269,231

Partnership Distribution	$ 500,000
Fiduciary's Tax Liability	(269,231)
Payable to the Beneficiary	$ 230,769

In addition, B will report $230,769 on his or her own personal income tax return, paying taxes of $80,769. Because Trust T withheld $269,231 to pay its taxes and B paid $80,769 taxes of its own, B bore the entire $350,000 tax burden on the $1 million of entity taxable income, including the $500,000 that the entity retained that presumably increased the value of the trust's investment entity.

If a trustee determines that it is appropriate to so, it should consider exercising the discretion granted in UPIA section 506 to adjust between income and principal. Alternatively, the trustee may exercise the power to adjust under UPIA section 104 to the extent it is available and appropriate under the circumstances, including whether a future distribution from the entity that would be allocated to principal should be reallocated to income because the income beneficiary already bore the burden of taxes on the reinvested income. In exercising the power, the trust should consider the impact that future distributions will have on any current adjustments.

§ 506. Adjustments Between Principal and Income Because of Taxes.

(a) A fiduciary may make adjustments between principal and income to offset the shifting of economic interests or tax benefits between income beneficiaries and remainder beneficiaries which arise from:

(1) elections and decisions, other than those described in subsection (b), that the fiduciary makes from time to time regarding tax matters;

(2) an income tax or any other tax that is imposed upon the fiduciary or a beneficiary as a result of a transaction involving or a distribution from the estate or trust; or

(3) the ownership by an estate or trust of an interest in an entity whose taxable income, whether or not distributed, is includable in the taxable income of the estate, trust, or a beneficiary.

(b) If the amount of an estate tax marital deduction or charitable contribution deduction is reduced because a fiduciary deducts an amount paid from principal for income tax purposes instead of deducting it for estate tax purposes, and as a result estate taxes paid from principal are increased and income taxes paid by an estate, trust, or beneficiary are decreased, each estate, trust, or beneficiary that benefits from the decrease in income tax shall reimburse the principal from which the increase in estate tax is paid. The total reimbursement must equal the increase in the estate tax to the extent that the principal used to pay the increase would have qualified for a marital deduction or charitable contribution deduction but for the payment. The proportionate share of the reimbursement for each estate, trust, or beneficiary whose income taxes are reduced must be the same as its proportionate share of the total decrease in income tax. An estate or trust shall reimburse principal from income.

---

[1] $D = (C-R*K)/(1-R) = (500,000 - 350,000)/(1 - .35) = $230,769$. (D is the amount payable to the income beneficiary, K is the entity's K-1 taxable income, R is the trust ordinary tax rate, and C is the cash distributed by the entity).

Comment

Discretionary adjustments. Section 506(a) permits the fiduciary to make adjustments between income and principal because of tax law provisions. It would permit discretionary adjustments in situations like these: (1) A fiduciary elects to deduct administration expenses that are paid from principal on an income tax return instead of on the estate tax return; (2) a distribution of a principal asset to a trust or other beneficiary causes the taxable income of an estate or trust to be carried out to the distributee and relieves the persons who receive the income of any obligation to pay income tax on the income; or (3) a trustee realizes a capital gain on the sale of a principal asset and pays a large state income tax on the gain, but under applicable federal income tax rules the trustee may not deduct the state income tax payment from the capital gain in calculating the trust's federal capital gain tax, and the income beneficiary receives the benefit of the deduction for state income tax paid on the capital gain. See generally Joel C. Dobris, Limits on the Doctrine of Equitable Adjustment in Sophisticated Postmortem Tax Planning, 66 Iowa L. Rev. 273 (1981).

Section 506(a)(3) applies to a qualified Subchapter S trust (QSST) whose income beneficiary is required to include a pro rata share of the S corporation's taxable income in his return. If the QSST does not receive a cash distribution from the corporation that is large enough to cover the income beneficiary's tax liability, the trustee may distribute additional cash from principal to the income beneficiary. In this case the retention of cash by the corporation benefits the trust principal. This situation could occur if the corporation's taxable income includes capital gain from the sale of a business asset and the sale proceeds are reinvested in the business instead of being distributed to shareholders.

Mandatory adjustment. Subsection (b) provides for a mandatory adjustment from income to principal to the extent needed to preserve an estate tax marital deduction or charitable contributions deduction. It is derived from New York's EPTL § 11-1.2(A), which requires principal to be reimbursed by those who benefit when a fiduciary elects to deduct administration expenses on an income tax return instead of the estate tax return. Unlike the New York provision, subsection (b) limits a mandatory reimbursement to cases in which a marital deduction or a charitable contributions deduction is reduced by the payment of additional estate taxes because of the fiduciary's income tax election. It is intended to preserve the result reached in *Estate of Britenstool v. Commissioner*, 46 T.C. 711 (1966), in which the Tax Court held that a reimbursement required by the predecessor of EPTL § 11-1.2(A) resulted in the estate receiving the same charitable contributions deduction it would have received if the administration expenses had been deducted for estate tax purposes instead of for income tax purposes. Because a fiduciary will elect to deduct administration expenses for income tax purposes only when the income tax reduction exceeds the estate tax reduction, the effect of this adjustment is that the principal is placed in the same position it would have occupied if the fiduciary had deducted the expenses for estate tax purposes, but the income beneficiaries receive an additional benefit. For example, if the income tax benefit from the deduction is $30,000 and the estate tax benefit would have been $20,000, principal will be reimbursed $20,000 and the net benefit to the income beneficiaries will be $10,000.

Irrevocable grantor trusts. Under Sections 671-679 of the Internal Revenue Code (the "grantor trust" provisions), a person who creates an irrevocable trust for the benefit of another person may be subject to tax on the trust's income or capital gains, or both, even though the settlor is not entitled to receive any income or principal from the trust. Because this is now a well-known tax result, many trusts have been created to produce this result, but there are also trusts that are unintentionally subject to this rule. The Act does not require or authorize a trustee to distribute funds from the trust to the settlor in these cases because it is difficult to establish a rule that applies only to trusts where this tax result is unintended and does not apply to trusts where the tax result is intended. Settlors who intend this tax result rarely state it as an objective in the terms of the trust, but instead rely on the operation of the tax law to produce the desired result. As a result it may not be possible to determine from the terms of the trust if the result was intentional or unintentional. If the drafter of such a trust wants the trustee to have the authority to distribute principal or income to the settlor to reimburse the settlor for taxes paid on the trust's income or capital gains, such a provision should be placed in the terms of the trust. In some situations the Internal Revenue Service may require that such a provision be placed in the terms of the trust as a condition to issuing a private letter ruling.

[ARTICLE] 6
MISCELLANEOUS PROVISIONS

§ 601. Uniformity of Application and Construction. In applying and construing this Uniform Act, consideration must be given to the need to promote uniformity of the law with respect to its subject matter among States that enact it.

§ 602. Severability Clause. If any provision of this [Act] or its application to any person or circumstance is held invalid, the invalidity does not affect other provisions or applications of this [Act] which can be given effect without the invalid provision or application, and to this end the provisions of this [Act] are severable.

§ 603. Repeal. The following acts and parts of acts are repealed:

(1) ....

(2) ....

(3) ....

§ 604. Effective Date. This [Act] takes effect on ....

§ 605. Application of [Act] to Existing Trusts and Estates. This [Act] applies to every trust or decedent's estate existing on [the effective date of this [Act]] except as otherwise expressly provided in the will or terms of the trust or in this [Act].

Former (1962) Version

§ 14. [Application of Act.] Except as specifically provided in the trust instrument or the will or in this Act, this Act shall apply to any receipt or expense received or incurred after the effective date of this Act by any trust or decedent's estate whether established before or after the effective date of this Act and whether the asset involved was acquired by the trustee before or after the effective date of this Act.

ALTERNATIVE A

§ 606. Transitional Matters. Section 409, as amended by this [act], applies to a trust described in Section 409(d) on and after the following dates:

(1) If the trust is not funded as of [the effective date of this [act]], the date of the decedent's death.

(2) If the trust is initially funded in the calendar year beginning January 1, _____ [insert year in which this [act] takes effect], the date of the decedent's death.

(3) If the trust is not described in paragraph (1) or (2), January 1, _____ [insert year in which this [act] takes effect].

ALTERNATIVE B

§ 606. Transitional Matters. Section 409 applies to a trust described in Section 409(d) on and after the following dates:

(1) If the trust is not funded as of [the effective date of this [act]], the date of the decedent's death.

(2) If the trust is initially funded in the calendar year beginning January 1, _____ [insert year in which this [act] takes effect], the date of the decedent's death.

(3) If the trust is not described in paragraph (1) or (2), January 1, _____ [insert year in which this [act] takes effect].

END OF ALTERNATIVES

Legislative Note: Use Alternative A if your state has already enacted the Uniform Principal and Income Act. Use Alternative B if your state has not enacted the Uniform Principal and Income Act.

UNIFORM PRUDENT INVESTOR ACT (1994)

Table of Sections

Prefatory Note

Over the quarter century from the late 1960's the investment practices of fiduciaries experienced significant change. The Uniform Prudent Investor Act (UPIA) undertakes to update trust investment law in recognition of the alterations that have occurred in investment practice. These changes have occurred under the influence of a large and broadly accepted body of empirical and theoretical knowledge about the behavior of capital markets, often described as "modern portfolio theory."

This Act draws upon the revised standards for prudent trust investment promulgated by the American Law Institute in its Restatement (Third) of Trusts: Prudent Investor Rule (1992) [hereinafter Restatement of Trusts 3d: Prudent Investor Rule; also referred to as 1992 Restatement].

Objectives of the Act. UPIA makes five fundamental alterations in the former criteria for prudent investing. All are to be found in the Restatement of Trusts 3d: Prudent Investor Rule.

(1) The standard of prudence is applied to any investment as part of the total portfolio, rather than to individual investments. In the trust setting the term "portfolio" embraces all the trust's assets. UPIA § 2(b).

(2) The tradeoff in all investing between risk and return is identified as the fiduciary's central consideration. UPIA § 2(b).

(3) All categoric restrictions on types of investments have been abrogated; the trustee can invest in anything that plays an appropriate role in achieving the risk/return objectives of the trust and that meets the other requirements of prudent investing. UPIA § 2(e).

(4) The long familiar requirement that fiduciaries diversify their investments has been integrated into the definition of prudent investing. UPIA § 3.

(5) The much criticized former rule of trust law forbidding the trustee to delegate investment and management functions has been reversed. Delegation is now permitted, subject to safeguards. UPIA § 9.

Literature. These changes in trust investment law have been presaged in an extensive body of practical and scholarly writing. See especially the discussion and reporter's notes by Edward C. Halbach, Jr., in Restatement of Trusts 3d: Prudent Investor Rule (1992); see also Edward C. Halbach, Jr., Trust Investment Law in the Third Restatement, 27 Real Property, Probate & Trust J. 407 (1992); Bevis Longstreth, Modern Investment Management and the Prudent Man Rule (1986); Jeffrey N. Gordon, The Puzzling Persistence of the Constrained Prudent Man Rule, 62 N.Y.U.L. Rev. 52 (1987); John H. Langbein & Richard A. Posner, The Revolution in Trust Investment Law, 62 A.B.A.J. 887 (1976); Note, The Regulation of Risky Investments, 83 Harvard L. Rev. 603 (1970). A succinct account of the main findings of modern portfolio theory, written for lawyers, is Jonathan R. Macey, An Introduction to Modern Financial Theory (1991) (American College of Trust & Estate Counsel Foundation). A leading introductory text on modern portfolio theory is R.A. Brealey, An Introduction to Risk and Return from Common Stocks (2d ed. 1983).

Legislation. Most states have legislation governing trust-investment law. This Act promotes uniformity of state law on the basis of the new consensus reflected in the Restatement of Trusts 3d: Prudent Investor Rule. Some states have already acted. California, Delaware, Georgia, Minnesota, Tennessee, and Washington revised their prudent investor legislation to emphasize the total-portfolio standard of care in advance of the 1992 Restatement. These statutes are extracted and discussed in Restatement of Trusts 3d: Prudent Investor Rule § 227, reporter's note, at 60-66 (1992).

Drafters in Illinois in 1991 worked from the April 1990 "Proposed Final Draft" of the Restatement of Trusts 3d: Prudent Investor Rule and enacted legislation that is closely modeled on the new Restatement. 760 ILCS § 5/5 (prudent investing); and § 5/5.1 (delegation) (1992). As the Comments to this Uniform Prudent Investor Act reflect, the Act draws upon the Illinois statute in several sections. Virginia revised its prudent investor act in a similar vein in 1992. Virginia Code § 26-45.1 (prudent investing) (1992). Florida revised its statute in 1993. Florida Laws, ch. 93-257, amending Florida Statutes § 518.11 (prudent investing) and creating § 518.112 (delegation). New York legislation drawing on the new Restatement and on a preliminary version of this Uniform Prudent Investor Act was enacted in 1994. N.Y. Assembly Bill 11683-B, Ch. 609 (1994), adding Estates, Powers and Trusts Law § 11-2.3 (Prudent Investor Act).

Remedies. This Act does not undertake to address issues of remedy law or the computation of damages in trust matters. Remedies are the subject of a reasonably distinct body of doctrine. See generally Restatement (Second) of Trusts §§ 197-226A (1959) [hereinafter cited as Restatement of Trusts 2d; also referred to as 1959 Restatement].

Implications for charitable and pension trusts. This Act is centrally concerned with the investment responsibilities arising under the private gratuitous trust, which is the common vehicle for conditioned wealth transfer within the family. Nevertheless, the prudent investor rule also bears on charitable and pension trusts, among others. "In making investments of trust funds the trustee of a charitable trust is under a duty similar to that of the trustee of a private trust." Restatement of Trusts 2d § 389 (1959). The Employee Retirement Income Security Act (ERISA), the federal regulatory scheme for pension trusts enacted in 1974, absorbs trust-investment law through the prudence standard of ERISA § 404(a)(1)(B), 29 U.S.C. § 1104(a). The Supreme Court has said: "ERISA's legislative history confirms that the Act's fiduciary responsibility provisions 'codif[y] and mak[e] applicable to [ERISA] fiduciaries certain principles developed in the evolution of the law of trusts.'" *Firestone Tire & Rubber Co. v. Bruch*, 489 U.S. 101, 110-11 (1989) (footnote omitted).

Other fiduciary relationships. The Uniform Prudent Investor Act regulates the investment responsibilities of trustees. Other fiduciaries - such as executors, conservators, and guardians of the property - sometimes have responsibilities over assets that are governed by the standards of prudent investment. It will often be appropriate for states to adapt the law governing investment by trustees under this Act to these other fiduciary regimes, taking account of such changed circumstances as the relatively short duration of most executorships and the intensity of court supervision of conservators and guardians in some jurisdictions. The present Act does not undertake to adjust trust-investment law to the special circumstances of the state schemes for administering decedents' estates or conducting the affairs of protected persons.

Although the Uniform Prudent Investor Act by its terms applies to trusts and not to charitable corporations, the standards of the Act can be expected to inform the investment responsibilities of directors and officers of charitable corporations. As the 1992 Restatement observes, "the duties of the members of the governing board of a charitable corporation are generally similar to the duties of the trustee of a charitable trust." Restatement of Trusts 3d: Prudent Investor Rule § 379, Comment *b*, at 190 (1992). See also id. § 389, Comment *b*, at 190-91 (absent contrary statute or other provision, prudent investor rule applies to investment of funds held for charitable corporations).

§ 1. Prudent Investor Rule.

(a) Except as otherwise provided in subsection (b), a trustee who invests and manages trust assets owes a duty to the beneficiaries of the trust to comply with the prudent investor rule set forth in this [Act].

(b) The prudent investor rule, a default rule, may be expanded, restricted, eliminated, or otherwise altered by the provisions of a trust. A trustee is not liable to a beneficiary to the extent that the trustee acted in reasonable reliance on the provisions of the trust.

Comment

This section imposes the obligation of prudence in the conduct of investment functions and identifies further sections of the Act that specify the attributes of prudent conduct.

Origins. The prudence standard for trust investing traces back to *Harvard College v. Amory*, 26 Mass. (9 Pick.) 446 (1830). Trustees should "observe how men of prudence, discretion and intelligence manage their own affairs, not in regard to speculation, but in regard to the permanent disposition of their funds, considering the probable income, as well as the probable safety of the capital to be invested." Id. at 461.

Prior legislation. The Model Prudent Man Rule Statute (1942), sponsored by the American Bankers Association, undertook to codify the language of the *Amory* case. See Mayo A. Shattuck, The Development of the Prudent Man Rule for Fiduciary Investment in the United States in the Twentieth Century, 12 Ohio State L.J. 491, at 501 (1951); for the text of the model act, which inspired many state statutes, see id. at 508-09. Another prominent codification of the *Amory* standard is Uniform Probate Code § 7-302 (1969), which provides that "the trustee shall observe the standards in dealing with the trust assets that would be observed by a prudent man dealing with the property of another . . . ."

Congress has imposed a comparable prudence standard for the administration of pension and employee benefit trusts in the Employee Retirement Income Security Act (ERISA), enacted in 1974. ERISA § 404(a)(1)(B), 29 U.S.C. § 1104(a), provides that "a fiduciary shall discharge his duties with respect to a plan solely in the interest of the participants and beneficiaries and . . . with the care, skill, prudence, and diligence under the circumstances then prevailing that a prudent man acting in a like capacity and familiar with such matters would use in the conduct of an enterprise of like character and with like aims . . . ."

Prior Restatement. The Restatement of Trusts 2d (1959) also tracked the language of the *Amory* case: "In making investments of trust funds the trustee is under a duty to the beneficiary . . . to make such investments and only such investments as a prudent man would make of his own property having in view the preservation of the estate and the amount and regularity of the income to be derived . . . ." Restatement of Trusts 2d § 227 (1959).

Objective standard. The concept of prudence in the judicial opinions and legislation is essentially relational or comparative. It resembles in this respect the "reasonable person" rule of tort law. A prudent trustee behaves as other trustees similarly situated would behave. The standard is, therefore, objective rather than subjective. Sections 2 through 9 of this Act identify the main factors that bear on prudent investment behavior.

Variation. Almost all of the rules of trust law are default rules, that is, rules that the settlor may alter or abrogate. Subsection (b) carries forward this traditional attribute of trust law. Traditional trust law also allows the beneficiaries of the trust to excuse its performance, when they are all capable and not misinformed. Restatement of Trusts 2d § 216 (1959).

§ 2. Standard of Care; Portfolio Strategy; Risk and Return Objectives.

(a) A trustee shall invest and manage trust assets as a prudent investor would, by considering the purposes, terms, distribution requirements, and other circumstances of the trust. In satisfying this standard, the trustee shall exercise reasonable care, skill, and caution.

(b) A trustee's investment and management decisions respecting individual assets must be evaluated not in isolation but in the context of the trust portfolio as a whole and as a part of an overall investment strategy having risk and return objectives reasonably suited to the trust.

(c) Among circumstances that a trustee shall consider in investing and managing trust assets are such of the following as are relevant to the trust or its beneficiaries:

(1) general economic conditions;

(2) the possible effect of inflation or deflation;

(3) the expected tax consequences of investment decisions or strategies;

(4) the role that each investment or course of action plays within the overall trust portfolio, which may include financial assets, interests in closely held enterprises, tangible and intangible personal property, and real property;

(5) the expected total return from income and the appreciation of capital;

(6) other resources of the beneficiaries;

(7) needs for liquidity, regularity of income, and preservation or appreciation of capital; and

(8) an asset's special relationship or special value, if any, to the purposes of the trust or to one or more of the beneficiaries.

(d) A trustee shall make a reasonable effort to verify facts relevant to the investment and management of trust assets.

(e) A trustee may invest in any kind of property or type of investment consistent with the standards of this [Act].

(f) A trustee who has special skills or expertise, or is named trustee in reliance upon the trustee's representation that the trustee has special skills or expertise, has a duty to use those special skills or expertise.

Comment

Section 2 is the heart of the Act. Subsections (a), (b), and (c) are patterned loosely on the language of the Restatement of Trusts 3d: Prudent Investor Rule § 227 (1992), and on the 1991 Illinois statute, 760 § ILCS 5/5a (1992). Subsection (f) is derived from Uniform Probate Code § 7-302 (1969).

Objective standard. Subsection (a) of this Act carries forward the relational and objective standard made familiar in the *Amory* case, in earlier prudent investor legislation, and in the Restatements. Early formulations of the prudent person rule were sometimes troubled by the effort to distinguish between the standard of a prudent person investing for another and investing on his or her own account. The language of subsection (a), by relating the trustee's duty to "the purposes, terms, distribution requirements, and other circumstances of the trust," should put such questions to rest. The standard is the standard of the prudent investor similarly situated.

Portfolio standard. Subsection (b) emphasizes the consolidated portfolio standard for evaluating investment decisions. An investment that might be imprudent standing alone can become prudent if undertaken in sensible relation to other trust assets, or to other nontrust assets. In the trust setting the term "portfolio" embraces the entire trust estate.

Risk and return. Subsection (b) also sounds the main theme of modern investment practice, sensitivity to the risk/return curve. See generally the works cited in the Prefatory Note to this Act, under "Literature." Returns correlate strongly with risk, but tolerance for risk varies greatly with the financial and other circumstances of the investor, or in the case of a trust, with the purposes of the trust and the relevant circumstances of the beneficiaries. A trust whose main purpose is to support an elderly widow of modest means will have a lower risk tolerance than a trust to accumulate for a young scion of great wealth.

Subsection (b) of this Act follows Restatement of Trusts 3d: Prudent Investor Rule § 227(a), which provides that the standard of prudent investing "requires the exercise of reasonable care, skill, and caution, and is to be applied to investments not in isolation but in the context of the trust portfolio and as a part of an overall investment strategy, which should incorporate risk and return objectives reasonably suitable to the trust."

Factors affecting investment. Subsection (c) points to certain of the factors that commonly bear on risk/return preferences in fiduciary investing. This listing is nonexclusive. Tax considerations, such as preserving the stepped up basis on death under Internal Revenue Code § 1014 for low-basis assets, have traditionally been exceptionally important in estate planning for affluent persons. Under the present recognition rules of the federal income tax, taxable investors, including trust beneficiaries, are in general best served by an investment strategy that minimizes the taxation incident to portfolio turnover. See generally Robert H. Jeffrey & Robert D. Arnott, Is Your Alpha Big Enough to Cover Its Taxes?, Journal of Portfolio Management 15 (Spring 1993).

Another familiar example of how tax considerations bear upon trust investing: In a regime of pass-through taxation, it may be prudent for the trust to buy lower yielding tax-exempt securities for high-bracket taxpayers, whereas it would ordinarily be imprudent for the trustees of a charitable trust, whose income is tax exempt, to accept the lowered yields associated with tax-exempt securities.

When tax considerations affect beneficiaries differently, the trustee's duty of impartiality requires attention to the competing interests of each of them.

Subsection (c)(8), allowing the trustee to take into account any preferences of the beneficiaries respecting heirlooms or other prized assets, derives from the Illinois act, 760 ILCS § 5/5(a)(4) (1992).

Duty to monitor. Subsections (a) through (d) apply both to investing and managing trust assets. "Managing" embraces monitoring, that is, the trustee's continuing responsibility for oversight of the suitability of investments already made as well as the trustee's decisions respecting new investments.

Duty to investigate. Subsection (d) carries forward the traditional responsibility of the fiduciary investor to examine information likely to bear importantly on the value or the security of an investment - for example, audit reports or records of title. E.g., *Estate of Collins*, 72 Cal. App. 3d 663, 139 Cal. Rptr. 644 (1977) (trustees lent on a junior mortgage on unimproved real estate, failed to have land appraised, and accepted an unaudited financial statement; held liable for losses).

Abrogating categoric restrictions. Subsection 2(e) clarifies that no particular kind of property or type of investment is inherently imprudent. Traditional trust law was encumbered with a variety of categoric exclusions, such as prohibitions on junior mortgages or new ventures. In some states legislation created so-called "legal lists" of approved trust investments. The universe of investment products changes incessantly. Investments that were at one time thought too risky, such as equities, or more recently, futures, are now used in fiduciary portfolios. By contrast, the investment that was at one time thought ideal for trusts, the long-term bond, has been discovered to

import a level of risk and volatility - in this case, inflation risk - that had not been anticipated. Accordingly, section 2(e) of this Act follows Restatement of Trusts 3d: Prudent Investor Rule in abrogating categoric restrictions. The Restatement says: "Specific investments or techniques are not per se prudent or imprudent. The riskiness of a specific property, and thus the propriety of its inclusion in the trust estate, is not judged in the abstract but in terms of its anticipated effect on the particular trust's portfolio." Restatement of Trusts 3d: Prudent Investor Rule § 227, Comment f, at 24 (1992). The premise of subsection 2(e) is that trust beneficiaries are better protected by the Act's emphasis on close attention to risk/return objectives as prescribed in subsection 2(b) than in attempts to identify categories of investment that are per se prudent or imprudent.

The Act impliedly disavows the emphasis in older law on avoiding "speculative" or "risky" investments. Low levels of risk may be appropriate in some trust settings but inappropriate in others. It is the trustee's task to invest at a risk level that is suitable to the purposes of the trust.

The abolition of categoric restrictions against types of investment in no way alters the trustee's conventional duty of loyalty, which is reiterated for the purposes of this Act in Section 5. For example, were the trustee to invest in a second mortgage on a piece of real property owned by the trustee, the investment would be wrongful on account of the trustee's breach of the duty to abstain from self-dealing, even though the investment would no longer automatically offend the former categoric restriction against fiduciary investments in junior mortgages.

Professional fiduciaries. The distinction taken in subsection (f) between amateur and professional trustees is familiar law. The prudent investor standard applies to a range of fiduciaries, from the most sophisticated professional investment management firms and corporate fiduciaries, to family members of minimal experience. Because the standard of prudence is relational, it follows that the standard for professional trustees is the standard of prudent professionals; for amateurs, it is the standard of prudent amateurs. Restatement of Trusts 2d § 174 (1959) provides: "The trustee is under a duty to the beneficiary in administering the trust to exercise such care and skill as a man of ordinary prudence would exercise in dealing with his own property; and if the trustee has or procures his appointment as trustee by representing that he has greater skill than that of a man of ordinary prudence, he is under a duty to exercise such skill." Case law strongly supports the concept of the higher standard of care for the trustee representing itself to be expert or professional. See Annot., Standard of Care Required of Trustee Representing Itself to Have Expert Knowledge or Skill, 91 A.L.R. 3d 904 (1979) & 1992 Supp. at 48-49.

The Drafting Committee declined the suggestion that the Act should create an exception to the prudent investor rule (or to the diversification requirement of Section 3) in the case of smaller trusts. The Committee believes that subsections (b) and (c) of the Act emphasize factors that are sensitive to the traits of small trusts; and that subsection (f) adjusts helpfully for the distinction between professional and amateur trusteeship. Furthermore, it is always open to the settlor of a trust under Section 1(b) of the Act to reduce the trustee's standard of care if the settlor deems such a step appropriate. The official comments

to the 1992 Restatement observe that pooled investments, such as mutual funds and bank common trust funds, are especially suitable for small trusts. Restatement of Trusts 3d: Prudent Investor Rule § 227, Comments *h*, *m*, at 28, 51; reporter's note to Comment *g*, id. at 83.

Matters of proof. Although virtually all express trusts are created by written instrument, oral trusts are known, and accordingly, this Act presupposes no formal requirement that trust terms be in writing. When there is a written trust instrument, modern authority strongly favors allowing evidence extrinsic to the instrument to be consulted for the purpose of ascertaining the settlor's intent. See Uniform Probate Code § 2-601 (1990), Comment; Restatement (Third) of Property: Donative Transfers (Preliminary Draft No. 2, ch. 11, Sept. 11, 1992).

§ 3. Diversification. A trustee shall diversify the investments of the trust unless the trustee reasonably determines that, because of special circumstances, the purposes of the trust are better served without diversifying.

Comment

The language of this section derives from Restatement of Trusts 2d § 228 (1959). ERISA insists upon a comparable rule for pension trusts. ERISA § 404(a)(1)(C), 29 U.S.C. § 1104(a)(1)(C). Case law overwhelmingly supports the duty to diversify. See Annot., Duty of Trustee to Diversify Investments, and Liability for Failure to Do So, 24 A.L.R. 3d 730 (1969) & 1992 Supp. at 78-79.

The 1992 Restatement of Trusts takes the significant step of integrating the diversification requirement into the concept of prudent investing. Section 227(b) of the 1992 Restatement treats diversification as one of the fundamental elements of prudent investing, replacing the separate section 228 of the Restatement of Trusts 2d. The message of the 1992 Restatement, carried forward in Section 3 of this Act, is that prudent investing ordinarily requires diversification.

Circumstances can, however, overcome the duty to diversify. For example, if a tax-sensitive trust owns an underdiversified block of low-basis securities, the tax costs of recognizing the gain may outweigh the advantages of diversifying the holding. The wish to retain a family business is another situation in which the purposes of the trust sometimes override the conventional duty to diversify.

Rationale for diversification. "Diversification reduces risk . . . [because] stock price movements are not uniform. They are imperfectly correlated. This means that if one holds a well diversified portfolio, the gains in one investment will cancel out the losses in another." Jonathan R. Macey, An Introduction to Modern Financial Theory 20 (American College of Trust and Estate Counsel Foundation, 1991). For example, during the Arab oil embargo of 1973, international oil stocks suffered declines, but the shares of domestic oil producers and coal companies benefitted. Holding a broad enough portfolio allowed the investor to set off, to some extent, the losses associated with the embargo.

Modern portfolio theory divides risk into the categories of "compensated" and "uncompensated" risk. The risk of owning shares in a mature and well-managed company in a settled industry is less than the risk of owning shares in a start-up high-technology venture. The investor requires a higher expected return to induce the investor to bear the greater risk of disappointment associated with the start-up firm. This is compensated risk—the firm pays the investor for bearing the risk. By contrast, nobody pays the investor for owning too few stocks. The investor who owned only international oils in 1973 was running a risk that could have been reduced by having configured the portfolio differently–to include investments in different industries. This is uncompensated risk–nobody pays the investor for owning shares in too few industries and too few companies. Risk that can be eliminated by adding different stocks (or bonds) is uncompensated risk. The object of diversification is to minimize this uncompensated risk of having too few investments. "As long as stock prices do not move exactly together, the risk of a diversified portfolio will be less than the average risk of the separate holdings." R.A. Brealey, An Introduction to Risk and Return from Common Stocks 103 (2d ed. 1983).

There is no automatic rule for identifying how much diversification is enough. The 1992 Restatement says: "Significant diversification advantages can be achieved with a small number of well-selected securities representing different industries . . . . Broader diversification is usually to be preferred in trust investing," and pooled investment vehicles "make thorough diversification practical for most trustees." Restatement of Trusts 3d: Prudent Investor Rule § 227, General Note on Comments *e-h*, at 77 (1992). See also Macey, supra, at 23-24; Brealey, supra, at 111-13.

Diversifying by pooling. It is difficult for a small trust fund to diversify thoroughly by constructing its own portfolio of individually selected investments. Transaction costs such as the round-lot (100 share) trading economies make it relatively expensive for a small investor to assemble a broad enough portfolio to minimize uncompensated risk. For this reason, pooled investment vehicles have become the main mechanism for facilitating diversification for the investment needs of smaller trusts.

Most states have legislation authorizing common trust funds; see 3 Austin W. Scott & William F. Fratcher, The Law of Trusts § 227.9, at 463-65 n.26 (4th ed. 1988) (collecting citations to state statutes). As of 1992, 35 states and the District of Columbia had enacted the Uniform Common Trust Fund Act (UCTFA) (1938), overcoming the rule against commingling trust assets and expressly enabling banks and trust companies to establish common trust funds. 7 Uniform Laws Ann. 1992 Supp. at 130 (schedule of adopting states). The Prefatory Note to the UCTFA explains: "The purposes of such a common or joint investment fund are to diversify the investment of the several trusts and thus spread the risk of loss, and to make it easy to invest any amount of trust funds quickly and with a small amount of trouble." 7 Uniform Laws Ann. 402 (1985).

Fiduciary investing in mutual funds. Trusts can also achieve diversification by investing in mutual funds. See Restatement of Trusts 3d: Prudent Investor Rule, § 227, Comment *m*, at 99-100 (1992) (endorsing trust investment in mutual funds). ERISA § 401(b)(1), 29 U.S.C. § 1101(b)(1), expressly authorizes pension trusts to invest in mutual funds, identified as securities "issued by an investment company registered under the Investment Company Act of 1940 . . . ."

§ 4. Duties at Inception of Trusteeship.

§ 4. Duties at Inception of Trusteeship. Within a reasonable time after accepting a trusteeship or receiving trust assets, a trustee shall review the trust assets and make and implement decisions concerning the retention and disposition of assets, in order to bring the trust portfolio into compliance with the purposes, terms, distribution requirements, and other circumstances of the trust, and with the requirements of this [Act].

Comment

Section 4, requiring the trustee to dispose of unsuitable assets within a reasonable time, is old law, codified in Restatement of Trusts 3d: Prudent Investor Rule § 229 (1992), lightly revising Restatement of Trusts 2d § 230 (1959). The duty extends as well to investments that were proper when purchased but subsequently become improper. Restatement of Trusts 2d § 231 (1959). The same standards apply to successor trustees, see Restatement of Trusts 2d § 196 (1959).

The question of what period of time is reasonable turns on the totality of factors affecting the asset and the trust. The 1959 Restatement took the view that "[o]rdinarily any time within a year is reasonable, but under some circumstances a year may be too long a time and under other circumstances a trustee is not liable although he fails to effect the conversion for more than a year." Restatement of Trusts 2d § 230, comment *b* (1959). The 1992 Restatement retreated from this rule of thumb, saying, "No positive rule can be stated with respect to what constitutes a reasonable time for the sale or exchange of securities."

Restatement of Trusts 3d: Prudent Investor Rule § 229, comment *b* (1992).

The criteria and circumstances identified in Section 2 of this Act as bearing upon the prudence of decisions to invest and manage trust assets also pertain to the prudence of decisions to retain or dispose of inception assets under this section.

§ 5. Loyalty. A trustee shall invest and manage the trust assets solely in the interest of the beneficiaries.

Comment

The duty of loyalty is perhaps the most characteristic rule of trust law, requiring the trustee to act exclusively for the beneficiaries, as opposed to acting for the trustee's own interest or that of third parties. The language of Section 4 of this Act derives from Restatement of Trusts 3d: Prudent Investor Rule § 170 (1992), which makes minute changes in Restatement of Trusts 2d § 170 (1959).

The concept that the duty of prudence in trust administration, especially in investing and managing trust assets, entails adherence to the duty of loyalty is familiar. ERISA § 404(a)(1)(B), 29 U.S.C. § 1104(a)(1)(B), extracted in the Comment to Section 1 of this Act, effectively merges the requirements of prudence and loyalty. A fiduciary cannot be prudent in the conduct of investment functions if the fiduciary is sacrificing the interests of the beneficiaries.

The duty of loyalty is not limited to settings entailing self-dealing or conflict of interest in which the trustee would benefit personally from the trust. "The trustee is under a duty to the beneficiary in administering the trust not to be guided by the interest of any third person. Thus, it is improper for the trustee to sell trust property to a third person for the purpose of benefitting the third person rather than the trust." Restatement of Trusts 2d § 170, comment *q*, at 371 (1959).

No form of so-called "social investing" is consistent with the duty of loyalty if the investment activity entails sacrificing the interests of trust beneficiaries - for example, by accepting below-market returns - in favor of the interests of the persons supposedly benefitted by pursuing the particular social cause. See, e.g., John H. Langbein & Richard Posner, Social Investing and the Law of Trusts, 79 Michigan L. Rev. 72, 96-97 (1980) (collecting authority). For pension trust assets, see generally Ian D. Lanoff, The Social Investment of Private Pension Plan Assets: May it Be Done Lawfully under ERISA?, 31 Labor L.J. 387 (1980). Commentators supporting social investing tend to concede the overriding force of the duty of loyalty. They argue instead that particular schemes of social investing may not result in below-market returns. See, e.g., Marcia O'Brien Hylton, "Socially Responsible" Investing: Doing Good Versus Doing Well in an Inefficient Market, 42 American U.L. Rev. 1 (1992). In 1994 the Department of Labor issued an Interpretive Bulletin reviewing its prior analysis of social investing questions and reiterating that pension trust fiduciaries may invest only in conformity with the prudence and loyalty standards of ERISA §§ 403-404. Interpretive Bulletin 94-1, 59 Fed. Regis. 32606 (Jun. 22, 1994), to be codified as 29 CFR § 2509.94-1. The Bulletin reminds fiduciary investors that they are prohibited from "subordinat[ing] the interests of participants and beneficiaries in their retirement income to unrelated objectives."

§ 6. Impartiality. If a trust has two or more beneficiaries, the trustee shall act impartially in investing and managing the trust assets, taking into account any differing interests of the beneficiaries.

Comment

The duty of impartiality derives from the duty of loyalty. When the trustee owes duties to more than one beneficiary, loyalty requires the trustee to respect the interests of all the beneficiaries. Prudence in investing and administration requires the trustee to take account of the interests of all the beneficiaries for whom the trustee is acting, especially the conflicts between the interests of beneficiaries interested in income and those interested in principal.

The language of Section 6 derives from Restatement of Trusts 2d § 183 (1959); see also id., § 232. Multiple beneficiaries may be beneficiaries in succession (such as life and remainder interests) or beneficiaries with simultaneous interests (as when the income interest in a trust is being divided among several beneficiaries).

The trustee's duty of impartiality commonly affects the conduct of investment and management functions in the sphere of principal and income allocations. This Act prescribes no regime for allocating receipts and expenses. The details of such allocations are commonly handled under specialized legislation, such as the Revised Uniform Principal and Income Act (1962) (which is presently under study by the Uniform Law Commission with a view toward further revision).

§ 7. Investment Costs.

In investing and managing trust assets, a trustee may only incur costs that are appropriate and reasonable in relation to the assets, the purposes of the trust, and the skills of the trustee.

Comment

Wasting beneficiaries' money is imprudent. In devising and implementing strategies for the investment and management of trust assets, trustees are obliged to minimize costs.

The language of Section 7 derives from Restatement of Trusts 2d § 188 (1959). The Restatement of Trusts 3d says: "Concerns over compensation and other charges are not an obstacle to a reasonable course of action using mutual funds and other pooling arrangements, but they do require special attention by a trustee. . . . [I]t is important for trustees to make careful cost comparisons, particularly among similar products of a specific type being considered for a trust portfolio." Restatement of Trusts 3d: Prudent Investor Rule § 227, comment m, at 58 (1992).

§ 8. Reviewing Compliance.

Compliance with the prudent investor rule is determined in light of the facts and circumstances existing at the time of a trustee's decision or action and not by hindsight.

Comment

This section derives from the 1991 Illinois act, 760 ILCS 5/5(a)(2) (1992), which draws upon Restatement of Trusts 3d: Prudent Investor Rule § 227, comment b, at 11 (1992). Trustees are not insurers. Not every investment or management decision will turn out in the light of hindsight to have been successful. Hindsight is not the relevant standard. In the language of law and economics, the standard is ex ante, not ex post.

§ 9. Delegation of Investment and Management Functions.

(a) A trustee may delegate investment and management functions that a prudent trustee of comparable skills could properly delegate under the circumstances. The trustee shall exercise reasonable care, skill, and caution in:

(1) selecting an agent;

(2) establishing the scope and terms of the delegation, consistent with the purposes and terms of the trust; and

(3) periodically reviewing the agent's actions in order to monitor the agent's performance and compliance with the terms of the delegation.

(b) In performing a delegated function, an agent owes a duty to the trust to exercise reasonable care to comply with the terms of the delegation.

(c) A trustee who complies with the requirements of subsection (a) is not liable to the beneficiaries or to the trust for the decisions or actions of the agent to whom the function was delegated.

(d) By accepting the delegation of a trust function from the trustee of a trust that is subject to the law of this State, an agent submits to the jurisdiction of the courts of this State.

Comment

This section of the Act reverses the much-criticized rule that forbad trustees to delegate investment and management functions. The language of this section is derived from Restatement of Trusts 3d: Prudent Investor Rule § 171 (1992), discussed infra, and from the 1991 Illinois act, 760 ILCS § 5/5.1(b), (c) (1992).

Former law. The former nondelegation rule survived into the 1959 Restatement: "The trustee is under a duty to the beneficiary not to delegate to others the doing of acts which the trustee can reasonably be required personally to perform." The rule put a premium on the frequently arbitrary task of distinguishing discretionary functions that were thought to be nondelegable from supposedly ministerial functions that the trustee was allowed to delegate. Restatement of Trusts 2d § 171 (1959).

The Restatement of Trusts 2d admitted in a comment that "There is not a clear-cut line dividing the acts which a trustee can properly delegate from those which he cannot properly delegate." Instead, the comment directed attention to a list of factors that "may be of importance: (1) the amount of discretion involved; (2) the value and character of the property involved; (3) whether the property is principal or income; (4) the proximity or remoteness of the subject matter of the trust; (5) the character of the act as one involving professional skill or facilities possessed or not possessed by the trustee himself." Restatement of Trusts 2d § 171, comment *d* (1959). The 1959 Restatement further said: "A trustee cannot properly delegate to another power to select investments." Restatement of Trusts 2d § 171, comment *h* (1959).

For discussion and criticism of the former rule see William L. Cary & Craig B. Bright, The Delegation of Investment Responsibility for Endowment Funds, 74 Columbia L. Rev. 207 (1974); John H. Langbein & Richard A. Posner, Market Funds and Trust-Investment Law, 1976 American Bar Foundation Research J. 1, 18-24.

The modern trend to favor delegation. The trend of subsequent legislation, culminating in the Restatement of Trusts 3d: Prudent Investor Rule, has been strongly hostile to the nondelegation rule. See John H. Langbein, Reversing the Nondelegation Rule of Trust-Investment Law, 59 Missouri L. Rev. 105 (1994).

The delegation rule of the Uniform Trustee Powers Act. The Uniform Trustee Powers Act (1964) effectively abrogates the nondelegation rule. It authorizes trustees "to employ persons, including attorneys, auditors, investment advisors, or agents, even if they are associated with the trustee, to advise or assist the trustee in the performance of his administrative duties; to act without independent investigation upon their recommendations; and instead of acting personally, to employ one or more agents to perform any act of administration, whether or not discretionary . . . ." Uniform Trustee Powers Act § 3(24), 7B Uniform Laws Ann. 743 (1985). The Act has been enacted in 16 states, see "Record of Passage of Uniform and Model Acts as of September 30, 1993," 1993-94 Reference Book of Uniform Law Commissioners (unpaginated, following page 111) (1993).

UMIFA's delegation rule. The Uniform Management of Institutional Funds Act (1972) (UMIFA), authorizes the governing boards of eleemosynary institutions, who are trustee-like fiduciaries, to delegate investment matters either to a committee of the board or to outside investment advisors, investment counsel, managers, banks, or trust companies. UMIFA § 5, 7A Uniform Laws Ann. 705 (1985). UMIFA has been enacted in 38 states, see "Record of Passage of Uniform and Model Acts as of September 30, 1993," 1993-94 Reference Book of Uniform Law Commissioners (unpaginated, following page 111) (1993).

ERISA's delegation rule. The Employee Retirement Income Security Act of 1974, the federal statute that prescribes fiduciary standards for investing the assets of pension and employee benefit plans, allows a pension or employee benefit plan to provide that "authority to manage, acquire or dispose of assets of the plan is delegated to one or more investment managers . . . ." ERISA § 403(a)(2), 29 U.S.C. § 1103(a)(2). Commentators have explained the rationale for ERISA's encouragement of delegation:

ERISA . . . invites the dissolution of unitary trusteeship. . . . ERISA's fractionation of traditional trusteeship reflects the complexity of the modern pension trust. Because millions, even billions of dollars can be involved, great care is required in investing and safekeeping plan assets. Administering such plans-computing and honoring benefit entitlements across decades of employment and retirement-is also a complex business. . . . Since, however, neither the sponsor nor any other single entity has a comparative advantage in performing all these functions, the tendency has been for pension plans to use a variety of specialized providers. A consulting actuary, a plan administration firm, or an insurance company may oversee the design of a plan and arrange for processing benefit claims. Investment industry professionals manage the portfolio (the largest plans spread their pension investments among dozens of money management firms).

John H. Langbein & Bruce A. Wolk, Pension and Employee Benefit Law 496 (1990).

The delegation rule of the 1992 Restatement. The Restatement of Trusts 3d: Prudent Investor Rule (1992) repeals the nondelegation rule of Restatement of Trusts 2d § 171 (1959), extracted supra, and replaces it with substitute text that reads:

> § 171. Duty with Respect to Delegation. A trustee has a duty personally to perform the responsibilities of trusteeship except as a prudent person might delegate those responsibilities to others. In deciding whether, to whom, and in what manner to delegate fiduciary authority in the administration of a trust, and thereafter in supervising agents, the trustee is under a duty to the beneficiaries to exercise fiduciary discretion and to act as a prudent person would act in similar circumstances.

Restatement of Trusts 3d: Prudent Investor Rule § 171 (1992). The 1992 Restatement integrates this delegation standard into the prudent investor rule of section 227, providing that "the trustee must . . . act with prudence in deciding whether and how to delegate to others . . . ." Restatement of Trusts 3d: Prudent Investor Rule § 227(c) (1992).

Protecting the beneficiary against unreasonable delegation. There is an intrinsic tension in trust law between granting trustees broad powers that facilitate flexible and efficient trust administration, on the one hand, and protecting trust beneficiaries from the misuse of such powers on the other hand. A broad set of trustees' powers, such as those found in most lawyer-drafted instruments and exemplified in the Uniform Trustees' Powers Act, permits the trustee to act vigorously and expeditiously to maximize the interests of the beneficiaries in a variety of transactions and administrative settings. Trust law relies upon the duties of loyalty and prudent administration, and upon procedural safeguards such as periodic accounting and the availability of judicial oversight, to prevent the misuse of these powers.

Delegation, which is a species of trustee power, raises the same tension. If the trustee delegates effectively, the beneficiaries obtain the advantage of the agent's specialized investment skills or whatever other attributes induced the trustee to delegate. But if the trustee delegates to a knave or an incompetent, the delegation can work harm upon the beneficiaries.

Section 9 of the Uniform Prudent Investor Act is designed to strike the appropriate balance between the advantages and the hazards of delegation. Section 9 authorizes delegation under the limitations of subsections (a) and (b). Section 9(a) imposes duties of care, skill, and caution on the trustee in selecting the agent, in establishing the terms of the delegation, and in reviewing the agent's compliance.

The trustee's duties of care, skill, and caution in framing the terms of the delegation should protect the beneficiary against overbroad delegation. For example, a trustee could not prudently agree to an investment management agreement containing an exculpation clause that leaves the trust without recourse against reckless mismanagement. Leaving one's beneficiaries remediless against willful wrongdoing is inconsistent with the duty to use care and caution in formulating the terms of the delegation. This sense that it is imprudent to expose beneficiaries to broad exculpation clauses underlies both federal and state legislation restricting exculpation clauses, e.g., ERISA §§ 404(a)(1)(D), 410(a), 29 U.S.C. §§ 1104(a)(1)(D), 1110(a); New York Est. Powers Trusts Law § 11-1.7 (McKinney 1967).

Although subsection (c) of the Act exonerates the trustee from personal responsibility for the agent's conduct when the delegation satisfies the standards of subsection 9(a), subsection 9(b) makes the agent responsible to the trust. The beneficiaries of the trust can, therefore, rely upon the trustee to enforce the terms of the delegation.

Costs. The duty to minimize costs that is articulated in Section 7 of this Act applies to delegation as well as to other aspects of fiduciary investing. In deciding whether to delegate, the trustee must balance the projected benefits against the likely costs. Similarly, in deciding how to delegate, the trustee must take costs into account. The trustee must be alert to protect the beneficiary from "double dipping." If, for example, the trustee's regular compensation schedule presupposes that the trustee will conduct the investment management function, it should ordinarily follow that the trustee will lower its fee when delegating the investment function to an outside manager.

§ **10. Language Invoking Standard of [Act].** The following terms or comparable language in the provisions of a trust, unless otherwise limited or modified, authorizes any investment or strategy permitted under this [Act]: "investments permissible by law for investment of trust funds," "legal investments," "authorized investments," "using the judgment and care under the circumstances then prevailing that persons of prudence, discretion, and intelligence exercise in the management of their own affairs, not in regard to speculation but in regard to the permanent disposition of their funds, considering the probable income as well as the probable safety of their capital," "prudent man rule," "prudent trustee rule," "prudent person rule," and "prudent investor rule."

Comment

This provision is taken from the Illinois act, 760 ILCS § 5/5(d) (1992), and is meant to facilitate incorporation of the Act by means of the formulaic language commonly used in trust instruments.

§ **11. Application to Existing Trusts.** This [Act] applies to trusts existing on and created after its effective date. As applied to trusts existing on its effective date, this [Act] governs only decisions or actions occurring after that date.

§ **12. Uniformity of Application and Construction.** This [Act] shall be applied and construed to effectuate its general purpose to make uniform the law with respect to the subject of this [Act] among the States enacting it.

§ **13. Short Title.** This [Act] may be cited as the "[Name of Enacting State] Uniform Prudent Investor Act."

§ **14. Severability.** If any provision of this [Act] or its application to any person or circumstance is held invalid, the invalidity does not affect other provisions or applications of this [Act] which can be given effect without the invalid provision or application, and to this end the provisions of this [Act] are severable.

§ **15. Effective Date.** This [Act] takes effect _____.

§ **16. Repeals.** The following acts and parts of acts are repealed:
   (1)
   (2)
   (3)

UNIFORM CUSTODIAL TRUST ACT (1987)

Table of Sections

Prefatory Note

This Uniform Act provides for the creation of a statutory custodial trust for adults to be governed by the provisions of the Act whenever property is delivered to another "as custodial trustee under the (Enacting state) Uniform Custodial Trust Act." The provisions of this Act are based on trust analogies to concepts developed and used in establishing custodianships for minors under the Uniform Transfers to Minors Act (UTMA). The Custodial Trust Act is designed to provide a statutory standby inter vivos trust for individuals who typically are not very affluent or sophisticated, and possibly represented by attorneys engaged in general rather than specialized estate practice. The most frequent use of this trust would be in response to the commonly occurring need of elderly individuals to provide for the future management of assets in the event of incapacity. The statute will also be available for accomplishing distribution of funds by judgment debtors and others to incapacitated persons for whom a conservator has not been appointed. Since this Act allows any person, competent to transfer property, to create custodial trusts for the benefit of themselves or others, with the beneficial interest in custodial trust property in the beneficiary and not in the custodial trustee, its potential for use is extensive. Although the most frequent use probably will be by elderly persons, it is also available for a parent to establish a custodial trust for an adult child who may be incapacitated; for adult persons in the military, or those leaving the country temporarily, to place their property with another for management without relinquishing beneficial ownership of their property; or for young people who have received property under the Uniform Transfers to Minors Act to continue a custodial trust as adults in order to obtain the benefit and convenience of management services performed by the custodial trustee.

This Act follows the approach taken by the Uniform Transfers to Minors Act and allows any kind of property, real or personal, tangible or intangible, to be made the subject of a transfer to a custodial trustee for the benefit of a beneficiary. However, the most typical transaction envisioned would involve a person who would transfer intangible property, such as securities or bank accounts, to a custodial trustee but with retention by the transferor of direction over the property. Later, this direction could be relinquished, or it could be lost upon incapacity. The objective of the statute is to provide a simple trust that is uncomplicated in its creation, administration, and termination. The potential for tax problems is minimized by permitting the beneficiary in most instances to retain control while the beneficiary has capacity to manage the assets effectively. The statute contains an asset specific transfer provision that it is believed will be simple to use and will gain the acceptance of the securities and financial industry. A simple transfer document, examples of which are set forth in the Act, and a receipt from the custodian, also in the Act, would provide for identification of beneficiaries or distributees upon death of the beneficiary. Protection is extended to third parties dealing with the custodian. Although the Act is patterned on the Uniform Transfers to Minors Act and meshes into the Uniform Probate Code, it is appropriate for enactment as well in states which have not adopted either UTMA or the UPC.

An adult beneficiary, who is not incapacitated, may: (1) terminate the custodial trust on demand (Section 2(e)); (2) receive so much of the income or custodial property as he or she may request from time to time (Section 9(a)); and (3) give the custodial trustee binding instructions for investment or management (Section 7(b)). In the absence of direction by the beneficiary, who is not incapacitated, the custodial trustee manages the property subject to the standard of care that would be observed by a prudent person dealing with the property of another and is not limited by other statutory restrictions on investments by fiduciaries. (Section 7).

A principal feature of the Custodial Trust under this Act is designed to protect the beneficiary and his or her dependents against the perils of the beneficiary's possible future incapacity without the necessity of a conservatorship. Under Section 10, the incapacity of the beneficiary does not terminate (1) the custodial trust, (2) the designation of a successor custodial trustee, (3) any power or authority of the custodial trustee, or (4) the immunities of third persons relying on actions of the custodial trustee. The custodial trustee continues to manage the property as a discretionary trust under the prudent person standard for the benefit of the incapacitated beneficiary.

Means of monitoring and enforcing the custodial trust include provisions requiring the custodial trustee to keep the beneficiary informed, requiring accounting by the custodial trustee (Section 15), providing for removal of the custodial trustee (Section 13), and the distribution of the assets on termination of the custodial trust (Section 17). The custodial trustee is protected in Section 16 by the statutes of limitation on proceedings against the custodial trustee.

Transactions with the custodial trustee should be executed readily and quickly by third parties because their rights and protections are determined by the Act and a third party acting in good faith has no need to determine the custodial trustee's authority to bind the beneficiary with respect to property and investment matters. (Section 11). The Act generally limits the claims of third parties to recourse against the custodial property, with the beneficiary insulated against personal liability unless he or she is personally at fault and the custodial trustee is similarly insulated unless the custodial trustee is personally at fault or failed to disclose the custodial capacity when entering into a contract (Section 12).

As a consequence of the mobility of our population, particularly the mature persons who are most likely to utilize this Act, uniformity of the laws governing custodial trusts is highly desirable, and the Act is designed to avoid conflict of laws problems. A custodial trust created under this Act remains subject to this Act despite a subsequent change in the residence of the transferor, the beneficiary, or the custodial trustee or the removal of the custodial trust property from the state of original location. (Section 19).

§ 1. Definitions. As used in this [Act]:

(1) "Adult" means an individual who is at least 18 years of age.

(2) "Beneficiary" means an individual for whom property has been transferred to or held under a

declaration of trust by a custodial trustee for the individual's use and benefit under this [Act].

(3) "Conservator" means a person appointed or qualified by a court to manage the estate of an individual or a person legally authorized to perform substantially the same functions.

(4) "Court" means the [_____] court of this State.

(5) "Custodial trust property" means an interest in property transferred to or held under a declaration of trust by a custodial trustee under this [Act] and the income from and proceeds of that interest.

(6) "Custodial trustee" means a person designated as trustee of a custodial trust under this [Act] or a substitute or successor to the person designated.

(7) "Guardian" means a person appointed or qualified by a court as a guardian of an individual, including a limited guardian, but not a person who is only a guardian ad litem.

(8) "Incapacitated" means lacking the ability to manage property and business affairs effectively by reason of mental illness, mental deficiency, physical illness or disability, chronic use of drugs, chronic intoxication, confinement, detention by a foreign power, disappearance, minority, or other disabling cause.

(9) "Legal representative" means a personal representative or conservator.

(10) "Member of the beneficiary's family" means a beneficiary's spouse, descendant, stepchild, parent, stepparent, grandparent, brother, sister, uncle, or aunt, whether of the whole or half blood or by adoption.

(11) "Person" means an individual, corporation, business trust, estate, trust, partnership, joint venture, association, or any other legal or commercial entity.

(12) "Personal representative" means an executor, administrator, or special administrator of a decedent's estate, a person legally authorized to perform substantially the same functions, or a successor to any of them.

(13) "State" means a state, territory, or possession of the United States, the District of Columbia, or the Commonwealth of Puerto Rico.

(14) "Transferor" means a person who creates a custodial trust by transfer or declaration.

(15) "Trust company" means a financial institution, corporation, or other legal entity, authorized to exercise general trust powers.

Comment

(1) "Adult" is a person 18 years of age for the purpose of custodial trusts. The result of this is that a person 18 years of age will be eligible to be a custodial trustee under this Act, although he or she may not be eligible under UTMA since minor custodianships under UTMA may run to age 21 and the minor could in some cases be older than the custodian. As the Comments under Section 1 of UTMA explain, the age of 21 was retained under that Act because the Internal Revenue Code continues to permit a "minority trust" under Section 2053(c), to continue in effect until age 21 and because it was believed that most transferors creating trusts or custodianships for minors would prefer to retain the property under management for the benefit of the young person as long as possible. The difference has little or no practical consequence and serves the purpose of each Act.

(3) "Conservator" is defined broadly to permit identification of a person functioning as a conservator.

(4) "Court" means _____ court. Here the likelihood is that most states would utilize the same court, e.g., the probate court, that deals with conservators and estates.

(5 and 6) The terms, "custodial trust property" and "custodial trustee," are used throughout to identify clearly the statutory trust property and trustee under this Act. The statutory trust concept is used throughout the Act.

(7) A definition of guardian has been included and is based on the Uniform Probate Code Section 5-103(6).

(8) A definition of incapacitated has been included,

for the purpose of this Act, because incapacity of the beneficiary converts the trust from a revocable trust to a discretionary trust. The definition is taken from the Uniform Probate Code Section 5-401(c) relating to the person who is unable to manage property. Compare Uniform Probate Code Section 5-103(7). Note that Section 10(a)(ii) permits a transferor to direct that the trust shall be administered as one for an incapacitated person. Section 10 deals specifically with the determination of incapacity.

(10) The beneficiary's family is broadly defined to identify persons who may have standing to seek judicial intervention or accounting (Sections 13 and 15).

(11) The definition of a person is taken from the Uniform Probate Code Section 1-201(29).

(12) Personal representative is broadly defined and the definition reflects that in the Uniform Probate Code Section 1-201(30).

§ 2. Custodial Trust; General.

(a) A person may create a custodial trust of property by a written transfer of the property to another person, evidenced by registration or by other instrument of transfer, executed in any lawful manner, naming as beneficiary, an individual who may be the transferor, in which the transferee is designated, in substance, as custodial trustee under the [Enacting state] Uniform Custodial Trust Act.

(b) A person may create a custodial trust of property by a written declaration, evidenced by registration of the property or by other instrument of declaration executed in any lawful manner, describing the property and naming as beneficiary an individual other than the declarant, in which the declarant as titleholder is designated, in substance, as custodial trustee under the [Enacting state] Uniform Custodial Trust Act. A registration or other declaration of trust for the sole benefit of the declarant is not a custodial trust under this [Act].

(c) Title to custodial trust property is in the custodial trustee and the beneficial interest is in the beneficiary.

(d) Except as provided in subsection (e), a transferor may not terminate a custodial trust.

(e) The beneficiary, if not incapacitated, or the conservator of an incapacitated beneficiary, may terminate a custodial trust by delivering to the custodial trustee a writing signed by the beneficiary or conservator declaring the termination. If not previously terminated, the custodial trust terminates on the death of the beneficiary.

(f) Any person may augment existing custodial trust property by the addition of other property pursuant to this [Act].

(g) The transferor may designate, or authorize the designation of, a successor custodial trustee in the trust instrument.

(h) This [Act] does not displace or restrict other means of creating trusts. A trust whose terms do not conform to this [Act] may be enforceable according to its terms under other law.

Comment

Section 2 is the principal provision authorizing the creation of a custodial trust and utilizes the concept of incorporation by reference when the transferee or titleholder of property is designated as custodial trustee under the Act. Section 2 sets forth the general effect of such a transfer. Section 18 provides forms which satisfy the requirements of this section and identifies customary methods of transferring assets to create a custodial trust.

Section 2(a) provides that a trust may be created by transfer to another for the benefit of the transferor or another. This is expected to be the most common way in which a custodial trust would be created. However, a custodial trust may also be created by declaration of trust by the owner of property to hold it for the benefit of another as is provided in Section 2(b). A declaration in trust by the owner of property for the sole benefit of the owner is not contemplated by this Act because such an attempt may be considered ineffective as a trust due to the total identity of the trustee and beneficiary. However, the doctrine of merger would not preclude an effective transfer under this Act for the benefit of the transferor and one or more other beneficiaries. See Section 6.

A custodial trust could be created by the exercise of a valid power of attorney or power of appointment given by the owner of property as one of the transfers "consistent with law."

These alternatives permit the major uses of the custodial trust to be accomplished expeditiously. For example, an older person, wishing to be relieved of management of property may transfer property to another for benefit of the transferor or of the transferor's spouse or child. The declaration may be used to establish a trust of which the owner is trustee to continue management of the property for benefit of another, such as a spouse or child. The trust may include a provision for distribution of assets remaining at the beneficiary's death directly to a named distributee.

This Act does not preclude the creation of trusts under other existing law, statutory or nonstatutory, but is designed to facilitate the creation of simple trusts incorporating the provisions of this Act. The written transfer or declaration "consistent with law" requires that the formalities of the transfer of particular property necessary under other law will be observed, e.g., if land is involved, the requirements of a proper deed and recording must be satisfied.

Section 2(c) provides for the retention of the beneficial interest in the custodial trust property in the beneficiary and, of course, not in the custodial trustee. The extensive control and benefit in the beneficiary who is not incapacitated maintains the simplicity of the trust and avoids tax complexity. The custodial trustee is given the title to the property and authority to act with regard to the property only as is authorized by the statute. The custodial trustee's powers are enumerated in Section 8.

Section 2(e) gives the adult beneficiary, who is not incapacitated, the power to terminate the custodial trust at any time during his or her lifetime. This power of termination exists in any beneficiary who is not incapacitated whether the beneficiary was or was not the transferor. A beneficiary may be determined to be incapacitated or the transferor may designate that the trust is to be administered as a trust for an incapacitated beneficiary under Section 10, in which event the beneficiary does not have the power to terminate. However, the designation of incapacity by the transferor can be modified by the trustee or the court by reason of changed circumstances pursuant to Section 10. The Act precludes termination by exercise of a durable power of attorney if the beneficiary is incompetent (Section 7(f)). If the donor prefers not to permit the beneficiary the power to terminate or to designate the beneficiary as incapacitated under Section 10, an individually drafted trust outside the scope of this Act would seem appropriate.

Upon termination of a custodial trust, the custodial trust property must be distributed as provided in Section 17.

A transfer under this Act is irrevocable except to the extent the beneficiary may terminate it. Hence, a transfer to a trustee for benefit of a person other than the transferor is not revocable by the transferor. If a power of revocation were retained by the transferor, that would be a trust outside the scope of this Act and enforceable under general law pursuant to subsection 2(h).

This Act does not provide for protection of the custodial trust assets from the claims of creditors of the beneficiary, whether those are general or governmental creditors. Other laws of the state remain unaffected. In this regard, unusual problems of handicapped persons and the coordination of resources and state or federal services call for special provision and planning outside the scope of this Act.

§ 3. Custodial Trustee for Future Payment or Transfer.

(a) A person having the right to designate the recipient of property payable or transferable upon a future event may create a custodial trust upon the occurrence of the future event by designating in writing the recipient, followed in substance by: "as custodial trustee for _____ (name of beneficiary) under the [Enacting state] Uniform Custodial Trust Act."

(b) Persons may be designated as substitute or successor custodial trustees to whom the property must be paid or transferred in the order named if the first designated custodial trustee is unable or unwilling to serve.

(c) A designation under this section may be made in a will, a trust, a deed, a multiple-party account, an insurance policy, an instrument exercising a power of appointment, or a writing designating a beneficiary of contractual rights. Otherwise, to be effective, the designation must be registered with or delivered to the fiduciary, payor, issuer, or obligor of the future right.

Comment

This section permits a future custodial trustee to be designated to receive property for the beneficiary of a custodial trust to be effective upon the occurrence of a future event or transfer. To accommodate changes in circumstances during the passage of time, one or more successors or substitute custodial trustees can also be designated. The designation of the future custodial trustee and the beneficiary can be made in an instrument which is revocable or irrevocable depending upon the nature of the transaction or transfer. Any person designated as a future custodial trustee may decline to serve before the transfer occurs or may resign under Section 13 after the transfer.

The source of this section is Section 3 of UTMA.

The enacting state's rule against perpetuities may limit or affect the creation of a custodial trust upon the occurrence of a future event, but because the use of a custodial trust usually contemplates dispositions for the benefit of living persons, perpetuity problems should rarely arise.

§ 4. Form and Effect of Receipt and Acceptance by Custodial Trustee, Jurisdiction.

(a) Obligations of a custodial trustee, including the obligation to follow directions of the beneficiary, arise under this [Act] upon the custodial trustee's acceptance, express or implied, of the custodial trust property.

(b) The custodial trustee's acceptance may be evidenced by a writing stating in substance:

CUSTODIAL TRUSTEE'S RECEIPT AND ACCEPTANCE

I, _____ (name of custodial trustee) acknowledge receipt of the custodial trust property described below or in the attached instrument and accept the custodial trust as custodial trustee for _____ (name of beneficiary) under the [Enacting state] Uniform Custodial Trust Act. I undertake to administer and distribute the custodial trust property pursuant to the [Enacting state] Uniform Custodial Trust Act. My obligations as custodial trustee are subject to the directions of the beneficiary unless the beneficiary is designated as, is, or becomes incapacitated. The custodial trust property consists of _____.

Dated: _____

_____
(Signature of Custodial Trustee)

(c) Upon accepting custodial trust property, a person designated as custodial trustee under this [Act] is subject to personal jurisdiction of the court with respect to any matter relating to the custodial trust.

Comment

Although a custodial trust is created by a transfer that satisfies Section 2 of the Act, the responsibility and obligations upon the trustee do not arise until the trustee has accepted the transfer. This detailed section is included to call the attention of the parties to the effective receipt and acceptance by the custodial trustee. Once a custodial trustee accepts the transfer of the custodial trust property, the custodial trustee assumes the obligation of a custodial trustee under this Act. The acceptance can be expressed or implied, but it is recommended that the written acceptance provided for in Section 4(b) be utilized. By the acceptance the custodial trustee submits to the personal jurisdiction of the courts of the enacting state for the purpose of the custodial trust, despite subsequent relocation of the parties or of the custodial trust property. The principal sources of these provisions are Sections 8 and 9 of UTMA and the analogous provisions under the Uniform Probate Code, Sections 3-602, 5-208, 5-307, 7-103.

§ 5. Transfer to Custodial Trustee by Fiduciary or Obligor; Facility of Payment.

(a) Unless otherwise directed by an instrument designating a custodial trustee pursuant to Section 3, a person, including a fiduciary other than a custodial trustee, who holds property of or owes a debt to an incapacitated individual not having a conservator may make a transfer to an adult member of the beneficiary's family or to a trust company as custodial trustee for the use and benefit of the incapacitated individual. If the value of the property or the debt exceeds [$20,000], the transfer is not effective unless authorized by the court.

(b) A written acknowledgment of delivery, signed by a custodial trustee, is a sufficient receipt and discharge for property transferred to the custodial trustee pursuant to this section.

Comment

This section is in the nature of a facility-of-payment provision that permits persons owing money to an incapacitated individual to discharge a fixed obligation by a payment to a custodial trustee under this Act. The section does not authorize the custodial trustee to settle claims for disputed amounts but only to acknowledge an effective receipt of property paid or delivered. It is based primarily on Sections 6 and 7 of UTMA and includes the protections of Section 8 of UTMA as well. It permits a custodial trust to be established as a substitute for a conservatorship to receive payments due an incapacitated individual. Also, see Section 11, which protects transferors and other third parties dealing with the custodial trustee.

§ 6. Multiple Beneficiaries; Separate Custodial Trusts; Survivorship.

(a) Beneficial interests in a custodial trust created for multiple beneficiaries are deemed to be separate custodial trusts of equal undivided interests for each beneficiary. Except in a transfer or declaration for use and benefit of spouses, for whom survivorship is presumed, a right of survivorship does not exist unless the instrument creating the custodial trust specifically provides for survivorship [or survivorship is required as to community or marital property].

(b) Custodial trust property held under this [Act] by the same custodial trustee for the use and benefit of the same beneficiary may be administered as a single custodial trust.

(c) A custodial trustee of custodial trust property held for more than one beneficiary shall separately account to each beneficiary pursuant to Sections 7 and 15 for the administration of the custodial trust.

Comment

This Act, unlike UTMA, does not preclude a custodial trust for more than one beneficiary. Adult persons creating custodial trusts are likely to set up custodial trusts in various forms, e.g., parents may wish to set up a custodial trust for their children or for themselves, then for a spouse, etc. However, the interests of each beneficiary are separate and the custodial trustee is obligated under subsection (c) to account separately to each beneficiary for administration of the beneficiary's interest in the custodial trust.

Subsection (b) allows a custodial trustee who is administering multiple custodial trusts for the same beneficiary to administer the custodial trusts as a single custodial trust. For example, if multiple trusts are created for an incapacitated beneficiary, the custodial trustee can administer them as a single custodial trust.

Historical Note. A technical amendment to subsection (a) was made in 2017 to replace "husband and wife" with "spouses."

§ 7. General Duties of Custodial Trustee.

(a) If appropriate, a custodial trustee shall register or record the instrument vesting title to custodial trust property.

(b) If the beneficiary is not incapacitated, a custodial trustee shall follow the directions of the beneficiary in the management, control, investment, or retention of the custodial trust property. In the absence of effective contrary direction by the beneficiary while not incapacitated, the custodial trustee shall observe the standard of care that would be observed by a prudent person dealing with property of another and is not limited by any other law restricting investments by fiduciaries. However, a custodial trustee, in the custodial trustee's discretion, may retain any custodial trust property received from the transferor. If a custodial trustee has a special skill or expertise or is named custodial trustee on the basis of representation of a special skill or expertise, the custodial trustee shall use that skill or expertise.

(c) Subject to subsection (b), a custodial trustee shall take control of and collect, hold, manage, invest, and reinvest custodial trust property.

(d) A custodial trustee at all times shall keep custodial trust property of which the custodial trustee has control, separate from all other property in a manner sufficient to identify it clearly as custodial trust property of the beneficiary. Custodial trust property, the title to which is subject to recordation, is so identified if an appropriate instrument so identifying the property is recorded, and custodial trust property subject to registration is so identified if it is registered, or held in an account in the name of the custodial trustee, designated in substance: "as custodial trustee for _____ (name of beneficiary) under the [Enacting state] Uniform Custodial Trust Act."

(e) A custodial trustee shall keep records of all transactions with respect to custodial trust property, including information necessary for the preparation of tax returns, and shall make the records and information available at reasonable times to the beneficiary or legal representative of the beneficiary.

(f) The exercise of a durable power of attorney for an incapacitated beneficiary is not effective to terminate or direct the administration or distribution of a custodial trust.

Comment

Subsection (b) restates and confirms the control by the beneficiary who is not incapacitated. However, the trustee has a reasonable obligation to act when the beneficiary has not directed him. Under Sections 9 and 10, when a beneficiary becomes incapacitated, the custodial trust becomes a discretionary trust and the trustee is subject to the control of the statute and not the beneficiary's direction. The custodial trustee is subject to the usual trustee's standard as taken from Section 7-302 of the Uniform Probate Code.

The statute also imposes a slightly higher standard on professional fiduciaries acting under the statute. Otherwise, much of this section is taken from Section 12 of UTMA. Whenever recordable assets, such as land, are in the custodial trust, the trustee would be expected to record title to the asset. The section is entitled "general duties" because there are additional specific duties identified in other sections such as Section 9.

§ 8. General Powers of Custodial Trustee.

(a) A custodial trustee, acting in a fiduciary capacity, has all the rights and powers over custodial trust property which an unmarried adult owner has over individually owned property, but a custodial trustee may exercise those rights and powers in a fiduciary capacity only.

(b) This section does not relieve a custodial trustee from liability for a violation of Section 7.

Comment

This section is taken from Section 13 of UTMA. It grants the trustee very broad powers over the property, subject, however, to the Prudent Person Rule and to the obligations set out in the Act. An alternative approach to subsection (a) that might be taken by an enacting state is to refer to the existing statutes granting powers to a trustee, such as the Uniform Trustee's Powers Act. For example: [(a) A custodial trustee has the powers of a trustee under the Uniform Trustee's Powers Act.]

§ 9. Use of Custodial Trust Property.

(a) A custodial trustee shall pay to the beneficiary or expend for the beneficiary's use and benefit so much or all of the custodial trust property as the beneficiary while not incapacitated may direct from time to time.

(b) If the beneficiary is incapacitated, the custodial trustee shall expend so much or all of the custodial trust property as the custodial trustee considers advisable for the use and benefit of the beneficiary and individuals who were supported by the beneficiary when the beneficiary became incapacitated, or who are legally entitled to support by the beneficiary. Expenditures may be made in the manner, when, and to the extent that the custodial trustee determines suitable and proper, without court order and without regard to other support, income, or property of the beneficiary.

(c) A custodial trustee may establish checking, savings, or other similar accounts of reasonable amounts under which either the custodial trustee or the beneficiary may withdraw funds from, or draw checks against, the accounts. Funds withdrawn from, or checks written against, the account by the beneficiary are distributions of custodial trust property by the custodial trustee to the beneficiary.

Comment

This section provides that the custodial trustee is obligated to follow the directions of the beneficiary who is not incapacitated in paying over or expending custodial trust property. If the beneficiary is incapacitated, this section imposes duties on the custodial trustee to apply funds for the beneficiary similar to those imposed on custodians for minors under Section 14 of UTMA. In addition, however, subsection (b) authorizes a custodial trustee to pay over or expend custodial trust property for the use and benefit of the incapacitated beneficiary's dependents who were supported by the beneficiary at the time the beneficiary became incapacitated or for whom there is a legal obligation to support.

The use-and-benefits standard for the expenditure of custodial property is intended to avoid any implication that the custodial trust property can be used only for the required support of the incapacitated beneficiary.

Subsection (c) allows a custodial trustee to maintain a bank account, of an amount reasonable under the circumstances, with the beneficiary whereby both the beneficiary and the custodial trustee may write checks on the account. This may be used as one method of making money available for the beneficiary's personal needs. Many incapacitated persons, unable to manage business affairs, are still competent to pay personal expenses. This type of arrangement would be important to them. A custodial trustee should maintain, of course, a separate bank account for use in managing the custodial trust property and investments.

An alternative approach might be taken to this section that refers to the distributive powers of a conservator under the laws of the enacting state, in the event that state should prefer that incorporation by reference. For example: [The custodial trustee has the distributive powers of a conservator under the Uniform Probate Code.]

§ 10. Determination of Incapacity; Effect.

(a) The custodial trustee shall administer the custodial trust as for an incapacitated beneficiary if (i) the custodial trust was created under Section 5, (ii) the transferor has so directed in the instrument creating the custodial trust, or (iii) the custodial trustee has determined that the beneficiary is incapacitated.

(b) A custodial trustee may determine that the beneficiary is incapacitated in reliance upon (i) previous direction or authority given by the beneficiary while not incapacitated, including direction or authority pursuant to a durable power of attorney, (ii) the certificate of the beneficiary's physician, or (iii) other persuasive evidence.

(c) If a custodial trustee for an incapacitated beneficiary reasonably concludes that the beneficiary's incapacity has ceased, or that circumstances concerning the beneficiary's ability to manage property and business affairs have changed since the creation of a custodial trust directing administration as for an incapacitated beneficiary, the custodial trustee may administer the trust as for a beneficiary who is not incapacitated.

(d) On petition of the beneficiary, the custodial trustee, or other person interested in the custodial trust property or the welfare of the beneficiary, the court shall determine whether the beneficiary is incapacitated.

(e) Absent determination of incapacity of the beneficiary under subsection (b) or (d), a custodial trustee who has reason to believe that the beneficiary is incapacitated shall administer the custodial trust in accordance with the provisions of this [Act] applicable to an incapacitated beneficiary.

(f) Incapacity of a beneficiary does not terminate (i) the custodial trust, (ii) any designation of a successor custodial trustee, (iii) rights or powers of the custodial trustee, or (iv) any immunities of third persons acting on instructions of the custodial trustee.

Comment

. This is one of the more important sections of the Act under which the custodial trustee may determine that the beneficiary is incapacitated so the trust will change from one subject to the control of the beneficiary to a discretionary trust for the beneficiary. Subsection (b) allows the custodial trustee to determine that the beneficiary is incapacitated provided the determination is based upon the certificate of the beneficiary's physician, the prior direction or authority of the beneficiary, or other reasonable evidence. That authority could be evidenced, for example, by a durable power of attorney executed by the beneficiary prior to becoming incapacitated even though that power of attorney is not otherwise effective to control management or termination of the custodial trust. Such a durable power of attorney could be given to a child, spouse, friend, or other trusted individual. In addition, specific authority is provided in subsection (d) for the beneficiary, the custodial trustee, or other interested person to seek a declaration from the court as to the capacity of the beneficiary for the purposes of this Act. This is important to the custodial trustee,

as his duties and responsibilities change on the event of the beneficiary's incapacity.

This section is not a proceeding for the appointment of a conservator, and it is not contemplated that such a declaration would lead to court appointment of a conservator or guardian unless other factors would warrant such appointment. The existence of a comprehensive and well-managed custodial trust would be one factor that would tend to avoid the necessity for the appointment of a conservator or guardian of the estate.

This section also does not provide a proceeding to attack the legal competence of a transferor in setting up a trust under Section 2. Rather, Section 10 relates to a management matter in a validly established custodial trust.

Subsection (f) provides that the incapacity of the beneficiary does not terminate the custodial trust. If the beneficiary becomes incapacitated, the authority of the custodial trustee continues and the custodial trustee must follow the statutory provisions of the Act relating to managing custodial trusts for incapacitated individuals.

§ 11. Exemption of Third Person from Liability.

A third person in good faith and without a court order may act on instructions of, or otherwise deal with, a person purporting to make a transfer as, or purporting to act in the capacity of, a custodial trustee. In the absence of knowledge to the contrary, the third person is not responsible for determining:

(1) the validity of the purported custodial trustee's designation;

(2) the propriety of, or the authority under this [Act] for, any action of the purported custodial trustee;

(3) the validity or propriety of an instrument executed or instruction given pursuant to this [Act] either by the person purporting to make a transfer or declaration or by the purported custodial trustee; or

(4) the propriety of the application of property vested in the purported custodial trustee.

Comment

This section is based upon Section 16 of the   UTMA and protects third persons who deal in good faith with the custodial trustee.

§ 12. Liability to Third Person.

(a) A claim based on a contract entered into by a custodial trustee acting in a fiduciary capacity, an obligation arising from the ownership or control of custodial trust property, or a tort committed in the course of administering the custodial trust, may be asserted by a third person against the custodial trust property by proceeding against the custodial trustee in a fiduciary capacity, whether or not the custodial trustee or the beneficiary is personally liable.

(b) A custodial trustee is not personally liable to a third person:

(1) on a contract properly entered into in a fiduciary capacity unless the custodial trustee fails to reveal that capacity or to identify the custodial trust in the contract; or

(2) for an obligation arising from control of custodial trust property or for a tort committed in the course of the administration of the custodial trust unless the custodial trustee is personally at fault.

(c) A beneficiary is not personally liable to a third person for an obligation arising from beneficial ownership of custodial trust property or for a tort committed in the course of administration of the custodial trust unless the beneficiary is personally in possession of the custodial trust property giving rise to the liability or is personally at fault.

(d) Subsections (b) and (c) do not preclude actions or proceedings to establish liability of the custodial trustee or beneficiary to the extent the person sued is protected as the insured by liability insurance.

Comment

This section is patterned after Section 17 of the UTMA and that section in turn was based upon Sections 5-428 and 7-306 of the Uniform Probate Code limiting the liability of conservators and trustees. See also Restatement of Trusts, 2d Sections 265 and 277. The effect of this section is to limit the claims of third parties to recourse against custodial trust property as both the custodial trustee and the beneficiary are protected from personal liability absent personal fault on their part. This section does not alter the obligations between the custodial trustee and the beneficiary arising out of the administration of the estate and the accounting for that administration.

There may be cases in which a custodial trustee or beneficiary may have a right to possession of custodial trust property and may insure against liability arising out of possession or control of the property as a named insured, e.g., under homeowner's or automobile liability insurance. In such a case, the beneficiary should be permitted as a party defendant under subsection (d) but only to the extent of the protection of the liability insurance.

§ 13. Declination, Resignation, Incapacity, Death, or Removal of Custodial Trustee, Designation of Successor Custodial Trustee.

(a) Before accepting the custodial trust property, a person designated as custodial trustee may decline to serve by notifying the person who made the designation, the transferor, or the transferor's legal representative. If an event giving rise to a transfer has not occurred, the substitute custodial trustee designated under Section 3 becomes the custodial trustee, or, if a substitute custodial trustee has not been designated, the person who made the designation may designate a substitute custodial trustee pursuant to Section 3. In other cases, the transferor or the transferor's legal representative may designate a substitute custodial trustee.

(b) A custodial trustee who has accepted the custodial trust property may resign by (i) delivering written notice to a successor custodial trustee, if any, the beneficiary and, if the beneficiary is incapacitated, to the beneficiary's conservator, if any, and (ii) transferring or registering, or recording an appropriate instrument relating to, the custodial trust property, in the name of, and delivering the records to, the successor custodial trustee identified under subsection (c).

(c) If a custodial trustee or successor custodial trustee is ineligible, resigns, dies, or becomes incapacitated, the successor designated under Section 2(g) or 3 becomes custodial trustee. If there is no effective provision for a successor, the beneficiary, if not incapacitated, may designate a successor custodial trustee. If the beneficiary is incapacitated, or fails to act within 90 days after the ineligibility, resignation, death, or incapacity of the custodial trustee, the beneficiary's conservator becomes successor custodial trustee. If the beneficiary does not have a conservator or the conservator fails to act, the resigning custodial trustee may designate a successor custodial trustee.

(d) If a successor custodial trustee is not designated pursuant to subsection (c), the transferor, the legal representative of the transferor or of the custodial trustee, an adult member of the beneficiary's family, the guardian of the beneficiary, a person interested in the custodial trust property, or a person interested in the welfare of the beneficiary, may petition the court to designate a successor custodial trustee.

(e) A custodial trustee who declines to serve or resigns, or the legal representative of a deceased or incapacitated custodial trustee, as soon as practicable, shall put the custodial trust property and records in the possession and control of the successor custodial trustee. The successor custodial trustee may enforce the obligation to deliver custodial trust property and records and becomes responsible for each item as received.

(f) A beneficiary, the beneficiary's conservator, an adult member of the beneficiary's family, a guardian of the person of the beneficiary, a person interested in the custodial trust property, or a person interested in the welfare of the beneficiary, may petition the court to remove the custodial trustee for cause and designate a successor custodial trustee, to require the custodial trustee to furnish a bond or other security for the faithful performance of fiduciary duties, or for other appropriate relief.

Comment

This section follows many of the provisions of Section 18 of UTMA with some substantive changes. It is designed to accommodate in a single section the circumstances in which a custodial trustee would be replaced by another custodial trustee. Under subsection (b), if the beneficiary is incapacitated, a custodial trustee who resigns must give written notice to both the beneficiary and the beneficiary's conservator if one exists. Under subsection (c), a beneficiary who is not incapacitated may designate, without limitation, a successor custodial trustee. If, however, the beneficiary fails to act or is incapacitated, the procedure to be followed is very similar to that found in UTMA except that the nonincapacitated beneficiary has 90 days to act and if

the beneficiary has no conservator or if the conservator declines to act, the custodial trustee may eventually designate a successor custodial trustee.

Under subsection (f), the beneficiary, whether or not incapacitated, can petition the court to remove the custodial trustee for cause and to designate a successor trustee, or the court may require the custodial trustee to give bond or other appropriate relief.

This section, unlike Section 18 of UTMA, does not give the custodial trustee the general power to designate a successor custodial trustee but rather limits that power to the situation in which the procedure for designating successor custodial trustees by others has been exhausted.

§ 14. Expenses, Compensation, and Bond of Custodial Trustee. Except as otherwise provided in the instrument creating the custodial trust, in an agreement with the beneficiary, or by court order, a custodial trustee:

(1) is entitled to reimbursement from custodial trust property for reasonable expenses incurred in the performance of fiduciary services;

(2) has a noncumulative election, to be made no later than six months after the end of each calendar

year, to charge a reasonable compensation for fiduciary services performed during that year; and

(3) need not furnish a bond or other security for the faithful performance of fiduciary duties.

Comment

This section follows the pattern of Section 15 of the UTMA except it does subject the arrangements for payment of expenses, compensation, and bond to provisions in the custodial trust instrument or agreement of the beneficiary or court order.

As in UTMA, the provisions with regard to compensation are designed to avoid imputed compensation to the custodian who waives compensation and also to avoid the accumulation of claims for compensation until the termination of the custodial trust. Although the ability to control these matters by the trust instrument or agreement of the beneficiary seems to be implied, as was assumed in UTMA, it is here expressly stated because of the possibility of informal arrangements with persons as trustees.

§ 15. Reporting and Accounting by Custodial Trustee; Determination of Liability of Custodial Trustee.

(a) Upon the acceptance of custodial trust property, the custodial trustee shall provide a written statement describing the custodial trust property and shall thereafter provide a written statement of the administration of the custodial trust property (i) once each year, (ii) upon request at reasonable times by the beneficiary or the beneficiary's legal representative, (iii) upon resignation or removal of the custodial trustee, and (iv) upon termination of the custodial trust. The statements must be provided to the beneficiary or to the beneficiary's legal representative, if any. Upon termination of the beneficiary's interest, the custodial trustee shall furnish a current statement to the person to whom the custodial trust property is to be delivered.

(b) A beneficiary, the beneficiary's legal representative, an adult member of the beneficiary's family, a person interested in the custodial trust property, or a person interested in the welfare of the beneficiary may petition the court for an accounting by the custodial trustee or the custodial trustee's legal representative.

(c) A successor custodial trustee may petition the court for an accounting by a predecessor custodial trustee.

(d) In an action or proceeding under this [Act] or in any other proceeding, the court may require or permit the custodial trustee or the custodial trustee's legal representative to account. The custodial trustee or the custodial trustee's legal representative may petition the court for approval of final accounts.

(e) If a custodial trustee is removed, the court shall require an accounting and order delivery of the custodial trust property and records to the successor custodial trustee and the execution of all instruments required for transfer of the custodial trust property.

(f) On petition of the custodial trustee or any person who could petition for an accounting, the court, after notice to interested persons, may issue instructions to the custodial trustee or review the propriety of the acts of a custodial trustee or the reasonableness of compensation determined by the custodial trustee for the services of the custodial trustee or others.

Comment

This section requires that the custodial trustee inform the beneficiary of the initiation of the trust and provide reasonably current reports of the administration of the custodial trust to the beneficiary or the beneficiary's legal representative. Even though some custodial trustees may act informally, it seems appropriate that both the trustee and the beneficiary be expected to exchange complete information concerning the administration of the trust at least once each year. In some cases, more frequent exchanges of information between the custodial trustee and beneficiary would be expected, e.g., when they use a bank account to which both have access. This is particularly true with regard to necessary information for tax reporting by the parties involved. This section assumes the usual minimum components of an account, i.e., assets and values at the beginning of the accounting period, receipts, and disbursements during the accounting period and assets and their values on hand or available for distribution at the close of the accounting period.

Subsection (a) identifies the necessary reports and accountings for the parties, and subsection (b) identifies a broad group of persons who may petition the court for an accounting by the custodial trustee or the custodial trustee's legal representative. Much of the section is drawn from Section 19 of the UTMA modified to fit the custodial trust. Subsection (f) recognizes the inherent power of the court to instruct trustees and review their actions. This paragraph is patterned after Uniform Probate Code Section 7-205.

§ 16. Limitations of Action Against Custodial Trustee.

(a) Except as provided in subsection (c), unless previously barred by adjudication, consent, or limitation, a claim for relief against a custodial trustee for accounting or breach of duty is barred as to a beneficiary, a person to whom custodial trust property is to be paid or delivered, or the legal representative of an incapacitated or deceased beneficiary or payee:

(1) who has received a final account or statement fully disclosing the matter unless an action or proceeding to assert the claim is commenced within two years after receipt of the final account or statement; or

(2) who has not received a final account or statement fully disclosing the matter unless an action or proceeding to assert the claim is commenced within three years after the termination of the custodial trust.

(b) Except as provided in subsection (c), a claim for relief to recover from a custodial trustee for fraud, misrepresentation, or concealment related to the final settlement of the custodial trust or concealment of the existence of the custodial trust, is barred unless an action or proceeding to assert the claim is commenced within five years after the termination of the custodial trust.

(c) A claim for relief is not barred by this section if the claimant:

(1) is a minor, until the earlier of two years after the claimant becomes an adult or dies;

(2) is an incapacitated adult, until the earliest of two years after (i) the appointment of a conservator, (ii) the removal of the incapacity, or (iii) the death of the claimant; or

(3) was an adult, now deceased, who was not incapacitated, until two years after the claimant's death.

Comment

In an effort to provide as comprehensive a statute as possible to inform the parties of substantially all of their obligations and rights, statutes of limitation are provided in this section. The limitations provided in this section are derived from the Uniform Probate Code, Sections 1-106 and 7-307, and from the Missouri Custodial Act.

The nature of the limitations imposed by the section are illustrated by the situation in which a custodial trustee is removed, resigns, or dies. If the former custodial trustee accounts as required under Section 13 on removal or resignation, or the deceased custodial trustee's personal representative accounts, the two-year limitation of subsection (a)(1) applies. Should the former custodial trustee or the personal representative fail to account, then, subsection (a)(2) would apply to limit the time in which a proceeding to assert the claim could be commenced. This time would begin to run on the date the trust terminated. Of course, if the claim is one for fraud or concealment, the longer time limitation of subsection (b) would apply. In any event, should the beneficiary become incapacitated or die before the applicable time limitation had expired, the tolling provision of subsection (c) could postpone the time bar until two years after removal of the disability or death.

§ 17. Distribution on Termination.

(a) Upon termination of a custodial trust, the custodial trustee shall transfer the unexpended custodial trust property:

(1) to the beneficiary, if not incapacitated or deceased;

(2) to the conservator or other recipient designated by the court for an incapacitated beneficiary; or

(3) upon the beneficiary's death, in the following order:

(i) as last directed in a writing signed by the deceased beneficiary while not incapacitated and received by the custodial trustee during the life of the deceased beneficiary;

(ii) to the survivor of multiple beneficiaries if survivorship is provided for pursuant to Section 6;

(iii) as designated in the instrument creating the custodial trust; or

(iv) to the estate of the deceased beneficiary.

(b) If, when the custodial trust would otherwise terminate, the distributee is incapacitated, the custodial trust continues for the use and benefit of the distributee as beneficiary until the incapacity is removed or the custodial trust is otherwise terminated.

(c) Death of a beneficiary does not terminate the power of the custodial trustee to discharge obligations of the custodial trustee or beneficiary incurred before the termination of the custodial trust.

Comment

This section controls distribution of the custodial trust property when the custodial trust is terminated under Section 2(e). It is designed to provide for efficient and certain distribution without judicial proceedings. Subsection (a)(3) is an important provision for avoiding complications on distribution and provides that distribution may be controlled first, by the direction of the deceased beneficiary or second, by the custodial trust instrument (see Sections 2, 6 and 18) and, only if no effective prior designation for the payment or distribution of the property on the death of the beneficiary has been made, shall it pass through the beneficiary's estate.

The direction to the custodial trustee by the beneficiary, who is not incapacitated, for distribution on termination of the custodial trust may be in any written form clearly identifying the distributee. For example, the following direction would be adequate under the statute:

I, _____ (name of beneficiary) hereby direct _____ (name of trustee) as custodial trustee, to transfer and pay the unexpended balance of the custodial trust property of which I am beneficiary to _____ as distibutee on the termination of the trust at my death. In the event of the prior death of _____ above named as distributee, I designate _____ as distributee of the custodial trust property.

Signed

Beneficiary

_____
(signature)

Date _____

Receipt Acknowledged

Custodial Trustee

_____
(signature)

Date _____

§ 18. Methods and Forms for Creating Custodial Trusts.

(a) If a transaction, including a declaration with respect to or a transfer of specific property, otherwise satisfies applicable law, the criteria of Section 2 are satisfied by:

681

(1) the execution and either delivery to the custodial trustee or recording of an instrument in substantially the following form:

TRANSFER UNDER THE [ENACTING STATE]
UNIFORM CUSTODIAL TRUST ACT

I, _____ (name of transferor or name and representative capacity if a fiduciary), transfer to _____ (name of trustee other than transferor), as custodial trustee for _____ (name of beneficiary) as beneficiary and _____ as distributee on termination of the trust in absence of direction by the beneficiary under the [Enacting state] Uniform Custodial Trust Act, the following: (insert a description of the custodial trust property legally sufficient to identify and transfer each item of property).

Dated: _____

_____
(Signature); or

(2) the execution and the recording or giving notice of its execution to the beneficiary of an instrument in substantially the following form:

DECLARATION OF TRUST UNDER THE [ENACTING STATE]
UNIFORM CUSTODIAL TRUST ACT

I, _____ (name of owner of property), declare that henceforth I hold as custodial trustee for _____ (name of beneficiary other than transferor) as beneficiary and _____ as distributee on termination of the trust in absence of direction by the beneficiary under the [Enacting state] Uniform Custodial Trust Act, the following: (Insert a description of the custodial trust property legally sufficient to identify and transfer each item of property).

Dated: _____

_____
(Signature)

(b) Customary methods of transferring or evidencing ownership of property may be used to create a custodial trust, including any of the following:

(1) registration of a security in the name of a trust company, an adult other than the transferor, or the transferor if the beneficiary is other than the transferor, designated in substance "as custodial trustee for _____ (name of beneficiary) under the [Enacting state] Uniform Custodial Trust Act";

(2) delivery of a certificated security, or a document necessary for the transfer of an uncertificated security, together with any necessary endorsement, to an adult other than the transferor or to a trust company as custodial trustee, accompanied by an instrument in substantially the form prescribed in subsection (a)(1);

(3) payment of money or transfer of a security held in the name of a broker or a financial institution or its nominee to a broker or financial institution for credit to an account in the name of a trust company, an adult other than the transferor, or the transferor if the beneficiary is other than

the transferor, designated in substance: "as custodial trustee for _____ (name of beneficiary) under the [Enacting state] Uniform Custodial Trust Act";

(4) registration of ownership of a life or endowment insurance policy or annuity contract with the issuer in the name of a trust company, an adult other than the transferor, or the transferor if the beneficiary is other than the transferor, designated in substance: "as custodial trustee for _____ (name of beneficiary) under the [Enacting state] Uniform Custodial Trust Act";

(5) delivery of a written assignment to an adult other than the transferor or to a trust company whose name in the assignment is designated in substance by the words: "as custodial trustee for _____ (name of beneficiary) under the [Enacting state] Uniform Custodial Trust Act";

(6) irrevocable exercise of a power of appointment, pursuant to its terms, in favor of a trust company, an adult other than the donee of the power, or the donee who holds the power if the beneficiary is other than the donee, whose name in the appointment is designated in substance: "as custodial trustee for _____ (name of beneficiary) under the [Enacting state] Uniform Custodial Trust Act";

(7) delivery of a written notification or assignment of a right to future payment under a contract to an obligor which transfers the right under the contract to a trust company, an adult other than the transferor, or the transferor if the beneficiary is other than the transferor, whose name in the notification or assignment is designated in substance: "as custodial trustee for _____ (name of beneficiary) under the [Enacting state] Uniform Custodial Trust Act";

(8) execution, delivery, and recordation of a conveyance of an interest in real property in the name of a trust company, an adult other than the transferor, or the transferor if the beneficiary is other than the transferor, designated in substance: "as custodial trustee for _____ (name of beneficiary) under the [Enacting state] Uniform Custodial Trust Act";

(9) issuance of a certificate of title by an agency of a state or of the United States which evidences title to tangible personal property:

(i) issued in the name of a trust company, an adult other than the transferor, or the transferor if the beneficiary is other than the transferor, designated in substance: "as custodial trustee for _____ (name of beneficiary) under the [Enacting state] Uniform Custodial Trust Act"; or

(ii) delivered to a trust company or an adult other than the transferor or endorsed by the transferor to that person, designated in substance: "as custodial trustee for _____ (name of beneficiary) under the [Enacting state] Uniform Custodial Trust Act"; or

(10) execution and delivery of an instrument of gift to a trust company or an adult other than the transferor, designated in substance: "as custodial trustee for _____ (name of beneficiary) under the [Enacting state] Uniform Custodial Trust Act."

Comment

This section largely follows Section 9 of UTMA. It provides instructional detail for forms and methods of transferring assets that satisfy the requirements of the statute. Although many of the customary methods of transferring assets are identified, these methods are not intended to be exclusive since any type of property that can be transferred by any legal means is intended to be within the scope of the statute, provided the requirements of Section 2 are met. The method of transfer or conveyance appropriate to the asset should be used, e.g., if land is involved, a deed or conveyance that satisfies the local requirements would be appropriate. In the effort to make the statute as self-contained and as fully explanatory as possible, these provisions for implementation are included in the statute rather than being appended or inserted in the Comments.

§ 19. Applicable Law.

(a) This [Act] applies to a transfer or declaration creating a custodial trust that refers to this [Act] if, at the time of the transfer or declaration, the transferor, beneficiary, or custodial trustee is a resident of or has its principal place of business in this State or custodial trust property is located in this State. The custodial trust remains subject to this [Act] despite a later change in residence or principal place of business of the transferor, beneficiary, or custodial trustee, or removal of the custodial trust property from this State.

(b) A transfer made pursuant to an act of another state substantially similar to this [Act] is governed by the law of that state and may be enforced in this State.

Comment

This section is designed to avoid confusion in the   event a party or assets are removed from the state.

§ 20. Uniformity of Application and Construction. This [Act] shall be applied and construed to effectuate its general purpose to make uniform the law with respect to the subject of this [Act] among states enacting it.

§ 21. Short Title. This [Act] may be cited as the "[Name of Enacting State] Uniform Custodial Trust Act."

§ 22. Severability. If any provision of this [Act] or its application to any person or circumstance is held invalid, the invalidity does not affect other provisions or applications of this [Act] which can be given effect without the invalid provision or application, and to this end the provisions of this [Act] are severable.

§ 23. Effective Date. This [Act] takes effect _____.

PART THREE: OTHER UNIFORM ACTS

Uniform Parentage Act (2017)

Revised Uniform Fiduciary Access to Digital Assets Act (2015)

Uniform Powers of Appointment Act (2013)

Uniform Premarital and Marital Agreements Act (2012)

Model Protection of Charitable Assets Act (2011)

Revised Uniform Anatomical Gift Act (2006, with
2007 Amendments)

Uniform Prudent Management of Institutional Funds Act (2006)

Uniform Health-Care Decisions Act (1993)

Uniform Simultaneous Death Act (1993)

Uniform Fraudulent Transfer Act (1984, with 2014 Amendments,
renamed the Uniform Voidable Transactions Act)

Uniform Transfers to Minors Act (1983, with 1986 Amendments)

Model Marital Property Act (1983)

PART THREE: OTHER UNIFORM ACTS

UNIFORM PARENTAGE ACT
(2017)

Table of Sections

[ARTICLE] 1
GENERAL PROVISIONS AND DEFINITIONS

[ARTICLE] 2
PARENT-CHILD RELATIONSHIP

[ARTICLE] 3
VOLUNTARY ACKNOWLEDGMENT OF PARENTAGE

[ARTICLE] 4
REGISTRY OF PATERNITY

688

[PART] 2
SPECIAL RULES FOR GESTATIONAL SURROGACY AGREEMENT

[PART] 3
SPECIAL RULES FOR GENETIC SURROGACY AGREEMENT

[ARTICLE] 9
INFORMATION ABOUT DONOR

[ARTICLE] 10
MISCELLANEOUS PROVISIONS

———

Prefatory Note

The Uniform Parentage Act (UPA) was originally promulgated in 1973 (UPA (1973)). UPA (1973) removed the legal status of illegitimacy and provided a series of presumptions used to determine a child's legal parentage. A core principle of UPA (1973) was to ensure that "all children and all parents have equal rights with respect to each other," regardless of the marital status of their parents. UPA (1973) § 2, Comment.

The UPA was revised in 2002 (UPA (2002)). UPA (2002) augmented and streamlined UPA (1973). UPA (2002) added provisions permitting a non-judicial acknowledgment of paternity procedure that is the equivalent of an adjudication of parentage in a court and added a paternity registry. UPA (2002) also included provisions governing genetic testing and rules for determining the parentage of children whose conception was not the result of sexual intercourse. Finally, UPA (2002) included a bracketed Article 8 to authorize surrogacy agreements.

UPA (2017) makes five major changes to the UPA. First, UPA (2017) seeks to ensure the equal treatment of children born to same-sex couples. UPA (2002) was written in gendered terms, and its provisions presumed that couples consist of one man and one woman. For example, Section 703 of UPA (2002) provided that "[a] man who provides sperm for, or consents to, assisted reproduction by a woman as provided in Section 704 with the intent to be the parent of her child, is a parent of the resulting child."

In *Obergefell v. Hodges*, 135 S. Ct. 2584 (2015), the United States Supreme Court held that laws barring marriage between two people of the same sex are unconstitutional. Even more recently, in June 2017, the Supreme Court held that a state may not, consistent with *Obergefell*, deny married same-sex couples recognition on their children's birth certificates that the state grants to married different-sex couples. *Pavan v. Smith*, 137 S. Ct. 2075, 2078-79 (2017). After *Obergefell* and *Pavan*, parentage laws that treat same-sex couples differently than different-sex couples may be unconstitutional. For example, in September 2017 the Arizona Supreme Court held that refusing to apply that state's marital presumption equally to same-sex spouses would violate the Due Process and Equal Protection Clauses of the United States Constitution. *McLaughlin v. Jones*, slip op. at 9 (Ariz. 2017) ("The marital paternity presumption is a benefit of marriage, and following *Pavan* and *Obergefell*, the state cannot deny same-sex spouses the same benefits afforded opposite-sex spouses."). *See also Roe v. Patton*, 2015 WL 4476734, *3 (D. Utah. 2015) (concluding that the plaintiffs were "highly likely to succeed in their claim" that extending the "benefits of the assisted reproduction statutes [which are based on UPA (2002)] to male spouses in opposite-sex couples but not for female spouses in same-sex couples" was unconstitutional). As the Arizona Supreme Court explained in *McLaughlin*, state legislatures, like state courts, are "obliged to follow the United States Constitution. . . . Through legislative enactments and rulemaking, [the] coordinate branches of government can forestall unnecessary litigation and help ensure that [state] law guarantees same-sex spouses the dignity and equality the Constitution requires—namely the same benefits afforded couples in opposite-sex marriages." *McLaughlin v. Jones*, slip op. at 13 (Ariz. 2017). UPA (2017) helps state legislatures address this potential constitutional infirmity by amending provisions throughout the act so that they address and apply equally to same-sex couples. These changes include broadening the presumption, acknowledgment, genetic testing, and assisted reproduction articles to make them gender-neutral.

UPA (2017) updates the act to address this potential constitutional infirmity by amending provisions throughout the act so that they address and apply equally to same-sex couples. These changes include broadening the presumption, acknowledgment, genetic testing, and assisted reproduction articles to make them gender-neutral.

Second, UPA (2017) includes a provision for the establishment of a de facto parent as a legal parent of a child. Most states recognize and extend at least some parental rights to people who have functioned as parents to children but who are unconnected to those children through either biology or marriage. These states span the country; ranging from Massachusetts, to West Virginia, to North and South Carolina, to Texas. Some states recognize such people under a variety of equitable doctrines – sometimes called de facto parentage, or in loco parentis, or the psychological parent doctrine. Other states extend rights to such people through broad third party standing statutes. And, more recently, states have begun to treat such people as legal parents under their parentage provisions. Two states – Delaware and Maine – achieve this result by including "de facto parents" in their definition of parent in their state versions of the Uniform Parentage Act. Other states, including California, Colorado, Kansas, New Hampshire, and New Mexico, reached this conclusion by applying their existing parentage provisions to such persons. New Section 609 provides a process for the establishment of parentage by those who claim to be de facto parents.

Third, UPA (2017) includes a provision that precludes establishment of a parent-child relationship by the perpetrator of a sexual assault that resulted in the conception of the child. The United States Congress adopted the Rape Survivor Child Custody Act in 2015, which provides incentives for states to enact "a law that allows the mother of any child that was conceived by rape to seek court-ordered termination of the parental rights of her rapist with regard to that child, which the court shall grant upon clear and convincing evidence of rape." In 2017, at least 17 state legislatures were considering bills to enact such statutes. New Section 614 provides language to implement the federal law.

Fourth, UPA (2017) updates the surrogacy provisions to reflect developments in that area. States have been particularly slow to enact Article 8 of UPA (2002). Eleven states adopted versions of UPA (2002).[1] Of these 11 states, only two – Texas and Utah – enacted the surrogacy provisions based on Article 8 of UPA (2002). At least five of the 11 states that enacted UPA (2002) enacted surrogacy provisions that are *not* premised on the 2002 UPA. These states include: Delaware (permitting) (enacted 2013); Illinois (permitting) (enacted 2004); Maine (permitting) (enacted 2015); North Dakota (banning) (enacted 2005); and Washington (banning

compensated) (enacted 1989).

The fact that very few states enacted Article 8 is likely the result of a confluence of factors. One likely factor is the controversial nature of surrogacy itself. But the fact that four of the states that enacted UPA (2002) have provisions permitting surrogacy that are not modeled on Article 8 of UPA (2002) suggests that the small number of enactments is also affected by the substance of Article 8. Accordingly, UPA (2017) updates the surrogacy provisions to make them more consistent with current surrogacy practice.

Finally, UPA (2017) includes a new article – Article 9 – that addresses the right of children born through assisted reproductive technology to access medical and identifying information regarding any gamete providers. Based on data from 2015, the CDC reports that "approximately 1.6% of all infants born in the United States every year are conceived using ART."[2] Data suggest that this percentage continues to increase. Gaia Bernstein, *Unintended Consequences: Prohibitions on Gamete Donor Anonymity and the Fragile Practice of Surrogacy*, 10 Ind. Health L. Rev. 291, 298 (2013) (noting that "from 2004 to 2008 the number of IVF cycles used for gestational surrogacy grew by 60%, the number of births by gestational surrogates grew by 53% and the number of babies born to gestational surrogates grew by 89%"). Accordingly, it is increasingly important for states to address the right of children to access information about their gamete donor. Article 9 does not require disclosure of the identity of a gamete donor, but it does require gamete banks and fertility clinics to ask donors if they want to have their identifying information disclosed when the resulting child attains 18 years of age. It does require disclosure of non-identifying medical history of the gamete donor.

---

[1] The eleven states are: Alabama, Delaware, Illinois, Maine, New Mexico, North Dakota, Oklahoma, Texas, Utah, Washington, and Wyoming. *See* Uniform Law Commission, *Legislative Fact Sheet – Parentage Act.*

[2] Centers for Disease Control, ART Success Rates, http://www.cdc.gov/art/reports/ (last updated May 4, 2017).

[ARTICLE] 1
GENERAL PROVISIONS

§ 101. Short Title. This [act] may be cited as the Revised Uniform Parentage Act (2017).

§ 102. Definitions. In this [act]:

(1) "Acknowledged parent" means an individual who has established a parent-child relationship under [Article] 3.

(2) "Adjudicated parent" means an individual who has been adjudicated to be a parent of a child by a court with jurisdiction.

(3) "Alleged genetic parent" means an individual who is alleged to be, or alleges that the individual is, a genetic parent or possible genetic parent of a child whose parentage has not been adjudicated. The term includes an alleged genetic father and alleged genetic mother. The term does not include:

    (A) a presumed parent;

    (B) an individual whose parental rights have been terminated or declared not to exist; or

    (C) a donor.

(4) "Assisted reproduction" means a method of causing pregnancy other than sexual intercourse. The term includes:

    (A) intrauterine or intracervical insemination;

    (B) donation of gametes;

    (C) donation of embryos;

    (D) in-vitro fertilization and transfer of embryos; and

    (E) intracytoplasmic sperm injection.

(5) "Birth" includes stillbirth.

(6) "Child" means an individual of any age whose parentage may be determined under this [act].

(7) "Child-support agency" means a government entity, public official, or private agency, authorized to provide parentage-establishment services under Title IV-D of the Social Security Act, 42 U.S.C. Sections 651 through 669.

(8) "Determination of parentage" means establishment of a parent-child relationship by a judicial or administrative proceeding or signing of a valid acknowledgment of parentage under [Article] 3.

(9) "Donor" means an individual who provides gametes intended for use in assisted reproduction, whether or not for consideration. The term does not include:

    (A) a woman who gives birth to a child conceived by assisted reproduction[, except as otherwise provided in [Article] 8]; or

    (B) a parent under [Article] 7[or an intended parent under [Article] 8].

(10) "Gamete" means sperm, egg, or any part of a sperm or egg.

(11) "Genetic testing" means an analysis of genetic markers to identify or exclude a genetic relationship.

(12) "Individual" means a natural person of any age.

(13) "Intended parent" means an individual, married or unmarried, who manifests an intent to be legally bound as a parent of a child conceived by assisted reproduction.

(14) "Man" means a male individual of any age.

(15) "Parent" means an individual who has established a parent-child relationship under Section 201.

(16) "Parentage" or "parent-child relationship" means the legal relationship between a child and a parent of the child.

(17) "Presumed parent" means an individual who under Section 204 is presumed to be a parent of a child, unless the presumption is overcome in a judicial proceeding, a valid denial of parentage is made under [Article] 3, or a court adjudicates the individual to be a parent.

(18) "Record" means information that is inscribed on a tangible medium or that is stored in an electronic or other medium and is retrievable in perceivable form.

(19) "Sign" means, with present intent to authenticate or adopt a record:

(A) to execute or adopt a tangible symbol; or

(B) to attach to or logically associate with the record an electronic symbol, sound, or process.

(20) "Signatory" means an individual who signs a record.

(21) "State" means a state of the United States, the District of Columbia, Puerto Rico, the United States Virgin Islands, or any territory or insular possession under the jurisdiction of the United States. The term includes a federally recognized Indian tribe.

(22) "Transfer" means a procedure for assisted reproduction by which an embryo or sperm is placed in the body of the woman who will give birth to the child.

(23) "Witnessed" means that at least one individual who is authorized to sign has signed a record to verify that the individual personally observed a signatory sign the record.

(24) "Woman" means a female individual of any age.

Comment

As was true of UPA (2002), UPA (2017) utilizes separate classifications of parents. Five of the classifications—acknowledged parents, adjudicated parents, alleged genetic parents, intended parents, and presumed parents—are largely carried over from UPA (2002), although the classifications have been made gender neutral.

As was true in UPA (2002), the terms "woman" and "man" are defined to clarify that any human,

regardless of age, can be a parent under the act.

UPA (2017) includes new definitions and amendments to existing definitions related to assisted reproduction. For example, the definition of the term "gamete" has been amended to include parts of gametes to reflect new technological developments. Definitions that are used in only one article have been moved into the relevant Article.

§ 103. Scope.

(a) This [act] applies to an adjudication or determination of parentage.

(b) This [act] does not create, affect, enlarge, or diminish parental rights or duties under law of this state other than this [act].

[(c) This [act] does not authorize or prohibit an agreement between one or more intended parents and a woman who is not an intended parent in which the woman agrees to become pregnant through assisted reproduction and which provides that each intended parent is a parent of a child conceived through assisted reproduction. If a birth results under the agreement and the agreement is unenforceable under [cite to law of this state regarding surrogacy agreements], the parent-child relationship is established as provided in [Articles] 1 through 6.]

Legislative Note: A state should enact subsection (c) if the state does not enact Article 8 or otherwise does not permit surrogacy agreements.

Comment

Source: UPA (2002) § 103.

UPA (2002) contained a single section—Section 103—that addressed both the scope of the act and the issue of choice of law under the act. UPA (2017)

follows the substance of UPA (2002), but addresses these concepts in two separate sections. The scope of the act is addressed in Section 103. Choice of law is addressed in Section 105.

§ 104. Authorized Court. The [designate court] may adjudicate parentage under this [act].

Comment

Source: UPA (2002) § 104.

The court and, if applicable, child-support agency having jurisdiction over parentage proceedings under the UPA should be identified here. As recognized in the comment to Section 402 of UIFSA, several states have laws that allow a child-support agency to determine parentage administratively in certain cases, such as when parentage is not contested, while other states rely solely on the judicial process for parentage adjudications. Section 466(a)(2) of the Social Security Act authorizes both administrative and judicial procedures for parentage establishment.

§ 105. Applicable Law. The court shall apply the law of this state to adjudicate parentage. The applicable law does not depend on:

(1) the place of birth of the child; or

(2) the past or present residence of the child.

Comment

Source: UPA (2002) § 103; UIFSA (2008) § 303; UIFSA (1996) § 303.

UPA (2017) follows the choice of law approach of UPA (2002) § 103, UIFSA (1996) § 303, and UIFSA (2008) § 303. These acts all direct the local court to apply local law. If this state is an inappropriate forum, dismissal for forum non-conveniens may be appropriate.

§ 106. Data Privacy. A proceeding under this [act] is subject to law of this state other than this [act] which governs the health, safety, privacy, and liberty of a child or other individual who could be affected by disclosure of information that could identify the child or other individual, including address, telephone number, digital contact information, place of employment, Social Security number, and the child's day-care facility or school.

Comment

Source: UPA (2002) § 105; UCCJEA (1997) § 209(e).

§ 107. Establishment of Maternity and Paternity. To the extent practicable, a provision of this [act] applicable to a father-child relationship applies to a mother-child relationship and a provision of this [act] applicable to a mother-child relationship applies to a father-child relationship.

Comment

Source: UPA (2002) § 106; UPA (1973) § 21.

This section carries over a principle followed in UPA (1973) § 21 and UPA (2002) § 106, that, where appropriate, a court may apply a gender-specific provision in a gender-neutral manner. Although UPA (2017) revised many provisions and concepts to make them gender neutral, some provisions of UPA (2017) remain written in terms applicable to one gender or the other. This section makes clear that a court has the authority to apply gendered provisions in a gender-neutral manner if appropriate.

[ARTICLE] 2
PARENT-CHILD RELATIONSHIP

§ 201. Establishment of Parent-child Relationship. A parent-child relationship is established between an individual and a child if:

(1) the individual gives birth to the child[, except as otherwise provided in [Article] 8];

(2) there is a presumption under Section 204 of the individual's parentage of the child, unless the presumption is overcome in a judicial proceeding or a valid denial of parentage is made under [Article] 3;

(3) the individual is adjudicated a parent of the child under [Article] 6;

(4) the individual adopts the child;

(5) the individual acknowledges parentage of the child under [Article] 3, unless the acknowledgment is rescinded under Section 308 or successfully challenged under [Article] 3 or 6;[or]

(6) the individual's parentage of the child is established under [Article] 7[; or]

(7) the individual's parentage of the child is established under [Article] 8].

Legislative Note: A state should include paragraph (7) if the state includes Article 8 in this act. If the state does not enact Article 8 but otherwise permits and recognizes surrogacy agreements by statute, the state should include a reference to the statute in paragraph (7).

Comment

Source: UPA (2002) § 201.

UPA (2017) updates the UPA so that it applies equally to children born to same-sex couples. Most of the mechanisms for establishing parentage apply equally without regard to gender. Accordingly, UPA (2017) merges into a single list what had been separate subsections for establishing the parentage of women and men. This approach removes unnecessary distinctions based on gender. This approach is also consistent with the approach taken by states that have amended their UPA-based parentage provisions to apply equally to children born to same-sex couples. *See, e.g.,* Me. Rev. Stat. tit. 19-a, § 1851; N.H. Rev. Stat. § 168-B:2.

In Section 201(2) and in other provisions of the act related to presumed parents, the UPA (2017) uses the term "overcome" in place of the term "rebuttal" that was used in prior versions of the act. The term "overcome" better captures the concept that the determination as to whether a presumed parent is a legal parent is a policy choice based on equitable considerations. Although the UPA (2017) uses a new term, the same principle animated earlier versions of the act. *See, e.g.,* UPA (2002), Section 608(a) (providing that a court can deny a presumed parent's challenge to his parentage "if the court determines that: (1) the conduct of the mother or . . . father estops that party from denying parentage; and (2) it would be inequitable to disprove the father-child relationship between the child and the presumed . . . father"); UPA (1973), Section 4(b) ("If two or more presumptions arise which conflict with each other, the presumption which on the facts is founded on the weightier considerations of policy and logic controls."). A court may draw upon case law regarding the term "rebuttal" when considering whether a presumption has been overcome.

§ 202. No Discrimination Based on Marital Status of Parent. A parent-child relationship extends equally to every child and parent, regardless of the marital status of the parent.

Comment

Source: UPA (2002) § 202; UPA (1973) § 2.

Historically, children born to unmarried women were extended fewer rights and protections than marital children. In the 1960s and 1970s, the Supreme Court decided cases in which it held unconstitutional rules that treated nonmarital children unequally. The nondiscrimination provision of UPA (1973), UPA 1973, § 2, was one of the "major substantive sections of the Act." UPA (1973), § 2, Comment. Section 2 of UPA (1973) was intended to "establish the principle that regardless of the marital status of the parents, all children and all parents have equal rights with respect to each other." UPA (1973) § 2, Comment. *See also* UPA (2002) § 202, Comment ("From a legal and social policy perspective, this is one of the most significant substantive provisions of the act, reaffirming the principle that regardless of the marital status of the parents, children and parents have equal rights with respect to each other.").

This provision reaffirms the principle that once a parent-child relationship has been established, that relationship is entitled to substantive equality, regardless of whether the child is a marital or a nonmarital child.

§ 203. Consequences of Establishing Parentage. Unless parental rights are terminated, a parent-child relationship established under this [act] applies for all purposes, except as otherwise provided by law of this state other than this [act].

Comment

Source: UPA (2002) § 203; USCACA (1988) § 10.

The qualifier "as otherwise provided by law of this state other than this [act]" is necessary because other statutes may restrict rights of a parent. For example, UPC (2008) § 2-114(a)(2) precludes a parent of a child (and the parent's family) from inheriting from the child by intestate succession if the child "died before reaching [18] years of age and there is clear and convincing evidence that immediately before the child's death the parental rights of the parent could have been terminated under the law of this state . . . "

§ 204. Presumption of Parentage.

(a) An individual is presumed to be a parent of a child if:

(1) except as otherwise provided under[[Article] 8 or] law of this state other than this [act]:

(A) the individual and the woman who gave birth to the child are married to each other and the child is born during the marriage, whether the marriage is or could be declared invalid;

(B) the individual and the woman who gave birth to the child were married to each other and the child is born not later than 300 days after the marriage is terminated by death, [divorce, dissolution, annulment, or declaration of invalidity, or after a decree of separation or separate maintenance], whether the marriage is or could be declared invalid; or

(C) the individual and the woman who gave birth to the child married each other after the birth of the child, whether the marriage is or could be declared invalid, the individual at any time asserted parentage of the child, and:

(i) the assertion is in a record filed with the [state agency maintaining birth records]; or

(ii) the individual agreed to be and is named as a parent of the child on the birth certificate of the child; or

(2) the individual resided in the same household with the child for the first two years of the life of the child, including any period of temporary absence, and openly held out the child as the individual's child.

(b) A presumption of parentage under this section may be overcome, and competing claims to parentage may be resolved, only by an adjudication under [Article] 6 or a valid denial of parentage under [Article] 3.

Legislative Note: *A state should use its own terms for the proceedings identified in the bracketed language in subsection (a)(1)(B).*

Comment

Source: UPA (2002) § 204; UPA (1973) § 4.

A network of presumptions was established by UPA (1973). Under UPA (1973), presumptions of parentage were established by previous marriage to the woman, subsequent marriage to the woman, and by the conduct of holding the child out as the individual's own child. Because, at the time of its drafting, marriage was permitted only between one man and one woman, and because few same-sex couples were raising children together, the presumptions were written to apply only to men.

These presumptions were largely carried over by UPA (2002), although UPA (2002) added an express durational requirement to the holding out presumption. As was true of UPA (1973), the presumptions remained gendered, referring only to men.

UPA (2017) carries over the substance of these presumptions, but revises them so that they apply equally to men and women. Revising the presumptions so that they apply equally to men and women may be required now that same-sex couples can marry in all states. *Obergefell v. Hodges*, 135 S. Ct. 2584 (2015). In *Obergefell*, and more recently in *Pavan v. Smith*, 137 S. Ct. 2075, 2078 (2017), the Supreme Court made clear that states not only are precluded from denying same-sex couples from the right to marry, they are also precluded from denying same-sex married spouses the "constellation of benefits" that are extended to married different-sex spouses. *See also McLaughlin v. Jones*, slip op. at 9 (Ariz. 2017) ("[T]he presumption of paternity . . . cannot, consistent with the Fourteenth Amendment's Equal Protection and Due Process Clauses, be restricted to only opposite-sex couples. The marital paternity presumption is a benefit of marriage, and following *Pavan* and *Obergefell*, the state cannot deny same-sex spouses the same benefits afforded opposite-sex spouses."). Several states recently have enacted similar revisions to parentage presumptions, making them apply equally to men and women. *See, e.g.*, Cal. Fam. Code § 7611; D.C. Code § 16-909; 750 Ill. Comp. Stat. Ann. § 46/204; Me. Rev. Stat. tit. 19-a, § 1881(1); N.H. Rev. Stat. § 168-B:2(V).

In addition, the holding out provision has been amended to account for situations where the person is absent only temporarily. The newly added language is modeled on the definition of "home state" in the Uniform Child Custody Jurisdiction and Enforcement Act. *See* UCCJEA § 102(7) ("A period of temporary absence of any of the mentioned persons is part of the period.").

Subsection (b) expressly addresses cases where multiple individuals have claims to parentage of a child under the act. UPA (1973) contained a provision for resolving cases involving multiple presumptions. Section 4(b) of UPA (1973) provided, in relevant part: "If two or more presumptions arise which conflict with each other, the presumption which on the facts is founded on the weightier considerations of policy and logic controls." UPA (1973) § 4(b). UPA (2002) omitted this provision and contained no provision expressly addressing how courts should resolve cases in which there are multiple presumptions of parentage. UPA (2017) provides express guidance for resolving such cases. Section 204(b) references the possibility that a court might have to resolve competing presumptions of parentage. Factors to be considered in such cases are set forth in Section 613.

[ARTICLE] 3
VOLUNTARY ACKNOWLEDGMENT OF PARENTAGE

Comment

Article 3 implements federal law. 42 U.S.C. § 666(a)(5)(C) provides that receipt of a federal subsidy by a state for its child-support enforcement program is contingent on state enactment of laws establishing specific procedures for "a simple civil process for voluntarily acknowledging paternity." If a state does not have such provisions or if its provisions are not in compliance with federal law, the state is at risk of losing its federal child-support subsidy. *See, e.g.,* 42 U.S.C. § 666(a) (providing that "each State must have in effect laws requiring the use of the following procedures, consistent with this section and with regulations of the Secretary"). *See also* 42 U.S.C. § 654(20). Today, all states have adopted procedures for voluntary acknowledgments of paternity. Indeed, "[v]oluntary acknowledgments have become the most common way to establish the legal paternity of children born outside marriage." Leslie Joan Harris, *Voluntary Acknowledgments of Parentage for Same-Sex Couples,* 20 AM. U. J. GENDER SOC. POL'Y & L. 467, 469-70 (2012) (footnotes omitted).

Article 3 of UPA (2002) referred only to the establishment of paternity through this administrative process. UPA (2017) makes Article 3 gender neutral and refers to the establishment of parentage through the acknowledgment process for an alleged genetic father, an intended parent, and a presumed parent, allowing Article 3 to apply to both men and women. The gender-neutral language and addition of the term "intended parent" is consistent with one of the goals of this revision process, which is to ensure that UPA (2017) applies equally to same-sex couples.

Revised Article 3 of UPA (2017) was drafted in close consultation with the federal Office of Child Support Enforcement (OCSE) to be consistent with Title IV-D requirements. State law determines what support rights exist and are legally enforceable. These changes ensure that all children can have parentage established regardless of a parent's gender and facilitate the establishment and enforcement of child support under state law.

Following is the text of portions of the Title IV-D statute most relevant to determinations of parentage:

42 U. S. C. § 666. Requirement of Statutorily Prescribed Procedures To Improve Effectiveness of Child Support Enforcement.

(a) **Types of procedures required.** In order to satisfy section 654(20)(A) of this title, each State must have in effect laws requiring the use of the following procedures, consistent with this section and with regulations of the Secretary, to increase the effectiveness of the program which the State administers under this part:

* * *

(5) **Procedures concerning paternity establishment.**

(A) **Establishment process available from birth until age 18.**

(i) Procedures which permit the establishment of the paternity of a child at any time before the child attains 18 years of age.

(ii) As of August 16, 1984, clause (i) shall also apply to a child for whom paternity has not been established or for whom a paternity action was brought but dismissed because a statute of limitations of less than 18 years was then in effect in the State.

(B) **Procedures concerning genetic testing.**

(i) Genetic testing required in certain contested cases. Procedures under which the State is required, in a contested paternity case (unless otherwise barred by State law) to require the child and all other parties (other than individuals found under section 654(29) of this title to have good cause and other exceptions for refusing to cooperate) to submit to genetic tests upon the request of any such party, if the request is supported by a sworn statement by the party:

(I) alleging paternity, and setting forth facts establishing a reasonable possibility of the requisite sexual contact between the parties; or

(II) denying paternity, and setting forth facts establishing a reasonable possibility of the nonexistence of sexual contact between the parties.

(ii) Other requirements. Procedures which require the State agency, in any case in which the agency orders genetic testing:

(I) to pay costs of such tests, subject to recoupment (if the State so elects) from the alleged father if paternity is established; and

(II) to obtain additional testing in any case if an original test result is contested, upon request and advance payment by the contestant.

(C) Voluntary paternity acknowledgment.

(i) Simple civil process. Procedures for a simple civil process for voluntarily acknowledging paternity under which the State must provide that, before a mother and a putative father can sign an acknowledgment of paternity, the mother and the putative father must be given notice, orally or through the use of audio or video equipment and in writing, of the alternatives to, the legal consequences of, and the rights (including, if 1 parent is a minor, any rights afforded due to minority status) and responsibilities that arise from, signing the acknowledgment.

(ii) Hospital-based program. Such procedures must include a hospital-based program for the voluntary acknowledgment of paternity focusing on the period immediately before or after the birth of a child.

(iii) Paternity establishment services.

(I) State-offered services. Such procedures must require the State agency responsible for maintaining birth records to offer voluntary paternity establishment services.

(II) Regulations.

(aa) Services offered by hospitals and birth record agencies. The Secretary shall prescribe regulations governing voluntary paternity establishment services offered by hospitals and birth record agencies.

(bb) Services offered by other entities. The Secretary shall prescribe regulations specifying the types of other entities that may offer voluntary paternity establishment services, and governing the provision of such services, which shall include a requirement that such an entity must use the same notice provisions used by, use the same materials used by, provide the personnel providing such services with the same training provided by, and evaluate the provision of such services in the same manner as the provision of such services is evaluated by, voluntary paternity establishment programs of hospitals and birth record agencies.

(iv) Use of paternity acknowledgment affidavit. Such procedures must require the State to develop and use an affidavit for the voluntary acknowledgment of paternity which includes the minimum requirements of the affidavit specified by the Secretary under section 652(a)(7) of this title for the voluntary acknowledgment of paternity, and to give full faith and credit to such an affidavit signed in any other State according to its procedures.

(D) Status of signed paternity acknowledgment.

(i) Inclusion in birth records. Procedures under which the name of the father shall be included on the record of birth of the child of unmarried parents only if:

(I) the father and mother have signed a voluntary acknowledgment of paternity; or

(II) a court or an administrative agency of competent jurisdiction has issued an adjudication of paternity.

Nothing in this clause shall preclude a State agency from obtaining an admission of paternity from the father for submission in a judicial or administrative proceeding, or prohibit the issuance of an order in a judicial or administrative proceeding which bases a legal finding of paternity on an admission of paternity by the father and any other additional showing required by State law.

(ii) Legal finding of paternity. Procedures under which a signed voluntary acknowledgment of paternity is considered a legal finding of paternity, subject to the right of any signatory to rescind the acknowledgment within the earlier of:

(I) 60 days; or

(II) the date of an administrative or judicial proceeding relating to the child (including a proceeding to establish a support order) in which the signatory is a party.

(iii) Contest. Procedures under which, after the 60-day period referred to in clause (ii), a signed voluntary acknowledgment of paternity may be challenged in court only on the basis of fraud, duress, or material mistake of fact, with the burden of proof upon the challenger, and under which the legal responsibilities (including child support obligations) of any signatory arising from the acknowledgment may not be suspended during the challenge, except for good cause shown.

(E) Bar on acknowledgment ratification proceedings. Procedures under which judicial or administrative proceedings are not required or permitted to ratify an unchallenged

acknowledgment of paternity.

(F) **Admissibility of genetic testing results.** Procedures:

(i) requiring the admission into evidence, for purposes of establishing paternity, of the results of any genetic test that is:

(I) of a type generally acknowledged as reliable by accreditation bodies designated by the Secretary; and

(II) performed by a laboratory approved by such an accreditation body;

(ii) requiring an objection to genetic testing results to be made in writing not later than a specified number of days before any hearing at which the results may be introduced into evidence (or, at State option, not later than a specified number of days after receipt of the results); and

(iii) making the test results admissible as evidence of paternity without the need for foundation testimony or other proof of authenticity or accuracy, unless objection is made.

(G) **Presumption of paternity in certain cases.** Procedures which create a rebuttable or, at the option of the State, conclusive presumption of paternity upon genetic testing results indicating a threshold probability that the alleged father is the father of the child.

(H) **Default orders.** Procedures requiring a default order to be entered in a paternity case upon a showing of service of process on the defendant and any additional showing required by State law.

(I) **No right to jury trial.** Procedures providing that the parties to an action to establish paternity are not entitled to a trial by jury.

(J) **Temporary support order based on probable paternity in contested cases.** Procedures which require that a temporary order be issued, upon motion by a party, requiring the provision of child support pending an administrative or judicial determination of parentage, if there is clear and convincing evidence of paternity (on the basis of genetic tests or other evidence).

(K) **Proof of certain support and paternity establishment costs.** Procedures under which bills for pregnancy, childbirth, and genetic testing are admissible as evidence without requiring third-party foundation testimony, and shall constitute prima facie evidence of amounts incurred for such services or for testing on behalf of the child.

(L) **Standing of putative fathers.** Procedures ensuring that the putative father has a reasonable opportunity to initiate a paternity action.

(M) **Filing of acknowledgments and adjudications in State registry of birth records.** Procedures under which voluntary acknowledgments and adjudications of paternity by judicial or administrative processes are filed with the State registry of birth records for comparison with information in the State case registry.

§ 301. **Acknowledgment of Parentage.** A woman who gave birth to a child and an alleged genetic father of the child, intended parent under [Article] 7, or presumed parent may sign an acknowledgment of parentage to establish the parentage of the child.

Comment

Source: 42 U.S.C. § 666(a)(5)(C); UPA (2002) § 301.

This section has been revised to permit an intended parent under Article 7 or a presumed parent to sign an acknowledgment of parentage, in addition to an alleged genetic parent. This change not only furthers the goal of ensuring that the act applies equally to children born to same-sex couples, but it also furthers the goal of establishing parentage quickly and with certainty.

§ 302. **Execution of Acknowledgment of Parentage.**

(a) An acknowledgment of parentage under Section 301 must:

(1) be in a record signed by the woman who gave birth to the child and by the individual seeking to establish a parent-child relationship, and the signatures must be attested by a notarial officer or witnessed;

(2) state that the child whose parentage is being acknowledged:

(A) does not have a presumed parent other than the individual seeking to establish the parent-child relationship or has a presumed parent whose full name is stated; and

(B) does not have another acknowledged parent, adjudicated parent, or individual who is a parent of the child under [Article] 7[or 8] other than the woman who gave birth to the child; and

(3) state that the signatories understand that the acknowledgment is the equivalent of an adjudication of parentage of the child and that a challenge to the acknowledgment is permitted only under limited circumstances and is barred two years after the effective date of the acknowledgment.

(b) An acknowledgment of parentage is void if, at the time of signing:

(1) an individual other than the individual seeking to establish parentage is a presumed parent, unless a denial of parentage by the presumed parent in a signed record is filed with the [state agency maintaining birth records]; or

(2) an individual, other than the woman who gave birth to the child or the individual seeking to establish parentage, is an acknowledged or adjudicated parent or a parent under [Article] 7[or 8].

Comment

Source: 42 U.S.C. § 666(a)(5)(C); UPA (2002) § 302.

Section 302 has been amended to apply equally to men and women.

UPA (2017) also effects a substantive change to Subsection (b): the acknowledgment is void if another person other than the woman who gave birth *is* a presumed, acknowledged, or adjudicated parent. Under UPA (2002), the acknowledgment was void only if it *stated* that there was another presumed, acknowledged, or adjudicated parent. Thus, under

UPA (2002), the acknowledgment was void only if the person knowingly lied on the form. As a result, under UPA (2002), the acknowledgment could cut off potential claims of other individuals so long as the signatories did not lie. UPA (2017) protects the rights of other individuals who are presumed, acknowledged, or adjudicated parents. What had been subsection (b)(3) of UPA (2002) § 302 has been eliminated because it is no longer necessary in light of this change to subsection (b).

§ 303. Denial of Parentage.

A presumed parent or alleged genetic parent may sign a denial of parentage in a record. The denial of parentage is valid only if:

(1) an acknowledgment of parentage by another individual is filed under Section 305;

(2) the signature of the presumed parent or alleged genetic parent is attested by a notarial officer or witnessed; and

(3) the presumed parent or alleged genetic parent has not previously:

(A) completed a valid acknowledgment of parentage, unless the previous acknowledgment was rescinded under Section 308 or challenged successfully under Section 309; or

(B) been adjudicated to be a parent of the child.

§ 304. Rules for Acknowledgment or Denial of Parentage.

(a) An acknowledgment of parentage and a denial of parentage may be contained in a single document or may be in counterparts and may be filed with the [state agency maintaining birth records] separately or simultaneously. If filing of the acknowledgment and denial both are required under this [act], neither is effective until both are filed.

(b) An acknowledgment of parentage or denial of parentage may be signed before or after the birth of the child.

(c) Subject to subsection (a), an acknowledgment of parentage or denial of parentage takes effect on the birth of the child or filing of the document with the [state agency maintaining birth records], whichever occurs later.

(d) An acknowledgment of parentage or denial of parentage signed by a minor is valid if the acknowledgment complies with this [act].

Comment

Source: 42 U.S.C. § 666(a)(5)(C)(i); UPA (2002) § 304.

§ 305. Effect of Acknowledgment or Denial of Parentage.

(a) Except as otherwise provided in Sections 308 and 309, an acknowledgment of parentage that complies with this [article] and is filed with the [state agency maintaining birth records] is equivalent to an adjudication of parentage of the child and confers on the acknowledged parent all rights and duties of a parent.

(b) Except as otherwise provided in Sections 308 and 309, a denial of parentage by a presumed parent or alleged genetic parent which complies with this [article] and is filed with the [state agency maintaining birth records] with an acknowledgment of parentage that complies with this [article] is equivalent to an adjudication of the nonparentage of the presumed parent or alleged genetic parent and discharges the presumed parent or alleged genetic parent from all rights and duties of a parent.

Comment

Source: 42 U.S.C. § 666(a)(5)(D)(ii), and 42 U.S.C. § 666(a)(5)(M); UPA (2002) § 305.

§ 306. No Filing Fee. The [state agency maintaining birth records] may not charge a fee for filing an acknowledgment of parentage or denial of parentage.

§ 307. Ratification Barred. A court conducting a judicial proceeding or an administrative agency conducting an administrative proceeding is not required or permitted to ratify an unchallenged acknowledgment of parentage.

Comment

This provision, which is carried over verbatim from UPA (2002), is required by federal law. *See* 42 U.S.C. § 666(a)(5)(E) ("procedures under which judicial administrative proceedings are not required or permitted to ratify an unchallenged acknowledgment of paternity.").

§ 308. Procedure for Rescission.

(a) A signatory may rescind an acknowledgment of parentage or denial of parentage by filing with the [relevant state agency] a rescission in a signed record which is attested by a notarial officer or witnessed, before the earlier of:

(1) 60 days after the effective date under Section 304 of the acknowledgment or denial; or

(2) the date of the first hearing before a court in a proceeding, to which the signatory is a party, to adjudicate an issue relating to the child, including a proceeding that establishes support.

(b) If an acknowledgment of parentage is rescinded under subsection (a), an associated denial of parentage is invalid, and the [state agency maintaining birth records] shall notify the woman who gave birth to the child and the individual who signed a denial of parentage of the child that the acknowledgment has been rescinded. Failure to give the notice required by this subsection does not affect the validity of the rescission.

Comment

UPA (2002) required a judicial process to rescind a voluntary acknowledgment of parentage. This is not required by the federal statute, 42 U.S.C. § 666(a)(5)(D)(ii), and many states allow the acknowledgment to be rescinded within the applicable timeframe by filing a rescission form with the child-support agency or vital records agency. UPA (2017) removes the judicial proceeding requirement to offer states flexibility in designing their rescission process.

§ 309. Challenge after Expiration of Period for Rescission.

(a) After the period for rescission under Section 308 expires, but not later than two years after the effective date under Section 304 of an acknowledgment of parentage or denial of parentage, a signatory of the acknowledgment or denial may commence a proceeding to challenge the acknowledgment or denial, including a challenge brought under Section 614, only on the basis of fraud, duress, or material mistake of fact.

(b) A challenge to an acknowledgment of parentage or denial of parentage by an individual who was not a signatory to the acknowledgment or denial is governed by Section 610.

Comment

Source: 42 U.S.C. § 666(a)(5)(D)(iii); UPA (2002) § 308.

The substance of subsection (a) is largely carried over from UPA (2002), § 308. This provision is consistent with federal law which permits a "challenge" to a voluntary acknowledgment of parentage, but only on the basis of alleged "fraud, duress, or material mistake of fact." 42 U.S.C. § 666(a)(5)(D)(iii). UPA (2017) does, however, add a cross-reference to the new Section 614 regarding children born as the result of sexual assault. If a woman establishes that the child was born as the result of sexual assault under Section 614, generally this showing will be sufficient to establish that she signed the acknowledgment under duress.

UPA (2017) also adds an express cross-reference to the provision governing challenges to an acknowledgment by a nonsignatory. The substantive rules governing such challenges were included in Article 6 of UPA (2002), but there was no cross-reference in Article 3 to the relevant provision.

§ 310. Procedure for Challenge by Signatory.

(a) Every signatory to an acknowledgment of parentage and any related denial of parentage must be made a party to a proceeding to challenge the acknowledgment or denial.

(b) By signing an acknowledgment of parentage or denial of parentage, a signatory submits to personal jurisdiction in this state in a proceeding to challenge the acknowledgment or denial, effective on the filing of the acknowledgment or denial with the [state agency maintaining birth records].

(c) The court may not suspend the legal responsibilities arising from an acknowledgment of parentage, including the duty to pay child support, during the pendency of a proceeding to challenge the acknowledgment or a related denial of parentage, unless the party challenging the acknowledgment or denial shows good cause.

(d) A party challenging an acknowledgment of parentage or denial of parentage has the burden of proof.

(e) If the court determines that a party has satisfied the burden of proof under subsection (d), the court shall order the [state agency maintaining birth records] to amend the birth record of the child to reflect the legal parentage of the child.

(f) A proceeding to challenge an acknowledgment of parentage or denial of parentage must be conducted under [Article] 6.

Comment

Source: UPA (2002) § 309.

The relevant provision of UPA (2002) addressed the procedure for both rescission and challenge. UPA (2017), however, removed the requirement that rescission be done through an adjudicatory process. Accordingly, references to rescission have been removed from this section. This section now addresses only the judicial procedures governing a challenge to an acknowledgment or denial of parentage.

UPA (2017) also places the responsibility to file the order described in subsection (e) with the agency maintaining birth records on the party who wants the record changed. If the party who wants the record changed does not file the order with the agency maintaining records and take any other required steps, the record will not be changed.

§ 311. Full Faith and Credit.

The court shall give full faith and credit to an acknowledgment of parentage or denial of parentage effective in another state if the acknowledgment or denial was in a signed record and otherwise complies with law of the other state.

Comment

Source: 42 U.S.C. § 666(a)(5)(C)(iv); UPA (2002) § 311.

The federal Personal Responsibility and Work Opportunity Reconciliation Act of 1996 requires states "to give full faith and credit to such an affidavit signed in any other State according to its procedures," 42 U.S.C. § 666(a)(5)(C)(iv), and that it have the same status as a judgment. This section, carried over from UPA (2002), implements these mandates.

§ 312. Forms for Acknowledgment and Denial of Parentage.

(a) The [state agency maintaining birth records] shall prescribe forms for an acknowledgment of parentage and denial of parentage.

(b) A valid acknowledgment of parentage or denial of parentage is not affected by a later modification of the form under subsection (a).

Comment

Source: 42 U.S.C. § 666(a)(5)(C)(i), (iv); UPA (2002) § 312.

§ 313. Release of Information.

The [state agency maintaining birth records] may release information relating to an acknowledgment of parentage or denial of parentage to a signatory of the acknowledgment or denial, a court, federal agency, and child-support agency of this or another state.

Comment

Source: UPA (2002) § 313.

[§ 314. Adoption of Rules.

The [state agency maintaining birth records] may adopt rules under [state administrative procedure act] to implement this [article].]

Legislative Note: A state should include Section 314 unless the provision is unnecessary or is inconsistent with other law of the state regarding agency rulemaking authority.

Comment

Source: UPA (2002) § 314.

Like UPA (2002), UPA (2017) makes this section optional to account for situations in which it may conflict with other rulemaking limitations in a particular state. States will implement acknowledgment procedures in a variety of ways, depending on local practice. This grant of rulemaking authority to carry out the provisions of this article may include electronic transmission of birth and acknowledgment data to the designated state agency.

[ARTICLE] 4
REGISTRY OF PATERNITY

Comment

The provisions establishing a paternity registry were added by UPA (2002). Signing a registry entitles the registrant to notice of and a right to oppose the adoption of an infant child; signing a paternity registry is *not* a means of establishing parentage. In *Lehr v. Robertson*, 463 U.S. 248 (1983), the Supreme Court upheld the constitutionality of a New York "putative father registry." A New York statute required a father of a nonmarital child to sign a paternity registry if he wished to be notified of a termination of parental rights or adoption proceeding. Thereafter, a series of well-publicized adoption cases occurred in which state courts held that nonmarital fathers had not been given proper notice of such proceedings and voided established adoptions. A substantial number of legislatures responded to these decisions by enacting paternity registries similar to the New York statute.

Like UPA (2002), UPA (2017) limits the effect of the registry to cases in which a child is less than one year of age at the time of the court hearing. This recognizes the need to expedite infant adoptions, while properly protecting the rights of those individuals who have not registered, but instead have established some relationship with the child following birth.

UPA (2017) does not make any substantive changes to Article 4. UPA (2017) does, however, replace gendered terms with gender-neutral ones where appropriate.

[PART] 1
GENERAL PROVISIONS

§ 401. Establishment of Registry. A registry of paternity is established in the [state agency maintaining the registry].

§ 402. Registration for Notification.

(a) Except as otherwise provided in subsection (b) or Section 405, a man who desires to be notified of a proceeding for adoption of, or termination of parental rights regarding, his genetic child must register in the registry of paternity established by Section 401 before the birth of the child or not later than 30 days after the birth.

(b) A man is not required to register under subsection (a) if[:

(1)] a parent-child relationship between the man and the child has been established under this [act] or law of this state other than this [act][; or

(2) the man commences a proceeding to adjudicate his parentage before a court has terminated his parental rights].

(c) A man who registers under subsection (a) shall notify the registry promptly in a record of any change in the information registered. The [state agency maintaining the registry] shall incorporate new information received into its records but need not seek to obtain current information for incorporation in the registry.

Source: UPA (2002) § 402.

Subsection (b)(2) addresses and eliminates a concern raised by *Lehr v. Robertson*, 463 U.S. 248 (1983). In *Lehr*, although the alleged genetic father did not avail himself of the New York putative fathers registry, he had filed a "visitation and paternity" petition in another local court. The trial judge in the adoption proceeding knew the identity of the genetic father, where he could be located, and that he was seeking to establish his parentage in another court. Nonetheless, the court granted the adoption and terminated the genetic father's parental rights without notice to him. Subsection (b)(2) exempts an alleged parent from the requirement of registration if the man "commences a proceeding to adjudicate his parentage before a court has terminated his parental rights."

§ 403. Notice of Proceeding. An individual who seeks to adopt a child or terminate parental rights to the child shall give notice of the proceeding to a man who has registered timely under Section 402(a) regarding the child. Notice must be given in a manner prescribed for service of process in a civil proceeding in this state.

§ 404. Termination of Parental Rights: Child under One Year of Age. An individual who seeks to terminate parental rights to or adopt a child is not required to give notice of the proceeding to a man who may be the genetic father of the child if:

(1) the child is under one year of age at the time of the termination of parental rights;

(2) the man did not register timely under Section 402(a); and

(3) the man is not exempt from registration under Section 402(b).

§ 405. Termination of Parental Rights: Child at Least One Year of Age. If a child is at least one year of age, an individual seeking to adopt or terminate parental rights to the child shall give notice of the proceeding to each alleged genetic father of the child, whether or not he has registered under Section 402(a) unless his parental rights have already been terminated. Notice must be given in a manner prescribed for service of process in a civil proceeding in this state.

[PART] 2
OPERATION OF REGISTRY

§ 406. Required Form.

(a) The [state agency maintaining the registry] shall prescribe a form for registering under Section 402(a). The form must state that:

(1) the man who registers signs the form under penalty of perjury;

(2) timely registration entitles the man who registers to notice of a proceeding for adoption of the child or termination of the parental rights of the man;

(3) timely registration does not commence a proceeding to establish parentage;

(4) the information disclosed on the form may be used against the man who registers to establish parentage;

(5) services to assist in establishing parentage are available to the man who registers through [the appropriate child-support agency];

(6) the man who registers also may register in a registry of paternity in another state if conception

or birth of the child occurred in the other state;

(7) information on registries of paternity of other states is available from [the appropriate state agency]; and

(8) procedures exist to rescind the registration.

(b) A man who registers under Section 402(a) shall sign the form described in subsection (a) under penalty of perjury.

§ 407. Furnishing Information; Confidentiality.

(a) The [state agency maintaining the registry] is not required to seek to locate the woman who gave birth to the child who is the subject of a registration under Section 402(a), but the [state agency maintaining the registry] shall give notice of the registration to the woman if the [state agency maintaining the registry] has her address.

(b) Information contained in the registry of paternity established by Section 401 is confidential and may be released on request only to:

(1) a court or individual designated by the court;

(2) the woman who gave birth to the child who is the subject of the registration;

(3) an agency authorized by law of this state other than this [act], law of another state, or federal law to receive the information;

(4) a licensed child-placing agency;

(5) a child-support agency;

(6) a party or the party's attorney of record in a proceeding under this [act] or in a proceeding to adopt or terminate parental rights to the child who is the subject of the registration; and

(7) a registry of paternity in another state.

§ 408. Penalty for Releasing Information.
An individual who intentionally releases information from the registry of paternity established by Section 401 to an individual or agency not authorized under Section 407(b) to receive the information commits a [appropriate level misdemeanor].

§ 409. Rescission of Registration.
A man who registers under Section 402(a) may rescind his registration at any time by filing with the registry of paternity established by Section 401 a rescission in a signed record that is attested by a notarial officer or witnessed.

§ 410. Untimely Registration.
If a man registers under Section 402(a) more than 30 days after the birth of the child, the [state agency maintaining the registry] shall notify the man who registers that, based on a review of the registration, the registration was not filed timely.

§ 411. Fees for Registry.

(a) The [state agency maintaining the registry] may not charge a fee for filing a registration under Section 402(a) or rescission of registration under Section 409.

(b) [Except as otherwise provided in subsection (c), the][The] [state agency maintaining the registry] may charge a reasonable fee to search the registry of paternity established by Section 401 and for furnishing a certificate of search under Section 414.

709

[(c) A child-support agency [is][and other appropriate agencies, if any, are] not required to pay a fee authorized by subsection (b).]

Legislative Note: *A state should include subsection (c) if the state does not require certain agencies to pay a fee authorized by subsection (b).*

[PART] 3
SEARCH OF REGISTRY

§ 412. Child Born Through Assisted Reproduction: Search of Registry Inapplicable. This [part] does not apply to a child born through assisted reproduction.

Comment

This section was added to clarify that individuals who have children through assisted reproduction are not required to conduct a search of the paternity registry, which was not designed or intended to address such situations.

§ 413. Search of Appropriate Registry.

If a parent-child relationship has not been established under this [act] between a child who is under one year of age and an individual other than the woman who gave birth to the child:

(1) an individual seeking to adopt or terminate parental rights to the child shall obtain a certificate of search under Section 414 to determine if a registration has been filed in the registry of paternity established by Section 401 regarding the child; and

(2) if the individual has reason to believe that conception or birth of the child may have occurred in another state, the individual shall obtain a certificate of search from the registry of paternity, if any, in that state.

§ 414. Certificate of Search of Registry.

(a) The [state agency maintaining the registry] shall furnish a certificate of search of the registry of paternity established by Section 401 on request to an individual, court, or agency identified in Section 407(b) or an individual required under Section 413(1) to obtain a certificate.

(b) A certificate furnished under subsection (a):

(1) must be signed on behalf of the [state agency maintaining the registry] and state that:

(A) a search has been made of the registry; and

(B) a registration under Section 402(a) containing the information required to identify the man who registers:

(i) has been found; or

(ii) has not been found; and

(2) if paragraph (1)(B)(i) applies, must have a copy of the registration attached.

(c) An individual seeking to adopt or terminate parental rights to a child must file with the court the certificate of search furnished under subsection (a) and Section 413(2), if applicable, before a proceeding to adopt or terminate parental rights to the child may be concluded.

§ 415. Admissibility of Registered Information. A certificate of search of a registry of paternity in this or another state is admissible in a proceeding for adoption of or termination of parental rights to a child and, if relevant, in other legal proceedings.

[ARTICLE] 5
GENETIC TESTING

§ 501. Definitions. In this [article]:

(1) "Combined relationship index" means the product of all tested relationship indices.

(2) "Ethnic or racial group" means, for the purpose of genetic testing, a recognized group that an individual identifies as the individual's ancestry or part of the ancestry or that is identified by other information.

(3) "Hypothesized genetic relationship" means an asserted genetic relationship between an individual and a child.

(4) "Probability of parentage" means, for the ethnic or racial group to which an individual alleged to be a parent belongs, the probability that a hypothesized genetic relationship is supported, compared to the probability that a genetic relationship is supported between the child and a random individual of the ethnic or racial group used in the hypothesized genetic relationship, expressed as a percentage incorporating the combined relationship index and a prior probability.

(5) "Relationship index" means a likelihood ratio that compares the probability of a genetic marker given a hypothesized genetic relationship and the probability of the genetic marker given a genetic relationship between the child and a random individual of the ethnic or racial group used in the hypothesized genetic relationship.

Comment

UPA (2017) amends terms that were used in UPA (2002) to reflect the fact that a court may need to adjudicate the parentage of an alleged genetic mother. UPA (2017) moves the relevant definitions from Section 102 to Section 501 because they are used only in this article.

The formula for calculating the probability of parentage is $100*AB/(AB-(1-B))$, where A is the combined relationship index and B is the prior probability (assumed to be 0.50).

§ 502. Scope of [Article]; Limitation on Use of Genetic Testing.

(a) This [article] governs genetic testing of an individual in a proceeding to adjudicate parentage, whether the individual:

(1) voluntarily submits to testing; or

(2) is tested under an order of the court or a child-support agency.

(b) Genetic testing may not be used:

(1) to challenge the parentage of an individual who is a parent under [Article] 7[or 8]; or

(2) to establish the parentage of an individual who is a donor.

Legislative Note: A state should include the bracketed reference to Article 8 if the state includes Article 8 in this act.

Comment

Source: UPA (2002) § 501.

The substance of Section 502(a) is carried over from UPA (2002) § 501.

Subsection (b) has been added to clarify that genetic testing cannot be used to challenge or argue against the parentage of an intended parent who is considered a parent under Articles 7 or 8. Because the parentage of an intended parent under Articles 7 and 8 is not premised on a genetic connection, the lack of a genetic connection should not be the basis of a challenge to the individual's parentage.

New subsection (b)(2) clarifies that an individual who is a donor under this act, and therefore is not a parent, is precluded from seeking to establish parentage by evidence of a genetic connection to the child.

§ 503. Authority to Order or Deny Genetic Testing.

(a) Except as otherwise provided in this [article] or [Article] 6, in a proceeding under this [act] to determine parentage, the court shall order the child and any other individual to submit to genetic testing if a request for testing is supported by the sworn statement of a party:

(1) alleging a reasonable possibility that the individual is the child's genetic parent; or

(2) denying genetic parentage of the child and stating facts establishing a reasonable possibility that the individual is not a genetic parent.

(b) A child-support agency may order genetic testing only if there is no presumed, acknowledged, or adjudicated parent of a child other than the woman who gave birth to the child.

(c) The court or child-support agency may not order in utero genetic testing.

(d) If two or more individuals are subject to court-ordered genetic testing, the court may order that testing be completed concurrently or sequentially.

(e) Genetic testing of a woman who gave birth to a child is not a condition precedent to testing of the child and an individual whose genetic parentage of the child is being determined. If the woman is unavailable or declines to submit to genetic testing, the court may order genetic testing of the child and each individual whose genetic parentage of the child is being adjudicated.

(f) In a proceeding to adjudicate the parentage of a child having a presumed parent or an individual who claims to be a parent under Section 609, or to challenge an acknowledgment of parentage, the court may deny a motion for genetic testing of the child and any other individual after considering the factors in Section 613(a) and (b).

(g) If an individual requesting genetic testing is barred under [Article] 6 from establishing the individual's parentage, the court shall deny the request for genetic testing.

(h) An order under this section for genetic testing is enforceable by contempt.

Comment

Source: 42 U.S.C. § 666(a)(5)(B)(i); UPA (2002) § 502 & § 608; UPA (1973) § 11.

Most of the substance of this section regarding genetic testing is carried over from UPA (2002). This section of UPA (2017) does, however, consolidate several subsections that had been included in different sections and in different articles of UPA (2002). Subsections (a) through (d) are carried over from UPA (2002) § 502, with some minor modifications to make the provisions gender neutral

where appropriate. Subsection (e) is carried over from UPA (2002) § 622(c). Subsection (h) is carried over from UPA (2002), § 622(a). Subsection (f) is similar in substance to Section 608 of UPA (2002).

Subsection (g) is new and is intended to clarify that if an individual is barred under Article 6 from establishing parentage, there is no use for the genetic testing under this act, which governs legal parentage. Accordingly, it directs a court to deny the request in such circumstances.

§ 504. Requirements for Genetic Testing.

(a) Genetic testing must be of a type reasonably relied on by experts in the field of genetic testing and performed in a testing laboratory accredited by:

(1) the AABB, formerly known as the American Association of Blood Banks, or a successor to its functions; or

(2) an accrediting body designated by the Secretary of the United States-Department of Health and Human Services.

(b) A specimen used in genetic testing may consist of a sample or a combination of samples of blood, buccal cells, bone, hair, or other body tissue or fluid. The specimen used in the testing need not be of the same kind for each individual undergoing genetic testing.

(c) Based on the ethnic or racial group of an individual undergoing genetic testing, a testing laboratory shall determine the databases from which to select frequencies for use in calculating a relationship index. If an individual or a child-support agency objects to the laboratory's choice, the following rules apply:

(1) Not later than 30 days after receipt of the report of the test, the objecting individual or child-support agency may request the court to require the laboratory to recalculate the relationship index using an ethnic or racial group different from that used by the laboratory.

(2) The individual or the child-support agency objecting to the laboratory's choice under this subsection shall:

(A) if the requested frequencies are not available to the laboratory for the ethnic or racial group requested, provide the requested frequencies compiled in a manner recognized by accrediting bodies; or

(B) engage another laboratory to perform the calculations.

(3) The laboratory may use its own statistical estimate if there is a question which ethnic or racial group is appropriate. The laboratory shall calculate the frequencies using statistics, if available, for any other ethnic or racial group requested.

(d) If, after recalculation of the relationship index under subsection (c) using a different ethnic or racial group, genetic testing under Section 506 does not identify an individual as a genetic parent of a child, the court may require an individual who has been tested to submit to additional genetic testing to identify a genetic parent.

Comment

Source: 42 U.S.C. § 666(a)(5)(B)(i) and § 666(a)(5)(F)(i); UPA (2002) § 503.

This substance of this section is largely carried over from UPA (2002). Section 504(a)(1), however, was revised because the listed entity now uses a different name. The reference to the American Society for Histocompatibility and Immunogenetics was deleted because that body is no longer accrediting laboratories for parentage testing.

§ 505. Report of Genetic Testing.

(a) A report of genetic testing must be in a record and signed under penalty of perjury by a designee of the testing laboratory. A report complying with the requirements of this [article] is self-authenticating.

(b) Documentation from a testing laboratory of the following information is sufficient to establish a reliable chain of custody and allow the results of genetic testing to be admissible without testimony:

(1) the name and photograph of each individual whose specimen has been taken;

(2) the name of the individual who collected each specimen;

(3) the place and date each specimen was collected;

(4) the name of the individual who received each specimen in the testing laboratory; and

(5) the date each specimen was received.

Comment

Source: 42 U.S.C. § 666(a)(5)(F).

§ 506. Genetic Testing Results; Challenge to Results.

(a) Subject to a challenge under subsection (b), an individual is identified under this [act] as a genetic parent of a child if genetic testing complies with this [article] and the results of the testing disclose:

(1) the individual has at least a 99 percent probability of parentage, using a prior probability of 0.50, as calculated by using the combined relationship index obtained in the testing; and

(2) a combined relationship index of at least 100 to 1.

(b) An individual identified under subsection (a) as a genetic parent of the child may challenge the genetic testing results only by other genetic testing satisfying the requirements of this [article] which:

(1) excludes the individual as a genetic parent of the child; or

(2) identifies another individual as a possible genetic parent of the child other than:

(A) the woman who gave birth to the child; or

(B) the individual identified under subsection (a).

(c) Except as otherwise provided in Section 511, if more than one individual other than the woman who gave birth is identified by genetic testing as a possible genetic parent of the child, the court shall order each individual to submit to further genetic testing to identify a genetic parent.

Comment

Source: 42 U.S.C. § 666(a)(5)(G); UPA (2002) § 505.

The use of a probability of parentage of 99.0% and a combined relationship index of 100 to 1 is consistent with accreditation standards in the year 2017 within the parentage-testing community.

The prior probability is expressed as a number, rather than a percentage, within the parentage-testing community and by applicable cases. *See, e.g., Butcher v.*

Commonwealth, 96 S.W.3d 3 (Ky. 2002); *Brown v. Smith*, 526 S.E.2d 686 (N.C. App. 2000); *Griffith v. State*, 976 S.W.2d 241 (Tex. Ct. App. 1998); *Plemel v. Walter*, 735 P.2d 1209 (Or. 1987).

Identification as a child's genetic parent does not, in and of itself, establish the child's legal parentage. The standards for adjudicating the parentage of a child are addressed in Article 6.

§ 507. Cost of Genetic Testing.

(a) Subject to assessment of fees under [Article] 6, payment of the cost of initial genetic testing must be made in advance:

(1) by a child-support agency in a proceeding in which the child-support agency is providing services;

(2) by the individual who made the request for genetic testing;

(3) as agreed by the parties; or

(4) as ordered by the court.

(b) If the cost of genetic testing is paid by a child-support agency, the agency may seek reimbursement from the genetic parent whose parent-child relationship is established.

Comment

Source: 42 U.S.C. § 666(a)(5)(B)(ii)(I); UPA (2002)
§ 506; UPA (1973) § 11.

§ 508. Additional Genetic Testing. The court or child-support agency shall order additional genetic testing on request of an individual who contests the result of the initial testing under Section 506. If initial genetic testing under Section 506 identified an individual as a genetic parent of the child, the court or agency may not order additional testing unless the contesting individual pays for the testing in advance.

Comment

Source: 42 U.S.C. § 666(a)(5)(B)(ii)(II); UPA (2002) § 507; UPA (1973) § 11.

§ 509. Genetic Testing When Specimen Not Available.

(a) Subject to subsection (b), if a genetic-testing specimen is not available from an alleged genetic parent of a child, an individual seeking genetic testing demonstrates good cause, and the court finds that the circumstances are just, the court may order any of the following individuals to submit specimens for genetic testing:

(1) a parent of the alleged genetic parent;

(2) a sibling of the alleged genetic parent;

(3) another child of the alleged genetic parent and the woman who gave birth to the other child; and

(4) another relative of the alleged genetic parent necessary to complete genetic testing.

(b) To issue an order under this section, the court must find that a need for genetic testing outweighs the legitimate interests of the individual sought to be tested.

Comment

Source: UPA (2002) § 508.

In the vast majority of cases, a genetic-testing specimen will be available from an alleged genetic parent of a child. In those circumstances when a specimen is not available, Section 509 gives the court authority to order genetic testing from other relatives of the alleged genetic parent in a limited set of circumstances. To order genetic testing of other relatives, the court must find that the circumstances are just, and the court must also find that that the need for genetic testing outweighs the legitimate interests, including the privacy and bodily integrity interests, of the individual sought to be tested.

§ 510. Deceased Individual. If an individual seeking genetic testing demonstrates good cause, the court may order genetic testing of a deceased individual.

Comment

Source: UPA (2002) § 509.

§ 511. Identical Siblings.

(a) If the court finds there is reason to believe that an alleged genetic parent has an identical sibling and evidence that the sibling may be a genetic parent of the child, the court may order genetic testing of the sibling.

(b) If more than one sibling is identified under Section 506 as a genetic parent of the child, the court may rely on nongenetic evidence to adjudicate which sibling is a genetic parent of the child.

Comment

Source: UPA (2002) § 510.

§ 512. Confidentiality of Genetic Testing.

(a) Release of a report of genetic testing for parentage is controlled by law of this state other than this [act].

(b) An individual who intentionally releases an identifiable specimen of another individual collected for genetic testing under this [article] for a purpose not relevant to a proceeding regarding parentage, without a court order or written permission of the individual who furnished the specimen, commits a [appropriate level misdemeanor].

Comment

Source: UPA (2002) § 511.

This provision is carried over from UPA (2002).

Subsection (a) refers to provisions other than this act that may regulate the disclosure of a genetic testing report that is part of the case record. In some states, the records of parentage proceedings are sealed. In these states, rules regarding disclosure of materials from a sealed proceeding would apply. In addition, there are also privacy rules in the federal regulations governing child support programs that may be applicable.

Subsection (b) expressly prohibits the intentional release of an identifiable specimen of another individual for a purpose not relevant to the parentage proceeding without proper authorization.

[ARTICLE] 6
PROCEEDING TO ADJUDICATE PARENTAGE

Comment

While largely retaining the substance of Article 6 of UPA (2002), UPA (2017) substantially reorganizes the content of former Article 6 to improve its clarity and flow.

[PART] 1
NATURE OF PROCEEDING

§ 601. Proceeding Authorized.

[(a)] A proceeding may be commenced to adjudicate the parentage of a child. Except as otherwise provided in this [act], the proceeding is governed by [cite to this state's rules of civil procedure].

[(b) A proceeding to adjudicate the parentage of a child born under a surrogacy agreement is governed by [Article] 8.]

Legislative Note: A state should include subsection (b) if the state includes Article 8 in the act.

Comment

Source: UPA (2002) § 601.

Subsection (b), which is new, clarifies that Article 8 governs proceedings to determine the parentage of a child born through surrogacy.

§ 602. Standing to Maintain Proceeding. Except as otherwise provided in [Article] 3 and Sections 608 through 611, a proceeding to adjudicate parentage may be maintained by:

(1) the child;

(2) the woman who gave birth to the child, unless a court has adjudicated that she is not a parent;

(3) an individual who is a parent under this [act];

(4) an individual whose parentage of the child is to be adjudicated;

(5) a child-support agency[or other governmental agency authorized by law of this state other than this [act]];

(6) an adoption agency authorized by law of this state other than this [act] or licensed child-placement agency; or

(7) a representative authorized by law of this state other than this [act] to act for an individual who otherwise would be entitled to maintain a proceeding but is deceased, incapacitated, or a minor.

Comment

Source: UPA (2002) § 602; UPA (1973) § 6.

§ 603. Notice of Proceeding.

(a) The [petitioner] shall give notice of a proceeding to adjudicate parentage to the following individuals:

(1) the woman who gave birth to the child, unless a court has adjudicated that she is not a parent;

(2) an individual who is a parent of the child under this [act];

(3) a presumed, acknowledged, or adjudicated parent of the child; and

(4) an individual whose parentage of the child is to be adjudicated.

(b) An individual entitled to notice under subsection (a) has a right to intervene in the proceeding.

(c) Lack of notice required by subsection (a) does not render a judgment void. Lack of notice does not preclude an individual entitled to notice under subsection (a) from bringing a proceeding under Section 611(b).

Comment

This new section is intended to ensure that steps are taken to give notice to all persons with a claim to parentage of a child. Giving such individuals notice of and a right to intervene in the proceeding is important because the rights of any absent individual with a claim to parentage of a child could be indirectly affected by the proceeding. Indeed, Section 623(d) provides that, "[e]xcept as otherwise provided in subsection (b), a determination of parentage may be a defense in a subsequent proceeding seeking to adjudicate parentage by an individual who was not a party to the earlier proceeding."

While a goal of the Section 603 is to ensure that steps are taken to permit all individuals with a claim to parentage of a child the opportunity to participate in the proceeding, another goal of the section is to permit parentage to be adjudicated even if such an individual declines to participate in the proceeding. Hence, the section does not require joinder of such individuals. Subsection (c) also clarifies that failure to comply with the notice requirement of this section does not render the judgment void.

The notice should include a copy of Section 603.

Section 603 does not require that notice be given to the child. This is consistent with the policy decision of UPA (2002) not to require that the child be joined as a necessary party to the proceeding. As the Comment to Section 602 of UPA (2002) explained, few states require children to be joined as necessary parties in parentage actions, and no states then required children born during a marriage to be named as parties to a divorce proceeding. Because the child need not be a party to the action, there is no obligation to notice the child of the proceeding. In addition, as provided in Section 623, the child is not bound during minority by the adjudication unless the order is consistent with the results of genetic testing or the child was represented by an attorney.

§ 604. Personal Jurisdiction.

(a) The court may adjudicate an individual's parentage of a child only if the court has personal jurisdiction over the individual.

(b) A court of this state with jurisdiction to adjudicate parentage may exercise personal jurisdiction over a nonresident individual, or the [guardian or conservator] of the individual, if the conditions prescribed in [cite to this state's Section 201 of the Uniform Interstate Family Support Act] are satisfied.

(c) Lack of jurisdiction over one individual does not preclude the court from making an adjudication of parentage binding on another individual.

Comment

Source: UPA (2002) § 604; UPA (1973) § 6(b).

This section is carried over from UPA (2002). UPA (2017) continues to take the position that, unlike child custody and visitation proceedings which are considered status adjudications that do not require personal jurisdiction over both parents, parentage proceedings require personal jurisdiction.

While the ideal scenario involves bringing all potential claimants together in a single proceeding, subsection (c) takes the approach that if the court lacks jurisdiction over an individual with a claim to parentage of a child, the court can still proceed.

§ 605. Venue. Venue for a proceeding to adjudicate parentage is in the [county] of this state in which:

(1) the child resides or is located;

(2) if the child does not reside in this state, the [respondent] resides or is located; or

(3) a proceeding has been commenced for administration of the estate of an individual who is or may be a parent under this [act].

Comment

Source: UPA (2002) § 605; UPA (1973) § 8(c).   UPA (1973) and UPA (2002).
The venue provision follows the approach taken by

[PART] 2

SPECIAL RULES FOR PROCEEDING TO ADJUDICATE PARENTAGE

§ 606. Admissibility of Results of Genetic Testing.

(a) Except as otherwise provided in Section 502(b), the court shall admit a report of genetic testing ordered by the court under Section 503 as evidence of the truth of the facts asserted in the report.

(b) A party may object to the admission of a report described in subsection (a), not later than [14] days after the party receives the report. The party shall cite specific grounds for exclusion.

(c) A party that objects to the results of genetic testing may call a genetic-testing expert to testify in person or by another method approved by the court. Unless the court orders otherwise, the party offering the testimony bears the expense for the expert testifying.

(d) Admissibility of a report of genetic testing is not affected by whether the testing was performed:

(1) voluntarily or under an order of the court or a child-support agency; or

(2) before, on, or after commencement of the proceeding.

Comment

Source: 42 U.S.C. § 666(a)(5)(F)(ii); UPA (2002) §
621(a), (b); UPA (1973) §§ 10, 13.

§ 607. Adjudicating Parentage of Child with Alleged Genetic Parent.

(a) A proceeding to determine whether an alleged genetic parent who is not a presumed parent is a parent of a child may be commenced:

(1) before the child becomes an adult; or

(2) after the child becomes an adult, but only if the child initiates the proceeding.

(b) Except as otherwise provided in Section 614, this subsection applies in a proceeding described in subsection (a) if the woman who gave birth to the child is the only other individual with a claim to parentage of the child. The court shall adjudicate an alleged genetic parent to be a parent of the child if the alleged genetic parent:

(1) is identified under Section 506 as a genetic parent of the child and the identification is not successfully challenged under Section 506;

(2) admits parentage in a pleading, when making an appearance, or during a hearing, the court

accepts the admission, and the court determines the alleged genetic parent to be a parent of the child;

(3) declines to submit to genetic testing ordered by the court or a child-support agency, in which case the court may adjudicate the alleged genetic parent to be a parent of the child even if the alleged genetic parent denies a genetic relationship with the child;

(4) is in default after service of process and the court determines the alleged genetic parent to be a parent of the child; or

(5) is neither identified nor excluded as a genetic parent by genetic testing and, based on other evidence, the court determines the alleged genetic parent to be a parent of the child.

(c) Except as otherwise provided in Section 614 and subject to other limitations in this [part], if in a proceeding involving an alleged genetic parent, at least one other individual in addition to the woman who gave birth to the child has a claim to parentage of the child, the court shall adjudicate parentage under Section 613.

Comment

This substance of this section is largely carried over from UPA (2002). This section, however, consolidates into a single provision concepts that were previously scattered throughout Article 6 of UPA (2002).

Subsection (a) is based on UPA (2002) § 606; UPA (2017), however, eliminates UPA (2002) § 606(2), which permitted a parentage action to be commenced at any time if an earlier proceeding had been dismissed based on the application of a statute of limitation then in effect. Because federal law requires states to permit parentage establishment any time before the child attains 18 years of age, that provision is no longer necessary. 42 U.S.C. § 666(a)(5)(A)(ii).

Subsection (b)(1) is based on UPA (2002) § 631(2).
Subsection (b)(2) is based on UPA (2002) § 623.
Subsection (b)(3) is based on UPA (2002) § 622(b).
Subsection (b)(4) is based on UPA (2002) § 634.
Subsection (b)(5) is based on UPA (2002) § 631(3).

Subsection (c) is arguably new, although its underlying principle – that a court may adjudicate an individual who is not a genetic parent to be a child's legal parent based on consideration of the child's best interest – is based on and consistent with UPA (2002) § 608.

§ 608. Adjudicating Parentage of Child with Presumed Parent.

(a) A proceeding to determine whether a presumed parent is a parent of a child may be commenced:

(1) before the child becomes an adult; or

(2) after the child becomes an adult, but only if the child initiates the proceeding.

(b) A presumption of parentage under Section 204 cannot be overcome after the child attains two years of age unless the court determines:

(1) the presumed parent is not a genetic parent, never resided with the child, and never held out the child as the presumed parent's child; or

(2) the child has more than one presumed parent.

(c) Except as otherwise provided in Section 614, the following rules apply in a proceeding to adjudicate a presumed parent's parentage of a child if the woman who gave birth to the child is the only other individual with a claim to parentage of the child:

(1) If no party to the proceeding challenges the presumed parent's parentage of the child, the court shall adjudicate the presumed parent to be a parent of the child.

(2) If the presumed parent is identified under Section 506 as a genetic parent of the child and that identification is not successfully challenged under Section 506, the court shall adjudicate the presumed parent to be a parent of the child.

(3) If the presumed parent is not identified under Section 506 as a genetic parent of the child and the presumed parent or the woman who gave birth to the child challenges the presumed parent's parentage of the child, the court shall adjudicate the parentage of the child in the best interest of the child based on the factors under Section 613(a) and (b).

(d) Except as otherwise provided in Section 614 and subject to other limitations in this [part], if in a proceeding to adjudicate a presumed parent's parentage of a child, another individual in addition to the woman who gave birth to the child asserts a claim to parentage of the child, the court shall adjudicate parentage under Section 613.

Comment

This substance of this section is largely carried over from UPA (2002). This section, however, consolidates into a single provision concepts that were previously included in several provisions of Article 6 of UPA (2002).

Subsection (a) is based on UPA (2002) § 607(a). Subsection (b) is based on UPA (2002) § 607(b)(1) and (2). Subsections (c) and (d) are based on UPA (2002) § 608.

§ 609. Adjudicating Claim of De Facto Parentage of Child.

(a) A proceeding to establish parentage of a child under this section may be commenced only by an individual who:

(1) is alive when the proceeding is commenced; and

(2) claims to be a de facto parent of the child.

(b) An individual who claims to be a de facto parent of a child must commence a proceeding to establish parentage of a child under this section:

(1) before the child attains 18 years of age; and

(2) while the child is alive.

(c) The following rules govern standing of an individual who claims to be a de facto parent of a child to maintain a proceeding under this section:

(1) The individual must file an initial verified pleading alleging specific facts that support the claim to parentage of the child asserted under this section. The verified pleading must be served on all parents and legal guardians of the child and any other party to the proceeding.

(2) An adverse party, parent, or legal guardian may file a pleading in response to the pleading filed under paragraph (1). A responsive pleading must be verified and must be served on parties to the proceeding.

(3) Unless the court finds a hearing is necessary to determine disputed facts material to the issue of standing, the court shall determine, based on the pleadings under paragraphs (1) and (2), whether the individual has alleged facts sufficient to satisfy by a preponderance of the evidence the requirements of paragraphs (1) through (7) of subsection (d). If the court holds a hearing under this subsection, the hearing must be held on an expedited basis.

(d) In a proceeding to adjudicate parentage of an individual who claims to be a de facto parent of the child, if there is only one other individual who is a parent or has a claim to parentage of the child, the court shall adjudicate the individual who claims to be a de facto parent to be a parent of the child if the individual demonstrates by clear-and-convincing evidence that:

(1) the individual resided with the child as a regular member of the child's household for a significant period;

(2) the individual engaged in consistent caretaking of the child;

722

(3) the individual undertook full and permanent responsibilities of a parent of the child without expectation of financial compensation;

(4) the individual held out the child as the individual's child;

(5) the individual established a bonded and dependent relationship with the child which is parental in nature;

(6) another parent of the child fostered or supported the bonded and dependent relationship required under paragraph (5); and

(7) continuing the relationship between the individual and the child is in the best interest of the child.

(e) Subject to other limitations in this [part], if in a proceeding to adjudicate parentage of an individual who claims to be a de facto parent of the child, there is more than one other individual who is a parent or has a claim to parentage of the child and the court determines that the requirements of subsection (d) are satisfied, the court shall adjudicate parentage under Section 613.

Comment

This section adds a new means by which an individual can establish a parent-child relationship. This section is modeled on provisions that were recently enacted in Delaware and Maine, two states that adopted UPA (2002), and it reflects trends in state family law.

In most states, if an individual can establish that he or she has developed a strong parent-child relationship with the consent and encouragement of a legal parent, the individual is entitled to some parental rights and possibly some parental responsibilities. Some states extend rights to such persons under equitable principles. *See, e.g., Bethany v. Jones*, 378 S.W.3d 731 (Ark. 2011) (in loco parentis); *Mullins v. Picklesimer*, 317 S.W.3d 569 (Ky. 2010) (in equity); *Boseman v. Harrell*, 704 S.E.2d 494 (N.C. 2010) (in equity); *McAllister v. McAllister*, 779 N.W.2d 652 (N.D. 2010) (psychological parent); *Marquez v. Caudill*, 656 S.E.2d 737 (S.C. 2008) (psychological parent); In re *Clifford K.*, 619 S.E.2d 138 (W. Va. 2005) (psychological parent). Other states extend rights to such individuals through broad third party custody and visitation statutes. *See, e.g.,* Minn. Stat. § 257C.01-08; Tex. Fam. Code § 102.003(9).

In addition, by statute and through case law, several states recognize such persons as legal parents. *See, e.g., Elisa B. v. Superior Court*, 117 P.3d 660 (Cal. 2005) (under the holding out provision of UPA (1973)); In re *Parentage of L.B.*, 122 P.3d 161 (Wash. 2005) (under Washington state constitution); In re *S.N.V.*, 2011 WL 6425562 (Colo. App. 2011) (under the holding out provision of UPA (1973)); Del. Code Ann., tit. 13, § 8-201(c) (by express statutory

provision); *Frazier v. Goudschaal*, 295 P.3d 542 (Kan. 2013) (under a provision based on UPA (1973)); *Partanen v. Gallagher*, 59 N.E.3d 1133 (Mass. 2016) (under a provision based on the holding out provision of UPA (1973)); Me. Rev. Stat. tit. 19-a, § 1891 (by express statutory provision); *Guardianship of Madelyn B.*, 98 A.3d 494 (N.H. 2014) (under the holding out provision of UPA (1973)); *Chatterjee v. King*, 280 P.3d 283 (N.M. 2012) (under the holding out provision of UPA (1973)).

To provide greater clarity to the parties and affected child, UPA (2017) addresses this issue through an express statutory provision. Under this new section, an individual who has functioned as a child's parent for a significant period such that the individual formed a bonded and dependent parent-child relationship may be recognized as a legal parent. This provision ensures that individuals who form strong parent-child bonds with children with the consent and encouragement of the child's legal parent are not excluded from a determination of parentage simply because they entered the child's life sometime after the child's birth. Consistent with the case law and the existing statutory provisions in other states, this section does not include a specific time length requirement. Instead, whether the period is significant is left to the determination of the court, based on the circumstances of the case. The length of time required will vary depending on the age of the child.

At the same time, however, the scope of this section is limited in several ways. First, this section includes a heightened standing requirement that must be satisfied by the individual claiming to be a de facto parent. This requirement is included to ensure that permitting proceedings by de facto parents does not subject parents to unwarranted and unjustified litigation. At the standing stage, under Section 609(c)(3), the requirements may be proved by only a preponderance of the evidence.

Second, the section sets forth a series of substantive requirements that must be satisfied before a court can adjudicate such an individual to be a parent. Some of these substantive requirements—the individual reside with the child for a significant period of time and the individual formed a bonded and dependent relationship with the child which is parental in nature—are based on factors developed under common law doctrine that is utilized in many states. See, e.g., In re Parentage of L.B., 122 P.3d 161, 176 (Wash. 2005), cert. denied, 547 U.S. 1143 (2006); V.C. v. J.M.B., 748 A.2d 539, 551 (N.J.), cert. denied, 531 U.S. 926 (2000); Custody of H.S.H.-K., 533 N.W.2d 419, 421 (Wis. 1995). Accordingly, a court

may look to those common law decisions for guidance.

Third, this section permits only the individual alleging himself or herself to be a de facto parent to initiate a proceeding under this section. This limitation was added to address concerns that stepparents might be held responsible for child support under this theory of parentage. Finally, this section requires the proceeding to establish de facto parentage be commenced before the death of the child and the death of the individual alleged to be a de facto parent, and before the child attains 18 years of age. These safeguards protect against unwarranted and unjustified litigation.

This section is not intended to preclude legal actions based on other legal theories. See, e.g., DeHart v. DeHart, 986 N.E.2d 85 (Ill. 2013) (recognizing a cause of action for equitable adoption and contract for adoption in an action contesting the validity of a will).

§ 610. Adjudicating Parentage of Child with Acknowledged Parent.

(a) If a child has an acknowledged parent, a proceeding to challenge the acknowledgment of parentage or a denial of parentage, brought by a signatory to the acknowledgment or denial, is governed by Sections 309 and 310.

(b) If a child has an acknowledged parent, the following rules apply in a proceeding to challenge the acknowledgment of parentage or a denial of parentage brought by an individual, other than the child, who has standing under Section 602 and was not a signatory to the acknowledgment or denial:

(1) The individual must commence the proceeding not later than two years after the effective date of the acknowledgment.

(2) The court may permit the proceeding only if the court finds permitting the proceeding is in the best interest of the child.

(3) If the court permits the proceeding, the court shall adjudicate parentage under Section 613.

Comment

Source: UPA (2002) § 609.

This section is based on UPA (2002) § 609. Section 609 of UPA (2002) addressed challenges both to adjudicated parents and to acknowledged parents. UPA (2017) separates these concepts into separate sections – Section 610, addressing challenges to acknowledged parents, and Section 611, addressing challenges to adjudicated parents.

As was true under UPA (2002), subsection (b)

imposes a two-year limitations period to challenges to an acknowledgment. This is consistent with the limitations periods in other sections of the UPA, including the time for challenging an acknowledgment of parentage by a signatory under Section 307. As was true under UPA (2002), a challenge brought within this limitations period is subject to considerations related to the best interest of the child.

§ 611. Adjudicating Parentage of Child with Adjudicated Parent.

(a) If a child has an adjudicated parent, a proceeding to challenge the adjudication, brought by an individual who was a party to the adjudication or received notice under Section 603, is governed by the rules governing a collateral attack on a judgment.

(b) If a child has an adjudicated parent, the following rules apply to a proceeding to challenge the adjudication of parentage brought by an individual, other than the child, who has standing under Section 602 and was not a party to the adjudication and did not receive notice under Section 603:

(1) The individual must commence the proceeding not later than two years after the effective date of the adjudication.

(2) The court may permit the proceeding only if the court finds permitting the proceeding is in the best interest of the child.

(3) If the court permits the proceeding, the court shall adjudicate parentage under Section 613.

Comment

Source: UPA (2002) § 609.

This section is based on UPA (2002) § 609. Section 609 of UPA (2002) addressed challenges both to adjudicated parents and to acknowledged parents. UPA (2017) separates these concepts into separate sections: Section 610, addressing challenges to acknowledged parents, and Section 611, addressing challenges to adjudicated parents.

Subsection (a) clarifies that if the individual received notice of the action under Section 603, a proceeding to challenge the adjudication by the individual is governed by the rules governing

collateral attacks on judgments.

As was true under UPA (2002), subsection (b) imposes a two-year limitations period on challenges to an adjudication of parentage of a child by an individual who was not a party to and did not receive notice of the prior proceeding. Other sections of the act likewise utilize a two-year limitations period. *See, e.g.*, Section 307; Section 608. As was true under UPA (2002), a challenge brought within this limitations period is subject to considerations related to the best interest of the child.

§ 612. Adjudicating Parentage of Child of Assisted Reproduction.

(a) An individual who is a parent under [Article] 7 or the woman who gave birth to the child may bring a proceeding to adjudicate parentage. If the court determines the individual is a parent under [Article] 7, the court shall adjudicate the individual to be a parent of the child.

(b) In a proceeding to adjudicate an individual's parentage of a child, if another individual other than the woman who gave birth to the child is a parent under [Article] 7, the court shall adjudicate the individual's parentage of the child under Section 613.

Comment

This new section specifically authorizes the filing of a proceeding to adjudicate the parentage of individuals who are intended parents under Article 7.

The rules regarding adjudications of parentage for individuals who are parents under Article 8 are set forth in Article 8.

§ 613. Adjudicating Competing Claims of Parentage.

(a) Except as otherwise provided in Section 614, in a proceeding to adjudicate competing claims of, or challenges under Section 608(c), 610, or 611 to, parentage of a child by two or more individuals, the court shall adjudicate parentage in the best interest of the child, based on:

(1) the age of the child;

(2) the length of time during which each individual assumed the role of parent of the child;

(3) the nature of the relationship between the child and each individual;

(4) the harm to the child if the relationship between the child and each individual is not

recognized;

(5) the basis for each individual's claim to parentage of the child; and

(6) other equitable factors arising from the disruption of the relationship between the child and each individual or the likelihood of other harm to the child.

(b) If an individual challenges parentage based on the results of genetic testing, in addition to the factors listed in subsection (a), the court shall consider:

(1) the facts surrounding the discovery the individual might not be a genetic parent of the child; and

(2) the length of time between the time that the individual was placed on notice that the individual might not be a genetic parent and the commencement of the proceeding.

Alternative A

(c) The court may not adjudicate a child to have more than two parents under this [act].

Alternative B

(c) The court may adjudicate a child to have more than two parents under this [act] if the court finds that failure to recognize more than two parents would be detrimental to the child. A finding of detriment to the child does not require a finding of unfitness of any parent or individual seeking an adjudication of parentage. In determining detriment to the child, the court shall consider all relevant factors, including the harm if the child is removed from a stable placement with an individual who has fulfilled the child's physical needs and psychological needs for care and affection and has assumed the role for a substantial period.

End of Alternatives

Legislative Note: A state should enact Alternative A if the state does not wish a child to have more than two parents. A state should enact Alternative B if the state wishes to authorize a court in certain circumstances to establish more than two parents for a child.

Comment

UPA (1973) contained a provision addressing situations in which multiple individuals have a claim to parentage of a child. Section 4(b) of UPA (1973) provided guidance in such situations, although the guidance was vague. UPA (1973) § 4(b) ("If two or more presumptions arise which conflict with each other, the presumption which on the facts is founded on the weightier considerations of policy and logic controls.").

UPA (2002) eliminated that provision and did not expressly address how a court should resolve cases involving competing presumptions or claims of parentage. UPA (2002) did, however, include a provision that implicitly acknowledged the possibility of multiple claimants. UPA (2002), § 608 authorized a court to deny a request for genetic testing in cases in which a party sought to challenge a presumption of parentage. The section provided a list of factors that a court was directed to consider in such cases. The

reality is, however, that whether or not the court orders genetic testing, the parties often know what the results of that genetic tests would reveal. In that way, the section concealed the purpose of the provision, which was to provide guidance to a court faced with competing claims of parentage between an alleged genetic parent and a presumed parent.

UPA (2017) addresses how to resolve cases between competing claimants directly. While UPA (2017) frames the issue differently, this section is consistent with the basic approach of UPA (2002) § 608. Thus, the factors included in this section are largely carried over from UPA (2002) § 608.

This section also expressly addresses another issue that UPA (2002) did not: whether a court may conclude that a child has more than two parents under the act. This is a question with which courts have increasingly been confronted.

The act provides two alternatives. Alternative A

provides that a child cannot have more than two legal parents. Alternative B permits a court, in rare circumstances, to find that a child has more than two legal parents.

Alternative B is consistent with an emerging trend permitting courts to recognize more than two people as a child's parents. Four states expressly permit a court to find that a child has more than two legal parents by statute. *See* Cal. Fam. Code 7612(c); Del. Code Ann. tit. 13, § 8-201(a)(4), (b)(6), (c); D.C. Code § 16-909(e); Me. Rev. Stat. tit. 19-a, § 1853(2). In addition, courts in several other states have reached that conclusion as a matter of common law. *See, e.g., Warren v. Richard*, 296 So.3d 813, 815 (La. 1974). In addition, courts in some states have concluded that a child had two legal parents and one equitable parent who was entitled to at least some rights and duties of a parent. *See, e.g., In Interest of P.S.*, 505 S.W.3d 106 (Tex. Ct. App. 2016) (3-way custody and visitation arrangement); *A.B. v. T.V.*, 2015 WL 7571451 (Pa. Super. Ct. 2015); In re *Parentage of J.B.R. Child*, 336 P.3d 648, 653 (Wash. App. Ct. 2014) ("The fact that [the child] has two living biological parents does not prohibit [the child's stepparent] from petitioning for de facto parentage."); *McAllister v. McAllister*, 779 N.W.2d 652 (N.D. 2010).

Again, Alternative B recognizes and reflects this trend in favor of recognizing the possibility that a child may have more than two legal parents. Alternative B, however, stakes out a narrow, limited approach to the issue by erecting a high substantive hurdle before the court can reach this conclusion: a court can determine that a child has more than two legal parents only when failure to do so would cause detriment to the child.

§ 614. Precluding Establishment of Parentage by Perpetrator of Sexual Assault.

(a) In this section, "sexual assault" means [cite to this state's criminal rape statutes].

(b) In a proceeding in which a woman alleges that a man committed a sexual assault that resulted in the woman giving birth to a child, the woman may seek to preclude the man from establishing that he is a parent of the child.

(c) This section does not apply if:

(1) the man described in subsection (b) has previously been adjudicated to be a parent of the child; or

(2) after the birth of the child, the man established a bonded and dependent relationship with the child which is parental in nature.

(d) Unless Section 309 or 607 applies, a woman must file a pleading making an allegation under subsection (b) not later than two years after the birth of the child. The woman may file the pleading only in a proceeding to establish parentage under this [act].

(e) An allegation under subsection (b) may be proved by:

(1) evidence that the man was convicted of a sexual assault, or a comparable crime in another jurisdiction, against the woman and the child was born not later than 300 days after the sexual assault; or

(2) clear-and-convincing evidence that the man committed sexual assault against the woman and the child was born not later than 300 days after the sexual assault.

(f) Subject to subsections (a) through (d), if the court determines that an allegation has been proved under subsection (e), the court shall:

(1) adjudicate that the man described in subsection (b) is not a parent of the child;

(2) require the [state agency maintaining birth records] to amend the birth certificate if requested by the woman and the court determines that the amendment is in the best interest of the child; and

(3) require the man pay to child support, birth-related costs, or both, unless the woman requests otherwise and the court determines that granting the request is in the best interest of the child.

Comment

According to the National Conference of State Legislatures (NCSL), it is estimated that there are between "17,000 and 32,000 rape-related pregnancies in the United States each year." In 2015, Congress enacted the Rape Survivor Child Custody Act. Title IV of that act provides for increased funding for states that have statutes permitting women who conceived children through rape to seek termination of the perpetrator's parental rights. According to NCSL, today "[a]pproximately 45 states and the District of Columbia have enacted legislation regarding the parental rights of perpetrators of sexual assault." Most states that have enacted legislation address the issue in one of two ways: (1) approximately 30 states have statutes that permit a court to terminate the parental rights of the perpetrator; (2) approximately 20 states permit courts to restrict the custodial or visitation rights of the perpetrator.

This section permits a court to declare that the perpetrator is not a parent if the person has been convicted of sexual assault or if the sexual assault is proved by clear and convincing evidence in the proceeding and the child was conceived as a result the sexual assault. The latter method of proof must be included to meet the requirements of the federal statute. 42 U.S.C. § 14043h-2.

In subsection (a), states must decide which criminal rape statutes should be included in this section. A state may, for example, want to exclude from coverage some forms of statutory rape where the individuals are close in age, or incest between consenting adults who do not have a parent-child relationship.

In most cases, an allegation that this section applies must be made within two years of the child's birth. This is consistent with several other provisions of UPA 2017 that also impose a two-year statute of limitations. *See, e.g.*, Sections 307, 608, 705. There is one exception to this two-year limitations period. In an action to adjudicate parentage when the child has no presumed, adjudicated, or acknowledged parent, the two-year statute of limitations does not apply.

Even if the action is timely filed, a court must deny the request to preclude the man's parentage of the child if the man has developed a bonded and dependent parent-child relationship with the child. This exception is consistent with the act's focus on the best interest of the child, and with the act's goal of protecting established parent-child bonds.

A woman may seek to preclude establishment of parentage of a child by an alleged perpetrator of sexual assault only in a proceeding to adjudicate parentage.

Subsection (c) provides that a woman may seek to preclude an establishment of parentage under this section. While most proceedings under this section will be brought by the woman, subsection (c) does not expressly limit such proceedings to ones initiated by the woman because there may be limited circumstances when someone acting on behalf of the woman may be permitted to bring a proceeding under this section. This may be the case, for example, if the woman is very young or if she is incapacitated.

[PART] 3
HEARING AND ADJUDICATION

§ 615. Temporary Order.

(a) In a proceeding under this [article], the court may issue a temporary order for child support if the order is consistent with law of this state other than this [act] and the individual ordered to pay support is:

(1) a presumed parent of the child;

(2) petitioning to be adjudicated a parent;

(3) identified as a genetic parent through genetic testing under Section 506;

(4) an alleged genetic parent who has declined to submit to genetic testing;

(5) shown by clear-and-convincing evidence to be a parent of the child; or

(6) a parent under this [act].

(b) A temporary order may include a provision for custody and visitation under law of this state other than this [act].

Comment

Source: 42 U.S.C. § 666(a)(5)(J); UPA (2002) § 624; UIFSA (1996) § 401.

This provision is carried over from UPA (2002) § 624. The provision requires that parentage be established by clear and convincing evidence to comply with federal law. *See* 42 U.S.C. § 666(a)(5)(J) (requiring states to adopt "[p]rocedures which require that a temporary order be issued, upon motion by a party, requiring the provision of child support pending an administrative or judicial determination of parentage, if there is clear and convincing evidence of paternity (on the basis of genetic tests or other evidence).").

The temporary orders referenced in both subsections (a) and (b) include interim orders.

§ 616. Combining Proceedings.

(a) Except as otherwise provided in subsection (b), the court may combine a proceeding to adjudicate parentage under this [act] with a proceeding for adoption, termination of parental rights, child custody or visitation, child support, [divorce, dissolution, annulment, declaration of invalidity, or legal separation or separate maintenance,] administration of an estate, or other appropriate proceeding.

(b) A [respondent] may not combine a proceeding described in subsection (a) with a proceeding to adjudicate parentage brought under [the Uniform Interstate Family Support Act].

Legislative Note: A state should use its own terms for the proceedings identified in the bracketed language in subsection (a).

Comment

Source: UPA (2002) § 610; UPA (1973) § 8.

This provision is carried over from UPA (2002), although the prior concept of "joining" proceeding has been replaced with the concept of "combining" various proceedings. As the comment to the UPA (2002) provision explained, it is common to have multiple proceedings regarding a single child pending at the same time, especially when a child-support agency seeks to establish paternity and fix child support.

This provision is intended to permit a court to combine such proceedings unless the court would not otherwise have jurisdiction over the proceeding. Accordingly, subsection (b) restricts counterclaims in those instances in which an initiating state sends proceeding to adjudicate parentage to the responding state. Because petitioner is "appearing" in the other forum, to permit counterclaims would serve as a major deterrent to bringing such proceedings. This bar does not prevent a separate proceeding for such matters, but there must be independent jurisdiction not arising from the petitioner's appearance in the parentage proceeding.

§ 617. Proceeding Before Birth.

[Except as otherwise provided in [Article] 8, a][A] proceeding to adjudicate parentage may be commenced before the birth of the child and an order or judgment may be entered before birth, but enforcement of the order or judgment must be stayed until the birth of the child.

Legislative Note: A state should include the bracketed phrase on Article 8 if the state wishes to recognize in statute surrogacy agreements and includes Article 8 in this act.

Comment

UPA (2002) provided that an action to determine parentage could be initiated prior to birth, but that it could not be concluded until after the birth of the child. UPA (2002) § 611.

UPA (2017) takes a slightly different position. This section permits a court to issue an order prior to birth, although the judgment is stayed until the birth of the child. This provision is based on a California provision. Cal. Fam. Code § 7633. In some instances, it may be very helpful for the parties to have a determination of parentage prior to birth, even if the order or judgment is not effective until after birth.

§ 618. Child as Party; Representation.

(a) A minor child is a permissive party but not a necessary party to a proceeding under this [article].

(b) The court shall appoint [an attorney, guardian ad litem, or similar person] to represent a child in a proceeding under this [article], if the court finds that the interests of the child are not adequately represented.

Legislative Note: A state should replace the bracketed language in subsection (b) for terms of persons authorized to represent a child in a proceeding under this article with terms for persons performing similar representation under law of the state other than this act.

Comment

Source: UPA (2002) § 612.

Section 618 follows UPA (2002). Unlike UPA (1973), UPA (2002) and UPA (2017) take the view that the child is not a necessary party. The court, however, is permitted to appoint an attorney or similar person to represent the child if the court finds that the child's interests are not adequately represented.

§ 619. Court to Adjudicate Parentage. The court shall adjudicate parentage of a child without a jury.

Comment

Source: 42 U.S.C. § 666(a)(5)(I); UPA (2002) § 632.

This provision is carried over from UPA (2002). This provision is consistent with federal law, which provides that "parties to an action to establish paternity are not entitled to a trial by jury." 42 U.S.C. § 666(a)(5)(I).

§ 620. Hearing[; Inspection of Records].

[(a)]On request of a party and for good cause, the court may close a proceeding under this [article] to the public.

[(b) A final order in a proceeding under this [article] is available for public inspection. Other papers and records are available for public inspection only with the consent of the parties or by court order.]

Legislative Note: A state should review the state's open records laws to determine if subsection (b) needs to be included or amended.

Comment

Source: UPA (2002) § 633; UPA (1973) § 20.

§ 621. Dismissal for Want of Prosecution. The court may dismiss a proceeding under this [act] for want of prosecution only without prejudice. An order of dismissal for want of prosecution purportedly with prejudice is void and has only the effect of a dismissal without prejudice.

Comment

Source: UPA (2002) § 635.

A major principle of UPA (2017) —and its predecessors—is that the child's right to have a determination of parentage is fundamental. This section, which is carried over from UPA (2002), confirms this right by declaring that the delinquency of another person, such as the mother or a support enforcement agency, in prosecuting such a proceeding may not permanently preclude the ultimate resolution of a parentage determination.

§ 622. Order Adjudicating Parentage.

(a) An order adjudicating parentage must identify the child in a manner provided by law of this state other than this [act].

(b) Except as otherwise provided in subsection (c), the court may assess filing fees, reasonable attorney's fees, fees for genetic testing, other costs, and necessary travel and other reasonable expenses incurred in a proceeding under this [article]. Attorney's fees awarded under this subsection may be paid directly to the attorney, and the attorney may enforce the order in the attorney's own name.

(c) The court may not assess fees, costs, or expenses in a proceeding under this [article] against a child-support agency of this state or another state, except as provided by law of this state other than this [act].

(d) In a proceeding under this [article], a copy of a bill for genetic testing or prenatal or postnatal health care for the woman who gave birth to the child and the child, provided to the adverse party not later than 10 days before a hearing, is admissible to establish:

(1) the amount of the charge billed; and

(2) that the charge is reasonable and necessary.

(e) On request of a party and for good cause, the court in a proceeding under this [article] may order the name of the child changed. If the court order changing the name varies from the name on the birth certificate of the child, the court shall order the [state agency maintaining birth records] to issue an amended birth certificate.

Comment

Source: UPA (2002) § 636; UPA (1973) §§ 15, 16, 23; UIFSA (1996) § 313.

§ 623. Binding Effect of Determination of Parentage.

(a) Except as otherwise provided in subsection (b):

(1) a signatory to an acknowledgment of parentage or denial of parentage is bound by the acknowledgment and denial as provided in [Article] 3; and

(2) a party to an adjudication of parentage by a court acting under circumstances that satisfy the jurisdiction requirements of [cite to this state's Section 201 of the Uniform Interstate Family Support Act] and any individual who received notice of the proceeding are bound by the adjudication.

(b) A child is not bound by a determination of parentage under this [act] unless:

(1) the determination was based on an unrescinded acknowledgment of parentage and the acknowledgment is consistent with the results of genetic testing;

(2) the determination was based on a finding consistent with the results of genetic testing, and the consistency is declared in the determination or otherwise shown;

(3) the determination of parentage was made under [Article] 7[or 8]; or

(4) the child was a party or was represented by [an attorney, guardian ad litem, or similar person] in the proceeding.

(c) In a proceeding for [divorce, dissolution, annulment, declaration of invalidity, legal separation, or separate maintenance], the court is deemed to have made an adjudication of parentage of a child if the court acts under circumstances that satisfy the jurisdiction requirements of [cite to this state's Section 201 of the Uniform Interstate Family Support Act] and the final order:

(1) expressly identifies the child as a "child of the marriage" or "issue of the marriage" or includes similar words indicating that both spouses are parents of the child; or

(2) provides for support of the child by a spouse unless that spouse's parentage is disclaimed specifically in the order.

(d) Except as otherwise provided in subsection (b) or Section 611, a determination of parentage may be asserted as a defense in a subsequent proceeding seeking to adjudicate parentage of an individual who was not a party to the earlier proceeding.

(e) A party to an adjudication of parentage may challenge the adjudication only under law of this state other than this [act] relating to appeal, vacation of judgment, or other judicial review.

Legislative Note: *A state should include the bracketed reference to Article 8 if the state wishes to recognize in statute surrogacy agreements and includes Article 8 in this act.*

A state should replace the bracketed language in subsection (b)(4) for terms of persons authorized to represent a child in a proceeding under this article with terms for persons performing similar representation under law of the state other than this act.

A state should use its own terms for the proceedings identified in the bracketed language in subsection (c).

Comment

Source: UPA (2002) § 637.

As explained in the comment to UPA (2002) § 637, a considerable amount of litigation involves who is bound by a final order determining parentage. This section codifies rules regarding the effect of such orders. Consistent with UPA (2002), subsection (a) provides that, if the order is issued under standards of personal jurisdiction of UIFSA (2008), the order is binding on all parties to the proceeding.

Subsection (b) follows UPA (2002) with regard to whether a child is bound by the terms of the order determining parentage. UPA (2017), as did UPA (2002), adopts the rule that a child is not bound during minority unless the order is consistent with the results of genetic testing or the child was represented by an attorney.

Subsection (c) follows UPA (2002) on whether a divorce decree constitutes a finding of parentage. Subsection (d) follows UPA (2002) by giving protection to third parties who may claim benefit of an earlier determination of parentage.

As was true of UPA (2002), this section is silent on whether state IV-D agencies are bound by prior determinations of parentage. This issue is left to other law of the state. Similarly, issues of collateral attack on final judgments are to be resolved by recourse to other state law.

[ARTICLE] 7
ASSISTED REPRODUCTION

Comment

The content of Article 7 is substantively similar to the content of Article 7 of UPA (2002). The primary changes to Article 7 are intended to update the article so that it applies equally to same-sex couples..

§ 701. Scope of [Article]. This [article] does not apply to the birth of a child conceived by sexual intercourse[or assisted reproduction under a surrogacy agreement under [Article] 8].

Legislative Note: *A state should include the bracketed phrase concerning a surrogacy agreement if the state wishes to recognize in statute surrogacy agreements and includes Article 8 in this act.*

§ 702. Parental Status of Donor. A donor is not a parent of a child conceived by assisted reproduction.

Comment

Source: UPA (2002) § 702.

§ 703. Parentage of Child of Assisted Reproduction. An individual who consents under Section 704 to assisted reproduction by a woman with the intent to be a parent of a child conceived by the assisted reproduction is a parent of the child.

§ 704. Consent to Assisted Reproduction.

(a) Except as otherwise provided in subsection (b), the consent described in Section 703 must be in a record signed by a woman giving birth to a child conceived by assisted reproduction and an individual who intends to be a parent of the child.

(b) Failure to consent in a record as required by subsection (a), before, on, or after birth of the child, does not preclude the court from finding consent to parentage if:

(1) the woman or the individual proves by clear-and-convincing evidence the existence of an express agreement entered into before conception that the individual and the woman intended they both would be parents of the child; or

(2) the woman and the individual for the first two years of the child's life, including any period of temporary absence, resided together in the same household with the child and both openly held out the child as the individual's child, unless the individual dies or becomes incapacitated before the child attains two years of age or the child dies before the child attains two years of age, in which case the court may find consent under this subsection to parentage if a party proves by clear-and-convincing evidence that the woman and the individual intended to reside together in the same household with the child and both intended the individual would openly hold out the child as the individual's child, but the individual was prevented from carrying out that intent by death or incapacity.

Comment

Source: UPA (2002) § 704; UPC (2010) § 2-120(f).

This section largely follows UPA (2002), in that it provides that an individual is a parent of a child born through assisted reproduction if the individual consents in writing to the assisted reproduction, or, in the absence of consent, if for the first two years of the child's life, the individual resided together in the same household with the child and both openly held out the child as the individual's child.

This section adds two new means by which an

individual can establish parentage of a child born through assisted reproduction. In the absence of written consent to the assisted reproduction, parentage can be established under subsection (b)(1) if the woman or the individual proves that the parties entered into an express agreement prior to conception that they intended that they would both be parents of the child. UPA (2017) continues to provide the most protection to those who have written consent. This protection encourages parties to obtain written consent, which helps avoid disputes and litigation.

Case law and experience make clear, however, that many parties do not consent in writing, even when the statute requires written consent and even when the evidence indicates that the parties intended that they would both be parents to the child. Some courts have relied on equitable or common law doctrines to do justice in such cases. *See, e.g., In re Parentage of M.J.*, 203 Ill. 3d 526, 541, 787 N.E.2d 144, 152 (2003) (holding that even though the assisted reproduction statute did not apply in the absence of written consent, a man who consented in fact to the woman's insemination was a parent under common law

principles and that "to hold otherwise would deprive the children of financial support merely because of deception and a technical oversight."). Some other courts, however, have rigidly applied written consent requirements, often producing results that seem inequitable and harmful to the child.

In light of this experience, UPA (2017) recognizes some non-written forms of consent. New subsection (b)(1) adds a new method of establishing parentage in the absence of written consent, but this new method imposes a high substantive bar: the express agreement must be proven by clear and convincing evidence.

In addition, subsection (b)(2) has been expanded to bring UPA (2017) more in line with the Uniform Probate Code. UPA (2002) provided that the failure to sign a written consent did not preclude a determination of parentage if the individual, during the first two years of the child's life, resided together in the same household with the child and openly held out the child as the individual's own. UPA (2017) also permits a determination of parentage when this two-year period is not fulfilled because of the death or incapacity of the individual or the death of the child.

§ 705. Limitation on Spouse's Dispute of Parentage.

(a) Except as otherwise provided in subsection (b), an individual who, at the time of a child's birth, is the spouse of the woman who gave birth to the child by assisted reproduction may not challenge the individual's parentage of the child unless:

(1) not later than two years after the birth of the child, the individual commences a proceeding to adjudicate the individual's parentage of the child; and

(2) the court finds the individual did not consent to the assisted reproduction, before, on, or after birth of the child, or withdrew consent under Section 707.

(b) A proceeding to adjudicate a spouse's parentage of a child born by assisted reproduction may be commenced at any time if the court determines:

(1) the spouse neither provided a gamete for, nor consented to, the assisted reproduction;

(2) the spouse and the woman who gave birth to the child have not cohabited since the probable time of assisted reproduction; and

(3) the spouse never openly held out the child as the spouse's child.

(c) This section applies to a spouse's dispute of parentage even if the spouse's marriage is declared invalid after assisted reproduction occurs.

Comment

Source: UPA (2002) § 705.

The substance of this section is carried over from UPA (2002). Like UPA (2002) § 705, this section applies even if the parties' marriage is annulled or

declared invalid after assisted reproduction occurs, and the term "spouse" includes parties who were in a marriage that was declared invalid after the assisted reproduction occurred.

§ 706. Effect of Certain Legal Proceedings Regarding Marriage. If a marriage of a woman who gives birth to a child conceived by assisted reproduction is [terminated through divorce or dissolution,

subject to legal separation or separate maintenance, declared invalid, or annulled] before transfer of gametes or embryos to the woman, a former spouse of the woman is not a parent of the child unless the former spouse consented in a record that the former spouse would be a parent of the child if assisted reproduction were to occur after a [divorce, dissolution, annulment, declaration of invalidity, legal separation, or separate maintenance], and the former spouse did not withdraw consent under Section 707.

Legislative Note: A state should use its own terms for the proceedings identified in the bracketed language.

Comment

Source: UPA (2002) § 706(a).

This section is largely carried over from UPA (2002) § 706(a). This section applies only to married couples and provides that the spouse is not a parent if the gamete or embryo transfer resulting in pregnancy occurs after annulment or dissolution unless the individual consented in a record that the individual would be a parent if assisted reproduction were to occur after divorce or annulment. The only substantive change made by UPA (2017) is to clarify that the principle established in UPA (2002) § 706(a) applies equally to divorces and annulments.

Like UPA (2002), § 706 of UPA (2017) provides rules for determining of parentage. Accordingly, in the event of a dissolution of marriage or the withdrawal of consent, this act does not address under what circumstances a transfer or gametes or embryos may or may not occur, or which party has the right to control any gametes or embryos.

§ 707. Withdrawal of Consent.

(a) An individual who consents under Section 704 to assisted reproduction may withdraw consent any time before a transfer that results in a pregnancy, by giving notice in a record of the withdrawal of consent to the woman who agreed to give birth to a child conceived by assisted reproduction and to any clinic or health-care provider facilitating the assisted reproduction. Failure to give notice to the clinic or health-care provider does not affect a determination of parentage under this [act].

(b) An individual who withdraws consent under subsection (a) is not a parent of the child under this [article].

Comment

Source: UPA (2002) § 706(b).

The substance of this provision is carried over from UPA (2002) § 706. UPA (2017), however, divides two concepts that had previously been included in a single section into two separate sections.

The substance of UPA (2002) § 706(b), regarding the rules for the withdrawal of consent by any individual, married or unmarried, is addressed in this section. The content of UPA (2002) § 706(a), regarding the effect of a dissolution or annulment of a marriage, is addressed in UPA (2017) § 706.

§ 708. Parental Status of Deceased Individual.

(a) If an individual who intends to be a parent of a child conceived by assisted reproduction dies during the period between the transfer of a gamete or embryo and the birth of the child, the individual's death does not preclude the establishment of the individual's parentage of the child if the individual otherwise would be a parent of the child under this [act].

(b) If an individual who consented in a record to assisted reproduction by a woman who agreed to give birth to a child dies before a transfer of gametes or embryos, the deceased individual is a parent of a child conceived by the assisted reproduction only if:

(1) either:

(A) the individual consented in a record that if assisted reproduction were to occur after the death of the individual, the individual would be a parent of the child; or

(B) the individual's intent to be a parent of a child conceived by assisted reproduction after the individual's death is established by clear-and-convincing evidence; and

(2) either:

(A) the embryo is in utero not later than [36] months after the individual's death; or

(B) the child is born not later than [45] months after the individual's death.

Comment

Source: UPA (2002) § 707; UPC (2008) § 2-120(f).

The rule stated in subsection (a) was implicit in UPA (2002), but UPA (2017) makes the rule explicit. The substance of subsection (b)(1)(A) is carried over from UPA (2002).

Subsection (b)(1)(B) was not included in UPA (2002), but is based on and consistent with the Uniform Probate Code. UPC § 2-120(f) provides that an individual is "treated as the other parent" if it can be shown, "considering all the facts and circumstances," that the individual consented to the assisted reproduction. Subsection (b)(2) was not included in UPA (2002), but, again, is based on and consistent with the approach of UPC § 2-120(k). *See also* 750 ILCS 46/705.

[[ARTICLE] 8
SURROGACY AGREEMENT

Legislative Note: A state should include Article 8 if the state wishes to recognize in statute surrogacy agreements.

Comment

UPA (2017) updates the surrogacy provisions of UPA (2002) to reflect developments that have occurred over the last 15 years. UPA (2002) included a bracketed Article 8 that authorized surrogacy agreements. States have been particularly reluctant to enact that article. Eleven states adopted versions of UPA (2000) or UPA (2002). However, of these 11 states, only two – Texas and Utah – enacted the surrogacy provisions based on Article 8 of UPA (2002).

The fact that very few states enacted Article 8 of UPA (2002) is likely the result of a confluence of factors. One likely factor is the controversial nature of surrogacy itself. To be clear, however, it is not simply resistance to surrogacy that explains states' reluctance to enact Article 8 of UPA (2002). Indeed, at least five of the 11 states that enacted UPA (2002) enacted statutory provisions permitting surrogacy that are *not* premised on UPA (2002). These states include: Delaware (permitting) (enacted 2013); Illinois (permitting) (enacted 2004); Maine (permitting) (enacted 2015). Thus, there appeared to be a lack of enthusiasm for the substance of the provisions themselves. Moreover, much has changed in this rapidly developing area of law and practice during the last 15 years. More states address surrogacy by statute, and more people are having children through surrogacy. Accordingly, UPA (2017) updates the surrogacy provisions to make them more consistent with current surrogacy practice.

As was true of UPA (2002), Article 8 of UPA (2017) regulates and permits both genetic (often referred to as "traditional") and gestational surrogacy agreements. But UPA (2017) differs in the way that it regulates these two types of surrogacy agreements. UPA (2002) set forth a single set of requirements that applied equally to genetic and gestational surrogacy agreements. While UPA (2017) continues to permit both types of surrogacy, UPA (2017) imposes additional safeguards or requirements on genetic surrogacy agreements. For example, while gestational surrogacy agreements are binding once the successful transfer has occurred, UPA (2017) allows genetic surrogates to withdraw their consent any time up until 72 hours after birth. This differentiation between genetic and gestational surrogacy is intended to reflect both the factual differences between the two types of surrogacy as well as the reality that policy makers view these two forms of surrogacy as being quite different. Of the states that permit surrogacy, most permit *only* gestational surrogacy agreements.

While UPA (2017) adds additional requirements that apply only to genetic surrogacy agreements, it simultaneously liberalizes the rules governing gestational surrogacy agreements. For example, UPA (2017) eliminates the requirement imposed under UPA (2002) that parties to a gestational agreement obtain court approval of the agreement before any medical procedures related to the agreement. The changes to the rules governing gestational surrogacy agreements are intended to bring UPA (2017) more in line with current practice and law.

Sections 801 through 807 establish the rules that apply to both types of surrogacy agreements. Sections 808 through 812 include rules that apply only to gestational surrogacy agreements. Sections 813 through 818 include rules that apply only to genetic surrogacy agreements.

[PART] 1
GENERAL REQUIREMENTS

§ 801. Definitions. In this [article]:

(1) "Genetic surrogate" means a woman who is not an intended parent and who agrees to become pregnant through assisted reproduction using her own gamete, under a genetic surrogacy agreement as provided in this [article].

(2) "Gestational surrogate" means a woman who is not an intended parent and who agrees to become pregnant through assisted reproduction using gametes that are not her own, under a gestational surrogacy agreement as provided in this [article].

(3) "Surrogacy agreement" means an agreement between one or more intended parents and a woman who is not an intended parent in which the woman agrees to become pregnant through assisted reproduction and which provides that each intended parent is a parent of a child conceived under the agreement. Unless otherwise specified, the term refers to both a gestational surrogacy agreement and a genetic surrogacy agreement.

§ 802. Eligibility to Enter Gestational or Genetic Surrogacy Agreement.

(a) To execute an agreement to act as a gestational or genetic surrogate, a woman must:

(1) have attained 21 years of age;

(2) previously have given birth to at least one child;

(3) complete a medical evaluation related to the surrogacy arrangement by a licensed medical doctor;

(4) complete a mental-health consultation by a licensed mental-health professional; and

(5) have independent legal representation of her choice throughout the surrogacy arrangement regarding the terms of the surrogacy agreement and the potential legal consequences of the agreement.

(b) To execute a surrogacy agreement, each intended parent, whether or not genetically related to the child, must:

(1) have attained 21 years of age;

(2) complete a medical evaluation related to the surrogacy arrangement by a licensed medical doctor;

(3) complete a mental-health consultation by a licensed mental health professional; and

(4) have independent legal representation of the intended parent's choice throughout the surrogacy arrangement regarding the terms of the surrogacy agreement and the potential legal consequences of the agreement.

Comment

This section is modeled on the more recently adopted surrogacy provisions, including those enacted in Delaware (enacted 2013); Maine (enacted 2015); Nevada (enacted 2013); New Hampshire (enacted 2014); Illinois (enacted 2004); and the District of Columbia (enacted 2017), among other states. *See, e.g.,* Del. Stat., tit. 13 §§ 8-801 to 8-809; Me. Rev. Stat. tit. 19-a, §§ 1931 to 1938; Nev. Rev. Stat. §§ 126.500 to 126.810; N.H. Rev. Stat. §§ 168-B:1 to 168-B:22; 750 ILCS 47/1 to 47/75; D.C. Code §§ 16-401 to 16-412.

Most of these recently adopted surrogacy provisions include similar requirements regarding age, medical and mental health evaluations, and independent counsel. *See, e.g.,* D.C. Code § 16-405 (age, medical and mental health evaluations); 16-406(3) (requiring affirmation that all parties had independent legal counsel); Me. Rev. Stat. tit. 19-a, § 1931; Nev. Rev. Code § 126.740; N.H. Rev. Code § 128-B:9. Another requirement included in some recently adopted statutes is that the surrogate have "given birth to at least one live child." *See, e.g.,* D.C. Code § 16-405(a)(2). *See also* Me. Rev. Stat. tit. 19-a, § 1931(1)(B). This requirement was not included in UPA (2002), but has been included here.

§ 803. Requirements of Gestational or Genetic Surrogacy Agreement: Process.

A surrogacy agreement must be executed in compliance with the following rules:

(1) At least one party must be a resident of this state or, if no party is a resident of this state, at least one medical evaluation or procedure or mental-health consultation under the agreement must occur in this state.

(2) A surrogate and each intended parent must meet the requirements of Section 802.

(3) Each intended parent, the surrogate, and the surrogate's spouse, if any, must be parties to the agreement.

(4) The agreement must be in a record signed by each party listed in paragraph (3).

(5) The surrogate and each intended parent must acknowledge in a record receipt of a copy of the agreement.

(6) The signature of each party to the agreement must be attested by a notarial officer or witnessed.

(7) The surrogate and the intended parent or parents must have independent legal representation throughout the surrogacy arrangement regarding the terms of the surrogacy agreement and the potential legal consequences of the agreement, and each counsel must be identified in the surrogacy agreement.

(8) The intended parent or parents must pay for independent legal representation for the surrogate.

(9) The agreement must be executed before a medical procedure occurs related to the surrogacy agreement, other than the medical evaluation and mental health consultation required by Section 802.

Comment

This section is modeled on several recently adopted surrogacy schemes, including those enacted in Delaware (enacted 2013); Maine (enacted 2015); Nevada (enacted 2013); New Hampshire (enacted 2014); Illinois (enacted 2004); and the District of Columbia (enacted 2017), among other states. *See, e.g.*, Del. Stat., tit. 13 §§ 8-801 to 8-809; Me. Rev. Stat. tit. 19-a, §§ 1931 to 1938; Nev. Rev. Stat. §§ 126.500 to 126.810; N.H. Rev. Stat. §§ 168-B:1 to 168-B:22; 750 ILCS 47/1 to 47/75; D.C. Code §§ 16-401 to 16-412.

One issue on which these recently adopted statutory schemes diverge is with regard to payment for the surrogate's counsel. As noted above, most recently adopted statutory schemes require the surrogate and the intended parent or parents to be represented by separate, independent counsel. That said, only a minority of states statutorily require the intended parents to pay for the surrogate's counsel. *See* Me. Rev. Stat. tit. 19-a, § 1931(1)(D). Contra cf. Nev. Rev. Stat. § 126.750(2) (requiring separate and independent counsel, but not addressing payment); N.H. Rev. Stat. § 168-B:11(III) (same); D.C. Code § 16-406(b) (same). UPA (2017) requires the intended parents to pay for the surrogate's counsel.

§ 804. Requirements of Gestational or Genetic Surrogacy Agreement: Content.

(a) A surrogacy agreement must comply with the following requirements:

(1) A surrogate agrees to attempt to become pregnant by means of assisted reproduction.

(2) Except as otherwise provided in Sections 811, 814, and 815, the surrogate and the surrogate's spouse or former spouse, if any, have no claim to parentage of a child conceived by assisted reproduction under the agreement.

(3) The surrogate's spouse, if any, must acknowledge and agree to comply with the obligations imposed on the surrogate by the agreement.

(4) Except as otherwise provided in Sections 811, 814, and 815, the intended parent or, if there are two intended parents, each one jointly and severally, immediately on birth will be the exclusive parent or parents of the child, regardless of number of children born or gender or mental or physical condition of each child.

(5) Except as otherwise provided in Sections 811, 814, and 815, the intended parent or, if there are two intended parents, each parent jointly and severally, immediately on birth will assume responsibility for the financial support of the child, regardless of number of children born or gender or mental or physical condition of each child.

(6) The agreement must include information disclosing how each intended parent will cover the surrogacy-related expenses of the surrogate and the medical expenses of the child. If health-care

coverage is used to cover the medical expenses, the disclosure must include a summary of the health-care policy provisions related to coverage for surrogate pregnancy, including any possible liability of the surrogate, third-party-liability liens, other insurance coverage, and any notice requirement that could affect coverage or liability of the surrogate. Unless the agreement expressly provides otherwise, the review and disclosure do not constitute legal advice. If the extent of coverage is uncertain, a statement of that fact is sufficient to comply with this paragraph.

(7) The agreement must permit the surrogate to make all health and welfare decisions regarding herself and her pregnancy. This [act] does not enlarge or diminish the surrogate's right to terminate her pregnancy.

(8) The agreement must include information about each party's right under this [article] to terminate the surrogacy agreement.

(b) A surrogacy agreement may provide for:

(1) payment of consideration and reasonable expenses; and

(2) reimbursement of specific expenses if the agreement is terminated under this [article].

(c) A right created under a surrogacy agreement is not assignable and there is no third-party beneficiary of the agreement other than the child.

Comment

This section is modeled on several recently adopted surrogacy provisions. *See, e.g.,* D.C. Code § 16-406; Me. Rev. Stat. tit. 19-a, § 1932(J); N.H. Rev. Stat. § 168-B:11.

Subsection (a)(6) is based on Cal. Fam. Code § 7692(a)(4).

The first sentence of subsection (a)(7) is modeled on UPA (2002) and the recently adopted provisions in Maine and D.C. *See, e.g.,* UPA (2002) § 801(f) ("A gestational agreement may not limit the right of the gestational mother to make decisions to safeguard her health or that of the embryos or fetus."); Me. Rev. Stat. tit. 19-a, § 1932(5) ("A gestational carrier agreement may not limit the right of the gestational carrier to make decisions to safeguard her health."); D.C. Code § 16-406(c) ("A surrogacy agreement may not limit the right of the surrogate to make decisions to safeguard the surrogate's health or that of the embryo or fetus."). The second sentence of subsection

(a)(7) reaffirms that the surrogate has a constitutionally protected right to decide whether to terminate the pregnancy within the limits of the law. *Cf.* D.C. Code § 16-406(4)(C) ("Agree that at all times during the pregnancy and until delivery, regardless of whether the court has issued an order of parentage, the surrogate shall maintain control and decision-making authority over the surrogate's body.").

Subsection (b) carries over the position of UPA (2002) by permitting compensated surrogacy agreements. Most states that permit surrogacy agreements by statute likewise permit compensated as well as uncompensated agreements.

Unless terminated as provided in this article, a gestational or genetic surrogacy agreement that complies with the requirements of Sections 802, 803, and 804 is enforceable; the agreement may contain additional requirements so long as they are not inconsistent with Sections 802, 803, and 804.

§ 805. Surrogacy Agreement: Effect of Subsequent Change of Marital Status.

(a) Unless a surrogacy agreement expressly provides otherwise:

(1) the marriage of a surrogate after the agreement is signed by all parties does not affect the validity of the agreement, her spouse's consent to the agreement is not required, and her spouse is not a presumed parent of a child conceived by assisted reproduction under the agreement; and

(2) the [divorce, dissolution, annulment, declaration of invalidity, legal separation, or separate maintenance] of the surrogate after the agreement is signed by all parties does not affect the validity of the agreement.

(b) Unless a surrogacy agreement expressly provides otherwise:

(1) the marriage of an intended parent after the agreement is signed by all parties does not affect the validity of a surrogacy agreement, the consent of the spouse of the intended parent is not required,

and the spouse of the intended parent is not, based on the agreement, a parent of a child conceived by assisted reproduction under the agreement; and

(2) the [divorce, dissolution, annulment, declaration of invalidity, legal separation, or separate maintenance] of an intended parent after the agreement is signed by all parties does not affect the validity of the agreement and, except as otherwise provided in Section 814, the intended parents are the parents of the child.

Legislative Note: A state should use its own terms for the proceedings identified in the bracketed language in subsections (a)(2) and (b)(2).

Comment

Source: UPA (2002) § 808; D.C. Code § 16-410.

In some states, the statutes address the effect of a subsequent marriage of the surrogate only. *See, e.g.,* Me. Rev. Stat. tit. 19-a, § 1937; Nev. Rev. Stat. § 126.770; N.H. Rev. Stat. § 168-B:14. *See also* UPA

(2002) § 808. To avoid ambiguity and unnecessary litigation, UPA (2017) expressly addresses the effect of any subsequent marriage or divorce by any party to the surrogacy agreement.

[**§ 806. Inspection of Documents.** Unless the court orders otherwise, a petition and any other document related to a surrogacy agreement filed with the court under this [part] are not open to inspection by any individual other than the parties to the proceeding, a child conceived by assisted reproduction under the agreement, their attorneys, and [the relevant state agency]. A court may not authorize an individual to inspect a document related to the agreement, unless required by exigent circumstances. The individual seeking to inspect the document may be required to pay the expense of preparing a copy of the document to be inspected.]

Legislative Note: A state should review the state's open records law to determine if this section needs to be included or amended.

Comment

Source: UPA (2002) § 804; Cal. Fam. Code § 7962(h); Nev. Rev. Stat. § 126.730.

In some states, family law matters are not open for inspection. In such a state, this provision may be

unnecessary. If, however, family law matters generally are open for inspection, a state may consider enacting Section 806.

§ 807. Exclusive, Continuing Jurisdiction. During the period after the execution of a surrogacy agreement until 90 days after the birth of a child conceived by assisted reproduction under the agreement, a court of this state conducting a proceeding under this [act] has exclusive, continuing jurisdiction over all matters arising out of the agreement. This section does not give the court jurisdiction over a child-custody or child-support proceeding if jurisdiction is not otherwise authorized by law of this state other than this [act].

Comment

Source: UPA (2002) § 805; Me. Rev. Stat. tit. 19-a, § 1935.

[PART] 2
SPECIAL RULES FOR GESTATIONAL SURROGACY AGREEMENT

Comment

As noted above, UPA (2002) applied the same substantive rules to gestational and genetic surrogacy agreements. Among other things, UPA (2002) required all agreements to be validated by a court prior to any medical treatments. UPA (2002) also required a home study of the intended parents unless waived by the court. These rules were not widely adopted by states, and they are not consistent with contemporary practice. Part 2, providing special rules for gestational surrogacy agreements, modernizes the rules regarding gestational surrogacy to make them more consistent with contemporary surrogacy practice and the laws in the states that permit surrogacy agreements.

§ 808. Termination of Gestational Surrogacy Agreement.

(a) A party to a gestational surrogacy agreement may terminate the agreement, at any time before an embryo transfer, by giving notice of termination in a record to all other parties. If an embryo transfer does not result in a pregnancy, a party may terminate the agreement at any time before a subsequent embryo transfer.

(b) Unless a gestational surrogacy agreement provides otherwise, on termination of the agreement under subsection (a), the parties are released from the agreement, except that each intended parent remains responsible for expenses that are reimbursable under the agreement and incurred by the gestational surrogate through the date of termination.

(c) Except in a case involving fraud, neither a gestational surrogate nor the surrogate's spouse or former spouse, if any, is liable to the intended parent or parents for a penalty or liquidated damages, for terminating a gestational surrogacy agreement under this section.

Comment

Source: UPA (2002) § 808; Me. Rev. Stat. tit. 19-a, § 1936.

Subsection (a) is largely carried over from UPA (2002). Subsection (a) permits a party to terminate the agreement before a successful transfer. This allows the parties some time to change their minds, but within a limited window that does not unduly prejudice the interests of other parties to the agreement.

Subsection (b) is new. The substance of subsection (b) is consistent with the implicit but unstated rule of UPA (2002). UPA (2017) states expressly that if a party properly terminates the agreement under this provision, that termination releases the parties from the obligations recited under the agreement—most importantly rights and duties with regard to the child—except with regard to expenses that are reimbursable under the agreement.

Subsection (c) clarifies that, except in cases involving fraud, the gestational carrier and her spouse, if any, are not liable for any penalties other than any expenses that are reimbursement under the agreement.

§ 809. Parentage under Gestational Surrogacy Agreement.

(a) Except as otherwise provided in subsection (c) or Section 810(b) or 812, on birth of a child conceived by assisted reproduction under a gestational surrogacy agreement, each intended parent is, by operation of law, a parent of the child.

(b) Except as otherwise provided in subsection (c) or Section 812, neither a gestational surrogate nor the surrogate's spouse or former spouse, if any, is a parent of the child.

(c) If a child is alleged to be a genetic child of the woman who agreed to be a gestational surrogate, the court shall order genetic testing of the child. If the child is a genetic child of the woman who agreed to be a gestational surrogate, parentage must be determined based on [Articles] 1 through 6.

(d) Except as otherwise provided in subsection (c) or Section 810(b) or 812, if, due to a clinical or laboratory error, a child conceived by assisted reproduction under a gestational surrogacy agreement is not genetically related to an intended parent or a donor who donated to the intended parent or parents, each intended parent, and not the gestational surrogate and the surrogate's spouse or former spouse, if any, is a parent of the child, subject to any other claim of parentage.

Comment

Source: Me. Rev. Stat. tit. 19-a, § 1933; Me. Rev. Stat. tit. 19-a, § 1938(4).

Subsections (a) and (b) expressly clarify the legal parentage of a child born through an enforceable gestational surrogacy agreement.

Subsection (c) clarifies how parentage should be determined if the child was not conceived through assisted reproduction. UPA (2002) § 807 acknowledged that possibility and provided for the ordering of genetic testing, but did not expressly state how parentage should be determined in such cases.

UPA (2017) includes a clear rule for determining parentage.

UPA (2002) did not expressly address cases involving clinic error. While such cases are rare, they have occurred. *See, e.g., Perry-Rogers v. Fasano*, 715 N.Y.S.2d 19 (N.Y. App. Div. 2000). UPA (2017) addresses such cases expressly in subsection (d). The substance of subsection (d) is based on the newly adopted provision in Maine.

§ 810. Gestational Surrogacy Agreement: Parentage of Deceased Intended Parent.

(a) Section 809 applies to an intended parent even if the intended parent died during the period between the transfer of a gamete or embryo and the birth of the child.

(b) Except as otherwise provided in Section 812, an intended parent is not a parent of a child conceived by assisted reproduction under a gestational surrogacy agreement if the intended parent dies before the transfer of a gamete or embryo unless:

(1) the agreement provides otherwise; and

(2) the transfer of a gamete or embryo occurs not later than [36] months after the death of the intended parent or birth of the child occurs not later than [45] months after the death of the intended parent.

Comment

Source: UPC (2010) § 2-121; D.C. Code § 16-409.

UPA (2002) did not specifically address the issue of parentage if an intended parent died during the arrangement. To avoid uncertainty and unnecessary litigation, UPA (2017) addresses this issue specifically.

The principle stated in subsection (a) is implicit with other provisions in Article 8. Subsection (b) is based on the relevant UPC provision, and is consistent with the analogous provision in Article 7 of the act.

§ 811. Gestational Surrogacy Agreement: Order of Parentage.

(a) Except as otherwise provided in Sections 809(c) or 812, before, on, or after the birth of a child conceived by assisted reproduction under a gestational surrogacy agreement, a party to the agreement may commence a proceeding in the [appropriate court] for an order or judgment:

(1) declaring that each intended parent is a parent of the child and ordering that parental rights and duties vest immediately on the birth of the child exclusively in each intended parent;

(2) declaring that the gestational surrogate and the surrogate's spouse or former spouse, if any, are not the parents of the child;

(3) designating the content of the birth record in accordance with [cite applicable law of this state other than this [act]] and directing the [state agency maintaining birth records] to designate each intended parent as a parent of the child;

(4) to protect the privacy of the child and the parties, declaring that the court record is not open to inspection[except as authorized under Section 806];

(5) if necessary, that the child be surrendered to the intended parent or parents; and

(6) for other relief the court determines necessary and proper.

(b) The court may issue an order or judgment under subsection (a) before the birth of the child. The court shall stay enforcement of the order or judgment until the birth of the child.

(c) Neither this state nor the [state agency maintaining birth records] is a necessary party to a proceeding under subsection (a).

Legislative Note: A state should include the bracketed language in subsection (a)(4) if the state enacts Section 806.

Comment
Source: D.C. Code § 16-408(d); Me. Rev. Stat. tit. 19-a, § 1934; N.H. Rev. Stat. § 168-B:12.

§ 812. Effect of Gestational Surrogacy Agreement.

(a) A gestational surrogacy agreement that complies with Sections 802, 803, and 804 is enforceable.

(b) If a child was conceived by assisted reproduction under a gestational surrogacy agreement that does not comply with Sections 802, 803, and 804, the court shall determine the rights and duties of the parties to the agreement consistent with the intent of the parties at the time of execution of the agreement. Each party to the agreement and any individual who at the time of the execution of the agreement was a spouse of a party to the agreement has standing to maintain a proceeding to adjudicate an issue related to the enforcement of the agreement.

(c) Except as expressly provided in a gestational surrogacy agreement or subsection (d) or (e), if the agreement is breached by the gestational surrogate or one or more intended parents, the non-breaching party is entitled to the remedies available at law or in equity.

(d) Specific performance is not a remedy available for breach by a gestational surrogate of a provision in the agreement that the gestational surrogate be impregnated, terminate or not terminate a pregnancy, or submit to medical procedures.

(e) Except as otherwise provided in subsection (d), if an intended parent is determined to be a parent of the child, specific performance is a remedy available for:

(1) breach of the agreement by a gestational surrogate which prevents the intended parent from exercising immediately on birth of the child the full rights of parentage; or

(2) breach by the intended parent which prevents the intended parent's acceptance, immediately on birth of the child conceived by assisted reproduction under the agreement, of the duties of parentage.

Comment
Source: Me. Rev. Stat. tit. 19-a, § 1938(3), (5); Nev. Rev. Stat. § 126.790(1), (2); N.H. Rev. Stat. § 168-B:18(I), (II).

Subsection (a) expressly declares that a gestational surrogacy agreement that complies with the requirements of this Article is enforceable.

Subsection (b), setting forth the rules for determining parentage in the event of a noncompliant agreement, is based on Me. Rev. Stat. tit. 19-a, § 1938(2); Nev. Rev. Stat. § 126.780(2). In such cases, a court must determine parentage by looking to the intent of the parties at the time of execution.

UPA (2002) did not address the rules that apply in the event of a breach of a surrogacy agreement. New subsection (c) follows the approach taken by several of the recently enacted comprehensive surrogacy statutes, providing that the parties are entitled to remedies available at law or in equity. *See, e.g.,* Me. Rev. Stat. tit. 19-a, § 1938(3); Nev. Rev. Stat. § 126.790(1), (2) (providing that, in the event of a breach, the intended parents or the gestational surrogate, as appropriate, are entitled to "any remedy available at law or equity."); N.H. Rev. Stat. § 168-

B:18(I), (II) (providing that, in the event of a breach, the intended parents or the gestational surrogate, as appropriate, are entitled to "all remedies available at law or equity").

Subsection (d) clarifies that certain forms of specific performance are precluded, including a court order requiring a surrogate be impregnated, terminate or not terminate a pregnancy, or submit to medical procedures. Such an order may violate the constitutional rights of the surrogate. *See also* Me.

Rev. Stat. tit 19-a, § 1938(5) (addressing impregnation and termination, but not submission to medical procedures); Nev. Rev. Stat. § 126.780 ("There must be no specific performance remedy available for breach of the gestational agreement by the gestational carrier that would require the gestational carrier to be impregnated.").

Subsection (e) provides some forms of specific performance that can be ordered.

[PART] 3
SPECIAL RULES FOR GENETIC SURROGACY AGREEMENT

Comment

UPA (2002) imposed the same rules on gestational and genetic surrogacy agreements. UPA (2017) departs from this approach. While there are some common requirements, UPA (2017) imposes additional requirements or safeguards on genetic surrogacy agreements. Among other things, UPA (2017) allows a genetic surrogate to withdraw her consent up until 72 hours after birth.

Currently, only a very small minority of states expressly permit genetic surrogacy through a comprehensive statutory scheme. These states include Florida, Maine (for close relatives only), Virginia, and the District of Columbia. The statutes in these states distinguish between genetic and gestational arrangements and several of these states permit genetic surrogates to withdraw consent after pregnancy has occurred. *See, e.g.,* Fla. Stat. Ann. § 63.213 (48 hours after birth); D.C. Code § 16-411(4) (48 hours after birth). *Cf.* Vir. Code Ann. § 20-161(B) (providing that in cases where the "surrogate ... is also a genetic parent" the surrogate may "terminate the agreement ... [w]ithin 180 days after the last performance of any assisted conception").

§ 813. Requirements to Validate Genetic Surrogacy Agreement.

(a) Except as otherwise provided in Section 816, to be enforceable, a genetic surrogacy agreement must be validated by the [designate court]. A proceeding to validate the agreement must be commenced before assisted reproduction related to the surrogacy agreement.

(b) The court shall issue an order validating a genetic surrogacy agreement if the court finds that:

(1) Sections 802, 803, and 804 are satisfied; and

(2) all parties entered into the agreement voluntarily and understand its terms.

(c) An individual who terminates under Section 814 a genetic surrogacy agreement shall file notice of the termination with the court. On receipt of the notice, the court shall vacate any order issued under subsection (b). An individual who does not notify the court of the termination of the agreement is subject to sanctions.

Comment

Source: UPA (2002) § 803, § 806(c).

UPA (2002) required pre-pregnancy validation for all agreements. This requirement is now imposed only on genetic surrogacy agreements. Section 813 makes changes to the requirements of UPA (2002). First, Section 813 eliminates the prior requirement of a home study of the intended parents unless waived by a court. Given that it was waivable by the court, in practice it often was not required of the parties. The inclusion in the provision, however, created uncertainty for the parties. Second, UPA (2002) provided that a court "may" issue an order validating the agreement upon a finding that the requirements were fulfilled. Thus, even if the parties complied with all of the statutory requirements, their right to obtain an order validating their agreement was within the discretion of the court. Again, this added uncertainty to the process. Accordingly, UPA (2017) requires the court to issue the order validating the agreement if the court finds that the requirements have been fulfilled.

§ 814. Termination of Genetic Surrogacy Agreement.

(a) A party to a genetic surrogacy agreement may terminate the agreement as follows:

(1) An intended parent who is a party to the agreement may terminate the agreement at any time before a gamete or embryo transfer by giving notice of termination in a record to all other parties. If a gamete or embryo transfer does not result in a pregnancy, a party may terminate the agreement at any time before a subsequent gamete or embryo transfer. The notice of termination must be attested by a notarial officer or witnessed.

(2) A genetic surrogate who is a party to the agreement may withdraw consent to the agreement any time before 72 hours after the birth of a child conceived by assisted reproduction under the agreement. To withdraw consent, the genetic surrogate must execute a notice of termination in a record stating the surrogate's intent to terminate the agreement. The notice of termination must be attested by a notarial officer or witnessed and be delivered to each intended parent any time before 72 hours after the birth of the child.

(b) On termination of the genetic surrogacy agreement under subsection (a), the parties are released from all obligations under the agreement except that each intended parent remains responsible for all expenses incurred by the surrogate through the date of termination which are reimbursable under the agreement. Unless the agreement provides otherwise, the surrogate is not entitled to any non-expense related compensation paid for serving as a surrogate.

(c) Except in a case involving fraud, neither a genetic surrogate nor the surrogate's spouse or former spouse, if any, is liable to the intended parent or parents for a penalty or liquidated damages, for terminating a genetic surrogacy agreement under this section.

Comment

Source: Fla. Stat. Ann. § 63.213 (providing that a genetic surrogacy agreement must permit "a right of rescission by the volunteer mother any time within 48 hours after the birth of the child, if the volunteer mother is genetically related to the child"); D.C. Code § 16-411(4) (providing that a genetic surrogate may withdraw consent "within 48 hours after the birth of the child").

UPA (2002) did not permit a genetic surrogate to withdraw her consent after validation of the agreement. No state, however, enacted a version of UPA (2002) that authorized genetic surrogacy agreements. Currently, only a very small minority of states expressly permit genetic surrogacy through a comprehensive statutory scheme. These states include Florida, Maine (for close relatives only), Virginia, and the District of Columbia. The statutes in several of these states similarly provide that the genetic surrogate can withdraw her consent up until some period shortly after the birth of the child. *See, e.g.,* Fla. Stat. Ann. § 63.213 (48 hours after birth); D.C. Code § 16-411(4) (48 hours after birth). *Cf.* Vir. Code Ann. § 20-161(B) (providing that in cases where the "surrogate … is also a genetic parent" the surrogate may "terminate the agreement … [w]ithin 180 days after the last performance of any assisted conception").

§ 815. Parentage under Validated Genetic Surrogacy Agreement.

(a) Unless a genetic surrogate exercises the right under Section 814 to terminate a genetic surrogacy agreement, each intended parent is a parent of a child conceived by assisted reproduction under an agreement validated under Section 813.

(b) Unless a genetic surrogate exercises the right under Section 814 to terminate the genetic surrogacy agreement, on proof of a court order issued under Section 813 validating the agreement, the court shall make an order:

(1) declaring that each intended parent is a parent of a child conceived by assisted reproduction under the agreement and ordering that parental rights and duties vest exclusively in each intended parent;

(2) declaring that the gestational surrogate and the surrogate's spouse or former spouse, if any, are not parents of the child;

(3) designating the contents of the birth certificate in accordance with [cite to applicable law of the state other than this [act]] and directing the [state agency maintaining birth records] to designate each intended parent as a parent of the child;

(4) to protect the privacy of the child and the parties, declaring that the court record is not open to inspection[except as authorized under Section 806];

(5) if necessary, that the child be surrendered to the intended parent or parents; and

(6) for other relief the court determines necessary and proper.

(c) If a genetic surrogate terminates under Section 814(a)(2) a genetic surrogacy agreement, parentage of the child conceived by assisted reproduction under the agreement must be determined under [Articles] 1 through 6.

(d) If a child born to a genetic surrogate is alleged not to have been conceived by assisted reproduction, the court shall order genetic testing to determine the genetic parentage of the child. If the child was not conceived by assisted reproduction, parentage must be determined under [Articles] 1 through 6. Unless the genetic surrogacy agreement provides otherwise, if the child was not conceived by assisted reproduction the surrogate is not entitled to any non-expense related compensation paid for serving as a surrogate.

(e) Unless a genetic surrogate exercises the right under Section 814 to terminate the genetic surrogacy agreement, if an intended parent fails to file notice required under Section 814(a), the genetic surrogate or [the appropriate state agency] may file with the court, not later than 60 days after the birth of a child conceived by assisted reproduction under the agreement, notice that the child has been born to the genetic surrogate. Unless the genetic surrogate has properly exercised the right under Section 814 to withdraw consent to the agreement, on proof of a court order issued under Section 813 validating the agreement, the court shall order that each intended parent is a parent of the child.

Legislative Note: *A state should include the bracketed language in subsection (b)(4) if the state enacts Section 806.*

Comment

Source: UPA (2002) § 807.

The substance of this section is largely carried over from UPA (2002). The content of this section does reflect, however, that UPA (2017) permits a genetic surrogate to withdraw consent any time up until 72 hours after the child's birth. Accordingly, new subsection (c) sets forth how parentage should be determined in the event the genetic surrogate withdraws consent within that time period.

§ 816. Effect of Nonvalidated Genetic Surrogacy Agreement.

(a) A genetic surrogacy agreement, whether or not in a record, that is not validated under Section 813 is enforceable only to the extent provided in this section and Section 818.

(b) If all parties agree, a court may validate a genetic surrogacy agreement after assisted reproduction has occurred but before the birth of a child conceived by assisted reproduction under the agreement.

(c) If a child conceived by assisted reproduction under a genetic surrogacy agreement that is not validated under Section 813 is born and the genetic surrogate, consistent with Section 814(a)(2), withdraws her consent to the agreement before 72 hours after the birth of the child, the court shall adjudicate the parentage of the child under [Articles] 1 through 6.

(d) If a child conceived by assisted reproduction under a genetic surrogacy agreement that is not validated under Section 813 is born and a genetic surrogate does not withdraw her consent to the agreement, consistent with Section 814(a)(2), before 72 hours after the birth of the child, the genetic surrogate is not automatically a parent and the court shall adjudicate parentage of the child based on the best interest of the child, taking into account the factors in Section 613(a) and the intent of the parties at the time of the execution of the agreement.

(e) The parties to a genetic surrogacy agreement have standing to maintain a proceeding to adjudicate parentage under this section.

Comment

This section sets forth the rules for determining parentage of children born through genetic surrogacy where the genetic surrogacy agreement was not properly validated.

Under subsection (b), even if the parties did not validate the agreement prior to pregnancy as required by Section 813, a court is authorized to validate the agreement thereafter if all parties are still in agreement.

Subsections (c) and (d) set forth the rules for determining parentage if the agreement is never validated. Subsection (c) confirms that a genetic surrogate retains the right to withdraw her consent up until 72 hours after the birth of the child, even if the agreement is not validated. If the genetic surrogate withdraws her consent within this time period, parentage is determined based on Articles 1 through 6 of the act. In cases involving an unvalidated genetic surrogacy agreement where the genetic surrogate does not withdraw her consent within that period, subsection (d) provides that the court must determine parentage based on the best interest of the child. In such cases, the genetic surrogate may or may not be determined to be the child's parent.

§ 817. Genetic Surrogacy Agreement: Parentage of Deceased Intended Parent.

(a) Except as otherwise provided in Section 815 or 816, on birth of a child conceived by assisted reproduction under a genetic surrogacy agreement, each intended parent is, by operation of law, a parent of the child, notwithstanding the death of an intended parent during the period between the transfer of a gamete or embryo and the birth of the child.

(b) Except as otherwise provided in Section 815 or 816, an intended parent is not a parent of a child conceived by assisted reproduction under a genetic surrogacy agreement if the intended parent dies before the transfer of a gamete or embryo unless:

(1) the agreement provides otherwise; and

(2) the transfer of the gamete or embryo occurs not later than [36] months after the death of the intended parent, or birth of the child occurs not later than [45] months after the death of the intended parent.

Comment

Source: UPC (2010) § 2-121; D.C. Code § 16-409.

UPA (2002) did not specifically address parentage in the event of the death of an intended parent. To avoid uncertainty and unnecessary litigation, UPA (2017) expressly addresses this scenario. The principle stated in subsection (a) is implicit in other provisions in Article 8, but UPA (2017) states the rule expressly.

Subsection (b) is based on the relevant UPC provision, and is consistent with the analogous provision in Article 7.

§ 818. Breach of Genetic Surrogacy Agreement.

(a) Subject to Section 814(b), if a genetic surrogacy agreement is breached by a genetic surrogate or one or more intended parents, the non-breaching party is entitled to the remedies available at law or in equity.

(b) Specific performance is not a remedy available for breach by a genetic surrogate of a requirement of a validated or non-validated genetic surrogacy agreement that the surrogate be impregnated, terminate or not terminate a pregnancy, or submit to medical procedures.

(c) Except as otherwise provided in subsection (b), specific performance is a remedy available for:

(1) breach of a validated genetic surrogacy agreement by a genetic surrogate of a requirement which prevents an intended parent from exercising the full rights of parentage 72 hours after the birth of the child; or

(2) breach by an intended parent which prevents the intended parent's acceptance of duties of parentage 72 hours after the birth of the child.]

Comment

Source: Me. Rev. Stat. tit. 19-a, § 1938(3), (5); Nev. Rev. Stat. § 126.790(1), (2); N.H. Rev. Stat. § 168-B:18(I), (II).

UPA (2002) did not address the applicable rules in the event of a breach of the agreement. New subsection (a) follows the approach taken by several of the recently enacted comprehensive surrogacy statutes, and provides that the parties are entitled to remedies available at law or in equity. *See, e.g.*, Me. Rev. Stat. tit. 19-a, § 1938(3); Nev. Rev. Stat. § 126.790(1), (2) (providing that, in the event of a breach, the intended parents or the gestational surrogate, as appropriate, are entitled to "any remedy available at law or equity."); N.H. Rev. Stat. § 168-B:18(I), (II) (providing that, in the event of a breach, the intended parents or the gestational surrogate, as appropriate, are entitled to "all remedies available at law or equity").

New subsection (b) expressly states that a court cannot order that a surrogate be impregnated, terminate or not terminate a pregnancy, or submit to medical procedures. Such an order may violate the constitutional rights of the surrogate. *See also* Me. Rev. Stat. tit 19-a, § 1938(5) (addressing impregnation and termination, but not submission to medical procedures); Nev. Rev. Stat. § 126.780 ("There must be no specific performance remedy available for breach of the gestational agreement by the gestational carrier that would require the gestational carrier to be impregnated.").

[ARTICLE] 9
INFORMATION ABOUT DONOR

Comment

Article 9 is a new addition to the UPA. The content of this article was not included in UPA (2002). The content of new Article 9 is premised on a Washington State provision. Wash. Rev. Code § 26.26.750.

§ 901. Definitions. In this [article]:

(1) "Identifying information" means:

(A) the full name of a donor;

(B) the date of birth of the donor; and

(C) the permanent and, if different, current address of the donor at the time of the donation.

(2) "Medical history" means information regarding any:

(A) present illness of a donor;

(B) past illness of the donor; and

(C) social, genetic, and family history pertaining to the health of the donor.

§ 902. Applicability. This [article] applies only to gametes collected on or after [the effective date of this [act]].

§ 903. Collection of Information. A gamete bank or fertility clinic licensed in this state shall collect from a donor the donor's identifying information and medical history at the time of the donation. If the gamete bank or fertility clinic sends the gametes of a donor to another gamete bank or fertility clinic, the sending gamete bank or fertility clinic shall forward any identifying information and medical history of the donor, including the donor's signed declaration under Section 904 regarding identity disclosure, to the receiving gamete bank or fertility clinic. A receiving gamete bank or fertility clinic licensed in this state shall collect and retain the information about the donor and each sending gamete bank or fertility clinic.

§ 904. Declaration Regarding Identity Disclosure.

(a) A gamete bank or fertility clinic licensed in this state which collects gametes from a donor shall:

(1) provide the donor with information in a record about the donor's choice regarding identity disclosure; and

(2) obtain a declaration from the donor regarding identity disclosure.

(b) A gamete bank or fertility clinic licensed in this state shall give a donor the choice to sign a declaration, attested by a notarial officer or witnessed, that either:

(1) states that the donor agrees to disclose the donor's identity to a child conceived by assisted reproduction with the donor's gametes on request once the child attains 18 years of age; or

(2) states that the donor does not agree presently to disclose the donor's identity to the child.

(c) A gamete bank or fertility clinic licensed in this state shall permit a donor who has signed a declaration under subsection (b)(2) to withdraw the declaration at any time by signing a declaration under subsection (b)(1).

Comment

Article 9 permits a donor to withdraw a declaration of non-disclosure and replace it with a declaration of identity disclosure. The Article does not permit, however, a donor to withdraw a declaration of identity disclosure. UPA (2017) makes this distinction because the recipients of identity disclosure gametes often chose those gametes at least in part because the donor had agreed to identity disclosure. While some donors may change their minds, the equities weigh in favor of holding the donor to his or her original position permitting identity disclosure.

§ 905. Disclosure of Identifying Information and Medical History.

(a) On request of a child conceived by assisted reproduction who attains 18 years of age, a gamete bank or fertility clinic licensed in this state which collected, stored, or released for use the gametes used in the assisted reproduction shall make a good-faith effort to provide the child with identifying information of the donor who provided the gametes, unless the donor signed and did not withdraw a declaration under Section 904(b)(2). If the donor signed and did not withdraw the declaration, the gamete bank or fertility clinic shall make a good-faith effort to notify the donor, who may elect under Section 904(c) to withdraw the donor's declaration.

(b) Regardless whether a donor signed a declaration under Section 904(b)(2), on request by a child conceived by assisted reproduction who attains 18 years of age, or, if the child is a minor, by a parent or guardian of the child, a gamete bank or fertility clinic licensed in this state shall make a good-faith effort to provide the child or, if the child is a minor, the parent or guardian of the child, access to nonidentifying medical history of the donor.

§ 906. Recordkeeping.
A gamete bank or fertility clinic licensed in this state which collects, stores, or releases gametes for use in assisted reproduction shall collect and maintain identifying information and medical history about each gamete donor. The gamete bank or fertility clinic shall collect and maintain records of gamete screening and testing and comply with reporting requirements, in accordance with federal law and applicable law of this state other than this [act].

[ARTICLE] 10
MISCELLANEOUS PROVISIONS

§ 1001. Uniformity of Application and Construction. In applying and construing this uniform act, consideration must be given to the need to promote uniformity of the law with respect to its subject matter among states that enact it.

§ 1002. Relation to Electronic Signatures in Global and National Commerce Act. This [act] modifies, limits, or supersedes the Electronic Signatures in Global and National Commerce Act, 15 U.S.C. Section 7001 et seq., but does not modify limit, or supersede Section 101(c) of that act, 15 U.S.C. Section 7001(c), or authorize electronic delivery of any of the notices described in Section 103(b) of that act, 15 U.S.C. Section 7003(b).

§ 1003. Transitional Provision. This [act] applies to a pending proceeding to adjudicate parentage commenced before [the effective date of this [act]] for an issue on which a judgment has not been entered.

[§ 1004. Severability. If any provision of this [act] or its application to any person or circumstance is held invalid, the invalidity does not affect other provisions or applications of this [act] which can be given effect without the invalid provision or application, and to this end the provisions of this [act] are severable.]

Legislative Note: Include this section only if this state lacks a general severability statute or a decision by the highest court of this state stating a general rule of severability.

§ 1005. Repeals; Conforming Amendments. The following are repealed:
    (1) [Uniform Act on Paternity (1960)];
    (2) [Uniform Parentage Act (1973)];
    (3) [Uniform Putative and Unknown Fathers Act (1988)];
    (4) [Uniform Status of Children of Assisted Conception Act (1988)];
    (5) [Uniform Parentage Act (2002)]; and
    (6) [other inconsistent statutes].

§ 1006. Effective Date. This [act] takes effect ....

REVISED UNIFORM FIDUCIARY ACCESS TO DIGITAL ASSETS ACT
(2015)

Table of Sections

Prefatory Note

The purpose of this act is twofold. First, it gives fiduciaries the legal authority to manage digital assets and electronic communications in the same way they manage tangible assets and financial accounts, to the extent possible. Second, it gives custodians of digital assets and electronic communications legal authority to deal with the fiduciaries of their users, while respecting the user's reasonable expectation of privacy for personal communications. The general goal of the act is to facilitate fiduciary access and custodian disclosure while respecting the privacy and intent of the account holder. It adheres to the traditional approach of trusts and estates law, which respects the intent of the account holder and promotes the fiduciary's ability to administer the account holder's property in accord with legally-binding fiduciary duties. The act removes barriers to a fiduciary's access to electronic records and property and leaves unaffected other law, such as fiduciary, probate, trust, banking, investment securities, agency, and privacy law. Existing law prohibits any fiduciary from violating fiduciary responsibilities by divulging or publicizing any information the fiduciary obtains while carrying out his or her fiduciary duties.

Revised UFADAA addresses four different types of fiduciaries: personal representatives of decedents' estates, conservators for protected persons, agents acting pursuant to a power of attorney, and trustees. It distinguishes the authority of fiduciaries, which exercise authority subject to this act only on behalf of the account holder, from any other efforts to access the digital assets. Family members or friends may seek such access, but, unless they are fiduciaries, their efforts are subject to other laws and are not covered by this act.

Digital assets are electronic records in which individuals have a right or interest. As the number of digital assets held by the average person increases, questions surrounding the disposition of these assets upon the individual's death or incapacity are

753

becoming more common. These assets, ranging from online gaming items to photos, to digital music, to client lists, can have real economic or sentimental value. Yet few laws exist on the rights of fiduciaries over digital assets. Holders of digital assets may not consider the fate of their online presences once they are no longer able to manage their assets, and may not expressly provide for the disposition of their digital assets or electronic communications in the event of their death or incapacity. Even when they do, their instructions may come into conflict with custodians' terms-of-service agreements. Some Internet service providers have explicit policies on what will happen when an individual dies, while others do not, and even where these policies are included in the terms of service agreement, consumers may not be fully aware of the implications of these provisions in the event of death or incapacity or how courts might resolve a conflict between such policies and a will, trust instrument, or power of attorney.

The situation regarding fiduciaries' access to digital assets is less than clear, and is subject to federal and state privacy and computer "hacking" laws as well as state probate law. A minority of states has enacted legislation on fiduciary access to digital assets, and numerous other states have considered, or are considering, legislation. Existing legislation differs with respect to the types of digital assets covered, the rights of the fiduciary, the category of fiduciary included, and whether the principal's death or incapacity is covered. A uniform approach among states will provide certainty and predictability for courts, account holders, fiduciaries, and Internet service providers. Revised UFADAA gives states precise, comprehensive, and easily accessible guidance on questions concerning fiduciaries' ability to access the electronic records of a decedent, protected person, principal, or a trust.

With regard to the general scope of the act, the act's coverage is inherently limited by the definition of "digital assets." The act applies only to electronic records in which an individual has a property right or interest, which do not include the underlying asset or liability unless it is itself an electronic record.

The act is divided into 21 sections. Section 2 contains definitions of terms used throughout the act.

Section 3 governs applicability, clarifying the scope of the act and the fiduciaries who have access to digital assets under Revised UFADAA, and carves out an exception for digital assets of an employer used by an employee during the ordinary course of business.

Section 4 provides ways for users to direct the disposition or deletion of their digital assets at their death or incapacity, and establishes a priority system in case of conflicting instructions.

Section 5 establishes that the terms-of-service governing an online account apply to fiduciaries as well as to users, and clarify that a fiduciary cannot take any action that the user could not have legally taken.

Section 6 gives the custodians of digital assets a choice for disclosing those assets to fiduciaries. A custodian may, but need not, comply with a request for access by allowing the fiduciary to reset the password and access the user's account. In many cases that will be the simplest method of compliance. However, a custodian may also comply without giving access to a user's account by simply giving a copy of all the user's digital assets to the fiduciary. That method may be preferred for a social media account when a fiduciary has no need for full access and control.

Sections 7-14 establish the rights of personal representatives, conservators, agents acting pursuant to a power of attorney, and trustees. Each of the fiduciaries is subject to different rules for the content of communications protected under federal privacy laws and for other types of digital assets. Generally, a fiduciary will have access to a catalogue of the user's communications, but not the content, unless the user consented to the disclosure of the content.

Section 15 contains general provisions relating to the rights and responsibilities of the fiduciary. Section 16 addresses compliance by custodians and grants immunity for any acts taken in order to comply with a fiduciary's request under this act. Sections 17-21 address miscellaneous topics, including retroactivity, the effective date of the act, and similar issues.

§ 1. Short Title. This [act] may be cited as the Revised Uniform Fiduciary Access to Digital Assets Act (2015).

§ 2. Definitions. In this [act]:

(1) "Account" means an arrangement under a terms-of-service agreement in which a custodian carries, maintains, processes, receives, or stores a digital asset of the user or provides goods or services to the user.

(2) "Agent" means an attorney-in-fact granted authority under a durable or nondurable power of attorney.

(3) "Carries" means engages in the transmission of an electronic communication.

(4) "Catalogue of electronic communications" means information that identifies each person with which a user has had an electronic communication, the time and date of the communication, and the electronic address of the person.

(5) "[Conservator]" means a person appointed by a court to manage the estate of a living individual. The term includes a limited [conservator].

(6) "Content of an electronic communication" means information concerning the substance or meaning of the communication which:

(A) has been sent or received by a user;

(B) is in electronic storage by a custodian providing an electronic communication service to the public or is carried or maintained by a custodian providing a remote computing service to the public; and

(C) is not readily accessible to the public.

(7) "Court" means the [insert name of court in this state having jurisdiction in matters relating to the content of this act].

(8) "Custodian" means a person that carries, maintains, processes, receives, or stores a digital asset of a user.

(9) "Designated recipient" means a person chosen by a user using an online tool to administer digital assets of the user.

(10) "Digital asset" means an electronic record in which an individual has a right or interest. The term does not include an underlying asset or liability unless the asset or liability is itself an electronic record.

(11) "Electronic" means relating to technology having electrical, digital, magnetic, wireless, optical, electromagnetic, or similar capabilities.

(12) "Electronic communication" has the meaning set forth in 18 U.S.C. Section 2510(12)[, as amended].

(13) "Electronic communication service" means a custodian that provides to a user the ability to send or receive an electronic communication.

(14) "Fiduciary" means an original, additional, or successor personal representative, [conservator], agent, or trustee.

(15) "Information" means data, text, images, videos, sounds, codes, computer programs, software, databases, or the like.

(16) "Online tool" means an electronic service provided by a custodian that allows the user, in an agreement distinct from the terms-of-service agreement between the custodian and user, to provide directions for disclosure or nondisclosure of digital assets to a third person.

(17) "Person" means an individual, estate, business or nonprofit entity, public corporation, government or governmental subdivision, agency, or instrumentality, or other legal entity.

(18) "Personal representative" means an executor, administrator, special administrator, or person that performs substantially the same function under law of this state other than this [act].

(19) "Power of attorney" means a record that grants an agent authority to act in the place of a principal.

(20) "Principal" means an individual who grants authority to an agent in a power of attorney.

(21) "[Protected person]" means an individual for whom a [conservator] has been appointed. The term includes an individual for whom an application for the appointment of a [conservator] is pending.

(22) "Record" means information that is inscribed on a tangible medium or that is stored in an electronic or other medium and is retrievable in perceivable form.

(23) "Remote computing service" means a custodian that provides to a user computer-processing services or the storage of digital assets by means of an electronic communications system, as defined in 18 U.S.C. Section 2510(14)[, as amended].

(24) "Terms of service agreement" means an agreement that controls the relationship between a user and a custodian.

(25) "Trustee" means a fiduciary with legal title to property under an agreement or declaration that creates a beneficial interest in another. The term includes a successor trustee.

(26) "User" means a person that has an account with a custodian.

(27) "Will" includes a codicil, testamentary instrument that only appoints an executor, and instrument that revokes or revises a testamentary instrument.

Legislative Note: In paragraphs (5) and (21), an enacting jurisdiction should replace the bracketed language with local terminology, if different. Enacting jurisdictions should insert the appropriate court in paragraph (7) that would have jurisdiction over matters relating to this act. In jurisdictions in which the constitution, or other law, does not permit the phrase "as amended" when federal statutes are incorporated into state law, the phrase should be deleted in paragraphs (12) and (23).

Comment

Many of the definitions are based on those in the Uniform Probate Code: agent (UPC Section 1 201(1)), conservator (UPC Section 5 102(1)), court (UPC Section 1 201(8)), electronic (UPC Section 5B 102(3)), fiduciary (UPC Section 1 201(15)), person (UPC Section 5B 101(6)), personal representative (UPC Section 1 201(35)), power of attorney (UPC Section 5B 102(7)), principal (UPC Section 5B 102(9)), protected person (UPC Section 5 102(8)), record (UPC Section 1 201(41)), and will (UPC Section 1 201(57)). The definition of "information" is based on that in the Uniform Electronic Transactions Act, Section 2, subsection (11). Many of the other definitions are either drawn from federal law, as discussed below, or are new for this act.

The definition of "account" is broadly worded to encompass any contractual arrangement subject to a terms-of-service agreement, but limited for the purpose of this act by the requirement that the custodian carry, maintain, process, receive, or store a digital asset of the user.

The definition of "digital asset" expressly excludes underlying assets such as funds held in an online bank account. Because records may exist in both electronic and non electronic formats, this definition clarifies the scope of the act and the limitation on the type of records to which it applies. The term includes types of electronic records currently in existence and yet to be invented. It includes any type of electronically stored information, such as: 1) information stored on a user's computer and other digital devices; 2) content uploaded onto websites; and 3) rights in digital property. It also includes records that are either the catalogue or the content of an electronic communication. See 18 U.S.C. Section 2702(a)(2); James D. Lamm, Christina L. Kunz, Damien A. Riehl and Peter John Rademacher, *The Digital Death Conundrum: How Federal and State Laws Prevent Fiduciaries from Managing Digital Property*, 68 U. Miami L. Rev. 385, 388 (2014) (available at: http://goo.gl/T9jX1d).

The term "catalogue of electronic communications" is designed to cover log type information about an electronic communication such as the email addresses of the sender and the recipient, and the date and time the communication was sent.

The term "content of an electronic communication" is adapted from 18 U.S.C. Section 2510(8), which provides that content: "when used with respect to any wire, oral, or electronic communication, includes any information concerning the substance, purport, or meaning of that communication." The definition is designed to cover only content subject to the coverage of Section 2702 of the Electronic Communications Privacy Act (ECPA), 18 U.S.C. Section 2510 et seq.; it does not include content not subject to ECPA. Consequently, the "content of an electronic communication", as used later throughout Revised UFADAA, refers only to information in the body of an electronic message that is not readily accessible to the public; if the information were readily accessible to the public, it would not be subject to the privacy protections of federal law under ECPA. See S. Rep. No. 99 541, at 36 (1986). Example: X uses a Twitter account to send a message. If the tweet is sent only to other people who have been granted access to X's tweets, then it meets Revised UFADAA's definition of "content of an electronic communication." But, if the tweet is completely public with no access restrictions, then it does not meet the act's definition of "content of an electronic communication." ECPA does not apply to private e mail service providers, such as employers and educational institutions. See 18 U.S.C. Section 2702(a)(2); James D. Lamm, Christina L. Kunz, Damien A. Riehl and Peter John Rademacher, *The Digital Death Conundrum: How Federal and State Laws Prevent Fiduciaries from Managing Digital Property*, 68 U. Miami L. Rev. 385, 404 (2014) (available at: http://goo.gl/T9jX1d).

A "user" is a person that has an account with a custodian, and includes a deceased individual that entered into the agreement while alive. A fiduciary can be a user when the fiduciary opens the account.

The definition of "carries" is drawn from federal law, 47 U.S.C. Section 1001(8).

A "custodian" includes any entity that provides or stores electronic data for an account holder.

The fiduciary's access to a record defined as a "digital asset" does not mean the fiduciary owns the asset or may engage in transactions with the asset. Consider, for example, a fiduciary's legal rights with respect to funds in a bank account or securities held with a broker or other custodian, regardless of whether the bank, broker, or custodian has a brick and mortar presence. This act affects electronic records concerning the bank account or securities, but does not affect the authority to engage in transfers of title or other commercial transactions in the funds or securities, even though such transfers or other transactions might occur electronically. Revised UFADAA only deals with the right of the fiduciary to access all relevant electronic communications and digital assets accessible through the online account.

An entity may not refuse to provide access to online records any more than the entity can refuse to provide the fiduciary with access to hard copy records.

An "electronic communication" is a particular type of digital asset subject to the privacy protections of the Electronic Communications Privacy Act. It includes email, text messages, instant messages, and any other electronic communication between private parties. The definition of "electronic communication" is that set out in 18 U.S.C. Section 2510(12):

"electronic communication" means any transfer of signs, signals, writing, images, sounds, data, or intelligence of any nature transmitted in whole or in part by a wire, radio, electromagnetic, photoelectronic or photooptical system that affects interstate or foreign commerce, but does not include-

(A) any wire or oral communication;

(B) any communication made through a tone-only paging device;

(C) any communication from a tracking device (as defined in section 3117 of this title); or

(D) electronic funds transfer information stored by a financial institution in a communications system used for the electronic storage and transfer of funds.

The definition of "electronic communication service" is drawn from 18 U.S.C. Section 2510(15): "any service which provides to users thereof the ability to send or receive wire or electronic communications." The definition of "remote computing service" is adapted from 18 U.S.C. Section 2711(2): "the provision to the public of computer storage or processing services by means of an electronic communications system." The definition refers to 18 U.S.C. Section 2510(14), which defines an electronic communications system as: "any wire, radio, electromagnetic, photooptical or photoelectronic facilities for the transmission of wire or electronic communications, and any computer facilities or related electronic equipment for the electronic storage of such communications."

A "fiduciary" under this act occupies a status recognized by state law, and a fiduciary's powers under this act are subject to the relevant limits established by other state laws.

An "online tool" is a mechanism by which a user names an individual to manage the user's digital assets after the occurrence of a future event, such as the user's death or incapacity. The named individual is referred to as the "designated recipient" in the act to differentiate the person from a fiduciary. A designated recipient may perform many of the same tasks as a fiduciary, but is not held to the same legal standard of conduct.

The term "record" includes information available on both tangible and electronic media. Revised UFADAA applies only to electronic records.

The "terms of service agreement" definition relies on the definition of "agreement" found in UCC Section 1 201(b)(3) ("the bargain of the parties in fact,

as found in their language or inferred from other circumstances, including course of performance, course of dealing, or usage of trade"). It refers to any agreement that controls the relationship between an account holder and a custodian, even though it might be called a terms of use agreement, a click wrap agreement, a click through license, or a similar term. State and federal law determine capacity to enter into a binding terms of service agreement.

§ 3. Applicability.

(a) This [act] applies to:

(1) a fiduciary acting under a will or power of attorney executed before, on, or after [the effective date of this [act]];

(2) a personal representative acting for a decedent who died before, on, or after [the effective date of this [act]];

(3) a [conservatorship] proceeding commenced before, on, or after [the effective date of this [act]]; and

(4) a trustee acting under a trust created before, on, or after [the effective date of this [act]].

(b) This [act] applies to a custodian if the user resides in this state or resided in this state at the time of the user's death.

(c) This [act] does not apply to a digital asset of an employer used by an employee in the ordinary course of the employer's business.

Legislative Note: In subsection (a)(3), an enacting jurisdiction should replace the bracketed language with local terminology, if different.

Comment

This act does not change the substantive rules of other laws, such as agency, banking, conservatorship, contract, copyright, criminal, fiduciary, privacy, probate, property, security, trust, or other applicable law except to vest fiduciaries with authority, according to the provisions of this act, to access or copy digital assets of a decedent, protected person, principal, settlor, or trustee.

Subsection (a)(2) covers the situations in which a decedent dies intestate, so it falls outside of subsection (a)(1), as well as the situations in which a state's procedures for small estates are used.

Subsection (b) clarifies that the act does not apply to a fiduciary's access to an employer's internal email system.

Example 1-Fiduciary access to an employee e mail account. D dies, employed by Company Y. Company Y has an internal e mail communication system, available only to Y's employees, and used by them in the ordinary course of Y's business. D's personal representative, R, believes that D used Company Y's

e mail system to effectuate some financial transactions that R cannot find through other means. R requests access from Company Y to the e mails.

Company Y is not a custodian subject to the act. Under Section 2(8), a custodian must carry, maintain or store a user's digital assets. A user, under Section 2(26) must have an account, and an account, in turn, is defined under Section 2(1) as a contractual arrangement subject to a terms of service agreement. Company Y, like most employers, did not enter into a terms of service agreement with D, so Y is not a custodian.

Example 2-Employee of electronic communication service provider. D dies, employed by Company Y. Company Y is an electronic communication service provider. Company Y has an internal e mail communication system, available only to Y's employees and used by them in the ordinary course of Y's business. D used the internal Company Y system. When not at work, D also used an electronic communication service system that Company Y provides to the public. D's personal representative, R, believes that D used Company Y's internal e mail system as well as Company Y's electronic communication system available to the public to effectuate some financial transactions. R seeks access to both communication systems.

As is true in Example 1, Company Y is not a

custodian subject to the act for purposes of the internal email system. The situation is different with respect to R's access to Company Y's system that is available to the public. Assuming that Company Y can disclose the communications under federal law and R meets the other requirements of this act, Company Y must disclose them to R.

§ 4. User Direction for Disclosure of Digital Assets.

(a) A user may use an online tool to direct the custodian to disclose or not to disclose some or all of the user's digital assets, including the content of electronic communications. If the online tool allows the user to modify or delete a direction at all times, a direction regarding disclosure using an online tool overrides a contrary direction by the user in a will, trust, power of attorney, or other record.

(b) If a user has not used an online tool to give direction under subsection (a) or if the custodian has not provided an online tool, the user may allow or prohibit in a will, trust, power of attorney, or other record, disclosure to a fiduciary of some or all of the user's digital assets, including the content of electronic communications sent or received by the user.

(c) A user's direction under subsection (a) or (b) overrides a contrary provision in a terms-of-service agreement that does not require the user to act affirmatively and distinctly from the user's assent to the terms of service.

Comment

This section addresses the relationship of online tools, other records documenting the user's intent, and terms-of-service agreements. In some instances, there may be a conflict between the directions provided by a user in an online tool that limits access by other parties to the user's digital assets, and the user's estate planning or other personal documents that purport to authorize access for specified persons in identified situations. The act attempts to balance these interests by establishing a three-tier priority system for determining the user's intent with respect to any digital asset.

Subsection (a) gives top priority to a user's wishes as expressed using an online tool. If a custodian of digital assets allows the user to provide directions for handling those digital assets in case of the user's

death or incapacity, and the user does so, that provides the clearest possible indication of the user's intent and is specifically limited to those particular digital assets.

If the user does not give direction using an online tool, but makes provisions in an estate plan for the disposition of digital assets, subsection (b) gives legal effect to the user's directions. The fiduciary charged with managing the user's digital assets must provide a copy of the relevant document to the custodian when requesting access. See Sections 7 through 14.

If the user provides no other direction, the terms-of-service governing the account will apply. If the terms-of-service do not address fiduciary access to digital assets, the default rules provided in this act will apply.

§ 5. Terms-of-Service Agreement.

(a) This [act] does not change or impair a right of a custodian or a user under a terms-of-service agreement to access and use digital assets of the user.

(b) This [act] does not give a fiduciary any new or expanded rights other than those held by the user for whom, or for whose estate, the fiduciary acts or represents.

(c) A fiduciary's access to digital assets may be modified or eliminated by a user, by federal law, or by a terms-of-service agreement if the user has not provided direction under Section 4.

Comment

This section clarifies that, to the extent that a custodian gives a fiduciary access to an account pursuant to Section 6, the account's terms-of-service agreement applies equally to the original user and to a fiduciary acting for the original user. A fiduciary is subject to the same terms and conditions of the user's agreement with the custodian. This section does not require a custodian to permit a fiduciary to assume a user's terms-of-service agreement if the custodian can otherwise comply with Section 6.

§ 6. Procedure for Disclosing Digital Assets.

(a) When disclosing digital assets of a user under this [act], the custodian may at its sole discretion:

(1) grant a fiduciary or designated recipient full access to the user's account;

(2) grant a fiduciary or designated recipient partial access to the user's account sufficient to perform the tasks with which the fiduciary or designated recipient is charged; or

(3) provide a fiduciary or designated recipient a copy in a record of any digital asset that, on the date the custodian received the request for disclosure, the user could have accessed if the user were alive and had full capacity and access to the account.

(b) A custodian may assess a reasonable administrative charge for the cost of disclosing digital assets under this [act].

(c) A custodian need not disclose under this [act] a digital asset deleted by a user.

(d) If a user directs or a fiduciary requests a custodian to disclose under this [act] some, but not all, of the user's digital assets, the custodian need not disclose the assets if segregation of the assets would impose an undue burden on the custodian. If the custodian believes the direction or request imposes an undue burden, the custodian or fiduciary may seek an order from the court to disclose:

(1) a subset limited by date of the user's digital assets;

(2) all of the user's digital assets to the fiduciary or designated recipient;

(3) none of the user's digital assets; or

(4) all of the user's digital assets to the court for review in camera.

Comment

This section governs a custodian's response to a request for disclosure of a user's digital assets.

Subsection (a) gives the custodian of digital assets a choice of methods for disclosing digital assets to an authorized fiduciary. Each custodian has a different business model and may prefer one method over another.

Subsection (b) allows a custodian to assess a reasonable administrative charge for the cost of disclosure. This is intended to be analogous to the charge any business may assess for administrative tasks outside the ordinary course of its business to comply with a court order.

Subsection (c) states that any digital asset deleted by the user need not be disclosed, even if recoverable by the custodian. Deletion is assumed to be a good indication that the user did not intend for a fiduciary to have access.

Subsection (d) addresses requests that are unduly burdensome because they require segregation of digital assets. For example, a fiduciary's request for disclosure of "any email pertaining to financial matters" would require a custodian to sort through the full list of emails and cull any irrelevant messages before disclosure. If a custodian receives an unduly burdensome request of this sort, it may decline to disclose the digital assets, and either the fiduciary or custodian may seek guidance from a court.

§ 7. Disclosure of Content of Electronic Communications of Deceased User.
If a deceased user consented or a court directs disclosure of the contents of electronic communications of the user, the custodian shall disclose to the personal representative of the estate of the user the content of an electronic communication sent or received by the user if the representative gives the custodian:

(1) a written request for disclosure in physical or electronic form;

(2) a [certified] copy of the death certificate of the user;

(3) a [certified] copy of [the letter of appointment of the representative or a small estate affidavit or court order];

(4) unless the user provided direction using an online tool, a copy of the user's will, trust, power of attorney, or other record evidencing the user's consent to disclosure of the content of electronic communications; and

(5) if requested by the custodian:

(A) a number, username, address, or other unique subscriber or account identifier assigned by the custodian to identify the user's account;

(B) evidence linking the account to the user; or

(C) a finding by the court that:

(i) the user had a specific account with the custodian, identifiable by the information specified in subparagraph (A);

(ii) disclosure of the content of electronic communications of the user would not violate 18 U.S.C. Section 2701 et seq.[, as amended], 47 U.S.C. Section 222[, as amended], or other applicable law;

(iii) unless the user provided direction using an online tool, the user consented to disclosure of the content of electronic communications; or

(iv) disclosure of the content of electronic communications of the user is reasonably necessary for administration of the estate.

Legislative Note: *In jurisdictions that certify legal documents, the word "certified" should be included in paragraphs (2) and (3). Other jurisdictions may substitute a word or phrase that conforms to the local practice for authentication. Enacting jurisdictions should insert into paragraph (3) the local term given to a document that authorizes a personal representative to administer a decedent's estate. In jurisdictions in which the constitution, or other law, does not permit the phrase "as amended" when federal statutes are incorporated into state law, the phrase should be deleted in paragraph (5)(C)(ii).*

Comment

The Electronic Communications Privacy Act (ECPA) distinguishes between the permissible disclosure of the "content" of an electronic communication, covered in 18 U.S.C. Section 2702(b), and of "a record or other information pertaining to a" subscriber or customer, covered in 18 U.S.C. Section 2702(c); *see* Matthew J. Tokson, *The Content/Envelope Distinction in Internet Law*, 50 Wm. & Mary L. Rev. 2105 (2009). Section 7 concerns disclosure of content; Section 8 covers disclosure of non-content and other digital assets of the user.

Content based material can, in turn, be divided into two types of communications: those received by the user and those sent. Federal law, 18 U.S.C. Section 2702(b) permits a custodian to divulge the contents of a communication "(1) to an addressee or intended recipient of such communication or an agent of such addressee or intended recipient" or "(3) with the lawful consent of the originator or an addressee or intended recipient of such communication, or the subscriber in the case of remote computing service."

Consequently, when the user is the "addressee or intended recipient," material can be disclosed either to that individual or to an agent for that person, 18 U.S.C. Section 2702(b)(1), and it can also be disclosed to third parties with the "lawful consent" of the addressee or intended recipient. 18 U.S.C. Section 2702(b)(3). Material for which the user is the "originator" (or the "subscriber" to a remote computing service) can be disclosed to third parties only with the account holder's "lawful consent." 18 U.S.C. Section 2702(b)(3). (Note that, when the user is the addressee or intended recipient, material can be disclosed under either (b)(1) or (b)(3), but that when the user is the originator, lawful consent is required under (b)(3).) See the Comments concerning the definition of "content" after Section 2. By contrast to content based material, non content material can be disclosed either with the lawful consent of the user or to any person (other than a governmental entity) even without lawful consent. This information includes material about any communication sent, such as the addressee, sender, date/time, and other subscriber data, which this act defines as the "catalogue of electronic communications." (Further discussion of this issue and examples are set out in the Comments to Section 15, *infra*.)

Therefore, Section 7 gives the personal representative access to digital assets if the user consented to disclosure or if a court orders disclosure. To obtain access, the personal representative must provide the documentation specified by Section 7. First, the personal representative must give the custodian a written request for disclosure, a copy of the death certificate, a document establishing the authority of the personal representative, and, in the absence of an online tool, a record evidencing the user's consent to disclosure. When requesting disclosure, the fiduciary must write or email the custodian. The form of the request is limited, and

does not, for example, include video, Tweet, instant message or other forms of communication.

Second, if the custodian requests, then the personal representative can be required to establish that the requested information is necessary for estate administration and the account is attributable to the decedent. Different custodians may have different procedures. Thus a custodian may request that the personal representative obtain a court order, and such an order must include findings that: 1) the user had a specific account with the custodian, 2) that disclosure of the content of electronic communications of the user would not violate the SCA or other law, 3) unless the user provided direction using an online tool, that the user consented to disclosure of the content of electronic communications, or 4) that disclosure of the content of electronic communications of a user is reasonably necessary for administration of the estate.

§ 8. Disclosure of Other Digital Assets of Deceased User. Unless the user prohibited disclosure of digital assets or the court directs otherwise, a custodian shall disclose to the personal representative of the estate of a deceased user a catalogue of electronic communications sent or received by the user and digital assets, other than the content of electronic communications, of the user, if the representative gives the custodian:

(1) a written request for disclosure in physical or electronic form;

(2) a [certified] copy of the death certificate of the user;

(3) a [certified] copy of [the letter of appointment of the representative or a small estate affidavit or court order]; and

(4) if requested by the custodian:

(A) a number, username, address, or other unique subscriber or account identifier assigned by the custodian to identify the user's account;

(B) evidence linking the account to the user;

(C) an affidavit stating that disclosure of the user's digital assets is reasonably necessary for administration of the estate; or

(D) a finding by the court that:

(i) the user had a specific account with the custodian, identifiable by the information specified in subparagraph (A); or

(ii) disclosure of the user's digital assets is reasonably necessary for administration of the estate.

Legislative Note: In jurisdictions that certify legal documents, the word "certified" should be included in paragraphs (2) and (3). Other jurisdictions may substitute a word or phrase that conforms to the local practice for authentication. Enacting jurisdictions should insert into paragraph (3) the local term given to a document that authorizes a personal representative to administer a decedent's estate.

Comment

As in Section 7, when requesting disclosure of non-content, the fiduciary must write or email the custodian.

Section 8 requires disclosure of all other digital assets, unless prohibited by the decedent or directed by the court, once the personal representative provides a written request, a death certificate and a certified copy of the letter of appointment. In addition, the custodian may request a court order, and such an order must include findings that the decedent had a specific account with the custodian and that disclosure of the decedent's digital assets is reasonably necessary for administration of the estate. Thus, Section 8 was intended to give personal representatives default access to the "catalogue" of electronic communications and other digital assets not protected by federal privacy law.

§ 9. Disclosure of Content of Electronic Communications of Principal. To the extent a power of attorney expressly grants an agent authority over the content of electronic communications sent or received by the principal and unless directed otherwise by the principal or the court, a custodian shall disclose to the agent the content if the agent gives the custodian:

(1) a written request for disclosure in physical or electronic form;

(2) an original or copy of the power of attorney expressly granting the agent authority over the content of electronic communications of the principal;

(3) a certification by the agent, under penalty of perjury, that the power of attorney is in effect; and

(4) if requested by the custodian:

(A) a number, username, address, or other unique subscriber or account identifier assigned by the custodian to identify the principal's account; or

(B) evidence linking the account to the principal.

Comment

An agent has access to the content of electronic communications only when the power of attorney explicitly grants access. Section 10 concerns disclosure of other digital assets of the principal.

When a power of attorney contains the consent of the principal, ECPA does not prevent the agent from exercising authority over the content of an electronic communication. See the Comments to Section 7. There should be no question that an explicit delegation of authority in a power of attorney constitutes authorization from the user to access digital assets and provides "lawful consent" to allow disclosure of the content of an electronic communication from an electronic communication service or a remote computing service pursuant to applicable law. Both authorization and lawful consent are important because 18 U.S.C. Section 2701 deals with intentional access without authorization and 18 U.S.C. Section 2702 allows a service provider to disclose with lawful consent. Federal courts have not yet interpreted how ECPA affects a fiduciary's efforts to access the content of an electronic communication. *E.g., In re Facebook, Inc.,* 923 F. Supp. 2d 1204 (N.D. Cal. 2012).

When requesting access, the agent must write or email the custodian (see the comments in Section 7). The agent must also give the custodian an original or copy of the power of attorney expressly granting the agent authority over the contents of electronic communications of the principal to the agent and a certification by the agent, under penalty of perjury, that the power of attorney is in effect. In addition, if requested by the custodian, the agent must provide a unique subscriber or account identifier assigned by the custodian to identify the principal's account or other evidence linking the account to the principal.

§ 10. Disclosure of Other Digital Assets of Principal. Unless otherwise ordered by the court, directed by the principal, or provided by a power of attorney, a custodian shall disclose to an agent with specific authority over digital assets or general authority to act on behalf of a principal a catalogue of electronic communications sent or received by the principal and digital assets, other than the content of electronic communications, of the principal if the agent gives the custodian:

(1) a written request for disclosure in physical or electronic form;

(2) an original or a copy of the power of attorney that gives the agent specific authority over digital assets or general authority to act on behalf of the principal;

(3) a certification by the agent, under penalty of perjury, that the power of attorney is in effect; and

(4) if requested by the custodian:

(A) a number, username, address, or other unique subscriber or account identifier assigned by the custodian to identify the principal's account; or

(B) evidence linking the account to the principal.

Comment

This section establishes that the agent has default authority over all of the principal's digital assets, other than the content of the principal's electronic communications. When requesting access, the agent must write or email the custodian (see the comments in Section 7).

The agent must also give the custodian an original or copy of the power of attorney and a certification by the agent, under penalty of perjury, that the power of attorney is in effect. Also, if requested by the custodian, the agent must provide a unique subscriber or account identifier assigned by the custodian to identify the principal's account, or some evidence linking the account to the principal.

§ 11. Disclosure of Digital Assets Held in Trust When Trustee Is Original User. Unless otherwise ordered by the court or provided in a trust, a custodian shall disclose to a trustee that is an original user of an account any digital asset of the account held in trust, including a catalogue of electronic communications of the trustee and the content of electronic communications.

Comment

Section 11 provides that trustees who are original account holders can access all digital assets held in the trust. There should be no question that a trustee who is the original account holder will have full access to all digital assets. This includes the content of electronic communications, as access to content is presumed with respect to assets for which the trustee is the initial account holder. A trustee may have title to digital assets when the trustee opens an account as trustee; under those circumstances, the trustee can access the content of each digital asset that is in an account for which the trustee is the original account holder, not necessarily each digital asset held in the trust.

§ 12. Disclosure of Contents of Electronic Communications Held in Trust When Trustee Not Original User. Unless otherwise ordered by the court, directed by the user, or provided in a trust, a custodian shall disclose to a trustee that is not an original user of an account the content of an electronic communication sent or received by an original or successor user and carried, maintained, processed, received, or stored by the custodian in the account of the trust if the trustee gives the custodian:

(1) a written request for disclosure in physical or electronic form;

(2) a certified copy of the trust instrument[or a certification of the trust under [cite trust certification statute, such as Uniform Trust Code Section 1013]] that includes consent to disclosure of the content of electronic communications to the trustee;

(3) a certification by the trustee, under penalty of perjury, that the trust exists and the trustee is a currently acting trustee of the trust; and

(4) if requested by the custodian:

(A) a number, username, address, or other unique subscriber or account identifier assigned by the custodian to identify the trust's account; or

(B) evidence linking the account to the trust.

Comment

For accounts that are transferred into a trust by the settlor or in another manner, a trustee is not the original user of the account, and the trustee's authority is qualified. Thus, Section 12, governing disclosure of content of electronic communications from those accounts, requires consent.

Section 12 addresses situations involving an inter vivos transfer of a digital asset into a trust, a transfer into a testamentary trust, or a transfer via a pourover will or other governing instrument of a digital asset into a trust. In those situations, a trustee becomes a successor user when the settlor transfers a digital asset into the trust. There should be no question that the trustee with legal title to the digital asset was authorized by the settlor to access the digital assets so transferred, including both the catalogue and content of an electronic communication, and this provides "lawful consent" to allow disclosure of the content of an electronic communication from an electronic communication service or a remote computing service pursuant to applicable law. See the Comments concerning the definitions of the "content of an electronic communication" after Section 2. Nonetheless, Sections 12 and 13 distinguish between the catalogue and content of an electronic communication in case there are any questions about

whether the form in which property transferred into a trust is held constitutes lawful consent. Both authorization and lawful consent are important because 18 U.S.C. Section 2701 deals with intentional access without authorization and because 18 U.S.C. Section 2702 allows a service provider to disclose with lawful consent.

The underlying trust documents and default trust law will supply the allocation of responsibilities between and among trustees. When requesting access, the trustee must write or email the custodian (see comments to Section 7). The trustee must also give the custodian an original or copy of the trust that includes consent to disclosure of the content of electronic communications to the trustee and a certification by the trustee, under penalty of perjury, that the trust exists and that the trustee is a currently acting trustee of the trust. Also, if requested by the custodian, the trustee must provide a unique subscriber or account identifier assigned by the custodian to identify the trust's account, or some evidence linking the account to the trust.

§ 13. **Disclosure of Other Digital Assets Held in Trust When Trustee Not Original User.** Unless otherwise ordered by the court, directed by the user, or provided in a trust, a custodian shall disclose, to a trustee that is not an original user of an account, a catalogue of electronic communications sent or received by an original or successor user and stored, carried, or maintained by the custodian in an account of the trust and any digital assets, other than the content of electronic communications, in which the trust has a right or interest if the trustee gives the custodian:

(1) a written request for disclosure in physical or electronic form;

(2) a certified copy of the trust instrument[or a certification of the trust under [cite trust certification statute, such as Uniform Trust Code Section 1013]];

(3) a certification by the trustee, under penalty of perjury, that the trust exists and the trustee is a currently acting trustee of the trust; and

(4) if requested by the custodian:

(A) a number, username, address, or other unique subscriber or account identifier assigned by the custodian to identify the trust's account; or

(B) evidence linking the account to the trust.

Comment

Section 13 governs digital assets other than the contents of electronic communications, so it does not require the settlor's consent.

When requesting access, the trustee must write or email the custodian (see Comments to Section 7).

The trustee must also give the custodian an original or copy of the trust, and a certification by the trustee,

under penalty of perjury, that the trust exists and that the trustee is a currently acting trustee of the trust. Also, if requested by the custodian, the trustee must provide a unique subscriber or account identifier assigned by the custodian to identify the trust's account, or some evidence linking the account to the trust.

§ 14. **Disclosure of Digital Assets to [Conservator] of [Protected Person].**

(a) After an opportunity for a hearing under [state conservatorship law], the court may grant a [conservator] access to the digital assets of a [protected person].

(b) Unless otherwise ordered by the court or directed by the user, a custodian shall disclose to a [conservator] the catalogue of electronic communications sent or received by a [protected person] and any digital assets, other than the content of electronic communications, in which the [protected person] has a right or interest if the [conservator] gives the custodian:

(1) a written request for disclosure in physical or electronic form;

(2) a [certified] copy of the court order that gives the [conservator] authority over the digital assets of the [protected person]; and

(3) if requested by the custodian:

(A) a number, username, address, or other unique subscriber or account identifier assigned by the custodian to identify the account of the [protected person]; or

(B) evidence linking the account to the [protected person].

(c) A [conservator] with general authority to manage the assets of a [protected person] may request a custodian of the digital assets of the [protected person] to suspend or terminate an account of the [protected person] for good cause. A request made under this section must be accompanied by a [certified] copy of the court order giving the [conservator] authority over the protected person's property.

Legislative Note: *Throughout this section, an enacting jurisdiction should replace the bracketed terms [conservator] and [protected person] with local terminology, if different. In jurisdictions that certify legal documents, the word "certified" should be included in subsections (b) and (c). Other jurisdictions may substitute a word or phrase that conforms to the local practice for authentication.*

Comment

When a conservator is appointed to represent a protected person's interests, the protected person may still retain some right to privacy in their personal communications. Therefore, Section 14 does not permit conservators to request disclosure of a protected person's electronic communications on the basis of the conservatorship order alone. To access a protected person's digital assets and a catalogue of electronic communications, a conservator must be specifically authorized by the court to do so. This requirement for express judicial authority over digital assets does not limit the fiduciary's authority over the underlying assets, such as funds held in a bank account. The meaning of the term "hearing" will vary from state to state according to state law and procedures.

State law will establish the criteria for when a court will grant power to the conservator. For example, UPC Section 5 411(c) requires the court to consider the decision the protected person would have made as well as a list of other factors. Existing state law may also set out the requisite standards for a conservator's actions. The conservator must exercise authority in the interests of the protected person. When requesting access to digital assets in which the protected person has a right or interest, the conservator must write or email the custodian (see comments to Section 7).

The conservator must also give the custodian a certified copy of the court order that gives the conservator authority over the protected person's digital assets. Also, if requested by the custodian, the conservator must provide a unique subscriber or account identifier assigned by the custodian to identify the protected person's account, or some evidence linking the account to the protected person. The custodian is required to disclose the digital assets so requested.

Under subsection (c), a conservator with general authority to manage the assets of the protected person may request suspension or termination of the protected person's account, for good cause.

§ 15. Fiduciary Duty and Authority.

(a) The legal duties imposed on a fiduciary charged with managing tangible property apply to the management of digital assets, including:

(1) the duty of care;

(2) the duty of loyalty; and

(3) the duty of confidentiality.

(b) A fiduciary's authority with respect to a digital asset of a user:

(1) except as otherwise provided in Section 4, is subject to the applicable terms of service;

(2) is subject to other applicable law, including copyright law;

(3) is limited by the scope of the fiduciary's duties; and

(4) may not be used to impersonate the user.

(c) A fiduciary with authority over the property of a decedent, [protected person], principal, or settlor has the right to access any digital asset in which the decedent, [protected person], principal, or settlor had a right or interest and that is not held by a custodian or subject to a terms-of-service agreement.

(d) A fiduciary acting within the scope of the fiduciary's duties is an authorized user of the property of the decedent, [protected person], principal, or settlor for the purpose of applicable computer fraud and unauthorized computer access laws, including [this state's law on unauthorized computer access].

(e) A fiduciary with authority over the tangible, personal property of a decedent, [protected person], principal, or settlor:

(1) has the right to access the property and any digital asset stored in it; and

(2) is an authorized user for the purpose of computer fraud and unauthorized computer access laws, including [this state's law on unauthorized computer access].

(f) A custodian may disclose information in an account to a fiduciary of the user when the information is required to terminate an account used to access digital assets licensed to the user.

(g) A fiduciary of a user may request a custodian to terminate the user's account. A request for termination must be in writing, in either physical or electronic form, and accompanied by:

(1) if the user is deceased, a [certified] copy of the death certificate of the user;

(2) a [certified] copy of the [letter of appointment of the representative or a small estate affidavit or court order,] court order, power of attorney, or trust giving the fiduciary authority over the account; and

(3) if requested by the custodian:

(A) a number, username, address, or other unique subscriber or account identifier assigned by the custodian to identify the user's account;

(B) evidence linking the account to the user; or

(C) a finding by the court that the user had a specific account with the custodian, identifiable by the information specified in subparagraph (A).

Legislative Note: *States with a computer trespass statute should cite to it in subsections (d) and (e), and may want to amend those statutes to be in accord with this act. In jurisdictions that certify legal documents, the word "certified" should be included in subsection (g). Other jurisdictions may substitute a word or phrase that conforms to the local practice for authentication. In subsections (c) and (e), an enacting jurisdiction should replace the bracketed language with local terminology, if different.*

Comment

The original version of UFADAA incorporated fiduciary duties by reference to "other law." This proved to be confusing and led to enactment difficulty. Section 15 specifies the nature, extent and limitation of the fiduciary's authority over digital assets. Subsection (a) expressly imposes all fiduciary duties to the management of digital assets, including the duties of care, loyalty and confidentiality. Subsection (b) specifies that a fiduciary's authority over digital assets is subject to the terms-of-service agreement, except to the extent the terms-of-service agreement provision is overridden by an action taken pursuant to Section 4, and it reinforces the applicability of copyright and fiduciary duties. Finally, subsection 15(b) prohibits a fiduciary's authority being used to impersonate a user. Subsection 15(c) permits the fiduciary to access all digital assets not in an account or subject to a terms-of-service agreement. Subsection 15(d) further specifies that the fiduciary is an authorized user under any applicable law on unauthorized computer access.

Subsection 15(g) gives the fiduciary the option of requesting that an account be terminated, if termination would not violate a fiduciary duty.

This issue concerning the parameters of the fiduciary's authority potentially arises in two situations: 1) the fiduciary obtains access to a password or the like directly from the account holder, as would be true in various circumstances such as for the trustee of an inter vivos trust or someone who has stored passwords in a written or electronic list and those passwords are then transmitted to the fiduciary; and 2) the fiduciary obtains access pursuant to this act.

This section clarifies that the fiduciary has the same authority as the user if the user were the one exercising the authority (note that, where the user has died, this means that the fiduciary has the same access as the user had immediately before death). This means that the fiduciary's authority to access the digital asset is the same as the user except where, pursuant to Section 4, the user has explicitly opted out of fiduciary access. In exercising its responsibilities, the fiduciary is subject to the duties and obligations established pursuant to state fiduciary law, and is liable for breach of those duties. Note that even if the digital asset were illegally obtained by the account holder, the fiduciary would still need access in order to handle that asset appropriately. There may, for example, be tax consequences that the fiduciary would be obligated to report.

However, this section does not require a custodian to permit a fiduciary to assume a user's terms-of-service agreement if the custodian can otherwise comply with Section 6.

In exercising its responsibilities, the fiduciary is subject to the same limitations as the user more generally. For example, a fiduciary cannot delete an account if this would be fraudulent. Similarly, if the user could challenge provisions in a terms of service agreement, then the fiduciary is also able to do so. *See Ajemian v. Yahoo!, Inc.*, 987 N.E.2d 604 (Mass.

2013).

Subsection (b) is designed to establish that the fiduciary is authorized to obtain or access digital assets in accordance with other applicable laws. The language mirrors that used in Title II of the Electronic Communications Privacy Act of 1986 (ECPA), also known as the Stored Communications Act, 18 U.S.C. Section 2701 *et seq.* (2006); *see, e.g.,* Orin S. Kerr, *A User's Guide to the Stored Communications Act, and a Legislator's Guide to Amending It,* 72 Geo. Wash. L. Rev. 1208 (2004). The subsection clarifies that state law treats the fiduciary as "authorized" under state laws criminalizing unauthorized access.

State laws vary in their coverage but typically prohibit unauthorized computer access. By defining the fiduciary as an authorized user in subsection (d), the fiduciary has authorization under applicable law to access the digital assets under state computer trespass laws.

Federal courts may look to these provisions to guide their interpretations of ECPA and the federal Computer Fraud and Abuse Act (CFAA), but fiduciaries should understand that federal courts may not view such provisions as dispositive in determining whether access to a user's account violated federal criminal law.

Subsection (e) clarifies that the fiduciary is authorized to access digital assets stored on tangible personal property of the decedent, protected person, principal, or settlor, such as laptops, computers, smartphones or storage media, exempting fiduciaries from application for purposes of state or federal laws on unauthorized computer access. For criminal law purposes, this clarifies that the fiduciary is authorized to access all of the account holder's digital assets, whether held locally or remotely.

Example 1–Access to digital assets by personal representative. D dies with a will that is silent with respect to digital assets. D has a bank account for which D received only electronic statements, D has stored photos in a cloud based Internet account, and D has an e mail account with a company that provides electronic communication services to the public. The personal representative of D's estate needs access to the electronic bank account statements, the photo account, and e mails.

The personal representative of D's estate has the authority to access D's electronic banking statements and D's photo account, which both fall under the act's definition of a "digital asset." This means that, if these accounts are password protected or otherwise unavailable to the personal representative, then the bank and the photo account service must give access to the personal representative when the request is made in accordance with Section 9. If the terms of service agreement permits D to transfer the accounts electronically, then the personal representative of D's estate can use that procedure for transfer as well.

The personal representative of D's estate is also able to request that the e mail account service provider grant access to e mails sent or received by D; ECPA permits the service provider to release the catalogue to the personal representative. The service provider also must provide the personal representative access to the content of an electronic communication sent or received by D if the service provider is permitted under 18 U.S.C. Section 2702(b) to disclose the content. The bank may release the catalogue of electronic communications or content of an electronic communication for which it is the originator or the addressee because the bank is not subject to the ECPA.

Example 2–Access to digital assets by agent. X creates a power of attorney designating A as X's agent. The power of attorney expressly grants A authority over X's digital assets, including the content of an electronic communication. X has a bank account for which X receives only electronic statements, X has stored photos in a cloud based Internet account, and X has a game character and in game property associated with an online game. X also has an e mail account with a company that provides electronic communication services to the public.

A has the authority to access X's electronic bank statements, the photo account, the game character and in game property associated with the online game, all of which fall under the act's definition of a "digital asset." This means that, if these accounts are password protected or otherwise unavailable to A as X's agent, then the bank, the photo account service provider, and the online game service provider must give access to A when the request is made in accordance with Section 9. If the terms of service agreement permits X to transfer the accounts electronically, then A as X's agent can use that procedure for transfer as well.

As X's agent, A is also able to request that the e mail account service provider grant access to e mails sent or received by X; ECPA permits the service provider to release the catalogue. The service provider also must provide A access to the content of

an electronic communication sent or received by X if the service provider is permitted under 18 U.S.C. Section 2702(b) to disclose the content. The bank may release the catalogue of electronic communications or content of an electronic communication for which it is the originator or the addressee because the bank is not subject to the ECPA.

Example 3–Access to digital assets by trustee. T is the trustee of a trust established by S. As trustee of the trust, T opens a bank account for which T receives only electronic statements. S transfers into the trust to T as trustee (in compliance with a terms of service agreement) a game character and in game property associated with an online game and a cloud based Internet account in which S has stored photos. S also transfers to T as trustee (in compliance with the terms of service agreement) an e mail account with a company that provides electronic communication services to the public.

T is an original user with respect to the bank account that T opened, and T has the ability to access the electronic banking statements. T, as successor user to S, may access the game character and in game property associated with the online game and the photo account, which both fall under the act's definition of a "digital asset." This means that, if these accounts are password protected or otherwise unavailable to T as trustee, then the bank, the photo account service provider, and the online game service provider must give access to T when the request is made in accordance with the act. If the terms of service agreement permits the user to transfer the accounts electronically, then T as trustee can use that procedure for transfer as well.

T as successor user of the e mail account for which S was previously the user is also able to request that the e mail account service provider grant access to e mails sent or received by S; the ECPA permits the service provider to release the catalogue. The service provider also must provide T access to the content of an electronic communication sent or received by S if the service provider is permitted under 18 U.S.C. Section 2702(b) to disclose the content. The bank may release the catalogue of electronic communications or content of an electronic communication for which it is the originator or the addressee because the bank is not subject to the ECPA.

§ 16. Custodian Compliance and Immunity.

(a) Not later than [60] days after receipt of the information required under Sections 7 through 14, a custodian shall comply with a request under this [act] from a fiduciary or designated recipient to disclose digital assets or terminate an account. If the custodian fails to comply, the fiduciary or designated recipient may apply to the court for an order directing compliance.

(b) An order under subsection (a) directing compliance must contain a finding that compliance is not in violation of 18 U.S.C. Section 2702[, as amended].

(c) A custodian may notify the user that a request for disclosure or to terminate an account was made under this [act].

(d) A custodian may deny a request under this [act] from a fiduciary or designated recipient for disclosure of digital assets or to terminate an account if the custodian is aware of any lawful access to the account following the receipt of the fiduciary's request.

(e) This [act] does not limit a custodian's ability to obtain or require a fiduciary or designated recipient requesting disclosure or termination under this [act] to obtain a court order which:

(1) specifies that an account belongs to the [protected person] or principal;

(2) specifies that there is sufficient consent from the [protected person] or principal] to support the requested disclosure; and

(3) contains a finding required by law other than this [act].

(f) A custodian and its officers, employees, and agents are immune from liability for an act or omission done in good faith in compliance with this [act].

Legislative Note: In jurisdictions in which the constitution, or other law, does not permit the phrase "as amended" when federal statutes are incorporated into state law, the phrase should be deleted in subsection (b). In subsection (e), an enacting jurisdiction should replace the bracketed language with local terminology, if different.

Comment

This section establishes that custodians are protected from liability when they act in accordance with the procedures of this act and in good faith. The types of actions covered include disclosure as well as transfer of copies. The critical issue in conferring immunity is the source of the liability. Direct liability is not subject to immunity; indirect liability is subject to immunity.

Direct liability could only arise from noncompliance with a judicial order issued under sections 7 to 15. Upon determination of a right of access under those sections, a court may issue an order to grant access under section 16. Section 16(b) requires that an order directing compliance contain a finding that compliance is not in violation of 18 U.S.C. Section 2702. Noncompliance with that order would give rise to liability for contempt. There is no immunity from this liability.

Indirect liability could arise from granting a right of access under this act. Access to a digital asset might invade the privacy or the harm the reputation of the decedent, protected person, principal, or settlor, it might harm the family or business of the decedent, protected person, principal, or settlor, and it might harm other persons. The grantor of access to the digital asset is immune from liability arising out of any of these circumstances if the grantor acted in good faith to comply with this act. If there is a judicial order under section 16, compliance with the order establishes good faith. Absent a judicial order under section 16, good faith must be established by the grantor's assessment of the requirements of this act.

Further, Section 16 (e) allows the custodian to verify that the account belongs to the person represented by the fiduciary.

§ 17. Uniformity of Application and Construction.
In applying and construing this uniform act, consideration must be given to the need to promote uniformity of the law with respect to its subject matter among states that enact it.

§ 18. Relation to Electronic Signatures in Global and National Commerce Act. This [act] modifies, limits, or supersedes the Electronic Signatures in Global and National Commerce Act, 15 U.S.C. Section 7001 et seq., but does not modify, limit, or supersede Section 101(c) of that act, 15 U.S.C. Section 7001(c), or authorize electronic delivery of any of the notices described in Section 103(b) of that act, 15 U.S.C. Section 7003(b).

[**§ 19. Severability.** If any provision of this [act] or its application to any person or circumstance is held invalid, the invalidity does not affect other provisions or applications of this [act] which can be given effect without the invalid provision or application, and to this end the provisions of this [act] are severable.]

Legislative Note: Include this section only if the jurisdiction lacks a general severability statute or a decision by the highest court of the jurisdiction stating a general rule of severability.

§ 20. Repeals; Conforming Amendments.
(a) ....
(b) ....
(c) ....

§ 21. Effective Date. This [act] takes effect....

UNIFORM POWERS OF APPOINTMENT ACT
(2013)

Table of Sections

§ 504. Creditor Claim: Nongeneral Power

Prefatory Note

Professor W. Barton Leach described the power of appointment as "the most efficient dispositive device that the ingenuity of Anglo-American lawyers has ever worked out." 24 A.B.A. J. 807 (1938). Powers of appointment are routinely included in trusts to add flexibility to the arrangement.

A power of appointment is the authority, acting in a nonfiduciary capacity, to designate recipients of beneficial ownership interests in, or powers of appointment over, the appointive property. An owner, of course, has this authority with respect to the owner's property. By creating a power of appointment, the owner typically confers this authority on someone else.

The power of appointment is a staple of modern estate-planning practice. However, many jurisdictions within the United States have very little statutory or case law on powers of appointment.

A comprehensive restatement of the law of powers of appointment was approved in 2010 and published in 2011 by the American Law Institute. See chapters 17-23 of the Restatement Third of Property: Wills and Other Donative Transfers.

This act draws heavily on that Restatement. The aim of this act is to codify the law of powers of appointment, or at least the portions of the law that are most amenable to codification.

The act is divided into six articles. Article 1 contains general provisions. Article 2 contains provisions concerning the creation, revocation, and amendment of a power of appointment. Article 3 addresses the exercise of a power of appointment. Article 4 contains provisions on the disclaimer or release of a power of appointment and on contracts to appoint or not to appoint. Article 5 concerns the rights of the powerholder's creditors in appointive property. Article 6 contains miscellaneous provisions.

After each section, there is a detailed Comment. The Comments explain, and should be read in conjunction with, the statutory text. The Comments also provide information and guidance about best practices in creating and exercising powers of appointment.

[ARTICLE] 1
GENERAL PROVISIONS

§ 101. **Short Title.** This [act] may be cited as the Uniform Powers of Appointment Act.

§ 102. **Definitions.** In this [act]:

(1) "Appointee" means a person to which a powerholder makes an appointment of appointive property.

(2) "Appointive property" means the property or property interest subject to a power of appointment.

(3) "Blanket-exercise clause" means a clause in an instrument which exercises a power of appointment and is not a specific-exercise clause. The term includes a clause that:

(A) expressly uses the words "any power" in exercising any power of appointment the powerholder has;

(B) expressly uses the words "any property" in appointing any property over which the powerholder has a power of appointment; or

(C) disposes of all property subject to disposition by the powerholder.

(4) "Donor" means a person that creates a power of appointment.

(5) "Exclusionary power of appointment" means a power of appointment exercisable in favor of any one or more of the permissible appointees to the exclusion of the other permissible appointees.

(6) "General power of appointment" means a power of appointment exercisable in favor of the powerholder, the powerholder's estate, a creditor of the powerholder, or a creditor of the powerholder's estate.

(7) "Gift-in-default clause" means a clause identifying a taker in default of appointment.

(8) "Impermissible appointee" means a person that is not a permissible appointee.

(9) "Instrument" means a [writing][record].

(10) "Nongeneral power of appointment" means a power of appointment that is not a general power of appointment.

(11) "Permissible appointee" means a person in whose favor a powerholder may exercise a power of appointment.

(12) "Person" means an individual, estate, trust, business or nonprofit entity, public corporation, government or governmental subdivision, agency, or instrumentality, or other legal entity.

(13) "Power of appointment" means a power that enables a powerholder acting in a nonfiduciary capacity to designate a recipient of an ownership interest in or another power of appointment over the appointive property. The term does not include a power of attorney.

(14) "Powerholder" means a person in which a donor creates a power of appointment.

(15) "Presently exercisable power of appointment" means a power of appointment exercisable by the powerholder at the relevant time. The term:

(A) includes a power of appointment not exercisable until the occurrence of a specified event, the satisfaction of an ascertainable standard, or the passage of a specified time only after:

(i) the occurrence of the specified event;

(ii) the satisfaction of the ascertainable standard; or

(iii) the passage of the specified time; and

(B) does not include a power exercisable only at the powerholder's death.

(16) ["Record" means information that is inscribed on a tangible medium or that is stored in an electronic or other medium and is retrievable in perceivable form.]

(17) "Specific-exercise clause" means a clause in an instrument which specifically refers to and exercises a particular power of appointment.

(18) "Taker in default of appointment" means a person that takes all or part of the appointive property to the extent the powerholder does not effectively exercise the power of appointment.

(19) "Terms of the instrument" means the manifestation of the intent of the maker of the instrument regarding the instrument's provisions as expressed in the instrument or as may be established by other evidence that would be admissible in a legal proceeding.

Legislative Note: *A state should choose in paragraph (9) whether to define "instrument" as a writing or as a record. The choice will determine what kind of instruments may be used to create, revoke, amend, or exercise a power of appointment. If a state defines "instrument" as a record, the state should include the definition of "record" as paragraph (16).*

Comment

Paragraph (1) defines an appointee as the person to which a powerholder makes an appointment of appointive property. For the definition of the related term, "permissible appointee," see paragraph 11.

Paragraph (2) defines appointive property as the property or property interest subject to a power of appointment. The effective creation of a power of appointment requires that there be appointive property. See Section 201.

Paragraphs (3) and (17) introduce the distinction between blanket-exercise and specific-exercise clauses. A specific-exercise clause exercises and specifically refers to the particular power of appointment in question, using language such as the following: "I exercise the power of appointment conferred upon me by my father's will as follows: I appoint [fill in details of appointment]." In contrast, a blanket-exercise clause exercises "any" power of appointment the powerholder may have, appoints "any" property over which the powerholder may have a power of appointment, or disposes of all property subject to disposition by the powerholder. The use of specific-exercise clauses is encouraged; the use of blanket-exercise clauses is discouraged. See Section 301 and the accompanying Comment.

Paragraphs (4) and (14) define the donor and the powerholder. The donor is the person who created the power of appointment. The powerholder is the person in whom the power of appointment was conferred or in whom the power was reserved. The traditional, but potentially confusing, term for powerholder is "donee." See Restatement of Property § 319 (1940); Restatement Second of Property: Donative Transfers § 11.2 (1986); Restatement Third of Property: Wills and Other Donative Transfers § 17.2 (2011). In the case of a reserved power, the same person is both the donor and the powerholder.

Paragraph (5) introduces the distinction between exclusionary and nonexclusionary powers of appointment. An exclusionary power is one in which the donor has authorized the powerholder to appoint to any one or more of the permissible appointees to the exclusion of the other permissible appointees. For example, a power to appoint "to such of my descendants as the powerholder may select" is exclusionary, because the powerholder may appoint to any one or more of the donor's descendants to the exclusion of the other descendants. In contrast, a nonexclusionary power is one in which the powerholder cannot make an appointment that excludes any permissible appointee, or one or more designated permissible appointees, from a share of the appointive property. An example of a nonexclusionary power is a power "to appoint to all and every one of my children in such shares and proportions as the powerholder shall select." Here,

the powerholder is not under a duty to exercise the power; but, if the powerholder does exercise the power, the appointment must abide by the power's nonexclusionary nature. See Sections 301 and 305. An instrument creating a power of appointment is construed as creating an exclusionary power unless the terms of the instrument manifest a contrary intent. See Section 203. The typical power of appointment is exclusionary. And in fact, only a power of appointment whose permissible appointees are "defined and limited" can be nonexclusionary. For elaboration of the well-accepted term of art "defined and limited," see Section 205 and the accompanying Comment.

Paragraphs (6) and (10) explain the distinction between general and nongeneral powers of appointment. A general power of appointment enables the powerholder to exercise the power in favor of one or more of the following: the powerholder, the powerholder's estate, the creditors of the powerholder, or the creditors of the powerholder's estate, regardless of whether the power is also exercisable in favor of others. A nongeneral power of appointment — sometimes called a "special" power of appointment — cannot be exercised in favor of the powerholder, the powerholder's estate, the creditors of the powerholder, or the creditors of the powerholder's estate. Estate planners often classify nongeneral powers as being either "broad" or "limited," depending on the range of permissible appointees. A power to appoint to anyone in the world except the powerholder, the powerholder's estate, and the creditors of either would be an example of a broad nongeneral power. In contrast, a power in the donor's spouse to appoint among the donor's descendants would be an example of a limited nongeneral power.

An instrument creating a power of appointment is construed as creating a general power unless the terms of the instrument manifest a contrary intent. See Section 203. A power to revoke, amend, or withdraw is a general power of appointment if it is exercisable in favor of the powerholder, the powerholder's estate, or the creditors of either. If the settlor of a trust empowers a trustee or another person to change a power of appointment from a general power into a nongeneral power, or vice versa, the power is either general or nongeneral depending on the scope of the power at any particular time.

Paragraph (7) defines the gift-in-default clause. In an instrument creating a power of appointment, the clause that identifies the taker in default is called the gift-in-default clause. A gift-in-default clause is not mandatory but is included in a well-drafted instrument.

Paragraphs (8) and (11) explain the distinction between impermissible and permissible appointees. The permissible appointees — known at common law as the "objects" — of a power of appointment may be narrowly defined (for example, "to such of the powerholder's descendants as the powerholder may select"), broadly defined (for example, "to such persons as the powerholder may select, except the powerholder, the powerholder's estate, the powerholder's creditors, or the creditors of the powerholder's estate"), or unlimited (for example, "to such persons as the powerholder may select"). A permissible appointee of a power of appointment does not, in that capacity, have a property interest that can be transferred to another. Otherwise, a permissible appointee could transform an impermissible appointee into a permissible appointee, exceeding the intended scope of the power and thereby violating the donor's intent. An appointment cannot benefit an impermissible appointee. See Section 307.

Paragraph (9) defines the term "instrument" as either a writing or a record, depending on the choice made by the enacting jurisdiction. The drafting committee had no clear preference between the two options. Interestingly, there is no pre-existing Uniform Law definition of "instrument" outside the commercial context. See Uniform Commercial Code §§ 3-104(b), 9-102(a)(47). The term is used without definition in, for example, the Uniform Probate Code, the Uniform Trust Code, and the Uniform Power of Attorney Act.

Paragraphs (12) and (16) contain the definitions of "person" and "record". With one exception, these are standard definitions approved by the Uniform Law Commission. The exception is that the word "trust" has been added to the definition of "person". Trust law in the United States is moving in the direction of viewing the trust as an entity, see Restatement Third of Trusts Introductory Note to Chapter 21, but does not yet do so.

Paragraph (13) defines a power of appointment. A power of appointment is a power enabling the powerholder, acting in a nonfiduciary capacity, to designate recipients of ownership interests in or powers of appointment over the appointive property. (Powers held in a fiduciary capacity, such a trustee's power to "decant" property from one trust to another, are the subject of other uniform legislation.)

A power to revoke or amend a trust or a power to withdraw income or principal from a trust is a power of appointment, whether the power is reserved by the transferor or conferred on another. See Restatement Third of Trusts § 56, Comment b. A power to withdraw income or principal subject to an ascertainable standard is a postponed power, exercisable upon the satisfaction of the ascertainable standard. See the Comment to paragraph (15), below.

A power to direct a trustee to distribute income or principal to another is a power of appointment.

In this act, a fiduciary distributive power is not a power of appointment. Fiduciary distributive powers include a trustee's power to distribute principal to or for the benefit of an income beneficiary, or for some other individual, or to pay income or principal to a designated beneficiary, or to distribute income or principal among a defined group of beneficiaries. Unlike the exercise of a power of appointment, the exercise of a fiduciary distributive power is subject to fiduciary standards. Unlike a power of appointment, a fiduciary distributive power does not lapse upon the death of the fiduciary, but survives in a successor fiduciary. Nevertheless, a fiduciary distributive power, like a power of appointment, cannot be validly exercised in favor of or for the benefit of someone who is not a permissible appointee.

A power over the management of property, sometimes called an administrative power, is not a power of appointment. For example, a power of sale coupled with a power to invest the proceeds of the sale, as commonly held by a trustee of a trust, is not a power of appointment but is an administrative power. A power of sale merely authorizes the person to substitute money for the property sold but does not authorize the person to alter the beneficial interests in the substituted property.

A power to designate or replace a trustee or other fiduciary is not a power of appointment. A power to designate or replace a trustee or other fiduciary involves property management and is a power to designate only the nonbeneficial holder of property.

A power of attorney is not a power of appointment. See Restatement of Property § 318, Comment h: "A power of attorney, in the commonest sense of that term, creates the relationship of principal and agent ... and is terminated by the death of the [principal]. In both of these characteristics such a power differs from a power of appointment. The latter does not create an agency relationship and, except in the case of a power reserved in the donor, it is usually expected that it will be exercised after the donor's death." The distinction is carried forward in Restatement Third of Property: Wills and Other Donative Transfers § 17.1, Comment j. See also Uniform Power of Attorney Act §§ 102(7) (defining the holder of a power of attorney as an agent), 110(a)(1) (providing that the principal's death terminates a power of attorney).

A power to create or amend a beneficiary designation, for example with respect to the proceeds of a life insurance policy or of a pension plan, is not a power of appointment. An instrument creating a power of appointment must, among other things, transfer the appointive property. See Section 201; Restatement Third of Property: Wills and Other Donative Transfers § 18.1.

On the authority of a powerholder to exercise the power of appointment by creating a new power of appointment, see Section 305. If a powerholder exercises a power by creating another power, the powerholder of the first power is the donor of the second power, and the powerholder of the second power is the appointee of the first power.

Paragraph (15) introduces the distinctions among powers of appointment based upon when the power can be exercised. (A power is exercised when the instrument of exercise is effective. Thus, a power exercised by deed is exercised when the deed is effective. The law of deeds typically requires, among other things, intent, delivery, and acceptance. A power exercised by will is exercised when the will is effective – at the testator's death, not when the will is executed.)

There are three categories here: a power of appointment is presently exercisable, postponed, or testamentary.

A power of appointment is presently exercisable if it is exercisable at the time in question. Typically, a presently exercisable power of appointment is exercisable at the time in question during the powerholder's life and also at the powerholder's death, e.g., by the powerholder's will. Thus, a power of appointment that is exercisable "by deed or will" is a presently exercisable power. To take another example, a power of appointment exercisable by the powerholder's last unrevoked instrument in writing is a presently exercisable power, because the powerholder can make a present exercise irrevocable by explicitly so providing in the instrument exercising the power. See Restatement Third of Property: Wills and Other Donative Transfers § 17.4, Comment a.

A power of appointment is presently exercisable even though, at the time in question, the powerholder can only appoint an *interest* that is revocable or subject to a condition. For example, suppose that a trust directs the trustee to pay the income to the powerholder for life, then to distribute the principal by representation to the powerholder's surviving descendants. The trust further provides that, if the powerholder leaves no surviving descendants, the principal is to be distributed "to such individuals as the powerholder shall appoint." The powerholder has a presently exercisable power of appointment, but the appointive property is a remainder interest that is conditioned on the powerholder leaving no surviving descendants.

A power is a postponed power – sometimes known as a deferred power – if it is not yet exercisable until the occurrence of a specified event, the satisfaction of an ascertainable standard, or the passage of a specified time. A postponed power becomes presently exercisable upon the occurrence of the specified event, the satisfaction of the ascertainable standard, or the passage of the specified time. The second sentence in paragraph (15) is modeled on Uniform Power of Attorney Act § 102(8).

A power is testamentary if it is not exercisable during the powerholder's life but only in the powerholder's will or in a nontestamentary instrument that is functionally similar to the powerholder's will, such as the powerholder's revocable trust that remains revocable until the powerholder's death. On the ability of a powerholder to exercise a testamentary power of appointment in such a revocable trust, see Section 304 and the accompanying Comment. See also Restatement Third of Property: Wills and Other Donative Transfers § 19.9, Comment b.

Paragraph (18) defines a taker in default of appointment. A taker in default of appointment – often called the "taker in default" – has a property interest that can be transferred to another. If a taker in default transfers the interest to another, the transferee becomes a taker in default.

Paragraph (19) defines the "terms of the instrument" as the manifestation of the intent of the maker of the instrument regarding the instrument's provisions as expressed in the instrument or as may be established by other evidence that would be admissible in a legal proceeding. The maker of an instrument creating a power of appointment is the donor. The maker of an instrument exercising a power of appointment is the powerholder. This definition is a slightly modified version of the definition of "terms of a trust" in Uniform Trust

Code § 103(18).

The definitions in this section are substantially consistent with, and this Comment draws on, Restatement Third of Property: Wills and Other Donative Transfers §§ 17.1 to 17.5 and the accompanying Commentary.

§ 103. Governing Law.

Unless the terms of the instrument creating a power of appointment manifest a contrary intent:

(1) the creation, revocation, or amendment of the power is governed by the law of the donor's domicile at the relevant time; and

(2) the exercise, release, or disclaimer of the power, or the revocation or amendment of the exercise, release, or disclaimer of the power, is governed by the law of the powerholder's domicile at the relevant time.

Comment

This section provides default rules for determining the law governing the creation and exercise of, and related matters concerning, a power of appointment.

Unless the terms of the instrument creating the power provide otherwise, the actions of the donor – the creation, revocation, or amendment of the power – are governed by the law of the donor's domicile; and the actions of the powerholder – the exercise, release, or disclaimer, or the revocation or amendment thereof – are governed by the law of the powerholder's domicile.

In each case, the domicile is determined *at the relevant time*. For example, a donor's creation of a power is governed by the law of the donor's domicile at the time of the power's creation; and a donor's amendment of a power is governed by the law of the donor's domicile at the time of the amendment. Similarly, a powerholder's exercise of a power is governed by the law of the powerholder's domicile at the time of the exercise.

The standard "public policy" rules of choice of law naturally continue to apply. See, for example, Restatement Second of Conflict of Laws § 187.

Paragraph (2) is a departure from older law. The older position was that the law of the donor's domicile governs acts both of the donor (such as the creation of the power) and of the powerholder (such as the exercise of the power). *See, e.g., Beals v. State Street Bank & Trust Co.*, 326 N.E.2d 896 (Mass. 1975); *Bank of New York v. Black*, 139 A.2d 393 (N.J. 1958).

Paragraph (2) adopts the modern view that acts of the powerholder should be governed by the law of the powerholder's domicile, because that is the law the powerholder (or the powerholder's lawyer) is likely to know. This approach is supported by Restatement Third of Property: Wills and Other Donative Transfers § 19.1, Comment e; Restatement Second of Conflict of Laws § 275, Comment c. It is also supported by *Estate of McMullin*, 417 A.2d 152 (Pa. 1980); *White v. United States*, 680 F.2d 1156 (7th Cir. 1982).

See generally, Restatement Third of Property: Wills and Other Donative Transfers § 19.1, Comment e; Restatement Second of Conflict of Laws § 275, Comment c.

§ 104. Common Law and Principles of Equity.

The common law and principles of equity supplement this [act], except to the extent modified by this [act] or law of this state other than this [act].

Comment

This act codifies those portions of the law of powers of appointment that are most amenable to codification. The act is supplemented by the common law and principles of equity. To determine the common law and principles of equity in a particular state, a court might look first to prior case law in the state and to more general sources, such as the Restatement Third of Property: Wills and Other Donative Transfers. The common law is not static but includes the contemporary and evolving rules of decision developed by the courts in exercise of their power to adapt the law to new situations and changing conditions. It also includes the traditional and broad equitable jurisdiction of the court, which the act in no way restricts.

The statutory text of the act is also supplemented

by these Comments, which, like the Comments to any Uniform Act, may be relied on as a guide for interpretation. *See Stern Oil Co. v. Brown,* 817 N.W.2d 395 (S.D. 2012) (interpreting Uniform Commercial Code); *Isbell v. Commercial Investment Associates, Inc.,* 644 S.E.2d 72 (Va. 2007) (interpreting Uniform Residential Landlord Tenant Act); *Yale University v. Blumenthal,* 621 A.2d 1304, 1307 (Conn. 1993) (interpreting Uniform Management of Institutional Funds Act); *GMAC v. Anaya,* 703 P.2d 169, 172 (N.M. 1985) (interpreting Uniform Commercial Code and describing the Comments as "persuasive" though "not binding"); Jack Davies, Legislative Law and Process in a Nutshell § 59-4 (3d ed. 2007).

The text of and Comment to this section are based on Uniform Trust Code § 106 and its accompanying Comment.

[ARTICLE] 2
CREATION, REVOCATION, AND AMENDMENT OF POWER OF APPOINTMENT

§ 201. Creation of Power of Appointment.

(a) A power of appointment is created only if:

(1) the instrument creating the power:

(A) is valid under applicable law; and

(B) except as otherwise provided in subsection (b), transfers the appointive property; and

(2) the terms of the instrument creating the power manifest the donor's intent to create in a powerholder a power of appointment over the appointive property exercisable in favor of a permissible appointee.

(b) Subsection (a)(1)(B) does not apply to the creation of a power of appointment by the exercise of a power of appointment.

(c) A power of appointment may not be created in a deceased individual.

(d) Subject to an applicable rule against perpetuities, a power of appointment may be created in an unborn or unascertained powerholder.

Comment

An instrument can only create a power of appointment if, under applicable law, the instrument itself is valid (or partially valid, see the next paragraph). Thus, for example, a *will* creating a power of appointment must be valid under the law — including choice of law (see Section 103) — applicable to wills. An *inter vivos trust* creating a power of appointment must be valid under the law — including choice of law (see Section 103) — applicable to inter vivos trusts. In part, this requirement of validity means that the instrument must be properly executed to the extent other law imposes requirements of execution. In addition, the creator of the instrument must have the capacity to execute the instrument and be free from undue influence and other wrongdoing. On questions of capacity, see Restatement Third of Property: Wills and Other Donative Transfers §§ 8.1 (Mental Capacity) and 8.2 (Minority). On freedom from undue influence and other wrongdoing, see,

e.g., Restatement Third of Property §§ 8.3 (Undue Influence, Duress, or Fraud). The ability of an agent or guardian to create a power of appointment on behalf of a principal or ward is determined by other law, such as the Uniform Power of Attorney Act or the Uniform Guardianship and Protective Proceedings Act.

The instrument need not be entirely valid. A partially valid instrument creates a power of appointment if the provisions creating the power are valid.

In addition to being valid in the relevant provisions, an instrument creating a power of appointment must transfer the appointive property. The creation of a power of appointment — unlike the creation of a power of attorney — requires a transfer. See Restatement Third of Property: Wills and Other Donative Transfers § 18.1 ("A power of appointment is created by a transfer that manifests an intent to create a power of appointment."). The term "transfer" includes a declaration by an owner of property that the owner holds the property as trustee. Such a declaration necessarily entails a transfer of legal title from the owner-as-owner to the owner-as-trustee; it also entails a transfer of all or some of the equitable interests in the property from the owner to the trust's beneficiaries. See Restatement Third of Property: Wills and Other Donative Transfers § 7.1, Comment a.

The requirement of a transfer presupposes that the donor has the right to transfer the property. An ordinary individual cannot create a power of appointment over the Brooklyn Bridge. Less fancifully, a donor cannot create a power of appointment if doing so would circumvent a valid restriction on the transfer of the property. For example, interests in unincorporated business organizations may have transfer restrictions arising from statute, contract, or both. A donor cannot use the creation of a power of appointment to circumvent a valid restriction on transfer.

The one exception to the requirement of a transfer is stated in subsection (b): by necessity, the requirement of a transfer does not apply to the creation of a power of appointment by the exercise of a power of appointment. On the ability of a powerholder to exercise the power by creating a new power of appointment, see Section 305.

In addition to the aforementioned requirements, an instrument creating a power of appointment must manifest the donor's intent to create in one or more powerholders a power of appointment over appointive property. This manifestation of intent does not require the use of particular words or phrases (such as "power of appointment"), but careful drafting should leave no doubt about the transferor's intent.

Sometimes the instrument is poorly drafted, raising the question whether the donor intended to create a power of appointment. In such a case, determining the donor's intent is a process of construction. On construction generally, see Chapters 10, 11, and 12 of the Restatement Third of Property: Wills and Other Donative Transfers. See also, more specifically, Restatement Third of Property: Wills and Other Donative Transfers § 18.1, Comments b-g, containing many illustrations of language ambiguous about whether a power of appointment was intended and, for each illustration, offering guidance about how to construe the language.

The creation of a power of appointment requires

that there be a donor, a powerholder (who may be the same as the donor), and appointive property. There must also be one or more permissible appointees, though these need not be restricted; a powerholder can be authorized to appoint to anyone. A donor is not required to designate a taker in default of appointment, although a well-drafted instrument will specify one or more takers in default.

Subsection (c) states the well-accepted rule that a power of appointment cannot be created in an individual who is deceased. If the powerholder dies before the effective date of an instrument purporting to confer a power of appointment, the power is not created, and an attempted exercise of the power is ineffective. (The effective date of a power of appointment created in a donor's will is the donor's death, not when the donor executes the will. The effective date of a power of appointment created in a donor's inter vivos trust is the date the trust is established, even if the trust is revocable. See Restatement Third of Property: Wills and Other Donative Transfers § 19.11, Comments b and c.)

Nor is a power of appointment created if all the possible permissible appointees of the power are deceased when the transfer that is intended to create the power becomes legally operative. If all the possible permissible appointees of a power die after the power is created and before the powerholder exercises the power, the power terminates.

A power of appointment is not created if the permissible appointees are so indefinite that it is impossible to identify any person to whom the powerholder can appoint. If the description of the permissible appointees is such that one or more persons are identifiable, but it is not possible to determine whether other persons are within the description, the power is validly created, but an appointment can only be made to persons who can be identified as within the description of the permissible appointees.

Subsection (d) explains that a power of appointment can be conferred on an unborn or unascertained powerholder, subject to any applicable rule against perpetuities. This is a postponed power. The power arises on the powerholder's birth or ascertainment. The language creating the power as well as other factors such as the powerholder's capacity under applicable law determine whether the power is then presently exercisable, postponed, or testamentary.

The rules of this section are consistent with, and this Comment draws on, Restatement Third of

Property: Wills and Other Donative Transfers §§ 18.1   and 19.9 and the accompanying Commentary.

§ 202. Nontransferability. A powerholder may not transfer a power of appointment. If a powerholder dies without exercising or releasing a power, the power lapses.

Comment

A power of appointment is nontransferable. The powerholder may not transfer the power to another person. (On the ability of the powerholder to exercise the power by conferring on a permissible appointee a new power of appointment over the appointive property, see Section 305.) If the powerholder dies without exercising or releasing the power, the power lapses. (If a power is held by multiple powerholders, which is rare, on the death of one powerholder that individual's power lapses but the power continues to be held by the surviving powerholders.) If the powerholder partially releases the power and dies without exercising the remaining part, the unexercised part of the power lapses. The power does not pass through the powerholder's estate to the powerholder's successors in interest.

The ability of an agent or guardian to create, revoke, exercise, or revoke the exercise of a power of appointment on behalf of a principal or ward is determined by other law, such as the Uniform Power of Attorney Act or the Uniform Guardianship and Protective Proceedings Act.

The rule of this section is consistent with, and this Comment draws on, the Restatement Third of Property: Wills and Other Donative Transfers § 17.1, Comment b.

§ 203. Presumption of Unlimited Authority. Subject to Section 205, and unless the terms of the instrument creating a power of appointment manifest a contrary intent, the power is:

(1) presently exercisable;

(2) exclusionary; and

(3) except as otherwise provided in Section 204, general.

Comment

In determining which type of power of appointment is created, the general principle of construction, articulated in this section, is that a power falls into the category giving the powerholder the maximum discretionary authority except to the extent the terms of the instrument creating the power restrict the powerholder's authority. Maximum discretion confers on the powerholder the flexibility to alter the donor's disposition in response to changing conditions.

In accordance with this presumption of unlimited authority, a power is general unless the terms of the creating instrument specify that the powerholder cannot exercise the power in favor of the powerholder, the powerholder's estate, or the creditors of either. A power is presently exercisable unless the terms of the creating instrument specify that the power can only be exercised at some later time or in some document such as a will that only takes effect at some later time. A power is exclusionary unless the terms of the creating instrument specify that a permissible appointee must receive a certain amount or portion of the appointive assets if the power is exercised.

This general principle of construction applies, unless the terms of the instrument creating the power of appointment provide otherwise. A well-drafted instrument intended to create a nongeneral or testamentary or nonexclusionary power will use clear language to achieve the desired objective. Not all instruments are well-drafted, however. A court may have to construe the terms of the instrument to discern the donor's intent. For principles of construction applicable to the creation of a power of appointment, see Restatement Third of Property: Wills and Other Donative Transfers Chapters 17 and 18, and the accompanying Commentary, containing many examples.

§ 204. Exception to Presumption of Unlimited Authority. Unless the terms of the instrument creating a power of appointment manifest a contrary intent, the power is nongeneral if:

(1) the power is exercisable only at the powerholder's death; and

(2) the permissible appointees of the power are a defined and limited class that does not include the powerholder's estate, the powerholder's creditors, or the creditors of the powerholder's estate.

Comment

This section is designed to remedy a recurring drafting mistake. A testamentary power of appointment created in a defined and limited class that happens to include the powerholder is usually intended to be a nongeneral power. For example, a testamentary power created in one of the donor's descendants (such as the donor's child or grandchild) to appoint among the donor's "descendants" or "issue" is typically intended to be a nongeneral power. See, for example, PLR 201229005 (stating the ruling

of the Internal Revenue Service that a testamentary power of appointment in the donor's son, exercisable in favor of the donor's "issue," is a nongeneral power for purposes of 26 U.S.C. § 2041). Accordingly, the presumption of this Section is that such a power is nongeneral.

On the meaning of the well-accepted term of art "defined and limited," see the Comment to Section 205. See also Restatement Third of Property: Wills and Other Donative Transfers § 17.5, Comment c.

§ 205. Rules of Classification.

(a) In this section, "adverse party" means a person with a substantial beneficial interest in property which would be affected adversely by a powerholder's exercise or nonexercise of a power of appointment in favor of the powerholder, the powerholder's estate, a creditor of the powerholder, or a creditor of the powerholder's estate.

(b) If a powerholder may exercise a power of appointment only with the consent or joinder of an adverse party, the power is nongeneral.

(c) If the permissible appointees of a power of appointment are not defined and limited, the power is exclusionary.

Comment

Subsection (b) states a well-accepted and mandatory exception to the presumption of unlimited authority articulated in Section 203. If a power of appointment can be exercised only with the consent or joinder of an adverse party, the power is not a general power. An adverse party is an individual who has a substantial beneficial interest in the trust or other property arrangement that would be adversely affected by the exercise or nonexercise of the power in favor of the powerholder, the powerholder's estate, or the creditors of either. In this context, the word "substantial" is not subject to precise definition but must be determined in light of all the facts and circumstances. Consider the following examples.

Example 1. D transferred property in trust, directing the trustee "to pay the income to D's son S for life, remainder in corpus to such person or persons as S, with the joinder of X, shall appoint; in default of appointment, remainder to X." S's power is not a general power because X meets the definition of an adverse party.

Example 2. Same facts as Example 1, except that S's power is exercisable with the joinder of Y rather than with the joinder of X. Y has no property interest that

could be adversely affected by the exercise of the power. Because Y is not an adverse party, S's power is general.

Whether the party whose consent or joinder is required is adverse or not is determined at the time in question. Consider the following example.

Example 3. Same facts as Example 2, except that, one month after D's creation of the trust, X transfers the remainder interest to Y. Before the transfer, Y is not an adverse party and S's power is general. After the transfer, Y is an adverse party and S's power is nongeneral.

Subsection (c) also states a longstanding mandatory rule. Only a power of appointment whose permissible appointees are defined and limited can be nonexclusionary. "Defined and limited" in this context is a well-accepted term of art. For elaboration and examples, see Restatement Third of Property: Wills and Other Donative Transfers § 17.5, Comment c. In general, permissible appointees are "defined and limited" if they are defined and limited to a reasonable number. Typically, permissible appointees who are defined and limited are described in class-gift terms: a single-generation class such as "children," "grandchildren," "brothers and sisters," or "nieces and nephews," or a multiple-generation class such as "issue" or "descendants" or "heirs." Permissible appointees need not be described in class-gift terms to be defined and limited, however. The permissible appointees are also defined and limited if one or more permissible appointees are designated by name or otherwise individually identified.

If the permissible appointees are not defined and limited, the power is exclusionary irrespective of the donor's intent. A power exercisable, for example, in favor of "such person or persons other than the powerholder, the powerholder's estate, the creditors of the powerholder, and the creditors of the powerholder's estate" is an exclusionary power. An attempt by the donor to require the powerholder to appoint at least $X to each permissible appointee of the power is ineffective, because the permissible appointees of the power are so numerous that it would be administratively impossible to carry out the donor's expressed intent. The donor's expressed restriction is disregarded, and the powerholder may exclude any one or more of the permissible appointees in exercising the power.

In contrast, a power to appoint only to the powerholder's creditors or to the creditors of the powerholder's estate is a power in favor of a defined and limited class. Such a power could be nonexclusionary if, for example, the terms of the instrument creating the power provide that the power is a power to appoint "to such of the powerholder's estate creditors as the powerholder shall by will appoint, but if the powerholder exercises the power,

the powerholder must appoint $X to a designated estate creditor or must appoint in full satisfaction of the powerholder's debt to a designated estate creditor."

If a power is determined to be nonexclusionary, it is to be inferred that the donor intends to require an appointment to confer a reasonable benefit upon each mandatory appointee. An appointment under which a mandatory appointee receives nothing, or only a nominal sum, violates this requirement and is forbidden. This doctrine is known as the doctrine forbidding illusory appointments. For elaboration, see Restatement Third of Property: Wills and Other Donative Transfers § 17.5, Comment j.

The terms of the instrument creating a power of appointment sometimes provide that no appointee shall receive any share in default of appointment unless the appointee consents to allow the amount of the appointment to be taken into account in calculating the fund to be distributed in default of appointment. This "hotchpot" language is used to minimize unintended inequalities of distribution among permissible appointees. Such a clause does not make the power nonexclusionary, because the terms do not prevent the powerholder from making an appointment that excludes a permissible appointee. See Restatement Third of Property: Wills and Other Donative Transfers § 17.5, Comment k.

The rules of this section are consistent with, and this Comment draws on, Restatement Third of Property: Wills and Other Donative Transfers §§ 17.3 to 17.5 and the accompanying Introductory Note and Commentary.

§ 206. Power to Revoke or Amend.

A donor may revoke or amend a power of appointment only to the extent that:

(1) the instrument creating the power is revocable by the donor; or

(2) the donor reserves a power of revocation or amendment in the instrument creating the power of appointment.

Comment

The donor of a power of appointment has the authority to revoke or amend the power only to the extent the instrument creating the power is revocable by the donor or the donor reserves a power of revocation or amendment in the instrument creating the power.

For example, the donor's power to revoke or amend a revocable inter vivos trust carries with it the authority to revoke or amend any power of appointment created in the trust. However, to the

extent an exercise of the power removes appointive property from the trust, the donor's authority to revoke or amend the power is eliminated, unless the donor expressly reserved authority to revoke or amend any transfer from the trust after the transfer is completed.

If an irrevocable inter vivos trust confers a presently exercisable power on someone who is not the settlor of the trust (the settlor being the donor of the power), the donor lacks authority to revoke or amend the power, except to the extent the donor reserved the authority to do so. If the donor did reserve the authority to revoke or amend the power, that authority is only effective until the powerholder irrevocably exercises the power.

If the same individual is both the donor and the powerholder, the donor in his or her capacity as powerholder can indirectly revoke or amend the power by a partial or total release of the power. See Section 402. After the power has been irrevocably exercised, however, the donor as donor is in no different position in regard to revoking or amending the exercise of the power than the donor would be if the donor and powerholder were different

individuals.

The ability of an agent or guardian to revoke or amend a power of appointment on behalf of a principal or ward is determined by other law, such as the Uniform Power of Attorney Act or the Uniform Guardianship and Protective Proceedings Act.

Other law of the state may permit the reformation of an otherwise irrevocable instrument. See, for example, Uniform Probate Code § 2-805; Uniform Trust Code § 415.

The rule of this section is consistent with, and this Comment draws on, Restatement Third of Property: Wills and Other Donative Transfers § 18.2 and the accompanying Commentary.

[ARTICLE] 3
EXERCISE OF POWER OF APPOINTMENT

§ 301. Requisites for Exercise of Power of Appointment. A power of appointment is exercised only:

(1) if the instrument exercising the power is valid under applicable law;

(2) if the terms of the instrument exercising the power:

    (A) manifest the powerholder's intent to exercise the power; and

    (B) subject to Section 304, satisfy the requirements of exercise, if any, imposed by the donor; and

(3) to the extent the appointment is a permissible exercise of the power.

Comment

Paragraph (1) states the fundamental principle that an instrument can only exercise a power of appointment if the instrument, under applicable law, is valid (or partially valid, see the next paragraph). Thus, for example, a *will* exercising a power of appointment must be valid under the law – including choice of law (see Section 103) – applicable to wills. An *inter vivos trust* exercising a power of appointment must be valid under the law – including choice of law (see Section 103) – applicable to inter vivos trusts. In part, this means that the instrument must be properly executed to the extent other law imposes requirements of execution. In addition, the creator of the instrument must have the capacity to execute the instrument and be free from undue influence and other wrongdoing. On questions of capacity, see Restatement Third of Property: Wills and Other Donative Transfers §§ 8.1 (Mental Capacity) and 8.2 (Minority). On freedom from undue influence and other wrongdoing, see, e.g., Restatement Third of Property §§ 8.3 (Undue Influence, Duress, or Fraud). The ability of an agent or guardian to exercise a

power of appointment on behalf of a principal or ward is determined by other law, such as the Uniform Power of Attorney Act or the Uniform Guardianship and Protective Proceedings Act.

The instrument need not be entirely valid. A partially valid instrument can exercise a power of appointment if the provisions exercising the power are valid.

Paragraph (2) requires the terms of the instrument exercising the power of appointment to manifest the powerholder's intent to exercise the power of appointment. Whether a powerholder has manifested an intent to exercise a power of appointment is a question of construction. See generally Restatement Third of Property: Wills and Other Donative Transfers § 19.2. For example, a powerholder's disposition of appointive property may manifest an intent to exercise the power even though the powerholder does not refer to the power. See Restatement Third of Property: Wills and Other Donative Transfers § 19.3. Paragraph (2) also requires that the terms of the instrument exercising the power must, subject to Section 304, satisfy the requirements of exercise, if any, imposed by the donor.

Language expressing an intent to exercise a power is clearest if it makes a specific reference to the creating instrument and exercises the power in unequivocal terms and with careful attention to the requirements of exercise, if any, imposed by the donor.

The recommended method for exercising a power of appointment is by a specific-exercise clause, using language such as the following: "I exercise the power of appointment conferred upon me by [my father's will] as follows: I appoint [fill in details of appointment]."

Not recommended is a blanket-exercise clause, which purports to exercise "any" power of appointment the powerholder may have, using language such as the following: "I exercise any power of appointment I may have as follows: I appoint [fill in details of appointment]." Although a blanket-exercise clause does manifest an intent to exercise any power of appointment the powerholder may have, such a clause raises the often-litigated question of whether it satisfies the requirement of specific reference imposed by the donor in the instrument creating the power.

A blending clause purports to blend the appointive property with the powerholder's own property in a common disposition. The exercise portion of a blending clause can take the form of a specific exercise or, more commonly, a blanket exercise. For example, a clause providing "All the residue of my estate, including the property over which I have a power of appointment under my mother's will, I devise as follows" is a blending clause with a specific exercise. A clause providing "All the residue of my estate, including any property over which I may have a power of appointment, I devise as follows" is a blending clause with a blanket exercise.

This act aims to eliminate any significance attached to the use of a blending clause. A blending clause has traditionally been regarded as significant in the application of the doctrines of "selective allocation" and "capture." This act eliminates the significance of such a clause under those doctrines. See Sections 308 (selective allocation) and 309 (capture). The use of a blending clause is more likely to be the product of the forms used by the powerholder's lawyer than a deliberate decision by the powerholder to facilitate the application of the doctrines of selective allocation or capture.

If the powerholder decides not to exercise a specific power or any power that the powerholder might have, it is important to consider whether to depend on mere silence to produce a nonexercise or to take definitive action to assure a nonexercise. Definitive action can take the form of a release during life (see Section 402) or a nonexercise clause in the powerholder's will or other relevant instrument. A nonexercise clause can take the form of a specific-nonexercise clause (for example, "I do not exercise the power of appointment conferred on me by my father's trust") or the form of a blanket-nonexercise clause (for example, "I do not exercise any power of appointment I may have").

In certain circumstances, different consequences depend on the powerholder's choice. Under Section 302, a residuary clause in the powerholder's will is treated as manifesting an intent to exercise a general power in certain limited circumstances if the powerholder silently failed to exercise the power, but not if the powerholder released the power or refrained in a record from exercising it. Under Section 310, unappointed property passes to the powerholder's estate in certain limited circumstances if the powerholder silently failed to exercise a general power, but passes to the donor or to the donor's successors in interest if the powerholder released the power.

Paragraph (3) provides that the exercise is valid only to the extent the exercise is permissible. On permissible and impermissible exercise, see Sections 305 to 307.

The rule of this section is consistent with, and this Comment draws on, Restatement Third of Property: Wills and Other Donative Transfers §§ 19.1, 19.8, and 19.9 and the accompanying Commentary.

§ 302. Intent to Exercise: Determining Intent from Residuary Clause.

(a) In this section:

(1) "Residuary clause" does not include a residuary clause containing a blanket-exercise clause or a specific-exercise clause.

(2) "Will" includes a codicil and a testamentary instrument that revises another will.

(b) A residuary clause in a powerholder's will, or a comparable clause in the powerholder's revocable trust, manifests the powerholder's intent to exercise a power of appointment only if:

(1) the terms of the instrument containing the residuary clause do not manifest a contrary intent;

(2) the power is a general power exercisable in favor of the powerholder's estate;

(3) there is no gift-in-default clause or the clause is ineffective; and

(4) the powerholder did not release the power.

Comment

This section addresses a question arising under Section 301(2)(A) — namely, whether the powerholder's intent to exercise a power of appointment is manifested by a garden-variety residuary clause such as "All the residue of my estate, I devise to ..." or "All of my estate, I devise to ...." (The section also applies to a comparable provision in the powerholder's revocable trust, such as a provision providing for the distribution of the trust corpus.) This section does not address the effect of a residuary clause that contains a blanket exercise or a specific exercise of a power of appointment. On blanket-exercise and specific-exercise clauses, see the Comment to Section 301.

The rule of this section is that *in most circumstances* a garden-variety residuary clause does *not* manifest an intent to exercise a power of appointment.

Such a clause manifests an intent to exercise a power of appointment only in the rare circumstance when (1) the terms of the instrument containing the residuary clause do not manifest a contrary intent, (2) the power in question is a general power exercisable in favor of the powerholder's estate, (3) there is no gift-in-default clause or it is ineffective, and (4) the powerholder did not release the power.

In a well-planned estate, a power of appointment, whether general or nongeneral, is accompanied by a gift in default. In a less carefully planned estate, on the other hand, there may be no gift-in-default clause. Or, if there is such a clause, the clause may be wholly or partly ineffective. To the extent the donor did not provide for takers in default or the gift-in-default clause is ineffective, it is more efficient to attribute to the powerholder the intent to exercise a general power in favor of the powerholder's residuary devisees. The principal benefit of attributing to the powerholder the intent to exercise a general power is that it allows the property to pass under the powerholder's will instead of as part of the donor's estate. Because the donor's death would normally have occurred before the powerholder died, some of the donor's successors might themselves have predeceased the powerholder. It is more efficient to avoid tracing the interest through multiple estates to determine who are the present successors. Moreover, to the extent the donor did not provide for takers in default, it is also more in accord with the donor's probable intent for the powerholder's residuary clause to be treated as exercising the power.

A gift-in-default clause can be ineffective or partially ineffective for a variety of reasons. The clause might cover only part of the appointive property. The clause might be invalid because it violates a rule against perpetuities or some other rule, or it might be ineffective because it conditioned the interest of the takers in default on an uncertain event that did not happen, the most common of which is an unsatisfied condition of survival.

Under no circumstance does a residuary clause manifest an intent to exercise a *nongeneral* power. A residuary clause disposes of the powerholder's own property, and a nongeneral power is not an ownership-equivalent power. Similarly, a residuary clause does not manifest an intent to exercise a general power which is general only because it is exercisable in favor of the creditors of the powerholder or the creditors of the powerholder's estate.

The rule of this section is consistent with, and this Comment draws on, Restatement Third of Property: Wills and Other Donative Transfers § 19.4 and the accompanying Commentary.

§ 303. Intent to Exercise: After-Acquired Power. Unless the terms of the instrument exercising a power of appointment manifest a contrary intent:

(1) except as otherwise provided in paragraph (2), a blanket-exercise clause extends to a power acquired by the powerholder after executing the instrument containing the clause; and

(2) if the powerholder is also the donor of the power, the clause does not extend to the power unless there is no gift-in-default clause or the gift-in-default clause is ineffective.

Comment

Nothing in the law prevents a powerholder from exercising an after-acquired power – in other words, from exercising a power in an instrument executed before acquiring the power. The only question is one of construction: whether the powerholder *intended* by the earlier instrument to exercise the after-acquired power. (The term "after-acquired power" in this section refers only to an after-acquired power acquired before the powerholder's death. A power of appointment cannot be conferred on a deceased powerholder. See Section 201.)

If the instrument of exercise specifically identifies the power to be exercised, then the question of construction is readily answered: the specific-exercise clause expresses an intent to exercise the power, whether the power is after-acquired or not. However, if the instrument of exercise uses only a *blanket-exercise clause*, the question of whether the powerholder intended to exercise an after-acquired power is often harder to answer. The presumptions in this section provide default rules of construction on the powerholder's likely intent.

Paragraph (1) states the general rule of this section. Unless the terms of the instrument indicate that the powerholder had a different intent, a blanket-exercise clause extends to a power of appointment acquired after the powerholder executed the instrument containing the blanket-exercise clause. General references to then-present circumstances, such as "all the powers I have" or similar expressions, are not a sufficient indication of an intent to exclude an after-acquired power. In contrast, more precise language,

such as "all powers I have at the date of execution of this will," does indicate an intent to exclude an after-acquired power.

It is important to remember that even if the terms of the instrument manifest an intent to exercise an after-acquired power, the intent may be ineffective, for example if the terms of the *donor's* instrument creating the power manifest an intent to preclude such an exercise. In the absence of an indication to the contrary, however, it is inferred that the time of the execution of the powerholder's exercising instrument is immaterial to the donor. Even if the donor declares that the property shall pass to such persons as the powerholder "shall" or "may" appoint, these terms do not suffice to indicate an intent to exclude exercise by an instrument previously executed, because these words may be construed to refer to the time when the exercising document becomes effective.

Paragraph (2) states an exception to the general rule of paragraph (1). If the powerholder is also the donor, a blanket-exercise clause in a preexisting instrument is rebuttably presumed *not* to manifest an intent to exercise a power later reserved in another donative transfer, unless the donor/powerholder did not provide for a taker in default of appointment or the gift-in-default clause is ineffective.

The black-letter of this section is consistent with, and this Comment draws on, Restatement Third of Property: Wills and Other Donative Transfers § 19.6 and the accompanying Commentary.

§ 304. Substantial Compliance with Donor-Imposed Formal Requirement. A powerholder's substantial compliance with a formal requirement of appointment imposed by the donor, including a requirement that the instrument exercising the power of appointment make reference or specific reference to the power, is sufficient if:

(1) the powerholder knows of and intends to exercise the power; and

(2) the powerholder's manner of attempted exercise of the power does not impair a material purpose of the donor in imposing the requirement.

Comment

This section adopts a substantial-compliance rule for donor-imposed formal requirements. This section only applies to formal requirements imposed *by the donor*. It does not apply to formal requirements imposed by law, such as the requirement that a will must be signed and attested. The section also does not apply to *substantive* requirements imposed by the donor, for example a requirement that the

powerholder attain a certain age before the power is exercisable.

Whenever the donor imposes formal requirements with respect to the instrument of appointment that exceed the requirements imposed by law, the donor's purpose in imposing the additional requirements is relevant to whether the powerholder's attempted exercise satisfies the rule of this section. To the extent the powerholder's failure to comply with the additional requirements will not impair the accomplishment of a material purpose of the donor, the powerholder's attempted appointment in a manner that substantially complies with a donor-imposed requirement does not fail for lack of perfect compliance with that requirement.

For example, a donor's formal requirement that the power of appointment is exercisable "by will" may be satisfied by the powerholder's attempted exercise in a nontestamentary instrument that is functionally similar to a will, such as the powerholder's revocable trust that remains revocable until the powerholder's death. See Restatement Third of Property: Wills and Other Donative Transfers § 19.9, Comment b ("Because a revocable trust operates in substance as a will, a power of appointment exercisable "by will" can be exercised in a revocable-trust document, as long as the revocable trust remained revocable at the [powerholder]'s death.").

A formal requirement commonly imposed by the donor is that, in order to be effective, the powerholder's attempted exercise must make specific reference to the power. Specific-reference clauses were a pre-1942 invention designed to prevent an inadvertent exercise of a general power. The federal estate tax law then provided that the value of property subject to a general power was included in the powerholder's gross estate if the general power was exercised. The idea of requiring specific reference was designed to thwart unintended exercise and, hence, estate taxation.

The federal estate tax law has changed. For a general power created after October 21, 1942, estate tax consequences do not depend on whether the power is exercised.

Nevertheless, donors continue to impose specific-reference requirements. Because the original purpose of the specific-reference requirement was to prevent an inadvertent exercise of the power, it seems reasonable to presume that that this is still the donor's purpose in doing so. Consequently, a specific-reference requirement still overrides any applicable state law that presumes that an ordinary residuary clause was intended to exercise a general power. Put differently: An ordinary residuary clause may manifest the powerholder's *intent to exercise* (under Section 301(2)(A)) but does not satisfy the *requirements of exercise* if the donor imposed a specific-reference requirement (this section and Section 301(2)(B)).

A more difficult question is whether a *blanket-exercise clause* satisfies a specific-reference requirement. If it could be shown that the powerholder had knowledge of and intended to exercise the power, the blanket-exercise clause would be sufficient to exercise the power, unless it could be shown that the donor's intent was not merely to prevent an inadvertent exercise of the power but instead that the donor had a material purpose in insisting on the specific-reference requirement. In such a case, the possibility of applying Uniform Probate Code § 2-805 or Restatement Third of Property: Wills and Other Donative Transfers § 12.1 to reform the powerholder's attempted appointment to insert the required specific reference should be explored.

This rule of this section is consistent with, but an elaboration of, Uniform Probate Code § 2-704: "If a governing instrument creating a power of appointment expressly requires that the power be exercised by a reference, an express reference, or a specific reference, to the power or its source, it is presumed that the donor's intent, in requiring that the [powerholder] exercise the power by making reference to the particular power or to the creating instrument, was to prevent an inadvertent exercise of the power."

The rule of this section is consistent with, and this Comment draws on, Restatement Third of Property: Wills and Other Donative Transfers § 19.10 and the accompanying Commentary.

§ 305. Permissible Appointment.

(a) A powerholder of a general power of appointment that permits appointment to the powerholder or the powerholder's estate may make any appointment, including an appointment in trust or creating a new power of appointment, that the powerholder could make in disposing of the powerholder's own property.

(b) A powerholder of a general power of appointment that permits appointment only to the creditors of the powerholder or of the powerholder's estate may appoint only to those creditors.

(c) Unless the terms of the instrument creating a power of appointment manifest a contrary intent, the powerholder of a nongeneral power may:

(1) make an appointment in any form, including an appointment in trust, in favor of a permissible appointee;

(2) create a general power in a permissible appointee; or

(3) create a nongeneral power in any person to appoint to one or more of the permissible appointees of the original nongeneral power.

Comment

When a donor creates a general power under which an appointment can be made outright to the powerholder or the powerholder's estate, the necessary implication is that the powerholder may accomplish by an appointment to others whatever the powerholder could accomplish by first appointing to himself and then disposing of the property, including a disposition in trust or in the creation of a further power of appointment.

A general power to appoint only to the powerholder (even though it says "and to no one else") does not prevent the powerholder from exercising the power in favor of others. There is no reason to require the powerholder to transform the appointive assets into owned property and then, in a second step, to dispose of the owned property. Likewise, a general power to appoint only to the powerholder's estate (even though it says "and to no one else") does not prevent an exercise of the power by will in favor of others. There is no reason to require the powerholder to transform the appointive assets into estate property and then, in a second step, to dispose of the estate property by will.

Similarly, a general power to appoint to the powerholder may purport to allow only one exercise of the power, but such a restriction is ineffective and does not prevent multiple partial exercises of the power. To take another example, a general power to appoint to the powerholder or to the powerholder's estate may purport to restrict appointment to outright interests not in trust, but such a restriction is ineffective and does not prevent an appointment in trust.

An additional example will drive home the point. A general power to appoint to the powerholder or to the powerholder's estate may purport to forbid the powerholder from imposing conditions on the enjoyment of the property by the appointee. Such a restriction is ineffective and does not prevent an appointment subject to such conditions.

As stated in subsection (b), however, a general power to appoint only to the powerholder's creditors or the creditors of the powerholder's estate permits an appointment only to those creditors.

Except to the extent the terms of the instrument creating the power manifest a contrary intent, the powerholder of a nongeneral power has the same breadth of discretion in appointment to permissible appointees that the powerholder has in the disposition of the powerholder's owned property to permissible appointees of the power.

Thus, unless the terms of the instrument creating the power manifest a contrary intent, the powerholder of a nongeneral power has the authority to exercise the power by an appointment in trust. In order to manifest a contrary intent, the terms of the instrument creating the power must specifically prohibit an appointment in trust. So, for example, a power to appoint "to" the powerholder's descendants includes the authority to appoint in trust for the benefit of one or more of those descendants.

Similarly, unless the terms of the instrument creating the power manifest a contrary intent, the powerholder of a nongeneral power has the authority to exercise the power by creating a general power in a permissible appointee. The rationale for this rule is a straightforward application of the maxim that the greater includes the lesser. A powerholder of a nongeneral power may appoint outright to a permissible appointee, so the powerholder may instead create in a permissible appointee a general power.

And finally, unless the terms of the instrument creating the power manifest a contrary intent, the powerholder of a nongeneral power may exercise the power by creating a new nongeneral power in *any* person, whether or not a permissible appointee, to appoint to some or all of the permissible appointees of the original nongeneral power. In order to manifest a contrary intent, the terms of the instrument creating the power must prohibit the creation of such powers. Language merely conferring the power of appointment on the powerholder does not suffice.

The rules of subsection (c) are default rules. The terms of the instrument creating the power may manifest a contrary intent. For example, a donor may choose to loosen the restriction in subsection (c)(3) by authorizing the powerholder of a nongeneral power to create a new nongeneral power with broader permissible appointees. Consider the following examples.

Example 1. D creates a nongeneral power in D's child, P1, to appoint among D's descendants. Under the default rule of subsection (c)(3), P1 may exercise this power to create a new nongeneral power in D's child, P2. Unless the terms of D's instrument manifest a contrary intent, however, the permissible appointees of P2's nongeneral power cannot be broader than the permissible appointees of P1's nongeneral power.

Example 2. Same facts as in Example 1, except that D's instrument states: "The nongeneral power of appointment granted to P1 may be exercised to create in one or more of my descendants a new nongeneral power. This new nongeneral power may have permissible appointees as broad as P1 sees fit." On these facts, the default rule of subsection (c)(3) is overridden by the terms of D's instrument. The permissible appointees of P2's nongeneral power may be broader than the permissible appointees of P1's nongeneral power.

The rules of this section are consistent with, and this Comment draws on, Restatement Third of Property: Wills and Other Donative Transfers §§ 19.13 and 19.14 and the accompanying Commentary.

§ 306. Appointment to Deceased Appointee or Permissible Appointee's Descendant.

(a) [Subject to [refer to state law on antilapse], an] [An] appointment to a deceased appointee is ineffective.

(b) Unless the terms of the instrument creating a power of appointment manifest a contrary intent, a powerholder of a nongeneral power may exercise the power in favor of, or create a new power of appointment in, a descendant of a deceased permissible appointee whether or not the descendant is described by the donor as a permissible appointee.

Legislative Note: A state that has extended antilapse protection to appointees should include the opening clause of subsection (a) ("Subject to..."). A state that has not extended antilapse protection to appointees is strongly encouraged to do so. See, e.g., Uniform Probate Code Sections 2-603(a)(5), 2-603(a)(6), and 2-707(a)(7).

Comment

Just as property cannot be transferred to an individual who is deceased (see Restatement Third of Property: Wills and Other Donative Transfers § 1.2), a power of appointment cannot be effectively exercised in favor of a deceased appointee.

However, an antilapse statute may apply to trigger the substitution of the deceased appointee's descendants (or other substitute takers), unless the terms of the instrument creating or exercising the power of appointment manifest a contrary intent. Antilapse statutes typically provide, as a default rule of construction, that devises to certain relatives who predecease the testator pass instead to specified substitute takers, usually the descendants of the predeceased devisee who survive the testator. See generally Restatement Third of Property: Wills and Other Donative Transfers § 5.5.

When an antilapse statute does not expressly address whether it applies to the exercise of a power of appointment, a court should construe it to apply to such an exercise. See Restatement Third of Property: Wills and Other Donative Transfers § 5.5, Comment

l. The rationale underlying antilapse statutes, that of presumptively attributing to the testator the intent to substitute the descendants of a predeceased devisee, applies equally to the exercise of a power of appointment.

The substitute takers provided by an antilapse statute (typically the descendants of the deceased appointee) are treated as permissible appointees even if the description of permissible appointees provided by the donor does not expressly cover them. This rule corresponds to the rule applying antilapse statutes to class gifts. Antilapse statutes substitute the descendants of deceased class members, even if the class member's descendants are not members of the class. See Restatement Third of Property: Wills and Other Donative Transfers § 19.12, Comment e.

The donor of a power, general or nongeneral, can prohibit the application of an antilapse statute to the powerholder's appointment and, in the case of a nongeneral power, can prohibit an appointment to the descendants of a deceased permissible appointee, but must manifest an intent to do so in the terms of the instrument creating the power of appointment. A traditional gift-in-default clause does not manifest a contrary intent in either case, unless the clause provides that it is to take effect instead of the descendants of a deceased permissible appointee.

Subsection (b) provides that the descendants of a deceased permissible appointee are treated as permissible appointees of a nongeneral power of appointment. This rule is a logical extension of the application of antilapse statutes to appointments. If an antilapse statute can substitute the descendants of a deceased appointee, the powerholder should be allowed to appoint in favor of, or to create a new power of appointment in, a descendant (meaning, one or more descendants; the Uniform Law Commission uses the singular to include the plural) of a deceased permissible appointee.

Who qualifies as a "descendant" is defined by state law. See, for example, Uniform Probate Code §§ 1-201(9), 2-103, 2-115 to 2-122, 2-705.

The rule of this section is consistent with, and this Comment draws on, Restatement Third of Property: Wills and Other Donative Transfers § 19.12 and the accompanying Commentary.

§ 307. Impermissible Appointment.

(a) Except as otherwise provided in Section 306, an exercise of a power of appointment in favor of an impermissible appointee is ineffective.

(b) An exercise of a power of appointment in favor of a permissible appointee is ineffective to the extent the appointment is a fraud on the power.

Comment

The rules of this section apply to the extent the powerholder attempts to confer a beneficial interest in the appointive property on an impermissible appointee. For example, a nongeneral power may not be exercised in favor of the powerholder. And a nongeneral power in favor of the donor's descendants may not be exercised in favor of the donor's spouse (assuming the usual scenario wherein the spouse is not also a descendant).

To the extent an appointment is ineffective, it is invalid. But it bears emphasizing that an appointment that is partially valid remains partially valid. Partial invalidity does not doom the entire appointment.

The rules of this section do not apply to an appointment of a *non*beneficial interest — for example, the appointment of legal title to a trustee — if the beneficial interest is held by permissible appointees.

Nor do the rules of this section prohibit beneficial appointment to an impermissible appointee if the intent to benefit the impermissible appointee is not the powerholder's but rather is the intent of a permissible appointee in whose favor the powerholder has decided to exercise the power. In other words, if the powerholder makes a decision to exercise the power in favor of a permissible appointee, the permissible appointee may request the powerholder to transfer the appointive assets directly to an impermissible appointee. The appointment directly to the impermissible appointee in this situation is effective, being treated for all purposes as an appointment first to the permissible appointee followed by a transfer by the permissible appointee to the impermissible appointee.

The donor of a power of appointment sets the range of permissible appointees by designating the permissible appointees of the power. The rules of this section are concerned with attempts by the powerholder to exceed that authority. Such an attempt is called a fraud on the power and is ineffective. The term "fraud on the power" is a well-accepted term of art. See Restatement Third of Property: Wills and Other Donative Transfers §§ 19.15 and 19.16.

Among the most common devices employed to commit a fraud on the power are: an appointment conditioned on the appointee conferring a benefit on an impermissible appointee; an appointment subject to a charge in favor of an impermissible appointee; an appointment upon a trust for the benefit of an impermissible appointee; an appointment in consideration of a benefit to an impermissible appointee; and an appointment primarily for the benefit of the permissible appointee's creditor if the creditor is an impermissible appointee. Each of these appointments is impermissible and ineffective.

The rules of this section are consistent with, and this Comment draws on, Restatement Third of Property: Wills and Other Donative Transfers §§ 19.15 and 19.16 and the accompanying Commentary.

§ 308. Selective Allocation Doctrine. If a powerholder exercises a power of appointment in a disposition that also disposes of property the powerholder owns, the owned property and the appointive property must be allocated in the permissible manner that best carries out the powerholder's intent.

Comment

The rule of this section is commonly known as the doctrine of selective allocation. This doctrine applies if the powerholder uses the same instrument to exercise a power of appointment and to dispose of property that the powerholder owns. For purposes of this section, the powerholder's will, any codicils to the powerholder's will, and any revocable trust created by the powerholder that did not become irrevocable before the powerholder's death are treated as the same instrument.

The doctrine of selective allocation provides that the owned property and the appointive property shall be allocated in the permissible manner that best carries out the powerholder's intent.

One situation that often calls for selective allocation is when the powerholder disposes of property to permissible and impermissible appointees. By allocating owned assets to the dispositions favoring impermissible appointees and allocating appointive assets to permissible appointees, the appointment is rendered effective. Consider the following example, drawn from the Restatement Third of Property: Wills and Other Donative Transfers.

Example. D died, leaving a will that devised property worth $100,000 to T in trust. T is directed to pay the net income to S (Donor's son) for life and then "to pay the principal to S's descendants as S shall by will appoint, and in default of appointment to pay the principal by representation to S's descendants then living, and if no descendant of S is then living, to pay the principal to X-Charity." S dies. The property over which S has the nongeneral power is worth $200,000 at his death. S's owned property at his death is worth $800,000. S's will provides as follows: "All property I own or over which I have any power of appointment shall be used first to pay my debts, expenses of administration, and death taxes, and the balance I give outright to my daughters." S's debts plus the death taxes payable on S's death plus the expenses of administering S's estate total $200,000. If S's owned property is allocated ratably to the payment of such $200,000, one-fifth of the $200,000 would be an ineffective appointment, because it would be to impermissible appointees. That one-fifth of $200,000 ($40,000 of the appointive assets) would pass in default of appointment, and the owned property would have to pick up the full payment of the debts, taxes, and expenses of administration. A selective allocation in the first instance of owned assets to the payment of debts, taxes, and expenses of administration leaves the appointive assets appointed only to permissible appointees of the nongeneral power and nothing passes in default of appointment.

The result of applying selective allocation is always one that the powerholder could have provided for in specific language, and one that the powerholder most probably would have provided for had he or she been aware of the difficulties inherent in the dispositive scheme. By the rule of selective allocation, courts undertake to prevent the dispositive plan from being frustrated by the ineptness of the powerholder or the powerholder's lawyer. For an early case adopting selective allocation, see Roe v. Tranmer, 2 Wils. 75, 95 Eng. Rep. 694 (C.P. 1757).

For further discussion of selective allocation, and illustrations of its application to various fact-patterns, see Restatement Third of Property: Wills and Other Donative Transfers § 19.19 and the accompanying Commentary. This rule of this Section is consistent with, and this Comment draws on, that Restatement.

On the distinction between selective allocation (a rule of construction based on the assumed intent of the powerholder) and the process sometimes known as "marshaling" (an outgrowth of general equitable principles), see the Restatement Second of Property: Donative Transfers, especially the Introductory Note to Chapter 22.

§ 309. Capture Doctrine: Disposition of Ineffectively Appointed Property under General Power. To the extent a powerholder of a general power of appointment, other than a power to withdraw property from, revoke, or amend a trust, makes an ineffective appointment:

(1) the gift-in-default clause controls the disposition of the ineffectively appointed property; or

(2) if there is no gift-in-default clause or to the extent the clause is ineffective, the ineffectively

appointed property:

(A) passes to:

(i) the powerholder if the powerholder is a permissible appointee and living; or

(ii) if the powerholder is an impermissible appointee or deceased, the powerholder's estate if the estate is a permissible appointee; or

(B) if there is no taker under subparagraph (A), passes under a reversionary interest to the donor or the donor's transferee or successor in interest.

Comment

This section applies when the powerholder of a general power makes an ineffective appointment. This section does not apply when the powerholder of a general power fails to exercise or releases the power. (On such fact-patterns, see instead Section 310.)

Nor does this section apply to an ineffective exercise of a power of revocation, amendment, or withdrawal — in each case, a power pertaining to a trust. To the extent a powerholder of one of these types of powers makes an ineffective appointment, the ineffectively appointed property remains in the trust.

The central rule of this section — in paragraph (1) and subparagraph (2)(A) — is a modern variation of the so-called "capture doctrine" adopted by a small body of case law and followed in Restatement Second of Property: Donative Transfers § 23.2. Under that doctrine, the ineffectively appointed property passed to the powerholder or the powerholder's estate, but only if the ineffective appointment manifested an intent to assume control of the appointive property "for all purposes" and not merely for the limited purpose of giving effect to the attempted appointment. If the ineffective appointment manifested such an intent, the ineffective appointment was treated as an implied alternative appointment to the powerholder or the powerholder's estate, and thus took effect even if the donor provided for takers in default and one or more of the takers in default were otherwise entitled to take.

The capture doctrine was developed at a time when the donor's gift-in-default clause was considered an afterthought, inserted just in case the powerholder failed to exercise the power. Today, the donor's gift-in-default clause is typically carefully drafted and intended to take effect, unless circumstances change that would cause the powerholder to exercise the power. Consequently, if the powerholder exercises the power effectively, the exercise divests the interest of the takers in default. But if the powerholder makes an ineffective appointment, the powerholder's intent

regarding the disposition of the ineffectively appointed property is problematic.

Whether or not the ineffective appointment manifested an intent to assume control of the appointive property "for all purposes" often depended on nothing more than whether the ineffective appointment was contained in a blending clause. The use of a blending clause rather than a direct-exercise clause, however, is typically the product of the drafting lawyer's forms rather than a deliberate choice of the powerholder.

This section alters the traditional capture doctrine in two ways: (1) the gift-in-default clause takes precedence over any implied alternative appointment to the powerholder or the powerholder's estate deduced from the use of a blending clause or otherwise; and (2) the ineffectively appointed property passes to the powerholder or the powerholder's estate only if there is no gift-in-default clause or to the extent the gift-in-default clause is ineffective. Nothing turns on whether the powerholder used a blending clause or somehow otherwise manifested an intent to assume control of the appointive property "for all purposes."

Subparagraph (2)(B) addresses the special case of a power of appointment that is general only because it is exercisable in favor of creditors, but not exercisable in favor of the powerholder or the powerholder's estate. This type of general power is sometimes used in generation-skipping transfer tax planning. However, this type of general power should not trigger the capture doctrine, because the powerholder and the powerholder's estate are impermissible appointees. Instead, ineffectively appointed property should pass under the gift-in-default clause (paragraph (1)) or, if there is no gift-in-default clause or it is ineffective, under a reversionary interest to the donor or the donor's transferee or successor in interest (subparagraph (2)(B)).

The rule of this section is essentially consistent with, and this Comment draws on, Restatement Third of Property: Wills and Other Donative

Transfers § 19.21 and the accompanying Commentary.

§ 310. Disposition of Unappointed Property under Released or Unexercised General Power.
To the extent a powerholder releases or fails to exercise a general power of appointment other than a power to withdraw property from, revoke, or amend a trust:

(1) the gift-in-default clause controls the disposition of the unappointed property; or

(2) if there is no gift-in-default clause or to the extent the clause is ineffective:

(A) except as otherwise provided in subparagraph (B), the unappointed property passes to:

(i) the powerholder if the powerholder is a permissible appointee and living; or

(ii) if the powerholder is an impermissible appointee or deceased, the powerholder's estate if the estate is a permissible appointee; or

(B) to the extent the powerholder released the power, or if there is no taker under subparagraph (A), the unappointed property passes under a reversionary interest to the donor or the donor's transferee or successor in interest.

Comment

The rules of this section apply to unappointed property under a general power of appointment. The rules do *not* apply to unappointed property under a power of revocation, amendment, or withdrawal — powers pertaining to a trust. If the powerholder releases or dies without exercising a power of revocation or amendment, the power to revoke expires and, unless someone else continues to have a power of revocation or amendment, the trust becomes irrevocable and unamendable. If the powerholder releases or dies without exercising a power to withdraw principal of a trust, the principal that the powerholder could have withdrawn, but did not, remains part of the trust.

The rationale for the rules of this section runs as follows. The gift-in-default clause controls the disposition of unappointed property to the extent the clause is effective. To the extent the gift-in-default clause is nonexistent or ineffective, the disposition of the unappointed property depends on whether the powerholder merely failed to exercise the power or whether the powerholder released the power. If the powerholder merely *failed to exercise* the power, the unappointed property passes to the powerholder or to the powerholder's estate (if these are permissible appointees). The rationale is the same as when the powerholder makes an ineffective appointment. If, however, the powerholder *released* the power, the powerholder has affirmatively chosen to reject the opportunity to gain ownership of the property, hence the unappointed property passes under a reversionary interest to the donor or to the donor's transferee or successor in interest.

These rules are illustrated by the following examples.

Example 1. D transfers property to T in trust, directing T to pay the income to S (D's son) for life, with a general testamentary power in S to appoint the principal of the trust, and in default of appointment the principal is to be distributed "to S's descendants who survive S, by representation, and if none, to X-Charity." S dies leaving a will that does not exercise the power. The principal passes under the gift-in-default clause to S's descendants who survive S, by representation.

Example 2. Same facts as Example 1, except that D's gift-in-default clause covered only half of the principal, and S died intestate. Half of the principal passes under the gift-in-default clause. The other half of the principal passes to S's estate for distribution to S's intestate heirs.

Example 3. Same facts as Example 2, except that S released the power before dying intestate. Half of the principal passes under the gift-in-default clause. The other half of the principal passes to D or to D's transferee or successor in interest.

In addition to governing a released general power, subparagraph (2)(B) also applies to the special case of an unexercised general power that is general only because it is exercisable in favor of creditors, but not exercisable in favor of the powerholder or the powerholder's estate. This type of general power is sometimes used in generation-skipping transfer tax planning. In such a case, unappointed property passes under the gift-in-default clause (paragraph (1)) or, if there is no gift-in-default clause or to the extent it is ineffective, under a reversionary interest to the donor or the donor's transferee or successor in interest (subparagraph (2)(B)).

The rules of this section are essentially consistent with, and this Comment draws on, Restatement Third of Property: Wills and Other Donative Transfers § 19.22 and the accompanying Commentary.

§ 311. Disposition of Unappointed Property under Released or Unexercised Nongeneral Power.

To the extent a powerholder releases, ineffectively exercises, or fails to exercise a nongeneral power of appointment:

(1) the gift-in-default clause controls the disposition of the unappointed property; or

(2) if there is no gift-in-default clause or to the extent the clause is ineffective, the unappointed property:

(A) passes to the permissible appointees if:

(i) the permissible appointees are defined and limited; and

(ii) the terms of the instrument creating the power do not manifest a contrary intent; or

(B) if there is no taker under subparagraph (A), passes under a reversionary interest to the donor or the donor's transferee or successor in interest.

Comment

To the extent the powerholder of a nongeneral power releases, ineffectively exercises, or fails to exercise the power, thus causing the power to lapse, the gift-in-default clause controls the disposition of the unappointed property to the extent the gift-in-default clause is effective.

To the extent the gift-in-default clause is nonexistent or ineffective, the unappointed property passes to the permissible appointees of the power — including those who are substituted for permissible appointees under an antilapse statute (see Section 306) — if the permissible appointees are "defined and limited" (on the meaning of this term of art, see the Comment to Section 205) and the donor has not manifested an intent that the permissible appointees shall receive the appointive property only so far as the powerholder elects to appoint it to them. This rule of construction is based on the assumption that the donor intends the permissible appointees of the power to have the benefit of the property. The donor focused on transmitting the appointive property to the permissible appointees through an appointment, but if the powerholder fails to carry out this particular method of transfer, the donor's underlying intent to pass the appointive property to the defined and limited class of permissible appointees should be carried out. Subparagraph (2)(A) effectuates the donor's underlying intent by implying a gift in default of appointment to the defined and limited class of permissible appointees.

If the defined and limited class of permissible appointees is a multigenerational class, such as "descendants," "issue," "heirs," or "relatives," the default rule of construction is that they take by representation. See Restatement Third of Property: Wills and Other Donative Transfers § 14.3, Comment b. If the defined and limited class is a single-generation class, the default rule of construction is that the eligible class members take equally. See Restatement Third of Property: Wills and Other Donative Transfers § 14.2.

No implied gift in default of appointment to the permissible appointees arises if the permissible appointees are identified in such broad and inclusive terms that they are not defined and limited. In such an event, the donor has no underlying intent to pass the appointive property to such permissible appointees. Similarly, if the donor manifests an intent that the defined and limited class of permissible appointees is to receive the appointive property only by appointment, the donor's manifestation of intent eliminates any implied gift in default to the permissible appointees. Subparagraph (2)(B) responds to these possibilities by providing for a reversionary interest to the donor or the donor's transferee or successor in interest.

The rules are illustrated by the following examples.

Example 1. D died, leaving a will devising property to T in trust. T is directed to pay the income to S (D's son) for life, and then to pay the principal "to such of S's descendants who survive S as S may appoint by will." D's will contains no gift-in-default clause. S dies without exercising the nongeneral power. The permissible appointees of the power constitute a defined and limited class. Accordingly, the principal of the trust passes at S's death to S's descendants who survive S, by representation.

Example 2. Same facts as Example 1, except that the permissible appointees of S's power of appointment are "such one or more persons, other than S, S's estate, S's creditors, or creditors of S's estate." The permissible appointees do not constitute a defined and limited class. Accordingly, the principal of the trust passes, at S's death, under a reversionary interest to D or D's transferee or successor in interest.

The rules of this section are consistent with, and this Comment draws on, Restatement Third of Property: Wills and Other Donative Transfers § 19.23 and the accompanying Commentary.

§ 312. Disposition of Unappointed Property If Partial Appointment to Taker in Default. Unless the terms of the instrument creating or exercising a power of appointment manifest a contrary intent, if the powerholder makes a valid partial appointment to a taker in default of appointment, the taker in default of appointment may share fully in unappointed property.

Comment

If a powerholder makes a valid partial appointment to a taker in default, leaving some propery unappointed, there is a question about whether that taker in default may also fully share in the unappointed property. In the first instance, the intent of the *donor* controls. In the absence of any indication of the donor's intent, it is assumed that the donor intends that the taker can take in both capacities. This rule presupposes that the donor contemplated that the taker in default who is an appointee could receive more of the appointive assets than a taker in default who is not an appointee. The donor can defeat this rule by manifesting a contrary intent in the instrument creating the power of appointment, thereby restricting the powerholder's freedom to benefit an appointee who is also a taker in default in both capacities. If the donor has not so manifested a contrary intent, the *powerholder* is free to exercise the power in favor of a taker in default who is a permissible appointee. Unless the powerholder manifests a contrary intent in the terms of the instrument exercising the power, it is assumed that the powerholder does not intend to affect in any way the disposition of any unappointed property.

The rule of this section is consistent with, and this Comment draws on, Restatement Third of Property: Wills and Other Donative Transfers § 19.24 and the accompanying Commentary.

§ 313. Appointment to Taker in Default. If a powerholder makes an appointment to a taker in default of appointment and the appointee would have taken the property under a gift-in-default clause had the property not been appointed, the power of appointment is deemed not to have been exercised and the appointee takes under the clause.

Comment

This section articulates the rule that, to the extent an appointee would have taken appointed property as a taker in default, the appointee takes under the gift-in-default clause rather than under the appointment.

Takers in default have future interests that may be defeated by an exercise of the power of appointment. To whatever extent the powerholder purports to appoint an interest already held in default of appointment, the powerholder does not exercise the power to alter the donor's disposition but merely declares an intent not to alter it. To the extent, however, that the appointed property *is different from* (e.g., is a lesser estate) or *exceeds the total of* the property the appointee would receive as a taker in default, the property passes under the appointment.

Usually it makes no difference whether the appointee takes as appointee or as taker in default. The principal difference arises in jurisdictions that follow the rule that the estate creditors of the powerholder of a general testamentary power that was conferred on the powerholder by another have no claim on the appointive property unless the powerholder has exercised the power. Although this act does not follow that rule regarding creditors' rights (see Section 502), some jurisdictions do.

The rule of this section is consistent with, and this Comment draws on, Restatement Third of Property: Wills and Other Donative Transfers § 19.25 and the accompanying Commentary.

§ 314. Powerholder's Authority to Revoke or Amend Exercise. A powerholder may revoke or amend an exercise of a power of appointment only to the extent that:

(1) the powerholder reserves a power of revocation or amendment in the instrument exercising the power of appointment and, if the power is nongeneral, the terms of the instrument creating the power of appointment do not prohibit the reservation; or

(2) the terms of the instrument creating the power of appointment provide that the exercise is revocable or amendable.

Comment

This section recognizes that a powerholder lacks the authority to revoke or amend an exercise of the power of appointment, except to the extent (1) the powerholder reserved a power of revocation or amendment in the instrument exercising the power of appointment and the terms of the instrument creating the power of appointment do not effectively prohibit the reservation, or (2) the donor provided that the exercise is revocable or amendable.

A powerholder who exercises a power of appointment is like any other transferor of property in regard to authority to revoke or amend the transfer. Hence, unless the powerholder (or the donor) in some appropriate manner manifests an intent that an appointment is revocable or amendable, the appointment is irrevocable.

The ability of an agent or guardian to revoke or amend the exercise of a power of appointment on behalf of a principal or ward is determined by other law, such as the Uniform Power of Attorney Act or the Uniform Guardianship and Protective Proceedings Act.

Other law of the state may permit the reformation of an otherwise irrevocable instrument. See, for example, Uniform Probate Code § 2-805; Uniform Trust Code § 415.

The rule of this section is essentially consistent with, and this Comment draws on, Restatement Third of Property: Wills and Other Donative Transfers § 19.7 and the accompanying Commentary.

[ARTICLE] 4
DISCLAIMER OR RELEASE; CONTRACT TO APPOINT
OR NOT TO APPOINT

§ 401. Disclaimer. As provided by [cite state law on disclaimer or the Uniform Disclaimer of Property Interests Act]:

(1) A powerholder may disclaim all or part of a power of appointment.

(2) A permissible appointee, appointee, or taker in default of appointment may disclaim all or part of an interest in appointive property.

Comment

A prospective powerholder cannot be compelled to accept the power of appointment, just as the prospective donee of a gift cannot be compelled to accept the gift.

A disclaimer is to be contrasted with a release. A release occurs after the powerholder accepts the power. A disclaimer prevents acquisition of the power, and consequently a powerholder who has accepted a power can no longer disclaim.

Disclaimer statutes frequently specify the time within which a disclaimer must be made. The Uniform Disclaimer of Property Interests Act (1999)

(UDPIA) does not specify a time limit, but allows a disclaimer until a disclaimer is barred (see UDPIA § 13).

Disclaimer statutes customarily specify the methods for filing a disclaimer. UDPIA § 12 provides that the statutory methods must be followed. In the absence of such a requirement, statutory formalities for making a disclaimer of a power are not construed as exclusive, and any manifestation of the powerholder's intent not to accept the power may also suffice.

A partial disclaimer of a power of appointment leaves the powerholder possessed of the part of the power not disclaimed.

Just as an individual who would otherwise be a powerholder can avoid acquiring the power by disclaiming it, a person who otherwise would be a permissible appointee, appointee, or taker in default of appointment can avoid acquiring that status by disclaiming it.

The ability of an agent or guardian to disclaim on behalf of a principal or ward is determined by other law, such as the Uniform Power of Attorney Act or the Uniform Guardianship and Protective Proceedings Act.

The rule of this section is consistent with, and this Comment draws on, Restatement Third of Property: Wills and Other Donative Transfers § 20.4 and the accompanying Commentary.

§ 402. Authority to Release. A powerholder may release a power of appointment, in whole or in part, except to the extent the terms of the instrument creating the power prevent the release.

Comment

Whether a power of appointment is general or nongeneral, presently exercisable or testamentary, the powerholder has the authority to release the power in whole or in part, in the absence of an effective restriction on release imposed by the donor. A partial release is a release that narrows the freedom of choice otherwise available to the powerholder but does not eliminate the power. A partial release may relate either to the manner of exercising the power or to the persons in whose favor the power may be exercised.

If the powerholder did not create the power, so that the powerholder and donor are different individuals, the donor can effectively impose a restraint on release, but the donor must manifest an intent in the terms of the creating instrument to impose such a restraint.

If the powerholder created the power, so that the powerholder is also the donor, the donor/powerholder cannot effectively impose a restraint on release. A self-imposed restraint on release resembles a self-imposed restraint on alienation, which is ineffective. See, for example, Restatement Third of Trusts § 58.

If the exercise of a power of appointment requires the action of two or more individuals, each powerholder has a power of appointment. If one but not the other joint powerholder releases the power, the power survives in the hands of the nonreleasing powerholder, unless the continuation of the power is inconsistent with the donor's purpose in creating the joint power. See Restatement Third of Property: Wills and Other Donative Transfers § 20.1, Comment f.

The ability of an agent or guardian to release a power of appointment on behalf of a principal or ward is determined by other law, such as the Uniform Power of Attorney Act or the Uniform Guardianship and Protective Proceedings Act.

The rule of this section is consistent with, and this Comment draws on, Restatement Third of Property: Wills and Other Donative Transfers §§ 20.1 and 20.2 and the accompanying Commentary.

§ 403. Method of Release.

[(a) In this section, "record" means information that is inscribed on a tangible medium or that is stored in an electronic or other medium and is retrievable in perceivable form.

(b)] A powerholder of a releasable power of appointment may release the power in whole or in part:

(1) by substantial compliance with a method provided in the terms of the instrument creating the power; or

(2) if the terms of the instrument creating the power do not provide a method or the method provided in the terms of the instrument is not expressly made exclusive, by a record manifesting the powerholder's intent by clear and convincing evidence.

Legislative Note: A state that defines "record" in Section 102 should delete the bracketed material in this section.

Comment

A powerholder may release the power of appointment by substantial compliance with the method specified in the terms of the instrument creating the power or any other method manifesting clear and convincing evidence of the powerholder's intent. Only if the method specified in the terms of the creating instrument is made exclusive is use of the other methods prohibited. Even then, a failure to comply with a technical requirement, such as required notarization, may be excused as long as compliance with the method specified in the terms of the creating instrument is otherwise substantial.

Examples of methods manifesting clear and convincing evidence of the powerholder's intent to release include: (1) delivering (by the same method of delivery that would make an instrument of transfer effective, see Restatement Third of Property: Wills and Other Donative Transfers § 20.3, Comment b) an instrument declaring the extent to which the power is released to an individual who could be adversely affected by an exercise of the power; (2) joining with some or all of the takers in default in making an otherwise effective transfer of an interest in the appointive property, in which case the power is released to the extent a subsequent exercise of the power would defeat the interest transferred; (3) contracting with an individual who could be adversely affected by an exercise of the power not to exercise the power, in which case the power is released to the extent a subsequent exercise of the power would violate the terms of the contract; and (4) communicating in a record an intent to release the power, in which case the power is released to the extent a subsequent exercise of the power would be contrary to manifested intent.

The black-letter of this section is based on Uniform Trust Code § 602(c). The rule of this section is fundamentally consistent with, and this Comment draws on, Restatement Third of Property: Wills and Other Donative Transfers § 20.3 and the accompanying Commentary.

§ 404. Revocation or Amendment of Release.

A powerholder may revoke or amend a release of a power of appointment only to the extent that:

(1) the instrument of release is revocable by the powerholder; or

(2) the powerholder reserves a power of revocation or amendment in the instrument of release.

Comment

A release is typically irrevocable. If a powerholder wishes to retain the power to revoke or amend the release, the powerholder should so indicate in the instrument executing the release.

The ability of an agent or guardian to revoke or amend the release of a power of appointment on behalf of a principal or ward is determined by other law, such as the Uniform Power of Attorney Act or the Uniform Guardianship and Protective Proceedings Act.

Other law of the state may permit the reformation of an otherwise irrevocable instrument. See, for example, Uniform Probate Code § 2-805; Uniform Trust Code § 415.

The rule of this section is consistent with, and this Comment draws on, Restatement Third of Property: Wills and Other Donative Transfers §§ 20.1 and 20.2 and the accompanying Commentary.

§ 405. Power to Contract: Presently Exercisable Power of Appointment.

A powerholder of a presently exercisable power of appointment may contract:

(1) not to exercise the power; or

(2) to exercise the power if the contract when made does not confer a benefit on an impermissible appointee.

Comment

A powerholder of a presently exercisable power may contract to make, or not to make, an appointment if the contract does not confer a benefit on an impermissible appointee. The rationale is that the power is presently exercisable, so the powerholder can presently enter into a contract concerning the appointment.

The contract may not confer a benefit on an impermissible appointee. Recall that a general power presently exercisable in favor of the powerholder or the powerholder's estate has no impermissible appointees. See Section 305(a). In contrast, a presently exercisable nongeneral power, or a general power presently exercisable only in favor of one or more of the creditors of the powerholder or the powerholder's estate, does have impermissible appointees. See Section 305(b)-(c).

A contract *not* to appoint assures that the appointive property will pass to the taker in default. A contract to appoint to a taker in default, if enforceable, has the same effect as a contract not to appoint.

The ability of an agent or guardian to contract on behalf of a principal or ward is determined by other law, such as the Uniform Power of Attorney Act or the Uniform Guardianship and Protective Proceedings Act.

The rule of this section is consistent with, and this Comment draws on, Restatement Third of Property: Wills and Other Donative Transfers § 21.1 and the accompanying Commentary.

§ 406. Power to Contract: Power of Appointment Not Presently Exercisable.

A powerholder of a power of appointment that is not presently exercisable may contract to exercise or not to exercise the power only if the powerholder:

(1) is also the donor of the power; and

(2) has reserved the power in a revocable trust.

Comment

Except in the case of a power reserved by the donor in a revocable inter vivos trust, a contract to exercise, or not to exercise, a power of appointment that is not presently exercisable is unenforceable, because the powerholder does not have the authority to make a current appointment. If the powerholder was also the donor of the power and created the power in a revocable inter vivos trust, however, a contract to appoint is enforceable, because the donor-powerholder could have revoked the trust and recaptured ownership of the trust assets or could have amended the trust to change the power onto one that is presently exercisable.

In all other cases, the donor of a power not presently exercisable has manifested an intent that the selection of the appointees and the determination of the interests they are to receive are to be made in the light of the circumstances that exist on the date that the power becomes exercisable. Were a contract to be enforceable, the donor's intent would be defeated.

The ability of an agent or guardian to contract on behalf of a principal or ward is determined by other law, such as the Uniform Power of Attorney Act or the Uniform Guardianship and Protective Proceedings Act.

The rule of this section is consistent with, and this Comment draws on, Restatement Third of Property: Wills and Other Donative Transfers § 21.2 and the accompanying Commentary.

§ 407. Remedy for Breach of Contract to Appoint or Not to Appoint.

The remedy for a powerholder's breach of a contract to appoint or not to appoint appointive property is limited to damages payable out of the appointive property or, if appropriate, specific performance of the contract.

Comment

This section sets forth a rule on remedy. The remedy for a powerholder's breach of an enforceable contract to appoint, or not to appoint, is limited to damages payable out of the appointive property or, if appropriate, specific performance. The powerholder's owned assets are not available to satisfy a judgment for damages. For elaboration and discussion, see Restatement Third of Property: Wills and Other Donative Transfers §§ 21.1 and 21.2, and especially id., § 21.1, Comments c and d. This section does not address the *amount* of damages, which is determined by other law of the state, such as contract law.

[ARTICLE] 5
RIGHTS OF POWERHOLDER'S CREDITORS IN APPOINTIVE PROPERTY

§ 501. Creditor Claim: General Power Created by Powerholder.

(a) In this section, "power of appointment created by the powerholder" includes a power of appointment created in a transfer by another person to the extent the powerholder contributed value to the transfer.

(b) Appointive property subject to a general power of appointment created by the powerholder is subject to a claim of a creditor of the powerholder or of the powerholder's estate to the extent provided in [cite state law on fraudulent transfers or the Uniform Fraudulent Transfers Act].

(c) Subject to subsection (b), appointive property subject to a general power of appointment created by the powerholder is not subject to a claim of a creditor of the powerholder or the powerholder's estate to the extent the powerholder irrevocably appointed the property in favor of a person other than the powerholder or the powerholder's estate.

(d) Subject to subsections (b) and (c), and notwithstanding the presence of a spendthrift provision or whether the claim arose before or after the creation of the power of appointment, appointive property subject to a general power of appointment created by the powerholder is subject to a claim of a creditor of:

(1) the powerholder, to the same extent as if the powerholder owned the appointive property, if the power is presently exercisable; and

(2) the powerholder's estate, to the extent the estate is insufficient to satisfy the claim and subject to the right of a decedent to direct the source from which liabilities are paid, if the power is exercisable at the powerholder's death.

Comment

Subsection (b) states a well-settled rule: a donor of a power of appointment cannot use a fraudulent transfer to avoid creditors. If a donor fraudulently transfers appointive property, retaining a power of appointment, the donor/powerholder's creditors and the creditors of the donor/powerholder's estate may reach the appointive property as provided in the law of fraudulent transfers.

Subsection (c) also states a well-settled rule: if there is no fraudulent transfer, and the donor/powerholder has made an irrevocable appointment to a third party of the appointive property, the appointed property is beyond the reach of the donor/powerholder's creditors or the creditors of the donor/powerholder's estate. In other words, an irrevocable and nonfraudulent exercise of the general power by the donor/powerholder in favor of someone other than the powerholder or the powerholder's estate eliminates the ability of the powerholder's creditors or the creditors of the powerholder's estate to reach those assets.

Subsection (d) establishes rules governing the remaining fact-pattern: the donor has retained a general power of appointment but has made neither a fraudulent transfer nor an irrevocable appointment. In such a case, the following rules apply. If the donor retains a presently exercisable general power of appointment, the appointive property is subject to a claim of — and is reachable by — a creditor of the powerholder to the same extent as if the powerholder owned the appointive property. If the donor retains a general power of appointment exercisable at death, the appointive property is subject to a claim of — and is reachable by — a creditor of the donor/powerholder's estate (defined with reference to other law, but including costs of administration, expenses of the funeral and disposal of remains, and statutory allowances to the surviving spouse and children) to the extent the estate is insufficient, subject to the decedent's right to direct the source from which liabilities are paid. For the same rules in the context of a retained power to revoke a revocable trust, see Uniform Trust Code § 505(a). The application of these rules is not affected by the presence of a spendthrift provision or by whether the claim arose before or after the creation of the power of appointment. See Restatement Third of Property: Wills and Other Donative Transfers § 22.2,

Comment a.

Subsection (a) enables all of these rules to apply even if the general power was not created in a transfer made by the powerholder. The rules will apply to the extent the powerholder contributed value to the transfer. See Restatement Third of Property: Wills and Other Donative Transfers § 22.2, Comment d. Consider the following examples, drawn from the Restatement.

Example 1. D purchases Blackacre from A. Pursuant to D's request, A transfers Blackacre "to D for life, then to such person as D may by will appoint." The rule of subsection (d) applies to D's general testamentary power, though in form A created the power.

Example 2. A by will transfers Blackacre "to D for life, then to such persons as D may by will appoint." Blackacre is subject to mortgage indebtedness in favor of X in the amount of $10,000. The value of Blackacre is $20,000. D pays the mortgage indebtedness. The rule of subsection (d) applies to half of the value of Blackacre, though in form A's will creates the general power in D.

Example 3. D, an heir of A, contests A's will on the ground of undue influence on A by the principal beneficiary under A's will. The contest is settled by transferring part of A's estate to Trustee in trust. Under the trust, Trustee is directed "to pay the net income to D for life and, on D's death, the principal to such persons as D shall by will appoint." The rule of subsection (d) applies to the transfer in trust, though in form D did not create the general power.

The provisions of this section are designed to be consistent with Uniform Trust Code § 505(a). The provisions and this Comment also rely in part on Restatement Third of Property: Wills and Other Donative Transfers § 22.2 and the accompanying Commentary.

§ 502. Creditor Claim: General Power Not Created by Powerholder.

(a) Except as otherwise provided in subsection (b), appointive property subject to a general power of appointment created by a person other than the powerholder is subject to a claim of a creditor of:

(1) the powerholder, to the extent the powerholder's property is insufficient, if the power is presently exercisable; and

(2) the powerholder's estate, to the extent the estate is insufficient, subject to the right of a decedent to direct the source from which liabilities are paid.

(b) Subject to Section 504(c), a power of appointment created by a person other than the powerholder which is subject to an ascertainable standard relating to an individual's health, education, support, or maintenance within the meaning of 26 U.S.C. Section 2041(b)(1)(A) or 26 U.S.C. Section 2514(c)(1), [on the effective date of this [act]][as amended], is treated for purposes of this [article] as a nongeneral power.

Legislative Note: *In states in which the constitution, or other law, does not permit the phrase "as amended" when federal statutes are incorporated into state law, the phrase should be deleted in subsection (b).*

Comment

Subsection (a) reaffirms the fundamental principle that a presently exercisable general power of appointment is an ownership-equivalent power. Consequently, subsection (b) provides that property subject to a presently exercisable general power of appointment is subject to the claims of the powerholder's creditors, to the extent the powerholder's property is insufficient. Furthermore, upon the powerholder's death, property subject to a general power of appointment is subject to creditors' claims against the powerholder's estate (defined with reference to other law, but including costs of administration, expenses of the funeral and disposal of remains, and statutory allowances to the surviving spouse and children) to the extent the estate is insufficient, subject to the decedent's right to direct the source from which liabilities are paid. In each case, whether the powerholder has or has not purported to exercise the power is immaterial.

Subsection (b) states an important exception. If the power is subject to an ascertainable standard within the meaning of 26 U.S.C. § 2041(b)(1)(A) or 26 U.S.C. § 2514(c)(1), the power is treated for purposes of this article as a nongeneral power, and the rights of the powerholder's creditors in the appointive property are governed by Sections 504(a) and (b).

§ 503. Power to Withdraw.

(a) For purposes of this [article], and except as otherwise provided in subsection (b), a power to withdraw property from a trust is treated, during the time the power may be exercised, as a presently exercisable general power of appointment to the extent of the property subject to the power to withdraw.

(b) On the lapse, release, or waiver of a power to withdraw property from a trust, the power is treated as a presently exercisable general power of appointment only to the extent the value of the property affected by the lapse, release, or waiver exceeds the greater of the amount specified in 26 U.S.C. Section 2041(b)(2) and 26 U.S.C. Section 2514(e) or the amount specified in 26 U.S.C. Section 2503(b), [on the effective date of this [act]][as amended].

Legislative Note: *In states in which the constitution, or other law, does not permit the phrase "as amended" when federal statutes are incorporated into state law, the phrase should be deleted in subsection (b).*

Comment

Subsection (a) treats a power of withdrawal as the equivalent of a presently exercisable general power of appointment, because the two are ownership-equivalent powers. Upon the lapse, release, or waiver of the power of withdrawal, subsection (b) follows the lead of Uniform Trust Code § 505(b)(2) in creating an exception for property subject to a Crummey or five and five power: the holder of the power of withdrawal is treated as a powerholder of a presently exercisable general power of appointment only to the extent the value of the property affected by the lapse, release, or waiver exceeds the greater of the amount specified in Internal Revenue Code §§ 2041(b)(2) and 2514(e) [greater of 5% or $5,000] or § 2503(b) [$13,000 in 2012].

§ 504. Creditor Claim: Nongeneral Power.

(a) Except as otherwise provided in subsections (b) and (c), appointive property subject to a nongeneral power of appointment is exempt from a claim of a creditor of the powerholder or the powerholder's estate.

(b) Appointive property subject to a nongeneral power of appointment is subject to a claim of a creditor of the powerholder or the powerholder's estate to the extent that the powerholder owned the property and, reserving the nongeneral power, transferred the property in violation of [cite state statute on fraudulent transfers or the Uniform Fraudulent Transfers Act].

(c) If the initial gift in default of appointment is to the powerholder or the powerholder's estate, a nongeneral power of appointment is treated for purposes of this [article] as a general power.

Comment

Subsection (a) states the general rule of this section. Appointive property subject to a nongeneral power of appointment is exempt from a claim of a creditor of the powerholder or the powerholder's estate. The rationale for this general rule is that a nongeneral power of appointment is not an ownership-equivalent power, so the powerholder's creditors have no claim to the appointive assets.

Subsection (b) addresses an important exception: the fraudulent transfer. A fraudulent transfer arises if the powerholder formerly owned the appointive property covered by the nongeneral power and transferred the property in fraud of creditors, reserving the nongeneral power. In such a case, the creditors can reach the appointive property under the rules relating to fraudulent transfers.

Subsection (c) also addresses an important exception, arising when the initial gift in default of appointment is to the powerholder or the powerholder's estate. In such a case, the power of appointment, though in form a nongeneral power, is in substance a general power, and the rights of the powerholder's creditors in the appointive property are governed by Sections 501 and 502.

The rules of this section are consistent with, and this Comment draws on, Restatement Third of Property: Wills and Other Donative Transfers § 22.1 and the accompanying Commentary.

[ARTICLE] 6
MISCELLANEOUS PROVISIONS

§ 601. Uniformity of Application and Construction. In applying and construing this uniform act, consideration must be given to the need to promote uniformity of the law with respect to its subject matter among states that enact it.

§ 602. Relation to Electronic Signatures in Global and National Commerce Act. This [act] modifies, limits, or supersedes the Electronic Signatures in Global and National Commerce Act, 15 U.S.C. Section 7001 et seq., but does not modify, limit, or supersede Section 101(c) of that act, 15 U.S.C. Section 7001(c), or authorize electronic delivery of any of the notices described in Section 103(b) of that act, 15 U.S.C. Section 7003(b).

§ 603. Application to Existing Relationships.
    (a) Except as otherwise provided in this [act], on and after [the effective date of this [act]]:
    (1) this [act] applies to a power of appointment created before, on, or after [the effective date of this [act]];
    (2) this [act] applies to a judicial proceeding concerning a power of appointment commenced on or after [the effective date of this [act]];
    (3) this [act] applies to a judicial proceeding concerning a power of appointment commenced before [the effective date of this [act]] unless the court finds that application of a particular provision of this [act] would interfere substantially with the effective conduct of the judicial proceeding or prejudice a right of a party, in which case the particular provision of this [act] does not apply and the superseded law applies;
    (4) a rule of construction or presumption provided in this [act] applies to an instrument executed before [the effective date of this [act]] unless there is a clear indication of a contrary intent in the terms of the instrument; and
    (5) except as otherwise provided in paragraphs (1) through (4), an action done before [the effective date of this [act]] is not affected by this [act].
    (b) If a right is acquired, extinguished, or barred on the expiration of a prescribed period that commenced under law of this state other than this [act] before [the effective date of this [act]], the law continues to apply to the right.

Comment

This act is intended to have the widest possible effect within constitutional limitations. Specifically, the act applies to all powers of appointment whenever created, to judicial proceedings concerning powers of appointment commenced on or after its effective date, and unless the court otherwise orders, to judicial proceedings in progress on the effective date. In addition, any rules of construction or presumption provided in the act apply to preexisting instruments unless there is a clear indication of a contrary intent in the instruments's terms. By applying the act to preexisting instruments, the need to know two bodies of law will quickly lessen.

This legislation cannot be fully retroactive, however. Constitutional limitations preclude retroactive application of rules of construction to alter property rights that became irrevocable prior to the effective date. Also, rights already barred under former law are not revived by a possibly more liberal rule under this act. Nor, except as otherwise provided in paragraphs (1) through (4) of subsection (a), is an action done before the effective date of the act affected by the act's enactment.

For comparable Uniform Law provisions, see Uniform Trust Code § 1106 and Uniform Probate Code § 8-101.

§ 604. Repeals; Conforming Amendments.

(a) ....

(b) ....

(c) ....

§ 605. Effective Date. This [act] takes effect ....

UNIFORM PREMARITAL AND MARITAL AGREEMENTS ACT
(2012)

Table of Sections

Prefatory Note

The purpose of this act is to bring clarity and consistency across a range of agreements between spouses and those who are about to become spouses. The focus is on agreements that purport to modify or waive rights that would otherwise arise at the time of the dissolution of the marriage or the death of one of the spouses.

Forty years ago, state courts generally refused to enforce premarital agreements that altered the parties' right at divorce, on the basis that such agreements were attempts to alter the terms of a status (marriage) or because they had the effect of encouraging divorce (at least for the party who would have to pay less in alimony or give up less in the division of property). Over the course of the 1970s and 1980s, nearly every state changed its law, and currently every state allows at least some divorce-focused premarital agreements to be enforced, though the standards for regulating those agreements vary greatly from state to state. The law relating to premarital agreements affecting the parties' rights at the death of a spouse had historically been less hostile than the treatment of such agreements affecting the right of the parties at divorce. The ability of a wife to waive her dower rights goes back to the 16th century English Statute of Uses. 27 Hen. VIII, c. 10, § 6 (1535). Other countries have also moved towards greater legal recognition of premarital agreements and marital agreements, though there remains a great diversity of approaches internationally. *See* Jens M. Scherpe (ed.), *Marital Agreements and Private Autonomy in Comparative Perspective* (Hart Publishing, 2012); *see also* Katharina Boele-Woelki, Jo Miles and Jens M. Scherpe (eds.), *The Future of Family Property in Europe* (Intersentia, 2011).

The Uniform Premarital Agreement Act was promulgated in 1983. Since then it has been adopted by 26 jurisdictions, with roughly half of those jurisdictions making significant amendments, either at the time of enactment or at a later date. *See* Amberlynn Curry, Comment, "The Uniform Premarital Agreement Act and Its Variations throughout the States," 23 *Journal of the American Academy of Matrimonial Lawyers* 355 (2010). Over the years, commentators have offered a variety of criticisms of that Act, many arguing that it was weighted too strongly in favor of enforcement, and was insufficiently protective of vulnerable parties. *E.g.*, Barbara Ann Atwood, "Ten Years Later: Lingering Concerns About the Uniform Premarital Agreement Act," 19 *Journal of Legislation* 127 (1993); Gail Frommer Brod, "Premarital Agreements and Gender Justice," 9 *Yale Journal of Law & Feminism* 229 (1994); J. Thomas Oldham, "With All My Worldly

Goods I Thee Endow, or Maybe Not: A Reevaluation of the Uniform Premarital Agreement Act After Three Decades," 19 *Duke Journal of Gender and the Law* 83 (2011). Whatever its faults, the Uniform Premarital Agreement Act has brought some consistency to the legal treatment of premarital agreements, especially as concerns rights at dissolution of marriage.

The situation regarding marital agreements has been far less settled and consistent. Some states have neither case law nor legislation, while the remaining states have created a wide range of approaches. Additionally, other legal standards relating to the waiver of rights at the death of the other spouse, by either premarital agreements or marital agreements, seem to impose somewhat different requirements. *See, e.g., Uniform Probate Code*, Section 2-213; *Restatement (Third) of Property*, Section 9.4 (2003); *Model Marital Property Act*, Section 10 (1983); and *Internal Revenue Code*, Sections 401 and 417 (stating when a surviving spouse's waiver of rights to a qualified plan would be valid).

The general approach of this act is that parties should be free, within broad limits, to choose the financial terms of their marriage. The limits are those of due process in formation, on the one hand, and certain minimal standards of substantive fairness, on the other. Because a significant minority of states authorizes some form of fairness review based on the parties' circumstances at the time the agreement is to be enforced, a bracketed provision in Section 9(f) offers the option of refusing enforcement based on a finding of substantial hardship at the time of enforcement. And because a few states put the burden of proof on the party seeking enforcement of marital (and, more rarely, premarital) agreements, a

Legislative Note after Section 9 suggests alternative language to reflect that burden of proof.

This act chooses to treat premarital agreements and marital agreements under the same set of principles and requirements. A number of states currently treat premarital agreements and marital agreements under different legal standards, with higher burdens on those who wish to enforce marital agreements. *See, e.g.,* Sean Hannon Williams, "Postnuptial Agreements," 2007 *Wisconsin Law Review* 827, 838-845; Brian H. Bix, "The *ALI Principles* and Agreements: Seeking a Balance Between Status and Contract," in *Reconceiving the Family: Critical Reflections on the American Law Institute's Principles of the Law of Family Dissolution* (Robin Fretwell Wilson, ed., Cambridge University Press, 2006), pp. 372-391, at pp. 382-387; Barbara A. Atwood, "Marital Contracts and the Meaning of Marriage," 54 *Arizona Law Review* 11 (2012). However, this act follows the American Law Institute, in its *Principles of the Law of Family Dissolution* (2002), in treating the two types of agreements under the same set of standards. While this act, like the American Law Institute's *Principles* before it, recognizes that different sorts of risks may predominate in the different transaction types – risks of unfairness based on bounded rationality and changed circumstances for premarital agreements, and risks of duress and undue influence for marital agreements (*Principles of the Law of Family Dissolution*, Section 7.01, comment *e*, at pp. 953-954) – this act shares the American Law Institute's view that the resources available through this act and common law principles are sufficient to deal with the likely problems related to either type of transaction.

§ 1. Short Title. This [act] may be cited as the Uniform Premarital and Marital Agreements Act.

§ 2. Definitions. In this [act]:

(1) "Amendment" means a modification or revocation of a premarital agreement or marital agreement.

(2) "Marital agreement" means an agreement between spouses who intend to remain married which affirms, modifies, or waives a marital right or obligation during the marriage or at separation, marital dissolution, death of one of the spouses, or the occurrence or nonoccurrence of any other event. The term includes an amendment, signed after the spouses marry, of a premarital agreement or marital agreement.

(3) "Marital dissolution" means the ending of a marriage by court decree. The term includes a divorce, dissolution, and annulment.

(4) "Marital right or obligation" means any of the following rights or obligations arising between spouses because of their marital status:

(A) spousal support;

(B) a right to property, including characterization, management, and ownership;

(C) responsibility for a liability;

(D) a right to property and responsibility for liabilities at separation, marital dissolution, or death of a spouse; or

(E) award and allocation of attorney's fees and costs.

(5) "Premarital agreement" means an agreement between individuals who intend to marry which affirms, modifies, or waives a marital right or obligation during the marriage or at separation, marital dissolution, death of one of the spouses, or the occurrence or nonoccurrence of any other event. The term includes an amendment, signed before the individuals marry, of a premarital agreement.

(6) "Property" means anything that may be the subject of ownership, whether real or personal, tangible or intangible, legal or equitable, or any interest therein.

(7) "Record" means information that is inscribed on a tangible medium or that is stored in an electronic or other medium and is retrievable in perceivable form.

(8) "Sign" means with present intent to authenticate or adopt a record:

(A) to execute or adopt a tangible symbol; or

(B) to attach to or logically associate with the record an electronic symbol, sound, or process.

(9) "State" means a state of the United States, the District of Columbia, Puerto Rico, the United States Virgin Islands, or any territory or insular possession subject to the jurisdiction of the United States.

Legislative Note: *If your state recognizes nonmarital relationships, such as civil unions and domestic partnerships, consider whether these definitions need to be amended.*

Comment

The definition of "amendment" includes "amendments" of agreements, narrowly understood, and also revocations.

The definitions of "premarital agreement" and "marital agreement" are part of the effort to clarify that this act is not intended to cover cohabitation agreements, separation agreements, or conventional day-to-day commercial transactions between spouses. Marital agreements and separation agreements (sometimes called "marital settlement agreements") are usually distinguished based on whether the couple at the time of the agreement intends for their marriage to continue, on the one hand, or whether a court-decreed separation, permanent physical separation or dissolution of the marriage is imminent or planned, on the other. To avoid deception of the other party or the court regarding intentions, one jurisdiction refuses to enforce a marital agreement if it is quickly followed by an action for legal separation or dissolution of the marriage. *See Minnesota Statutes* § 519.11, subd. 1a(d)(marital agreement presumed to be unenforceable if separation or dissolution sought

within two years; in such a case, enforcement is allowed only if the spouse seeking enforcement proves that the agreement was fair and equitable).

While most premarital agreements and marital agreements will be stand-alone documents, a fragment of a writing that deals primarily with other topics could also constitute a premarital agreement or marital agreement for the purpose of this act.

With premarital agreements, the nature and timing of the agreement (between parties who are about to marry) reduces the danger that the act's language will accidentally include types of transactions that are not thought of as premarital agreements and should not be treated as premarital agreements (but see the discussion of *Mahr* agreements, below). There is a greater concern with marital agreements, since (a) spouses enter many otherwise enforceable financial transactions, most of which are not problematic and should not be made subject to special procedural or substantive constraints; and (b) there are significant questions about how to deal with agreements whose primary intention may not be to waive one spouse's rights at dissolution of the marriage or the other spouse's death, but where the agreement nonetheless has that effect. In the terms of another uniform act, the purpose of the definition of "marital agreement" is to exclude from coverage "acts and events that have significance apart from their effect" upon rights at dissolution of the marriage or at the death of one of the spouses. *See Uniform Probate Code*, Section 2-512 ("Events of Independent Significance"). Such transactions might include the creation of joint and several liability through real estate mortgages, motor vehicle financing agreements, joint lines of credit, overdraft protection, loan guaranties, joint income tax returns, creation of joint property ownership with a right of survivorship, joint property with payment-on-death provisions or transfer-on-death provisions, durable power of attorney or medical power of attorney, buy-sell agreements, agreements regarding the valuation of property, the placing of marital property into an irrevocable trust for a child, etc.

The shorter definition of "premarital agreement" used by the Uniform Premarital Agreement Act (in its Section 1(1): "an agreement between prospective spouses made in contemplation of marriage and to be effective upon marriage") had the disadvantage of encompassing agreements that were entered by couples about to marry but that were not intended to affect the parties' existing legal rights and obligations upon divorce or death, e.g., Islamic marriage contracts, with their deferred *Mahr* payment

provisions. See Nathan B. Oman, "Bargaining in the Shadow of God's Law: Islamic *Mahr* Contracts and the Perils of Legal Specialization," 45 *Wake Forest Law Review* 579 (2010); Brian H. Bix, "*Mahr* Agreements: Contracting in the Shadow of Family Law (and Religious Law) – A Comment on Oman," 1 *Wake Forest Law Review Online* 61 (2011), available at http://wakeforestlawreview.com/.

The definition of "property" is adapted from the *niform Trust Code*, Section 103(12).

This act does not define "separation agreement," leaving this to the understanding, rules, and practices of the states, noting that the practices do vary from state to state (*e.g.*, that in many states separation agreements require judicial approval while in other states they can be valid without judicial approval).

A premarital agreement or marital agreement may include terms not in violation of public policy of this state, including terms relating to: (1) rights of either or both spouses to interests in a trust, inheritance, devise, gift, and expectancy created by a third party; (2) appointment of fiduciary, guardian, conservator, personal representative, or agent for person or property; (3) a tax matter; (4) the method for resolving a dispute arising under the agreement; (5) choice of law governing validity, enforceability, interpretation, and construction of the agreement; or (6) formalities required to amend the agreement in addition to those required by this act.

§ 3. Scope.

(a) This [act] applies to a premarital agreement or marital agreement signed on or after [the effective date of this [act]].

(b) This [act] does not affect any right, obligation, or liability arising under a premarital agreement or marital agreement signed before [the effective date of this [act]].

(c) This [act] does not apply to:

(1) an agreement between spouses which affirms, modifies, or waives a marital right or obligation and requires court approval to become effective; or

(2) an agreement between spouses who intend to obtain a marital dissolution or court-decreed separation which resolves their marital rights or obligations and is signed when a proceeding for marital dissolution or court-decreed separation is anticipated or pending.

(d) This [act] does not affect adversely the rights of a bona fide purchaser for value to the extent that this [act] applies to a waiver of a marital right or obligation in a transfer or conveyance of property by a spouse to a third party.

Comment

This section distinguishes marital agreements, which are subject to this act, both from agreements that parties might enter at a time when they intend to obtain a divorce or legal separation or to live permanently apart, and also from the conventional transfers of property in which state law requires one or both spouses waive rights that would otherwise accrue at the death of the other spouse.

Subsection (c) is meant to exclude "separation agreements" and "marital settlement agreements" from the scope of the act. These tend to have their own established standards for enforcement. The reference to "a waiver of a marital right or obligation" in Subsection (d) would include the release of dower, curtesy, or homestead rights that often accompanies the conveyance of real property. In general, the enforceability of agreements in Subsections (b), (c) and (d) is left to other law in the state. This section is not meant to restrict third-party beneficiary standing where it would otherwise apply.

§ 4. Governing Law. The validity, enforceability, interpretation, and construction of a premarital agreement or marital agreement are determined:

(1) by the law of the jurisdiction designated in the agreement if the jurisdiction has a significant relationship to the agreement or either party and the designated law is not contrary to a fundamental public policy of this state; or

(2) absent an effective designation described in paragraph (1), by the law of this state, including the choice-of-law rules of this state.

Comment

This section is adapted from the *Uniform Trust Code*, Section 107. It is consistent with *Uniform Premarital Agreement Act*, Section 3(a)(7), but is broader in scope. The section reflects traditional conflict of laws and choice of law principles relating to the enforcement of contracts. *See Restatement (Second) of Conflict of Laws*, Sections 186-188 (1971). Section 187(2)(a) of that *Restatement* expressly states that the parties' choice of law is not to be enforced if "the chosen state has no substantial relationship to the parties or the transaction and there is no other reasonable basis for the parties' choice...." Section 187(2)(b) of the same *Restatement* holds that the parties' choice of law is not to be enforced if "application of the law of the chosen state would be contrary to a fundamental policy of a state which has a materially greater interest than the chosen state in the determination of the particular issue ...." The limitation of choice of law provisions to jurisdictions having some connection with the parties or the transaction tracks a similar restriction in the *Uniform Commercial Code*, which restricts choice of law provisions to states with a reasonable relation to the transaction (this was Section 1-105 under the UCC before the 2001 revisions; and Section 1-301 in the (2001) Revised UCC Article 1).

"Significant relation" and "fundamental public policy" are to be understood under existing state principles relating to conflict of laws, and "contrary to ... fundamental public policy" means something more than that the law of the other jurisdiction differs from that of the forum state. *See, e.g., International Hotels Corporation v. Golden*, 15 N.Y.2d 9, 14, 254 N.Y.S.2d 527, 530, 203 N.E.2d 210, 212-13 (1964); *Capital One Bank v. Fort*, 255 P.3d 508, 510-513 (Or. App. 2011) (court refused to apply law under choice of law provision because contrary to "fundamental public policy" of forum state); Russell J. Weintraub, *Commentary on the Conflict of Laws* 118-125 (6th ed., Foundation Press, 2010).

For examples of choice of law and conflict of law principles operating in this area, see, *e.g., Bradley v. Bradley*, 164 P.3d 537, 540-544 (Wyo. 2007) (premarital agreement had choice of law provision selecting Minnesota law; amendment to agreement held invalid because it did not comply with Minnesota law for modifying agreements); *Gamache v. Smurro*, 904 A.2d 91, 95-96 (Vt. 2006) (applying California law to prenuptial agreement signed in California); *Black v. Powers*, 628 S.E.2d 546, 553-556 (Va. App. 2006) (Virginia couple drafted agreement in Virginia, but signed it during short stay in the Virgin Islands before their wedding there; the agreement was held to be covered by Virgin Islands law because there was no clear party intention that Virginia law apply and because Virgin Island law was not contrary to the forum state's public policy); *cf. Davis v. Miller*, 7 P.3d 1223, 1229-1230 (Kan. 2000) (parties can use choice of law provision to choose the state version of the Uniform Premarital Agreement

Act to apply to a marital agreement, even though that Act would otherwise not apply).

§ 5. Principles of Law and Equity.

Unless displaced by a provision of this [act], principles of law and equity supplement this [act].

Comment

This section is similar to Section 106 of the *Uniform Trust Code* and Section 1-103(b) of the *Uniform Commercial Code*, and incorporates the case-law that has developed to interpret and apply those provisions. Because this act contains broad, amorphous defenses to enforcement like "voluntariness" and "unconscionability" (Section 9), there is a significant risk that parties, and even some courts, might assume that other conventional doctrinal contract law defenses are not available because preempted. This section is intended to make clear that common law contract doctrines and principles of equity continue to apply where this act does not displace them. Thus, it is open to parties, e.g., to resist enforcement of premarital agreements and marital agreements based on legal incompetency, misrepresentation, duress, undue influence, unconscionability, abandonment, waiver, etc. For example, a premarital agreement presented to one of the parties for the first time hours before a marriage (where financial commitments have been made and guests have arrived from far away) clearly raises issues of duress, and might be voidable on that ground. *Cf.* In re *Marriage of Balcof*, 141 Cal.App.4th 1509, 1519-1527, 47 Cal.Rptr.3d 183, 190-196 (2006) (marital agreement held unenforceable on the basis of undue influence and duress); *Bakos v. Bakos*, 950 So.2d 1257, 1259 (Fla. App. 2007) (affirming trial court conclusion that premarital agreement was voidable for undue influence).

The application of doctrines like duress varies greatly from jurisdiction to jurisdiction: *e.g.*, on whether duress can be shown even in the absence of an illegal act, e.g. *Farm Credit Services of Michigan's Heartland v. Weldon*, 591 N.W.2d 438, 447 (Mich. App. 1998) (illegal act required for claim of duress under Michigan law), and whether the standard of duress should be applied differently in the context of domestic agreements compared to commercial agreements. This act is not intended to change state law and principles relating to these matters.

Rules of construction, including rules of severability of provisions, are also to be taken from state rules and principles. *Cf. Rivera v. Rivera*, 243 P.3d 1148, 1155 (N.M. App. 2010), *cert. denied*, 243 P.3d 1146 (N.M. 2010) (premarital agreement that improperly waived the right to alimony and that contained no severability clause deemed invalid in its entirety); *Sanford v. Sanford*, 694 N.W.2d 283, 291-294 (S.D. 2005) (applying state principles of severability to conclude that invalid alimony waiver in premarital agreement severable from valid provisions relating to property division); *Bratton v. Bratton*, 136 S.W.3d 595, 602 (Tenn. 2004) (property division provision in marital agreement not severable from provision waiving alimony). Additionally, state rules and principles will govern the ability of parties to include elevated formalities for the revocation or amendment of their agreements.

§ 6. Formation Requirements.

A premarital agreement or marital agreement must be in a record and signed by both parties. The agreement is enforceable without consideration.

Comment

This section is adapted from *Uniform Premarital Agreement Act*, Section 2. Almost all jurisdictions currently require premarital agreements to be in writing. A small number of courts have indicated that an oral premarital agreement might be enforced based on partial performance, *e.g.*, In re *Marriage of Benson*, 7 Cal. Rptr. 3d 905 (App. 2003), *rev'd*, 36 Cal.4th 1096, 116 P.3d 1152 (Cal. 2005) (ultimately holding that the partial performance exception to statute of

frauds did not apply to transmutation agreement), and at least one jurisdiction has held that a premarital agreement could be amended or rescinded by actions alone. *Marriage of Baxter*, 911 P.2d 343, 345-346 (Or. App. 1996), review denied, 918 P.2d 847 (Or. 1996). One court, in an unpublished opinion, enforced an oral agreement that a written premarital agreement would become void upon the birth of a child to the couple. *Ehlert v. Ehlert*, No. 354292, 1997 WL 53346

(Conn. Super. 1997). While this act affirms the traditional rule that formation, amendment, and revocation of premarital agreements and marital agreements need to be done through signed written documents, states may obviously construe their own equitable doctrines (application through Section 5) to warrant enforcement or modification without a writing in exceptional cases.

It is the consensus view of jurisdictions and commentators that premarital agreements are or should be enforceable without (additional) consideration (the agreement to marry or the act of marrying is often treated as sufficient consideration). Additionally, most modern approaches to premarital agreements have by-passed the consideration requirement entirely: e.g., *Uniform Premarital Agreement Act*, Section 2; American Law Institute, *Principles of the Law of Family Dissolution*, Section 7.01(4) (2002); *Restatement (Third) of Property*, Section 9.4(a) (2003).

In some states, courts have raised concerns relating to the consideration for marital agreements. The view of this act is that marital agreements, otherwise valid, should not be made unenforceable on the basis of lack of consideration. As the American Law Institute wrote on the distinction (not requiring additional consideration for enforcing premarital agreements, but requiring it for marital agreements): "This distinction is not persuasive in the context of a legal regime of no-fault divorce in which either spouse is legally entitled to end the marriage at any time." *Principles of the Law of Family Dissolution*, Section 7.01, Comment c, at 947-948 (2002). The consideration doctrine is sometimes used as an indirect way to ensure minimal fairness in the agreement, and the seriousness of the parties. *See, e.g.,* Lon L. Fuller, "Consideration and Form," 41 *Columbia Law Review* 799 (1941). Those concerns for marital agreements are met in this act directly by other provisions. On the conclusion that consideration should not be required for marital agreements, see also *Restatement (Third) of Property*, Section 9.4(a) (2003), and *Model Marital Property Act*, Section 10 (1983).

§ 7. When Agreement Effective. A premarital agreement is effective on marriage. A marital agreement is effective on signing by both parties.

Comment

This section is adapted from *Uniform Premarital Agreement Act*, Section 4. The effective date of an agreement (premarital agreement at marriage, marital agreement at signing) does not foreclose the parties from agreeing that certain provisions within the agreement will not go into force until a later time, or will go out of force at that later time. For example, a premarital agreement may grant a spouse additional rights should the marriage last a specified number of years.

Parties sometimes enter agreements that are part cohabitation agreement and part premarital agreement. This act deals only with the provisions triggered by marriage, without undermining whatever enforceability the cohabitation agreement has during the period of cohabitation.

§ 8. Void Marriage. If a marriage is determined to be void, a premarital agreement or marital agreement is enforceable to the extent necessary to avoid an inequitable result.

Comment

This section is adapted from *Uniform Premarital Agreement Act*, Section 7. For example, if John and Joan went through a marriage ceremony, preceded by a premarital agreement, but, unknown to Joan, John was still legally married to Martha, the marriage between John and Joan would be void, and whether their premarital agreement should be enforced would be left to the discretion of the court, taking into account whether enforcement in whole or in part would be required to avoid an inequitable result.

This section is intended to apply primarily to cases where a marriage is void due to the pre-existing marriage of one of the partners. Situations where one partner is seeking a civil annulment (see Section 2(3)) relating to some claims of misrepresentation or mutual mistake would usually be better left to the main enforcement provisions of Sections 9 and 10.

§ 9. Enforcement.

(a) A premarital agreement or marital agreement is unenforceable if a party against whom enforcement is sought proves:

    (1) the party's consent to the agreement was involuntary or the result of duress;

      (2) the party did not have access to independent legal representation under subsection (b);

    (3) unless the party had independent legal representation at the time the agreement was signed, the agreement did not include a notice of waiver of rights under subsection (c) or an explanation in plain language of the marital rights or obligations being modified or waived by the agreement; or

    (4) before signing the agreement, the party did not receive adequate financial disclosure under subsection (d).

(b) A party has access to independent legal representation if:

    (1) before signing a premarital or marital agreement, the party has a reasonable time to:

      (A) decide whether to retain a lawyer to provide independent legal representation; and

      (B) locate a lawyer to provide independent legal representation, obtain the lawyer's advice, and consider the advice provided; and

    (2) the other party is represented by a lawyer and the party has the financial ability to retain a lawyer or the other party agrees to pay the reasonable fees and expenses of independent legal representation.

(c) A notice of waiver of rights under this section requires language, conspicuously displayed, substantially similar to the following, as applicable to the premarital agreement or marital agreement:

"If you sign this agreement, you may be:

Giving up your right to be supported by the person you are marrying or to whom you are married.

Giving up your right to ownership or control of money and property.

Agreeing to pay bills and debts of the person you are marrying or to whom you are married.

Giving up your right to money and property if your marriage ends or the person to whom you are married dies.

Giving up your right to have your legal fees paid."

(d) A party has adequate financial disclosure under this section if the party:

    (1) receives a reasonably accurate description and good-faith estimate of value of the property, liabilities, and income of the other party;

    (2) expressly waives, in a separate signed record, the right to financial disclosure beyond the disclosure provided; or

    (3) has adequate knowledge or a reasonable basis for having adequate knowledge of the information described in paragraph (1).

(e) If a premarital agreement or marital agreement modifies or eliminates spousal support and the modification or elimination causes a party to the agreement to be eligible for support under a program of public assistance at the time of separation or marital dissolution, a court, on request of that party, may require the other party to provide support to the extent necessary to avoid that eligibility.

(f) A court may refuse to enforce a term of a premarital agreement or marital agreement if, in the context of the agreement taken as a whole[:]

    [(1)] the term was unconscionable at the time of signing[; or

    (2) enforcement of the term would result in substantial hardship for a party because of a material change in circumstances arising after the agreement was signed].

(g) The court shall decide a question of unconscionability [or substantial hardship] under subsection (f) as a matter of law.

Legislative Note: *Section 9(a) places the burden of proof on the party challenging a premarital agreement or a marital agreement. Amendments are required if your state wants to (1) differentiate between the two categories of agreements and place the burden of proof on a party seeking to enforce a marital agreement, or (2) place the burden of proof on a party seeking to enforce either a premarital agreement or marital agreement.*

If your state wants to permit review for "substantial hardship" caused by a premarital agreement or marital agreement at the time of enforcement, Section 9(f), including the bracketed language, should be enacted.

Comment

This section is adapted from *Uniform Premarital Agreement Act*, Section 6. While this section gives a number of defenses to the enforcement of premarital agreements and marital agreements, other defenses grounded in the principles of law and equity also are available. See Section 5.

The use of the phrase "involuntary or the result of duress" in Subsection (a)(1) is not meant to change the law. There is significant and quite divergent caselaw that has developed under the "voluntariness" standard of the Uniform Premarital Agreement Act and related law – *e.g., compare Marriage of Bernard*, 204 P.3d 907, 910-913 (Wash. 2009) (finding agreement "involuntary" when significantly revised version of premarital agreement was presented three days before the wedding) *and Peters-Riemers v. Riemers*, 644 N.W.2d 197, 205-207 (N.D. 2002) (agreement presented three days before wedding found to be "involuntary"; court also emphasized absence of independent counsel and adequate financial disclosure) *with Brown v. Brown*, No. 2050748, 19 So.3d 920 (Table) (Ala. App. 2007) (agreement presented day before wedding; court held assent to be "voluntary"), *aff'd sub. nom* Ex parte *Brown*, 26 So.3d 1222, 1225-1228 (Ala. 2009) *and Binek v. Binek*, 673 N.W.2d 594, 597-598 (N.D. 2004) (agreement sufficiently "voluntary" to be enforceable despite being presented two days before the wedding); *see also Mamot v. Mamot*, 813 N.W.2d 440, 447 (Neb. 2012) (summarizing five-factor test many courts use to evaluate "voluntariness" under the UPAA); *see generally* Judith T. Younger, "Lovers' Contracts in the Courts: Forsaking the Minimal Decencies," 13 *William & Mary Journal of Women and the Law* 349, 359-400 (2007) (summarizing the divergent interpretations of "voluntary" and related concepts under the UPAA); Oldham, "With All My Worldly Goods," *supra*, at 88-99 (same). This act is not intended either to endorse or override any of those decisions. One factor that courts should certainly consider: the presence of domestic violence would be of obvious relevance to any conclusion about whether a party's consent to an agreement was "involuntary or the result of duress."

The requirement of "access to independent counsel" in Subsections (a)(2) and (b) represents the view that representation by independent counsel is crucial for a party waiving important legal rights. The act stops short of requiring representation for an agreement to be enforceable, *cf. California Family Code* § 1612(c) (restrictions on spousal support allowed only if the party waiving rights consulted with independent counsel); *California Probate Code* § 143(a) (waiver of rights at death of other spouse unenforceable unless the party waiving was represented by independent counsel); *Ware v. Ware*, 687 S.E.2d 382, 387-391 (W. Va. 2009) (*access to independent counsel required, and presumption of validity* for premarital agreement available only where party challenging the agreement actually consulted with independent counsel). When a party has an obligation to make funds available for the other party to retain a lawyer, under Subsection (b)(2), this refers to the cost of a lawyer competent in this area of law, not necessarily the funds needed to retain as good or as many lawyers as the first party may have.

The notice of waiver of rights of Subsections (a)(3) and (c) is adapted from the *Restatement (Third) of Property*, Section 9.4(c)(3) (2003), and it is also similar in purpose to *California Family Code* §1615(c)(3). It creates a safe harbor when dealing with unrepresented parties by use of the applicable designated warning language of Subsection (c), or language substantially similar, but also allows enforcement where there has been an explanation in plain language of the rights and duties being modified or waived by the agreement.

The requirement of reasonable financial disclosure of Subsection (a)(4) and (d) pertains only to assets of which the party knows or reasonably should know. There will be occasions where the valuation of an asset can only be approximate, or may be entirely unknown, and this can and should be noted as part of a reasonable disclosure. Disclosure will qualify as "reasonably accurate" even if a value is approximate or difficult to determine, and even if there are minor inaccuracies. As the Connecticut Supreme Court stated, after reviewing cases from many jurisdictions on the comparable standard of "fair and reasonable disclosure," "[t]he overwhelming majority of jurisdictions that apply this standard do not require financial disclosure to be exact or precise. ... [The standard] requires each contracting party to provide the other with a general approximation of their income, assets and liabilities...." *Friezo v. Friezo*, 914 A.2d 533, 549, 550 (Conn. 2007). Under Subsection (d)(1), an estimate of value of property, liabilities, and income made in good faith would satisfy this act even if it were later found to be inaccurate.

Some commentators have urged that a waiver of the right of financial disclosure (or the right of financial disclosure beyond what has already been disclosed) be valid only if the waiver were signed after receiving legal advice. The argument is that it is too easy to persuade an unrepresented party to sign or initial a waiver provision, and that the party waiving that right would then likely be ignorant of the magnitude of what was being given up. Even when notified in the abstract of the rights being given up, it would make a great deal of difference if the party thinks that what was being given up was a claim to a portion of $80,000, when in fact what was being given up was a claim to a portion of $80,000,000. However, this act follows the current consensus among the states in not requiring legal representation for a waiver. One reason for not requiring legal advice is that this might effectively require legal representation for all premarital agreements and marital agreements. Under a requirement of legal representation, parties entering agreements might reasonably worry that even if there were significant disclosure, it would always be open to the other party at the time of enforcement to challenge the agreement on the basis that the disclosure was not sufficient, and that any waiver of disclosure beyond the amount given was invalid because of a lack of legal representation. In general, there was a concern that a requirement of legal representation would create an invitation to strategic behavior and unnecessary litigation.

"Conspicuously displayed" in Subsection (c) follows the language and standard of Uniform Commercial Code § 1-201(10), and incorporates the case-law regarding what counts as "conspicuous." Reference in Subsection (d)(3) to "adequate knowledge" includes at least approximate knowledge of the value of the property, liabilities, and income in question.

Subsection (e) as adapted from the *Uniform Premarital Agreement Act*, Section 6(b). Other jurisdictions have in the past chosen even more significant protections for vulnerable parties. *See, e.g.,* N.M. *Stat.* § 40-3A-4(B) (premarital agreement may not affect spouse's right to support); *Matter of Estate of Spurgeon*, 572 N.W.2d 595, 599 (Iowa 1998) (widow's spousal allowance could be awarded, even in the face of express provision in premarital agreement waiving that right); In re *Estate of Thompson*, No. 11-0940, 812 N.W.2d 726 (Table), 2012 WL 469985 (Iowa App. 2012) (same); *Hall v. Hall*, 4 So.3d 254, 256-257 (La. App. 2009), writ denied, 9 So.3d 166 (La. 2009) (waiver of interim support in premarital agreement unenforceable as contrary to public policy). This act attempts to give vulnerable parties significant procedural and substantive protections (protections far beyond what was given in the original *Uniform Premarital Agreement Act*), while maintaining an appropriate balance between such protection and freedom of contract.

The reference in Subsection (f) to the unconscionability of (or substantial hardship caused by) a term is meant to allow a court to strike particular provisions of the agreement while enforcing the remainder of the agreement – consistent with the normal principles of severability in that state (see Section 5 and its commentary). However, this language is not meant to prevent a court from concluding that the agreement was unconscionable as a whole, and to refuse enforcement to the entire agreement.

Subsection (f) includes a bracketed provision for states that wish to include a "second look," considering the fairness of enforcing an agreement relative to the time of enforcement. The suggested standard is one of whether "enforcement of the term would result in substantial hardship for a party because of a material change in circumstances arising after the agreement was signed." This language broadly reflects the standard applied in a number of states. *E.g., Connecticut Code* § 46b-36g(2) (whether premarital agreement was "unconscionable . . . when enforcement is sought"); *New Jersey Statutes* § 37:2-38(b) (whether premarital agreements was "unconscionable at the time enforcement is sought"); *North Dakota Code* § 14-03.1-07 ("enforcement of a premarital agreement would be clearly unconscionable"); *Ansin v. Craven-Ansin*, 929 N.E.2d 955, 964 (Mass. 2010) ("the terms of the [marital] agreement are fair and reasonable ... at the time of divorce"); *Bedrick v. Bedrick*, 17 A.3d 17, 27 (Conn. 2011) ("the terms of the [marital] agreement are . . . not unconscionable at the time of dissolution"). However, it should be noted that even in such "second look" states, case law invalidating premarital agreements and marital agreements at the time of enforcement almost universally concerns rights at divorce. There is little case law invalidating waivers of rights arising at the death of the other spouse grounded on the unfairness at the time of enforcement.

Among the states that allow challenges based on the circumstances at the time of enforcement, the terminology and the application vary greatly from state to state. Courts characterize the inquiry differently, referring variously to "fairness," "hardship," "undue burden," "substantial injustice" (the term used by the American Law Institute's *Principles of the Law of Family Dissolution* § 7.05 (2002)), or just "unconscionability" at the time of enforcement. In determining whether to enforce the agreement or not under this sort of review, courts generally look to a variety of factors, including the duration of the marriage, the purpose of the agreement, the current income and earning capacity of the parties, the parties' current obligations to children of the marriage and children from prior marriages, the age and health of the parties, the parties' standard of living during the marriage, each party's financial and home-making contributions during the marriage, and the disparity between what the parties would receive under the agreement and what they would likely have received under state law in the absence of an agreement. *See* Brett R. Turner & Laura W. Morgan, *Attacking and Defending Marital Agreements* (2nd ed., ABA Section of Family Law, 2012), p. 417. The American Law Institute argued that courts generally were (and should be) more receptive to claims when the marriage had lasted a long time, children had been born to or adopted by the couple, or there had been "a change of circumstances that has a substantial impact on the parties ... [and that] the parties probably did not anticipate either the change, or its impact" at the time the agreement was signed. American Law Institute, *Principles of the Law of Family Dissolution* § 7.05(2) (2002). One court listed the type of circumstances under which enforcement might be refused as including: "an extreme health problem requiring considerable care and expense; change in employability of the spouse; additional burdens placed upon a spouse by way of responsibility to children of the parties; marked changes in the cost of providing the necessary maintenance of the spouse; and changed circumstance of the standards of living occasioned by the marriage, where a return to the prior living standard would work a hardship upon a spouse." *Gross v. Gross*, 464 N.E.2d 500, 509-510 n.11 (Ohio 1984).

Subsection (g) characterizes questions of unconscionability (or substantial hardship) as questions of law for the court. This follows the treatment of unconscionability in conventional commercial contracts. *See* UCC § 2-302(1) & Comment 3; *Restatement (Second) of Contracts* § 208, comment f (1981). This subsection is not intended to establish or modify the standards of review under which such conclusions are considered on appeal under state law.

Waiver or modification of claims relating to a spouse's pension is subject to the constraints of applicable state and federal law, including ERISA (Employee Retirement Income Security Act of 1974, 29 U.S.C. 1001 *et seq.*). *See, e.g., Robins v. Geisel*, 666 F.Supp.2d 463, 467-468 (D. N.J. 2009) (wife's premarital agreement waiving her right to any of her husband's separate property did not qualify as a waiver of her spousal rights as beneficiary under ERISA); *Strong v. Dubin*, 901 N.Y.S.2d 214, 217-220 (N.Y. App. Div. 2010) (waiver in premarital agreement conforms with ERISA waiver requirement and is enforceable).

In contrast to the approach of the act, some jurisdictions put the burden of proof on the party seeking enforcement of an agreement. *See, e.g., Randolph v. Randolph*, 937 S.W.2d 815, 820-821 (Tenn. 1996) (party seeking to enforce premarital agreement had burden of showing, in general, that other party entered agreement "knowledgeably": in particular, that a full and fair disclosure of assets was given or that it was not necessary due to the other party's independent knowledge); *Stancil v. Stancil*, No. E2011-00099-COA-R3-CV, 2012 WL 112600 (Tenn. Ct. App., Jan. 13, 2012) (same); In re *Estate of Cassidy*, 356 S.W.3d 339, 345 (Mo. App. 2011) (parties seeking to enforce waivers of rights at the death of the other spouse have the burden of proving that procedural and substantive requirements were met). The Legislative Note directs a state to amend Subsection (a) appropriately if the state wants to place the burden of proof on the party seeking enforcement of a marital agreement, a premarital agreement, or both. In those jurisdictions, Subsection (a) should provide that the agreement is unenforceable unless the party seeking to enforce the agreement proves each of the required elements.

Many jurisdictions impose greater scrutiny or higher procedural safeguards for marital agreements as compared to premarital agreements. *See, e.g., Ansin v. Craven-Ansin*, 929 N.E.2d 955, 961-964 (Mass. 2010); *Bedrick v. Bedrick*, 17 A.3d 17, 23-25 (Conn. 2011). Those jurisdictions view agreements in the midst of marriage as being especially at risk of coercion (the analogue of a "hold up" in a commercial arrangement) or overreaching. Additionally, these conclusions are sometimes based on the view that parties already married are in a fiduciary relationship in a way that parties about to marry, and considering a premarital agreement, are

not. Linda J. Ravdin, *Premarital Agreements: Drafting and Negotiation* (American Bar Association, 2011), pp. 16-18. Also, some jurisdictions have distinguished "reconciliation agreements" entered during marriage with other marital agreements, giving more favorable treatment to reconciliation agreements. *See, e.g., Bratton v. Bratton*, 136 S.W.3d 595, 599-600 (Tenn. 2004) (summarizing the prior law in Tennessee under which reconciliation agreements were enforceable but other marital agreements were void). Many other jurisdictions and The American Law Institute (in its *Principles of the Law of Family Dissolution*, Section 7.01(3) & Comment *b* (2002)) treat marital agreements under the same standards as premarital agreements. This is the approach adopted by this act.

§ 10. Unenforceable Terms.

(a) In this section, "custodial responsibility" means physical or legal custody, parenting time, access, visitation, or other custodial right or duty with respect to a child.

(b) A term in a premarital agreement or marital agreement is not enforceable to the extent that it:

(1) adversely affects a child's right to support;

(2) limits or restricts a remedy available to a victim of domestic violence under law of this state other than this [act];

(3) purports to modify the grounds for a court-decreed separation or marital dissolution available under law of this state other than this [act]; or

(4) penalizes a party for initiating a legal proceeding leading to a court-decreed separation or marital dissolution.

(c) A term in a premarital agreement or marital agreement which defines the rights or duties of the parties regarding custodial responsibility is not binding on the court.

Legislative Note: A state may vary the terminology of "custodial responsibility" to reflect the terminology used in the law of this state other than this act.

Comment

This section lists provisions that are not binding on a court (this contrasts with the agreements mentioned in Section 3, where the point was to distinguish agreements whose regulation fell outside this act). They include some provisions (*e.g.*, regarding the parents' preferences regarding custodial responsibility) that, even though not binding on a court, a court might consider by way of guidance.

There is a long-standing consensus that premarital agreements may not bind a court on matters relating to children: agreements cannot determine custody or visitation, and cannot limit the amount of child support (though an agreed *increase* of child support may be enforceable). *E.g.*, In re *Marriage of Best*, 901 N.E.2d 967, 970 (Ill. App. 2009) ("Premarital

agreements limiting child support are ... improper"), appeal denied, 910 N.E.2d 1126 (Ill. 2009); *cf. Pursley v. Pursley*, 144 S.W.3d 820, 823-826 (Ky. 2004) (agreement by parties in a separation agreement to child support well in excess of guideline amounts is enforceable; it is not unconscionable or contrary to public policy). The basic point is that parents and prospective parents do not have the power to waive the rights of third parties (their current or future children), and do not have the power to remove the jurisdiction or duty of the courts to protect the best interests of minor children. Subsection (b)(1) applies also to step-children, to whatever extent the state imposes child-support obligation on step-parents.

There is a general consensus in the caselaw that

courts will not enforce premarital agreement provisions relating to topics beyond the parties' financial obligations *inter se*. And while some courts have refused to enforce provisions in premarital agreements and marital agreements that regulate (or attach financial penalties to) conduct during the marriage, *e.g.*, *Diosdado v. Diosdado*, 118 Cal. Rptr.2d 494, 496-497 (Cal. App. 2002) (refusing to enforce provision in agreement imposing financial penalty for infidelity); In re *Marriage of Mehren & Dargan*, 118 Cal.App.4th 1167, 13 Cal.Rptr.3d 522 (Cal. App. 2004) (refusing to enforce provision that penalized husband's drug use by transfer of property); *see also* Brett R. Turner and Laura W. Morgan, *Attacking and Defending Marital Agreements* 379 (2nd ed., ABA Section on Family Law, 2012) ("It has been generally held that antenuptial agreements attempting to set the terms of behavior during the marriage are not enforceable" (footnote omitted)), this act does not expressly deal with such provisions, in part because a few courts have chosen to enforce premarital agreements relating to one type of marital conduct: parties' cooperating in obtaining religious divorces or agreeing to appear before a religious arbitration board. *E.g.*, *Avitzur v. Avitzur*, 446 N.E.2d 136, 138-139 (N.Y. 1983) (holding enforceable religious premarital agreement term requiring parties to appear before religious tribunal and accept its decision regarding a religious divorce). Also, while there appear to be scattered cases in the distinctly different context of separation agreements where a court has enforced the parties' agreement to avoid fault grounds for divorce, e.g., *Massar v. Massar*, 652 A.2d 219, 221-223 (N.J. App. Div. 1994); *cf. Eason v. Eason*, 682 S.E.2d 804, 806-808 (S.C. 2009) (agreement not to use adultery as defense to alimony claim enforceable); see generally Linda J. Ravdin, *Premarital Agreements: Drafting and Negotiation* (ABA, 2011), p. 111 ("In some fault states, courts may enforce a provision [in a premarital agreement] that waives fault"), there appears to be no case law enforcing an agreement to avoid *no-fault* grounds. This act follows the position of the American Law Institute (*Principles of the Law of Family Dissolution*, Section 7.08(1) (2002)), that agreements affecting divorce grounds in any way should not be enforceable.

It is common to include escalator clauses and sunset provision in premarital agreements and marital agreements, making parties' property rights vary with the length of the marriage. *Cf. Peterson v. Sykes-Peterson*, 37 A.3d 173, 177-178 (Conn. App. 2012), cert. denied, 42 A.3d 390 (Conn. 2012) (rejecting argument that sunset provision in premarital agreement is unenforceable because contrary to public policy). Subsection (b)(4), which makes provisions unenforceable that penalize one party's initiating an action that leads to the dissolution of a marriage, does not cover such escalator clauses. Additionally, nothing in this provision is intended to affect the rights of parties who enter valid covenant marriages in states that make that alternative form of marriage available.

Section 10 does not purport to list all the types of provisions that are unenforceable. Other provisions which are contrary to public policy would also be unenforceable. See Section 5.

§ 11. Limitation of Action. A statute of limitations applicable to an action asserting a claim for relief under a premarital agreement or marital agreement is tolled during the marriage of the parties to the agreement, but equitable defenses limiting the time for enforcement, including laches and estoppel, are available to either party.

Comment

This Section is adapted from *Uniform Premarital Agreement Act*, Section 8. As the Comment to that Section stated: "In order to avoid the potentially disruptive effect of compelling litigation between the spouses in order to escape the running of an applicable statute of limitations, Section 8 tolls any applicable statute during the marriage of the parties .... However, a party is not completely free to sit on his or her rights because the section does preserve certain equitable defenses."

§ 12. Uniformity of Application and Construction. In applying and construing this uniform act, consideration must be given to the need to promote uniformity of the law with respect to its subject matter among states that enact it.

§ 13. Relation to Electronic Signatures in Global and National Commerce Act. This [act] modifies, limits, or supersedes the Electronic Signatures in Global and National Commerce Act, 15 U.S.C. Section 7001 et seq., but does not modify, limit, or supersede Section 101(c) of that act, 15 U.S.C. Section 7001(c), or authorize electronic delivery of any of the notices described in Section 103(b) of that act, 15 U.S.C. Section 7003(b).

[§ 14. Repeals; Conforming Amendments.

(a) [Uniform Premarital Agreement Act] is repealed.

(b) [Uniform Probate Code Section 2-213 (Waiver of Right to Elect and of Other Rights)] is repealed.

(c) [....]]

§ 15. Effective Date. This [act] takes effect ....

Restatement (Third) of Property: Wills and Other Donative Transfers (2003)

§ 9.4 Premarital or Marital Agreement

(a) The elective share and other statutory rights accruing to a surviving spouse may be waived, wholly or partially, or otherwise altered, before or during marriage, by a written agreement that was signed by both parties. An agreement that was entered into before marriage is a premarital agreement. An agreement that was entered into during marriage is a marital agreement. Consideration is not necessary to the enforcement of a premarital or a marital agreement.

(b) For a premarital or a marital agreement to be enforceable against the surviving spouse, the enforcing party must show that the surviving spouse's consent was informed and was not obtained by undue influence or duress.

(c) A rebuttable presumption arises that the requirements of subsection (b) are satisfied, shifting the burden of proof to the surviving spouse to show that his or her consent was not informed or was obtained by undue influence or duress, if the enforcing party shows that:

(1) before the agreement's execution, (i) the surviving spouse knew, at least approximately, the decedent's assets and asset values, income, and liabilities; or (ii) the decedent or his or her representative provided in timely fashion to the surviving spouse a written statement accurately disclosing the decedent's significant assets and asset values, income, and liabilities; and either

(2) the surviving spouse was represented by independent legal counsel; or

(3) if the surviving spouse was not represented by independent legal counsel, (i) the decedent or the decedent's representative advised the surviving spouse, in timely fashion, to obtain independent legal counsel, and if the surviving spouse was needy, offered to pay for the costs of the surviving spouse's representation; and (ii) the agreement stated, in language easily understandable by an adult of ordinary intelligence with no legal training, the nature of any rights or claims otherwise arising at death that were altered by the agreement, and the nature of that alteration.

Uniform Premarital Agreement Act (1983)

§ 1. Definitions. As used in this Act:

(1) "Premarital agreement" means an agreement between prospective spouses made in contemplation of marriage and to be effective upon marriage.

(2) "Property" means an interest, present or future, legal or equitable, vested or contingent, in real or personal property, including income and earnings.

§ 2. Formalities. A premarital agreement must be in writing and signed by both parties. It is enforceable without consideration.

§ 3. Content.

(a) Parties to a premarital agreement may contract with respect to:

(1) the rights and obligations of each of the parties in any of the property of either or both of them whenever and wherever acquired or located;

(2) the right to buy, sell, use, transfer, exchange, abandon, lease, consume, expend, assign, create a security interest in, mortgage, encumber, dispose of, or otherwise manage and control property;

(3) the disposition of property upon separation, marital dissolution, death, or the occurrence or nonoccurrence of any other event;

(4) the modification or elimination of spousal support;

(5) the making of a will, trust, or other arrangement to carry out the provisions of the agreement;

(6) the ownership rights in and disposition of the death benefit from a life insurance policy;

(7) the choice of law governing the construction of the agreement; and

(8) any other matter, including their personal rights and obligations, not in violation of public policy or a statute imposing a criminal penalty.

(b) The right of a child to support may not be adversely affected by a premarital agreement.

§ 4. Effect of Marriage. A premarital agreement becomes effective upon marriage.

§ 5. Amendment, Revocation. After marriage, a premarital agreement may be amended or revoked only by a written agreement signed by the parties. The amended agreement or the revocation is enforceable without consideration.

§ 6. Enforcement.

(a) A premarital agreement is not enforceable if the party against whom enforcement is sought proves that:

(1) that party did not execute the agreement voluntarily; or

(2) the agreement was unconscionable when it was executed and, before execution of the agreement, that party:

(i) was not provided a fair and reasonable disclosure of the property or financial obligations of the other party;

(ii) did not voluntarily and expressly waive, in writing, any right to disclosure of the property or financial obligations of the other party beyond the disclosure provided; and

(iii) did not have, or reasonably could not have had, an adequate knowledge of the property or financial obligations of the other party.

(b) If a provision of a premarital agreement modifies or eliminates spousal support and that modification or elimination causes one party to the agreement to be eligible for support under a program of public assistance at the time of separation or marital dissolution, a court, notwithstanding the terms of the agreement, may require the other party to provide support to the extent necessary to avoid that eligibility.

(c) An issue of unconscionability of a premarital agreement shall be decided by the court as a matter of law.

§ 7. Enforcement: Void Marriage. If a marriage is determined to be void, an agreement that would otherwise have been a premarital agreement is enforceable only to the extent necessary to avoid an inequitable result.

§ 8. Limitation of Actions. Any statute of limitations applicable to an action asserting a claim for relief under a premarital agreement is tolled during the marriage of the parties to the agreement. However, equitable defenses limiting the time for enforcement, including laches and estoppel, are available to either party.

§ 9. Application and Construction. This [Act] shall be applied and construed to effectuate its general purpose to make uniform the law with respect to the subject of this [Act] among states enacting it.

§ 10. Short Title. This [Act] may be cited as the Uniform Premarital Agreement Act.

§ 11. Severability. If any provision of this [Act] or its application to any person or circumstance is held invalid,

the invalidity does not affect other provisions or applications of this [Act] which can be given effect without the invalid provision or application, and to this end the provisions of this [Act] are severable.

§ 12. Time of Taking Effect. This [Act] takes effect and applies to any premarital agreement executed on or after that date.

§ 13. Repeal. The following acts and parts of acts are repealed:

   (a)

   (b)

   (c)

MODEL PROTECTION OF CHARITABLE ASSETS ACT
(2011)

Table of Sections

Prefatory Note

The Model Protection of Charitable Assets Act (the "Act") states and clarifies the role of the Attorney General in the protection of charitable assets. In addition, the Act requires some persons holding charitable assets to register with the Attorney General, file annual reports, and provide notice of certain fundamental changes or significant events. These requirements apply only to persons with assets above a threshold amount and exemptions further limit the number of persons subject to these duties. These registration and reporting requirements will facilitate performance of the Attorney General's responsibility to protect the public interest in charitable assets.

The Charitable Sector. American charities provide a wide variety of services and benefits through a range of charitable purposes, from art and health care to education and environmental protection. The sector also helps to relieve poverty through a variety of social services. The sector continues to grow, with the reported total number of U.S. charities in 2009, 1,581,111, representing a 31.5% increase in 10 years. *See* Urban Institute, National Center for Charitable Statistics, Number of Public Charities in the United States, 2010, http://nccsdataweb.urban.org/Pub Apps/profile1.php. Charities manage substantial funds in conjunction with carrying out their charitable purposes, over $3 trillion in assets in 2010. *See id.* at http://nccsdataweb.urban.org/PubApps/profileDrillDown.php?state=US&rpt=PC; http://nccsdataweb.urban.org/PubApps/profileDrillDown

.php?state=US&rpt=PF. Charities carry out important functions, improving the quality of life for many people and in many cases supplementing or complementing government programs.

Charitable organizations are formed and operate under state law. Although some are large and operate across state lines, most are local or regional in nature. These local charities provide a significant opportunity for the public to participate in the improvement of local community life. They represent an integral component of our culture.

Public confidence in charities maintains the vibrancy of the charitable sector. If potential donors worry that charities will misuse contributed funds, donors are unlikely to contribute. The good work charities do will suffer if reports of abuse, fraud, or other types of misbehavior reduce public confidence in the sector.

The regulation of charities remains minimal, and yet the importance of public confidence in the sector points to the need for some modicum of protection for the assets entrusted to charities. In the charitable sector, self-regulation has always been and will continue to be important. *See* Panel on the Nonprofit Sector: Principles for Good Governance and Ethical Practice: A Guide for Charities and Foundations (2007), www.nonprofitpanel.org/Report/principles/Principles_Guide.pdf (outlining 33 recommendations for good governance by charitable organizations).

The Internal Revenue Service ("IRS") has begun to increase its role in charitable supervision, and in 2008 the IRS redesigned its Form 990 (Return of Organizations Exempt from Income Tax), which must be filed annually by certain charitable organizations, to request more governance information. The IRS, however, does not have the authority, the resources, or the ability to oversee these myriad charitable entities. Historically, the states have had that authority. The goal of this Act is to acknowledge and protect the role of the states with respect to charitable assets, by clarifying the role of the state Attorney General.

Attorneys General in states that take an active role in protecting charitable assets report the need for information so they can do their jobs. Providing information about charitable assets in other states will allow the Attorneys General in those states to do a better job. Examples of problems with charitable assets demonstrate the need for the Act in states that do not yet have reporting requirements.

The Attorney General in Massachusetts identified charities that needed to establish and follow conflict of interest policies. The Attorney General helped Suffolk University develop a conflict of interest policy and procedures for following the policies. *See* http://www.mass.gov/ago/docs/nonprofit/suffolk-university-070909.pdf. The Attorney General investigated a charity called Angel Flight and required independent directors so those in control of the organization were not in a position to benefit financially. *See* http://www.mass.gov/ago/news-and-updates/press-releases/2010/ag-coakleys-office-and-angel-flight-of-new.html. The Massachusetts Attorney General also investigated problems with a charity called Touched By Angels. The founder and the charity were indicted for fraud, embezzlement, and labor violations. *See* http://www.mass.gov/ago/news-and-updates/press-releases/2011/founder-of-defunct-charity-indicted.html.

Newspaper stories from August 2011 demonstrate the need for oversight of charitable assets. Many more examples exist, and these stories, all posted within a three-day period, merely provide a snapshot of the problems. Concerns about the Kauai Independent Food Bank focused on alleged mismanagement of funds and a conflict of interest that resulted from its purchase of food from a for-profit company owned by members of the food bank. The for-profit company allegedly benefitted by marking up food before selling it to the food bank. *See* http://www.midweek.com/content/columns/

justthoughts_article/kauai_food_bank_misuses_779000/. In Oregon, a jury convicted Pete Seda for fraud for using a charity, Al-Haramain USA, to launder money being sent to Saudi Arabia. *See* http://special.registerguard.com/web/newslocalnews/26695741-41/seda-judge-trial-government-hogan.html.csp.

Described as a "criminal enterprise of mammoth proportion," U.S. Navy Veterans Association raised millions of dollars in several states but did little for veterans. Attorneys General in Florida, Hawaii, Minnesota, Missouri, New Mexico, Ohio, Oregon, and Virginia brought actions against the founder, an employee, companies soliciting on behalf of the organization, and the organization itself. *See* http://www.tampabay.com/news/courts/criminal/key-player-in-navy-vets-scam-to-be-sentenced-today/1185227.

Many charities fall victim to embezzlers. In Pennsylvania, the office manager of the York Symphony Orchestra wrote checks to herself and disguised them as payments to vendors and guest artists. She was charged with embezzling $58,000. *See* http://www.pennlive.com/midstate/index.ssf/2011/08/woman_charged_with_embezzling.html. The director of administration of a New York charity, the Abert Eliss Institute, was accused of embezzling $2.5 million by shifting funds into bank accounts he controlled. *See* http://philanthropy.com/blogs/philanthropytoday/former-chair-of-n-y-nonprofit-board-accused-of-embezzlement/38427. The Gilroy Dispatch, from Gilroy California, reports that a consultant allegedly embezzled $52,000 from the South County Collaborative. *See* http://www.gilroydispatch.com/news/278138-nonprofits-keenly-aware-of-money-trail. In Hartford, Connecticut, the Mark Twain House and Museum struggled to survive while an employee embezzled $1 million. *See* http://articles.courant.com/2011-08-10/news/hc-ed-twain-house-bleeding-20110810_1_nonprofits-museum-restitution. A bookkeeper at Anderson Ranch Arts Center in Snowmass, Colorado embezzled $700,000. *See* http://www.snowmasssun.com/article/20110810/NEWS/110819997/1064&ParentProfile=1039, and in Wyoming $100,000 disappeared from the Genesee Falls Fire Department books. *See* http://thedailynewsonline.com/news/article_63cfbe64-c2ff-11e0-8261-001cc4c03286.html.

These examples, just a sample of the problems that

can arise, indicate the need for protection of charitable assets. For more examples of wrongdoing committed against charities and charitable assets, see Marion R. Fremont-Smith and Andras Kosaras, *Wrongdoing by Officers and Directors of Charities: A Survey of Press Reports 1995-2002*, THE EXEMPT ORGANIZATION TAX REVIEW, October 2003, Vol. 42, No. 1.

The Role of the Courts and the Attorney General under Existing Law. The courts, using their broad equity powers, have long played an important role in determining the scope of charitable purposes and powers in the United States. MARION R. FREMONT-SMITH, GOVERNING NONPROFIT ORGANIZATIONS 302-3 (2004). The duty of the Attorney General to protect assets held for charitable purposes "is stated in the legal texts as an absolute duty and is recognized in almost all of the states either by statute or judicial decision." *Id.* at 306. As Professor Fremont-Smith explains: "Both the enforcement power, exercised by the attorney general, and the regulatory power, exercised by the courts, extend to all assets dedicated to charitable purpose, regardless of the legal form - corporation, trust, or voluntary association - in which they are held." *Id.* at 301.

Thirty-seven states have statutes related to the Attorney General's duty with respect to charitable assets. In a few states - Florida, Mississippi, Missouri, Nebraska, and Wyoming - the statutory authority is limited to corporate transactions of nonprofit corporations, and in Indiana the authority of the Attorney General is limited to petitioning for a trust accounting. In all six of those states, the power to enforce charitable trusts is recognized in the case law. *See id.* at 306. When the Supreme Court of Virginia held that the Attorney General did not have power to enforce charitable corporations but only to enforce charitable trusts, *Virginia v. The JOCO Foundation*, 558 S.E.2d 280 (Va. 2002), the legislature responded quickly to clarify that the assets of a charitable corporation "shall be deemed to be held in trust for the public" and "[t]he attorney general shall have the same authority to act on behalf of the public with respect to such assets as he has with respect to assets held by unincorporated charitable trusts and other charitable entities, including the authority to seek such judicial relief as may be necessary to protect the public interest in such assets." VA. CODE ANN. §2.2-507.1 (2011). The legislature confirmed that the courts had jurisdiction over charitable corporations as well as other charitable entities. VA. CODE ANN.

§17.1-513.01 (2011). In Louisiana, no case or statute describes the Attorney General's role with respect to charitable assets, although the statute providing for cy pres proceedings requires notice to the Attorney General. In all other states the duty to protect charitable funds exists either in the Attorney General or in another public official. *See* FREMONT-SMITH, *supra*, 306-7 (2004).

The states have generally provided minimal resources for the protection of charitable assets. According to one source, in 2007 attorneys staffing state offices (generally those of the Attorneys General) varied from 20.5 attorneys in New York, to 12 in California and Pennsylvania, to no attorneys assigned to this function in 17 states. Some 79% of the states had one or fewer full-time equivalent attorneys devoted to charitable oversight. Garry W. Jenkins, Incorporation Choice, Uniformity, and the Reform of Nonprofit State Law, 41 GA. L. REV. 1113, 1128-1129 (2007). These officials are dedicated professionals but the limited number of these officials and the limited information available in most states make it difficult, if not impossible, to focus on cases warranting attention, or even to respond to complaints. State charity officials have formed the National Association of State Charity Officials (NASCO), which provides an important means of exchanging information, promoting professional education, and upgrading procedures. In addition, the Charities Regulation and Oversight Project of the National State Attorneys General Program at Columbia Law School provides a resource to state attorneys general in fulfilling their responsibilities with regard to charities and charitable assets. Among other things, the project facilitates communication among attorneys general and institutionalizes the dialogue between attorneys general, the regulated communities, and legal scholars specializing in charities and nonprofit studies.

Members of NASCO participated actively in the work of the Drafting Committee for this Act, providing invaluable advice and information based on their experiences. The regulators and charitable organizations, which also played an active role in the work of the committee, represent the key components necessary to a healthy and productive charitable community in our states. Organizations holding charitable assets are typically creatures of state law, subject to state law requirements and expectations. Without more attention to these issues at the state level, increased regulatory activity on the federal level is likely. A healthy federal system requires the states to clarify and exercise their responsibilities over charitable assets. This Act is designed to provide a minimal statutory framework necessary to this effort. States can enhance these requirements as their experiences dictate.

Private rights of action are not addressed in this Act and are left to other statutes and common law. *See, e.g.*, RESTATEMENT (THIRD) OF TRUSTS § 94 (T.D. No. 5, 2009). The rights and the duties of trustees of charitable trusts and directors and officers of nonprofit corporations and unincorporated associations are the subject of other recent products of the Uniform Law Commission ("ULC") (also known as the National Conference of Commissioners of Uniform State Laws or NCCUSL), notably the Uniform Trust Code (2000) and the Uniform Prudent Management of Institutional Funds Act (2006). Important new efforts by the American Law Institute concerning state law are contained in the new Restatement (Third) of Trusts and Principles of the Law of Nonprofit Organizations (partly now in draft).

The authority of the Attorney General to protect charitable assets exists in some form throughout the country, but a procedure for reporting the existence of charitable assets and providing identifying and contact information for persons holding such assets has been lacking in many states. In 1954 the ULC approved the Uniform Supervision of Trustees for Charitable Purposes Act ("1954 Act"), an attempt to rectify the problem by creating registration and reporting requirements. The 1954 Act defines "trustee" to mean anyone, including a corporation, holding assets for charitable purposes. The 1954 Act excluded government agencies, and, in an alternative provision, excluded charities organized and operated exclusively for educational or religious purposes. The Act provided that all covered charities (with no threshold amount) had to register and provide annual reports. The Act also gave the Attorney General authority to investigate charities and request information from the persons managing them.

Arkansas, California, Illinois, Massachusetts, Michigan, Minnesota, New Hampshire, New York, Ohio, Oregon, Pennsylvania, Rhode Island, and Washington all have registration statutes separate from solicitation statutes. *See* ARK. CODE ANN. § 4-28-401 (2011); CAL. [GOV'T] CODE § 12580 et seq. (West 2011) (no threshold amount; exempts religious organizations, educational institutions, hospitals, health care service plans, and cemetery corporations); 760 IL. COMP. STAT. 55/1 et seq. (2011) (more than

$4,000 in assets); MASS. GEN. LAWS ch. 12, § 8E (2011) (no threshold amount); MICH. COMP. LAWS § 14.251 et seq. (2011) (no threshold amount; exempts religious organizations, educational institutions, and hospitals); MINN. STAT. § 501B.33 et seq. (2011) (assets of $25,000 or more; exempts religious associations, split-interest trusts); N.H. REV. STAT. ANN. § 7:19 (2011) (no threshold amount); N.Y. [EST. POWERS & TRUSTS] LAW § 8-1.4 (2011) (total receipts or total assets more than $25,000); OHIO REV. CODE ANN. § 109.26 (West 2011) (no threshold amount; exempts charitable remainder trusts and agricultural societies); OR. REV. STAT. ANN. § 128.610 et seq. (2011) (no threshold amount; exempts religious organizations, cemeteries, and certain child care agencies); 10 PA. CONS. STAT. ANN. § 379 (2011) ($25,000 or more of contributions a year or program service revenue equal to or exceeding $5 million; exempts religious institutions and organizations forming an integral part of a religious institution); R.I. GEN. LAWS § 18-9-6 (2010 (no threshold amount); WASH. REV. CODE ANN. § 11.110.051 (2011) (no threshold amount; exempts religious organizations and educational institutions with programs of instruction comparable to Washington public schools and universities).

Although Idaho does not require registration, it provides by statute that the Attorney General has the duty to supervise any person holding property subject to a charitable or public trust and to enforce the purpose of the trust. IDAHO CODE ANN. § 67-1401 (2011). Idaho also provides that each person holding charitable assets is subject to examination by the Attorney General "to ascertain the condition of its affairs and to what extent, if at all, said trustee or trustees may have failed to comply with trusts said trustee or trustees have assumed or may have departed from the general purpose for which it was formed." *Id. See also* NEV. REV. STAT. ANN. § 82.536 (West 2010); N.H. REV. STAT. ANN. § 7:24 (2011); S.D. CODIFIED LAWS § 55-9-5 (2010); TEX. [GOV'T] CODE ANN. § 402.021 (Vernon 2011) (*See Hill v. Lower Colo. River Auth.*, 568 S.W.2d 473 (Tex. Civ. App. 1978) for case law that affords the Texas Attorney General authority to protect public charity trusts); VT. STAT. ANN. tit. 9, § 2479(b) (2011); WYO. STAT. ANN. § 17-19-170 (2010).

Many states require charities to register if they intend to solicit charitable contributions. Alabama: ALA. CODE § 13A-9-71 (2011); Alaska: ALASKA STAT. § 45.68.010 (2010); Arizona: ARIZ. REV. STAT. ANN. § 44-6552 (2011); Colorado: COLO. REV. STAT. ANN.

§ 6-16-104 (West 2011); Connecticut: CONN. GEN. STAT. §21a-190b (2011); Florida: FLA. STAT. ANN. § 496.405 (West 2011); Georgia: GA. CODE ANN. § 43-17-5 (West 2011); Hawaii: HAW. REV. STAT. § 467B-2.1 (2011); Illinois: 225 ILL. COMP. STAT. 460/2 (2011); Kansas: KAN. STAT. ANN. § 17-1761 (2010); Kentucky: KY. REV. STAT. ANN. § 367.657 (West 2010); Maryland: MD. CODE ANN., [BUS. REG.] § 6-401 (West 2011); Maine: ME. REV. STAT. ANN. tit. 9, § 5004 (2010); Massachusetts: MASS. GEN. LAWS ch. 68, § 19 (2011); Michigan: MICH. COMP. LAWS § 14.303 (2011); Minnesota: MINN. STAT. § 309.52 (2011); Mississippi: MISS. CODE ANN. § 79-11-503 (West 2010); Missouri: MO. ANN. STAT. § 407.462 (West 2011); New Jersey: N.J. STAT. ANN. § 45:17A (West 2011); New Mexico: N.M. STAT. ANN. § 57-22-6 (West 2011); New York: N.Y. [Executive] LAW § 172 (2011); North Carolina: N.C. GEN. STAT. ANN. § 131F-5 (West 2010); North Dakota: N.D. CENT. CODE § 50-22-02 (2009); Ohio: OHIO REV. CODE ANN. § 1716.01 et seq. (West 2011); Oklahoma: OKLA. STAT. ANN. tit. 18, § 552.3 (West 2011); Pennsylvania: PA. CONS. STAT. ANN. 10 P.S. § 162.1 et seq. (West 2011); Rhode Island: R.I. GEN. LAWS § 5-53.1-1 et seq. (2010); South Carolina: S.C. CODE ANN. § 33-56-10 et seq. (2010); Utah: UTAH CODE ANN. § 13-22-1 et seq. (West 2011); Virginia: VA. CODE ANN. § 57-48 et seq. (West 2011); Washington: WASH. REV. CODE ANN. § 19.09.010 et seq. (West 2011); West Virginia: W. VA. CODE ANN. § 29-19-1 et seq. (West 2011); Wisconsin: WIS. STAT. ANN. § 440.42 (West 2011).

A few states require professional fundraising firms that solicit for charities, but not the charities themselves, to register. Indiana: IND. CODE § 23-7-8-2(a) (West 2011); Iowa: IOWA CODE § 13C.2 (2011); Louisiana: LA. REV. STAT. ANN. §51:1901.1 (2011) (the charity must furnish information to substantiate claims that it is charitable if requested by the Attorney General, *id.* at § 51:1902); Oregon: OR. REV. STAT. ANN. § 128.802 (West 2011).

Registration is a common requirement for charities in the United Kingdom and the Republic of Ireland. The laws relating to the registration and administration of charities acts in these jurisdictions have all been redone in the past ten years. In addition to broad registration requirements, with certain exceptions they require detailed financial accounts to be filed with a central regulatory agency that is separate from the taxing authorities. In England and Wales, the Charities Act of 2006 is the governing statutory authority, Scotland has the

Charities and Trustee Investment Act of 2005, Northern Ireland has the Charities Act of 2008, and the Republic of Ireland has the Irish Charities Act of 2009. These jurisdictions maintain arrangements for informal cooperation since many charities in the British Isles operate across regulatory boundaries. In essence, these jurisdictions require all charities to keep proper accounting records, to publish annual statement of accounts, and to register with the relevant regulator. There are income thresholds applicable in England and Wales for the filing of annual reports and accounts, and the requirement for accounts to be independently examined by a lay examiner applies only for charities with higher levels of activity. Higher thresholds are required for full audits in each of these jurisdictions. *See, generally, Cross-Border Issues in the Regulation of Charities Experiences from the UK and Ireland,* 11 INTERNATIONAL JOURNAL FOR NOT FOR PROFIT LAW, Issue 3 (May 2009).

Goals of the Act. The Model Protection of Charitable Assets Act articulates and confirms the role of the state Attorney General in protecting charitable assets. The Attorney General's existing authority is broad and this Act does not limit or narrow that authority. In some states, however, the scope of the authority is unclear. In the great majority of states, the Act will provide a helpful statutory articulation of that authority.

The Act adopts registration, reporting, and notice requirements that will enable the Attorney General to fulfill the responsibility of that office to represent the public interest by protecting charitable assets. The requirements are designed so as not to overburden either the Attorneys General or those with the duty to report. The Act is based on a minimalist or basic platform.

It is useful to remember that the Attorney General has an educational role and a facilitative role in addition to the responsibility to protect charitable assets from waste, diversion, or mismanagement. Currently, many Attorneys General educate charities and work with charities to help them become more efficient and more effective. The Attorney General will be better able to perform these roles with more adequate information about the charities operating in the state.

Model v. Uniform Act. Because some states have substantial statutes in this area of the law, while others have little or no statutory authority with respect to the protection of charitable assets, the prospect of uniformity in statutory language is limited. The approach of this Act is to create a model, all or part of which would be useful to all of the states. As a whole, it is designed to produce a minimalist structure for those states without significant structures presently in place. While uniformity is desirable, adoption by states presently without significant legislation in this area will foster uniform understanding of the role of the Attorney General and ways in which that role can be supported. It should also enhance cooperation among the states.

Who Does the Act Cover? The Attorney General of a state has a duty to protect charitable assets located and used in the state and all charitable assets held by entities incorporated or organized in the state, so the Act has broad applicability. However, certain sections of the Act (registration, reporting, and notice) apply more narrowly due to threshold amounts or exemptions based on policy. The threshold amounts that apply to the duty to register, to file an annual report, and to provide notices are in brackets, indicating that a state can change the amounts to apply the duties more broadly or to limit the duties to fewer organizations. The Act does not cover assets held by governmental bodies or entities. It does not cover private businesses, except to the extent that those entities hold charitable assets. The Act does not use the term "charity," because that term has a variety of meanings in statutes and common parlance so using the term with a definition specific to the Act could be confusing.

General Authority of the Attorney General. The Act states the broad duty of the Attorney General to represent the public interest in the protection of charitable assets. The Act states that the Attorney General may enforce the use of charitable assets for the purposes for which the assets were given; may take action to prevent or correct a breach of a fiduciary duty in connection with the administration of the entity holding the assets or with respect to the charitable assets; and may intervene in an action brought to correct a misapplication of charitable assets, a departure from the purpose of the entity holding the charitable assets, or a breach of a fiduciary duty.

Registration. The Act provides that a person that holds, or within the preceding 12 months has received, charitable assets with a value in the aggregate of more than a suggested $50,000 must register with the Attorney General within a specified period of time after the charity initially receives property. The information required for the registration is brief but will provide the Attorney General's office with basic information about the organization (name, address, statutory agent, federal identification number, and contact person) and information about the charitable purpose of the organization. Section 4 contains several exemptions from the registration requirement, including exemptions for a government or governmental subdivision, agency or instrumentality, and an organization the primary purpose of which is to influence elections. Section 4 further contains, in brackets, exemptions for the states to consider, including alternatives dealing with churches and religious organizations and an exemption for an organization that has as its primary activity advocacy on issues of public or governmental policy. The Comments to Section 4 include a one-page registration form.

Annual Reports. An organization with charitable assets or receipts above the threshold amount and that is required to register under Section 4 must file an annual report with the Attorney General. The annual report will provide basic information and requires that the charity attach a copy of any report the charity files with the IRS (e.g., a Form 990, Form 990-EZ, or Form 990-PF). The Comments to Section 5 include a two-page annual report form. If an organization holds charitable assets above the threshold amount but was exempt from registration under Section 4, the person is not required to file an annual report.

Notice of "Life Events." One of the concerns the Act seeks to address was the problem that occurs when an Attorney General learns about the loss of charitable assets after a person holding the assets disposes of them. The Act requires a person holding charitable assets to file a notice with the Attorney General of certain planned events, a specified number of days before the event is to occur. Events that require notice represent fundamental changes and include the following:

- A dissolution or termination;
- The disposition of all or substantially all of its property;
- A merger, conversion, or domestication;
- A removal of the charity or of significant charitable assets from the state.

The transfer of assets without providing notice or, after providing notice, before the passage of the time prescribed in the Act, will be considered a violation of the Act unless the person receives written consent from the Attorney General or notice that the

Attorney General will take no action with respect to the event. Approval by the Attorney General is not required, but the Act provides the Attorney General the opportunity to determine whether there is a need to take action to protect charitable assets before the event occurs.

In addition, if a decedent's estate or a revocable trust after the settlor's death involves the distribution of property to a person holding charitable assets, the personal representative of the estate or the trustee of the trust must send the Attorney General a copy of the will or a description of the charitable interests in the trust. A person holding charitable assets must also send notice to the Attorney General of revocation or modification of its federal, state, or local tax exemption.

Any person who asserts a claim in a proceeding involving charitable assets or a person holding charitable assets must give written notice to the Attorney General. This may be the charitable person itself or some other person. The notice must include a copy of the initial pleading. The proceedings that require notice are the following:

- An action seeking to enforce a term relating to a gift of a charitable asset;
- An action seeking to enforce the use of charitable assets or involving the breach of a duty owed to the person holding charitable assets;
- A proceeding seeking instructions relating to the management, use, or distribution of charitable assets;
- A proceeding to construe a document under which charitable assets are held or to modify the terms under which charitable assets are held;
- A proceeding to remove, appoint, or replace a trustee of a charitable trust;
- A proceeding involving a trust or decedent's estate in which matters affecting charitable assets may be decided; or
- A proceeding for bankruptcy or receivership.

Waiver of Filing Requirements. The Act addresses concerns about excessive filing requirements in two ways. First, the Act limits registration and annual report requirements to persons holding more than a suggested $50,000 of assets. This threshold is significantly higher than that used by existing state registration statutes and by the federal government and should serve to remove a significant number of persons from the reporting requirements of the Act. Second, the Attorney General can decide to waive certain filing requirements under the Act. The goal is to limit the need to make duplicate filings. In a state with a solicitation statute, annual reports filed under that statute may contain information similar to that required under this Act. One filing may be sufficient for the purposes of the solicitation statute and the purposes of this Act, and the Attorney General may choose to waive the filing of annual reports under this Act. The Act does not attempt to coordinate with solicitation statutes, but a state may choose to do so.

The Attorney General may waive the registration requirement for a person holding charitable assets that is registered in another state under a under a law substantially similar to this Act and require instead the filing of a copy of the registration filed with the other state. If a person holding charitable assets is not required to register, it will not be required to file annual reports.

Cooperation with Other Officials. The Act permits the Attorney General to cooperate with any official of the state, another state, the United States, or a foreign government. The Attorney General can provide information or documents concerning an investigation or proceeding to the other official in connection with the official's role in the oversight of charities and charitable assets, but cannot provide information kept confidential by law. The Attorney General can also acquire information or documents from the other official.

Resources and Enactment. A state without the resources to manage the filings required under Sections 4-7 may want to adopt only Sections 1-3. The Act will still provide valuable guidance if the state adopts only Section 3, providing clarification of Attorney General authority. A state may also choose to require registration but not require annual reports. If a state adopts only Sections 1-3, the state will want to delete Section 2(5), the definition of responsible person, used only in Sections 4 and 5.

§ 1. **Short Title.** This [act] may be cited as the Model Protection of Charitable Assets Act.

§ 2. **Definitions.** In this [act]:

(1) "Charitable asset" means property that is given, received, or held for a charitable purpose. The

term does not include property acquired or held for a for-profit purpose.

(2) "Charitable purpose" means the relief of poverty, the advancement of education or religion, the promotion of health, the promotion of a governmental purpose, or any other purpose the achievement of which is beneficial to the community.

(3) "Person" means an individual, corporation, estate, trust, business trust, statutory trust, partnership, limited liability company, association, joint venture, public corporation, government or governmental subdivision, agency, or instrumentality, or any other legal or commercial entity.

(4) "Record" means information that is inscribed on a tangible medium or that is stored in an electronic or other medium and is retrievable in perceivable form.

(5) "Responsible individual" means an individual who, with respect to a person holding charitable assets:

(A) is generally familiar with the affairs of the person; and

(B) participates, directly or indirectly, in the control or management of the person.

(6) "State" means a state of the United States, the District of Columbia, Puerto Rico, the United States Virgin Islands, or any territory or insular possession subject to the jurisdiction of the United States.

Comment

Subsection (1). Charitable Asset. The term "property" includes all interests in real property or tangible or intangible personal property, including cash, remainder interests, land, and conservation or preservation easements or restrictions. The remainder interest in a charitable remainder trust is property held for a charitable purpose, as is the current interest in a charitable lead trust, property held for ten years in a building fund, and property given to a charitable organization subject to a restriction on its use. Property held in a revocable trust that provides a remainder interest for a charitable purpose is not a charitable asset while the settlor is alive because the settlor can revoke or change the interest.

Property held with a for-profit purpose is not a charitable asset, even if the purpose is one that could be considered charitable if held on a nonprofit basis. For example, education is a purpose that has long been considered a charitable purpose. Many colleges operate as nonprofits and their educational purpose is considered charitable, but some educational institutions – University of Phoenix is an example – operate on a for-profit basis. A for-profit university is not operating for a charitable purpose even if its purpose is educational. The same is true for a for-profit hospital. The second sentence to the definition is included to avoid any misunderstanding that somehow a business purpose could be considered a charitable purpose.

The word "asset" does not have the meaning it would have in an accounting context, for example on a balance sheet.

Subsection (2). Charitable Purposes. The definition of charitable purposes follows that of Uniform Trust Code § 405, Restatement (Third) of Trusts § 28 (2003), and Uniform Prudent Management of Institutional Funds Act § 2(1) (2006). This long-familiar standard in U.S. trust law derives from the English Statute of Charitable Uses, enacted in 1601. As used in this Act the definition means the definition of charitable purpose that has developed under the common law. A charitable purpose is a nonprofit purpose (and not a purpose for private benefit) that benefits an indefinite class of the public.

The definition includes purposes "beneficial to the community" because that concept is part of the traditional definition of charitable purposes. The definition means purposes considered charitable and not merely beneficial. Many activities and organizations, such as social welfare organizations, cooperative associations, and business entities, benefit the community. Nonetheless, these organizations and the activities they carry on are not charitable within the meaning of the Act because their earnings inure to the benefit of private persons such as members or shareholders. *Attorney General v. Weymouth Agricultural & Industrial Society*, 400 Mass. 475, 479, 509 N.E.2d 1193, 1195 (1987). The definition of charitable has long been limited to those beneficial purposes that fit within one of the other categories of charitable, for example educational, that relate to the relief of poverty, or that provide some general good such as improvement of the environment. By using the standard definition, the Act intends to include the case law that has developed around the term "charitable" in trust law.

Case law has distinguished between purposes that are charitable and those that are merely beneficial. For example, in *Shenandoah Valley National Bank v. Taylor*, 192 Va. 135, 63 S.E.2d 786 (1951), a settlor attempted to create a trust to provide small amounts of money to children just before winter and spring holidays. The distributions were not restricted in their purpose and were not limited based on the financial need of the recipients. The court concluded that the purpose was beneficial and not charitable. As the court explained, "charitable" means either distributions in response to financial need or distributions that support an educational purpose or one of the other identified charitable purposes.

Something that is now considered charitable but does not fit neatly in one of the other delineated categories is environmental protection. Thus, for example, organizations that protect watersheds, wildlife habitat, or biodiversity will be considered charitable even though they do not provide for the relief of poverty, the advancement of education or religion, the promotion of health (except, perhaps, tangentially), or the promotion of a governmental purpose (although governments may become involved in the protection of such resources), because achievement of its purpose will be beneficial to the community. The phrase "beneficial to the community" as used in the definition of "charitable purpose" allows some development of the term "charitable" in the case law, but the phrase should not be read to mean that anything that is beneficial to some people benefits the community and is charitable for purposes of this Act. An activity with a charitable purpose is one that benefits a sufficiently large and indefinite class of persons-the community and not just a fortunate few-and the earnings from the activity cannot be distributed to private persons. *Attorney General v. Weymouth Agricultural & Industrial Society*, 400 Mass. at 479, 509 N.E.2d at 1195. Nor does the Act apply to organizations whose primary purpose is political advocacy. *Workmen's Circle Educational Center of Springfield v. Board of Assessors*, 314 Mass. 616, 619, 51 N.E.2d 313, 316 (1943).

Some states have created statutory definitions of charitable purpose for various reasons. See, e.g., 10 Pa. Cons. Stat. § 162.3 (2005) (defining charitable purpose within the Solicitation of Funds for Charitable Purposes Act to include "humane," "patriotic," "social welfare and advocacy," and "civic" purposes). The definition in subsection (2) applies for purposes of this Act and does not affect definitions of charitable purpose in other legislation. If a state has another definition of charitable purpose, the state may consider substituting the other definition for the definition in the Act. However, because definitions in different contexts serve different purposes, the state should consider any substitution carefully. For example, some states have narrowed the definition of charity for tax purposes, but protection of assets devoted to a charitable purpose might be appropriate even if the purpose does not qualify for tax exemption under state law. Weymouth Agricultural & Industrial Society, 400 Mass. at 477 n.3, 509 N.E.2d at 1194.

Subsection (3). Person. Person is defined using the standard ULC definition and includes individuals as well as entities. Charitable entities organized as nonprofit corporations, charitable trusts or unincorporated associations are included within this definition.

Subsection (4). Record. Record is defined using the standard ULC definition. The term allows the use of one word instead of several when the act deals with traditional forms of paper, as well as information in electronic form.

Subsection (5). Responsible Individual. This term describes someone the Attorney General could contact for information about the charity. Often the Attorney General will be able to resolve a question about a charity's use of assets informally, and having someone identified as a contact person for the charity will make that informal discussion more efficient and effective. A responsible individual should be someone who is generally familiar with, among other things, how the charity is managed, but the person need not be a director or trustee. The definition is based on one in the Uniform Law Enforcement Access to Entity Information Act (2009).

§ 3. Authority of [Attorney General] to Protect Charitable Assets.

(a) The [Attorney General] shall represent the public interest in the protection of charitable assets and may:

(1) enforce the application of a charitable asset in accordance with:

(A) the law and terms governing the use, management, investment, distribution, and expenditure of the charitable asset; and

    (B) the charitable purpose of the person holding the asset;

  (2) act to prevent or remedy:

    (A) the misapplication, diversion, or waste of a charitable asset; or

    (B) a breach of fiduciary or other legal duty in the governance, management, or administration of a charitable asset; and

  (3) commence or intervene in an action to:

    (A) prevent, remedy, or obtain damages for:

      (i) the misapplication, diversion, or waste of a charitable asset; or

      (ii) for a breach of fiduciary or other legal duty in the governance, management, or administration of a charitable asset;

    (B) enforce this [act]; or

    (C) determine that an asset is a charitable asset.

(b) If the [Attorney General] has reason to believe an investigation is necessary to determine whether action is advisable under this [act], the [Attorney General] may conduct an investigation, including exercising administrative subpoena power under [law of this state providing for administrative subpoena power].

(c) This [act] does not limit the powers and duties of the [Attorney General] under law of this state other than this [act].

(d) The [Attorney General] shall promulgate rules to implement [this [act]] [Sections 4(a) and (e), 5(a), 6, 7(b), and 8].

Legislative Note: *States that detail Attorney General subpoena power in statutes dealing broadly with Attorney General power will not need to add provisions regarding subpoena power to Section 3. States that do not provide specific statutory authority for the Attorney General will need to add a subsection to do so. States that provide in their statutes for Attorney General civil subpoena power specifically in connection with another Attorney General function (such as consumer protection) may want to add that language to Section 3 with any necessary adaptations.*

<h2 style="text-align:center">Comment</h2>

One of the major goals of the Act is to articulate the Attorney General's duty to represent the public interest in the protection of charitable assets. The duty exists in the common law and in statutes in many states, but the scope of the duty is sometimes uncertain. The Act declares and clarifies the scope of the duty and what the Attorney General is authorized to do to fulfill it, although the Act does not limit the authority or powers that already exist.

The Attorney General's duty has sometimes been described as the "parens patriae" power – the duty to protect the public interest in property that has been committed to charitable purposes. Unlike a private corporation or a private trust, no shareholder or private beneficiary has a financial incentive to supervise the proper management of assets held for charitable purposes. A donor or charitable beneficiary may be interested in the management of the assets, but under the common law the Attorney General has standing to sue or take action to protect the public's interest in charitable assets. A Massachusetts statute, first enacted in 1847, describes the duty as the duty to "enforce the due application of funds given or appropriated to public charities . . . and prevent breaches in the administration thereof . . . ." MASS. GEN. LAWS ch. 12, §8. A court in Pennsylvania recently explained:

The Commonwealth has parens patriae standing whenever it asserts quasi-sovereign interests, which are interests that the Commonwealth has in the well-being of its populace. Here, the Commonwealth's interest in the well-being of the public that Citizens was created to serve is a clear example of such a quasi-sovereign interest. In fact, "*in every proceeding which affects a charitable trust,* whether the action concerns invalidation, administration, termination or enforcement, the attorney general must be made a party of record because the public as the real party in interest in the trust is otherwise not properly represented." In re Pruner's Estate, 390 Pa. 529, 532-33, 136 A.2d 107, 110 (1957) (emphasis added). It is the duty of the Attorney General to ensure that the purpose of the charity remains charitable. *Commonwealth v. Citizens Alliance for Better Neighborhoods, Inc., et al.*, 983 A. 2d 1274, 1278 (Pa. Cmwlth. 2009). *See also* JAMES J. FISHMAN & STEPHEN SCHWARZ, NONPROFIT ORGANIZATIONS 226 (4th ed. FOUNDATION PRESS 2010) (stating, "the attorney general represents the state and the public, promoting accountability by charities and fiduciaries").

The Attorney General's authority over charitable assets does not depend on the organizational form of the person holding the assets. Charitable assets may be held by nonprofit corporations or unincorporated associations, as well as by trustees of charitable trusts, and the Attorney General will protect the interests of the public in these assets, however held. In a recent case a defendant tried to distinguish between cases involving charitable trusts and the defendant's organization, a nonprofit corporation. Applying Massachusetts law, the court simply noted: "Charitable corporations and trusts are both considered 'public charities' under Massachusetts law and, as such, are subject to the Attorney General's supervisory authority." *Lifespan Corp. v. New England Medical Center*, 2010 WL 3718952, at 3 (D.R.I. Sept. 20, 2010). The Attorney General's authority also extends over charitable assets held by for-profit entities.

The Attorney General protects the public interest in charitable assets, but assets held by a charitable organization are not converted to public (governmental) assets. Restrictions imposed by donors and the governing documents of the organization control the use of the assets and the government cannot take over and manage the organization. Rather, the Attorney General may take appropriate action to enforce the restrictions and to prevent self-dealing and mismanagement of the property. In *Dartmouth College v. Woodward*, the U.S. Supreme Court held that the constitutional restriction on the impairment of contracts applied to the "contract" that created Dartmouth College – the granting of its corporate charter by the Crown. The opinion by Justice Marshall explains that because Dartmouth College is a charitable organization the legislature cannot change the use of the funds held by the trustees. The fact that the government had

granted the charter did not make the college a government-controlled entity. A concurrence by Justice Story explains:

A private donation, vested in a trustee, for objects of a general nature, does not thereby become a public trust, which the government may, at its pleasure, take from the trustee, and administer in its own way. . . .The only authority remaining to the government is judicial, to ascertain the validity of the grant, to enforce its proper uses, to suppress frauds, and, if the uses are charitable, to secure their regular administration, through the means of equitable tribunals, in cases where there would otherwise be a failure of justice. Dartmouth College v. Woodward, 17 U.S. 518, 697-98 (1819).

Thus, the role of the state in protecting charitable assets has long been recognized. The state cannot substitute its own judgment as to how an organization should be managed or who should manage it, and the legislature cannot convert charitable assets to government assets, but the state can, and should, protect assets from mismanagement, misapplication, diversion, or waste. The Attorney General is charged with this authority. If the Attorney General finds a breach of fiduciary duty or identifies mismanagement of charitable assets, a court can impose sanctions.

Subsection (a). Duty of Attorney General and Powers. Subsection (a) states the duty of the Attorney General concerning charitable assets. This subsection follows existing law in most states and may serve as a declaration of the role of the Attorney General in states in which the duty has not been stated explicitly. Subsection (a) states the duty to preserve and protect charitable assets and ensure their proper use and administration and lists the powers within the discretion of the Attorney General. To carry out the duty to protect charitable assets, the Attorney General may take action to enforce the purposes or terms for which an asset was given to a charity and may act to prevent or remedy a breach of a duty owed to a charity by a fiduciary or by another person. The Attorney General may begin or intervene in an action to protect charitable assets.

Donor Restrictions. Subsection (a)(1)(A) provides that the Attorney General may enforce the terms governing a gift of charitable assets. These terms include provisions in a gift agreement specifying the charitable purpose of the gift or the terms of its administration. UPMIFA § 2(3), reflecting thoughtful case law, provides that written documents used at the time of a gift, including solicitation materials or organizational documents, can be considered part of a "gift instrument" creating the terms of a gift. Subsection (a)(1)(A) uses "terms of the gift" with the UPMIFA definition in mind and also with the intent to incorporate other state law regarding donor restrictions on gifts. The doctrines of cy pres and deviation, for example, provide rules for modifying restrictions imposed by the donor at the time of a gift.

The Act does not directly address the question of whether an entity holding charitable assets can change its purposes and thereby change the way it uses unrestricted donations already received. It seems likely that a donor who contributes money or other property to an organization expects the organization to use the gift for the purposes for which the entity is organized and operating at the time the gift is made, even if the donor does not enter into a formal gift agreement. An entity organized as a nonprofit corporation can, however, change its purposes by amending its articles of incorporation and bylaws. Accordingly, a question arises as to whether an organization can apply unrestricted gifts received before a change in its corporate purpose to its new or expanded purpose. Some courts have held that unrestricted gifts are "impressed with a charitable trust" and must be used in a manner consistent with the charity's purpose at the time the gift was made. *See, e.g., Queen of Angels Hosp. v. Younger*, 66 Cal. App. 3d 359, 365 (Ct. App. 1977); *Holt v. College of Osteopathic Physicians and Surgeons*, 61 Cal. 2d 750, 755 (1964). Other courts have similarly held, even though the unrestricted gifts were not deemed to technically be held in trust. *See, e.g., Attorney Gen. v. Hahnemann Hosp.*, 494 N.E. 2d 1011, 1020-21 (Mass. 1986) (in which the court stated that the nonprofit corporation could broaden its purposes by amending its articles, but the hospital could not use unrestricted donations received prior to the amendment for the new purposes).

Whether the governing documents of a nonprofit corporation impose purpose restrictions on otherwise unrestricted gifts may depend on evolving case law. The draft ALI Principles of the Law of Nonprofit Organizations take the position that a charity can change the purpose to which unrestricted assets are devoted by amending its governing documents to change its corporate purpose, regardless of the extent of the change. *See* PRINCIPLES OF THE LAW OF NONPROFIT ORGS. §400, cmt. (d)(3) (The American Law Institute Preliminary Draft No. 5 2009) (stating, "a facially unrestricted gift made to a charity having a single, narrow purpose is not viewed as a restricted

gift. Rather, a donor's desire that the gift be used for a specific purpose must be expressed, in writing, in order for the recipient charity to be bound to use that gift for that purpose.").

Whether an Attorney General will object to the application of unrestricted gifts received before a change in the organization's corporate purpose to the organization's new or expanded purpose will depend on specific facts. An Attorney General is not likely to seek to enforce the use of the gifts for the original purpose where the change in the organization's governing documents is minor or necessary to comply with changing laws. For example, an Attorney General might not be concerned about donor intent when a charitable hospital established to provide acute care is expanded to add sub-acute care. However, the court in *Hahnemann* notes a different sort of example: "As the Attorney General, colorfully, but no doubt correctly, observes in his reply brief, 'those who give to a home for abandoned animals do not anticipate a future board amending the charity's purpose to become research vivisectionists.'" Attorney Gen. v. Hahnemann Hosp., 494 N.E. 2d 1011, 1021 n. 18 (Mass. 1986).

The Attorney General protects charitable assets whether held by an entity organized for charitable purposes or by an entity or individual not so organized. Although subsection (a)(1)(B) refers to the charitable purpose of the person holding the assets, a non-charitable entity or an individual will not have a charitable purpose. A separate fund managed by a business corporation might have a charitable purpose, such as when assets are sold with the representation that a percentage of the proceeds will be used for a charitable purpose. That fund should be administered in accordance with that charitable purpose. The fact that a business entity or an individual does not have a charitable purpose means that the reference to the "charitable purpose of the person" will not apply in those cases.

Subsection (b). Power to Investigate. Subsection (b) states the authority of the Attorney General to conduct an investigation under the Act. The Attorney General must have a reason to believe the investigation is necessary to determine whether further action under the Act is appropriate. In conducting investigations, an Attorney General will also be limited under the Fourth Amendment to issuing administrative subpoenas sufficiently limited in scope, relevant in purpose, and specific in direction so that compliance will not be unreasonably burdensome. *Becker v. Kroll*, 494 F.3d 904, 916 (7th

Cir. 2007).

Oftentimes, the Attorney General will be able to resolve an issue with a charity through the exchange of information followed by discussion without the need for a court proceeding. The Attorney General's authority to investigate will make non-judicial resolution of matters involving charities more likely, so that more assets will be preserved for charitable purposes. Of course, if the Attorney General and the charity cannot agree on appropriate steps, a court will be the final arbiter.

Subsection (c). Other Authority. Subsection (c) reflects the intention that the Act not replace any common law or other statutory powers the Attorney General may have. For example, some states regulate charitable solicitation through other statutes.

Subsection (d). Regulations. The Attorney General may need to issue regulations to carry out the terms of this Act and to provide guidance about compliance. If an Attorney General is not otherwise authorized to promulgate regulations, a state will want to include this subsection, giving the Attorney General that authority.

Investigative Authority. States vary with respect to process and procedure relating to Attorney General's investigative authority. In many states the Attorney General has civil jurisdiction but another agency has criminal jurisdiction. For example, the Connecticut Attorney General is the civil charitable regulator but if the Attorney General wishes to initiate a criminal proceeding, the Attorney General must do so through the chief state's attorney. In other states (e.g. Maryland), the county state's attorney has general criminal jurisdiction. For examples of state statutes that provide for the power to issue subpoenas or orders with the effect of subpoenas in connection with investigations of charitable organizations, see HAW. REV. STAT. § 467B-9.3 (2010); MASS. GEN. LAWS Ch. 12, § 8 H (2010; MICH. COMP. LAWS § 400.291 (2010); N.H. REV. STAT. ANN. § 7:24 (2011).

Relators. A few states provide for the use of relators. A relator is a private person who is authorized to sue a charitable organization on behalf of the Attorney General. A California statute permits persons granted relator status by the California Attorney General to sue a charitable organization on behalf of the Attorney General. CAL. CORP. CODE §5142(a)(5) (2011). Pursuant to the regulations, Cal. Code Regs. Tit.11 §§ 1-10 (2011), a private person

can notify the Attorney General of abuse by the charity or its fiduciaries. The suit must be one that the Attorney General could have brought, and the Attorney General must authorize the suit before the relator can proceed. The private relator pays the court costs, but the attorney general remains in control of the action. The Act does not provide for relators, but states are free to add such provisions.

Standing of Others. The Act does not, either expressly or by implication, affect existing law concerning the rights of persons other than the Attorney General to standing in connection with a matter involving charitable assets. As stated in the Prefatory Note, in some states courts or legislatures have recognized limited standing for someone other than the Attorney General. For example, the Uniform Trust Code grants standing to settlors of charitable trusts. UNIF. TRUST CODE § 405(c). See also, RESTATEMENT (THIRD) OF TRUSTS § 94 (T.D. No. 5, 2009).

Religious Organizations. The Act does not exclude trusts held for religious purposes from oversight by the Attorney General. Due to Constitutional protections, the Attorney General would not determine whether an organization used property for a religious purpose. For example, if a rabbi kept paintings in the offices used by the rabbi and others, it would not be appropriate for the Attorney General to try to determine whether the paintings had religious significance and were used for religious purposes. In contrast, if a religious body decided to divide into two and a dispute developed between the two factions about property owned by the original body, the Attorney General might be involved to ensure that the property stayed with the two successor organizations and did not end up in private hands. The Attorney General is properly concerned that property committed to religious purposes not be taken for an individual's personal purposes. See Sherri Buri McDonald, CEO *Wrongly Enriched, Judge Says*, THE REGISTER GUARD, Dec. 15, 2011 (The Oregon Attorney General has been involved in a case brought be members of a Sikh religious community against administrative leaders who unjustly enriched themselves by transferring a business held by the religious community to themselves for a grossly undervalued amount.).

§ 4. Registration.

(a) The [Attorney General] shall establish and maintain a public registry of persons registered under this section.

(b) Except as otherwise provided in subsection (c), a person is required to register if the person holds, or within the preceding 12 months received, charitable assets with a value in the aggregate exceeding $[50,000] and:

(1) is formed under the law of this state or, if the person is a trust, has its principal place of administration in this state;

(2) has its principal place of business in this state;

(3) holds charitable assets with a value in excess of $[50,000] in this state other than assets held primarily for investment purposes; or

(4) subject to subsection (d), conducts activities in this state for a charitable purpose.

(c) The following are exempt from the requirement in subsection (b) to register:

(1) a government or governmental subdivision, agency, or instrumentality;

(2) an organization the primary purpose of which is to influence elections or legislation;

(3) with respect to charitable assets that belong to another person, a financial institution, attorney's trust account, investment company, licensed escrow agent, or storage facility;

(4) a [personal representative] of a decedent's estate that holds a charitable asset, during the period of administration of the estate; [and]

(5) a trustee of a revocable trust that becomes irrevocable because of the settlor's death, during a period of administration following the settlor's death not to exceed two years[.][;] [; and]

[(6) a person that has as its primary activity advocacy on issues of public or governmental policy][.][; and]

Alternative A

[(7)] a religious organization, an organization operated, supervised, or controlled by or in connection with a religious organization, or an officer or director of, or a trustee that holds property in an official capacity for an organization described in this paragraph.]

Alternative B

[(7)] a [church][house of worship], a convention or association of [churches][houses of worship], or an integrated auxiliary of a [church][house of worship].]

Alternative C

[(7)] a religious organization as defined by [insert statute].]

Alternative D

[(7)] a person that holds assets for the advancement of religion and is not required to report to the Internal Revenue Service, to the extent of those assets.]

End of Alternatives

(d) The following activities, without more, do not constitute conducting activities in this state for a charitable purpose:

(1) maintaining, defending, mediating, arbitrating, or settling an action or proceeding;

(2) holding a meeting of trustees, directors, or members;

(3) maintaining an account in a financial institution or an investment account;

(4) holding real or personal property;

(5) engaging in an isolated activity that is not in the course of similar activities; [and]

(6) making a grant, scholarship, or award to a person in this state[.][; and]

(7) soliciting or accepting contributions.]

(e) Unless the [Attorney General] grants a waiver under Section 8(a), a person required by this section to register shall register with the [Attorney General] not later than [three] months after the date charitable assets held by the person exceed the value of $[50,000].

(f) The registration required by subsection (b) must provide:

(1) the name and address of the person;

(2) the name and address of the statutory agent of the person for service of process or the individual on whom service of process may be made;

(3) the name and contact information of a responsible individual of the person;

(4) the federal employer identification number, if any, for the person; [and]

(5) information concerning the federal tax status of the person[.][;][; and]

[(6) a copy of the record, however denominated, that describes the charitable purposes of the person and the use and administration of charitable assets held by the person[.][; and

(7) the name under which the person has registered under [the state's solicitation statute] and the registration number, if any.]

(g) A registration pursuant to subsection (b) is terminated on the filing with the [Attorney General] by the person registered of:

(1) a written notice of termination of registration that states the person no longer holds a charitable asset and has no reasonable expectation it will hold charitable assets with a value in the aggregate exceeding $[50,000] in the next 12 months; and

(2) an annual report for the current year.

Legislative Note: *If the state has a solicitation statute, the state should include Section 4(f)(7) and may include the optional Section 4(d)(7). If the state does not have a solicitation statute, the state should not include those sections.*

Comment

The Act requires persons holding charitable assets to register with the Attorney General so the Attorney General will have basic information about the charitable assets the Attorney General has a duty to protect. The Act directs the Attorney General to maintain a registry of the persons who must register, and the registry will serve as a resource for the public as well as for the Attorney General. The registration requires minimal information to avoid overburdening either charitable organizations or Attorneys General. The hope is that states will be able to move to an electronic system for registration and reporting, thereby reducing some of the burden on persons required to register. While a large organization that operates in many states will likely have an obligation to register in multiple states, the Act's move toward uniformity will minimize the burden of multiple registrations. Electronic registration, when it comes, will further ease the burden. These Comments include a statutory form of registration to enable states to adopt a requirement that is consistent across states.

Registration is important for several reasons. First, the list of registered entities can serve as a quick resource of information for the Attorney General and for the public. If the Attorney General receives a question from a member of the public, the Attorney General may be able to answer the question simply by reviewing the information provided in the registration. No further inquiry may be necessary, and both the Attorney General and the registered entity will save time and expense.

Second, a potential donor may consult the list of registered entities to determine whether an organization requesting a donation is current in its filings with the Attorney General. If the organization is not registered, the donor will want to investigate further before making a donation. If the organization has consistently made the required filings, that information suggests the organization is more likely to be well managed by fiduciaries who comply with their duties.

Finally, the requirement to register serves as a reminder to someone organizing an entity to hold charitable assets of the seriousness of the fiduciary duties an individual undertakes when acting as a director or trustee. If the individual does not want to assume the duties associated with managing charitable assets, the individual can give the assets to an existing organization or start a donor advised fund.

Subsection (b). Who Must Register. Subsection (b) limits registration in a number of ways, creating both a threshold amount for registration and limiting registration to organizations with significant contacts with the state.

The threshold created by subsection (b) applies whether a person "holds, or within the preceding 12 months received" assets above the threshold amount. The duty to register will apply after an organization passes the threshold amount and holds assets in that amount, and the duty will also apply if an organization raises money, uses it for charitable purposes, and then raises more money. After the total amount raised by the organization exceeds the threshold, the duty to register applies, even if the organization uses the assets raised and does not hold more than the threshold amount at any one time.

Subsection (b). Threshold Amount. Persons holding charitable assets in money or value in excess of the amount fixed in the adopting legislation must register under the Act. The Act suggests $50,000 as the floor for requiring registration, but places that amount in brackets to indicate that a state may use a larger or smaller number.

The threshold for filing Form 1023, Recognition of Exempt Status, with the IRS is $5,000. The information required to register with the Attorney General is significantly less detailed than the information required to complete a Form 1023, so an organization required to file with the IRS should not face an undue burden if required to register with the Attorney General. The advantage of a threshold as low as $5,000 is that a smaller organization may be more likely than a larger organization to encounter difficulties due to the lack of adequate checks and balances within the organization or lack of expertise on the part of the founding directors. The Attorney General can provide education and other assistance that may be particularly beneficial for smaller organizations.

The Act has $50,000 rather than $5,000 as the suggested figure to minimize the burdens on smaller charities and in recognition of the limited resources in some Attorney General offices. The committee chose $50,000 because that number is the threshold at which organizations must file significant financial information with the IRS (charities with annual gross receipts of $50,000 or less must file an on-line e-postcard called 990-N with the IRS; charities with receipts over $50,000 must file Form 990-EZ, Form 990, or Form 990-PF).

The National Center for Charitable Statistics

reports that in 2008, 1,071,851 charities had registered with the IRS. Of that number, fewer than half (458,963) filed annual returns reporting financial information. See http://nccsdataweb.urban.org/PubApps/reports.php?rid=35. In 2008, the filing threshold for reporting financial information was $25,000, so with the increase in the threshold to $50,000, the number of returns that contain significant financial information should decrease. The National Center for Charitable Statistics reports the number of charitable organizations filing returns by state, so a state can determine the number of potential filers by examining that data. Illinois, which currently requires annual returns for persons holding charitable assets in excess of $4,000, receives about 26,000 returns a year from entities operating in Illinois.

Of the states that have registration requirements apart from solicitation requirements, California, Massachusetts, Michigan, New Hampshire, Oregon, Rhode Island and Washington have no threshold amount. Illinois requires registration when a charity has more than $4,000 in assets; Minnesota requires registration when assets exceed $25,000; New York requires registration when assets or receipts exceed $25,000; and Pennsylvania requires registration when contributions exceed $25,000. Registration requirements in England and Wales, Scotland, the Irish Republic and Northern Ireland generally require registration without regard to annual receipts. See Prefatory Note.

A state enacting Section 4 and the other sections requiring reports to the Attorney General (Sections 5-7) should make its decision on the appropriate threshold amount by considering the resources available in that state for managing the filings. States should be aware that the $50,000 amount in the Act is a higher number than the number used in existing statutes.

Fair Market Value. The valuation of assets held for charitable purposes, should be made based on the fair market value of the assets, reasonably determined. The Act does not use the term "fair market value" because the Drafting Committee did not want to suggest that appraisals were required to determine value. A person holding charitable assets can estimate the value, as long as the estimate is reasonable. Because the determination of value is used only for deciding whether a person meets the thresholds for registration and reporting, a reasonable estimate of value is sufficient. The value determined for purposes of the Act should be the value to the charitable organization and not the value on the market, and should be based on the value of the property assuming its use is not restricted. For example, a parcel of land given to an organization to be used as a nature preserve, or artwork given to a museum to be displayed and not sold or loaned, should be valued for registration purposes at its unrestricted value (what a willing buyer would pay a willing seller for the land or artwork assuming it was not subject to a use restriction). The value of a conservation easement for registration purposes should be the difference between the fair market value of the subject property encumbered and unencumbered by the easement.

Subsection (b). Significant Contacts. The Act requires registration of only those organizations that have significant contacts in the state. The inclusions and exclusions strike an appropriate balance between the risk of overburdening entities that have little contact with a particular state and the need for the Attorney General to be alerted to the existence of charitable organizations and assets in the state.

Although the types of contact listed in subsection (b) are not limited by the terms "substantial" or "significant," the intention is that a negligible level of activity or other contact not be considered sufficient to cause an Attorney General to assert protection powers. The state constitution will control the level of activity necessary for Attorney General protection.

Subsection (b)(1). A nonprofit corporation must register in its state of incorporation, even if the nonprofit corporation conducts all of its activities in another state (the nonprofit will also need to register in the other state). A trust must register in its principal place of administration. A trust's principal place of administration is typically where the trustee is located. If the trust has trustees located in more than one jurisdiction, then other factors, including the location of assets and activities, will be used to determine the principal place of administration. *See* UNIF. TRUST CODE §108, cmt. (2010). UTC §108 provides that the terms of a trust can name the place of administration, so long as the trustee's principal place of business or residence is in the state named or all or part of the administration of the trust occurs in that state. If a trustee moves the principal place of administration, the trustee will have to register in the new state.

The trustee of an irrevocable trust with a charitable organization as a beneficiary must register. For example, the trustee of a charitable remainder trust or a charitable lead trust must register if the value of the charitable interest exceeds $50,000. The charitable organization named in the trust is not required to register because the trustee, and not the organization, is the person holding the charitable assets.

Subsection (b)(2). The term "principal place of business" is used to mean principal place of administration, governance, activities, and operation. Although using the term "business" for charitable activities sounds odd, the term is used to bring with it the substantial case law connected with the term.

Subsection (b)(3). If a person holds investment assets located in a state and has no other contacts with the state, the person need not register. If a person holds assets used for its charitable purposes, however, the person must register. In most cases, if the person holds assets for its charitable purposes it will also be conducting charitable activities in the state. For example, an entity organized in Chicago might own land in Wisconsin that it uses as a summer camp for disadvantaged children.

If an organization holds an asset in a state only until the asset can be sold and the proceeds used for charitable purposes, the asset will not trigger the duty to register. For example, an organization operating in Illinois might be given land in Michigan. If the organization continues to hold the land as an investment, subsection (b)(3) applies and that asset will not create a duty to register. If the Illinois organization holds the land only until it can be sold, subsection (b)(3) does not require registration even though the organization is not holding the land as a long-term investment.

Subsection (b)(4). If an organization conducts its principal activities in one state but also conducts activities in another state, the organization must register in both states (under (b)(2) and (b)(4)). An organization with minimal contacts in a state does not need to register there, but if the organization conducts significant activities, the organization should register. For example, an organization incorporated in Philadelphia might operate homeless shelters in Philadelphia and across the state border in New Jersey. The organization would register in Pennsylvania and New Jersey. If the organization purchased property in Delaware to use for a homeless shelter but was not yet operating a shelter there, the organization would not need to register in Delaware under subsection (b)(4) because subsection (d)(4) provides that holding property, without more, will not be considered conducting activities. Of course, if the value of the property exceeded the threshold in subsection (b)(3), and if the property was acquired for charitable activities (eventual use as a shelter) and not for investment, then subsection (b)(3) would require registration.

Subsection (c). Exemptions. Subsection (c) exempts a number of entities and individuals from the registration requirement.

Subsection (c)(1). Governmental Subdivisions. The Attorney General already represents government subdivisions, so the Act excludes government subdivisions and agencies from registration. This exemption applies even if a government agency holds a fund for charitable purposes that are not usually governmental purposes, for example a scholarship fund. If a separate organization supports a government activity, for example an education fund created by a community to support local schools, that separate organization will register, even if under federal tax law it qualifies as a supporting organization to the government subdivision.

Subsections (c)(2) and (c)(6). Political, Lobbying and Advocacy Groups. Organizations created primarily to influence elections, to lobby, or as political advocacy organizations are not primarily charitable organizations. These exclusions may be unnecessary, because these organizations would not be included under (b) in most circumstances. These exclusions are provided in the Act to clarify that organizations engaged primarily in these activities are not required to register, even if they hold assets for a charitable purpose.

Subsection (c)(3). Financial Institutions. Financial institutions and investment companies are not included within the definition by virtue of having accounts owned by charitable organizations. If a bank or trust company serves as trustee for a trust holding charitable assets, the trustee must register based on the other subsections of Section 4(b).

Subsections (c)(4), (c)(5). Wills and Revocable Trusts. If an individual provided a gift to a charitable organization under a will or through a revocable trust that acts as a will substitute at death, the personal representative of the decedent's estate or the trustee of the trust must notify the Attorney General after the individual's death under Section 6, but they do not need to register under Section 4. The exclusion for a decedent's estate applies for the period of administration of the estate, and the exclusion for a revocable trust applies for two years from the date of the settlor's death. Because a revocable trust does not have an identifiable period of administration, the two-year time period serves as an approximation of the time needed for administration.

Subsection (c)(7). Religious Organizations.

Charitable assets held by religious organizations fall within the scope of the Attorney General's duty to protect charitable assets, but a state may decide not to require religious organizations to register or report. A state can require religious organizations to register or choose one of four exceptions to exclude religious groups or organizations. Defining which organizations to exclude proved difficult, so the Act provides four alternatives for the exclusion. A fifth alternative appears in these Comments.

Alternative A creates a broad exemption that includes religious organizations as well as organized religions. Under Alternative A, a United Church of Christ congregation, a Jewish synagogue, a Buddhist temple, and a Muslim mosque would all be exempt, as would a K-12 school, food pantry, or homeless shelter operated by any religious organization. This broad definition is not limited to organized worship. It excludes significant assets, particularly with respect to education.

Alternative B tracks the concept and language of the Internal Revenue Code. Although there is concern about using the word "church" to mean groups of people practicing a religion and the assets used in doing so, Alternative B is drafted to match the language the IRS uses. Obviously, "church" excludes a lot of religions practiced in the U.S. IRS publication 1828 titled "Churches and Religious Organizations" explains its use of the term:

> The term church is found, but not specifically defined, in the Internal Revenue Code (IRC). The term is not used by all faiths; however, in an attempt to make this publication easy to read, we use it in its generic sense as a place of worship including, for example, mosques and synagogues. With the exception of the special rules for church audits, the use of the term church throughout this publication also includes conventions and associations of churches as well as integrated auxiliaries of a church. Because special tax rules apply to churches, it is important to distinguish churches from other religious organizations. Therefore, when this publication uses the term "religious organizations," it is not referring to churches or integrated auxiliaries. Religious organizations that are not churches typically include nondenominational ministries, interdenominational and ecumenical organizations, and other entities whose principal purpose is the study or advancement of religion.

Alternative B provides "house of worship" as an option, but that term is problematic as well. Either "church" or "house of worship" might exclude something like a mickva - a ritual bath used by Orthodox Jews. *See Combined Congregations of District of Columbia v. Dent*, 140 F.2d 9, 10 (C.A.D.C. 1943) ("Since the statute [pertaining to a property tax exemption] refers to the building rather than to the institution it is difficult to see how a structure which contains only a ceremonial bath can come within the ordinary meaning of the word 'church' or 'synagogue'"). The terms do not mean merely a building, but instead require a group of people organized to practice a religion (to qualify as a "church" or "house of worship" it is necessary to have a congregation or group). Therefore, "church" and "house of worship" are used as stand-ins for the idea of a group of people engaged in the practice of a religion.

Alternative B includes "integrated auxiliaries," a term that comes from the Internal Revenue Code and includes organizations that are closely tied to a particular church or churches, but does not include free-standing religious organizations without such ties. Thus, Alternative B would include a K-12 school run by a particular church but not a free-standing religious school.

Alternative C suggests that a state use its own state definition of religious organization or cross-reference that definition.

Alternative D was added to link the exclusion to the Internal Revenue Code's definition while avoiding the use of the word "church." Yet another alternative that attempts to reach the same result as Alternatives B and D, would be "a religious corporation, association, or society." *See Mordecai F. Ham Evangelistic Ass'n v. Matthews*, 189 S.W.2d 524, (Ky. 1945) (referring to "an association or body of [religious] communicants ... usually meeting in some stated place for worship or for instruction, or organized for the accomplishment of religious purposes such as instruction or dissemination of some tenet or particular faith or otherwise furthering its teachings"). A state could also consider New Mexico's version: "A church, organization or group organized for the purpose of divine worship or religious teaching or other specific religious activity or any other organization that is formed in association with or to primarily encourage, support or promote the work worship, fellowship, or teaching of the church, organization, or group." N. M. Stat. Ann. § 57-22-3.

All of the alternatives are intended to include a corporation sole in a state that has that organizational form. Corporations sole are legal entities intended to promote continuity between office holders of a corporation, usually a religious organization. This structure allows an organization to maintain nonprofit status without establishing bylaws or maintaining a Board of Directors. See http://www.irs.gov/charities/article/0,,id=128736,00.html.

The Internal Revenue Code does not require houses of worship to register with the Internal Revenue Service. I.R.C. § 6033. However, this section does not exempt religious organizations that are not houses of worship, conventions or associations, or integrated auxiliaries from filing for recognition of their exempt status and making annual reports.

The Constitutional protections of the free exercise of religion mean that the government cannot interfere with the exercise of tenets of religious doctrine. The Constitution does not prohibit registration and reporting by religious organizations.

Subsection (d). Minimal Activities. This subsection lists a number of activities a charitable organization might engage in that do not rise to the level of activity that requires registration. The goal is to limit registration to states in which the organization has sufficient activity or assets for the Attorney General to be concerned about proper administration. Even if an organization engages in several of these activities, the organization need not register unless required to do so for another reason. Each charitable organization will register in at least one state because the organization will register in the state in which it is formed or, if a trust, administered.

For example, a university located in Connecticut would register in Connecticut. The university might hold alumni events throughout the country, and registration in other states would depend on the activity and on the event's organizer. A one-time event held in another state would not require registration, because subsection (d)(5) excludes isolated activities. If the alumni events were held every year, the organization holding the event might need to register. The alumni association, rather than the university itself, might be the organization conducting activities in the state, or a state alumni organization might be the responsible organization. Registration will depend on the extent of the activities. Subsection (d)(7) excludes mere solicitation, but social activities that include solicitation could trigger the duty to register.

Subsection (e). Time for Registration. The duty to

register depends on the date the person's charitable assets exceed the value set in the enacted statute (the Act suggests $50,000). The person must register within three months of that date. Even if the person holding charitable assets does not hold the value set at any one time, if the person receives assets that total the set figure in a 12-month period, the person must register.

Subsection (f). Registration Information. The Act requires minimal registration information. Some states that currently provide for registration of persons holding charitable assets ask for more information. If a state wants to consider more extensive registration requirements, the state can look at California, Illinois, Massachusetts, or New York for examples. *See* CAL. [GOV'T] CODE § 12580 et seq. (West 2011); 760 IL. COMP. STAT. 55/1 et seq. (2011); MASS. GEN. LAWS ch. 12, § 8E (2011) (no threshold amount); N.Y. [EST. POWERS & TRUSTS] LAW § 8-1.4 (2011).

Subsections (f)(1)-(3). The registration must include an address, which can be the address of the organization and need not be the address of an individual. In addition to the statutory agent, the organization must provide the name of a "responsible individual" who can answer questions about the organization. If the Attorney General has a question or receives a complaint, the Attorney General can often resolve the issue with a phone call if the Attorney General is able to reach a person who is knowledgeable about the organization. Resolving issues quickly in this way saves time and resources for both the Attorney General and the organization.

Subsection (f)(4). The registration includes the federal employer identification number of the person holding charitable assets. This number should be the EIN for the person (the nonprofit corporation, charitable trust, or other organization) and not for an individual associated with the person. If the person for some reason does not have an EIN, the individual filing the registration should so indicate and should not provide a social security number.

Subsection (f)(5). Most new organizations will need to register before they receive their determination letters from the IRS indicating that they are tax exempt. The registration can state that the organization has applied for recognition of its tax-exempt status and the request is pending.

Subsection (f)(6). This subsection is in brackets to indicate that some states may not want to include this provision. Subsection (f)(6) requires the person registering to provide documents that describe its

charitable purposes and how it will use and administer its assets. Most persons registering will provide articles and bylaws or a copy of the trust instrument. Organizing documents are not specifically required because those documents depend on the organizational structure of the person, and because not all persons who hold charitable assets are nonprofit corporations or trusts. The intent is for the person holding charitable assets to provide documentation indicating the charitable purposes for the assets and any restrictions on use of the assets so the Attorney General will have notice of the purposes for which they were solicited or given.

If a person holding charitable assets is a business corporation that has set aside assets in a charitable fund, the business need only furnish the portions of its documents that relate to the charitable assets. The business corporation need not provide its articles and bylaws in their entirety because most of the content of those documents will not apply to the charitable assets. The same is true for a trust if part of the trust applies to private beneficiaries and part has a charitable purpose. Only the portions of the trust applicable to the charitable assets need be provided and the rest of the trust instrument can be redacted.

Subsection (f)(7). If a state has a solicitation statute that requires registration, the registration filed under this Act should include information that will enable the state to link the two registrations. This Act requires registration of all organizations that meet the threshold requirements, whether or not the organization solicits, so a solicitation statute by itself does not address the need for this Act.

Subsection (g). A person holding charitable assets will continue to be registered until the person dissolves, but if an entity holding charitable assets is not a charitable organization, the entity may want to terminate its registration once the charitable assets have been used. For example, a business corporation might create a scholarship fund for students at a local high school. If the fund had more than $50,000 the corporation would register, file annual reports, and provide notices required under Section 6. If after several years the corporation distributed all the money and closed the fund, the corporation would provide that information to the Attorney General and might want to terminate its registration. If the corporation did not terminate its registration, the corporation would have an ongoing duty to provide notices under Section 6, even though it no longer held charitable assets.

Website Benefits. An organization required to

register in a state may benefit from posting its registration on its website. Although registration by itself does not indicate Attorney General approval, knowing that an organization is registered and current with its annual reports may make potential donors more likely to contribute.

Form. A form for registration appears in these

Comments. The form can be reproduced on one page. The committee encourages states to use this form so persons registering can use one form for multiple filings. Because a person holding charitable assets may need to register in multiple states, having the same form used in all states will save time and expense.

REGISTRATION UNDER PROTECTION OF CHARITABLE ASSETS ACT

Name of Organization: _____
Federal Employer Identification Number (EIN): _____
Street Address: _____
City, State, and ZIP Code: _____
Phone number: _____ Website: _____
Name of Statutory Agent or Individual on Whom Service of Process May Be Made:

_____
Street Address: _____
City, State, and ZIP Code: _____
Name of Responsible Individual to Contact: _____
Street Address: _____
City, State, and ZIP Code: _____
Phone number: _____ E-mail address: _____

Tax-Exempt Status

Which of the following describes the organization's tax-exempt status application with the Internal Revenue Service? Please note that an application for tax-exempt status is different from an application for an employer identification number.

( )   The organization holds IRS tax-exempt status.

( )   The organization applied for tax-exempt status on _____/_____/_____ but a determination letter has not been received from the IRS.

( )   The organization has not applied for tax-exempt status. Explain the reason for not applying on an attached page.

( )   The organization applied for tax-exempt status and the IRS denied the application.

[Registration Under Charitable Solicitation Act

If the organization is registered under [the state's solicitation statute]:
Name registered: _____
Registration number: _____]

[Required Documents

Attach to this registration form a copy of the document (articles of incorporation, bylaws, articles of association, trust agreement, or other document) that describes the organization's charitable purpose and the use and administration of its charitable assets.]

§ 5. Annual Report.

(a) [Unless the [Attorney General] grants a waiver under Section 8(b),] [A] [a] person required to register under Section 4 which holds charitable assets with a value exceeding $[50,000] at the end of the person's most recent annual accounting period or receives charitable assets with a value in the aggregate exceeding $[50,000] during the period shall file with the [Attorney General], not later than the later of four months and 15 days after the end of the period or the date authorized for filing an informational return with the Internal Revenue Service, including all extensions, an annual report providing [and verifying][and certifying the accuracy of] the following information:

(1) the name and address of the person;

(2) the name and address of the statutory agent of the person for service of process or the individual on whom service of process may be made;

(3) the name and contact information of a responsible individual of the person during the period;

(4) a description of the person's most significant charitable activities, not exceeding three, during the period;

(5) whether during the period the person:

(A) engaged in an event described in Section 6(a) or (b);

(B) entered into a contract, loan, lease, or other financial transaction with an officer, director, trustee, or other fiduciary of the person, or a [family member] of an officer, director, trustee, or other fiduciary of the person, either directly or with an entity in which the officer, director, trustee, other fiduciary, or [family member] had a material financial interest;

(C) became aware of an embezzlement, theft, or diversion of a charitable asset of the person;

(D) became aware of use of a charitable asset of the person to pay a penalty, fine, or judgment;

(E) became aware of the payment by an officer, director, trustee, or other fiduciary of the person of a penalty, fine, or judgment with respect to the person;

(F) became aware of the use of restricted funds of the person for a purpose other than the charitable purpose specified in the restriction; or

(G) received notice of revocation, modification, or denial of its federal or [state][local] charitable [income] tax exemption;

(6) an explanation of an affirmative answer reported under paragraph (5)[.][;][; and]

[(7) the person's total revenue relating to its charitable assets for the period; [and]

(8) the value of the person's charitable assets as of the last day of the period[.][;][; and]

[(9)] a change to any information provided under Section 4 [.][; and

(10) the name under which the person has registered under [the state's solicitation statute] and the registration number, if any.]

(b) If a person required to file an annual report under subsection (a) is required to file a federal information return with the IRS, the person shall attach to the annual report a copy of the publicly available part of the most recently filed return.

Legislative Note: *In subsection (a)(5)(B), "family member" is not a precise term, and a state may want to use a specific definition here or refer to a definition in other law in the state. For example, the state may want to clarify whether the term includes, with respect to an individual, a spouse, descendants, ascendants, siblings, spouses of family members, an unmarried domestic partner, or step-relatives.*

In subsection (a)(5)(G), "income" is in brackets to indicate that a state may want to limit reporting to situations in which action taken involves an organization's exempt status for income tax purposes or may want to expand the reporting requirement to include action taken with respect to exempt status for other state taxes, such as a state or local property tax or sales tax. A state should choose "state" or "local" to reflect the taxes the state has and wants to include in the reporting requirement.

Comment

A person with charitable assets in excess of the amount a state provides or that receives assets in excess of that amount during the accounting period, must file an annual report providing basic information about its revenue, assets, and activities during the year. The Act requires that each person that meets the filing threshold file a short annual report and attach a copy of the person's federal tax filing. The annual report form filed in addition to the federal form should allow the Attorney General to review quickly the information provided by the person filing the form. The annual report requires minimal information, and if states adopt the annual report form uniformly, the burden on persons required to file in multiple states will be reduced. The report is due four months and 15 days after the end of the accounting period ~ the due date for the annual reporting to the IRS. The Act adds "or such later date as the Attorney General authorizes" because many organizations receive extensions for filing their annual forms with the IRS. The assumption is that the Attorney General will authorize extensions for state filings to match due dates for federal filings.

The annual report should cover the organization's total revenue, assets, and activities and not just those in the state. The Attorney General will be concerned about charitable assets in the state, but it is not necessary for the organization to separate out the information on a per-state basis. The organization will be able to use the same information for federal purposes as well as in each state in which the organization needs to report.

The reporting requirement can encourage good governance. The annual report can serve an educational purpose, providing a reminder of some of the duties owed with respect to charitable assets. The Attorney General needs to receive information in a timely fashion to be able to address problems before charitable assets are lost. The registration and reporting requirements are important in promoting appropriate protection of charitable assets. Further, timely filing of annual reports will give the public confidence that an organization is being managed properly.

The filing threshold for the annual report is consistent with the threshold for registration. Although some committee members noted that small organizations are often the ones that suffer most from improper management, the committee decided on the $50,000 threshold to minimize the impact on organizations and the Attorneys General. If a state decides to lower the threshold for registration, the state can choose to keep the threshold for the annual report at $50,000 or lower it. Some states with current registration and reporting statutes have different thresholds for the two requirements. For example, in Illinois the threshold to register is $4,000 and the threshold to file an annual report is $25,000. 760 IL. COMP. STAT. 55/7 (2011).

States that require annual reporting under a statute that regulates charitable solicitation may want to coordinate the report required here with the report required by the solicitation statute and may find the reporting requirement in Section 5 duplicative and unnecessary.

Subsection (a).   Information to Report. Subsection (a) lists the items to be included in the report. The subsection begins with the person's name, the name of a statutory agent, and the name of a responsible person. A state can decide what information to include in the report, but this Act recommends the inclusion of all the items in subsection (a). The committee used brackets on some of the items with the recognition that some states will want less information.

Subsection (a)(4) requires the person to describe the three (or fewer) most significant charitable activities during the reporting period.

Subsection (a)(5) asks the person to indicate whether the person engaged in certain activities or became aware of certain incidents, any of which might indicate a problem in the management or use of the charitable assets. The person checks "yes" or "no" on the annual report form for each item, so in most cases this part of the report will take little time. If the person answers "yes" for any item, then subsection (6) asks the person to explain. The information will give the Attorney General a quick way to determine whether the Attorney General should take a closer look at something involving the person.

Subsection (a)(7) asks for the person's total revenue for its most recent accounting period. The intention here is to have the person report the same number reported on line 12 of Part I of IRS Form 990, so that only one computation is necessary. Subsection (a)(8) asks for the asset value on the last day of the reporting period. The committee decided not to include a requirement to report disbursements because that information can be determined by comparing asset value from year to year.

Subsection (a)(9) requires the person to update the information provided on its registration. A state with a solicitation statute should include Subsection (10), which asks for the name under which the person registered under the other statute.

Subsection (b).   Federal Information Return. Subsection (b) asks the person to attach to the annual report a copy of its federal filing. Although federal filings are public records and are eventually posted on Guidestar, obtaining a copy of the form immediately after it is filed can be difficult. The benefits to the

Attorney General of having immediate access to the federal form outweigh the burden on charities of a requirement to file a photocopy of the federal form.

Form. A form of annual report that includes all the items listed in subsection (a) appears in these Comments. The form can be reproduced on one page, using both the front and the back of the page.

The committee encourages states to use this form for the annual report to enable persons filing an annual report in more than one state to use one form for multiple filings. Because a person may need to file an annual report in multiple states, having the same form used in all states will save time and expense.

ANNUAL REPORT UNDER PROTECTION OF CHARITABLE ASSETS ACT

Name of Organization: _____

Federal Employer Identification Number (EIN): _____

Street Address: _____

City, State, and ZIP Code: _____

Phone number: _____Website: _____

Name of Statutory Agent or Individual on Whom Service of Process may Be Made:

_____

Street address: _____

City, State, and ZIP Code: _____

Name of Responsible Individual to Contact: _____

Street Address: _____

City, State, and ZIP Code: _____

Phone number: _____E-mail address: _____

Check if:

( )   Change of name   ( )   Change of address

( )   Change in statutory agent   ( )   Change in individual to contact

( )   Amendment of document (articles of incorporation, bylaws, articles of association, trust agreement, or other document) changing charitable purpose or use and administration of charitable assets (attach copy of amendment)

[( ) Registered Under Charitable Solicitation Act, Registration Number _____]

PART A - ACTIVITIES

For your most recent full accounting period beginning _____/_____/_____ and ending

_____/_____/_____, list:

Total revenue: $ _____   Total assets at end of period: $ _____

Description of most significant program activities, not to exceed three:

_____

_____

_____

PART B - STATEMENTS ABOUT ORGANIZATION DURING THE PERIOD OF THIS REPORT

Note: If you answer "yes" to any of the questions below, attach an explanation of each "yes" response. During this accounting period:

                  Yes No

1. Were there any contracts, loans, leases, or other financial transactions between   ( ) ( )
the organization and an officer, director, trustee, or other fiduciary or family member of an officer, director, trustee, or other fiduciary of the organization, either directly or with an entity in which the fiduciary or family member had a material financial interest?

2. Did the organization become aware of any embezzlement, theft, or diversion of   ( ) ( )
of the organization's charitable assets?

3. Did the organization become aware of the use of a charitable asset of the organization to pay any penalty, fine, or judgment? ( ) ( )

4. Did the organization become aware of the payment by an officer, director, trustee, or other fiduciary of the organization of a penalty, fine, or judgment with respect to the organization? ( ) ( )

5. Did the organization become aware of the use of restricted funds of the organization for a purpose other than the purpose specified in the restriction? ( ) ( )

6. Did the organization dissolve? ( ) ( )

7. Did the organization terminate? ( ) ( )

8. Did the organization dispose of all or substantially all of its charitable assets? ( ) ( )

9. Did the organization leave the jurisdiction of this state? ( ) ( )

10. Did the organization remove significant charitable assets of the organization from this state? ( ) ( )

11. Did the organization enter into or begin the process of entering into a merger, conversion, or domestication? ( ) ( )

12. Did the organization receive notice of revocation, modification, or denial of its federal or state [income] tax exemption? ( ) ( )

I declare [under penalty of perjury] that I have examined this report, including accompanying documents, and to the best of my knowledge and belief, it is true, correct, and complete.

Signature of authorized individual: _____

Name and Title: _____

Date: _____

§ 6. Notice to [Attorney General] of Reportable Event.

(a) A person required to register under Section 4 shall give notice in a record to the [Attorney General] not later than [20] days before any of the following events:

(1) dissolution of the person;

(2) termination of the person;

(3) disposition by the person of all or substantially all of the charitable assets of the person;

(4) removal of the person from the jurisdiction of this state;

(5) removal of significant charitable assets of the person from this state; or

(6) an amendment of the record that describes the charitable purposes of the person and the use and administration of charitable assets held by the person.

(b) A person required to register under Section 4 shall give notice in a record to the [Attorney General] not later than [90] days before the consummation of a merger, conversion, or domestication of the person.

(c) A transfer of a charitable asset in connection with an event described in subsection (a) or (b) which occurs earlier than [20] days after giving the notice required by subsection (a) or earlier than [90] days after giving the notice required by subsection (b) is a violation of this [act] unless, before the transfer, the person receives from the [Attorney General] in a record consent to the event or notice that the [Attorney General] will take no action regarding the event.

(d) If a decedent's estate opened by a court in this state involves, or may involve, the distribution of property to a person holding charitable assets, unless the distribution is a nonresiduary devise with a value of less than $[50,000] to a named person, the [personal representative] shall deliver to the [Attorney General] not later than [90] days after the date the [personal representative] is appointed:

(1) a copy of the will;

(2) a copy of the [application] [petition] for probate; and

(3) a copy of the inventory or, if none is filed with the court, a statement of the value of the estate.

(e) If a revocable trust becomes irrevocable because of the settlor's death, has its principal place of administration in this state after the settlor's death, and provides for a distribution of property to a person holding charitable assets, unless the distribution is a nonresiduary devise with a value of less than $[50,000] to a named person, the trustee shall deliver to the [Attorney General] not later than [90] days after the date of the settlor's death:

(1) a description of the charitable interests; and

(2) a statement of the value of the trust assets.

(f) A person required to register under Section 4 shall give notice in a record to the [Attorney General] not later than [20] days after receipt of a notice of revocation, modification, or denial of its federal or [state][local] charitable [income] tax exemption.

Comment

The Act requires notice to the Attorney General of a limited number of significant events that might occur in the life of a person holding charitable assets. The events that trigger the notice requirement are those that raise particular opportunities for misapplication of charitable assets. Notice is intended to give the Attorney General an opportunity to monitor the events in time to prevent problems or to correct problems that have already arisen. Some states require notice of certain proposed changes that could trigger concerns over breach of the Charitable Trust Doctrine but do not require a court proceeding. For example, the Attorney General of New Hampshire requires notice of certain proposed amendments to restrictions in conservation easements. *See* http://clca.forestsociety.org/pdf/amending-or-terminating-conservation-easements.pdf. States may wish to consider adding provisions to Section 6, but adequate staffing is a significant issue in many states so requiring additional notices may not be feasible. Any modification that requires a court proceeding, for example a *cy pres* proceeding, will necessitate notification under Section 7.

Some states require notice to the Attorney General of actions that may involve a breach of an organization's fiduciary duties in administering the conservation easements it holds. In Maine, the holder of a conservation easement that is organized or doing business in the state must file an annual report with the Executive Department's State Planning Office regarding the conservation easements it holds, and the State Planning Office must report to the Attorney General any failure of a holder disclosed by the filing or otherwise known to the office. *See* ME. REV. STAT. ANN. tit. 33, § 479-C. In addition, conservation easements in the state may not be terminated or amended in such a manner as to materially detract from the conservation values

intended for protection without the prior approval of the court in an action in which the Attorney General is made a party, regardless of the manner in which the easements were acquired (as charitable gifts or by purchase, exaction, or otherwise). *See id.* § 477-A.2.B. Rhode Island has a similar statutory provision governing the termination or amendment of conservation easements, and further provides that the Attorney General, pursuant to his or her inherent authority, may bring an action in the superior court to enforce the public interest in conservation restrictions. *See* R.I. GEN. LAWS §§ 34-39-5(c), -3(d). Recognizing the status of many conservation easements as charitable gifts made for a specific purpose, the Attorney General of New Hampshire has requested that notice be provided to its Division of Charitable Trusts of certain proposed amendments to or the termination of conservation easements in the state. *See* http://clca.forestsociety.org/pdf/amending-or-terminating-conservation-easements.pdf. Given the importance of land use and land use planning to a state, as well as the status of conservation easements as unique and often irreplaceable charitable or public assets, states may wish to consider similar approaches, consistent with their resources.

Subsections (a) - (c). Disposition or Removal of All or Significantly All Assets. If an entity holding charitable assets will terminate, dispose of substantially all of its assets, or move to another state, the entity must notify the Attorney General before the entity gives up control of the assets or removes them from the jurisdiction. This notice provision gives the Attorney General time to review the proposed transaction and recommend changes if necessary while the assets can still be reached. If the Attorney General objects to the proposed transaction, the Attorney General must deliver the objection to the entity in writing. These subsections give the Attorney General the information needed to work with the entity on an appropriate plan of distribution or other transfer. If the Attorney General and the entity cannot reach agreement, they can request a court determination to resolve the issue.

Subsection (d). Decedent's Estate. If a decedent's estate contains a gift to a charitable organization or creates a new organization through a gift under the will, the personal representative must notify the Attorney General. This notice is included to protect the charitable bequest because it could be adversely affected if an heir contests the will or if the personal representative or others take excessive fees in managing the estate. An exception exists for a nonresiduary bequest to a named charitable beneficiary in an amount less than $50,000, because the named beneficiary will have an incentive to monitor the bequest. An exception for residuary gifts to named beneficiaries was not created because the Attorney General may need to monitor fees that would reduce the value of the residue. A beneficiary may be reluctant to challenge fees because of concerns about public goodwill or the hope of future gifts from the same family.

Subsection (e). Revocable Trust. Many property owners use a revocable trust rather than a will to distribute property at death. This subsection applies the same notice requirement that applies to property distributed under a will to property distributed through a revocable trust. Notice should be given to the Attorney General of the state in which the trust has its principal place of administration after the settlor's death. Upon the death of the settlor of a revocable trust, a new trustee typically is appointed or succeeds to the position, and if that trustee is in a different state, the place of administration may move. The appropriate state for notice is the state in which the trust will be administered during the period immediately following the settlor's death.

Subsection (f). Action Affecting Tax Exemption. The revocation of a federal or state tax exemption may signal problems that the Attorney General should consider. This subsection requires notice to the Attorney General of revocation or modification of an organization's exempt status for any tax purpose. A state may want to limit notice to actions affecting only a particular state tax exemption. In some states the important state tax exemption may be an income tax exemption, but in other states the property tax exemption may be of greater importance. The Attorney General may not need notification of action affecting every state tax exemption. The notification required under this subsection does not require notice of administrative proceedings prior to revocation of exemption of tax-exempt status, but Section 7 requires notice of the proceeding.

§ 7. Notice to Attorney General of Action or Proceeding.

(a) This section applies to an action or proceeding in this state in a federal or state court:

(1) by, against, or on behalf of a person holding a charitable asset in which the relief sought relates to a gift of a charitable asset;

(2) concerning the use of a charitable asset or a breach of duty or other obligation owed to a person holding a charitable asset;

(3) by, against, or on behalf of a person holding a charitable asset in which the relief sought includes:

(A) instruction, injunction, or declaratory relief relating to the management, use, or distribution of a charitable asset;

(B) construction of a record under which a charitable asset is held;

(C) modification, reformation, interpretation, or termination of the terms of a record under which a charitable asset is held;

(D) removal, appointment, or replacement of a trustee of a charitable trust; or

(E) a challenge to the administration of or a distribution from a decedent's estate or a trust in which matters affecting a charitable asset may be decided; and

(4) for bankruptcy under federal law, receivership under [state receivership statute] or a similar receivership statute of another state, or relief in any other insolvency proceeding.

(b) If an action or proceeding to which this section applies is commenced by or brought against a person in this state, the party seeking relief shall give notice in a record to the [Attorney General]. The notice must include a copy of the initial pleading. An order, decree, or judgment rendered in an action in which notice is required by this section is not binding on the [Attorney General] if the notice has not been given.

Legislative Note: In states where the Attorney General is a necessary party to any of the actions addressed in this section, part or all of the section may be unnecessary.

Comment

The Attorney General ought to be made aware of a wide range of proceedings that might affect charitable assets or the structure or governance of a person holding charitable assets. The information will be beneficial to the Attorney General, but a state without the resources to receive and review all of the notices provided for in this section may not want to adopt every part of this section. At a minimum, states will benefit from requiring that the Attorney General be provided notice of and an opportunity to participate in *cy pres* or deviation proceedings or their equivalent in the state.

State law may already require notice to the Attorney General of some of the actions identified in this section. For example, the Uniform Prudent Management of Institutional Funds Act, adopted in all but two states, requires notice to the Attorney General before a charitable organization subject to UPMIFA modifies a donor-imposed restriction or asks a court to modify a restriction. UPMIFA §6. If other law requires notice to the Attorney General under certain circumstances, a state should modify the requirement of notice in this section accordingly but not remove the requirement entirely. For

example, UPMIFA requires notice in certain circumstances, but applies only to those organizations that fall within its definition of "institution" and only to the "institutional funds" managed by those institutions.

The intention of this section is for the applicable statute of limitations, if any, to control. In some states, the common law bars the application of a statute of limitations to the Attorney General's enforcement of fiduciary duties in connection with charities. *See, e.g., Lifespan Corp. v. New England Medical Center, Inc.,* 731 F.Supp.2d 232 (D.R.I. 2010), clarification order 2010 WL 3718952 (Sept. 20, 2010) (applying Massachusetts law); *Com. ex. rel. Corbett v. Citizens Alliance for Better Neighborhoods, Inc.,* 983 A.2d 1274, 1278 (Pa. Cmwlth. Ct. 2009). The equitable doctrine of laches also does not bar Attorney General enforcement of fiduciary duties in some states, *FDIC v. Gladstone,* 44 F. Supp. 2d 81, 90 (D. Mass. 1999), although it may apply in other states if the delay in bringing a suit is inexcusable and would significantly prejudice the defendant. *Com. ex rel. Corbett,* at 1279.

§ 8. Waiver of Filing of Registration [Or Annual Report].

[(a)] The [Attorney General] may waive registration under Section 4 by a person required to register only under Section 4(b)(3) or (4) if the person is registered in another state under a law that is substantially similar to this [act] and files with the [Attorney General] a copy of the registration filed in the other state.

[(b) The [Attorney General] may waive the requirement to file an annual report under Section 5 if the person required to make the filing files a report pursuant to [insert state charitable solicitation statute or other statute].]

Comment

Subsection a. Registration. If a person holds or has received during a 12-month period charitable assets with an aggregate value exceeding $50,000, the person will need to register in its state of incorporation or administration and in the state in which it has its principal place of business. If the person holds charitable assets in another state or

conducts activities in another state, the person will have to register in that other state, but the Attorney General in that other state can waive the duty to register and require the person to file instead a copy of the registration filed in the state of incorporation or principal place of business. Even if the Attorney General waives the duty to register, the person may be required to file annual reports under Section 5.

Subsection b. Annual Report. The Attorney General can agree to waive the filing of an annual report if a person holding charitable assets files a report with similar information in the same state. For example, in a state that requires an annual report in connection with solicitation, that filing may provide the same information required under Section 5. If so, the Attorney General can waive the duty to file an annual report. This Act does not attempt to coordinate with solicitation statutes, but a state may choose to do so. Even if the Attorney General waives the duty to file annual reports, the organization will still be required to register under Section 4, unless subsection (a) of this Section 8 applies, and will be required to file the notices provided for in Sections 6 and 7.

Additional Waivers. A state may choose to authorize the Attorney General to waive requirements under Sections 5, 6, and 7 by substituting for Section 8(a) the following: "The [Attorney General] shall waive the registration required under Section 4 and the filings required under Sections 5, 6, and 7, if a person required to register under Section 4 is registered in another state under a law that is substantially similar to this [act] and files with the [Attorney General] a copy of the registration filed in the other state."

§ 9. Fees.

Alternative A

(a) A person required to register under Section 4 shall pay a fee of $[15] with the registration and, if the registration is not filed timely, a late fee of $[100].

(b) A person required to file a report under Section 5 shall pay a fee of $[15] with the report and, if the report is not filed timely, a late fee of $[100].

Alternative B

The [Attorney General] shall adopt rules in accordance with [this state's administrative procedure act] setting fees for filing, and for late filing, of a registration under Section 4 and an annual report under Section 5.

End of Alternatives

Comment

The Act provides limited provisions for fees, and a state may want to delete these requirements or add more. The alternative provision directs the Attorney General to set fees. Some states with current registration statutes use a sliding scale based on gross support and revenue received during the fiscal year. *See* Mass. G.L. c. 12, § 8F.

§ 10. Cooperation with Other Official.

(a) The [Attorney General] may cooperate with an official of this state, another state, the United States, a foreign government, or a governmental subdivision, agency, or instrumentality of any of the foregoing charged with protecting charitable assets.

(b) The [Attorney General] may:

(1) notify an official described in subsection (a) of the commencement, status, or resolution of an investigation or proceeding pursuant to this [act];

(2) make available to the official information relating to a charitable asset which is relevant to the official's protection of charitable assets; or

(3) request from the official information relevant to an investigation pursuant to Section 3.

Comment

This section authorizes cooperation between a state Attorney General and relevant officials of other states, the federal government, and foreign governments. In some states a person holding charitable assets submits reports to the Secretary of State or to other state offices. This section allows the Attorney General to coordinate with any other state agency and provide information to other agencies as well as request information from other agencies.

[**§ 11. Public Records.** A registration filed under Section 4 and an annual report filed under Section 5 are public records. The [Attorney General], on the written request of a person required to register under Section 4, shall withhold from public inspection any part of the person's registration or annual report which does not relate to a charitable purpose or charitable assets and is not otherwise a public record.]

Legislative Note: *In some states, the state's Freedom of Information Act may require additional statutory language in Section 11. In other states this section will be unnecessary because the state's Freedom of Information Act will apply without a provision in this statute.*

§ 12. Relation to Electronic Signatures in Global and National Commerce Act. This [act] modifies, limits, and supersedes the Electronic Signatures in Global and National Commerce Act, 15 U.S.C. Section 7001, et seq., but does not modify, limit, or supersede Section 101(c) of that act, 15 U.S.C. Section 7001(c), or authorize electronic delivery of any of the notices described in Section 103(b) of that act, 15 U.S.C. Section 7003(b).

§ 13. Repeals. The following are repealed:

§ 14. Effective Date. This [act] takes effect . . . .

REVISED UNIFORM ANATOMICAL GIFT ACT
(2006, with 2007 Amendments)

Table of Sections

Prefatory Note

As of January, 2006 there were over 92,000 individuals on the waiting list for organ transplantation, and the list keeps growing. It is estimated that approximately 5,000 individuals join the waiting list each year. See "Organ Donation: Opportunities for Action," Institute of Medicine of the National Academies (2006) www.nap.edu. Every hour another person in the United States dies because of the lack of an organ to provide a life saving organ transplant.

The lack of organs results from the lack of organ donors. For example, according to the Scientific Registry of Transplant Recipients in 2005 when there were about 90,000 people on the organ transplant waiting list, there were 13,091 individuals who died under the age of 70 using cardiac and brain death criteria and who were eligible to be organ donors. Of these, only 58% or 7,593 were actual donors who provided just over 23,000 organs. Living donors, primarily of kidneys, contributed about 6,800 more organs. Between them about 28,000 organs were transplanted into patients on the waiting list in 2005. (See www.optn.org).

The 2005 data on cadaveric organ donors suggests there were 5,498 individuals who died that year that could have been donors who weren't and that had they been organ donors there would have been approximately 17,000 additional organs potentially available for transplantation. (See generally, www.unos.org and www.ustransplant.org). However, these numbers to some extent are only estimates. First, they exclude individuals dying over the age of 70. Second, the data are self reported for eligible donors. Indicative of the absence of precision in this area is the report from the Institute of Medicine. According to the IOM, it has been estimated that donor-eligible deaths range between 10,500 and 16,800 per year. See Organ Donation: Opportunities for Action," Institute of Medicine of the National Academies (2006) at page 27. www.nap.edu Using the 2005 figures for deceased organ donors, this would suggest that between approximately 3,000 and 9,000 decedents could have been donors but weren't. Further, if one assumes an average of three solid organs recovered from each of them, there could be between 9,000 and 27,000 more organs that might have been available to transplant into individuals on the waiting list.

The data for eye and tissue is, however, more encouraging. On an annual basis there are approximately 50,000 eye donors and tissue donors and over 1,000,000 ocular and tissue transplants.

This Revised Uniform Anatomical Gift Act ("UAGA") is promulgated by the National Conference of Commissioners on Uniform State Laws ("NCCUSL") to address in part the critical organ shortage by providing additional ways for making organ, eye, and tissue donations. The original UAGA was promulgated by NCCUSL in 1968 and promptly enacted by all states. In 1987, the UAGA was revised and updated, but only 26 states adopted that version. Since 1987, many states have adopted non-uniform amendments to their anatomical gift acts. The law among the various states is no longer uniform and harmonious, and the diversity of law is an impediment to transplantation. Furthermore the federal government has been increasingly active in the organ transplant process.

Since 1987, there also have been substantial improvements in the technology and practice of organ, eye, and tissue transplantation and therapy. And, the need for organs, eyes, and tissue for research and education has increased to assure more successful transplantations and therapies. The improvements in technology and the growing needs of the research community have correspondingly increased the need for more donors.

This 2006 Revised UAGA is promulgated with the substantial and active participation of the major stakeholders representing donors, recipients, doctors, procurement organizations, regulators, and others affected. The Drafting Committee held four meetings with the stakeholders beginning on Friday morning and ending Sunday noon, reading and discussing each section of the drafts word by word (Chicago, December 3-5, 2004; Philadelphia, March 18-20, 2005; Chicago, November 2-4, 2005; and Detroit, April 21-23, 2006). The following stakeholders were actively engaged in the dialogue working for a consensus that could and should be adopted on a uniform basis to facilitate the anatomical gifts of human bodies and parts: American Bar Association, American Medical Association, American Lung Association, Association of Organ Procurement Organizations, American Association of Tissue Banks, Eye Bank Association of America, Health Law Institute and Center for Race and Bioethics, Life Alaska Donor Services, Musculoskeletal Transplant Foundation, National Association of Medical Examiners, National Disease Research Interchange, National Kidney Foundation, North American Transplant Coordinators Organization, RTI Donor Services, United Network for Organ Sharing (UNOS) and United States Department of Health & Human Services. In addition, there were many who contributed their views and comments by correspondence, including the Funeral Consumers Alliance, Inc. and Funeral Ethics Organization.

This [act] adheres to the significant policy determinations reflected in existing anatomical gift acts. First, the [act] is designed to encourage the making of anatomical gifts. Second, the [act] is designed to honor and respect the autonomy interest of individuals to make or not to make an anatomical gift of their body or parts. Third, the [act] preserves the current anatomical gift system founded upon altruism by requiring a positive affirmation of an intent to make a gift and prohibiting the sale and purchase of organs. This [act] includes a number of provisions, discussed below, that enhance these policies.

History of 1968 and 1987 Acts

The first reported medical transplant occurred in the third century. However, medical miracles flowing from transplants are truly a modern story beginning in the first decade of the twentieth century with the first successful transplant of a cornea. But, not until three events occurred in the twentieth century, in addition to the development of surgical techniques to effectuate a transplant, could transplants become a viable option to save and meaningfully extend lives.

The first event was the development in the late 1960s of the first set of neurological criteria for determining death. These criteria allowed persons to be declared dead upon the cessation of all brain activity. Ultimately these criteria, together with the historic measure of determining death by cessation of circulation and respiration, were incorporated into Section 1 of the Uniform Determination of Death Act providing that: "An individual who has sustained either (1) irreversible cessation of circulatory and respiratory function, or (2) irreversible cessation of all functions of the entire brain, including the brain stem, is dead."

The second event, following shortly after Dr. Christian Barnard's successful transplant of a heart in November, 1967, was this Conference's adoption of the first Uniform Anatomical Gift Act. In short order, every jurisdiction uniformly adopted the 1968 Act. The most significant contribution of the 1968 Act was to create a right to donate organs, eyes, and tissue. This right was not clearly recognized at common law. By creating this right, individuals became empowered to donate their parts or their loved one's parts to save or improve the lives of others.

The last event was the development of immunosuppressive drugs that prevented organ recipients from rejecting transplanted organs. This permitted many more successful organ transplants, thus contributing to the rapid growth in the demand for organs and the need for changes in the law to facilitate the making of anatomical gifts.

In 1987, a revised Uniform Anatomical Gift Act was promulgated to address changes in circumstances and in practice. Only 26 jurisdictions enacted the 1987 revision. Consequently, there is significant non-uniformity between states with the 1968 Act and those with the 1987 revisions. Neither of those acts comports with changes in federal law adopted subsequent to the 1987 Act relating to the role of hospitals and procurement organization in securing organs, eyes, and tissues for transplantation. And, both of them have impediments that are inconsistent with a policy to encourage donation.

The two previous anatomical gift acts, as well as this [act], adhere to an "opt in" principle as its default rule. Thus, an individual becomes a donor only if the donor or someone acting on the donor's behalf affirmatively makes an anatomical gift. The system universally adopted in this country is contrary to the system adopted in some countries, primarily in Europe, where an individual is deemed to be a donor unless the individual or another person acting on the individual's behalf "opts out." This other system is known as "presumed consent." While there are proponents of presumed consent who believe the concept of presumed consent could receive in the future a favorable reception in this country, the professional consensus appears to be not to replace the present opt-in principle at this time. See "Organ Donation: Opportunities in Action," Institute of Medicine of the National Academies (2006) at page 12.

Scope of the 2006 Revised Act

This [act] is limited in scope to donations from deceased donors as a result of gifts made before or after their deaths. Although recently there has been a significant increase in so-called "living donations," where a living donor immediately donates an organ (typically a kidney or a section of a liver) to a recipient, donations by living donors are not covered in this [act] because they raise distinct and difficult legal issues that are more appropriate for a separate act.

A majority of donors or prospective donors are candidates for donation of eyes or tissue, but only a small percentage of individuals die under circumstances that permit an anatomical gift of an organ. To procure an anatomical gift for transplantation, therapy, research, or education, a donor or prospective donor must be declared dead (see Uniform Determination of Death Act). In cases of potential organ donation, measures necessary to ensure the medical suitability of an organ for transplantation or therapy are administered to a patient who is dead or near death to determine if the patient could be a prospective donor.

Pursuant to federal law, when a donor or a patient who could be a prospective donor is dead or near death, a procurement organization, or a designee, must be notified. The organization begins to develop a medical and social history to determine whether the dying or deceased individual's body might be medically suitable for donation. If the body of a dying or deceased person might be medically suitable for donation, the procurement organization checks for evidence of a donation, if not otherwise known, and seeks consent to donation from authorized persons, if necessary. In the case of an organ, the organ procurement organization obtains from the Organ Procurement and Transplantation Network

("OPTN") a prioritized list of potential recipients from the national organ waiting list and takes the necessary steps to see that the organ finds its way to the appropriate recipient. If eye or tissue is donated, the appropriate procurement organization procures the eye or tissue and takes the necessary steps to screen, test, process, store, or distribute them as required for transplantation, therapy, research, or education. All must be done expeditiously.

Recent technological innovations have increased the types of organs that can be transplanted, the demand for organs, and the range of individuals who can donate or receive an organ, thereby increasing the number of organs available each year and the number of transplantations that occur each year. Nonetheless, the number of deaths for lack of available organs also has increased. While the Commissioners are under no illusion that any anatomical gift act can fully satisfy the need for organs, any change that could increase the supply of organs and thus save lies is an improvement.

Transplantation occurs across state boundaries and requires speed and efficiency if the organ is to be successfully transplanted into a recipient. There simply is no time for researching and conforming to variations of the laws among the states. Thus, uniformity of state law is highly desirable. Furthermore, the decision to be a donor is a highly personal decision of great generosity and deserves the highest respect from the law. Because current state anatomical gift laws are out of harmony with both federal procurement and allocation policies and do not fully respect the autonomy interests of donors, there is a need to harmonize state law with federal policy as well as to improve the manner in which anatomical gifts can be made and respected.

Summary of the Changes in the Revised Act

This revision retains the basic policy of the 1968 and 1987 anatomical gift acts by retaining and strengthening the "opt-in" system that honors the free choice of an individual to donate the individual's organ (a process known in the organ transplant community as "first person consent" or "donor designation"). This revision also preserves the right of other persons to make an anatomical gift of a decedent's organs if the decedent had not made a gift during life. And, it strengthens the right of an individual not to donate the individual's organs by signing a refusal that also bars others from making a gift of the individual's organs after the individual's death. This revision:

1. Honors the choice of an individual to be or not to be a donor and strengthens the language barring others from overriding a donor's decision to make an anatomical gift (Section 8);

2. Facilitates donations by expanding the list of those who may make an anatomical gift for another individual during that individual's lifetime to include health-care agents and, under certain circumstances, parents or guardians (Section 4);

3. Empowers a minor eligible under other law to apply for a driver's license to be a donor (Section 4);

4. Facilitates donations from a deceased individual who made no lifetime choice by adding to the list of persons who can make a gift of the deceased individual's body or parts the following persons: the person who was acting as the decedent's agent under a power of attorney for health care at the time of the decedent's death, the decedent's adult grandchildren, and an adult who exhibited special care and concern for the decedent (Section 9) and defines the meaning of "reasonably available" which is relevant to who can make an anatomical gift of a decedent's body or parts (Section 2(23));

5. Permits an anatomical gift by any member of a class where there is more than one person in the class so long as no objections by other class members are known and, if an objection is known, permits a majority of the members of the class who are reasonably available to make the gift without having to take account of a known objection by any class member who is not reasonably available (Section 9);

6. Creates numerous default rules for the interpretation of a document of gift that lacks specificity regarding either the persons to receive the gift or the purposes of the gift or both (Section 11);

7. Encourages and establishes standards for donor registries (Section 20);

8. Enables procurement organizations to gain access to documents of gifts in donor registries, medical records, and the records of a state motor vehicle department (Sections 14 and 20);

9. Resolves the tension between a health-care directive requesting the withholding or withdrawal of life support systems and anatomical gifts by permitting measures necessary to ensure the medical suitability of organs for intended transplantation or therapy to be administered (Sections 14 and 21);

10. Clarifies and expands the rules relating to cooperation and coordination between procurement organizations and coroners or medical examiners (Sections 22 and 23);

11. Recognizes anatomical gifts made under the

laws of other jurisdictions (Section 19); and

12. Updates the [act] to allow for electronic records and signatures (Section 25).

In addition, Section 2 provides a number of new definitions that are used in the substantive provisions of the [act] to clarify and expand the opportunities for anatomical gifts. These include: adult, agent, custodian, disinterested witness, donee, donor registry, driver's license, eye bank, guardian, know, license, minor, organ procurement organization, parent, prospective donor, reasonably available, recipient, record, sign, tissue, tissue bank, and transplant hospital.

Section 4 authorizes individuals to make anatomical gifts of their bodies or parts. It also permits certain persons, other than donors, to make an anatomical gift on behalf of a donor during the donor's lifetime. The expanded list includes agents acting under a health-care power of attorney or other record, parents of unemancipated minors, and guardians. The section also recognizes that it is appropriate that minors who can apply for a driver's license be empowered to make anatomical gifts, but, under Section 8(g), either parent can revoke the gift if the minor dies under the age of 18.

Section 5 recognizes that, since the adoption of the previous versions of this [act], some states and many private organizations have created donor registries for the purpose of making anatomical gifts. Thus, in addition to evidencing a gift on a donor card or driver's license, this [act] allows for the making of anatomical gifts on donor registries. It also permits gifts to be made on state-issued identification cards and, under limited circumstances, to be made orally. Except for oral gifts, there is no witnessing requirement to make an anatomical gift.

Section 6 permits anatomical gifts to be amended or revoked by the execution of a later-executed record or by inconsistent documents of gifts. It also permits revocation by destruction of a document of gift and, under limited circumstances, permits oral revocations.

Section 7 permits an individual to sign a refusal that bars all other persons from making an anatomical gift of the individual's body or parts. A refusal generally can be made by a signed record, a will, or, under limited circumstances, orally. By permitting refusals, this [act] recognizes the autonomy interest of an individual either to be or not to be a donor. The section also recognizes that a refusal can be revoked.

Section 8 substantially strengthens the respect due a decision to make an anatomical gift. While the 1987 Act provided that a donor's anatomical gift was irrevocable (except by the donor), until quite recently it had been a common practice for procurement organizations to seek affirmation of the gift from the donor's family. This could result in unnecessary delays in the recovery of organs as well as a reversal of a donor's donation decision. Section 8 intentionally disempowers families from making or revoking anatomical gifts in contravention of a donor's wishes. Thus, under the strengthened language of this [act], if a donor had made an anatomical gift, there is no reason to seek consent from the donor's family as they have no right to give it legally. See Section 8(a). Of course, that would not bar, nor should it bar, a procurement organization from advising the donor's family of the donor's express wishes, but that conversation should focus more on what procedures will be followed to carry out the donor's wishes and on answering a family's questions about the process rather than on seeking approval of the donation. A limited exception applies if the donor is a minor at the time of death. In this case, either parent may amend or revoke the donor's anatomical gift. See Section 8(g).

Section 8 also recognizes that some decisions of a donor are inherently ambiguous, making it appropriate to adopt rules that favor the making of anatomical gifts. For example, a donor's revocation of a gift of a part is not to be construed as a refusal for others to make gifts of other parts. Likewise, a donor's gift of one part is not to be construed as a refusal that would bar others from making gifts of other parts absent an express, contrary intent.

Section 9 sets forth a prioritized list of classes of persons who can make an anatomical gift of a decedent's body or part if the decedent was neither a donor nor had signed a refusal. The list is more expansive than under previous versions of this [act]. It includes persons acting as agents at the decedent's death, adult grandchildren, and close friends.

Section 10 deals with the manner of making, amending, or revoking an anatomical gift following the decedent's death.

Section 11 deals with the passing of parts to named persons and more generally to eye banks, tissue banks, and organ procurement organizations. In part, the section is designed to harmonize this [act] with federal law, particularly with respect to organs donated for transplantation or therapy. The National Organ Transplant Act created the Organ

Procurement and Transplantation Network ("OPTN") to facilitate the nationwide, equitable distribution of organs. Currently, United Network Organ Sharing ("UNOS") operates the OPTN under contract with the U.S. Department of Health and Human Services. When an organ donor dies, the donor's organs, barring the rare instance of a donation to a named individual, are recovered by the organ procurement organization for the service area in which the donor dies, as custodian of the organs, to be allocated by it either locally, regionally, or nationally in accordance with allocation policies established by the OPTN.

Section 11 includes two important improvements to previous versions of this [act]. First, it creates a priority for transplantation or therapy over research or education when an anatomical gift is made for all four purposes in a document of gift that fails to establish a priority.

Second, it specifies the person to whom a part passes when the document of gift merely expresses a "general intent" to be an "organ donor." This type of general designation is common on a driver's license. Under Section 11(f) a general statement of intent to be a donor results only in an anatomical gift of the donor's eyes, tissues, and organs (not the whole body) for transplantation or therapy. Since a general statement of intent to be an organ donor does not result in the making of an anatomical gift of the whole body, or any part, for research or education, more specific language is required to make such a gift.

Section 11(b) provides that, if an anatomical gift of the decedent's body or parts does not pass to a named person designated in a document of gift, it passes to a procurement organization typically for transplantation or therapy and possibly for research or education. Custody of a body or part that is the subject of an anatomical gift that cannot be used for any intended purpose passes to the "person under obligation to dispose of the body or parts." See Section 11(i).

Section 11(j) prohibits a person from accepting an anatomical gift if the person knows that the gift was not validly made. For this purpose, if a person knows that an anatomical gift was made on a document of gift, the person is deemed to know of a refusal to make a gift if the refusal is on the same document of gift.

Lastly, Section 11(k) clarifies that nothing in this [act] affects the allocation of organs for transplantation or therapy except to the extent there has been a gift to a named recipient. See Section

11(a)(2). The allocation of organs is administered exclusively under policies of the Organ Procurement and Transplantation Network.

In part, Section 14 has been redrafted to accord with controlling federal law when applicable. The federal rules require hospitals to notify an organ procurement organization or third party designated by the organ procurement organization of an individual whose death is imminent or who has died in the hospital to increase donation opportunity, and thus, transplantation. See 42 CFR § 482.45 (Medicare and Medicaid Programs: Conditions of Participation: Identification of Potential Organ, Tissue, and Eye Donors and Transplant Hospitals' Provision of Transplant-Related Data). The right of the procurement organization to inspect a patient's medical records in Section 14(e) does not violate HIPAA. See 45 CFR § 164.512(h) ("A covered entity may use or disclose protected health information to organ procurement organizations or other entities engaged in the procurement, banking, or transplantation of cadaveric organs, eyes, or tissue for the purpose of facilitating organ, eye, or tissue donation and transplantation"). Section 14(c) permits measures necessary to ensure the medical suitability of parts to be administered to a patient who is being evaluated to determine whether the patient has organs that are medically suitable for transplantation.

Section 17 and Section 18 deal with liability and immunity, respectively. (Section 16, dealing with the sale of parts, also provides for potential liabilities but is essentially the same as prior law). Section 17 includes a new provision establishing criminal sanctions for falsifying the making, amending, or revoking of an anatomical gift. Section 18, in substance, is the same as the 1987 Act providing immunity for "good faith" efforts to comply with this [act]. However, while the [act] contains no provisions relating to bad faith it is important to note that other laws of the state and federal governments may provide for further remedies and sanctions for bad faith, including those under regulatory rules, licensing requirements, Unfair and Deceptive Practices acts, and the common law.

Section 18(c) provides that in determining whether an individual has a right to make an anatomical gift under Section 9, a person, such as an organ procurement organization, may rely on the individual's representation regarding the individual's relationship to the donor or prospective donor.

Section 19 sets forth rules relating to the validity of documents of gift executed outside of the state while providing that any document of gift shall be interpreted in accordance with the laws of the state.

Section 20 authorizes an appropriate state agency to establish or contract for the establishment of a donor registry. It also provides that a registry can be established without a state contract. While this [act] does not specify in great detail what could or should be on a donor registry, it does mandate minimum requirements for all registries. First, the registry must provide a database that allows a donor or other person authorized to make an anatomical gift to include in the registry a statement or symbol that the donor has made a gift. Second, at or near the death of a donor or prospective donor, the registry must be accessible to all procurement organizations to obtain information relevant to determine whether the donor or prospective donor has made, amended, or revoked an anatomical gift. Lastly, the registry must be accessible on a twenty four hour, seven day a week basis.

Section 21 creates a default rule to adjust the tension that might exist between preserving organs to assure their medical suitability for transplantation or therapy and the expression of intent by a prospective donor in either a declaration or advance health-care directive not to have life prolonged by use of life support systems. The default rule under this [act] is that measures necessary to ensure the medical suitability of an organ for transplantation or therapy may not be withheld or withdrawn from the prospective donor. A prospective donor could expressly provide otherwise in the declaration or advance health-care directive.

Sections 22 and 23 represent a complete revision of the relationship of the [coroner] [medical examiner] to the anatomical gift process. Previous versions of this [act] permitted the [coroner] [medical examiner], under limited circumstances, to make anatomical gifts of the eyes of a decedent in the [coroner's] [medical examiner's] possession. In light of a series of Section 1983 lawsuits in which the [coroner's] [medical examiner's] actions were held to violate the property rights of surviving family members, see, e.g., Brotherton v. Cleveland, 923 F.2d 477 (6th Cir. 1991), the authority of the [coroner] [medical examiner] to make anatomical gifts was deleted from this [act]. Parts, with the rare exception discussed in the comments to Section 9, can be recovered for the purpose of transplantation, therapy, research, or education from a decedent whose body is under the jurisdiction of the [coroner] [medical examiner] only if there was an anatomical gift of those parts under Section 5 or Section 10 of this [act].

This [act] includes a series of new provisions in Sections 22 and 23 relating to the relationship between the [coroner] [medical examiner] and procurement organizations. These provisions should encourage meaningful cooperation between these groups in hopes of increasing the number of anatomical gifts. Importantly, the section does not permit a [coroner] [medical examiner] to make an anatomical gift.

§ 1. Short Title. This [act] may be cited as the Revised Uniform Anatomical Gift Act.

§ 2. Definitions. In this [act]:

(1) "Adult" means an individual who is at least [18] years of age.

(2) "Agent" means an individual:

(A) authorized to make health-care decisions on the principal's behalf by a power of attorney for health care; or

(B) expressly authorized to make an anatomical gift on the principal's behalf by any other record signed by the principal.

(3) "Anatomical gift" means a donation of all or part of a human body to take effect after the donor's death for the purpose of transplantation, therapy, research, or education.

(4) "Decedent" means a deceased individual whose body or part is or may be the source of an anatomical gift. The term includes a stillborn infant and, subject to restrictions imposed by law other than this [act], a fetus.

(5) "Disinterested witness" means a witness other than the spouse, child, parent, sibling, grandchild, grandparent, or guardian of the individual who makes, amends, revokes, or refuses to make an anatomical gift, or another adult who exhibited special care and concern for the individual. The term does not include a person to which an anatomical gift could pass under Section 11.

(6) "Document of gift" means a donor card or other record used to make an anatomical gift. The term includes a statement or symbol on a driver's license, identification card, or donor registry.

(7) "Donor" means an individual whose body or part is the subject of an anatomical gift.

(8) "Donor registry" means a database that contains records of anatomical gifts and amendments to or revocations of anatomical gifts.

(9) "Driver's license" means a license or permit issued by the [state department of motor vehicles] to operate a vehicle, whether or not conditions are attached to the license or permit.

(10) "Eye bank" means a person that is licensed, accredited, or regulated under federal or state law to engage in the recovery, screening, testing, processing, storage, or distribution of human eyes or portions of human eyes.

(11) "Guardian" means a person appointed by a court to make decisions regarding the support, care, education, health, or welfare of an individual. The term does not include a guardian ad litem.

(12) "Hospital" means a facility licensed as a hospital under the law of any state or a facility operated as a hospital by the United States, a state, or a subdivision of a state.

(13) "Identification card" means an identification card issued by the [state department of motor vehicles].

(14) "Know" means to have actual knowledge.

(15) "Minor" means an individual who is under [18] years of age.

(16) "Organ procurement organization" means a person designated by the Secretary of the United States Department of Health and Human Services as an organ procurement organization.

(17) "Parent" means a parent whose parental rights have not been terminated.

(18) "Part" means an organ, an eye, or tissue of a human being. The term does not include the whole body.

(19) "Person" means an individual, corporation, business trust, estate, trust, partnership, limited liability company, association, joint venture, public corporation, government or governmental subdivision, agency, or instrumentality, or any other legal or commercial entity.

(20) "Physician" means an individual authorized to practice medicine or osteopathy under the law of any state.

(21) "Procurement organization" means an eye bank, organ procurement organization, or tissue bank.

(22) "Prospective donor" means an individual who is dead or near death and has been determined by a procurement organization to have a part that could be medically suitable for transplantation, therapy, research, or education. The term does not include an individual who has made a refusal.

(23) "Reasonably available" means able to be contacted by a procurement organization without undue effort and willing and able to act in a timely manner consistent with existing medical criteria necessary for the making of an anatomical gift.

(24) "Recipient" means an individual into whose body a decedent's part has been or is intended to be transplanted.

(25) "Record" means information that is inscribed on a tangible medium or that is stored in an electronic or other medium and is retrievable in perceivable form.

(26) "Refusal" means a record created under Section 7 that expressly states an intent to bar other persons from making an anatomical gift of an individual's body or part.

(27) "Sign" means, with the present intent to authenticate or adopt a record:

(A) to execute or adopt a tangible symbol; or

(B) to attach to or logically associate with the record an electronic symbol, sound, or process.

(28) "State" means a state of the United States, the District of Columbia, Puerto Rico, the United States Virgin Islands, or any territory or insular possession subject to the jurisdiction of the United

States.

(29) "Technician" means an individual determined to be qualified to remove or process parts by an appropriate organization that is licensed, accredited, or regulated under federal or state law. The term includes an enucleator.

(30) "Tissue" means a portion of the human body other than an organ or an eye. The term does not include blood unless the blood is donated for the purpose of research or education.

(31) "Tissue bank" means a person that is licensed, accredited, or regulated under federal or state law to engage in the recovery, screening, testing, processing, storage, or distribution of tissue.

(32) "Transplant hospital" means a hospital that furnishes organ transplants and other medical and surgical specialty services required for the care of transplant patients.

Legislative Note: If this state does not license "hospitals", the definition of "hospital" should include a reference to the facility or facilities with equivalent functions by an additional sentence such as the following: "The term includes an acute care facility."

§ 3. Applicability. This [act] applies to an anatomical gift or amendment to, revocation of, or refusal to make an anatomical gift, whenever made.

§ 4. Who May Make Anatomical Gift Before Donor's Death. Subject to Section 8, an anatomical gift of a donor's body or part may be made during the life of the donor for the purpose of transplantation, therapy, research, or education in the manner provided in Section 5 by:

(1) the donor, if the donor is an adult or if the donor is a minor and is:

(A) emancipated; or

(B) authorized under state law to apply for a driver's license because the donor is at least [insert the youngest age at which an individual may apply for any type of driver's license] years of age;

(2) an agent of the donor, unless the power of attorney for health care or other record prohibits the agent from making an anatomical gift;

(3) a parent of the donor, if the donor is an unemancipated minor; or

(4) the donor's guardian.

§ 5. Manner of Making Anatomical Gift Before Donor's Death.

(a) A donor may make an anatomical gift:

(1) by authorizing a statement or symbol indicating that the donor has made an anatomical gift to be imprinted on the donor's driver's license or identification card;

(2) in a will;

(3) during a terminal illness or injury of the donor, by any form of communication addressed to at least two adults, at least one of whom is a disinterested witness; or

(4) as provided in subsection (b).

(b) A donor or other person authorized to make an anatomical gift under Section 4 may make a gift by a donor card or other record signed by the donor or other person making the gift or by authorizing that a statement or symbol indicating that the donor has made an anatomical gift be included on a donor registry. If the donor or other person is physically unable to sign a record, the record may be signed by another individual at the direction of the donor or other person and must:

(1) be witnessed by at least two adults, at least one of whom is a disinterested witness, who have signed at the request of the donor or the other person; and

(2) state that it has been signed and witnessed as provided in paragraph (1).

(c) Revocation, suspension, expiration, or cancellation of a driver's license or identification card upon which an anatomical gift is indicated does not invalidate the gift.

(d) An anatomical gift made by will takes effect upon the donor's death whether or not the will is probated. Invalidation of the will after the donor's death does not invalidate the gift.

§ 6. Amending or Revoking Anatomical Gift Before Donor's Death.

(a) Subject to Section 8, a donor or other person authorized to make an anatomical gift under Section 4 may amend or revoke an anatomical gift by:

(1) a record signed by:

(A) the donor;

(B) the other person; or

(C) subject to subsection (b), another individual acting at the direction of the donor or the other person if the donor or other person is physically unable to sign; or

(2) a later-executed document of gift that amends or revokes a previous anatomical gift or portion of an anatomical gift, either expressly or by inconsistency.

(b) A record signed pursuant to subsection (a)(1)(C) must:

(1) be witnessed by at least two adults, at least one of whom is a disinterested witness, who have signed at the request of the donor or the other person; and

(2) state that it has been signed and witnessed as provided in paragraph (1).

(c) Subject to Section 8, a donor or other person authorized to make an anatomical gift under Section 4 may revoke an anatomical gift by the destruction or cancellation of the document of gift, or the portion of the document of gift used to make the gift, with the intent to revoke the gift.

(d) A donor may amend or revoke an anatomical gift that was not made in a will by any form of communication during a terminal illness or injury addressed to at least two adults, at least one of whom is a disinterested witness.

(e) A donor who makes an anatomical gift in a will may amend or revoke the gift in the manner provided for amendment or revocation of wills or as provided in subsection (a).

§ 7. Refusal to Make Anatomical Gift; Effect of Refusal.

(a) An individual may refuse to make an anatomical gift of the individual's body or part by:

(1) a record signed by:

(A) the individual; or

(B) subject to subsection (b), another individual acting at the direction of the individual if the individual is physically unable to sign;

(2) the individual's will, whether or not the will is admitted to probate or invalidated after the individual's death; or

(3) any form of communication made by the individual during the individual's terminal illness or injury addressed to at least two adults, at least one of whom is a disinterested witness.

(b) A record signed pursuant to subsection (a)(1)(B) must:

(1) be witnessed by at least two adults, at least one of whom is a disinterested witness, who have signed at the request of the individual; and

(2) state that it has been signed and witnessed as provided in paragraph (1).

(c) An individual who has made a refusal may amend or revoke the refusal:

(1) in the manner provided in subsection (a) for making a refusal;

(2) by subsequently making an anatomical gift pursuant to Section 5 that is inconsistent with the refusal; or

(3) by destroying or canceling the record evidencing the refusal, or the portion of the record used to make the refusal, with the intent to revoke the refusal.

(d) Except as otherwise provided in Section 8(h), in the absence of an express, contrary indication by the individual set forth in the refusal, an individual's unrevoked refusal to make an anatomical gift of the individual's body or part bars all other persons from making an anatomical gift of the individual's body or part.

§ 8. Preclusive Effect of Anatomical Gift, Amendment, or Revocation.

(a) Except as otherwise provided in subsection (g) and subject to subsection (f), in the absence of an express, contrary indication by the donor, a person other than the donor is barred from making, amending, or revoking an anatomical gift of a donor's body or part if the donor made an anatomical gift of the donor's body or part under Section 5 or an amendment to an anatomical gift of the donor's body or part under Section 6.

(b) A donor's revocation of an anatomical gift of the donor's body or part under Section 6 is not a refusal and does not bar another person specified in Section 4 or 9 from making an anatomical gift of the donor's body or part under Section 5 or 10.

(c) If a person other than the donor makes an unrevoked anatomical gift of the donor's body or part under Section 5 or an amendment to an anatomical gift of the donor's body or part under Section 6, another person may not make, amend, or revoke the gift of the donor's body or part under Section 10.

(d) A revocation of an anatomical gift of a donor's body or part under Section 6 by a person other than the donor does not bar another person from making an anatomical gift of the body or part under Section 5 or 10.

(e) In the absence of an express, contrary indication by the donor or other person authorized to make an anatomical gift under Section 4, an anatomical gift of a part is neither a refusal to give another part nor a limitation on the making of an anatomical gift of another part at a later time by the donor or another person.

(f) In the absence of an express, contrary indication by the donor or other person authorized to make an anatomical gift under Section 4, an anatomical gift of a part for one or more of the purposes set forth in Section 4 is not a limitation on the making of an anatomical gift of the part for any of the other purposes by the donor or any other person under Section 5 or 10.

(g) If a donor who is an unemancipated minor dies, a parent of the donor who is reasonably available may revoke or amend an anatomical gift of the donor's body or part.

(h) If an unemancipated minor who signed a refusal dies, a parent of the minor who is reasonably available may revoke the minor's refusal.

§ 9. Who May Make Anatomical Gift of Decedent's Body or Part.

(a) Subject to subsections (b) and (c) and unless barred by Section 7 or 8, an anatomical gift of a decedent's body or part for purpose of transplantation, therapy, research, or education may be made by any member of the following classes of persons who is reasonably available, in the order of priority listed:

(1) an agent of the decedent at the time of death who could have made an anatomical gift under Section 4(2) immediately before the decedent's death;

(2) the spouse of the decedent;

(3) adult children of the decedent;

(4) parents of the decedent;

(5) adult siblings of the decedent;

(6) adult grandchildren of the decedent;

(7) grandparents of the decedent;

(8) an adult who exhibited special care and concern for the decedent;

(9) the persons who were acting as the [guardians] of the person of the decedent at the time of death; and

(10) any other person having the authority to dispose of the decedent's body.

(b) If there is more than one member of a class listed in subsection (a)(1), (3), (4), (5), (6), (7), or (9) entitled to make an anatomical gift, an anatomical gift may be made by a member of the class unless that member or a person to which the gift may pass under Section 11 knows of an objection by another member of the class. If an objection is known, the gift may be made only by a majority of the members of the class who are reasonably available.

(c) A person may not make an anatomical gift if, at the time of the decedent's death, a person in a prior class under subsection (a) is reasonably available to make or to object to the making of an anatomical gift.

§ 10. Manner of Making, Amending, or Revoking Anatomical Gift of Decedent's Body or Part.

(a) A person authorized to make an anatomical gift under Section 9 may make an anatomical gift by a document of gift signed by the person making the gift or by that person's oral communication that is electronically recorded or is contemporaneously reduced to a record and signed by the individual receiving the oral communication.

(b) Subject to subsection (c), an anatomical gift by a person authorized under Section 9 may be amended or revoked orally or in a record by any member of a prior class who is reasonably available. If more than one member of the prior class is reasonably available, the gift made by a person authorized under Section 9 may be:

(1) amended only if a majority of the reasonably available members agree to the amending of the gift; or

(2) revoked only if a majority of the reasonably available members agree to the revoking of the gift or if they are equally divided as to whether to revoke the gift.

(c) A revocation under subsection (b) is effective only if, before an incision has been made to remove a part from the donor's body or before invasive procedures have begun to prepare the recipient, the procurement organization, transplant hospital, or physician or technician knows of the revocation.

§ 11. Persons That May Receive Anatomical Gift; Purpose of Anatomical Gift.

(a) An anatomical gift may be made to the following persons named in the document of gift:

(1) a hospital; accredited medical school, dental school, college, or university; organ procurement organization; or other appropriate person, for research or education;

(2) subject to subsection (b), an individual designated by the person making the anatomical gift if the individual is the recipient of the part;

(3) an eye bank or tissue bank.

(b) If an anatomical gift to an individual under subsection (a)(2) cannot be transplanted into the individual, the part passes in accordance with subsection (g) in the absence of an express, contrary indication by the person making the anatomical gift.

(c) If an anatomical gift of one or more specific parts or of all parts is made in a document of gift that does not name a person described in subsection (a) but identifies the purpose for which an anatomical gift may be used, the following rules apply:

(1) If the part is an eye and the gift is for the purpose of transplantation or therapy, the gift passes to the appropriate eye bank.

(2) If the part is tissue and the gift is for the purpose of transplantation or therapy, the gift passes to the appropriate tissue bank.

(3) If the part is an organ and the gift is for the purpose of transplantation or therapy, the gift passes to the appropriate organ procurement organization as custodian of the organ.

(4) If the part is an organ, an eye, or tissue and the gift is for the purpose of research or education, the gift passes to the appropriate procurement organization.

(d) For the purpose of subsection (c), if there is more than one purpose of an anatomical gift set forth in the document of gift but the purposes are not set forth in any priority, the gift must be used for transplantation or therapy, if suitable. If the gift cannot be used for transplantation or therapy, the gift may be used for research or education.

(e) If an anatomical gift of one or more specific parts is made in a document of gift that does not name a person described in subsection (a) and does not identify the purpose of the gift, the gift may be used only for transplantation or therapy, and the gift passes in accordance with subsection (g).

(f) If a document of gift specifies only a general intent to make an anatomical gift by words such as "donor", "organ donor", or "body donor", or by a symbol or statement of similar import, the gift may be used only for transplantation or therapy, and the gift passes in accordance with subsection (g).

(g) For purposes of subsections (b), (e), and (f) the following rules apply:

(1) If the part is an eye, the gift passes to the appropriate eye bank.

(2) If the part is tissue, the gift passes to the appropriate tissue bank.

(3) If the part is an organ, the gift passes to the appropriate organ procurement organization as custodian of the organ.

(h) An anatomical gift of an organ for transplantation or therapy, other than an anatomical gift under subsection (a)(2), passes to the organ procurement organization as custodian of the organ.

(i) If an anatomical gift does not pass pursuant to subsections (a) through (h) or the decedent's body or part is not used for transplantation, therapy, research, or education, custody of the body or part passes to the person under obligation to dispose of the body or part.

(j) A person may not accept an anatomical gift if the person knows that the gift was not effectively made under Section 5 or 10 or if the person knows that the decedent made a refusal under Section 7 that was not revoked. For purposes of the subsection, if a person knows that an anatomical gift was made on a document of gift, the person is deemed to know of any amendment or revocation of the gift or any refusal to make an anatomical gift on the same document of gift.

(k) Except as otherwise provided in subsection (a)(2), nothing in this [act] affects the allocation of organs for transplantation or therapy.

§ 12. Search and Notification.

(a) The following persons shall make a reasonable search of an individual who the person reasonably believes is dead or near death for a document of gift or other information identifying the individual as a donor or as an individual who made a refusal:

(1) a law enforcement officer, firefighter, paramedic, or other emergency rescuer finding the individual; and

(2) if no other source of the information is immediately available, a hospital, as soon as practical after the individual's arrival at the hospital.

(b) If a document of gift or a refusal to make an anatomical gift is located by the search required by subsection (a)(1) and the individual or deceased individual to whom it relates is taken to a hospital, the person responsible for conducting the search shall send the document of gift or refusal to the hospital.

(c) A person is not subject to criminal or civil liability for failing to discharge the duties imposed by this section but may be subject to administrative sanctions.

§ 13. Delivery of Document of Gift Not Required; Right to Examine.

(a) A document of gift need not be delivered during the donor's lifetime to be effective.

(b) Upon or after an individual's death, a person in possession of a document of gift or a refusal to make an anatomical gift with respect to the individual shall allow examination and copying of the document of gift or refusal by a person authorized to make or object to the making of an anatomical gift with respect to the individual or by a person to which the gift could pass under Section 11.

§ 14. Rights and Duties of Procurement Organization and Others.

(a) When a hospital refers an individual at or near death to a procurement organization, the organization shall make a reasonable search of the records of the [state department of motor vehicles] and any donor registry that it knows exists for the geographical area in which the individual resides to ascertain whether the individual has made an anatomical gift.

(b) A procurement organization must be allowed reasonable access to information in the records of the [state department of motor vehicles] to ascertain whether an individual at or near death is a donor.

(c) When a hospital refers an individual at or near death to a procurement organization, the organization may conduct any reasonable examination necessary to ensure the medical suitability of a part that is or could be the subject of an anatomical gift for transplantation, therapy, research, or education from a donor or a prospective donor. During the examination period, measures necessary to ensure the medical suitability of the part may not be withdrawn unless the hospital or procurement organization knows that the individual expressed a contrary intent.

(d) Unless prohibited by law other than this [act], at any time after a donor's death, the person to which a part passes under Section 11 may conduct any reasonable examination necessary to ensure the medical suitability of the body or part for its intended purpose.

(e) Unless prohibited by law other than this [act], an examination under subsection (c) or (d) may include an examination of all medical and dental records of the donor or prospective donor.

(f) Upon the death of a minor who was a donor or had signed a refusal, unless a procurement organization knows the minor is emancipated, the procurement organization shall conduct a reasonable search for the parents of the minor and provide the parents with an opportunity to revoke or amend the anatomical gift or revoke the refusal.

(g) Upon referral by a hospital under subsection (a), a procurement organization shall make a reasonable search for any person listed in Section 9 having priority to make an anatomical gift on behalf of a prospective donor. If a procurement organization receives information that an anatomical gift to any other person was made, amended, or revoked, it shall promptly advise the other person of all relevant information.

(h) Subject to Sections 11(i) and 23, the rights of the person to which a part passes under Section 11 are superior to the rights of all others with respect to the part. The person may accept or reject an anatomical gift in whole or in part. Subject to the terms of the document of gift and this [act], a person that accepts an anatomical gift of an entire body may allow embalming, burial or cremation, and use of remains in a funeral service. If the gift is of a part, the person to which the part passes under Section 11, upon the death of the donor and before embalming, burial, or cremation, shall cause the part to be removed without unnecessary mutilation.

(i) Neither the physician who attends the decedent at death nor the physician who determines the time of the decedent's death may participate in the procedures for removing or transplanting a part from the decedent.

(j) A physician or technician may remove a donated part from the body of a donor that the physician or technician is qualified to remove.

§ 15. Coordination of Procurement and Use. Each hospital in this state shall enter into agreements or affiliations with procurement organizations for coordination of procurement and use of anatomical gifts.

§ 16. Sale or Purchase of Parts Prohibited.

(a) Except as otherwise provided in subsection (b), a person that for valuable consideration, knowingly purchases or sells a part for transplantation or therapy if removal of a part from an individual is intended to occur after the individual's death commits a [[felony] and upon conviction is subject to a fine not exceeding [$50,000] or imprisonment not exceeding [five] years, or both][class[ ] felony].

(b) A person may charge a reasonable amount for the removal, processing, preservation, quality control, storage, transportation, implantation, or disposal of a part.

§ 17. Other Prohibited Acts. A person that, in order to obtain a financial gain, intentionally falsifies, forges, conceals, defaces, or obliterates a document of gift, an amendment or revocation of a document of gift, or a refusal commits a [[felony] and upon conviction is subject to a fine not exceeding [$50,000] or imprisonment not exceeding [five] years, or both] [class[ ] felony].

§ 18. Immunity.

(a) A person that acts in accordance with this [act] or with the applicable anatomical gift law of another state, or attempts in good faith to do so, is not liable for the act in a civil action, criminal prosecution, or administrative proceeding.

(b) Neither the person making an anatomical gift nor the donor's estate is liable for any injury or damage that results from the making or use of the gift.

(c) In determining whether an anatomical gift has been made, amended, or revoked under this [act], a person may rely upon representations of an individual listed in Section 9(a)(2), (3), (4), (5), (6), (7), or (8) relating to the individual's relationship to the donor or prospective donor unless the person knows that the representation is untrue.

§ 19. Law Governing Validity; Choice of Law as to Execution of Document of Gift; Presumption of Validity.

(a) A document of gift is valid if executed in accordance with:

(1) this [act];

(2) the laws of the state or country where it was executed; or

(3) the laws of the state or country where the person making the anatomical gift was domiciled, has a place of residence, or was a national at the time the document of gift was executed.

(b) If a document of gift is valid under this section, the law of this state governs the interpretation of the document of gift.

(c) A person may presume that a document of gift or amendment of an anatomical gift is valid unless that person knows that it was not validly executed or was revoked.

§ 20. Donor Registry.

(a) The [insert name of appropriate state agency] may establish or contract for the establishment of a donor registry.

(b) The [state department of motor vehicles] shall cooperate with a person that administers any donor registry that this state establishes, contracts for, or recognizes for the purpose of transferring to the donor registry all relevant information regarding a donor's making, amendment to, or revocation of an anatomical gift.

(c) A donor registry must:

(1) allow a donor or other person authorized under Section 4 to include on the donor registry a statement or symbol that the donor has made, amended, or revoked an anatomical gift;

(2) be accessible to a procurement organization to allow it to obtain relevant information on the donor registry to determine, at or near death of the donor or a prospective donor, whether the donor or prospective donor has made, amended, or revoked an anatomical gift; and

(3) be accessible for purposes of paragraphs (1) and (2) seven days a week on a 24-hour basis.

(d) Personally identifiable information on a donor registry about a donor or prospective donor may not be used or disclosed without the express consent of the donor, prospective donor, or person that made the anatomical gift for any purpose other than to determine, at or near death of the donor or prospective donor, whether the donor or prospective donor has made, amended, or revoked an anatomical gift.

(e) This section does not prohibit any person from creating or maintaining a donor registry that is not established by or under contract with the state. Any such registry must comply with subsections (c) and (d).

Legislative Note: *If the state has an existing donor registry statute, it should consider whether this section is necessary. It should also consider whether subsections (c) and (d), and Section 14(g)(last sentence), should be incorporated into its existing statute. Subsection (b) may be deleted if the state department of motor vehicles is the agency specified in subsection (a).*

§ 21. Effect of Anatomical Gift on Advance Health-Care Directive.

(a) In this section:

(1) "Advance health-care directive" means a power of attorney for health care or a record signed or authorized by a prospective donor containing the prospective donor's direction concerning a health-care decision for the prospective donor.

(2) "Declaration" means a record signed by a prospective donor specifying the circumstances under which a life support system may be withheld or withdrawn from the prospective donor.

(3) "Health-care decision" means any decision regarding the health care of the prospective donor.

(b) If a prospective donor has a declaration or advance health-care directive and the terms of the declaration or directive and the express or implied terms of a potential anatomical gift are in conflict with regard to the administration of measures necessary to ensure the medical suitability of a part for transplantation or therapy, the prospective donor's attending physician and prospective donor shall confer to resolve the conflict. If the prospective donor is incapable of resolving the conflict, an agent acting under the prospective donor's declaration or directive, or, if none or the agent is not reasonably available, another person authorized by law other than this [act] to make health-care decisions on behalf of the prospective donor, shall act for the donor to resolve the conflict. The conflict must be resolved as expeditiously as possible. Information relevant to the resolution of the conflict may be obtained from the appropriate procurement organization and any other person authorized to make an anatomical gift for the prospective donor under Section 9. Before resolution of the conflict, measures necessary to ensure the medical suitability of the part may not be withheld or withdrawn from the prospective donor if withholding or withdrawing the measures is not contraindicated by appropriate end-of-life care.

§ 22. Cooperation Between [Coroner] [Medical Examiner] and Procurement Organization.

(a) A [coroner] [medical examiner] shall cooperate with procurement organizations to maximize the opportunity to recover anatomical gifts for the purpose of transplantation, therapy, research, or education.

(b) If a [coroner] [medical examiner] receives notice from a procurement organization that an anatomical gift might be available or was made with respect to a decedent whose body is under the jurisdiction of the [coroner] [medical examiner] and a post-mortem examination is going to be performed, unless the [coroner] [medical examiner] denies recovery in accordance with Section 23, the [coroner] [medical examiner] or designee shall conduct a post-mortem examination of the body or the part in a manner and within a period compatible with its preservation for the purposes of the gift.

(c) A part may not be removed from the body of a decedent under the jurisdiction of a [coroner] [medical examiner] for transplantation, therapy, research, or education unless the part is the subject of an anatomical gift. The body of a decedent under the jurisdiction of the [coroner] [medical examiner] may not be delivered to a person for research or education unless the body is the subject of an anatomical gift. This subsection does not preclude a [coroner] [medical examiner] from performing the medicolegal investigation upon the body or parts of a decedent under the jurisdiction of the [coroner] [medical examiner].

§ 23. Facilitation of Anatomical Gift from Decedent Whose Body Is under Jurisdiction of [Coroner] [Medical Examiner].

(a) Upon request of a procurement organization, a [coroner] [medical examiner] shall release to the procurement organization the name, contact information, and available medical and social history of a decedent whose body is under the jurisdiction of the [coroner] [medical examiner]. If the decedent's body or part is medically suitable for transplantation, therapy, research, or education, the [coroner] [medical examiner] shall release post-mortem examination results to the procurement organization. The procurement organization may make a subsequent disclosure of the post-mortem examination results or other information received from the [coroner] [medical examiner] only if relevant to transplantation or therapy.

(b) The [coroner] [medical examiner] may conduct a medicolegal examination by reviewing all medical records, laboratory test results, x-rays, other diagnostic results, and other information that any person possesses about a donor or prospective donor whose body is under the jurisdiction of the [coroner] [medical examiner] which the [coroner] [medical examiner] determines may be relevant to the investigation.

(c) A person that has any information requested by a [coroner] [medical examiner] pursuant to subsection (b) shall provide that information as expeditiously as possible to allow the [coroner] [medical examiner] to conduct the medicolegal investigation within a period compatible with the preservation of parts for the purpose of transplantation, therapy, research, or education.

(d) If an anatomical gift has been or might be made of a part of a decedent whose body is under the jurisdiction of the [coroner] [medical examiner] and a post-mortem examination is not required, or the [coroner] [medical examiner] determines that a post-mortem examination is required but that the recovery of the part that is the subject of an anatomical gift will not interfere with the examination, the [coroner] [medical examiner] and procurement organization shall cooperate in the timely removal of the part from the decedent for the purpose of transplantation, therapy, research, or education.

(e) If an anatomical gift of a part from the decedent under the jurisdiction of the [coroner] [medical examiner] has been or might be made, but the [coroner] [medical examiner] initially believes that the recovery of the part could interfere with the post-mortem investigation into the decedent's cause or manner of death, the [coroner] [medical examiner] shall consult with the procurement organization or physician or technician designated by the procurement organization about the proposed recovery.

After consultation, the [coroner] [medical examiner] may allow the recovery.

(f) Following the consultation under subsection (e), in the absence of mutually agreed-upon protocols to resolve conflict between the [coroner] [medical examiner] and the procurement organization, if the [coroner] [medical examiner] intends to deny recovery, the [coroner] [medical examiner] or designee, at the request of the procurement organization, shall attend the removal procedure for the part before making a final determination not to allow the procurement organization to recover the part. During the removal procedure, the [coroner] [medical examiner] or designee may allow recovery by the procurement organization to proceed, or, if the [coroner] [medical examiner] or designee reasonably believes that the part may be involved in determining the decedent's cause or manner of death, deny recovery by the procurement organization.

(g) If the [coroner] [medical examiner] or designee denies recovery under subsection (f), the [coroner] [medical examiner] or designee shall:

(1) explain in a record the specific reasons for not allowing recovery of the part;

(2) include the specific reasons in the records of the [coroner] [medical examiner]; and

(3) provide a record with the specific reasons to the procurement organization.

(h) If the [coroner] [medical examiner] or designee allows recovery of a part under subsection (d), (e), or (f), the procurement organization, upon request, shall cause the physician or technician who removes the part to provide the [coroner] [medical examiner] with a record describing the condition of the part, a biopsy, a photograph, and any other information and observations that would assist in the post-mortem examination.

(i) If a [coroner] [medical examiner] or designee is required to be present at a removal procedure under subsection (f), upon request the procurement organization requesting the recovery of the part shall reimburse the [coroner] [medical examiner] or designee for the additional costs incurred in complying with subsection (f).

Legislative Note: Section 23 could be incorporated into the provisions of the state's code where the provisions relating to a coroner or medical examiner are codified rather than included in this act. If codified in that manner, the definitions in Section 2 of "anatomical gift", "donor", "eye bank", "organ procurement organization", "part", "procurement organization", "prospective donor" (first sentence only), "tissue", and "tissue bank" also should be included.

§ 24. Uniformity of Application and Construction. In applying and construing this uniform act, consideration must be given to the need to promote uniformity of the law with respect to its subject matter among states that enact it.

§ 25. Relation to Electronic Signatures in Global and National Commerce Act. This act modifies, limits, and supersedes the Electronic Signatures in Global and National Commerce Act, 15 U.S.C. Section 7001 et seq., but does not modify, limit or supersede Section 101(a) of that act, 15 U.S.C. Section 7001, or authorize electronic delivery of any of the notices described in Section 103(b) of that act, 15 U.S.C. Section 7003(b).

§ 26. Repeals. The following acts and parts of acts are repealed:

(1) [Uniform Anatomical Gift Act];

(2)

(3)

§ 27. Effective Date. This [act] takes effect _____.

UNIFORM PRUDENT MANAGEMENT OF INSTITUTIONAL FUNDS ACT (2006)

Table of Sections

Prefatory Note

Reasons for Revision. The Uniform Prudent Management of Institutional Funds Act (UPMIFA) replaces the Uniform Management of Institutional Funds Act (UMIFA). The National Conference of Commissioners on Uniform State Laws approved UMIFA in 1972, and 47 jurisdictions have enacted the act. UMIFA provided guidance and authority to charitable organizations within its scope concerning the management and investment of funds held by those organizations, UMIFA provided endowment spending rules that did not depend on trust accounting principles of income and principal, and UMIFA permitted the release of restrictions on the use or management of funds under certain circumstances. The changes UMIFA made to the law permitted charitable organizations to use modern investment techniques such as total-return investing and to determine endowment fund spending based on spending rates rather than on determinations of "income" and "principal."

UMIFA was drafted almost 35 years ago, and portions of it are now out of date. The prudence standards in UMIFA have provided useful guidance, but prudence norms evolve over time. The new Act provides modern articulations of the prudence standards for the management and investment of charitable funds and for endowment spending. The Uniform Prudent Investor Act (UPIA), an Act promulgated in 1994 and already enacted in 43 jurisdictions, served as a model for many of the revisions. UPIA updates rules on investment decision

making for trusts, including charitable trusts, and imposes additional duties on trustees for the protection of beneficiaries. UPMIFA applies these rules and duties to charities organized as nonprofit corporations. UPMIFA does not apply to trusts managed by corporate and other fiduciaries that are not charities, because UPIA provides management and investment standards for those trusts.

In applying principles based on UPIA to charities organized as nonprofit corporations, UPMIFA combines the approaches taken by UPIA and by the Revised Model Nonprofit Corporation Act (RMNCA). UPMIFA reflects the fact that standards for managing and investing institutional funds are and should be the same regardless of whether a charitable organization is organized as a trust, a nonprofit corporation, or some other entity. See Bevis Longstreth, Modern Investment Management and the Prudent Man Rule 7 (1986) (stating "[t]he modern paradigm of prudence applies to all fiduciaries who are subject to some version of the prudent man rule, whether under ERISA, the private foundation provisions of the Code, UMIFA, other state statutes, or the common law."); Harvey P. Dale, Nonprofit Directors and Officers - Duties and Liabilities for Investment Decisions, 1994 N.Y.U. Conf. Tax Plan. 501(c)(3) Org's. Ch. 4.

UPMIFA provides guidance and authority to charitable organizations concerning the management and investment of funds held by those organizations, and UPMIFA imposes additional duties on those who manage and invest charitable funds. These duties provide additional protections for charities and also protect the interests of donors who want to see their contributions used wisely.

UPMIFA modernizes the rules governing expenditures from endowment funds, both to provide stricter guidelines on spending from endowment funds and to give institutions the ability to cope more easily with fluctuations in the value of the endowment.

Finally, UPMIFA updates the provisions governing the release and modification of restrictions on charitable funds to permit more efficient management of these funds. These provisions derive from the approach taken in the Uniform Trust Code (UTC) for modifying charitable trusts. Like the UTC provisions, UPMIFA's modification rules preserve the historic position of the attorneys general in most states as the overseers of charities.

As under UMIFA, the new Act applies to charities organized as charitable trusts, as nonprofit corporations, or in some other manner, but the rules do not apply to funds managed by trustees that are not charities. Thus, the Act does not apply to trusts managed by corporate or individual trustees, but the Act does apply to trusts managed by charities.

Prudent Management and Investment. UMIFA applied the 1972 prudence standard to investment decision making. In contrast, UPMIFA will give charities updated and more useful guidance by incorporating language from UPIA, modified to fit the special needs of charities. The revised Act spells out more of the factors a charity should consider in making investment decisions, thereby imposing a modern, well accepted, prudence standard based on UPIA.

Among the expressly enumerated prudence factors in UPMIFA is "the preservation of the endowment fund," a standard not articulated in UMIFA.

In addition to identifying factors that a charity must consider in making management and investment decisions, UPMIFA requires a charity and those who manage and invest its funds to:

1. Give primary consideration to donor intent as expressed in a gift instrument,

2. Act in good faith, with the care an ordinarily prudent person would exercise,

3. Incur only reasonable costs in investing and managing charitable funds,

4. Make a reasonable effort to verify relevant facts,

5. Make decisions about each asset in the context of the portfolio of investments, as part of an overall investment strategy,

6. Diversify investments unless due to special circumstances, the purposes of the fund are better served without diversification,

7. Dispose of unsuitable assets, and

8. In general, develop an investment strategy appropriate for the fund and the charity.

UMIFA did not articulate these requirements. Thus, UPMIFA strengthens the rules governing management and investment decision making by charities and provides more guidance for those who manage and invest the funds.

Donor Intent with Respect to Endowments. UPMIFA improves the protection of donor intent with respect to expenditures from endowments. When a donor expresses intent clearly in a written gift instrument, the Act requires that the charity follow the donor's instructions. When a donor's intent is not so expressed, UPMIFA directs the charity to spend an amount that is prudent, consistent with the purposes of the fund, relevant economic factors, and the donor's intent that the fund continue in perpetuity. This approach allows the charity to give effect to donor intent, protect its endowment, assure generational equity, and use the endowment to support the purposes for which the endowment was created.

Retroactivity. Like UMIFA, UPIA, the Uniform Principal and Income Act of 1961, and the Uniform Principal and Income Act of 1997, UPMIFA applies retroactively to institutional funds created before and prospectively to institutional funds created after enactment of the statute. Regarding the considerations motivating this treatment of the issues, see the comment to Section 4.

Endowment Spending. UPMIFA improves the endowment spending rule by eliminating the concept of historic dollar value and providing better guidance regarding the operation of the prudence standard. Under UMIFA a charity can spend amounts above historic dollar value that the charity determines to be prudent. The Act directs the charity to focus on the purposes and needs of the charity rather than on the purposes and perpetual nature of the fund. Amounts below historic dollar value cannot be spent. The Drafting Committee concluded that this endowment spending rule created numerous problems and that restructuring the rule would benefit charities, their donors, and the public. The problems include:

1. Historic dollar value fixes valuation at a moment in time, and that moment is arbitrary. If a donor provides for a gift in the donor's will, the date of

valuation for the gift will likely be the donor's date of death. (UMIFA left uncertain what the appropriate date for valuing a testamentary gift was.) The determination of historic dollar value can vary significantly depending upon when in the market cycle the donor dies. In addition, the fund may be below historic dollar value at the time the charity receives the gift if the value of the asset declines between the date of the donor's death and the date the asset is actually distributed to the charity from the estate.

2. After a fund has been in existence for a number of years, historic dollar value may become meaningless. Assuming reasonable long term investment success, the value of the typical fund will be well above historic dollar value, and historic dollar value will no longer represent the purchasing power of the original gift. Without better guidance on spending the increase in value of the fund, historic dollar value does not provide adequate protection for the fund. If a charity views the restriction on spending simply as a direction to preserve historic dollar value, the charity may spend more than it should.

3. The Act does not provide clear answers to questions a charity faces when the value of an endowment fund drops below historic dollar value. A fund that is so encumbered is commonly called an "underwater" fund. Conflicting advice regarding whether an organization could spend from an underwater fund has led to difficulties for those managing charities. If a charity concluded that it could continue to spend trust accounting income until a fund regained its historic dollar value, the charity might invest for income rather than on a total-return basis. Thus, the historic dollar value rule can cause inappropriate distortions in investment policy and can ultimately lead to a decline in a fund's real value. If, instead, a charity with an underwater fund continues to invest for growth, the charity may be unable to spend anything from an underwater endowment fund for several years. The inability of a charity to spend anything from an endowment is likely to be contrary to donor intent, which is to provide current benefits to the charity.

The Drafting Committee concluded that providing clearly articulated guidance on the prudence rule for spending from an endowment fund, with emphasis on the permanent nature of the fund, would provide the best protection of the purchasing power of endowment funds.

Presumption of Imprudence. UPMIFA includes as an optional provision a presumption of imprudence

if a charity spends more than seven percent of an endowment fund in any one year. The presumption is meant to protect against spending an endowment too quickly. Although the Drafting Committee believes that the prudence standard of UPMIFA provides appropriate and adequate protection for endowments, the Committee provided the option for states that want to include a mechanical guideline in the statute. A major drawback to any statutory percentage is that it is unresponsive to changes in the rate of inflation or deflation.

Modification of Restrictions on Charitable Funds. UPMIFA clarifies that the doctrines of cy pres and deviation apply to funds held by nonprofit corporations as well as to funds held by charitable trusts. Courts have applied trust law rules to nonprofit corporations in the past, but the Drafting Committee believed that statutory authority for applying these principles to nonprofit corporations would be helpful. UMIFA permitted release of restrictions but left the application of cy pres uncertain. Under UPMIFA, as under trust law, the court will determine whether and how to apply cy pres or deviation and the attorney general will receive notice and have the opportunity to participate in the proceeding. The one addition to existing law is that UPMIFA gives a charity the authority to modify a restriction on a fund that is both old and small. For these funds, the expense of a trip to court will often be prohibitive. By permitting a charity to make an appropriate modification, money is saved for the charitable purposes of the charity. Even with respect to small, old funds, however, the charity must notify the attorney general of the charity's intended action. Of course, if the attorney general has concerns, he or she can seek the agreement of the charity to change or abandon the modification, and if that fails, can commence a court action to enjoin it. Thus, in all types of modification the attorney general continues to be the protector both of the donor's intent and of the public's interest in charitable funds.

Other Organizational Law. For matters not governed by UPMIFA, a charitable organization will continue to be governed by rules applicable to charitable trusts, if it is organized as a trust, or rules applicable to nonprofit corporations, if it is organized as a nonprofit corporation.

Relation to Trust Law. Although UPMIFA applies a number of rules from trust law to institutions organized as nonprofit corporations, in two respects UPMIFA creates rules that do not exist under the common law applicable to trusts. The endowment spending rule of Section 4 and the provision for modifying a small, old fund in subsection (d) of Section 6 have no counterparts in the common law or the UTC. The Drafting Committee believes that these rules could be useful to charities organized as trusts, and the Committee recommends conforming amendments to the UTC and the Principal and Income Act to incorporate these changes into trust law.

§ 1. Short Title. This [act] may be cited as the Uniform Prudent Management of Institutional Funds Act.

§ 2. Definitions. In this [act]:

(1) "Charitable purpose" means the relief of poverty, the advancement of education or religion, the promotion of health, the promotion of a governmental purpose, or any other purpose the achievement of which is beneficial to the community.

(2) "Endowment fund" means an institutional fund or part thereof that, under the terms of a gift instrument, is not wholly expendable by the institution on a current basis. The term does not include assets that an institution designates as an endowment fund for its own use.

(3) "Gift instrument" means a record or records, including an institutional solicitation, under which property is granted to, transferred to, or held by an institution as an institutional fund.

(4) "Institution" means:

(A) a person, other than an individual, organized and operated exclusively for charitable purposes;

(B) a government or governmental subdivision, agency, or instrumentality, to the extent that it holds funds exclusively for a charitable purpose; and

(C) a trust that had both charitable and noncharitable interests, after all noncharitable interests have terminated.

(5) "Institutional fund" means a fund held by an institution exclusively for charitable purposes. The term does not include:

(A) program-related assets;

(B) a fund held for an institution by a trustee that is not an institution; or

(C) a fund in which a beneficiary that is not an institution has an interest, other than an interest that could arise upon violation or failure of the purposes of the fund.

(6) "Person" means an individual, corporation, business trust, estate, trust, partnership, limited liability company, association, joint venture, public corporation, government or governmental subdivision, agency, or instrumentality, or any other legal or commercial entity.

(7) "Program-related asset" means an asset held by an institution primarily to accomplish a charitable purpose of the institution and not primarily for investment.

(8) "Record" means information that is inscribed on a tangible medium or that is stored in an electronic or other medium and is retrievable in perceivable form.

§ 3. Standard of Conduct in Managing and Investing Institutional Fund.

(a) Subject to the intent of a donor expressed in a gift instrument, an institution, in managing and investing an institutional fund, shall consider the charitable purposes of the institution and the purposes of the institutional fund.

(b) In addition to complying with the duty of loyalty imposed by law other than this [act], each person responsible for managing and investing an institutional fund shall manage and invest the fund in good faith and with the care an ordinarily prudent person in a like position would exercise under similar circumstances.

(c) In managing and investing an institutional fund, an institution:

(1) may incur only costs that are appropriate and reasonable in relation to the assets, the purposes of the institution, and the skills available to the institution; and

(2) shall make a reasonable effort to verify facts relevant to the management and investment of the fund.

(d) An institution may pool two or more institutional funds for purposes of management and investment.

(e) Except as otherwise provided by a gift instrument, the following rules apply:

(1) In managing and investing an institutional fund, the following factors, if relevant, must be considered:

(A) general economic conditions;

(B) the possible effect of inflation or deflation;

(C) the expected tax consequences, if any, of investment decisions or strategies;

(D) the role that each investment or course of action plays within the overall investment portfolio of the fund;

(E) the expected total return from income and the appreciation of investments;

(F) other resources of the institution;

(G) the needs of the institution and the fund to make distributions and to preserve capital; and

(H) an asset's special relationship or special value, if any, to the charitable purposes of the institution.

(2) Management and investment decisions about an individual asset must be made not in isolation but rather in the context of the institutional fund's portfolio of investments as a whole and as a part of an overall investment strategy having risk and return objectives reasonably suited to the fund and to the institution.

(3) Except as otherwise provided by law other than this [act], an institution may invest in any kind of property or type of investment consistent with this section.

(4) An institution shall diversify the investments of an institutional fund unless the institution reasonably determines that, because of special circumstances, the purposes of the fund are better served without diversification.

(5) Within a reasonable time after receiving property, an institution shall make and carry out decisions concerning the retention or disposition of the property or to rebalance a portfolio, in order to bring the institutional fund into compliance with the purposes, terms, distribution requirements of the institution or necessary to meet other circumstances of the institution and the requirements of this [act].

(6) A person that has special skills or expertise, or is selected in reliance upon the person's representation that the person has special skills or expertise, has a duty to use those skills or that expertise in managing and investing institutional funds.

§4. Appropriation for Expenditure or Accumulation of Endowment Fund; Rules of Construction.

(a) Subject to the intent of a donor expressed in the gift instrument [and to subsection (d)], an institution may appropriate for expenditure or accumulate so much of an endowment fund as the institution determines is prudent for the uses, benefits, purposes, and duration for which the endowment fund is established. Unless stated otherwise in the gift instrument, the assets in an endowment fund are donor-restricted assets until appropriated for expenditure by the institution. In making a determination to appropriate or accumulate, the institution shall act in good faith, with the care that an ordinarily prudent person in a like position would exercise under similar circumstances, and shall consider, if relevant, the following factors:

(1) the duration and preservation of the endowment fund;

(2) the purposes of the institution and the endowment fund;

(3) general economic conditions;

(4) the possible effect of inflation or deflation;

(5) the expected total return from income and the appreciation of investments;

(6) other resources of the institution; and

(7) the investment policy of the institution.

(b) To limit the authority to appropriate for expenditure or accumulate under subsection (a), a gift instrument must specifically state the limitation.

(c) Terms in a gift instrument designating a gift as an endowment, or a direction or authorization in the gift instrument to use only "income", "interest", "dividends", or "rents, issues, or profits", or "to preserve the principal intact", or words of similar import:

(1) create an endowment fund of permanent duration unless other language in the gift instrument limits the duration or purpose of the fund; and

(2) do not otherwise limit the authority to appropriate for expenditure or accumulate under subsection (a).

[(d) The appropriation for expenditure in any year of an amount greater than seven percent of the fair market value of an endowment fund, calculated on the basis of market values determined at least quarterly and averaged over a period of not less than three years immediately preceding the year in which the appropriation for expenditure was made, creates a rebuttable presumption of imprudence. For an endowment fund in existence for fewer than three years, the fair market value of the endowment fund must be calculated for the period the endowment fund has been in existence. This subsection does not:

(1) apply to an appropriation for expenditure permitted under law other than this [act] or by the gift instrument; or

(2) create a presumption of prudence for an appropriation for expenditure of an amount less than or equal to seven percent of the fair market value of the endowment fund.]

[§ 5. Delegation of Management and Investment Functions.

(a) Subject to any specific limitation set forth in a gift instrument or in law other than this [act], an institution may delegate to an external agent the management and investment of an institutional fund to the extent that an institution could prudently delegate under the circumstances. An institution shall act in good faith, with the care that an ordinarily prudent person in a like position would exercise under similar circumstances, in:

(1) selecting an agent;

(2) establishing the scope and terms of the delegation, consistent with the purposes of the institution and the institutional fund; and

(3) periodically reviewing the agent's actions in order to monitor the agent's performance and compliance with the scope and terms of the delegation.

(b) In performing a delegated function, an agent owes a duty to the institution to exercise reasonable care to comply with the scope and terms of the delegation.

(c) An institution that complies with subsection (a) is not liable for the decisions or actions of an agent to which the function was delegated.

(d) By accepting delegation of a management or investment function from an institution that is subject to the laws of this state, an agent submits to the jurisdiction of the courts of this state in all proceedings arising from or related to the delegation or the performance of the delegated function.

(e) An institution may delegate management and investment functions to its committees, officers, or employees as authorized by law of this state other than this [act].]

§ 6. Release or Modification of Restrictions on Management, Investment, or Purpose.

(a) If the donor consents in a record, an institution may release or modify, in whole or in part, a restriction contained in a gift instrument on the management, investment, or purpose of an institutional fund. A release or modification may not allow a fund to be used for a purpose other than a charitable purpose of the institution.

(b) The court, upon application of an institution, may modify a restriction contained in a gift instrument regarding the management or investment of an institutional fund if the restriction has become impracticable or wasteful, if it impairs the management or investment of the fund, or if, because of circumstances not anticipated by the donor, a modification of a restriction will further the purposes of the fund. The institution shall notify the [Attorney General] of the application, and the [Attorney General] must be given an opportunity to be heard. To the extent practicable, any modification must be made in accordance with the donor's probable intention.

(c) If a particular charitable purpose or a restriction contained in a gift instrument on the use of an institutional fund becomes unlawful, impracticable, impossible to achieve, or wasteful, the court, upon application of an institution, may modify the purpose of the fund or the restriction on the use of the fund in a manner consistent with the charitable purposes expressed in the gift instrument. The institution shall notify the [Attorney General] of the application, and the [Attorney General] must be given an opportunity to be heard.

(d) If an institution determines that a restriction contained in a gift instrument on the management, investment, or purpose of an institutional fund is unlawful, impracticable, impossible to achieve, or wasteful, the institution, [60 days] after notification to the [Attorney General], may release or modify the restriction, in whole or part, if:

(1) the institutional fund subject to the restriction has a total value of less than [$25,000];

(2) more than [20] years have elapsed since the fund was established; and

(3) the institution uses the property in a manner consistent with the charitable purposes expressed in the gift instrument.

§ 7. Reviewing Compliance. Compliance with this [act] is determined in light of the facts and circumstances existing at the time a decision is made or action is taken, and not by hindsight.

§ 8. Application to Existing Institutional Funds. This [act] applies to institutional funds existing on or established after [the effective date of this act]. As applied to institutional funds existing on [the effective date of this act] this [act] governs only decisions made or actions taken on or after that date.

§ 9. Relation to Electronic Signatures in Global and National Commerce Act. This [act] modifies, limits, and supersedes the Electronic Signatures in Global and National Commerce Act, 15 U.S.C. Section 7001 et seq., but does not modify, limit, or supersede Section 101 of that act, 15 U.S.C. Section 7001(a), or authorize electronic delivery of any of the notices described in Section 103 of that act, 15 U.S.C. Section 7003(b).

§ 10. Uniformity of Application and Construction. In applying and construing this uniform act, consideration must be given to the need to promote uniformity of the law with respect to its subject matter among states that enact it.

§ 11. Effective Date. This [act] takes effect . . . .

§ 12. Repeal. The following acts and parts of acts are repealed:
   (a) [The Uniform Management of Institutional Funds Act]

UNIFORM HEALTH-CARE DECISIONS ACT (1993)

Table of Sections

Prefatory Note

Since the Supreme Court's decision in *Cruzan v. Commissioner, Missouri Department of Health*, 497 U.S. 261 (1990), significant change has occurred in state legislation on health-care decision making. Every state now has legislation authorizing the use of some sort of advance health-care directive. All but a few states authorize what is typically known as a living will. Nearly all states have statutes authorizing the use of powers of attorney for health care. In addition, a majority of states have statutes allowing family members, and in some cases close friends, to make health-care decisions for adult individuals who lack capacity.

This state legislation, however, has developed in fits and starts, resulting in an often fragmented, incomplete, and sometimes inconsistent set of rules. Statutes enacted within a state often conflict and conflicts between statutes of different states are common. In an increasingly mobile society where an advance health-care directive given in one state must frequently be implemented in another, there is a need for greater uniformity.

The Health-Care Decisions Act was drafted with this confused situation in mind. The Act is built around the following concepts.

First, the Act acknowledges the right of a competent individual to decide all aspects of his or her own health care in all circumstances, including the right to decline health care or to direct that health care be discontinued, even if death ensues. An individual's instructions may extend to any and all health-care decisions that might arise and, unless limited by the principal, an agent has authority to make all health-care decisions which the individual could have made. The Act recognizes and validates an individual's authority to define the scope of an instruction or agency as broadly or as narrowly as the individual chooses.

Second, the Act is comprehensive and will enable an enacting jurisdiction to replace its existing legislation on the subject with a single statute. The Act authorizes health-care decisions to be made by an agent who is designated to decide when an individual cannot or does not wish to; by a designated surrogate, family member, or close friend when an individual is unable to act and no guardian or agent has been appointed or is reasonably available; or by a court having jurisdiction as decision maker of last resort.

Third, the Act is designed to simplify and facilitate the making of advance health-care directives. An instruction may be either written or oral. A power of attorney for health care, while it must be in writing, need not be witnessed or acknowledged. In addition, an optional form for the making of a directive is provided.

Fourth, the Act seeks to ensure to the extent possible that decisions about an individual's health care will be governed by the individual's own desires concerning the issues to be resolved. The Act requires an agent or surrogate authorized to make health-care decisions for an individual to make those decisions in accordance with the instructions and other wishes of the individual to the extent known. Otherwise, the agent or surrogate must make those decisions in accordance with the best interest of the individual but in light of the individual's personal values known to the agent or surrogate. Furthermore, the Act requires a guardian to comply with a ward's previously given instructions and prohibits a guardian from revoking the ward's advance health-care directive without express court approval.

Fifth, the Act addresses compliance by health-care providers and institutions. A health-care provider or institution must comply with an instruction of the patient and with a reasonable interpretation of that instruction or other health-care decision made by a person then authorized to make health-care decisions for the patient. The obligation to comply is not absolute, however. A health-care provider or institution may decline to honor an instruction or decision for reasons of conscience or if the instruction or decision requires the provision of medically ineffective care or care contrary to applicable health-care standards.

Sixth, the Act provides a procedure for the resolution of disputes. While the Act is in general to be effectuated without litigation, situations will arise where resort to the courts may be necessary. For that reason, the Act authorizes the court to enjoin or direct a health-care decision or order other equitable relief and specifies who is entitled to bring a petition.

The Health-Care Decisions Act supersedes the Commissioners' Model Health-Care Consent Act (1982), the Uniform Rights of the Terminally Ill Act (1985), and the Uniform Rights of the Terminally Ill Act (1989). A state enacting the Health-Care Decisions Act which has one of these other acts in force should repeal it upon enactment.

§ 1. Definitions. In this [Act]:

(1) "Advance health-care directive" means an individual instruction or a power of attorney for health care.

(2) "Agent" means an individual designated in a power of attorney for health care to make a health-care decision for the individual granting the power.

(3) "Capacity" means an individual's ability to understand the significant benefits, risks, and alternatives to proposed health care and to make and communicate a health-care decision.

(4) "Guardian" means a judicially appointed guardian or conservator having authority to make a health-care decision for an individual.

(5) "Health care" means any care, treatment, service, or procedure to maintain, diagnose, or otherwise affect an individual's physical or mental condition.

(6) "Health-care decision" means a decision made by an individual or the individual's agent, guardian, or surrogate, regarding the individual's health care, including:

(i) selection and discharge of health-care providers and institutions;

(ii) approval or disapproval of diagnostic tests, surgical procedures, programs of medication, and orders not to resuscitate; and

(iii) directions to provide, withhold, or withdraw artificial nutrition and hydration and all other forms of health care.

(7) "Health-care institution" means an institution, facility, or agency licensed, certified, or otherwise authorized or permitted by law to provide health care in the ordinary course of business.

(8) "Health-care provider" means an individual licensed, certified, or otherwise authorized or permitted by law to provide health care in the ordinary course of business or practice of a profession.

(9) "Individual instruction" means an individual's direction concerning a health-care decision for the individual.

(10) "Person" means an individual, corporation, business trust, estate, trust, partnership, association,

joint venture, government, governmental subdivision, agency, or instrumentality, or any other legal or commercial entity.

(11) "Physician" means an individual authorized to practice medicine [or osteopathy] under [appropriate statute].

(12) "Power of attorney for health care" means the designation of an agent to make health-care decisions for the individual granting the power.

(13) "Primary physician" means a physician designated by an individual or the individual's agent, guardian, or surrogate, to have primary responsibility for the individual's health care or, in the absence of a designation or if the designated physician is not reasonably available, a physician who undertakes the responsibility.

(14) "Reasonably available" means readily able to be contacted without undue effort and willing and able to act in a timely manner considering the urgency of the patient's health-care needs.

(15) "State" means a State of the United States, the District of Columbia, the Commonwealth of Puerto Rico, or a territory or insular possession subject to the jurisdiction of the United States.

(16) "Supervising health-care provider" means the primary physician or, if there is no primary physician or the primary physician is not reasonably available, the health-care provider who has undertaken primary responsibility for an individual's health care.

(17) "Surrogate" means an individual, other than a patient's agent or guardian, authorized under this [Act] to make a health-care decision for the patient.

§ 2. Advance Health-Care Directives.

(a) An adult or emancipated minor may give an individual instruction. The instruction may be oral or written. The instruction may be limited to take effect only if a specified condition arises.

(b) An adult or emancipated minor may execute a power of attorney for health care, which may authorize the agent to make any health-care decision the principal could have made while having capacity. The power must be in writing and signed by the principal. The power remains in effect notwithstanding the principal's later incapacity and may include individual instructions. Unless related to the principal by blood, marriage, or adoption, an agent may not be an owner, operator, or employee of [a residential long-term health-care institution] at which the principal is receiving care.

(c) Unless otherwise specified in a power of attorney for health care, the authority of an agent becomes effective only upon a determination that the principal lacks capacity, and ceases to be effective upon a determination that the principal has recovered capacity.

(d) Unless otherwise specified in a written advance health-care directive, a determination that an individual lacks or has recovered capacity, or that another condition exists that affects an individual instruction or the authority of an agent, must be made by the primary physician.

(e) An agent shall make a health-care decision in accordance with the principal's individual instructions, if any, and other wishes to the extent known to the agent. Otherwise, the agent shall make the decision in accordance with the agent's determination of the principal's best interest. In determining the principal's best interest, the agent shall consider the principal's personal values to the extent known to the agent.

(f) A health-care decision made by an agent for a principal is effective without judicial approval.

(g) A written advance health-care directive may include the individual's nomination of a guardian of the person.

(h) An advance health-care directive is valid for purposes of this [Act] if it complies with this [Act], regardless of when or where executed or communicated.

Comment

The individual instruction authorized in subsection (a) may but need not be limited to take effect in specified circumstances, such as if the individual is dying. An individual instruction may be either written or oral.

Subsection (b) authorizes a power of attorney for health care to include instructions regarding the principal's health care. This provision has been included in order to validate the practice of designating an agent and giving individual instructions in one document instead of two. The authority of an agent falls within the discretion of the principal as expressed in the instrument creating the power and may extend to any health-care decision the principal could have made while having capacity.

Subsection (b) excludes the oral designation of an agent. Section 5(b) authorizes an individual to orally designate a surrogate by personally informing the supervising health-care provider. A power of attorney for health care, however, must be in writing and signed by the principal, although it need not be witnessed or acknowledged.

Subsection (b) also limits those who may serve as agents to make health-care decisions for another. The subsection addresses the special vulnerability of individuals in residential long-term health-care institutions by protecting a principal against those who may have interests that conflict with the duty to follow the principal's expressed wishes or to determine the principal's best interest. Specifically, the owners, operators or employees of a residential long-term health-care institution at which the principal is receiving care may not act as agents. An exception is made for those related to the principal by blood, marriage or adoption, relationships which are assumed to neutralize any consequence of a conflict of interest adverse to the principal. The phrase "a residential long-term health-care institution" is placed in brackets to indicate to the legislature of an enacting jurisdiction that it should substitute the appropriate terminology used under local law.

Subsection (c) provides that the authority of the agent to make health-care decisions ordinarily does not become effective until the principal is determined to lack capacity and ceases to be effective should the principal recover capacity. A principal may provide, however, that the authority of the agent becomes effective immediately or upon the happening of some event other than the loss of capacity but may do so only by an express provision in the power of attorney. For example, a mother who does not want to make

her own health-care decisions but prefers that her daughter make them for her may specify that the daughter as agent is to have authority to make health-care decisions immediately. The mother in that circumstance retains the right to later revoke the power of attorney as provided in Section 3.

Subsection (d) provides that unless otherwise specified in a written advance health-care directive, a determination that a principal has lost or recovered capacity to make health-care decisions must be made by the primary physician. For example, a principal might specify that the determination of capacity is to be made by the agent in consultation with the primary physician. Or a principal, such as a member of the Christian Science faith who relies on a religious method of healing and who has no primary physician, might specify that capacity be determined by other means. In the event that multiple decision makers are specified and they cannot agree, it may be necessary to seek court instruction as authorized by Section 14.

Subsection (d) also provides that unless otherwise specified in a written advance health-care directive, the existence of other conditions which affect an individual instruction or the authority of an agent must be determined by the primary physician. For example, an individual might specify that an agent may withdraw or withhold treatment that keeps the individual alive only if the individual has an incurable and irreversible condition that will result in the individual's death within a relatively short time. In that event, unless otherwise specified in the advance health-care directive, the determination that the individual has that condition must be made by the primary physician.

Subsection (e) requires the agent to follow the principal's individual instructions and other expressed wishes to the extent known to the agent. To the extent such instructions or other wishes are unknown, the agent must act in the principal's best interest. In determining the principal's best interest, the agent is to consider the principal's personal values to the extent known to the agent. The Act does not prescribe a detailed list of factors for determining the principal's best interest but instead grants the agent discretion to ascertain and weigh the factors likely to be of importance to the principal. The legislature of an enacting jurisdiction that wishes to add such a list may want to consult the Maryland Health-Care Decision Act, Md. Health-Gen. Code Ann. § 5-601.

Subsection (f) provides that a health-care decision

made by an agent is effective without judicial approval. A similar provision applies to health-care decisions made by surrogates (Section 5(g)) or guardians (Section 6(c)).

Subsection (g) provides that a written advance health-care directive may include the individual's nomination of a guardian of the person. A nomination cannot guarantee that the nominee will be appointed but in the absence of cause to appoint another the court would likely select the nominee. Moreover, the mere nomination of the agent will reduce the likelihood that a guardianship could be used to thwart the agent's authority.

Subsection (h) validates advance health-care directives which conform to the Act, regardless of when or where executed or communicated. This includes an advance health-care directive which would be valid under the Act but which was made prior to the date of its enactment and failed to comply with the execution requirements then in effect. It also includes an advance health-care directive which was made in another jurisdiction but which does not comply with that jurisdiction's execution or other requirements.

§ 3. Revocation of Advance Health-care Directive.

(a) An individual may revoke the designation of an agent only by a signed writing or by personally informing the supervising health-care provider.

(b) An individual may revoke all or part of an advance health-care directive, other than the designation of an agent, at any time and in any manner that communicates an intent to revoke.

(c) A health-care provider, agent, guardian, or surrogate who is informed of a revocation shall promptly communicate the fact of the revocation to the supervising health-care provider and to any health-care institution at which the patient is receiving care.

(d) A decree of annulment, divorce, dissolution of marriage, or legal separation revokes a previous designation of a spouse as agent unless otherwise specified in the decree or in a power of attorney for health care.

(e) An advance health-care directive that conflicts with an earlier advance health-care directive revokes the earlier directive to the extent of the conflict.

Comment

Subsection (b) provides that an individual may revoke any portion of an advance health-care directive at any time and in any manner that communicates an intent to revoke. However, a more restrictive standard applies to the revocation of the portion of a power of attorney for health care relating to the designation of an agent. Subsection (a) provides that an individual may revoke the designation of an agent only by a signed writing or by personally informing the supervising health-care provider. This higher standard is justified by the risk of a false revocation of an agent's designation or of a misinterpretation or miscommunication of a principal's statement communicated through a third party. For example, without this higher standard, an individual motivated by a desire to gain control over a patient might be able to assume authority to act as agent by falsely informing a health-care provider that the principal no longer wishes the previously designated agent to act but instead wishes to appoint the individual.

Subsection (c) requires any health-care provider, agent, guardian or surrogate who is informed of a revocation to promptly communicate that fact to the supervising health-care provider and to any health-care institution at which the patient is receiving care. The communication triggers the Section 7(b) obligation of the supervising health-care provider to record the revocation in the patient's health-care record and reduces the risk that a health-care provider or agent, guardian or surrogate will rely on a health-care directive that is no longer valid.

Subsection (e) establishes a rule of construction permitting multiple advance health-care directives to be construed together in order to determine the individual's intent, with the later advance health-care directive superseding the former to the extent of any inconsistency.

The section does not specifically address amendment of an advance health-care directive because such reference is not necessary. Subsection (b) specifically authorizes partial revocation, and subsection (e) recognizes that an advance health-care directive may be modified by a later directive.

§ 4. Optional Form. The following form may, but need not, be used to create an advance health-care directive. The other sections of this [Act] govern the effect of this or any other writing used to create an advance health-care directive. An individual may complete or modify all or any part of the following form:

ADVANCE HEALTH-CARE DIRECTIVE

Explanation

You have the right to give instructions about your own health care. You also have the right to name someone else to make health-care decisions for you. This form lets you do either or both of these things. It also lets you express your wishes regarding donation of organs and the designation of your primary physician. If you use this form, you may complete or modify all or any part of it. You are free to use a different form.

Part 1 of this form is a power of attorney for health care. Part 1 lets you name another individual as agent to make health-care decisions for you if you become incapable of making your own decisions or if you want someone else to make those decisions for you now even though you are still capable. You may also name an alternate agent to act for you if your first choice is not willing, able, or reasonably available to make decisions for you. Unless related to you, your agent may not be an owner, operator, or employee of [a residential long-term health-care institution] at which you are receiving care.

Unless the form you sign limits the authority of your agent, your agent may make all health-care decisions for you. This form has a place for you to limit the authority of your agent. You need not limit the authority of your agent if you wish to rely on your agent for all health-care decisions that may have to be made. If you choose not to limit the authority of your agent, your agent will have the right to:

(a) consent or refuse consent to any care, treatment, service, or procedure to maintain, diagnose, or otherwise affect a physical or mental condition;

(b) select or discharge health-care providers and institutions;

(c) approve or disapprove diagnostic tests, surgical procedures, programs of medication, and orders not to resuscitate; and

(d) direct the provision, withholding, or withdrawal of artificial nutrition and hydration and all other forms of health care.

Part 2 of this form lets you give specific instructions about any aspect of your health care. Choices are provided for you to express your wishes regarding the provision, withholding, or withdrawal of treatment to keep you alive, including the provision of artificial nutrition and hydration, as well as the provision of pain relief. Space is also provided for you to add to the choices you have made or for you to write out any additional wishes.

Part 3 of this form lets you express an intention to donate your bodily organs and tissues following your death.

Part 4 of this form lets you designate a physician to have primary responsibility for your health care.

After completing this form, sign and date the form at the end. It is recommended but not required that you request two other individuals to sign as witnesses. Give a copy of the signed and completed form to your physician, to any other health-care providers you may have, to any health-care institution at which you are receiving care, and to any health-care agents you have named. You should talk to the person you have named as agent to make sure that he or she understands your wishes and is willing to take the responsibility.

You have the right to revoke this advance health-care directive or replace this form at any time.

* * * * * * * * * * * * * * * * * * * *

PART 1
POWER OF ATTORNEY FOR HEALTH CARE

(1) DESIGNATION OF AGENT: I designate the following individual as my agent to make health-care decisions for me:

_____

(name of individual you choose as agent)

_____

(address)   (city)   (state)   (zip code)

_____

(home phone)   (work phone)

OPTIONAL: If I revoke my agent's authority or if my agent is not willing, able, or reasonably available to make a health-care decision for me, I designate as my first alternate agent:

_____

(name of individual you choose as first alternate agent)

_____

(address)   (city)   (state)   (zip code)

_____

(home phone)   (work phone)

OPTIONAL: If I revoke the authority of my agent and first alternate agent or if neither is willing, able, or reasonably available to make a health-care decision for me, I designate as my second alternate agent:

_____

(name of individual you choose as second alternate agent)

_____

(address)   (city)   (state)   (zip code)

_____

(home phone)   (work phone)

(2) AGENT'S AUTHORITY: My agent is authorized to make all health-care decisions for me, including decisions to provide, withhold, or withdraw artificial nutrition and hydration and all other forms of health care to keep me alive, except as I state here:

_____

_____

(Add additional sheets if needed.)

(3) WHEN AGENT'S AUTHORITY BECOMES EFFECTIVE: My agent's authority becomes effective when my primary physician determines that I am unable to make my own health-care decisions unless I mark the following box. If I mark this box [ ], my agent's authority to make health-care decisions for me takes effect immediately.

(4) AGENT'S OBLIGATION: My agent shall make health-care decisions for me in accordance with this power of attorney for health care, any instructions I give in Part 2 of this form, and my other wishes to the extent known to my agent. To the extent my wishes are unknown, my agent shall make health-care decisions for me in accordance with what my agent determines to be in my best interest. In determining my best interest, my agent shall consider my personal values to the extent known to my agent.

(5) NOMINATION OF GUARDIAN: If a guardian of my person needs to be appointed for me by a court, I nominate the agent designated in this form. If that agent is not willing, able, or reasonably available to act as guardian, I nominate the alternate agents whom I have named, in the order designated.

PART 2
INSTRUCTIONS FOR HEALTH CARE

If you are satisfied to allow your agent to determine what is best for you in making end-of-life decisions, you need not fill out this part of the form. If you do fill out this part of the form, you may strike any wording you do not want.

(6) END-OF-LIFE DECISIONS: I direct that my health-care providers and others involved in my care provide, withhold, or withdraw treatment in accordance with the choice I have marked below:

[ ] (a)   Choice Not To Prolong Life

I do not want my life to be prolonged if (i) I have an incurable and irreversible condition that will result in my death within a relatively short time, (ii) I become unconscious and, to a reasonable degree of medical certainty, I will not regain consciousness, or (iii) the likely risks and burdens of treatment would outweigh the expected benefits, OR

[ ] (b)   Choice To Prolong Life

I want my life to be prolonged as long as possible within the limits of generally accepted health-care standards.

(7) ARTIFICIAL NUTRITION AND HYDRATION: Artificial nutrition and hydration must be provided, withheld, or withdrawn in accordance with the choice I have made in paragraph (6) unless I mark the following box. If I mark this box [ ], artificial nutrition and hydration must be provided regardless of my condition and regardless of the choice I have made in paragraph (6).

(8) RELIEF FROM PAIN: Except as I state in the following space, I direct that treatment for alleviation of pain or discomfort be provided at all times, even if it hastens my death:

_____

_____

(9) OTHER WISHES: (If you do not agree with any of the optional choices above and wish to write your own, or if you wish to add to the instructions you have given above, you may do so here.) I direct that:

_____

_____

(Add additional sheets if needed.)

886

PART 3
DONATION OF ORGANS AT DEATH

(OPTIONAL)

(10) Upon my death (mark applicable box)

[ ] (a)   I give any needed organs, tissues, or parts, OR

[ ] (b)   I give the following organs, tissues, or parts only

_____

_____

   (c)   My gift is for the following purposes (strike any of the following you do not want)
     (i) Transplant
     (ii) Therapy
     (iii) Research
     (iv) Education

PART 4
PRIMARY PHYSICIAN

(OPTIONAL)

(11) I designate the following physician as my primary physician:

_____
(name of physician)

_____
(address)   (city)   (state)   (zip code)

_____
(phone)

OPTIONAL: If the physician I have designated above is not willing, able, or reasonably available to act as my primary physician, I designate the following physician as my primary physician:

_____
(name of physician)

_____
(address)   (city)   (state)   (zip code)

_____
(phone)

* * * * * * * * * * * * * * * * * * * *

(12) EFFECT OF COPY: A copy of this form has the same effect as the original.

(13) SIGNATURES: Sign and date the form here:

_____   _____
(date)   (sign your name)

_____   _____
(address)   (print your name)

(city)	(state)

(Optional) SIGNATURES OF WITNESSES:

First witness   Second witness

_____   _____
(print name)   (print name)

_____   _____
(address)   (address)

_____   _____
(city)   (state)   (city)   (state)

_____   _____
(signature of witness)   (signature of witness)

_____   _____
(date)   (date)

Comment

The optional form set forth in this section incorporates the Section 2 requirements applicable to advance health-care directives. There are four parts to the form. An individual may complete all or any parts of the form. Any part of the form left blank is not to be given effect. For example, an individual may complete the instructions for health care part of the form alone. Or an individual may complete the power of attorney for health care part of the form alone. Or an individual may complete both the instructions and power of attorney for health care parts of the form. An individual may also, but need not, complete the parts of the form pertaining to donation of bodily organs and tissue and the designation of a primary physician.

Part 1, the power of attorney for health care, appears first on the form in order to ensure to the extent possible that it will come to the attention of a casual reader. This reflects the reality that the appointment of an agent is a more comprehensive approach to the making of health-care decisions than is the giving of an individual instruction, which cannot possibly anticipate all future circumstances which might arise.

Part 1 (1) of the power of attorney for health care form requires only the designation of a single agent, but with opportunity given to designate a single first alternate and a single second alternate, if the individual chooses. No provision is made in the form for the designation of co-agents in order not to encourage the practice. Designation of co-agents is discouraged because of the difficulties likely to be encountered if the co-agents are not all readily available or do not agree. If co-agents are appointed, the instrument should specify that either is authorized to act if the other is not reasonably available. It should also specify a method for resolving disagreements.

Part 1 (2) of the power of attorney for health care form grants the agent authority to make all health-care decisions for the individual subject to any limitations which the individual may state in the form. Reference is made to artificial nutrition and hydration and other forms of treatment to keep an individual alive in order to ensure that the individual is aware that those are forms of health care that the agent would have the authority to withdraw or withhold absent specific limitation.

Part 1 (3) of the power of attorney for health care form provides that the agent's authority becomes effective upon a determination that the individual lacks capacity, but as authorized by Section 2(c) a box is provided for the individual to indicate that the authority of the agent takes effect immediately.

Part 1 (4) of the power of attorney for health care form directs the agent to make health-care decisions in accordance with the power of attorney, any instructions given by the individual in Part 2 of the form, and the individual's other wishes to the extent known to the agent. To the extent the individual's wishes in the matter are not known, the agent is to make health-care decisions based on what the agent determines to be in the individual's best interest. In determining the individual's best interest, the agent is to consider the individual's personal values to the extent known to the agent. Section 2(e) imposes this standard, whether or not it is included in the form, but its inclusion in the form will bring it to the attention of the individual granting the power, to the agent, to any guardian or surrogate, and to the individual's health-care providers.

Part 1 (5) of the power of attorney for health care form nominates the agent, if available, able, and willing to act, otherwise the alternate agents in order of priority stated, as guardians of the person for the individual. This provision is included in the form for two reasons. First, if an appointment of a guardian becomes necessary the agent is the one whom the individual would most likely want to serve in that role. Second, the nomination of the agent as guardian will reduce the possibility that someone other than the agent will be appointed as guardian who could use the position to thwart the agent's authority.

Because the variety of treatment decisions to which health-care instructions may relate is virtually unlimited, Part 2 of the form does not attempt to be comprehensive, but is directed at the types of treatment for which an individual is most likely to have special wishes. Part 2(6) of the form, entitled "End-of-Life Decisions", provides two alternative choices for the expression of wishes concerning the provision, withholding, or withdrawal of treatment. Under the first choice, the individual's life is not to be prolonged if the individual has an incurable and irreversible condition that will result in death within a relatively short time, if the individual becomes unconscious and, to a reasonable degree of medical certainty, will not regain consciousness, or if the likely risks and burdens of treatment would outweigh the expected benefits. Under the second choice, the individual's life is to be prolonged within the limits of generally accepted health-care standards. Part 2(7) of the form provides a box for an individual to mark if the individual wishes to receive artificial nutrition and hydration in all circumstances. Part 2(8) of the form provides space for an individual to specify any circumstance when the individual would prefer not to receive pain relief. Because the choices provided in Parts 2(6) to 2(8) do not cover all possible situations, Part 2(9) of the form provides space for the individual to write out his or her own instructions or to supplement the instructions given in the previous

subparts of the form. Should the space be insufficient, the individual is free to add additional pages.

The health-care instructions given in Part 2 of the form are binding on the agent, any guardian, any surrogate, and, subject to exceptions specified in Section 7(e)-(f), on the individual's health-care providers. Pursuant to Section 7(d), a health-care provider must also comply with a reasonable interpretation of those instructions made by an authorized agent, guardian, or surrogate.

Part 3 of the form provides the individual an opportunity to express an intention to donate bodily organs and tissues at death. The options provided are derived from a suggested form in the Comment to Section 2 of the Uniform Anatomical Gift Act (1987).

Part 4 of the form provides space for the individual to designate a primary physician should the individual choose to do so. Space is also provided for the designation of an alternate primary physician should the first designated physician not be available, able, or willing to act.

Paragraph (12) of the form conforms with the provisions of Section 12 by providing that a copy of the form has the same effect as the original.

The Act does not require witnessing, but to encourage the practice the form provides space for the signatures of two witnesses.

The form does not require formal acceptance by an agent. Formal acceptance by an agent has been omitted not because it is an undesirable practice but because it would add another stage to executing an advance health-care directive, thereby further reducing the number of individuals who will follow through and create directives. However, practitioners who wish to adapt this form for use by their clients are strongly encouraged to add a formal acceptance. Designated agents have no duty to act until they accept the office either expressly or through their conduct. Consequently, requiring formal acceptance reduces the risk that a designated agent will decline to act when the need arises. Formal acceptance also makes it more likely that the agent will become familiar with the principal's personal values and views on health care. While the form does not require formal acceptance, the explanation to the form does encourage principals to talk to the person they have named as agent to make certain that the designated agent understands their wishes and is willing to take the responsibility.

§ 5. Decisions by Surrogate.

(a) A surrogate may make a health-care decision for a patient who is an adult or emancipated minor if the patient has been determined by the primary physician to lack capacity and no agent or guardian has been appointed or the agent or guardian is not reasonably available.

(b) An adult or emancipated minor may designate any individual to act as surrogate by personally informing the supervising health-care provider. In the absence of a designation, or if the designee is not reasonably available, any member of the following classes of the patient's family who is reasonably available, in descending order of priority, may act as surrogate:

(1) the spouse, unless legally separated;

(2) an adult child;

(3) a parent; or

(4) an adult brother or sister.

(c) If none of the individuals eligible to act as surrogate under subsection (b) is reasonably available, an adult who has exhibited special care and concern for the patient, who is familiar with the patient's personal values, and who is reasonably available may act as surrogate.

(d) A surrogate shall communicate his or her assumption of authority as promptly as practicable to the members of the patient's family specified in subsection (b) who can be readily contacted.

(e) If more than one member of a class assumes authority to act as surrogate, and they do not agree on a health-care decision and the supervising health-care provider is so informed, the supervising health-care provider shall comply with the decision of a majority of the members of that class who have communicated their views to the provider. If the class is evenly divided concerning the health-care decision and the supervising health-care provider is so informed, that class and all individuals having lower priority are disqualified from making the decision.

(f) A surrogate shall make a health-care decision in accordance with the patient's individual instructions, if any, and other wishes to the extent known to the surrogate. Otherwise, the surrogate shall make the decision in accordance with the surrogate's determination of the patient's best interest. In determining the patient's best interest, the surrogate shall consider the patient's personal values to the extent known to the surrogate.

(g) A health-care decision made by a surrogate for a patient is effective without judicial approval.

(h) An individual at any time may disqualify another, including a member of the individual's family, from acting as the individual's surrogate by a signed writing or by personally informing the supervising health-care provider of the disqualification.

(i) Unless related to the patient by blood, marriage, or adoption, a surrogate may not be an owner, operator, or employee of [a residential long-term health-care institution] at which the patient is receiving care.

(j) A supervising health-care provider may require an individual claiming the right to act as surrogate for a patient to provide a written declaration under penalty of perjury stating facts and circumstances reasonably sufficient to establish the claimed authority.

Comment

Subsection (a) authorizes a surrogate to make a health-care decision for a patient who is an adult or emancipated minor if the patient lacks capacity to make health-care decisions and if no agent or guardian has been appointed or the agent or guardian is not reasonably available. Health-care decision making for unemancipated minors is not covered by this section. The subject of consent for treatment of minors is a complex one which in many states is covered by a variety of statutes and is therefore left to other state law.

While a designation of an agent in a written power of attorney for health care is preferred, situations may arise where an individual will not be in a position to execute a power of attorney for health care. In that event, subsection (b) affirms the principle of patient autonomy by allowing an individual to designate a surrogate by personally informing the supervising health-care provider. The supervising health-care provider would then, in accordance with Section 7(b), be obligated to promptly record the designation in the individual's health-care record. An oral designation of a surrogate made by a patient directly to the supervising health-care provider revokes a previous designation of an agent. See Section 3(a).

If an individual does not designate a surrogate or if the designee is not reasonably available, subsection (b) applies a default rule for selecting a family member to act as surrogate. Like all default rules, it is not tailored to every situation, but incorporates the presumed desires of a majority of those who find themselves so situated. The relationships specified in subsection (b) include those of the half-blood and by adoption, in addition to those of the whole blood.

Subsection (c) permits a health-care decision to be made by a more distant relative or unrelated adult with whom the individual enjoys a close relationship but only if all family members specified in subsection (b) decline to act or are otherwise not reasonably available. Consequently, those in non-traditional relationships who want to make certain that health-care decisions are made by their companions should execute powers of attorney for health care designating them as agents or, if that has not been done, should designate them as surrogates.

Subsections (b) and (c) permit any member of a class authorized to serve as surrogate to assume authority to act even though there are other members in the class.

Subsection (d) requires a surrogate who assumes authority to act to immediately so notify the members of the patient's family who in given circumstances would be eligible to act as surrogate. Notice to the specified family members will enable them to follow health-care developments with respect to their now incapacitated relative. It will also alert them to take appropriate action, including the appointment of a guardian or the commencement of judicial proceedings under Section 14, should the need arise.

Subsection (e) addresses the situation where more than one member of the same class has assumed authority to act as surrogate and a disagreement over a health-care decision arises of which the supervising health-care provider is informed. Should that occur, the supervising health-care provider must comply with the decision of a majority of the members of that class

who have communicated their views to the provider. If the members of the class who have communicated their views to the provider are evenly divided concerning the health-care decision, however, then the entire class is disqualified from making the decision and no individual having lower priority may act as surrogate. When such a deadlock arises, it may be necessary to seek court determination of the issue as authorized by Section 14.

Subsection (f) imposes on surrogates the same standard for health-care decision making as is prescribed for agents in Section 2(e). The surrogate must follow the patient's individual instructions and other expressed wishes to the extent known to the surrogate. To the extent such instructions or other wishes are unknown, the surrogate must act in the patient's best interest. In determining the patient's best interest, the surrogate is to consider the patient's personal values to the extent known to the surrogate.

Subsection (g) provides that a health-care decision made by a surrogate is effective without judicial approval. A similar provision applies to health-care decisions made by agents (Section 2(f)) or guardians (Section 6(c)).

Subsection (h) permits an individual to disqualify any family member or other individual from acting as the individual's surrogate, including disqualification of a surrogate who was orally designated.

Subsection (i) disqualifies an owner, operator, or employee of a residential long-term health-care institution at which a patient is receiving care from acting as the patient's surrogate unless related to the patient by blood, marriage, or adoption. This disqualification is similar to that for appointed agents. See Section 2(b) and Comment.

Subsection (j) permits a supervising health-care provider to require an individual claiming the right to act as surrogate to provide a written declaration under penalty of perjury stating facts and circumstances reasonably sufficient to establish the claimed relationship. The authority to request a declaration is included to permit the provider to obtain evidence of claimed authority. A supervising health-care provider, however, does not have a duty to investigate the qualifications of an individual claiming authority to act as surrogate, and Section 9(a) protects a health-care provider or institution from liability for complying with the decision of such an individual, absent knowledge that the individual does not in fact have such authority.

§ 6. Decisions by Guardian.

(a) A guardian shall comply with the ward's individual instructions and may not revoke the ward's advance health-care directive unless the appointing court expressly so authorizes.

(b) Absent a court order to the contrary, a health-care decision of an agent takes precedence over that of a guardian.

(c) A health-care decision made by a guardian for the ward is effective without judicial approval.

Comment

The Act affirms that health-care decisions should whenever possible be made by a person whom the individual selects to do so. For this reason, subsection (b) provides that a health-care decision of an agent takes precedence over that of a guardian absent a court order to the contrary, and subsection (a) provides that a guardian may not revoke the ward's power of attorney for health care unless the appointing court expressly so authorizes. Without these subsections, a guardian would in many states have authority to revoke the ward's power of attorney for health care even though the court appointing the guardian might not be aware that the principal had made such alternate arrangement.

The Act expresses a strong preference for honoring an individual instruction. Under the Act, an individual instruction must be honored by an agent, by a surrogate, and, subject to exceptions specified in Section 7(e)-(f), by an individual's health-care providers. Subsection (a) extends this principle to guardians by requiring that a guardian effectuate the ward's individual instructions. A guardian may revoke the ward's individual instructions only if the appointing court expressly so authorizes.

Courts have no particular expertise with respect to health-care decision making. Moreover, the delay attendant upon seeking court approval may undermine the effectiveness of the decision ultimately made, particularly but not only when the patient's condition is life-threatening and immediate decisions concerning treatment need to be made. Decisions should whenever possible be made by a patient, or the patient's guardian, agent, or surrogate in consultation with the patient's health-care providers without outside interference. For this reason, subsection (c) provides that a health-care decision made by a guardian for the ward is effective without judicial approval, and the Act includes similar provisions for health-care decisions made by agents (Section 2(f)) or surrogates (Section 5(g)).

§ 7. Obligations of Health-Care Provider.

(a) Before implementing a health-care decision made for a patient, a supervising health-care provider, if possible, shall promptly communicate to the patient the decision made and the identity of the person making the decision.

(b) A supervising health-care provider who knows of the existence of an advance health-care directive, a revocation of an advance health-care directive, or a designation or disqualification of a surrogate, shall promptly record its existence in the patient's health-care record and, if it is in writing, shall request a copy and if one is furnished shall arrange for its maintenance in the health-care record.

(c) A primary physician who makes or is informed of a determination that a patient lacks or has recovered capacity, or that another condition exists which affects an individual instruction or the authority of an agent, guardian, or surrogate, shall promptly record the determination in the patient's health-care record and communicate the determination to the patient, if possible, and to any person then authorized to make health-care decisions for the patient.

(d) Except as provided in subsections (e) and (f), a health-care provider or institution providing care to a patient shall:

(1) comply with an individual instruction of the patient and with a reasonable interpretation of that instruction made by a person then authorized to make health-care decisions for the patient; and

(2) comply with a health-care decision for the patient made by a person then authorized to make health-care decisions for the patient to the same extent as if the decision had been made by the patient while having capacity.

(e) A health-care provider may decline to comply with an individual instruction or health-care decision for reasons of conscience. A health-care institution may decline to comply with an individual instruction or health-care decision if the instruction or decision is contrary to a policy of the institution which is expressly based on reasons of conscience and if the policy was timely communicated to the patient or to a person then authorized to make health-care decisions for the patient.

(f) A health-care provider or institution may decline to comply with an individual instruction or health-care decision that requires medically ineffective health care or health care contrary to generally accepted health-care standards applicable to the health-care provider or institution.

(g) A health-care provider or institution that declines to comply with an individual instruction or health-care decision shall:

(1) promptly so inform the patient, if possible, and any person then authorized to make health-care decisions for the patient;

(2) provide continuing care to the patient until a transfer can be effected; and

(3) unless the patient or person then authorized to make health-care decisions for the patient refuses assistance, immediately make all reasonable efforts to assist in the transfer of the patient to another health-care provider or institution that is willing to comply with the instruction or decision.

(h) A health-care provider or institution may not require or prohibit the execution or revocation of an advance health-care directive as a condition for providing health care.

Comment

Subsection (a) further reinforces the Act's respect for patient autonomy by requiring a supervising health-care provider, if possible, to promptly communicate to a patient, prior to implementation, a health-care decision made for the patient and the identity of the person making the decision.

The recording requirement in subsection (b) reduces the risk that a health-care provider or institution, or agent, guardian or surrogate, will rely on an outdated individual instruction or the decision of an individual whose authority has been revoked.

Subsection (c) imposes recording and communication requirements relating to determinations that may trigger the authority of an agent, guardian or surrogate to make health-care decisions on an individual's behalf. The determinations covered by these requirements are those specified in Sections 2(c)-(d) and 5(a).

Subsection (d) requires health-care providers and institutions to comply with a patient's individual instruction and with a reasonable interpretation of that instruction made by a person then authorized to make health-care decisions for the patient. A health-care provider or institution must also comply with a health-care decision made by a person then authorized to make health-care decisions for the patient to the same extent as if the decision had been made by the patient while having capacity. These requirements help to protect the patient's rights to

autonomy and self-determination and validate and seek to effectuate the substitute decision making authorized by the Act.

Not all instructions or decisions must be honored, however. Subsection (e) authorizes a health-care provider to decline to comply with an individual instruction or health-care decision for reasons of conscience. Subsection (e) also allows a health-care institution to decline to comply with a health-care instruction or decision if the instruction or decision is contrary to a policy of the institution which is expressly based on reasons of conscience and if the policy was timely communicated to the patient or to an individual then authorized to make health-care decisions for the patient.

Subsection (f) further authorizes a health-care provider or institution to decline to comply with an instruction or decision that requires the provision of care which would be medically ineffective or contrary to generally accepted health-care standards applicable to the provider or institution. "Medically ineffective health care", as used in this section, means treatment which would not offer the patient any significant benefit.

Subsection (g) requires a health-care provider or institution that declines to comply with an individual instruction or health-care decision to promptly communicate the refusal to the patient, if possible, and to any person then authorized to make health-care decisions for the patient. The provider or institution also must provide continuing care to the patient until a transfer can be effected. In addition, unless the patient or person then authorized to make health-care decisions for the patient refuses assistance, the health-care provider or institution must immediately make all reasonable efforts to assist in the transfer of the patient to another health-care provider or institution that is willing to comply with the instruction or decision.

Subsection (h), forbidding a health-care provider or institution to condition provision of health care on execution, non-execution, or revocation of an advance health-care directive, tracks the provisions of the federal Patient Self-Determination Act (42 U.S.C. § 1395cc(f)(1)(C) (Medicare); 42 U.S.C. § 1396a(w)(1)(C) (Medicaid)).

§ 8. Health-Care Information. Unless otherwise specified in an advance health-care directive, a person then authorized to make health-care decisions for a patient has the same rights as the patient to request, receive, examine, copy, and consent to the disclosure of medical or any other health-care information.

§ 9. Immunities.

(a) A health-care provider or institution acting in good faith and in accordance with generally accepted health-care standards applicable to the health-care provider or institution is not subject to civil or criminal liability or to discipline for unprofessional conduct for:

(1) complying with a health-care decision of a person apparently having authority to make a health-care decision for a patient, including a decision to withhold or withdraw health care;

(2) declining to comply with a health-care decision of a person based on a belief that the person then lacked authority; or

(3) complying with an advance health-care directive and assuming that the directive was valid when made and has not been revoked or terminated.

(b) An individual acting as agent or surrogate under this [Act] is not subject to civil or criminal liability or to discipline for unprofessional conduct for health-care decisions made in good faith.

§ 10. Statutory Damages.

(a) A health-care provider or institution that intentionally violates this [Act] is subject to liability to the aggrieved individual for damages of $[500] or actual damages resulting from the violation, whichever is greater, plus reasonable attorney's fees.

(b) A person who intentionally falsifies, forges, conceals, defaces, or obliterates an individual's advance health-care directive or a revocation of an advance health-care directive without the individual's consent, or who coerces or fraudulently induces an individual to give, revoke, or not to give an advance health-care directive, is subject to liability to that individual for damages of $[2,500] or actual damages resulting from the action, whichever is greater, plus reasonable attorney's fees.

§ 11. Capacity.

(a) This [Act] does not affect the right of an individual to make health-care decisions while having capacity to do so.

(b) An individual is presumed to have capacity to make a health-care decision, to give or revoke an advance health-care directive, and to designate or disqualify a surrogate.

§ 12. Effect of Copy. A copy of a written advance health-care directive, revocation of an advance health-care directive, or designation or disqualification of a surrogate has the same effect as the original.

§ 13. Effect of [Act].

(a) This [Act] does not create a presumption concerning the intention of an individual who has not made or who has revoked an advance health-care directive.

(b) Death resulting from the withholding or withdrawal of health care in accordance with this [Act] does not for any purpose constitute a suicide or homicide or legally impair or invalidate a policy of insurance or an annuity providing a death benefit, notwithstanding any term of the policy or annuity to the contrary.

(c) This [Act] does not authorize mercy killing, assisted suicide, euthanasia, or the provision, withholding, or withdrawal of health care, to the extent prohibited by other statutes of this State.

(d) This [Act] does not authorize or require a health-care provider or institution to provide health care contrary to generally accepted health-care standards applicable to the health-care provider or institution.

[(e) This [Act] does not authorize an agent or surrogate to consent to the admission of an individual to a mental health-care institution unless the individual's written advance health-care directive expressly so provides.]

[(f) This [Act] does not affect other statutes of this State governing treatment for mental illness of an individual involuntarily committed to a [mental health-care institution under appropriate statute].]

§ 14. Judicial Relief. On petition of a patient, the patient's agent, guardian, or surrogate, a health-care provider or institution involved with the patient's care, or an individual described in Section 5(b) or (c), the [appropriate] court may enjoin or direct a health-care decision or order other equitable relief. A proceeding under this section is governed by [here insert appropriate reference to the rules of procedure or statutory provisions governing expedited proceedings and proceedings affecting incapacitated persons].

§ 15. Uniformity of Application and Construction. This [Act] shall be applied and construed to effectuate its general purpose to make uniform the law with respect to the subject matter of this [Act] among States enacting it.

§ 16. Short Title. This [Act] may be cited as the Uniform Health-Care Decisions Act.

§ 17. Severability Clause. If any provision of this [Act] or its application to any person or circumstance is held invalid, the invalidity does not affect other provisions or applications of this [Act] which can be given effect without the invalid provision or application, and to this end the provisions of this [Act] are severable.

§ 18. Effective Date. This [Act] takes effect on _____
_____.

§ 19. Repeal. The following acts and parts of acts are repealed:

(1)

(2)

(3)

UNIFORM SIMULTANEOUS DEATH ACT (1993)

Table of Sections

Prefatory Note

The Uniform Simultaneous Death Act (USDA) was first promulgated in 1940. It was amended in 1953 and has been enacted in the District of Columbia and all but three of the States.

The original USDA provided that, when there is no sufficient evidence that two individuals died otherwise than simultaneously, each individual's property is distributed as if he or she survived the other. The advantages of this approach are that each individual's property passes to that individual's relatives rather than to the other individual's relatives and that double administrative costs are avoided because property does not pass from one estate to another estate.

This revision of the USDA does not alter the result of the original Act. Rather, it expands the narrow application of the original Act so that, as revised, it no longer is restricted to situations in which there is no sufficient evidence that two individuals died otherwise than simultaneously. In cases in which both individuals caught in a common tragedy have died by the time third parties arrive at the scene, or shortly thereafter, the narrow application of the original Act has sometimes led to unfortunate litigation in which the representative of one of the individuals attempts, through the use of gruesome medical evidence, to prove that the one he or she represents survived the other by an instant or two. Examples include Janus v. Tarasewicz, 482 N.E.2d 418 (Ill. App. Ct.1985) (husband's brother died as result of ingesting Tylenol capsules laced with cyanide by unknown perpetrator prior to sale in stores; after learning of his death, but before the cause of his death had been determined,

husband and wife returned from their honeymoon and each ingested contaminated Tylenol capsules; upon their arrival at intensive care unit of emergency room, neither showed visible vital signs; hospital personnel never succeeded in establishing in husband any spontaneous blood pressure, pulse, or signs of respiration and pronounced him dead; hospital personnel did succeed in establishing in wife a measurable, though unsatisfactory, blood pressure; although she had very unstable vital signs, remained in a coma, and had fixed and dilated pupils, she was placed on mechanical respirator and remained on the respirator for two days before she was pronounced dead; USDA found inapplicable because there was sufficient evidence that wife survived husband); In re Bucci's Will, 57 Misc.2d 1001, 293 N.Y.S.2d 994 (N.Y.Surr.Ct.1968) (husband and wife found dead when removed from wreckage of their small airplane, which crashed and burned after having collided in air with large airplane; existence of carbon monoxide in wife's blood found sufficient evidence to establish wife's survival of husband, whose skull was fractured and in whose blood no carbon monoxide was found).

Even in cases in which it is indisputable that one of the two survived the other, such as a case in which one is clearly dead at the scene of the accident and the other clearly dies in the ambulance on the way to the hospital, the policy of the original Act plainly should apply.

This version of the USDA, then, extends the application of the original Act to situations in which there *is* sufficient evidence that one of the individuals survived the other one, but the period of survival was insubstantial. This version originated in Sections 2-104 and 2-601 of the Uniform Probate Code of 1969, which imposed a 120-hour requirement of survival for intestate and testate succession, and in the revisions of Article I and II of the Uniform Probate Code that were approved in 1990 and 1991, which extend the 120-hour requirement of survival to provisions of a "governing instrument" and to "co-owners with right of survivorship," as those terms are defined in Section 1. A clear and convincing evidence standard of proof of survival by 120 hours is imposed throughout in order to reduce litigation and to resolve close cases in favor of non-survival.

The sections specifically pertaining to community property and insurance policies contained in the original Act are unnecessary and omitted from the 1991 version. If a decedent spouse dies owning community property, those community property interests are covered by the general provisions of Sections 2 and/or 3. Similarly, insurance is covered by the general provisions of Section 3.

Section 5 of this version, titled "Evidence of Death or Status," covers an area not covered in the original Act. Subsection (1) of Section 5 defines death by reference to the Uniform Determination of Death Act. Subsections (2) through (6) are drawn from Section 1-107 of the Uniform Probate Code as revised in 1991 and provide for evidence of death or status. Note that subsection (6) is made desirable by the introduction of the requirement that survival by 120 hours must be established by clear and convincing evidence. Subsection (6) provides that, in the absence of evidence disputing the time of death stipulated on a document such as a certified copy of a death certificate, such a document that stipulates a time of death 120 hours or more after the time of death of another individual, however the time of death of the other individual is determined, establishes by clear and convincing evidence that the individual survived the other individual by 120 hours.

Section 7 of this version is a new section made desirable by the extension of a 120-hour requirement of survival to all governing instruments, such as life-insurance beneficiary designations, and to co-ownership arrangements with right of survivorship, such as joint tenancies and joint checking accounts. Section 7 grants protection to payors and other third parties who, before receiving written notice of a claimed lack of entitlement under the Act, pay off or in other ways rely on a survivor's apparent entitlement to succeed to property.

This version of the USDA is appropriate for enactment in states that have not enacted Sections 1-107, 2-104, and 2-702 of the Uniform Probate Code (1991)....

Reference. This Act is discussed in Halbach & Waggoner, "The UPC's New Survivorship and Antilapse Provisions," 55 Alb.L.Rev. 1091, 1091-99 (1992).

§ 1. Definitions. In this [Act]:

(1) "Co-owners with right of survivorship" includes joint tenants, tenants by the entireties, and other co-owners of property or accounts held under circumstances that entitles one or more to the whole of the property or account on the death of the other or others.

(2) "Governing instrument" means a deed, will, trust, insurance or annuity policy, account with POD designation, pension, profit-sharing, retirement, or similar benefit plan, instrument creating or exercising a power of appointment or a power of attorney, or a dispositive, appointive, or nominative instrument of any similar type.

(3) "Payor" means a trustee, insurer, business entity, employer, government, governmental agency or subdivision, or any other person authorized or obligated by law or a governing instrument to make payments.

§ 2. Requirement of Survival by 120 Hours Under Probate Code. Except as provided in Section 6, if the title to property, the devolution of property, the right to elect an interest in property, or the right to exempt property, homestead or family allowance depends upon an individual's survivorship of the death of another individual, an individual who is not established by clear and convincing evidence to have survived the other individual by 120 hours is deemed to have predeceased the other individual. This section does not apply if its application would result in a taking of intestate estate by the state.

Comment

By 1993 technical amendment, an anomalous exemption of securities registered under the Uniform TOD Security Registration Act from the 120-hour survival requirement of this section and of Section 3 was eliminated. The exemption reflected a temporary concern attributable to UTODSRA's preparation prior to discussion of inserting a 120-hour survival requirement in this Act.

Former (1953) Version

§ 1. No Sufficient Evidence of Survivorship. Where title to property or the devolution thereof depends upon priority of death and there is no sufficient evidence that the persons have died otherwise than simultaneously, the property of each person shall be disposed of as if he had survived, except as provided otherwise in this act.

§ 4. Community Property. Where a husband and wife have died, leaving community property, and there is no sufficient evidence that they have died otherwise than simultaneously, one-half of all the community property shall pass as if the husband had survived [and as if said one-half were his separate property,] and the other one-half thereof shall pass as if the wife had survived [and as if said other one-half were her separate property.]

---

§ 3. Requirement of Survival by 120 Hours Under Governing Instruments. Except as provided in Section 6, for purposes of a provision of a governing instrument that relates to an individual surviving an event, including the death of another individual, an individual who is not established by clear and convincing evidence to have survived the event by 120 hours is deemed to have predeceased the event.

Former (1953) Version

§ 2. Survival of Beneficiaries. If property is so disposed of that the right of a beneficiary to succeed to any interest therein is conditional upon his surviving another person, and both persons die, and there is no sufficient evidence that the two have died otherwise than simultaneously, the beneficiary shall be deemed not to have survived. If there is no sufficient evidence that two or more beneficiaries have died otherwise than simultaneously and property has been disposed of in such a way that at the time of their death each of such beneficiaries would have been entitled to the property if he had survived the others, the property shall be divided into as many equal portions as there were such beneficiaries and these portions shall be distributed respectively to those who would have taken in the event that each of such beneficiaries had survived.

§ 5. Insurance Policies. Where the insured and the beneficiary in a policy of life or accident insurance have died and there is no sufficient evidence that they have died otherwise than simultaneously the proceeds of the policy shall be distributed as if the insured had survived the beneficiary, [except if the policy is community property of the insured and his spouse, and there is no alternative beneficiary except the estate or personal representatives of the insured, the proceeds shall be distributed as community property under Section 4.]

---

§ 4. Co-owners With Right of Survivorship; Requirement of Survival by 120 Hours. Except as provided in Section 6, if (i) it is not established by clear and convincing evidence that one of two co-owners with right of survivorship survived the other co-owner by 120 hours, one-half of the property passes as if one had survived by 120 hours and one-half as if the other had survived by 120 hours and (ii) there are more than two co-owners and it is not established by clear and convincing evidence that at least one of them survived the others by 120 hours, the property passes in the proportion that one bears to the whole number of co-owners.

Comment

This section applies to property or accounts held by co-owners with right of survivorship. As defined in Section 1, the term "co-owners with right of survivorship" includes multiple-party accounts with right of survivorship. In the case of a joint checking account registered in the name of the decedent and his or her spouse with right of survivorship, the 120-hour requirement of survivorship imposed by this section will not interfere with the surviving spouse's ability to withdraw funds from the account during the

120-hour period following the decedent's death if the state has a facility-of-payment statute such as Section 6-222(1) of the Uniform Probate Code. A state without such a facility-of-payment statute should consider enacting one in conjunction with the enactment of this Act.

Former (1953) Version

§ 3. Joint Tenants or Tenants by the Entirety. Where there is no sufficient evidence that two joint tenants or tenants by the entirety have died otherwise than simultaneously the property so held shall be distributed one-half as if one had survived and one-half as if the other had survived. If there are more than two joint tenants and all of them have so died the property thus distributed shall be in the proportion that one bears to the whole number of joint tenants.

The term "joint tenants" includes owners of property held under circumstances which entitled one or more to the whole of the property on the death of the other or others.

---

§ 5. Evidence of Death or Status. In addition to the rules of evidence in courts of general jurisdiction, the following rules relating to a determination of death and status apply:

(1) Death occurs when an individual [is determined to be dead under the Uniform Determination of Death Act] [has sustained either (1) irreversible cessation of circulatory and respiratory functions or (2) irreversible cessation of all functions of the entire brain, including the brain stem. A determination of death must be made in accordance with accepted medical standards].

(2) A certified or authenticated copy of a death certificate purporting to be issued by an official or agency of the place where the death purportedly occurred is prima facie evidence of the fact, place, date, and time of death and the identity of the decedent.

(3) A certified or authenticated copy of any record or report of a governmental agency, domestic or foreign, that an individual is missing, detained, dead, or alive is prima facie evidence of the status and of the dates, circumstances, and places disclosed by the record or report.

(4) In the absence of prima facie evidence of death under paragraph (2) or (3), the fact of death may be established by clear and convincing evidence, including circumstantial evidence.

(5) An individual whose death is not established under the preceding paragraphs who is absent for a continuous period of five years, during which he [or she] has not been heard from, and whose absence is not satisfactorily explained after diligent search or inquiry, is presumed to be dead. His [or her] death is presumed to have occurred at the end of the period unless there is sufficient evidence for determining that death occurred earlier.

(6) In the absence of evidence disputing the time of death stipulated on a document described in paragraph (2) or (3), a document described in paragraph (2) or (3) that stipulates a time of death 120 hours or more after the time of death of another individual, however the time of death of the other individual is determined, establishes by clear and convincing evidence that the individual survived the other individual by 120 hours.

Comment

States that have enacted the Uniform Determination of Death Act should enact the first set of bracketed language in paragraph (1). States that have not enacted the Uniform Determination of Death Act should enact the second set of bracketed language in paragraph (1).

§ 6. Exceptions. Survival by 120 hours is not required if:

(1) the governing instrument contains language dealing explicitly with simultaneous deaths or deaths in a common disaster and that language is operable under the facts of the case;

(2) the governing instrument expressly indicates that an individual is not required to survive an event, including the death of another individual, by any specified period or expressly requires the

individual to survive the event for a specified period; but survival of the event or the specified period must be established by clear and convincing evidence;

(3) the imposition of a 120-hour requirement of survival would cause a nonvested property interest or a power of appointment to [be invalid under the Rule Against Perpetuities] [fail to qualify for validity under Section 1(a)(1), (b)(1), or (c)(1) or to become invalid under Section 1(a)(2), (b)(2), or (c)(2), of the Uniform Statutory Rule Against Perpetuities]; but survival must be established by clear and convincing evidence; or

(4) the application of a 120-hour requirement of survival to multiple governing instruments would result in an unintended failure or duplication of a disposition; but survival must be established by clear and convincing evidence.

Comment

Subsection (1). Subsection (1) provides that the 120-hour requirement of survival is inapplicable if the governing instrument "contains language dealing explicitly with simultaneous deaths or deaths in a common disaster and that language is operable under the facts of the case." The application of this provision is illustrated by the following example.

Example. G died leaving a will devising her entire estate to her husband, H, adding that "in the event he dies before I do, at the same time that I do, or under circumstances as to make it doubtful who died first," my estate is to go to my brother Melvin. H died about 38 hours after G's death, both having died as a result of injuries sustained in an automobile accident.

Under this section, G's estate passes under the alternative devise to Melvin because H's failure to survive G by 120 hours means that H is deemed to have predeceased G. The language in the governing instrument does not, under subsection (1), nullify the provision that causes H, because of his failure to survive G by 120 hours, to be deemed to have predeceased G. Although the governing instrument does contain language dealing with simultaneous deaths, that language is not operable under the facts of the case because H did not die before G, at the same time as G, or under circumstances as to make it doubtful who died first.

Subsection (2). Subsection (2) provides that the 120-hour requirement of survival is inapplicable if "the governing instrument expressly indicates that an individual is not required to survive an event, including the death of another individual, by any specified period or expressly requires the individual to survive the event for a stated period."

Mere words of survivorship in a governing instrument do not expressly indicate that an individual is not required to survive an event by any specified period. If, for example, a trust provides that the net income is to be paid to A for life, remainder in corpus to B if B survives A, the 120-hour requirement of survival would still apply. B would have to survive A by 120 hours. If, however, the trust expressly stated that B need not survive A by any specified period, that language would negate the 120-hour requirement of survival.

Language in a governing instrument requiring an individual to survive by a specified period also renders the 120-hour requirement of survival inapplicable. Thus, if a will devises property "to A if A survives me by 30 days," the express 30-day requirement of survival overrides the 120-hour survival period provided by this Act.

Subsection (4). Subsection (4) provides that the 120-hour requirement of survival is inapplicable if "the application of this section to multiple governing instruments would result in an unintended failure or duplication of a disposition." The application of this provision is illustrated by the following example.

Example. Pursuant to a common plan, H and W executed mutual wills with reciprocal provisions. Their intention was that a $50,000 charitable devise would be made on the death of the survivor. To that end, H's will devised $50,000 to the charity if W predeceased him. W's will devised $50,000 to the charity if H predeceased her. Subsequently, H and W were involved in a common accident. W survived H by 48 hours.

Were it not for subsection (4), not only would the charitable devise in W's will be effective, because H in fact predeceased W, but the charitable devise in H's will would also be effective, because W's failure to survive H by 120 hours would result in her being deemed to have predeceased H. Because this would result in an unintended duplication of the $50,000 devise, subsection (4) provides that the 120-hour requirement of survival is inapplicable. Thus, only the $50,000 charitable devise in W's will is effective.

Subsection (4) also renders the 120-hour requirement of survival inapplicable had H and W died in circumstances in which it could not be established by clear and convincing evidence that either survived the other. In such a case, an appropriate result might be to give effect to the common plan by paying half of the intended $50,000 devise from H's estate and half from W's estate.

Historical Note. This comment was revised in 1993. For the prior version, see 8B U.L.A. 261 (1993).

Former (1953) Version

§ 6. Act Does Not Apply if Decedent Provides Otherwise. This act shall not apply in the case of wills, living trusts, deeds, or contracts of insurance, or any other situation where provision is made for distribution of property different from the provisions of this act, or where provision is made for a presumption as to survivorship which results in a distribution of property different from that here provided.

---

§ 7. Protection of Payors, Bona Fide Purchasers, and Other Third Parties; Personal Liability of Recipient.

(a) [Protection of Payors and Other Third Parties.]

(1) A payor or other third party is not liable for having made a payment or transferred an item of property or any other benefit to a person designated in a governing instrument who, under this [Act], is not entitled to the payment or item of property, or for having taken any other action in good faith reliance on the person's apparent entitlement under the terms of the governing instrument, before the payor or other third party received written notice of a claimed lack of entitlement under this [Act]. A payor or other third party is liable for a payment made or other action taken after the payor or other third party received written notice of a claimed lack of entitlement under this [Act].

(2) Written notice of a claimed lack of entitlement under paragraph (1) must be mailed to the payor's or other third party's main office or home by registered or certified mail, return receipt requested, or served upon the payor or other third party in the same manner as a summons in a civil action. Upon receipt of written notice of a claimed lack of entitlement under this [Act], a payor or other third party may pay any amount owed or transfer or deposit any item of property held by it to or with the court having jurisdiction of the probate proceedings relating to the decedent's estate, or if no proceedings have been commenced, to or with the court having jurisdiction of probate proceedings relating to decedents' estates located in the county of the decedent's residence. The court shall hold the funds or item of property and, upon its determination under this [Act], shall order disbursement in accordance with the determination. Payments, transfers, or deposits made to or with the court discharge the payor or other third party from all claims for the value of amounts paid to or items of property transferred to or deposited with the court.

(b) [Protection of Bona Fide Purchasers; Personal Liability of Recipient.]

(1) A person who purchases property for value and without notice, or who receives a payment or other item of property in partial or full satisfaction of a legally enforceable obligation, is neither obligated under this [Act] to return the payment, item of property, or benefit nor liable under this [Act] for the amount of the payment or the value of the item of property or benefit. But a person who, not for value, receives a payment, item of property, or any other benefit to which the person is not entitled under this [Act] is obligated to return the payment, item of property, or benefit, or is personally liable for the amount of the payment or the value of the item of property or benefit, to the person who is entitled to it under this [Act].

(2) If this [Act] or any part of this [Act] is preempted by federal law with respect to a payment, an

item of property, or any other benefit covered by this [Act], a person who, not for value, receives the payment, item of property, or any other benefit to which the person is not entitled under this [Act] is obligated to return the payment, item of property, or benefit, or is personally liable for the amount of the payment or the value of the item of property or benefit, to the person who would have been entitled to it were this [Act] or part of this [Act] not preempted.

§ 8. Uniformity of Application and Construction. This [Act] shall be applied and construed to effectuate its general purpose to make uniform the law with respect to the subject of this [Act] among states enacting it.

§ 9. Short Title. This [Act] may be cited as the Uniform Simultaneous Death Act (1993).

§ 10. Repeal. The following acts and parts of acts are repealed:
  (1)
  (2)
  (3)

§ 11. Severability Clause. If any provision of this [Act] or its application to any persons or circumstance is held invalid, the invalidity does not affect other provisions or applications of the [Act] which can be given effect without the invalid provision or application, and to this end the provisions of this [Act] are severable.

§ 12. Effective Date
  (a) This [Act] takes effect _____.
  (b) On the effective date of this [Act]:

  (1) an act done before the effective date in any proceeding and any accrued right is not impaired by this [Act]. If a right is acquired, extinguished, or barred upon the expiration of a prescribed period of time that has commenced to run by the provisions of any statute before the effective date, the provisions remain in force with respect to that right; and

  (2) any rule of construction or presumption provided in this [Act] applies to instruments executed and multiple-party accounts opened before the effective date unless there is a clear indication of a contrary intent.

Comment

Subsection (b) is adapted from Section 8-101(b)(4) and (5) of the Uniform Probate Code.

Application to Pre-Existing Governing Instruments. For decedents dying after the effective date of enactment, the provisions of this Act apply to governing instruments executed prior to as well as on or after the effective date of enactment. The Joint Editorial Board for the Uniform Probate Code has issued a statement concerning the constitutionality under the Contracts Clause of this feature. The statement, titled "Joint Editorial Board Statement Regarding the Constitutionality of Changes in Default Rules as Applied to Pre-Existing Documents," can be found at 17 ACTEC Notes 184 (1991) or can be obtained from the headquarters office of the National Conference of Commissioners on Uniform State Laws, 676 N. St. Clair St., Suite 1700, Chicago, IL 60611, Phone 312/915-0195, FAX 312/915-0187.

Historical Note. This comment was revised in 1993. For the prior version, see 8B U.L.A. 266 (1993).

UNIFORM FRAUDULENT TRANSFER ACT (1984, with 2014 Amendments, renamed the UNIFORM VOIDABLE TRANSACTIONS ACT)

Table of Sections

Prefatory Note

Note (2014): The following version of the 1984 Prefatory Note was edited in connection with the 2014 Amendments to the Act and differs slightly from the original. It continues to speak to the Act as originally promulgated in 1984, but references to sections of the Act and its comments have been updated to the 2014 numbering.

The Uniform Fraudulent Conveyance Act was promulgated by the National Conference of Commissioners on Uniform State Laws in 1918. As of 1984 it has been adopted in 25 jurisdictions, including the Virgin Islands. it has also been adopted in the sections of the Bankruptcy Act of 1938 and the Bankruptcy Reform Act of 1978 that deal with fraudulent transfers and obligations.

The Uniform Fraudulent Conveyance Act was a codification of the "better" decisions applying the Statute of 13 Elizabeth. See Analysis of H.R. 12339, 74th Cong., 2d Sess. 213 (1936). The English statute was enacted in some form in many states, but, whether or not so enacted, the voidability of fraudulent transfers was part of the law of every American jurisdiction. Because intent to hinder, delay, or defraud creditors is seldom susceptible of direct proof, courts have relied on badges of fraud. The weight given these badges varied greatly from jurisdiction to jurisdiction, and the Conference sought to minimize or eliminate the diversity by providing that proof of certain fact combinations would conclusively establish fraud. In the absence of evidence of the existence of such facts, proof of a fraudulent transfer was to depend on evidence of actual intent. An important reform effected by the Uniform Fraudulent Conveyance Act was the elimination of any requirement that a creditor have obtained a judgment or execution returned unsatisfied before bringing an action to avoid a transfer as fraudulent. See American Surety Co. v. Conner, 251 N.Y. 1, 166 N.E. 783, 67 A.L.R. 244 (1929) (per C.J. Cardozo).

The Conference was persuaded in 1979 to appoint a committee to undertake a study of the Uniform Fraudulent Conveyance Act with a view to preparing the draft of a revision. The Conference was influenced by the following considerations:

(1) The Bankruptcy Reform Act of 1978 has made numerous changes in the section of that Act dealing with fraudulent transfers and obligations, thereby substantially reducing the correspondence of the provisions of the federal bankruptcy law on fraudulent transfers with the Uniform Fraudulent Conveyance Act.

(2) The Committee on Corporate Laws of the Section of Corporations, Banking & Business Law of

the American Bar Association, engaged in revising the Model Corporation Act, suggested that the Conference review provisions of the Uniform Fraudulent Conveyance Act with a view to determining whether the Acts are consistent in respect to the treatment of dividend distributions.

(3) The Uniform Commercial Code, enacted at least in part by all 50 states, had substantially modified related rules of law regulating transfers of personal property, notably by facilitating the making and perfection of security transfers against attack by unsecured creditors.

(4) Debtors and trustees in a number of cases have avoided foreclosure of security interests by invoking the fraudulent transfer
section of the Bankruptcy Reform Act.

(5) The Model Rules of Professional Conduct adopted by the House of Delegates of the American Bar Association on August 2, 1983, forbid a lawyer to counsel or to assist a client in conduct that the lawyer knows is fraudulent.

The Drafting Committee appointed by the Conference held its first meeting in January of 1983. A first reading of a draft of the revision of the Uniform Fraudulent Conveyance Act was had at the Conference's meeting in Boca Raton, Florida, on July 27, 1983. The Committee held four meetings in addition to a meeting held in connection with the Conference meeting in Boca Raton. Meetings were also attended by the following representatives of interested organizations:

Robert Rosenberg, Esq., of the American Bar Association;

Richard Cherin, Esq., of the Commercial Financial Services Committee of the Corporation, Banking and Business Law Section of the American Bar Association;

Robert Zinman, Esq., of the American College of Real Estate Lawyers;

H. Bruce Bernstein, Esq., of the National Commercial Finance Association;

Ernest E. Specks, Esq., of the Real Property, Probate and Trust Law Section of the American Bar Association.

The Committee determined to name the new Act the Uniform Fraudulent Transfer Act in recognition of its applicability to transfers of personal property as well as real property, "conveyance" having a connotation restricting it to a transfer of real property. As noted in Comment (2) accompanying § 1(2) and Comment (8) accompanying § 4, however, the new Act, like the original Uniform Fraudulent Conveyance Act, does not purport to cover the whole law of voidable transfers and obligations. The limited scope of the original Act did not impair its effectiveness in achieving uniformity in the areas covered. See McLaughlin, Application of the Uniform Fraudulent Conveyance Act, 46 Harv.L.Rev. 404, 405 (1933).

The basic structure and approach of the Uniform Fraudulent Conveyance Act are preserved in the Uniform Fraudulent Transfer Act. There are two sections in the new Act delineating what transfers and obligations are fraudulent. Section 4(a) is an adaptation of three sections of the U.F.C.A.; § 5(a) is an adaptation of another section of the U.F.C.A.; and § 5(b) is new. One section of the U.F.C.A. (§ 8) is not carried forward into the new Act because deemed to be redundant in part and in part susceptible of inequitable application. Both Acts declare a transfer made or an obligation incurred with actual intent to hinder, delay, or defraud creditors to be fraudulent. Provisions of the new Act, carried forward with little change from the Uniform Fraudulent Conveyance Act, render a transfer made or obligation incurred without adequate consideration to be constructively fraudulent - i.e., without regard to the actual intent of the debtor - under one of the following conditions:

(1) the debtor was left by the transfer or obligation with unreasonably small assets for a transaction or the business in which the debtor was engaged or was about to engage;

(2) the debtor intended to incur, or believed or reasonably should have believed that the debtor would incur, more debts than the debtor would be able to pay; or

(3) the debtor was insolvent at the time or as a result of the transfer or obligation.

As under the Uniform Fraudulent Conveyance Act a transfer or obligation that is constructively fraudulent because insolvency concurs with or follows failure to receive adequate consideration (clause (3) above) is voidable only by a creditor in existence at the time the transfer occurs or the obligation is incurred. Either an existing or subsequent creditor may avoid a transfer or obligation for inadequate consideration when accompanied by a condition referred to in clause (1) or (2) above.

Reasonably equivalent value is required in order to constitute adequate consideration under the new Act. The new Act follows the Bankruptcy Code in eliminating good faith on the part of the transferee or obligee as an issue in the determination of whether adequate consideration is given by a transferee or obligee. The new Act, like the Bankruptcy Code, allows the transferee or obligee to show good faith in defense after a creditor establishes that a fraudulent transfer has been made or a fraudulent obligation has been incurred. Thus a showing by a defendant that a reasonable equivalent has been given in good faith for a transfer or obligation is a complete defense although the debtor is shown to have intended to hinder, delay, or defraud creditors.

A good faith transferee or obligee that has given less than a reasonable equivalent is nevertheless allowed a reduction in liability to the extent of the value given. The new Act, like the Bankruptcy Code, eliminates the provision of the Uniform Fraudulent Conveyance Act that enables a creditor to attack a security transfer on the ground that the value of the property transferred is disproportionate to the debt secured. The premise of the new Act is that the value of the interest transferred for security is measured by and thus corresponds exactly to the debt secured. Foreclosure of a debtor's interest by a regularly conducted, noncollusive sale on default under a mortgage or other security agreement may not be avoided under the new Act as a transfer for less than a reasonably equivalent value.

The definition of insolvency under the new Act is adapted from the definition of the term in the Bankruptcy Code. Insolvency is presumed from proof of a failure generally to pay debts as they become due.

The new Act adds a new category of fraudulent transfer, namely, a preferential transfer by an insolvent debtor to a creditor that is an insider of the debtor and that has reasonable cause to believe the debtor to be insolvent. An insider is defined in much the same way as in the Bankruptcy Code and includes a relative, also defined as in the Bankruptcy Code, a director or officer of a corporate debtor, a general partner, or a person in control of a debtor. This provision is available only to an existing creditor. Its premise is that an insolvent debtor is obliged to pay debts to creditors not related to the debtor before paying insiders that have reason to know of the debtor's financial distress.

The new Act omits any provision directed particularly at transfers or obligations of insolvent partnership debtors. Under § 8 of the Uniform Fraudulent Conveyance Act any transfer made or obligation incurred by an insolvent partnership to a partner is fraudulent without regard to intent or adequacy of consideration. So categorical a condemnation of a partnership transaction with a partner may unfairly prejudice the interests of a

partner's separate creditors. The new Act also omits as redundant a provision in the Uniform Fraudulent Conveyance Act that makes fraudulent a transfer made or obligation incurred by an insolvent partnership for less than a fair consideration to the partnership.

Section 7 lists the remedies available to creditors under the new Act. It eliminates as unnecessary and confusing a differentiation made in the Uniform Fraudulent Conveyance Act between the remedies available to holders of matured claims and those holding unmatured claims. Since promulgation of the Uniform Fraudulent Conveyance Act the Supreme Court has imposed restrictions on the availability and use of prejudgment remedies. As a result many states have amended their statutes and rules applicable to such remedies, and it is frequently unclear whether a state's procedures include a prejudgment remedy against a fraudulent transfer or obligation. Section 7 accommodates prejudgment remedies if available under applicable law.

Section 8 prescribes the measure of liability of a transferee or obligee under the new Act and enumerates defenses. Defenses against avoidance of a preferential transfer to an insider under § 5(b) include an adaptation of defenses available under § 547(c)(2) and(4) of the Bankruptcy Code when such a transfer is sought to be avoided as a preference by the trustee in bankruptcy. In addition a preferential transfer may be justified when shown to be made pursuant to a good-faith effort to stave off forced liquidation and rehabilitate the debtor. Section 8 also precludes avoidance, as a constructively fraudulent transfer, of the termination of a lease on default or the enforcement of a security interest in compliance with Article 9 of the Uniform Commercial Code.

The new Act includes a new section specifying when a transfer is made or an obligation is incurred. The section specifying the time when a transfer occurs is adapted from § 548(d) of the Bankruptcy Code. Its premise is that if the law prescribes a mode for making the transfer a matter of public record or notice, it is not deemed to be made for any purpose under the new Act until it has become such a matter of record or notice.

The new Act also includes a statute of limitations that bars the right rather than the remedy on expiration of the statutory periods prescribed. The law governing limitations on actions to avoid fraudulent transfers among the states is unclear and full of diversity.

The Act recognizes that laches and estoppel may

operate to preclude a particular creditor from pursuing a remedy against a fraudulent transfer or obligation even though the statutory period of limitations has not run.

Prefatory Note (2014 Amendments)

In 2014 the Uniform Law Commission approved a set of amendments to the Uniform Fraudulent Transfer Act. The amendments changed the title of the Act to the Uniform Voidable Transactions Act. The amendment project was instituted to address a small number of narrowly-defined issues, and was not a comprehensive revision. The principal features of the amendments are listed below. Further explanation of provisions added or revised by the amendments may be found in the comments to those provisions.

Choice of Law. The amendments add a new § 10, which sets forth a choice of law rule applicable to claims for relief of the nature governed by the Act.

Evidentiary Matters. New §§ 4(c), 5(c), 8(g), and 8(h) add uniform rules allocating the burden of proof and defining the standard of proof with respect to claims for relief and defenses under the Act. Language in the former comments to § 2 relating to the presumption of insolvency created by § 2(b) has been moved to the text of that provision, the better to assure its uniform application.

Deletion of the Special Definition of "Insolvency" for Partnerships. Section 2(c) of the Act as originally written set forth a special definition of "insolvency" applicable to partnerships. The amendments delete original § 2(c), with the result that the general definition of "insolvency" in § 2(a) now applies to partnerships. One reason for this change is that original § 2(c) gave a partnership full credit for the net worth of each of its general partners. That makes sense only if each general partner is liable for all debts of the partnership, but such is not necessarily the case under modern partnership statutes. A more fundamental reason is that the general definition of "insolvency" in § 2(a) does not credit a non-partnership debtor with any part of the net worth of its guarantors. To the extent that a general partner is liable for the debts of the partnership, that liability is analogous to that of a guarantor. There is no good reason to define "insolvency" differently for a partnership debtor than for a non-partnership debtor whose debts are guaranteed by contract.

Defenses. The amendments refine in relatively minor respects several provisions relating to defenses available to a transferee or obligee, as follows:

(1) As originally written, § 8(a) created a complete defense to an action under § 4(a)(1) (which renders voidable a transfer made or obligation incurred with actual intent to hinder, delay, or defraud any creditor of the debtor) if the transferee or obligee takes in good faith and for a reasonably equivalent value. The amendments add to § 8(a) the further requirement that the reasonably equivalent value must be given the debtor.

(2) Section 8(b), derived from Bankruptcy Code §§ 550(a), (b) (1984), creates a defense for a subsequent transferee (that is, a transferee other than the first transferee) that takes in good faith and for value, and for any subsequent good-faith transferee from such a person. The amendments clarify the meaning of § 8(b) by rewording it to follow more closely the wording of Bankruptcy Code §§ 550(a), (b) (which is substantially unchanged as of 2014). Among other things, the amendments make clear that the defense applies to recovery of or from the transferred property or its proceeds, by levy or otherwise, as well as to an action for a money judgment.

(3) Section 8(e)(2) as originally written created a defense to an action under § 4(a)(2) or § 5 to avoid a transfer if the transfer results from enforcement of a security interest in compliance with Article 9 of the Uniform Commercial Code. The amendments exclude from that defense acceptance of collateral in full or partial satisfaction of the obligation it secures (a remedy sometimes referred to as "strict foreclosure").

Series Organizations. A new § 11 provides that each "protected series" of a "series organization" is to be treated as a person for purposes of the Act, even if it is not treated as a person for other purposes. This change responds to the emergence of the "series organization" as a significant form of business organization.

Medium Neutrality. In order to accommodate modern technology, the references in the Act to a "writing" have been replaced with "record," and related changes made.

Style. The amendments make a number of stylistic changes that are not intended to change the meaning of the Act. For example, the amended Act consistently uses the word "voidable" to denote a transfer or obligation for which the Act provides a remedy. As originally written the Act sometimes inconsistently used the word "fraudulent." No change in meaning is intended. See § 15, Comment 4. Likewise, the retitling of the Act is not intended to change its meaning. See § 15, Comment 1.

Official Comments. Comments were added explaining provisions added or revised by the amendments, and the original comments were supplemented and otherwise refreshed.

§ 1. Definitions. As used in this [Act]:

(1) "Affiliate" means:

(i) a person that directly or indirectly owns, controls, or holds with power to vote, 20 percent or more of the outstanding voting securities of the debtor, other than a person that holds the securities:

(A) as a fiduciary or agent without sole discretionary power to vote the securities; or

(B) solely to secure a debt, if the person has not in fact exercised the power to vote;

(ii) a corporation 20 percent or more of whose outstanding voting securities are directly or indirectly owned, controlled, or held with power to vote, by the debtor or a person that directly or indirectly owns, controls, or holds with power to vote, 20 percent or more of the outstanding voting securities of the debtor, other than a person that holds the securities:

(A) as a fiduciary or agent without sole discretionary power to vote the securities; or

(B) solely to secure a debt, if the person has not in fact exercised the power to vote;

(iii) a person whose business is operated by the debtor under a lease or other agreement, or a person substantially all of whose assets are controlled by the debtor; or

(iv) a person that operates the debtor's business under a lease or other agreement or controls substantially all of the debtor's assets.

(2) "Asset" means property of a debtor, but the term does not include:

(i) property to the extent it is encumbered by a valid lien;

(ii) property to the extent it is generally exempt under nonbankruptcy law; or

(iii) an interest in property held in tenancy by the entireties to the extent it is not subject to process by a creditor holding a claim against only one tenant.

(3) "Claim", except as used in "claim for relief", means a right to payment, whether or not the right is reduced to judgment, liquidated, unliquidated, fixed, contingent,matured, unmatured, disputed, undisputed, legal, equitable, secured, or unsecured.

(4) "Creditor" means a person that has a claim.

(5) "Debt" means liability on a claim.

(6) "Debtor" means a person that is liable on a claim.

(7) "Electronic" means relating to technology having electrical, digital, magnetic, wireless, optical, electromagnetic, or similar capabilities.

(8) "Insider" includes:

(i) if the debtor is an individual:

(A) a relative of the debtor or of a general partner of the debtor;

(B) a partnership in which the debtor is a general partner;

(C) a general partner in a partnership described in clause (B); or

(D) a corporation of which the debtor is a director, officer, or person in control;

(ii) if the debtor is a corporation:

(A) a director of the debtor;

(B) an officer of the debtor;

(C) a person in control of the debtor;

(D) a partnership in which the debtor is a general partner;

(E) a general partner in a partnership described in clause (D); or

(F) a relative of a general partner, director, officer, or person in control of the debtor;

(iii) if the debtor is a partnership:

(A) a general partner in the debtor;

(B) a relative of a general partner in, or a general partner of, or a person in control of the debtor;

(C) another partnership in which the debtor is a general partner;

(D) a general partner in a partnership described in clause (C); or

(E) a person in control of the debtor;

(iv) an affiliate, or an insider of an affiliate as if the affiliate were the debtor; and

(v) a managing agent of the debtor.

(9) "Lien" means a charge against or an interest in property to secure payment of a debt or performance of an obligation, and includes a security interest created by agreement, a judicial lien obtained by legal or equitable process or proceedings, a common-law lien, or a statutory lien.

(10) "Organization" means a person other than an individual.

(11) "Person" means an individual, estate, business or nonprofit entity, public corporation, government or governmental subdivision, agency, or instrumentality, or other legal entity.

(12) "Property" means anything that may be the subject of ownership.

(13) "Record" means information that is inscribed on a tangible medium or that is stored in an electronic or other medium and is retrievable in perceivable form.

(14) "Relative" means an individual related by consanguinity within the third degree as determined by the common law, a spouse, or an individual related to a spouse within the third degree as so determined, and includes an individual in an adoptive relationship within the third degree.

(15) "Sign" means, with present intent to authenticate or adopt a record:

(i) to execute or adopt a tangible symbol; or

(ii) to attach to or logically associate with the record an electronic symbol, sound, or process.

(16) "Transfer" means every mode, direct or indirect, absolute or conditional, voluntary or involuntary, of disposing of or parting with an asset or an interest in an asset, and includes payment of money, release, lease, license, and creation of a lien or other encumbrance.

(17) "Valid lien" means a lien that is effective against the holder of a judicial lien subsequently obtained by legal or equitable process or proceedings.

Comment

1. The definition of "affiliate" is derived from Bankruptcy Code § 101(2) (1984).

2. The definition of "asset" is substantially to the same effect as the definition of "assets" in § 1 of the Uniform Fraudulent Conveyance Act. The definition in this Act, unlike that in the earlier Act, does not, however, require a determination that the property is liable for the debts of the debtor. Thus, for example, an unliquidated claim for damages resulting from personal injury or a contingent claim of a surety for reimbursement, subrogation, restitution, contribution, or the like may be counted as an asset for the purpose of determining whether the holder of the claim is solvent as a debtor under § 2 of this Act, even if applicable law does not allow such an asset to be levied on and sold by a creditor. Cf. Manufacturers & Traders Trust Co. v. Goldman (In re Ollag Construction Equipment Corp.), 578 F.2d 904, 907-09 (2d Cir. 1978).

Subparagraphs (i), (ii), and (iii) provide clarification by excluding from the term not only generally exempt property but also an interest in a tenancy by the entirety in many states and an interest that is generally beyond reach by unsecured creditors because subject to a valid lien. This Act, like the Uniform Fraudulent Conveyance Act and the Statute of 13 Elizabeth, declares rights and provides remedies for unsecured creditors against transfers that impede them in the collection of their claims. The laws protecting valid liens against impairment by levying creditors, exemption statutes, and the rules restricting levyability of interest in entireties property are limitations on the rights and remedies of unsecured creditors, and it is therefore appropriate to exclude property interests that are beyond the reach of unsecured creditors from the definition of "asset" for the purposes of this Act.

A creditor of a joint tenant or tenant in common

may ordinarily collect a judgment by process against the tenant's interest, and in some states a creditor of a tenant by the entirety may likewise collect a judgment by process against the tenant's interest. See 2 American Law of Property 10, 22, 28-32 (1952); Craig, An Analysis of Estates by the Entirety in Bankruptcy, 48 Am.Bankr.L.J. 255, 258-59 (1974). The levyable interest of such a tenant is included as an asset under this Act.

The definition of "assets" in the Uniform Fraudulent Conveyance Act excluded property that is exempt from liability for debts. The definition did not, however, exclude all property that cannot be reached by a creditor through judicial proceedings to collect a debt. Thus, it included the interest of a tenant by the entirety although in nearly half the states such an interest cannot be subjected to liability for a debt unless it is an obligation owed jointly by the debtor with his or her cotenant by the entirety. See 2 American Law of Property 29 (1952); Craig, An Analysis of Estates by the Entirety in Bankruptcy, 48 Am.Bankr.L.J. 255, 258 (1974). The definition in this Act requires exclusion of interests in property held by tenants by the entirety that are not subject to collection process by a creditor without a right to proceed against both tenants by the entirety as joint debtors.

The reference to "generally exempt" property in § 1(2)(ii) recognizes that all exemptions are subject to exceptions. Creditors having special rights against generally exempt property typically include claimants for alimony, taxes, wages, the purchase price of the property, and labor or materials that improve the property. See Uniform Exemptions Act § 10 (1979) and the accompanying Comment. The fact that a particular creditor may reach generally exempt property by resorting to judicial process does not warrant its inclusion as an asset in determining whether the debtor is insolvent.

Because this Act is not an exclusive law on the subject of voidable transfers and obligations (see Comment 9 to § 4), it does not preclude the holder of a claim that may be collected by process against property generally exempt as to other creditors from obtaining relief from a transfer of such property that hinders, delays, or defrauds the holder of such a claim. Likewise the holder of an unsecured claim enforceable against tenants by the entirety is not precluded by the Act from pursuing a remedy against a transfer of property held by the entirety that hinders, delays, or defrauds the holder of such a claim.

Nonbankruptcy law is the law of a state or federal law that is not part of the Bankruptcy Code, Title 11 of the United States Code. The definition of an "asset" thus does not include property that would be subject to administration for the benefit of creditors under the Bankruptcy Code unless it is subject under other applicable law, state or federal, to process for the collection of a creditor's claim against a single debtor.

3. The definition of "claim" is derived from Bankruptcy Code § 101(4) (1984). Because the purpose of this Act is primarily to protect unsecured creditors against transfers and obligations injurious to their rights, the words "claim" and "debt" as used in the Act generally have reference to an unsecured claim and debt. As the context may indicate, however, usage of the terms is not so restricted. See, e.g. §§ 1(1)(i)(B) and 1(9).

4. The definition of "creditor" in combination with the definition of "claim" has substantially the same effect as the definition of "creditor" under § 1 of the Uniform Fraudulent Conveyance Act. As under that Act, the holder of an unliquidated tort claim or a contingent claim may be a creditor protected by this Act.

5. The definition of "debt" is derived from Bankruptcy Code § 101(11) (1984).

6. The definition of "debtor" had no analogue in the Uniform Fraudulent Conveyance Act.

7. The definition of "electronic" is the standard definition of that term used in acts prepared by the Uniform Law Commission as of 2014.

8. The definition of "insider" is derived from Bankruptcy Code § 101(28) (1984). In this Act, as in the Bankruptcy Code, the definition states that the term "includes" certain listed persons; it does not state that the term "means" the listed persons. Hence the definition is not exclusive, and the statutory list is merely exemplary. See also Bankruptcy Code § 102(3) (1984). Accordingly, a person may be an "insider" of a debtor that is an individual, corporation or partnership even though the person is not designated as such by the statutory list. For example, a trust may be found to be an "insider" of a beneficiary. Similarly, a court may find a person living with an individual debtor for an extended time in the same household or as a permanent companion to have the kind of close relationship intended to be covered by the term "insider." See also, e.g., Browning Interests v. Allison (In re Holloway), 955 F.2d 1008 (5th Cir.1992) (former spouse of debtor was an "insider" because of their close and continued personal relationship, even

though they had long ago divorced and remarried others).

The differences between the definition in this Act and that in the Bankruptcy Code are slight. In this Act, the definition has been restricted in clauses (i)(C), (ii)(E), and (iii)(D) to make clear that a partner is not an insider of an individual, corporation, or partnership if any of these latter three persons is only a limited partner. The definition of "insider" in the Bankruptcy Code does not purport to make a limited partner an insider of the partners or of the partnership with which the limited partner is associated, but it is susceptible of a contrary interpretation and one which would extend unduly the scope of the defined relationship when the limited partner is not a person in control of the partnership. The definition of "insider" in this Act also omits the reference in Bankruptcy Code § 101(28)(D) (1984) to an elected official or relative of such an official as an insider of a municipality.

9. The definition of "lien" is derived from paragraphs (30), (31), (43), and (45) of Bankruptcy Code § 101 (1984), which define "judicial lien," "lien," "security interest," and "statutory lien" respectively.

10. The definition of "organization" is derived from Uniform Commercial Code § 1-201(b0(25) (2014).

11. The definition of "person" is the standard definition of that term used in acts prepared by the Uniform Law Commission as of 2014. Section 11 renders a "protected series" of a "series organization" a "person" for purposes of this Act, even though the "protected series" may not qualify as a "person" under paragraph (11) of this section.

12. The definition of "property" is derived from Uniform Probate Code § 1-201(33) (1969). Property includes both real and personal property, whether tangible or intangible, and any interest in property, whether legal or equitable.

13. The definition of "record" is the standard definition of that term used in acts prepared by the Uniform Law Commission as of 2014.

14. The definition of "relative" is derived from Bankruptcy Code § 101(37) (1984) but is explicit in its references to the spouse of a debtor in view of uncertainty as to whether the common law determines degrees of relationship by affinity.

15. The definition of "sign" is the standard definition of that term used in acts prepared by the Uniform Law Commission as of 2014.

16. The definition of "transfer" is derived principally from Bankruptcy Code § 101(48) (1984). The definition of "conveyance" in § 1 of the Uniform Fraudulent Conveyance Act was similarly comprehensive, and the references in this Act to "payment of money, release, lease, and the creation of a lien or encumbrance" are derived from the Uniform Fraudulent Conveyance Act. While the definition in the Uniform Fraudulent Conveyance Act did not explicitly refer to an involuntary transfer, the decisions under that Act were generally consistent with an interpretation that covered such a transfer. See, e.g., Hearn 45 St. Corp. v. Jano, 283 N.Y. 139, 27 N.E.2d 814, 128 A.L.R. 1285 (1940) (execution and foreclosure sales); Lefkowitz v. Finkelstein Trading Corp., 14 F.Supp. 898, 899 (S.D.N.Y. 1936) (execution sale); Langan v. First Trust & Deposit Co., 277 App.Div. 1090, 101 N.Y.S.2d 36 (4th Dept. 1950), aff'd, 302 N.Y. 932, 100 N.E.2d 189 (1951) (mortgage foreclosure); Catabene v. Wallner, 16 N.J.Super. 597, 602, 85 A.2d 300, 302 (1951) (mortgage foreclosure). The 2014 amendments add a reference to transfer by "license," which is derived from the definition of "proceeds" in Uniform Commercial Code § 9-102(a)(64)(A) (2014).

17. The definition of "valid lien" had no analogue in the Uniform Fraudulent Conveyance Act. A valid lien includes an equitable lien that may not be defeated by a judicial lien creditor. See, e.g., Pearlman v. Reliance Insurance Co., 371 U.S. 132, 136 (1962) (upholding a surety's equitable lien in respect to a fund owing a bankrupt contractor).

§ 2. Insolvency.

(a) A debtor is insolvent if, at a fair valuation, the sum of the debtor's debts is greater than the sum of the debtor's assets.

(b) A debtor that is generally not paying the debtor's debts as they become due other than as a result of a bona fide dispute is presumed to be insolvent. The presumption imposes on the party against which the presumption is directed the burden of proving that the nonexistence of insolvency is more probable than its existence.

(c) Assets under this section do not include property that has been transferred, concealed, or removed with intent to hinder, delay, or defraud creditors or that has been transferred in a manner making the transfer voidable under this [Act].

(d) Debts under this section do not include an obligation to the extent it is secured by a valid lien on property of the debtor not included as an asset.

Comment

1. Subsection (a) is derived from the definition of "insolvent" in Bankruptcy Code § 101(29)(A) (1984). The definition in subsection (a) contemplates a fair valuation of the debts as well as the assets of the debtor. The 2014 amendments reword subsection (a) in order to eliminate the elegant variation in the original text between "the sum of" debts and "all of" assets, and to make clearer that "fair valuation" applies to debts as well as to assets. No change in meaning is intended.

Financial accounting standards may permit or require fair value measurement of an asset or a debt. The fair value of an asset or a debt for financial accounting purposes may be based on standards that are not appropriate for use in subsection (a). For example, Fin. Accounting Standards Bd., Accounting Standards Codification ¶¶ 820-10-35-17 to -18 (2014) (formerly Statement of Financial Accounting Standards No. 157: Fair Value Measurement ¶ 15 (2006)) requires for financial accounting purposes that the "fair value" of a liability reflect nonperformance risk (i.e., the risk that the debtor will not pay the liability as and when due). By contrast, proper application of subsection (a) excludes any adjustment to the face amount of a liability on account of nonperformance risk. Such an adjustment would be contrary to the purpose of subsection (a), which is to assess the risk that the debtor will not be able to satisfy its liabilities. Only in unusual circumstances would the "fair valuation" for the purpose of subsection (a) of a liquidated debt be other than its face amount. Examples of such circumstances include discounting the face amount of a contingent debt to reflect the probability that the contingency will not occur, and discounting the face amount of a non-interest-bearing debt that is due in the future in order to reduce the debt to its present value.

As under the definition of the term "insolvent" in § 2 of the Uniform Fraudulent Conveyance Act, exempt property is excluded from the computation of the value of the assets. See § 1(2). For similar reasons interests in valid spendthrift trusts and interests in tenancies by the entireties that are not subject to process by a creditor of only one tenant are not included. See Comment 2 to § 1. Because a valid lien also precludes an unsecured creditor from collecting the creditor's claim from the encumbered interest in a debtor's property, both the encumbered interest and the debt secured thereby are excluded from the computation of insolvency under this Act. See § 1(2) and subsection (d) of this section.

2. Subsection (b) establishes a rebuttable presumption of insolvency from the fact of general nonpayment of debts as they become due. Such general nonpayment is a ground for the filing of an involuntary petition under Bankruptcy Code § 303(h)(1) (1978). See also U.C.C. § 1-201(23) (1962) (defining a person to be "insolvent" who "has ceased to pay his debts in the ordinary course of business"). The 2014 amendments to this Act clarify that general nonpayment of debts does not count nonpayment as a result of a bona fide dispute. That was the intended meaning of the language before 2014, as stated in the official comments, and the cited provisions of the Bankruptcy Code and the Uniform Commercial Code have been similarly clarified. See Bankruptcy Code § 303(h)(1) (2014); U.C.C. § 1-203(b)(23) (2014) (defining "insolvent" to include "having generally ceased to pay debts in the ordinary course of business other than as a result of bona fide dispute").

Subsection (b) defines the effect of the presumption to be (in paraphrase) that the burden of persuasion on the issue of insolvency shifts to the defendant. That conforms to the default definition of the effect of a presumption in civil cases set forth in Uniform Rules of Evidence (1974 Act), Rule 301(a) (later Rule 302(a) (1999 Act as amended 2005)). It also conforms to the Final Draft of Federal Rule 301 as submitted to the United States Supreme Court by the Advisory Committee on Federal Rules of Evidence in 1973. "The so-called 'bursting bubble' theory, under which a presumption vanishes upon the introduction of evidence which would support a finding of the nonexistence of the presumed fact, even though not believed, is rejected as according presumptions too 'slight and evanescent' an effect." Advisory Committee's Note to Rule 301, 56 F.R.D. 183, 208 (1973). See also 1 J. Weinstein & M. Berger, Evidence ¶ 301[01] (1982). It should be noted that the Federal Rule of Evidence as finally enacted gave by default a different effect to presumptions in civil cases, in effect adopting the "bursting bubble" definition. See Fed. R. Evid. 301 (1975) (carried forward in the 2011 revision). The statement of the effect of the presumption in subsection (b) was added by the 2014 amendments to this Act, but subsection (b) was intended to have the same meaning before 2014, as stated in the official comments.

The presumption is established in recognition of the difficulties typically imposed on a creditor in proving insolvency in the bankruptcy sense, as provided in subsection (a). See generally Levit, The Archaic Concept of Balance-Sheet Insolvency, 47 Am.Bankr.L.J. 215 (1973). Not only is the relevant information in the possession of a debtor that is apt to be noncooperative, but the debtor's records are apt to be incomplete and inaccurate. As a practical matter, insolvency is most cogently evidenced by a general cessation of payment of debts, as has long been recognized by the laws of other countries and is now reflected in the Bankruptcy Code. See Honsberger, Failure to Pay One's Debts Generally as They Become Due: The Experience of France and Canada, 54 Am.Bankr.L.J. 153 (1980); J. MacLachlan, Bankruptcy 13, 63-64, 436 (1956). In determining whether a debtor is paying its debts generally as they become due, the court should look at more than the amount and due dates of the indebtedness. The court should also take into account such factors as the number of the debtor's debts, the proportion of those debts not being paid, the duration of the nonpayment, and the existence of bona fide disputes or other special circumstances alleged to constitute an explanation for the stoppage of payments. The court's determination may be affected by a consideration of the debtor's payment practices prior to the period of alleged nonpayment and the payment practices of the trade or industry in which the debtor is engaged. The case law that has developed under Bankruptcy Code § 303(h)(1) (1984) has not required a showing that a debtor has failed or refused to pay a majority in number and amount of the debtor's debts in order to prove general nonpayment of debts as they become due. See, e.g., Hill v. Cargill, Inc. (In re Hill), 8 B.R. 779, 3 C.B.C.2d 920 (Bankr. D.Minn. 1981) (nonpayment of three largest debts held to constitute general nonpayment, although small debts were being paid); In re All Media Properties, Inc., 5 B.R. 126, 6 B.C.D. 586, 2 C.B.C.2d 449 (Bankr. S.D.Tex. 1980) (missing significant number of payments or regularly missing payments significant in amount said to constitute general nonpayment; missing payments on more than 50% of aggregate of claims said not to be required to show general nonpayment; nonpayment for more than 30 days after billing held to establish nonpayment of a debt when it is due); In re Kreidler Import Corp., 4 B.R. 256, 6 B.C.D. 608, 2 C.B.C.2d 159 (Bankr. D.Md. 1980) (nonpayment of one debt constituting 97% of debtor's total indebtedness held to constitute general nonpayment).

3. Subsection (c) follows the approach of the definition of "insolvency" in Bankruptcy Code § 101(29) (1984) by excluding from the computation of the value of the debtor's assets any value that can be realized only by avoiding a transfer of an interest formerly held by the debtor or by discovery or pursuit of property that has been concealed or removed with intent to hinder, delay, or defraud creditors.

4. Subsection (d) has no analogue in Bankruptcy Code § 101(29) (1984). It makes clear that a person is not rendered insolvent under this section by counting as a debt an obligation secured by property of the debtor that is not counted as an asset. See also Comment 2 to § 1 and Comment 1 to § 2.

§ 3. Value.

(a) Value is given for a transfer or an obligation if, in exchange for the transfer or obligation, property is transferred or an antecedent debt is secured or satisfied, but value does not include an unperformed promise made otherwise than in the ordinary course of the promisor's business to furnish support to the debtor or another person.

(b) For the purposes of Section 4(a)(2) and Section 5, a person gives a reasonably equivalent value if the person acquires an interest of the debtor in an asset pursuant to a regularly conducted, noncollusive foreclosure sale or execution of a power of sale for the acquisition or disposition of the interest of the debtor upon default under a mortgage, deed of trust, or security agreement.

(c) A transfer is made for present value if the exchange between the debtor and the transferee is intended by them to be contemporaneous and is in fact substantially contemporaneous.

Comment

1. This section defines when "value" is given for a transfer or obligation. "Value" is used in that sense in various contexts in this Act, frequently with a qualifying adjective. The word appears in the following sections:

4(a)(2) ("reasonably equivalent value");
4(b)(8) ("value ... reasonably equivalent);
5(a) ("reasonably equivalent value");
5(b) ("present, reasonably equivalent value");
8(a) ("reasonably equivalent value");
8(b)(1)(ii)(A) and (d) ("value");
8(f)(1) ("new value"); and
8(f)(3) ("present value").

"Value is also used in other senses in this Act, to which this section is not relevant. See, e.g., §§ 8(b)(1), 8(c) ("value" in the sense of the value of a transferred asset).

2. Section 3(a) is adapted from Bankruptcy Code § 548(d)(2)(A) (1984). See also § 3(a) of the Uniform Fraudulent Conveyance Act. The definition in Section 3 is not exclusive. "Value" is to be determined in light of the purpose of the Act to protect a debtor's estate from being depleted to the prejudice of the debtor's unsecured creditors. Consideration having no utility from a creditor's viewpoint does not satisfy the statutory definition. The definition does not specify all the kinds of consideration that do not constitute value for the purposes of this Act - e.g., love and affection. See, e.g., United States v. West, 299 F.Supp. 661, 666 (D.Del. 1969).

3. Section 3(a) does not indicate what is "reasonably equivalent value" for a transfer or obligation. Under this Act, as under Bankruptcy Code § 548(a)(2) (1984), a transfer for security is ordinarily for a reasonably equivalent value notwithstanding a discrepancy between the value of the asset transferred and the debt secured, because the amount of the debt is the measure of the value of the interest in the asset that is transferred. See, e.g., Peoples-Pittsburgh Trust Co. v. Holy Family Polish Nat'l Catholic Church, Carnegie, Pa., 341 Pa. 390, 19 A.2d 360 (1941). If the debt is a voidable obligation under this Act, a transfer to secure it as well as the obligation would be vulnerable to attack as voidable. A transfer to satisfy or secure an antecedent debt owed an insider is also subject to avoidance under the conditions specified in Section 5(b).

4. Section 3(a) of the Uniform Fraudulent Conveyance Act has been thought not to recognize that an unperformed promise could constitute fair consideration. See McLaughlin, Application of the Uniform Fraudulent Conveyance Act, 46 Harv.L.Rev. 404, 414 (1933). Courts construing these provisions of the prior law nevertheless have held unperformed promises to constitute value in a variety of circumstances. See, e.g., Harper v. Lloyd's Factors, Inc., 214 F.2d 662 (2d Cir. 1954) (transfer of money for promise of factor to discount transferor's purchase-money notes given to fur dealer); Schlecht v. Schlecht, 168 Minn. 168, 176-77, 209 N.W. 883, 886-87 (1926) (transfer for promise to make repairs and improvements on transferor's homestead); Farmer's Exchange Bank v. Oneida Motor Truck Co., 202 Wis. 266, 232 N.W. 536 (1930) (transfer in consideration of assumption of certain of transferor's liabilities); see also Hummel v. Cernocky, 161 F.2d 685 (7th Cir. 1947) (transfer in consideration of cash, assumption of a mortgage, payment of certain debts, and agreement to pay other debts). Likewise a transfer in consideration of a negotiable note discountable at a commercial bank, or the purchase from an established, solvent institution of an insurance policy, annuity, or contract to provide care and accommodations clearly appears to be for value. On the other hand, a transfer for an unperformed promise by an individual to support a parent or other transferor has generally been held not to constitute value. See, e.g., Springfield Ins. Co. v. Fry, 267 F.Supp. 693 (N.D.Okla. 1967); Sandler v. Parlapiano, 236 App.Div. 70, 258 N.Y.Supp. 88 (1st Dep't 1932); Warwick Municipal Employees Credit Union v. Higham, 106 R.E. 363, 259 A.2d 852 (1969); Hulsether v. Sanders, 54 S.D. 412, 223 N.W. 335 (1929); Cooper v. Cooper, 22 Tenn.App. 473, 477, 124 S.W.2d 264, 267 (1939); Note, Rights of Creditors in Property Conveyed in Consideration of Future Support, 45 Iowa L.Rev. 546, 550-62 (1960). This Act adopts the view taken in the cases cited in determining whether an unperformed promise is value.

5. Subsection (b) rejects the rule of such cases as Durrett v. Washington Nat. Ins. Co., 621 F.2d 201 (5th Cir. 1980) (nonjudicial foreclosure of a mortgage avoided as a voidable transfer when the property of an insolvent mortgagor was sold for less than 70% of its fair value); and Abramson v. Lakewood Bank & Trust Co., 647 F.2d 547 (5th Cir. 1981), cert. denied, 454 U.S. 1164 (1982) (nonjudicial foreclosure held to be voidable transfer if made without fair consideration). Subsection (b) adopts the view taken in Lawyers Title Ins. Corp. v. Madrid (In re Madrid),

21 B.R. 424 (B.A.P. 9th Cir. 1982), aff'd on another ground, 725 F.2d 1197 (9th Cir. 1984), that the price bid at a regularly conducted and noncollusive foreclosure sale determines the fair value of the property sold for purposes of voidable transfer law. See also BFP v. Resolution Trust Corp., 511 U.S. 531, 537 n.3 (1994) (similarly construing Bankruptcy Code § 548; opinion expressly limited to foreclosure of real estate mortgages).

Subsection (b) prescribes the effect of a sale meeting its requirements, whether the asset sold is personal or real property. It applies only to a sale under a mortgage, deed of trust, or security agreement. Subsection (b) thus does not apply to a sale foreclosing a nonconsensual lien, such as a tax lien. However, the subsection does apply to a foreclosure by sale of the interest of a vendee under an installment land contract in accordance with applicable law that requires or permits the foreclosure to be effected by a sale in the same manner as the foreclosure of a mortgage. See G.Osborne, G.Nelson, & D.Whitman, Real Estate Finance Law 83-84, 95-97 (1979).

If a lien given an insider for a present consideration is not perfected as against a subsequent bona fide purchaser or is so perfected after a delay following an extension of credit secured by the lien, foreclosure of the lien may result in a transfer for an antecedent debt that is voidable under Section 5(b) infra. Subsection (b) does not apply to an action under Section 4(a)(1) to avoid a transfer or obligation because made or incurred with actual intent to hinder, delay, or defraud any creditor.

(6) Subsection (c) is an adaptation of Bankruptcy Code § 547(c)(1) (1984). A transfer to an insider for an antecedent debt may be voidable under § 5(b).

§ 4. Transfer or Obligation Voidable as to Present or Future Creditor.

(a) A transfer made or obligation incurred by a debtor is voidable as to a creditor, whether the creditor's claim arose before or after the transfer was made or the obligation was incurred, if the debtor made the transfer or incurred the obligation:

(1) with actual intent to hinder, delay, or defraud any creditor of the debtor; or

(2) without receiving a reasonably equivalent value in exchange for the transfer or obligation, and the debtor:

(i) was engaged or was about to engage in a business or a transaction for which the remaining assets of the debtor were unreasonably small in relation to the business or transaction; or

(ii) intended to incur, or believed or reasonably should have believed that the debtor would incur, debts beyond the debtor's to pay as they became due.

(b) In determining actual intent under subsection (a)(1), consideration may be given, among other factors, to whether:

(1) the transfer or obligation was to an insider;

(2) the debtor retained possession or control of the property transferred after the transfer;

(3) the transfer or obligation was disclosed or concealed;

(4) before the transfer was made or obligation was incurred, the debtor had been sued or threatened with suit;

(5) the transfer was of substantially all the debtor's assets;

(6) the debtor absconded;

(7) the debtor removed or concealed assets;

(8) the value of the consideration received by the debtor was reasonably equivalent to the value of the asset transferred or the amount of the obligation incurred;

(9) the debtor was insolvent or became insolvent shortly after the transfer was made or the obligation was incurred;

(10) the transfer occurred shortly before or shortly after a substantial debt was incurred; and

(11) the debtor transferred the essential assets of the business to a lienor who transferred the assets to an insider of the debtor.

(c) A creditor making a claim for relief under subsection (a) has the burden of proving the elements of the claim for relief by a preponderance of the evidence.

Comment

1. Section 4(a)(1) is derived from § 7 of the Uniform Fraudulent Conveyance Act, which in turn was derived from the Statute of 13 Elizabeth, c. 5 (1571). Factors appropriate for consideration in determining actual intent under Section 4(a)(1) are specified in subsection (b).

2. Section 4, unlike § 5, protects creditors of a debtor whose claims arise after as well as before the debtor made or incurred the challenged transfer or obligation. Similarly, there is no requirement in § 4(a)(1) that the intent referred to be directed at a creditor existing or identified at the time of transfer or incurrence. For example, promptly after the invention in Pennsylvania of the spendthrift trust, the assets and beneficial interest of which are immune from attachment by the beneficiary's creditors, courts held that a debtor's establishment of a spendthrift trust for the debtor's own benefit is a voidable transfer under the Statute of 13 Elizabeth, without regard to whether the transaction is directed at an existing or identified creditor. Mackason's Appeal, 42 Pa. 330, 338-39 (1862); see also, e.g., Ghormley v. Smith, 139 Pa. 584, 591-94 (1891); Patrick v. Smith, 2 Pa. Super. 113, 119 (1896). Cf. Restatement (Third) of Trusts § 58(2) (2003) (setting forth a substantially similar rule as a matter of trust law). Likewise, for centuries § 4(a)(1) and its predecessors have been employed to invalidate nonpossessory property interests that are thought to be potentially deceptive, without regard to whether the deception is directed at an existing or identified creditor. See, e.g., McGann v. Capital Sav. Bank & Trust Co., 89 A.2d 123, 183-84 (Vt. 1952) (seller's retention of possession of goods after sale held voidable); Superior Partners v. Prof'l Educ. Network, Inc., 485 N.E.2d 1218, 1221 (Ill. App. Ct. 1985) (similar); Clow v. Woods, 5 Serg. & Rawle 275 (Pa. 1819) (holding that a nonpossessory chattel mortgage is voidable, in the absence of a system for giving public notice of such interests such as is today supplied by Article 9 of the Uniform Commercial Code).

Section 4(a)(1) has the meaning elaborated in the preceding paragraph, but it is of course possible that a jurisdiction in which this Act is in force might enact other legislation that modifies the results of the particular examples given to illustrate that meaning. For example, some states have enacted legislation authorizing the establishment and funding of self-settled spendthrift trusts, subject to specified conditions. In such a state, such legislation will supersede the historical interpretation referred to in the preceding paragraph, either expressly or by necessary implication, with respect to allowed transfers to such a statutorily-validated trust. See, e.g., Del. Code. Ann. tit. 12, § 3572(a), (b) (2014). See also Comment 8. Likewise, the historical skepticism of nonpossessory property interests has been superseded as to security interests in personal property by the Uniform Commercial Code. See Comment 9.

3. Section 4(a)(2) is derived from §§ 5 and 6 of the Uniform Fraudulent Conveyance Act but substitutes "reasonably equivalent value" for "fair consideration." The transferee's good faith was an element of "fair consideration" as defined in § 3 of the Uniform Fraudulent Conveyance Act, and lack of fair consideration was one of the elements of a fraudulent transfer as defined in four sections of the Uniform Fraudulent Conveyance Act. The transferee's good faith is irrelevant to a determination of the adequacy of the consideration under this Act, but lack of good faith may be a basis for withholding protection of a transferee or obligee under § 8.

4. Unlike the Uniform Fraudulent Conveyance Act, this Act does not prescribe different tests for voidability of a transfer that is made for the purpose of security and a transfer that is intended to be absolute. The premise of this Act is that when a transfer is for security only, the equity or value of the asset that exceeds the amount of the debt secured remains available to unsecured creditors and thus cannot be regarded as the subject of a voidable transfer merely because of the encumbrance resulting from an otherwise valid security transfer. Disproportion between the value of the asset securing the debt and the size of the debt secured does not, in the absence of circumstances indicating a purpose to hinder, delay, or defraud creditors, constitute an impermissible hindrance to the enforcement of other creditors' rights against the debtor-transferor. Cf. U.C.C. § 9-401(b) (2014) (providing that a debtor's interest in collateral subject to a security interest is transferable notwithstanding an agreement with the secured party prohibiting transfer).

5. Subparagraph (i) of § 4(a)(2) is an adaptation of § 5 of the Uniform Fraudulent Conveyance Act but substitutes "unreasonably small [assets] in relation to the business or transaction" for "unreasonably small capital." The reference to "capital" in the Uniform Fraudulent Conveyance Act might be interpreted, incorrectly, to refer to the par value of stock or to the consideration received for stock issued. The special meanings of "capital" in corporation law have no

relevance in the law of voidable transfers. The subparagraph focuses attention on whether the amount of all the assets retained by the debtor was inadequate, i.e., unreasonably small, in light of the needs of the business or transaction in which the debtor was engaged or about to engage.

Subparagraph (ii) of § 4(a)(2) is an adaptation of § 6 of the Uniform Fraudulent Conveyance Act, which relates to a debtor that has or will have debts beyond the debtor's ability to pay as they become due (a condition that is sometimes referred to as "insolvency in the equity sense"). Subparagraph (ii) carries forward the previous Act's language capturing a debtor that "intends" or "believes" that the debtor is or will be unable to pay the debtor's debts as they become due, and adds to that language capturing a debtor that "reasonably should have believed" the same. The added language makes clear that subparagraph (ii) also captures a debtor that, on the basis of objective assessment, has or will have debts beyond the debtor's ability to pay as they become due, regardless of the debtor's subjective belief.

6. Subsection (b) is a nonexclusive catalogue of factors appropriate for consideration by the court in determining whether the debtor had an actual intent to hinder, delay, or defraud one or more creditors. Proof of the existence of any one or more of the factors enumerated in subsection (b) may be relevant evidence as to the debtor's actual intent but does not create a presumption that the debtor has made a voidable transfer or incurred a voidable obligation. The list of factors includes most of the so-called "badges of fraud" that have been recognized by the courts in construing and applying the Statute of 13 Elizabeth and § 7 of the Uniform Fraudulent Conveyance Act. Proof of the presence of certain badges in combination establishes voidability conclusively—i.e., without regard to the actual intent of the debtor—when they concur as provided in § 4(a)(2) or in § 5. The fact that a transfer has been made to a relative or to an affiliated corporation has not been regarded as a badge of fraud sufficient to warrant avoidance when unaccompanied by any other evidence of intent to hinder, delay, or defraud creditors. The courts have uniformly recognized, however, that a transfer to a closely related person warrants close scrutiny of the other circumstances, including the nature and extent of the consideration exchanged. See 1 G. Glenn, Fraudulent Conveyances and Preferences § 307 (Rev. ed. 1940). The second, third, fourth, and fifth factors listed are all adapted from the classic catalogue of badges of fraud provided

by Lord Coke in Twyne's Case, 3 Coke 80b, 76 Eng.Rep. 809 (Star Chamber 1601). Lord Coke also included the use of a trust and the recitation in the instrument of transfer that it "was made honestly, truly, and bona fide," but the use of the trust is voidable only when accompanied by indicia of intent to hinder, delay, or defraud creditors, and recitals of "good faith" can no longer be regarded as significant evidence of intent to hinder, delay, or defraud creditors.

7. In considering the factors listed in § 4(b) a court should evaluate all the relevant circumstances involving a challenged transfer or obligation. Thus the court may appropriately take into account all indicia negativing as well as those suggesting intent to hinder, delay, or defraud creditors, as illustrated in the following reported cases:

(a) Whether the transfer or obligation was to an insider: Salomon v. Kaiser (In re Kaiser), 722 F.2d 1574, 1582-83 (2d Cir. 1983) (insolvent debtor's purchase of two residences in the name of his spouse and the creation of a dummy corporation for the purpose of concealing assets held to evidence intent to hinder, delay, or defraud creditors); Banner Construction Corp. v. Arnold, 128 So.2d 893 (Fla.Dist.App. 1961) (assignment by one corporation to another having identical directors and stockholders constituted a badge of fraud); Travelers Indemnity Co. v. Cormaney, 258 Iowa 237, 138 N.W.2d 50 (1965) (transfer between spouses said to be a circumstance that shed suspicion on the transfer and that with other circumstances warranted avoidance); Hatheway v. Hanson, 230 Iowa 386, 297 N.W. 824 (1941) (transfer from parent to child said to require a critical examination of surrounding circumstances, which, together with other indicia of intent to hinder, delay, or defraud creditors, warranted avoidance); Lumpkins v. McPhee, 59 N.M. 442, 286 P.2d 299 (1955) (transfer from daughter to mother said to be indicative of intent to hinder, delay, or defraud creditors, but transfer held not to be voidable due to adequacy of consideration and delivery of possession by transferor).

(b) Whether the transferor retained possession or control of the property after the transfer: Harris v. Shaw, 224 Ark. 150, 272 S.W.2d 53 (1954) (retention of property by transferor said to be a badge of fraud and, together with other badges, to warrant avoidance of transfer); Stephens v. Reginstein, 89 Ala. 561, 8 So. 68 (1890) (transferor's retention of control and management of property and business after transfer held material in determining transfer to be voidable); Allen v. Massey, 84 U.S. (17 Wall.) 351 (1872) (joint possession of furniture by transferor and transferee considered in holding transfer to be voidable); Warner v. Norton, 61 U.S. (20 How.) 448 (1857) (surrender of possession by transferor deemed to negate allegations of intent to hinder, delay, or defraud creditors).

(d) Whether, before the transfer was made or obligation was incurred, a creditor sued or threatened to sue the debtor: Harris v. Shaw, 224 Ark. 150, 272 S.W.2d 53 (1954) (transfer held to be voidable when causally connected to pendency of litigation and accompanied by other badges of fraud); Pergrem v. Smith, 255 S.W.2d 42 (Ky.App. 1953) (transfer in anticipation of suit deemed to be a badge of fraud; transfer held voidable when accompanied by insolvency of transferor who was related to transferee); Bank of Sun Prairie v. Hovig, 218 F.Supp. 769 (W.D.Ark. 1963) (although threat or pendency of litigation said to be an indicator of intent to hinder, delay, or defraud creditors, transfer was held not to be voidable when adequate consideration and good faith were shown).

(e) Whether the transfer was of substantially all the debtor's assets: Walbrun v. Babbitt, 83 U.S. (16 Wall.) 577 (1872) (sale by insolvent retail shop owner of all of his inventory in a single transaction held to be voidable); Cole v. Mercantile Trust Co., 133 N.Y. 164, 30 N.E. 847 (1892) (transfer of all property before plaintiff could obtain a judgment held to be voidable); Lumpkins v. McPhee, 59 N.M. 442, 286 P.2d 299 (1955) (although transfer of all assets said to indicate intent to hinder, delay, or defraud creditors, transfer held not to be voidable because full consideration was paid and transferor surrendered possession).

(f) Whether the debtor had absconded: In re Thomas, 199 F. 214 (N.D.N.Y. 1912) (when debtor collected all of his money and property with the intent to abscond, intent to hinder, delay, or defraud creditors was held to be shown).

(g) Whether the debtor had removed or concealed assets: Bentley v. Young, 210 F. 202 (S.D.N.Y. 1914), aff'd, 223 F. 536 (2d Cir. 1915) (debtor's removal of goods from store to conceal their whereabouts and to sell them held to render sale voidable); Cioli v. Kenourgios, 59 Cal.App. 690, 211 P. 838 (1922) (debtor's sale of all assets and shipment of proceeds out of the country held to be voidable notwithstanding adequacy of consideration).

(h) Whether the value of the consideration received by the debtor was reasonably equivalent to the value of the asset transferred or the amount of the obligation incurred: Toomay v. Graham, 151 S.W.2d 119 (Mo.App. 1941) (although mere inadequacy of consideration said not to be a badge of fraud unless it is grossly inadequate, transfer held to be voidable when accompanied by other badges of fraud); Texas Sand Co. v. Shield, 381 S.W.2d 48 (Tex. 1964) (inadequate consideration said to be an indicator of intent to hinder, delay, or defraud creditors, and transfer held to be voidable because of inadequate consideration, pendency of suit, family relationship of transferee, and fact that all nonexempt property was transferred); Weigel v. Wood, 355 Mo. 11, 194 S.W.2d 40 (1946) (although inadequate consideration said to be a badge of fraud, transfer held not to be voidable when inadequacy not gross and not accompanied by any other badge; fact that transfer was from father to son held not sufficient to establish intent to hinder, delay, or defraud creditors).

(i) Whether the debtor was insolvent or became insolvent shortly after the transfer was made or obligation was incurred: Harris v. Shaw, 224 Ark. 150, 272 S.W.2d 53 (1954) (insolvency of transferor said to be a badge of fraud and transfer held voidable when accompanied by other badges of fraud); Bank of Sun Prairie v. Hovig, 218 F.Supp. 769 (W.D. Ark. 1963) (although the insolvency of the debtor said to be a badge of fraud, transfer held not voidable when debtor was shown to be solvent, adequate consideration was paid, and good faith was shown, despite the pendency of suit); Wareheim v. Bayliss, 149 Md. 103, 131 A. 27 (1925) (although insolvency of debtor acknowledged to be an indicator of intent to hinder, delay, or defraud creditors, transfer held not to be voidable when adequate consideration was paid and whether debtor was insolvent in fact was doubtful).

(j) Whether the transfer occurred shortly before or shortly after a substantial debt was incurred: Commerce Bank of Lebanon v. Halladale A Corp., 618 S.W.2d 288, 292 (Mo.App. 1981) (when transferors incurred substantial debts near in time to the transfer, transfer was held to be voidable due to inadequate consideration, close family relationship, the debtor's retention of possession, and the fact that almost all the debtor's property was transferred).

(k) Whether the debtor transferred the essential assets of the business to a lienor that transferred the assets to an insider of the debtor: The wrong addressed by § 4(b)(11) is collusive and abusive use of a lienor's superior position to eliminate junior creditors while leaving equity holders in place, perhaps unaffected. The kind of disposition sought to be reached is exemplified by that found in Northern Pacific Co. v. Boyd, 228 U.S. 482, 502-05 (1913), the leading case in establishing the absolute priority doctrine in reorganization law. There the Court held that a reorganization whereby the secured creditors and the management-owners retained their economic interests in a railroad through a foreclosure that cut off claims of unsecured creditors against its assets was in effect a voidable disposition. See Bruce A. Markell, Owners, Auctions and Absolute Priority in Bankruptcy Reorganizations, 44 Stan.L.Rev. 69, 74-83 (1991). For cases in which an analogous injury to unsecured creditors was inflicted by a lienor and a debtor, see Voest-Alpine Trading USA Corp. v. Vantage Steel Corp., 919 F.2d 206 (3d Cir. 1990) (lender foreclosed on assets of steel company at 5:00 p.m. on a Friday, then transferred the assets to an affiliate of the debtor; lender made a loan to the affiliate to enable it to purchase at the foreclosure sale on almost the same terms as the old loan; new business opened Monday morning); Jackson v. Star Sprinkler Corp. of Florida, 575 F.2d 1223, 1231-34 (8th Cir. 1978); Heath v. Helmick, 173 F.2d 157, 161-62 (9th Cir. 1949); Toner v. Nuss, 234 F.Supp. 457, 461-62 (E.D.Pa. 1964); and see In re Spotless Tavern Co., Inc., 4 F.Supp. 752, 753, 755 (D.Md. 1933).

8. The phrase "hinder, delay, or defraud" in § 4(a)(1), carried forward from the primordial Statute of 13 Elizabeth, is potentially applicable to any transaction that unacceptably contravenes norms of creditors' rights. Section 4(a)(1) is sometimes said to require "actual fraud," by contrast to § 4(a)(2) and § 5(a), which are said to require "constructive fraud." That shorthand is highly misleading. Fraud is not a necessary element of a claim for relief under any of those provisions. By its terms, § 4(a)(1) applies to a transaction that "hinders" or "delays" a creditor, even if it does not "defraud" the creditor. See, e.g., Shapiro v. Wilgus, 287 U.S. 348, 354 (1932); Means v. Dowd, 128 U.S. 273, 288-89 (1888); Consove v. Cohen (In re Roco Corp.), 701 F.2d 978, 984 (1st Cir. 1983); Empire Lighting Fixture Co. v. Practical Lighting

Fixture Co., 20 F.2d 295, 297 (2d Cir. 1927); Lippe v. Bairnco Corp., 249 F. Supp. 2d 357, 374 (S.D.N.Y. 2003). "Hinder, delay, or defraud" is best considered to be a single term of art describing a transaction that unacceptably contravenes norms of creditors' rights. Such a transaction need not bear any resemblance to common-law fraud. Thus, the Supreme Court held a given transfer voidable because made with intent to "hinder, delay, or defraud" creditors, but emphasized: "We have no thought in so holding to impute to [the debtor] a willingness to participate in conduct known to be fraudulent.... [He] acted in the genuine belief that what [he] planned was fair and lawful. Genuine the belief was, but mistaken it was also. Conduct and purpose have a quality imprinted on them by the law." Shapiro v. Wilgus, 287 U.S. 348, 357 (1932).

Diminution of the assets available to the debtor's creditors is not necessarily required to "hinder, delay, or defraud" creditors. For example, the age-old legal skepticism of nonpossessory property interests, which stems from their potential for deception, has often resulted in their avoidance under § 4(a)(1) or its predecessors. See Comments 2 and 7(b); cf. Comment 9. A transaction may "hinder, delay, or defraud" creditors although it neither reduces the assets available to the debtor's creditors nor involves any potential deception. See, e.g., Shapiro v. Wilgus, 287 U.S. 348 (1932) (holding voidable a solvent individual debtor's conveyance of his assets to a wholly-owned corporation for the purpose of instituting a receivership proceeding not available to an individual).

A transaction that does not place an asset entirely beyond the reach of creditors may nevertheless "hinder, delay, or defraud" creditors if it makes the asset more difficult for creditors to reach. Simple exchange by a debtor of an asset for a less liquid asset, or disposition of liquid assets while retaining illiquid assets, may be voidable for that reason. See, e.g., Empire Lighting Fixture Co. v. Practical Lighting Fixture Co., 20 F.2d 295, 297 (2d Cir. 1927) (L. Hand, J.) (credit sale by a corporation to an affiliate of its plant, leaving the seller solvent with ample accounts receivable, held voidable because made with intent to hinder creditors of the seller, due to the comparative difficulty of creditors realizing on accounts receivable under then-current collection practice). Overcollateralization of a debt that is made with intent to hinder the debtor's creditors, by rendering the debtor's equity in the collateral more difficult for creditors to reach, is similarly voidable. See Comment 4. Likewise, it is voidable for a debtor intentionally to hinder creditors by transferring assets to a wholly-owned corporation or other organization, as may be the case if the equity interest in the organization is more difficult to realize upon than the assets (either because the equity interest is less liquid, or because the applicable procedural rules are more demanding). See, e.g., Addison v. Tessier, 335 P.2d 554, 557 (N.M. 1959); First Nat'l Bank. v. F. C. Trebein Co., 52 N.E. 834, 837-38 (Ohio 1898); Anno., 85 A.L.R. 133 (1933).

Under the same principle, § 4(a)(1) would render voidable an attempt by the owners of a corporation to convert it to a different legal form (e.g., limited liability company or partnership) with intent to hinder the owners' creditors, as may be the case if an owner's interest in the alternative organization would be subject only to a charging order, and not to execution (which would typically be available against stock in a corporation). See, e.g., Firmani v. Firmani, 752 A.2d 854, 857 (N.J. Super. Ct. App. Div. 2000); cf. Interpool Ltd. v. Patterson, 890 F. Supp. 259, 266-68 (S.D.N.Y. 1995) (similar, but relying on a "good faith" requirement of the former Uniform Fraudulent Conveyance Act rather than that act's equivalent of § 4(a)(1)). If such a conversion is done with intent to hinder creditors, it contravenes § 4(a)(1) regardless of whether it is effected by conveyance of the corporation's assets to a new entity or by conversion of the corporation to the alternative form. In both cases the owner begins with the stock of the corporation and ends with an ownership interest in the alternative organization, a property right with different attributes. Either is a "transfer" under the designedly sweeping language of § 1(16), which encompasses "every mode...of...parting with an asset or an interest in an asset." Cf., e.g., United States v. Sims (In re Feiler), 218 F.3d 948 (9th Cir. 2000) (debtor's irrevocable election under the Internal Revenue Code to waive carryback of net operating losses is a "transfer" under the substantially similar definition in the Bankruptcy Code); Weaver v. Kellogg, 216 B.R. 563, 573-74 (S.D. Tex. 1997) (exchange of notes owed to the debtor for new notes having different terms is a "transfer" by the debtor under that definition).

In § 4(a)(1), the phrase "hinder, delay, or defraud," like the word "intent," is a term of art whose words do not have their dictionary meanings. For example, every grant of a security interest "hinders" the debtor's unsecured creditors in the dictionary sense of that word. Yet it would be absurd to suggest that every grant of a security interest contravenes § 4(a)(1). The

line between permissible and impermissible grants cannot coherently be drawn by reference to the debtor's subjective mental state, for a rational person knows the natural consequences of his actions, and that includes the adverse consequences to unsecured creditors of any grant of a security interest. See, e.g., Dean v. Davis, 242 U.S. 438, 444 (1917) (equating an act whose "obviously necessary effect" is to hinder, delay, or defraud creditors with an act intended to hinder, delay, or defraud creditors); United States v. Tabor Court Realty Corp., 803 F.3d 1288, 1305 (3rd Cir. 1986) (holding that the trial court's finding of intent to hinder, delay, or defraud creditors properly followed from its finding that the debtor could have foreseen the effect of its act on its creditors, because "a party is deemed to have intended the natural consequences of his acts"); In re Sentinel Management Group Inc., 728 F.3d 660, 667 (7th Cir. 2013). Whether a transaction is captured by § 4(a)(1) ultimately depends upon whether the transaction unacceptably contravenes norms of creditors' rights, given the devices legislators and courts have allowed debtors that may interfere with those rights. Section 4(a)(1) is the regulatory tool of last resort that restrains debtor ingenuity to decent limits.

Thus, for example, suppose that entrepreneurs organize a business as a limited liability company, contributing assets to capitalize it, in the ordinary situation in which none of the owners has particular reason to anticipate personal liability or financial distress and no other unusual facts are present. Assume that the LLC statute has the creditor-thwarting feature of precluding execution upon equity interests in the LLC and providing only for charging orders against such interests. Notwithstanding that feature, the owners' transfers of assets to capitalize the LLC is not voidable under § 4(a)(1) as in force in the same state. The legislature in that state, having created the LLC vehicle having that feature, must have expected it to be used in such ordinary circumstances. By contrast, if owners of an existing business were to reorganize it as an LLC under such a statute when the clouds of personal liability or financial distress have gathered over some of them, and with the intention of gaining the benefit of that creditor-thwarting feature, the transfer effecting the reorganization should be voidable under § 4(a)(1), at least absent a clear indication that the legislature truly intended the LLC form, with its creditor-thwarting feature, to be available even in such circumstances.

Because the laws of different jurisdictions differ in

their tolerance of particular creditor-thwarting devices, choice of law considerations may be important in interpreting § 4(a)(1) as in force in a given jurisdiction. For example, as noted in Comment 2, the language of § 4(a)(1) historically has been interpreted to render voidable a transfer to a self-settled spendthrift trust. Suppose that jurisdiction X, in which this Act is in force, also has in force a statute permitting an individual to establish a self-settled spendthrift trust and transfer assets thereto, subject to stated conditions. If an individual Debtor whose principal residence is in X establishes such a trust and transfers assets thereto, then under § 10 of this Act the voidable transfer law of X applies to that transfer. That transfer cannot be considered voidable in itself under § 4(a)(1) as in force in X, for the legislature of X, having authorized the establishment of such trusts, must have expected them to be used. (Other facts might still render the transfer voidable under X's enactment of § 4(a)(1).) By contrast, if Debtor's principal residence is in jurisdiction Y, which also has enacted this Act but has no legislation validating such trusts, and if Debtor establishes such a trust under the law of X and transfers assets to it, then the result would be different. Under § 10 of this Act, the voidable transfer law of Y would apply to the transfer. If Y follows the historical interpretation referred to in Comment 2, the transfer would be voidable under § 4(a)(1) as in force in Y.

9. This Act is not an exclusive law on the subject of voidable transfers and obligations. See § 1, Comment 2. For example, the Uniform Commercial Code supplements or modifies the operation of this Act in numerous ways. Instances include the following:

(a) U.C.C. § 2-402(2) (2014) recognizes the generally prevailing rule that retention of possession of goods by a seller may be voidable, but limits the application of the rule by negating any imputation of voidability from "retention of possession in good faith and current course of trade by a merchant-seller for a commercially reasonable time after a sale or identification." (Indeed, independently of § 2-402(2), retention of possession of goods in good faith and current course of trade by a merchant-seller for a commercially reasonable time after a sale or identification should not in itself be considered to "hinder, delay, or defraud" any creditor of the merchant-seller under § 4(a)(1).)

(b) Section 2A-308(1) provides a rule analogous to § 2-402(2) for situations in which a lessor retains possession of goods that are subject to a lease

contract. Section 2A-308(3) provides that retention of possession of goods by the seller-lessee in a sale-leaseback transaction does not render the transaction voidable by a creditor of the seller-lessee if the buyer bought for value and in good faith.

(c) This Act does not preempt statutes governing bulk transfers, including Article 6 of the Uniform Commercial Code in jurisdictions in which it remains in force.

(d) Section 9-205 precludes treating a security interest in personal property as voidable on account of various enumerated features it may have. Among other things, § 9-205 immunizes a security interest in tangible property from being avoided on account of the secured party not being in possession of the property, notwithstanding the historical skepticism of nonpossessory property interests.

This Act operates independently of rules in an organic statute applicable to a business organization that limit distributions by the organization to its equity owners. Compliance with those rules does not insulate such a distribution from being voidable under this Act. It is conceivable that such an organic statute might contain a provision preempting the application of this Act to such distributions. Cf. Model Business Corporation Act § 152 (optional provision added in 1979 preempting the application of "any other statutes of this state with respect to the legality of distributions"; deleted 1984). Such a preemptive statute of course must be respected if applicable, but choice of law considerations may well render it inapplicable. See, e.g., Faulkner v. Kornman (In re The Heritage Organization, L.L.C.), 413 B.R. 438, 462-63 (Bankr. N.D. Tex. 2009) (action under the Texas enactment of this Act challenging a distribution by a Delaware limited liability company to its members; held, a provision of the Delaware LLC statute imposing a three-year statute of repose on an action under "any applicable law" to recover a distribution by a Delaware LLC did not apply, because choice of law rules directed application of the voidable transfer law of Texas).

10. Subsection (c) was added in 2014. Sections 2(b), 4(c), 5(c), 8(g), and 8(h) together provide uniform rules on burdens and standards of proof relating to the operation of this Act.

Pursuant to subsection (c), proof of intent to "hinder, delay, or defraud" a creditor under § 4(a)(1) is sufficient if made by a preponderance of the evidence. That is the standard of proof ordinarily applied in civil actions. Subsection (c) thus rejects cases that have imposed an extraordinary standard, typically "clear and convincing evidence," by analogy to the standard commonly applied to proof of common-law fraud. That analogy is misguided. By its terms, § 4(a)(1) applies to a transaction that "hinders" or "delays" a creditor even if it does not "defraud," and a transaction to which § 4(a)(1) applies need not bear any resemblance to common-law fraud. See Comment 8. Furthermore, the extraordinary standard of proof commonly applied to common-law fraud originated in cases that were thought to involve a special danger that claims might be fabricated. In the earliest such cases, a court of equity was asked to grant relief on claims that were unenforceable at law for failure to comply with the Statute of Frauds, the Statute of Wills, or the parol evidence rule. In time, extraordinary proof also came to be required in actions seeking to set aside or alter the terms of written instruments. See Herman & MacLean v. Huddleston, 459 U.S. 375, 388-89 (1983) and sources cited therein. Those reasons for extraordinary proof do not apply to claims for relief under § 4(a)(1).

For similar reasons, a procedural rule that imposes extraordinary pleading requirements on a claim of "fraud," without further gloss, should not be applied to a claim for relief under § 4(a)(1). The elements of a claim for relief under § 4(a)(1) are very different from the elements of a claim of common-law fraud. Furthermore, the reasons for such extraordinary pleading requirements do not apply to a claim for relief under § 4(a)(1). Unlike common-law fraud, a claim for relief under § 4(a)(1) is not unusually susceptible to abusive use in a "strike suit," nor is it apt to be of use to a plaintiff seeking to discover unknown wrongs. Likewise, a claim for relief under § 4(a)(1) is unlikely to cause significant harm to the defendant's reputation, for the defendant is the transferee or obligee, and the elements of the claim do not require the defendant to have committed even an arguable wrong. See Janvey v. Alguire, 846 F.Supp.2d 662, 675-77 (N.D. Tex. 2011); Carter-Jones Lumber Co. v. Benune, 725 N.E.2d 330, 331-33 (Ohio App. 1999). Cf. Federal Rules of Civil Procedure, Appendix, Form 21 (2010) (illustrative form of complaint for a claim for relief under § 4(a)(1) or similar law, which Rule 84 declares sufficient to comply with federal pleading rules).

11. Subsection (c) allocates to the party making a claim for relief under § 4 the burden of persuasion as to the elements of the claim. Courts should not apply nonstatutory presumptions that reverse that allocation, and should be wary of nonstatutory presumptions that would dilute it. The command of § 13—that this Act is to be applied so as to effectuate its purpose of making uniform the law among states enacting it—applies with particular cogency to nonstatutory presumptions. Given the elasticity of key terms of this Act (e.g., "hinder, delay, or defraud") and the potential difficulty of proving others (e.g., the financial condition tests in § 4(a)(2) and § 5), employment of divergent nonstatutory presumptions by enacting jurisdictions may render the law nonuniform as a practical matter. It is not the purpose of subsection (c) to forbid employment of any and all nonstatutory presumptions. Indeed, in some instances a judicially-crafted presumption applied under this Act or its predecessors has won such favor as to be codified as a separate statutory creation. Examples include the bulk sales laws, the absolute priority rule applicable to reorganizations under Bankruptcy Code § 1129(b)(2)(B)(ii) (2014), and the so-called "constructive fraud" provisions of § 4(a)(2) and § 5(a) of this Act itself. However, subsection (c) and § 13 mean, at the least, that a nonstatutory presumption is suspect if it would alter the statutorily-allocated burden of persuasion, would upset the policy of uniformity, or is an unwarranted carrying-forward of obsolescent principles. An example of a nonstatutory presumption that should be rejected for those reasons is a presumption that the transferee bears the burden of persuasion as to the debtor's compliance with the financial condition tests in § 4(a)(2) and § 5, in an action under those provisions, if the transfer was for less than reasonably equivalent value (or, as another example, if the debtor was merely in debt at the time of the transfer). See Fidelity Bond & Mtg. Co. v. Brand, 371 B.R. 708, 716-22 (E.D. Pa. 2007) (rejecting such a presumption previously applied in Pennsylvania).

§ 5. Transfer or Obligation Voidable as to Present Creditor.

(a) A transfer made or obligation incurred by a debtor is voidable as to a creditor whose claim arose before the transfer was made or the obligation was incurred if the debtor made the transfer or incurred the obligation without receiving a reasonably equivalent value in exchange for the transfer or obligation and the debtor was insolvent at that time or the debtor became insolvent as a result of the transfer or obligation.

(b) A transfer made by a debtor is voidable as to a creditor whose claim arose before the transfer was made if the transfer was made to an insider for an antecedent debt, the debtor was insolvent at that time, and the insider had reasonable cause to believe that the debtor was insolvent.

(c) Subject to Section 2(b), a creditor making a claim for relief under subsection (a) or (b) has the burden of proving the elements of the claim for relief by a preponderance of the evidence.

Comment

1. Subsection (a) is derived from § 4 of the Uniform Fraudulent Conveyance Act. It adheres to the limitation of the protection of that section to a creditor whose claim arose before the transfer or obligation described. As pointed out in Comment 3 accompanying § 4, this Act substitutes "reasonably equivalent value" for "fair consideration."

2. Subsection (b) renders a preferential transfer—i.e., a transfer by an insolvent debtor for or on account of an antecedent debt—to an insider voidable when the insider had reasonable cause to believe that the debtor was insolvent. This subsection adopts for general application the rule of such cases as Jackson Sound Studios, Inc. v. Travis, 473 F.2d 503 (5th Cir. 1973) (security transfer of corporation's equipment to corporate principal's mother perfected on eve of bankruptcy of corporation held to be voidable); In re Lamie Chemical Co., 296 F. 24 (4th Cir. 1924) (corporate preference to corporate officers and directors held voidable by receiver when corporation was insolvent or nearly so and directors had already voted for liquidation); Stuart v. Larson, 298 F. 223 (8th Cir. 1924), noted 38 Harv.L.Rev. 521 (1925) (corporate preference to director held voidable). See generally 2 G. Glenn, Fraudulent Conveyances and Preferences 386 (Rev. ed. 1940). Subsection (b) overrules such cases as Epstein v. Goldstein, 107 F.2d 755, 757 (2d Cir. 1939) (transfer by insolvent husband to wife to secure his debt to her sustained against attack by husband's trustee); Hartford Accident & Indemnity Co. v. Jirasek, 254 Mich. 131, 139, 235 N.W. 836, 839 (1931) (mortgage given by debtor to his brother to secure an antecedent debt owed the brother sustained as not voidable).

3. Subsection (b) does not extend as far as § 8(a) of the Uniform Fraudulent Conveyance Act and Bankruptcy Code § 548(b) (1984) in rendering voidable a transfer made by an insolvent partnership to a partner. A general partner is an insider of the partnership, but a transfer by the partnership to the partner nevertheless is not vulnerable to avoidance under § 5(b) unless the transfer is for an antecedent debt and the partner has reasonable cause to believe that the partnership is insolvent. By contrast, the cited provisions of the Uniform Fraudulent Conveyance Act and the Bankruptcy Code make any transfer by an insolvent partnership to a general partner voidable. Avoidance of the partnership transfer without reference to the partner's state of mind and the nature of the consideration exchanged would be unduly harsh treatment of the creditors of the partner and unduly favorable to the creditors of the partnership.

4. Subsection (c) was added in 2014. Sections 2(b), 4(c), 5(c), 8(g), and 8(h) together provide uniform rules on burdens and standards of proof relating to the operation of this Act. The principles stated in Comment 11 to § 4 apply to subsection (c).

§ 6. When Transfer Is Made or Obligation Is Incurred. For the purposes of this [Act]:

(1) a transfer is made:

(i) with respect to an asset that is real property other than a fixture, but including the interest of a seller or purchaser under a contract for the sale of the asset, when the transfer is so far perfected that a good-faith purchaser of the asset from the debtor against whom applicable law permits the transfer to be perfected cannot acquire an interest in the asset that is superior to the interest of the transferee; and

(ii) with respect to an asset that is not real property or that is a fixture, when the transfer is so far perfected that a creditor on a simple contract cannot acquire a judicial lien otherwise than under this [Act] that is superior to the interest of the transferee;

(2) if applicable law permits the transfer to be perfected as provided in paragraph (1) and the transfer is not so perfected before the commencement of an action for relief under this [Act], the

transfer is deemed made immediately before the commencement of the action;

(3) if applicable law does not permit the transfer to be perfected as provided in paragraph (1), the transfer is made when it becomes effective between the debtor and the transferee;

(4) a transfer is not made until the debtor has acquired rights in the asset transferred;

(5) an obligation is incurred:

(i) if oral, when it becomes effective between the parties; or

(ii) if evidenced by a record, when the record signed by the obligor is delivered to or for the benefit of the obligee.

Comment

1. One of the uncertainties in the law governing the avoidance of transfers and obligations of the nature governed by this Act is the time at which the cause of action arises. Section 6 clarifies that point in time. For transfers of real property other than a fixture, paragraph (1)(i) fixes the time as the date of perfection against a good-faith purchaser from the transferor. For transfers of fixtures and assets constituting personalty, paragraph (1)(ii) fixes the time as the date of perfection against a judicial lien creditor not asserting rights under this Act. Perfection under paragraph (1) typically is effected by notice-filing, recordation, or delivery of unequivocal possession. See U.C.C. §§ 9-310, 9-313 (2014) (security interest in personal property generally is perfected by notice-filing or delivery of possession to transferee); 4 American Law of Property §§ 17.10-17.12 (1952) (recordation of transfer or delivery of possession to grantee required for perfection against bona fide purchaser from grantor). The provision for postponing the time a transfer is made until its perfection is an adaptation of Bankruptcy Code § 548(d)(1) (1984). When no steps are taken to perfect a transfer that applicable law permits to be perfected, the transfer is deemed by paragraph (2) to be perfected immediately before the filing of an action to avoid it; without such a provision to cover that eventuality, an unperfected transfer arguably would be immune to attack. Some transfers may not be amenable to perfection as against a bona fide purchaser or judicial lien creditor. In the event that a transfer may not be perfected as provided in paragraph (1), paragraph (3) provides that the transfer occurs for the purpose of this Act when the transferor effectively parts with an interest in the asset.

2. Paragraph (4) requires the transferor to have rights in the asset transferred before the transfer is made for the purpose of this section. This provision makes clear that the purpose of this section may not be circumvented by notice-filing or recordation of a document evidencing an interest in an asset to be acquired in the future. Cf. Bankruptcy Code § 547(e) (1984); U.C.C. § 9-203(b)(2) (2014).

3. Paragraph (5) had no analogue in the Uniform Fraudulent Conveyance Act. It is intended to resolve uncertainty arising from Rubin v. Manufacturers Hanover Trust Co., 661 F.2d 979, 989-91, 997 (2d Cir. 1981), insofar as that case holds that an obligation of guaranty may be deemed to be incurred when advances covered by the guaranty are made rather than when the guaranty first became effective between the parties. Compare Rosenberg, Intercorporate Guaranties and the Law of Fraudulent Conveyances: Lender Beware, 125 U.Pa.L.Rev. 235, 256-57 (1976).

An obligation may be avoided under this Act if it is incurred under the circumstances specified in § 4(a) or § 5(a). The debtor may receive reasonably equivalent value in exchange for an obligation incurred even though the benefit to the debtor is indirect. See Rubin v. Manufacturers Hanover Trust Co., 661 F.2d at 991-92; Williams v. Twin City Co., 251 F.2d 678, 681 (9th Cir. 1958); Rosenberg, supra, at 243-46.

Under paragraph (5), an oral obligation is incurred when it becomes effective between the parties, and later confirmation of the oral obligation by a record does not reset the time of incurrence to that later time.

§ 7. Remedies of Creditor.

(a) In an action for relief against a transfer or obligation under this [Act], a creditor, subject to the limitations in Section 8, may obtain:

(1) avoidance of the transfer or obligation to the extent necessary to satisfy the creditor's claim;

(2) an attachment or other provisional remedy against the asset transferred or other property of the transferee if available under applicable law; and

(3) subject to applicable principles of equity and in accordance with applicable rules of civil procedure:

(i) an injunction against further disposition by the debtor or a transferee, or both, of the asset transferred or of other property;

(ii) appointment of a receiver to take charge of the asset transferred or of other property of the transferee; or

(iii) any other relief the circumstances may require.

(b) If a creditor has obtained a judgment on a claim against the debtor, the creditor, if the court so orders, may levy execution on the asset transferred or its proceeds.

Comment

1. This section is derived from §§ 9 and 10 of the Uniform Fraudulent Conveyance Act. Section 9 of that Act specified the remedies of creditors whose claims have matured, and § 10 enumerated the remedies available to creditors whose claims have not matured. A creditor holding an unmatured claim may be denied the right to receive payment from the proceeds of a sale on execution until the claim has matured, but the proceeds may be deposited in court or in an interest-bearing account pending the maturity of the creditor's claim. The remedies specified in this section are not exclusive.

2. The availability of an attachment or other provisional remedy has been restricted by amendments of statutes and rules of procedure in response to Connecticut v. Doehr, 501 U.S. 1 (1991), Sniadach v. Family Finance Corp., 395 U.S. 337 (1969), and their progeny. This judicial development and the procedural changes that followed in its wake do not preclude resort to attachment by a creditor in seeking avoidance of a transfer or obligation. See, e.g., Britton v. Howard Sav. Bank, 727 F.2d 315, 317-20 (3d Cir. 1984); Computer Sciences Corp. v. Sci-Tek Inc., 367 A.2d 658, 661 (Del. Super. 1976); Great Lakes Carbon Corp. v. Fontana, 54 A.D.2d 548, 387 N.Y.S.2d 115 (1st Dep't 1976). Section 7(a)(2) continues the authorization for the use of attachment contained in § 9(b) of the Uniform Fraudulent Conveyance Act, or of a similar provisional remedy, when applicable law provides therefor, subject to the constraints imposed by the due process clauses of the United States and state constitutions.

3. Subsections (a) and (b) of § 10 of the Uniform Fraudulent Conveyance Act authorized the court, in an action on a voidable transfer or obligation, to restrain the defendant from disposing of his property, to appoint a receiver to take charge of his property, or to make any order the circumstances may require.

Section 10, however, applied only to a creditor whose claim was unmatured. There is no reason to restrict the availability of these remedies to such a creditor, and the courts have not so restricted them. See, e.g., Lipskey v. Voloshen, 155 Md. 139, 143-45, 141 A. 402, 404-05 (1928) (judgment creditor granted injunction against disposition of property by transferee, but appointment of receiver denied for lack of sufficient showing of need for such relief); Matthews v. Schusheim, 36 Misc.2d 918, 922-23, 235 N.Y.S.2d 973, 976-77, 991-92 (Sup.Ct. 1962) (injunction and appointment of receiver granted to holder of claims for fraud, breach of contract, and alimony arrearages; whether creditor's claim was mature said to be immaterial); Oliphant v. Moore, 155 Tenn. 359, 362-63, 293 S.W. 541, 542 (1927) (tort creditor granted injunction restraining alleged tortfeasor's disposition of property).

4. As under the Uniform Fraudulent Conveyance Act, a creditor is not required to obtain a judgment against the debtor-transferor or to have a matured claim in order to proceed under subsection (a). See §§ 1(3) and 1(4) ; American Surety Co. v. Conner, 251 N.Y. 1, 166 N.E. 783, 65 A.L.R. 244 (1929); 1 G. Glenn, Fraudulent Conveyances and Preferences 129 (Rev. ed. 1940).

5. The provision in subsection (b) for a creditor to levy execution on a transferred asset continues the availability of a remedy provided in § 9(b) of the Uniform Fraudulent Conveyance Act. See, e.g., Doland v. Burns Lbr. Co., 156 Minn. 238, 194 N.W. 636 (1923); Montana Ass'n of Credit Management v. Hergert, 181 Mont. 442, 449, 453, 593 P.2d 1059, 1063, 1065 (1979); Corbett v. Hunter, 292 Pa.Super. 123, 128, 436 A.2d 1036, 1038 (1981); see also American Surety Co. v. Conner, 251 N.Y. 1, 6, 166 N.E. 783, 784, 65 A.L.R. 244, 247 (1929) ("In such circumstances he [the creditor] might find it necessary

to indemnify the sheriff and, when the seizure was erroneous, assumed the risk of error"); McLaughlin, Application of the Uniform Fraudulent Conveyance Act, 46 Harv.L.Rev. 404, 441-42 (1933).

6. The remedies specified in § 7, like those enumerated in §§ 9 and 10 of the Uniform Fraudulent Conveyance Act, are cumulative. Lind v. O. N. Johnson Co., 204 Minn. 30, 40, 282 N.W. 661, 667, 119 A.L.R. 940 (1939) (Uniform Fraudulent Conveyance Act held not to impair or limit availability of the "old practice" of obtaining judgment and execution returned unsatisfied before proceeding in equity to set aside a transfer); Conemaugh Iron Works Co. v. Delano Coal Co., Inc., 298 Pa. 182, 186, 148 A. 94, 95 (1929) (Uniform Fraudulent Conveyance Act held to give an "additional optional remedy" and not to "deprive a creditor of the right, as formerly, to work out his remedy at law"); 1 G. Glenn, Fraudulent Conveyances and Preferences 120, 130, 150 (Rev. ed. 1940).

7. If a transfer or obligation is voidable under § 4 or § 5, the basic remedy provided by this Act is its avoidance under subsection (a)(1). "Avoidance" is a term of art in this Act, for it does not mean that the transfer or obligation is simply rendered void. It has long been established that a transfer avoided by a creditor under this Act or its predecessors is nevertheless valid as between the debtor and the transferee. For example, in the case of a transfer of property worth $100 by Debtor to Transferee, held voidable in a suit by Creditor-1 who is owed $80 by Debtor, "avoidance" of the transfer leaves the $20 surplus with Transferee. Debtor is not entitled to recover the surplus. Nor is Debtor's Creditor-2 entitled to pursue the surplus by reason of Creditor-1's action (though Creditor-2 may be entitled to bring its own avoidance action to pursue the surplus). The foregoing principle is embedded in the language of subsection (a)(1), which prescribes "avoidance" only "to the extent necessary to satisfy the creditor's claim." Section 9(a) of the Uniform Fraudulent Conveyance Act was similarly limited. See, e.g., Becker v. Becker, 416 A.2d 156, 162 (Vt. 1980); De Martini v. De Martini, 52 N.E.2d 138, 141 (Ill. 1943); Markward v. Murrah, 156 S.W.2d 971, 974 (Tex. 1941); Society Milion Athena, Inc. v. National Bank of Greece, 22 N.E.2d 374, 377 (N.Y. 1939); National Radiator Corp. v. Parad, 8 N.E.2d 794, 796-97 (Mass. 1937); 1 G. Glenn, Fraudulent Conveyances and Preferences § 114, at 225 (Rev. ed. 1940). The transferee's mental state is irrelevant to the foregoing, but a good-faith transferee may also be afforded protection by § 8.

It follows that "avoidance" of an obligation under subsection (a)(1) likewise should not mean its cancellation, but rather a remedy that recognizes the existence of the obligation and the superiority of the plaintiff creditor's interest over the obligee's interest. Ordinarily that should mean subordination of the obligation to the plaintiff creditor's claim against the debtor. That would entail disgorgement by the obligee of any payments received or receivable on the obligation, to the extent necessary to satisfy the plaintiff creditor's claim, with the obligee being subrogated to the plaintiff creditor when the latter's claim is paid. Of course, if the obligation is unenforceable for reasons other than contravention of this Act, contravention of this Act does not render the obligation enforceable.

This Comment relates to the meaning of subsection (a)(1). If this Act is invoked in a bankruptcy proceeding, the remedial entitlements provided by the Bankruptcy Code may differ from those provided by this Act.

§ 8. Defenses, Liability, and Protection of Transferee or Obligee.

(a) A transfer or obligation is not voidable under Section 4(a)(1) against a person that took in good faith and for a reasonably equivalent value given the debtor or against any subsequent transferee or obligee.

(b) To the extent a transfer is avoidable in an action by a creditor under Section 7(a)(1), the following rules apply:

(1) Except as otherwise provided in this section, the creditor may recover judgment for the value of the asset transferred, as adjusted under subsection (c), or the amount necessary to satisfy the creditor's claim, whichever is less. The judgment may be entered against:

(i) the first transferee of the asset or the person for whose benefit the transfer was made; or

(ii) an immediate or mediate transferee of the first transferee, other than:

(A) a good-faith transferee that took for value; or

(B) an immediate or mediate good-faith transferee of a person described in clause (A).

(2) Recovery pursuant to Section 7(a)(1) or (b) of or from the asset transferred or its proceeds, by levy or otherwise, is available only against a person described in paragraph (1)(i) or (ii).

(c) If the judgment under subsection (b) is based upon the value of the asset transferred, the judgment must be for an amount equal to the value of the asset at the time of the transfer, subject to adjustment as the equities may require.

(d) Notwithstanding voidability of a transfer or an obligation under this [Act], a good-faith transferee or obligee is entitled, to the extent of the value given the debtor for the transfer or obligation, to:

(1) a lien on or a right to retain an interest in the asset transferred;

(2) enforcement of an obligation incurred; or

(3) a reduction in the amount of the liability on the judgment.

(e) A transfer is not voidable under Section 4(a)(2) or Section 5 if the transfer results from:

(1) termination of a lease upon default by the debtor when the termination is pursuant to the lease and applicable law; or

(2) enforcement of a security interest in compliance with Article 9 of the Uniform Commercial Code, other than the acceptance of collateral in full or partial satisfaction of the obligation it secures.

(f) A transfer is not voidable under Section 5(b):

(1) to the extent the insider gave new value to or for the benefit of the debtor after the transfer was made, except to the extent the new value was secured by a valid lien;

(2) if made in the ordinary course of business or financial affairs of the debtor and the insider; or

(3) if made pursuant to a good-faith effort to rehabilitate the debtor and the transfer secured present value given for that purpose as well as an antecedent debt of the debtor.

(g) The following rules determine the burden of proving matters referred to in this section:

(1) A party that seeks to invoke subsection (a), (d), (e), or (f) has the burden of proving the applicability of that subsection.

(2) Except as otherwise provided in paragraphs (3) and (4), the creditor has the burden of proving each applicable element of subsection (b) or (c).

(3) The transferee has the burden of proving the applicability to the transferee of subsection (b)(1)(ii)(A) or (B).

(4) A party that seeks adjustment under subsection (c) has the burden of proving the adjustment.

(h) The standard of proof required to establish matters referred to in this section is preponderance of the evidence.

Comment

1. Subsection (a) sets forth a complete defense to an action for avoidance under § 4(a)(1). The subsection is an adaptation of the exception stated in § 9 of the Uniform Fraudulent Conveyance Act. Pursuant to subsection (g), the person invoking this defense carries the burden of establishing good faith and the reasonable equivalence of the consideration exchanged.

2. Subsection (b) is derived from Bankruptcy Code §§ 550(a), (b) (1984). The value of the asset transferred is limited to the value of the levyable interest of the transferor, exclusive of any interest encumbered by a valid lien. See § 1(2).

The requirement of Bankruptcy Code § 550(b)(1) (1984) that a transferee be "without knowledge of the voidability of the transfer" in order to be protected has been omitted as inappropriate. Knowledge of the facts rendering the transfer voidable would be inconsistent with the good faith that is required of a protected transferee. Knowledge of the voidability of a transfer would seem to involve a legal conclusion. Determination of the voidability of the transfer ought not to require the court to inquire into the legal sophistication of the transferee.

A transfer of property by the transferee of a voidable transfer might, on appropriate facts, be avoidable for reasons independent of the original voidable transfer. In such a case the subsequent transferee may be entitled to a defense under § 8(b) to an action based on the original voidable transfer, but that defense would not apply to an action based on the subsequent transfer that is independently voidable. For example, suppose that X transfers property to Y in a transfer voidable under this Act, and that Y later transfers the property to Z, who is a good-faith transferee for value. In general, C-1, a creditor of X, would have the right to a money judgment against Y pursuant to § 8(b), but C-1 could not recover under this Act from Z, who would be protected by § 8(b)(1)(ii)(A). However, it might be the case that Y's transfer to Z is independently voidable as to Y's creditors (including C-1, as creditor of Y by dint of its rights under this Act). Such might be the case if, for example, the value received by Y in exchange for the transfer is not reasonably equivalent and Y is in financial distress, or if Y made the transfer with intent to hinder, delay, or defraud any of its creditors. In such a case creditors of Y may pursue remedies against Z with respect to that independently voidable transfer, and the defense afforded to Z by § 8(b)(1)(ii)(A) would not apply to that action. Of course choice of law must be considered in such a situation: the jurisdiction whose law governs the voidability of the original transfer from X to Y and the consequent liability of Y and subsequent transferees need not be the same as the jurisdiction whose law governs the voidability of the independently voidable transfer from Y to Z and the consequent liability of Z and subsequent transferees.

3. Subsection (c) has no analogue in Bankruptcy Code § 550(a), (b) (1984). The measure of the recovery of a creditor against a transferee is usually limited to the value of the asset transferred at the time of the transfer. See, e.g., United States v. Fernon, 640 F.2d 609, 611 (5th Cir. 1981); Hamilton Nat'l Bank of Boston v. Halstead, 134 N.Y. 520, 31 N.E. 900 (1892); cf. Buffum v. Peter Barceloux Co., 289 U.S. 227 (1932) (transferee's objection to trial court's award of highest value of asset between the date of the transfer and the date of the decree of avoidance rejected because an award measured by value as of time of the transfer plus interest from that date would have been larger). The premise of § 8(c) is that changes in value of the asset transferred that occur after the transfer should ordinarily not affect the amount of the creditor's recovery. Circumstances may require a departure from that measure of the recovery, however, as the cases decided under the Uniform Fraudulent Conveyance Act and other laws derived from the Statute of 13 Elizabeth illustrate. Thus, if the value of the asset at the time of levy and sale to enforce the judgment of the creditor has been enhanced by improvements of the asset transferred or discharge of liens on the property, a good-faith transferee should be reimbursed for the outlay for such a purpose to the extent the sale proceeds were increased thereby. See Bankruptcy Code § 550(d) (1984); Janson v. Schier, 375 A.2d 1159, 1160 (N.H. 1977); Anno., 8 A.L.R. 527 (1920). If the value of the asset at the time of the transfer has been diminished by severance and disposition of timber or minerals or fixtures, the transferee should be liable for the amount of the resulting reduction. See Damazo v. Wahby, 269 Md. 252, 257, 305 A.2d 138, 142 (1973). If the transferee has collected rents, harvested crops, or derived other income from the use or occupancy of the asset after the transfer, the liability of the transferee should be limited in any event to the net income after deduction of the expense incurred in earning the income. Anno., 60 A.L.R.2d 593 (1958). On the other hand, adjustment for the equities does not warrant an award to the creditor of consequential damages alleged to accrue from mismanagement of the asset after the transfer.

4. Subsection (d) is an adaptation of Bankruptcy Code § 548(c) (1984). An insider that receives property or an obligation from an insolvent debtor as security for or in satisfaction of an antecedent debt of the transferor or obligor is not a good-faith transferee or obligee if the insider has reasonable cause to believe that the debtor was insolvent at the time the transfer was made or the obligation was incurred. If a foreclosure sale is voidable and does not qualify for the benefit of § 3(b) or § 8(e)(2) because it was not conducted in accordance with the requirements of applicable law, the buyer, if in good faith, will still be entitled to the benefit of subsection (d) to the extent of the price paid by the buyer.

5. Subsection (e)(1) rejects the rule adopted in Darby v. Atkinson (In re Farris), 415 F.Supp. 33, 39-41 (W.D.Okla. 1976), that termination of a lease on default in accordance with its terms and applicable law may constitute a voidable transfer.

Subsection (e)(2) protects a transferee that acquires a debtor's interest in an asset as a result of the enforcement by a secured party (which may but need not be the transferee) of rights pursuant to and in compliance with the provisions of Part 6 of Article 9 of the Uniform Commercial Code. Cf. Calaiaro v. Pittsburgh Nat'l Bank (In re Ewing), 33 B.R. 288, 9

C.B.C.2d 526, CCH B.L.R. ¶ 69,460 (Bankr. W.D.Pa. 1983) (sale of pledged stock held subject to avoidance under § 548 of the Bankruptcy Code), rev'd, 36 B.R. 476 (W.D.Pa. 1984) (transfer held not voidable because deemed to have occurred more than one year before bankruptcy petition filed). The global requirement of Article 9 that the secured party enforce its rights in good faith, and the further requirement of Article 9 that certain remedies be conducted in a commercially reasonable manner, provide substantial protection to the other creditors of the debtor. See U.C.C. §§ 1-304, 9-607(b), 9-610(b) (2014). The exemption afforded by subsection (e)(2) does not extend to acceptance of collateral in full or partial satisfaction of the obligations it secures. That remedy, contemplated by U.C.C. §§ 9-620–9-622 (2014), is sometimes referred to as "strict foreclosure." An exemption for strict foreclosure is inappropriate because compliance with the rules of Article 9 relating to strict foreclosure may not sufficiently protect the interests of the debtor's other creditors if the debtor does not act to protect equity the debtor may have in the asset.

6. Subsection (f) provides additional defenses against the avoidance of a preferential transfer to an insider under § 5(b).

Paragraph (1) is adapted from Bankruptcy Code § 547(c)(4) (1984), which permits a preferred creditor to set off the amount of new value subsequently advanced against the recovery of a voidable preference by a trustee in bankruptcy to the debtor without security. The new value may consist not only of money, goods, or services delivered on unsecured credit but also of the release of a valid lien. See, e.g., In re Ira Haupt & Co., 424 F.2d 722, 724 (2d Cir. 1970); Baranow v. Gibraltor Factors Corp. (In re Hygrade Envelope Co.), 393 F.2d 60, 65-67 (2d Cir.), cert. denied, 393 U.S. 837 (1968); In re John Morrow & Co., 134 F. 686, 688 (S.D.Ohio 1901). It does not include an obligation substituted for a prior obligation. If the insider receiving the preference thereafter extends new credit to the debtor but also takes security from the debtor, the injury to the other creditors resulting from the preference remains undiminished by the new credit. On the other hand, if a lien taken to secure the new credit is itself voidable by a judicial lien creditor of the debtor, the new value received by the debtor may appropriately be treated as unsecured and applied to reduce the liability of the insider for the preferential transfer.

Paragraph (2) is derived from Bankruptcy Code § 547(c)(2) (1984), which excepts certain payments made in the ordinary course of business or financial affairs from avoidance by the trustee in bankruptcy as preferential transfers. Whether a transfer was in the "ordinary course" requires a consideration of the pattern of payments or secured transactions engaged in by the debtor and the insider prior to the transfer challenged under § 5(b). See Tait & Williams, Bankruptcy Preference Laws: The Scope of Section 547(c)(2), 99 Banking L.J. 55, 63-66 (1982). The defense provided by paragraph (2) is available, irrespective of whether the debtor or the insider or both are engaged in business, but the prior conduct or practice of both the debtor and the insider-transferee are relevant.

Paragraph (3) has no analogue in Bankruptcy Code § 547 (1984). It reflects a policy judgment that an insider who has previously extended credit to a debtor should not be deterred from extending further credit to the debtor in a good-faith effort to save the debtor from a forced liquidation in bankruptcy or otherwise. A similar rationale has sustained the taking of security from an insolvent debtor for an advance to enable the debtor to stave off bankruptcy and extricate itself from financial stringency. Blackman v. Bechtel, 80 F.2d 505, 508-09 (8th Cir. 1935); Olive v. Tyler (In re Chelan Land Co.), 257 F. 497, 5 A.L.R. 561 (9th Cir. 1919); In re Robin Bros. Bakeries, Inc., 22 F.Supp. 662, 663-64 (N.D.Ill. 1937); see Dean v. Davis, 242 U.S. 438, 444 (1917). The amount of the present value given, the size of the antecedent debt secured, and the likelihood of success for the rehabilitative effort are relevant considerations in determining whether the transfer was in good faith.

7. Subsections (g) and (h) were added in 2014. Sections 2(b), 4(c), 5(c), 8(g), and 8(h) together provide uniform rules on burdens and standards of proof relating to the operation of this Act. The principles stated in Comment 11 to § 4 apply to subsections (g) and (h).

8. The provisions of § 8 are integral elements of the rights created by this Act. Accordingly, they should apply if this Act is invoked in a bankruptcy proceeding pursuant to Bankruptcy Code § 544(b) (2014). That follows from the fundamental principle that property rights in bankruptcy should be the same as outside bankruptcy, unless a federal interest compels a different result. See Butner v. United States, 440 U.S. 48, 55 (1979). Section 8(b) limits damages under this Act to the amount of the plaintiff creditor's claim, and that limitation is overridden in bankruptcy by the rule of Moore v. Bay, 284 U.S. 4 (1931), which Congress unmistakably maintained

when it enacted the Bankruptcy Code. In the absence of a clear override by the Bankruptcy Code or other federal law, however, other aspects of § 8 should apply if this Act is invoked in bankruptcy. See, e.g., Decker v. Tramiel (In re JTS Corp.), 617 F.3d 1102, 1110-16 (9th Cir. 2010) (holding that § 8(d) applies to a claim for relief brought under this Act in a bankruptcy proceeding pursuant to Bankruptcy Code § 544(b)).

§ 9. Extinguishment of Claim for Relief.

A claim for relief with respect to a transfer or obligation under this [Act] is extinguished unless action is brought:

(a) under Section 4(a)(1), not later than four years after the transfer was made or the obligation was incurred or, if later, not later than one year after the transfer or obligation was or could reasonably have been discovered by the claimant;

(b) under Section 4(a)(2) or 5(a), not later than four years after the transfer was made or the obligation was incurred; or

(c) under Section 5(b), not later than one year after the transfer was made.

Comment

1. This section had no analogue in the Uniform Fraudulent Conveyance Act. Its purpose is to make clear that lapse of the statutory periods prescribed by the section bars the right and not merely the remedy. The section rejects the rule applied in United States v. Gleneagles Inv. Co., 565 F.Supp. 556, 583 (M.D.Pa. 1983) (state statute of limitations held not to apply to action by United States based on Uniform Fraudulent Conveyance Act). Another consequence of barring the right and not merely the remedy is that, under Restatement (Second) of Conflict of Laws § 143 (1971), if an action is brought in jurisdiction A and the action is determined to be governed by this Act as enacted in jurisdiction B, the action cannot be maintained if it is time-barred in jurisdiction B. The 1988 revision of §§ 142 and 143 of the Restatement (Second) of Conflict of Laws, which eliminated the right/remedy distinction, should not be applied to this Act. Because a voidable transfer or obligation may injure all of a debtor's many creditors, there is need for a uniform and predictable cutoff time.

2. Statutes of limitations applicable to the avoidance of transfers and obligations vary widely from state to state and are frequently subject to uncertainties in their application. See Hesson, The Statute of Limitations in Actions to Set Aside Fraudulent Conveyances and in Actions Against Directors by Creditors of Corporations, 32 Cornell L.Q. 222 (1946); Annos., 76 A.L.R. 864 (1932), 128 A.L.R. 1289 (1940), 133 A.L.R. 1311 (1941), 14 A.L.R.2d 598 (1950), and 100 A.L.R.2d 1094 (1965). Together with § 6, this section should mitigate the uncertainty and diversity that have characterized the decisions applying statutes of limitations to actions to avoid transfers and obligations. The periods prescribed apply, whether the action under this Act is brought by a creditor or by a purchaser at a sale on execution levied pursuant to § 7(b) and whether the action is brought against the original transferee or subsequent transferee. The prescription of statutory periods of limitation does not preclude the barring of an avoidance action for laches. See § 12 and the accompanying Comment.

3. Subsection (a) provides that the four-year period ordinarily applicable to a claim for relief under § 4(a)(1) is extended to "one year after the transfer or obligation was or could reasonably have been discovered by the claimant." Antecedents to that "discovery rule" have long existed in common law and in other statutes, and courts may take different approaches to filling out the meaning of subsection (a) by reference to such precedents. Thus, subsection (a) literally starts the one-year period when the transfer was or could reasonably have been discovered by the claimant, but cases applying subsection (a) have held that the period starts only when the transfer and its wrongful nature were or could reasonably have been discovered. See, e.g., Freitag v. McGhie, 947 P.2d 1186 (Wash. 1997); State Farm Mut. Auto. Ins. Co. v. Cordua, 834 F.Supp.2d 301, 306-08 (E.D. Pa. 2011). A recurring situation to which that distinction may be relevant is Spouse X's transfer of assets beyond the reach of creditors, made in anticipation of divorcing Spouse Y after the four-year period has elapsed and made for the purpose of thwarting Spouse Y's economic interests in the divorce. Spouse Y may well know of the transfer long before Spouse Y learns its wrongful purpose. Of course, even if the period specified in subsection (a) is held to have lapsed in a given case, law other than this Act might

allow the transferred assets to be considered in making a division of assets in the ensuing divorce case.

§ 10. Governing Law.

(a) In this section, the following rules determine a debtor's location:

(1) A debtor who is an individual is located at the individual's principal residence.

(2) A debtor that is an organization and has only one place of business is located at its place of business.

(3) A debtor that is an organization and has more than one place of business is located at its chief executive office.

(b) A claim for relief in the nature of a claim for relief under this [Act] is governed by the local law of the jurisdiction in which the debtor is located when the transfer is made or the obligation is incurred.

Comment

1. Section 10, added in 2014, is a simple and predictable choice of law rule applicable to claims for relief of the nature governed by the Act. It provides that a claim for relief in the nature of a claim for relief under the Act is governed by the local law of the jurisdiction in which the debtor is "located" at the time the challenged transfer is made or the challenged obligation is incurred. "Local" law means the substantive law of the referenced jurisdiction, and not its choice of law rules. Section 6 determines the time at which a transfer is made or obligation is incurred for purposes of the Act, including this section. Section 10 applies equally to a candidate jurisdiction that is a sister state and to a candidate jurisdiction that is a foreign nation.

Basing choice of law on the location of the debtor is analogous to the rule set forth in U.C.C. § 9-301 (2014), which provides that the priority of a security interest in intangible property is generally governed by the local law of the jurisdiction in which the debtor is located. The analogy is apt, because the substantive rules of this Act are a species of priority rule, in that they determine the circumstances in which a debtor's creditors, rather than the debtor's transferee, have superior rights in property transferred by the debtor. In keeping with that analogy, the definition of the debtor's "location" in subsection (a) is identical to the baseline definition of that term in U.C.C. § 9-307(b) (2014). Subsection (a) does not include any of the exceptions to the baseline definition that are set forth in Article 9 of the Uniform Commercial Code, such as U.C.C. § 9-307(e) (2014) (providing that the location of a domestic corporation or other "registered organization" is its jurisdiction of organization), and

U.C.C. § 9-307(c) (2014) (providing in effect that if the baseline definition would locate a debtor in a jurisdiction that lacks an Article 9-style filing system, then the debtor is instead located in the District of Columbia). Those exceptions are not included in subsection (a) because their primary purpose relates to the operation of Article 9's perfection rules, which have no analogue in this Act.

2. The choice of law rule set forth in § 10(b) applies to any claim for relief in the nature of a claim for relief under this Act—in other words, any claim for relief sufficiently similar to a claim for relief under this Act as to warrant the application of this Act's choice of law rule. "This Act" of course refers to the enactment of this Act that is in force in the jurisdiction whose enactment of § 10(b) is being applied. Section 10(b) could not properly have been written to apply merely to "a claim for relief under this Act," for such a formulation would presuppose the applicability of the substantive provisions of this Act as in force in that jurisdiction. If a question should arise as to whether a given claim for relief is sufficiently similar to a claim for relief under this Act that § 10(b) should apply to it, the answer is left to judicial determination.

3. As used in subsection (a), the terms "principal residence," "place of business," and "chief executive office" are to be evaluated on the basis of authentic and sustained activity, not on the basis of manipulations employed to establish a location artificially (e.g., by such means as establishing a notional "chief executive office" by use of straw-man officers or directors in a jurisdiction in which creditors' rights are substantially debased, or establishing a notional "principal residence" for a

short term in such a jurisdiction for the purpose of making an asset transfer while there). Notwithstanding the adaptation of subsection (a) from U.C.C. § 9-307(b) (2014), the foregoing terms need not necessarily have the same meanings in both statutes. Debtors are likely to have greater incentive and ability to employ "asset tourism" for the purpose of seeking to evade the substantive rules of this Act than for the purpose of seeking to manipulate the perfection and priority rules of secured transactions law. Interpretation and application of this Act should so recognize.

4. "Location" under this Act is completely independent from the concept of "center of main interests" ("COMI"), as that term is used in Chapter 15 of the Bankruptcy Code. Chapter 15, which applies to transnational insolvency proceedings, requires United States courts to defer in various ways to a foreign proceeding in the jurisdiction of the debtor's COMI. Those consequences are quite different from the consequences of "location" under this Act. Furthermore, if the debtor is an organization, the debtor's jurisdiction of organization has no bearing on the debtor's "location" under subsection (a), by contrast to the presumption in Bankruptcy Code § 1516(c) (2014) that the jurisdiction in which the debtor has its registered office (i.e., its jurisdiction of organization) is its COMI.

5. Section 10(b) determines the governing law only for a claim for relief in the nature of a claim for relief under this Act. Furthermore, this Act, like the earlier Uniform Fraudulent Conveyance Act, has never purported to be an exclusive law on the subject of voidable transfers and obligations. See Comment 2 to § 15. Accordingly, the choice of law rule set forth in this § 10 is by no means applicable to all assertions that a transfer was made or an obligation incurred in contravention of law.

For example, suppose that the principal residence of Spouse X is State A and the principal residence of Spouse Y is State B. Spouse Y, anticipating a future divorce, transfers assets to Transferee for the purpose of thwarting X's economic interests in the divorce. Later a divorce action between X and Y is properly brought in the courts of State A, which has enacted this Act. Law other than this Act (presumably the family law of State A) will govern such matters as the classification of the transferred property as marital or separate and the remedies available against Y for wrongful dissipation of assets, such as awarding a larger share of marital property to X or imposing a lien on the separate property of Y. The choice of law rule set forth in § 10 does not apply to those matters, for they do not involve a claim for relief in the nature of a claim for relief under this Act. However, if Transferee is subject to personal jurisdiction in State A and X brings an action in State A against Transferee seeking avoidance of the transfer, or a money judgment against Transferee in lieu of avoidance, on the ground that the transfer had been made by Y with intent to hinder, delay, or defraud X, the choice of law rule set forth in § 10 would apply to that action, and as a result that action would be governed by the voidable transfer law of State B.

§ 11. Application to Series Organization.

(a) In this section:

(1) "Protected series" means an arrangement, however denominated, created by a series organization that, pursuant to the law under which the series organization is organized, has the characteristics set forth in paragraph (2).

(2) "Series organization" means an organization that, pursuant to the law under which it is organized, has the following characteristics:

(i) The organic record of the organization provides for creation by the organization of one or more protected series, however denominated, with respect to specified property of the organization, and for records to be maintained for each protected series that identify the property of or associated with the protected series.

(ii) Debt incurred or existing with respect to the activities of, or property of or associated with, a particular protected series is enforceable against the property of or associated with the protected series only, and not against the property of or associated with the organization or other protected series of the organization.

(iii) Debt incurred or existing with respect to the activities or property of the organization is enforceable against the property of the organization only, and not against the property of or associated with a protected series of the organization.

(b) A series organization and each protected series of the organization is a separate person for purposes of this [Act], even if for other purposes a protected series is not a person separate from the organization or other protected series of the organization.

Legislative Note: This section should be enacted even if the enacting jurisdiction does not itself have legislation enabling the creation of protected series. For example, in such an enacting jurisdiction this section will apply if a protected series of a series organization organized under the law of a different jurisdiction makes a transfer to another protected series of that organization and, under applicable choice of law rules, the voidability of the transfer is governed by the law of the enacting jurisdiction.

Comment

This section, added in 2014, accommodates developments in business organization statutes exemplified by the Uniform Statutory Trust Entity Act §§ 401-404 (2009) and Del. Code Ann. tit. 6, § 18-215 (2012) (pertaining to Delaware limited liability companies). The definition of "series organization" in subsection (a)(2) is adapted from §§ 401-402 of the Uniform Statutory Trust Entity Act. If the statute under which an organization is organized permits it to divide its assets and debts among "protected series" (however denominated), such that assets and debts of, or associated with, each "protected series" are separated in accordance with subsections (a)(2)(ii) and (iii), and if the organization does so, then the provisions of this Act apply to each "protected series" as if it were a legal entity, regardless of whether it is considered to be a legal entity for other purposes. The conditions referred to in subsections (a)(2)(ii) and (iii) are satisfied if the law under which the organization is organized so provides. It does not matter whether the separation of assets and debts described in subsections (a)(2)(ii) and (iii) would be respected by another jurisdiction in which the organization does business, or would be given effect by the Bankruptcy Code in the bankruptcy of the organization. An organization may be a "series organization" having "protected series," as those terms are used in this section, even though the statute under which the organization is organized uses different terminology. This section uses the term "protected series," which is not used in either the Uniform Statutory Trust Entity Act or the Delaware provisions cited above, to emphasize that the application of this section does not depend upon the terminology used by the applicable statute.

The addition of this section to the Act does not imply any judgment about the desirability of legislation enabling the creation of protected series.

§ 12. Supplementary Provisions.

§ 12. Supplementary Provisions. Unless displaced by the provisions of this [Act], the principles of law and equity, including the law merchant and the law relating to principal and agent, estoppel, laches, fraud, misrepresentation, duress, coercion, mistake, insolvency, or other validating or invalidating cause, supplement its provisions.

Comment

This section is derived from § 11 of the Uniform Fraudulent Conveyance Act and Uniform Commercial Code § 1-103 (1984) (later § 1-103(b) (2014)). The section adds a reference to "laches" in recognition of the particular appropriateness of the application of this equitable doctrine to an untimely action to avoid a transfer under this Act. See Louis Dreyfus Corp. v. Butler, 496 F.2d 806, 808 (6th Cir. 1974) (action to avoid transfers to debtor's wife when debtor was engaged in speculative business held to be barred by laches or applicable statutes of limitations); Cooch v. Grier, 30 Del.Ch. 255, 265-66, 59 A.2d 282, 287-88 (1948) (action under the Uniform Fraudulent Conveyance Act held barred by laches when the creditor was chargeable with inexcusable delay and the defendant was prejudiced by the delay).

§ 13. Uniformity of Application and Construction. This [Act] shall be applied and construed to effectuate its general purpose to make uniform the law with respect to the subject of this [Act] among states enacting it.

§ 14. Relation to Electronic Signatures in Global and National Commerce Act. This [Act] modifies, limits, or superseded the Electronic Signatures in Global and National Commerce Act, 15 U.S.C. Section 7001 et seq., but does not modify, limit, or supersede Section 101(c) of that act, 15 Section 7001(c), or authorize electronic delivery of any of the notices described in Section 103(b) of that act, 15 U.S.C. 7003(b).

§ 15. Short Title. This [Act], which was formerly cited as the Uniform Fraudulent Transfer Act, may be cited as the Uniform Voidable Transactions Act.

Comment

1. The 2014 amendments change the short title of the Act from "Uniform Fraudulent Transfer Act" to "Uniform Voidable Transactions Act." The change of title is not intended to effect any change in the meaning of the Act. The retitling is not motivated by the substantive revisions made by the 2014 amendments, which are relatively minor. Rather, the word "Fraudulent" in the original title, though sanctioned by historical usage, was a misleading description of the Act as it was originally written. Fraud is not, and never has been, a necessary element of a claim for relief under the Act. The misleading intimation to the contrary in the original title of the Act led to confusion in the courts. See, e.g., § 4, Comment 10. The misleading insistence on "fraud" in the original title also contributed to the evolution of widely-used shorthand terminology that further tends to distort understanding of the provisions of the Act. Thus, several theories of recovery under the Act that have nothing whatever to do with fraud (or with intent of any sort) came to be widely known by the oxymoronic and confusing shorthand tag "constructive fraud." See §§ 4(a)(2), 5(a). Likewise, the primordial theory of recovery under the Act, set forth in § 4(a)(1), came to be widely known by the shorthand tag "actual fraud." That shorthand is misleading, because that provision does not in fact require proof of fraudulent intent. See § 4, Comment 8.

In addition, the word "Transfer" in the original title of the Act was underinclusive, because the Act applies to incurrence of obligations as well as to transfers of property.

2. The Act, like the earlier Uniform Fraudulent Conveyance Act, has never purported to be an exclusive law on the subject of voidable transfers and obligations. See Prefatory Note (1984), ¶5; § 1, Comment 2, ¶6; § 4, Comment 9, ¶1; § 10, Comment 5. It remains the case that the Act is not the exclusive law on the subject of voidable transfers and obligations.

3. The retitling of the Act should not be construed to affect references to the Act in other statutes or international instruments that use the former terminology. See, e.g., Convention on International Interests in Mobile Equipment, art. 30(a)(3), opened for signature Nov. 16, 2001, 49 S. Treaty Doc. No. 108-10 (referring to "any rules of law applicable in insolvency proceedings relating to the avoidance of a transaction as a ... transfer in fraud of creditors").

4. The 2014 amendments also make a correction to the text of the Act that is consonant with the change of the Act's title. As originally written, the Act inconsistently used different words to denote a transfer or obligation for which the Act provides a remedy: sometimes "voidable" (see original § 2(d), §§ 8(a), (d), (e), (f)), and sometimes "fraudulent" (see original § 4(a), §§ 5(a), (b), § 9). The amendments resolve that inconsistency by using "voidable" consistently or deleting the word as unnecessary. No change in meaning is intended.

5. The Act does not address the extent to which a person who facilitates the making of a transfer or the incurrence of an obligation that is voidable under the Act may be subject to liability for that reason, whether under a theory of aiding and abetting, civil conspiracy, or otherwise. The Act leaves that subject to supplementary principles of law. See § 12. Cf. § 8(b)(1)(i) (imposing liability upon, inter alia, "the person for whose benefit the transfer was made"). Other law also governs such matters as (i) the

circumstances in which a lawyer who assists a debtor in making a transfer or incurring an obligation that is voidable under the Act violates rules of professional conduct applicable to lawyers, (ii) the circumstances in which communications between the debtor and the lawyer in respect of such a transfer or obligation are excepted from attorney-client privilege, and (iii) the extent to which criminal sanctions apply to a debtor, transferee, obligee, or person who facilitates the making of a transfer or the incurrence of an obligation that is voidable under the Act. Neither the retitling of the Act, nor the consistent use of "voidable" in its text per Comment 4, effects any change in the meaning of the Act, and those amendments should not be construed to affect any of the foregoing matters.

§ 16. Repeals; Conforming Amendments.

    (a) ....

    (b) ....

    (c) ....

Comment

If enacted by this State, the Uniform Fraudulent Conveyance Act should be listed among the statutes repealed.

Legislative Note: *The legislation enacting the 2014 amendments in a jurisdiction in which the act is already in force should provide as follows: (i) the amendments apply to a transfer made or obligation incurred on or after the effective date of the enacting legislation, (ii) the amendments do not apply to a transfer made or obligation incurred before the effective date of the enacting legislation, (iii) the amendments do not apply to a right of action that has accrued before the effective date of the enacting legislation, and (iv) for the foregoing purposes a transfer is made and an obligation is incurred at the time provided in Section 6 of the act. In addition, the enacting legislation should revise any reference to the act by its former title in other permanent legislation of the enacting jurisdiction.*

UNIFORM TRANSFERS TO MINORS ACT
(1983, with 1986 Amendments)

Table of Sections

Prefatory Note

This Act revises and restates the Uniform Gifts to Minors Act (UGMA), one of the Conference's most successful products, some version of which has been enacted in every American jurisdiction.

The original version of UGMA was adopted by the Conference in 1956 and closely followed a model "Act concerning Gifts of Securities to Minors" which was sponsored by the New York Stock Exchange and the Association of Stock Exchange Firms and which had been adopted in 14 states. The 1956 version of UGMA broadened the model act to cover gifts of money as well as securities but made few other changes.

In 1965 and 1966 the Conference revised UGMA to expand the types of financial institutions which could serve as depositories of custodial funds, to facilitate the designation of successor custodians, and to add life insurance policies and annuity contracts to the types of property (cash and securities) that could be made the subject of a gift under the Act.

Not all states adopted the 1966 revisions; some 11 jurisdictions retained their versions of the 1956 Act. More importantly, however, many states since 1966 have substantially revised their versions of UGMA to expand the kinds of property that may be made the subject of a gift under the Act, and a few states permit transfers to custodians from other sources, such as trusts and estates, as well as lifetime gifts. As a result, a great deal of non-uniformity has arisen among the states. Uniformity in this area is important, for the Conference has cited UGMA as an example of an act designed to avoid conflicts of law when the laws of more than one state may apply to a transaction or a series of transactions.

This Act follows the expansive approach taken by several states and allows any kind of property, real or personal, tangible or intangible, to be made the subject of a transfer to a custodian for the benefit of a minor (SECTION 1(6)). In addition, it permits such transfers not only by lifetime outright gifts (SECTION 4), but also from trusts, estates and guardianships, whether or not specifically authorized in the governing instrument (SECTIONS 5 and 6), and from other third parties indebted to a minor who does not have a conservator, such as parties against whom a minor has a tort claim or judgment, and depository institutions holding deposits or insurance companies issuing policies payable on death to a minor (SECTION 7). For this reason, and to distinguish the enactment of this statute from the 1956 and 1966 versions of UGMA, the title of the Act has been changed to refer to "Transfers" rather than to "Gifts," a much narrower term.

As so expanded, the Act might be considered a statutory form of trust or guardianship that continues until the minor reaches 21. Note, however, that unlike a trust, a custodianship is not a separate legal entity or taxpayer. Under SECTION 11(b) of this Act, the custodial property is indefeasibly vested in the minor, not the custodian, and thus any income received is attributable to and reportable by the minor, whether or not actually distributed to the minor.

The expansion of the Act to permit transfers of any kind of property to a custodian creates a significant problem of potential personal liability for the minor or the custodian arising from the ownership of property such as real estate, automobiles, general partnership interests, and business proprietorships.

This problem did not exist under UGMA under which custodial property was limited to bank deposits, securities and insurance. In response, SECTION 17 of this Act generally limits the claims of third parties to recourse against the custodial property, with the minor insulated against personal liability unless he is personally at fault. The custodian is similarly insulated unless he is personally at fault or fails to disclose his custodial capacity in entering into a contract.

Nevertheless, the Act should be used with caution with respect to property such as real estate or general partnership interests from which liabilities as well as benefits may arise. Many of the possible risks can and should be insured against, and the custodian has the power under SECTION 13(a) to purchase such insurance, at least when other custodial assets are sufficient to do so. If the assets are not sufficient, there is doubt that a custodian will act, or there are significant uninsurable risks, a transferor should consider a trust with spendthrift provisions, such as a minority trust under Section 2503(c), IRC, rather than a custodianship, to make a gift of such property to a minor.

The Act retains (or reverts to) 21 as the age of majority or, more accurately, the age at which the custodianship terminates and the property is distributed. Since tax law permits duration of Section 2503(c) trusts to 21, even though the statutory age of majority is 18 in most states, this age should be retained since most donors and other transferors wish to preserve a custodianship as long as possible.

Finally, the Act restates and rearranges, rather than amends, the 1966 Act. The addition of other forms of property and other forms of dispositions made adherence to the format and language of the prior act very unwieldy. In addition, the 1966 and 1956 Acts closely followed the language of the earlier model act, which had already been adopted in several states, even though it did not conform to Conference style. It is hoped that this rewriting and revision of UGMA will improve its clarity while also expanding its coverage.

§ 1. Definitions. In this [Act]:

(1) "Adult" means an individual who has attained the age of 21 years.

(2) "Benefit plan" means an employer's plan for the benefit of an employee or partner.

(3) "Broker" means a person lawfully engaged in the business of effecting transactions in securities or commodities for the person's own account or for the account of others.

(4) "Conservator" means a person appointed or qualified by a court to act as general, limited, or temporary guardian of a minor's property or a person legally authorized to perform substantially the

same functions.

(5) "Court" means [_____ court].

(6) "Custodial property" means (i) any interest in property transferred to a custodian under this [Act] and (ii) the income from and proceeds of that interest in property.

(7) "Custodian" means a person so designated under Section 9 or a successor or substitute custodian designated under Section 18.

(8) "Financial institution" means a bank, trust company, savings institution, or credit union, chartered and supervised under state or federal law.

(9) "Legal representative" means an individual's personal representative or conservator.

(10) "Member of the minor's family" means the minor's parent, stepparent, spouse, grandparent, brother, sister, uncle, or aunt, whether of the whole or half blood or by adoption.

(11) "Minor" means an individual who has not attained the age of 21 years.

(12) "Person" means an individual, corporation, organization, or other legal entity.

(13) "Personal representative" means an executor, administrator, successor personal representative, or special administrator of a decedent's estate or a person legally authorized to perform substantially the same functions.

(14) "State" includes any state of the United States, the District of Columbia, the Commonwealth of Puerto Rico, and any territory or possession subject to the legislative authority of the United States.

(15) "Transfer" means a transaction that creates custodial property under Section 9.

(16) "Transferor" means a person who makes a transfer under this [Act].

(17) "Trust company" means a financial institution, corporation, or other legal entity, authorized to exercise general trust powers.

Comment

To reflect the broader scope and the unlimited types of property to which the new Act will apply, a number of definitional changes have been made from the 1966 Act. In addition, several definitions specifically applicable to the limited types of property (cash, securities and insurance policies) subject to the 1966 Act have been eliminated as unnecessary. These include the definitions of "bank," "issuer," "life insurance policy or annuity contract," "security," and "transfer agent." No change in the meaning or construction of these terms as used in this Act is intended by such deletions.

The definitions of "domestic financial institution" and "insured financial institution" have been eliminated because few if any states limit deposits by custodians to local institutions, and the prudent person rule of SECTION 12(b) of this Act may dictate the use of insured institutions as depositories, without having the Act so specify.

The principal changes or additions to the remaining definitions are discussed below.

Paragraph (2). The definition of "benefit plan" is intentionally very broad and is meant to cover any contract, plan, system, account or trust such as a pension plan, retirement plan, death benefit plan, deferred compensation plan, employment agency arrangement or, stock bonus, option or profit sharing plan.

Paragraph (4). The term "conservator" rather than "guardian of the estate" has been employed in the Act to conform to Uniform Probate Code terminology. The term includes a guardian of the minor's property, whether general, limited or temporary, and includes a committee, tutor, or curator of the minor's property.

Paragraph (6). The definition of "custodial property" has been generalized and expanded to encompass every conceivable legal or equitable interest in property of any kind, including real estate and tangible or intangible personal property. The term is intended, for example, to include joint interests with right of survivorship, beneficial interests in land trusts, as well as all other intangible interests in property. Contingent or expectancy interests such as the designation as a beneficiary under insurance policies or benefit plans become "custodial property" only if the designation is irrevocable, or when it becomes so, but the Act specifically authorizes the "nomination" of a future custodian as beneficiary of such interests (see SECTION 3). Proceeds of custodial property, both immediate and remote, are themselves custodial property, as is the case under UGMA.

Custodial property is defined without reference to the physical location of the property, even if it has one. No useful purpose would be served by restricting the application of the Act to, for example, real estate "located in this state," since a conveyance recorded in the state of the property's location, if done with proper formalities, should be effective even if that state has not enacted this Act. The rights, duties and powers of the custodian should be determined by reference to the law of the state under which the custodianship is created, assuming there is sufficient nexus under SECTION 2 between that state and the transferor, the minor or the custodian.

Paragraph (11). This definition of "minor" retains the historical age of 21 as the age of majority, even though most states have lowered the age for most other purposes, as well as in their versions of the 1966 Act. Nevertheless, because the Internal Revenue Code continues to permit "minority trusts" under Section 2503(c), IRC, to continue in effect until age 21, and because it is believed that most donors creating minority trusts or custodianships prefer to retain the property under management for the benefit of the young person as long as possible, it is strongly suggested that the age of 21 be retained as the age of majority under this Act. For states that have reduced the age of majority in their versions of the 1966 Act,

SECTION 22(c) of this Act provides that a change back to 21 will not affect custodianships that have already terminated at an earlier age.

Paragraph (13). The definition of the term "personal representative" is based upon that definition in Sec. 1-201(30) of the Uniform Probate Code.

Paragraph (15). The new definition of "transfer" is necessary to reflect the application of the Act not only to gifts, but also to distributions from trusts and estates, obligors of the minor, and transfers of the minor's own assets to a custodianship by the legal representative of a minor, all of which are now permitted by this Act.

Paragraph (16). The new definition of "transferor" is required because the term includes not only the maker of a gift, i.e., a donor in the usual sense, but also fiduciaries and obligors who control or own property that is the subject of the transfer. Nothing in this Act requires that a transferor be an "adult." If permitted under other law of the enacting state relating to emancipation or competence to make a will, gift, or other transfer, a minor may make an effective transfer of property to a custodian for his benefit or for the benefit of another minor.

Paragraph (17). Only entities authorized to exercise "general" trust powers qualify as "trust companies"; that is, the authority to exercise only limited fiduciary responsibilities, such as the authority to accept Individual Retirement Account deposits, is not sufficient.

§ 2. Scope and Jurisdiction.

(a) This [Act] applies to a transfer that refers to this [Act] in the designation under Section 9(a) by which the transfer is made if at the time of the transfer, the transferor, the minor, or the custodian is a resident of this State or the custodial property is located in this State. The custodianship so created remains subject to this [Act] despite a subsequent change in residence of a transferor, the minor, or the custodian, or the removal of custodial property from this State.

(b) A person designated as custodian under this [Act] is subject to personal jurisdiction in this State with respect to any matter relating to the custodianship.

(c) A transfer that purports to be made and which is valid under the Uniform Transfers to Minors Act, the Uniform Gifts to Minors Act, or a substantially similar act, of another state is governed by the law of the designated state and may be executed and is enforceable in this State if at the time of the transfer, the transferor, the minor, or the custodian is a resident of the designated state or the custodial property is located in the designated state.

Comment

This section has no counterpart in the 1966 Act. It attempts to resolve uncertainties and conflicts-of-laws questions that have frequently arisen because of the present non-uniformity of UGMA in the various states and which may continue to arise during the transition from UGMA to this Act.

The creation of a custodianship must invoke the law of a particular state because of the form of the transfer required under SECTION 9(a). This section provides that a choice of the UTMA of the enacting state is appropriate and effective if any of the nexus factors specified in subsection (a) exists at the time of the transfer. This Act continues to govern, and subsection (b) makes the custodian accountable and subject to personal jurisdiction in the courts of the enacting state for the duration of the custodianship, despite subsequent relocation of the parties or the property.

Subsection (c) recognizes that residents of the enacting state may elect to have the law of another state apply to a transfer. That choice is valid if a nexus with the chosen state exists at the time of the transfer. If personal jurisdiction can be obtained in the enacting state under other law apart from this Act, the custodianship may be enforced in its courts, which are directed to apply the law of the state elected by the transferor.

If the choice of law under subsection (a) or (c) is ineffective because of the absence of the required nexus, the transfer may still be effective under the Act of another state with which a nexus does exist. See SECTION 21.

§ 3. Nomination of Custodian.

(a) A person having the right to designate the recipient of property transferable upon the occurrence of a future event may revocably nominate a custodian to receive the property for a minor beneficiary upon the occurrence of the event by naming the custodian followed in substance by the words: "as custodian for _____ (name of minor) under the [name of Enacting State] Uniform Transfers to Minors Act." The nomination may name one or more persons as substitute custodians to whom the property must be transferred, in the order named, if the first nominated custodian dies before the transfer or is unable, declines, or is ineligible to serve. The nomination may be made in a will, a trust, a deed, an instrument exercising a power of appointment, or in a writing designating a beneficiary of contractual rights which is registered with or delivered to the payor, issuer, or other obligor of the contractual rights.

(b) A custodian nominated under this section must be a person to whom a transfer of property of that kind may be made under Section 9(a).

(c) The nomination of a custodian under this section does not create custodial property until the nominating instrument becomes irrevocable or a transfer to the nominated custodian is completed under Section 9. Unless the nomination of a custodian has been revoked, upon the occurrence of the future event the custodianship becomes effective and the custodian shall enforce a transfer of the custodial property pursuant to Section 9.

Comment

This section is new and permits a future custodian for a minor to be nominated to receive a distribution under a will or trust, or as a beneficiary of a power of appointment, or of contractual rights such as a life or endowment insurance policy, annuity contract, P.O.D. Account, benefit plan, or similar future payment right. Nomination of a future custodian does not constitute a "transfer" under this Act and does not create custodial property. If it did, the nomination and beneficiary designation would have to be permanent, since a "transfer" is irrevocable and indefeasibly vests ownership of the interest in the minor under SECTION 11(b).

Instead, this section permits a revocable beneficiary designation that takes effect only when the donor dies, or when a lifetime transfer to the custodian for the minor beneficiary occurs, such as a distribution under an inter vivos trust. However, an unrevoked nomination under this section is binding on a personal representative or trustee (see SECTION 5(b)) and on insurance companies and other obligors who contract to pay in the future (see SECTION 7(b)).

The person making the nomination may name

contingent or successive future custodians to serve, in the order named, in the event that the person first nominated dies, or is unable, declines, or is ineligible to serve. Such a substitute future custodian is a custodian "nominated ... under Section 3" to whom the transfer must be made under SECTIONS 5(b) and 7(b).

Any person nominated as future custodian may decline to serve before the transfer occurs and may resign at any time after the transfer. See SECTION 18.

§ 4. Transfer by Gift or Exercise of Power of Appointment. A person may make a transfer by irrevocable gift to, or the irrevocable exercise of a power of appointment in favor of, a custodian for the benefit of a minor pursuant to Section 9.

Comment

To emphasize the different kinds of transfers that create presently effective custodianships under this Act, they are separately described in SECTIONS 4, 5, 6 and 7. This section in part corresponds to Section 2(a) of the 1966 Act and covers the traditional lifetime gift that was the only kind of transfer authorized by the 1966 Act. It also covers an irrevocable exercise of a power of appointment in favor of a custodian, as distinguished from the exercise of a power in a revocable instrument that results only in the nomination of a future custodian under SECTION 3.

§ 5. Transfer Authorized by Will or Trust.

(a) A personal representative or trustee may make an irrevocable transfer pursuant to Section 9 to a custodian for the benefit of a minor as authorized in the governing will or trust.

(b) If the testator or settlor has nominated a custodian under Section 3 to receive the custodial property, the transfer must be made to that person.

(c) If the testator or settlor has not nominated a custodian under Section 3, or all persons so nominated as custodian die before the transfer or are unable, decline, or are ineligible to serve, the personal representative or the trustee, as the case may be, shall designate the custodian from among those eligible to serve as custodian for property of that kind under Section 9(a).

Comment

This section is new and has no counterpart in the 1966 Act. It is based on nonuniform provisions adopted by Connecticut, Illinois, Wisconsin and other states to validate distributions from trusts and estates to a custodian for a minor beneficiary, when the use of a custodian is expressly authorized by the governing instrument. It also covers the designation of the custodian whenever the settlor or testator fails to make a nomination, or the future custodian nominated under SECTION 3 (and any alternate named) fails to qualify.

§ 6. Other Transfer by Fiduciary.

(a) Subject to subsection (c), a personal representative or trustee may make an irrevocable transfer to another adult or trust company as custodian for the benefit of a minor pursuant to Section 9, in the absence of a will or under a will or trust that does not contain an authorization to do so.

(b) Subject to subsection (c), a conservator may make an irrevocable transfer to another adult or trust company as custodian for the benefit of the minor pursuant to Section 9.

(c) A transfer under subsection (a) or (b) may be made only if (i) the personal representative, trustee, or conservator considers the transfer to be in the best interest of the minor, (ii) the transfer is not prohibited by or inconsistent with provisions of the applicable will, trust agreement, or other governing instrument, and (iii) the transfer is authorized by the court if it exceeds [$10,000] in value.

Comment

This section is new and has no counterpart in the 1966 Act. It covers a new concept, already authorized by the law of some states through nonuniform amendments to the 1966 Act, to permit custodianships to be used as guardianship or conservator substitutes, even though not specifically authorized by the person whose property is the subject of the transfer. It also permits the legal representative of the minor, such as a conservator or guardian, to transfer the minor's own property to a new or existing custodianship for the purposes of convenience or economies of administration.

A custodianship may be created under this section even though not specifically authorized by the transferor, the testator, or the settlor of the trust if three tests are satisfied. First, the fiduciary making the transfer must determine in good faith and in his fiduciary capacity that a custodianship will be in the best interests of the minor. Second, a custodianship may not be prohibited by, or inconsistent with, the terms of any governing instrument. Inconsistent terms would include, for example, a spendthrift clause in a governing trust, provisions terminating a governing trust for the minor's benefit at a time other than the time of the minor's age of majority, and provisions for mandatory distributions of income or principal at specific times or periodic intervals. Provisions for other outright distributions or bequests would not be inconsistent with the creation of a custodianship under this section. Third, the amount of property transferred (as measured by its value) must be of such relatively small amount that the lack of court supervision and the typically stricter investment standards that would apply to the conservator otherwise required will not be important. However, if the property is of significant size, transfer to a custodian may still be made if the court approves and if the other two tests are met.

The custodianship created under this section without express authority in the governing instrument will terminate upon the minor's attainment of the statutory age of majority of the enacting state apart from this Act, i.e., at the same age a conservatorship of the minor would end. See SECTION 20(b) and the Comment thereto.

§ 7. Transfer by Obligor.

(a) Subject to subsections (b) and (c), a person not subject to Section 5 or 6 who holds property of or owes a liquidated debt to a minor not having a conservator may make an irrevocable transfer to a custodian for the benefit of the minor pursuant to Section 9.

(b) If a person having the right to do so under Section 3 has nominated a custodian under that section to receive the custodial property, the transfer must be made to that person.

(c) If no custodian has been nominated under Section 3, or all persons so nominated as custodian die before the transfer or are unable, decline, or are ineligible to serve, a transfer under this section may be made to an adult member of the minor's family or to a trust company unless the property exceeds [$10,000] in value.

Comment

This section is new and, like SECTION 6, permits a custodianship to be established as a substitute for a conservator to receive payments due a minor from sources other than estates, trusts, and existing guardianships covered by SECTIONS 5 and 6. For example, a tort judgment debtor of a minor, a bank holding a joint or P.O.D. account of which a minor is the surviving payee, or an insurance company holding life insurance policy or benefit plan proceeds payable to a minor may create a custodianship under this section.

Use of this section is mandatory when a future custodian has been nominated under SECTION 3 as a named beneficiary of an insurance policy, benefit plan, deposit account, or the like, because the original owner of the property specified a custodianship (and a future custodian) to receive the property. If that custodian (or any alternate named) is not available, if none was nominated, or none could have been nominated (as in the case of a tort judgment payable to the minor), this section is permissive and does not preclude the obligor from requiring the appointment of a conservator to receive payment. It allows the obligor to transfer to a custodian unless the property exceeds the stated value, in which case a conservator must be appointed to receive it.

§ 8. Receipt for Custodial Property. A written acknowledgment of delivery by a custodian constitutes a sufficient receipt and discharge for custodial property transferred to the custodian pursuant to this [Act].

Comment

This section discharges transferors from further responsibility for custodial property delivered to and receipted for by the custodian. See also SECTION 16 which protects transferors and other third parties dealing with custodians. Because a discharge or release for a donative transfer is not necessary, this section had no counterpart in the 1966 Act.

This section does not authorize an existing custodian, or a custodian to whom an obligor makes a transfer under SECTION 7, to settle or release a claim of the minor against a third party. Only a conservator, guardian ad litem or other person authorized under other law to act for the minor may release such a claim.

§ 9. Manner of Creating Custodial Property and Effecting Transfer; Designation of Initial Custodian; Control.

(a) Custodial property is created and a transfer is made whenever:

(1) an uncertificated security or a certificated security in registered form is either:

(i) registered in the name of the transferor, an adult other than the transferor, or a trust company, followed in substance by the words: "as custodian for _____ _____ (name of minor) under the [Name of Enacting State] Uniform Transfers to Minors Act"; or

(ii) delivered if in certificated form, or any document necessary for the transfer of an uncertificated security is delivered, together with any necessary endorsement to an adult other than the transferor or to a trust company as custodian, accompanied by an instrument in substantially the form set forth in subsection (b);

(2) money is paid or delivered, or a security held in the name of a broker, financial institution, or its nominee is transferred, to a broker or financial institution for credit to an account in the name of the transferor, an adult other than the transferor, or a trust company, followed in substance by the words: "as custodian for _____ __ (name of minor) under the [Name of Enacting State] Uniform Transfers to Minors Act";

(3) the ownership of a life or endowment insurance policy or annuity contract is either:

(i) registered with the issuer in the name of the transferor, an adult other than the transferor, or a trust company, followed in substance by the words: "as custodian for _____ _____ (name of minor) under the [Name of Enacting State] Uniform Transfers to Minors Act"; or

(ii) assigned in a writing delivered to an adult other than the transferor or to a trust company whose name in the assignment is followed in substance by the words: "as custodian for _____ (name of minor) under the [Name of Enacting State] Uniform Transfers to Minors Act";

(4) an irrevocable exercise of a power of appointment or an irrevocable present right to future payment under a contract is the subject of a written notification delivered to the payor, issuer, or other obligor that the right is transferred to the transferor, an adult other than the transferor, or a trust company, whose name in the notification is followed in substance by the words: "as custodian for _____ (name of minor) under the [Name of Enacting State] Uniform Transfers to Minors Act";

(5) an interest in real property is recorded in the name of the transferor, an adult other than the transferor, or a trust company, followed in substance by the words: "as custodian for _____ (name of minor) under the [Name of Enacting State] Uniform Transfers to

Minors Act";

(6) a certificate of title issued by a department or agency of a state or of the United States which evidences title to tangible personal property is either:

(i) issued in the name of the transferor, an adult other than the transferor, or a trust company, followed in substance by the words: "as custodian for _____ _____ (name of minor) under the [Name of Enacting State] Uniform Transfers to Minors Act"; or

(ii) delivered to an adult other than the transferor or to a trust company, endorsed to that person followed in substance by the words: "as custodian for _____ _____ (name of minor) under the [Name of Enacting State] Uniform Transfers to Minors Act"; or

(7) an interest in any property not described in paragraphs (1) through (6) is transferred to an adult other than the transferor or to a trust company by a written instrument in substantially the form set forth in subsection (b).

(b) An instrument in the following form satisfies the requirements of paragraphs (1)(ii) and (7) of subsection (a):

"TRANSFER UNDER THE [NAME OF ENACTING STATE]
UNIFORM TRANSFERS TO MINORS ACT

I, _____ (name of transferor or name and representative capacity if a fiduciary) hereby transfer to _____ (name of custodian), as custodian for _____
(name of minor) under the [Name of Enacting State] Uniform Transfers to Minors Act, the following: (insert a description of the custodial property sufficient to identify it).
Dated: _____

_____
(Signature)

_____ (name of custodian) acknowledges receipt of the property described above as custodian for the minor named above under the [Name of Enacting State] Uniform Transfers to Minors Act.
Dated: _____

_____
(Signature of Custodian)

(c) A transferor shall place the custodian in control of the custodial property as soon as practicable.

Comment

The 1966 Act contained optional bracketed language permitting an adopting state to limit the class of eligible initial custodians to an adult member of the minor's family or a guardian of the minor. This optional limitation has been deleted because it would preclude the use of an individual and uncompensated custodian if no qualified or willing family member is available.

Otherwise, with respect to transfers of securities, cash, and insurance or annuity contracts, this section tracks the cognate provisions of subsection 2(a) of the 1966 Act, with one exception. Under subsection (a)(1)(ii) of this section, a transfer of securities in registered form may be accomplished without registering the transfer in the name of the custodian so that transfers may be accomplished more expeditiously, and so that securities may be held by custodians in street name. In other words, subsection (a)(1)(i) is not the exclusive manner for making effective transfers of securities in registered form.

In addition, subsection (a) creates new procedures for handling the additional types of property now subject to the Act; specifically:

Paragraph (3) covers the irrevocable transfer of ownership of life and endowment insurance policies and annuity contracts.

Paragraph (4) covers the irrevocable exercise of a power of appointment and the irrevocable present assignment of future payment rights, such as royalties, interest and principal payments under a promissory note, or beneficial interests under life or endowment or annuity insurance contracts or benefit plans. The payor, issuer, or obligor may require additional formalities such as completion of a specific assignment form and an endorsement, but the transfer is effective upon delivery of the notification. See SECTION 3 and the Comment thereto for the procedure for revocably "nominating" a future custodian as a beneficiary of a power of appointment or such payment rights.

Paragraph (5) is the exclusive method for the transfer of real estate and includes a disposition effected by will. Under the law of those states in which a devise of real estate vests in the devisee without the need for a deed from the personal representative of the decedent, a document such as the will must still be "recorded" under this provision to make the transfer effective. For inter vivos transfers, of course, a conveyance in recordable form would be employed for dispositions of real estate to a custodian.

Paragraph (6) covers the transfer of personal property such as automobiles, aircraft, patent rights, and other property subject to registration of ownership with a state or federal agency. Either registration of the transfer in the name of the custodian or delivery of the endorsed certificate in registerable form makes the transfer effective.

Paragraph (7) is a residual classification, covering all property not otherwise covered in the preceding paragraphs. Examples would include nonregistered securities, partnership interests, and tangible personal property not subject to title certificates.

The form of transfer document recommended and set forth in subsection (b) contains an acceptance that must be executed by the custodian to make the disposition effective. While such a form of written acceptance is not specifically required in the case of registered securities under subsection (a)(1), money under (a)(2), insurance contracts or interests under (a)(3) or (4), real estate under (a)(5), or titled personal property under (a)(6), it is certainly the better and recommended practice to obtain the acknowledgment, consent, and acceptance of the

designated custodian on the instrument of transfer, or otherwise.

A transferor may create a custodianship by naming himself as custodian, except for transfers of securities under subsection (a)(1)(ii), insurance and annuity contracts under (a)(3)(ii), and titled personalty under (a)(6)(ii), which are made without registering them in the name of the custodian, and transfers of the residual class of property covered by (a)(7). In all of these cases a transfer of possession and control to a third party is necessary to establish donative intent and consummation of the transfer, and designation of the transferor as custodian renders the transfer invalid under SECTION 11(a)(2).

Note, also, that the Internal Revenue Service takes the position that custodial property is includable in the gross estate of the donor if he appoints himself custodian and dies while serving in that capacity before the minor attains the age of 21. Rev. Rul. 57-366, C.B. 1957-2, 618; Rev. Rul. 59-357, C.B. 1959-2, 212; Rev. Rul. 70-348, C.B. 1970-2, 193; *Estate of Prudowsky v. Comm'r*, 55 T.C. 890 (1971), *affd. per curiam*, 465 F.2d 62 (7th Cir. 1972).

This Act has been drafted in an attempt to avoid income attribution to the parent or inclusion of custodial insurance policies on a custodian's life in the estate of the custodian through the changes made in the standards for expenditure of custodial property and the custodian's incidents of ownership in custodial property. See SECTIONS 13 and 14 and the Comments thereto. However, the much greater problem of inclusion of custodial property in the estate of the donor who serves as custodian remains. Therefore, despite the fact that this section of the Act permits it in the case of registered securities, money, life insurance, real estate, and personal property subject to titling laws, it is generally still inadvisable for a donor to appoint himself custodian or for a parent of the minor to serve as custodian. See, generally Sections 2036 and 2038 I.R.C. and Rulings and cases cited above; with respect to gifts of closely held stock when a donor retains voting rights by serving as custodian, see Section 2036(b), I.R.C., overruling *U.S. v. Byrum*, 408 U.S. 125 (1972), rehearing denied 409 U.S. 898.

Subsection (c) tracks in substance Section 2(c) of the 1966 Act. However, it replaces the requirement that the transferor "promptly do all things within his power" to complete the transfer, with the requirement that such action must be taken "as soon as practicable." This change is intended only to reflect the fact that possession and control of property transferred from an estate can rarely be accomplished with the immediacy that the term "promptly" may have implied. In the case of inter vivos transfers, no relaxation of the former requirement is intended, since "prompt" transfer of dominion is usually practicable.

§ 10. Single Custodianship. A transfer may be made only for one minor, and only one person may be the custodian. All custodial property held under this [Act] by the same custodian for the benefit of the same minor constitutes a single custodianship.

Comment

The first sentence follows Section 2(b) of the 1966 Act. The second sentence states what was implicit in the 1966 Act, that additional transfers at different times and from different sources may be made to an existing custodian for the minor and do not create multiple custodianships. This provision also permits an existing custodian to be named as successor custodian by another custodian for the same minor who resigns under SECTION 18 for the purpose of consolidating the assets in a single custodianship.

Note, however, that these results are limited to transfers made "under this Act." Gifts previously made under the enacting state's UGMA or under the UGMA or UTMA of another state must be treated as separate custodianships, even though the same custodian and minor are involved, because of possible differences in the age of distribution and custodian's powers under those other Acts.

Even when all transfers to a single custodian are made "under this Act" and a single custodianship results, custodial property transferred under SECTIONS 6 and 7 must be accounted for separately from property transferred under SECTIONS 4 and 5 because the custodianship will terminate sooner with respect to the former property if the enacting state has a statutory age of majority lower than 21. See SECTION 20 and the Comment thereto.

§ 11. Validity and Effect of Transfer.

(a) The validity of a transfer made in a manner prescribed in this [Act] is not affected by:

(1) failure of the transferor to comply with Section 9(c) concerning possession and control;

(2) designation of an ineligible custodian, except designation of the transferor in the case of property for which the transferor is ineligible to serve as custodian under Section 9(a); or

(3) death or incapacity of a person nominated under Section 3 or designated under Section 9 as custodian or the disclaimer of the office by that person.

(b) A transfer made pursuant to Section 9 is irrevocable, and the custodial property is indefeasibly vested in the minor, but the custodian has all the rights, powers, duties, and authority provided in this [Act], and neither the minor nor the minor's legal representative has any right, power, duty, or authority with respect to the custodial property except as provided in this [Act].

(c) By making a transfer, the transferor incorporates in the disposition all the provisions of this [Act] and grants to the custodian, and to any third person dealing with a person designated as custodian, the respective powers, rights, and immunities provided in this [Act].

Comment

Subsection (a) generally tracks Section 2(c) of the 1966 Act, except that the transferor's designation of himself as custodian of property for which he is not eligible to serve under SECTION 9(a) makes the transfer ineffective. See Comment to SECTION 9.

The balance of this section generally tracks Section 3 of the 1966 Act with a number of necessary, and perhaps significant, changes required by the new kinds of property subject to custodianships. The 1966 Act provides that a transfer made in accordance with its terms "conveys to the minor indefeasibly vested legal title to the [custodial property]." Because equitable interests in property may be the subject of a transfer under this Act, the reference to "legal title" has been deleted, but no change concerning the effect or finality of the transfer is intended.

However, subsection (b) qualifies the rights of the minor in the property, by making them subject to "the rights, powers, duties and authority" of the custodian under this Act, a concept that may have been implicit and intended in the 1966 Act, but not expressed. The concept is important because of the kinds of property, particularly real estate, now subject to custodianship. If the minor is married, it would be possible for homestead, dower, or community property rights to attach to real estate (or other property) acquired after marriage by the minor through a transfer to a custodianship for his benefit. The quoted language qualifying the minor's interest in the property is intended to override these rights insofar as they may conflict with the custodian's ability and authority to manage, sell, or transfer such property while it is custodial property. Upon termination of the custodianship and transfer of the custodial property to the former minor, the custodial property would then become subject to such spousal rights for the first time.

For a list of the immunities enjoyed by third persons under subsection (c), see SECTION 16 and the Comment thereto.

Because a custodianship under this Act can extend beyond the age of majority in many states, or beyond emancipation of a minor through marriage or otherwise, the Drafting Committee considered the addition of a spendthrift clause to this section. The idea was rejected because neither the 1966 Act nor its predecessors had such a provision, because spendthrift protection would extend only until 21 in any event and judgments against the minor would then be enforceable, and because the spendthrift qualification on the interest of the minor in the property may be inconsistent with the theory of the Act to convey the property indefeasibly to the minor.

§ 12. Care of Custodial Property.

(a) A custodian shall:

(1) take control of custodial property;

(2) register or record title to custodial property if appropriate; and

(3) collect, hold, manage, invest, and reinvest custodial property.

(b) In dealing with custodial property, a custodian shall observe the standard of care that would be observed by a prudent person dealing with property of another and is not limited by any other statute restricting investments by fiduciaries. If a custodian has a special skill or expertise or is named custodian on the basis of representations of a special skill or expertise, the custodian shall use that skill or expertise. However, a custodian, in the custodian's discretion and without liability to the minor or the minor's estate, may retain any custodial property received from a transferor.

(c) A custodian may invest in or pay premiums on life insurance or endowment policies on (i) the life of the minor only if the minor or the minor's estate is the sole beneficiary, or (ii) the life of another person in whom the minor has an insurable interest only to the extent that the minor, the minor's estate, or the custodian in the capacity of custodian, is the irrevocable beneficiary.

(d) A custodian at all times shall keep custodial property separate and distinct from all other property in a manner sufficient to identify it clearly as custodial property of the minor. Custodial property consisting of an undivided interest is so identified if the minor's interest is held as a tenant in common and is fixed. Custodial property subject to recordation is so identified if it is recorded, and custodial property subject to registration is so identified if it is either registered, or held in an account designated, in the name of the custodian, followed in substance by the words: "as a custodian for _____ (name of minor) under the [Name of Enacting State] Uniform Transfers to Minors Act."

(e) A custodian shall keep records of all transactions with respect to custodial property, including information necessary for the preparation of the minor's tax returns, and shall make them available for inspection at reasonable intervals by a parent or legal representative of the minor or by the minor if the minor has attained the age of 14 years.

Comment

Subsection (a) expands Section 4(a) of the 1966 Act to include the duties to take control and appropriately register or record custodial property in the name of the custodian.

Subsection (b) restates and makes somewhat stricter the prudent man fiduciary standard for the custodian, since it is now cast in terms of a prudent person "dealing with property of another" rather than one "who is seeking a reasonable income and the preservation of his capital," as under the 1966 Act. The rule also adds a slightly higher standard for professional fiduciaries. The rule parallels section 7-302 of the Uniform Probate Code in order to refer to the existing and growing body of law interpreting that standard. The 1966 Act permitted a custodian to retain any security or bank account received, without the obligation to diversify investment. This subsection extends that rule to any property received.

In order to eliminate any uncertainty that existed under the 1966 Act, subsection (c) grants specific authority to invest custodial property in life insurance on the minor's life, provided the minor's estate is the sole beneficiary, or on the life of another person in whom the minor has an insurable interest, provided the minor, the minor's estate, or the custodian in his custodial capacity is made the beneficiary of such policies.

Subsection (d) generally tracks Section 4(g) of the 1966 Act but adds the provision requiring that custodial property consisting of an undivided interest be held as a tenant in common. This provision permits the custodian to invest custodial property in common trust funds, mutual funds, or in a proportional interest in a "jumbo" certificate of deposit. Investment in property held in joint tenancy with right of survivorship is not permitted, but the Act does not preclude a transfer of such an interest to a custodian, and the custodian is authorized under subsection (b) to retain a joint tenancy interest so received.

Subsection (e) follows Section 4(h) of the 1966 Act, but adds the requirement that income tax information be maintained and made available for preparation of the minor's tax returns. Because the custodianship is not a separate legal entity or taxpayer, the minor's tax identification number should be used to identify all custodial property accounts.

§ 13. Powers of Custodian.

(a) A custodian, acting in a custodial capacity, has all the rights, powers, and authority over custodial property that unmarried adult owners have over their own property, but a custodian may exercise those rights, powers, and authority in that capacity only.

(b) This section does not relieve a custodian from liability for breach of Section 12.

Comment

Subsection (a) replaces the specific list of custodian's powers in Section 4(f) of the 1966 Act which related only to securities, money, and insurance, then the only permitted kinds of custodial property. It was determined not to expand the list to try to deal with all forms of property now covered by the Act and to specify all powers that might be appropriate for each kind of property, or to refer to an existing body of state law, such as the Trustee's Powers Act, since such powers would not be uniform. Instead, this provision grants the custodian the very broad and general powers of an unmarried adult owner of the property, subject to the prudent person rule and to the duties of segregation and record keeping specified in SECTION 12. This approach permits the Act to be self-contained and more readily understandable by volunteer, non-professional fiduciaries, who most often serve as custodians. It is intended that the authority granted includes the powers most often suggested for custodians, such as the power to borrow, whether at interest or interest free, the power to invest in common trust funds, and the power to enter contracts that extend beyond termination of the custodianship.

Subsection (a) further specifies that the custodian's powers or incidents of ownership in custodial property such as insurance policies may be exercised only in his capacity as custodian. This provision is intended to prevent the exercise of those powers for the direct or indirect benefit of the custodian, so as to avoid as nearly as possible the result that a custodian who dies while holding an insurance policy on his own life for the benefit of a minor will have the policy taxed in his estate. See, Section 2042, I.R.C.; but compare *Terriberry v. U.S.*, 517 F.2d 286 (5th Cir. 1975), and *Rose v. U.S.*, 511 F.2d 259 (5th Cir. 1975).

§ 14. Use of Custodial Property.

(a) A custodian may deliver or pay to the minor or expend for the minor's benefit so much of the custodial property as the custodian considers advisable for the use and benefit of the minor, without court order and without regard to (i) the duty or ability of the custodian personally or of any other person to support the minor, or (ii) any other income or property of the minor which may be applicable or available for that purpose.

(b) On petition of an interested person or the minor if the minor has attained the age of 14 years, the court may order the custodian to deliver or pay to the minor or expend for the minor's benefit so much of the custodial property as the court considers advisable for the use and benefit of the minor.

(c) A delivery, payment, or expenditure under this section is in addition to, not in substitution for, and does not affect any obligation of a person to support the minor.

Comment

Subsections (a) and (b) track subsections (b) and (c) of Section 4 of the 1966 Act, but with two significant changes. The standard for expenditure of custodial property has been amended to read "for the use and benefit of the minor," rather than "for the support, maintenance, education and benefit of the minor" as specified under the 1966 Act. This change is intended to avoid the implication that the custodial property can be used only for the required support of the minor.

The IRS has taken the position that the income from custodial property, to the extent it is used for the support of the minor-donee, is includable in the gross income of any person who is legally obligated to support the minor-donee, whether or not that person or parent is serving as the custodian. Rev. Rul. 56-484, C.B. 1956-2, 23; Rev. Rul. 59-357, C.B. 1959-2, 212. However, Reg. 1.662(a)-4 provides that the term "legal obligation" includes a legal obligation to support another person if, and only if, the obligation is not affected by the adequacy of the dependent's own resources. Thus, if under local law a parent may use the resources of a child for the child's support in lieu of supporting the child himself or herself, no obligation of support exists, whether or not income is actually used for support, at least if the child's resources are adequate. See, Bittker, *Federal Taxation of Income Estates and Gifts*, ¶ 80.4.4 (1981).

For this reason, new subsection (c) has been added to specify that distributions or expenditures may be made for the minor without regard to the duty or ability of any other person to support the minor and that distributions or expenditures are not in substitution for, and shall not affect, the obligation of any person to support the minor. Other possible methods of avoiding the attribution of custodial property income to the person obligated to support the minor would be to prohibit the use of custodial property or its income for that purpose, or to provide that any such use gives rise to a cause of action by the minor against his parent to the extent that custodial property or income is so used. The first alternative was rejected as too restrictive, and the second as too cumbersome.

The "use and benefit" standard in subsections (a) and (b) is intended to include payment of the minor's legally enforceable obligations such as tax or child support obligations or tort claims. Custodial property could be reached by levy of a judgment creditor in any event, so there is no reason not to permit custodian or court-ordered expenditures for enforceable claims.

An "interested person" entitled to seek court ordered distributions under subsection (b) would include not only the parent or conservator or guardian of the minor and a transferor or a transferor's legal representative, but also a public agency or official with custody of the minor and a third party to whom the minor owes legally enforceable debts.

§ 15. Custodian's Expenses, Compensation, and Bond.

(a) A custodian is entitled to reimbursement from custodial property for reasonable expenses incurred in the performance of the custodian's duties.

(b) Except for one who is a transferor under Section 4, a custodian has a non-cumulative election during each calendar year to charge reasonable compensation for services performed during that year.

(c) Except as provided in Section 18(f), a custodian need not give a bond.

Comment

This section parallels and restates Section 5 of the 1966 Act. It deletes the statement that a custodian may act without compensation for services, since that concept is implied in the retained provision that a custodian has an "election" to be compensated. However, to prevent abuse, the latter provision for permissive compensation is denied to a custodian who is also the donor of the custodial property.

The custodian's election to charge compensation must be exercised (although the compensation need not be actually paid) at least annually or it lapses and may not be exercised later. This provision is intended to avoid imputed income to the custodian who waives compensation, and also to avoid the accumulation of a large unanticipated claim for compensation exercisable at termination of the custodianship.

This section deletes as surplusage the bracketed optional standards contained in the 1966 Act for determining "reasonable compensation" which included, "in the order stated," a direction by the donor, statutes governing compensation of custodians or guardians, or court order. While compensation of custodians becomes a more likely occurrence and a more important issue under this Act because property requiring increased management may now be subject to custodianship, compensation can still be determined by agreement, by reference to a statute or by court order, without the need to so state in this Act.

§ 16. Exemption of Third Person from Liability.

A third person in good faith and without court order may act on the instructions of or otherwise deal with any person purporting to make a transfer or purporting to act in the capacity of a custodian and, in the absence of knowledge, is not responsible for determining:

(1) the validity of the purported custodian's designation;

(2) the propriety of, or the authority under this [Act] for, any act of the purported custodian;

(3) the validity or propriety under this [Act] of any instrument or instructions executed or given either by the person purporting to make a transfer or by the purported custodian; or

(4) the propriety of the application of any property of the minor delivered to the purported custodian.

Comment

This section carries forward, but shortens and simplifies, Section 6 of the 1966 Act, with no substantive change intended. The 1966 revision permitted a 14-year old minor to appoint a successor custodian and specifically provided that third parties were entitled to rely on the appointment. Because this section refers to any custodian, and "custodian" is defined to include successor custodians (SECTION 1(7)), a successor custodian appointed by the minor is included among those upon whom third parties may rely.

Similarly, because this section protects any third "person," it is not necessary to specify here or in SECTION 11(c) that it extends to any "issuer, transfer agent, bank, life insurance company, broker, or other person or financial institution," as did the 1966 Act. See the definition of "person" in SECTION 1(12).

This section excludes from its protection persons with "knowledge" of the irregularity of a transaction, a concept not expressed but probably implied in Section 6 of the 1966 Act. See, *e.g.*, *State ex rel Paden v. Currel*, 597 S.W.2d 167 (Mo. App. 1980) disapproving the pledge of custodial property to secure a personal loan to the custodian.

Similarly, this section does not alter the requirements for bona fide purchaser or holder in due course status under other law for persons who acquire from a custodian custodial property subject to recordation or registration.

§ 17. Liability to Third Persons.

(a) A claim based on (i) a contract entered into by a custodian acting in a custodial capacity, (ii) an obligation arising from the ownership or control of custodial property, or (iii) a tort committed during the custodianship, may be asserted against the custodial property by proceeding against the custodian in the custodial capacity, whether or not the custodian or the minor is personally liable therefor.

(b) A custodian is not personally liable:

(1) on a contract properly entered into in the custodial capacity unless the custodian fails to reveal that capacity and to identify the custodianship in the contract; or

(2) for an obligation arising from control of custodial property or for a tort committed during the custodianship unless the custodian is personally at fault.

(c) A minor is not personally liable for an obligation arising from ownership of custodial property or for a tort committed during the custodianship unless the minor is personally at fault.

Comment

This section has no counterpart in the 1966 Act and is based upon Section 5-429 of the Uniform Probate Code, relating to limitations on the liability of conservators. Because some forms of custodial property now permitted under this Act can give rise to liabilities as well as benefits (*e.g.*, general partnership interests, interests in real estate or business proprietorships, automobiles, etc.) the Committee believes it is necessary to protect the minor and other assets he might have or acquire from such liabilities, since the minor is unable to disclaim a transfer to a custodian for his benefit. Similar protection for the custodian is necessary so as not to discourage nonprofessional or uncompensated persons from accepting the office. Therefore this section generally limits the claims of third parties to recourse against the custodial property, as third

parties dealing with a trust are generally limited to recourse against the trust corpus.

The custodian incurs personal liability only as provided in subsection (b) for actual fault or for failure to disclose his custodial capacity "in the contract" when contracting with third parties. In oral contracts, oral disclosure of the custodial capacity is sufficient. The minor, on the other hand, incurs personal liability under subsection (c) only for actual fault.

When custodial property is subjected to claims of third parties under this section, the minor or his legal representative, if not a party to the action by which the claim is successfully established, may seek to recover the loss from the custodian in a separate action. See SECTION 19 and the Comment thereto.

§ 18. Renunciation, Resignation, Death, or Removal of Custodian; Designation of Successor Custodian.

(a) A person nominated under Section 3 or designated under Section 9 as custodian may decline to serve by delivering a valid disclaimer [under the Uniform Disclaimer of Property Interests Act of the Enacting State] to the person who made the nomination or to the transferor or the transferor's legal representative. If the event giving rise to a transfer has not occurred and no substitute custodian able, willing, and eligible to serve was nominated under Section 3, the person who made the nomination may nominate a substitute custodian under Section 3; otherwise the transferor or the transferor's legal representative shall designate a substitute custodian at the time of the transfer, in either case from among the persons eligible to serve as custodian for that kind of property under Section 9(a). The custodian so designated has the rights of a successor custodian.

(b) A custodian at any time may designate a trust company or an adult other than a transferor under Section 4 as successor custodian by executing and dating an instrument of designation before a subscribing witness other than the successor. If the instrument of designation does not contain or is not accompanied by the resignation of the custodian, the designation of the successor does not take effect until the custodian resigns, dies, becomes incapacitated, or is removed.

(c) A custodian may resign at any time by delivering written notice to the minor if the minor has attained the age of 14 years and to the successor custodian and by delivering the custodial property to the successor custodian.

(d) If a custodian is ineligible, dies, or becomes incapacitated without having effectively designated a successor and the minor has attained the age of 14 years, the minor may designate as successor custodian, in the manner prescribed in subsection (b), an adult member of the minor's family, a conservator of the minor, or a trust company. If the minor has not attained the age of 14 years or fails to act within 60 days after the ineligibility, death, or incapacity, the conservator of the minor becomes successor custodian. If the minor has no conservator or the conservator declines to act, the transferor, the legal representative of the transferor or of the custodian, an adult member of the minor's family, or any other interested person may petition the court to designate a successor custodian.

(e) A custodian who declines to serve under subsection (a) or resigns under subsection (c), or the legal representative of a deceased or incapacitated custodian, as soon as practicable, shall put the custodial property and records in the possession and control of the successor custodian. The successor custodian by action may enforce the obligation to deliver custodial property and records and becomes responsible for each item as received.

(f) A transferor, the legal representative of a transferor, an adult member of the minor's family, a guardian of the person of the minor, the conservator of the minor, or the minor if the minor has attained the age of 14 years may petition the court to remove the custodian for cause and to designate a successor custodian other than a transferor under Section 4 or to require the custodian to give appropriate bond.

Comment

This section tracks but condenses Section 7 of the 1966 Act to provide that the custodian, or if the custodian does not do so, the minor if he is 14, may appoint the successor custodian, or failing that, that the conservator of the minor or a court appointee shall serve. It also covers disclaimer of the office by designated or successor custodians or by nominated future custodians who decline to serve.

This Act broadens the category of persons who may be designated by the initial custodian as successor custodian from an adult member of the minor's family, his conservator, or a trust company to any adult or trust company. However, the minor's designation remains limited to an adult member of his family (expanded to include a spouse and a stepparent, see SECTION 1(10)), his conservator, or a trust company.

§ 19. Accounting by and Determination of Liability of Custodian.

(a) A minor who has attained the age of 14 years, the minor's guardian of the person or legal representative, an adult member of the minor's family, a transferor, or a transferor's legal representative may petition the court (i) for an accounting by the custodian or the custodian's legal representative; or (ii) for a determination of responsibility, as between the custodial property and the custodian personally, for claims against the custodial property unless the responsibility has been adjudicated in an action under Section 17 to which the minor or the minor's legal representative was a party.

(b) A successor custodian may petition the court for an accounting by the predecessor custodian.

(c) The court, in a proceeding under this [Act] or in any other proceeding, may require or permit the custodian or the custodian's legal representative to account.

(d) If a custodian is removed under Section 18(f), the court shall require an accounting and order delivery of the custodial property and records to the successor custodian and the execution of all instruments required for transfer of the custodial property.

Comment

This section carries forward Section 8 of the 1966 Act, but expands the class of parties who may require an accounting by the custodian to include any person who made a transfer to him (or any such person's legal representative), the minor's guardian of the person, and the successor custodian.

Subsection (b) authorizes but does not obligate a successor custodian to seek an accounting by the predecessor custodian. Since the minor and other persons mentioned in subsection (a) may also seek an accounting from the predecessor at any time, it is anticipated that the exercise of this right by the successor should be rare.

Subsection (a) also gives the same parties (other than a successor custodian) the right to seek recovery from the custodian for loss or diminution of custodial property resulting from successful claims by third persons under SECTION 17, unless that issue has already been adjudicated in an action under that section to which the minor was a party.

This section does not contain a separate statute of limitations precluding petitions for accounting after termination of the custodianship. Because custodianships can be created without the knowledge of the minor, a person might learn of a custodian's failure to turn over custodial property long after reaching majority, and should not be precluded from asserting his rights in the case of such fraud. In addition, the 1966 Act has no such preclusion and seems to have worked well. Other law, such as general statutes of limitation and the doctrine of laches, should serve adequately to protect former custodians from harassment.

§ 20. Termination of Custodianship. The custodian shall transfer in an appropriate manner the custodial property to the minor or to the minor's estate upon the earlier of:

(1) the minor's attainment of 21 years of age with respect to custodial property transferred under Section 4 or 5;

(2) the minor's attainment of [majority under the laws of this State other than this [Act]] [age 18 or other statutory age of majority of Enacting State] with respect to custodial property transferred under Section 6 or 7; or

(3) the minor's death.

Comment

This section tracks Section 4(d) of the 1966 Act, but provides that custodianships created by fiduciaries without express authority from the donor of the property under SECTION 6 and by obligors of the minor under SECTION 7 terminate upon the minor's attaining the age of majority under the general laws of the state, since these custodianships are substitutes for conservatorships that would otherwise terminate at that time. Because property in a single custodianship may be distributable at different times, separate accounting for custodial property by source may be required. See Comment to SECTION 10.

§ 21. Applicability. This [Act] applies to a transfer within the scope of Section 2 made after its effective date if:

(1) the transfer purports to have been made under [the Uniform Gifts to Minors Act of the Enacting State]; or

(2) the instrument by which the transfer purports to have been made uses in substance the designation "as custodian under the Uniform Gifts to Minors Act" or "as custodian under the Uniform Transfers to Minors Act" of any other state, and the application of this [Act] is necessary to validate the transfer.

Comment

This section is new and has two purposes. First, it operates as a "savings clause" to validate transfers made after its effective date which mistakenly refer to the enacting state's UGMA rather than to this Act. Second, it validates transfers attempted under the UGMA of another state which would not permit transfers from that source or of property of that kind or under the UTMA of another state with no nexus to the transaction, provided in each case that the enacting state has a sufficient nexus to the transaction under SECTION 2.

§ 22. Effect on Existing Custodianships.

(a) Any transfer of custodial property as now defined in this [Act] made before [the effective date of this Act] is validated notwithstanding that there was no specific authority in [the Uniform Gifts to Minors Act of the Enacting State] for the coverage of custodial property of that kind or for a transfer from that source at the time the transfer was made.

(b) This [Act] applies to all transfers made before the effective date of this [Act] in a manner and form prescribed in [the Uniform Gifts to Minors Act of the Enacting State], except insofar as the application impairs constitutionally vested rights or extends the duration of custodianships in existence on the effective date of this [Act].

[(c) Sections 1 and 20 with respect to the age of a minor for whom custodial property is held under this [Act] do not apply to custodial property held in a custodianship that terminated because of the minor's attainment of the age of [18] after [date prior Act was amended to specify [18] as age of majority] and before [the effective date of this Act].]

Comment

Subsection (a) is new and is based on Section 45-109a of the Connecticut Act which validates gifts of real estate and partnership interests made prior to their inclusion as "custodial property" under that Act. However, this provision goes further and purports also to validate prior transfers of the kind now covered by the Act, i.e., transfers from estates, trusts, guardianships, and obligors.

All states have previously enacted some version of UGMA, and it will be more orderly to subject gifts or other transfers under the prior Act to the procedures of this Act, rather than to keep both Acts in force, presumably for 18 or 21 years until all custodianships created under prior law have terminated. Subsection (b) is intended to apply this Act to prior gifts and existing custodianships insofar as it is constitutionally permissible to do so. However, prior custodianships will continue to terminate at the age prescribed under the prior Act.

Optional subsection (c) is also new and is based upon Section 45-109b of the Connecticut Act. It is intended for adoption in those states that amended their Acts to reduce the age of majority to 18, but which adopt the recommended return to 21 as the age at which custodianships terminate. Its purpose is to avoid resurrecting custodianships for persons not yet 21 which terminated during the period that the age of 18 governed termination.

§ 23. Uniformity of Application and Construction. This [Act] shall be applied and construed to effectuate its general purpose to make uniform the law with respect to the subject of this [Act] among states enacting it.

§ 24. Short Title. This [Act] may be cited as the "[Name of Enacting State] Uniform Transfers to Minors Act."

§ 25. Severability. If any provisions of this [Act] or its application to any person or circumstance is held invalid, the invalidity does not affect other provisions or applications of this [Act] which can be given effect without the invalid provision or application, and to this end provisions of this [Act] are severable.

§ 26. Effective Date. This [Act] takes effect _____ _____.

§ 27. Repeals. [Insert appropriate reference to the existing Gifts to Minors Act of the Enacting State or other jurisdiction] is hereby repealed. To the extent that this [Act], by virtue of Section 22(b), does not apply to transfers made in a manner prescribed in [the Gifts to Minors Act of the Enacting State] or to the powers, duties, and immunities conferred by transfers in that manner upon custodians and persons dealing with custodians, the repeal of [the Gifts to Minors Act of the Enacting State] does not affect those transfers or those powers, duties, and immunities.

MODEL MARITAL PROPERTY ACT (1983)

(Formerly the Uniform Marital Property Act)

Table of Sections

Prefatory Note

"The institution of property is the embodiment of accidents, events, and the wisdom of the past. It is before us as clay into which we can introduce the coloration and configuration representing our wisdom. How great, how useful this new ingredient may be will largely determine the future happiness, and perhaps the continued existence of our society." Powell, *The Law of Real Property* (Rohan 4th ed. 1977).

Marriages have beginnings and endings. For their participants, the period between these points *is* the marriage. This Act is a property law. It functions to recognize the respective contributions made by men and women during a marriage. It discharges that function by raising those contributions to the level of defined, shared and enforceable property rights at the time the contributions are made.

The challenge to create such a framework is not new. Basic differences in approaches to marital economics go back for many centuries. *See* Donahue, *What Causes Fundamental Legal Ideas? Marital Property in England and France in the Thirteenth Century,* 78 Mich. L. Rev. 59 (1979); Younger, *Marital Regimes: A Story of Compromise and Demoralization, Together with Criticism and Suggestions for Reform,* 67 Cornell L. Rev. 45 (1981). In modern times the challenge was well articulated twenty years ago by the Report of the Committee on Civil and Political Rights to the President's Commission on the Status of Women. In 1963 that Report said:

Marriage is a partnership to which each spouse makes a different but equally important

957

contribution. This fact has become increasingly recognized in the realities of American family living. While the laws of other countries have reflected this trend, family laws in the United States have lagged behind. Accordingly, the Committee concludes that during marriage each spouse should have a legally defined and substantial right in the earnings of the other spouse and in the real and personal property acquired as a result of such earnings, as well as in the management of such earnings and property. Such right should survive the marriage and be legally recognized in the event of its termination by annulment, divorce, or death. This policy should be appropriately implemented by legislation which would safeguard either spouse against improper alienation of property by the other.

In the twenty years after those words much has changed regarding the institution of marriage, even though the challenge has not been fully met.

A prime example is the very demography of marriage and its terminal events. In 1963, 66.31% of all terminated marriages ended by death and 33.69% by divorce. By 1979 only 42.77% terminated by death, while 57.23% ended by dissolution. For half a decade the ratio of marriages to dissolution has been about two to one. The latest figures were 2,438,000 marriages and 1,219,000 divorces in 1981. The two to one ratio contrasts with 1930, when there were six marriages to every dissolution.

Statistics are not the only evidence of dramatic change. Statehouses have reflected it. Beginning with California at the end of the 60's and promulgation of the Uniform Marriage and Divorce Act in the early 70's, no-fault divorce has swept the statute books. In 1983 Illinois and South Dakota stand alone in adhering to fault-based divorce, and efforts to change to no-fault continue in Illinois. "Equitable distribution" of property became the handmaiden of no-fault divorce in the Uniform Marriage and Divorce Act and in most other reforms. Forty-one traditional common law jurisdictions now use some form of *property division* as a principal means of resolving economic dilemmas on dissolution. Adding the eight community property jurisdictions in which such a division is an inherent aspect of spousal property rights yields a total of 49. The one state missing on the property division roster is Mississippi. These property division developments address and typically adopt sharing concepts and bring many common law jurisdictions close to a deferred community property approach to divorce. Cheadle, *The Development of Sharing Principles in Common Law Marital Property States*, 28 UCLA L.Rev. 1269 (1981); *see also* Younger, *op. cit., supra.*

The ferment of change has not been limited to dissolution. The Uniform Probate Code was promulgated in 1969. Fourteen states are now listed as Code states or as substantially conforming states. Article II of the Code contains the concept of an augmented estate. It borrows heavily from New York's 1966 version of the idea. It is an advance on traditional forced-share procedures, operating by the creation of a larger universe of property against which a spousal right of election is exercisable. It accomplishes this by penetrating the veil of title and other techniques which have developed to insulate assets from the reach of forced-share statutes. In the official comment to the Code the augmented estate provisions are described as preventing arrangements by the owner of wealth which would transmit property to others than a surviving spouse by means other than probate for the deliberate purpose of defeating the rights of a surviving spouse.

It is worth noting that the Code's provisions, as well as conventional forced-share provisions in common law states, leave a gap. They transform assets into a sharing mode in a meaningful way only when the "have-not" spouse survives. If the sequence of death is the opposite, the have-not spouse has no power to dispose of assets over which he or she has no title in any common law jurisdiction.

The long-arm augmented estate provisions of the Uniform Probate Code may not go far enough to accommodate the perception of most laymen. A significant empirical study published in 1978 indicates a widespread public preference for a distribution of an *entire* intestate estate to a surviving spouse, whether or not there are surviving children. Fellows, Simon & Rau, *Public Attitudes About Distribution At Death And Intestate Succession Laws In The United States*, 1978 Am. B. Found. Research J. 319.

Obviously the "everything to each other" mode is confined to dispositions at death. An imposing body of case law testifies to a paradigm shift in this view when the question of "Who should get what and when?" is asked at a dissolution! And it is the equitable distribution court's demanding role in the judicial process to monitor and referee the ensuing contests in the divorce courts. Burgeoning advance sheets clearly indicate just how difficult the referee's job is when it must be done well over a million times a year!

In 1981 yet another shift was added to the catalog of change. After years of debate, tax-free interspousal transfers entered the stage under the auspices of the Economic Recovery Tax Act of 1981. *Wall Street Journal* columnist Vermont Royster furnished a characteristically succinct summary of it all:

> "The marriage ceremony may say you two are now one and even include that phrase about with all my worldly goods I thee endow. The Internal Revenue Service has always taken a different view. It's wanted its share.
>
> ... wait until January 1, 1982, and ... after that magic date you can share with your spouse as much as you please of those worldly goods ... without so much as a by-your-leave from the federal tax man. In 1982 no more gift and estate taxes between spouses." Wall St. J., Sept. 2, 1981.

Heavy economic responsibilities of married couples and methods of coping with them point to yet another trendline of the last few decades. It is that of the two-worker households in which sharing the burden of producing family income is becoming routine. In more than half of American marriages with two spouses present there is a working wife and the number is growing. When there are children, the ratio is even higher. In more than two-thirds of current upper income marriages ($24,000 or more) there are two wage earners. Sharing of responsibility for wages from *outside* the home is altering traditional spousal roles and particularly economic roles rights, and responsibilities.

Thus the stage is set by substantial social and legislative change in the duration of marriages and in the economics of the termination of marriages by dissolution and death.

The Uniform Marital Property Act makes its appearance on that stage to offer a means of establishing present shared property rights of spouses *during* the marriage. This approach is bottomed on two propositions. The first is creation of an immediate sharing mode of ownership. The second proposition is that the sharing mode during marriage is an ownership right already in existence at the end of a marriage. Thus recognition and perfection of shared and vested ownership rights in marital property are in place at divorce or death. They do not have to come to fruition as a result of a court-ordained and possibly adversary "division" or by a statutorily-sanctioned "transfer."

Is the Uniform Marital Property Act a panacea for the malaise of marriage? Will it lower the divorce rate? Save the family? Eliminate marital violence? Be fully comprehensible? Be welcomed by all? Lower the cost of the family house? Create better parents? Solve child abuse? Avoid probate? Lower the cost of death or divorce?

Perhaps some but certainly not all of the above. If it does affect any of those considerations, it will take time and the process will be subtle. The disintegrating forces operating on marriages and families are many and complex. It would be a bold claim to suggest that any legislation could fully identify and rectify the problems in such an area. But the obvious and apparent existence of problems in the economic area of marriage certainly justifies an effort to identify and rectify them. The Uniform Marital Property Act is precisely such an effort.

What are the root concepts?

FIRST: Property acquired during marriage by the effort of spouses is shared and is something the couple can truly style as "ours." Rather than an evanescent hope, the idea of sharing implicit in viewing property as "ours" becomes reality as a result of a present, vested ownership right which each spouse has in all property acquired by the personal efforts of either during the marriage. That property is "marital property." (Section 4).

Except for its income, property brought into the marriage or acquired afterward by gift or devise is not marital but "individual property." Its *appreciation* remains individual property. However, the *income* of that property becomes marital property, so that *all* income of a couple is marital property. (Section 4).

Property already owned when the Act becomes effective or owned by couples moving into an adopting state will take on the characteristics of marital property only at death or marital dissolution and then only if it would have been marital property under the Act had the Act been in effect when and where the property was acquired. Prior to death or dissolution the Act ordains no change in the classification of property of a couple acquired at a time when the Act did not apply. (Sections 4(h), 17 and 18).

SECOND: The system which the Act creates to manage and control marital property accords a considerable measure of individual option. "Management and control" is a phrase of art in the Act. Basically management and control rights flow from the form in which title to property is held. If only one spouse holds property there is no requirement for the other spouse to participate in management and control functions. If both spouses hold property they must both participate in management and control unless the holding is in an alternative ("A *or* B") form. Couples can select their own options as they deem appropriate. (Sections 3, 5, 10 and 11). Management and control is different from ownership. Ownership rights are not lost by relinquishing or even neglecting management and control rights. In essence, the Act's management and control system is substantially similar to the existing procedures of title based management in common law states. (Section 5).

To guard against possible abuses by a spouse with sole title, a court can implement the addition of the name of the other spouse to marital property so that it is held, managed and controlled by both spouses. (Section 15).

The rule on gifts of marital property to third parties provides a safe harbor for smaller gifts. Unless aggregate gifts of marital property by one spouse to a third party in a calendar year are less than a specified dollar amount or are reasonable in amount with respect to the economic position of the spouses when made, both spouses must join in making the gift. A failure to procure that joinder renders the gift voidable at the option of the non-participating spouse. (Section 6).

THIRD: The varying patterns of today's marriages are accommodated by an opportunity to create custom systems by "marital property agreements." Full freedom to contract with respect to virtually all property matters is possible under the Act. By a marital property agreement a couple could opt out of the provisions of the Act in whole or in part. Conversely, they could opt in by agreeing that the Act's provisions will apply to all or a part of the property they own before they became subject to its terms.

As a protection and to ease matters of proof, the Act requires that marital property agreements be made in writing and signed by both spouses. (Section 10). Marital property agreements are enforceable without consideration.

FOURTH: On dissolution the structure of the Act as a *property statute* comes into full play. The Act takes the parties "to the door of the divorce court" only. It leaves to existing dissolution procedures in the several states the selection of the appropriate procedures for dividing property. On the other hand the Act has the function of confirming the *ownership* of property as the couple enters the process. Thus reallocation of

property derived from the effort of both spouses during the marriage starts from a basis of the equal undivided ownership that the spouses share in their marital property. A given state's equitable distribution or other property division procedures could mean that the ownership will end that way, or that it could be substantially altered, but that will depend on other applicable state law and judicial determinations. An analogous situation obtains at death, with the Act operating primarily as a property statute rather than a probate statute.

At divorce and death special provisions will apply to property of a couple acquired before the Act applied to that couple. If any of that property would have been marital property under the Act, had the Act been in effect when and where it was acquired, then such property will be treated as if it were marital property at divorce. Property of the deceased spouse having that characteristic will be treated in that manner at death. This represents a deferred approach to reclassification of the property of spouses which does not otherwise have the characteristics of marital property due to the time or place of its acquisition. The deferral is to the time of marital termination at divorce or death. Those are events at which states have long altered the classification of their citizens' property by equitable distribution provisions or by forced share and augmented estate provisions. The Act builds on those established patterns already followed by the states by creating the deferred classification with respect to property owned by couples before the Act applied to them. A provision effecting automatic reclassification of such property with the passage of the Act would amount to retroactive legislation and would risk constitutional attack. *See* Irish, *A Common Law State Considers A Shift to Community Property*, 5 Community Prop. J. 227 (1978). On the other hand, the deferred approach of the Act operates only prospectively, tracking the procedure of the bulk of existing state legislation that prescribes forms of marital sharing effective only at divorce or death. (Sections 17 and 18).

FIFTH: Creditors may have claims that arise before marriage and after marriage. The premarital creditor is denied a bonanza by a marriage. (Section 8(b)(iii)). That creditor can only reach what would have been reached had there been no marriage. Postmarital obligations may subject both marital and individual property to claims. Obligations incurred by a spouse during marriage are presumed to be incurred in the interest of the marriage and the family and those obligations may be satisfied from all marital property and the other property of the incurring spouse. (Section 8(a) and (b)(ii)).

SIXTH: Bona fide purchasers of property for value are protected in their transactions with spouses by reliance on the manner in which property is held. They are under no duty to look "underneath" the manner of holding and are fully protected for not doing so. (Section 9).

In addition to those root concepts, a series of enabling provisions offer convenient support for the system. These include special methods of holding property, including a survivorship form of ownership (Section 11); dispositions by a probate avoidance feature in marital property agreements (Section 10(c)(6)); and remedies for disputes between the spouses affecting their property, including interspousal property accountings (Section 15). There are procedures to deal with marital and individual property which becomes intermixed. (Section 14). Special rules deal with complex property rights in life insurance and deferred employee benefits. (Sections 12 and 13). Conventional concurrent and survivorship forms may be used for marital property. (Section 11(d)). As an option for use in states that recognize tenancy by the entireties, existing tenancy by the entireties property continues to be available to perpetuate the creditor protection it affords. (Section 19).

Some of the root concepts can be traced to the sharing ideal which is at the center of the historical community property approach. The fundamental principle that ownership of all of the economic rewards from the personal effort of each spouse during marriage is shared by the spouses in vested, present, and equal interests is the heart of the community property system. It is also the heart of the Uniform Marital Property Act. Common law states have been moving closer and closer to the sharing concept in both divorce and probate legislation, and the Uniform Marital Property Act builds on the direction of that movement. Sharing is seen as a system of elemental fairness and justice so that those who share in the many and diverse forms of work involved in establishing and maintaining a marriage will have a protected share in the material acquisitions of that marriage. The Act creates and protects that share without forcing a spouse to await the completion of a gift from the other spouse or the garnering of proof of dollar-for-dollar contributions to the purchase price of assets acquired over the years of marriage. Under the Act, the sharing of property is recognized by creation of a present interest simultaneously with acquisition of property by effort during marriage. The interest is legally defined and enforceable. It permeates assets as they are acquired and continues to permeate them as they are invested and reinvested, as they are exchanged and transferred, and as they grow or diminish.

Such a law translates the emotional and perceived concept of "ours" into a verified legal reality. And while that parallels sharing under community property systems, the Act is more accurately characterized as a *sui generis* approach, and as one which utilizes equally useful ideas developed in common law jurisdictions, such as title based management and control. In addition, it is a response to the twenty-year-long challenge of the President's Commission on the Status of Women issued in 1963 to face the reality that each spouse makes a different but equally important contribution in a marriage. Though drafted with an awareness of various community property statutes and cases, the Uniform Marital Property Act is not an image of any of them. It is a statute speaking to the realities and equities of marriages in America in the Eighties.

§ 1. General Definitions In this [Act]:

(1) "Acquire" in relation to property includes reduction of indebtedness on encumbered property and obtaining a lien on or security interest in property.

(2) "Appreciation" means a realized or unrealized increase in the value of property.

(3) "Decree" means a judgment or other order of a court.

(4) "Deferred employment benefit" means a benefit under a plan, fund, program, or other arrangement under which compensation or benefits from employment are expressly, or as a result of surrounding circumstances, deferred to a later date or the happening of a future event. Such an arrangement includes a pension, profit sharing, or stock-bonus plan; an employee stock-ownership or stock-purchase plan; a savings or thrift plan; an annuity plan; a qualified bond-purchase plan; a self-employed retirement plan; a simplified employee pension; and a deferred compensation agreement or plan. It does not include life, health, accident, or other insurance, or a plan, fund, program, or

other arrangement providing benefits comparable to insurance benefits, except to the extent that benefits under the arrangement: (i) have a present value that is immediately realizable in cash at the option of the employee; (ii) constitute an unearned premium for the coverage; (iii) represent a right to compensation for loss of income during disability; or (iv) represent a right to payment of expenses incurred before time of valuation.

(5) "Determination date" means the last to occur of the following: (i) marriage; (ii) 12:01 a.m. on the date of establishment of a marital domicile in this State; or (iii) 12:01 a.m. on the effective date of this [Act].

(6) "Disposition at death" means transfer of property by will, intestate succession, nontestamentary transfer, or other means that take effect at the transferor's death.

(7) "Dissolution" means: (i) termination of a marriage by a decree of dissolution, divorce, annulment, or declaration of invalidity; or (ii) entry of a decree of legal separation or separate maintenance.

(8) "During marriage" means a period that begins at marriage and ends at dissolution or at the death of a spouse.

(9) Property is "held" by a person only if a document of title to the property is registered, recorded, or filed in a public office in the name of the person or a writing that customarily operates as a document of title to the type of property is issued for the property in the person's name.

(10) "Income" means wages, salaries, commissions, bonuses, gratuities, payments in kind, deferred employment benefits, proceeds, other than death benefits, of a health, accident, or disability insurance policy, or of a plan, fund, program, or other arrangement providing benefits comparable to those forms of insurance, other economic benefits having value which are attributable to the effort of a spouse, dividends, interest, income from trusts, and net rents and other net returns attributable to investment, rental, licensing, or other use of property, unless attributable to a return of capital or to appreciation.

(11) "Management and control" means the right to buy, sell, use, transfer, exchange, abandon, lease, consume, expend, assign, create a security interest in, mortgage, encumber, dispose of, institute or defend a civil action regarding, or otherwise deal with, property as if it were property of an unmarried person.

(12) "Marital property agreement" means an agreement that complies with Section 10.

(13) A person has "notice" of a fact if the person has knowledge of it, receives a notification of it, or has reason to know that it exists from the facts and circumstances known to the person.

(14) "Presumption" or a "presumed" fact means the imposition on the person against whom the presumption or presumed fact is directed of the burden of proving that the nonexistence of the presumed condition or fact is more probable than its existence.

(15) "Property" means an interest, present or future, legal or equitable, vested or contingent, in real or personal property.

(16) "Written consent" means a document signed by a person against whose interests it is sought to be enforced.

§ 2. Responsibility Between Spouses

(a) Each spouse shall act in good faith with respect to the other spouse in matters involving marital property or other property of the other spouse. This obligation may not be varied by a marital property agreement.

(b) Management and control by a spouse of that spouse's property that is not marital property in a manner that limits, diminishes, or fails to produce income from that property does not violate subsection (a).

Spouses are not trustees or guarantors toward each other. Neither are they simple parties to a contract endeavoring to further their individual interests. The duty is between, and is one of good faith....

§ 3. Variation by Marital Property Agreement. Except as provided in Sections 2, 8(e), 9(c) and 10(b), a marital property agreement may vary the effect of this [Act].

§ 4. Classification of Property of Spouses

(a) All property of spouses is marital property except that which is classified otherwise by this [Act].

(b) All property of spouses is presumed to be marital property.

(c) Each spouse has a present undivided one-half interest in marital property.

(d) Income earned or accrued by a spouse or attributable to property of a spouse during marriage and after the determination date is marital property.

(e) Marital property transferred to a trust remains marital property.

(f) Property owned by a spouse at a marriage after the determination date is individual property.

(g) Property acquired by a spouse during marriage and after the determination date is individual property if acquired:

(1) by gift or a disposition at death made by a third person to the spouse and not to both spouses;

(2) in exchange for or with the proceeds of other individual property of the spouse;

(3) from appreciation of the spouse's individual property except to the extent that the appreciation is classified as marital property under Section 14;

(4) by a decree, marital property agreement, written consent, or reclassification under Section 7(b) designating it as the individual property of the spouse;

(5) as a recovery for damage to property under Section 15, except as specifically provided otherwise in a decree, marital property agreement, or written consent; or

(6) as a recovery for personal injury except for the amount of that recovery attributable to expenses paid or otherwise satisfied from marital property.

(h) Except as provided otherwise in this [Act] the enactment of this [Act] does not alter the classification and ownership rights of property acquired before the determination date.

(i) Except as provided otherwise in this [Act] and to the extent it would affect the ownership rights of the spouse that existed in the property before the determination date, during marriage the interest of a spouse in property owned immediately before the determination date is treated as if it were individual property.

The Section creates the heart of the Act. It contains a general presumption, a series of property rules, an income rule, classification rules, and transition rules.

Classification: "Classification" is an essential process in applying the Act. In classification the essential sorting process is taking place: What is a given item or aggregation of property? Marital property? Individual property? Property owned before the determination date which had a wholly different set of ownership incidents not established by the Act at all? All property has a classification—a generic and basic set of characteristics—and the process is devoted to establishing those precise characteristics and answering those questions. The most important parts of the answer depend on *source* and *time of acquisition.* Title is *not* an answer since title functions under the Act principally to establish management and control rights and the facilitation of third party transactions flowing from the exercise of management and control rights. Under the Act title does *not* function as a classification index. Reclassification is just what the word implies—it is a change in classification, generally from marital to individual or vice versa.

The General Presumption: The first building block in the Act's operation is the general presumption in Subsection (b). The bias of the presumption favors classifying spousal assets as marital property. Thus at the beginning of any process of classifying spousal assets, everything is presumed to be marital property. When there is adequate proof to overcome the general presumption, then the proof will prevail and classification will be otherwise. But the "easy way," when there are no records or proof, will result in the operation of the presumption and in the classification of all spousal property as marital.

The Present Interest: A second building block is the creation of a *present* equal undivided interest for each spouse. This is a distinct departure from existing versions of "marital property" arising out of equitable distribution developments in family law. Those family-law interests set forth in marital property definitions in equitable distribution statutes are delayed-action in nature and come to maturity only during the dissolution process. Marital property under the Act is created *as assets are acquired* by the spouses, whether from income from the effort of either spouse during marriage, as income attributable to passive or investment sources, or as appreciation of or in an exchange for or rollover of existing marital property. When the assets are acquired from such sources, the incidents and attributes of marital property, including the creation of a present legal interest, attach simultaneously with the acquisition. The assets so acquired are instantly classified or characterized as marital property. The classification persists until the marriage terminates by dissolution or death, or until occurrence of a "reclassification" by one or another of the methods provided in the Act.

The Income Rule: The third feature is an income rule, creating an easily comprehended system. By treating all income from any source as marital property, the Act affords a simple and understandable arrangement. In the majority of marriages, most income will be spent sooner or later. In those so affluent that this does not happen, the rule can either be followed or changed by marital property agreement. In the latter group of marriages, some extra record-keeping following an agreed bifurcation of income from marital and individual property should not pose an undue burden.

The income rule poses some "front-end" and "tail-end" problems. The "front-end" problem pertains to income received shortly after the determination date from effort or accrual of rights before the determination date. Actual ownership of such income became fixed before the determination date and it should not be and is not classified as marital property. This is handled by providing that income is marital only if "earned or accrued" after the determination date *and* during marriage.

With a disintegrating marriage in a state which has had the Act for a reasonable period of time, a cash basis or actual receipt rule at dissolution could give rise to significant abuses. This is the potential "tail-end" problem. Receipt of income under the management and the control of one spouse could be delayed voluntarily until the dissolution was complete, to the prejudice of the former spouse who was not in such a position of control. Hence the earned or accrued rule of the Act also addresses this problem. The accounting and classification problems of the accrual or constructive receipt system used in the Act to deal with the tail-end problem obviously could necessitate tracing activities, but the potential for manipulation and diversion with a cash basis rule is such that the difficulty is justified.

Transition to the Income Rule: There is an additional important element in the treatment of income. All property of couples already married when the Act becomes law in an adopting state has a set of characteristics not created by the Act. The Act has been drafted to avoid altering those characteristics during the on-going marriage as far as the *principal* of the pre-adoption property is concerned. However the income rule obviously affects post-adoption income, classifying it as marital property. Post-adoption income is just that. It is not principal, and it is received and regulated by the Act's provisions only when the claim of right to it occurs by virtue of its having been earned or accrued *after* adoption. Hence the Act's income rule is not retroactive.

Trusts: Marital property transferred to a trust remains marital property and does not become "something else" under Subsection (e). A marital property agreement could provide otherwise. The subsection's principal enabling function is to permit the creation of revocable living trusts by one or both spouses without any automatic reclassification of property committed to the trust. If the trust is created by both spouses, or if created by one and consented to by the other, it would itself be a sufficient written form of marital property agreement to effect any reclassification directed by its terms if the other requirements of Section 10 are met. A trust created by one spouse would necessarily be measured by the good faith provisions of Section 2. The subsection would have no application to testamentary trusts, since marital property is the property of spouses. When a former spouse dies leaving a will that creates a trust, the property funding the trust can no longer be marital property. It could, and ordinarily would, be the decedent's share of *former* marital property.

Appreciation of Individual Property: Individual property definitions for post-determination date acquisitions are furnished in a listed format. In addition to such acquisitions by gift or inheritance, there are other obvious inclusions. One of special importance concerns *appreciation* of individual property. Assume that one spouse comes to a marriage subject to the Act as the owner of a valuable piece of real estate. It is individual property. If it quadruples in value, it is *still* individual property. While its income is marital property, the property itself *and* its appreciation in value is almost always individual property. One exception is the special rule announced in Section 14(b). That rule is concerned with the application to the individual property of one spouse of personal effort by the other spouse. It could apply in limited situations, but establishing it requires a very strong showing. Another possible exception could arise from mixing marital property with the individual property, also dealt with in Section 14. If the components of the mixed property can be traced, then no reclassification will occur. Monetary contributions to real estate acquisition or improvement are typically traceable, so that this form of reclassification regarding real estate should not be a frequent issue.

Donated Property: The rule treating property received by gift as individual property applies to gifts made to only one spouse. If a gift is made to both spouses, the donated property is marital property. This would apply to gifts to both in any form, including transfers to them as joint tenants, tenants in common, or in one of the title forms included in Section 11.

Effect on Existing Property: Subsection (h) states an important transitional rule. It can be assumed that in an adopting state one spouse might own property absolutely, and that a couple might also own property concurrently or as community property. The latter would be true of a couple which moved into an adopting state from one of the existing community property states as well as a couple in an adopting community property state. All of the property of a married couple in an adopting state on hand at the determination date would have a particular classification. Certain incidents would already have attached to the manner of ownership. Survivorship would be an incident of jointly held or entireties property. A tenancy in common would consist of undivided interests, with each interest subject to individual rights of disposition. Community property

would have the incidents described in the *Uniform Disposition of Community Property Rights at Death Act,* and possibly others developed between the spouses by agreement. Trust interests would be regulated by governing instruments. The Act is *not* designed to alter these various incidents of ownership or to reclassify such property.

With minor exceptions, the arrival of the determination date for such a couple would neither reclassify any of their property as marital property nor as *any* type of property other than what it was prior to the determination date. The exceptions all operate on that property only *after* the determination date. They are limited and include only the "deferred marital property" approach at dissolution and death set forth in Sections 17 and 18, the income treatment set forth in Subsection (d), and the specific provisions of Subsection (i).

Note that Subsection (h) applies to property of *spouses* owned before the determination date. On the other hand Subsection (f) deals specifically with property owned *before marriage* by persons marrying in an adopting state after the Act is effective. It follows the traditional pattern of community property and dissolution-based marital property statutes in clearly classifying solely owned property owned before marriage as individual property effective with the marriage. Except for its income, individual property under the Act is analogous to solely owned property in a common law state or to separate property in an American community property state. Texas, Louisiana and Idaho separate property is even more kindred, since the income of separate property in those states is community property.

The "As If" Treatment: Subsection (i) is a statutory statement to identify pre-determination date property that is solely owned as functioning with a "fraternal twin" relationship to individual property under the Act. It is a transitional rule, stated as it is to avoid a direct substantive reclassification of pre-determination date property, but to clarify the functional treatment of it in applying the Act. It is important that it be read as the "as if" rule that it is, and not as a reclassification statute.

The exceptions in Subsection (i) are intended to avoid any interference with actual ownership incidents in property owned prior to the determination date. For example, community property owned prior to the determination date should not be treated functionally as individual property in applying the Act. On the other hand, tenancy in common property could function as if it were individual property under the Act's provisions with each owner's undivided interest being treated as though it were individual property. A tenancy in common of individual property of the respective spouses is possible under the Act.

Property "that is not marital property": There are references in the Act to property of a spouse "... that is not marital property ..." (Sections 8(b) and 14(a)); property "... having any other classification ..." (Section 14(a)); "... property of the designated owner of the policy ..." (Section 12(c)(4)); "... all property then owed by the spouses ... which would have been marital property ..." (Section 17(1)); or "... all property then owned by the spouse ... which would have been marital property ..." (Section 18(a)). It is reasonable to ask why such references are not to *individual* property and to ask further whether the Act fractionalizes all property of spouses into marital *or* individual

property. The explanation is part of the transition problem and is consonant with Subsections (b) and (i). Property in existence prior to adoption is *not* individual property, by definition, since the classification of individual property is a creation of the Act. Property in existence prior to adoption of the Act is whatever it is without the Act. Subsection (h) makes it clear that the Act does not go about reclassifying that property. Hence there will be a multitude of couples that will have property that is "something else" than marital property or the individual property established by the Act. That "something else" type of property is property of a spouse that "... is not marital property ..." property, "... having any other classification ..." and the like. Hence such descriptions are intentional in the reference they make to the "something else" or predetermination date property to which they point.

§ 5. Management and Control of Property of Spouses

(a) A spouse acting alone may manage and control:

(1) that spouse's property that is not marital property;

(2) except as provided in subsections (b) and (c), marital property held in that spouse's name alone or not held in the name of either spouse;

(3) a policy of insurance if that spouse is designated as the owner on the records of the issuer of it;

(4) the rights of an employee under an arrangement for deferred employment benefits that accrue as a result of that spouse's employment;

(5) a claim for relief vested in that spouse by other law; and

(6) marital property held in the names of both spouses in the alternative, including a manner of holding using the names of both spouses and the word "or".

(b) Spouses may manage and control marital property held in the names of both spouses other than in the alternative only if they act together.

(c) The right to manage and control marital property transferred to a trust is determined by the terms of the trust.

(d) The right to manage and control marital property does not determine the classification of property of the spouses and does not rebut the presumption of Section 4(b).

(e) The right to manage and control marital property permits gifts of that property only to the extent provided in Section 6.

(f) The right to manage and control any property of spouses acquired before the determination date is not affected by this [Act].

(g) A court may appoint a [conservator, guardian] to exercise a disabled spouse's right to manage and control marital property.

Comment

Title Based System: If Section 4 is the heart of the Act, then Section 5 and its management and control system is its aorta. Management and control is a title based system and to that extent will parallel the management and control rights which typically follow title in common law states. However, there is a very basic difference. While title is virtually synonymous with ownership in the common law system, it is perhaps best understood as a *nominee* relationship under the Act. Title can be viewed as something of a permeable membrane that presents one state of affairs to third parties while encompassing an ownership relationship between the spouses within that relationship which may well be different from the title-side of the membrane. To lawyers long attuned to common law concepts of the impermeable membrane view of title, the thrust is a new one. A fairly useful illustrative analogy is the fractionalization of title which occurs when a trust is created. A trustee has "legal title" (and management rights) while a beneficiary (usually undisclosed on legal title) has equitable and beneficial rights. Two sets of rights coexist, yet the outside world need deal only with the trustee as apparent owner, notwithstanding the beneficiary's completely valid, enforceable, coexisting, but usually undisclosed rights. In the marital property situation, the spouses as co-owners are analogous to the beneficiaries and a spouse as sole holder of marital property is analogous to the trustee as title holder. This comment is *not* intended to imply that marital property creates a trust, but simply to use an analogy to illustrate the coexisting relationships that are present in both situations.

Sole Management: Under Section 5 either spouse has sole management and control rights of a marital property asset which that spouse "holds" alone. No joinder for management and control functions would be required for that property. Holding is defined in Section 1(9) and that definition and this Section

function together to treat conventional title as the method of determining holding.

Concurrent Holding: Management and control of concurrently held assets is dealt with specifically. The rights are related to the use of "and" or "or" in the title. If "and" is used in the concurrent title, *both* spouses manage and control, and joinder of both is required to discharge management and control functions. If "or" is used, it means what it says, and either spouse may manage and control the asset. Section 11(c) effectively applies the provisions on management and control of concurrent property not only to the special optional forms authorized by Section 11, but to conventional forms already in use in adopting states.

Bearer property and other property not "held" can be managed and controlled by either spouse, and no joinder is required. (Section 5(a)(2)). Section 5(a)(2) permits a spouse to manage and control property not held in the name of either spouse; this covers bearer property. The term "held" in Section 1(9) does not extend to bearer property, and the provisions of Section 5(a)(2) integrate with that by permitting one spouse to manage and control any marital property that does not come within the purview of the holding definition in Section 1(9).

Special rules apply to insurance and employee benefits, and claims for relief. Insurance is managed and controlled by its owner. Employee benefits are managed and controlled by the employee on whose behalf they accrue. A claim for relief is managed and controlled by the spouse in whom the claim is vested by other law. (Section 5(a)(3), (4) and (5)).

§ 6. Gifts of Marital Property to Third Persons

(a) A spouse acting alone may give to a third person marital property that the spouse has the right to manage and control only if the value of the marital property given to the third person does not aggregate more than [$500] in a calendar year, or a larger amount if, when made, the gift is reasonable in amount considering the economic position of the spouses. Any other gift of marital property to a third person is subject to subsection (b) unless both spouses act together in making the gift.

(b) If a gift of marital property by a spouse does not comply with subsection (a), the other spouse may bring an action to recover the property or a compensatory judgment in place of the property, to the extent of the noncompliance. The other spouse may bring the action against the donating spouse, the recipient of the gift, or both. The action must be commenced within the earlier of one year after the other spouse has notice of the gift or 3 years after the gift. If the recovery occurs during marriage, it is marital property. If the recovery occurs after a dissolution or the death of either spouse, it is limited to one-half of the value of the gift and is individual property.

§ 7. Property Transactions Between Spouses

(a) Restrictions on the power of spouses to enter into property transactions with each other are abolished.

(b) Spouses may reclassify their property by gift or marital property agreement.

§ 8. Obligations of Spouses

(a) An obligation incurred by a spouse during marriage, including one attributable to an act or omission during marriage, is presumed to be incurred in the interest of the marriage or the family.

(b) After the determination date:

(i) a spouse's obligation to satisfy a duty of support owed to the other spouse or to a child of the marriage may be satisfied only from all marital property and all other property of the obligated spouse that is not marital property;

(ii) an obligation incurred by a spouse in the interest of the marriage or the family may be satisfied only from all marital property and all other property of that spouse that is not marital property;

(iii) an obligation incurred by a spouse before or during marriage that is attributable to an obligation arising before marriage or to an act or omission occurring before marriage may be satisfied only from property of that spouse that is not marital property and that part of marital property which would have been the property of that spouse, but for the marriage; and

(iv) any other obligation incurred by a spouse during marriage, including one attributable to an act or omission during marriage, may be satisfied only from property of that spouse that is not marital property and that spouse's interest in marital property and in that order.

(c) This [Act] does not alter the relationship between spouses and their creditors with respect to any property or obligation in existence on the determination date.

(d) Provisions of a written consent signed by a creditor which diminish the rights of the creditor provided in this section are binding on the creditor.

(e) No provision of a marital property agreement adversely affects the interest of a creditor unless the creditor had actual knowledge of that provision when the obligation to that creditor was incurred. The effect of this subsection may not be varied by a marital property agreement.

(f) This [Act] does not affect the exemption of any property of spouses under other law.

§ 9. Protection of Bona Fide Purchasers Dealing With Spouses

(a) In this section:

(1) "Bona fide purchaser" means a purchaser of property for value who: (i) has not knowingly been a party to fraud or illegality affecting the interest of the spouses or other parties to the transaction; (ii) does not have notice of an adverse claim by a spouse; and (iii) has acted in the transaction in good faith.

(2) "Purchase" means to acquire property by sale, lease, discount, negotiation, mortgage, pledge, or lien or otherwise to deal with property in a voluntary transaction other than a gift.

(3) A purchaser gives "value" for property acquired: (i) in return for a binding commitment to extend credit; (ii) as security for or in total or partial satisfaction of a pre-existing claim; (iii) by accepting delivery pursuant to a pre-existing contract for purchase; or (iv) generally, in return for any other consideration sufficient to support a simple contract.

(b) Notice of the existence of a marital property agreement, a marriage, or the termination of a marriage does not affect the status of a purchaser as a bona fide purchaser.

(c) Marital property purchased by a bona fide purchaser from a spouse having the right to manage and control the property under Section 5 is acquired free of any claim of the other spouse. The effect of this subsection may not be varied by a marital property agreement.

§ 10. Marital Property Agreement

(a) A marital property agreement must be a document signed by both spouses. It is enforceable without consideration.

(b) A marital property agreement may not adversely affect the right of a child to support.

(c) Except as provided in Sections 2, 8(e), and 9(c) and in subsection (b), in a marital property agreement spouses may agree with respect to:

(1) rights and obligations in any of their property whenever and wherever acquired or located;

(2) management and control of any of their property;

(3) disposition of any of their property on dissolution, death, or the occurrence or nonoccurrence of any other event;

(4) modification or elimination of spousal support;

(5) making a will, trust, or other arrangement to carry out the agreement;

(6) a provision that upon the death of either of them, any of their property, including after-acquired property, will pass without probate to a designated person, trust, or other entity by nontestamentary disposition;

(7) choice of law governing construction of the agreement; and

(8) any other matter affecting their property not in violation of public policy or a statute imposing a criminal penalty.

(d) A marital property agreement may be amended or revoked only by a later marital property agreement. The amended agreement or the revocation is enforceable without consideration.

(e) Persons intending to marry each other may enter into a marital property agreement as if married, but the agreement becomes effective only upon their marriage.

(f) A marital property agreement executed during marriage is not enforceable if the spouse against whom enforcement is sought proves that:

(1) the agreement was unconscionable when made; or

(2) that spouse did not execute the agreement voluntarily; or

(3) before execution of the agreement, that spouse:

(i) was not provided a fair and reasonable disclosure of the property or financial obligations of the other spouse;

(ii) did not voluntarily sign a written consent expressly waiving any right to disclosure of the property or financial obligations of the other spouse beyond the disclosure provided; and

(iii) did not have notice of the property or financial obligations of the other spouse.

(g) A marital property agreement executed before marriage is not enforceable if the spouse against whom enforcement is sought proves that:

(1) that spouse did not execute the agreement voluntarily; or

(2) the agreement was unconscionable when made and before execution of the agreement that spouse:

(i) was not provided a fair and reasonable disclosure of the property or financial obligations of the other spouse;

(ii) did not voluntarily sign a written consent expressly waiving any right to disclosure of the property or financial obligations of the other spouse beyond the disclosure provided; and

(iii) did not have notice of the property or financial obligations of the other spouse.

(h) An issue of unconscionability of a marital property agreement is for decision by the court as a matter of law.

(i) If a provision of a marital property agreement modifies or eliminates spousal support and that modification or elimination causes one spouse to be eligible for support under a program of public assistance at the time of dissolution, the court may require the other spouse to provide support to the extent necessary to avoid that eligibility, notwithstanding the terms of the agreement.

(j) A document signed before the effective date of this [Act] by spouses or unmarried persons who subsequently married each other which affects the property of either of them and is enforceable by either of them without reference to this [Act] is not affected by this [Act] except as provided otherwise in a marital property agreement made after the determination date.

§ 11. Optional Forms of Holding Property, Including Use of "And" or "Or"; Survivorship Ownership

(a) Spouses may hold marital property in a form that designates the holders of it by the words "(name of one spouse) or (name of other spouse) as marital property." Marital property held in that form is subject to Section 5(a)(6).

(b) Spouses may hold marital property in a form that designates the holder of it by the words "(name of one spouse) and (name of other spouse) as marital property." Marital property held in that form is subject to Section 5(b).

(c) A spouse may hold individual property in a form that designates the holder of it by the words "(name of spouse) as individual property." Individual property held in that form is subject to Section 5(a)(1).

(d) Spouses may hold property in any other form permitted by law, including a concurrent form or a form that provides for survivorship ownership.

(e) If the words "survivorship marital property" are used instead of the words "marital property" in the form described in subsection (a) or (b), marital property so held is survivorship marital property. On the death of a spouse, the ownership rights of that spouse in survivorship marital property vest solely in the surviving spouse by nontestamentary disposition at death. The first deceased spouse does not have a right of disposition at death of any interest in survivorship marital property. Holding marital property in a form described in subsection (a) or (b) does not alone establish survivorship ownership between the spouses with respect to the property held in that form.

§ 12. Classification of Life Insurance Policies and Proceeds

(a) In this section:

(1) "Owner" means a person appearing on the records of the policy issuer as the person having the ownership interest or, if no person other than the insured appears on those records as a person having that interest, it means the insured.

(2) "Ownership interest" means the rights of an owner under a policy.

(3) "Policy" means an insurance policy insuring the life of a spouse and providing for payment of death benefits at the spouse's death.

(4) "Proceeds" means the death benefit from a policy and all other economic benefits from it, whether they accrue or become payable as a result of the death of an insured person or upon the occurrence or nonoccurrence of another event.

(b) If a policy issuer makes payments or takes actions in accordance with the policy and the issuer's records, the issuer is not liable because of those payments or actions unless, at the time of the payments or actions, it had actual knowledge of inconsistent provisions of a decree or marital property agreement or of an adverse claim by a spouse, former spouse, surviving spouse, or persons claiming under a deceased spouse's disposition at death.

(c) Except as provided in subsections (d), (e), and (f):

(1) The ownership interest and proceeds of a policy issued after the determination date which designates the insured as the owner are marital property without regard to the classification of property used to pay premiums on the policy.

(2) The ownership interest and proceeds of a policy issued before the determination date which designates the insured as the owner are mixed property if a premium on the policy is paid from marital property after the determination date without regard to the classification of property used to pay premiums on that policy after the initial payment of a premium on it from marital property. The marital property component of the ownership interest and proceeds is the part resulting from multiplying the entire ownership interest and proceeds by a fraction of which the numerator is the period during marriage that the policy was in effect after the date on which a premium was paid from marital property and the denominator is the entire period the policy was in effect.

(3) The ownership interest and proceeds of a policy issued during marriage which designates the spouse of the insured as the owner are individual property of its owner without regard to the classification of property used to pay premiums on the policy.

(4) The ownership interest and proceeds of a policy that designates a person other than either of the spouses as the owner are not affected by this [Act] if no premium on the policy is paid from marital property after the determination date. If a premium on the policy is paid from marital property after the determination date, the ownership interest and proceeds of the policy are in part property of the designated owner of the policy and in part marital property of the spouses without regard to the classification of property used to pay premiums on that policy after the initial payment of a premium on it from marital property. The marital property component of the ownership interest and proceeds is the part resulting from multiplying the entire ownership interest and proceeds by a fraction of which the numerator is the period during marriage that the policy was in effect after the date on which a premium was paid from marital property and the denominator is the entire period the policy was in effect.

(5) Written consent by a spouse to the designation of another person as the beneficiary of the proceeds of a policy is effective to relinquish that spouse's interest in the ownership interest and proceeds of the policy without regard to the classification of property used by a spouse or another to pay premiums on that policy. A designation by either spouse of a parent or child of either of the spouses as the beneficiary of the proceeds of a policy is presumed to have been made with the consent of the other spouse.

(6) Unless the spouses provide otherwise in a marital property agreement, designation of a trust as the beneficiary of the proceeds of a policy with a marital property component does not reclassify that component.

(d) This section does not affect a creditor's interest in the ownership interest or proceeds of a policy assigned or made payable to the creditor as security.

(e) The interest of a person as owner or beneficiary of a policy acquired under a decree or property settlement agreement incident to a prior marriage or parenthood is not marital property without regard to the classification of property used to pay premiums on that policy.

(f) This section does not affect the ownership interest or proceeds of a policy if neither spouse is designated as an owner in the policy or the records of the policy issuer and no marital property is used to pay a premium on the policy.

§ 13. Classification of Deferred Employment Benefits

(a) A deferred employment benefit attributable to employment of a spouse occurring after the determination date is marital property.

(b) A deferred employment benefit attributable to employment of a spouse occurring during marriage and partly before and partly after the determination date is mixed property. The marital property component of that mixed property is the part resulting from multiplying the entire benefit by a fraction of which the numerator is the period of employment giving rise to the benefit that occurred after the determination date and during marriage and the denominator is the total period of the employment. Unless provided otherwise in a decree, marital property agreement, or written consent, valuation of a deferred employment benefit that is mixed property shall be made as of the death of a spouse or a dissolution.

(c) Ownership or disposition provisions of a deferred employment benefit which conflict with subsections (a) and (b) are ineffective between spouses, former spouses, or between a surviving spouse and a person claiming under a deceased spouse's disposition at death.

(d) If an administrator of an arrangement for deferred employment benefits makes payments or takes actions in accordance with the arrangement and the administrator's records, the administrator is not liable because of those payments or actions unless, at the time of the payments or actions, it had actual knowledge of inconsistent provisions of a decree or marital property agreement or of an adverse claim by a spouse, former spouse, surviving spouse, or a person claiming under a deceased spouse's disposition at death.

§ 14. Mixed Property

(a) Except as provided otherwise in Sections 12 and 13, mixing marital property with property having any other classification reclassifies the other property to marital property unless the component of the mixed property which is not marital property can be traced.

(b) Application by one spouse of substantial labor, effort, inventiveness, physical or intellectual skill, creativity, or managerial activity on individual property of the other spouse creates marital property attributable to that application if:

(i) reasonable compensation is not received for the application; and

(ii) substantial appreciation of the individual property of the other spouse results from the application.

§ 15. Interspousal Remedies

(a) A spouse has a claim against the other spouse for breach of the duty of good faith imposed by Section 2 resulting in damage to the claimant spouse's present undivided one-half interest in marital property.

(b) A court may order an accounting of the property and obligations of the spouses and may determine rights of ownership in, beneficial enjoyment of, or access to, marital property and the classification of all property of the spouses.

(c) A court may order that the name of a spouse be added to marital property held in the name of the other spouse alone, except with respect to:

(1) a partnership interest held by the other spouse as a general partner;

(2) an interest in a professional corporation, professional association, or similar entity held by the other spouse as a stockholder or member;

(3) an asset of an unincorporated business if the other spouse is the only spouse involved in operating or managing the business; or

(4) any other property if the addition would adversely affect the rights of a third person.

(d) Except as provided otherwise in Section 6(b), a spouse must commence an action against the other spouse under subsection (a) not later than 3 years after acquiring actual knowledge of the facts giving rise to the claim.

Comment

The section will create a change in the law of those states which prohibit litigation between spouses regarding property rights during an ongoing marriage....

§ 16. Invalid Marriages. If a marriage is invalidated by a decree, a court may apply so much of this [Act] to the property of the persons who were parties to the invalid marriage as is necessary to avoid an inequitable result.

§ 17. Treatment of Certain Property at Dissolution. Except as provided in Section 16:

(1) In a dissolution, all property then owned by the spouses that was acquired during marriage and before the determination date which would have been marital property under this [Act] if acquired after the determination date must be treated as if it were marital property.

(2) In a dissolution, any property of either spouse which can be traced to property received by a spouse after the determination date as a recovery for a loss of earning capacity during marriage must be treated as if it were marital property.

(3) After a dissolution, each former spouse owns an undivided one-half interest in the former marital property as a tenant in common except as provided otherwise in a decree or written consent.

[(4) In an action for legal separation, the court may decree the extent to which property acquired by the spouses after the legal separation is marital property and the responsibility of each spouse for obligations incurred after the decree of legal separation.]

§ 18. Treatment of Certain Property at Death of Spouse

(a) At the death of a spouse domiciled in this State, all property then owned by the spouse that was acquired during marriage and before the determination date which would have been marital property under this [Act] if acquired after the determination date must be treated as if it were marital property.

(b) At the death of a spouse domiciled in this State, any property of the spouse which can be traced to property received by the spouse after the determination date as a recovery for a loss of earning capacity during marriage must be treated as if it were marital property.

[**§ 19. Estate by Entireties.** This [Act] does not affect the relationship between spouses and their creditors with respect to property held by spouses in an estate by entireties after the determination date.]

§ 20. Rules of Construction. Unless displaced by this [Act], the principles of law and equity supplement its provisions.

§ 21. Uniformity of Application and Construction. This [Act] shall be applied and construed to effectuate its general purpose to make uniform the law with respect to the subject of this [Act] among states enacting it.

§ 22. Short Title. This [Act] may be cited as the "Uniform Marital Property Act."

§ 23. Severability. If any provision of this [Act] or its application to any person or circumstance is held invalid, the invalidity does not affect other provisions or applications of this [Act] which can be given effect without the invalid provision or application, and to this end the provisions of this [Act] are severable.

§ 24. Time of Taking Effect. This [Act] takes effect on January 1, 19[–].

§ 25. Repeal. The following Acts and parts of Acts are repealed:

§ 26. Laws Not Repealed. This [Act] does not repeal:

    (1)

    (2)

    (3)

Mental Capacity

Mental capacity to make a will

- understand Act
- Knows Extent of property
- understands disposition
- Knows natural objects of bounty
- will reps her wishes

Insane Delusion

Elements: 1. Insane Delusion — false perception of Reality
2. Produced the will

Insane Delusion Tests:

- persistent belief w/ no existance in Fact & adheared to W/ out against all evidence

- must prove insane delusion and that created the will

Under Influence

Testators free will is overcome by someone's influence that causes the testator to make bequests they normally wouldn't.

Standard

- Donor susceptible to Undue Infl
- wrongdoer had opprtunt to exert UI
- had Disposition to exert UI, and
- The result appears to be effect of UI

Common Law

- Confidential Relationship
- Suspicious Circumstance
    - person helped prep will & Benefican

Statutory

Attorney, Beneficary, Caregiver, Fiduciary, presumed of UI, unless blood Relation to 4th Degree

Mistake & Ambiguity

- Extrinsic evidence Allowed to clear Ambiguity
- Clear and convincing evidence of the mistake and what the Intent was — then Reformed

Fraud in Execution — not aware they are signing a will
    — extrinsic is allowed

Fraud in Inducement — false info to change the ben

fevy

Secret Trusts

only Arises from resulting Trust

"50K to A"

- Then Evidence shows was to be kept for B in trust

Semi - Secret Trust

"

"

"50K to A to hold in trust"
- unknown Beneficiary

• no Evidence allowed

- Creates resulting trust for Residuary/Intestacy

Revokable Trust

All trusts are presumed to be Revokable unless its stated that it is irrevokable

Power of Appointment

Power Role that can appoint Beneficiarys
• General or Non-General
• present or postponed

• Non-General
- Creditors cant reach

• Presently Exerciseable General power
- Creditors Can Reach
- Powers property for Taxes

• Postponed General
- Creditors Reach if/once can take

UPC allows Blanket Clause
Clear Testator Knows also
and intent

Trust Fiduciary Duties

Loyalty
- Sole Benefit of Benefits
- No Self dealing

Prudence
- act as prudent person
- make Reasonable Inquiry
- Duty to diversify
  - excuse Texas

Duty To Earmark
- ~~Keep Trust property~~ Separate
  Mark trust property as such

Duty to not Commingle
- Keep property separate
  from own

Duty to administer trust according to terms
- Cant Quit w/o Court permission

Duty of Impartiality
- Cant act impartial between Beneficiary
- Treat lifetime & residual benefit

Delegations
- Trustee to Delegate Functs
  - must use prudence
    in hiring
- CA Liable for actions

Exculpation

Presumption language drafting is wrong if Trustee.

UPC 2-101 - Intestate Estate

UPC 2-102 - Share of Spouse

UP2 2-103 - Share of heirs other than surviving spouse

UPC - 2-104 - Requirement of survival

UPC 2-105 - No taker

UPC 2-109 - Advancement

UPC 2-803 - Slayer rule

English

(D)

(A) (B) (C)

E F
1/4 1/4

G 1/2

I

E
1/4   F
       1/4

Modern

(D)

(A) (B) (C)

E   F
1/3 1/3

G 1/3

I

UPC

(D)

(A) (B) (C)

1/3 E (F)

(G)

I   J
2/9 2/9

K
2/9

$\left(\frac{1}{3} \times \frac{2}{3} = \frac{2}{9}\right)$